The SAGE
Handbook of
Industrial Relations

The SAGE
Handbook of
Industrial Relations

Edited by
Paul Blyton
Nicolas Bacon
Jack Fiorito
and Edmund Heery

Los Angeles • London • New Delhi • Singapore

First published 2008

SAGE Publications Ltd
1 Oliver's Yard
55 City Road
London EC1Y 1SP

SAGE Publications Inc.
2455 Teller Road
Thousand Oaks, California 91320

SAGE Publications India Pvt Ltd
B 1/I 1 Mohan Cooperative Industrial Area
Mathura Road
New Delhi 110 044

SAGE Publications Asia-Pacific Pte Ltd
33 Pekin Street #02-01
Far East Square
Singapore 048763

Library of Congress Control Number: 2007934979

British Library Cataloguing in Publication data

A catalogue record for this book is available from
the British Library

ISBN 978-1-4129-1154-2

Typeset by CEPHA Imaging Pvt. Ltd., Bangalore, India
Printed in India at Replika Press Pvt. Ltd
Printed on paper from sustainable resources

Contents

List of Figures

List of Tables

Notes on Contributors

Peter Ackers is Professor of Industrial Relations and Labour History at Loughborough University Business School. During 2005–06 he was Leverhulme Visiting Fellow at the Indian Institute of Management, Calcutta. His current research is on British Industrial Relations History, including a biographical study of Professor Hugh Clegg, and Indian Industrial Relations. He has edited *Understanding Work and Employment: Industrial Relations in Transition* (Oxford University Press 2003) with Adrian Wilkinson and *The New Workplace and Trade Unionism* (Routledge 1996) with Chris Smith and Paul Smith.

Nicolas Bacon is Professor of Human Resource Management at Nottingham University Business School, UK. His current research on trade unions includes partnership agreements, negotiations to change working practices and union learning representatives; the employment effects of buyouts and shareholder value management; and employment practices in small and medium-sized enterprises. He is currently editor of the *Industrial Relations Journal*.

Devasheesh Bhave is a PhD candidate in the Human Resources and Industrial Relations department at the Carlson School of Management, University of Minnesota. His research interests include the areas of electronic performance monitoring, relational demography, and employment relationships.

Paul Blyton is Professor of Industrial Relations and Industrial Sociology at Cardiff University, UK. His research interests include employees' experience of work restructuring, working time developments, and work-life balance concerns. His recent publications include *The Realities of Work* with Mike Noon (Palgrave Macmillan) and *Key Concepts in Work* with Jean Jenkins (Sage).

Peter Boxall is Professor of Human Resource Management at the University of Auckland. His research is concerned with both management and employee strategies in contemporary workplaces and their respective outcomes. He is co-editor (with John Purcell and Patrick Wright) of the Oxford University Press *Handbook of Human Resource Management* and co-editor (with Richard Freeman and Peter Haynes) of *What Workers Say: Employee Voice in the Anglo-American Workplace* (Cornell University Press).

William Brown is Professor of Industrial Relations in the Economics Faculty at Cambridge University and Master of Darwin College. He was previously Director of the Industrial Relations Research Unit at Warwick University. An active arbitrator, he was a member of the council of the UK's Advisory, Conciliation and Arbitration Service (ACAS), and was a founder member of the Low Pay Commission which established, and maintains, the UK national minimum wage.

His research interests include collective bargaining, pay systems, trade unions, and the effects of legal intervention in the labor market.

Alex Bryson is a Research Director at the Policy Studies Institute. He has been at the institute since 1991, during which time his research has focused on the evaluation of welfare-to-work programs and industrial relations. Recently he has been applying techniques common in the evaluation literature to problems in industrial relations. He is an editor of the *British Journal of Industrial Relations* and the Manpower Research Fellow at the Centre for Economic Performance.

John W. Budd is a Professor in the Industrial Relations Center at the University of Minnesota's Carlson School of Management. He is the author of *Employment with a Human Face: Balancing Efficiency, Equity, and Voice* (Cornell University Press), *Labor Relations: Striking a Balance* (McGraw-Hill/Irwin), and a co-editor of *The Ethics of Human Resources and Industrial Relations* (Labor and Employment Relations Association). His current research interests include industrial relations theory, employment-related public policies, and conceptualizations of work.

Ali Dastmalchian is Professor of Organizational Analysis and Dean, Faculty of Business, University of Victoria, Canada. His recent research interests include organizational change, organizational design in health care, and healthy organizations. His recent publications include *Work-Life Integration* with Paul Blyton, Ken Reed, and Betsy Blunsdon (Palgrave Macmillan). His work has appeared in journals such as the *British Journal of Industrial Relations*, *Industrial and Labor Relations Review* and *Human Relations*.

Simon Deakin is Professor of Law at the University of Cambridge. He specializes in the economics and sociology of law, focusing on labor, company and private law. His books include *The Law of the Labour Market* (2005, with Frank Wilkinson). He is a member of the editorial boards of the *British Journal of Industrial Relations*, the *Industrial Law Journal*, and the *Cambridge Journal of Economics*.

John T. Delaney is Professor of Management and Dean of the Joseph M. Katz Graduate School of Business and College of Business Administration at the University of Pittsburgh. His research focuses on dispute resolution, high performance work practices, and labor relations. His recent publications include *Organized Labor's Political Scorecard* (with Marick Masters), *Ethical Challenges in Labor Relations*, and *Change to Win: Can Structural Change Revitalize the American Labor Movement* (with Jack Fiorito and Paul Jarley).

Jack Fiorito is J. Frank Dame Professor of Management at Florida State University and Principal Research Fellow at the University of Hertfordshire. His research interests include worker attitudes toward unions and employers, and how unions function as organizations. His recent publications include 'The State of the Unions in the United States', *Journal of Labor Research* (2007), and 'Change to Win: Can Structural Reform Revitalize the American Labor Movement?' *Advances in Industrial and Labor Relations* (2007).

Robert J. Flanagan is the Konosuke Matsushita Professor of International Labor Economics and Policy Analysis at the Graduate School of Business, Stanford University. His current research interests include the relationship between globalization, working conditions, and labor rights around the world and the economics of symphony orchestras. His most recent book is *Globalization and Labor Conditions* (Oxford University Press, 2006).

John Forth is a Research Fellow at the National Institute of Economic and Social Research. He works on a range of labor market issues including employment relations, equality, and skills. He is co-author of *Inside the Workplace* and *All Change at Work?*, both arising from his involvement in the Workplace Employment Relations Survey series. Other recent publications have focused on topics such as pay determination, 'high involvement management', and productivity, with a particular emphasis on the role of trade unions.

Richard B. Freeman is Professor of Economics at Harvard University, Labor Studies Program Director at NBER, and Professorial Research Fellow at the Centre for Economic Performance, London School of Economics. His research interests include the growth and decline of unions; self-organizing non-unions in the labor market; restructuring European welfare states; international labor standards; Chinese labor markets; crime; employee involvement programs; globalization; income distribution and equity in the marketplace; immigration and trade; and the job market for scientists and engineers. His recent publications include *What Workers Want* (Cornell 2nd edition), *Can Labor Standards Improve Under Globalization?* (IIE), and *America Works: The Exceptional Labor Market* (Sage).

Carola M. Frege is a Reader in Employment Relations at the London School of Economics and Political Science. She is the author of *Employment Research and State Traditions* (Oxford University Press 2007) and co-editor of *Varieties of Unionism* (OUP, 2004). She has published widely in academic journals and edited collections on comparative employment relations and is the editor of the *British Journal of Industrial Relations*.

Ann C. Frost is Associate Professor at the Richard Ivey School of Business, University of Western Ontario. Her main research focus has been in the area of workplace restructuring and high performance forms of work organization. Articles from this research have appeared in *Advances in Industrial and Labor Relations*, the *British Journal of Industrial Relations*, and the *Industrial and Labor Relations Review*. Her current research interests include models of labor-management co-operation, restructuring in the health care sector, the impact of recent changes in work organization on the careers of low wage workers, and employment practices in Canadian call centers.

Gregor Gall is Professor of Industrial Relations and Director of the Centre for Research in Employment Studies at the University of Hertfordshire, UK. His research interests revolve around trade unionism and worker mobilization. His recent books include *Sex Worker Union Organizing: An International Study* (Palgrave Macmillan) and *The Political Economy of Scotland: Red Scotland? Radical Scotland?* (University of Wales Press). Also, he is the editor of two volumes on union recognition (with Routledge) and a forthcoming one (with Palgrave Macmillan).

Daniel G. Gallagher is the CSX Corporation Professor of Management at James Madison University in Harrisonburg, Virginia. His current research interests include a variety of topics related to the study of independent contracting and other forms of work outside of the traditional employer–employee relationship. He also has an ongoing interest in the study of union member attitudes and behaviors. He is currently an Associate Editor of *Human Relations*, and serves on the editorial boards of *Industrial Relations* and the *Journal of Management*.

Ray Gibney is an Assistant Professor of Management at the Pennsylvania State University at Harrisburg. His primary research interests are positive and negative employee-collective social exchange relationships. In addition, Ray is interested in labor unions in the political process and employee self-service technology in organizations.

John Godard is Professor at the Faculty of Management, the University of Manitoba. His work focuses on state policies and labor law, on comparative institutional environments, and on the implications of work and human resource practices for workers and their unions. It has been published in a number of edited books and in numerous academic journals, appearing most frequently in the *Industrial and Labor Relations Review* and the *British Journal of Industrial Relations*. He is a former editor of the *British Journal of Industrial Relations*, and serves on the boards of a number of scholarly journals.

Irena Grugulis is Professor of Employment Studies and head of the HR/OB teaching group at Bradford University School of Management. Her research interests cover most areas of skill, particularly the impact that national and organizational systems have on the people who experience them. Her latest book, published by Palgrave Macmillan in 2007 is *Skills, Training and Human Resource Development: A Critical Text*. Her current projects include research into employment in the film and TV industry and retail work in Britain. She is an associate fellow of SKOPE and edits the *Debates and Controversies* section of *Work, Employment and Society*.

David Guest is Professor of Organizational Psychology and Human Resource Management at King's College, London. His current research interests are the relationship between human resource management, organizational performance, and employee well-being in the public and private sectors; the individualization of employment relations and the role of the psychological contract; flexibility and employment contracts; partnership at work; and the future of the career.

Rebecca Gumbrell-McCormick is Lecturer in Management at Birkbeck, University of London, UK. She is a former international trade union official and official of the ILO. Her main research areas are international and European industrial relations and equal opportunities. Her most recent publications include 'Embedded Collectivism? Workplace Representation in France and Germany', in *Industrial Relations Journal*, 37(5), September 2006 (with Richard Hyman) and 'The ICFTU and the World Economy: A Historical Perspective', in R Munck (2003) (ed.) *Labour and Globalisation: Results and Prospects* (Liverpool University Press).

Kerstin Hamann is Professor of Political Science at the University of Central Florida in Orlando, US. Her research focuses on comparative political economy and industrial relations in Western Europe, and on Spanish politics and labor unions. Her work has been published in journals such as the *British Journal of Industrial Relations*, the *European Journal of Industrial Relations*, *Comparative Political Studies*, and *Industrial and Labor Relations Review*. Her current collaborative research with John Kelly analyzes the political dynamics of the origins of social pacts in Western Europe.

Robert Hebdon is the Chair of the Faculty Program in Industrial Relations and Associate Professor in the Desautels Faculty of Management of McGill University. His research interests include public sector restructuring and workplace conflict. His recent publications include articles on strike duration with Mike Campoletti and Doug Hyatt (*Industrial and Labor Relations Review*), workplace conflict (*Advances in Industrial Relations*), and comparative local government restructuring with Patrice Jalette (*Environment and Planning C*).

Edmund Heery is Professor of Employment Relations and Joint Director (with Peter Fairbrother) of the Centre for Global Labor Research at Cardiff University. His primary research interest in recent years has been union strategies of revitalization, which has included study of union organizing, union representation of contingent workers, and union bargaining over equality and work-life balance. His current research is a study of worker representation through 'civil society organizations'; charities, advocacy, and campaigning organizations. His recent publications include *The Future of Worker Representation* (edited with Geraldine Healy, Phil Taylor, and William Brown), Palgrave MacMillan, 2004.

Charles Heckscher is a Professor at Rutgers University and Director of the Center for Workplace Transformation. His research focuses on organization change and the changing nature of employee representation. His books include *The New Unionism, White-Collar Blues*, and *The Collaborative Enterprise*.

Richard Hyman is Professor of Industrial Relations at the London School of Economics and Political Science (LSE) and is founding editor of the *European Journal of Industrial Relations*. He has written extensively on the themes of industrial relations, collective bargaining, trade unionism, industrial conflict, and labor market policy, and is author of many books, including *Strikes* and *Industrial Relations: A Marxist Introduction*. He co-edited the 17-country text *Changing Industrial Relations in Europe* (Blackwell, 1998). His comparative study *Understanding European Trade Unionism: Between Market, Class and Society* was published by Sage in 2001.

Paul Jarley is Professor of Management and Dean of the College of Business at the University of Nevada Las Vegas. His research interests focus on trade union structures and strategies, interest arbitration, and social capital at work. His recent publications include *Unions as Social Capital, Justice and Union Participation* (with Nancy Brown Johnson), and *Change to Win: Can Structural Change Revitalize the American Labor Movement?* (with Jack Fiorito and John T. Delaney).

Jean Jenkins is Lecturer in HRM at Cardiff University. Her research interests center on employment relations in the manufacturing sector, particularly in the clothing sector, and employees' experiences in the increasingly internationalized market for labor. Her recent publications include *Key Concepts in Work* (with Paul Blyton), Sage 2007.

John Kelly is Professor of Industrial Relations in the School of Management Birkbeck College, University of London. His main areas of research are comparative labor relations, labor unions, and industrial relations theory and recent publications include *Varieties of Unionism* (OUP, 2004, co-editor), *Union Organization and Activity* (Routledge 2004, co-editor), and *Rethinking Industrial Relations* (Routledge, 1998).

Russell D. Lansbury is Professor of Work and Organizational Studies and Associate Dean (Research) in the Faculty of Economics and Business at the University of Sydney. He is the current President of the International Industrial Relations Association. His major research contributions have been in the fields of international and comparative studies of employment relations and management.

David Lewin is the Neil Jacoby Professor of Management, Human Resources and Organizational Behavior in the UCLA Anderson School of Management. His research interests include workplace/organizational conflict, human resource management and business performance, pay and rewards, and new challenges to old wage and hour law. His recent publications include *Contemporary Issues in Employment Relations* (2006) and *Advances in Industrial and Labor Relations, Volume 15* (2007).

Marick F. Masters is a Professor of Business Administration and of Public and International Affairs at the University of Pittsburgh, where he directs the Center on Conflict Resolution and Negotiation. He has written more than 100 articles and several books. His current interests lie in negotiations, conflict resolution, the role of interest groups in politics, and the management of political campaigns. He is a senior partner with AIM Consultants, a management consulting firm, with offices in New London, CT and Pittsburgh, PA.

Wanjiru Njoya is Lecturer in Law at Oxford University, and a Fellow of Wadham College Oxford. Her publications include *Property in Work: The Employment Relationship in the Anglo-American Firm* (Aldershot, Ashgate Publishing, 2007). She specializes in labor law and corporate governance, and her research has appeared in the *British Journal of Industrial Relations*, the *Industrial Law Journal*, and the *Law Quarterly Review*.

Barbara Pocock is Director of the Centre for Work + Life at the University of South Australia. She has worked in a range of industries. Her past research includes analysis of trade unions, gender politics at work, the regulation of industrial relations systems, and effects on inequality. At present she is studying the changing nature of work and its intersections with changing household and social life, with Australia as her primary focus. Her latest books are *The Work/Life Collision* (2003) and *The Labour Market Ate My Babies* (2006), both published by Federation Press.

Stephen Procter is Alcan Professor of Management and Director of Research at Newcastle University Business School. His chief area of research interest is new patterns of work in the public sector, particularly teamworking and workplace flexibility. He is currently involved in projects looking at new working patterns in the mental health services workforce, multi-agency working in public services, and the management of public sector mergers. He is co-founder and co-organizer of the International Workshop on Teamworking, Chair of the Editorial Advisory Board of *Personnel Review*, and, in 2007–08, Chair of the British Academy of Management Special Interest Group on HRM.

Iryna Shevchuk is a PhD candidate at the University of Pittsburgh. Her research interests include the employer–employee relationship, employee turnover, and quantitative research methods and design.

George Strauss is Professor Emeritus at the Haas School of Management at the University of California, Berkeley. He is also a member of the Institute for Research on Labor and Employment (previously the Institute for Industrial Relations), also at UCB. He is the co-author (with Keith Whitfield) of *Researching the World of Work: Strategies and Methods of Studying Industrial Relations* (ILR Press).

Franz Traxler is Professor of Industrial Sociology at the University of Vienna. His research focuses on comparative industrial relations and organized interests. Book publications include *National Labour Relations in Internationalized Markets* (with S. Blaschke and B. Kittel) (Oxford University Press 2001), and *Handbook of Business Interest Associations, Firm Size and Governance* (with G. Huemer) (Routledge 2007).

Nick Wailes is a Senior Lecturer in Work and Organizational Studies at the University of Sydney, Australia. He teaches comparative industrial relations and strategic management. His two main areas of research are the impact of globalization on national relations systems and the study of organizational change associated with information and communications technology.

Keith Whitfield is Professor of Human Resource Management and Economics at Cardiff University, UK. His research focuses on the impact of human resource policies and practices on employee and organizational outcomes. He was recently a member of the steering group for the Fifth British Workplace Employment Relations Survey, and is currently the principal investigator for a project examining a quarter century of change in British Employment Relations.

Adrian Wilkinson is Professor of Employment Relations at Griffith University, Australia. His research interests include employee participation, high performance workplaces, and industrial relations and human resource management theory. Recent publications include *Human Resource Management at Work* (CIPD) with Mick Marchington and *Understanding Work and Employment* (OUP) with Peter Ackers.

Tom Zagenczyk is an Assistant Professor of Management at Clemson University. His research interests include the employer–employee relationship, social influence processes in organizations, developmental relationships, and the relationship between IT and employee attitudes.

Preface

The purpose of this Handbook is to provide readers with an overview of current knowledge from Industrial Relations scholarship, and consider what issues and questions still need to be addressed. The scope of the different contributions is testament to a subject area that has broadened its perspective far beyond what many in the past considered the central areas of Industrial Relations interest: trade unions, collective bargaining, and strikes. It is now widely recognized that the different aspects of the employment relationship are what define the field of industrial relations: the various elements that comprise the employment relationship; the bases and assumptions on which employment relationships are formed and modified; the significance of different institutional arrangements within which those employment relationships are situated; and the relevance of broader economic, social, and technological developments that fundamentally affect contemporary society. Questions and concerns that first gave rise to industrial relations enquiry have not disappeared, but have been augmented by the recognition of a much broader set of issues and developments impacting on people's experience of work.

The international group of contributors brought together here are the leading experts of their fields and this provides them both with a solid base from which to review what is known about their area of study, but also what we as yet do not sufficiently know: what questions we have failed to answer satisfactorily to date, and what issues still clamor for attention.

It is a highly appropriate time to produce such a collection. With profound changes occurring within industrial relations practice over the past two decades – not least, changes in trade union presence, the coverage of union-management relations, and the state's role within the employment relationship – coupled with fundamental developments in national and international product and labor markets, it is apposite to take stock of what these developments signify for the field of industrial relations and what new questions and challenges they pose.

In bringing this collection to fruition, we wish to acknowledge the help we have had from various different quarters. First, our thanks to all the contributors who not only agreed to fit this task into their already busy schedules, but to respond willingly to comments on drafts that helped create a more cohesive and comprehensive collection that otherwise wouldn't have been the case. Second, thanks to the administrative efforts of Sue O'Brien and Penny Smith at Cardiff University who endeavored to keep a hold on where everything was, as drafts moved back and forth. Third, our thanks to the team at Sage – Chris Rojek, Mila Steele, and Kay Bridger – for putting the idea of the Handbook to us in the first place, for being patient as the delays that are probably inevitable in a large project of this kind duly occurred, and for allowing us the opportunity to work with such a thought-provoking group of academics.

Introduction: The Field of Industrial Relations

Edmund Heery, Nicholas Bacon, Paul Blyton
and Jack Fiorito

INTRODUCTION

The purpose of this Handbook is to profile the academic field of industrial relations (IR) at the start of the twenty-first century. To this end we have assembled an international roster of subject experts to reflect on the multiple facets of IR scholarship, summarize bodies of knowledge and theory and identify current developments and likely future trends. IR was a product of the great class compromise of the twentieth century between ruling elites and the rising working class. Many of its founding scholars were exercised by the 'labor problem' and the need for a practically oriented field of study to support the creation of new institutions that would regulate industrial conflict and integrate the working population into liberal democratic societies (Kaufman, 1993: 4–9; Lyddon, 2003). Much of this impulse (though not all) has faded as the decades have passed but the field of IR continues to evolve and address a broad and continually shifting set of issues within the employment relationship. This collection we believe, attests to the continuing vigor of, what is now, a mature academic field and its continuing relevance at the start of a new century, very different from the old.

The purpose of this introduction is to provide a platform for the 33 chapters that follow. It does so by providing an overview of three core aspects of contemporary IR scholarship. We consider in turn the definition and scope of academic industrial relations, the multi-disciplinary nature of IR and the theoretical perspectives that shape its research program, and the normative orientations of IR scholars that provide a standard for evaluating IR practice and underpin the advice to governments, employers, unions and others that issue from an applied, policy-oriented field. In each of these areas our aim is to identify classic positions and defining characteristics of IR but also point to contemporary themes and developments. Our purpose is to show how the enduring features of the field continue to evolve. To conclude the introduction, we also describe the structure of the Handbook and introduce the separate chapters that comprise the volume.

DEFINITION AND SCOPE

Twenty-five years ago Marsden (1982: 232) declared that, 'Everyone, instinctively it seems, knows what industrial relations is about, even those who have never studied the subject. It is "about" trade unions, managers and collective bargaining.' Undoubtedly many outside the field, if pressed, would provide a similar definition and it is certainly the case that the core of IR scholarship has focused, for a long time, on collective industrial relations. Studies of trade unions, collective employment law, collective bargaining and state–trade union relations continue to feature prominently in the field (Frege, 2005).

Definitions offered from within the field, however, typically cast their net much wider and effectively claim the non-union as well as the unionized segment of the economy as IR's province. This was true of some of the first attempts to specify the bounds of IR as an academic subject. Thus, in Dunlop's 1958 formulation of a 'general theory of industrial relations', the subject matter is defined as the 'industrial relations system', a distinct institutional domain within developed economies, comprising actors, processes, context and outcomes (Dunlop, 1993). Crucially, this definition includes but is not confined to the examination of trade unions and collective bargaining; the roster of actors embraces workers and their informal work groups as well as formal representative institutions, the list of processes covers management decision and legal regulation as well as bilateral regulation by unions and employers.

More recent attempts to designate the object of the study of IR have followed a similar tack and tend to define the field as the study of the employment relationship. This is true of authoritative statements by Kaufman (2004a: 45), who states that IR is 'the study of the employment relationship and all the behaviors, outcomes, practices, and institutions that emanate from or impinge on the relationship', and Edwards (2003: 1–2), who declares that the 'focus is employment:

all forms of economic activity in which an employee works under the authority of an employer and receives a wage for his or her labor.' Both authors state that 'employment relations' is a more satisfactory label for the field, if only because it has less connotations with smoke-stack industry, and in some parts of the world IR has begun to yield to this newer label.[1] We are sympathetic to this change of usage but have retained the established term to minimize possible confusion, as do Edwards and Kaufman.

Defining IR as the study of the employment relationship is only an initial step and the next is to identify the component elements of the employment relationship in order to further specify IR's domain. In our view, four elements can usefully be identified.

Actors

Much IR research is focused on the parties to the employment relationship, typically labeled since Dunlop the industrial relations 'actors'. These include workers and their representative institutions, including trade unions and left political parties; employers, their managerial representatives within the firm and their collective organizations, employers' associations; and the state and its multiple agencies involved in the formation and regulation of employment relationships. The latter includes legislatures, judicial and police authorities and specialist agencies engaged in training and development and dispute resolution. As traditional, collective actors have declined in significance in many countries so the field has begun to research 'new actors in industrial relations' (Heery and Frege, 2006). With regard to employees there has been a growth of interest in non-union representatives, including work councilors elected or appointed under statutory provisions and representatives operating under voluntary arrangements established by employers (Frege, 2002; Kaufman and Taras, 2000). There has also been a growth of interest in identity-groups and social movement organizations that campaign on behalf of particular categories of employee, for example, women, lesbian, gay and bisexuals, migrants, the disabled or older workers (Fine, 2006; Piore and Safford, 2006). A similar trend is apparent on the employers' side. Here there has been a growth of interest in organizations that can be regarded as forming and expressing the collective interests of employers, including management consultants developing new practice, employment agencies and other labor market intermediaries, and organizations providing standards and inspection in the field of corporate social responsibility (Kuruvilla and Verma, 2006: 48–51; Logan, 2006; Osterman et al., 2001: 144–6).

IR research focused on actors deals with a broad range of substantive issues. If one considers the classic subject matter of trade unions then the following main areas of research can be identified:

1) the formation and reproduction of unions including trends in membership and the basis of union joining;
2) the internal structure and functioning of unions including union democracy, governance and management; ·
3) the external structure of unions including the nature of union 'job territories' (enterprise, occupation, industry or general) and the degree of integration of the national trade union movement;
4) union functions and areas of activity including direct service provision to members, collective bargaining and dispute handling, legal advocacy and political action;
5) union strategies particularly in the context of union decline and attempts of renewal; and
6) union effects on business, economy and society and their effectiveness in representing their members.

Equivalent lists can be compiled readily for other IR actors though perhaps in all cases the key distinction that can be drawn is between the organizational characteristics of any given actor and the nature of its intervention within the IR system; that is between structure and strategy. Thus, for employers IR researchers are interested in the degree of centralization or decentralization of the management hierarchy and its composition, with a particular interest

in the presence and power of specialist HR managers. But they are interested also in management strategies of labor use and the multiple initiatives pursued to secure the compliance of workers or their active commitment to employer goals (Purcell and Ahlstrand, 1994).

Processes

The second main focus of IR research is the processes through which the employment relationship is governed. Again according to Dunlop, it is common to define these processes in terms of rule-making or 'job regulation', with two primary types of rule being generated: substantive rules that specify the content of the employment relationship (wages, hours of work, methods of working, staffing levels, etc.) and procedural rules that govern the interaction and behavior of the parties (bargaining, consultation, information disclosure and dispute resolution). Both types of rule may be formal, inscribed in company policies, collective agreements or statutes, or informal, enshrined in customary expectations and relationships. The main way of classifying these regulatory processes is in terms of their authorship – which actor or combination of actors is the creator of rules. It is usual to distinguish unilateral regulation by employers (and less frequently) trade unions, joint regulation through collective bargaining, legal regulation by the state and tripartite regulation, in which government, employers and unions formulate 'social pacts' that govern the economy, including wage growth, welfare expenditure and employment (Hassel, 2006).

From this starting point theoretical and research work on IR processes has followed a number of avenues. One course has been to identify the component elements of each rule-making process; to break it down into its constituent elements. A classic venture of this kind was Clegg's (1976) identification of the structural components of national systems of collective bargaining, which varied in terms of bargaining coverage, level, depth, scope and degree of employer support for trade unions.

More recent contributions have identified the elements of other IR processes. Sisson and Marginson (2002), for example, have developed a framework that is similar to Clegg's for analyzing 'co-ordinated bargaining', the process through which discrete episodes of bargaining are linked in broader sectoral, national or, indeed, international systems of regulation.

A second development has been to identify separate forms of each process. Thus, with regard to legal regulation, it is common to distinguish 'hard' and 'soft' forms of regulation (Kuruvilla and Verma, 2006). The former consists of rights and employment standards established by statute and enforced both through application to courts and inspection by government agencies. The latter, in contrast, consists of opinions, advice, guidance, charters and codes of practice, which are issued by legislative bodies and intended to encourage the adoption of good practice but which are not reinforced by direct sanctions. Scholars have further refined this typology, identifying other forms of legal regulation. In the European Union (EU), for instance, there has been a growth of what has been labeled 'reflexive governance' (Barnard and Deakin, 2002), in which employers can derogate from legal standards and tailor regulations to their particular circumstances provided this occurs through consultation with employee representatives.

A third line of development has been to explore the relationship between different forms and the degree to which they supplant or complement one another. National economies contain multiple processes of job regulation with management decision, collective bargaining, legal regulation and the inclusion of social partners, business and worker representatives, in government policy-making existing alongside one another, applied variously to different issues, different segments of the workforce or different industrial sectors. The separate processes may reinforce one another, with particular regulations establishing boundaries and ensuring integration. Thus, collective agreements frequently contain 'management rights' clauses that specify those elements of the employment relationship that are subject to collective bargaining and those that are regulated through management decision (Sisson, 1987). A similar interface can be identified between collective bargaining and employment law. In Anglophone countries the prime function of the latter through much of the twentieth century was to serve as 'auxiliary legislation' (Davies and Freedland, 1993: 29), providing legal support for trade unions and collective bargaining rather than directly regulating the terms of the employment relationship. In Britain, auxiliary legislation famously took the form of 'statutory immunities', legal protection for trade unions from civil action under the common law if they organized industrial action that disrupted employers' business (Howell, 2005: 61–4, 149–50).

The decline of collective bargaining over the past two decades in many countries, however, has generated a fresh interest in the relationship between different forms of job regulation. It is asked with increasing frequency whether the rise of other forms is implicated in the decline of bargaining and researchers have focused on the interaction between joint regulation and both new forms of management regulation and the expanding volume of employment law. The central questions have been whether alternative regulatory processes supplant bargaining or whether collective bargaining and other forms can hybridize and support one another? Answers differ. For some writers the spread of human resource management and high-performance work systems poses a threat to joint regulation and is implicated in the de-unionization of industrial relations, essentially because it realigns worker and management interests and provides the basis for 'mutual gains' (Dickson et al., 1988; Fiorito, 2001). For others collective bargaining can support new work systems, union pressure serving to ensure that benefits are shared equitably between company and workforce and thereby helping to sustain innovation (Bacon and Blyton, 2006; Frost, 2001). A similar debate has emerged over the 'juridification' of the employment relationship, the growth of individual employment law. On the one hand, it is argued that individual rights diminish worker need for collective bargaining (Metcalf, 2005: 114), while on the other hand it is suggested that new law can support collective bargaining, the platform of rights providing minima above which collective agreements can build and the threat of union-sponsored legal action serving as a lever to open up negotiations (Heery and Conley, 2007). Whichever of these positions is correct, the relationship between new and old forms of job regulation has emerged as one of the central themes in current IR research.[2]

Outcomes

IR is also, indeed increasingly, concerned with assessing the outcomes of processes. The classic expression of this concern can be seen in the very substantial body of research exploring the relationship between trade union presence and collective bargaining and a broad range of economic, psychological and social phenomena. The latter include rates of productivity and profit, job satisfaction and organizational commitment and levels of income inequality (Turnbull, 2003). Although a well-established research theme, development continues with new datasets, new theories, and new research techniques adding to an established body of work (for example Belman and Voos, 2006; Fairris, 2006). Another area where outcomes research has blossomed in recent years is that concerned with the impact of HR practices on business performance. This work lies at the center of what Godard (2004a) has termed the 'high performance paradigm' within current IR research. Its distinguishing feature is the use of large datasets and econometric methods to establish a statistical relationship between measures of sophisticated human resource management, often expressed as the use of 'high performance work systems', and a variety of indicators of business performance (Wall and Wood, 2005; Whitfield and Poole, 1997). The broad aim is to validate employer

investment in the human resource and confirm that good management practice can have a bottom-line pay-off.

Research on outcomes within IR research has a number of dimensions. One marked feature is the emphasis on evaluating outcomes from the perspective of multiple stakeholders. Unlike other subjects taught in business schools, in IR there is no unreflexive adoption of the perspective of the employer and research on business outcomes sits alongside research on outcomes for workers and others. This is even apparent in the high-performance paradigm, where a notable development has been the growth of research on the effect of new work systems on employees, sometimes from a highly critical perspective that seeks to debunk the claim that all parties benefit from innovation (Thompson and Harley, 2007). In a related development researchers have also begun to apply ethical frameworks to employment issues, using normative criteria drawn from moral philosophy to judge IR outcomes (for example Budd, 2004; Guest, 2007; Legge, 2007). Another distinction that can be drawn in outcomes research relates to the issue of scale. A great deal of work is focused on the proximate effects of IR processes, such as the impact of work organization or union presence on job satisfaction. The distal effects of IR processes are also considered, however, and in a tradition that reaches back to the origins of the subject, there is a continuing interest in the contribution of IR to social integration and inclusion, the civilizing of the market order and the reproduction of liberal democracy (for example Adams, 1995; Estlund, 2003; Green, 2006). IR scholars are not just concerned with the minutiae of the workplace order, important though these are, but with the contribution of IR institutions to the making of a good society.

A final point to note about research on IR outcomes is that it is often comparative, in the sense that it seeks to evaluate the effects of *different* IR processes. Perhaps the clearest example today can be seen in the literature on gender equality. The outcomes of interest in this research include measures of pay inequality, vertical and horizontal job segregation and the degree to which employment systems remain predicated on a male 'norm' of continuous, full-time employment (Blau et al., 2006). Researchers are interested in the contribution to narrowing these indicators of inequality of management decision, persuaded by a 'business case' for equality, unions prioritizing the needs of women workers through 'equality bargaining' and equal opportunity and other bodies of employment law (Dickens, 1999). For each process, moreover, researchers have tried to identify the conditions under which it is more or less effective. Management policy may be more developed and significant where there is a professional HR function that includes equality specialists (Colling and Dickens, 1998; Hoque and Noon, 2004), bargaining may be more effective when it is centralized or where women occupy negotiating positions (Colling and Dickens, 1989; Hunter and Rimmer, 1995) and law may be more effective when it imposes obligations on employers not to discriminate, backed up by inspection (Dickens, 2007). Whatever the precise question, however, the key thing is that in research of this stamp the central concern is comparative, to evaluate competing routes to the achievement of desired IR outcomes.

Levels

Another feature of IR research is that it is conducted at different scales or levels, stretching from the workplace to the global and encompassing many points in-between (see Kochan et al., 1986: 15–20). Table 1.1 illustrates this range and identifies typical actors, processes and outcomes that are researched at each of four analytical levels. Thus, at the workplace or enterprise level, IR researchers have focused on workplace representation, bargaining and dispute-resolution and examined outputs such as productivity growth and innovation in working practices and work quality and employee well-being. At the meso-level, encompassing studies of particular industries, occupations or localities, researchers have examined industry and occupational unions, employers' associations and

industry or pattern bargaining. A particularly important branch of IR scholarship at this level has examined public sector industrial relations and the distinctive patterns of worker behavior and attitudes, union representation and employer policy within public service organizations (for example Bach et al., 1999). At the national level key actors have been national labor movements and union confederations, peak-level business organizations and state policies and institutions, with a pronounced emphasis in European IR research on the relationship between government and social partners (Teague, 2006; Traxler et al., 2002). Finally, and increasingly, IR research has focused on the supra-national level. There is an increasing volume of regional research examining the industrial relations of particular trading and political blocs, such as the EU and the North American Free Trade Area (NAFTA) and a growing body of work that examines IR at a global scale. The latter encompasses research on multi-national enterprises and their supply-chains, global trade unions and non-governmental organizations (NGOs) that campaign for workers' rights and the activities of international regulatory bodies, such as the International Labour Organization.

Throughout IR's history as a field of study each of these levels has attracted research and scholarship. At different points in the subject's development, however, certain levels have attracted particular attention. In the 1960s and 1970s, for example, often regarded as a golden age of IR scholarship in some countries, there was a pronounced focus on workplace studies (Ackers and Wilkinson, 2003a: 11). This was partly driven by the changing nature of the 'problem of order'. The growth of workplace militancy, often beyond the control of official union representatives, prompted a search for the origins of 'disorder' and for policy solutions that would more effectively regulate workplace relations (for example Maitland, 1983). In addition, however, there was a growing volume of left scholarship in IR that was attracted to the rank-and-file challenge and sought both to record and identify the potential for social change of the

Table 1.1 Levels of industrial relations analysis

Levels	Actors			Processes			Outcomes	
	Worker	Employer	State	Management decision	Joint decision	State regulation	Business and performance	Social and justice
Workplace and enterprise	Work groups, shop stewards and works councilors	Supervisory and general management; HR function	Inspectorates, mediators and labor courts adjudicating workplace disputes	HR policies and practices; employee involvement	Workplace and enterprise level bargaining; consultation and co-determination	Third party mediation and arbitration	Labor productivity; innovation and quality enhancement; financial performance	Work quality and employee well-being
Industry, occupation and locality	Industry and occupational unions; professional associations; living wage and other local coalitions	Employers' associations; consultancy firms and labor market intermediaries	Industry and occupational regulatory bodies; occupational licensing authorities	Public sector management; state as 'model' employer	Industry-level and pattern bargaining	Training, educational and economic development programmes	Diffusion of high performance practices within industry sectors	Impact of privatization and deregulation on labor standards
National economy	Union confederations; social movements addressing issues at work	Peak-level business organizations	National legislature, judiciary and regulatory bodies	National systems of corporate governance and their impact on labor management	Economy-wide bargaining and the coordination of bargaining outcomes across sectors	National systems of labor law and vocational education and training; social partnership and social pacts	IR institutions and national economic performance	Wage and income inequality; gender, race and other forms of identity-based inequality
Regional and global	Global unions and international union federations; European and global works councils; NGOs monitoring labor standards	International employers' associations; multinational enterprises	European Union and other supra-state institutions; International Labour Organization	Diffusion of management policies within MNEs; corporate social responsibility within supply chains	International framework agreements; international bargaining and consultation within MNEs	Creation and enforcement of international labor standards	Labor standards and economic development; varieties of capitalism and relative economic performance	Diffusion and effectiveness of global labor standards

wave of workplace militancy that erupted at the end of the 1960s (for example Beynon, 1984; Herding,1972). A feature of much of this work was a claim that workplace research possessed greater authenticity and generated a deeper insight into the nature of capitalist social relations. As such, it could be contrasted with an earlier tradition that focused on formal institutions erected above the workplace level – trade unions, employers' associations and industry-wide collective agreements and disputes procedures. As these institutions were challenged in the 1960s and 1970s so IR research switched focus and explored the source of that challenge at the point of production.

In the intervening period the focus of research has switched again and there has been a revival of work examining formal institutions, particularly at national level. As the long post-war boom faltered in the 1970s and as mass unemployment re-emerged, so academic attention switched to the forces shaping national economic performance. There was a growth of research on 'corporatism' and the systems of industrial relations in Northern Europe that co-ordinated wage bargaining and generated relatively low inflation and low unemployment (Goldthorpe, 1985). Although interest in corporatism has waned as the performance of once successful economies has faltered, the focus on national institutions of industrial relations has survived (Baccaro, 2003). This is most apparent in the 'varieties of capitalism' literature (Hall and Soskice, 1998) and its attempt to identify different types of national comparative advantage in a globalized economy. In this work a distinction is drawn between 'liberal market economies', such as the US, that excel at innovation and the development of new industries, and 'co-ordinated market economies', such as Germany and Japan, that dominate mature industries through incremental product and process development. In both types of economy, it is suggested, a complex of institutions embracing the financing and governance of industry, skill formation and wage bargaining reinforce one another and, in combination, underpin the trajectory of national economic

development. In this approach IR forms part of a broader comparative political economy that seeks to map and explain national sources of comparative advantage.

Another recent trend has been the growth of international IR research that examines the employment relationship on a regional or global scale. Much of this work is motivated by the threat to national systems of job regulation posed by globalization and the increasingly transnational scope of both product and labor markets. In the developed world there has been an export of jobs in manufacturing and an erosion of the position of trade unions as previously sheltered markets have been opened to competition. The result has been a policy interest in re-building or extending job regulation at an international level, which has generated academic research in its wake. There has been a growth of research on international unionism (Anner et al., 2006; Gordon and Turner, 2000), international collective bargaining (Lillie, 2006), the policies of multinational enterprises, including corporate codes of conduct on labor standards (Ferner et al., 2006; Tsogas, 2001: 61–85), and international regulatory bodies at regional and global levels (Marginson and Sisson, 2004; van Roozendaal, 2002). Like the research on gender equality described above, much of this work seeks to assess different ways of dealing with the same basic problem – establishing effective international labor standards that limit downward pressure on employment conditions from global competition.

The shifting focus of IR research, moving from different levels of analysis, as different types of 'labor problem' come into view, underlines the nature of IR as an applied, policy-oriented field (Ackers and Wilkinson, 2003a: 11; Hyman, 2004: 272). The research agenda for IR scholars has often been set by policy-makers or by the labor movement, seeking insight into pressing issues and help with institution building or reform. This is only one aspect of the field, however, IR research is also driven by an evolving theoretical impulse and the field contributes to the application, testing, refinement and development of social theory. It is to this aspect of IR that we now turn.

THEORY AND EXPLANATION

IR is commonly described as an academic field, rather than an academic discipline (for example Müller-Jentsch, 2004: 1). It has provided a territory that has been occupied by different core disciplines, which have entered, exerted influence and occasionally withdrawn to be replaced by rivals. One way of telling the theoretical story of IR therefore is to track the oscillating contribution of different core disciplines to the field. Indeed, in several recent collections the contribution to the study of the employment relationship of economics, psychology, sociology, law, geography and other subjects has been examined and assessed (Ackers and Wilkinson, 2003b; Coyle-Shapiro et al., 2004; Korczynski et al., 2006). Many scholars in the field, however, identify themselves as 'industrial-relationists' or as employment specialists who have long abandoned their home-discipline address (Adams, 1993: 128–31). A second way of telling IR's theoretical history, therefore, is to identify the theoretical positions that IR specialists have developed or made on their own, regardless of their disciplinary provenance. This option necessarily takes us to the ground of middle-range theory and an attempt to categorize the models that IR specialists have used to analyze trade unions, management strategy, state policy and other areas of substantive inquiry (for example Heery, 2003). Neither narrative strategy can be fully attempted here but at the risk of over-heroic generalization we examine some of the current disciplinary influences on IR and the main types of explanatory argument developed by its practitioners.

Disciplinary influences

The academic discipline that has exerted most influence over IR, at least in the US, is economics. The relationship of IR to economics is a complex one, however, with different traditions within economics having influence at different times. According to Kaufman (1993: 30–5; see also Adams, 1993: 122), a key role was played in the foundation of IR by heterodox economists who rejected the assumptions of neo-classical orthodoxy and favored instead realistic accounts and inductive theorizing of the institutions that regulated the labor market. This branch of institutional economics focused on the solution of practical 'labor problems' and was broadly sympathetic to trade unions and other regulatory institutions that tamed both employer power and market forces. In John R. Commons, Selig Perlman, John T. Dunlop, Clerk Kerr and others it provided key figures in the founding and development of the field (Kaufman, 1993: 84–91).

From the 1960s, however, the institutional tradition lost ground within labor economics and neo-classical orthodoxy reasserted itself. The focus of labor economics switched from the analysis of labor problems to the analysis of the labor market with an associated methodological turn toward deductive theorizing and the statistical testing of models using secondary datasets. The earlier sympathy with the regulation of management and market diminished (Kaufman, 1993: 121–5). It is economics on this conventional model that now exerts influence over IR. Particularly in the US, IR journals are replete with articles based on conventional neo-classical assumptions that examine core issues within the field (Kaufman, 2004b: 365; see also Machin, 2006; Turnbull, 2003). *Inter alia* these include the economic effects of trade unions, the impact of minimum wage regulation on earnings and employment, the gender pay gap, the causes of rising income inequality and the basis of investment decisions in training and the returns to employers and employees. In a recent development economists have also begun to enter territory once occupied by psychologists, undertaking research on job satisfaction and the determinants of work quality (for example Clark, 2005; Green and Tsitisanis, 2005).

While economics is probably the strongest disciplinary influence in IR it is not the only one and aspects of the field continue to be shaped by sociology, psychology, law, political studies and history. These non-economics influences are particularly apparent outside the US (Frege, 2005: 186–8). Other disciplines continue to be added to the list. Corporate strategy and other applied fields based alongside IR in business schools now exert influence (for example Bacon et al., 2004; Purcell and Ahlstrand, 1994) while there has been a recent surge of interest in social geography and the analysis of the spatial dimension of employment relations (Ellem, 2002; Rainnie et al., 2007; Turnbull, 2006).

It is not possible for us to trace these diverse influences and show how they have added to IR theory. What we can do, however, is demonstrate the continuing shaping of the field by outside disciplines in two particular areas. The first is the body of theory developed by political scientists and sociologists, which is variously labeled 'contentious politics' or 'social movement theory' (McAdam et al., 1996; McAdam et al., 2001; Tarrow, 1998). The purpose of this field is to understand and account for the origins of social movements, their development and degree of success in challenging political elites. Among the core propositions developed by scholars in this tradition are the following:

1) that social movements arise in response to a 'political opportunity structure', often characterized by a division within the elite that reduces state capacity for repression and allows movements to form alliances with alienated elite politicians;
2) while movements have a spontaneous element and emerge in deeply held grievances they rely also on a 'mobilizing structure', an organizational framework comprised of 'movement entrepreneurs', activists and networks that builds collective action amongst supporters;
3) the work of mobilization has a discursive component and movement leaders develop ideological 'frames' that legitimate grievances, attribute them to an oppressor and articulate means of redress;
4) movements often develop distinctive 'repertoires of contention'; that is forms of mobilization and

protest that embrace both the exertion of power against opponents (for example strikes, boycotts, riots, harassment, media scrutiny) and the use of symbols that generate emotional attachment to the movement among its adherents (for example street theatre, costumes, songs, graffiti).

This set of ideas has begun to influence IR scholars, with a key bridge being supplied by Kelly's (1998) landmark book on IR theory, *Rethinking Industrial Relations: Mobilization, Collectivism and Long Waves*. Kelly used what he termed 'mobilization theory' to analyze a broad set of developments in British industrial relations and others have followed in his wake. The social movement framework has been applied to studies of union organizing, union participation, employer counter-mobilization and the changing internal politics of trade unions (for example Badigannavar and Kelly, 2004; Brown Johnson and Jarley, 2004; Foley, 2003; Heery and Conley, 2007). It has been used to revitalize the study of workers' collective action and to move beyond the stale opposition between rank-and-file and bureaucracy that for so long has underpinned analysis of unions on the radical wing of IR scholarship.

The second influence lies in the field of 'political economy' or 'socio-economics'. This is a field developed by a new wave of institutional economists, political scientists and economic sociologists that is concerned with the institutional 'embeddedness' of capitalist economies. Central themes include the formation and shaping of markets by state and other institutions and the plasticity of the capitalist economy, which assumes a wide variety of forms across and within nation states and which generates highly variable outcomes (Coates, 2005). The Varieties of Capitalism school, described above, is one expression of this literature, which has attracted particular attention within IR (for example Godard, 2004b). A line of research that has emerged under this influence has focused on the relationship between IR actors, processes and outcomes and other (varying) institutions of the capitalist economy, including modes of finance, corporate governance and different types of business enterprise. The link between forms of governance and IR has been a particular focus of research (for example Armour et al., 2003; Gospel and Pendleton, 2005; Konzelmann et al., 2006). Work of this kind updates the classic interest of IR scholars in the institutions of the labor market but links it to a broader resurgence of comparative political economy across several social science disciplines.

Explanatory models

The other way of looking at IR theory is to identify themes in the substantive, middle-range theories scholars use to account for IR phenomena. Of course, a colossal amount of theory of this kind has been accumulated over the decades. Nevertheless, we feel that this can be sorted into different types of explanatory model without doing excessive violence to the diversity of the subject and below identify four of these. These are: 1) societal models that account for IR developments in terms of adaptation to long-run social and economic change; 2) institutional models that offer explanations grounded in the structural characteristics of the IR system itself or the broader configuration of the national political economy; 3) organizational models that explain the behavior (strategy) of IR actors in terms of their organizational characteristics (structure); and 4) agency models that develop typologies of IR strategy and explore the identities of agents who promote them (see Heery et al., 2004).

Societal

There is a long tradition in IR of explaining the behavior of actors and shifting processes and outcomes as an adaptation to long-run change in economy and society. Causal variables identified in this tradition range from technical change, the globalization of product markets and the feminization of the workforce to less tangible developments such as the emergence of a more reflexive, individualistic population. It is also common to identify discrete stages of development in the evolution of capitalist societies with each calling forth a set of matching IR institutions and practices. The current stage of capitalist development has been variously labeled, 'post-industrial', 'post-Fordist', 'neo-Fordist', 'the network society', 'disorganized capitalism' and an age of 'flexible specialization'. Assessments of its implications for IR diverge sharply. From one perspective, the diffusion of new high-performance practices presents an opportunity to recast IR on a more co-operative basis within the 'mutual gains enterprise' (Kochan and Osterman, 1994). From another, the latest stage of capitalist development threatens many of the achievements secured by working people in the twentieth century and the function of IR is to retard its evolution or mitigate its worst effects. A group of American writers has argued that the defining feature of 'post-industrialism' is the emergence of a more market-based system of employment relations, characterized by the hollowing out of large corporations, sub-contracting, the erosion of internal labor markets, the growth of contingent labor, de-unionization, rising income inequality and the collapse of employment standards (for example Cobble, 1991; Fine, 2006; Milkman, 2006).[3] Faced with this challenge, it is believed there is a need to develop new institutions to re-regulate the labor market and take wages out of competition. Accordingly, researchers have examined emerging practices, such as living wage ordinances, community-based movements of low-wage workers and labor-market organizing by trade unions, seeking to identify their potential to diffuse and contribute to a broader regulation of the new economy.

Institutional

A second form of explanation stresses the role of institutional structures in shaping the behavior of IR actors and the outcomes of IR processes. A classic statement of this argument was Clegg's (1976) comparative analysis of trade unions, which claimed that forms of union organization and patterns of activity, including internal democracy and involvement in industrial conflict, were determined primarily by the structure of collective bargaining. Contemporary analysts of trade unions continue to make this type of argument, the best known example of which is Fairbrother's (1996) union renewal thesis with its claim that the decentralization of bargaining can prompt the revitalization of workplace unionism. Another example can be seen in comparative research on the gender pay gap, which indicates that progress in narrowing the gap between female and male earnings is a function of industry-wide pay bargaining and relatively strong minimum wage regulations (Almond and Rubery, 1998). These examples focus on the relationship between the structure of IR processes and patterns of actor behavior and outcomes. Other theoretical explanations focus on institutional structures beyond IR narrowly conceived. This is a feature of both of the new disciplinary influences outlined above. Those influenced by social movement theory, for instance, emphasize the role of broader political structures – the political opportunity structure – in channeling union behavior (Turnbull, 2006); those influenced by the Varieties of Capitalism school identify a causal link between union strategies and the institutional constraints imposed respectively by liberal- and co-ordinated-market economies (Frege and Kelly, 2004: 37–9). As these examples indicate, institutional models are frequently comparative, identifying differences in actor behavior and outcomes across national boundaries and explaining these in terms of distinctive national, institutional contexts. Unlike societal models, which stress broad, underlying causes that are universal in their effects (at least across developed societies), institutional models stress contingency and (particularly cross-national) variation.

Organizational

In the third type of model the central interest lies in the causal relationship between the organizational structure of IR actors

and their patterns of behavior and effects. A classic illustration can be seen in the long-standing interest in the relationship between trade union democracy (and trade union oligarchy) and forms of union activity and effectiveness. Concern with this relationship continues to feature strongly in research on trade unions. An example can be seen in the examination of the link between union attempts to promote the interests of women and minorities – believed by many to be a precondition for union revitalization – and the reform of union governance structures to allow for gender democracy and the clearer expression of minority interests. There is a growing body of research on this linkage with different positions being adopted. In some contributions new democratic institutions within unions, such as women's committees and self-organized groups, remain marginalized and exert little influence over union bargaining and political activity (McBride, 2001). In others their effectiveness in pushing significant changes in union policy, which in turn have fed through into legal change and new collective agreements, is accepted (Heery and Conley, 2007). The same type of analysis, linking organizational characteristics to patterns of action, can be seen in research on IR actors besides unions. Thus, in research on management there is an interest in the influence of business structure and internal planning and control procedures on the content of IR policies. The trend toward the decentralization of collective bargaining in large, multi-divisional enterprises has been explained by the spread of new financial controls over operating divisions, in which corporate office monitors performance through financial ratios while conceding autonomy over operational matters, including pay determination, to business unit managers (Purcell and Ahlstrand, 1994: 75–7). Another example can be seen in the theory of corporatism, where it has long been argued that the capacity of states to develop effective tripartite regulation of the economy depends on the presence of strong, centralized and encompassing peak organizations of business and labor (Baccaro, 2003). Whichever actor is considered, however, the common feature of this type of model remains the same; patterns of activity and their effects within the IR system are dependent on a particular form of organization being adopted – strategy flows from structure.

Agency

The final type of model departs from the structural argument common to the other three and is voluntarist in its assumptions, holding that IR actors have scope for strategic choice (Kochan et al., 1986: 3–20). Choice is exercised within constraints but is not reducible to an external and structured context. For adherents of this position, indeed, strategic choices themselves shape organizational and wider institutional structures. Theory development within this strategic choice tradition has followed two broad avenues. The first has led to the elaboration of typologies of strategy; a listing of the options available to strategic actors. There are many, many examples developed for all of the main IR actors. Thus, Boxall and Haynes (1997) commenting on the renewal strategies of New Zealand trade unions identify two underpinning, dimensions of choice. Unions can adopt an adversarial or co-operative stance toward employers and an organizing or servicing approach to members. From this starting point a menu of four strategic options can be identified: 'classic unionism' (adversarialism plus organizing); 'partnership unionism' (cooperation plus organizing); 'paper-tiger unionism' (adversarialism plus servicing) and 'consultancy unionism' (cooperation plus servicing). A well-known equivalent for employers is Guest and Conway's (1999) typology of management strategy that rests on the extent to which unions are accepted and recognized and the degree to which managers follow a sophisticated, high commitment approach to HRM. Once again four options are identified: 'the new realism' (sophisticated HRM plus union recognition); 'traditional collectivism' (union recognition with traditional HR practices); 'individualized HRM' (non-union with sophisticated HRM)

and 'the black hole' (non-union with poor HR practice).

The second avenue leads to an examination of choice-makers and choice-making. Explanation here is directed both at the identities of those leading organizations and deciding strategy and at the internal political and discursive practices that lead to the selection and legitimization of a particular strategic choice. The focus on choice-makers is most readily apparent in research on trade unions, where there is a wealth of material that explains patterns of union activity in terms of the gender, generation or ideological stamp of union leaders and activists (see Heery, 2003: 290–5). There has been a particular emphasis on gender, with the feminization of union policy and the recreation of union democratic and management structures to better represent diversity, being seen as dependent on the prior mobilization of feminist activists within unions (Ledwith and Colgan, 2002). Equivalent work on the employer side is perhaps less developed though analogous explanations can be found. They exist, for instance, in attempts to explain company cultures in terms of the imprint of charismatic founding fathers or mothers, whether Victorian Quakers or New Age entrepreneurs, like Anita Roddick of Body Shop, contriving a deliberate informality and seeking employee commitment to ethical standards (Purcell and Sisson, 1983: 116–7). They can also be seen in attempts to explain variation in HRM within multi-nationals through a parent-country effect; that HR is shaped by the transfer of a distinctive corporate identity from one national culture to another (Gunnigle et al., 2006).

Theories that focus on choice-making allocate a central part to the (frequently conflictual) social processes through which strategic choices are made. In a study of the emergence of social pacts in Ireland, Italy and South Korea, for example, Baccaro and Lim (2007) noted that the outcome of a fierce dispute between moderates and more radical elements in the labor movement was a crucial stage in each process. Decisive victories for the moderate, partnership wing ensured the development of pacts in Ireland and Italy, while a radical victory in South Korea led to the pact's instability. There are numerous other examples. To take one, Ledwith and Colgan (2002: 16–18) identify a key stage of 'usurpation' in the feminization of unions, through which new activists challenge and overcome the resistance of the incumbent, male-dominated elite. There is also an element in this body of work that emphasizes discursive practice and the deployment of legitimizing frames for new strategic choices. Thus, Heery and Conley's (2007) study of union policy on part-time work in the UK, stresses the significance of distinct 'instrumental' and 'solidarity' frames in garnering support for new policy and rendering opposition non-legitimate.

The four types of explanation we have identified are in certain respects competing. They offer different accounts of IR phenomena and many empirical studies in IR seek to weigh the explanatory power of different structural explanations – societal, institutional and organizational – or the relative strength of structural and strategic choice perspectives. An example of this type of contest can be seen in the different explanations put forward of a widespread IR trend, the decentralization of collective bargaining to enterprise and workplace levels. On the one hand, this has been explained, as we have seen, as an artifact of the diffusion of new financial control systems within the management hierarchies of multidivisional firms – an organizational account. On the other hand, it has been explained as an adjustment within IR to the diffusion of more flexible forms of production that require tailor-made, plant-specific systems of job regulation – a societal account (Katz, 1993). If pushed to their extreme, neither of these explanations can accommodate the other and much routine academic work within IR involves assembling evidence to choose between seemingly equally plausible explanatory models.

If extremes are avoided, however, then the different types of explanation can be combined; assembled in a complex, multifactor model. This is also a common development within IR theory. Again, we can provide a single illustrative case. Baccaro and Lim's (2007) full explanatory model for the emergence of social pacts combines different types of explanation. The search for a pact typically originates in a broad economic and social crisis, reflects a particular institutional context defined by a weak government that needs allies to develop a response to crisis, and depends on a strategic choice to co-operate within the labor movement which, in turn, is the outcome of a choice-making conflict between moderates and radicals. The latter also has an organizational dimension and Baccaro and Lim (2007) emphasize the importance of balloting procedures in both Ireland and Italy in registering union-member support for social pacts and isolating the opposition. Finally, social pacts become institutionalized if there is a subsequent buy-in by employers, which depends on the authority of employers' confederations (organizational), political opportunities to shape pacts (institutional) and calculations of strategic advantage amongst different employer groups (strategic choice). The supporting conditions, Baccaro and Lim (2007) note, were fully in place only in Ireland and it is in this single case that the social pact has been institutionalized and become an enduring feature of the IR system – in the other two cases the experiment faltered albeit after a period of success in Italy.[4] The essential point, however, is that a complex, abstract model, combining different types of explanation, has been devised to account for a significant IR development.

NORMATIVE ORIENTATION

The dominant normative orientation amongst IR scholars is one of pluralism. This 'frame of reference' comprises core beliefs about the nature of the employment relationship, which provide a standard for evaluating IR practice and serve as a guide to developing policy advice, an essential component of an applied field. At the heart of the pluralist position is a conviction that the employment relationship embraces two equally legitimate sets of interests, those of employers and those of employees. It is further believed that, while these interests are congruent in very large degree, there is an irreducible core of conflict. A preparedness to acknowledge conflicting interests at work and accept that the expression of conflict is not a pathological symptom has been held to be a defining feature of IR (Kochan, 1998: 37–9). A third core belief of pluralists is that there is an imbalance of power within the employment relationship and that the dependence of workers on employers for the means of subsistence places them in a vulnerable position. A fourth belief follows; that workers have the right to combine in trade unions and other types of collectivity in order to accumulate power, provide a counterweight to the otherwise dominant position of the employer and pursue their separate, legitimate interests (Budd, 2004: 26). The final component of the pluralist position is a conviction that collective organization by employees and the creation of a pluralist IR system based on trade unionism, collective bargaining and the regulation of conflict serves not only the interests of employees but can also serve a wider, general or public interest. The classic expression of this belief in the twentieth century was the claim that the IR system was functional for the wider society, addressing the 'labor problem' and successfully integrating the working population into liberal democratic societies (Budd, 2004: 4).

Several features of IR flow from this pluralist conception of the employment relationship. One is that the research agenda has often focused on the experiences, concerns and needs of workers and their institutions and has not slavishly reflected the interests of employers. This aspect of IR, moreover, has persisted despite the fact that most of the field's members now work in business schools. Research on the quality of work experienced by individual employees (for example Barley and Kunda, 2004; Green, 2006) or exploring the revitalization strategies of unions (for example Wheeler, 2002) is testament to the continuing vitality of the pluralist tradition. Another feature is that a considerable body of IR research is critical of employers and their practices, identifying unethical, exploitative, oppressive and inefficient aspects of management practice, particularly in a context of light regulation or non-unionism. Sisson's (1993: 207) judgement on the non-union workplace in Britain as something of a 'bleak house' is indicative of a much wider orientation amongst IR scholars.[5] There is little faith in employers' capacity to manage the employment system for the benefit of multiple stakeholders and IR commentators frequently identify market failures that arise from employers pursuing sectional or short-term interests. Partly for this reason there is broad acceptance of the need for intervention in both the market order and the order of management control within firms. IR pluralists have a bias toward regulation of employer behavior through law but also through collective representation of workers and the joint regulation of the employment relationship.

The classic policy position adopted by IR pluralists, therefore, has been support for collective bargaining and the associated auxiliary legislation that can underpin it (Ackers, 2007). The main qualification to this position has occurred when pluralists have identified a tension between collective organization and a putative general interest; a tension that was particularly apparent in the long period of full-employment and relatively strong trade unionism after the Second World War. Pluralists have accepted constraints on collective action by employees to minimize general economic costs (for example restricting collective bargaining to reduce inflationary wage pressure) or preserve state functions and sovereignty (for example restricting strikes in essential services). Indeed, much policy ink has been spilt designing IR systems that retain collective organization by employees while reducing dysfunctional effects for the wider society. For much of the second half of the twentieth century IR pluralists were quintessential reformists, seeking to update and eliminate the flaws from established IR institutions founded on collective bargaining.

Challenge and critique

While pluralism has been the dominant orientation, it has not gone unchallenged. This challenge has been threefold and has come from Marxism, feminism and neo-liberalism. In each case, it should be noted, the critique has been fundamental in that it has targeted the core beliefs of IR pluralists and offered a different interpretation of interests within the employment relationship. The main elements of this three-headed critique are as follows.

Marxism

Marxism shares pluralism's focus on the dyadic relationship between employers and employees and a belief that interests are separate and conflicting, but it differs in one fundamental aspect. For Marxists there is only one set of *legitimate* interests, those of workers. Thus, in Kelly's (1998: 4–15) attempt to recast the field of IR around mobilization theory the starting point are the interests of workers, with main themes being the accumulation of power resources by workers and the strategies of counter-mobilization adopted by state and employers in response. The other distinctive feature of the Marxist normative position is a belief that workers' fundamental interest lies in challenging and overturning the capitalist mode of production. Two orientations flow from this belief. On the one hand, there is criticism of institutions that stabilize the economic order and integrate the working population into society. Unlike pluralists, Marxists do not believe that a 'balance is best' (Budd et al., 2004) and are typically highly critical of the regulatory institutions of capitalist societies that channel industrial conflict into compromise solutions while leaving the broader configuration of the economy unchanged (Hyman, 1975). Thus, since Lenin, Marxists have sharply criticized trade unionism, recognizing it as an expression of worker rebellion against capital but decrying its limited goals. On the other hand, there is a celebration of industrial conflict (Darlington and Lyddon, 2001) and a continual searching for new points of challenge to capital beyond the established institutions of IR. The policy prescription for Marxists is typically one of militancy and support for rank-and-file movements that promise the renewal of trade unionism from below (Darlington, 1994; Fairbrother, 2000). The challenge to pluralist IR from Marxists has diminished somewhat as Marxism has lost influence generally in the social sciences since the 1980s. The division between pluralists and Marxists is still an active front, however, and continues to structure debate in IR. It is a particularly notable feature of the field in Britain with pluralists and Marxists offering competing interpretations of contemporary phenomena, such as the vogue for labor-management partnership agreements (cf. Samuel, 2005; Tailby et al., 2004) or the record of the Labour Government elected in 1997 (cf. Brown, 2000; Smith and Morton, 2006).

Feminism

The distinctive feature of the feminist critique is that it has not accepted the dyadic relationship between employer and employee as a satisfactory basis for the subject. In particular, it is argued that a focus on the gender-neutral category of 'worker' obscures the fact that the employment relationship is profoundly gendered and that the experiences of men and women employees are divergent and their interests often conflicting.[6] Accordingly, the separate and gendered interests of male and female workers must be acknowledged and incorporated within the core research and normative concerns of IR scholars. However, feminist commentators have also problematized the category of 'women' and noted that 'multiple "women" exist' (Pocock, 1997a: 3), as a consequence of the 'intersectionality' of gender and other forms of social identity (Holgate et al., 2006: 310). A critique that started with a call to acknowledge distinct gender interests, therefore, has progressed to encompass diversity of interests based in multiple identities: race, ethnicity, faith, age, disability and sexuality.[7] All of these must now receive their due recognition within IR scholarship.

An extensive research agenda has developed from this attempt to reorient the subject toward gender and minority interests. One course has been to map and seek explanations of patterns of inequality at work. In many cases this has focused on the strategies used by men to maintain the subordination of women; whether male workers seeking to monopolize skilled trades, male-dominated unions prioritizing a traditional bargaining agenda or male employers designing low-skilled, part-time jobs for women workers (for example Beechey and Perkins, 1987; Cockburn, 1983; Colling and Dickens, 1989). A second course has been to broaden the subject matter of IR in two distinct ways. On the one hand, feminist researchers have noted that the gendered employment contracts of men and women reflect a prior 'sexual contract' and rest on an unequal domestic division of labor (Wacjman, 2000: 193–5). This has encouraged work on the interrelationship of the domestic sphere and forms and experiences of paid work, a theme that has been given added impetus by public policy interest in the issue of work-life integration. On the other hand, there has been a drive to examine questions of sexuality and emotion at work that has encompassed research on the design of jobs to incorporate emotional and sexual display and the issue of sexual harassment (Forrest, 1993: 424; Wacjman, 2000: 192–3).

A third theme in feminist IR research has been to uncover women's resistance to oppression at work; to rediscover events, actors and movements that have been 'hidden from history' and neglected systematically by a male-dominated field (Forrest, 1993: 416). This concern has generated a substantial volume of work on women's trade unionism, which has emerged as a major theme in IR research in recent years (for example Briskin and McDermott, 1993; Cobble, 1993; Colgan and Ledwith, 2002; Pocock, 1997b). A fourth main area of research identified by feminist IR scholars is the evaluation of equality and diversity policies developed by states, unions and employers. Much of this work is highly critical, pointing to the persistence of gender inequality at work and

the superficial character of policies to deal with it. Nevertheless, a body of work has been accumulated that can inform evidence-based policy-making. This work points to the conditions under which employment law, collective bargaining and management policy are more or less likely to contribute to the narrowing of workplace inequality (for example Grimshaw and Rubery, 2001).

A characteristic that feminist IR scholars share with the pluralist mainstream is a belief in the need for law and collective bargaining to shape the behavior of employers. There is often a deep skepticism about the potential for employer policy to secure significant advancement toward equality, which is expressed in a critique of the 'business case' for equal opportunities and the 'diversity management' programs to which it gives rise (Kirton and Green, 2000). Effective external regulation (and the mobilization of women and minority groups themselves against employers), are deemed necessary because business pressures to eliminate inequality will only be felt by a proportion of employers. The ugly fact motivating much feminist comment on IR policy is that many employers gain from unequal treatment and consequently cannot be relied upon to act as agents for social justice. Partly for this reason the main feminist orientation to policy stresses the continual strengthening of legal regulation in particular to make it more exacting from the employers' perspective. An international manifestation of this orientation is the pressure to rewrite equality law so that it not only confers rights not to suffer discrimination but imposes a positive duty on employers to provide for equality at work (McColgan, 1994).

Feminist commentators differ in their evaluation of trade unions but there is a strong current of belief that 'social regulation' through unions and collective bargaining can supplement law and indeed ensure that it is more effectively 'mediated' at workplace level (Dickens, 1999). The policy advocated for unions is twofold. On the one hand, it is suggested that there must be more effective 'external' representation of women and minorities by unions through the development of 'equality bargaining' (Colling and Dickens, 1989); that is through the incorporation of issues of discrimination, equality and diversity into the routine representative work of unions. On the other hand, it is argued that there must be more effective 'internal' representation of women and minorities through the reform of union government systems to ensure that their interests gain expression. Each type of reform can reinforce the other and both are deemed essential (Bercusson and Dickens, 1996).

Calls for legal and union-based regulation have to do with the means to ends – how the cause of equality can be advanced. Feminist IR scholars have also written extensively on the objectives of policy. Several themes stand out from this work. Perhaps the most fundamental is the need for policy to extend beyond mere equality of opportunity and secure equality of outcome, if needs be through positive/reverse discrimination. A second theme derives from the identification of the separate and distinct interests of women and minorities, the corollary of which is the need to tailor work and employment systems and surrounding regulations to accommodate this diversity (for example Baird, 2006). While feminists have developed a critique of 'diversity management', there is nevertheless a common policy emphasis on difference and the need to develop flexible systems of employment that accommodate the distinct interests of women and minorities(Dickens, 2005: 201–3).[8] A third theme extends beyond the world of work and targets the domestic sphere through policies that socialize childcare and either encourage or require men to assume a greater domestic workload (for example through state paternity and family leave policies). As the origins of workplace inequality have been located in a broader 'sexual contract', so IR policy has leaned toward social and family policy and sought to reconstruct domestic as well as workplace relations. This, in turn, reflects an abiding theme of feminist IR scholarship; in both its analysis and in its normative stance it has extended the scope of the subject and tried to erase the lines that separate IR from adjacent fields of (gendered) social life.

Neo-liberalism

The third challenge to pluralist orthodoxy has come from the neo-liberal right and although its proponents constitute only a tiny minority of IR scholars the ideas they expound reflect major themes in recent public policy in the US, Britain, Australia, New Zealand and other countries. In certain respects this normative orientation is the mirror image of Marxism, choosing to privilege the interests of employers rather than labor. This is not fully the case, however. Neo-liberals accept that employees have legitimate interests that they inevitably will pursue but suggest that inefficiencies will result and the interests of consumers suffer, if they are not restrained by a combination of competitive markets and management hierarchy. Competition and control, from this perspective, are the necessary disciplines that must keep 'producer' interests in check. It follows that, regulatory institutions which inhibit competition or which restrict the operation of management hierarchies are inevitably viewed with suspicion, if not hostility. The actions of the state in regulating the labor market and of trade unions in raising wages and challenging management prerogative have been particular targets. The same institutions that are seen to offer solutions to labor market problems in pluralist analysis are viewed as the source of problems by neo-liberals.

Following Hirschman (1991), we can identify the main types of argument that neo-liberals have mounted against pluralist industrial relations. One response has been to question the severity of the social problems that are the target of regulatory intervention by pluralists. Thus, it has been suggested that there is less need for unions to redress the power imbalance in the employment relationship when second jobs, self-employment and the ownership of shares and other private property render workers less dependent on wages earned from a single employer (Hanson and Mather,

1988: 36). An equivalent argument made against minimum wage legislation is to point to the fact that many low-wage workers live in multi-income households and so are not solely dependent on their own income. A second response, labeled the 'futility thesis' by Hirschman (1991), questions the capacity of regulation to moderate market outcomes, at least in the longer term. Examples of the futility thesis include the claim that minimum wage laws simply displace employment into the informal sector or Troy's (1999: 24) argument that union pattern-bargaining can never truly 'take wages out of competition' and simply displaces employment into the non-union economy. A third response, the 'perversity thesis', states that regulation rebounds against the very group it is intended to help, in most versions of the argument by destroying the jobs of unionized workers or those protected by legal regulation. To quote from Troy (2004: 70), '...high Franco-German unemployment, lower productivity, downsizing, and the export of production to other countries...can be traced to an important extent, to the works councils (and unionism) that [pluralists] extol and urge [the USA] to impose on its own workplaces'. The final argument, the 'jeopardy thesis', submits that regulation destroys other desirable states, such as national competitiveness. To quote once more from Troy (2004: 72) the effect of strong trade unions in the American school system is to raise the costs of education and impose 'externalities', including 'uneducated children who are ill-equipped to compete in America's labor markets...' For Troy, as for many neo-liberals, the effect of unionism is to create low quality and inefficiency by imposing work rules on managers that elevate producer interests above those of the consumers of goods and services.

The prescription which flows from this analysis is for the deregulation of industrial relations. Neo-liberals routinely call for the withdrawal or weakening of legislation that interferes with market forces or inhibits the capacity of managers to respond to market signals. Where regulation is unavoidable, as is the case in the UK required to implement European social policy directives, there is a preference for 'soft law' or other, relatively weak forms of regulation. Employment legislation is continually weighed in the balance to identify potential costs and dysfunctional consequences. An even closer scrutiny has been directed at regulation stemming from trade unions and collective bargaining (Minford, 1985) and the weakening of union capacity to regulate labor markets has been a notable feature of jurisdictions where neo-liberalism has shaped public policy. The long catalogue of anti-union reform in Britain under Margaret Thatcher in the 1980s or the more recent Work Choices policy of John Howard's government in Australia, provide examples. For some neo-liberal commentators the only legitimate role for trade unions is in providing labor market services to their members; that is in helping the labor market to operate more efficiently through the provision of skills and information (Roberts, 1987; Shenfield 1986).

If deregulation is the negative side of neo-liberal prescription for industrial relations, what is the positive element? Perhaps the clearest neo-liberal agenda for reconstructing work relations focuses on the use of financial incentives to alleviate principal-agent problems and re-align the interests of shareholders, managers and employees. Thus, one of the reasons Troy inveighs against the actions of educational unions in the US is because of their opposition to incentive and merit pay. Many neo-liberals have a particular enthusiasm for profit-sharing and employee share-ownership (for example Bell and Hanson, 1987) and the diffusion of neo-liberal ideas has been accompanied by an international trend to promote worker shareholding through tax incentives and other policy instruments (see Vaughan-Whitehead, 1995). The objective of re-aligning worker and employer interests was cogently expressed by the late President Reagan, 'Could there be a better answer to the stupidity of Karl Marx than millions of workers individually sharing in the means of production?' (quoted in Bradley and Gelb, 1986: 22).

Pluralist responses

Notwithstanding the challenge from Marxism, feminism and neo-liberalism, pluralism remains the dominant normative orientation within academic IR. The mainstream has stretched to accommodate aspects of each critique, however, and many recent developments in the field have emerged from the tension between pluralism and its opponents.

The classic pluralist response to the Marxist challenge has been to point to the effectiveness of IR reform in civilizing the market order, both in a material sense of raising workers' living standards and in a procedural sense of protecting workers from arbitrary treatment and importing due process into the employment relationship. Thus, Flanders (1970) defending UK unions in the 1960s from the Marxist charge of economism, declared that, 'by doggedly sticking to their immediate ends and refusing to be captured and exploited by any political party, they have gradually transformed society'. This search for evidence of reform, and for the capacity of capitalist economies to undergo significant reform, continues within the pluralist tradition. Its clearest contemporary expression can be seen in the attraction of many IR scholars to the Varieties of Capitalism literature. Particularly for IR pluralists in Anglophone countries, evidence of sustainable alternative forms of capitalism, which are more receptive to the interests of workers or which foster less adversarial relations between managers and employees, is deeply appealing (for example Adams, 1995). In recent years the labor market institutions of 'coordinated market economies' have served as a menu for Anglophone IR reformists, a new set of recipes for civilizing capitalism. German works councils, in particular, have been identified as an institution that can provide a model for reform, helping to create 'the mutual gains enterprise' in the USA and other 'liberal market economies' (Kochan and Osterman, 1994: 204–207).[9]

The response to feminism has been more accommodating and, as some feminist critics of mainstream IR acknowledge, there has been greater recognition of gender and the issue of equality in textbooks and research literature (Healy et al., 2006). IR may still lag behind other fields of social inquiry in drawing from feminist theory and the accommodation may be limited (and largely ignore the gendered experience of men) but a shift has occurred. There remains a line of division, however, that has recently been sketched by Edwards (2003: 28–30). He makes two key points. The first is that the field of IR will lose its coherence if it extends too far beyond the employment relationship to embrace the domestic sphere and the wider cultural expression of gender relations. Edwards likens the walls of the workplace to a 'semi-permeable membrane', which 'filters influences from outside and also shapes how processes within the workplace affect relations elsewhere'. Clearly relations at work are shaped by forces beyond, including the sexual division of labor within the home, but they are not reducible to them and for this reason the proper focus of IR scholarship should remain the employment relationship. The second point is that the extent to which institutions involved in regulating the workplace are gendered is a matter of degree and to be established by empirical research. Edwards is at pains to concede that the use of gender-neutral categories by IR academics has often shielded important features of working life from inquiry, but holds that their use may be legitimate in particular circumstances. A related theme has recently appeared in empirical work asking if gender is of 'declining significance'; that is, if sex differences are becoming less apparent in the distribution of earnings and other indicators of workers' experiences (Blau et al., 2006).

If many pluralists have wanted to accommodate a feminist perspective, the typical response to neo-liberalism has been defensive, striving to rebut elements of the neo-liberal attack. One important service discharged by pluralist IR researchers has been to disprove the wilder claims of free marketers that protective regulation of the labor market generates perverse and other effects. For example, a series of careful studies of the UK's cautious experiment with minimum wage regulation in recent years have shown little evidence of significant job losses (Dickens and Manning, 2003). A more offensive position has been to develop 'business case' arguments in support of the regulatory institutions favored by pluralists. One of the earliest and best known examples of this type of argument was Freeman and Medoff's (1984: 162–80) defense of US trade unionism, particularly on the grounds that it stimulated higher productivity. Since then other researchers have trod the same path, using empirical data to make a positive case for trade unionism and employment law (for example Turnbull et al., 2004). At a theoretical level pluralists have also developed the concept of 'beneficial constraints', as a counterweight to the neo-liberal predilection for perversity (Streeck, 1997). Institutions that inhibit the market or management decision, it is suggested, promote long-term efficiency by shutting off the low-road to cost-minimization and encouraging managers to forge long-term, co-operative relations with employees. The final and most ambitious pluralist response has been not to accept but to transcend the standards of evaluation employed by neo-liberals. There has been a turn to ethical reasoning and the revival of social justice arguments as a basis for labor market regulation, independently of economic effects (Budd, 2004). While many pluralists have fought neo-liberals on their own ground, there is a growing trend to reach beyond their Gradgrind values to mount the case for decent conditions for working men and women.

THE STRUCTURE OF THE HANDBOOK

The themes, developments and issues outlined above are reflected in the chapters that follow. In the first part, the contributors provide an overview of the theoretical and ideological underpinnings of the field, its interconnections with other disciplines, links with developments taking place both within and outside the work organization and the questions these raise for optimum ways of studying contemporary industrial relations. In Chapter 2, Carola M. Frege considers the historical development of industrial relations research, examining to what extent the approach and focus of that research reflects particular national conditions. She highlights significant variation in the influence of particular disciplines in different countries (most notably the relative strengths of economic vs. sociological approaches to industrial relations) and the continuing influence of different academic structures, epistemological traditions and political discourses on the ways in which industrial relations research is pursued. The theme of the relationship of industrial relations to social science disciplines is developed further by Peter Ackers and Adrian Wilkinson in Chapter 3. They argue the case for a renewed dialogue not only with economics, politics, sociology and history, but also with psychology, law and geography. A key contribution of industrial relations to this dialogue is seen to be an institutional analysis of the employment relationship that incorporates much more than trade unionism and collective bargaining.

In Chapter 4, Edmund Heery considers different theoretical approaches to industrial relations. He contrasts 'cross-sectional' models that specify the different elements comprising the industrial relations field, their interrelationships and outcomes, with other models that focus more on types and rates of change occurring over time. Given evident shortcomings in the former approach, which has dominated the field in the past (mainly in the form of systems theory), Heery identifies the need for an approach that incorporates a sophisticated model of change, combining elements of the different models of change he outlines. In Chapter 5, John Budd and Devasheesh Bhave explore the different underlying values, ideologies and frames of reference held by those studying and practicing industrial relations. They view the different frames of reference existing within the field as both a weakness and strength of the subject: a weakness when it leads to different groups 'talking past each other' and a strength when it helps to interpret the complexity of the world of work. For the latter to thrive however, Budd and Bhave emphasize the need for a clearer exposure of the values and ideologies within industrial relations discourse.

In Chapter 6, William Brown draws on three decades of research into pay setting to examine the central influence of product market conditions on industrial relations. He explores the relationship between greater competition and increased unwillingness on the part of employers to reach the sort of agreements with unions that were widespread in the past. In the light of this, Brown notes the growing importance of other means for workers to seek influence, including working to secure more state support for employment standards and gaining consumer backing for fair labor conditions.

In Chapter 7, Kerstin Hamman and John Kelly broaden the theme of influences on industrial relations systems by considering the links between different models of capitalism (focusing particularly on the Varieties of Capitalism typology) and the characteristics and trajectories of different national systems of industrial relations. While their analysis points to a number of identifiable clusters of industrial relations systems, they demonstrate the inability of simple dichotomous classifications – such as between liberal market economies and co-ordinated market economies – adequately to categorize patterns and developments in industrial relations. Hamman and Kelly argue that systematic comparisons of industrial relations systems need a greater sensitivity to, for example, the particular roles of national states, political parties and different welfare systems than is represented by the broad Varieties of Capitalism categories.

In Chapter 8, Stephen Procter shortens the horizon of analysis to consider changes occurring within the workplace. This is one of a number of contributions in the volume that draw on current debates regarding human resource practices and firm performance. In exploring what is known (and less known) in this area, Procter argues that the employment relationship has yet to be fully considered in questions such as the factors influencing

the diffusion of human resource practices, or more generally how management actions have 'effects' on practice and performance.

In the final chapter in Part One, George Strauss and Keith Whitfield discuss recent trends in research approaches by industrial relations scholars. Analyses of journal contents are used to gauge the extent of change in industrial relations research: the trend toward more deductive and less inductive approaches, for example and the growing use of large data sets and multivariate statistical methods. To avoid the danger of becoming too detached from the people and contexts they are purporting to study, Strauss and Whitfield discuss the potential for designing studies that benefit from both qualitative and quantitative approaches.

Part Two focuses on developments among the different actors engaged in industrial relations, considering not only the 'usual suspects' of employers and management, trade unions and national state institutions, but also other relevant actors such as transnational institutions, works councils and a range of other actors whose activities have a bearing on industrial relations processes and outcomes. In the first of two chapters on trade unions, Jack Fiorito and Paul Jarley consider in Chapter 10 the main developments in union structure, including trends toward general unionism and how union governance and administrative structures relate to outcomes. Implications of 'organizing model' and 'social network' conceptions of unions are also considered. In noting the difficulties facing many individual unions and national trade union movements, Fiorito and Jarley advocate greater investigation both of the relationship between union structure and practice and the relationship between local and national union structures and outcomes, together with a more thorough evaluation of the consequences of different union choices. This latter aspect is considered in detail by Peter Boxall in Chapter 11, in which he examines the strategic choices facing trade unions in the difficult environments many now confront. Drawing on the notion of organizational life cycles, Boxall argues the inappropriateness of universal union renewal strategies, such as 'organizing' or 'servicing' strategies. He contends that different types of worker, facing diverse conditions and working for employers who have varying responses to trade union representation, require union revitalization strategies that are capable of responding to these different conditions.

In Chapter 12, Franz Traxler examines the relevance of the changing structure of employer organizations for the conduct of industrial relations. He notes the inevitable tensions that exist within employer organizations, and the extent to which the incentives for employers to join such organizations have declined, reflecting not only widespread reductions in union power, but also the internationalization of markets and the reduced significance of multi-employer agreements. Traxler argues that broadening their range of activities and developing roles in ways encouraged by the state, could become increasingly significant for the maintenance of employer organizations in the future.

In Chapter 13 Nicolas Bacon explores management's central position within industrial relations and the scope for, and constraints upon management in developing particular industrial relations approaches, such as those designed to build a 'high commitment' workplace. He emphasizes the need for greater understanding of the degree to which management can exercise choice in their approach to industrial relations given the constraints imposed by, among other things, product markets (and nature of competition), labor markets, financial systems and institutional contexts.

In the first of three chapters examining different aspects of the state's role in industrial relations, Richard Hyman in Chapter 14 points to the peripheral way in which the state has been investigated much in industrial relations research. He argues that this has acted to underplay the close interrelationship between states and markets and the centrality of the state within industrial relations, as employer, legislator, economic manager and welfare provider. Hyman develops a threefold typology of the way that states shape

industrial relations, each representing a different balance of priorities in the weight attached to pursuing economic efficiency, social stability and the rights and standards accorded to its citizens.

In Chapter 15 Simon Deakin and Wanjiru Njoya reassess the position of labor law within broader industrial relations inquiry. Drawing on the examples of several countries, they trace the development of labor law and the different interests and wide range of objectives that it attempts to regulate. Identifying a continuing diversity across different national systems, Deakin and Njoya also point to common challenges facing established legal concepts and categories stemming from, for example, changes occurring in organizational forms and the global spread of business operations.

In Chapter 16, Marick Masters, Ray Gibney, Iryna Shevchuk and Tom Zagenczyk focus on developments in the state's role as an employer. The picture drawn is again one of substantial change, not least in the spread of different business practices from the private into the public sector, and increased pressures on public sector workers to improve their performance. They anticipate these pressures intensifying further, potentially signaling important industrial relations implications regarding work pressure, and the nature of the work-effort bargain among public sector workers. In Chapter 17, Rebecca Gumbrell-McCormick turns her attention to the international regulation of the employment relationship, through the influence of such bodies as the International Labour Organization, the World Bank and the World Trade Organization, as well as international federations of trade unions and employers' organizations. She identifies significant areas of development of an international industrial relations system; such developments are judged to have been restricted, however, by the limited powers ceded to organizations such as international trade union federations by national constituent members concerned to maintain their autonomy.

In Chapter 18, Jean Jenkins and Paul Blyton examine the development and prospects for works councils within industrial relations systems. While they identify a number of factors potentially challenging the future of works councils, other developments appear to signal fresh impetus for the expansion of works council arrangements. However, without active support from the different industrial relations parties, the prospects for the latest generation of works councils exerting significant influence are seen to be limited.

In Chapter 19, Charles Heckscher charts the emergence of new industrial relations actors, distinguishing between issue groups (such as consumers and environmentalists) and identity groups (based on race, sex or disability, for example). Though such groups show a growing preparedness to press their own demands, for the most part he notes the lack of adaptation of existing industrial relations processes to integrate these different stakeholders. Heckscher identifies a need for improved internal and external organization among the new actors, as well as for increased attention by trade unions to building effective relations and coalitions with these emerging stakeholders.

Part Three of the Handbook focuses mainly on processes of industrial relations. In Chapter 20, John Godard considers the factors influencing the formation of trade unions, particularly what determines individuals to seek collective representation. He reviews the different evidence on individual predispositions, the role of trade unions and employers, and the broader relevance of legal structures and economic and political contexts. Godard's analysis points to a long list of influencing factors, but also how different national institutional environments – and the norms that these give rise to – shape the particular influence of specific factors in different circumstances.

In Chapter 21, Robert Flanagan assesses the impact of changing bargaining structures on the exercise of bargaining power. He considers the widespread trend toward more decentralized industrial relations arrangements, that in turn have contributed to increased pay dispersion and a broadening of the agenda discussed within more localized industrial relations. Pressures for decentralization are seen by Flanagan as continuing, giving rise to an expected greater industrial relations focus on productivity issues, and more generally signaling a degree of convergence among industrial relations systems toward more decentralized structures. In Chapter 22, Ann C. Frost picks up the theme of high performance work systems and considers the impact on the broader field of industrial relations. In questioning the longevity and diffusion of such human resource initiatives, she points to the general lack of evidence of accompanying mutual gains relationships, or significantly greater worker autonomy over decisions, particularly in many low-paid service environments. Frost highlights the need for more research involving a broader range of work sectors, better to reflect the diversity of working environments and the growing scale of non-union settings.

The issue of employee involvement in decision-making is also addressed in Chapter 23 by Russell D. Lansbury and Nick Wailes, who consider the extent to which certain institutional systems are more conducive to employee participation than others. They also cast doubt on the sustainability of work reorganization initiatives based on greater worker participation, particularly in those (liberal market) economies that otherwise do not provide an environment conducive to extending worker influence over decision-making. Looking to the future, Lansbury and Wailes note that even within coordinated market economies, participation traditions may be more difficult to sustain as pressures on firms increase for short-term financial returns.

In Chapter 24, David Lewin examines different theories of why employer-employee conflict occurs and charts the changes taking place in patterns of conflict resolution. He notes the significance of the shift away from collective toward more individual expressions of conflict, and the resulting expansion of conflict resolution methods outside collectively-agreed grievance procedures. In reviewing the different individual methods of conflict resolution, Lewin points to a need for further evaluation of the effectiveness of different procedures, for individuals' and organizations.

The contributors to Part Four primarily address the outcomes of industrial relations. The nature of these outcomes varies considerably and the ten chapters in this part reflect this diversity. In Chapter 25 Daniel Gallagher reviews trends in workforce structure and how that structure is shaped by the system of industrial relations. He particularly explores the development of different forms of temporary work contract and the implications of these for our understanding of the 'typical' employer-employee relationship or indeed the 'typical' organization. One of the future research issues identified is the need for further assessment of different union strategies being adopted for increasing recruitment among temporary workers. In Chapter 26 Alex Bryson and John Forth examine the different explanations of wage determination. They identify the many variables that impact on pay setting, giving rise among other things, to continuing wage inequality between the sexes, full- and part-time workers, and across occupations. Bryson and Forth emphasize the importance for those researching pay determination, of incorporating a sufficient degree of complexity into their analyses.

In Chapter 27, Paul Blyton considers another major focus of union-management relations: the determination of working time patterns. He examines the shifting influence of different forms of regulation over working time by the state, collective agreement, management and by employees themselves. Blyton also assesses the centrality of working time within the current debate over work-life balance, and the way in which current trends in working time potentially act both to facilitate and to inhibit workers achieving a successful work-life balance. In Chapter 28, David Guest broadens the discussion of industrial relations outcomes by considering worker well-being, with a particular focus on job satisfaction, insecurity, workload and stress. He identifies little relationship between trade union presence and aspects of well-being, and notes that traditional industrial relations have rarely directly addressed questions of worker well-being in the past. However, with growing concerns over issues such as workplace stress, Guest identifies worker well-being as a potential area for greater attention by trade unions and industrial relations in the future.

In Chapter 29 Ali Dastmalchian reviews the research conducted on industrial relations climates. Drawing insights on the climate concept from organizational theory, he highlights a number of methodological issues which remain unresolved. Dastmalchian nonetheless identifies the influence of industrial relations climate on the outcomes of union-management relations, and notes the significance of the research on climate for current debates, including the question of whether unions and management should pursue greater 'partnership' relations. In Chapter 30 Barbara Pocock considers inequalities in employment outcomes. She emphasizes the multiple sources and manifestations of inequality and the ways in which recent developments both in industrial relations (such as decollectivization and decentralization) and labor markets (for example increased casualization) have contributed to widening inequalities. Pocock highlights the importance of a perspective that incorporates international as well as national and local comparisons; the chapter also underlines the broader importance of maintaining a focus on inequality in a field where it is prone to being crowded out by other issues such as economic performance.

In Chapter 31, Gregor Gall and Robert Hebdon examine issues surrounding how conflict is manifested at work. In reviewing the range of forms that conflict can take, and the widespread decline in strike levels that has taken place over the past two decades, they highlight the increased significance of more individualized conflict expressions and the degree to which these are currently substituting for other, more collective forms. In considering the future, Gall and Hebdon anticipate the continuation of both collective and individual forms of conflict, and the possible further development of cross-national conflict expression coordinated through international trade union campaigns.

In Chapter 32, Irena Grugulis notes the central role that 'skill' has played within industrial relations, acting as a basis for union formation, wage demands and pay differentials, among other things. She examines national variations in skill formation systems, together with firm-level and trade union influences. Grugulis explores the factors that are putting established systems of vocational education and training under pressure, and identifies the dangers of weaker skill formation systems for continuing job quality. In Chapter 33, John Delaney considers the evidence on the relationship between industrial relations and business performance. While noting the overall lack of evidence that industrial relations enhance business performance, he questions the significance of this in terms of measuring the contribution that industrial relations actually makes. Rather than relying on a yardstick of economic efficiency, he identifies the need for developing other measures of performance, such as worker well-being or social justice, and poses the broader question of how industrial relations can be developed to make a more significant contribution in a rapidly-changing world.

In the final chapter, Richard Freeman questions to what extent differences in economic performance between countries can be attributed to differences in labor market institutions. While he finds clear evidence that centralized wage setting is associated with narrower pay gaps, more generally the results on any broader relationships between labor institutions and, for example, economic efficiency, growth and employment, are inconclusive, despite previous pronouncements and even policy advice based on seeming consensus. Freeman calls for more firm-level and other types of evidence, together with the development of more sophisticated theories concerning the contribution of labor institutions.

Together the chapters provide a wide-ranging review of the issues currently shaping and challenging the industrial relations field.

They identify too a series of questions about the future purpose and contribution of industrial relations within contemporary society. These questions underline the continuing importance of the subject in a world of work in which vital issues concerning the conditions under which that work is undertaken, remain to be resolved.

NOTES

1 Fiorito (2005) notes that although the term 'industry' or 'industrial' connotes heavy industry for many, its use by IR scholars serves to differentiate 'industrial' or developed societies, from agrarian societies based largely on peasant production. Service businesses, public services, small enterprises and, indeed, contemporary agricultural production all exhibit industrial relations, to the extent that economic activity rests on the hiring of formally free labor to perform work tasks on the employer's behalf. Fiorito also notes that, while independent production for the market by the self-employed falls beyond IR's purview, bogus self-employment, in which dependent self-employed work for larger enterprises, and various forms of contingent labor, such as those based on the supply of contractors to employers through agencies, do not. In fact the study of contingent labor has been a notable theme in recent IR literature (for example Carré et al., 2000; Forde and Slater, 2005). In developed economies the employment relationship is the dominant institution through which work is organized – Edwards (2003: 2) estimates that 88 per cent of the UK's economically active population is engaged in an employment relationship – a fact that, in principle, underlines the continuing relevance of the study of industrial relations.

2 Another case can be identified along the boundary between state regulation and management decision. It is often suggested that managers (at least in Anglophone liberal market economies) are now the dominant actor in employment relations with the freedom to design systems of human resource management in a largely non-union context. Much of the prescriptive writing on HRM echoes this analysis with its emphasis on managers designing HR policies and practices that complement particular business strategies (see Legge, 2005: 19–25). In an important series of empirical articles, however, Dobbin and colleagues have cast doubt on this interpretation (Dobbin et al., 1993; Dobbin and Sutton, 1998; Kelly and Dobbin, 1999; Sutton et al., 1994). They argue essentially that the development of HR systems in US business since the early 1960s has been driven by the passage of equality law, which prompted US corporations to strengthen

the HR function and formalize and professionalize HR practice. The elaboration of HR systems, on this analysis, therefore, flowed from the interaction of management decision with legal regulation (see also Piore and Safford, 2006).

3 Stage-models seem to be used particularly by US writers. The scale of the US, the size of its economy and its dominance in the world system encourages indigenous scholars to treat it as a paradigmatic case. In Europe, in contrast, a continent crammed full of nation states each with their own traditions (Crouch, 1993), there is more emphasis on comparative studies and institutional analysis.

4 In Italy, although there was union support secured by a moderate victory, employer buy-in was limited and evaporated once Berlusconi's strong right-wing government was elected. Italian employers at that point had no need of a social pact to secure their objectives: 'When the 2001 elections gave a right-wing government the strongest majority of the post-war period, employers chose the more confrontational strategy of lobbying government for labor market deregulation'. (Baccaro and Lim, 2007: 40).

5 We note in passing, however, that despite this orientation there is little interest in IR amongst those engaged in what has come to be labeled 'critical management studies'.

6 Thus, Holgate et al. (2006: 325) note that, '...a dominant theme throughout has been the way in which "mainstream" IR has often reduced workers' experiences to the manifestation of class relations that are defined purely in economic terms, or which are theorized in terms of a single conflict between managers and employees'. Forrest (1993: 410) similarly observes both pluralism and Marxism that, '...these diverse approaches share a world-view that discounts the importance of gender as an analytical concept. Both presume that workers and trade unionists are quintessentially male; neither analyzes the way in which social relations at work are rooted in gender relations'.

7 Healy et al. (2006: 293) describe the contribution of feminist research within IR in terms of, 'putting women, and gender, and more recently, race/ethnicity, sexuality, disability and age, back in...'

8 Dickens writes of the need to abandon the 'Procrustean bed' of full-time continuous employment, designed to match the needs of male workers supported by a dependent care-giver. It must be pointed out, however, that feminist commentators are often critical of the actual work-life balance or family-friendly policies employers develop to accommodate diversity. Systems of flexible working time that allow women better to integrate paid and domestic labor, for instance, may simply reinforce a 'sexual contract' in which male interests are dominant.

9 The response of Marxists, in turn, has been to argue that differences between the 'varieties of capitalism' are exaggerated or that the force of globalization will in due course erode institutional differences with an accompanying leveling down of employment standards (see Coates, 2000).

REFERENCES

Ackers, P. (2007) 'Collective bargaining as industrial democracy: Hugh Clegg and the political foundations of British Industrial Relations pluralism', *British Journal of Industrial Relations*, 45 (1): 77–101.

Ackers, P. and Wilkinson, A. (2003a) 'Introduction: the British industrial relations tradition – formation, breakdown and salvage', in P. Ackers and A. Wilkinson (eds) *Understanding Work and Employment: Industrial Relations in Transition*. Oxford, Oxford University Press. pp. 1–27.

Ackers, P. and Wilkinson, A. (eds) (2003b) *Understanding Work and Employment: Industrial Relations in Transition*. Oxford, Oxford University Press.

Adams, R.J. (1993) '"All aspects of people at work": unity and division in the study of labor and labor management', in R.J. Adams and N.M. Meltz (eds) *Industrial Relations Theory: Its Nature, Scope and Pedagogy*. Metuchen NJ and London, IMLR Press/Rutgers University and the Scarecrow Press. pp. 119–60.

Adams, R.J. (1995) *Industrial Relations under Liberal Democracy: North America in Comparative Perspective*. Columbia SC, University of South Carolina Press.

Almond, P. and Rubery, J. (1998) 'The gender impact of recent European trends in pay determination', *Work, Employment and Society*, 12 (4): 675–93.

Anner, M., Greer, I., Hauptmeier, M., Lillie, N. and Winchester, N. (2006) 'The industrial determinants of transnational solidarity: global interunion politics in three sectors', *European Journal of Industrial Relations*, 12 (1): 7–27.

Armour, J., Deakin, S. and Konzelmann, S.J. (2003) 'Shareholder primacy and the trajectory of UK corporate governance', *British Journal of Industrial Relations*, 41 (3): 531–55.

Baccaro, L. (2003) 'What is alive and what is dead in the theory of corporatism', *British Journal of Industrial Relations*, 41 (4): 683–706.

Baccaro, L. and Lim, S-H. (2007) 'Social pacts as coalitions of the weak and moderate: Ireland, Italy and South Korea in comparative perspective', *European Journal of Industrial Relations*, 13 (1): 27–46.

Bach, S., Bordogna, L., Della Roca, G. and Winchester, D. (eds) (1999) *Public Service Employment Relations in Europe*. London, Routledge.

Bacon, N. and Blyton, P. (2006) 'Union co-operation in a context of job insecurity: negotiated outcomes from teamworking', *British Journal of Industrial Relations*, 44 (2): 215–38.

Bacon, N., Wright, M. and Demina, N. (2004) 'Management buyouts and human resource management', *British Journal of Industrial Relations*, 42 (2): 325–47.

Badigannavar, V., and Kelly, J. (2004) 'Union organizing', in J. Kelly and P. Willman (eds) *Union Organization and Activity*. London, Routledge. pp. 32–50.

Baird, M. (2006) 'The gender agenda: women, work and maternity leave', in M. Hearn and G. Patmore (eds) *Rethinking Work: Time, Space and Discourse*. Melbourne, Cambridge University Press. pp. 39–59.

Barley, S.R. and Kunda, G. (2004) *Gurus, Hired Guns and Warm Bodies: Itinerant Experts in a Knowledge Economy*. Princeton and Oxford, Princeton University Press.

Barnard, C. and Deakin, S. (2002) 'Corporate governance, European governance and social rights', in B. Hepple (ed.) *Social and Labour Rights in a Global Context: International and Comparative Perspectives*. Cambridge, Cambridge University Press. pp. 122–50.

Beechey, V. and Perkins, T. (1987) *A Matter of Hours: Part-time Work and the Labour Market*. Cambridge, Polity Press.

Bell, D.W. and Hanson, C.G. (1987) *Profit-sharing and Profitability*. London, Kogan Page.

Belman, D. and Voos, P. (2006) 'Union wages and union decline: evidence from the construction industry', *Industrial and Labor Relations Review*, 60 (1): 67–87.

Bercusson, B. and Dickens, L. (1996) *Equal Opportunities and Collective Bargaining in Europe: Defining the Issues*. Dublin, European Foundation for the Improvement of Living and Working Conditions.

Beynon, H. (1984) *Working for Ford*, 2nd edition. Harmondsworth, Penguin.

Blau, F.D., Brinton, M.C. and Grusky, D.B. (eds) (2006) *The Declining Significance of Gender?* New York, Russell Sage Foundation.

Boxall, P. and Haynes, P. (1997) 'Strategy and trade union effectiveness in a neo-liberal environment', *British Journal of Industrial Relations*, 35 (4): 567–91.

Bradley, K .and Gelb, A. (1986) *Share Ownership for Employees*. London, Public Policy Centre.

Briskin, L. and McDermott, P. (eds) (1993) *Women Challenging Unions: Feminism, Democracy and Militancy*. Toronto, University of Toronto Press.

Brown, W. (2000) 'Putting partnership into practice in Britain', *British Journal of Industrial Relations*, 38 (2): 299–316.

Brown Johnson, N. and Jarley, P. (2004) 'Justice and union participation: an extension and test of mobilization theory', *British Journal of Industrial Relations*, 42 (3): 543–62.

Budd, J.W. (2004) *Employment with a Human Face: Balancing Efficiency, Equity and Voice*. London and Ithaca NY, ILR Press.

Budd, J.W., Gomez, R. and Meltz, N.M. (2004) 'Why a balance is best: the pluralist industrial relations paradigm of balancing competing interests', in B.E. Kaufman (ed.) *Theoretical Perspectives on Work and the Employment Relationship*. University of Illinois at Urbana-Champaign, Industrial Relations Research Association. pp. 195–227.

Carré, F., Ferber, M.A., Golden, L. and Herzenberg, S.A. (eds) (2000) *Nonstandard Work: The Nature and Challenges of Changing Employment Arrangements*. University of Illinois, Urbana-Champaign IL, Industrial Relations Research Association.

Clark, A.E. (2005) 'Your money or your life: changing job quality in OECD countries', *British Journal of Industrial Relations*, 43 (3): 377–400.

Clegg, H.A. (1976) *Trade Unionism under Collective Bargaining: A Theory Based on Comparisons of Six Countries*. Oxford, Basil Blackwell.

Coates, D. (2000) *Models of Capitalism: Growth and Stagnation in the Modern Era*. Cambridge, Cambridge University Press.

Coates, D. (ed.) (2005) *Varieties of Capitalism, Varieties of Approaches*. Basingstoke, Palgrave MacMillan.

Cobble, D.S. (1991) 'Organizing the post-industrial workforce: lessons from the history of waitress unionism', *Industrial and Labor Relations Review*, 44 (3): 419–36.

Cobble, D.S. (ed.) (1993) *Women and Unions: Forging a Partnership*. Ithaca and London, ILR Press.

Cockburn, C. (1983) *Brothers: Male Dominance and Technological Change*. London, Pluto Press.

Colgan, F. and Ledwith, S. (eds) (2002) *Gender, Diversity and Trade Unions: International Perspectives*. London, Routledge.

Colling, T. and Dickens, L. (1989) *Equality Bargaining – Why Not?* Equal Opportunities Commission Research Series, London, Her Majesty's Stationery Office.

Colling, T. and Dickens, L. (1998) 'Selling the case for gender equality: deregulation and equality bargaining', *British Journal of Industrial Relations*, 36 (3): 389–411.

Coyle-Shapiro, J. A-M., Shore, L.M., Taylor, M.S. and Tetrick, L.E. (eds) (2004) *The Employment Relationship: Examining Psychological and Contextual Perspectives*. Oxford, Oxford University Press.

Crouch, C. (1993) *Industrial Relations and European State Traditions*. Oxford, Oxford University Press.

Darlington, R. (1994) *The Dynamics of Workplace Trade Unionism*. London and New York, Mansell.

Darlington, R. and Lyddon, D. (2001) *Glorious Summer: Class Struggle in Britain 1972*. London, Chicago and Sydney, Bookmarks.

Davies, P. and Freedland, M. (1993) *Labour Legislation and Public Policy*. Oxford, Clarendon Press.

Dickens, L. (1999) 'Beyond the business case: a three-pronged approach to equality action', *Human Resource Management Journal*, 9 (1): 9–20.

Dickens, L. (2005) 'Walking the talk? Equality and diversity in employment', in S. Bach (ed.) *Managing Human Resources: Personnel Management in Transition*. Oxford, Blackwell Publishing. pp. 178–208.

Dickens, L. (2007) 'The road is long: thirty years of equality legislation in Britain', *British Journal of Industrial Relations*, 45 (3): 463–94.

Dickens, R. and Manning A. (2003) 'Minimum wage, minimum impact', in R. Dickens, P. Gregg and J. Wadsworth (eds) *The Labour Market under New Labour: The State of Working Britain*. Basingstoke, Palgrave MacMillan. pp. 201–13.

Dickson, T., McLachlan, H.V., Prior, P. and Swales, K. (1988) 'Big Blue and the unions: IBM, individualism and trade union strategy', *Work, Employment and Society*, 2 (4): 506–20.

Dobbin, F., Sutton, J.R., Meyer, J.W. and Scott, R. (1993) 'Equal opportunity law and the construction of internal labor markets', *American Journal of Sociology*, 99 (2): 396–427.

Dobbin, F. and Sutton, J.R. (1998) 'The strength of a weak state: the rights revolution and the rise of human resource management divisions', *American Journal of Sociology*, 104 (2): 441–76.

Dunlop, J.T. (1993) *Industrial Relations Systems*, revised edition. Boston MA, Harvard Business School Press.

Edwards, P. (2003) 'The employment relationship and the field of industrial relations', in P. Edwards (ed.) *Industrial Relations: Theory and Practice*, second edition, Oxford, Blackwell Publishing. pp. 1–36.

Ellem, B. (2002) 'Power, place and scale: union recognition in the Pilbara, 1999–2002', *Labour and Industry*, 13 (2): 67–89.

Estlund, C. (2003) *Working Together: How Workplace Bonds Strengthen a Diverse Democracy*. Oxford, Oxford University Press.

Fairbrother, P. (1996) 'Workplace trade unionism in the state sector', in P. Ackers, C. Smith and P. Smith (eds) *The New Workplace and Trade Unionism*. London, Routledge. pp. 110–48.

Fairbrother, P. (2000) *Trade Unions at the Crossroads*. London and New York, Mansell.

*Fairris, D. (2006) 'Union voice effects in Mexico', *British Journal of Industrial Relations*, 44 (4): 781–800.

Ferner, A., Qintanilla, J. and Sánchez-Runde, C. (eds) (2006) *Multinationals, Institutions and the Construction of Transnational Practices: Convergence and Diversity in the Global Economy*. Basingstoke, Palgrave MacMillan.

Fine, J. (2006) *Worker Centers: Organizing Communities at the Edge of the Dream*. Ithaca and London, ILR Press.

Fiorito, J. (2005) 'Industrial relations', in S. Cartright (ed.) *The Blackwell Encyclopedia of Management*, second edition. Malden, MA, Blackwell. pp. 183–85.

Fiorito, J. (2001) 'Human resource management practices and worker desires for union representation', *Journal of Labor Research*, 22 (2): 335–54.

Flanders, A. (1970) *Management and Unions: The Theory and Reform of Industrial Relations*. London, Faber and Faber.

Foley, J.R. (2003) 'Mobilization and change in a trade union setting: environment, structures and action', *Work, Employment and Society*, 17 (2): 247–68.

Forde, C. and Slater, G. (2005) 'Agency working in Britain: character, consequence and regulation', *British Journal of Industrial Relations*, 43 (2): 249–72.

Forrest, A. (1993) 'Women and IR theory: no room in the discourse', *Relations Industrielles*, 48 (3): 409–40.

Freeman, R. and Medoff, J. (1984) *What Do Unions Do?* New York, Basic Books.

Frege, C.M. (2002) 'A critical assessment of the theoretical and empirical research on works councils', *British Journal of Industrial Relations*, 40 (2): 221–48.

Frege, C.M. (2005) 'Varieties of industrial relations research: take-over, convergence or divergence?', *British Journal of Industrial Relations*, 43 (2): 179–207.

Frege, C.M. and Kelly, J. (2004) 'Union strategies in comparative context', in C.M. Frege and J. Kelly (eds) *Varieties of Unionism: Strategies of Union Revitalization in a Globalizing Economy*. Oxford, Oxford University Press. pp. 31–44.

Frost, A. (2001) 'Reconceptualising local union responses to workplace restructuring in North America', *British Journal of Industrial Relations*, 39 (4): 307–33.

Godard, J. (2004a) 'A critical assessment of the high performance paradigm', *British Journal of Industrial Relations*, 42 (2): 349–78.

Godard, J. (2004b) 'The new institutionalism, capitalist diversity and industrial relations', in B.E. Kaufman (ed.) *Theoretical Perspectives on Work and the Employment Relationship*. Champaign IL, Industrial Relations Research Association. pp. 229–64.

Goldthorpe, J.H. (1985) 'The end of convergence: corporatist and dualist tendencies in modern western societies', in B. Roberts, R. Finnegan and D. Gallie (eds) *New Approaches to Economic Life*. Manchester, Manchester University Press. pp. 124–53.

Gordon, M.E. and Turner, L. (eds) (2000) *Transnational Cooperation among Labor Unions*. Ithaca and London, ILR Press.

Gospel, H. and Pendleton, A. (eds) (2005) *Corporate Governance and Labour Management*. Oxford, Oxford University Press.

Green, F. (2006) *Demanding Work: The Paradox of Job Quality in the Affluent Economy*. Princeton and Oxford, Princeton University Press.

Green, F. and Tsitsianis, N. (2005) 'An investigation of national trends in job satisfaction in Britain and Germany', *British Journal of Industrial Relations*, 43 (3): 401–29.

Grimshaw, D. and Rubery, J. (2001) *The Gender Pay Gap: a Research Review*. Research Discussion Series, Manchester, Equal Opportunities Commission.

Guest, D. (2007) 'HRM and performance: can partnership address the ethical dilemmas?' in A. Pinnington, R. Macklin and T. Campbell (eds) *Human Resource Management: Ethics and Employment*. Oxford, Oxford University Press. pp. 52–65.

Guest, D. and Conway, N. (1999) 'Peering into the Black Hole: the downside of new employment relations in the UK', *British Journal of Industrial Relations*, 37 (3): 367–89.

Gunnigle, P., Collings, D.C. and Morley, M.J. (2006) 'Accomodating global capitalism? State policy and industrial relations in American MNCs in Ireland', in A. Ferner, J. Qunitanilla and C. Sánchez-Runde (eds) *Multinationals, Institutions and the Construction of Transnational Practices: Convergence and Diversity in the Global Economy*. Basingstoke, Palgrave MacMillan. pp. 86–108.

Hall, P.A. and Soskice, D. (1998) 'An introduction to varieties of capitalism', in P.A. Hall and D. Soskice (eds) *Varieties of Capitalism: The Institutional Foundations of Comparative Advantage*. Oxford, Oxford University Press. pp. 1–70.

Hanson, C. G. and Mather, G. (1988) *Striking out Strikes: Changing Employment Relations in the British Labour Market*. Hobart Paper 110, London, The Institute of Economic Affairs.

Hassel, A. (2006) *Wage-Setting, Social Pacts and the Euro*. Amsterdam, Amsterdam University Press.

Healy, G., Hansen, L.L. and Ledwith, S. (2006) 'Editorial: still uncovering gender in industrial relations', *Industrial Relations Journal*, 37 (4): 290–8.

Heery, E. (2003) 'Trade unions and industrial relations', in P. Ackers and A. Wilkinson (eds) *Understanding Work and Employment: Industrial Relations in Transition*. Oxford, Oxford University Press. pp. 278–304.

Heery, E. and Conley, H. (2007) 'Frame extension in a mature social movement: British trade unions and part-time work', *The Journal of Industrial Relations*, 48 (1): 5–29.

Heery, E. and Frege, C. (2006) 'New actors in industrial relations', *British Journal of Industrial Relations*, 44 (4): 601–4.

Heery, E., Healy, G. and Taylor, P. (2004) 'Representation at work: themes and issues', in G. Healy, E. Heery, P. Taylor and W. Brown (eds) *The Future of Worker Representation*. Basingstoke, Palgrave MacMillan. pp. 1–36.

Herding, R. (1972) *Job Control and Union Structure*. Rotterdam, University of Rotterdam Press.

Hirschman, A.O. (1991) *The Rhetoric of Reaction: Perversity, Futility, Jeopardy*. Cambridge MA and London, The Belknap Press of Harvard University Press.

Holgate, J., Hebson, G. and McBride, A. (2006) 'Why gender and "difference" matters: a critical appraisal of industrial relations research', *Industrial Relations Journal*, 37 (4): 310–28.

Hoque, K. and Noon, M. (2004) 'Equal opportunities policy and practice in Britain: evaluating the "empty shell" hypothesis', *Work, Employment and Society*, 18 (3): 481–506.

Howell, C. (2005) *Trade Unions and the State: The Construction of Industrial Relations Institutions in Britain, 1890–2000*. Princeton and Oxford: Princeton University Press.

Hunter, L.C. and Rimmer, S. (1995) 'An economic exploration of the UK and Australian experiences', *Gender, Work and Organization*, 2 (3): 140–56.

Hyman, R. (1975) *Industrial Relations: A Marxist Introduction*. London and Basingstoke, The MacMillan Press.

Hyman, R. (2004) 'Is industrial relations theory always ethnocentric?', in B.E. Kaufman (ed.) *Theoretical Perspectives on Work and the Employment Relationship*. University of Illinois at Urbana-Champaign, Industrial Relations Research Association. pp. 265–92.

Katz, H.C. (1993) 'The decentralization of collective bargaining: a literature review and comparative analysis', *Industrial and Labor Relations Review*, 47 (1): 3–22.

Kaufman, B.E. (1993) *The Origins and Evolution of the Field of Industrial Relations in the United States*. Ithaca NY, ILR Press.

Kaufman, B.E. (2004a) 'Employment relations and the employment relations system: a guide to theorizing', in B.E. Kaufman (ed.) *Theoretical Perspectives on Work and the Employment Relationship*. Champaign IL, Industrial Relations Research Association. pp. 41–75.

Kaufman, B.E. (2004b) *The Global Evolution of Industrial Relations: Events, Ideas and the IIRA*. Geneva, International Labour Office.

Kaufman, B.E. and Taras, D.G. (eds) (2000) *Nonunion Employee Representation: History, Contemporary Practice and Policy*. Armonk, NY, M.E. Sharpe.

Kelly, E. and Dobbin, F. (1999) 'Civil rights law at work: sex discrimination and the rise of maternity leave policies', *American Journal of Sociology*, 105 (2): 455–92.

Kelly, J. (1998) *Rethinking Industrial Relations: Mobilization, Collectivism and Long Waves*. London, Routledge.

Kirton, G. and Greene, A-M. (2000) *The Dynamics of Managing Diversity: A Critical Approach*. London, Butterworth-Heinemann.

Kochan, T.A. (1998) 'What is distinctive about industrial relations research?', in K. Whitfield and G. Strauss (eds) *Researching the World of Work: Strategies and Methods in Studying Industrial Relations*. Ithaca and London, ILR Press. pp. 31–45.

Kochan, T.A., Katz, H.C., McKersie, R.B. (1986) *The Transformation of American Industrial Relations*. New York, Basic Books.

Kochan, T.A. and Osterman, P. (1994) *The Mutual Gains Enterprise: Forging a Winning Partnership among Labor, Management and Government*. Cambridge MA, Harvard Business School Press.

Konzelmann, S.J., Conway, N., Trenberth, L. and Wilkinson, F. (2006) 'Corporate governance and human resource management', *British Journal of Industrial Relations*, 44 (3): 541–67.

Korczynski, M., Hodson, R. and Edwards, P. (eds) (2006) *Social Theory at Work*. Oxford, Oxford University Press.

Kuruvilla, S. and Verma, A. (2006) 'International labor standards, soft regulation and national government roles', *The Journal of Industrial Relations*, 48 (1): 41–58.

Ledwith, S. and Colgan, F. (2002) 'Tackling gender, diversity and trade union democracy: a worldwide project?', in F. Colgan and S. Ledwith (eds) *Gender, Diversity and Trade Unions: International Perspectives*. London, Routledge. pp. 1–27.

Legge, K. (2005) *Human Resource Management; Rhetorics and Realities*, anniversary edition. Basingstoke and New York, Palgrave MacMillan.

Legge, K. (2007) 'The ethics of HRM in dealing with individual employees without collective representation', in A. Pinnington, R. Macklin and T. Campbell (eds) *Human Resource Management: Ethics and Employment*. Oxford, Oxford University Press. pp. 35–41.

Lillie, N. (2006) *A Global Union for Global Workers: Collective Bargaining and Regulatory Politics in Maritime Shipping*. New York and London, Routledge.

Logan, J. (2006) 'The union avoidance industry in the United States', *British Journal of Industrial Relations*, 44 (4): 651–76.

Lyddon, D. (2003) 'History and industrial relations', in P. Ackers and A. Wilkinson (eds) *Understanding Work and Employment: Industrial Relations in Transition*. Oxford, Oxford University Press. pp. 89–118.

McAdam, D., McCarthy, J.D. and Zald, M.N. (eds) (1996) *Comparative Perspectives on Social Movements: Political Opportunities, Mobilizing Structures, and Cultural Framings*. Cambridge and New York, Cambridge University Press.

McAdam, D., Tarrow, S. and Tilly, C. (eds) (2001) *Dynamics of Contention*. Cambridge and New York, Cambridge University Press.

McBride, A. (2001) 'Making it work: supporting group representation in a liberal democratic organization', *Gender, Work and Organization*, 8 (4): 411–29.

Machin, S. (2006) 'The economic approach to analysis of the labor market', in M. Korczynski, R. Hodson and P. Edwards (eds) *Social Theory at Work*. Oxford, Oxford University Press. pp. 182–207.

McColgan, A. (1994) *Pay Equity – Just Wages for Women?* London: The Institute of Employment Rights.

Maitland, I. (1983) *The Causes of Industrial Disorder: A Comparison of a British and German Factory*. London, Routledge and Kegan Paul.

Marginson, P. and Sisson, K. (2004) *European Integration and Industrial Relations: Multi-level Governance in the Making*. Basingstoke, Palgrave MacMillan.

Marsden, R. (1982) 'Industrial relations: a critique of empiricism', *Sociology*, 16 (2): 232–50.

Metcalf, D. (2005) 'Trade unions: resurgence or perdition?', in S. Fernie and D. Metcalf (eds) *Trade Unions: Resurgence or Demise?* London and New York, Routledge. pp. 83–117.

Milkman, R. (2006) *L.A. Story: Immigrant Workers and the Future of the U.S. Labor Movement*. New York, Russell Sage Foundation.

Minford, P. (1985) 'Trade unions destroy a million jobs', in W.E.J. McCarthy (ed.) *Trade Unions: Selected Readings*. Harmondsworth, Penguin. pp. 365–75.

Müller-Jentsch, W. (2004) 'Theoretical approaches to industrial relations', in B.E. Kaufman (ed.) *Theoretical Perspectives on Work and the Employment Relationship*. University of Illinois at Urbana-Champaign, Industrial Relations Research Association. pp. 1–40.

Osterman, P., Kochan, T.A., Locke, R.M. and Piore, M.J. (2001) *Working in American: A Blueprint for the New Labor Market*. Cambridge MA, The MIT Press.

Piore, M.J. and Safford, S. (2006) 'Changing regimes of workplace governance: shifting axes of social mobilization and the challenge to industrial relations theory', *Industrial Relations*, 45 (3): 299–325.

Pocock, B. (1997a) 'Gender and Australian industrial relations theory and research practice', *Labour and Industry*, 8 (1): 1–19.

Pocock, B. (ed.) (1997b) *Strife, Sex and Politics in Labour Unions*. St Leonards, Allen and Unwin.

Purcell, J. and Ahlstrand, B. (1994) *Human Resource Management in the Multi-divisional Company*. Oxford, Oxford University Press.

Purcell, J. and Sisson, K. (1983) 'Strategies and practice in the management of industrial relations', in G.S. Bain (ed.) *Industrial Relations in Britain*. Oxford, Basil Blackwell. pp. 95–120.

Rainnie, A., Herod, A. and McGrath Champ, S. (2007) 'Spatializing industrial relations', *Industrial Relations Journal*, 38 (2): 102–18.

Roberts, B. (1987) *Mr Hammond's Cherry Tree: The Morphology of Union Survival*. Eighteenth Wincott Memorial Lecture, Occasional Paper 76, London, The Institute of Economic Affairs.

Samuel, P. (2005) 'Partnership working and the cultivated activist', *Industrial Relations Journal*, 36 (1): 59–76.

Shenfield, A. (1986) *What Right to Strike?* Hobart Paper 106, London, The Institute for Economic Affairs.

Sisson, K. (1987) *The Management of Collective Bargaining: An International Comparison*. Oxford, Basil Blackwell.

Sisson, K. (1993) 'In search of HRM', *British Journal of Industrial Relations*, 31 (2): 201–10.

Sisson, K. and Marginson, P. (2002) 'Co-ordinated bargaining: a process for our times?', *British Journal of Industrial Relations*, 40 (2): 197–220.

Smith, P. and Morton, G. (2006) 'Nine years of New Labour: Neoliberalism and workers' rights', *British Journal of Industrial Relations*, 44 (3): 401–20.

Streeck, W. (1997) 'Beneficial constraints: on the economic limits of rational voluntarism', in J.R. Hollingsworth and R. Boyer (eds) *Contemporary Capitalism: The Embeddedness of Institutions*. Cambridge, Cambridge University Press. pp. 197–219.

Sutton, J.R., Dobbin, F., Meyer, J.W. and Scott, W.R. (1994) 'The legalization of the workplace', *American Journal of Sociology*, 99 (4): 944–71.

Tailby, S., Richardson, M., Stewart, P., Danford, A. and Upchurch, M. (2004) 'Partnership at work and worker participation: an NHS case study', *Industrial Relations Journal*, 35 (5): 403–18.

Tarrow, S. (1998) *Power in Movement: Social Movements and Contentious Politics*, second edition. Cambridge and New York, Cambridge University Press.

Teague, P. (2006) 'Social partnership and local development in Ireland: the limits to deliberation', *British Journal of Industrial Relations*, 44 (3): 421–43.

Thompson, P. and Harley, B. (2007) 'HRM and the worker: labor process perspectives', in P. Boxall, J. Purcell and P. Wright (eds) *The Oxford Handbook of Human Resource Management*. Oxford, Oxford University Press. 147–65.

Traxler, F., Blaschke, S. and Kittel, B. (2002) *National Labour Relations in Internationalized Markets: A Comparative Study of Institutions, Change, and Performance*. Oxford, Oxford University Press.

Troy, L. (1999) *Beyond Unions and Collective Bargaining*. Armonk, NY, M.E. Sharpe.

Troy, L. (2004) *The Twilight of the Old Unionism*. Armonk, NY, M.E. Sharpe.

Tsogas, G. (2001) *Labor Regulation in a Global Economy*. Armonk, NY, M.E. Sharpe.

Turnbull, P.J. (2003) 'What do unions do now?', *Journal of Labor Research*, 24 (3): 492–526.

Turnbull, P.J. (2006) 'The war on Europe's waterfront – repertoires of power in the port transport industry', *British Journal of Industrial Relations*, 44 (2): 305–26.

Turnbull, P.J., Blyton, P. and Harvey, G. (2004) 'Cleared for take-off? Management-labor partnership in the European civil aviation industry', *European Journal of Industrial Relations*, 10 (3): 287–307.

Van Roozendaal, G. (2002) *Trade Unions and Global Governance*. London and New York, Continuum.

Vaughan-Whitehead, D. (ed.) (1995) *Workers' Financial Participation: East-West Experiences*. Geneva, International Labour Office.

Wacjman, J. (2000) 'Feminism facing industrial relations in Britain', *British Journal of Industrial Relations*, 38 (2): 183–201.

Wall, T. and Wood, S. (2005) 'The romance of HRM and business performance, and the case for Big Science', *Human Relations*, 58 (4): 429–62.

Wheeler, H.N. (2002) *The Future of the American Labor Movement*. Cambridge, Cambridge University Press.

Whitfield, K. and Poole, M. (1997) 'Organizing employment for high performance: theories, evidence and policy', *Organization Studies*, 18 (5): 745–64.

PART ONE

Perspectives and Approaches

2

The History of Industrial Relations as a Field of Study

Carola M. Frege

Industrial relations (IR) broadly defined as the study of work and employment, was established as an independent academic field in the 1920s in the US and subsequently after WWII in Britain and other Anglophone countries.[1] Though originally established by US institutional economists it soon became to be seen as an interdisciplinary field incorporating labor economists, social psychologists, personnel management scholars, industrial sociologists, labor lawyers as well as political scientists working on labor issues. In continental Europe and indeed in the rest of the world research on work and employment remained, however, a subject within those social science disciplines.

This chapter starts by outlining the different historical developments of IR research in the US and Britain as two examples of Anglophone countries with the longest traditions in IR research. It is then contrasted with the developments in Germany as an example of continental Europe. A major finding is that research traditions and outcomes differ from country to country and challenge the classical notion of the universality of scientific research. This chapter argues instead for the embeddedness of IR research in national-specific path dependencies.

INSTITUTIONAL HISTORIES OF IR RESEARCH

The industrial revolution and its social consequences in Europe and the US in the nineteenth and early twentieth century increasingly drew scholars from a variety of emerging social sciences (for example law, economics, political science, sociology) to engage in the analysis of the mechanics of capitalism and the 'social question', in particular the 'labor problem' (poverty and social unrest related to the industrialization) (Katznelson, 1996). In the US and Britain (and subsequently in other Anglophone regions) an independent field of study of employment, industrial or labor relations, developed at the beginning of the twentieth century.

As outlined before, this development did not occur in the rest of the world, in particular not in continental Europe, where IR research remained multi-disciplinary, conducted mainly by sociologists, political scientists and lawyers. The different institutional developments across countries are accompanied by specific research traditions exemplified in different methods, theories and paradigms.

In the following sections I will briefly outline the historical development of IR research in the three countries.[2] Generalizing and classifying national traditions is a potentially problematic task. Research is never homogeneous and there are always alternative lines of research. Note that this chapter does not attempt to achieve a complete coverage of the field of study in each country but merely wishes to outline its main, comparatively distinctive features.

United States

The first IR course in the US was created at the University of Wisconsin in 1920. Other universities such as the University of Pennsylvania (Wharton Business School, 1921) and Princeton (1922) and Harvard (1923) followed. In the same year the National Association of Employment Managers changed its name to the IRAA (Industrial Relations Association of America), which was a forerunner of the current professional association, IRRA/LERA (Labor and Employment Relations Association), which was created in 1947. After the end of World War II IR became increasingly institutionalized as an independent field of study in various US universities.

Historically IR as an academic field was founded in the US by institutional or political economists, such as Richard Ely, Henry Carter Adams and John Commons (the founder of the Wisconsin School), who were heavily influenced by the German historical school of economics and felt increasingly alienated in their economics departments which began to turn towards neo-classical paradigms at the beginning of the twentieth century

(Hodgson, 2001). One can argue therefore that the 'new political economy' or institutional economics arose in reaction to the ascendance of the laissez-faire perspective within economics. The institutional economists found in IR a niche to pursue pragmatic, behaviorist, public-policy oriented research which took institutional constraints in the labor market into account (Jacoby, 1990; Kaufman, 1993). Ideally, this perspective focused on the rules and norms underpinning economic activity, viewing institutions of work and employment as embedded within, and largely inseparable from, broader social, economic, and political institutions (Godard, 1994: 1).

One should note that these early theorists were not radical progressives however, but liberals and conservatives at the same time. They were liberals in their desire for reforming some of the social processes operating in the US society and conservatives in their desire to preserve the contours of a capitalist system and the parameters of wealth and power therein (DeBrizzi, 1983: 8). As Commons would have put it, they wanted to preserve capitalism by making it good. It comes as no surprise that when the IRAA was established in 1920 the top positions were taken over by pro-management conservatives. Their publication *personnel* became dominated by the conservatives and adopted a strident anti-communist tone that spilled over into more general anti-labor sentiments (in particular against militant workers) but continued to remain agnostic on the question of collective bargaining (Kimmel, 2000: 197).

Moreover, the pioneers of the field in the Anglophone world, Commons in the US and the Webbs in Britain, were heavily engaged in the world of public policy (Hyman, 2001). IR was therefore developed as a policy-oriented field of research, thus devoted to problem-solving (Kaufman, 2004: 117).

IR in the US arose as a relatively pragmatic, socially progressive reform movement, thus

occupying a position in the progressive centre to moderate left on issues of politics and economics, and spanning a diverse and not entirely consistent range of opinion with liberal business leaders on the more conservative side of the field and moderate socialists on the more radical side. (Kaufman, 2004: 2)

The aim was to solve the labor problem without threatening capitalism. As Kaufman (2004: 121) states 'the goals of efficiency, equity and human self-development were mutually served by an active, broad-ranging program of social and industrial reform'. In other words, IR sought major change in the legal rights, management, and conditions of labor in industry, but at the same time was conservative and non-Marxist in that it sought to reform the existing social order rather than replace it with a new one. In fact, Marxists were antagonistic to the new field of IR since it sought to save through reform what they hoped to replace by revolution (Kaufman, 1993: 5).

At the same time, HR practitioners (or what was formerly called personnel management) and managerial scholars also became interested in the wider field of work and employment (Kaufman, 1993: 19). Already in the 1910s there was increasing interest in the scientific engineering of human capital, as symbolized in the work by Frederick W. Taylor (*Principles of Scientific Management*, 1911). According to Kimmel (2000: 5), by the end of WWI, however, academic researchers and practitioners in personnel management split in two camps, the 'reformists' and 'managerialists'. The reformists adopted liberal values and continued to support progressive ideas of capitalist reforms and saw a role for personnel managers to meditate between workers and employers interests. 'They defined their professional task as the regulation of labor relations in the public interest and the oversight of collective dealings between employers and employees' (Kimmel, 2000: 6). These scholars and practitioners would borrow from the theory and methods of the institutional labor economists. They were part of a wider progressive group of policy makers and scholars from different disciplines who came to the joint conviction that modern industries would need reform such as an employment department which would promote employee welfare, for example (Commons, 1919: 167).

The managerialists, on the other side of the spectrum, embraced, according to Kimmel (2000), scientific expertise and objectivity as the defining features of their profession and assumed a harmony between employers and employees. Their task was to discover the source of problems in 'sick' companies where workplace relations were not harmonious and then to cure them. They used scientific techniques for 'adjusting' workers to industry, drawing in particular on industrial and social psychology. The idea was to improve workplace relations by a special profession which would apply in particular the new science of psychology to the 'human factor' in industry.

Over time, the more reform-oriented HR members of the management profession found themselves increasingly marginalized (Shenhav, 2002: 187). The triumph of managerialists meant a sharp split between psychological approaches and political and economic approaches to the study of IR. Managerialists favored psychological approaches which were seen as more objective. Industrial psychology became very popular during WWI and thereafter and was increasingly regarded as the solution to the labor problem (Shenhav, 2002: 183). This shift of the new profession of personnel management away from reform and toward 'science' also entailed a move away from a broad treatment of work and employment as involving economic and political, as well as psychological and social factors, towards a narrow treatment of IR/HR as a fundamentally psychological concern (Kimmel, 2000: 311). This approach gained dominance during the 1930s and 1940s. In 1922 business leaders even found their own rival organization to promote the field of employment/personnel management. The American Management Association (AMA), as it was named, campaigned vigorously for the open shop and against organized labor. Thus, increasingly in the early twentieth century the rising academic field of management excluded concerns with labor from their industry and personnel studies and pushed those reformist scholars interested to the evolving field of study of IR (Shenhav, 2002: 187).

As a consequence, institutional economists interested in IR and reformist HR scholars shared in the beginning a common interest in pragmatic research leading to solutions of the labor problems. However, over time disagreements arose in particular over trade unions and collective bargaining (as one possible regulatory solution) and the two factions eventually split but learnt to co-exist and to divide the problem of work and employment between them, with personnel types handling the 'human element' and IR experts handling the material and collective aspects of labor relations (Kimmel, 2000: 312). For Kaufman (1993: 20), this divide remained a characteristic feature of the field over the following decades. These complicated developments partly explain why today there are two sorts of HR scholars in the US: the ones in the IR field under the umbrella of LERA and the HR and OB scholars which belong to the Academy of Management. Another reason may also be the growing divide between business schools and free-standing schools of labor relations.

It comes as no surprise that the broad field of IR was perceived as an interdisciplinary study rather than a distinctive discipline (Kaufman, 1993: 12). For example, as the director of the IR section at Princeton 1926–1954, J. D. Brown, states, IR should include 'all factors, conditions, problems and policies involved in the employment of human resources in organized production or service' (quoted in Kaufman, 1993: 201). However, interdisciplinarity was in reality pretty narrowly defined. The leading assumption was that the field should investigate a broad terrain by combining economics as well as psychology (see for example the Committee on Industrial Relations in their overview of the field of study in 1926, quoted in Kimmel, 2000: 304). Interdisciplinary research did not mean the dynamic interplay of related disciplines such as political science, sociology or history and their different methodologies and paradigms. Labor economics and social psychology

(in the tradition of the Hawthorne experiments) were clearly the leading disciplines in the field of IR in the US.

After WWII the split between the two economic and psychological groups became larger and the field became increasingly dominated by labor economists and other institutionally oriented scholars interested in collective bargaining (Jacoby, 2003; Kaufman, 1993). Thus, the quasi-stable co-existence of HR and IR started to disintegrate in the 1970s and 1980s when the New Deal system of collective labor relations began to break down. Labor economists have since then increasingly dominated the LERA activities and research programs as well as publications (Kaufman, 1993: 193). According to Kaufman (ibid.: 155) it is no surprise that the past academic presidents of the LERA were all labor economists. Similarly, Mitchell (2001: 375) agrees that IR research in the US was always dominated by labor economic paradigms, and probably now even more than in its high days, in the 1950s and 1970s.

As mainstream economics developed during the 1970s toward a sharply focused analytical discipline with a strong methodological consensus centering on model-building and on the statistical-empirical verification of largely mathematical theoretical hypotheses (Solow, 1997) this unsurprisingly also had an impact on labor economics and IR and ended up marginalizing the institutionalists. Thus, labor economics developed from an original institutional focus towards increasingly neo-classical (rational choice) paradigms (Boyer and Smith, 2001; Jacoby, 1990). Strauss and Feuille (1978: 535) argue that 'if collective bargaining represents industrial relations central core, then labor economics has largely divorced itself from that core'. Labor economists are currently more interested in micro level studies such as skill-wage differentials, labor contracts or training (for example the leading Cambridge School in US labor economics) than institutional research. Thus, institutionalism may have lost its theoretical link to labor economics (Jacoby, 2003). This development can be linked to the declining importance of institutions in the US labor market such as trade unions or collective bargaining.

In sum, it comes as no surprise that labor economics has dominated much of US IR research from its very beginning. Not only are most authors of American IR publications labor economists but research methods, theories and paradigms of the majority of US publications are also shaped by labor economics (Frege, 2005). As outlined above, this does not deny the existence of a large contingent of US labor scholars who use non-economic, multi-disciplinary theories and methodologies, but compared to other countries the share of labor economists dominates the field. Thus, mainstream American IR research is commonly character-ized by empirical, quantitative, deductive research with multi-variant statistics and mid-range hypotheses and focused on the micro-level (individual or groups of employees) (Frege, 2005; Mitchell, 2001; Whitfields and Strauss, 2000). Moreover, most IR theories are borrowed from economics or psychology and produce rational choice or strategic choice hypotheses or behavioristic, social-psychological approaches (Cappelli, 1985: 98; Godard, 1994). There is also evidence that research published in American IR journals, has increasingly focused on HR rather than IR issues (Frege, 2005). Finally, with regard to the underlying research paradigms it is commonly suggested that mainstream US research has generally inter-preted IR as a labor market outcome and has been driven by a paradigm of contractual laissez-faire which was traditionally defined as free collective bargaining and is now increasingly perceived as an individualistic contractual system (Finkin, 2002).

Britain

British universities were initially more reluc-tant than their US counterparts to welcome a new field of social science research and the first university course in IR appeared in the early 1930s when the Nobel-prize economist John Hicks offered a lecture series at the London School of Economics (LSE) entitled 'Economic problems of industrial relations'. Only in the 1950s were academic appoint-ments in IR made, first at the LSE, and then Manchester and Oxford. The British counter-part to LERA, BUIRA (British Universities Industrial Relations Association), was estab-lished in 1950 and in the beginning only targeted academics and hesitated to accept practitioners for a long time. This was very different to LERA, respectively IRAA, of course which in the beginning was composed largely of business people with an interest in HR (Kaufman, 1993: 5).

Scholarly work on IR issues in Britain however started much earlier with Beatrice and Sidney Webb, who wrote the first classics in the field (*Industrial Democracy*, 1897; *History of Trade Unionism*, 1920) with their insights into the dynamics of unionism and bargaining and which have been constantly referred to by later generations of IR scholars. It could easily be argued that the Webbs were the true founders of the Anglophone field of IR rather than Commons (Gospel, 2005: 5). Also G. D. H. Cole, the outstanding Fabian of the post-Webb generation (McCarthy, 1994: 201) had a huge influence on the field. Cole founded Labor Studies in Oxford. Cole's early 'memorandum' advocated public ownership and workers' control (McCarthy, 1994: 202). However, most of these scholars, though utterly political and interested in transforming the country by reforming the institutions of capitalism ultimately stayed within the parameters of liberalism similar to their counterparts in the US (Katznelson, 1996: 27).

In contrast with the US however, though British economists had an interest in the field, IR as a more institutionalized study was mainly developed by a heterogeneous group of scholars who founded the so-called Oxford School of Industrial Relations, such as Fox and Clegg who studied PPE (Politics, Philosophy and Economics) in Oxford and Flanders (who did not have an undergraduate degree at all). The field was characterized by 'a strong current of positivist Fabian social engineering, common sense and Anglophone empiricism' not too dissimilar to the early US research (Ackers and Wilkinson, 2003: 8) though it stayed more inter-disciplinary and kept its institutional and historical approach to IR for much longer. Gospel (2005: 3) characterized this approach as mainly focused on the 'institutions of job regulation', especially trade unions and collective bargaining.

There was no real split between IR and HR scholars in Britain. This was partly because the field was less under the control of institutional economists than in the US, partly because behavioral sciences such as industrial psychology were much less developed in British universities at that time. Moreover, the leading paradigm was a pluralistic approach to IR, thus the acceptance of different interests between labor and capital and the conviction that conflict can be regulated benefiting both parties (positive sum game). This pluralistic perception of the labor market and of industrial unrest became a defining characteristic of the academic field in Britain, more so than in the US. It was also more accepted by the wider British public.

The 1970s saw the rise of a more radical Marxist frame of reference which opposed the pluralist desire of reaching stable employment relations and focused instead on class struggle and the subversion of the capitalist system. The radicalization of the 1968 student revolution affected IR scholars and a new generation of academics, in particular sociologists, rejuvenated the personnel of the discipline and added much needed rigor to its theoretical and methodological approaches (Gall, 2003). Prominent examples are Hyman's *Industrial Relations: A Marxist Introduction* (1975), or Fox's later work *Beyond Contract: Work, Power and Trust Relations* (1974). This Marxist stream was much less dominant in the US. The general absence of Marxist social sciences in the US has been widely documented (Ross, 1991) and British social sciences are commonly perceived as more progressive and ideological than those in the US (but less progressive and more pragmatic compared to continental Europe) (Katznelson, 1996: 18 and 40).

What developed from this Marxist approach were sophisticated ethnographic case studies mainly by industrial sociologists such as Batstone et al. (1977), for example, and studies of the 'Labor Process' school. Yet, this radicalization did not last. As Wood (2000: 3) describes, 'in the 1980s sociology as the key discipline within IR tended to give way to economics. This partly reflected the advent of neo-liberalism, as well as the past failings of the institutionalists to analyze economic problems such as productivity'. Ackers and Wilkinson (2003: 12) put it into a political perspective:

> the discipline's best response to [Thatcher and] the New Right was a skeptical empiricism. Following political defeat, and in the absence of any new ideas, there grew a highly quantitative new empiricism, centered around the Workplace Industrial Relations Surveys (Cully et al., 1998; Millward et al., 2000), a unique national, longitudinal data set on the state of British workplace relations. IR spent much of the 1980s and early 1990s counting, measuring, and at times denying, the very obvious dismantling of Clegg's 'system of industrial relations'.

In a nutshell, British IR developed a coexistence of sociological qualitative and econometric quantitative studies, the latter being as exemplified in particular in the publications of the *British Journal of Industrial Relations*.

Finally, with regard to the research practices there is evidence to suggest that the field has been traditionally dominated by IR/HR scholars rather than by labor economists as in the US but also that the field remains more inter-disciplinary than in the US. Based on a longitudinal cross-country survey of IR journal publications during the 1970s and 1990s authors publishing in the UK are mostly affiliated as HR/IR scholars rather than economists but that there is nevertheless a wider range of other affiliations compared to the US (Frege, 2005). Also, there is no evidence that the decline of traditional IR institutions such as trade unions and collective bargaining in Britain has lead to a declining academic interest. In contrast, research on IR issues such as unions has been stronger during the 1990s in British publication outlets compared to the 1970s, for example. Moreover, the majority of British IR research has been characterized as mainly empirical but more qualitative, inductive and if quantitative then less based on econometrical analysis compared to the US (Capelli, 1985). The major focus of research tends to be the level of the firm rather than of the individual as in the US (Frege, 2005). Finally, IR has been traditionally defined as labor market outcomes as in the US though over the years the state and legislation became to be seen as increasingly important in shaping IR. Moreover, there is a long tradition of analyzing workplace relations in political terms (labor process debate). The traditional research paradigm can be described using Kahn-Freund's famous terminology 'collective laissez-faire' (Davies and Freedland, 2002) though individual employment contracts are increasingly taking over collective regulations.

Germany

In Germany employment studies have a long tradition going back to Karl Marx, Max Weber, Lujo Brentano and Goetz Briefs. During the twentieth century the field became dominated by law, political science, but most prominently by sociology with the first university institute specializing in industrial sociology in 1928 at the Technical University Berlin (Keller, 1996; Mueller-Jentsch, 2001). Despite the fact that the relationship between capital and labor and the emergence of interest institutions were discussed in German social sciences from the mid-nineteenth century, IR was, however, not established as an independent academic discipline (Keller, 1996: 199). There is no IR department in any German university. The same is true for all other continental European countries.

Research on work and employment issues remained the subject of various social science disciplines. A few indicators should suffice to support this observation. First, although there have been increasing attempts in recent years to establish an IR discipline in Germany (for example the establishment of *Industrielle Beziehungen* – the German journal of industrial relations) the academic community directly associated with IR is still quite small. The German section of the IIRA (GIRA, established in 1970) counted 80 members in 1995 (verses 520 BUIRA members in Britain or 3850 LERA members in the US in 1995). Of those members virtually all are affiliated with a department of sociology or another social science discipline.

Moreover, an overview of *Industrielle Beziehungen*, the only specialized IR journal in Germany, between 1994 (its founding date) and 2004 reveals that published research has been conducted by researchers with a wide array of specializations: industrial sociologists, labor lawyers, political scientists, business administration scholars and economists (Frege, 2005). Rarely does anyone call themself an IR scholar. Industrial sociologists are in the clear majority. One should also note that there is hardly any cross-disciplinary communication. Business administration or law scholars for example are rarely cited in the industrial sociology literature and vice-versa (Muller, 1999: 468). The field is really multi- rather than inter-disciplinary.

Industrial sociology has made the most significant contribution to the study of IR (Keller, 1996). Its central focus are core IR issues such as bargaining policies, working time, technical change and rationalization, and their impact on work organization and social structure, but not labor market issues (Baethge and Overbeck, 1986; Kern and Schumann, 1984; Schumann et al., 1994). From its very beginning industrial sociology included a much larger field of topics compared to industrial sociology in Anglophone countries. German industrial sociology was closely connected to social philosophy and general sociology and in fact regarded as its major sub-discipline (Mueller-Jentsch, 2001: 222; Schmidt et al., 1982). It positioned itself within the broader societal context of industrialization, and focused in particular on the role of organized labor.

Max Weber initiated the first systematic sociological research on German industry under the patronage of the 'Verein fuer Socialpolitik' (first empirical research on industrial work in large German firms) in the late nineteenth century. The famous 'Verein fuer Socialpolitik', founded in 1872 by academics of the German historical school, intended to establish social fairness between capital and labor (Mueller-Jentsch 2001: 223). Goetz Briefs developed the field of 'Betriebssoziologie' (sociology of the firm), later subsumed under 'Industriesoziologie' (industrial sociology) which became a major approach of research during the 1920s and 1930s (Mueller-Jentsch, 2001: 222). Another major research project of the 'Verein' was launched in the first decade of the twentieth century on the selection and adjustment of workers in different segments of German industry (1910–15). According to Mueller-Jentsch (ibid.: 224) this was the beginning of systematic industrial research in Germany. The core question was what kind of men are shaped by modern industry and which job prospects (and indirectly life chances) do big enterprises offer them? Weber wrote a long introduction to the research project and outlined various questions to be addressed: social and geographical origins of the workforce; the principles of their selection; the physical and psychological conditions of the work process; job performance; preconditions and prospects of careers; how workers adjust to factory life; their family situation and leisure time (Mueller-Jentsch ibid.: 224). Methodology was based on interviews and participant observation in selected companies.

Mueller-Jentsch (2001) argues that industrial sociology at that time was heavily shaped by the notion of workers exploitation and this was advanced not just by Marxists but also by liberal scholars. Lujo Brentano, for example, was an early liberal economist and antipode of Marx and Engels but argued that 'trade unions play a constitutional role in capitalist economies since they empower employees to behave like sellers of commodities. Only the unions enable workers to adjust their supply according to market conditions' (ibid: 225).

After WWII sociology was gradually (re)established as an academic discipline (Mueller-Jentsch, 2001: 229). Industrial sociology quickly became a major focus (Maurer, 2004: 7). In the early years after the war sociologists were primarily concerned with whether the political democracy introduced by the Allies would stabilize in Germany. There was a common conviction that democracy is not only about institutions but that it also needs a cultural basis in society. According to v. Friedeburg (1997: 26) the fear was that class conflicts either become too strong that they endanger the democratization process or that they become too weak and endanger the reform potential of the labor movement. Thus, the belief was that only self-conscious workers could be a counterweight to the restorative forces in post-war Germany. As a consequence many sociologists focused on exploring worker consciousness and beliefs, traditional IR topics.

The first explicit project on IR after WWII was conducted by industrial sociologists in the late 1970s at the Institute for Social Research in Frankfurt (Bergmann et al., 1979). The project entailed a large empirical project on trade unions in Germany from an explicitly sociological point of view (Mueller-Jentsch, 1982: 408). In the same year IR was first introduced as an official topic at the German sociological congress (Berliner Soziologentag, 1979). It is also symptomatic that the first German textbook on IR was written by an industrial sociologist, Walther Mueller-Jentsch (1986) and called *Sociology of Industrial Relations*.

To conclude, German IR research has traditionally been dominated by industrial sociologists. Research focuses on IR rather than HR issues, is more theoretical or essayistic than empirical and if empirical favors qualitative, inductive research (Frege, 2005; Hetzler, 1995). The focus is on the firm level like in Britain. The dominant paradigm is to interpret IR as a socio-political process, thus as being shaped by economic as well as political forces, and the emphasis is on corporatist social partnership approaches rather than collective bargaining (Hyman, 1995: 39; 2004).

RESEARCH VARIATIONS AND THEIR NATIONAL EMBEDDEDNESS

The above brief overview has revealed different national developments in the IR research field. In the US labor economics was, from the early days, the leading discipline in IR research, initially with a strong institutional, policy orientation which was subsequently taken over by a more neo-classical approach to labor markets. In Britain prominent social reformers started the field and hence IR developed a strongly pragmatic public policy orientation which was less influenced by labor economists. Moreover, it received a strong Marxist influence during the 1970s which was unparalleled in the US. The field became more inter-disciplinary than its US counterpart and became dominated by scholars who received a degree in IR. Finally, Germany has a long intellectual (Marxist and liberal) tradition on researching work and employment issues which has been traditionally dominated by industrial sociologists. Whereas the field has not established institutional independence in Germany but remains multi-disciplinary, IR became an independent academic field in the US and Britain.

At the same time it comes to no surprise that all three countries reveal variations in their research practices: their major methodologies, theories and research paradigms. These variations have been shown to be long-standing national academic profiles (Frege, 2005; Kaufman, 2004; Whitfield and Strauss, 2000). Such diversity of research styles undermines assumptions of a universal, linear evolution of social sciences and it also challenges recent claims that globalization will evoke a convergence of scientific research to a universal, if not US-led model. Thus, at this stage there is evidence of a continuing national embeddedness of IR research despite the growing internationalization of academia (international conferences, cross-national research collaborations, exchange programs etc.) and despite the increasing globalization of IR practices throughout the advanced industrialized world. To conclude, there remains distinctive national research patterns which seem, so far, astonishingly resistant to processes of universalization.

How then can we explain the ongoing diversity and persistence of national research traditions? The chapter now turns to explore the longstanding roots of national IR research profiles in specific structural, institutional and political constellations within which social scientists have tried to develop discursive understandings of their IR systems. For example, a theory may gain acceptance in the field not simply because it provides the most 'adequate' explanation for a phenomenon, but, rather, because the explanation it does offer is in a form that is particularly attractive to a specific national culture or a particular group of scholars who are leading in the field.

Explaining research variation is of course an ambitious enterprise. No one single factor can explain the variations across the different research traditions. The inquiry seems to require a complex set of multiple factors, reaching into various disciplines, and in need of a historical and comparative analysis. Thus, for the study of IR research, ideally, it seems one would need a comparative history of IR and its ideas in Britain, Germany and the US, a history of knowledge production, a history of the relations between IR and related disciplines, a history of influential academics in the field and a social history (students and their background). We would also need a theory to interconnect historical, structural and cognitive determinants and the actions of scientific community (Weingart, 1976). However, as Fourcade-Gourinchas (2001: 398) argues, we do not yet have a satisfactory encompassing theory of knowledge formation that would allow us to account simultaneously for the social structures and institutions of knowledge production and for the latter's intrinsic, substantive ideational nature. And we have no theoretical framework to analyze cross-cultural variations between social science disciplines.

The remaining part of this chapter, therefore, introduces three preliminary approaches which highlight the embeddedness of IR research in its national-specific context.

These are heuristic tools rather than a tight theoretical framework, exploring interrelations between variables rather than determining causalities. The first provides a substantive approach and focuses on how the subject field of academic inquiry and national IR practices, shape research traditions. The second approach highlights the institutional embeddedness of IR research in national scientific traditions. The third and final approach discusses the relationship between national political traditions, in particular the conception of political and industrial democracy, and IR research.

IR practices

This approach provides a contextual explanation of cross-country research variations by linking 'external' IR practices to 'internal' research practices. It is assumed that in particular research topics, author affiliations and academic paradigms will mirror the development and practice of IR institutions in a specific country. This position is essentially functionalist since it assumes an independent scientific space organized around specific self-referential understandings of the subject field, thus in our case IR practices (Wagner, 1990: 478). In other words, academic disciplines and specializations develop essentially as structural reactions to changes in the external environment.

This assumption is widely acknowledged among social scientists today and is in stark contrast to the original positivist position which argued that scientific inquiry is independent of the phenomenon observed (Delanty, 1997). Moreover, because IR is a problem-oriented field of study it is even more likely to be shaped by the real world of IR which differs from country to country. As Dunlop states, 'different interests of academic experts seem largely a reflection of their type of IR system' (1958: 329). Hyman (2001) points out that the different national IR systems provoke different research topics: for example an emphasis of Anglophone research on collective bargaining and in Germany on social partnership and co-determination.

Thus, the traditional lack of academic interest in the state or in social partnership in the US can be explained by the traditional absence of the state and of workplace democracy in American IR, whereas their dominance in German research mirrors their continuing relevance for the German employment system.

In a similar vein, scholars have highlighted that research follows changing policy questions (Derber, 1964; Dunlop, 1977; Strauss and Feuille, 1978). In particular, Capelli (1985) argues that shifts in research topics easily occur as a reaction to shifts in government, union or employer policies. For example, the increasing interest in HR issues in the US can be understood as a reaction to the increasing number of non-union workplaces and anti-union employer and/or state strategies. Moreover, should IR regulations and practices increasingly converge in a globalizing world (see Chapter 7) one would expect a simultaneous convergence of research patterns across countries. So far however this does not seem to have happened (Frege, 2005).

There can be no doubt that this approach helps to explain research shifts over time in one particular country (for example the decline of IR and the increase of HR topics in the US) but also cross-country variations in research. Moreover, this approach provides an explanation of why different professions get interested in researching IR topics. For example, the more legalistic and corporatist IR systems in continental Europe attract more legal scholars, political scientists and sociologists whereas labor economists are primarily attracted in Anglophone countries where market forces play a larger and more accepted role in determining IR outcomes. The substantive approach is not a sufficient explanation, however, and for example is not helpful in exploring the different development of the field of study, thus its institutionalization.

Scientific traditions

A second approach is introduced which is historical in nature and embraces the embeddedness of IR research within national social science traditions.

It is now widely recognized that social sciences and their disciplines are social constructs, embedded in specific historical contexts and shaped by national cultures and philosophies (Levine, 1995: 100). They are not just the outcome of a universal, automatic progress of science, nor are they natural, pre-determined categories, but can vary from country to country. In Ross' words (1991: 1), 'the content and borders of the disciplines that resulted in the beginning of the twentieth century were as much the product of national cultures, local circumstances and accidental opportunities as intellectual logic'. In particular, the development of social sciences was closely connected to the rise of modern universities and were shaped by national epistemological traditions.

University structures

It is during the late-nineteenth century in particular that universities were resurrected as primary knowledge-producing institutions and that the idea of a research-oriented university became predominant in Europe and the US (Wittrock, 1993: 305). This development was closely related to the rise of the modern nation-state and the new economic capitalist order. Universities therefore came to be key institutions both for knowledge production, in particular technological progress and for strengthening a sense of national and cultural identity (ibid.: 321). As we will see, however, they developed in different ways in different countries. Major questions which were debated in all countries were, for example, between the pros and cons of a liberal versus vocational education and pure versus applied research.

The national-specific structures of universities are useful in explaining the institutional differences within IR research, thus its institutionalization as a field of study in the Anglophone world but not in continental Europe.

The close relationship between knowledge structures and research practices has been widely accepted in the literature. Already Merton (1968: 521) observed that research patterns are influenced by specific forms of knowledge organization. Fourcade-Gourinchas (2001: 400) points out that 'scientific discourses [research patterns] are inevitably driven by broader, nationally constituted, cultural frameworks embodied in specific institutions of knowledge production'. And Ringer (1992: 26) convincingly proposes that intellectual communities such as academic disciplines cannot be adequately discussed without reference to the history of educational systems in each country which are heavily dependent on the specific relationship between state and society.

Applied to our context, this trajectory links the existence or absence of the institutionalization of the IR field to the different national university structures. Arguably, the development of the German university structure of professorial chairs enabled a broader research agenda for the individual professors but hindered the institutionalization of inter-disciplinary fields. In contrast, the more formal departmental structure as developed in the US in the early-twentieth century, which was later also introduced to British universities, narrowed the individual's research area but facilitated the creation of institutionalized inter-disciplinary fields.

In other words, the strict classification of disciplines in US universities, which became more dominant than in Europe (Wagner, 1990: 236), made it more difficult for individual scholars to integrate IR topics into their own discipline but on the other hand created the opportunity to establish specific inter-disciplinary programs. US social science disciplines tend to follow a strict methodological and theoretical canon and are more likely to discriminate alternative views. In Ross' (1991: 10) words,

the importance of disciplines and disciplinary professions to stabilize academic positions in the US system lead frequently to an ontological purification of disciplinary discourses by excluding outside factors to strengthen disciplinary identification whereas in Europe disciplines were less inhibited to use theoretical concepts from other disciplines.

The fact that in the US, IR institutes were first created by institutional economists who felt increasingly left out of their own discipline, substantiates this point.

In Germany, the Humboldtian reforms in the second part of the nineteenth century supported an organizational structure around chairs which traditionally allowed a slightly less rigid definition of the disciplines. Individual professors were more able to follow their own interests independent of the mainstream. Thus, a sociology or law professor interested in labor found it easier to follow this research topic even if it did not fit completely with disciplinary boundaries. Therefore there was less need to establish inter-disciplinary forums. An additional reason was that inter-disciplinary, specialized or vocational fields had less chance to get accepted because of the traditional German emphasis on general, pure knowledge creation which was fostered by Humboldt.

Finally, Britain is characterized by a less rigid disciplinary structure than the US but also by weaker professorial chairs than in Germany. Britain for a long time almost exclusively focused on elitist undergraduate education dominated by colleges and neglecting the development of graduate or professional schools like in the US (Fourcade-Gourinchas, 2001: 165). The great British universities in the nineteenth century were strongly anti-professional. Professional education was dominated by practitioners outside universities (Burrage, 1993: 155). Moreover, British universities for a long time developed as relatively insular, elitist institutions emphasizing the classical subjects while neglecting natural as well as social sciences. The first social science research which arose out of a response to the increasing social problems of industrialization developed outside the university such as in the famous Manchester Statistical Society (1833) (Manicas, 1987: 196). Thus, all these factors help to explain why IR as an inter-disciplinary study was delayed for a long time in Britain.

Epistemological traditions

In addition to the university structures, epistemological traditions also shaped the development and patterns of scientific disciplines in each country. These traditions help explain, for example, why a German and a US sociologist working on similar labor issues may use different research tools, in particular different methodologies, despite their shared profession. And why a British economist and a British sociologist may have something in common despite their different professions. In other words, it may provide an explanation as to why the US is generally leaning toward quantitative empirical research whereas German IR research is usually characterized by qualitative research and Britain exhibits traces of both; or why both US and British IR research tend to produce intermediate, middle-range theories whereas Germany is biased toward more abstract, general social science theories (Bulmer, 1991).

Modern philosophies of knowledge developed during the eighteenth and nineteenth centuries and influenced the countries' conception of knowledge creation. In short, the idealist philosophy and humanistic university reforms during the nineteenth century in Germany were strongly oriented toward science for its own sake ('pure science') rather than to be an instrument for larger societal purposes (for example improving social conditions) as it became the norm in particular in the US. There was an emphasis on holistic thinking in broad historical cultural categories and being informed by a philosophy which rejected narrow-minded specialization which provided a challenge to mechanistic and compositional thinking prevalent in Europe at that time. As a consequence, when social sciences (including the academic treatment of work and employment) were slowly established at the end of the nineteenth century they became mostly concerned with elaborating a coherent theoretical framework for societal analysis based on philosophical foundations (Wittrock et al., 1991: 41). Social sciences were originally interpreted as historical sciences embedded in the humanities. This shaped the tendency of the social sciences toward descriptive, historical, qualitative and theoretical research as we can still observe today, for example in the case of IR research. Efforts at empirical research were very fragmented as well as policy-oriented research which could hardly develop in the shadow of formal theorizing (Wittrock, ibid.). This may have induced the strong presence of hermeneutic and Marxist epistemological approaches and heuristic methodologies in German social sciences. In a nutshell, one can argue that these traditions may have facilitated a more political and critical awareness of social conditions and problems. Social science was understood as a tool to explore the genesis of modern society and it fostered the importance of academic freedom and supported the pursuit of pure knowledge rather than of instrumental, pragmatic research.

In Britain social sciences were caught in the bind between the positivistic heritage of moralistic reformism and administrative (empirical) knowledge (Delanty, 1997: 26). Thus, they were characterized by a strong positivist-utilitarian tradition, methodological individualism and a naturalistic morality. British social sciences essentially go back to Hobbes' utilitarianism and his ideas based on the methods of natural science (Halevy, 1966: 153). J. S. Mill for example, who was heavily influenced by Hobbes, was critical of scientific politics and stood for a model of 'useful' knowledge. Empiricism was praised as an inductive science of general causal laws. On the other side, British social science was characterized by a moral focus and science was linked to the idea of moral improvement and a humane secular ethic (Delanty, 1997: 26). As Manicas (1987: 197) highlights, the social problems of the industrializing British Empire were interpreted by the British academic elite as a moral problem and were, accordingly, a problem of how to restore the morals of individuals.

The US developed in similar ways to Britain but with a more scientist, pragmatic approach to the sciences, in particular social sciences which was seen as a tool to improve the social conditions of modern society. Thus, whereas British social sciences started as a fusion of analysis and (moral) prescription, the US eventually favored a more scientific, detached approach to social questions which was modeled upon natural sciences (Bulmer, 1991: 152). This ultimately induced a bias toward an empiricist ideology with a focus on quantitative scientific methods in the US (Ross, 1991).

In sum, these national knowledge systems, which originated in the nineteenth century, shape the different ways in which social sciences and therefore IR research have been organized and practiced in the three countries. British IR research, for example, always had a stronger public-policy agenda than the US and was less interested in perfecting econometric tools for measuring IR practices and outcomes. German IR research on the other hand has been heavily theory driven and if empirical has mainly pursued hermeneutic, descriptive methods.

Political traditions

The cross-national variation of subject fields, as well as, the scientific traditions are a necessary but not sufficient explanation for cross-national research variation. For example, similar research topics can be researched in very different ways. The fact that the US traditionally has a strong interest in HR policy whereas German academics are more interested in the labor process – both approaches look at the workplace – indicates the existence of different paradigms and aims of research. German social scientists have traditionally been more concerned about the labor process and its outcomes for workers as a social class than their mainstream US counterparts who are more interested in individual work attitudes and workplace efficiency. These variations cannot be sufficiently explained on the basis of different subject fields or scientific traditions.

A third and final factor then, is the political embeddedness of the research field. The assumption is that political traditions have a certain independence of their subject matter and of their academic institutionalization and can shape research patterns in different ways. In particular research paradigms, aims and also theories are likely to be influenced by political ideas.

I focus on the national political discourse on work and democracy which originates in the nineteenth century. I argue that the philosophical traditions of idealism in Germany or of liberalism and positivism in Britain and the US shaped the political understanding and subsequent writings on the state, democracy and the economy during the nineteenth century. In particular, the relationship between political and industrial democracy crucially influenced the development of different research paradigms. The three countries developed during the nineteenth century rather different political traditions on the relationship between state, society and economy which shaped two different streams of interpretations of industrial democracy: an Anglophone and a German (continental European) stream. Germany developed a legalistic, state-oriented approach (co-determination) whereas Britain and the US developed a free collective bargaining approach (and eventually voluntary, employer-led direct participation schemes). Both constitutional traditions are based on two distinct concepts of industrial democracy which I call 'contractual' and 'communal'.

In essence, the US and Britain regarded the capitalist enterprise as a 'private affair' (firm as private property) and the economy as an assembly of free individuals joining in contractual relationships. Private contracts rule. Industrial democracy is therefore focused on the free bargaining between employers and employees. Moreover, the law privileges individual rather than collective employment rights. One should note the differences between Britain and the US: between a social democratic and a liberal divide on industrial democracy the US emerge virtually exclusively on the liberal side of the line (Katznelson, 1996: 40). Britain, on the other hand, is slightly more infatuated with markets and experienced times, in particular after WWI and II, of socialist attempts to

nationalize important industries and is in general more committed to state intervention than the US (Jacoby, 2003: 49).

In Germany, the main understanding was to perceive the firm as a 'quasi-public affair', as a social community, a state within the state, a constitutional monarchy, where workers would receive certain democratic rights and the monarch/owner would not have absolute power as in a constitutional monarchy. 'The employment relationship is not seen as one of free subordination but of democratization'. This was the declaration of the famous Weimar labor law scholar, Hugo Sinzheimer (Finkin, 2002: 621). One could also say that the US and Britain focused on 'private contracts' whereas Germany focused on a 'social contract' within the firm, to adopt Rousseau's phrase.

The distinction between a private and public view of the firm has a clear reminiscence to the mechanic and organic state theories and to civil and common law traditions. The role of the entrepreneur is seen differently in both traditions. In the Anglophone common law tradition the enterprise is the property of the entrepreneur with workers relegated to contractual claims, at best, on the surplus from production (Deakin, 2005: 12). The continental or in our case German entrepreneurs are members of the enterprise community and share duties and privileges that this position entails.

One can conclude therefore that democracy in the US and to a lesser extent in Britain has been mainly conceptualized at a political level and developed a much weaker place in economic life where democracy is limited to certain individual rights and a minimum of collective rights (for example free labor contracts and collective bargaining). In other words, the individual has only very limited democratic rights at work, the main right being to be in a free contractual relationship and therefore to be able to leave the contract. The focus of Anglophone labor law on individual rights therefore has a long tradition. Today this is emphasized even more in the increasing decline of collective labor law and the dominance of identity-based employee rights in particular in the US. In contrast, in Germany industrial democracy has been much more linked to the development of political democracy and has legally restrained managerial discretion. The focus of labor law is on collective rights.

In sum, this approach highlights the importance of linking national research patterns to the historically embedded discourses on democracy at work. The different state philosophies as they developed in Germany, Britain and the US during the nineteenth century shaped the perception of the capitalist firm and subsequently the conception of industrial democracy.

Applied to the context of IR the different intellectual traditions of political and industrial democracy can explain certain cross-national research differences. For example, the fact that German scholars traditionally work on topics related to worker participation may not just be due to their labor institutions promoting democracy at work ('subject field'), but also because of a long-standing intellectual tradition in German social sciences to interpret industrial democracy as an important adjunct to political democracy and hence as a value itself. This also explains the interest of German political scientists and lawyers in IR research. In contrast, industrial democracy in the US for example has not generally been seen as a precondition or attribute of political democracy and has been traditionally perceived as individual rights, property rights on one side and no forced labor on the other side. Recent discussions on employee voice (Freeman and Rogers, 1999) exemplify this individualistic conception of industrial democracy (but see exceptions such as Derber, 1964).

CONCLUSION

This chapter has offered a brief description of the historical development of IR as a field of research in Britain, Germany and the US, which represent trends in the Anglophone world as well as in continental Europe. It suggested that social sciences, such as the

IR field, do not necessarily develop in similar ways across countries but are embedded in broader national-specific cultures. There is no reason to assume that these varying research styles are deviations from a standard, or delays in reaching that standard. On the contrary, the persistence of national intellectual profiles over time undermines assumptions of a universal, linear evolution of the social sciences and instead highlights their national historical embeddedness.

This chapter further explored the embeddedness of these research patterns in their national contexts. On one hand it highlighted the significance of national institutions and practices of IR in shaping research outcomes. On the other hand, the chapter also reminded us to conceptualize IR research as a social scientific field of study which is inevitably embedded in long-standing national traditions of scientific knowledge production, such as university structures and philosophical traditions of knowledge creation. Finally, the chapter outlined the importance of intellectual conceptions of political and industrial democracy and to what extent and how the workplace was regarded as part of a wider political democracy.

To conclude, IR research has developed differently in different countries and there is reason to suggest that this will continue for some time. As of today there is no evidence of a significant convergence of research styles across countries. Sustained divergence is the result so far. This also challenges predictions of various globalization and convergence theories of the diminishing significance of the nation state. This chapter argues instead for the nation state's enduring importance at least for the field of scientific knowledge creation.

However, this does not mean that research patterns should be seen as historically deterministic. They are potentially open for change. Scholars may have had good reasons for choosing their scientific path, which was subsequently institutionalized, but there were reasons consistently shaped by specific historical and cultural intentions (Ross, 1991). Given hindsight, we may find that there are better reasons for choosing differently in the future, in particular given the increasing academic crisis of the IR discipline. Becoming aware of different national approaches, and thus of different research options, is a first step. What should follow is a dialogue between the research patterns; how one could benefit from each other to ensure the long-term viability of the discipline.

NOTES

1 For the purposes of this paper, I use this term to refer to the following countries: Great Britain, Ireland, United States of America, Canada, Australia and New Zealand (see Crouch 2005).

2 For more detailed country overviews see Frege (2007) and Kaufman (2004).

REFERENCES

Ackers, P. and Wilkinson, A. (eds) (2003) *Understanding Work and Employment: Industrial Relations in Transition*. Oxford: Oxford University Press.

Baethge, M. and Overbeck, H. (1986*) Zukunft der Angestellten. Neue Technologien und berufliche Perspektiven in Büro und Verwaltung*. Frankfurt: Campus.

Batstone, E., Boraston, I. and Frenkel, S. (1977) *Shop Stewards in Action: The Organization of Workplace Conflict and Accommodation*. Oxford: Blackwell.

Bergmann, J., Jakobi, O. and Mueller-Jentsch, W. (1979) *Gewerkschaften in der BRD*. Frankfurt am Main: Suhrkamp.

Boyer, G. and Smith, R. (2001) 'The development of the neoclassical tradition in labor economics', *Industrial and Labor Relations Review*, 54 (2).

Bulmer, M. (1991) 'National context for the development of social-policy research: British and American research on poverty and social welfare compared', in P. Wagner, C. Hirschon Weiss, B. Wittrock and H. Wollmann (eds) *Social Sciences and Modern States*. Cambridge: Cambridge University Press. pp. 148–67.

Burrage, M. (1993) 'From practice to school-based professional education: patterns of conflict and accommodation in England, France and the United States', in S. Rothblatt and B. Wittrock (eds) *The European and American University Since 1800: Historical and Sociological Essays*. Cambridge: Cambridge University Press.

Capelli, P. (1985) 'Theory construction in IR and some implications for research', *Industrial Relations*, 24 (1): 90–112.

Committee on Industrial Relations (1926) Advisory committee on industrial relations, memorandum, 'to the Committee on Policy and Problems', August 1926, Box 59, Folder 331. R.G. 1.8 SSRC. RAC.

Commons, J. (1919) *Industrial Goodwill*. New York: McGraw-Hill.

Crouch, C. (2005) *Capitalist Diversity and Change: Recombinant Governance and Institutional Entrepreneurs*. Oxford: Oxford University Press.

Cully, M., Woodland, S., O'Reilly, A. and Dix, G. (1998) *Britain at work: as depicted by the 1998 Workplace Employee Relations Survey*. London: Routledge.

Davies, P. and Freedland, M. (2002) 'National styles in labor law scholarship', *Comparative Labor Law and Policy Journal*, 23 (3).

Deakin, S. (2005) 'Coevolution of law and the economy: industrialization and labor law in Britain and Continental Europe', conference paper, *Workshop on Making Markets Through the Law: Legal Claim and Economic Possibility*. Paris, June 2005.

DeBrizzi, J. (1983) *Ideology and the Rise of Labor Theory in America*. Westport: Greenwood Press.

Delanty, G. (1997) *Social Science: Beyond Con-structivism and Realism*. Minneapolis: Minnesota University Press.

Derber, M. (1964) 'Divergent tendencies in IR Research', *Industrial and Labor Relations Review*, XVII, July: 598–616.

Dunlop, J. (1958) *Industrial Relations Systems*. New York: Henry Holt & Co.

Dunlop, J. (1977) 'Policy decisions and research in economics and industrial relations', *Industrial and Labor Relations Review*, April: 275–82.

Finkin, M. (2002) 'Menschenbild: the conception of the employee as a person in western law', *Comparative Labor Law and Policy Journal*, 23 (2): 577–637

Fourcade-Gourinchas, M. (2001) 'Politics, institutional structures, and the rise of economics: a comparative study', *Theory and Society*, 30: 397–447.

Fox, A. (1974) *Beyond Contract: Work, Power and Trust Relations*. London: Faber.

Freeman, R. and Rogers, J. (1999) *What Workers Want*. Ithaca: Cornell University Press.

Frege, C.M. (2005) 'Varieties of industrial relations research: take-over, convergence or divergence?', *British Journal of Industrial Relations*, 43 (2): 179–207.

Frege, C.M. (2007) *Employment Research and State Tra-ditions. A Comparative History of Britain, Germany, and the United States*. Oxford: Oxford University Press.

Gall, G. (2003) 'Marxism and Industrial Relations', in P. Ackers and A. Wilkinson (eds) *Understanding Work and Employment*. Oxford: Oxford University Press.

Godard, J. (1994) 'Beyond empiricism: towards a reconstruction of IR theory and research', *Advances in Industrial and Labor Relations*, (6): 1–35.

Gospel, H. (2005) 'A British and historical perspective on workplace governance'. kaufman and 'the global evolution of industrial relations', *Industrielle Beziehungen*, 12 (4): 1–10.

Halevy, E. (1966) *The growth of philosophical radicalism*. Boston: Beacon press.

Hetzler, H.W. (1995) '25 Jahre Deutsche Sektion der International Industrial Relations Association - Erinnerungen, Erfahrungen und Erwartungen', *Industrielle Beziehungen*, 2 (3): 312–334.

Hodgson, G. (2001) *How economics forgot history*. London: Routledge.

Hyman, R. (1975) *Industrial Relations: A Marxist Introduction*. Basingstoke: MacMillan.

Hyman, R. (1995) 'Industrial relations in Europe: theory and practice', *European Journal of Industrial Relations*. 1 (1): 17–46.

Hyman, R. (2001) *Theorizing Industrial Relations: Anglo-American Individualism versus the European Social Model*. Working paper, London School of Economics.

Hyman (2004) 'Is Industrial relations theory always ethnocentric?' in B. Kaufman (ed.) *Theoretical perspectives on Work and the Employment Relationship*. Champaign-Urbana: IRRA Publications. pp. 265–92.

Jacoby, S.M. (2003) 'Economic ideas and the labor market: Origins of the Anglo-American Model and prospects for global diffusion', *Comparative Labor Law and Policy Journal*, 25 (1): 43–78.

Jacoby, S.M. (1990) 'The new institutionalism: what can it learn from the old?', *Industrial Relations*, 29 (2): 316–359.

Katznelson, I. (1996) 'Knowledge about What? Policy Intellectuals and the New Liberalism', in D. Rueschemeyer and T. Skocpol, (eds) *States, social knowledge, and the origins of modern social policies*. Princeton: Princeton University Press

Kaufman, B. (1993) *The Origins and Evolution of the Field of Industrial Relations in the United States*. Ithaca: ILR Press.

Kaufman, B. (2004) *The Global Evolution of Industrial Relations*. Geneva: ILO.

Keller, B. (1996) 'The German approach to industrial relations: a literature review', *European Journal of Industrial Relations*, 2 (2): 199–210.

Kern, H. and Schumann, M. (1984) *Das Ende der Arbeitsteilung? Rationalisierung in der industriellen Produktion*, 3rd edn. München: Beck.

Kimmel, J. (2000) *Creating A Real Science of Human Relations: Personnel Management and the Politics of Professionalism, 1910–1940*, PhD Thesis. John Hopkins University.

Levine, D. (1995) *Visions of the Sociological Tradition*. Chicago: Chicago University Press.

McCarthy, W. (1994) 'The involvement of academics in British industrial relations', *British Journal of Industrial Relations*, 32 (2).

Manicas, P. (1987) *A History and Philosophy of the Social Sciences*. New York: Basil Blackwell.

Maurer, A. (2004) 'Elend und Ende der Arbeits- und Industriesoziologie', *Soziologie*, 33 (4): 7–19.

Merton, R. (1968) *Social Theory and Social Structure*. New York: Free Press.

Millward, N., Bryson, A. and Forth, J. (1992) *All Change at Work?: British Employee Relations, 1980–1998, Portrayed by the Workplace Industrial Relations Survey Series*. London: Routledge.

Mitchell, D. (2001) 'IR journal and conference literature from the 1960s to the 1990s: what can HR learn from it? Where is it headed?', *Human Resource Management Review*, 11: 375–93.

Muller, M. (1999) 'Enthusiastic embrace or critical reception?: The German HRM debate', *Journal of Management Studies,* 35 (4): 465–82.

Mueller-Jentsch, W. (1982) 'Gewerkschaften als intermediäre Organisationen', *Kölner Zeitschrift für Soziologie und Sozialpsychologie*, Sonderheft 'Materialien zur Industriesoziologie', 34: 408–32.

Mueller-Jentsch, W. (1986) *Soziologie der industriellen Beziehungen*. Frankfurt: Campus.

Mueller-Jentsch, W. (2001) Germany, chp 11, in D. Cornfield and R. Hodson (eds) *Worlds of Work: Building an International Sociology of Work*. New York: Kluwer.

Ringer, F. (1992) *Fields of Knowledge: French Academic Culture in Comparative Perspective*. Cambridge: Cambridge University Press.

Ross, D. (1991) *The Origins of American Social Science*. Cambridge: Cambridge University Press.

Schmidt, G., Braczyk, H.J., Knesebeck, J.v.d., (1982) Materialien zur Industriesoziologie', *Koelner Zeitschrift fuer Soziologie und Sozialpsychologie*. Sonderheft 24.

Schumann, M., Baethge-Kinsky, V., Kuhlmann, M., Kurz, C. and Neumann, U. (1994) *Trendreport Rationalisierung. Automobilindustrie, Werkmaschinenbau, Chemische Industrie* 2nd edn. Berlin: Sigma.

Shenav, Y. (2000) *Manufacturing Rationality: The Engineering Foundations of the Managerial Revolution*. Oxford: Oxford University Press.

Solow, R. (1997) 'How did Economics get that way and what way did it get?', in Th. Bender and C.E. Schorske (eds) *American Academic Culture in Transformation: Fifty Years, Four Disciplines*. Princeton: Princeton University Press. pp. 57–76.

Strauss, G. and Feuille, P. (1978) 'Industrial Relations Research: A Critical Analysis', *Industrial Relations*, XVII, October: 259–77.

Taylor, F. W. (1911) *Principles of Scientific Management*. Elibron Classics: Norwood, MA., USA: Plimpton Press.

v. Friedeburg, L. (1997) 'Kooperation und Konkurrenz', *SOFI-Mitteilungen*, 25, July: 25–32.

Wagner, P. (1990) *Sozialwissenschaften und Staat. Frankreich, Italien, Deutschland 1890–1980*. Frankfurt/M: Campus.

Weingart, P. (1976) *Wissensproduktion und soziale Struktur*. Frankfurt/M: Suhrkamp.

Whitfield, K. and Strauss, G. (2000), 'Methods matter: changes in industrial relations research and their Implications', *British Journal of Industrial Relations*, 38 (1): 141–52.

Wittrock, B. (1993) 'The modern university: the three transformations', in S. Rothblatt and B. Wittrock, (eds) *The European and American University Since 1800: Historical and Sociological Essays*. Cambridge: Cambridge University Press. pp. 303–63.

Wittrock, B. and Wollmann, H. (1991) 'Social science and the modern state: policy knowledge and political institutions in Western Europe and the United States', in P. Wagner, C. Hirschon Weiss, B. Wittrock and H. Wollmann (eds) *Social Sciences and Modern States: National Experiences and Theoretical Crossroads*. Cambridge: Cambridge University Press.

Wood, St. (2000) 'The BJIR and industrial relations in the new millennium', *British Journal of Industrial Relations*, 38 (1): 1–5.

3

Industrial Relations and the Social Sciences

Peter Ackers and Adrian Wilkinson

INTRODUCTION

We begin with a paradox. The broad subject matter of Industrial Relations (IR) – the regulation of work and employment – is as topical today as it ever was. Yet IR as a traditional academic field of study, centered on trade unions and collective bargaining, now touches only a very limited part of contemporary working life (Ackers, 2004). As Gospel (2006) notes, it is important to keep in mind the distinction between the *real world subject* and the *field of study*, while recognizing that there is a dynamic relationship between the two. This is particularly true of the applied social sciences, where the dialogue between academic ideas and public policy is especially intimate. Just as social policy was shaped, as an academic field, by the post-war development of welfare systems, so in western economies and beyond academic IR was developed in response to the growth of trade unions and collective bargaining. Today that tide has ebbed and turned, such that much of the world's working population are now well beyond the reach of joint regulation and

the old IR models appear almost everywhere of decreasing policy relevance. Even for those in the shrinking unionized sphere, the scope of union influence has been much reduced and many of the things that matter to managers and workers are left to state and employer regulation. As Mike Emmott (2005) of the British Chartered Institute of Personnel and Development (CIPD) has argued, the central role of management in working life has marginalized the traditional IR analysis of joint regulation (see also Sisson's dissenting 2006 response).

How can we characterize in broad-brush terms the way that this real world subject has changed, assuming that there are deeper sociological reasons for the global decline of trade unions and collective bargaining? The IR community is justifiably uncomfortable with vague prophetic theories of post-modernity that are immune to empirical testing. However, there are other more grounded, historical ways of stating the problem. The real world occasion for the birth of IR was the emergence of the organized working class, labor movement in the late-nineteenth-century industrial society of Britain and the US (Ackers and Wilkinson, 2003; Kaufman, 2004; Wilkinson, 2007). With the benefit of hindsight and historical perspective, we can see this as a particular period of industrial society, which, in America and Europe, has evolved into the *post-industrial economy* of recent decades. In the private sector, large factory concentrations of male, manual workers have given way to a predominantly service economy, which is highly feminized and based on smaller work units in close contact with customers: a very different employment relationship (Korczynski, 2003). By itself, this doesn't explain everything: not the survival of unions among public sector professionals, or the failure of unions to thrive in the new industrial economies like China, nor the uneven pattern of union decline.

Much of this seems to be accounted for by state politics and political choice, but still there appears to be an inexorable IR pattern emerging. The term *neo-liberalism* best captures the conjuncture of global market pressures and ideological choices that is driving this. The latter relates to the cultural decline of traditional social democratic politics (and the collapse of Communism), so that while, in Britain, we still have a Labour Party and a quarter of the workforce are members of trade unions, it now sounds anachronistic and nostalgic to speak of the 'labor movement' or 'the working class'. Our assumption is that in advanced post-industrial economies, we have reached 'the end of labor history', as traditionally understood, whereby the problem of labor has lost its former political, institutional and international dimension. Governments everywhere think less and less of improving workforce commitment, skills and training through a relationship with an identifiable labor movement. Even a society like India, with its huge working poor, seems to have moved in the same direction. While poverty and social strife continue, the labor movement and labor relations no longer form the primary conduit through which these problems are represented and resolved (Ackers, 2006b). Once we allow for the persistence of different varieties of capitalism

(Hall and Soskice, 2001), there remains some sense of a neo-liberal consensus, which has displaced the post-war social democratic consensus. This has shifted the dominant economic policy emphasis from the state to the business enterprise and markets; while within employment relations a combination of employer regulation and 'minimum' legal regulation has taken the central place formerly occupied by collective bargaining. Arguably, this new policy emphasis reaches across the global economy and embraces mainstream social democracy, such that the range of government policy debate has contracted to the political right's 'minimalist state' versus the political left's 'enabling state' (Hennessy, 2006: 71).

Within these terms, this chapter is not a plea for the old IR to launch a counter-offensive to recapture lost ground. Rather, we argue that such a fundamental shift in 'events' and 'ideas' (Ackers, 2005b; 2006a; Kaufman, 2004) means that IR analysis can only be reconstituted in dialogue with surrounding social science disciplines; not as institutional analysis of a shrinking collective bargaining 'system', but as a theory-and-policy paradigm that speaks to the wider business school and social science communities. Our discussion is centered on the British case, reflecting both the Anglo-Saxon origins of the subject (Frege, 2004) and an attempt to take an alternative view to that of the American approach; but we use this to illuminate broader themes for social scientists all over the world.

IR has always centered on the study of social institutions. It began with the Webbs as an administrative social science and, in Britain, the work of the Oxford School carried forward this enthusiasm for accumulating historical detail about trade unions, collective bargaining and employers associations as the central realities of IR analysis. Even IR radicals, who have often expressed exasperation with this conservative institutional agenda, have adopted many aspects of it. Today, however, IR institutionalism is besieged, on all sides, by an army of academic critics from neo-classical economics, managerial psychology and post-modernist social theory. IR is criticized (or just ignored) not just for its obsession with a highly limited range of social institutions – trade unions and collective bargaining – which are becoming less and less central to the sociology of contemporary society; but for its emphasis on institutions *per se*. According to 'science building' positivists, IR does not generate predictive theory, but only piles up description (see Kaufman, 2003). For post-modernists, IR confuses the linguistically-constructed nature of our knowledge of society with something much more solid and accessible (see Eldridge, 2003). In both cases, institutional context is downplayed in the quest to understand organizational behavior (OB).

The IR tradition has many faults. At times, it has accumulated description for its own sake, made a fetish of facts and confused the content of union agreements with the much richer social dynamics swirling around them. However, the critics also have their Achilles heel, and while they come from opposite poles of social science – positivist and anti-positivist, managerial and critical management – theirs is a shared intellectual weakness: the neglect of 'real' socio-economic context and the institutions which constitute it and, crucially, can change it. Thus for us, IR's institutional analysis of the employment relationship needs to be re-thought and re-tooled, within a broader social science tradition of institutional theory and critical realism (Ackroyd and Fleetwood, 2004; Edwards, 2005) – rather than simply abandoned. This chapter concentrates on the former strand.

Viewed from within the academic IR community, the twin dangers are that either the academic study of employment lifts entirely free from its old IR mooring, jettisoning a rich tradition of concepts and empirical studies; or alternatively that IR scholars continue to work within the comfortable but shrinking walls of its established paradigm and ignore the changing outside world of work and ideas. These extreme options may be expressed as *liquidation* versus *anachronism*. In the first case, already evident in American IR journals and departments, the words, Industrial

Relations, may remain for reasons of tradition and inertia, while the content is hollowed-out and replaced by other disciplinary approaches, typically drawn from neo-classical economics or managerial psychology. In the second case, strongly represented in the British radical tradition, academics continue to write and teach exclusively about trade unions, strikes and collective bargaining; even though these issues affect a declining number of employees and have become marginal subjects of wider intellectual debate.

This chapter seeks a middle way between these ultimately terminal cases. We begin by recalling the social science genesis of Anglo-American IR and assessing the academic disciplines that flowed into it. Next, we consider the current dominant *academic context* of IR scholarship, throughout the world: largely practised in business schools and intermingled with the new core curriculum of HRM and OB. Finally, we sketch a possible extended future life for IR, through an engagement with a wider social science tradition of institutional theory; one which enables IR to continue drawing on its own disciplinary past while moving forward confidently and combatively into a very different real world and academic context.

THE INTER-DISCIPLINARY GENESIS OF IR

Sidney and Beatrice Webb's *Industrial Democracy* (1897) was the intellectual foundation stone of academic IR (see Ackers, 2005a). Characteristically, the Webbs' tied together IR theory and public policy at a time when Economics, Politics and Sociology, in particular, were in the early stages of development (see Bulmer, 1985). The Webb's own career, as Fabian social democrats, as formative figures in many of these new disciplines and as founders of the London School of Economics, embedded IR in the interdisciplinary movement for social reform. After World War Two, British and American social scientists, each in their own way, worked out a stable academic division of labor – famously orchestrated by Talcott Parsons for the US – but this was also closely linked to the dynamics and requirement of public policy. The management of a post-war social democratic consensus in a largely industrial society threw up problems like strikes and incomes policy. IR academics, such as Hugh Clegg at Warwick, both built academic IR departments and sat on numerous public enquiries and commissions (Ackers, 2007).

In Britain at least, the election of Margaret Thatcher in 1979 marked a fairly abrupt end to the IR theory-public policy nexus. The combination of a post-industrial economy and neo-liberalism has disrupted the interdisciplinary social science status quo. Alongside the predictable rise of expansionist and individualistic academic traditions, such as neo-classical economics and managerial psychology – closely attuned to the new public policy mood – have come the more exotic cross-disciplinary growths associated with post-modernism. As the old academic division of labor unravels, it is worth reflecting again on the interdisciplinary mix that went into the old IR and how this has changed – a task we began in an earlier book (Ackers and Wilkinson, 2003). In our view, any attempt to identify a single disciplinary basis for IR is misguided. Nor do we foresee a single model or integrative theory, as Kaufman (2003) does. Instead, we regard one central theme and approach, the study of society through social institutions, as the unifying force that can give academic IR a new interdisciplinary social science identity.

In the US, the root discipline of IR was economics, drawing especially on the work of Commons (see Kaufman, 2004). Notwithstanding the growth of neo-classical economics, which focused on perfect competition market models and either ignored institutional factors like trade unions and collective bargaining or deprecated the distortions to economic efficiency, Roosevelt's New Deal and the central public policy role it gave trade unions, propelled a distinctive tradition of Institutional Labor Economics (ILE) and the empirical study of real rather

than hypothetical labor markets. In Britain, by contrast, the Oxford IR school showed little interest in economic analysis – though this was already a significant strand of academic IR – and Clegg famously insisted that it would contribute little to the understanding of labor market behavior. Important figures, such as H. A. Turner, remained outside the pluralist mainstream and when Marxism became an influence, through the work of Vic Allen and Richard Hyman, it was animated more by politics and sociology.

Since the early 1980s, however, institutional economics has exercised a growing influence on British IR, as witnessed both by the contents of the *British Journal of Industrial Relations* and the key IR text by Edwards (2003). The Workplace Employment Relation Surveys (WERS) have provided a focus for this new quantitative emphasis challenging the longstanding case-study approach (Wood, 2000). A promising strand of work on different varieties of capitalism has encouraged institutional economists to move beyond traditional labor market debates about trade unions and collective bargaining to look at other intervening institutions. Some have called for IR to link to the fields of political economy and socio-economics (Godard, 2004). This type of analysis provides us with new concepts such as path dependency, social embeddedness and institutional complementarities – all bulwarks against neo-classical theory – even if there are dangers of institutional determinism, as Crouch (2001) has pointed out. This said institutional economics alone cannot drive the renaissance of IR because its theoretical development draws on sociological and political analyses of economic phenomena.

In Britain, politics was the primary post-war discipline, though this was not widely recognized even within the field, once the political assumptions became an unspoken normative background to work for public policy reform and institutional analysis. Both Clegg and Flanders were driven by strong Fabian-style social democratic political convictions forged out of their experience of Fascism and Communism. For them, IR pluralism was primarily an exercise in non-totalitarian industrial democracy – as it became too in the US. This political analysis was pushed into the background during the 1960s and early 1970s, until Hyman's (1975) New Left brand of Marxist political sociology forced it back to the surface. The IR academics of the New Deal era in the US and the social democratic consensus in Britain tended to take the political context for granted.

Following the 1980s rise of the New Right, IR has not only been marginalized by neo-liberalism in general; it has also lost contact with 'revisionist' political developments in social democracy as that movement has sought to adapt to global, post-industrial society. For example, the British IR community has been reluctant to engage with the rethinking of Tony Blair's Third Way, largely because this explicitly recognizes the reduced role trade unions are likely to play in the future (see Ackers, 2002). Current British IR academics play a significant policy role in the areas of arbitration and conciliation, minimum-wage setting and equal opportunities. Even so, there are signs that a strongly normative and problem-solving field has become detached from progressive left-of-center thinking and new policy solutions. The post-war IR generations were influential in both academic and public policy terms because they offered credible, policy solutions, such as incomes policy or the reform of workplace bargaining, that seemed relevant to mainstream political actors at that time. Likewise, American 'golden age' IR was intimately involved with the New Deal reform package (see Kaufman, 2004, Chapter 4). Contemporary IR needs to engage constructively with the new political reality, rather than remain nostalgic for a social democratic consensus that has long gone. Thus the renaissance of IR rests partly on the development of a new realistic politics of employment relations.

Sociology was a late arrival within British IR theory and has remained weakly represented in American IR. In both countries, there was a suspicion of Human Relations as managerial and de-contextualized and of Marxism as totalitarian and ideological, which acted as a barrier to the development of any sociological analysis. Thus leading sociological figures in IR, such as Alan Fox and Richard Hyman, began within trade union history and institutional IR and then developed their own distinctive sociological analyses. Only from the 1970s did greater emphasis on workplace conflict and bargaining open new space for the industrial sociologists like Eric Batstone. Today British IR is an integral part of the empirical sociology of work, as represented by the radical Labor Process Conference and the journal *Work Employment and Society*. So far this seems a story of belated success, as sociology overtakes politics in IR research from the late 1970s onwards. There are problems, however. Much of radical IR sociology remains trapped in a Braverman-style Marxist fundamentalism in which all employers degrade, intensify and de-skill work. At the same time, IR pluralists have been slow to develop a more convincing political sociology of how managers and employees establish, negotiate and change workplace rules that reaches across union and non-union workplaces and beyond the narrowing band of union-centered joint regulation. There is plenty of scope here to draw on the earlier work of Dahrendorf, Fox and Batstone or the classical theories of Durkheim and Weber.

At the same time, work, economic analysis and empirical research has become deeply unfashionable in British sociology, broadly defined. On the one hand, this means IR/HRM in Business Schools has become *the* center for the empirical sociology of work. On the other, IR and the sociology of work has virtually vanished from many Sociology departments, while even in Business Schools, the field of OB is often dominated by either psychologists or post-modern social theorists. Much early IR case study research was an unreflective, unconscious amateur brand of sociology. In our view, a theoretically-informed, but steadfastly empirical sociology of work can become one central pillar for a new IR paradigm centered on the new institutionalism. The real sociological opportunity for IR may be to forge theoretical common ground with other applied fields, such as Social Policy, which share with IR an empirical, problem-solving approach (see Bulmer, 1985).

It is easy to forget that History was a central influence on early IR. The Webbs published their *History of Trade Unionism* in 1893 and since then IR scholars, all over the world, have contributed to an institutional, trade union history sub-genre within labor and social history; one which has been especially strong in Australia. In Britain, the once steady flow of trade union histories has become a trickle. Few pluralist IR academics today write history or are engaged with the mainstream historical community. Radical IR history is more active, but prone to a socialist antiquarianism, centered on long catalogues of strikes. More generally, the preoccupation with trade union history has long occluded other important historical IR subjects: employers and management, state employment and social policy, non-union employees, women and ethnic minorities, private service sector workers and so on. It has stood in the way of a more rounded social history of the experience of work or a more integrated history of IR. The current IR emphasis on varieties of capitalism and path dependency, as a foil against neo-liberal convergence theory, if it is to be more than rhetoric, calls out for more historical studies. Jacoby's (1997) work on American Welfare Capitalism, Hyman's (2001) study of European trade unionism or Howells' (2005) analysis of the role of the state in the evolution of the British IR system are all examples of the potentially important role history has to play in linking IR' old paradigm to its new one. Lyddon (2003) suggests that contemporary academic HRM has encouraged a sort of historical amnesia, whereby old IR concepts and studies have been abandoned in the pursuit of novelty. This may be one side of the problem, but the other is that much IR history is deeply conservative in method and topic area and reluctant to ask new, more topical questions about the past.

The remaining disciplines can be dispensed more cursorily mainly because their engagement with IR has been fleeting. The sub-field of Labor Geography has recently drawn a small but influential group of scholars into the ambit of IR (see Herod et al., 2003). Their emphasis on the spatial nature of the employment relationship in an era of globalization has helped take IR beyond the closed national systems of the post-war period. Law was sidelined in IR's preference for voluntary collective bargaining. The jurifidication of employment regulation over recent decades has drawn British academics increasingly into analysis of legal developments such as the national minimum wage, trade union recognition and European works councils (Ewing, 2003). Intellectually, this calls for IR to explore in more depth the nature of law, including differences between 'hard' and 'soft' law and relationships with the field of socio-legal studies. Psychology is often seen as one of the two principal enemies of IR (along with neo-classical economics), and an alternative root discipline for HRM and its understanding of the employment relationship. Yet psychologists, such as Guest (1998), continue to contribute to the IR field. And while the notion of a psychological contract does provide an individualistic and (possibly) managerial challenge to IR collectivism, the renaissance of IR within the field of management depends upon producing theories that explain the behavior of individual managers and employees.

Traditional IR was a distinctive synthesis of various social science influences, with certain disciplines predominating in different periods. Thus American IR became locked into ILE while 1950s and 1960s British IR drew mainly from politics and history. Indian IR remains more influenced by economics than sociology. In the 1970s, industrial sociology became the main discipline of British IR, often centered on factory conflict, while since the 1980s an empirical, analytical institutional economics has gained prominence through the WERS surveys. In our view, the global renaissance of IR calls for an active and open-minded re-engagement with all these surrounding disciplines in the search for concepts that can be synthesized into a new

IR paradigm centered on the contemporary employment relationship.

IR AND HRM IN THE BUSINESS SCHOOL CONTEXT

Even a single generation ago, the academic IR map of the world of work was badly skewed (Ackers, 1994; Redman and Wilkinson, 2006). It neglected substantial areas of the economy where joint regulation was non-existent or weak and emphasized collective bargaining at the expense of other modes of regulation, such as joint consultation and especially legal regulation. With the odd exception (see Goodman et al., 1977), it highlighted conflict rather than co-operation. But above all, it almost completely ignored the most crucial and pervasive form of employment regulation: employer and management regulation. Only late in his career did Clegg recognize the extent to which employers shaped collective bargaining and launch the research programme that led to the belated re-discovery of Personnel Management as HRM (see Sisson, 1989; Storey, 1989). In this respect, the field of study of the old academic IR was always a highly partial theorization of the real world subject of the employment relationship and its regulation.

Before HRM, Personnel Management had been a marginal field in both Britain and the US, partly because it was neglected by IR (see Kaufman, 2004). Pioneers like Flanders and Clegg (1954) had ignored and dismissed the subject and the former was noted for his 'frank disdain of personnel management' (Brown, 1998: 850). By and large, management activity outside collective bargaining, including non-union companies and consultation, was viewed through the normative prism of joint regulation and accorded marginal status. Despite the protests of some veteran IR academics that management had always been a key concern to them, their real primary preoccupation had been with collective bargaining, as the key texts testify. While Clegg and Flanders originally included non-union forms and non-formal methods

of regulation in his definition of IR, this was rarely operationalized in IR research until the 1980s. Phelps Brown (1959:114) opens his chapter on the 'Development of Industrial Relations' with the declaration that 'The story of modern British industrial relations begins with the beginnings of the unions'. For a long time it ended there too; and for some it still does. As Kaufman (2004: 610) notes, IR 'regarded non-union employers and unitarist employment systems with varying degrees of aversion, suspicion and opprobrium'.

Yet management has always been central to the employment relationship. By overlooking this, traditional academic IR not only left a gap in its theory, but in its public policy mission. It did so by failing to recognize the crucial role that employer regulation plays in employees' lives and the gaps in employment regulation left by concentrating exclusively on voluntary collective bargaining. To take the British example, Perkins (1989) notes the failure of unions to 'professionalize' working class life through excessive dependence on collective bargaining about money wages. As a result, the state was late in legislating for universal provisions or in raising the status of hourly paid work in relation to job security, holiday entitlements, pensions and equal opportunities – areas where Britain lagged behind the best continental European countries. With the death of institutional IR proclaimed over a decade ago (Purcell, 1993) and the end of joint regulation (Terry, 2004) more recently, contemporary IR badly needs HRM to fill in much of what matters in working life today. By neglecting the central business actor, academic IR missed out on much of the crucial fine grain of employment regulation. As Bach and Sisson (2000, p. 3) note: 'It is easy to forget in the current avalanche of literature that, as late as 1989, there was very little analysis of and information of personnel management in practice'. Any applied problem-solving academic field that ignores such central issues and such crucial policy actors is bound to find itself overtaken by events.

Seen in this light, the emergence of HRM as a central topic of IR research is not a threat to the field – as has so often been mooted – but its potential salvation. With the benefit of hindsight, it is clear that the real threat to IR as a distinctive academic paradigm came not from the influence of American business school ideology, but from fundamental real world changes in the nature of work and the institutional context of academic life. These widened still further the gap between academic field of study and real world subject; while policy makers and other social scientists began to notice what IR left out. Once the calls for better trained and educated managers were finally met by a massive expansion of university business schools, changes in the real world subject and the academic context of its study marched hand-in-hands. Similar instances of this twin-track change can be found across the globe, in countries as different as India since market liberalization in 1991 (see Ackers, 2006b). In Britain, the combination of 1970s economic crisis and pluralist IR crisis, created the impression that academic IR had little to contribute to a successful market economy. Into this intellectual and policy vacuum came HRM, with a more economically relevant agenda, an aspirational vision and a new set of tools of analysis that are widely seen as more 'relevant' to the world of work today, presenting indeed 'a new orthodoxy' (Guest, 1998). With or without HRM, IR would have entered a decline. At least the advent of HRM raised the profile of people management within businesses and business schools and extended the field of enquiry into areas that IR had previously neglected and has now begun to grasp.

HRM brings to IR not only a broader employment canvass, but also new concepts, such as strategy, from management disciplines that barely existed during the IR golden age. As Kaufman (2004: 625) observes, 'industrial relations has fallen out of step with the modern workplace because its toolkit of institutional "fixes" is no longer regarded as very effective'. Today the field needs to demonstrate its own contribution to business performance and employee well-being, in addition to its enduring and distinctive emphasis on questions of power and conflict in the employment relationship. In this task, IR is well positioned as an academic tradition that is now interested in management, but remains sympathetic to employees, concerned about social justice and the needs of the wider society and suspicious of authoritarian management ideologies and pop management prescriptions. HRM is addressed critically, as a field of empirical enquiry, not a cure-all set of ready-made prescriptions. HRM-without-IR is the real social science problem. Here Bacon (2003: 84) identifies an excessive individualism that overlooks the collective aspects of employment and underplays the contested terrain in which management choices are made. This version of HRM does exaggerate the currency of enlightened, high commitment management, and ignores the role of power and conflict in the employment relationship. The business organization appears able to create its own organizational climate unrestrained by institutions and context. For all these reasons, HRM is where the major public policy debate on the future of work takes place.

To flourish, academic IR must be relevant to both its real world and academic contexts. The future of the field is far from guaranteed. The global IR academic community today is overwhelmingly concentrated in business schools, though many of these have no recognizable IR presence. To make sense of this we need to appreciate the wider institutional context within which the IR academic community resides. Business schools have been a global success story over the last 20 years with a dramatic expansion not only in domestic undergraduate students but also of mainly overseas, postgraduate MSc and MBA students. The demand from these students is not for traditional IR: the study of a small corner of what was once England. All MBA courses have HRM/OB modules, under these or other labels, but they are taught from a variety of perspectives: by psychologists, post-modernists or by orthodox OB sociologists. In other words IR has to compete for space and its position is not privileged. While marketing, accounting, finance and HRM/OB are guaranteed a place at the table – as core business school academic disciplines and management functions – IR is not. As the American model of Business School spreads globally through the influence of AACSB accreditation, this is especially problematic – particularly given the decline of the once powerful American IR community.

Continued academic centrality demands a stronger intellectual rationale, perhaps linked to notions of human capital and high performance. Budd (2004: 191) advocates a meta-paradigm or organizing map (not theory) which defines the parameters of an integrated IR and HRM field, with *efficiency* and *voice* and *equity* as the key objectives. As he argues, the standard narrow HRM focus on efficiency must be balanced by IR's normative insistence on employees' entitlement to fair treatment and the opportunity to have a meaningful input into decisions. This thematic approach would define a 'common vision of the unique domain of the field' (Budd, 2004:12) embracing HRM and IR, with the emphasis shifting between different poles of the triad. The normative tradition of IR has been seen as a scientific weakness (Kaufman, 2004) and an exclusive sympathy for trade unions no longer serves as an adequate or meaningful social philosophy in the new economy. By returning to core general values, rather than fixing on any specific institution, Budd positions IR to contribute to the modern debate about the morality of business schools. Ghoshal (2005: 76–7) has written a stinging critique of their reliance on 'ideologically inspired amoral themes which have actively freed students from any sense of moral responsibility', and which view the purpose of social theory as 'solving the "negative problem" of restricting the social costs arising from human imperfections'. The popularity of critical management studies in Britain shows the scope for this revived normative role.

According to Roethlisberger (1977), the positivist preference for modeling and 'science' has squeezed out the notion of theory,

not as scientific law, but as temporary 'walking sticks' to aid sense making as we go along – something akin to Popper's idea of piecemeal social engineering discussed below. Once IR broadens its horizons, beyond the institutions and solutions of industrial society, there is renewed scope to play a part in the 'rational reconstruction of society' (Coleman, 1993). The narrow scientific model often excludes human ethical choices, just as causal determinism dehumanizes management practice. Here again, HRM draws IR into the major debates about the future role of business schools (AIM, 2006). Should they follow a social science model or a professional model akin to medicine? The IR field bridges both: it is both a critical, normative approach to management but also brings a strong pragmatic orientation with the emphasis on useful knowledge and reform. In this new more ambitious guise, IR could aim to set the social science agenda for management studies.

REJOINING THE MAINSTREAM: IR AS INSTITUTIONAL THEORY

Once personnel management is drawn back into a new combined IR/HRM fold and the normative assumptions of the old academic IR have been redefined and restated, there remains the question of which bundle of concepts and approaches can drive academic IR, as an *applied social science*, with a coherent research programme and a repertoire of new problem-solving policy solutions. The answer, at the level of theory, seems to lie in stripping the old academic IR back to its essential core as the *institutional analysis of the employment relationship*, and then looking both for allies and ways of taking this approach forward.

Scott's (2001) *Institutions and Organizations* suggest the potential for a re-engagement between IR and one central strand of the social sciences. His institutional tradition is highly inclusive with space for traditional IR as well as Marx, Weber, Durkheim, Parsons, Giddens and even Geertz. Scott provides a welcome analytical clarity, distinguishing three main institutional pillars: *regulative* (coercive rule-making), *normative* (values); and *cultural-cognitive* (symbols, meaning, routines, ways of doing). In these terms, IR has been a center for *old institutionalism*, which centered on regulative and normative institutions; though 'custom and practice' has always played a significant, if rather defensive, role in IR analysis. The *new institutionalism*, by contrast, centers more on cultural-cognitive institutions. This third dimension could add something new and important to IR analysis, as collective bargaining contracts and the search is on for new more fine grain forms of institutional analysis. The cultural-cognitive approach to institutions also contributes something new to IR as a problem solving rather than science building field. Arguably it suggests useful new approaches to practical policy questions, such as how to diffuse HRM 'best practice' or achieve regulatory compliance. In addition to the established coercive and normative strategies, new institutionalism suggests the importance of mimetic influences and organizational isomorphism; and may illuminate novel forms of voluntary regulation as alternatives to blunt state regulation.

According to Godard (2004: 236), while there are several types of new institutionalism, they all fall within a 'broader paradigm united by a common focus on the importance of rules that undergird economic, social and political arrangements forming the institutional environment within which the parties act'. This may be too complacent, however. Certain types of new institutional turn pose problems for IR institutional theory, as we normally understand it, demanding that we set our own boundaries. In our view, if new institutionalism is to contribute to the rejuvenation of IR, we must engage with it critically and selectively and not just buy the whole package off the shelf. For instance, one weakness of Scott's sociological perspective is that none of his three pillars really reflect the *economic context* of labor and product markets – a wider weakness of much organizational

theory. Two other important boundary issues stand out.

One concerns the important distinction raised by Scott between *variance* and *process* approaches to institutions. Process analysis, once more, is what IR has always done. It embraces real-life institutions, like trade unions, bargaining committees and team briefings, and describes and analyzes their operation in real, natural settings. It concerns the relations between events not variables and in this 'history matters' (Gospel, 2005). Variance analysis has stronger pretensions to hard predictive science, like neo-classical economics and occupational psychology, and treats institutions as 'abstract variables'. This is the road taken by the new institutionalism, 'transaction costs' economics (see Jacoby, 1990). Full-scale adoption of variance institutionalism would destroy everything that the IR research tradition has stood for. IR institutionalism stands or falls by its adherence to critical realist ontology and the importance of real, naturalistic context. Any theory that either argues we cannot reach or research institutional context (post-structuralism/ post-modernism), or that some adapted rational choice model is a substitute for doing so (positivist variance theory), denies the importance of real social and historical context. In this light, process theory is genuine institutionalism, while variant theories with their contrived and synthetic responses are not.

In addition, while IR desperately needs a broader sociological view of institutions (see Ackers, 2002), we still need to deal with relatively stable 'bodies' that are recognizable as institutions. For IR theory, institutions must be both real and substantial. They do not need to be formal bodies, but nor can they be fleeting social encounters. This is not an argument for returning to the old, descriptive 'brick and mortar' institutional IR theory. That approach lacked sociological sensitivity and often failed to develop either theory or analysis, because it confused the tip of the iceberg – hard institutional information – with the fuller understanding that comes from looking below the surface. Institutions are part of social reality, and often a crucial doorway into grasping social reality, but they alone cannot give us a rounded picture of the employment relationship. On the other hand, institutions have a double social science value, as the place where social problems or issues are identified *and* the practical means whereby these can be solved. Without real-life social institutions society is like sand that slips through our fingers. By combining an institutional focus – which may include certain types of survey research – with a case-study method that grasps the fine grain of socio-economic life, we can do full justice to context.

Blyton and Turnbull (2004) suggest that institutionalism makes IR inherently conservative through the association with a functionalist antipathy to social change Here our response is twofold. Certainly, institutional theory is better for reformers than revolutionaries, and mainstream IR has always stood firmly in the former camp. Moreover, the critique of functionalism is from another era when, in the 1960s, the New Left challenged the stable institutions of industrial society. Today it is the New Right that thrives on chaos and free markets (Ackers, 1994). Arguably, new institutional theory provides an array of instruments to socially regulate runaway capitalism. This still leaves the problem of human agency and the charge that institutional analysis reifies what are in effect relations between people. There is another defensible border that separates institutional theory from the methodological individualism of neo-classical economics and managerial psychology. But it remains important to ask how institutional accounts integrate the actions of the individuals and groups that constitute them.

Many IR academics are already doing new institutionalism without knowing it. To illustrate this we take two examples from our own research.

When IR researchers of our generation found themselves not in the familiar pasture of unions, collective bargaining and strikes, but looking at the new Employee Involvement (EI) in the late 1980s, they carried their ontological road map with them (Ackers et al., 2006c; Marchington et al., 1992). Instead of beginning, as a psychologist would, by asking individual employees if they 'felt involved', they looked for institutions and they found them: old ones like trade unions and joint consultation committees; and new ones such as quality circles, team briefings and TQM programmes. These activities exhibited regularity and had formal structures with specific managerial roles to support them. They were never, however, a full picture of the nature of EI. Many small companies explicitly claimed that they had few structures, but that involvement operated through a dynamic informal culture, an open door policy, and management by walking about – all claims that are hard to assess using traditional institutional measures (Wilkinson et al., 2007). For large organizations, however, the formal institutions were a useful starting point: an *institutional focus* or doorway into the wider social relations. It allowed us to ask questions about the gap between rhetoric and reality and to seek the true meaning of interview and questionnaire responses, in the context of both what institutions management had created, how much money they had spent on them, how often they met and so on. To this could be added other contextual information about the labor and product markets of the firm. In this sense, institutions framed a broader, qualitative research agenda. And it is a short step from assessing the regulative and normative impact of New Labour policies and European Works Council legislation, to exploring the cultural-cognitive influence of benchmarks like Investors in People or the CBI's Excellence initiative, or simply the voluntary, mimetic spread of TQM.

A still more recent issue in UK IR research is Work-Life Balance and Family-Friendly policies, and once more this displays the familiar combination of coercive statutory regulation, government normative injunction and the cultural-cognitive copying of best practice. Here institutions are societal as well as organizational and without them, researchers can 'lose' crucial factors that shape thought and behaviour. For example, Merlilainen et al. (2004) compare management careers and work-life balance in Finland and Britain using a post-modern discourse approach. They show convincingly that the discourse of the two groups was very different. The British managers were driven by work and downgraded their children and private lives, working very long hours. By contrast, the Finns sought work-life balance and valued time spent with their children. In explanation, the authors refer to a discursive or 'cultural context' that shapes the way these management consultants 'talk about their work and careers' (Ibid: 540). We would suggest that very often 'culture' – the ether of post-modernism – is really no explanation at all (see Kahn and Ackers, 2004; Kuper, 1999). And Merlilainen et al. later reach for 'societal context' (Ibid: 547), 'public policy' (551), 'public childcare facilities' (554) and 'institutionalized arrangements' (558) – all suggesting the explanatory limitations of discourse analysis.

If the question is: why do managers in different national states develop different ways of thinking and behaving? the answer, very probably, is due to institutions. The Scandinavian employment and welfare model is replete with well-funded regulative, normative and cultural-cognitive institutions, which both make responsible parenthood materially easy and morally desirable. State day-care systems are institutions, but so are strong trade unions that help to shape this 'social market' culture. The corollary is that the organizations, institutions and actors that operate at that level, and the interaction with wider societal supports, are crucial to understanding the choices individual actors make. On the opposite side of the sociological spectrum, a similar criticism can be made of Hakim's (2000) important positivist work on women's choices (Hantrais and Ackers, 2005). In short, without a grasp of real institutional context we fail to understand why people behave in a certain way or what could be done to change this behavior.

CONCLUSION: REAL CONTEXT AND SOCIAL DEMOCRATIC REFORM

For IR scholars institutional theory is both very old and very new. They have always coupled scientific and normative justifications. In most cases, to gain an adequate theory of social life, we need to combine institutional context with the actors' social meanings that inhabit this. Without either our analysis is likely to be incomplete. Beyond this, however, there is a strong reformist, social democratic (in the broadest sense) public policy case for institutional social science. You need to be an institutionalist to improve society, because if we do not start with institutions we do not reach any collective agency or public policy position that will structurally change society for the better. We can wish society will collapse, like a pack of cards, as some radicals do. We can train managers and employees on how to adapt to the status quo, as constructed by the institutional power holders we refuse to see, as managerial psychology and neo-classical economics does. We can urge individuals to free themselves, at least in their hearts, as some critical management studies scholars advocate. But without some institutional focus, we can't reform society in a purposeful and piecemeal way.

In the wake of Communism, there has been an understandable reaction against grand theories of social change. Tietze et al. (2003), for instance, argue:

Concomitant with the demise of metanarratives, we can observe a return of the 'little' narrative' (Lyotard, 1979/1986: 61) of the everyday. These little narratives focus on the stories of (organizational) lives in terms that emphasize the situation and temporal embeddedness of (moral) choices. *The onus of responsibility is on each individual/ individual organization – rather than on institutions and bodies.* This includes the responsibility to make sense of the complexities of (organizational) circumstance: the 'big questions' – if answerable at all – are to be addressed not within universalist and potentially totalitarian ideologies, but within the contingencies and expediences of an increasingly complex world (our emphasis).

Within IR and many other applied social sciences, however, the main alternative to Marxist grand theory has been 'institutions and bodies'. Karl Popper, no less, did not fear the institutional solution, but saw it as the main bulwark against totalitarianism. In *The Open Society and its Enemies* (1945, 1995 edition: 354) he posed the question thus:

What have we to say to Marx's analysis? Are we to believe that politics, or the framework of legal institutions, are intrinsically impotent to remedy such a situation, and that only a complete social revolution, a complete change of the 'social system' can help? Or are we to believe the defenders of an unrestrained 'capitalist' system who emphasize (rightly, I think) the tremendous benefit to be gained from the mechanism of free markets, and who conclude from this that a truly free labor market would be of the greatest benefit to all concerned.

In common cause with Anglo-American IR pluralists of the same generation, Popper chose a third, social democratic option of 'piecemeal social engineering' (1995: 364) and institutional reform through the legal framework, starting with labor legislation. In his view, 'the principle of non-intervention, of an unrestrained economic system, has to be given up', so that we can 'construct social institutions, enforced by the power of the state, for the protection of the economically weak from the economically strong' (1995: 355). He contrasts two methods of rule, one by 'institutional' or 'indirect' intervention, the other by 'personal' or 'direct' intervention, and judges that 'from the point of view of democratic control' the first is clearly preferable (1995: 361–3). With Weber he regards personal authority as 'irrational' and institutional or rule-governed authority as 'rational' particularly because:

The legal framework can be known and understood by the individual citizen; and it should be designed to be so understandable. Its functioning is predictable. It introduces a factor of certainty and security into social life ... As opposed to this, the method of personal intervention must introduce an ever-growing element of unpredictability into social life, and with it will develop the feeling that social life is irrational and insecure.

Popper was specifically addressing state power, but the IR parallels are apparent. As Flanders (1975:137) argued:

In labour relations, control by the 'rule of law' is more than control by legislation. Every instrument of regulation that compels management to respect rules in making its decisions has to be included: the provisions of collective agreements and unwritten custom and practice as much as the statutory requirements of protective labour legislation. Even the rules which management makes unilaterally regulate its use of power, though it is not a matter of indifference to workers whether they have participated in making these rules. Only then have they any assurance that their interests have been taken into account and can they feel any responsibility for seeing that the rules are observed.

For these reasons, institutional schools like IR are potentially unique in their ability to carry theory into practice. Today, European social policy is another illustration of the continuing relevance of institutional theory. Law is active in regulating business, but the experience of numerous EU directives shows the implementation is at once problematic and crude, unless it works with the grain of local conditions. Hence policy moves down from national framework policies, on working time or equal opportunities, to detailed implementation by institutional actors in localities and organizations. In this respect, institutional theory is both a description of how policy making works and a prescription about how it can be improved. Legal regulation has always had a normative element, but as we move from hard to soft regulation, the cultural-cognitive approach to spreading HRM 'best practice' becomes ever more critical.

In conclusion, Anglo-American IR has never been a closed academic discipline engaged in pure 'science building'; but nor has it been an entirely open inter-disciplinary field responding to employment problems in a completely *ad hoc* way. Rather, as we have argued before, the IR academic community has constructed a hybrid paradigm by selectively synthesizing concepts and approaches from other social sciences in response to contemporary issues (Ackers and Wilkinson, 2005). This paradigm has both mirrored and shaped the understanding of employment problems and their policy solutions in the real world. In the post-war era of industrial society and the social democratic consensus, the IR public policy tool-kit centered on a very narrow range of social institution – trade unions and voluntary collective bargaining – and tended to ignore both legal regulation and personnel management. As advanced post-industrial societies have changed dramatically in recent decades, joint regulation has become incapable of playing this central policy role, which, in turn, has undermined the hinterland of IR theory that centered on this specific approach. This exhaustion of the old institutionalism appears to be an increasingly global trend. Our argument here is that IR can only regain its theory and policy cutting edge by: first, expanding its range to include HRM; second, rethinking and reviving its traditional normative goals and, third, deepening its analysis of social institutions. All three tasks entail an outgoing, open-minded engagement with the contemporary inter-disciplinary social sciences. The outcome should be better theory, driving more compelling research and more relevant public policy.

REFERENCES

Ackers, P. (1994) 'Back to Basics: Industrial Relations and the Enterprise Culture', *Employee Relations*, 16 (8): 32–47.

Ackers, P. (2002) 'Reframing employment relations: the case for neo-pluralism', *Industrial Relations Journal*, 33 (1): 2–19.

Ackers, P. (2004) 'Haunted by History: Industrial Relations Faces the Future', *Organization Studies*, 25 (9): 1623–29.

Ackers, P. (2005a) 'Between the Devil and the Deep Blue Sea: Global History, the British Tradition, and the European Renaissance', *Comparative Labor Law and Policy Journal*, 27 (1): 93–104.

Ackers, P. (2005b) 'Theorizing the Employment Relationships: Materialists and Institutionalists', *British Journal of Industrial Relations*, 43 (3), September: 537–43.

Ackers, P. (2006a) 'Commentary: The History of Occupational Psychology: A View from Industrial Relations', *Journal of Occupational and Organizational Psychology*, 79 (2): 213–16.

Ackers, P. (2006b), 'Leaving Labour? Some British Impressions of Indian Academic Employment Relations', *Economic and Political Weekly* (India), XLI: 39: 30.

Ackers, P. (2007) 'Collective Bargaining as Industrial Democracy: Hugh Clegg and the Political Foundations of British Industrial Relations Pluralism', *British Journal of Industrial Relations*, 45 (1), March: 77–101.

Ackers, P., Marchington, M., Wilkinson, A. and Dundon, T. (2006c) 'Employee participation in Britain: From Collective Bargaining and Industrial Democracy to Employee Involvement and Social partnership – Two Decades of Manchester/Loughborough Research', *Decision* (Indian Institute of Management, Calcutta), 33 (1), January–June: 75–88.

Ackers, P. and Wilkinson, A. (2003) (eds) *Understanding Work and Employment: Industrial Relations In Transition*. Oxford University Press.

Ackers, P. and Wilkinson, A. (2005) 'The British Industrial Relations Paradigm: a critical outline and prognosis', *Journal of Industrial Relations*, 47 (4), December: 443–56.

Ackroyd, S. and Fleetwood, S. (2004) *Critical Realist Applications in Organization and Management Studies*. London: Routledge.

AIM (2006) *UK Business Schools: Historical Contexts and Future Scenarios*. London: AIM research.

Bacon, N. (2003) 'Human Resource Management and Industrial Relations', in P. Ackers and A. Wilkinson (eds) *Understanding Work and Employment: Industrial Relations In Transition*. Oxford: Oxford University Press. pp. 71–88.

Blyton, P. and Turnbull, P. (2004), *The Dynamics of Employee Relations*, 3rd edition, Basingstoke: Palgrave MacMillan.

Brown, W. (1998) 'Clegg, Hugh Armstrong', in M. Poole and M.Warner (eds) *IEBM The Handbook of Human Resource Management*. London: ITP.

Bulmer, M. (1985) 'The development of sociology and empirical social science in Britain', in M. Bulmer (ed) *Essays on the History of the British Sociological Research*. Cambridge: Cambridge University Press.

Budd, J. (2004) *Employment with a Human Face*. Ithaca, NY: Cornell University Press.

Coleman, J. S. (1993) 'The Rational Reconstruction of Society', *American Sociological Review*, 58 (1): 1–15.

Edwards, P. (ed) (2003) *Industrial Relations*, 2nd edition, Oxford: Blackwell.

Edwards, P. (2005) 'The Promising Future of Industrial Relations: Developing the Connections Between

Theory and Relevance', *Industrial Relations Journal*, 36 (4): 264–82.

Eldridge, J. (2003) 'Post-Modernism and IR', in P. Ackers and A. Wilkinson (eds) *Understanding Work and Employment: Industrial Relations In Transition*. Oxford: Oxford University Press. pp. 325–36.

Emmott, M. (2005) 'What is Employee Relations'. London: CIPD (Change Agenda).

Ewing, K. (2003) 'Industrial Relations and the Law', in P. Ackers and A. Wilkinson (eds) *Understanding Work and Employment: Industrial Relations In Transition*. Oxford: Oxford University Press. pp. 138–60

Flanders, A. (1975) *Management and Unions: The Theory and Reform of Industrial Relations*. London: Faber.

Flanders, A. and Clegg, H.A. (1954) (eds) *The System of Industrial Relations in Great Britain: Its History Law and Institutions*. Oxford: Blackwell.

Frege, C. (2004) 'Varieties of Industrial Relations Research', *British Journal of Industrial Relations*, 43 (2): 179–207.

Ghoshal, S. (2005) 'Bad management theories are destroying good management practices', *Academy of Management Learning and Education*, 4 (1): 75–91.

Godard, J. (2004) 'The New Institutionalism, Capitalist Diversity and Industrial Relations', in B. Kaufman, *Theoretical Perspectives on Work and the Employment Relationship*. Champaign, IL: IRRA. pp. 229–64.

Godard, J. and Delaney, J. (2000) 'Reflections on the high performance paradigm's implications for IR as a field', *Industrial and Labor Relations Review*, 53 (3): 482–503.

Goodman, J. F. B., Armstrong, E. G. A., Davis, J. E. and Wagner, A. (1977) *Rule-making and Industrial Peace*. London: Croom Helm.

Gospel, H. (2005) 'Markets, Firms and Unions: Historical and Institutionalist Perspectives in the Future of Unions', in D. Metcalf and S. Fernie (eds) *Unions and Performance*. London: Routledge.

Gospel, H. (2006) 'A British and Historical Perspective on Workplace Governance: Kaufman and the Global Evolution of Industrial Relations?', *Industrielle Beziehungen*, 13 (1): 2006, pp. 57–66.

Guest, D. (1990) 'Human Resource Management and Industrial Relations', *Journal of Management Studies*, 27 (4): 377–98.

Guest, D. (1998) 'Beyond HRM', in P. Sparrow and M. Marchington (eds) *HRM: the New Agenda*, FT/Pitman.

Hakim, C. (2000) *Work-Lifestyle Choices in the 21st Century: Preference Theory*, Oxford: Oxford University Press.

Hall, P. and Soskice, D. (2001) *Varieties of Capitalism*. Oxford: Oxford University Press.

Hantrais, L. and Ackers, P. (2005) 'Women's Choices in Europe: Striking the Work-Life Balance', *European Journal of Industrial Relations*, 11 (2): 197–212.

Hennessy, P. (2006) *Having It So Good: Britain in the Fifties*. London: Allen Lane.

Herod, A., Peck, J. and Wills, J. (2003) Geography and Industrial Relations, in P. Ackers and A. Wilkinson (eds) *Understanding Work and Employment: Industrial Relations In Transition*. Oxford: Oxford University Press. pp. 175–94.

Howells, C. (2005) *Trade Unions and the State: The Construction of Industrial Relations Institutions in Britain, 1890–2000*. New Jersey: Princeton University Press.

Hyman, R. (1975) *Industrial Relations: A Marxist Introduction*. Basingstoke: MacMillan.

Hyman, R. (2001) *Understanding European Trade Unionism: Between Market, Class and Society*. London: Sage.

Jacoby, S. (1990) 'The New Institutionalism: What it Can Learn from the Old', *Industrial Relations*, 29 (2): 316–40.

Jacoby, S (1997) *Modern Manors: Welfare Capitalism since the New Deal*. New Jersey: Princeton University Press. (reviewed by Ackers, P. in *Historical Studies in Industrial Relations*, 8, Autumn 1999, 188–93).

Kahn, A.S. and Ackers, P. (2004) 'Neo-pluralism as a theoretical framework for understanding HRM in sub-Saharan Africa', *International Journal of Human Resource Management*, 15 (7), November: 1330–53.

Kaufman, B. (2003) *Theoretical perspectives on work and the employment relationship*. Champaign, IL: IRRA.

Kaufman, B. (2004) *The Global Evolution of Industrial Relations*. Geneva: ILO.

Korczynski, M. (2003) 'Consumer Capitalism and Industrial Relations' in P. Ackers and A. Wilkinson (eds) *Understanding Work and Employment: Industrial Relations In Transition*. Oxford: Oxford University Press. pp. 265–77.

Kuper, A. (1999) *Culture*. Cambridge, MA: Harvard.

Lyddon, D. (2003) 'History and Industrial Relations' in P. Ackers and A. Wilkinson (eds) *Understanding Work and Employment: Industrial Relations In Transition*. Oxford: Oxford University Press. pp. 89–118.

Marchington, M., Goodman, J., Wilkinson, A. and Ackers, P. (1992) *New Developments in Employee Involvement*, Employment Department, UK, Research series. London: HMSO.

Merilainen, S., Tienari, J., Thomas, R. and Davies, A. (2004) 'Management Consultant Talk: A Cross-Cultural Comparison of Normalizing Discourse and Resistance', *Organization*, 11 (4): 539–64.

Perkins, H. (1989) *The Rise of Professional Society.* London: Routledge.

Phelps Brown, H. (1959) *The Growth Of British Industrial Relations.* London: Macmillan.

Popper, K. (1995) *The Open Society and its Enemies.* London: Routledge.

Purcell, J. (1993) 'The End of Institutional Industrial Relations', *Political Quarterly,* 64 (1): 6–23

Redman, T. and Wilkinson, A. (2006) (eds) *Contemporary Human Resource Management.* London: FT/Prentice Hall.

Roethlisberger, F.J. (1977) *The Elusive Phenomena.* Boston: Harvard University Press.

Scott, R. (2001) *Institutions and Organizations,* 2nd edition, London: Sage.

Sisson, K. (1989) *Personnel Management in Britain.* Oxford: Blackwell.

Sisson, K. (2006) 'Responding to Mike Emmott' (unpublished).

Stern, R. N. and Barley, S. R. (1996) 'Organizations and social systems: Organization theory's neglected mandate', *Administrative Science Quarterly,* 41: 146–62.

Storey, J. (1989) *New Perspectives on Human Resource Management.* London: Routledge.

Terry, M. (2004) 'Can Partnership Reverse the decline of British trade unions?', *Work, Employment and Society,* 17 (3): 450–72.

Tietze, S., Cohen, L. and Musson, G. (2003) *Understanding Organizations through Language.* London: Sage.

Webb, B and Webb, S. (1897) *Industrial Democracy.* London: Longman.

Wilkinson A. (2007) 'Industrial relations', in S. Clegg and J. Bailey, *International Encyclopedia of Organization Studies.* London: Sage.

Wilkinson A., Dundon, T. and Grugulis, I. (2007) 'Information but not consultation: exploring employee involvement in SMES', *International Journal Of Human Resource Management,* 18 (7): 1279–97.

Wood, S. (2000) 'The BJIR and Industrial Relations in the New Millennium', *British Journal of Industrial Relations,* 38 (1): March: 1–5.

4

System and Change in Industrial Relations Analysis

Edmund Heery

INTRODUCTION

This chapter is concerned with two types of model-building in industrial relations (IR). The first type comprises what might be thought of as 'cross-sectional' models and is illustrated by the tradition of systems-thinking in IR. The distinctive feature of these models is that they seek to delineate the object of study of IR, including the definition of its constituent elements, such as actors and institutions, their interrelationship through social processes and the economic, social, moral and other effects that are thereby generated. In this tradition the constitutive elements of the IR system tend to be abstracted from a particular place or time; this is an approach to theory-building that is relatively ahistorical.

The second type puts history to the fore and comprises models of change over time. Models of this kind tend to be less frequently articulated in IR theory though on occasion theorists have tried to identify and evaluate underpinning models of change within IR (Blyton and Turnbull, 2004: 12–18; Erickson and Kuruvilla, 1998). Despite their relative

invisibility, these models lurk behind much empirical IR analysis and assumptions about the nature and rhythms of change shape much middle-range IR theory. Key distinctions that appear within these models concern the pattern of change and whether it is cyclical or directional, gradual or catastrophic, and its origin; whether it is generated endogenously within the employment relationship or has an exogenous source in the wider economy, society or polity.

Systems thinking

Discussion of systems thinking must begin with Dunlop's (1993) seminal text, *Industrial Relations Systems*, first published in 1958 and arguably the most influential IR book ever written (Kaufman, 2004b: 250–251). The explicit purpose of Dunlop's book was to designate the object of study of industrial relations and establish the field as an independent discipline, equivalent to economics (Dunlop, 1993: 9–10; 45–46). Whereas the subject of the latter was the economic system the subject of IR was the 'industrial relations system', conceived as a distinct and relatively autonomous, but integral, component of the wider social system. In Dunlop's (1993: 45) own words, 'An industrial relations system is to be viewed as an analytical subsystem of an industrial society on the same logical plane as an economic system, regarded as another analytical subsystem'.

The IR system itself comprised a number of elements. At its core were three sets of actors: workers and their institutions, including trade unions, works councils and political parties; a management hierarchy and the collective organizations of employers; and specialist institutions of the state, such as the US National Labor Relations Board (Dunlop, 1993: 47–8). The interaction of these actors generated two types of rule, procedural rules that governed their interaction, including procedures for collective bargaining and dispute resolution, and substantive rules that specified the terms of the employment relationship, including pay, hours of work, work organization and working practices. This web of rules was the vital output of the IR system in Dunlop's schema (Dunlop, 1993: 51). Its function was largely integrative, to allow the regulation of conflict and in doing so promote the stability of industrial society. Influenced by the functionalist sociology of Talcott Parsons (Kaufman, 2004b: 254; Hyman, 2004: 265), Dunlop regarded the IR sub-system as discharging a broadly integrative function for society as a whole.

There were two additional elements to Dunlop's schema, both of which shaped the behavior of IR actors. On the one hand, the IR context influenced IR actors and the procedural and substantive rules they created. Three contexts were regarded as critical:

- the 'technological characteristics of the workplace';
- the 'product and factor markets or budgetary constraints that impinge on the actors'; and
- 'the locus and distribution of power in the wider society' (Dunlop, 1993: 48).

As these 'inputs' to the IR system altered so the web of rules adjusted in order to maintain its regulatory function. On the other hand, the actors were bound by a common ideology, an acceptance of the rules of the IR game that further helped 'to bind or to integrate the system as a whole' (Dunlop, 1993: 53). A key feature of this ideology for Dunlop was that it conferred legitimacy on all of the actors, such that each accepted the rightful existence and entitlement to action within the system of the others.

Critique

Dunlop's systems model has cast a long shadow over IR. Analogous, though less abstract, definitions of the field have been developed by other theorists, from other countries (Clegg, 1975; Flanders, 1965). Scholars have also returned to the original schema and sought to update it for the present (Kaufman, 2004a; Meltz, 1993). More generally, Dunlop's conceptual map of IR as a system comprised of context, actors, processes and outcomes has been hard-wired into IR thinking and is followed repeatedly in course syllabi and textbooks (for example, Blyton and Turnbull, 2004).

Dunlop's system has also been subject to challenge and there is now an extensive critical literature that ranges from revisionist to fundamental critique. The purpose of what follows is not to review this critical literature in its totality (see Kaufman, 2004b: 252–5) but rather, themes within it are identified and used to highlight developments in the definition of the field and its constituent elements since Dunlop was writing. It should also be noted that Dunlop's text was both sophisticated and often qualified in its arguments but that many of the subtleties of his work have been overlooked by later writers. The focus here, however, is on his critics' reading of *Industrial Relations Systems* rather than an exposition of the book itself.

System boundaries

The cornerstone of Dunlop's system was the claim that IR was comprised of a discrete sub-system of industrial society and one avenue of critique has been to challenge the accuracy of this formulation (Hyman, 2004: 267). Critics have wanted to push back the boundary Dunlop drew around the subject and in some cases erase it altogether. Recently, two attempts at boundary extension have been prominent. On the one hand, there has been an attempt to erase the line between politics and IR, joining the latter to a broader field of political economy. Thus, Howell (2005), in a review of the history of the British trade union movement, has argued that union power, membership and strategies were not derived primarily from markets or technology or developed within an autonomous system of industrial relations. Rather, they were powerfully determined by the policies of the British state and its successive modes of intervention in industrial relations. On the other hand, there has been an attempt to connect IR, the sphere of the employment relationship, to the domestic sphere and the analysis of family structure and relationships. This originates largely in a feminist critique of IR for abstracting the workplace from other areas of social life and assuming it is populated by gender-neutral subjects (Greene, 2003; Wacjman, 2000). In fact, it is asserted, the substantive rules governing the work of men and women are gendered and rest on the domestic division of labor, which *inter alia* generates different patterns of labor market participation for the sexes. For those adopting this position a fruitful line of research has developed examining the relationship between paid work and domestic and private life. This has embraced studies of work-life (im)balance, family-friendly practices and the links between employment and stages of the life-cycle, the latter particularly in the context of an ageing workforce (for example Appelbaum et al., 2005; Blyton et al., 2006; Duncan et al., 2000).[1]

System actors

Dunlop's roll-call of industrial relations actors was quite extensive. In his own work, however, and in the tradition of IR scholarship of which he was a part, there tended to be a narrower focus on collective actors, trade unions, employers and state bureaucracies,

engaged in formal processes of rule-making, particularly collective bargaining (Hyman, 1975; Kaufman, 2004b: 254). The critical response, once more, has been to push back the boundaries and extend the roster of IR actors. One early line of revision was to focus on workplace actors, particularly informal work groups and union stewards, whose militancy posed a 'challenge from below' to official IR institutions in many countries in the 1960s and 1970s (Bain and Clegg, 1974; Hyman, 1975: 16–7). More recently, this argument has been restated with a feminist twist. The relative exclusion of women's interests from the formal institutions of IR, it has been suggested, requires a focus on the workplace, on women's workgroups and women activists, if these are to be adequately researched (Greene, 2003: 309).

Another response has been to focus on new institutional actors in industrial relations, whose activities have risen to prominence since Dunlop was writing or whose significance did not register in the intellectual concerns of his day. One group of actors that have begun to attract the attention of IR scholars is social movement organizations that seek to represent workers' interests. As unions – a central actor in Dunlop's schema – have declined in membership and power there has been a growth of interest in campaigning, advocacy, advisory and service-providing institutions that discharge some of their functions, often for a particular segment of the workforce or an identity group (for example Abbott, 2006; Fine, 2006; Osterman, 2006). Many of these bodies are rooted in the new social movements that have emerged since Dunlop's time and which have exerted a powerful influence, particularly over the system of legal regulation (Piore and Safford, 2006). Another set of actors that has attracted some attention are the organizations of end-users – clients or customers – which may shape patterns of service and the work and employment relations that underpin them (for example Bellemare, 2000).[2] Dunlop operated within a 'production-based paradigm' (Korczynski, 2003: 266), which restricted its concern to the relative interests of workers and employers. Many IR specialists retain this restricted view but this has become less tenable in a period when the figure of the consumer, and the organizations that give expression to consumer interests, have risen in importance. A final point to note about the interest of IR specialists in new actors is that it embraces their relationship with the 'old', particularly trade unions. There has been a growth of research on worker-consumer and worker-community coalitions and the degree to which trade unions can enlist the resources of new actors as a counter to employers and to promote their own revitalization (for example Foster and Scott, 1998; Frege et al., 2004; Ogden, 1991; Tattersall, 2005).

Causation

Critics of systems theory have also targeted Dunlop's approach to the explanation of IR phenomena. One target has been the determinism that many authors detect in Dunlop's model with its emphasis on the adaptation of IR rules particularly to the forces of technical change and market pressures (Godard, 2004: 230; for a contrary assessment of this aspect of Dunlop's work see Fiorito, 1990). An associated target has been the celebrated 'convergence thesis', developed by Dunlop in collaboration with Clark Kerr, Fred Harbison and Charles Myers in another classic text of early American IR, *Industrialism and Industrial Man* (Kerr et al., 1955). This declared that, as countries underwent technological development and industrialized so they developed a common form of social and economic order, 'characterized by an open and mobile society, an educated and technocratic workforce, a pluralistic set of organized interest groups, a reduced level of industrial conflict, and increasing government regulation of the labor market' (Kaufman, 2004b: 259).

Two responses to this perceived combination of determinism and convergence have been forthcoming, both of which emphasize the diversity of IR at common levels of economic development. Thomas Kochan, Harry Katz and Robert McKersie have emphasized the roles of 'strategic choice' and the values and ideology of managers in shaping the response of firms to environmental pressures. The latter 'do not strictly determine industrial relations outcomes' (Kochan et al., 1986: 14) but leave scope for choice, which is exercised in accordance with the ideologically-shaped preferences of managerial decision-makers. The logical inference is that patterns of IR will vary under common technological, market and institutional conditions as managers interpret the business environment and exercise discretion within a framing ideology. While this first response emphasizes variation within national economies, the second emphasizes variation across countries. Drawing on the new institutionalist literature, Godard (2004) has stressed the enduring differences in the configuration and outcomes of national systems of IR despite common technical and market pressures. The logical inference here is that the institutional form of capitalist economies carries greater explanatory weight than do the conditioning effects of technology and market and, indeed, that the latter are themselves shaped by the institutional matrix in which they operate. For institutionalists the capacity to exploit new technologies and develop a sustained presence in particular product markets will reflect the institutional form of a particular 'variety of capitalism', including labor market (IR) institutions which generate particular sets of skills and support particular forms of work organization.

Integrative ideology

Dunlop's claim that the IR system was knitted together by an integrative ideology has been another object of criticism, with critics offering alternative understandings of the role of ideology within IR. One alternative position has been effectively to accept the substantive content of Dunlop's argument but evaluate the effects of ideology from a competing normative position. Richard Hyman and Ian Brough, in *Social Values and Industrial Relations* (1975), argued that the effect of accepted notions of fair payment and occupational worth was to shorten worker objectives and contribute to the stabilization of an oppressive economic order. Essentially, this is a variant of what sociologists have labeled the 'dominant ideology thesis' (Hill, 1990), a belief that values and interpretative schema play a critical part in social reproduction and reconcile those who are exploited to their condition.

A second position was developed by writers, such as Alan Fox and John Goldthorpe (see Gilbert, 1986: 19–49), and stressed the anomic character of industrial relations, the absence of normative constraints on distributional conflict within advanced industrial societies. For these writers the decay of the traditional status order through forces of modernity had unleashed a spiral of competition for material resources, which under the conditions of the 1970s of full employment and strong trade unions when they were writing, stoked the rate of inflation.[3] The hallmark of this position, therefore, was a de-emphasis of the role of ideology within IR and an associated stress on the instability of the IR system.

A third position differs again and places ideology back at the center of IR analysis but casts it as a corrosive force, attacking the established IR system, rather than supporting it. Thus, Kochan et al. (1986) argued that American business ideology has been a major force behind the transformation of the Dunlopian industrial relations system in the US and noted that a central characteristic of that ideology has been a failure to accept or accord legitimacy to trade unions (see also Logan, 2006). A similar development can be seen in the analysis of the trade union movement. Drawing on the sociology of social movements, John Kelly (1998) has argued that the ideological framing of grievances by vanguard militants is an essential component of worker mobilization through unions. On this view, ideologies that legitimize grievances, attribute their source to the actions of employers and present plausible solutions to their resolution play a key part in mobilizing workers in periodic waves of conflict that challenge the existing IR system. A key function of ideology in this formulation, once again, is to delegitimize other actors in

the industrial relations system, in this case by undermining the authority of employers.

System outcomes

A final component of Dunlop's cross-sectional model that has attracted criticism is his conception of IR outcomes as a web of substantive and procedural rules that promote social integration. Attack here has followed two avenues. On the one hand, it has been suggested that Dunlop mis-specifies the outcomes of the IR system. The web of rules should be conceived, not as defining outcomes themselves but as 'independent or mediating variables' that potentially shape the 'various outcomes and behaviors' in which scholars are interested, such as 'wage rates, strikes, work effort and union organizing success' (Kaufman, 2004a: 48–9). Since Dunlop wrote, under the tutelage of labor economics, there has been an explosion of work that seeks to explain substantive outcomes of this kind and determine the extent to which they are shaped by particular institutional configurations (for example Freeman and Medoff, 1984; Metcalf, 1989; Rubery et al., 1999). Much of this work has focused on business outcomes, such as productivity, financial performance and competitiveness, whether measured at the level of the individual firm or that of the national economy (see Nolan and O'Donnell, 2003). But increasingly, IR scholars have assessed outcomes for workers, such as decent work or workplace well-being, using the same basic methodology (for example Brown et al., 2006; Green, 2006). There has also been a recent growth in attempts to evaluate IR outcomes from an explicitly ethical perspective, reflecting the emergence of the corporate social responsibility movement and the rise of business ethics as a distinct field of inquiry (for example Budd and Scoville, 2005).

On the other hand, scholars have challenged the functionality of the IR system, what many believe to have been Dunlop's core proposition. This attack has come from each of the main normative positions within IR. From the radical wing it has been argued that Dunlop over-estimated the capacity of the IR system to regulate conflict. The deep fissures of interest running through the employment relationship, on this view, make any accommodation unstable and prone to collapse (Hyman, 1975: 12). The pluralist center has been more accepting of Dunlop's position, granting that a functional equivalence between the IR system and the economic and social order is theoretically possible, while spending much effort identifying the dysfunctions of actually existing systems. A common position adopted by pluralists, from the British authors of the Donovan report (Fox, 1966) to those wishing to adapt IR to the flexible, high-performance economy (Osterman et al., 2001), is to posit an 'institutional lag', an urgent need to reform IR institutions to match a changed economy.

Perhaps the most severe critique, however, has come from a unitary perspective of a neo-liberal stamp. From the New Right the rules of the IR system – whether these be joint decision-making with worker representatives, collective agreements or minimum wage laws – have been the sustained target of what Hirschman (1991) identifies as the three main forms of the 'rhetoric of reaction', futility, perversity and jeopardy. Regulation through the IR system has been condemned as futile, a form of 'mock bureaucracy' unable to buck market forces or, when its potency is accepted, said to generate perverse effects that harm the interests of workers by generating unemployment or jeopardize other desirable conditions, such as competitiveness or liberty (see Richardson, 1996). In the face of this critique, indeed, there has been something of a retreat to Dunlop's functionalist argument amongst the opponents of neo-liberalism. Pluralists have argued that the rules of the IR system impose a benign constraint, shutting off the low road of price competition (Streeck, 1992: 29–35), that trade unions and collective bargaining generate productivity improvements and other benefits (Freeman, 1992; Freeman and Medoff, 1984), and that deregulation poses a threat to social integration (Clark, 1993). While Dunlop's belief in the functionality of the IR system

has possibly been the most attacked element of his schema, it has experienced a curious, though little acknowledged revival (see Budd et al., 2004).

RECENT DEVELOPMENTS

The tradition of systems thinking epitomized by Dunlop continues to exert influence and be developed within IR. Today, it is possible to identify three broad positions or perspectives on that tradition. The first rejects it utterly and holds that the attempt by Dunlop to establish a general theory of IR that defines its object of study, constituent elements and function is irredeemably flawed. This argument has recently been powerfully made by Richard Hyman who declares, 'it is neither possible nor desirable to pursue a self contained theory *of* industrial relations …' (2004: 267). Hyman's rejection of the systems tradition rests on a number of grounds, some of which have been identified above. He is critical of its roots in the conservative sociology of the 1950s, its technical determinism, conception of IR as a bounded, largely self-contained sub-system and assumption that human agents unreflexively perform the roles allocated to them by the system's functional imperative. He also makes two additional criticisms, however, which are directed at any general theory of IR, even one purged of the unsatisfactory elements in Dunlop's conception. First, he argues that the historical origins of IR deny its theoretical coherence. The field, he argues, has developed in an *ad hoc* fashion in response to the changing needs of states and employers rather than 'to any underlying intellectual rationale' and for this reason cannot be endowed with 'analytical coherence after the event' (2004: 266).[4] Second, he argues that both the practice and study of IR vary so greatly across national boundaries as to make the quest for a general specification of the IR system pointless. The object of study varies, embracing social policy as well as employment in some European countries, as do research traditions, including different patterns of disciplinary demarcation.

'We industrial relations scholars', Hyman notes, 'cannot assume that we have counterparts in other countries' (2004: 272).

Hyman is not content to leave IR as a pragmatic, policy-oriented field and calls for greater theoretical sophistication (2004: 267–9). Specifically, he suggests that IR scholars need to have more regard to the theory of theory and, in particular, address the attributes of effective theorizing. Following Przeworski and Teune (1970), he argues that theories should be judged on the extent to which they satisfy four competing (and to a degree contradictory) criteria, generality, parsimony, accuracy and causality, the latter defined in terms of the explanation rather than mere observation of 'a relationship among factors' (Hyman, 1994: 173). Hyman's position therefore declares a need for theory *in* IR, as opposed to the Dunlopian project of a theory *of* IR. Essentially it is a call for IR to connect with meta-theory, the concern with the ontological status of the social world and the epistemic status of social theory, which is central to other fields of social science but typically remote from pragmatic, empiricist IR (see also Edwards, 2005; Godard, 1993).

Employment relations system

The second position is occupied by those who would purge Dunlop's legacy of its undesirable elements and renew the systems tradition. For writers in this camp, such as Meltz (1993) and Kaufman (2004a), the creation of a *general* theory of IR remains a viable project. Kaufman's recent attempt to lay the basis of an 'integrative theory of industrial relations' is particularly noteworthy and deals with three issues: defining the object of study of IR, identifying the primary outcomes and behaviors to be explained and listing the 'key explanatory components ... and processes that must be included in the theory' (2004a: 42). The analytical core of IR, in Kaufman's model, is the employment relationship, in which formally free labor is hired by an employer to engage in a labor process. From this starting point, he elaborates an 'employment relations system' (ERS) that

embraces three institutional domains that regulate or govern that relationship. Most proximate is the institution of the firm with its management hierarchy and internal labor market, next are the product and labor markets in which the firm operates, and third are collective institutions, including the representative organs of capital and labor, state agencies and civil society organizations. Beyond this institutional sphere the employment relationship is shaped by more distant environmental factors, including social forces (for instance culture, class, ideology, ethics, history), law and science and technology (Kaufman, 2004a: 49–62).

Unlike Dunlop, Kaufman is not prescriptive about the explanandum of IR, the dependent variables, empirical regularities or behaviors it seeks to explain. What he does suggest is that the phenomena to be explained by IR can be ordered hierarchically and depends on the level of analysis. At the highest level, the purpose is to explain the existence of the employment relationship itself and identify the complex of exogenous forces that formed that relationship and institutionalized it within developed societies. At the next level the 'institutional structure and configuration of the employment relationship' is to be explained, at the next the 'form, operation and performance of individual institutions' and so on until at the final level the focus is on 'all the individual personal and organizational outcomes and behaviors that emanate from the employment relationship'. The latter include the common foci of research studies published in IR journals, 'such as job satisfaction, work effort, plant-level productivity, extent of high performance work practices, compensation and benefit levels, worker desire for union representation and many others besides' (Kaufman, 2004a: 69).

Neither is Kaufman prescriptive about the causal factors that should guide IR analysis. His ERS model clearly implies an interest in the causal links between the broad social and technical context, the three institutional domains (firms, markets and collective institutions) and the nature of the employment relationship. But there is no assumption of causal priority being allocated to a particular level and the model leaves ample scope for feedback loops and for phenomena at different levels to interact and condition each other. What Kaufman does state, however, is that IR is a boundary-spanning field that is concerned both with the functioning of markets and the workings of hierarchies, the domains respectively of economics and organization studies. In seeking to develop explanations the field should seek to draw on both of these fields and Kaufman believes that theoretical work in IR is best derived from the tradition of institutional economics most strongly associated with the work of Oliver Williamson (Kaufman, 2004a: 72).

Kaufman's ERS model is developed from a critique of Dunlop's earlier conception of the IR system and seeks to correct what are seen by many as the defects of that conception. In Kaufman's formulation the field is broadened beyond trade unions and collective bargaining, there are no assumptions about the functionality of IR and there is a deliberate attempt to allow for strategic actors who interact with and shape their institutional and wider environment. Like Dunlop the main concern is to provide a descriptive map of IR, to list the component elements of the subject so that its bounds are clear and differentiated from other fields. To this author, reflective stock-taking of this kind performs a useful service but the strength of Kaufman's model is also its weakness. It comprises a much fuller listing of the elements of IR (context, processes and outcomes) than that found in Dunlop, which better reflects the nature of contemporary employment relations. But the result is a rather anodyne, contentless model, with which it is difficult to find fault but which provides only a preliminary guide to analysis.[5] To use Hyman's terms, generality has been pursued at the expense of parsimony, accuracy and causality.

Varieties of capitalism

The third contemporary perspective on systems thinking effectively tries to strike a more even balance between generality and accuracy and has been developed by IR comparativists (for example Marsden, 1999). The intention here is not to develop a general model of the IR system but to identify different national types; to map and account for variation. It is in this guise that systems-thinking currently exerts most influence over IR scholarship, particularly through the Varieties of Capitalism (VoC) school, founded by Peter A. Hall and David Soskice (1998). The main elements of the latter are dealt with elsewhere in this volume (see Chapter 7) but its primary characteristic is the identification of two main forms of capitalist economy that solve problems of co-ordination (between firms themselves and between firms and investors and firms and employees) in different ways. In 'liberal market economies', exemplified by the US, co-ordination is primarily through lightly regulated markets, while in 'co-ordinated market economies', such as Germany, formal encompassing institutions and other non-market mechanisms play a much greater role. Both types of economy are characterized by an interlocking and stable set of institutional mechanisms that govern the financing of firms, skill formation, wage determination, labor processes and inter-firm relations. Each of these institutional combinations possesses functionality and market and non-market forms of co-ordination are held to confer equivalent though different forms of comparative advantage on their respective national economies. In liberal market economies firms have greater capacity for innovation and have successfully developed new industries, while in co-ordinated market economies, long-term, high trust relations between firms, investors and employees, support incremental change and competition on the basis of high value added in mature manufacturing (Hall and Soskice, 1998: 14–7).

Hall and Soskice's theory is a contribution to comparative political economy rather than IR as such though it has attracted increasing attention from IR scholars (for example, Godard, 2004). It is a perspective that erodes the boundary between IR and other fields of analysis and seeks to examine IR as an integral part of a national business system rather than as a distinct sub-system, sufficient to itself. Thus, drawing on this literature, Gospel and Pendleton (2003) have examined the implications for IR of 'insider' and 'outsider' forms of business financing and corporate governance, which are representative respectively of coordinated and liberal market economies. They identify six features of management that vary between these two types, all of which have major implications for the conduct of IR. These are:

1. the responsiveness of enterprise management to the relative interests of capital and labor;
2. the time-frame of managerial decision-making;
3. the nature of business strategies;
4. the importance allocated to financial measures in management decision-making;
5. the approach to securing employee commitment; and
6. the degree of cooperation with other firms (Gospel and Pendleton, 2003: 565).

Simplifying, it is argued that in market outsider (liberal) economies managers are driven by considerations of shareholder value and regard employees as a factor of production; time-frames are shorter reducing the scope for investment in skills or partnership with employees; business strategies are finance driven and emphasize cost reduction; the use of financial ratios to guide management decision-making discourages the development of less tangible assets such as trust or firm-specific skills; commitment is sought through financial incentives; and weak ties between firms are reflected in devolved, plant-level bargaining. The reverse pattern, characterized by longer-term decision-making and less emphasis on financial controls, is held to be characteristic of 'insider' or 'coordinated' systems and provides the basis for a less adversarial, investment orientation to the workforce.

Having delineated the place of IR in different types of national business system, Gospel and Pendleton immediately enter a qualification. They note that the practice of labor management varies enormously within

liberal and co-ordinated economies and that scope for 'strategic choice' remains. The 'emphasis on institutional complementarities and isomorphic processes' in Hall and Soskice's approach, they say, 'tends to downgrade the elements of national systems that do not fit the core characteristics of the model' (2003: 571). This argument is reminiscent of that developed in response to Dunlop's systems theory by Kochan et al. (1986) in *The Transformation of American Industrial Relations*, which also hinged on an actor-based account of within-system variation.

Other commentators on Hall and Soskice have applied elements of the classic critique of systems theory to their work. Perhaps the most noteworthy is Colin Crouch in his book *Capitalist Diversity and Change* (2005a; see also Crouch, 2005b). Among other criticisms, Crouch attacks the VoC model for its functionalism, determinism and conception of firms as 'institution takers'; actors that repeatedly enact the roles that each type of business system requires. His central target, however, is one that has frequently been identified in the critique of systems theory, the inability of the model to allow for or explain change over time. Crouch notes the strong emphasis on path determinacy within the VoC approach and the tendency of its adherents to account for social change through exogenous forces that disrupt the established institutional pattern (Crouch, 2005a: 16; see also Streeck and Thelen, 2005).

In response Crouch makes two points, one methodological the other substantive. The methodological point refers to the form of case analysis that VoC writers employ, which Crouch characterizes as 'the labeling method' (2005b: 452). In this approach,

> the neo-institutionalist researcher ... inspects the characteristics of an empirical case and decides which of a limited number of theoretical models ... it most closely resembles. The case is then considered to be 'an example' of that model and labeled accordingly, all features of it which do not fit the model being considered as 'noise' and disregarded.

The alternative favored by Crouch is the 'analytical method', in which cases are not conflated with theoretical models but are assumed to consist of an amalgam of principles of social organization each capable of theoretical description in a separate ideal type.[6] The complexity of cases then provides the ground on which change can occur. Crouch's substantive argument is that institutional change occurs within societies through the action of 'institutional entrepreneurs' who typically combine previously discrete forms of practice to create new forms. Change is always *recombinant*, therefore, drawing upon complexity to develop new institutions.

An example can be seen in the changing repertoire of trade unions in the light of the growing juridification of the employment relationship. In Britain, unions have responded to the opportunity afforded by a growing volume of law to make greater use of the method of legal regulation and pursue strategic cases through the courts, particularly in the area of discrimination and equality law. Cases, however, have been integrated with the established method of representation through collective bargaining and a form of pattern bargaining has emerged in which legal action (or the threat of legal action) has been used to establish precedents that are then diffused through collective agreements (Heery et al., 2004: 147). Entrepreneurs within the labor movement, therefore, have developed a new, post-voluntarist form of interest representation that combines previously distinct institutions.

Much of Crouch's response to the VoC school echoes the critical reaction to earlier systems models within IR. As systems theory has re-emerged in this latest form so the established elements of critique have been articulated; that systems models are determinist, functionalist, allow minimal scope for action and choice, are neglectful of variation and fail to explain change. This contest is perennial in social theory. On one side stand those who prioritize the explanation of order and on the other are those who seek to explain change, typically by identifying conflict, contradiction or complexity as defining elements of the social world. It is to a fuller account of

models of change that have been elaborated within IR that we now turn.

MODELS OF CHANGE

Much IR research in the positivist tradition is modeled on the nomothetic natural sciences: it seeks to establish regularities between variables abstracted from time and space. There is an alternative conception of IR as a quintessentially historical subject, however, which, like the historical natural sciences of geology and biology, is concerned with the evolution of forms (for example, forms of labor process, management control systems, trade unionism and modes of state regulation) through time.[7] Adherents of this position have urged IR scholars repeatedly to be sensitive to the historical origins of the institutions they study and have recommended that historical subjects and historical methods be included within IR (for example, Lyddon, 2004). In what follows this historical imperative is accepted but it is also accepted that change can proceed with different rhythms and under different kinds of propulsive force. Accordingly, there is an attempt to map the models of historical change that are employed by IR scholars and which are embedded in their empirical work.

This typology is shown in Table 4.1 and is comprised of three dichotomous elements. In the first place a distinction is drawn between processes of change that are cyclical and those that are directional or non-repetitive. In the second, a distinction is drawn between directional models of change that are gradualist or disjunctive; in the former change is steady and cumulative while in the latter it is catastrophic with sudden episodes of change disrupting long periods of stability. This disjunctive pattern is frequently described as 'punctuated equilibrium' (see Erickson and Kuruvilla, 1998: 9). The third dichotomy embraces the causes of change and is based on the familiar distinction between change that is endogenous, originating within IR, and change that is exogenous, driven by forces beyond. In combination these variables

Table 4.1   Models of change underpinning theories of union revitalization

	Directional		Cyclical
	Gradual	Disjunctive	
Exogenous	1. *Stages of development* Labor-management partnership a response to selective pressure exerted by technical change (high performance work systems) or the widening scope of product markets (globalization)	2. *Historical compromise* Social movement unionism a response to the neo-liberal turn in politics and the collapse of an earlier accommodation between state and labor	3. *Long waves* Periodic mobilization of the labor movement generated by Kondratieff long waves that lead both to the accumulation of grievances and the organizational capacity for mobilization
Endogenous	6. *Social learning* New union strategies are diffused by processes of social learning between and within national labor movements; key processes include mimetic and normative isomorphism	5. *Strategic choice* Union revitalization a product of strategic choice, reflecting political competition and the incursion of new waves of activist into positions of power within unions	4. *Unfolding contradiction* Union renewal a function of the perennial contest between the forces of accommodation and challenge within the labor movement

generate six types or models of historical change, each of which can be illustrated by the literature on 'union revitalization'; one of the prime foci of recent IR scholarship that is concerned explicitly with explaining changes in behavior over time (see Heery et al., 2004: 3–21).

Exogenous models

The first of the six types emphasizes gradual, cumulative change driven by forces beyond the employment relationship. Models of this type have been an enduring feature of IR and underpinned some of the classic statements of its founding fathers. Commons' analysis of the growth of national unions and national systems of bargaining in the USA in response to the growing scale of product markets provides one example (see Brown, Chapter 6 of this volume). Another is provided by Kerr et al.'s *Industrialism and Industrial Man* (1955), in which the creation of a 'mature' system of industrial relations is presented as a functional adaptation to industrialization. Both types of argument continue to be made today and can be seen in the contemporary literature on union revitalization, particularly that concerned with union use of 'partnership' or 'mutual gains' strategies to reconstitute their relations with employers. In much of

this literature partnership is conceived as an adaptive response to selective pressure emanating in some versions from technical change, particularly the spread of high performance work systems, and in others from the globalization of product markets.

The argument from technical change has been developed by North American writers influenced by theories of post-Fordism or post-industrialism (Appelbaum and Batt, 1994: 123–45; Bélanger et al., 2002: 45). In this formulation the spread of high performance work systems requires employers to invest in high commitment management to secure the necessary levels of skill, commitment and flexibility. This, in turn, provides new scope for identifying shared interests between employers and employees. Accordingly, a new unionism can emerge that centers on advancing employees' interests in development, involvement and job satisfaction and which makes use of partnership to embed new forms of production, and their associated management practices, in the economy (Frost, 2001). A second, less upbeat account of partnership can be found in the work of British writers who emphasize the widening scale of product markets. According to Brown and colleagues (Brown et al., 1998: 73; Brown et al., 2000: 616–9; Oxenbridge et al., 2003: 324–32), exposure of domestic markets to international competition has led to two broad changes in interest representation. On the one hand, distributive bargaining by unions to secure a wage premium has become less tenable. On the other hand, the heightened competitive threat encourages workers and their representatives to develop a 'productivity coalition' with employers, in which security of employment is exchanged for flexibility. The product of the first change is a union search for a new *modus vivendi* while the effect of the second is to channel that search toward either formal or informal partnership arrangements with employers, based on an exchange of cooperative work relations for job stability.

The second model emphasizes discontinuity, episodes of change interspersed by periods of stability; with change itself triggered by the irruption of outside forces into the employment relationship. Models of this kind are perhaps less common in IR than those that stress the gradual evolution of forms through a sequence of stages but they do have a place. The best example can be seen in the argument that national systems of IR originate in a broad political and economic crisis that results in an 'historic compromise', an accommodation between capital and labor enshrined in a set of IR institutions (for example Sisson, 1987). Developments subsequent to this episode of institution-building are then channeled along established paths by the force of path dependency; that is until a new crisis disrupts the system. This may originate in geo-political events that overwhelm existing IR institutions, requiring a search for a fresh accommodation between the stakeholders in the employment relationship. An example can be seen in the impact of Second World War, which generated new institutions to help mobilize the working population in the victorious states and the transplant of institutions to defeated states. Another is the collapse of the Soviet Empire, which prompted a search for new IR institutions across the previously subject states of Eastern Europe (for example Frege, 1999; Turner, 1998). The key features of this model, however, remain the same whatever the nature of the external shock: short bursts of institution-building prompted by crisis, which give way to long periods of inertia or gradual change.

The argument in the literature on union revitalization that approximates most closely to this model is that which relates experiment with 'social movement unionism' to the rise of neo-liberalism (Robinson, 2002). In this argument the latter is identified as a political and ideological construct, the carriers of which have secured control of governments often through fortuitous or contingent circumstances. They have then proceeded to attack the institutional and ideological foundations of the existing compromise between state, capital and labor, through a policy of 'labor exclusion', of denying unions access to established channels of influence over government and employers (Crouch, 1985; see also Howell, 2005: 141–58). This militant strategy of shutting down the institutional resources of the labor movement, in time, can generate a militant response and the attempt to recreate unions as social movements. The characteristics of the latter include an increased emphasis on recruiting and organizing, seeking to raise the 'willingness to act' of workers through mobilization strategies and discursive frames that emphasize the pursuit of social justice, the broadening of union goals beyond quantitative workplace demands and a renewed commitment to acting on the terrain of civil society, particularly through union-community coalitions (for example Turner and Hurd, 2001; Wills, 2001). Fundamental to this strategy is an attempt to develop new power resources by organizing more workers, deepening their attachment to unions and capacity for mobilization and forging alliances with other progressive forces in civil society. At its heart is an attempt to compensate for the collapse of external sources of power, resulting from the neo-liberal assault, through a revitalization strategy focused on building fresh, 'internal' sources of power. The key point to note, however, is that the origins of social movement unionism are seen to lie in a 'catastrophic' event, the neo-liberal challenge, which has rendered established patterns of union action ineffective and encouraged a new departure.

In the catastrophic model there is an emphasis on historical contingency, with the evolution of trade unions and other IR institutions jolted onto unanticipated lines of development as they encounter crisis. In the third model, in contrast, there is an assumption that change follows a repeating cycle of decline and renewal as IR institutions adapt to cyclical pressures in their external environment. The source of these pressures has been variously identified in middle-range IR theories. From economics the business cycle has been identified as a key factor explaining the rise and fall of union membership and other IR indices (for example Bain and Elsheikh, 1976). From politics it has been suggested that union-government relations in periods of left government follow a cyclical pattern; moving from tension to accommodation as the reciprocal need to re-elect a non-hostile government and secure union election funding becomes apparent (Ludlam and Taylor, 2003). And from sociology the periodic organizational crises of American labor, including the recent split in the AFL–CIO, have been explained by reference to waves of mass immigration and the tensions these impose on established union structures (Cornfield, 2006).

Within the union revitalization literature a notable example of this kind of argument can be found in John Kelly's (1998: 83–107) use of Kondratieff cycles or 'long waves' to explain recurrent episodes of union militancy. Kelly's starting point is the empirical observation by a variety of scholars that the world economy appears to move through extended cycles of approximately 50 years in duration. In a sequence that stretches back into the nineteenth century an upswing, distinguished by above average growth, is followed after about 25 years by a downswing, during which growth slackens. Kelly remains non-committal on the causal mechanism underpinning these long waves but notes that the transition points in the cycle are associated with periodic strike waves. The latter are particularly apparent at the end of upswings

(for example 1968–1974) when states and employers challenge entrenched union movements in order to re-establish profit and growth levels. They can also be observed, in at least some countries, at the end of downswings when more favorable economic conditions generate power resources for organized labor. The relevance of this argument to the debate over union revitalization appears to be twofold. First, it suggests that the current period of labor 'quiescence' cannot be extrapolated into the future; at key transition-points militancy may re-emerge. Second, the argument is determinist in character and suggests that waves of worker mobilization will only emerge under particular conditions when the world economy moves into or out of an extended upswing. On this analysis it is the rise and fall of the world economy that fundamentally determines the revitalization of the labor movement not the strategies or tactics of its constituent institutions.[8]

Endogenous models

Cyclical processes also lie at the core of the fourth model though in this case they originate in the employment relationship itself. Theories of endogenous cyclical change are typically rooted in a claim that the employment relationship embodies contradictory elements; competing impulses that push actors in different directions. For example, it is often suggested that the employment relationship is both adversarial, reflecting the opposing interests of employer and worker, and cooperative, reflecting the mutual dependence of the two parties (Edwards et al., 2006). One inference that can be drawn from this conceptualization is that management strategies of labor use that assume the relation has a single, dominant characteristic will encounter problems of implementation as they confront neglected features. Thus, adversarial strategies of labor control may be subverted by workers who retain tacit skills and elements of discretion in even the most tightly regulated labor process, while attempts to build worker commitment to management goals may be undermined by the periodic requirement to control costs or restructure the employing organization. In Hyman's (1987: 30) famous phrase management strategy can be regarded as 'the programmatic choice between alternatives none of which can prove satisfactory'. A further inference that can be drawn is that management strategy will follow a cyclical or oscillating pattern, prioritizing control or cooperation at one point but switching direction when the limits of each approach become apparent. Contradiction, that is, implies cyclical development.

The same line of argument can be seen in the analysis of trade unions, particularly in the influential model of trade union renewal that has been put forward by Peter Fairbrother (for example Fairbrother, 1996; 2000: 3–22). The starting point of this analysis is the identification of a similarly contradictory impulse within trade unions: toward accommodation with employers on the one hand and toward challenge and resistance on the other. The latter is generated in the immediate labor process where workers experience exploitative conditions, while the former stems from the pressure on representatives to seek institutional security from employers and state agencies. It follows that the impulse to accommodation will be stronger when unions are oligarchic and representatives insulated from the potentially militant pressure of the union rank- and-file. Insulation can never be complete, however, and the iron law of oligarchy potentially can fail. This may be because employers intensify the rate of exploitation and so generate a higher level of worker grievance or it may be because the decentralization of bargaining to workplace level brings union decision-making closer to workers and more susceptible to influence. Both factors are believed to be significant in Fairbrother's analysis and have promoted the 'renewal' of public service unions in Britain in recent years, understood both as a process of democratization and as a growth of militancy. Whatever the trigger, however, the key underlying point is that internal union politics follows a cyclical pattern, in which accommodation is challenged, re-established and challenged

once more.[9] Union revitalization on this view, therefore, is expressed initially within unions and takes the form of a rank-and-file challenge to an established and accommodative oligarchy.

The fifth model emphasizes disjunctive change that is generated within IR and is perhaps best illustrated by theories of strategic choice. As we have seen these have grown in popularity in recent years and are distinguished by allocating a zone of discretion to strategic actors (states, employers, unions), in which they exercise choice within a context of constraint. Episodes of choice therefore are the key points of disjuncture at which new forms emerge; whether these are new management policies, new collective agreements, new systems of union government or new forms of employment law. The field of IR is now replete with typologies of management and union strategy that seek to specify the menu of choices available to strategic actors (for example Boxall and Haynes, 1997; Purcell and Ahlstrand, 1994). There has also been a growth of research into the characteristics of actors that lead them to exercise choice in a particular way, to select a particular option from the menu. In research on management, for instance, there has been a focus on the composition of the management team and the relative power of the different functional groups represented within it (for example Colling and Dickens, 1998). The presence of HR managers and the existence of a strong HR function have been identified in a number of studies as a key factor shaping management policy and practice, particularly in the area of equality (for example Hoque and Noon, 2004; Kelly and Dobbin, 1999). In studies of union strategy a similar line of development is visible, with researchers variously identifying the influence of gender, generational change and ideology in shaping strategic choice (see Heery, 2003: 293–5). On this view, disjunctive change in union behavior is likely to stem from the replacement of incumbent office holders and activists with those of a different stamp.

In the literature on union revitalization a stress on internally-generated disjunctive change can be seen in the work of feminist IR scholars Fiona Colgan and Sue Ledwith (Ledwith and Colgan, 2002). They are concerned with explaining the increasing influence of women and minority groups in unions, a development that is visible across the globe and which has led to significant changes (albeit incomplete and contested) in internal union government and in the policies unions pursue toward employers and state. Colgan and Ledwith note that unions have often pursued policies of exclusion or demarcation with regard to women and minority groups. Under the former they are denied union membership and the benefits it provides, while under the latter they are accepted as a secondary category of members confirming their secondary position in the labor market. Both policies have been challenged by the mobilization of women and minorities within unions. Colgan and Ledwith note that 'usurpation' has often been a key stage in this process, defined as 'where a subordinate group mobilizes through strategies of social change to challenge the dominant group, and succeeds in changing the structure of positions and balance of leadership between the groups' (ibid: 16). They note also that 'usurpation strategies' are about 'replacing men with women, white members with black and so on' and consequently have often been fiercely resisted. The end result of this process can include 'transformation', that is the creation of radical new structures to mainstream equality initiatives within unions, and 'coalition', understood as the development of horizontal linkages between identity groups inside unions and collaboration with social movement organizations in wider civil society. Much of this model of revitalization resembles the union renewal thesis; they have a shared emphasis on mobilization from below. The key difference is that the change described by Colgan and Ledwith is unidirectional not cyclical; they are seeking to map the permanent impact on the 'old' social movement of labor of the new social movements grounded in gender and other diverse identities. For these writers union revitalization is dependent on the successful

conclusion of this process, of unions changing to represent diversity.

The final model of change emphasizes gradual transformation, driven by forces internal to IR. In one version there is a stress on IR institutions maturing over time, such that they become more complex and pursue more differentiated goals. An example might be the famous 'iron law of oligarchy', developed by Robert Michels (see Crouch, 1982: 163–5) to explain the retreat from revolutionary politics in trade unions and left political parties. In this argument the bureaucratization of labor institutions leads inexorably and irreversibly to goal displacement, as incumbent leaders develop interests separate from the membership and use their leadership position both to pursue these interests and insulate themselves from membership pressure. In a second version there is an emphasis on social learning and the gradual diffusion of forms across an institutional field. Key processes here might include normative and mimetic isomorphism; that is the creation of standards of good IR practice and their adoption by exemplars that provide a model for other organizations.

In the literature on union revitalization the latter argument is illustrated by studies of the 'organizing model' and its international diffusion (Cooper, 2000; Heery et al., 2002; Hurd, 1998; 2004; Oxenbridge, 1997). The concept of an 'organizing model' was coined by American trade unionists in the late 1980s and has since influenced policy debate and practice in unions across North America, Australia, New Zealand, Britain and, more latterly, the countries of continental Europe. It designates a conception of union good practice that comprises both core principles and a number of specific organizing techniques. The principles include prioritizing organizing, seeking to develop collective organization and capacity amongst workers and a stress on mobilization through a framing discourse that calls for 'dignity, justice and respect' at work. The techniques include selecting strategic organizing targets, mounting planned campaigns, mapping workforces to identify members and activists, using a representative 'organizing committee' to ensure member involvement, and the use of escalating pressure tactics to foster mobilization and demonstrate union effectiveness. The literature on the diffusion of this model has identified a number of factors that have encouraged its spread both within and between national labor movements and emphasizes gradual change through processes of deliberate learning. Among the factors that have been identified has been the role of national union confederations in sponsoring the organizing model and encouraging its diffusion by arranging seminars, conferences and visits to other countries and by establishing training programs for organizers. The latter include the Organizing Institute in the USA, Organizing Works in Australia and the Organizing Academy in Britain (Foerster, 2001; Heery et al., 2002). There has also been a focus on the structural features of unions that facilitate receptiveness to the organizing model. Thus, Voss and Sherman (2000) note that revived union locals in the US that have prioritized organizing tend to have relatively strong links to the union center; that is, diffusion follows lines of articulation between union headquarters and constituent branches. The essential point to note in this model of union revitalization, however, is that change is conceived as diffusion, a gradual process, and that it occurs through a process of deliberate knowledge transfer; the latter being conducted through both formal institutional ties and informal networks within the labor movement.

CONCLUSION

This chapter has reviewed two types of model-building within IR through two, separate processes of examination. On the one hand, it has considered cross-sectional models that seek to designate the object of study of IR, list the component elements of the IR system and identify its functional outcomes. The procedure in this case has been to review the subject's long dialogue with Dunlop's *Industrial Relations Systems* (1993), which despite its vintage continues to provide a point

of reference for those reflecting on the nature of the subject (for example Piore and Safford, 2006). On the other hand, there has been an attempt to illuminate the models of historical change that underpin much IR analysis but which are often not articulated. The procedure here has been to develop a typology of models of change in IR and to illustrate this through the literature on union revitalization.

Critical engagement with Dunlop has itself followed two routes, reflecting the dual purpose of his scheme. Commentators have asked if it continues to provide a satisfactory cross-section of IR; a descriptive mapping of the field's object study. They have also engaged with the causal elements of the model – what Hyman (2004: 269) terms the genuine 'theoretical content'; that is, its stress on technically-driven change, system integration through a binding ideology and assumption of functionality.

As we have seen many IR scholars continue to conceive of the field as a system comprising actors, processes, outcomes and context. Even amongst those sympathetic to the initial formulation, however, there is a concern to update and extend Dunlop's list of elements. The empirical substance of the field has become less coherent but more extensive since Dunlop first published his book in 1958 and much of the first line of engagement has been concerned to identify a greater complexity in IR's object of study. This drive to complexity can be seen in attempts to lower the boundary walls between Dunlop's neatly defined IR system and other, adjacent fields of inquiry, whether these are political economy, the domestic sphere or the system of corporate governance. It can also be seen in the changing specification of each of the elements of Dunlop's study. Thus, there has been a focus on 'new actors' that articulate interests, such as those of consumers or identity groups that were largely disregarded at the time when Dunlop was writing. Other developments include reduced attention to collective bargaining as a rule-making process with a corresponding growth of attention to management policy and the regulatory function of the state, an increased focus on the quantifiable outcomes of IR processes and a change in perceptions of the context of IR to give greater weight both to the institutional sources of difference between national systems and the strategic choices of firms that underpin within-country variation. Dunlop's first purpose was to specify clearly the object of study of IR, the IR system, and identify its constituent elements. The response to his work in the intervening period points to the frustration of this purpose as the bounds of the subject have become more ragged and its empirical subject matter has grown. Coherence has been sacrificed for complexity but to my mind this is a welcome development reflecting real changes in the world of work.

The substantive argument that many believe to be at the heart of Dunlop's book was that an integrated and institutionally distinct IR system was a necessary element of industrial society, serving to regulate economic conflict. This argument has been repeatedly attacked in the intervening 50 years though perhaps surprisingly his assumption about the functionality of the IR system has found fresh support as pluralist scholars have sought to defend IR from neo-liberal attack. It is also the case that systems-thinking that is analogous to that of Dunlop continues to be developed within IR. The clearest example can be seen in the work of IR comparativists influenced by Hall and Soskice's models of liberal and co-ordinated varieties of capitalism. Like Dunlop, there is an emphasis in these models on the fixed, determined nature of business systems though it is path dependency rather than economic development that is the determining force. There is also a stress on the integrated, mutually reinforcing character of different system elements, albeit extending beyond the employment sphere, and on the functionality of competing business systems. Both liberal and co-ordinated market economies can prosper in the world economy. This revival of systems-thinking has had a positive impact on IR, boosting comparative work, encouraging scholars to examine the links between IR institutions and other institutional domains

of national economies and serving as a corrective to convergence theses, whether grounded in technical or market determinism. Nevertheless, they share some of the same weaknesses of Dunlop's systems theory. The most persuasive critique is that of Crouch, who notes the inability of VoC theory to allow for significant change. For Crouch, innovation can only be theorized if social theory holds a place for contradiction and complexity. VoC models, with their emphasis on the synergy between institutions, deny such a place. Allowing that societies include a variety of social practices that can be recombined by institutional entrepreneurs compromises the elegance of systems models but, once again, imports necessary complexity.

In Dunlop's other great book, *Industrialism and Industrial Man* (1960), there is arguably a Whiggish conception of history, in which change advances gradually toward a desirable state.[10] The IR system appears as the natural precipitation of a maturing capitalist democracy, called into being by the need for a social sub-system to regulate conflict. Many other early IR texts carry this assumption; that industrial citizenship through trade unions and collective bargaining, like political citizenship before it, slowly spreads and civilizes the economy. The substantial erosion of IR institutions in recent decades means that this optimistic interpretation of the past is no longer tenable. In its place can be identified a series of models of historical change. In the empirical work of IR scholars change is regarded variously as gradual, disjunctive and cyclical and may be prompted by forces that are internal or external to the employment relationship. In much work these different models are opposed, as is illustrated by the work on union revitalization. For some, the latter can only occur if unions adapt to secular trends in work organization or the widening scale of product markets, while for others it will be prompted by the periodic crises of capitalism or a challenge to incorporated union leaders from below. But models of historical change can also be combined, such that cyclical processes occur between episodes of 'catastrophic' reconstruction or a secular trend exists beneath short-term cyclical fluctuation. Historians have increasingly recognized that change occurs at variable speeds, from Braudel's classic distinction between the history of events, conjunctures and the *longue durée* (Abrams, 1982: 334) to recent attempts to combine 'continuitist' and 'catastrophic' readings of the past (Wickham, 2006: 10–4). All of the models of historical change outlined in this chapter have validity and can generate empirical and practical insights for IR scholars; they can be combined. Like historians, IR scholars should recognize the complexity of historical processes and the fact that change occurs in different rhythms and at variable speeds.

ACKNOWLEDGMENTS

I would like to thank Paul Blyton, Paul Edwards and Jack Fiorito for challenging but helpful comments on an earlier draft of this chapter.

NOTES

1 These two examples constitute attempts to broaden the scope of IR but there has been another line of criticism, developed by Marxist writers, that seeks to deepen IR analysis. The central claim here is that the institutions and processes of the IR system are epiphenomenal and that analysis must begin at a deeper level with the generative structures of the capitalist mode of production. For Hyman (1975: 18–19), 'the crucial fact about the economies of Western Europe and North America – where most studies of industrial relations have had their focus – is their *capitalist* character (emphasis in original)' (see also Hyman, 1989: 125). The exploitative condition of wage labor and the class conflict, which it generates, is the source of the uncertain accommodation of capital and labor in the formal system of IR, described by Dunlop. In recognition of this fact, the field should be relabeled 'the study of processes of control over work relations' (Hyman, 1975: 12).

2 To provide one example, the campaigning UK charity, Public Concern at Work, has lobbied successfully for legislation protecting whistleblowers and advises employers and trade unions on public interest disclosure procedures. Its origins lie in the consumer movement, however, and its ultimate purpose in facilitating public interest disclosure by employees is to protect citizens and consumers from hazard or unscrupulous action by service providers and manufacturers.

3 This perspective continues to be articulated within IR. Peter Ackers' call for a 'neo-pluralism' (2002) is based on a diagnosis of social disintegration, the prescription for which is the rebuilding of the workplace status order through an ideology of stakeholding reinforced by the institutional practices of worker involvement and labor-management partnership.

4 This is perhaps a demanding standard to apply and invites a comparison – do other fields of social inquiry differ both in terms of their responsiveness to socially constituted interests and their intellectual coherence? All fields have an external, social history and are shaped by interests and the changing definition of social problems, while also possessing an internal, logical history in which practitioners add knowledge and engage in debate (see Hawthorn, 1976). Whether IR's social history is such as to disqualify its pretension to the status of an autonomous field is a difficult question to resolve.

5 To provide an example, one of Kaufman's conditioning social forces is 'history' and the point is made that national systems of IR exhibit a path dependency in which traditions and behavioral patterns endure (Kaufman, 2004a: 59). This is clearly an important initial observation but leaves more demanding questions about the origins, nature and strength of historical traditions to be posed and resolved.

6 Crouch (2005b: 449) notes that the labeling method in comparative analysis is often defended in terms of its parsimony. His response, using Hyman's terms, is to note the tension between parsimony and accuracy in social theory and to contend that the accuracy of the analytical approach, in which cases are regarded as 'amalgams of types', is an acceptable price to pay for greater complexity.

7 The parallels between the historical sciences, whatever their object of study, is a theme developed by the great evolutionary biologist, the late Stephen Jay Gould. Gould is perhaps best known to social scientists for his development (with Niles Eldredge) of the model of punctuated equilibrium, which has since diffused across many areas of social and natural inquiry. However, he also developed a useful typology of models of change in his book on the history of geology, *Time's Arrow, Time's Cycle* (Gould, 1987). Gould's typology is the inspiration for much of what follows.

8 Kelly qualifies this determinist argument and earlier in the same book stresses the role of union leaders and activists in mobilizing workers. This seems to express the classic division in Leninist thought between the laws of motion of the capitalist mode of production (understood here as a cyclical process rather than a directional movement toward collapse),

which operate beyond the control of social actors, and the space for deliberate and decisive action that is reserved for a revolutionary vanguard.

9 This cyclical process of challenge and accommodation is at the heart of many interpretations of change in trade unions (for example Turner, 2003). A particularly graphic example can be seen in the changing interpretation of workplace shop stewards by left commentators on British trade unions in the 1970s and 1980s. While the steward movement of the 1960s was initially regarded as a 'challenge from below' driving the renewal of UK unions, by the end of the 1970s observers were noting the 'bureaucratization of the rank and file' as the militant impulse flagged (Hyman, 1979). In Beynon's (1984: 371) classic study of the Ford Motor Company in the UK, it is noted that a new rank-and-file movement then began to emerge in opposition to the 'convenor system' of 'official' workplace representatives and which labeled itself the 'workers' combine committee'.

10 Elsewhere in Dunlop's work, however, alternative models of change are deployed and, interestingly, he was perhaps the earliest IR analyst to develop an interest in Kondratieff cycles (Dunlop, 1948).

REFERENCES

Abbott, B. (2006) 'Determining the significance of the Citizens' Advice Bureau as an industrial relations actor', *Employee Relations*, 28 (5): 435–48.

Abrams, P. (1982) *Historical Sociology*. West Compton House near Shepton Mallet: Open Books.

Ackers, P. (2002) 'Reframing employment relations: the case for neo-pluralism', *Industrial Relations Journal*, 33 (1): 2–19.

Appelbaum, E. and Batt, R. (1994) *The New American Workplace*. Ithaca and London: ILR Press.

Appelbaum, E., Bailey, T., Berg, P. and Kalleberg, A. (2005) 'Organizations and the intersection of work and family: a comparative perspective', in S. Ackroyd, R. Batt, P. Thompson and P.S. Tolbert (eds) *The Oxford Handbook of Work and Organization*. Oxford: Oxford University Press. pp. 52–73.

Bain, G.S. and Clegg, H.A. (1974) 'A strategy for industrial relations research in Britain', *British Journal of Industrial Relations*, 12 (1): 91–113.

Bain, G.S. and Elsheikh, F. (1976) *Union Growth and the Business Cycle: An Econometric Analysis*. Oxford: Basil Blackwell.

Bélanger, P.R., Lapointe, P.A. and Lévesque, B. (2002) 'Workplace innovation and the role of institutions', in G. Murray, J. Bélanger. A. Giles and P.A. Lapointe (eds) *Work and Employment Relations in the High Performance Workplace*. London and New York: Continuum. pp. 150–80.

Bellemare, G. (2000) 'End users: actors in the industrial relations system?', *British Journal of Industrial Relations*, 38 (3): 383–405.

Beynon, H. (1984) *Working for Ford*, second edition. Harmondsworth: Penguin.

Blyton, P., Blunsdon, B., Reed, K. and Dastmalchian, A. (eds) (2006) *Work-Life Integration: International Perspectives on the Balancing of Multiple Roles*. Basingtoke: Palgrave MacMillan.

Blyton, P. and Turnbull, P. (2004) *The Dynamics of Employee Relations*, third edition. Basingstoke: Palgrave MacMillan.

Boxall, P. and Haynes, P. (1997) 'Strategy and trade union effectiveness in a neo-liberal environment', *British Journal of Industrial Relations*, 35 (4): 567–91.

Brown, A., Charlwood, A., Forde, C. and Spencer, D. (2006) *Changing Job Quality in Great Britain 1998–2004*. Employment Relations Research Series No.70. London: Department of Trade and Industry.

Brown, W., Deakin, S., Hudson, M., Pratten, C. and Ryan, P. (1998) *The Individualization of Employment Contracts in Britain*. Employment Relations Research Series No. 4. London: Department of Trade and Industry.

Brown, W., Deakin, S., Nash, D. and Oxenbridge, S. (2000) 'The employment contract: from collective procedures to individual rights', *British Journal of Industrial Relations*, 38 (4): 299–316.

Budd, J.W., Gomez, R. and Meltz, N.M. (2004) 'Why a balance is best: the pluralist industrial relations paradigm of balancing competing interests', in B.E. Kaufman (ed.) *Theoretical Perspectives on Work and the Employment Relationship*. Urbana-Champaign IL: Industrial Relations Research Association. pp. 195–227.

Budd, J.W. and Scoville, J.G. (eds) (2005) *The Ethics of Human Resources and Industrial Relations*. Urbana-Champaign IL: Labor and Employment Relations Association.

Clark, J. (1993) 'Procedures and consistency versus flexibility and commitment: a comment on Storey', *Human Resource Management Journal*, 4 (1): 79–81.

Clegg, H.A. (1975) 'Pluralism in industrial relations', *British Journal of Industrial Relations* 13 (3): 309–16.

Colling, T. and Dickens, L. (1998) 'Selling the case for gender equality: deregulation and equality bargaining', *British Journal of Industrial Relations*, 36 (3): 389–411.

Cooper, R. (2000) 'Organize, organize, organize. ACTU conference 2000', *Journal of Industrial Relations*, 42 (4): 582–94.

Cornfield, D. (2006) 'Immigration, economic restructuring, and labor ruptures: from the Amalgamated to Change to Win', *Working USA*, 9 (2): 215–23.

Crouch, C. (1982) *Trade Unions: The Logic of Collective Action*. Glasgow: Fontana.

Crouch, C. (1985) 'Conservative industrial relations policy: towards labour exclusion', in O. Jacobi, B. Jessop, H. Kastendiek and M. Regini (eds) *Economic Crisis, Trade Unions and the State*. London: Croom Helm. pp. 131–53.

Crouch, C. (2005a) *Capitalist Diversity and Change: Recombinant Governance and Institutional Entrepreneurs*. Oxford: Oxford University Press.

Crouch, C. (2005b) 'Models of capitalism', *New Political Economy*, 10 (4): 441–56.

Duncan, C., Loretto, W. and White, P. (2000) 'Ageism, early exit and British trade unions', *Industrial Relations Journal*, 31 (3): 220–34.

Dunlop, J.T. (1948) 'The development of labor organizations: a theoretical framework', in R.A. Lester and J. Shister (eds) *Insights into Labor Issues*. New York: MacMillan Co. pp. 163–93.

Dunlop, J., Harbison, F., Kerr, C., and Myers, C. (1960) *Industrialism and Industrial Man*, Princeton: Princeton University Press.

Dunlop, J.T. (1993) *Industrial Relations Systems*, revised edition. Boston MA: Harvard Business School Press.

Edwards, P. (2005) 'The challenging but promising future of industrial relations: developing theory and method in context-sensitive research', *Industrial Relations Journal*, 36 (4): 264–82.

Edwards, P., Bélanger, J. and Wright, M. (2006) 'The bases of compromise in the workplace: a theoretical framework', *British Journal of Industrial Relations*, 44 (1): 125–45.

Erickson, C.L. and Kuruvilla, S. (1998) 'Industrial relations system transformation', *Industrial and Labor Relations Review*, 52 (1): 3–21.

Fairbrother, P. (1996) 'Workplace trade unionism in the state sector', in P. Ackers, C. Smith and P. Smith (eds) *The New Workplace and Trade Unionism*. London: Routledge. pp. 110–48.

Fairbrother, P. (2000) *Trade Unions at the Crossroads*. London and New York: Continuum.

Fine, J. (2006) *Worker Centers: Organizing Communities at the Edge of the Dream*. Ithaca and London: ILR Press.

Fiorito, J. (1990) 'Comments: the wider bounds of IR systems', in J. Chelins and J. Dworkin (eds) *Reflections on the Transformation of Industrial Relations*. Metuchen NJ and London: IMLR Press/Rutgers University and Scarecrow Press. pp. 96–106.

Flanders, A. (1965) 'Industrial relations: what is wrong with the system?', in A. Flanders, *Management and Unions: The Theory and Reform of Industrial Relations*. London: Faber and Faber. pp. 83–128.

Foerster, A. (2001) 'Confronting the dilemmas of organizing: obstacles and innovations at the AFL-CIO's Organizing Institute', in L. Turner, H.C. Katz and R.W. Hurd (eds) *Rekindling the Movement: Labor's Quest for Relevance in the 21st Century*. Ithaca and London: ILR Press. pp. 155–81.

Foster, D. and Scott, J. (1998) 'Conceptualizing union responses to contracting municipal services, 1979–1997', *Industrial Relations Journal*, 29 (2): 137–50.

Fox, A. (1966) *Industrial Sociology and Industrial Relations*, Research Paper 3, Royal Commission on Trade Unions and Employers' Associations. London: HMSO.

Freeman, R. (1992) 'Is declining unionization of the US good, bad or irrelevant?', in L. Mishel and P.B. Voos (eds) *Unions and Economic Competitiveness*. Armonk NY: M.E. Sharpe. pp. 143–69.

Freeman, R. and Medoff, J.L. (1984) *What Do Unions Do?* New York: Basic Books.

Frege, C.M. (1999) *Social Partnership at Work: Workplace Relations in Post-unification Germany*. London: Routledge.

Frege, C.M., Heery, E. and Turner, L. (2004) 'The new solidarity? Trade union coalition-building in five countries', in C.M. Frege and J. Kelly (eds) *Varieties of Unionism: Strategies for Union Revitalization in a Global Economy*. Oxford: Oxford University Press. pp. 137–58.

Frost, A. (2001) 'Reconceptualising local union responses to workplace restructuring in North America', *British Journal of Industrial Relations*, 39 (4): 307–33.

Gilbert, M. (1986) *Inflation and Social Conflict: A Sociology of Economic Life in Advanced Societies*. Brighton: Wheatsheaf Books.

Godard, J. (1993) 'Theory and method in industrial relations: modernist and postmodernist alternatives', in R.J. Adams and N.M. Meltz (eds) *Industrial Relations Theory: Its Nature, Scope and Pedagogy*. Metuchen NJ and London: IMLR Press/Rutgers University and The Scarecrow Press. pp. 283–306.

Godard, J. (2004) 'The new institutionalism, capitalist diversity and industrial relations', in B.E. Kaufman (ed.) *Theoretical Perspectives on Work and the Employment Relationship*. Champaign IL: Industrial Relations Research Association. pp. 229–64.

Gospel, H. and Pendleton, A. (2003) 'Finance, corporate governance and the management of labour: a conceptual and comparative analysis', *British Journal of Industrial Relations*, 41 (3): 557–82.

Gould, S.J. (1987) *Time's Arrow, Time's Cycle: Myth and Metaphor in the Discovery of Geological Time.* Harmondsworth: Penguin.

Green, F. (2006) *Demanding Work: The Paradox of Job Quality in the Affluent Economy.* Princeton and Oxford: Princeton University Press.

Greene, A-M. (2003) 'Women and industrial relations', in P. Ackers and A. Wilkinson (eds) *Understanding Work and Employment: Industrial Relations in Transition.* Oxford: Oxford University Press. pp. 305–15.

Hall, P.A. and Soskice, D. (1998) 'An introduction to varieties of capitalism', in P.A. Hall and D. Soskice (eds) *Varieties of Capitalism: The Institutional Foundations of Comparative Advantage.* Oxford: Oxford University Press. pp. 1–70.

Hawthorn, G. (1976) *Enlightenment and Despair: A History of Sociology.* Cambridge: Cambridge University Press.

Heery, E. (2003) 'Trade unions and industrial relations', in P. Ackers and A. Wilkinson (eds) *Understanding Work and Employment: Industrial Relations in Transition.* Oxford: Oxford University Press. pp. 278–304.

Heery, E., Conley, H., Delbridge, R., Simms, M. and Stewart, P. (2004) 'Trade union responses to non-standard work', in G. Healy, E. Heery, P. Taylor and W. Brown (eds) *The Future of Worker Representation.* Basingstoke: Palgrave. pp. 127–50.

Heery, E., Delbridge, R., Salmon, J., Simms, M. and Simpson, D. (2002) 'Global labour? The transfer of the organizing model to the United Kingdom', in Y.A. Debrah and I.G. Smith (eds) *Globalization, Employment and the Workplace: Diverse Impacts.* London: Routledge. pp. 41–68.

Heery, E., Healy, G. and Taylor, P. (2004) 'Union revitalization: themes and issues', in G. Healy, E. Heery, P. Taylor and W. Brown (eds) *The Future of Worker Representation.* Basingstoke: Palgrave. pp. 1–36.

Hill, S. (1990) 'The dominant ideology thesis after a decade', in N. Abercrombie, S. Hill and B.S. Turner (eds) *Dominant Ideologies.* London: Unwin Hyman. pp. 1–37.

Hirschman, A.O. (1991) *The Rhetoric of Reaction: Perversity, Futility, Jeopardy.* Cambridge MA: Harvard University Press.

Hoque, K. and Noon, M. (2004) 'Equal opportunities policy and practice in Britain: evaluating the "empty shell" hypothesis', *Work, Employment and Society,* 18 (3): 481–506.

Howell, C. (2005) *Trade Unions and the State: The Construction of Industrial Relations Institutions in Britain, 1890–2000.* Princeton NJ and Oxford: Princeton University Press.

Hurd, R.W. (1998) 'Contesting the dinosaur image: the labor movement's search for a future', *Labor Studies Journal,* 23 (4): 5–30.

Hurd, R.W. (2004) 'The failure of organizing: the New Unity Partnership and the future of the labor movement', *Working USA,* 8 (1): 5–25.

Hyman, R. (1975) *Industrial Relations: A Marxist Introduction.* London and Basingstoke: MacMillan.

Hyman, R. (1979) 'The politics of workplace trade unionism', *Capital and Class,* 8: 54–67.

Hyman, R. (1987) 'Strategy or structure: capital, labour and control', *Work, Employment and Society,* 1 (1): 35–55.

Hyman, R. (1989) 'Theory in industrial relations: towards a materialist analysis', in R. Hyman (ed.) *The Political Economy of Industrial Relations.* Basingstoke: MacMillan. pp. 120–46.

Hyman, R. (2004) 'Theory and industrial relations', *British Journal of Industrial Relations,* 32 (2): 165–80.

Hyman, R. (2004) 'Is industrial relations theory always ethnocentric?', in B.E. Kaufman (ed.) *Theoretical Perspectives on Work and the Employment Relationship.* Champaign IL: Industrial Relations Research Association. pp. 265–92.

Hyman, R. and Brough, I. (1975) *Social Values and Industrial Relations.* Oxford: Basil Blackwell.

Kaufman, B.E. (2004a) 'Employment relations and the employment relations system: a guide to theorizing', in B.E. Kaufman (ed.) *Theoretical Perspectives on Work and the Employment Relationship.* Champaign IL: Industrial Relations Research Association. pp. 41–75.

Kaufman, B.E. (2004b) *The Global Evolution of Industrial Relations: Events, Ideas and the IIRA.* Geneva: International Labor Office.

Kelly, E. and Dobbin, F. (1999) 'Civil rights law at work: sex discrimination and the rise of maternity leave policies', *American Journal of Sociology,* 105 (2): 455–92.

Kelly, J. (1998) *Rethinking Industrial Relations: Mobilization, Collectivism and Long Waves.* London: Routledge.

Kerr, C., Dunlop, J.T., Harbison, F. and Myers, C. (1955) *Industrialism and Industrial Man.* Cambridge MA: Harvard University Press.

Kochan, T.A., Katz, H.C. and McKersie, R.B. (1986) *The Transformation of American Industrial Relations.* New York: Basic Books.

Korczynski, M. (2003) 'Consumer capitalism and industrial relations', in P. Ackers and A. Wilkinson (eds) *Understanding Work and Employment: Industrial Relations in Transition.* Oxford: Oxford University Press. pp. 265–77.

Ledwith, S. and Colgan, F. (2002) 'Tackling gender, diversity and trade union democracy: a worldwide project?', in F. Colgan and S. Ledwith (eds) *Gender, Diversity and Trade Unions: International Perspectives*. London: Routledge. pp. 1–27.

Logan, J. (2006) 'The union avoidance industry in the United States', *British Journal of Industrial Relations*, 44 (4): 651–76.

Ludlam, S. and Taylor, A. (2003) 'The political representation of the labour interest in Britain', *British Journal of Industrial Relations*, 41 (4): 727–49.

Lyddon, D. (2004) 'History and industrial relations', in P. Ackers and A. Wilkinson (eds) *Understanding Work and Employment: Industrial Relations in Transition*. Oxford: Oxford University Press. pp. 89–118.

Marsden, D. (1999) *A Theory of Employment Systems: Micro-foundations of Societal Diversity*. Oxford: Oxford University Press.

Meltz, N.M. (1993) 'Industrial relations systems as a framework for organizing contributions to industrial relations theory', in R.J. Adams and N.M. Meltz (eds) *Industrial Relations Theory: Its Nature, Scope and Pedagogy*. Metuchen NJ and London: IMLR Press/Rutgers University and The Scarecrow Press. pp. 161–82.

Metcalf, D. (1989) 'Water notes dry up: the impact of the Donovan reform proposals and Thatcherism at work on labour productivity in British manufacturing industry', *British Journal of Industrial Relations*, 27 (1): 1–31.

Nolan, P. and O'Donnell, K. (2003) 'Industrial relations, HRM and performance', in P. Edwards (ed.) *Industrial Relations: Theory and Practice*, second edition. Oxford: Blackwell Publishing. pp. 489–512.

Ogden, S. (1991) 'The trade union campaign against water privatization', *Industrial Relations Journal*, 22 (1): 20–34.

Osterman, P. (2006) 'Community organizing and employee representation', *British Journal of Industrial Relations*, 44 (4): 629–49.

Osterman, P., Kochan, T.A., Locke, R.M. and Piore, M.J. (2001) *Working in America: A Blueprint for the New Labor Market*. Cambridge MA and London: The MIT Press.

Oxenbridge, S. (1997) 'Organizing strategies and organizing reform in New Zealand service sector unions', *Labor Studies Journal*, 22 (3): 3–27.

Oxenbridge, S., Brown, W., Deakin, S. and Pratten, C. (2003) 'Initial responses to the Employment Relations Act 1999', *British Journal of Industrial Relations*, 41 (2): 315–34.

Piore, M.J. and Safford, S. (2006) 'Changing regimes of workplace governance: shifting axes of social mobilization and the challenge to industrial relations theory', *Industrial Relations*, 45 (3): 299–325.

Przeworski, A. and Teune, H. (1970) *The Logic of Comparative Social Inquiry*. New York: Jonathan Wiley.

Purcell, J. and Ahlstrand, B. (1994) *Human Resource Management in the Multi-divisional Company*. Oxford: Oxford University Press.

Richardson, R. (1996) 'Coercion and trade unions: a reconsideration of Hayek', *British Journal of Industrial Relations*, 34 (2): 219–36.

Robinson, I. (2002) 'Does neo-liberal restructuring promote social movement unionism? US developments in comparative perspective', in B. Nissen (ed.) *Unions in a Globalized Environment: Changing Borders, Organizational Boundaries and Social Roles*. Armonk NY: ME Sharpe. pp. 189–235.

Rubery, J., Smith, M. and Fagan, C. (1999) *Women's Employment in Europe: Trends and Prospects*. London: Routledge.

Sisson, K. (1987) *The Management of Collective Bargaining: An International Comparison*. Oxford: Basil Blackwell.

Streeck, W. (1992) *Social Institutions and Economic Performance: Studies of Industrial Relations in Advanced Capitalist Economies*. London: Sage.

Streeck, W. and Thelen, K. (2005) 'Introduction: institutional change in advanced political economies', in W. Streeck and K. Thelen (eds) *Beyond Continuity: Institutional Change in Advanced Political Economies*. Oxford: Oxford University Press. pp. 1–39.

Tattersall, A. (2005) 'There is power in coalition: a framework for assessing how and when union-community coalitions are effective and enhance union power', *Labor and Industry*, 16 (2): 97–112.

Turner, L. (1998) *Fighting for Partnership: Labor and Politics in Unified Germany*. Ithaca and London: ILR Press.

Turner, L. (2003) 'Reviving the labor movement: a comparative perspective', in D. Cornfield and H. McCammon (eds) *Labor Revitalization: Global Perspectives and New Initiatives*. Research in the Sociology of Work Volume 11. Amsterdam: Elsevier. pp. 23–58.

Turner, L. and Hurd, R.W. (2001) 'Building social movement unionism: the transformation of the American labor movement', in L. Turner, H.C. Katz and R.W. Hurd (eds) *Rekindling the Movement: Labor's Quest for Relevance in the 21st Century*. Ithaca and London: ILR Press. pp. 9–26.

Voss, K. and Sherman, R. (2000) 'Breaking the iron law of oligarchy: union revitalization in the American labor movement', *American Journal of Sociology*, 106 (2): 303–49.

Wacjman, J. (2000) 'Feminism facing industrial relations in Britain', *British Journal of Industrial Relations*, 38 (2): 183–202.

Wickham, C. (2006) *Framing the Early Middle Ages*. Oxford: Oxford University Press.

Wills, J. (2001) 'Community unionism and trade union renewal in the UK: moving beyond the fragments at last?', *Transactions of the Institute of British Geographers*, 26 (4): 465–83.

5

Values, Ideologies, and Frames of Reference in Industrial Relations

John W. Budd and Devasheesh Bhave

Industrial relations – or what some might now call employment relations, and what others might call human resources and industrial relations – is a multidisciplinary field studying all aspects of work and the employment relationship (Ackers and Wilkinson, 2003; Budd, 2004; Kaufman, 2004). A multidisciplinary approach means that competing values and assumptions underlie the analyses, policies, and practices of employment relations scholars, practitioners, and policymakers. Unfortunately, these underlying beliefs are often implicit rather than explicit, or, with the long-standing focus on how industrial relations (IR) processes work, sometimes ignored altogether. But understanding the industrial relationship, corporate human resource management practices, labor union strategies, and work-related public policies and laws requires understanding how values and assumptions form the ideologies and frames of reference used by scholars, practitioners, and policymakers.

According to Kochan and Katz, 'The primary thread running through industrial relations research and policy prescriptions is that labor is more than a commodity ... and more than a set of human resources' and 'a critical assumption underlying industrial relations research is that there is an inherent conflict of interest between employees and employers' that comes from a 'clash of economic interests' (1988: 6). From this perspective, labor unions and government policies such as minimum wage laws are seen as socially beneficial because they can moderate the unequal bargaining power between employees and employers. This passage, therefore, is a good illustration of the importance of underlying values and assumptions in employment relations. At the same time, it only describes one perspective (the pluralist perspective). In contrast, labor unions and government regulations are seen as detrimental when one assumes that perfectly competitive labor markets are optimal (an egoist perspective), as unnecessary when employers and employees are viewed as always having common interests (a unitarist perspective), and as insufficient when one sees the employment relationship as an unequal power relation embedded in greater social and political inequalities (a critical perspective). These four views of unions and government regulation – harmful, unnecessary, socially beneficial, and insufficient – are firmly rooted in four different theories on the employment relationship that embody different values and assumptions (Budd, 2005).

These four key theories are the egoist, unitarist, pluralist, and critical models of the employment relationship.[1] They serve as the central ideologies and frames of reference for scholars, practitioners, and policymakers who deal with all aspects of work. These ideologies and frames of reference are packages of values and assumptions pertaining to the interests of the parties to the employment relationship – that is, the needs, wants, and aspirations of employees, employers, and the state – and the degree to which these interests are compatible. Outlining the important conceptualizations of these interests is, therefore, a major part of this chapter. The section that follows this discussion considers the different assumptions about the compatibility of these interests and integrates this analysis with a description of the four key theories. The importance of these values, assumptions, ideologies, and frames of reference is then explored. But first, these important concepts need to be defined.

DEFINING CONCEPTS

Values, ideology, and frame of reference are dangerous terms. Everyone has their own view of what these terms mean and it's common to use these terms without defining them. The term ideology is particularly problematic in being used in many different ways (e.g., see Eagleton, 1994). Figure 5.1 summarizes our definitions.[2] At the center of our discussion are theories of the employment relationship – coherent models of how the employment relationship works.

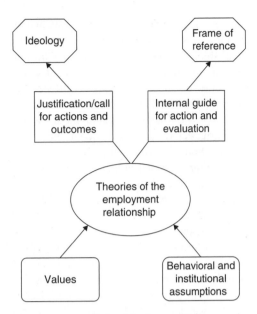

Figure 5.1   Defining ideology and frame of reference
Note: This diagram provides schematic definitions, not a causal model.

Each theory is built upon a collection of values and assumptions. Values are fundamental principles that ought to be true, such as the belief that labor should be treated as more than a commodity. Assumptions are beliefs about human behavior and the nature of various institutions such as markets, laws, corporations, and unions that are presumed to be true, such as the belief that there is an inherent conflict of interest in the employment relationship. Depending on how each theory is used, it can serve as an ideology or a frame of reference.

Thelen and Withall define frame of reference as a 'conceptual structure of generalizations or contexts, postulates about what is essential, assumptions of what is valuable, attitudes about what is possible, and ideas about what will work effectively' in which each individual 'perceives and interprets events' (1949: 159). Fox notes more simply that actors 'perceive and define social phenomena' (1974: 271) through frames of reference. More recently, *The Norton Dictionary of Modern Thought* defines frame of reference as 'the context, viewpoint, or set of presuppositions or of evaluative criteria within which a person's perception and thinking seem always to occur, and which constrains selectively the course and outcome of these activities' (Bullock and Trombley, 1999: 334). In other words, a frame of reference 'determines judgment, which in turn determines subsequent behavior' (Fox, 1966: 2). The themes of perception, evaluation, and individual action in these definitions are central to our definition of frame of reference.[3] More specifically, we define frame of reference as a theory used to guide and evaluate behaviors, outcomes, and institutions. To distinguish ideology from frame of reference, we adopt a definition of ideology that emphasizes public exposition rather than private evaluation. More specifically, we define ideology as a theory that is used to advocate and justify behaviors, outcomes, and institutions. This is consistent with *The Oxford Companion to Philosophy*: 'the most important usage [of ideology] in contemporary philosophy and politics' is as 'a collection of beliefs and values held by an individual or group for other than purely epistemic reasons' (Honderich, 2005: 419) and with Fox's (1966: 5) 'instrument of persuasion' function of ideology.[4]

In other words, a frame of reference is how one sees the world; an ideology is how one wants others to see the world. When a decline in union density troubles a policymaker because of a concern for protecting employees when employers have greater bargaining power, the pluralist model is being used as a frame of reference. When business leaders deploy the egoist model of the employment relationship to call for deregulating labor law and to justify relocating jobs to low wage countries, this model is being used as an ideology (the liberal market ideology). Admittedly, one's ideology and frame of reference might involve the same underlying theory – for example, a radical scholar might evaluate outcomes and advocate for reforms using a frame of reference and an ideology both based on a Marxist conception of the employment relationship. But our definitions allow for

the possibility that individuals preach from one ideology while practicing another. In particular, an important belief in some schools of Marxist thought is that ideology serves as a false consciousness in which the dominant class uses ideology to disguise their control. Managerial statements emphasizing individualism, cooperation, and competition are therefore seen as a strategy to legitimize a hierarchical and unequal workplace and to promote the continued managerial control of work (Anthony, 1977; Bendix, 1956; Fox, 1966; Kunda, 1992). A definition of ideology therefore needs to distinguish itself from frame of reference and allow for the *possibility* that actors say one thing, but do another. At the same time, it is important to remember that ideologies and frames of reference draw upon the same theories of the employment relationship. It is to those theories that we now turn, starting with a discussion of the various assumptions and values about the interests of the parties to the employment relationship.

EMPLOYEE INTERESTS

Employees are obviously a critical part of the employment relationship. But what do employees want to get out of work? Intellectually, how should we model employees as actors in the employment relationship (Kaufman, 1999)? Employees have diverse interests (Ciulla, 2000; Kelloway et al., 2004; Kelly, 1998). But the four theories of the employment relationship emphasize some interests over the others. It is therefore instructive to consider four categories of employee interests:

- survival and income;
- equity and voice;
- fulfillment and social identity; and
- power and control.

Survival and income

Most people need to work to survive. Our ancient ancestors used basic stone tools to butcher animals, cut firewood, and build basic shelters as many as 2.5 million years ago. In modern societies, wage or salary income is the means to purchase the basic necessities of life. In its most primal state, then, a worker's interest is survival. This survival imperative is reflected in Maslow's (1943) model of work motivation based on a hierarchy of needs in which individuals are posited to first seek the satisfaction of physiological needs before pursuing other desires and is also reflected in Wheeler's (1985) model in which workplace conflict stems from the deprivation of necessary material resources. Both Adam Smith (1776/2003) and Karl Marx (1844/1988) also hypothesized that wages for common laborers would fall to levels that just support subsistence so individuals end up working simply to survive.

In a more contemporary vein, one of the key foundations of mainstream neoclassical economics is modeling individuals as seeking to maximize their personal utility functions (Varian, 1984). Utility is generally seen as dependent on consumption which means that work is an activity tolerated by individuals to earn income to buy goods, services, and leisure (Killingsworth, 1983). As a purely income-earning activity, labor is viewed as any other commodity and is exchanged through impersonal transactions as determined by supply and demand (Kaufman, 2005). At its core, then, neoclassical economics equates employees' interests to income; while not typically seen as mere survival, the implications for the employment relationship are largely the same because the focal point of work is the self-interested acquisition of material or pecuniary benefits.

Equity and voice

An alternative conceptualization of employee interests is that employees not only want income, but also seek fairness. This is perhaps most simply demonstrated by organized labor's longtime pursuit of 'a fair day's pay for a fair day's work'. Human resource management scholars and industrial-organizational psychologists also believe that fairness is a critical dimension of employment. For example, Adams's (1965) equity theory has been widely applied to employment issues. Most simply, workers are posited to reduce work effort if they feel that they are working harder than others who are paid the same. More generally, organizational justice – that is, employee perceptions of and reactions to fairness – has become a key construct in the human resource management and industrial-organizational psychology literatures (Folger and Cropanzano, 1998).

For others, the concern with fairness is rooted more in human dignity and liberty than in the behavioral sciences. The International Labour Organization's (ILO) 1944 Declaration of Philadelphia, for example, asserts that, 'All human beings, irrespective of race, creed or sex, have the right to pursue both their material well-being and their spiritual development in conditions of freedom and dignity, of economic security and equal opportunity'. To this end, the ILO promotes labor standards pertaining to equal pay for equal work, reasonable working hours, periodic paid holidays, unemployment and disability insurance, the right to form labor unions, and many other aspects of work. As human dignity is a critical theological concept, the Catholic Church through papal encyclicals such as *Rerum Novarum* and other major religions advocate similar standards and reinforce fairness as an employee interest in the employment relationship (Budd, 2004; Peccoud, 2004). Ethical theories in the Aristotelian and Kantian traditions also support the importance of respecting human dignity in the employment relationship (Bowie, 1999; Budd, 2004; Solomon, 1992). In fact, basic labor standards are increasingly argued to be human rights (Adams, 2001; Gross, 1998; Wheeler, 1994).

Such standards have traditionally been grouped together under a broad heading of equity (e.g., Barbash, 1987). More recently, Budd (2004) articulates the key employee interests as equity and voice where equity is fair employment standards for both material outcomes (such as wages and safety) and personal treatment (especially nondiscrimination) and voice is the ability to have meaningful input into decisions. A similar distinction in the research on justice in the behavioral sciences is between distributive and procedural justice – that is, between fairness in outcomes and in procedures (Folger and Cropanzano, 1998). Whether seen as equity and voice or as distributive and procedural justice, the implication for employee interests is the same – survival and income are too narrow as the basis of employee interests; rather, employees seek fairness not only in work-related outcomes, but also in how these outcomes are produced.

Fulfillment and social identity

Another view of employee interests is based on the premise that individuals use work to provide psychological fulfillment and social identity. This is clearly reflected in the large literature in psychology on work motivation that emphasizes intrinsic work rewards over pay and other extrinsic rewards (Donovan, 2001; Latham and Pinder, 2005). Perhaps most famously, Maslow (1943) theorized that workers seek love, esteem, and self-actualization after their physiological and security needs are met. Thus, work provides employees with a basic outlet to channel their intrinsic motivation for achievement of desired objectives and personal fulfillment – or more simply, joy in work (De Man, 1929). A parallel stream of research in psychology examines the psychological importance of paid work. Building on Freud's claim that man's strongest link to reality is work, Jahoda (1982) argues that employment provides psychological fulfillment by providing time structure boundaries, a wider spectrum of social activities than those provided by family life, and involvement in a broader collective endeavor.

Similar themes are echoed by theorists in other disciplines (Ciulla, 2000; Leidner, 2006; Muirhead, 2004). In fact, Karl Marx, Emile Durkheim, and Max Weber all emphasize the importance of fulfillment through their concern with the loss of human dignity that accompanied the denial of human fulfillment in the then-emerging modern employment relationship (Hodson, 2001). For Marx (1844/1988), the defining feature of being human is freely working to create things, but under capitalism, workers do not control the means of production and are therefore alienated from their labor, and denied their essential dignity as humans. Durkheim (1893/1933) sees the division of labor as eroding social norms and therefore allowing the exploitation of workers while Weber (1925/1978) sees the bureaucracy of modern corporations as undermining dignity and fulfillment through the depersonalization of work.

The importance of work for individual fulfillment and dignity is also believed to provide the foundation for the importance of work for creating social identities and spiritual fulfillment. To help define themselves and where they fit into society, people classify themselves in occupational groupings (Ashforth and Mael, 1989; Tajfel, 1978; Turner, 1987). In other words, work contributes to employees' development of their self-concept by providing them with a social identity and thus another meaning to their employment beyond that of pay. On a spiritual level, as famously articulated by Weber (1904; 1976), the Protestant work ethic is based on Martin Luther's concept of work as a 'calling' (serving God by doing good work in whatever occupation you are suited for) and molded by John Calvin into a belief that hard work is the path to salvation. In Islam, Buddhism, and Hinduism, work also serves a higher motive that allows fulfillment of duty toward God such that individuals' interests in work are other than solely economic (Ali, 1988; Nord et al., 1990; Schumacher, 1974).

Power and control

A fourth perspective on employee interests is the belief that workers seek power and control in the workplace. Recall from the previous section that for Marx and some other theorists, 'labor in the sense of free productive activity is the essence of human life' (Singer, 2000: 35). Meaningful work is therefore seen as critical for fulfillment and dignity, but under capitalism, workers are alienated because the product of their labor does not belong to them, they have no control over what is produced and how it is produced, and work becomes less of a social activity (Hodson, 2001; Marx, 1844/1988). To achieve dignity, a key worker interest is power: 'the ability of an individual or group to control his (their) physical and social environment; and, as part of this process, the ability to influence the decisions which are and are not taken by others' (Hyman, 1975: 26).

Power and control can be pursued in various ways. Around the turn of the twentieth century in the US, craft unions developed work rules pertaining to apprenticeship standards, ownership over specific job duties, exclusion of undesirable or unskilled job duties, work allocation procedures, and other standards (Perlman, 1928). These work rules were often established unilaterally by the unions and enforced by having members refuse to work on any other terms and by fining or expelling members who undermined these standards (Montgomery, 1979). Today, some element of power and control are pursued by workers through various forms of solidarity and resistance (such as reduced work effort, absenteeism, and sabotage) (Edwards, 1986; Hodson, 2001; Kelly, 1998). Political theories in which capitalism is seen as inferior to socialism or syndicalism are at least partly rooted in a perception that workers lack sufficient power and control in a capitalist society. In addition to class struggles between labor and capital, struggles for workplace power and control can also take place along gender and racial lines (Amott and Matthaei, 1996; Delgado and Stefancic, 2001; Gottfried, 2006; Lustig, 2004). Lastly, industrial relations theories that embrace employees' interests in power and control are often derived from a belief that the primary employer interest is power and control over the workplace; this is discussed in next section.

EMPLOYER INTERESTS

One of the primary actors in the modern employment relationship is the employer. It is typical to see the employer's interests as those of shareholders, executives, and managers, or alternatively as those of the organization as an entity in its own right (which might be peculiar except that US law treats a corporation as a person with its own rights and obligations). We generally follow these approaches, but it should be noted that there is some danger in treating an employer as a monolithic entity. Executives or managers might have their own goals independent of those of the organization or the shareholders which can lead to principal-agent problems in which the agent does not always act in the best interests of the principal that hired him or her (Fama, 1980; Jensen and Meckling, 1976). When we speak of the employer's interests, we are referring to the organization's interests which will also be assumed to be consistent with the interests of the shareholders, executives, and managers. To the extent that executives and managers are agents that follow their self-interest rather than the organization's interests, the reader is referred back to the previous section on employee interests. After all, executives and managers are also employees in the employment relationship – they are hired, fired, and are concerned with income, fulfillment, and the like.

In modeling the employment relationship, there are three primary views on the interests of employers. The first is profit maximization – a firm's objective is to structure work so as to generate the highest profit level possible to the exclusive benefit of the firm's owners. The second broadens the objective of profit maximization to include consideration of other stakeholders such as employees. And the third is the pursuit of power and control over employees that goes beyond what is necessary to maximize profits in some technical sense. In the first conceptualization, profit maximization is seen as legitimate. In the second conceptualization, the pursuit of profits is legitimate when tempered by a respect for the interests of other stakeholders. In the third view, a primacy of profits over other concerns is rejected as illegitimate.

Before turning to each of these conceptualizations, the reader is reminded to not confuse employer strategies with employer interests. In practice, we observe a multitude of employment conditions ranging from abusive sweatshops to workplaces with generously-rewarded employees that have extensive decision-making authority. This does not mean that there are a large number of employer interests; rather, this diversity reflects a multitude of strategies for pursuing the three basic employer interests: profit maximization, stakeholder value, or power and control. Moreover, these three interests are not intended to simply capture how employers express their interests; rather we are also considering different ways of conceptualizing or modeling employer interests. Employers likely state that they are pursuing profits in a legitimate fashion or balancing the needs of various stakeholders while radical scholars will see employers as pursuing their interests through a more critical lens. The discussion here is intended to capture this wide range of alternatives.

Profit maximization

In economic thought, firms are assumed to maximize profits (the difference between revenue and costs) (Varian, 1984). Different types of workers are hired up to the point at which hiring one more worker costs more than the revenue generated. There are differing views on the extent to which labor markets are competitive, to which transaction costs are important, and to which there are principal-agent problems between workers and firms because of asymmetric information (such as the firm not being able to perfectly observe worker effort), but these complications do not change the basic foundation that each firm's objective is to maximize profits (Manning, 2003; Wachter, 2004). The real-world importance of profit maximization is reflected in the Anglo-American shareholder model of corporate governance. In this system, shareholders are residual claimants and everyone else is seen as receiving fixed payments for their services, such as wages and salaries. Since shareholders single-handedly bear the risk of making a profit or loss, they are seen as the key group and economic performance will be optimized when corporate decisions maximize shareholder value (Blair, 1995). Maximizing profits and shareholder value therefore go hand in hand.

Many features of the modern employment relationship are linked to the profit motive. Frederick Winslow Taylor's development of scientific management in the early-twentieth century through carefully studying work tasks and scientifically determining the one best way of completing a task can be seen as driven by the pursuit of greater efficiency, and therefore profitability (Kanigel, 1997). As articulated by Weber (1919/1946), the rise of the bureaucratic organizational form was a rational solution to decision-making problems in the face of significant organizational complexity (March and Simon, 1958). The bureaucratic form of organization is therefore geared toward the profit motive that is the prime employer interest. The contemporary movement away from the narrowly-defined tasks of Taylorism and the iron cage of Weber's bureaucracy reflects an attempt to boost profitability by creating more flexible employment practices (Applebaum and Batt, 1994). Layoffs, outsourcing, moving production to low-wage countries, and reducing employee benefits are also all done in the pursuit of enhancing profitability for the benefit of shareholders.

Stakeholder value

Note carefully that the shareholder model of corporate governance assumes that labor markets are perfectly competitive. As such, employees face little risk – if managers mismanage the business and it goes bankrupt, the assumption of perfectly competitive labor markets means that workers who lose their jobs can always find equivalent jobs elsewhere at no cost. Shareholders, however, lose their investment so the shareholder model holds managers liable for serving shareholder interests. But what if labor markets are not perfectly competitive? Employees invest their own human capital in a corporation and therefore, just like shareholders, make significant contributions and face risky returns (Blair, 1995). Employees might not be able to recoup their investment or find an equivalent job elsewhere if the business is mismanaged. As a result, stakeholder theory asserts that all stakeholders – not only shareholders and owners, but also employees, customers, suppliers, local communities, and others – are sufficiently affected by corporate actions to deserve the right to be considered in corporate decision-making. Stakeholder theory can also be rooted in property rights: even in the US with strong restrictions against harming others, property rights are not unlimited, so, the argument goes, a corporation must take multiple interests into account (Donaldson and Preston, 1995). In other words, a corporation does not exist just for the benefit of shareholders, and should be operated for the benefit of all those who have a stake in it. Supporters of stakeholder theory believe that shareholders deserve a fair rate of return, but also that the ideal of maximizing shareholder value without regard for other interests (as in the shareholder model) rests on questionable foundations and should not be used to elevate the importance of corporations over other stakeholders (Ghoshal, 2005).

In this vein, then, the interest of employers in the employment relationship should be serving the interests of shareholders, employees, and other stakeholders. In the US, 32 states have constituency statutes in which company directors are explicitly allowed to consider interests beyond those of the shareholders (Adams and Matheson, 2000). In Europe, codetermination policies institutionalize stakeholder theory by requiring employee representation on corporate boards of directors while social norms in Japan also foster a concern for stakeholder value (Jacoby, 2001; 2005).

Power and control

For another set of industrial relations scholars, characterizing the interest of employers simply as profit maximization, or even as increasing stakeholder value, is too benign. Rather, employer interests are modeled as seeking power and control over labor. This dominance serves not only to boost profits, but to promote capital accumulation, the amassing of wealth, and sociopolitical control (including, in the extreme, preventing a workers' revolution) by the owners of capital.

For Marx, this dominance is an integral feature of capitalism. As capitalists control the means of production, they are able to extract labor's surplus value which further empowers the capitalists at the expense of workers, not only in the economic arena, but in the sociopolitical realm as well. Rather than employers benignly seeking profit maximization by competing for workers in neutral labor markets, employers are seen as controlling and dominating labor through their superior economic and sociopolitical power (Hyman, 1975). In this vein, corporations are seen as using their political clout to promote their own interests by obtaining government subsidies and contracts and by shaping legislation that placates workers enough to avoid a broader working class threat while channeling labor conflict into tightly-regulated channels preferred by business rather than labor (e.g., witness the US restrictions on secondary boycotts) (Domhoff, 1990).

In the workplace, the de-skilling and division of labor that accompany Taylorism are not seen as a win-win situation in which labor works more efficiently, but rather as managerial strategies to decompose both skilled craft and clerical occupations into simplified, routine, low-skilled jobs in order to gain control over the workplace (Braverman, 1974; Montgomery, 1979). Bureaucracy is not seen simply as an efficient structure for managing complexity; rather, bureaucracy is seen as a strategy to routinize all aspects of management and to consolidate the power to establish rules and procedures in order to control the operations of an entire organization (Edwards, 1979). More generally, labor process theory emphasizes the importance of control mechanisms in the workplace (Thompson and Newsome, 2004). In addition to issues of control along class (labor and capital) lines, control methods can also occur along gender, racial, and ethnic lines, such as with occupational sex segregation (Greene, 2003). All of these are examples where employer interests are modeled as power and control beyond that needed to benignly pursue profits.

STATE INTERESTS

The third major actor in the employment relationship is the state. The state has five roles in the employment relationship (Godard, 2005). In the regulative role, laws regulate workers, unions, and companies. In the employer role, the state is a public sector organization with its own employees. In the facilitative role, the state establishes social norms and provides support services for the employment relationship. The structural role consists of economic policies that shape the economic environment. And in the constitutive role, the state determines how the employment relationship is constituted by the type of economic system embraced by the state (such as a market-based capitalist economy). But what are the interests of the state in the employment relationship that determine how the state acts in these five roles? In other words, what is the state trying to achieve? We present three broad alternatives: a focus on freedom and the rule of law, an interest in promoting equitable outcomes, and an objective to support the domination of the elite. As with the discussion of employer interests, these three interests are intended to capture different ways of conceptualizing or modeling state interests; they do not simply describe how the state expresses its interests.

In all three conceptualizations of the state's interests, it's possible that the state does not have independent interests; rather, its policies might simply mediate the political pressures of workers and employers in a pluralistic model or reflect and implement the political wishes of the dominant class in a Marxist model. For example, promoting freedom and the rule of law might be seen as an extension of employer interests, not an independent interest of the state. However, some research emphasizes the possibility of autonomous state action, especially as rooted in international connections of state officials, the need to maintain domestic stability, and the ability of government officials to use resources to pursue their own ends (Skocpol, 1985). In industrial relations circles, it is widely believed that the anti-union policies of the Reagan administration, in the US, and Thatcher government, in the UK, were more aggressive than would have been dictated if these administrations were simply reflecting business lobbying. Either as reflections or as independent interests, we believe the following three categories are instructive.

Freedom and the rule of law

In the liberal market paradigm, the interest of the state is in protecting freedom and the rule of law. As applied to the employment relationship, the law's role is to promote and protect the operation of free markets with voluntary exchange between companies, investors, consumers, and workers. In the US, this view manifests itself in an emphasis on common law principles that support economic transactions, especially well-defined property rights, liberty of contract, and the law of torts to protect against property damage (Posner, 1986). As captured by a report from the Bush administration:

> By providing a legal foundation for transactions, the government makes the market system reliable: it gives people certainty about what they can trade and keep, and it allows people to establish terms of trade that will be honored by both sellers and buyers. The absence of any one of these elements—competition, enforceable property rights, or an ability to form mutually advantageous contracts—can result in inefficiency and lower living standards (Council of Economic Advisors, 2004: 149).

Equitable outcomes

In pluralist political thought, the state responds to the power of competing interest groups and, in the variant most relevant here, enforces existing rules while also ensuring fair outcomes (Dunleavy and O'Leary, 1987; Faulks, 1999). An alternative vision of the state's interest in the employment relationship is therefore the promotion of equitable outcomes. As articulated by Sidney and Beatrice Webb, two of the founders of industrial relations, the state must balance various interests:

> [I]ndustrial administration is, in the democratic state, a more complicated matter than is naively imagined by the old-fashioned capitalist, demanding the 'right to manage his own business in his own way.'...In the interests of the community as a whole, no one of the interminable series of decisions can be allowed to run counter to the consensus of expert opinion representing the consumers on the one hand, the producers on the other, and the nation that is paramount over both (1897: 821–3).

In contrast to liberal market proponents then, in this paradigm there is greater support for government intervention to reduce market imperfections (such as unemployment), to equalize bargaining power between employers and employees through unionization and social safety nets, and to provide workers with greater voice through works councils. At an international level, there is support for the International Labour Organization (ILO) and its promotion of labor standards. For those that see labor rights as human rights, the state has the responsibility to guarantee these rights.

Dominance of the elite

A third view on the interests of the state in the employment relationship is that the capitalist state perpetuates the dominance of the ruling class. This view is most clearly articulated in Marxist thought in which social change is driven by capitalism rather than the behavior of the state so that the state is viewed as an instrument of the capitalists who are then society's ruling class (Faulks, 1999; Pierson, 1996). Even though the state appears

to be acting autonomously and neutrally, given its role of protection of ownership it is in effect intertwined with particular economic interests (Hyman, 1975; King, 1986). To wit, Kelly (1998) discusses how government repression of strikers, and the protection of strike replacements, reduces the effectiveness of collective action and thereby favors capital over labor.

THE (IN)COMPATABILITY OF INTERESTS

The framework developed in this chapter asserts that the ideologies and frames of reference of industrial relations are rooted in two key dimensions: the interests of the parties to the employment relationship and the degree of compatibility of these interests. The compatibility or incompatibility of interests, in turn, depends on how markets and the employment relationship work. Now that the interests have been described, consider four different views on the compatibility of these interests and the nature of the employment relationship.

1. Employers and employees freely pursue their own self-interest in competitive labor markets; when these interests align, they consummate an economic transaction, when they do not align, they keep searching for mutually-beneficial exchanges.
2. Although labor markets might not be perfect, employers and employees share a unity of interests, especially in that treating employees well improves the company's bottom line and vice versa.
3. Employers and employees interact as unequals with some shared and some conflicting interests, but these conflicts are economic in nature and limited to the employment relationship.
4. Employers and employees interact as unequals with significant power differentials that are pervasive through all social relations.

These differing views on the compatibility or incompatibility of the interests of employers and employees, as possibly shaped, mediated, or reflected by the interests of the state, define the four theories that underlie the essential

Table 5.1　Four theories of the employment relationship

Theory	Employer interests	Employee interests	State interests	Key beliefs
Egoist	Profit-maximization	Utility-maximization (survival and income)	Freedom and rule of law	Freedom and individual self-interest yield optimal outcomes through free market transactions.
Unitarist	Profit-maximization	Fulfillment	Freedom and rule of law	Corporate policies can align the interests of employers and employees.
Pluralist	Profit-maximization or stakeholder value	Equity and voice	Equitable outcomes	Optimal outcomes are achieved when there is a balance between employer and employee interests.
Critical				
Political economy	Power and control	Power and control	Dominance of the elite	Capital dominates labor in the employment relationship and in broader societal institutions.
Feminist	Power and control	Power and control	Dominance of the elite	Male concerns dominate female concerns in the employment relationship and in broader societal institutions.
Race	Power and control	Power and control	Dominance of the elite	Concerns of one ethnic group dominate other groups' concerns in the employment relationship and in broader societal institutions.

ideologies and frames of reference for most industrial relations scholars, policymakers, and practitioners – the egoist, unitarist, pluralist, and critical employment relationships (see Table 5.1).

The egoist employment relationship

The egoist employment relationship is rooted in the pursuit of individual self-interest by rational agents in economic markets. Labor is conceptualized as a commodity like any other productive resource. Employees are seen as interested in income while firms pursue profit maximization. The state promotes economic transactions through protecting property rights and enforcing contracts. As such, there isn't a conflict between employers and employees; rather, they simply engage in voluntary, mutually-beneficial transactions to buy and sell units of productive labor based on what the market will bear. Wages are never too low or too high, they simply

reflect each worker's productive contributions. If workers and employers are equal in terms of economic power, legal expertise and protections, and political influence, then neoclassical economic theory shows that abuses and exploitation are prevented by perfect competition in the labor market.

Employment-at-will – that is, the right to hire and fire, or take a job and quit, at anytime for any reason – is a key feature of the egoist employment relationship. Employers and employees should be able to enter into any explicit or implicit agreement involving any mutually-agreeable terms and conditions of employment, including compensation, hours, duration of employment, job duties, and the like. In the interests of both economic optimization and individual freedom, employers and employees should likewise be able to end these arrangements when conditions or preferences change, or if a better deal comes along (Epstein, 1984). Labor unions and government-mandated labor standards are seen as interfering with the invisible hand of the free market and distort employment and output levels throughout the economic system (Reynolds, 1984). Unions are also seen as interfering with the discipline of the market by protecting lazy workers. Note carefully that the egoist employment relationship critically depends on embracing a value system in which efficiency is the primary objective of the employment relationship and whatever the market bears is best.

The three remaining theories place less emphasis on market determinism; markets are seen as useful for allocating scarce resources to productive uses, but as also imperfect because of information problems, mobility and transactions costs, unequal access to financial and legal resources, the importance of behavioral concerns such as fairness or social pressure in individual decision-making, and other real-world complications (Manning, 2003). The three remaining theories are also rooted in a different set of values (based on embracing different employee interests), especially in that workers are seen as human beings with psychological and physical needs and aspirations, and in the last two theories, with moral worth and democratic rights, too.

The unitarist employment relationship

The second theory embraces a unitarist view of the employment relationship – the right employment policies and practices will align the interests of employers and employees (Bacon, 2003; Fox, 1974; Lewin, 2001). In other words, labor and management have a unity of interests; any conflict in practice stems from poor employment practices. This frame of reference underlies contemporary human resource management which focuses on creating policies that simultaneously benefit employers (through their interest in profit maximization) and employees (through their interest in fulfillment) (Pfeffer, 1998; Ulrich and Brockbank, 2005).

In practice, there are a number of variants of the human resource management model ranging from hierarchical, paternalistic approaches to high-commitment approaches to strategic approaches (Appelbaum and Batt, 1994; Katz and Darbishire, 2000). The underlying common denominator, however, is the attempt to devise human resources policies that are seen as aligning the interests of employees and employers. Some common examples include valid and reliable selection measures to hire and promote employees; training and development opportunities; respectful methods of supervision; compensation that provides more than a living wage while also rewarding performance; benefits that foster personal growth, security, and work-life balance; and informal or formal dispute resolution procedures.[5] As reflected by the emphasis on employees' interest in fulfillment, psychology is arguably the dominant disciplinary influence in the unitarist camp.

The unitarist emphasis is generally on individual rather than collective identities, behaviors, and practices. In fact, in the unitarist employment relationship, labor unions and government-mandated labor standards are unnecessary. If companies are following the human resource management school's ideas of effective management, then workers will be satisfied and will not support a union or need mandated labor standards. Such institutions are also largely seen as unnecessary because the unitarist view emphasizes fulfillment and intrinsic rewards. The role of the state is limited – while some scholars advocate government policies to promote high performance work practices (e.g., Levine, 1995), human resources professionals are more likely to lobby against rather than for additional regulation; instead, the state's role is seen as promoting the rule of law and economic transactions because this serves organizational performance. As with the other theories, this perspective is rooted in specific values and assumptions pertaining to the interests of the employment relationship and the nature of conflict within this relationship, and is often used as an important ideology and frame of reference by industrial relations actors.

The pluralist employment relationship

The pluralist employment relationship consists of workers and employers bargaining in imperfect labor markets in the presence of pluralist conflict – that is, in an employment relationship consisting of multiple, sometimes-conflicting interests (employers might want lower labor costs, flexibility, and an intense pace of work while employees might want higher wages, employment security, and a safe work environment) as well as shared interests (such as quality products, productive workers, and profitable companies) (Clegg, 1975; Fox, 1974).

The pluralist view of conflict is intimately related to a belief that labor markets are not perfectly competitive. Sidney and Beatrice Webb, John R. Commons, and other early institutionalists attributed the exploitive Anglo-American employment conditions of the early twentieth century to the superior power of large corporations over individual employees (Kaufman, 1997). This power advantage was believed to be rooted in market imperfections such as isolated company towns, mobility costs, lack of family savings or other resources, segmented markets, and excess labor supply. Moreover, a core pluralist value is the rejection that labor is simply a commodity (Kaufman, 2005) and therefore that labor is entitled to equity and voice in the employment relationship (Budd, 2004). As such, the role of the state is to promote equitable outcomes. Because inequitable outcomes are seen as stemming from imperfect labor markets and unequal bargaining power, unions and mandated labor standards are viewed as mechanisms for leveling the playing field between employers and employees thereby promoting the optimal operation of markets rather than interfering with it (as predicted by theories rooted in competitive markets). Also, because of the belief that there are at least some conflicts of interests, the pluralist industrial relations school rejects the unitarist reliance on corporate self-interest and goodwill to protect workers. Rather, labor unions are seen as a productive counterweight to corporate power; social insurance and mandated minimum standards also help protect all workers against the vagaries of the business cycle and corporate power.

The critical employment relationship

The critical employment relationship is rooted in the power and control interests of employers and employees and therefore sees the employment relationship as a struggle for power and control (Gall, 2003; Hyman, 1975; 2006). The schools of thought subscribing to this frame of reference can be grouped together under the umbrella of critical industrial relations and encompass Marxist, feminist, and other sociological theories based on the division and control of labor. While sharing the view that labor is more than just a commodity, unlike the pluralist view in which employer-employee conflict is confined to the employment relationship, the critical perspective is that employment relations conflict is part of a broader societal clash between competing groups (Kelly, 1998). A Marxist perspective assumes that employer-employee conflict is one element of unequal power relations between the capitalist and working classes throughout society. A feminist perspective focuses on unequal power relations between men and women; a critical race perspective emphasizes segregation and control along racial lines (Amott and Matthaei, 1996; Delgado and Stefancic, 2001; Gottfried, 2006; Greene, 2003; Lustig, 2004).

In the critical employment relationship, the labor market is not seen as a neutral forum for matching self-interested workers with self-interested firms (as in the egoist employment relationship); rather it is seen as a socially-based instrument of power and control (Hyman, 1975). The employment relationship is therefore not a voluntary exchange but rather is a contested exchange (Bowles and Gintis, 1990). Because of the socially-rooted, ongoing conflict between labor and capital, human resource management practices are not seen as methods for aligning worker and employer interests, but rather as disguised rhetoric that quietly undermines labor power and perpetuates the dominance of capital (Legge, 1995). Strong, militant labor unions are seen as important advocates for workers' interests in the workplace and in the political arena. But ultimately, relying on collective bargaining to advance workers' interests is inadequate because of the structural inequalities that pervade the workplace and the greater sociopolitical context. That conflict between competing groups is not limited to the employment relationship also means that the state is largely concerned with perpetuating the dominance of the powerful group, whether it be capitalists, men, or a dominant ethnic group. As with the other theories, the key to understanding the critical employment relationship is through an analysis of the interests of the employment relations actors paired with an understanding of how the parties interact and the extent to which the various interests are compatible.

FROM THEORY TO IDEOLOGY AND FRAME OF REFERENCE

Ideologies and frames of reference related to work and industrial relations are pervasive, from portrayals of labor in the paintings of Victorian England to the coverage of contemporary events in the mainstream media (Barringer, 2005; Martin, 2004). Under Mao, the authoritarian communist regime in China until the late 1970s emphasized unitarist employment themes because communism is supposed to resolve the conflicts of interest believed to be inherent in capitalism (Taylor et al., 2003). In the Western workplace, business executives and managers use ideology to legitimatize employment practices (Anthony, 1977; Bendix, 1956; Kunda and Ailon-Souday, 2005); unions and workers use ideology to justify their own behaviors and actions. The various actors use their frames of reference to evaluate the ideologies and actions of others. When another's ideology is unconvincing (because it is rejected by your frame of reference), it is tempting to dismiss

that ideology as hollow rhetoric to support a special interest. We believe, however, that it is more instructive to see these ideologies (and frames of reference) as rooted in the four theories of the employment relationship. Depending on the application, all four theories can serve as an ideology and as a frame of reference. Many of the examples used here follow the rest of the literature and focus on managerial ideologies and frames of reference, but it again bears emphasizing that all industrial relations actors have ideologies and frames of reference. This is implicit in Dunlop's (1958) assertion that an industrial relations system is stable only if the actors share a common ideology.

Management discourse currently emphasizes market ideals (Kunda and Ailon-Souday, 2005). The ideal corporation is portrayed as a nimble network of empowered entrepreneurial work groups that focus on core competencies; excess layers of management are supposed to be downsized; low value added activities are supposed to be outsourced. This ideology is grounded in the egoist employment relationship model and its laissez-faire ideals. Scholars that believe the values and assumptions that underlie the egoist model and use it as their frame of reference see the calls for more flexible business organizations as legitimate and wise. The power of the four models is in illuminating alternative perspectives. Scholars that analyze the employment relationship through a critical frame of reference see this market-based ideology as a mechanism of control that causes workers to buy into a system that doesn't serve their interests because employer and employee interests are fundamentally opposed.

Similarly, unitarist corporate ideologies are seen as valid frames of reference by unitarist actors, but are seen as disguised coercion and union busting by actors who look at human resources policies through the lenses of pluralist and critical frames of reference. Differing views on labor unions – from harmful to unnecessary to beneficial to inadequate – are clearly rooted in the four frames of reference presented here (Budd, 2005). Contrasting perspectives on ownership and control rights also flow from these frames of reference. In the egoist model, property rights are paramount so a firm's owners should have complete control rights. In the pluralist model, stakeholders merit full consideration, and in the critical model, even stakeholder rights are insufficient to overcome the structural inequalities of capitalism. In advocating such positions, the underlying theories are being used as ideologies; in evaluating ownership and control rights, the underlying theories are being employed as frames of reference.

The importance of ideologies and frames of reference is also apparent in the legal arena. In the US, for example, the *Lochner*-era Supreme Court in the early 1900s is well-known for striking down labor and employment laws on the basis that they interfered with the liberty of contract. In the critical frame of reference, the liberty of contract might be viewed as a rhetorical justification for rulings that favored capital, but there is some evidence that judges truly believed that liberty of contract benefited capital and labor as in the egoist frame of reference (Forbath, 1985). As a second example, Dannin (2006) shows how contemporary US judges decide labor law cases using common law principles pertaining to property rights as the basis for their legal analyses. This is consistent with their legal training so it is not surprising that it forms the basis of their egoist frame of reference.

Empirical work on ideologies and frames of reference is rare, but a few studies support the approach outlined here. In surveys of US and Canadian employment relations scholars, Godard (1992, 1995) finds that significant fractions of scholars use each of our four theories as a frame of reference. Moreover the evaluations of different employment relations issues are consistent within a frame which supports the coherence of these models. Godard (1997) further finds that managerial ideologies/frames of reference are an important determinant of managerial actions pertaining to industrial relations.

Kochan et al. (1986) ascribe the rise of the nonunion employment relationship in the United States largely to managerial frames of reference. Poole et al. (2005) find that the attitudes of British managers are linked to broader political and economic trends while Barley and Kunda (1992) present qualitative evidence that US managerial ideologies differ between economic expansions and contractions. There are likely many other complex factors that determine what ideology is dominant, how ideology shapes frames of reference and values, and many other important questions. There is therefore a need for more research on the dynamics of ideologies and frames of reference. For industrial relations, the starting point is the four theories presented here.

CONCLUSION: VALUES AT WORK

The chapter presents four theories as a starting point for understanding the major perspectives within the study and practice of industrial relations. When these theories are used to analyze employment relations and to determine one's actions, they become the four key frames of reference in industrial relations. When these theories are employed to advocate a certain viewpoint, they become the central ideologies in the field. Distinguishing between ideologies and frames of reference allows us to readily analyze situations in which some actors express one view but other actors see those actions differently. Union leaders may express an ideology of employee voice and balancing interests; employers may see this in their frame of reference as rhetoric covering up the union's selfish pursuit of better wages for union members at the expense of others. Rooting these ideologies and frames of reference in four theories of the employment relationship allows us to readily appreciate where these differing ideologies and frames of reference are coming from. Continuing with the previous example, the union leader's ideology might be rooted in a pluralist model whereas the employer's frame of reference is an egoist or unitarist model.

The postmodern emphasis on discourse underscores the importance' of explicitly recognizing the power of language in the world of work (Burrell, 2006; Hearn and Michelson, 2006). By rooting the analysis of industrial relations ideologies and frames of reference in the four theories of the employment relationship, it becomes apparent that clashes in discourse and practice between different ideologies or frames of reference stem from divergent underlying values and assumptions, especially as they pertain to the interests of the parties in the modern employment relationship. One of the key values of industrial relations outside the egoist model is that labor is more than just a commodity (Kaufman, 2005). In contrast, in the egoist model one of the key values is that laissez-faire market outcomes have particular worth because they are produced by voluntary free exchange. These differing values go a long way toward explaining divergent ideologies and frames of reference in employment relations and approaching industrial relations in this way reveals these underlying differences.

Values and ideologies are defined here (and elsewhere) with a large normative component – they represent principles and systems that *ought* to be true. Adherents to the egoist model lobby for the deregulation of the employment relationship. Believers in the unitarist model argue that companies should use certain human resources practices. Subscribers to the pluralist theory support public policy reforms that make it easier for workers to unionize. Adherents to the critical school seek more fundamental changes in ownership and control rights. But at the same time, it is essential to recognize the theoretical or analytical aspects that are rooted in the values and assumptions of industrial relations. The egoist model predicts that market-based relationships maximize welfare. The unitarist model implies that providing opportunities for individual fulfillment boosts employee productivity. The pluralist model hypothesizes that unions can improve productivity. The critical model predicts that managers will pursue strategies that increase their control in the workplace. Contrary to the characterization of even some industrial relations scholars (e.g., Kochan, 1998), values do not comprise just the normative foundations of the field; rather, values and assumptions underlie views on how the employment relationship works analytically as much as how it should work normatively (Budd et al., 2004).

On both a normative and positive level, as the support for various values and assumptions wax and wane, the four ideologies and frames of reference exhibit an uneven trajectory during the development of the field and practice of Anglo-American industrial relations (Ackers and Wilkinson, 2005; Kaufman, 1993; 2004). The egoist employment relationship was firmly cemented by the end of the nineteenth century in the US with the development of the employment-at-will doctrine and the rejection of mandated labor standards on the grounds that it interfered with free contracting. Cycles of economic depressions and widespread sweatshop working conditions, however, sparked the development of Marx's views on work and capitalism in the mid-1800s, and the later development of the pluralist model around the turn of the twentieth century, and the creation of the unitarist model shortly thereafter. The pluralist model was embraced on an international scale with the creation of the ILO at the end of First World War. During the 1920s, the four models competed for dominance, but the Great Depression discredited the egoist and unitarist models in the US. During the 1930s, then, the New Deal policies of the Roosevelt administration were rooted in the pluralist model. In Great Britain, the centrality of the pluralist model was reflected in the *Donovan Royal Commission on Trade Unions and Employers' Associations* in the 1960s. Fast forward to the twenty-first century and we see that with the rise of the liberal market paradigm, the egoist model has made a comeback; its ideology is certainly spoken with the loudest voice in popular discourse. In spite of ideas for revitalizing pluralist (Ackers, 2002; Budd, 2004) and critical (Kelly, 1998) industrial relations, the field is in flux as the pluralist and critical models face significant challenges from the egoist and unitarist perspectives (Ackers and Wilkinson, 2003, 2005; Kaufman, 2004).

With respect to evaluating corporate policies or shaping public policy, competition among these ideologies and frames of reference are to be expected since, as illustrated here, the models embrace different visions of the interests of the employment relationship and of their compatibility or incompatibility. But as an intellectual endeavor, the diversity of industrial relations is both a strength and a weakness. It is a weakness when adherents of different views are isolated and talk past each other. It is a strength when diverse perspectives can help us understand the complex issues inherent across the entire spectrum of the world of work. To foster this strength, competing and shared values, ideologies, and frames of reference must be given explicit recognition in our scholarship and discourse. For those new to the field, a true understanding of industrial relations requires an appreciation for the diverse values, ideologies, and frames of reference in the world of work.

ACKNOWLEDGMENTS

We gratefully acknowledge the helpful comments of Nicolas Bacon and Jack Fiorito.

NOTES

1 The broad scope and concise length of this review precludes a detailed examination of significant variations and details within the theories and perspectives outlined here. For example, Godard (1992: 244; 2005) includes a fifth model based on a pluralist economic and political system which is 'far more egalitarian in opportunities and outcomes and which provides workers with far greater rights' than in what he terms the orthodox pluralist perspective. While these two views perhaps envision different reforms and ideal institutions, they are rooted in similar assumptions and values so we consider them as one model. The interested reader is referred to the references cited herein and to the other chapters of this Handbook for more nuanced discussions of various theories and perspectives.

2 It should be emphasized that Figure 5.1 is intended to capture our definitions; it is not presented as a theoretical model of the determinants of any of the components of the figure. The popularity of an ideology, for example, might shape values and assumptions. While it's important to understand the determinants of dominant ideologies, such theoretical issues are beyond the scope of what Figure 5.1 is intended to portray.

3 These themes are also consistent with the construct of framing in psychology (Tversky and Kahneman, 1986) and collective action frames in sociology (Benford and Snow, 2000).

4 Definitions of ideology that emphasize assessment and understanding (e.g. Godard, 1995) are frames of reference under our definitions.

5 So-called low road strategies rooted in low wages and managerial control are better captured by the egoist theory of the employment relationship in that they are rooted in a narrow conception of employee interests and in an emphasis on what the labor market will bear.

REFERENCES

Ackers, Peter (2002) 'Reframing Employment Relations: The Case for Neo-Pluralism,' *Industrial Relations Journal*, 33 (1): 2–19.

Ackers, Peter and Wilkinson, Adrian (eds.) (2003) *Understanding Work and Employment: Industrial Relations in Transition*. Oxford: Oxford University Press.

Ackers, Peter and Wilkinson, Adrian (2005) 'British Industrial Relations Paradigm: A Critical Outline History and Prognosis,' *Journal of Industrial Relations*, 47 (4): 443–56.

Adams, Edward S. and Matheson, John H. (2000) 'A Statutory Model for Corporate Constituency Concerns,' *Emory Law Journal*, 49 (4): 1085–135.

Adams, Stacy J. (1965) 'Inequity in Social Exchange,' in Leonard Berkowitz (ed.), *Advances in Experimental Social Psychology, Volume 2*. New York: Academic Press. pp. 267–99.

Adams, Roy J. (2001) 'Choice or Voice? Rethinking American Labor Policy in Light of the International Human Rights Consensus,' *Employee Rights and Employment Policy Journal*, 5 (2): 521–48.

Ali, Abbas (1988) 'Scaling an Islamic Work Ethic,' *The Journal of Social Psychology*, 128 (5): 575–83.

Amott, Teresa and Matthaei, Julie (eds.) (1996) *Race, Gender, and Work: A Multicultural Economic History of Women in the United States*. Revised edn. Boston: South End Press.

Anthony, P.D. (1977) *The Ideology of Work*. London: Tavistock.

Appelbaum, Eileen and Batt, Rosemary (1994) *The New American Workplace: Transforming Work Systems in the United States*. Ithaca, NY: ILR Press.

Ashforth, Blake E. and Mael, Fred (1989) 'Social Identity Theory and the Organization,' *Academy of Management Review*, 14 (1): 20–39.

Bacon, Nicolas (2003) 'Human Resource Management and Industrial Relations,' in Peter Ackers and Adrian Wilkinson, (eds.), *Understanding Work and Employment: Industrial Relations in Transition*. Oxford: Oxford University Press. pp. 71–88.

Barbash, Jack (1987) 'Like Nature, Industrial Relations Abhors a Vacuum: The Case of the Union-Free Strategy,' *Industrial Relations/Relations Industrielles*, 42 (1): 168–79.

Barley, Stephen and Kunda, Gideon (1992) 'Design and Devotion: Surges of Rational and Normative Ideologies of Control in Managerial Discourse,' *Administrative Science Quarterly*, 37 (3): 363–99.

Barringer, Tim (2005) *Men at Work: Art and Labour in Victorian Britain*. New Haven: Yale University Press.

Bendix, Reinhard (1956) *Work and Authority in Industry*. New York: Harper & Row.

Benford, Robert D. and Snow, David A. (2000) 'Framing Processes and Social Movements: An Overview and Assessment,' *Annual Review of Sociology*, 26: 611–39.

Blair, Margaret M. (1995) *Ownership and Control: Rethinking Corporate Governance for the Twenty-First Century*. Washington, D.C.: Brookings.

Bowie, Norman E. (1999) *Business Ethics: A Kantian Perspective*. Malden, MA: Blackwell Publishers.

Bowles, Samuel and Gintis, Herbert (1990) 'Contested Exchange: New Microfoundations for the Political Economy of Capitalism,' *Politics and Society*, 18 (2): 165–222.

Braverman, Harry (1974) *Labor and Monopoly Capital: The Degradation of Work in the Twentieth Century*. New York: Monthly Review Press.

Budd, John W. (2004) *Employment with a Human Face: Balancing Efficiency, Equity, and Voice*. Ithaca, NY: Cornell University Press.

Budd, John W. (2005) *Labor Relations: Striking a Balance*. Boston: McGraw-Hill/Irwin.

Budd, John W., Gomez, Rafael and Meltz, Noah M. (2004) 'Why a Balance is Best: The Pluralist Industrial Relations Paradigm of Balancing Competing Interests,' in Bruce E. Kaufman (ed.), *Theoretical Perspectives on Work and the Employment Relationship*. Champaign, IL: Industrial Relations Research Association. pp. 195–227.

Bullock, Alan and Trombley, Stephen (eds.) (1999) *The Norton Dictionary of Modern Thought*. 2nd Revised edn. New York : W.W. Norton & Company.

Burrell, Gibson (2006) 'Foucauldian and Postmodern Thought and the Analysis of Work,' in Marek Korczynski, Randy Hodson, and Paul Edwards (eds.), *Social Theory at Work*. Oxford: Oxford University Press. pp. 155–81.

Ciulla, Joanne B. (2000) *The Working Life: The Promise and Betrayal of Modern Work*. New York: Three Rivers Press.

Clegg, H.A. (1975) 'Pluralism in Industrial Relations,' *British Journal of Industrial Relations*, 13 (3): 309–16.

Council of Economic Advisors (2004) *Economic Report of the President*. Washington, D.C.: U.S. Government Printing Office.

Dannin, Ellen. (2006) *Taking Back the Workers' Law: How to Fight the Assault on Labor Rights*. Ithaca, NY: Cornell University Press.

Delgado, Richard and Stefancic, Jean (2001) *Critical Race Theory: An Introduction*. New York: New York University Press.

De Man, Hendrik (1929) *Joy in Work*. Tr. Eden and Cedar Paul. New York: Henry Holt.

Domhoff, William G. (1990) *The Power Elite and the State: How Policy is Made in America*. New York: Aldine De Gruyter.

Donaldson, Thomas and Preston, Lee E. (1995) 'The Stakeholder Theory of the Corporation: Concepts, Evidence, and Implications,' *Academy of Management Review*, 20 (1): 65–91.

Donovan, John J. (2001) 'Work Motivation,' in Neil Anderson, et al. (eds.), *Handbook of Industrial, Work, and Organizational Psychology, Volume 2*. London: Sage. pp. 53–76.

Dunleavy, Patrick and O'Leary, Brendan (1987) *Theories of the State: The Politics of Liberal Democracy*. London: Macmillian Education.

Dunlop, John T. (1958) *Industrial Relations Systems*. New York: Henry Holt.

Durkheim, Emile (1893/1933) *The Division of Labor in Society*. Tr. George Simpson. New York: Macmillan.

Eagleton, Terry (1994) *Ideology*. New York: Longman.

Edwards, P.K. (1986) *Conflict at Work: A Materialist Analysis of Workplace Relations*. Oxford: Basil Blackwell.

Edwards, Richard (1979) *Contested Terrain*. New York: Basic Books.

Epstein, Richard A. (1984) 'In Defense of the Contract at Will,' *University of Chicago Law Review*, 51 (4): 947–82.

Fama, Eugene (1980) 'Agency Problems and the Theory of the Firm,' *Journal of Political Economy*, 88 (2): 288–307.

Faulks, Keith (1999) *Political Sociology: A Critical Introduction*. Edinburgh: Edinburgh University Press.

Folger, Robert and Cropanzano, Russell (1998) *Organizational Justice and Human Resource Management.* Thousand Oaks, CA: Sage.

Forbath William E. (1985) 'The Ambiguities of Free Labor: Labor and the Law in the Gilded Age,' *Wisconsin Law Review*, 1985 (4): 767–817.

Fox, Alan (1966) 'Industrial Sociology and Industrial Relations,' *Royal Commission on Trade Unions and Employers' Associations Research Papers 3.* London: HMSO.

Fox, Alan (1974) *Beyond Contract: Work, Power and Trust Relations.* London: Farber and Farber.

Gall, Gregor (2003) 'Marxism and Industrial Relations,' in Peter Ackers and Adrian Wilkinson (eds.), *Understanding Work and Employment: Industrial Relations in Transition.* Oxford: Oxford University Press. pp. 316–24.

Ghoshal, Sumantra (2005) 'Bad Management Theories are Destroying Good Management Practices,' *Academy of Management Learning and Education*, 4 (1): 75–91.

Godard, John (1992) 'Contemporary Industrial Relations Ideologies: A Study of Canadian Academics,' *Relations Industrielles*, 47 (2): 239–66.

Godard, John (1995) 'The Ideologies of U.S. and Canadian IR Scholars: A Comparative Analysis and Construct Validation,' *Journal of Labor Research*, 16 (2): 127–47.

Godard, John (1997) 'Whither Strategic Choice: Do Managerial IR Ideologies Matter?,' *Industrial Relations*, 36 (2): 206–28.

Godard, John (2005) *Industrial Relations, the Economy, and Society.* 3rd edn. Concord, Ontario: Captus Press.

Gottfried, Heidi (2006) 'Feminist Theories of Work,' in Marek Korczynski, Randy Hodson, and Paul Edwards (eds.), *Social Theory at Work.* Oxford: Oxford University Press. pp. 121–54.

Greene, Anne-Marie (2003) 'Women and Industrial Relations,' in Peter Ackers and Adrian Wilkinson, (eds.), *Understanding Work and Employment: Industrial Relations in Transition.* Oxford: Oxford University Press. pp. 305–15.

Gross, James A. (1998) 'The Broken Promises of the National Labor Relations Act and the Occupational Safety and Health Act: Conflicting Values and Conceptions of Rights and Justice,' *Chicago-Kent Law Review*, 73 (1): 351–87.

Hearn, Mark and Michelson, Grant (eds.) (2006) *Rethinking Work: Time, Space, and Discourse.* Melbourne: Cambridge University Press.

Hodson, Randy (2001) *Dignity at Work.* Cambridge: Cambridge University Press.

Honderich, Ted (ed.) (2005) *The Oxford Companion to Philosophy.* 2nd edn. Oxford: Oxford University Press.

Hyman, Richard (1975) *Industrial Relations: A Marxist Introduction.* London: Macmillan.

Hyman, Richard (2006) 'Marxist Thought and the Analysis of Work,' in Marek Korczynski, Randy Hodson, and Paul Edwards (eds.), *Social Theory at Work.* Oxford: Oxford University Press. pp. 26–55.

Jacoby, Sanford M. (2001) 'Employee Representation and Corporate Governance: A Missing Link,' *University of Pennsylvania Journal of Labor and Employment Law*, 3 (3): 449–89.

Jacoby, Sanford M. (2005) *The Embedded Corporation: Corporate Governance and Employment Relations in Japan and the United States.* Princeton, NJ: Princeton University Press.

Jahoda, Marie (1982) *Employment and Unemployment: A Social-Psychological Analysis.* Cambridge, MA: Cambridge University Press.

Jensen, Michael C. and Meckling, William H. (1976) 'Theory of the Firm: Managerial Behavior, Agency Costs, and Ownership Structure,' *Journal of Financial Economics*, 3 (4): 305–60.

Kanigel, Robert (1997) *The One Best Way: Frederick Winslow Taylor and the Enigma of Efficiency.* New York: Penguin.

Katz, Harry C. and Darbishire, Owen (2000). *Converging Divergences: Worldwide Changes in Employment Systems.* Ithaca, NY: ILR Press.

Kaufman, Bruce E. (1993) *The Origins and Evolution of the Field of Industrial Relations in the United States.* Ithaca, NY: ILR Press.

Kaufman, Bruce E. (1997) 'Labor Markets and Employment Regulation: The View of the "Old" Institutionalists,' in Bruce E. Kaufman (ed.), *Government Regulation of the Employment Relationship.* Madison, WI: Industrial Relations Research Association. pp. 11–55.

Kaufman, Bruce E. (1999) 'Expanding the Behavioral Foundations of Labor Economics,' *Industrial and Labor Relations Review*, 52 (3): 361–92.

Kaufman, Bruce E. (2004) *The Global Evolution of Industrial Relations: Events, Ideas, and the IIRA.* Geneva: International Labour Office.

Kaufman, Bruce E. (2005) 'The Social Welfare Objectives and Ethical Principles of Industrial Relations,' in John W. Budd and James G. Scoville (eds.), *The Ethics of Human Resources and Industrial Relations.* Champaign, IL: Labor and Employment Relations Association. pp. 23–59.

Kelloway, Kevin E., Gallagher, Daniel G., and Barling, Julian (2004) 'Work, Employment, and the Individual,' in Bruce E. Kaufman (ed.), *Theoretical Perspectives on Work and the Employment Relationship.* Champaign, IL: Industrial Relations Research Association. pp. 105–31.

Kelly, John (1998) *Rethinking Industrial Relations: Mobilization, Collectivism and Long Waves*. London: Routledge.

Killingsworth, Mark R. (1983) *Labor Supply*. Cambridge: Cambridge University Press.

King, Roger (1986). *The State in Modern Society: New Directions in Political Sociology*. Chatham, NJ: Chatham House Publishers.

Kochan, Thomas A. (1998) 'What is Distinctive About Industrial Relations Research?,' in George Strauss and Keith Whitfield (eds.), *Researching the World of Work: Strategies and Methods in Studying Industrial Relations*. Ithaca, NY: ILR Press. pp. 31–45.

Kochan, Thomas A. and. Katz, Harry C. (1988) *Collective Bargaining and Industrial Relations: From Theory to Policy and Practice*. 2nd edn. Homewood, IL: Irwin.

Kochan, Thomas A., Katz, Harry C., and McKersie, Robert B. (1986) *The Transformation of American Industrial Relations*. New York: Basic Books.

Kunda, Gideon (1992) *Engineering Culture: Control and Commitment in a High-Tech Corporation*. Philadelphia: Temple University Press.

Kunda, Gideon and Ailon-Souday, Galit (2005), 'New Designs: Design and Devotion Revisited,' in Stephen Ackroyd, Rosemary Batt, Paul Thompson, and Pamela S. Tolbert (eds.), *The Oxford Handbook of Work and Organization*. Oxford: Oxford University Press. pp. 200–19.

Latham, Gary P. and Pinder, Craig C. (2005) 'Work Motivation Theory and Research at the Dawn of the Twenty-First Century,' *Annual Review of Psychology*, 56: 485–516.

Legge, Karen (1995) *Human Resource Management: Rhetorics and Realities*. Basingstoke: Macmillan Press.

Leidner, Robin (2006) 'Identity and Work,' in Marek Korczynski, Randy Hodson, and Paul Edwards (eds.), *Social Theory at Work*. Oxford: Oxford University Press. pp. 424–63.

Levine, David I. (1995) *Reinventing the Workplace: How Business and Employees Can Both Win*. Washington, D.C.: Brookings Institution.

Lewin, David (2001) 'IR and HR Perspectives on Workplace Conflict: What Can Each Learn from the Other?,' *Human Resource Management Review*, 11 (4): 453–85.

Lustig, Jeffrey R. (2004) 'The Tangled Knot of Race and Class in America,' in Michael Zweig (ed.), *What's Class Got To Do With It? American Society in the Twenty-First Century*. Ithaca: Cornell University Press. pp. 45–60.

Manning, Alan (2003) *Monopsony in Motion: Imperfect Competition in Labor Markets*. Princeton, NJ: Princeton University Press.

March, James G. and Simon, Herbert A. (1958) *Organizations*. New York: John Wiley & Sons.

Martin, Christopher R. (2004) *Framed! Labor and the Corporate Media*. Ithaca, NY: ILR Press.

Marx, Karl (1844/1988) *Economic and Philosophic Manuscripts of 1844*. Tr. Martin Milligan Amherst, NY: Prometheus Books.

Maslow, Abraham H. (1943) 'A Theory of Human Motivation,' *Psychological Review*, 50 (4): 370–96.

Montgomery, David (1979) *Workers' Control in America: Studies in the History of Work, Technology, and Labor Struggles*. Cambridge: Cambridge University Press.

Muirhead, Russell (2004) *Just Work*. Cambridge: Harvard University Press.

Nord, Walter R., Brief, Arthur P., Atieh, Jennifer M., and Doherty, Elizabeth M. (1990) 'Studying Meanings of Work: The Case of Work Values,' in Arthur P. Brief and Walter R. Nord (eds.), *Meanings of Occupational Work*. Lexington, MA: Lexington Books. pp. 21–64.

Peccoud, Dominique (ed.) (2004) *Philosophical and Spiritual Perspectives on Decent Work*. Geneva: International Labour Office.

Perlman, Selig (1928) *A Theory of the Labor Movement*. New York: Macmillan.

Pfeffer, Jeffrey (1998) *The Human Equation: Building Profits by Putting People First*. Boston: Harvard Business School Press.

Pierson, C. (1996) *The Modern State*. New York: Routledge.

Poole, Michael, Mansfield, Roger, Gould-Williams, Julian, and Mendes, Priya (2005) 'British Managers' Attitudes and Behavior in Industrial Relations: A Twenty-Year Study,' *British Journal of Industrial Relations*, 43 (1): 117–34.

Posner, Richard A. (1986) *Economic Analysis of Law*. 3rd edn. Boston: Little, Brown.

Reynolds, Morgan O. (1984) *Power and Privilege: Labor Unions in America*. New York: Universe Books.

Schumacher, E. F. (1974) 'Economics from the Buddhist Point of View,' *Management Review*, 63 (5): 39–42.

Singer, Peter (2000) *Marx: A Very Short Introduction*. Oxford: Oxford University Press.

Skocpol, Theda. (1985) 'Bringing the State Back in: Strategies of Analysis in Current Research,' in Peter B. Evans, Dietrich Rueschemeyer, and Theda Skocpol (eds.), *Bringing the State Back In*. Cambridge: Cambridge University Press. pp. 3–37.

Smith, Adam (1776/2003) *An Inquiry Into the Nature and Causes of the Wealth of Nations*. New York: Bantam Books.

Solomon, Robert C. (1992) *Ethics and Excellence: Cooperation and Integrity in Business*. New York: Oxford University Press.

Tajfel, Henri (1978) 'Social Categorization, Social Identity, and Social Comparison,' in Henri Tajfel (ed.), *Differentiation Between Social Groups*. New York: Academic Press. pp. 61–76.

Taylor, Bill, Kai, Chang, and Qi, Li (2003) *Industrial Relations in China*. Cheltenham: Edward Elgar.

Thelen, Herbert and Withall, John (1949) 'Three Frames of Reference: The Description of Climate,' *Human Relations*, 2 (2):159–76.

Thompson, Paul and Newsome, Kirsty (2004) 'Labor Process Theory, Work, and the Employment Relation,' in Bruce E. Kaufman (ed.), *Theoretical Perspectives on Work and the Employment Relationship*. Champaign, IL: Industrial Relations Research Association. pp. 133–62.

Turner, John.C. (1987) *Rediscovering the Social Group: A Self-Categorization Theory*. Oxford: Basil Blackwell.

Tversky, Amos and Kahneman, Daniel (1986) 'The Framing of Decisions and the Psychology of Choice,' *Science*, 211 (4481): 453–58.

Ulrich, Dave and Brockbank, Wayne (2005) *The HR Value Proposition*. Boston: Harvard Business School Press.

Varian, Hal. R (1984) *Microeconomic Analysis*. 2nd edn. New York: W.W. Norton and Company.

Wachter, Michael L. (2004) 'Theories of the Employment Relationship: Choosing Between Norms and Contracts,' in Bruce E. Kaufman (ed.), *Theoretical Perspectives on Work and the Employment Relationship*. Champaign, IL: Industrial Relations Research Association. pp. 163–93.

Webb, Sidney, and Webb, Beatrice (1897) *Industrial Democracy*. London: Longmans, Green, and Co.

Weber, Max (1919/1946) *From Max Weber: Essays in Sociology*. Tr. H.H. Gerth and C. Wright Mills. New York, NY: Oxford University Press.

Weber, Max (1904/1976) *Protestant Work Ethic and the Spirit of Capitalism*. Tr. Talcott Parsons. London: Allen and Unwin.

Weber, Max (1925/1978) *Economy and Society: An Outline of Interpretive Sociology*. Tr. E. Fischoff. Guenther Roth and Claus Wittich (eds.), Berkeley: University of California Press.

Wheeler, Hoyt N. (1985) *Industrial Conflict: An Integrative Theory*. Columbia: University of South Carolina Press.

Wheeler, Hoyt N. (1994) 'Employee Rights as Human Rights,' in Jacques Rojot and Hoyt Wheeler (eds.), *Employee Rights and Industrial Justice*, special issue of *Bulletin of Comparative Labour Relations*, 28: 9–18.

6

The Influence of Product Markets on Industrial Relations

William Brown

Industrial relations are profoundly affected by the nature of the markets in which firms compete. The relationships between employers and workers cannot avoid being influenced by the competitive pressures bearing down on the employers, whether those pressures are light and permissive, or tight and unforgiving. How employers respond to these pressures is another matter. There may be many different ways of managing labor that allow firms to keep afloat in a given competitive situation. There will be consequent differences in their industrial relations (IR). But whatever style of labor management is adopted, an important and unavoidable constraint on that style is whether, and with what urgency, the firm's business is under competitive threat.

This chapter is concerned with the relationship between IR and the intensity of competition for a firm's goods and services – that is to say, the competitiveness of what is known generically as its 'product market'. The chapter first considers the development

of bargaining structures, designed in large part to manage these competitive pressures. It explores how this has influenced trade unions because, as the labor economist Nickell has observed, 'what unions do depends upon what they *can* do, and this depends on the extent of product market competition' (Boeri et al., 2001: 296). Attention is also given to public sector employment that, despite its insulation from normal price mechanisms, is now heavily influenced by comparable constraints. The chapter next considers survey-based economic evidence of the link between industrial relations and product markets. It then focuses in to look at ethnographic case study evidence. This sheds light on how competitive pressures are translated into the varied patterns of managerial control or complacency under which great diversity of industrial relations has developed in different industries and at different times. Finally, it considers the impact of the geographical widening of product market competition in an increasingly international economy, and the implications of this for contemporary IR institutions, which were rarely intended to reach beyond national frontiers.

COMPETITIVE INFLUENCES ON BARGAINING STRUCTURE

Product markets have, in a world of more or less imperfect competition, always had a huge influence on bargaining structures. The reasons lie in the nature of trade union activity. Unions attract and retain members by negotiating and protecting improvements in their pay and conditions of work. They have traditionally done this either directly by using the threat of strike action, or by controlling the supply of labor. The consequence is that, if they are successful, and unless there are off-setting productivity improvements, they increase unit wage costs for the firms that employ their members. But this in turn implies that they reduce those firms' capacity to compete successfully in their product markets. So the organizational challenge facing unions is how to reduce the jeopardy in which members' jobs are placed as a result of increasing the cost of their labor.

The argument that this would be best met by unions' organizing the whole product market was explored by the institutional economist John Commons. In 1909, in a study of the development of the shoe industry in the US, he drew attention to the historical emergence of a gap separating the wage bargain (between the employer and workers) from the price bargain (between the retailer and the consumer). Relationships between journeymen, masters, and customers that, in a restricted local economy, had regulated not only wages, but also prices and quality, gave way to increasing domination by merchant retailers who fixed prices by reference to the cheapest labor market from which they could obtain substitute goods, wherever that might be. The employment standards of the local labor market become threatened by those of the relevant product market, however great

its geographical extent. He described how what he called the 'competitive menace' is the marginal producer '... with the lowest standards of living and cost and quality of work, he is the producer whose competition tends to drag down the level of others toward his own' (Commons, 1964: 251).

'Throughout the course of industrial evolution the part played by the merchant stands out as the determining factor. The key to the situation is at all times the price-bargain', Commons argues. 'It is the merchant who controls both capital and labor. If the merchant has a market, he can secure capital. The 'conflict of capital and labor' is a conflict of market and labor, of merchant and wage-earner, of prices and wages' (Ibid: 261). Associations of manufacturers are primarily price-regarding. An extension of the product market, to include lower-paying marginal producers, is likely to provoke conflict, because established wage-earners may try to protect their wages through trade union action, When this happens, '... the manufacturer turns, for the time, from the market and faces the workman. His "employers' association" is wholly different in method, object and social significance, and usually in *personnel* from his "manufacturers' association"' (Ibid: 262).

Power in industrial relations thus follows the contours of the markets for the goods and services produced, and not just the contours of the market for labor. It is not that the labor market is irrelevant. Indeed, the state of the labor market is of great importance to the relative power of employers and unions. Other things being equal, unions generally become stronger if the labor they organize becomes scarcer. But what they and employers have to fight over is decided by the employers' profits. They consequently do battle on a field delineated by the employers' product market.

The implications for unions are summarized by Kochan. He describes how Commons:

showed that as transportation systems improved and it became feasible for employers to manufacture products in low labor cost cities and transport them to sell in high labor cost cities, it became necessary for unions to organize all competing employers in these various cities. The basic principle involved here is that unless unions organize all the substitutes for union labor, any increases in wage costs in the unionized portion of the market will result in a loss of employment to the non-union sector. Similarly, a strike by employees in the unionized sector will lead consumers to shift their demand to the non-union sector (Kochan, 1980: 50).

Irrespective of whether labor is organized in trade unions, the management of it has been shaped by the predisposition of employers to see labor market issues as secondary to the price-driven pressures of the product market. Clegg notes that from very early on, many trade associations

> ... interfered with the laws of supply and demand on their own, even undertaking to regulate wages without any pressure from unions. This was true of both coal and iron. In coalmining the regulation of prices and wages on a county basis by the coal-owners was the general practice long before stable unions were established (Clegg, 1970: 122).

In the present, as in the past, employers constantly monitor their local labor markets to ensure their own firm's pay levels are sufficiently competitive to attract and retain workers. But they have a quite different concern with the cost implications of what their commercial competitors are paying, a concern which predisposes them, if possible, to 'take wages out of competition' by colluding with those competitors. It was Adam Smith who observed, over 200 years ago, that 'Masters are always and everywhere in a sort of tacit, but constant and uniform combination, not to raise wages of labor over their actual rate' (Smith, 1776: 59).

Thus, while it is in the interest of unions to organize all the workers in a given product market, the employers whom they confront are predisposed to collude with each other as product market competitors. They do this in order to bring stability to employment, which is always a sensitive and potentially volatile aspect of any firm's operations. It might seem surprising that there should be this congruence in employer and trade union

organizational interests. But in practice it compounds into a broader collusion by both sides against the consumer of the product in question. Providing that all the employers in the product market are united, collectively they maintain a monopoly position which permits them to charge the consumer higher prices than would otherwise be the case. The resulting monopoly profits (referred to by economists as 'rents') may then, in effect, be shared with the union members by means of a collective agreement that establishes pay levels that are higher than would otherwise have been the case. This is where the state of the labor market and the organizational strength of the union become important; they influence what share of rents the union can win.

By combining against the consumer across the full extent of their product market, both sides benefit. The unions gain employer recognition and also relatively favorable, and stable, terms of employment for their members. Individual employers have the tricky problem of managing pay and conditions looked after by their employers' association. They are then free to concentrate on competing with each other by other means. Nor need such collusion be to the detriment of the consumer. By reinforcing training and other institutions at the industrial level, it can uphold quality standards for goods and services. It is likely to prevent a degrading 'race to the bottom' in employment conditions.

In Europe and some other countries, the result, in due course, was a remarkably stable organizational arrangement: the industrial agreement. Sometimes called a 'multi-employer' or 'sectoral' agreement, this became the foundation of collective bargaining in European industrialized countries for much of the twentieth century. Such arrangements often started on a local basis. Clegg notes that in Britain 'until the last quarter of the nineteenth century, most employers' associations were limited to a single town or region' (Clegg, 1970: 121). But they generally developed, in response to wider industrial conflict, and depending on the ease of transport of the product, to regional or national level. In his study of the cotton industry, Turner notes that such development tended to be more unstable when the employers had a strong cartel or monopoly element, 'but once it is clear that the unions are established, the employing body may move to a quite opposite attitude, of accommodation to collective organization among its workers' (Turner, 1962: 378). And once such bargaining structures were established as the main means of fixing pay rates, working hours, holiday entitlements, and so on, they would typically become powerfully reinforced with their own distinct apprenticeship arrangements, dispute procedures and, in most European countries, legal support.

Despite the fact that these industrial agreements were technically in constraint of trade, they commanded considerable governmental support. In effect, government tolerated the restraint they placed on competition because of the benefits they offered in terms of industrial peace and good employment standards. From the late-nineteenth century onward, industry-based collective bargaining was officially encouraged by British governments, typically as arrangements that were generally called National Joint Industrial Councils. In industries where the unions were too weak for these, then the Wages Boards (later Wages Councils) were established, on the bases of the distinct product markets where labor exploitation was seen to be a problem – Coffin Furniture; Cotton Waste Reclamation; Keg and Drum manufacture; Lace Finishing, or whatever. As recently as 1961, the Ministry of Labor's official Industrial Relations Handbook could say:

> When the agreement is made by a number of different employers or, as is often the case, by an employers' association acting on behalf of the whole or the greater part of the firms in a given industry within a wide area, all the workers employed by the employers concerned are secured equality of treatment, while each employer is protected against unfair competition by reason of lower wages costs in so far as his competitors are parties to the agreement. For many years collective agreements have played a most important part in

the regulation of working conditions in this country (Ministry of Labour, 1961: 18).

In effect, European governments accepted the implied inefficiencies arising from this officially blessed, industry-wide collusion against the consumer, in return for the public benefits in terms of industrial peace, effective training management, and a raft of individual employment rights. In Britain there were adverse inflationary implications that first emerged in the late 1950s, exacerbated by declining productivity growth, but it was not until the late 1980s that government ministers were publicly to criticize industrial agreements as a source of inefficiency and uncompetitiveness. As a senior government minister, Kenneth Clarke, put it, in urging the abandonment of pay rises linked to industrial agreements:

> If we move to a system where pay increases are based primarily on performance, merit, company profitability, and demand and supply in the local labor market, we will dethrone once and for all the annual pay round and the belief that pay increases do not have to be earned (Financial Times, 12th February 1987).

The benefits of collusion in the product market as a basis for managing labor relations were substantial. Trade unions whose organizational logic was tied to a particular skill or occupation, rather than product market, (such as those based on craft) would accommodate to industrial collective bargaining by becoming, for these purposes alone, members of union federations, such as the Confederation of Shipbuilding and Engineering Unions. In industries characterized by considerable heterogeneity of product market – such as engineering – employers would exercise substantial discretion at workplace level but, on the key issues of basic wage rates and hours of work, they would follow the industrial agreement (Marsh, 1965: 176).

The grip of the industry agreement was usually tighter in industries characterized by homogeneity of production technique and product, such as the manufacture of hosiery, or ceramics, or carpets, or newspapers. Some employers' associations imposed considerable discipline, including the enforcement of lock-outs. In cotton, for instance, they fined mill owners who continued to run their mills when their association was in dispute with unions; they refused help to member firms who paid above or below agreed wage-rates; and as late as 1950, they expelled firms which paid unauthorized bonuses on wages (Turner, 1962: 377). Even today some continue to exercise discipline over their members, such as the association that organizes electrical contractors for the construction industry, where licensing and safety issues are dominant.

Because labor can itself be so contentious and troublesome to manage, competing employers have a strong incentive to take it out of contention as an issue between themselves. Despite this, there have always been some employers who have pursued their own independent, enlightened employment practices as a distinctive means of product market competition. A number of Quaker-owned British firms come to mind that invested heavily in long-term relationships with employees and in their broader social welfare. Thereby they undoubtedly gained competitive advantage. But for most of the nineteenth and twentieth centuries this sort of benign, employee-oriented independence remained very much more the exception than the rule (Donkin, 2001).

THE BREAK UP OF PRODUCT MARKET BASED BARGAINING STRUCTURE

The starting point of this account of the underlying market dynamics of industrial relations was the predisposition of firms to concentrate, whether in competition or collusion, on the market in which their goods and services are traded. Wages are secondary to prices. If employees organize themselves into trade unions, sooner or later they have to come to terms with the employers' primary concern with the product market, and organize accordingly. As a consequence, firms' normal response, for most of the twentieth century, and for most developed economies (with the

notable exception of the US), was to confront the unions with employers' associations and to negotiate product market based, and hence industry based, collective agreements.

This was a satisfactory compromise so long as two conditions prevailed. The first was that the rival firms were sufficiently evenly matched within their product market, and gaining sufficiently from their collusion, for there to be inadequate net benefit to induce one or more larger firms to break away and deal with trade unions on their own (Ulman, 1974). The second condition was that trade unions were able to organize all relevant workers across the whole of the appropriate product market, in order to ensure that the firms they dealt with would not be undercut by competitors, able to gain advantage from employing cheaper labor.

The first condition prevailed in Europe, but it was not sustainable in Japan and the US. European governments of the first part of the twentieth century generally provided substantial legislative support for industry-based collective bargaining and also often for the associated training arrangements, welfare and employment rights. In large part this was because these countries had political parties backed by trade unions, whose periods in government sustained this legal support. Thus both trade union security and employer solidarity received statutory support, and strong industrial agreements were a consequence. Japan and the US, by contrast, not only lacked union-backed political parties with a commitment to collective bargaining, but had major industries that were, from early on, characterized by a relatively small number of dominant firms for which there were no net benefits from industry-based collective bargaining (Sisson, 1987).

In Europe, it was in Britain that industry-based bargaining first started to crumble. Initially this was because Britain's very *laissez-faire* legal structure provided little reinforcement to industrial bargaining and training institutions. These came under particular pressure when labor markets were tight in the 1950s and 1960s, creating exceptional strains between employers seeking to attract and retain scarce labor. One after another, industrial agreements began to break up, usually when dominant employers felt that they would gain more by controlling their own industrial relations strategy, most commonly by improving the motivational power of their internal pay structure and by paying higher rates. Early examples were Cadbury leaving the confectionary makers, Dunlop leaving the rubber manufacturers, and Esso leaving the petroleum refiners (Brown and Terry, 1978: 130). Here we have cases of mainly labor market pressures causing the break up of employer solidarity and hence of industrially based bargaining units. But this was happening firmly within the bounds of a secure national product market. By contrast, the second precondition is challenged by threats to the integrity of national product markets themselves.

The second precondition for industry-based collective bargaining is a trade union organization that is sufficiently comprehensive to encompass the whole product market. As has been noted, the early expansion of product markets as transport improved *within* countries brought no insurmountable problems. Unions and employer associations connived to out-flank and match each other in expanding the geographic scope of collective agreements. But once agreements reached national frontiers this process of joint regulation stopped. Extending further was no problem for what Commons described as the 'merchant retailers'. They simply bought wherever abroad price and transport costs provided the cheapest package. Nor did expanding overseas necessarily impede the established national producers who, as the twentieth century drew to a close, increasingly outsourced abroad or became multi-national and established their own production facilities in cheap labor countries.

For trade unions, however, the challenge of incoming, cheaper product substitutes from beyond national frontiers has been severe and often insuperable. There is over a 100 years of history of attempts at international trade union co-operation. Ten industry-specific 'global union federations' are currently associated with the International Trade Union Confederation. They cover broad separate industrial areas such as transport, journalism, metalworking, and chemicals, energy and mining (Levinson, 1972). But whatever they contribute in terms of communication, lobbying, and the spread of good practice, there is no evidence that they have made a major contribution to the exercise of power in collective bargaining (Borgers, 2000; Cooke, 2005). Of the many obstacles that confront attempts to build international trade union solidarity, the greatest challenge is probably simply that of getting workers in one country to make sacrifices and worsen their own job prospects in defense of workers in another country whose jobs are under threat. Even in domestic disputes, collective action makes tough demands on worker altruism; the evidence is that such demands become unsustainable when extended across frontiers. International trade union co-operation can, through political action and consumer bans, play a part in inhibiting the irresponsible use of exploited labor in other countries. There has recently been some development of cross-frontier union co-operation within the European Union (EU) (Marginson and Sisson, 2004). But experience suggests that the international use of direct coercion by collective sanctions is not an available option.

The challenge facing trade unions is growing massively. Product markets have, in recent decades, become substantially more exposed to international competitive pressures. This is because the world economy has become steadily more open to trade. The annual growth of international trade since World War Two has been consistently higher than the annual growth in world output, and over the past 20 or so years has been twice as great. Quite apart from this relative growth of trade between nations, the number of major trading nations and the size of the world's competitive base have increased. The emergence of China, India, and the old Soviet nations as serious competitors since about 1990 has roughly doubled the worldwide reservoir of employees competing for jobs.

These 'new' trading countries threaten exceptionally tough competition not only in terms of low wage rates but also, and of greater long-term significance, in terms of relatively high standards of education.

The internationalization of product markets has also been increased by the internationalization of company ownership. Foreign direct investment has over the past 20 years increased at twice the annual rate of world trade, facilitated by technological developments that have improved long-distance transport, communication, and control systems (Acocella, 2005; Singh and Zammit, 2004). The movement of jobs between countries, even while still within individual enterprises, becomes ever easier. Companies can easily move to sources of labor beyond the reach of both trade unions and legal employment protections.

From the trade union point of view, the prospects of gaining any effective bargaining leverage on ever more sprawling product markets are bleak. There have, of course, always been some unionized industrial sectors that have been exposed to foreign competition. A feature of the trade unions most affected is that they have often shown considerable sensitivity to this source of vulnerability. Thus, for example, in the 1960s and 1970s, the export-oriented metal-working unions took the lead in promoting counter-inflationary domestic economic policies in Germany, Switzerland and Australia (Crouch, 1993: 268; Kitay and Lansbury, 1997: 225). But in the twentieth century the challenge was often from unionized labor elsewhere, and in a relatively limited number of sectors of manufactures. More recently, international competition has intruded into an increasing range of both manufactures and services, and it has been much less constrained by trade unions, not least because their coverage has been diminishing in most countries. There are still some sheltered sectors. Unions are responding to the fact that many personal services are, by their nature, not amenable to overseas substitution, and thus offer substantial organizational potential (Milkman, 2004). But elsewhere they are finding ever

fewer sectors tenable for effective industrial collective agreements.

In Britain this has been partly reflected in the steady contraction in the coverage of industrial (multi-employer) collective agreements as the main basis of pay fixing in the private sector. They had covered the majority of the private sector workforce in 1960. By 2004, however, industrial agreements covered only 4 per cent of private sector workers (in workplaces with ten or more employees). Another 17 per cent of the workers in such workplaces were covered by enterprise-based (single-employer) agreements. But the remaining four-fifths of the private sector workforce had lost the support of any collective bargaining whatsoever (Kersley et al., 2006: 186).

Product market circumstances have also influenced the manner of this radical restructuring of collective bargaining. A survey of UK multi-plant enterprises was conducted in 1985, at a time when industrial agreements were already in retreatment, and when the single-employer bargaining, at that time to some extent replacing them, was close to its peak (Marginson et al., 1988). This confirmed that their adjustment was influenced by their exposure to international competition: '... it is employers whose companies compete primarily within the UK who appear to be most interested in taking wages 'out of competition' either on an intra-enterprise or an intra-industry basis'. (Marginson et al., 1988: 150).

Firms' internal arrangements are strongly influenced by their product markets. The survey by Marginson et al. showed that, as employers withdrew from industrial agreements (whether or not they continued to recognize trade unions), they tended to restructure their internal pay-fixing arrangements along product market lines so that pay could be linked more directly to the performance of specific business units, whether profit centers, divisions, or individual establishments. As a result, for any particular establishment in one of these multi-plant companies, what tended to matter in terms of pay levels depended not on where the establishment was in the country geographically – that is on its local labor market – but where it was situated in the business i.e on its product market. Thus, even when divorced from collusion with their competitors, and when free to manage their own employment policies, employers remain focused primarily upon the demands of the market for their product, rather than the demands of the market for their labor.

THE USE OF PROXY PRODUCT MARKETS IN THE PUBLIC SECTOR

When we turn to the public sector, the influence of product markets on industrial relations was traditionally notable for its absence. This was simply because, operating in non-traded goods and services, these large and, in most countries, highly unionized industries were unconstrained by normal market forces. Their labor markets are distinctive because the employer is usually the dominant provider and purchaser of specialist skills – whether soldiering, teaching, nursing, fire-fighting, or whatever. Their product markets are even more aberrant because, quite apart from the absence of any price-fixing mechanism, questions of quality and distribution are by their nature politically determined. This tends to place trade unions in a strong bargaining position, although they have traditionally been reluctant (and in some countries legally unable) to use it. Pay is usually fixed by reference to external comparison with the private sector. 'Rent' is reflected in levels of job security, manning levels, and job control. If public sector employment were preserved in this isolation from the traded sector, its industrial relations would remain a very large 'special case' on the margins of the present discussion.

Product market change has, however, become a crucial issue for the public sectors of most western industrialized countries in recent years. In large part this has been because there has been widespread privatization. For political, fiscal, strategic, and economic reasons, a variety of usually highly unionized industries have been sold to the private sector. In Britain, this has included railways, bus transport, road haulage, telecommunications, docks, vehicle, aircraft and ship manufacture, steel, gas, water, electricity, coal, munitions, airlines, research laboratories, recruitment services, waste disposal, airports, publishing, and much else. For most of these, the transition, since the 1980s, to the demands of a more-or-less competitive product market was traumatic and often strike-ridden. In Australia, as in Britain, trade union membership has usually fallen substantially, and established patterns of job control and work organization have been changed beyond recognition (Brown et al., 1998; Kitay and Lansbury, 1997).

The chastening effect of the introduction of product market pressures on both trade union and managerial behavior has had a substantial influence over British government policy toward those public services that have remained in state ownership. Since the 1980s, governments have introduced a number of devices to mimic or partially create similar stimuli. Those that introduced direct competition include: compulsory outsourcing of, and compulsory tendering for, non-core activities, such as catering and cleaning in hospitals and schools; building and highways maintenance for local government; pilot training for the armed forces; and prisoner transport for goals. One of the clearest examples where partial exposure to markets has had a fundamental impact on industrial relations was the creation, since the 1990s, of some privately owned and managed prisons. Covering about 10 per cent of the British prison population at time of writing, the existence of these, and the threat of more, has permitted the relatively peaceful introduction of a number of procedural constraints on the use of collective action by previously often militant prison officers.

Much quasi-market intervention in Britain has been less direct. Throughout the health and education sectors, a proliferation of league tables and associated performance measures has been used to try to channel funds and users in ways that might stimulate efficient labor management. The civil service has seen its once monolithic pay structure broken up – mimicking private sector multi-divisional enterprises – into mock product market fragments reflecting the domains of different departments and agencies. The net effects of these changes across public services, in terms of efficiency and service delivery, remain highly controversial. Industrial relations have certainly become more overtly conflictual by comparison with the private sector. While public services accounted for a small minority of strike action until the 1990s, during the years 2000–2005 they consistently accounted for at least a half of all strikes and three-quarters of all working days lost through strikes in the UK (ONS, 2006: 186). Some trade union opposition to quasi-market innovations has been successful. An example was the teachers' success in blunting the impact of performance-related pay in 1999. But generally the introduction of proxies for product markets has had the government's desired effect of diminishing the influence of public sector trade unions.

It was noted earlier that the condition of the labor market is of great importance to the relative power of employers and unions, but that they do battle on a field delineated by the employers' product market. It was also noted that the labor market for the public sector, which in Britain now largely means the public services, was highly constrained, with the state being the main provider and the main purchaser of the specialist skills required. This places the state, as employer, in a relatively weak position with regard to its employees, not least because of the political costs arising from the disruption of public services. The radical changes in public sector industrial relations of the past 20 or so years can be seen as a response to this. There has been a restructuring of incentives by the state in an effort to ensure, to use the previous metaphor, that power follows the contours of the market for the services delivered, not those of the market for labor delivering them, and thereby to rebuild the authority of the state as an employer.

THE ECONOMIC EVIDENCE OF PRODUCT MARKET EFFECTS

In a perfectly competitive product market, the role of trade unions is highly constrained. They may engage in co-operative behavior aimed at improving a firm's productivity. Sometimes called 'partnership' in Britain and 'mutual gains' in the US, this has become more evident in the past decade in response to tighter competition. But any more confrontational action that succeeded in raising wages or improving work conditions without compensating productivity improvements may threaten the survival of the firm and its jobs by rendering it uncompetitive. Most product markets are, however, to varying extents, imperfectly competitive. The firms that operate successfully within them receive the resulting rents as monopoly profits. Whether trade unions are able to obtain a share of those rents, and thereby benefit their members, depends upon the organizational issues discussed earlier.

Even if unions cannot organize the whole product market, the degree of its imperfection has considerable bearing on their strategy. An imperfect product market implies that the individual firms operating in it have some monopoly power. This may arise, among other things, from a distinctive product, a good reputation for service, or a familiar brand name. If unions can organize firms that have monopoly power, they should be able to extract some of the rent as benefits for their members. Even if the firm is in such a competitive situation that there is no rent, or if there is rent but the union cannot mobilize the strength to bargain a share of it, the union may still maintain employer recognition and employee members through co-operative strategies that, for example, facilitate superior quality of service.

Similarly, in a perfect labor market, employees of like skills and other attributes would be paid the same, irrespective of the profitability of their employers. But in practice, labor markets are also imperfect. As we have seen, one reason for this is the active role that employers play in 'taking wages out of competition' in order to bring stability to labor management. But the ending of the collusive fixing of wages with industrial collective agreements does not end the manipulation of wages by employers. Employers when bereft of employers' associations do not necessarily become passive 'price takers'. For all but the smallest firms, or those dealing in transitory and relatively unskilled labor, employers remain, within fairly broad labor market constraints, active 'price makers'. But they do so with the objective of maximizing the productivity of their labor. Internal pay structures are delicate motivational devices, whether or not they include performance-related pay and other explicit incentives. Notions of 'fair pay' are essentially concerned with relative pay, and the pay comparisons most intensely felt by workers arise within the enterprise. The demotivating consequences of internal pay mismanagement can rapidly corrode labor productivity. Internal pay structures require constant management attention.

Once away from an industrial agreement, employers thus place great emphasis on the integrity of their firms' internal pay structures, adapting them to the particular needs of their businesses, while keeping a weather eye on their local labor market pay levels in order to keep broadly in line with other employers. The effects of this were clearly demonstrated by a study of employees in seven occupations in 25 firms in the Coventry engineering industry over the decade of the 1970s, a watershed period in which these firms were breaking away from industrial collective bargaining into managing their own pay (Nolan and Brown, 1983). The study showed clearly how, as the decade progressed, the size of the annual pay rise an individual received owed less and less to their occupation, and more and more to the firm they were in. For the increasingly independent employers, in toughly competitive product markets, the labor market was a loose constraint. The important determinant of pay was '... the way in which employers manage work and pay so as to maximize their control over unit costs and output' (Ibid: 284).

In Britain's private sector during the post-war years of relatively high trade union strength, employees' pay did generally reflect their firm's profitability (Carruth and Oswald, 1989: 166). But while this is consistent with a link between product market circumstances and industrial relations outcomes, it is far from sufficient evidence, because firms have many reasons for success other than the product market in which they are placed. One study that explored this further exploited the peculiar characteristics of Australia's wage-fixing system that made it possible to identify, by occupation and establishment, informal establishment-negotiated pay increases over and above the quasi-judicially established industrial rates (Brown et al., 1984). The survey was conducted in 1974 of nearly 20,000 employees in 44 occupations in 198 establishments across nine industries in the urban labor market of Adelaide. The analysis suggested, as had the Coventry time-series study cited above, that pay settlements at establishment level owed more to the circumstances of the employer than to the occupation of the employee. More important, the analysis also suggested that the variance in the size of these establishment settlements correlated with the concentration ratio of the industry they were in. The less competitive was the industry, the less were the establishment-specific determinants of pay. It was concluded that wages paid by individual employers in excess of the industrial rates could only partly be explained in terms of meeting the needs of the local labor market. They also appeared to reflect '... employers' efforts, within the bounds of their product market power, to construct internal pay structures that will placate their employees, and motivate them to work productively' (Ibid: 175).

The influence of product markets is also reflected in the changing impact of collective bargaining. In a review of the micro-economic effects of trade unions, Metcalf notes that several studies in the 1980s had reported a negative association between union presence and financial performance. But by 1990 there were distinctive product market effects. Research suggested that 'over the course of the 1980s this negative impact weakened such that by 1990 the overall union effect was halved as compared to 1984 and unionized establishments had lower financial performance only where the union was strong and the establishment had some market power' (Wilkinson, 2000: 3). 'This tempering of the impact of unions was confirmed by Machin and Stewart (1996) who concluded that by 1990 unions only impacted adversely on profitability where there was a closed shop and/or weak competition in the product market' (Metcalf, 2003: 146).

'The intensity of competition has a profound effect on what unions can do ... It is well known that non-competitive product markets permit unions to raise wages. But unions can capture product market rents in forms other than wages', observes Metcalf, citing their propensity to protect members by introducing rigidities in work organization, rigidities which may incidentally discourage innovation and thus productivity growth (Ibid: 155). His own analysis of the 1998 British WERS (using over 1100 workplaces in the trading sector) permitted him to investigate this in unusual detail (controlling for a substantial number of workplace and workforce variables) because the survey contained comparative measures of labor productivity and of financial performance. When there is relatively low competition, with the firm reporting five or fewer competitors, 'the probability of above average labor productivity is 14 per cent lower for a unionized workplace than its non-union counterpart. But when there are six or more competitors the corresponding figure is 0.6 per cent (not statistically significant). And when there is little product market competition the likelihood of above average financial performance is 12.4 per cent lower for a union than non-union workplace, yet the corresponding figure is 7.4 per cent higher with a more competitive product market' (Ibid: 157). This is powerful evidence that product market competition plays a crucial role in determining union influence over both working practices and pay levels: the tighter the competition, the less the union influence.

The longer-term implications for trade unions are serious. Noting Blanchard's observation that across OECD countries 'rents are getting smaller, leading to less room for rent extraction ... this decrease in attractiveness [of unions to members] is reflected, in nearly all countries, by decreased membership and support' (Boeri et al., 2001: 295), Metcalf concludes that 'more intense product market competition implies a corrosion of the impact of union recognition in the workplace which suggests that in the longer term unions may need to find a different role if they are to prosper' (Metcalf, 2003: 157). It is a conclusion arrived at by the very different route of economic modeling of recent labor market performance in the US and Europe by Ebell et al. (2004: 11) which concludes that the decline in unionization in the US and UK might have been a direct consequence of product market reforms of the 1980s.

The picture that emerges from these quantitative studies is consistent with the earlier more descriptive account. As product markets become more internationally exposed, employers find it increasingly difficult to manage labor through employers' associations. If they cannot exercise control over wages by collusion with each other, they have the option of going alone, and making more active use of their payment systems as motivational devices. If employers' associations do break up, the ending of the industrial collective agreements associated with them has severe implications for trade union recognition. Bargaining may continue with employers on an individual basis, but its success is dependent upon the extent of those employers' monopoly power, as well as the union's organizational strength. Recent years have seen a reduction in trade unions' capacity to bargain a share of rents, both because those rents may have diminished and because unions are less able to mobilize effective bargaining power over geographically extended product markets. In the public services, the largely monopolistic and exclusively national nature of the product market ensures that the role of public employees' unions is relatively secure. But the scope for private sector trade unions in sectors exposed to foreign competition is becoming increasingly curtailed.

THE TRANSMISSION OF PRODUCT MARKET CIRCUMSTANCES INTO WORKPLACE RELATIONS

Thus, so far this discussion has been concerned with the broad structures of industrial relations and how they are shaped by product market circumstances. But product markets also impact upon day-to-day industrial relations in a much more immediate way. By what means do product markets actually change behavior and thereby shape the ways employers treat workers?

A study conducted in the heavy bargaining environment of the British engineering industry of the 1960s permitted a close examination of this question (Brown, 1973). The subject of inquiry was the individual piecework payment systems that were then prevalent in the industry. They were widely perceived to be a major cause of wage inflation through 'wage drift' processes that involved no formal negotiation. What were the origins of piecework pay rises, and why did their pace differ substantially between factories? Case studies of ten factories provided detailed individual wage data over several years, as well as opportunities for extensive interviews and observation. A close relationship was identified between the pace of informally derived piecework pay rises, on the one hand, and, on the other, the widely understood but unwritten, local workshop 'rules' that in effect regulated the informal bargaining over piecework 'prices'. These rules were not formally negotiated but developed as 'custom and practice'. This was primarily as a result of low-level managerial errors that, once accepted as desirable by workers, tended to become taken as binding precedents by their shop stewards and defended by threats of strike action. The relevant rules concerned questions such as the criteria for re-evaluating piecework prices, the appropriate level of compensation payment when

machines broke down, and the restrictions placed on the managerial staff who set the prices.

What determined the leniency, from the pieceworker's point of view, of these 'custom and practice' rules? Two influences were identified. One was the slackness of management controls over work: over such matters as the recording of working time, the foreman's freedom to compensate for lost piece-working time, and departmental cost controls. The other was the authority and coherence of the factories' shop stewards' committees, which had a potential role in controlling unruly bargaining that might jeopardize union solidarity. Both influences, the slackness of controls and the lack of authority of the shop steward organization, were then shown to correlate with a composite measure of the constraints exercised by product market and technological factors.

The relevant conclusions drawn were, first, that the rules governing the bargaining process are '… heavily influenced by the control systems that managements see fit to install in their factories'. Second, that 'the principal pressures influencing management control systems are those of the product market, and different product markets can vary considerably in both the degree and the character of their competitiveness' (Brown, 1973: 175). Third, that '… the organizational and bargaining characteristics of the workforce are not the root causes of poor management controls; a weakly integrated workforce may exacerbate the weaknesses of a control system further but it will have been the initial inadequacy of the controls which made the integration of the shop steward body difficult in the first place' (Ibid: 171). And, finally, that '… under relatively full employment and trade union organization, it is the product market rather than the labor market which has the major economic impact upon piecework wage determination' (Ibid: 175).

The chain of influence described here is fairly straight-forward. An uncompetitive product market does not directly cause poor management, but it does increase the probability of it because it provides an environment in which management has little incentive to devote resources to building and maintaining effective controls over labor and production. Sloppy controls give rise to inconsistency of payment and treatment of workers that generates discontents and encourages worker constraints on the organization of work. Loss of control is manifest in many ways, and the firm unwittingly concedes to its workers much of the rent accruing from its partial monopoly position. For the workers, the rent they thereby gain takes various largely haphazard forms: inequitably distributed 'windfall' pay rises, substantial control over the pace and conduct of work, discretion over job mobility, control over overtime, and so on. A loss of focus on competition in the product market leads to a loss of control over the management of the labor market.

The post-war British engineering industry was far from unique in this response to weak product market competition. Other major industries have seen similar development of haphazard workplace rent sharing arising from weak managerial controls. This was perhaps most notable in the decade or so of slack competition that followed the devastation of potential overseas competitors during Second World War. Thus the docks industry saw its workforce develop diverse localized controls over manning, piecework, and work allocation (Mellish, 1972). National newspapers allowed their union chapels to exercise almost complete control over work patterns, overtime and manning levels, a level of restriction that must have provided a barrier to new entrants from which the owners probably benefited (Sisson, 1975). The petroleum refining and distribution industry allowed middle managers repeatedly to concede aspects of the management of overtime to local union branches (Ahlstrand, 1990; Flanders, 1964). One could go on. A lack of financial restraint on employers is often associated with poor labor management – the stable lads employed by race-horse trainers and the household staff of the British royalty provide well-documented examples – because

the employer has little financial incentive to respond positively to the needs and capabilities of employees.

The more recent history of British industrial relations has been dominated by varied responses to tightening product markets. For some industries the shock has been so great, and the response so inadequate, that they have contracted almost to the point of vanishing in the face of overseas competition – coal-mining, ceramics, ship-building, footwear, textiles and clothing are examples. Some companies have responded by derecognizing unions, sometimes also out-sourcing work to non-union organizations – television, facilities management, newspapers, and banking provide examples. A common response has been to maintain formal union recognition but implicitly to reduce it substantially by reducing both the range of issues subject to negotiation and the influence that unions can have over them (Brown et al., 1998; Brown et al., 2000). Increasingly this has been combined with explicit co-operative bargaining arrangements (Oxenbridge and Brown, 2002). In all cases the primary driver for change has been heightened product market competition, and an accompanying feature has been a much-weakened trade union, less capable of accessing rents for its members other than through co-operative strategies.

CONCLUSION

This chapter has argued that product markets form the foundation upon which industrial relations institutions are built. Trade union strength with respect to employers is, of course, much affected by the tightness of the labor market, whether that arises from an economic boom, or from effective union controls over labor supply, or whatever else. But it is pre-existing imperfections in the product market that permit collective bargaining to deliver benefits to workers. The greater the imperfections, the greater the scope for union members to benefit, provided their union can exercise effective leverage over all suppliers to the product market, or over individual employers who occupy a sufficiently monopolistic position within it.

It has been argued here that the configuration of product markets has been moving in ways that are increasingly adverse for collective bargaining. This is of less significance in the public sector. Although even there the state has been eroding the bargaining position of public sector trade unions by mimicking product market incentives in order to weaken the employers' focus on labor. But the changing nature of product markets is of deep significance for the private sector, where so much employment is now exposed to competition from parts of the world where neither trade unions nor statutory minimum labor standards offer significant constraints.

Denied effective coercive bargaining power because of tighter product market competition, trade unions in many sectors are obliged to focus increasingly on strategies which in the past have tended to augment, rather than replace, confrontational bargaining. One of these is co-operative working with employers through the arrangements sometimes referred to as 'partnership' and 'mutual gains' . The success of this depends very much upon the willingness of the employer to make it effective and to encourage trade union membership as a means of upholding good employment practice.

Another strategy that is well-established in Europe is that of lobbying the government to improve statutory support for employment standards. Legal enforcement of improved terms and conditions is directly as important to union members as to any other employees. It also establishes a floor on which collective bargaining can be build without fear of being seriously under-cut. The improvement of statutory rights such as minimum wages and maximum working hours is of particular importance to unions seeking to organize those large numbers of workers in the private services, where international competition does not pose a threat. A major stimulus since the 1970s has come from the European Union, but the addition of poorer new member

states of Eastern Europe since 2004 will slow this down.

A third strategy, aimed at tackling the huge difficulties raised by the globalization of product markets, is that of consumer campaigns, whereby adverse publicity is given to those brand names which use suppliers with poor labor standards. During the past decade such campaigns have prompted a substantial increase in the use of publicly reported 'ethical trading audits' by both major consumer good brand names and major supermarket chains. The challenge such campaigns face is formidable. Because trading enterprises steer by the commercial imperatives of their product markets then, to the extent that their markets are global, the standards of employment for increasing numbers of workers will tend to be dragged down by the depth of inequality of labor across the world economy. The campaigners have to counter this by appealing to the consciences of consumers, and thereby threatening the reputation of the brand names and supermarkets. It is a vivid vindication of John Commons' emphasis, a 100 years ago, on the pivotal role of the 'merchant retailer'.

This chapter has been concerned with the interaction of markets and institutions. A major role of trade unions has always been to build institutions to provide the agreements and other protections that might insulate their members from the harsh vagaries of the market for their labor. Such vagaries have, in turn, depended heavily upon the markets for the goods and services that their labor produced. Ensuring that the geographic reach of union organization equaled that of their members' labor markets was relatively straight-forward. Doing the same for their employers' product markets was more difficult. But it suited the employers' own desire to remove employment as an issue of competitive contention and, with state support, provided the basis for nationally based employment regulation for many countries for most of the twentieth century.

Collective bargaining, and national statutory labor standards, tamed labor markets so long as product markets were predominantly nation-based. It has been the increasingly international nature of the world economy that has thrown these systems into disarray. Product markets that extend beyond the reach of either union movements or national governments now threaten the security and well-being of workers world-wide. The challenge for the twenty-first century is to develop new international institutions, capable of protecting decent labor standards and of diminishing the inequalities that will otherwise destroy them.

ACKNOWLEDGMENTS

The author is grateful for helpful comments from David Metcalf, Peter Nolan, Jon Trevor, and the editors.

REFERENCES

Acocella, N. (2005) *Economic Policy in the Age of Globalization*. Cambridge: CUP.

Ahlstrand, B. (1990) *The Quest for Productivity*. Cambridge: CUP.

Boeri, T., Brugiavivi, A., and Clamfors, L. (eds), (2001) *The Role of Unions in the Twenty-First Century*. Oxford: OUP.

Borgers, F. (2000) 'Global unionism: organizational challenges', in Hanami, T. (ed.), *Universal Wisdom through Globalisation*. Tokyo: Japan Institute of Labor.

Brown, W. (1973) *Piecework Bargaining*. London: Heinemann.

Brown, W. and Terry, M. (1978) 'The changing nature of national wage agreements', *Scottish Journal of Political Economy*, 25 (2): 119–34.

Brown, W., Hayles, J., Hughes, B., and Rowe, L. (1984) 'Product and labor markets in wage determination: some Australian evidence', *British Journal of Industrial Relations*, XXII (2): 169–76.

Brown, W., Deakin, S., Hudson, M., Pratten, C. and Ryan, P. (1998) *The Individualisation of Employment Contracts in Britain*. London: DTI.

Brown, W., Deakin, S., Nash, D., and Oxenbridge, S. (2000) 'The employment contract: from collective procedures to individual rights', *British Journal of Industrial Relations*, 38 (4): 611–30.

Carruth, A. A. and Oswald, A. J. (1989) *Pay Determination and Industrial Prosperity*. Oxford: Clarendon Press.

Clegg, H. A. (1970) *The System of Industrial Relations in Great Britain*. Oxford: Blackwell.

Commons, J. R. (1964) 'American Shoemakers, 1648–1895: A Sketch of Industrial Evolution' *Labor and Administration*. A. M. Kelley: New York, reprinted from *Quarterly Journal of Economics*, November, 1909.

Cooke, W. N. (2005) 'Exercising power in a prisoner's dilemma: transnational collective bargaining in an era of corporate globalisation?', *Industrial Relations Journal*, 36 (4): 283–302.

Crouch, C. (1993) *Industrial Relations and European State Traditions*. Oxford: Clarendon.

Donkin, R. (2001) *Blood, Sweat and Tears: the Evolution of Work*. New York: Texere.

Ebell, M., Doppelhofer, G., and Haefke, C. (2004) *Product market regulation in the presence of unions: quantitative implications*. Discussion paper.

Financial Times, 12th February 1987.

Flanders, A. (1964) *The Fawley Productivity Agreements*. London: Faber and Faber.

Kersley, B., Alpin, C., Forth, J., Bryson, A., Bewley, H., Dix, G., and Oxenbridge, S. (2006) *Inside the Workplace: Findings from the 2004 Workplace Employment Relations Survey*. London: Routledge.

Kitay, J. and Lansbury, R. (1997) *Changing Employment Relations in Australia*. Oxford: OUP.

Kochan, T. (1980) *Collective Bargaining and Industrial Relations*. R. D. Homewood: Irwin.

Levinson, C. (1972) *International Trade Unionism*. London: Allen and Unwin.

Machin, S. and Stewart, M. (1996) 'Trade unions and financial performance', *Oxford Economic Papers*, 48 (2): 213–41.

Marginson, P., Edwards, P. K., Martin, R., Purcell, J., and Sisson, K. (1988) *Beyond the Workplace: Managing Industrial Relations in the Multi-Establishment Enterprise*. Oxford: Blackwell.

Marginson, P. and Sisson, K. (2004) *European Integration and Industrial Relations*. Basingstoke: Palgrave.

Marsh, A. (1965) *Industrial Relations in Engineering*. Oxford: Pergamon.

Mellish, M. (1972) *The Docks after Devlin*. London: Heinemann.

Metcalf, D. (2003) 'Unions and productivity, financial performance and investment: international evidence', in Addison, J. T. and Schnabel, C. (eds), *International Handbook of Trade Unions*. Cheltenham: Elgar.

Milkman, R. (2004) *Organizing Immigrants in California*. Cornell: ILR Press.

Ministry of Labour (1961) *Industrial Relations Handbook*. London: HMSO.

Nolan, P. and Brown, W. (1983) 'Competition and workplace wage determination', *Oxford Bulletin of Economics and Statistics*, 45 (3): 269–88.

Office for National Statistics (2006) 'Labor disputes in 2005', *Labor Market Trends*, 114 (6): 174–90.

Oxenbridge, S. and Brown, W. (2002) 'The two faces of partnership? An assessment of partnership and co-operative employer/trade union relationships', *Employee Relations*, 24 (3): 262–76.

Singh, A. and Zammit, A. (2004) 'Labor standards and the "race to the bottom": rethinking globalization and workers' rights from developmental and solidaristic perspectives', *Oxford Review of Economic Policy*, 20 (1): 85–104.

Sisson, K. (1975) *Industrial Relations in Fleet Street*. Oxford: Blackwell.

Sisson, K. (1987) *The Management of Collective Bargaining*. Oxford: Blackwell.

Smith, A. (1776) *The Wealth of Nations*. London: Strahan and Cadell.

Turner, H. A. (1962) *Trade Union Growth, Structure and Policy*. London: Allen & Unwin.

Ulman, L. (1974) 'Connective bargaining and competitive bargaining', *Scottish Journal of Political Economy*, 21 (2): 97–109.

Wilkinson, D. (2000) 'Collective bargaining and workplace financial performance in Britain', mimeo, Policy Studies Institute, April.

7

Varieties of Capitalism and Industrial Relations

Kerstin Hamann and John Kelly

INTRODUCTION

Industrial relations systems have long been classified into different groups, such as the Anglo-Saxon, the Scandinavian, or the continental European model. Similarly, welfare states have also been sorted into several categories, such as Christian-democratic, liberal, or social-democratic. The Varieties of Capitalism (VoC) approach has grouped capitalist systems – especially those of the OECD – into several categories, such as Liberal Market Economies (LMEs) and Coordinated Market Economies (CMEs). Given the parallel existence of these classifications of capitalist political economies, this chapter discusses to what extent the VoC approach is congruent with or different from industrial relations classifications. It also analyzes whether and how the VoC approach contributes to the study of industrial relations. The next section reviews the literature on national models of industrial relations and; the third section outlines the main variants of the VoC approach. The chapter then assesses the theoretical links between industrial relations and varieties of capitalism. The fifth section evaluates the correspondence between national patterns of industrial relations and varieties of capitalism empirically. The chapter concludes by suggesting directions for further research.

NATIONAL DIFFERENCES IN THE INDUSTRIAL RELATIONS LITERATURE

Much of the research into national patterns of industrial relations has engaged with the long-standing debate over the degree of convergence or divergence between advanced capitalist economies. The seminal statement of the convergence hypothesis by Kerr et al. (*Industrialism and Industrial Man*, 1960) was a critique of the Marxist argument that the development of technology would generate increasing strains and conflicts in the relations between labor and capital and facilitate the transition to a socialist society. Kerr et al. argued that technological development in a context of competitive product markets would produce convergent 'pluralistic industrialism' instead of socialism. The defining attributes of this society were increased affluence and social mobility, class dealignment in voting behavior and party politics, and an industrial relations system based around group, not class, interests and regulated primarily by collective bargaining.

The world strike wave of 1968–1974 and the associated problems of stagflation, declining profitability and industrial and political disorder called into question both the predictions and the underlying assumptions of the original convergence hypothesis (see Armstrong et al., 1991: 169–220; Kelly, 1998: 83–107). Even more troubling for convergence theorists was the variety of government responses to the economic and industrial relations problems of the 1970s. In a number of countries leftist governments initiated what Pizzorno (1978) described as a process of 'political exchange' in which they offered increased legal rights to unions in return for union commitment to wage moderation. One of the major themes in the analysis of political exchange (increasingly described as corporatist policymaking) was the classification of differences between countries. Italy and Sweden, for example, had well developed corporatist arrangements compared to the 'pluralistic fragmentation' of the UK and the US, where corporatism was weak or non-existent (Goldthorpe, 1984; Regini, 1984). The increased globalization of production, trade, and investment through the 1980s revived the convergence hypothesis. Piore and Sabel (1984) charted the evolution of production systems throughout the twentieth century from Fordism to post-Fordism (or 'flexible specialization'), a superior form of economic organization to its mass production predecessor. Womack et al. (1990) built on this work to argue that Japanese 'lean production' and shop floor participation had demonstrated its economic superiority to other forms of work organization and workplace industrial relations. In their view competition would force other firms to adopt the 'Japanese model' or go under (see also Oliver and Wilkinson, 1992 but cf.; Bélanger et al., 1994; Kochan et al., 1997).

Analyzing production at the national level, however, some commentators found that the economic superiority of US capitalism could force the economies and industrial relations systems of Europe and Japan to converge on the US model (Dore et al., 1999). This revival of interest in converging production systems was short-lived because comparative industrial relations scholars were increasingly taking a broader approach and describing and analyzing differences between national systems of employment regulation. For example, Visser (1992) drew attention to the stability of union density in Scandinavia and Belgium compared to the rest of the advanced capitalist world, a fact he explained by reference to the role of unions in the provision of unemployment benefit (see also Western, 1997). Hyman's (2001) framework for analyzing trade union behavior and strategy develops three ideal types of union movement. Unions can function as labor market actors (as in the UK), as class actors (for example Italy), or as social actors (for example Germany) although in practice unions display varying degrees of each of these tendencies. The distinction between coordinated economies and liberal market economies (see below) has informed a number of IR studies, such as Gospel and Pendleton (2003) on trends in corporate governance or Turnbull et al.'s (2004) analysis of British, Irish, and German airlines.

Perhaps the most systematic typology of national systems of industrial relations was developed by Crouch (1993), who categorized industrial relations along two dimensions, power of organized labor (high-low) and degree of centralization of labor and capital (high-low), resulting in a 2 x 2 matrix. He labeled these neo-corporatism (strong labor), for example Scandinavia; neo-corporatism (weak labor), for example Germany, Netherlands; contestational bargaining (strong labor), for example the UK, Italy; and pluralistic bargaining (weak labor), for example France, Spain (Crouch, 1993: 43, 289–90; see also Regini, 1984). While the analysis focuses on the roles of unions, the country cases are broadly comparable to VoC categories, as discussed below.

This brief review reveals a striking parallel between the analyses of industrial relations scholars and those of political economists. The distinction between a 'liberal' model of industrial relations and some form of European model is commonplace and co-exists with more elaborate typologies. The next section shows how political economists have attempted to construct national patterns and clusters.

APPROACHES TO THE VARIETIES OF CAPITALISM SINCE THE 1990s

A series of events and developments in the 1990s led to renewed interest in understanding the systematic differences and similarities across the economies of Western democracies: the decline of neo-corporatism and varied national responses to external pressures, including European economic unification and globalization, demographic changes in advanced industrialized economies, and the replacement of the Keynesian consensus by neo-liberal ideas and policies. The political economy literature broadly distinguishes between two approaches: one addresses primarily types and origins of welfare states, while the second one looks at economic systems more generally by taking the complex interaction between sets of institutions and actors as its starting point for analysis (see Ebbinghaus and Manow, 2001).

Welfare-state centered approaches

Welfare state regimes are of great importance to industrial relations because they link to issues germane to unions, such as (un)employment protection. Some of the foremost studies analyzing types of welfare systems are Esping-Andersen's works, especially his seminal book *The Three Worlds of Welfare Capitalism* (1990). He identifies three distinct types of welfare state, social-democratic, liberal, and conservative and reasons these regime types are the result of

working-class mobilization and cross-class coalitions (Esping-Andersen, 1990: 31). The social-democratic type emphasizes universalism and decommodification of social rights to the working and the middle classes and is found primarily in Scandinavia. The liberal model emphasizes welfare measures that are means-tested and provides only modest universal transfers and social insurance plans; this regime is predominant in the US, Canada, and Australia. The conservative regime is present in highly corporatist countries, such as Austria, Germany, or France, and while in this welfare regime the state rather than the market provides most of the welfare, it also emphasizes status differences and thus offers few redistributive policies (Esping-Andersen, 1990: 26–8).

Other authors have developed slightly different categories. Hicks and Kenworthy (2003), for instance, identify two welfare state dimensions, 'progressive liberalism' and 'traditional conservatism'. The difference in classification matters when the relationship between the types of welfare state is related to economic performance in three areas, income redistribution, jobs, and gender equality.

Based on an empirical analysis of OECD countries, the authors conclude that thinking of welfare states in terms of dimensions rather than categories is a more useful approach because it allows for 'more elegant and fine-grained analyses of cross-regime differences in parameters explaining welfare state phenomena' (Hicks and Kenworthy, 2003: 31).

The development and crisis of welfare states form the central focus of Huber and Stephens (2001a, b), who understand the welfare state to be closely linked to the balance of power between different groups and political institutions. They differ from Esping-Andersen (1990) in that they re-label the conservative welfare state as 'Christian democratic' to denote the pivotal role of partisan politics. They also separate Australia and New Zealand into a fourth type, the 'wage earner welfare state' (Huber and Stephens, 2001a: 87). Huber and Stephens identify political parties as the motor of welfare state development. The ideology, or 'political coloring', of the parties was instrumental in shaping the welfare state; which parties were holding elected office, in turn, reflected social cleavages and the distribution of power, especially the strength of organized labor and religious cleavages (Huber and Stephens, 2001a: 1). The country's position in the international economy and its production regime were also pivotal factors in developing welfare systems. Furthermore, welfare state development and retrenchment are intrinsically political processes and are facilitated or constrained by political institutions that distribute power within the political system. For example, where multiple veto points exist, such as in Switzerland or Germany, welfare retrenchment was very limited, while those constitutions that have few built-in veto points allow for more rapid and dramatic retrenchment (Huber and Stephens, 2001a: 1–5).

Huber and Stephens (2001a) also find that some labor market parameters correspond broadly to welfare state types: for example, social-democratic countries (Scandinavia) generally feature high union density; Christian-democratic countries (for example Germany, Netherlands, Belgium) have lower union density, but high bargaining coverage. Corporatism and bargaining centralization similarly differ across types of welfare states – the social democratic and Christian democratic welfare states have relatively high scores on the corporatism index, while corporatism is less prevalent in the liberal welfare states, despite some variation within the categories. Liberal welfare states (for example Ireland, the UK, and US) have lower skill levels while social democratic systems have the highest skill levels; wage dispersion is highest in the liberal welfare states and much less so in the other two types, and social democratic welfare states show considerably higher levels of active labor market policies than the other welfare state types (Huber and Stephens, 2001a: 85–99). Similarly, types of welfare regimes and varieties of capitalism overlap: liberal

welfare states lack coordination and broadly correspond to the category of liberal market economies (see below). In this approach, industrial relations play a central part as the strength, organization, and representation of the working class forms a core component of the explanation for the emergence of the welfare and industrial relations institutions.

Going beyond types of welfare states, some authors have combined the analysis of types of capitalist systems and adjustment to new economic pressures with the insights from the literatures on welfare states and on political institutions and processes. Swank (2002) examines how these different aspects are related and finds that it is not just economic institutions and actors that determine how capitalist states respond to globalization, but also political institutions and processes. The three different types of welfare state – social democratic, corporatist-conservative and liberal – changed in different ways because of the differing forms of interest representation and the varying strengths of left and right political parties in these countries (Swank, 2002: 280–2).

Actor- and institution-centered approaches

The second approach to understanding differences and similarities across advanced industrialized economies looks at a variety of economic institutions and actors emphasizing the way in which coordination is organized. Several of these studies thus include industrial relations and production systems as well as welfare protection systems (for example Rhodes, 2005; Schmidt, 2002: 113; Swank, 2002: 41–4). Many of these studies use these frameworks to understand how national economies have responded to the challenges of demographic changes, European economic integration, and globalization. They find that the organization of the national economy has much to contribute to our understanding of national responses. This approach links together distinct spheres of the political economy – and sometimes the political system – and understands these parts to be connected as 'complementarities', (see Hall and Soskice, 2001a; Höpner, 2005). Authors differ in the emphasis they place on various actors and institutions, the range of countries they use as their empirical base, and the types of classifications they develop.

Maybe the most prominent analysis of varieties of capitalism is the edited volume with the same title by Peter Hall and David Soskice (2001b). In particular the editors' Introduction (Hall and Soskice, 2001a) provides a comprehensive framework outlining the differences between two main types of capitalist economies – liberal market economies (LMEs) and co-ordinated market economies (CMEs) – while also briefly mentioning a third variant, the Mediterranean economies (MEs). The authors emphasize that their interpretation of political economies relies on an actor-centered approach that focuses on how these institutions affect actors' strategic interactions (Hall and Soskice, 2001a: 5).

In a context of economic globalization and restructuring, firms act as 'key agents of adjustment' and therefore constitute the centerpiece of the analysis (2001a: 5). Hall and Soskice adopt a 'relational' conception of firms according to which firms engage in coordination processes in five spheres: industrial relations, vocational training and education, corporate governance, inter-firm relations, and employees. The different institutions in these spheres are not isolated, but instead are interconnected, producing what Hall and Soskice label 'institutional complementarities', where different institutions reinforce and complement each other. Institutions, in this view, are important because they provide support for firms as they attempt to resolve coordination problems (Hall and Soskice, 2001a: 9).

Together, the interlocking, mutually reinforcing institutions and the way firms interact with other actors in these five spheres co-vary systematically to produce two ideal types of capitalist political economy, LMEs and CMEs, and the Mediterranean economies,

which are not systematically discussed. LMEs are characterized by the fact that 'firms coordinate their activities primarily via hierarchies and competitive market arrangements' (Hall and Soskice, 2001a: 8), and the market mechanism based on supply and demand is, by and large, driven by factors identified in the liberal or neoclassical economic model. The US and the UK serve as standard ideal-type cases of this type of economy. In CMEs, by contrast, firms' coordination depends more heavily on non-market relationships (Hall and Soskice, 2001a: 8). Thus, compared to LMEs, CMEs display higher levels of cooperation among actors, which takes time to develop (Hall and Soskice, 2001a: 13). Hall and Soskice do not provide any normative evaluation about which system is better or preferable. Instead, they conclude that each of these ideal types has comparative advantages that are used by specific industries. For example, high-skill, high-wage industries find that CMEs with their patient capital, generous welfare systems and publicly-supported training regimes provide a better economic environment, while low-wage, low-skill industries that respond quickly to changing market demands find LMEs more advantageous (2001a: 40–1).

Hall and Soskice's approach grounds comparative analysis in a clear theoretical framework and directs attention to a wide range of economic institutions (*pace* Albert, 1993). However, the approach has been criticized from various perspectives. For example, one of the criticisms of VoC has been the fact that industrial relations play only a minor part in firms' coordination strategies, and that power relationships between unions and employers as well as class conflict are underemphasized (Crouch, 2005: 80; Howell, 2003; 2005). While Hall and Soskice (2001a) have little to say about class conflict in LMEs, the assumption of the congruency of class interests is particularly evident in the volume's discussion of CMEs: organized production systems and their complementary welfare protection systems benefit not just labor, but also employers, who see comparative advantages in such arrangements. This emphasis on a minimum of cross-class consensus in coordinated economies is mirrored in research focused on the role of employers in the creation of these systems including their welfare states (for example Mares, 2001; Swenson, 2002).[1]

A second main criticism of Hall and Soskice is that in assigning a central role to the firm they downplay the role of the state. Howell (2005) argues that the British state played a key role in the reconstruction of industrial relations throughout the twentieth century. More generally, Weiss (2003) contends that states continue to play a key role in the regulation of economic policy, constructing the fiscal and other environments within which firms make decisions. Finally, while Hall and Soskice's approach is able to explain institutional stability through the notion of complementarities, it is perhaps less well equipped to account for the type of radical institutional change witnessed in the UK after 1979 or in Ireland after the first social pact in 1987 (for these and additional critiques, see Crouch, 2005: 80–2; Hamann and Kelly, 2007; Howell, 2005; Pontusson, 2005).

Other authors have responded to these weaknesses by constructing their own typologies. Schmidt (2002) identifies three types of capitalist economies: market capitalism, embodied by the US and the UK; managed capitalism, practiced by central and northern European countries (for example Germany, Netherlands, Sweden); and state capitalism, prevalent in France and Italy. These types are distinct along three dimensions: business relations, including inter-firm relations, industry-finance relations, and investment patterns; the role of the government in the economy and the characteristics of the state; and the structure of the wage bargaining system and the role of the government in labor regulation (Schmidt, 2002: 113). She thus adds an in-depth analysis of cases outside of the LME–CME classification, and by looking at case studies over time rather than cross-sectional 'slices', also incorporates dynamics of change (Schmidt, 2002: 111).

Amable (2003) develops five models of capitalism and tests the robustness of his classification against a large number of indicators. Based on a combination of five institutional spheres – 'product-market competition; the wage-labor nexus and labor-market institutions; the financial intermediation sector and corporate governance; social protection and the welfare state; and the education sector' (Amable, 2003: 14) – he establishes a set of linkages and institutional complementarities between these spheres. The resulting clusters are identified as the market-based model, the continental European model, the Social-Democratic model, the Mediterranean model, and the Asian model (cf. Kitschelt et al., 1999: 430–4 for a similar, fourfold typology but without the Mediterranean model). Coates (2000: 9–11) contends that different 'models of capitalism' can be distinguished according to the actors that control decisions about production and investment: in market-led capitalisms it is the firm that predominates; in state-led capitalisms, economic decision making is shared between firms and the state, as in Japan or South Korea; and finally in 'negotiated or consensual capitalism', economic decisions involve the three social partners, firms, trade unions and the state, as in Germany or Scandinavia.

These and other classifications and typologies (see for example Boyer, 2005; Whitley, 1999) agree on a distinct variety of capitalism, variously called liberal market or market-led capitalism and typified by the US and UK. Where there is disagreement is over how to classify the remaining advanced capitalist countries, particularly those in Western Europe. Do these countries constitute two groups, the co-ordinated market economies and the Mediterranean economies, or should the Scandinavian economies be grouped as an additional type? Similar disagreement concerns the theoretical basis for classification. Some analyses start from a theoretical framework, such as the transaction costs model of coordination, and proceed to construct a logical typology based on modes of coordination (Hall and Soskice, 2001a). Others proceed inductively, examining a large body of evidence on institutions and outcomes and attempting to fit a typology to the data

(Amable, 2003). Of particular interest here is the way industrial relations are woven into the analyses of capitalism, and the extent to which the VoC approach furthers our understanding of industrial relations.

LINKS BETWEEN VARIETIES OF CAPITALISM AND INDUSTRIAL RELATIONS INSTITUTIONS

How, then, are the types of capitalism linked to industrial relations? What is the use of establishing typologies of capitalism in the context of industrial relations? Although Hall and Soskice claim there are no sustained and dramatic macro-economic performance differences between CMEs and LMEs, they also point to significant *labor market* differences. Specifically, LMEs are likely to show higher rates of employment and of income inequality than CMEs (Hall and Soskice, 2001a: 21–2). Soskice (1999) presents a more dynamic approach and examines whether different varieties of capitalism have affected how labor relations have changed since the 1980s. He finds that organized labor has remained 'incorporated', in some fashion, in the non-market coordination processes present in CMEs, whereas organized labor has been progressively excluded in the LMEs, which rely on market coordination between employers while the state remains at 'arm's length' (Soskice, 1999: 103). According to Hall and Soskice (2001a), the types of capitalism have distinctive industrial relations. For instance, LMEs tend to feature less regulated and more flexible labor markets with weaker unions, less centralized bargaining and less employment protection. The lack of employer coordination means that it is difficult for the state to negotiate with business collectively (Soskice, 1999: 110). Union strength is critical because in LMEs, strong unions are considered to weaken competitiveness by driving up production costs (King and Wood, 1999: 387). By contrast in CMEs, employers have an interest in strong unions because they 'form an essential part of productive strategies

focusing on high-skill, high-quality export manufacturing goods' (King and Wood, 1999: 387). Looking at industrial relations in more detail, we find that the VoC classifications can assist research on industrial relations in six ways.

First, because of variations in the role of markets across countries we would expect corresponding variations in the forms and degree of organization of the industrial relations actors and their relationships. Amable (2003) in particular posits we would expect significant differences in bargaining coordination, union density, and industrial conflict between the five varieties of capitalism he identifies. Hall and Soskice (2001a: 24–25), in contrast, find that CMEs display higher levels of bargaining coordination and coverage, as well as lower levels of industrial conflict, but will not necessarily show higher union density compared to LMEs (see also Thelen, 2001). Furthermore, CMEs rely on 'industrial relations systems in which unions play an important part and which allow *cooperative industrial relations* within the company and coordinated wage bargaining across companies' (Soskice, 1999: 106–7, emphasis in the original).

Second, differences in welfare state regimes across VoCs are associated with differences in labor supply and labor force composition. Liberal welfare states typically have a larger low-wage sector compared to Christian democratic welfares states. As the low-wage sector tends to employ relatively large numbers of women, female participation rates are often higher in the liberal welfares states (Huber and Stephens, 2001b: 117–8). In other words, social policy is instrumental in shaping labor supply (Esping-Andersen, 1990: 150).

Third, varieties of capitalism differ systematically in the skill composition of their labor forces, which in turn are linked to the business strategies of firms. For instance, the generous unemployment benefits found in the CMEs provide incentives for individuals to go through industry-specific training at low wages, which in turn makes it possible and profitable for employers to invest in high-skill industries (Estevez-Abe et al., 2001). LMEs, in contrast, operate with lower skill levels and flexible labor markets and less generous unemployment benefits (Mares, 2001). Thus, industrial relations factors (wage protection) interact with welfare systems (employment and unemployment protection) in the area of skill formation and are associated with different types of production regimes.

Fourth, differences in the training and welfare regimes of national capitalism are linked to wage bargaining institutions: coordinated wage bargaining systems would be expected where industry-specific skills are important, while weakly coordinated systems would be found where general skills matter most. This is because wage determination systems are related to wage protection, which 'reinforces the effects of *employment* and *unemployment protection* by reducing the risk that the wage levels for specific skills might drop radically in the future' (Estevez-Abe et al., 2001:153; emphasis in the original). Within CMEs, production strategies centered around highly skilled workers face the problem that those workers can be 'poached' by other firms (Hall and Soskice, 2001a: 24). Industrial relations institutions need to address this problem through wage bargaining institutions and extension mechanisms that assure comparable wages for specific skill levels across an industry. Coordinated bargaining should therefore enhance worker job tenure at firms and preempt inflationary trends (Hall and Soskice, 2001a: 24–5). Empirical evidence from 18 OECD countries broadly supports these theoretically developed linkages.

Fifth, varieties of capitalism may be useful in understanding labor market outcomes such as wage inequality (see Huber and Stephens, 2001b; Rueda and Pontusson, 2000). Since trade unions promote pay equality the more rapid demise of union density in the LMEs might result in greater pay inequality compared to the CMEs. However, it could also be the case that bargaining coverage, either as well as or instead of union density, has the greater impact on pay inequality. Insofar as centralized bargaining takes wages out of competition between firms it would be expected to yield less wage inequality than under more decentralized arrangements. Also, pay trends might be affected, directly or indirectly, by the higher unemployment often found in the LMEs.

And finally, Höpner (2005: 334) points out that the understanding of industrial relations as part of a larger web of institutions can have important policy ramifications. Proponents of particular reforms thus need to exercise caution when attempting to import success strategies from other countries. What 'works' in one particular institutional setting might not necessarily have the same effect in a different set of economic institutions; functional equivalents might need to be carefully defined and sought. Moreover, changing one part of the set of 'complementary' institutions might have ramifications for some or all of those institutions as well. To illustrate, Heery and Adler (2004) have shown that where bargaining coverage is high and uncoupled from union density, unions have relatively weak incentives to invest resources in recruiting and organizing new members. In contrast, where coverage is closely tied to density, as in the LMEs, unions have far more powerful incentives to engage in organizing.

DO VARIETIES OF INDUSTRIAL RELATIONS CORRESPOND TO VARIETIES OF CAPITALISM?

While Hall and Soskice (2001a) suggest that IR should systematically vary across types of capitalism as they form part of an interconnected set of complementary institutions, some of the contributions in their edited volume hint that IR do not always fit neatly into the different varieties of capitalism. Italy is a case in point: while labeled an 'ambiguous' case that is classed as a 'Mediterranean' economy in the introductory chapter (Hall and Soskice, 2001a: 21), Thelen in her chapter on labor politics in the same volume characterizes Italy as a CME. She reasons that Italy's industrial relations system resembles that of CMEs rather than that of

LMEs, in particular with respect to bargaining patterns (Thelen, 2001: 88–9). Thus, while industrial relations are part of a set of complementary institutions, sometimes they apparently take on a character of their own that does not necessarily mesh well with the other institutions. This might be particularly the case for the understudied 'Mediterranean' cases that are sometimes characterized by a lack of institutional complementarities (see Crouch, 2005: 71–2). We observed earlier that several authors (Amable, 2003; Hyman, 2004) argue that the Northern and Southern European economies should be distinguished from the prototypical coordinated economies, such as Germany, and from the LMEs. To see whether this fourfold typology rather than a threefold classification scheme makes sense for industrial relations, we have examined 20 OECD countries along a series of indicators commonly used in the industrial relations literature (Perraton and Clift, 2004): union density and union structure, bargaining structure and bargaining coverage, employment protection, income inequality, industrial conflict, and unemployment rates. We address three questions: are there continuing and significant differences in patterns of industrial relations between varieties of capitalism? Is there evidence of convergence? And how can we account for significant changes over time? We rely on comparisons of means and medians because the small number of cases in each group precludes meaningful statistical testing (cf also Huber and Stephens, 2001a: Tables 4.2– 4.4). Overall the data have produced a broad clustering of four groups as presented in the following tables and discussion.

According to Golden et al. (1999) the type of capitalist system had little systematic effect on changes in union density between 1950 and 1989. Union density decline was most pronounced in Austria (CME), the US (LME), France and Italy (ME), and Japan (considered by Hall and Soskice as a particular type of CME, 2001a: 34). However, these data cover only 12 countries and do not go beyond 1989. If we include additional cases and take the time series up to 2000, the evidence fits better with the VoC approach (see Table 7.1).

Broadly, countries fall into three clusters with respect to union density: the LMEs, the four Scandinavian countries – three of which operate the Ghent system of unemployment insurance (Western, 1997: 193) – and a much more heterogeneous CME group. Table 7.1 suggests that density decline has indeed been steeper in the six LMEs for the 1980–2000 time period compared to the remaining 14 non-LMEs (median percentage point declines were 20 and 9 respectively). However, also striking are the differences within the 'non-LME' group. The four Scandinavian economies stand out here because density rose in one of them and fell only slightly in the other three. Equally striking is the variation within pairs of countries that are otherwise very similar. For example, since the late 1980s density has risen in Spain but fallen in Portugal. If we look at changes over time, Table 7.1 shows that the gap between the Scandinavian economies and the other countries has actually widened: there is no evidence of convergence.

Union structure displays even more systematic variation across countries and again the evidence suggests that countries can be meaningfully grouped into several categories. Unitary confederations are largely confined to the LMEs but are also found in Austria and Greece. Occupational divisions are found both in the four Scandinavian countries and in a number of CMEs. Political and religious cleavages are more prevalent in the Mediterranean economies and in some of the CMEs (Belgium and the Netherlands for example) (Ebbinghaus and Visser, 2000).

Bargaining structure is increasingly difficult to measure because bargaining is often conducted at multiple levels within national economies and because of significant variation in the coordinating capacity of the social partners. Nonetheless Visser and colleagues (cited in Calmfors et al., 2001) have attempted to produce a composite measure that takes into account the degree of centralization of bargaining as well as the degree of coordination exercised by the unions at each level (Table 7.2).[2] The data show that a significant degree of bargaining

Table 7.1 Union density (%) and density change in 20 OECD countries 1980–2000

Country	1980	1990	2000	Absolute change 1980–2000, % points	Relative change 1980–2000, %
Denmark	79	75	74	−5	−6
Finland	69	72	76	+7	+10
Norway	58	59	54	−4	−7
Sweden	80	80	79	−1	−1
Mean N. Europe	**71.5**	**71.5**	**71**	**−0.5**	
France	18	10	10	−8	−44
Greece	39	32	27	−12	−31
Italy	50	39	35	−15	−30
Portugal	61	32	24	−37	−61
Spain	7	11	15	+8	+114
Mean MEs	**35**	**25**	**22**	**−12.8**	
Austria	57	47	37	−20	−35
Belgium	54	54	56	+2	+4
Germany	35	31	25	−10	−29
Netherlands	35	25	23	−12	−34
Switzerland	31	24	18	−13	−42
Mean C. Europe	**42**	**36**	**32**	**−10.6**	
Australia	48	40	25	−23	−48
Canada	35	33	28	−7	−20
Ireland	57	51	38	−19	−33
New Zealand	69	51	23	−46	−67
UK	51	39	31	−20	−39
USA	22	15	13	−9	−41
Mean LMEs	**47**	**38**	**26**	**−20.7**	

Source: OECD 2004a, Table 3.3.

Table 7.2 Bargaining coordination index and rankings in 15 OECD countries 1973–77 and 1993–97

Country	1973–77	1993–97
Denmark	0.639 (4)	0.341 (9)
Finland	0.642 (3)	0.465 (3)
Norway	0.419 (6)	0.419 (5)
Sweden	0.745 (2)	0.389 (7)
Mean N. Europe	**0.616 (3.75)**	**0.404 (6.0)**
France	0.104 (15)	0.079 (15)
Italy	0.382 (8)	0.324 (10)
Spain	0.395 (7)	0.343 (8)
Portugal	0.223 (13)	0.284 (11)
Mean MEs	**0.276 (10.75)**	**0.258 (11.0)**
Austria	0.823 (1)	0.648 (2)
Belgium	0.521 (5)	0.442 (4)
Germany	0.346 (11)	0.243 (12)
Netherlands	0.340 (12)	0.393 (6)
Switzerland	0.209 (14)	0.194 (13)
Mean C. Europe	**0.448 (8.6)**	**0.384 (7.4)**
Ireland	0.365 (10)	0.759 (1)
UK	0.370 (9)	0.141 (14)
Mean LMEs	**0.368 (9.5)**	**0.450 (7.5)**

Source: Calmfors et al., 2001: Table 4.2. 0 =Low, 1 =High.

decentralization has occurred and that the differences between types of capitalism have shrunk. On the other hand the rank ordering of countries and types of countries has remained remarkably stable over a 25-year period (with the exception of one or two countries such as Ireland and the Netherlands) so that the Scandinavian and the Mediterranean economies clearly stand out from the rest and from each other.

Bargaining coverage rates are somewhat more clear-cut in that they remained quite stable and high during the 1980s and 1990s in most non-LMEs compared to the LMEs. Within the latter group, they fell significantly in the UK and New Zealand and to a lesser degree in the US (Table 7.3). It is also evident that levels of bargaining coverage are diverging, not converging, across the varieties of capitalism. Over the past 20 years, coverage has risen slightly in the Scandinavian and Mediterranean economies, remained stable

Table 7.3 Collective bargaining coverage (%) in 20 OECD countries 1980–2000

Country	1980	1990	2000	Change 1980–2000
Denmark	70+	70+	80+	+10
Finland	90+	90+	90+	0
Norway	70+	70+	70+	0
Sweden	80+	80+	90+	+10
Mean N. Europe	**78**	**78**	**83**	**+5**
France	80+	90+	90+	+10
Greece	N/a	N/a	N/a	N/a
Italy	80+	80+	80+	0
Portugal	70+	70+	80+	+10
Spain	60+	70+	80+	+20
Mean MEs	**73**	**78**	**83**	**+10**
Austria	95+	95+	95+	0
Belgium	90+	90+	90+	0
Germany	80+	80+	68	−12
Netherlands	70+	70+	80+	+10
Switzerland	50+	50+	40+	−10
Mean C. Europe	**77**	**77**	**75**	**−2**
Australia	80+	80+	80+	0
Canada	37	38	32	−5
Ireland	N/a	N/a	N/a	N/a
New Zealand	60+	60+	25+	−35
UK	70+	40+	30+	−40
USA	26	18	14	−12
Mean LMEs	**55**	**47**	**36**	**−19**

Source: OECD 2004a, Table 3.3.

in the central European CMEs but declined sharply in the LMEs.

We turn now to the degree of protection for employees in the labor market embodied in the legal regulation of dismissal and redundancy. As Table 7.4 shows two groups of countries stand out: the Mediterranean economies still provide a relatively high degree of protection for employees while the LMEs, on the other hand, provide far fewer rights. Looking at trends we find a degree of convergence, with some relaxation of legislation in the Mediterranean economies and a mild increase in the level of employment protection in the LMEs.

Another labor market outcome that has been extensively investigated by IR researchers is the degree of income inequality both at a point in time across countries and over time. Hall and Soskice (2001a) posit that pay inequality would be one of the main areas in which varieties of capitalism would show systematic differences. According to recent OECD data,

a combination of union density and bargaining structure (not bargaining coverage) appears to best predict earnings inequality (OECD, 2004a: 160–161). Table 7.5 shows that the most distinctive profiles and the clearest trends are to be found in the Scandinavian countries and in the LMEs while developments in the CMEs and the Mediterranean economies are less clear. In the Scandinavian countries pay inequality was relatively low in the early 1980s and has more or less remained stable through the late 1990s. In the LMEs, by contrast, pay inequality was already high in the early 1980s and has increased still further in the intervening years. If we return to Table 7.1 it is clear that these inequality profiles are strongly associated with trends in union density. Where density has remained high – as in Scandinavia – inequality has remained low; where union density has fallen most sharply, as in the LMEs, inequality has dramatically increased. As with density we observe a degree of divergence, not

Table 7.4 Employment protection legislation in 19 OECD countries, late 1980s–2003

Country	Late 1980s	Late 1990s	2003	Change late 1980s–2003
Denmark	1.5	1.5	1.5	0
Finland	2.8	2.3	2.2	−0.5
Norway	2.3	2.3	2.3	0
Sweden	2.9	2.9	2.9	0
Mean N. Europe	**2.4**	**2.3**	**2.2**	**−0.2**
France	2.3	2.3	2.5	+0.2
Greece	2.5	2.3	2.4	−0.1
Italy	1.8	1.8	1.8	0
Portugal	4.8	4.3	4.2	−0.6
Spain	3.9	2.6	2.6	−1.3
Mean MEs	**3.1**	**2.7**	**2.7**	**−0.4**
Austria	2.9	2.9	2.4	−0.5
Belgium	1.7	1.7	1.7	0
Germany	2.6	2.7	2.7	+0.1
Netherlands	3.1	3.1	3.1	0
Switzerland	1.2	1.2	1.2	0
Mean C. Europe	**2.3**	**2.3**	**2.2**	**−0.1**
Australia	1.0	1.5	1.5	+0.5
Canada	1.3	1.3	1.3	0
Ireland	1.6	1.6	1.6	0
New Zealand	N/a	1.4	1.7	+0.3
UK	0.9	0.9	1.1	+0.2
USA	0.2	0.2	0.2	0
Mean LMEs	**1.0**	**1.2**	**1.2**	**+0.2**

Source: OECD 2004b, Table 2.A2.1. Scale from 0 (Low) to 6 (High).

Table 7.5 Gross earnings inequality (90:10 ratios) for full time employees in 19 OECD countries 1980–1984 to 1995–1999

Country	1980–1984	1990–1994	1995–1999	Change, 1st to last period
Denmark	2.17	2.16	N/a	−0.1
Finland	2.49	2.39	2.36	−0.13
Norway	N/a	N/a	1.96	N/a
Sweden	2.01	2.11	2.23	+0.22
Mean N. Europe	**2.22**	**2.22**	**2.18**	**−0.04**
France	3.18	3.21	3.07	−0.11
Greece	N/a	N/a	N/a	N/a
Italy	2.29*	2.35	2.40	+0.11
Portugal	3.56*	3.76	N/a	+0.20
Spain	N/a	N/a	N/a	N/a
Mean MEs	**3.01**	**3.11**	**N/a**	**+0.10**
Austria	3.45	3.56	N/a	+0.11
Belgium	2.40*	2.28	N/a	−0.12
Germany	2.88	2.79	2.87	−0.01
Netherlands	2.47	2.60	2.85	+0.38
Switzerland	N/a	2.71	2.69	−0.02
Mean C. Europe	**2.80**	**2.79**	**2.80**	**0**
Australia	2.88	2.82	2.94	+0.06
Canada	N/a	N/a	3.65	N/a
Ireland	N/a	4.06	3.97	−0.09
New Zealand	2.89	3.06	3.28	+0.39
UK	3.09	3.39	3.45	+0.36
USA	3.91	4.39	4.59	+0.68
Mean LMEs	**3.19**	**3.54**	**3.65**	**+0.46**

*1985–1989
Source: OECD 2004a, Table 3.2.

Table 7.6 Industrial conflict in selected OECD countries 1985–2003 (days lost per 1000 workers)

Country	1985–1989	1994–1998	1999–2003	Change (%, 1985–1989 to 1999–2003)
Denmark	240	309	43	−82.1
Finland	340	183	49	−85.6
Norway	140	103	63	−55.0
Sweden	120	43	38	−68.3
Median N. Europe	**190**	**143**	**46**	**−75.2**
France	60	97	N/a	N/a
Greece	1480	N/a	N/a	N/a
Italy	300	113	126	−58.0
Portugal	90	24	17	−81.1
Spain	650	256	203	−68.8
Median MEs	**300**	**61**	**126**	**−68.8**
Austria	0	1	81	N/a
Belgium	N/a	29	N/a	N/a
Germany	0	4	4	N/a
Netherlands	10	26	11	N/a
Switzerland	0	3	3	N/a
Median C. Europe	**0**	**4**	**8**	**N/a**
Australia	230	87	57	−75.2
Canada	280	209	163	−41.8
Ireland	290	73	70	−75.9
New Zealand	500	30	19	−96.2
UK	180	22	24	−86.7
USA	90	43	45	−50.0
Median LMEs	**255**	**58**	**51**	**−75.6**

Sources: Bird 1991, Table 1; Monger 2005, Table 1.

convergence, among the advanced capitalist countries.

Does the level of industrial conflict vary across the varieties of capitalism (Amable, 2003; Hall and Soskice, 2001a: 24–25)? Table 7.6 suggests that the picture is again complex. Measured by days lost per 1000 workers in recent years (1999–2003), the level of industrial conflict in 6 LMEs – 51 days lost per 1000 workers – was only a little higher than in 11 non-LMEs (43 days lost per 1000). However, if the non-LME countries are divided into three groups a different pattern emerges. The central European CMEs are less conflict-prone than the LMEs but the highest levels of conflict are found in several Scandinavian (Denmark and Finland) and Mediterranean economies (Spain and Italy) as well as in the LMEs. Looking at changes over time it is clear that while strike activity has generally declined in most countries, trends in the central European economies have moved in the opposite direction, with a modest rise

in days lost through strikes over the past 20 years.

Finally we examine levels and trends in unemployment, one of the most widely-used indicators of labor market functioning (Table 7.7). The data indicate that the Mediterranean economies have operated at relatively high rates of unemployment for many years, while the Scandinavian economies have generally displayed the lowest levels of unemployment (Portugal and Finland excepted in each category). In general, unemployment was lower in most countries in recent years (1999–2003) compared to the early 1990s.

Interpreting the evidence

What does this evidence suggest about the utility of the VoC approach as a way of understanding cross-national variations in industrial relations? For some indicators the distinction between LMEs and 'other' types of capitalism does make sense.

Table 7.7   Standardized unemployment rates (%) in selected OECD countries 1985–2003

Country	1985–1989	1994–1998	1999–2003
Denmark	6.3	6.2	4.8
Finland	5.0	14.1	9.4
Norway	3.0	4.7	3.7
Sweden	2.2	9.2	5.5
Mean N. Europe	**4.1**	**8.6**	**5.9**
France	10.0	11.7	9.3
Greece	N/a	9.7	10.8
Italy	9.3	11.5	9.8
Portugal	7.3	6.6	4.8
Spain	20.0	17.8	11.5
Median MEs	**11.7**	**11.4**	**9.3**
Austria	N/a	4.2	4.0
Belgium	9.4	9.5	7.5
Germany	6.4	8.7	8.4
Netherlands	7.8	5.6	3.0
Switzerland	N/a	3.8	3.1
Median C. Europe	**7.9**	**6.4**	**5.2**
Australia	7.4	8.4	6.5
Canada	8.9	9.4	7.4
Ireland	16.2	11.1	4.6
New Zealand	5.0	6.9	5.6
UK	9.9	7.8	5.3
USA	5.8	5.3	4.9
Mean LMEs	**8.9**	**8.2**	**5.7**

Sources: OECD 2004a Statistical Annex Table A; OECD 2001 Statistical Annex Table 22.

Bargaining coverage shows a clear divide between LMEs and non-LME countries whereas industrial conflict shows an equally clear divide between the central European CMEs and the rest. Beyond these comparisons the binary divide is of little value because the advanced capitalist countries more commonly fall into four groups rather than two. In addition to the LMEs and central European economies, the Mediterranean economies and the Scandinavian economies show distinct patterns of unionism and industrial relations structures and outcomes.

Second, the data raise questions about the logic of using specific indicators as a basis for classification. This includes concerns about between-group and within-group variation. For instance, profound differences are visible between Ireland and the UK, although both are commonly classed as liberal market economies. Which indicators are most important in assigning countries to categories?

Third, the data point to convergence on some dimensions of industrial relations but divergence on others. In four areas the evidence clearly indicates convergence in recent years: bargaining structures have become more decentralized almost everywhere; employment protection laws have been relaxed in the strictest regimes but tightened in the weakest regimes, producing convergence toward a moderate level of protection; strike rates have fallen in most, though not all, countries; and the dispersion in unemployment rates is now far lower than in the 1980s or 1990s. On the other hand union density rates, bargaining coverage, and earnings inequality have all diverged and the gaps between the different varieties of capitalism have increased. But given that capitalist economies change over time, how can we judge whether the changes produce more coherent and cohesive categories or blur the distinctions between categories? Again, the answer will most likely depend on the indicators that are chosen as most significant. Thus, the convergence-divergence debate is unlikely to be resolved by empirical evidence alone.

Fourth, how are we to account for significant changes over time? In line with some of the evidence on divergence, Thelen (2001) argues that the changes in industrial relations that can be observed across advanced economies are different in LMEs compared to CMEs. In LMEs, the logic of production and competition means that firms are interested in weakening 'overarching institutions for the collective representation of labor' since plant-level bargaining flexibility without strong sectoral or national unions and bargaining structures better meshes with internal labor markets (Thelen, 2001: 72). Firms in CMEs, on the other hand, continue to rely on highly skilled workers for 'their competitive strategies around high-quality, high value-added production that depends on a high degree of stability and cooperation with labor' (Thelen, 2001: 73). Therefore, employers, much like workers, are supportive of collective representation of labor above the firm level (Thelen, 2001: 73). While deregulation is an appropriate term to describe the developments in IR in LMEs and reflects the low coordination capacity among employers, CMEs are much more aptly described by a process of 'controlled decentralization' or 're-regulation', where coordination continues, albeit often at lower levels, and matches non-market coordination among employers (Thelen, 2001: 78–80).

The most dramatic declines in union density and bargaining coverage have occurred in LMEs, which might reflect the increased role of market regulation and the power of employers. But bargaining coverage has not declined in all of the LMEs and union membership decline varies considerably. In addition most LMEs have been operating at historically low levels of unemployment, which ought to have facilitated some recovery of union membership, but generally this has not happened.

DIRECTIONS FOR FURTHER RESEARCH: A DYNAMIC PERSPECTIVE ON POLITICS, VoC, AND INDUSTRIAL RELATIONS

Overall, the VoC literature has been criticized for taking on a relatively static view of economic institutions, and for being poorly equipped to account for change (Streeck and Thelen, 2005: 5; and see above). It has also been criticized for downplaying the role of politics and political actors. These two issues, however, are linked because a focus on political parties and the state makes it possible to account better for significant change in industrial relations systems.

The VoC approach centers on institutional equilibria of interconnected institutions and does not systematically incorporate an account of change. This does not mean, however, that the framework *could* not encompass mechanisms of institutional change. For example, institutional change may be the outcome of incremental change resulting

from ongoing contestation among a number of actors with competing interests (Hall and Thelen, 2005). In other cases, however, it may result from government action. Governments have the power not just to pass economic policies that may indirectly result in institutional change, but can more directly modify the institutional makeup of the economy, as well as the structure and outcomes of industrial relations, such as wage inequality. One additional variable to account for variation in such outcomes is party composition of the government. Rueda and Pontusson (2000: 380), for example, find that whether the government is dominated by the left or the right matters for wage inequality, particularly in LMEs. This is because in CMEs (roughly equivalent to SMEs in Rueda and Pontusson, 2000) wage bargaining is more widely institutionalized and less dominated by governmental policies such as minimum wage legislation than in LMEs. In other words, due to the scope of collective bargaining, governments in CMEs have less opportunity to influence wages directly, and consequently, partisanship matters less. Where bargaining is less encompassing, as in LMEs, on the other hand, parties in government have more of an influence on legislating wages, which makes partisanship more meaningful. Iversen and Cusack (2000: 346), in contrast, find that governments have expanded welfare states through transfer payments and social services provision regardless of party ideology, but 'partisanship continues to be important in the redistributive aspect of the welfare state'. Together with labor market institutions, partisanship of the government helps explain the responses of governments to the pressures of deindustrialization (Iversen and Cusack, 2000: 316).

To explain welfare expenditures, Swank (2002) finds that it is not just economic institutions and actors that determine how capitalist states respond to globalization, but also political institutions and processes. He distinguishes between Nordic social democracies, corporatist conservative welfare states, and liberal welfare states, similar to the models established by Esping-Andersen (1990).

Swank (2002: 5) contends that welfare state retrenchment can be expected to be most pronounced in the small liberal welfare states since their 'political institutions and pro-grammatic structures' facilitate retrenchment policies, while those of the larger West European welfare states are more likely to blunt pressures for retrenchment produced by global capital flows (see also Iversen, 2005).

A focus on partisanship and party com-position of governments can also provide important insights into the question of how change in economic institutions and types of capitalism comes about, or why institutions are stable (cf also Golden et al., 1999: 223; Huber and Stephens, 2001a). This is not to deny that economic actors sometimes have vested interests in modifying existing institutions, or that much change results from the actions of economic actors. Rather, we want to point to the linkages between economic and political actors and institutional change (or stability) that are sometimes neglected in the IR literature. For instance, union membership decline in the LMEs was not simply the result of changing labor and product markets because these changes were themselves influenced by governments' eco-nomic and labor relations policies paralleling Huber and Stephens' observations on the importance of party leanings for welfare state policies. Golden et al. (1999: 223), for instance, suspect that 'government policy and politics played at least as important a role as the market in promoting such catastrophic collapse' of union membership in the UK and the US (cf also King and Wood, 1999).

Prior to the 1980s, the political-economic institutions and processes present in the UK can be loosely described as a 'mixed form' in Hall and Soskice's (2001a) ideal-type con-figuration of LMEs and CMEs. This 'hybrid' constellation combined CME characteristics of industry-wide bargaining and coverage rates of around 70 per cent; training was similarly coordinated at the industry level; and internal labor markets within many large firms helped retain employees. These features were coupled with LME characteristics in the

spheres of corporate governance and inter-firm relations (Howell, 2005; Kelly, 2006). Only when Margaret Thatcher, elected as Prime Minister in 1979, legislated a series of sweeping reforms in the political economy did Britain metamorphose into a paradigmatic example of an LME. These reforms were not the result of some inherent movement of economic institutions into a system where the parts fit together more coherently than before, or some internal movement toward an equilibrium state. Instead, they were the result of governmental action and legislation (see Walsh and Crawford, 2003 for details of the equally far-reaching legislative assault on unions in New Zealand; and see Hamann, 2005 for an explanation of institutional stability in Spain focused on politics).

Ireland presents an interesting contrasting case, where an economy that is generally described as a classic LME has adopted some coordination strategies rather typical of CMEs. The 1987 Programme for National Recovery (PNR) was the first in a series of social pacts that would not have been expected in a liberal market economy. It was the government that pushed for a social pact in response to economic problems and electoral pressures (Hamann and Kelly, 2007). While the overall organization of the Irish economy might still, by and large, reflect LME characteristics, wage restraint is now coordinated centrally by political and economic actors, which questions the classification of Ireland as an ideal-type LME. The Irish case again demonstrates that shifts in economic institutions can be initiated by governments, and that the electoral interests of governing parties can play an active role in changing economic institutions.

Austria is another striking illustration of the importance of government partisanship and interests in modifying economic institutions (see Hamann and Kelly, 2007). Austria has been one of the most corporatist coun-tries in Western Europe in the post-war period, and the social partners were heavily involved and integrated in political economy institutions and decision-making until the populist-right Freedom Party (FPÖ) joined the conservative People's Party (ÖVP) in a coalition government in 2000. Soon after, the government for the first time passed policies unilaterally that previously would have been negotiated through the corporatist structures, such as a major pension reform, sparking an unprecedented wave of strikes and mobilizations. In addition, the government attacked some of the institutional foundations of corporatism in an attempt to diminish the power of the unions (and also employers) in the policy-making process. Again, governmental ideology and policy was instrumental in altering the institutions and processes of Austria's political economy.

CONCLUSION

The VoC literature continues to generate both debate and criticism. In our view, it facilitates a rigorous and systematic comparative study of both national capitalisms and national systems of industrial relations. It does so by grounding comparative analysis in a theoretical framework, although Hall and Soskice's version privileges the firm at the expense of other actors. The VoC literature is also valuable for IR researchers because of its insistence on looking at the interconnections between institutions, such as welfare systems, wage bargaining systems, and skill levels.

Even though the evidence reinforces the value of grouping national IR systems into clusters, it calls into question the utility of the widely-used CME vs. LME dichotomy. The empirical data indicate that it is meaningful to distinguish the Northern, Central and Southern European economies in addition to the LMEs. Are these different types of IR systems converging or diverging? Industrial relations are actually more complex and cannot be reduced to a simple trend in one direction or the other. On some dimensions, IR systems appear to be converging while on others, they are diverging. Consequently, we need to start asking more precise and better theorized questions about IR, linked to other spheres of national political economies,

to move beyond what is becoming a rather sterile debate.

For future research we propose to focus on the role of the state and political parties in order to understand the reproduction and transformation of IR systems. Despite existing claims that globalization will reduce and heavily constrain the role of national political actors, a growing body of evidence indicates that such actors retain considerable power and must therefore comprise a key part of the explanation for both the persistence and change in IR systems.

NOTES

1 We concentrate here on criticisms of the VoC approach that are closely linked to industrial relations. Many other criticisms have been leveled against the approach, and in particular against Hall and Soskice (2001b) and work based on that volume; see, for example, Allen (2004); Blyth (2003); Coates (2005); Goodin (2003); Höpner (2005); and Watson (2003).

2 The Visser scale incorporates union density and so hence the very low score for France despite the high degree of centralized bargaining. Siaroff (1999) uses an even wider array of measures including strike days lost, union policy and economic performance. But the sheer breadth and inclusiveness of his corporatism measure makes it very difficult to correlate it with other variables.

REFERENCES

Albert, Michel (1993) *Capitalism Against Capitalism.* London: Whurr Publishers.

Allen, Matthew (2004) 'The varieties of capitalism paradigm: not enough variety?', *Socio-Economic Review,* 2 (1): 87–108.

Amable, Bruno (2003) *The Diversity of Modern Capitalism.* Oxford: Oxford University Press.

Armstrong, Philip, Glyn, Andrew and Harrison, John (1991) *Capitalism Since 1945.* Oxford: Blackwell.

Bélanger, Jacques, Edwards, P.K. and Haiven, Larry (eds) (1994) *Workplace Industrial Relations and the Global Challenge.* Ithaca, NY: ILR Press.

Bird, Derek (1991) 'International comparisons of industrial disputes in 1989 and 1990', *Employment Gazette,* 99 (12): 653–58.

Blyth, Mark (2003) 'Same as it never was: Temporality and typology in the varieties of capitalism', *Comparative European Politics,* 1 (2): 215–25.

Boyer, Robert (2005) 'How and why capitalisms differ', *Economy and Society*, 34 (4): 509–57.

Calmfors, Lars, Booth, Alison, Burda, Michael, Checchi, Daniele, Naylor, Robin and Visser, Jelle (2001) 'The future of collective bargaining in Europe', in Tito Boeri, Agar Brugiavini and Lars Calmfors (eds), *The Role of Unions in the Twenty-First Century*. Oxford: Oxford University Press. pp. 1–155.

Coates, David (2000) *Models of Capitalism: Growth and Stagnation in the Modern Era*. Cambridge: Polity Press.

Coates, David (ed.) (2005) *Varieties of Capitalism, Varieties of Approaches*. Houndmills: Palgrave Macmillan.

Crouch, Colin (1993) *Industrial Relations and European State Traditions*. Oxford: Clarendon Press.

Crouch, Colin (2005) *Capitalist Diversity and Change: Recombinant Governance and Institutional Entrepreneurs*. Oxford: Oxford University Press.

Dore, Ronald, Lazonick, William and O'Sullivan, Mary (1999) 'Varieties of capitalism in the twentieth century', *Oxford Review of Economic Policy*, 15 (4): 102–20.

Ebbinghaus, Bernhard and Philip Manow (2001) 'Introduction: studying varieties of welfare capitalism', in Bernhard Ebbinghaus and Philip Manow (eds), *Comparing Welfare Capitalism*. London: Routledge. pp. 1–24.

Ebbinghaus, Bernhard and Visser, Jelle (2000) *Trade Unions in Western Europe Since 1945*. London: Macmillan Reference.

Esping-Andersen, Gøsta (1990) *The Three Worlds of Welfare Capitalism*. Princeton: Princeton University Press.

Estevez-Abe, Margarita, Iversen, Torben and Soskice, David (2001) 'Social protection and the formation of skills: a re-interpretation of the welfare state', in Peter Hall and David Soskice (eds), *Varieties of Capitalism: The Institutional Foundations of Comparative Advantage*. Oxford: Oxford University Press. pp. 145–83.

Golden, Miriam, Wallerstein, Michael and Lange, Peter (1999) 'Postwar trade-union organization and industrial relations in twelve countries', in Herbert Kitschelt, Peter Lange, Gary Marks and John D. Stephens (eds), *Continuity and Change in Contemporary Capitalism*. New York: Cambridge University Press. pp. 194–230.

Goldthorpe, John H. (1984) 'The end of convergence: corporatist and dualist tendencies in modern Western societies', in John H. Goldthorpe (ed.), *Order and Conflict in Contemporary Capitalism: Studies in the Political Economy of Western European Nations*. Oxford: Clarendon Press. pp. 315–43.

Goodin, Robert E. (2003) 'Choose your capitalism?', *Comparative European Politics*, 1 (2): 202–13.

Gospel, Howard and Pendleton, Andrew (2003) 'Finance, corporate governance and the management of labour: A conceptual and comparative analysis', *British Journal of Industrial Relations*, 41 (3): 557–82.

Hall, Peter and Soskice, David (2001a) 'An introduction to varieties of capitalism', in Peter Hall and David Soskice (eds), *Varieties of Capitalism: The Institutional Foundations of Comparative Advantage*. Oxford: Oxford University Press. pp. 1–68.

Hall, Peter and Soskice, David (eds) (2001b) *Varieties of Capitalism: The Institutional Foundations of Comparative Advantage*. Oxford: Oxford University Press.

Hall, Peter and Thelen, Kathleen (2005) 'Institutional change in varieties of capitalism', paper presented at the *American Political Science Association Meeting*, Washington, D.C., September.

Hamann, Kerstin (2005) 'Third-Way Conservatism? The Popular Party and labour relations in Spain', *International Journal of Iberian Studies*, 18 (2): 67–82.

Hamann, Kerstin and Kelly, John (2007) 'Party politics and the re-emergence of social pacts in Western Europe', *Comparative Political Studies*, 40 (8): 971–94.

Heery, Edmund and Adler, Lee (2004) 'Organizing the unorganized', in Carola Frege and John Kelly (eds), *Varieties of Unionism: Strategies for Union Revitalization in a Globalizing Economy*. Oxford: Oxford University Press. pp. 45–69.

Hicks, Alexander and Kenworthy, Lane (2003) 'Varieties of welfare capitalism', *Socio-Economic Review*, 1 (1): 27–61.

Höpner, Martin (2005) 'What connects industrial relations and corporate governance? Explaining institutional complementarity', *Socio-Economic Review*, 3 (2): 331–58.

Howell, Chris (2003) 'Review article: varieties of capitalism: and then there was one?', *Comparative Politics*, 36 (1): 103–24.

Howell, Chris (2005) *Trade Unions and the State: The Construction of Industrial Relations Institutions in Britain, 1890–2000*. Princeton: Princeton University Press.

Huber, Evelyne and Stephens, John D. (2001a) *Development and Crisis of the Welfare State*. Chicago: University of Chicago Press.

Huber, Evelyne and Stephens, John D. (2001b) 'Welfare state and production regimes in the era of retrenchment', in Paul Pierson (ed.), *The New Politics of the Welfare State*. New York: Oxford University Press. pp. 107–45.

Hyman, Richard (2001) *Understanding European Trade Unionism*. London: Sage.

Hyman, Richard (2004) 'Varieties of capitalism, national industrial relations systems and transnational challenges', in Anne-Wit Harzing and Joris van Ruysseveldt (eds), *International Human Resource Management: Managing People Across Borders*. London: Sage. pp. 411–32.

Iversen, Torben (2005) *Capitalism, Democracy, and Welfare*. New York: Cambridge University Press.

Iversen, Torben and Cusack, Thomas R. (2000) 'The causes of welfare state expansion: deindustrialization or globalization?', *World Politics*, 52 (April): 313–49.

Kelly, John (1998) *Rethinking Industrial Relations: Mobilization, Collectivism and Long Waves*. London: Routledge.

Kelly, John (2006) 'Bringing the state back in', *Labor History*, 47 (2): 252–58.

Kerr, Clark, Dunlop, John T., Harbison, Frederick and Myers, Charles A. (1960) *Industrialism and Industrial Man*, 2nd edition 1973. Harmondsworth: Penguin.

King, Desmond and Wood, Stewart (1999) 'The political economy of neoliberalism: Britain and the United States in the 1980s', in Herbert Kitschelt, Peter Lange, Gary Marks and John D. Stephens (eds), *Continuity and Change in Contemporary Capitalism*. New York: Cambridge University Press. pp. 371–97.

Kitschelt, Herbert, Lange, Peter, Marks, Gary and Stephens, John D. (1999) 'Convergence and divergence in advanced capitalist democracies', in Herbert Kitschelt, Peter Lange, Gary Marks and John D. Stephens (eds), *Continuity and Change in Contemporary Capitalism*. New York: Cambridge University Press. pp. 427–60.

Kochan, Thomas A., Lansbury, Russell D. and MacDuffie, John Paul (eds) (1997) *After Lean Production: Evolving Employment Practices in the World Auto Industry*. Ithaca, NY: ILR Press.

Mares, Isabela (2001) 'Firms and the welfare state: when, why, and how does social policy matter to employers?', in Peter Hall and David Soskice (eds), *Varieties of Capitalism: The Institutional Foundations of Comparative Advantage*. Oxford: Oxford University Press. pp. 184–212.

Monger, Joanne (2005) 'International comparisons of labour disputes in 2003', *Labour Market Trends*, 113 (4): 159–204.

OECD (2001) *OECD Employment Outlook 2001*. Paris: Organisation for Economic Cooperation and Development.

OECD (2004a) 'Wage-setting institutions and economic performance', in OECD *Employment Outlook 2004*. Paris: OECD. pp. 127–81.

OECD (2004b) 'Employment protection regulation and labour market performance', in OECD *Employment Outlook 2004*. Paris: OECD. pp. 61–125.

Oliver, Nick and Wilkinson, Barry (1992) *The Japanisation of British Industry, 2nd edition*. Oxford: Blackwell.

Perraton, Jonathan and Clift, Ben (2004) 'So where are national capitalisms now?', in Jonathan Perraton and Ben Clift (eds), *Where Are National Capitalisms Now?* London: Palgrave Macmillan. pp. 195–261.

Piore, Michael F. and Sabel, Charles F. (1984) *The Second Industrial Divide*. New York: Basic Books.

Pizzorno, Alessandro (1978) 'Political exchange and collective identity in industrial conflict', in Colin Crouch and Alessandro Pizzorno (eds), *The Resurgence of Class Conflict in Western Europe Vol 1*. London: Macmillan. pp. 277–98.

Pontusson, Jonas (2005) '"Varieties and commonalities" of capitalism', in David Coates (ed.), *Varieties of Capitalism, Varieties of Approaches*. London: Palgrave Macmillan. pp. 163–88.

Regini, Marino (1984) 'The conditions for political exchange: How concertation emerged and collapsed in Italy and Great Britain', in John H. Goldthorpe (ed.), *Order and Conflict in Contemporary Capitalism: Studies in the Political Economy of Western European Nations*. Oxford: Clarendon Press. pp. 124–42.

Rhodes, Martin (2005) '"Varieties of capitalism" and the political economy of European welfare states', *New Political Economy*, 10 (3): 363–70.

Rueda, David and Pontusson, Jonas (2000) 'Wage inequality and varieties of capitalism', *World Politics*, 52 (April): 350–83.

Schmidt, Vivien (2002) *The Futures of European Capitalism*. New York: Oxford University Press.

Siaroff, Alan (1999) 'Corporatism in 24 industrial democracies: meaning and measurement', *European Journal of Political Research*, 36 (2): 175–205.

Soskice, David (1999) 'Divergent production regimes: coordinated and uncoordinated market economies in the 1980s and 1990s', in Herbert Kitschelt, Peter Lange, Gary Marks and John D. Stephens (eds), *Continuity and Change in Contemporary Capitalism*. New York: Cambridge University Press. pp. 101–34.

Streeck, Wolfgang and Thelen, Kathleen (2005) 'Introduction: institutional change in advanced political economies', in Wolfgang Streeck and Kathleen Thelen (eds), *Beyond Continuity: Institutional Change in Advanced Political Economies*. Oxford: Oxford University Press. pp. 1–39.

Swank, Duane (2002) *Global Capital, Political Institutions, and Policy Change in Developed Welfare States*. Cambridge: Cambridge University Press.

Swenson, Peter (2002) *Capitalists Against Markets: The Making of Labor Markets and Welfare States in the United States and Sweden*. New York: Oxford University Press.

Thelen, Kathleen (2001) 'Varieties of labor politics in the developed democracies', in Peter Hall and David Soskice (eds), *Varieties of Capitalism: The Institutional Foundations of Comparative Advantage*. Oxford: Oxford University Press, pp. 71–103.

Turnbull, Peter, Blyton, Paul and Harvey, Geraint (2004) 'Cleared for take-off? Management-labour partnership in the European civil aviation industry', *European Journal of Industrial Relations*, 10 (3): 287–307.

Visser, Jelle (1992) 'The strength of labour movements in advanced capitalist democracies: Social and organizational variations', in Marino Regini (ed.), *The Future of Labour Movements*. London: Sage. pp. 17–52.

Walsh, Pat and Crawford, Aaron (2003) 'From organizational breadth to depth? New Zealand's trade unions under the Employment Contracts Act',

in Peter Fairbrother and Charlotte A. B. Yates (eds), *Trade Unions in Renewal: A Comparative Study*. London: Continuum. pp. 117–34.

Watson, Matthew (2003) 'Ricardian political economy and the "varieties of capitalism" approach', *Comparative European Politics*, 1 (2): 227–40.

Weiss, Linda (2003) 'Introduction: bringing domestic institutions back in' in Linda Weiss (ed.), *States in the Global Economy: Bringing Domestic Institutions Back In*. Cambridge: Cambridge University Press. pp. 1–33.

Western, Bruce (1997) *Between Class and Market: Postwar Unionization in the Capitalist Democracies*. Princeton: Princeton University Press.

Whitley, Richard (1999) *Divergent Capitalisms: The Social Structuring and Change of Business Systems*. Oxford: Oxford University Press.

Womack, James P., Jones, Daniel T. and Roos, Daniel (1990) *The Machine That Changed the World*. New York: Rawson Associates.

8

New Forms of Work and the High Performance Paradigm

Stephen Procter

INTRODUCTION

We can date the emergence of the high performance model to a series of studies published in the US in the mid-1990s (Appelbaum and Batt, 1994; Delery and Doty, 1996; Huselid, 1995; Ichniowski et al., 1997; MacDuffie, 1995; Osterman, 1994; Pfeffer, 1994). Their basic concern was to see whether new ways of organizing work and managing people were having an effect on the performance of organizations. For some, this represents a new research paradigm, in which more traditional institutional concerns are played down or neglected completely (Godard and Delaney, 2000). Others see it as a more natural reflection of the shift in the balance of power in the employment relationship in favor of management and employers.

Although reaching a precise definition would be difficult and probably counter-productive, the new forms of work being investigated are likely to involve the following:

- an extension of employee involvement or participation in decision-making, often in the form of the establishment of semi-autonomous teams;
- a division of labour such that employees are required to perform a range or a wider range of tasks.

A full account of the high performance model would also take into consideration the following broader organizational aspects:

- a conception of organizational performance that does not consist of nor largely rely upon the minimisation or reduction of the costs associated with employees;
- a recognition – or, at least, the hope or intention – that the management of work and people has a direct and significant effect on organizational performance;

- an acknowledgment that issues of work organization cannot be separated from considerations more usually associated with production management.

To examine the idea of 'high performance' this chapter divides into five main parts. Following this brief introductory section, the second part looks at what we mean by 'high performance', examining issues of terminology and definition and attempting to put the idea in its broader context. The third part looks at the 'high performance model' itself, highlighting the major works in this area and showing how they stand in relation to each other. The fourth section looks at a series of issues raised by the model. This covers the overall conclusion to be drawn from the volume of research, the diffusion and importance of the model, the role played by the institutional context, the implications of the model for employees and, finally, some of the more basic theoretical and methodological issues it faces.

The fifth part brings all these considerations together and offers some judgment on the model and its implications. Our argument here is that an understanding of many of the issues identified in the fourth section would benefit from contributions made from an industrial relations (IR) perspective. Rather than dismissing the high performance model and taking some delight in the difficulties in which it finds itself, the current situation offers those working in an industrial relations tradition the opportunity to shape the development of research and practice in this area.

THE HIGH PERFORMANCE MODEL: DEFINITION AND CONTEXT

Terminology

A first set of problems facing anyone approaching these issues for the first time are those of terminology and definition. A lot of the work in this area has coalesced around the term 'high performance work system' (HPWS) (see, for example Appelbaum

et al., 2000). In the mid-1990s, however, when these ideas were coming to prominence, a wide range of expressions was in use. Osterman (1994), for example, both refers to and makes use of the 'variety of labels' (173), with 'flexible work practices' perhaps being the most common expression in his own paper. Ichniowski et al. (1996), on the other hand, are among those who use 'workplace innovations' or 'innovative work practices'. The situation is made more complicated by the tendency of European-based academics to avoid the term 'high performance' altogether, and instead see things in terms of Human Resource Management (HRM) and its link with performance (see, for example, Guest, 1997; Paauwe, 2004).

Some of the explanation for, and implications of, these differences in terminology will emerge at various points in this chapter. Despite the differences, there is enough commonality in the substance of what is being considered to let us examine all of these things under the same heading. In the course of the present chapter we shall rely largely on the different terms used by the different authors; where an over-arching term is required for the sake of clarity of exposition, we shall use the terms 'high performance model' or 'high performance management' or, as a more general expression, 'HR management'.

High performance management

This is not to say, of course, that these and other expressions are simply different ways of describing exactly the same thing. This becomes clear if we move from terminology to definition. A key issue here is whether we are talking about high performance *practices* or high performance *systems*. If the former, then this suggests that a number of different practices can be identified as such, and that each will have an independent effect on performance. For those who emphasise the idea of systems, however, it is the combined effect of a particular set of practices that is important. The problem then is to identify the component parts of such a system and, on top of that, to establish whether there is a single high performance system or a number of systems, each appropriate to a different situation. We will approach these issues more systematically in the third section of this chapter.

Whether they are better seen as individual practices or system components, there is still the question of what should be included under the 'high performance' heading. The issue is perhaps best illustrated by Becker and Gerhart's (1996: 785) review of just 5 papers in this area. There were a total of 27 'high performance work practices' considered across the 5 papers. Of these 27, none was common to all the studies; just 2 were common to as many as 4 papers; and 20 of the practices were included in just 1 of the 5 papers.

As we noted in the introduction, central to the idea of high performance work is the extension of employee autonomy, often in the form of semi-autonomous team working. Osterman's (1994) influential study was based on four work organization practices: self-directed work teams, job rotation, problem-solving groups and Total Quality Management. Although not able to discern patterns in the distribution of these practices, he was able to identify the first of them as an 'anchoring practice' (1994: 177), in that more than 70 per cent of establishments with at least 1 of the 4 practices had self-directed teams. For Appelbaum et al. (2000: 102), '[the] opportunity to participate in substantive decisions is an essential element of an HPWS'. Just as for Osterman, this had four main parts: worker autonomy, communication, self-directed work teams and problem-solving groups. Again, it was the team working element provided by the latter two of these that was central, providing the conditions in which the former two could be made to work most effectively.

There is then the issue of where high performance management stands in relation to HRM. What makes things difficult here, of course, is that HRM itself has no settled definition. In broad terms, however, we can agree with Boxall and Purcell (2003) and say that while considerations of work organization would be central to a definition

of a high performance model, a definition of HRM is unlikely to include them. How far a high performance model might extend into more recognisably HRM territory – to include, say, training and appraisal – would then seem to be something that could be looked at only on a case-by-case basis. The danger of taking this too far is that 'high performance' becomes conflated with traditional 'good' HRM practice (Godard and Delaney, 2000) and thus loses any distinctiveness it might have. One way out of this is for the high performance model to focus on issues of work organization and for HRM policies to be treated as important or essential supports. This is the approach taken by Osterman (1994), for example, but it is certainly far from universally applied.

Similar issues arise when we look at the relationship between high performance work practices or systems and production management policies such as lean production and Total Quality Management. Wood's (1999) review of the 'HRM and performance' literature is perhaps the most direct attempt to address this question. He introduces the notions of high commitment management (HCM), which, following the work of Walton (1985), works exclusively through commitment; and high involvement management (HIM), a less restrictive version of HCM where high commitment policies are augmented by those aimed at skill acquisition and knowledge. High performance management (HPM) can then simply mean either HCM/HIM or the combination of HIM and production management policies such as TQM or lean production. We shall return to this relationship when we look at 'universal super-bundles' in the third part of this chapter.

Performance

The picture is no more straightforward when we turn to the other side of the equation. Here we ask the question: on the basis of what idea of performance should the effectiveness of the high performance model be judged? At first sight there seems to be a number of advantages in using financial measures. At least for large, private sector organizations they are easily obtainable and directly comparable across organizations. Ichniowski et al. (1996) argue that financial performance is important because this is what organizations themselves are focused on. On the other hand, financial measures might be thought of as quite remote from high performance management when such practices might be applied only to those employees directly involved in production (Ichniowski et al., 1996).

Some of the difficulties become apparent when we look at specific financial measures. Profit is perhaps the most obvious but its use in this context is far from straightforward. Quite apart from the issue of its availability, using current levels of profit might underestimate the performance of those organizations that are in pursuit of more long-term, growth-oriented objectives (Becker and Gerhart, 1996). Perhaps the most important objection, however, is that the level of profit might be a measure not so much of organizational success as of the ability of management to prevail in a distributional struggle with employees.

A number of studies use measures that are more closely related to the changes being applied, and these are often of an industry-specific nature. In Appelbaum et al.'s (2000) three-industry study in the US, for example, each industry emphasized a different performance measure: 'uptime' of capital in the steel industry, for example, and throughput time in apparel. This in some ways provides a truer test of effectiveness, since these are the kind of measures that the managers themselves are directing their efforts toward. The disadvantage is that it makes it difficult to compare results and to make generalizations.

These difficulties are compounded if we allow for organizations with multiple goals. Paauwe (2004) calls for a multi-dimensional approach to performance, arguing that it should be concerned not just with economic or strategic rationality but should also take into account wider societal demands such as fairness and legitimacy. Boxall and Purcell (2003) argue along similar lines. Although they

see the goals of the firm as, first, survival and, then, sustained competitive advantage, they argue that there are, in addition, the objectives of organizational flexibility and social legitimacy.

Historical context

Although itself dating only from the mid-1990s, the high performance model needs to be considered in the context of other attempts to understand the restructuring of work and employment relations. Two sets of debates are particularly important here: the 'what do unions do?' debate of the 1980s and 1990s; and the more prolonged debates around the concept of flexibility. The high performance model is closely related to the first of these. Based on Freeman and Medoff's (1984) examination of the nature and effects of trade unionism in the US, the possibility was advanced that union power would enhance rather than detract from economic performance. Rather than appearing simply as a residual, the link between union strength and economic performance became the subject of a more explicit and systematic analysis. Despite Freeman and Medoff's (1984) findings in the US, empirical work in the UK failed to provide support for this hypothesis (Fernie and Metcalf, 1995).

The emergence of the high performance model in the mid-1990s needs to be seen in this context, since both it and the work inspired by Freeman and Medoff are centrally concerned with the relationship between employment relations and economic performance. In both, we see an emphasis on the employment relations side of the equation. The change that occurs is that what happens on this side of the equation is seen as being determined by management rather than labor. At the same time, we see a shift away from concern for national-level measures of productivity and what they might imply for government policy, and their replacement by a concern for profit and what this implies for corporate-level strategies. As we shall see, the high performance model in fact makes very little reference to the 'what do unions do?' debate.

A whole range of other attempts to understand workplace and organizational restructuring have centered on the concept of flexibility (see Kalleberg, 2001; Vallas, 1999). In some cases, the idea of flexibility is operationalized in a quite specific way. In the UK context, for example, debate in the 1980s and early 1990s centered on the notion of the 'flexible firm', which claimed that employers were achieving flexibility by dividing their labor force into core and peripheral groups and managing each group in a different way (Atkinson, 1984). This idea provoked a long and lively debate (see Pollert, 1991; Procter et al., 1994) but, despite its immediate plausibility, the flexible firm suffered ultimately from a lack of supporting empirical evidence (Cully et al., 1999; see also Cappelli, 1995, for the US). In the UK, at least, it seemed that any restructuring of employment was taking place on the basis of broader corporate strategies with regard to products and customers (Ackroyd and Procter, 1998; Batt, 2000).

More ambitious approaches to the concept of flexibility were based on the idea that its pursuit marked an epochal change in the development of capitalism (Vallas, 1999). This was often characterized as a transition from Fordism to post-Fordism. This took a variety of forms but perhaps the most important of these attempts to conceptualize and explain the restructuring of work and production was Piore and Sabel's (1984) 'flexible specialization' thesis. They argued that the capitalist world faced a fundamental choice between persisting with an economy based on mass production and returning to one based on craft production in its new guise of flexible specialization. Under flexible specialization, production was based on flexible networks of technologically sophisticated manufacturing firms.

Partly as a result of its appeal from a policy point of view, flexible specialization did attract a number of adherents (Hirst and Zeitlin, 1989). A substantial part of the reaction it generated, however, was either skeptical or actively hostile (Vallas, 1999; Williams et al., 1987). Although flexible specialization is portrayed as the revival of craft production, Piore and Sabel did not explore in any real depth its implications for the nature of work. The assumption was that the use of more flexible capital equipment would be associated with the development of a highly flexible, multi-skilled workforce. As a way of understanding what was happening to management and work inside organizations, it provided little more than unsubstantiated generalizations.

THE HIGH PERFORMANCE MODEL: DIFFERENT APPROACHES

Classifying different approaches

Within the broad field we can identify a number of different approaches to the link between practice and performance. Two main classificatory devices have been developed. The first of these is provided by Delery and Doty (1996), whose concern was to show that the field of Strategic Human Resource Management (SHRM) was not an 'atheoretical wasteland' (1996: 828). They distinguished between three broad approaches.

- The universalistic approach, in which certain strategic HR practices can be identified that, in all circumstances will result in enhanced organizational performance.
- The contingency approach, in which HR policies are effective to the extent they are consistent with other aspects of the organization – in particular, its competitive or business strategy.
- The configurational approach, in which the important thing is not individual HR practices but their configuration in particular patterns or 'clusters'. What is required is both the 'horizontal fit' between the different practices and the 'vertical fit' between the cluster of practices and other organizational characteristics.

A second classification makes a twofold distinction between 'best practice' and 'best fit' approaches (see e.g. Purcell, 1999). The former equates roughly to Delery and

Doty's (1996) universalistic approach; while the latter stresses the 'fit' aspects of their configurational approach, encompassing both the horizontal and the vertical aspects.

In fact, neither of these classification devices is entirely satisfactory. An examination of Delery and Doty's classification reveals that their three approaches cannot be regarded as mutually exclusive. In particular, the 'vertical fit' in the configurational approach is difficult to distinguish from the contingency approach; and there also seems to be no logical reason why an approach cannot be both universalistic and configurational. The best practice/best fit distinction, on the other hand, makes no explicit reference to the idea of configurations or clusters of practices, although in usage this configurational aspect tends to be associated with best fit, leaving best practice to be equated with the universalistic approach.

The best practice/best fit debate also tends to get confused with the issue of bundles or systems. The issue here is the relationship between different practices. As Ichniowski et al. (1996) point out, different pairs of practices might be substitutes or complements. If the former (say, self-directed work teams and problem-solving groups) then one will have no effect if the other is present, and there might even be a negative impact. If two practices are complements (say, self-directed work teams and team-based pay), then the opposite applies: the effect of one depends upon the presence of the other.

The difficulties with the classification systems seem to arise from their attempt to force what is essentially a two-dimensional picture into one dimension. These two dimensions are represented in Table 8.1. On the vertical

axis we represent the relationship between the different practices in their proposed effect on performance. Using the same terminology as MacDuffie (1995) we can distinguish between additive and multiplicative effects. The former suggests that the effect of each practice is independent of the presence of other practices: to arrive at the overall effect on performance we simply add them up. A multiplicative effect implies that the impact of each individual practice depends on what other practices it is combined with. In the extreme case, the absence of one practice (that is, it has a value of zero) would mean that all the other practices would have zero effect. This is one way of expressing what Delery and Doty (1996) describe as the configurational (or cluster or bundle or system) approach; the additive effect, on the other hand, we can describe as non-configurational.

On the horizontal axis on Table 8.1 we have what we call the 'scope of application'. Are any effects (configurational or not) posited to apply universally or are they contingent upon certain conditions?

Reconsidering Delery and Doty's (1996) classification in these terms allows us to see that the configurational approach can be combined with either the universalistic or the contingent. It also allows us to see some of the limitations of the best practice/best fit classification. If best practice is equated with universalism, and best fit with configurational, then the two overlap in cell 3 in Table 8.1; if, however, best practice is restricted to cell 1 (that is, universal *and* additive) and best fit to cell 2 (contingent *and* configurational), then cell 3 is effectively ignored. Using Table 8.1 to provide the structure, we will now look at some of the most notable attempts to examine

Table 8.1 Classification device for studies linking HR practice and organizational performance

| | | Scope of application | |
		Universal	Contingent
Relationships between practices and/or systems	Non-configurational practices (additive)	1	4
	Configurational bundles (multiplicative)	3	2

the relationship between HR practice and organizational performance.

Universal practices

We start in cell 1 of Table 8.1 with the idea that innovative work and HR practices are universal in application and additive in effect. This kind of approach is often associated with the work of Pfeffer (1994), who provided a list of 16 HR practices that he saw as common to successful US organizations. The list of items was subsequently reduced to seven (Pfeffer, 1998). More rigorous support for the idea of universally applicable practices was provided by Huselid (1995), whose study of a large sample of US corporations across a number of industries concluded that firms can obtain substantial financial benefits from investment in high performance work practices. Having constructed an index of high performance work practices, he estimated that an increase of one standard deviation implied US$ 27,044 more in sales/employee, US$ 18,641 more in market value and US$ 3,814 more in profits.

Osterman's (1994) study was concerned with the extent to which 'flexible work practices' (work teams, job rotation, quality circles and Total Quality Management) were being adopted in the US. The performance of organizations is implicit rather than explicit in this study, but Osterman's analysis of how the practices were combined in individual establishments led him to the conclusion that there were no natural clusters: it was practices rather than systems that were important. In a UK context, West et al. (2002) took mortality rates as a measure of hospitals' performance. Their survey examined three areas of management: training, team working and appraisal. An increase of one standard deviation in their measure of appraisal, for example, was estimated to result in 1090 fewer deaths after hip fracture (per 100,000 admissions).

Contingent bundles

Turning to cell 2 focuses our attention on the notion of 'fit'. As already noted, we can identify two basic forms of fit: internal and external. Internal or 'horizontal' fit refers to individual practices fitting together into some kind of coherent system or 'bundle': the effect depends on the combination rather than the practices individually. External or 'vertical' fit, on the other hand, refers to the fit between the practices and other aspects of the organization. Logically, this is independent of internal fit (this would be cell 4 in Table 8.1), but the two are more often considered together: can different bundles of practices be identified *and* can their existence be explained by an external factor?

Something of the idea of internal fit is captured by Appelbaum and Batt (1994), who identify two high performance work systems in the US: American Lean Production, a version of lean production that omits the HRM and industrial relations institutions present in the original Japanese model (Womack et al., 1990); and American Team Production, which combines self-directed teams on the sociotechnical or Swedish model (Berggren, 1993) with an emphasis on quality engineering. Similarly, Appelbaum et al.'s (2000) four 'essential dimensions' could exist in isolation, but, it was argued, 'combining them increases the chance that they will have an effect' (p.104). Appelbaum et al. found evidence for a high performance work system having significant impact on 'uptime' in the steel industry; for 'team sewing' to reduce throughput time and costs in the apparel industry; and for 'cell production' to improve plant performance in medical imaging. Their study is unusual in being conducted across a small number of industries, but it does suggest a certain degree of industry-based specificity in the system-performance link.

In looking at the notion of external fit, perhaps the greatest attention has been paid to what Wood (1999) calls 'strategic fit'. The basic question here is whether the success of a high performance system is contingent upon the broader business strategy of an organization. Schuler and Jackson's (1987) work represents an early and influential attempt to look at the link between HRM practices and competitive strategies. Taking Porter's (1980, 1985) distinction between three strategies of innovation, quality enhancement and cost reduction, they looked at the employees' necessary 'role behaviors' for each and, in turn, the implications for HR management in such areas as job design, appraisal and compensation. Drawing on qualitative US case study data, their conclusion was that 'effectiveness can be increased by systematically melding human resource practices with the selected competitive strategy' (Schuler and Jackson, 1987: 217).

The idea of strategic fit is also given some support by Youndt et al.'s (1996) study of what they call 'human-capital-enhancing HR systems', but here the main effect on performance came through a link with manufacturing strategy rather than corporate strategy *per se*. More broadly, although this approach has some intuitive appeal, it does raise a dilemma. On the one hand, the idea of 'strategic fit' might be taken to highlight the part work organization and HR management can play in organizational strategy; on the other, it does tend to cast them in very much a secondary role (Wood, 1999). We shall return to this issue in the fourth part of this chapter.

Universal bundles

We turn now to cell 3 of Table 8.1. Again we have systems or bundles but the claim or the implication is that these are of universal application. Arthur's (1994) study of manufacturing performance in US steel minimills can be looked at in this light. He identifies and distinguishes between two human resource systems: one based on employee commitment, the other on control. His main aim is to test empirically the hypothesis that the steel plants with a 'commitment' system will outperform those with 'control'. Data from 30 US plants showed that those with the commitment system performed better than those with control in terms of labor inputs, scrap rates and labor turnover. As one of the early studies in this area, Arthur provided backing to the more general arguments of Walton (1985) and others.

Ichniowski et al.'s (1997) study of steel finishing lines in the US likewise claims to provide 'consistent support for the conclusions that groups or clusters of human resource management practices have large effects on productivity, while changes in individual work practices have little or no effect on productivity' (p.291). Looking at one part of the steel production process, they identified four different HRM systems. These ranged from the most traditional (system 4), where work was closely supervised and pay was based on the quantity of production, to the most innovative (system 1), where there were high levels of employee involvement and problem-solving teams. Taking production line 'uptime' as their measure of productivity, they found system 1 to be the most productive.

In the UK context the WIRS/WERS (Workplace Industrial/Employee Relations Survey) series has been used to follow a similar line. This quasi-official series of surveys, begun in 1980, provides comprehensive and reliable data on a variety of aspects of workplace-level employee relations and HR management. This has allowed researchers to develop classifications for workplaces on the basis of their employee relations characteristics, which can then be used with survey's measures of workplace performance (in terms of productivity, quality and finance) to see if there is any connection between the two. Fernie and Metcalf (1995) used the data from the third survey in the series (WIRS3), conducted in 1990, to look at the performance implications of different forms of what they called workplace governance. In terms of both productivity and productivity growth, they found that the 'collective bargaining' workplace was outperformed by its 'employee involvement' counterpart. In Fernie et al. (1994) the data are used to address the impact of HRM. Their own findings show that the 'strong union' workplace is out-performed by the 'strong HRM' workplace.

The idea of the HPWS was the explicit focus of attention for Ramsay et al. (2000) in their analysis of the 1998 WERS4 data. In an attempt to address the question of whether practices worked together in bundles, they subjected a set of 24 likely HRM practices to factor analysis. On this basis they were able to identify three groups of practices, one of which proved to have some association with measures of workplace performance. Although this offers some support for the idea of a 'universal bundle', the support would be stronger if, rather than simply emerging from the data, the three sets of practices were more deeply rooted in more conceptual considerations.

Universal super-bundles

We can take this argument a stage further by saying that what might be important is not so much an HR system or bundle itself, but how the system fits with other organizational systems. Extending the idea of internal fit in this way is what Wood (1999) calls 'organizational fit'. Here we give it the name 'universal super-bundle'. The fit now covers a wider area but is still horizontal or configurational in nature; and the application is still claimed to be universal rather than contingent. In terms of Table 8.1 we again find ourselves in cell 3.

It is in this light that we can consider Wood's (1999) main conclusion that, while the evidence does seem to support some version of the universalistic hypothesis, it is just as strong for the hypothesis that the key to performance is the link between 'high involvement' work practices and such techniques or philosophies as TQM and lean production. His main support for this is drawn from the two US studies of Lawler et al. (1995, 1998) – although he does stress that the evidence is certainly not overwhelming. In Wood's view it is this combination of HR management and the management of production that explains the positive impact on performance that tends to be attributed to the universal effect of HR management alone.

We can see something of this if we look at the idea of lean production. The term arose out of the US-based International Motor Vehicle Program, a US$ 5 million, 14-country project which resulted in the publication of *The Machine that Changed the World* (Womack et al., 1990). Based on the production system

that had been developed in Toyota, lean production was essentially the application of a just-in-time (JIT) system, in which stock or inventory is reduced to the minimum possible level. A comparison between a Toyota plant in Japan and a US automotive producer showed the former to have twice the level of productivity or to require 'half the human effort' to make a car.

Although significant doubt has been cast on the validity of these figures (Williams et al., 1992), two aspects of the claims made by the advocates of lean production are of particular interest to us here. A lean plant, it was claimed (Womack et al., 1990: 99), 'transfers the maximum number of tasks and responsibilities to those workers actually adding value to the car on the line'. Thus, 'in the end, it is the dynamic work team that emerges as the heart of the lean factory' (1990: 99). In other words, what might appear to be a system based on the management of operations (in particular, the flow of materials) is, in fact, a system that relies heavily on the management of people.

But what kind of work team would operate under lean production? The idea of team working is usually associated with a group's ability to act with some degree of autonomy, but any control over the pace of production would be severely circumscribed by the removal of buffer stocks which lean production implies (Klein, 1989). Delbridge et al.'s (2000) examination of teams in 'lean' plants in the automotive components sector found that the role of production workers was quite limited to the areas of maintenance and production management. More generally, Benders and Van Hootegem (2000) identify the key characteristics of the 'lean' team as: the focal position of foreman; the minute description and rigorous regulation of work through Standard Operating Procedures (SOPs); and the use of continuous improvement (*kaizen*) techniques to effect marginal improvement in these SOPs.

A second aspect of lean production is the claim that its principles are of universal application. Despite their argument that it emerged in response to specific conditions faced by the Japanese economy, Womack et al. (1990: 88) maintain that 'lean production can be introduced anywhere in the world'. MacDuffie (1995) provides some development of what we have called here the universal super-bundle. Although drawing on data from the International Motor Vehicle Program (IMVP), he argues that Womack et al. (1990) did not explain in sufficient depth how the HR practices they identified achieved the necessary degree of integration with production. In MacDuffie's view, what he calls the 'flexible' (rather than lean) production system in automotive assembly has an 'organizational logic' that provides this integration. Using multiplicative relationships between individual work practices, and also between the resultant work systems and HR and production systems, MacDuffie found strong support for the effects of these processes of bundling and integration: the flexible production systems formed in this way outperformed mass production in terms of both productivity and quality. This is to be taken together with other findings from the same project (MacDuffie and Pil, 1997) that gave qualified support to the idea that firms in the automotive sector across a range of countries were converging on the lean production model.

HIGH PERFORMANCE MANAGEMENT: THE ISSUES

The advocates of the high performance model thus find themselves in something of a quandary. On the one hand, the previous section of this chapter shows that in a relatively short period of time a strong, positive link seems to have been established between certain HR practices or systems and the performance of organizations. On the other hand, a number of important issues remain to be resolved, and it is these we consider now.

Overall assessment

The first of these issues is perhaps the most basic: can we say that the relationship

between practice and performance has in fact been established? In the previous section of this chapter we have looked at some of the most important attempts to address the question of the practice-performance link and, notwithstanding their differences in method and approach, all seem to at least point in the same direction.

For Godard (2004), however, this entire 'high performance paradigm' should be called into question. He points to a number of studies which offer the paradigm little support. These include his own longitudinal study of Canadian enterprises, which revealed few positive associations and even some negative ones (Godard, 1998). There has been a tendency, he argues, 'to emphasize results that appear to support the high performance paradigm while skating over those that do not' (Godard, 2004: 354; see also Wood, 1999). Overall, he claims, 'we should treat broad-brush claims about the performance effect of HPPs [high performance practices], and about research findings claiming to observe them, with a healthy degree of scepticism' (Godard, 2004: 355). Thus while not going so far as to dismiss the high performance model completely, he does suggest that the issues we examine in this part of the chapter should not be regarded merely as minor issues capable of being quickly and easily resolved. We can see this quite clearly when we turn to the issue of the model's diffusion.

Diffusion of the model

For Pil and MacDuffie (1996: 423) there is a 'striking paradox' to be explained: despite the strong links that research has been able to establish between practice and performance, the so-called 'high performance' practices had not been diffused widely and quickly. This was a particular concern of Osterman (1994), whose 1992 survey of US establishments examined the extent to which each of his four practices (self-directed work teams, job rotation, problem-solving groups and Total Quality Management) was present in an establishment's 'core' workforce. Taking as his criterion the presence of at least two of the practices across at least 50 per cent of the core workforce, he found that 37 per cent of workplaces could be considered 'transformed'. Repeating this survey in 1998, Osterman (2000) found that his headline figure for diffusion had risen to 71 per cent. As Lawler et al. (1995) and others (Ichniowski et al., 1996) had earlier pointed out, this and other figures refer more to individual work practices (or their aggregation) than to the existence of high performance work *systems*.

So how can the slow rate of diffusion be explained? Osterman (1994) himself looked at a range of possibilities for trying to identify which establishments were likely to become 'transformed'. Some of these proved statistically significant (especially 'managerial values') and some did not (including the presence of a trade union). Other authors have taken a more negative approach, and instead tried to identify *barriers* to diffusion. Among those tentatively suggested by Ichniowski et al. (1996) were: the limited performance gain for some businesses; the need to make radical change if 'bundles' are required; labor-management distrust; and the constraints imposed by institutional and public policy. Appelbaum and Batt (1994) provide a similar list, considering the barriers under three headings: the dilemmas facing firms and managers; union and worker ambivalence; and institutional barriers. Neither Ichniowski et al. (1996) nor Appelbaum and Batt (1994) undertake any systematic investigation of these possibilities.

Pil and MacDuffie (1996) try to understand the lack of diffusion in terms of ideas drawn from evolutionary economics and innovation theory. They suggest that pre-existing organizational 'routines' can make it difficult to effect radical changes. Their 'competence-destroying' nature means that performance might actually worsen when such changes are made, making new working practices difficult to persist with or unlikely to be introduced in the first place. Pil and MacDuffie's (1996) own study of the worldwide automotive assembly industry provides some support for this idea. Looking at take-up over the period

1989–1993/94, their strongest finding is that adoption of a set of innovative work practices is linked to the existence of a complementary set of practices in HR management. They are to some degree supported by the study of steel finishing lines carried out by Ichniowski et al. (1997), who found that in older lines there has been investment in other systems of skill and work relationships.

For Godard (2004) the issue is not so much lack of diffusion across organizations as lack of diffusion within them. Interpreting Osterman's (2000) study as showing that relatively few organizations fully adopt the high-performance model, he argues that this suggests that for most employers the overall benefits of adoption begin to level-off after a certain point is reached. Part of the problem here is that many studies look only at the benefit derived from new practices, ignoring any consideration of their cost. One exception to this is Cappelli and Neurmark (2001), whose US study showed that while there was weak evidence of high performance practices raising productivity, the evidence on increased labour costs was much stronger. Guthrie's (2001) study of the effects of high involvement work practices in New Zealand companies also cautioned against simply advocating their more extensive use. As employees became more valuable and more important in the organization's performance, he concluded, 'greater use of these practices is associated with significant productivity losses in the face of mounting employee turnover' (Guthrie, 2001: 188).

Importance of high performance management

Some light on our second issue – the limited rate of diffusion – might also be cast by consideration of our third: how important are the management of HR and work in overall organizational performance?

Becker and Gerhart (1996) argue that we should be concerned not just with the existence of a positive relationship – which many studies had been able to establish – but with the magnitude of any positive effect.

A number of other commentators have pointed to this as an important issue (Godard and Delaney, 2000; Guest, 1997; Ichniowski et al., 1996).

From studies that have looked at this in a more or less direct way, a range of answers has emerged. Amongst these is the Arthur Andersen 'Worldwide Manufacturing Competitiveness Survey', which looked at the use of the principles of lean production by companies in the automotive components industry (Lowe et al., 1997; Oliver et al., 1996). Taking three areas – seats, exhausts and brakes – they explored what they defined as 'world-class performance' in terms of both productivity and quality. The key factor in explaining performance, it was argued, was whether a company was located in a supply chain that was operated in a disciplined manner. The study found no convincing evidence of the universal applicability and superiority of any particular system of work organization and human resource management: it was location and ownership that were the important explanatory factors.

As we have seen, Ramsay et al.'s (2000) analysis of the 1998 UK WERS data provided some support for the idea of a universal bundle. Their regression equation as a whole, however, was able to explain less than 4 per cent of the total extent to which productivity differed between workplaces. Likewise, Huselid's (1995) results for the US explained only 1–3 per cent of the variation in financial performance.

On the other hand, Delery and Doty (1996) found HR factors to account for quite large differences in financial performance in the US banking sector. Three HR practices were found to be significant in terms of performance, and the average level of each of these across the sector was calculated. Compared to banks with the average level of adoption, banks whose level was one standard deviation above this enjoyed a 30 per cent better performance. As proportions of the total variation in performance, moreover, 11, 10 and 6 per cent were claimed respectively by the universalistic, contingency and configurational approaches.

Institutional/cultural context

Cutting across all the issues we have considered so far in this section is the question of institutional or cultural context. We observed in the introduction to this chapter that the idea of the high performance workplace was one that was developed out of the experience of US companies in the 1980s and 1990s. We have also seen that the greater part of research on this subject continues to be US-based. To the extent that we can identify the impact of the high performance model, therefore, we must ask to what degree this is confined to a particular setting.

Research on the link between practice and performance has been carried out in a wide variety of national and regional settings. Amongst European countries, Rodriguez and Ventura (2003) found internal human resource systems to have a positive impact on the financial performance of manufacturing companies in Spain, with more support offered to a universalistic interpretation than to a contingent one; d'Arcimoles (1997) also found some relationship between performance and certain HR indicators amongst large French companies in the 1980s; Lahteenmaki et al. (1998), however, found barely any such relationship in a study of Finnish organizations, their chief argument being that many studies failed to take into account the stage of the economic cycle at which research was undertaken.

Research in emerging economies also reveals a variety of findings. Bae and Lawler's (2000) research in Korean firms gave support to their main hypothesis, that high involvement HRM strategies improved economic performance, with their results favoring a best practice rather than a best fit approach. Bae et al. (2003) extended this work in a comparative study of Korea, Taiwan, Singapore and Thailand. Their results were broadly supportive of the effectiveness of HPWSs' right across this range of settings. A particular feature of the work was the difference they identified between locally owned companies and MNC subsidiaries: perhaps surprisingly, the new work system has slightly more effect in the former.

Huang's (1997) findings in Taiwan alone were rather more mixed than this; while Fey et al.'s (2000) study of foreign firms operating in Russia focused on HR outcomes, giving support to the idea that they could be used as mediating variables between HRM practices and firm performance.

There have been few attempts, however, to make a systematic analysis of this growing volume of international data. We can observe differences in findings across countries, but we don't know to what degree these simply reflect the same differences in approach that result in different findings *within* countries. Looked at from the other direction, we might ask what particular differences in cultural or institutional context might explain the differences in the findings. Godard's (2004) proposed 'political economy' approach, for example, suggests that we concentrate on the nature of economic institutions. He argues that, without reform of the institutional conditions, it would be misguided to advocate the widespread adoption of the high performance 'paradigm' in liberal market economies such as the US and the UK.

Mutual gains

We turn now to the question of the distribution of gains from the adoption of high performance management. In particular, to what degree do employees benefit from the performance gains available? As Osterman (2000) points out, there are strong reasons to expect that employees will gain, since to some degree the whole high performance model is posited on an enhancement of employee discretion and skill. Godard and Delaney (2000) argue that the high performance paradigm considers these things only insofar as they are the means through which the performance outcomes are achieved. We shall look at these 'transmission mechanisms' in more detail in the next section. Here we consider work that has looked explicitly at the question of mutual gain.

Osterman's (2000) 1997 survey looked at how employees had fared in those US workplaces designated 'transformed' in 1992

(Osterman, 1994). The presence of high performance practices was associated with a higher probability of lay-offs and no gains in real wages. 'The bottom line,' he concluded, 'is that there is very little evidence that HPWOs [High Performance Work Organizations] have delivered on the promise of "mutual gains"' (Osterman, 2000: 191).

Others have found that mutual gains can be identified. Godard's (2001) survey of Canadian employees found that team-based work had positive associations with belongingness, task involvement, job satisfaction, empowerment, commitment and citizenship behavior. Appelbaum et al.'s (2000) three-sector US study found that HPWSs increase workers' trust in their managers and enhance their intrinsic rewards from work; also that the opportunity to participate in decision-making was associated with an improvement in wages. For Appelbaum et al. (2000: 115) there were 'win-win outcomes for plants and workers'.

Another way of looking at this issue is to address the claim that, to the extent they are effective, high performance practices operate through work intensification and employee stress rather than involvement and commitment. Barker (1993), for example, sees self-managed teams as being effective through the notion of concertive control; and lean production has been accused of constituting management-by-stress (Parker and Slaughter, 1988).

Direct evidence on this issue is mixed. Appelbaum et al. (2000) found no evidence that HPWS practices amount to a 'speed-up' that negatively affects workers' stress. Their findings suggested that the opportunity for substantive participation is related to lower, not higher, levels of job stressors. Godard (2001), by contrast, found that alternative work practices were associated with more stressful work. This finding is supported by Ramsay et al. (2000) who also found high performance work practices to be positively related to job strain. This, they argued, raised questions about the widely held assumption that positive performance outcomes from HPWS flow via positive employee outcomes.

There is also the question of what the high performance model implies for organized labor. Perhaps as a reflection of the model's US roots, trade unions hardly feature at all in a large number of studies. As we have seen in the section on the diffusion of the high performance model, they tend to appear on the periphery of analysis, either as one possible characteristic of a high performance organization or as a barrier to the model's diffusion. The central and potentially performance-enhancing role that trade unions enjoyed in the debates surrounding Freeman and Medoff's (1984) *What do Unions Do?* seems largely to have disappeared.

As Godard (2004) demonstrates, however, there is a still a body of work that addresses more systematically the relationship between trade unions and the high performance model. His own study of Canadian 'high performance' organizations (Godard, 1998) showed that union avoidance was not a major motivation in the adoption of such a model. Whether the high performance model provides the vehicle for trade unions to take part in and derive benefit from a strategy of 'partnership' with employers is less clear. In line with broader considerations of this strategy, Godard (2004) suggests that only where unions have the opportunity and also the strength to be involved in something more than a superficial partnership, can this be to their advantage.

Transmission mechanisms

As the preceding section makes clear, the issue of mutual gains can also be seen in the context of – or as part of – the issue concerning the 'transmission mechanisms' of the high performance model. While research seems to have been successful in establishing the existence of a positive association between HR practice and organizational performance, it has been less so in explaining how that relationship comes about. According to Boselie et al.'s (2005: 77) comprehensive survey of journal articles in this area, the linking mechanisms are 'largely disregarded'. The general assumption is that any relationship

works through changing employees' attitudes and behaviors. Guest (1997), for example, has attempted to construct a framework that links HRM strategy and practice, on the one hand, with performance and financial outcomes, on the other, through the intermediation of, first, the HRM outcomes of commitment, quality and flexibility, and then the behavior outcomes of effort, co-operation, involvement and citizenship.

Interesting questions are raised, therefore, when practice and performance appear to have an association in the absence of these intermediating variables. Although Ramsay et al. (2000) could use the 1998 UK WERS data to establish an association between a high performance work system and certain measures of performance, this could not be explained by 'employee outcomes' such as commitment and job discretion. These findings in some ways echo what Fernie et al. (1994) found from WERS3: that although HRM workplaces outperformed their more unionised counterparts, they did so despite having worse industrial relations.

This might suggest that other transmission mechanisms are at work. This possibility is allowed for by Ichniowski et al. (1996), who identify three basic explanations of the practice-performance link. As well as the possibilities that individual workers work harder (as a result of heightened levels of motivation) and work smarter (as greater involvement means they are able to make their jobs more efficient), Ichniowski et al. also allow for improvements in performance to be the result of more structural changes which can accompany changes in work.

A greater emphasis on this possibility would certainly be in line with the universal super-bundle approach we identified earlier, and a number of researchers seem to be moving in this direction. Purcell (1999) suggests that operational strategies can be a key intervening variable, and amongst types of economic gain from high performance workplace practices identified by Appelbaum et al. (2000) are a reduction in the total number of employees and a reduction in interruptions to production.

Underpinning theory

Consideration of transmission mechanisms inevitably brings with it questions concerning the theory underpinning the link between HR practice and performance. Some of these we have already touched on in our attempt to classify the different ways of approaching this issue. Both Boxall (1992) and Purcell (1999) have criticized the idea of 'best fit' between HR and corporate strategy. Purcell (1999) points to the difficulties involved in operationalizing the concept, while both authors are concerned with its theoretical shortcomings, especially its reliance on the concepts of strategy developed by Porter. They also argue that the best practice/best fit debate has its limitations as a means of providing the basic structure to the debate. Boxall and Purcell (2003) argue for combining the two, with best practice providing a 'base-line' set of practices and best fit the means by which organizations can differentiate themselves beyond that.

In general, the development or application of theory has often taken second place to the methodological sophistication required to manipulate large, complex data-sets. Boselie et al.'s (2005: 71) survey article tried to identify which theoretical framework was being used in each case, but found that 'this proved far from obvious in many of the articles'. Other authors have used specific theoretical concepts for specific purposes. In addressing the issue of the complementarity of practices, for example, Ichniowski et al. (1997) argue this could be done on the basis of economic ideas of incentive contract theories, which stress the importance of interactive effects. Likewise, Pil and MacDuffie (1996) try to understand the issue of diffusion in terms of ideas about organizational 'routines' drawn from evolutionary economics and innovation theory.

More recently we have seen attempts to redress the rather atheoretical nature of the practice-performance debate by looking at in terms of the resource-based view (RBV) of the firm (see Boxall and Purcell, 2003; Purcell, 1999; Wright et al., 1994). Under the RBV, the chief concern of an organization is to identify and develop the internal resources that might generate a sustained competitive advantage. The theory requires that this resource has a number of qualities, prime amongst which is inimitability. What is required, in other words, is something that other organizations are unable to copy.

Boxall and Purcell (2003) argue that neither the human resources themselves nor the HR policies or practices can provide the means necessary to generate a sustained competitive advantage. The human resources or the people themselves can be moved from one organization to another; likewise, the policies or practices by which to manage them can also easily be adopted. The real source of inimitability and differentiation, it is argued, exists at a higher level, with the idea of 'social architecture'. HRM is to be seen as the creator of an organization's distinctiveness rather than the distinctiveness itself. A universally applicable set of principles might thus result in a number of different sets of practices (Becker and Gerhart, 1996).

Boxall and Steeneveld (1999) use this approach in their study of New Zealand engineering consultancies. Following a detailed longitudinal study, they are able to establish how the more successful companies differ from the less successful in term of 'human capital' or people, but they claim that it was much more difficult to discern the 'social architecture' or 'human process advantage' required for sustained competitive success. While this might illustrate the long-term, strategic importance of high performance management, the inability to draw definite conclusions even at the end of an in-depth, long-term project would seem to limit the predictive or prescriptive capacity of this approach.

Despite the apparent status it gives to HRM or high performance management, the implications of the RBV need to be examined carefully. The fact that the necessary contribution made by management in this area is, by definition, unique is something of a double-edged sword. While it seems to emphasize the importance to an organization of how its employees are managed, it makes it more difficult to see exactly what form that management should take. It would seem to undermine any claim that HPM or HRM might have to provide something that is of universal application (Wood, 1999).

The danger also, especially from an industrial relations point of view, is that the focus is very much internal to the firm. Quite apart from its management focus, the danger is of neglecting the institutional context within which organizations are operating. Paauwe (2004) tries to get this round by combining the RBV with institutionalist theory in his context-based human resource theory (CBHRT) (see also Paauwe and Boselie, 2005). While this might be welcomed as an attempt to temper the RBV and its impact, it is less easy to see how these two different approaches can be brought together either in theory or in its application.

Methodological issues

As well as the theoretical issues, the high performance model continues to face a number of methodological ones. Many of these stem from the fact that a large part of the work devoted to identifying the existence and nature of a practice-performance link has been in the form of large-scale, cross-sectional questionnaire surveys. Ichniowski et al. (1996) describe what an ideal research design would be in these circumstances, involving, for example, the random assignment of innovative work practices and a sample which closely resembles the population. They also show why such an ideal is unlikely to be attained.

A number of issues arise in the generation of data. The first of these is response bias. With response to most questionnaire surveys being of a voluntary nature, it might be the case that the more successful firms are more likely to respond. More than this, bias would arise as a result of high performance practices being more likely to be retained in firms where the benefits exceed the costs (Godard and Delaney, 2000). There is also the issue of the nature of the questions. By their nature, questionnaire surveys rely on questions that can be answered easily within a structured framework. 'Box-ticking' questions of this nature, however, will tend to focus attention on observable structures at the expense of organizational processes (Purcell, 1999). Other issues in the generation of the data include a reliance on subjective judgments on such things as innovative work practices and organizational performance, and the fact that data from a large organization or establishment might come from a single respondent (Ichniowski et al., 1996). Osterman (1994) argues that senior HR managers, the likely recipients of questionnaire surveys in this area, are very often ignorant of how employees' work is organized.

Just as serious are the issues involved in the interpretation of the data (see Godard, 2004; Boselie et al., 2005). The most basic of these is that cross-sectional work can identify an association between variables but cannot establish whether that association is based on a particular causal relationship (Godard and Delaney, 2000). It is conventional in cross-sectional research to acknowledge this (see, for example, Arthur, 1994; Delery and Doty, 2000) but, implicitly or explicitly, causal relationships are attributed to the findings. In looking at the practice-performance link it is assumed that practice causes performance. It could plausibly be argued that the direction of causality runs the other way: that better-performing companies are in a position to make investments in certain working practices. Schneider et al. (2003) take this one stage further, by showing how the 'reverse causality' might operate through employee attitudes. They studied the relationship between employee attitudes and firm performance across a number of US companies over a number of years, and concluded that it could not simply be assumed that attitudes lead to performance: 'some do and some do not, and some employee attitudes apparently are the *result* [emphasis added] of financial and market performance' (Schneider et al., 2003).

Another possibility is that there is a third variable involved, one that explains both practice and performance. As Ichniowski et al. (1996) point out, an ideal situation would be one in which the extent of high performance management was uncorrelated with other characteristics that affect performance. But could it be the case, for example, that organizations that are good at managing human resources will be good at other aspects of management? In order to guard against the 'omitted variable' problem, longitudinal studies might be preferred to cross sectional ones (Ichniowski et al., 1996).

An attempt to engage with these issues of causality has been made by Guest et al. (2003) (see also Wright et al., 2003). Using data on HR practice in the UK in 1999, they found that while an association could be established between HR practices and performance, the same could not be said for HR practices and subsequent *changes* in performance. Rather than practice causing performance, there was, argued Guest et al. (2003), stronger support for the idea of reverse causality. On this basis they could not support the view that 'greater application of HRM is likely to result in improved corporate performance' (311).

In Wood's (1999) view, part of the confusion arises as a result of having too many studies that adopt too simplistic a view of what hypotheses to test. The implication of this is that there should be a more synergistic relationship between, on the one hand, hypothesis-testing, quantitative surveys and, on the other, hypothesis-generating, qualitative case studies. There are, however, very few case studies that address in a direct way the relationship between HR practice and performance (Boselie et al., 2005). From the ones that do, moreover, it is difficult to get any feel for potential conceptual development. As we have already seen, it might be argued that Boxall and Steeneveld's (1999) account of New Zealand engineering consultancies reveals more of the weaknesses than the strengths of the resource-based view of the firm; while Truss' (2001) study of Hewlett-Packard, though interesting in itself, does not carry with it any important theoretical implications.

CONCLUSIONS

What can we conclude from our review of the high performance model? We can see first of all that, although they can be a source of confusion, issues of terminology and definition are not anything like insuperable difficulties. There exists enough common ground and common focus for a range of terms and definitions to co-exist. It would serve little purpose to try and impose too rigid a distinction between what is and what isn't 'high performance'.

Where some change might be made is how the different approaches to the issue might be classified. There appears in any case to be a move away from the best-practice/best-fit distinction that had achieved some currency. As the analysis presented in this chapter suggests, explicit account needs to be taken of both of the dimensions (the scope of the application of HPM practices and the relationship between them) along which studies might be classified.

More fundamentally than this, it seems to be generally recognized that there is a range of issues that still need to be addressed. These we have identified as follows:

- overall assessment of the model;
- its rate of diffusion;
- its importance in an organization's performance;
- the institutional/cultural context;
- the issue of mutual gains;
- the model's 'transmission mechanisms';
- underpinning theory;
- methodological issues.

Our argument here is that an industrial relations perspective is in a good position to generate understanding of these issues and thus to shape the future development of the debate around the high performance model. If we look at the issue of diffusion, for example, then, here as elsewhere, attempts to isolate particular factors as 'barriers' have not proved particularly fruitful. Understanding diffusion in terms of the labor-management relationships within particular workplaces appears to offer much more promise. Similarly, existing research has been weak on identifying and explaining the importance of the national or regional context. It might be argued that much of the literature in the broad HRM area is of this nature, amounting to little more than bemusement at why other settings are not the same as the US. Again, an understanding of the most important features of institutional context is something that emerges naturally from an industrial relations perspective.

The contribution industrial relations might make is perhaps most obvious in the area of mutual gains. This is not just a question of establishing the proportions in which any performance gains are divided. Irrespective of the extent to which they gain either financially or through having greater discretion at work, employees at the moment enter into this picture as passive recipients. A more explicit focus on employees' attitudes and strategies might not just allow us to see how any gains are generated and divided; it might also allow us to say more about the diffusion and impact of the high performance model. Overlapping with this is a need to look more deeply at the 'transmission mechanism' between practice and performance. This is a rather crude way of approaching what is essentially a system of social relations. A better understanding of management-employee relations might generate a less mechanistic understanding of how management actions have 'effects'.

All of this points to a more fundamental reconsideration of theoretical and methodological issues. The whole debate might be accused of being rather atheoretical in nature. Recent attempts have been made to remedy this, by promoting the RBV as the means by which the relationship between HR management and performance is best understood. Not only might this make generalization difficult, but it also downplays any role that the employment relationship might play in the analysis. The main methodological issues stem from the widespread reliance on the cross-sectional survey as the means of identifying the practice-performance relationship, and we can echo those such as Wood (1999) who call

for a more synergistic relationship between, on the one hand, hypothesis-testing, quantitative surveys and, on the other, hypothesis-generating, qualitative case studies.

The methodological and the theoretical issues might indeed be addressed simultaneously. What a more qualitative, case-study approach would do is not simply establish that the direction of causality ran one way or the other; it would reveal much more of the dynamics of the situation. What would be important then is not so much management action but the relationship between management and employees. It might only be when organizational performance is considered in the context of the employment relationship that it can fully be understood.

REFERENCES

Ackroyd, S. and Procter, S. (1998) 'British Manufacturing Organization and Workplace Industrial Relations: Some Attributes of the New Flexible Firm', *British Journal of Industrial Relations*, 36 (2): 163–83.

Appelbaum, E. and Batt, R. (1994) *The New American Workplace: Transforming Work Systems in the United States*. Ithaca, NY: ILR Press.

Appelbaum, E., Bailey, T., Berg, P. and Kalleberg, A. (2000) *Manufacturing Advantage: Why High-Performance Work Systems Pay Off*. Ithaca, NY: Cornell University Press.

d'Arcimoles, C. (1997) 'Human Resource Policies and Company Performance: a Quantitative Approach Using Longitudinal Data', *Organization Studies*, 18 (5): 857–74.

Arthur, J. (1994) 'Effects of Human Resource Systems on Manufacturing Performance and Turnover', *Academy of Management Journal*, 37 (3): 670–87.

Atkinson, J. (1984) 'Manpower Strategies for Flexible Organizations', *Personnel Management*, Aug: 28–31.

Bae, J. and Lawler, J. (2000) 'Organizational and HRM Strategies in Korea: Impact on Firm Performance in an Emerging Economy', *Academy of Management Journal*, 43 (3): 502–17.

Bae, J., Chen, S., Wan, T., Lawler, J. and Walumbwa, F. (2003) 'Human Resource Strategy and Firm Performance in Pacific Rim Countries', *International Journal of Human Resource Management*, 14 (8): 1308–22.

Barker, J. (1993) 'Tightening the Iron Cage: Concertive Control in Self-Managing Teams', *Administrative Science Quarterly*, 38 (3): 408–37.

Batt, R. (2000) 'Strategic Segmentation in Front-line Services: Matching Customers, Employees and Human Resource Systems', *International Journal of Human Resource Management*, 11 (3): 540–61.

Becker, B. and Gerhart, B. (1996) 'The Impact of Human Resource Management on Organizational Performance: Progress and Prospects', *Academy of Management Journal*, 39 (4): 779–801.

Benders, J. and Van Hootegem, G. (2000) 'How the Japanese Got Teams', in Procter, S. and Mueller, F. (eds) *Teamworking*. London: Macmillan. pp. 43–59.

Berggren, C. (1993) *The Volvo Experience: Alternatives to Lean Production in the Swedish Auto Industry*. London: Macmillan.

Boselie, P., Dietz, G. and Boon, C. (2005) 'Common-alities and Contradictions in HRM and Performance Research', *Human Resource Management Journal*, 15 (3): 67–94.

Boxall, P. (1992) 'Strategic Human Resource Management: Beginnings of a New Theoretical Sophistica-tion?', *Human Resource Management Journal*, 2 (3): 60–78.

Boxall, P. and Steeneveld, M. (1999) 'Human Resource Strategy and Competitive Advantage: a Longitudinal Study of Engineering Consultancies', *Journal of Management Studies*, 36 (4): 443–63.

Boxall, P. and Purcell, J. (2003) *Strategy and Human Resource Management*. Basingstoke: Palgrave.

Cappelli, P. (1995) 'Rethinking Employment', *British Journal of Industrial Relations*, 33 (4): 563–602.

Cappelli, P. and Neurmark, D. (2001) 'Do "High Performance" Work Practices Improve Establishment-level Outcomes?', *Industrial and Labor Relations Review*, 54 (4): 737–75.

Cully, M., Woodland, S., O'Reilly, A. and Dix, G. (1999) *Britain at Work: As Depicted by the 1998 Workplace Employee Relations Survey*. London: Routledge.

Delbridge, R., Lowe, J. and Oliver, N. (2000) 'Worker Autonomy in Lean Teams: Evidence from the World Automotive Components Industry', in Procter, S. and Mueller, F. (eds) *Teamworking*. London: Macmillan. pp. 125–42.

Delery, J. and Doty, H. (1996) 'Modes of Theorizing in Strategic Human Resource Management: Tests of Universalistic, Contingency and Configurational Performance Predictions', *Academy of Management Journal*, 39 (4): 802–35.

Fernie, S. and Metcalf, D. (1995) 'Participation, Contingent Pay, Representation and Workplace Performance: Evidence from Great Britain', *British Journal of Industrial Relations*, 33 (3): 379–415.

Fernie, S., Metcalf, D. and Woodland, S. (1994) 'What has Human Resource Management Achieved in the Workplace?' *Employment Policy Institute Economic Report*, 8 (3).

Fey C., Bjorkman, I. and Pavlovskaya, A. (2000) 'The Effect of Human Resource Management Practices on Firm Performance in Russia', *International Journal of Human Resource Management*, 11 (1): 1–18.

Freeman, R. and Medoff, J. (1984) *What Do Unions Do?* New York: Basic Books.

Godard, J. (1998) 'Workplace Reforms, Managerial Objectives, and Managerial Outcomes', *International Journal of Human Resource Management*, 9 (1): 18–40.

Godard, J. (2001) 'High Performance *and* the Trans-formation of Work? The Implications of Alternative Work Practices for the Experience and Outcomes of Work', *Industrial and Labor Relations Review*, 54 (4): 776–805.

Godard, J. (2004) 'A Critical Assessment of the High-Performance Paradigm', *British Journal of Industrial Relations*, 42 (2): 349–78.

Godard, J. and J. Delaney (2000) 'Reflections on the "High Performance" Paradigm's Implications for Industrial Relations as a Field', *Industrial and Labor Relations Review*, 53 (3): 482–502.

Guest, D. (1997) 'Human Resource Management and Performance: a Review and Research Agenda', *International Journal of Human Resource Management*, 8 (3): 263–76.

Guest, D., Michie, J., Conway, N. and Sheehan, M. (2003) 'Human Resource Management and Cor-porate Performance in the UK', *British Journal of Industrial Relations*, 41 (2): 291–314.

Guthrie, J. (2001) 'High Involvement Work Prac-tices, Turnover and Productivity: Evidence from New Zealand', *Academy of Management Review*, 44 (1): 180–90.

Hirst, P. and Zeitlin, J. (1989) 'Flexible Specialization and the Competitive Failure of UK Manufacturing', *Political Quarterly*, 60 (2): 164–78.

Huang, T. (1997) 'The Effect of Participative Manage-ment on Organizational Performance: the Case of Taiwan', *International Journal of Human Resource Management*, 8 (5): 677–89.

Huselid, M. (1995) 'The Impact of Human Resource Management Practices on Turnover, Productivity, and Corporate Performance', *Academy of Management Journal*, 38 (3): 635–72.

Ichniowski, C., Kochan, T., Levine, D., Olson, C. and Strauss, G. (1996) 'What Works at Work: Overview and Assessment', *Industrial Relations*, 35 (3): 299–333.

Ichniowski, C., Shaw, K. and Prennushi, G. (1997) 'The Effects of Human Resource Management

Practices on Productivity: a Study of Steel Finishing Lines', *American Economic Review*, 87 (3): 291–313.

Kalleberg, A. (2001) 'Organizing Flexibility: the Flexible Firm in the New Century', *British Journal of Industrial Relations*, 39 (4): 479–504.

Klein, J. (1989) 'The Human Costs of Manufacturing Reform', *Harvard Business Review*, Mar–Apr: 60–6.

Lahteenmaki, S., Storey, J. and Vanhala, S. (1998) 'HRM and Company Performance: the Use of Measurement and the Influence of Economic Cycles', *Human Resource Management Journal*, 8 (2): 51–65.

Lawler, E., Mohrman, S. and Ledford, G. (1995) *Creating High Performance Organizations*. San Francisco: Jossey Bass.

Lawler, E., Mohrman, S. and Ledford, G. (1998) *Strategies for High Performance Organizations*. San Francisco: Jossey Bass.

Lowe, J., Delbridge, R. and Oliver, N. (1997) 'High-performance Manufacturing: Evidence from the Automotive Components Industry', *Organization Studies*, 18 (5): 783–98.

MacDuffie, J. (1995) 'Human Resource Bundles and Manufacturing Performance: Organizational Logic and Flexible Production Systems in the World Auto Industry', *Industrial and Labor Relations Review*, 48 (2): 197–221.

MacDuffie, J. and Pil, F. (1997) 'Changes in Auto Industry Employment Practices: an International Overview', in T. Kochan, R. Lansbury, and J. MacDuffie, (eds) *After Lean Production*. Ithaca, New York: Cornell University Press. pp. 9–42.

Oliver, N., Delbridge, R. and Lowe, J. (1996) 'Lean Production Practices: International Comparisons in the Auto Components Industry', *British Journal of Management*, 7, special issue, 29–44.

Osterman, P. (1994) 'How Common is Workplace Transformation and Who Adopts It?', *Industrial and Labor Relations Review*, 47 (2): 173–88.

Osterman, P. (2000) 'Work Reorganization in an Era of Restructuring: Trends in Diffusion and Effects on Employee Welfare', *Industrial and Labor Relations Review*, 53 (2): 179–86.

Paauwe, J. (2004) *HRM and Performance: Achieving Long Term Viability*. Oxford: Oxford University Press.

Paauwe, J. and Boselie, P. (2003) 'Challenging "Strategic HRM" and the Relevance of the Institutional Setting', *Human Resource Management Journal*, 13 (5): 56–70.

Paauwe, J. and Boselie, P. (2005) 'HRM and Performance: What Next?', *Human Resource Management Journal*, 15 (4): 68–83.

Parker, M. and Slaughter, J. (1988) *Choosing Sides: Unions and the Team Concept*. Boston: South End Press.

Pfeffer, J. (1994) *Competitive Advantage through People*. Boston, MA: Harvard Business School Press.

Pfeffer, J. (1998) *The Human Equation: Building Profits by Putting People First*. Boston, MA: Harvard Business School Press.

Pil, F. and MacDuffie, J. (1996) 'The Adoption of High-Involvement Work Practices', *Industrial Relations*, 35 (3): 423–55.

Piore, M. and Sabel, C. (1984) *The Second Industrial Divide: Possibilities for Prosperity*. New York: Basic Books.

Pollert, A. (ed.) (1991) *Farewell to Flexibility?* Oxford: Blackwell.

Porter, M. (1980) *Competitive Strategy*. New York: Free Press.

Porter, M. (1985) *Competitive Advantage*. New York: Free Press.

Procter, S., Rowlinson, M., McArdle, L., Hassard, J. and Forrester, P. (1994) 'Flexibility, Politics and Strategy: in Defence of the Model of the Flexible Firm', *Work, Employment and Society*, 8 (2): 221–42.

Purcell, J. (1999) 'Best Practice and Best Fit: Chimera or Cul-de-sac?', *Human Resource Management Journal*, 9 (3): 26–41.

Ramsay, H., Scholarios, D. and Harley, B. (2000) 'Employees and High Performance Work Systems: Testing Inside the Black Box', *British Journal of Industrial Relations*, 38 (4): 501–31.

Rodriguez, J. and Ventura, J. (2003) 'Human Resource Management Systems and Organizational Performance: an Analysis of the Spanish Manufacturing Industry', *International Journal of Human Resource Management*, 14 (7): 1206–26.

Schneider, B., Hanges, P., Smith, D. and Salvaggio, A. (2003) 'Which Comes First: Employee Attitudes or Organizational Financial and Market Performance?', *Journal of Applied Psychology*, 88 (5): 836–51.

Schuler, R. and Jackson, S. (1987) 'Linking Competitive Strategies with Human Resource Management Practices', *Academy of Management Executive*, 1 (3): 207–19.

Truss, C. (2001) 'Complexities and Controversies in Linking HRM with Organizational Outcomes', *Journal of Management Studies*, 38 (8): 1121–49.

Vallas, S. (1999) 'Rethinking Post-Fordism: the Meaning of Workplace Flexibility', *Sociological Theory*, 17 (1): 68–101.

Walton, R. (1985) 'From Control to Commitment in the Workplace', *Harvard Business Review*, Mar–Apr: 76–84.

West, M. A., Borrill, C., Dawson, J., Scully, J., Carter, M., Anelay, S., Patterson, M. and Waring, J. (2002) 'The Link Between the Management of Employees and Patient Mortality in Acute Hospitals', *International Journal of Human Resource Management*, 13 (8): 1299–310.

Williams, K., Cutler, T., Williams, J. and Haslam, C. (1987) 'The End of Mass Production?', *Economy and Society*, 16 (3): 405–39.

Williams, K., Haslam, C., Williams, J. and Cutler, T. (1992) 'Against Lean Production', *Economy and Society*, 21 (3): 321–54.

Womack, J., Jones, D. and Roos, D. (1990) *The Machine that Changed the World*. New York: Rawson Associates.

Wood, S. (1999) 'Human Resource Management and Performance', *International Journal of Management Reviews*, 1 (4): 367–413.

Wright, P., Gardner, T. and Moynihan, L. (2003) 'The Impact of HR Practices on the Performance of Business Units', *Human Resource Management Journal*, 13 (3): 21–36.

Wright, P., McMahan, G. and McWilliams, A. (1994) 'Human Resources and Sustained Competitive Advantage: a Resource-based Perspective', *International Journal of Human Resource Management*, 5 (2): 301–26.

Youndt, M. A., Snell, S. A., Dean, J. W. and Lepak, D. P. (1996) 'Human Resource Management, Manufacturing Strategy and Firm Performance', *Academy of Management Journal*, 39 (4): 836–66.

9

Changing Traditions in Industrial Relations Research

George Strauss and Keith Whitfield

INTRODUCTION

In *Researching the World of Work: Strategies and Methods in Studying Industrial Relations Research* (Whitfield and Strauss, 1998), we made a number of points about the way in which Industrial Relations (IR) research is undertaken, and how it might respond to the challenges it currently faces. In particular, we stated that the

> ... tide engulfing industrial relations is strong... but we feel that allied to changes in conceptual tools, a broadening of scope, and possibly a modification of the field's title, the development of a distinctive and powerful approach to research design can contribute to a renaissance in the field ... (Whitfield and Strauss, 1998: 294).

Since then, we have undertaken a content analysis of the field's main academic journals covering almost half a century (Whitfield and Strauss, 2000), oriented around the themes developed in the book. The analysis was quite narrowly focused, but allowed us to check whether our perceptions were mirrored in the main journals, albeit only those which are more empirically tractable. It was followed by a not dissimilar paper by Carola M. Frege (2005), which examined similar themes and addressed some new issues.

We also listened closely to the views of those who reviewed the book, to see if there were any profound disagreements with our views. Most readers seemed to accept our caricature of the past, present, and future of the field. Less encouragingly, however, few of those reacting to our rather pessimistic views of the future offered suggestions as to how it might be made brighter.

This chapter has three main objectives. The first is to outline the arguments we made in our 1998 book. Our treatment is deliberately concise; those wanting more depth can consult the original. The second objective is to examine our assertions in the light of the two journal content analyses, ours and Frege's. Third, we address the question of where IR goes from here.

A FIELD IN FLUX

The academic field of IR faces some difficult dilemmas, and its future depends on how it responds. These dilemmas originate from a number of key shifts in the topics that the field seeks to understand, in the structure of academia, and in the opportunities open to researchers.

It is something of a cliché to say that research in IR is in a state of flux. There are, however, probably stronger grounds for saying this now than ever before. The field's subject matter is changing ever more markedly, its conceptual framework is under increasing scrutiny, boundaries between it and related fields of study are becoming ever more blurred, and new research techniques are continuously being developed. These changes are broadly linked to a series of transformations in how work and the employment relationship are perceived. There is a much wider recognition of the importance of what some call 'labor' (and others 'human resources' or 'human capital') to the prosperity of modern economies and the development of a 'good society'. Organizations are much more likely to recognize that the utilization of human resources is pivotal in attaining competitive advantage in ever-more-complex product markets.

Seventy years ago, academic IR covered broadly both what Kaufman (2004) called 'Institutional Labor Economics' and 'Personnel Management'. Gradually, as Kaufman documents, it narrowed its scope to primarily union-management relations. But more recently there is some evidence that its scope is once again broadening. Issues such as 'high-performance' work practices, occupational health and safety, employment discrimination, employee satisfaction, job security, and comparative international industrial relations have come to play an important role in the research agenda. This broadening of scope has been associated with a greater interchange between IR researchers and scholars from other fields. Topics such as the decline in union density are covered increasingly by scholars who are not normally

identified with IR (for example, Clawson, 2003; Voss and Sherman, 2000). Inevitably, there has developed a questioning of the efficacy of differing approaches to examining the employment relationship.

Just as the problems which academic IR deals with have changed, so have the research techniques used to study them. The advent of the computer has made the quick and cheap analysis of massive data-sets possible. This has caused major changes in research mehtodology throughout most of the social sciences. As a consequence, academic discourse has become increasingly quantitative.

Changing problems

One of the distinctive characteristics of IR has been its focus on socially defined problems. For example, before 1940, IR research in the US concentrated on the legitimization of unions and the case for social insurance (Millis and Montgomery, 1938–45). During the immediate postwar period, there was much industrial unrest and the focus turned to strikes and inflation (Strauss and Feuille, 1978). During the 1960s, it was training and race relations. More recently, the dominant themes have been the decline of unions, the attempts to reinvigorate them (Voss and Sherman, 2000), and the impact of participation schemes (Ichniowski et al., 2000).

British IR research focused on unions and union-management relations during the 1960s, on shop-floor labour-management relations during the 1970s, and, more recently, on the role of management and work organization. The heightened interest in human resource management (HRM) has contributed to the recent burst of British scholarship in that area. The decentralization of bargaining in contemporary Australia has been accompanied by a greater research emphasis on workplace issues.

The perceived nature of problems also affects the funding that is available, and this greatly influences the kind of research done. In the early 1970s, there was liberal government financing of poverty and training studies in the US. More recently, Sloan Foundation funding has paved the way for extensive research on 'high-commitment' workplaces. Perceived social problems led to the establishment of the Donovan Commission in Britain (Royal Commission on Unions and Employers' Associations, 1968), the Hancock Committee in Australia (Hancock, 1985), and the Dunlop Commission in the US (Commission on the Future of Worker-Management Relations, 1994). Each sponsored important research, and also inspired a host of related funding opportunities and research studies.

From policy to theory

Compared with related fields and disciplines, IR research has traditionally been strongly focused on the major policy issues of the time. As a consequence, relative to more theoretically-inclined fields, it has tended to:

1) be more multidisciplinary;
2) be more focused on a number of different organizational levels;
3) be more based on representative samples;
4) more often involve respondents who are role holders rather than private individuals; and
5) be more likely to examine complex causal processes.

In recent years, however, IR research has shown an increasing tendency to become more oriented toward issues that are of more interest to fellow academicians than policy-makers, potentially weakening the link between research and policy.

Less inductive, more deductive

The highly inductive tradition of context-specific research, once dominant in IR research in English-speaking countries, is clearly under siege (Cappelli, 1985). The earlier approach was predominantly based on intensive studies of individual situations, typically with the purpose of coming to focused policy recommendations, and possibly a contribution to middle-range theory.

It was perhaps best known for its extensive use of the case method. In the US, the pioneering study of this type was John R. Commons' single case study of shoemakers (Commons, 1909). In Britain, a similar impact resulted from the work of Sidney and Beatrice Webb. Theories were relatively unimportant, but to the extent they developed, they emerged from the facts, not as logical deductions from other theories.

Now dominant in the US, and increasingly important in other English speaking countries, is a more deductive approach that is far less grounded in specific research contexts. The deductive approach seeks general laws that apply in every situation to some extent, even though they may explain only part of any given situation. The search for such laws starts from hypotheses (for this reason it is sometimes called the 'hypothetico-deductive' approach). In IR, these hypotheses were traditionally drawn from economics, but increasingly they have come from psychology or one of the other social sciences. Hypotheses developed logically from such assumptions are tested against empirical facts as rigorously as possible. In short, facts are used to test theories, not to develop them. This type of research tends to be quantitative rather than qualitative, and to make use of large data-sets and often complex multivariate statistical analysis. Many of these data are economic in orientation, though there is increasing use of more employment-focused data-sets, particularly a range of workplace surveys in a growing number of countries.

In some areas, the two traditions have developed in unison, with secondary analysis of large-scale survey data being deployed alongside complementary case studies (Edwards, 2005). As Marginson (1998) points out, in Britain, large scale surveys have been widely used in the inductive mode to raise questions. Thus it would be incorrect to see the more abstract, newer style of research as simply crowding out the more traditional type. Nonetheless, there does seem to have been a distinct shift toward more deductive, less context-specific, and more theory-oriented inquiry.

Forms of validity

One of the key differences among the various research strategies is the attention given to the validation of constructs, models, and findings. Distinctions are often made among three major forms of validity: construct, internal, and external (Schwab, 2005).

- *Construct* validity concerns the degree to which the variables considered accurately reflect the factors composing the underlying conceptual model (or hypothesis), for example, the degree to which IQ scores are good measures of cognitive ability.
- *Internal* validity relates to the causal model (the hypothesized relationship) itself and concerns the degree to which the empirical model estimated is consistent on its own terms, for example, whether the relationship between union presence and pay is solely due to the impact of the former on the latter and can therefore be estimated in (determined by) a single statistical equation.
- *External* validity concerns the degree to which the results can be generalized beyond the particular situation studied.

Attaining high levels of all three forms of validity in a single project is rare. Typically, they are traded off against each other, and against more practical considerations such as cost and time. The nature of the trade-off reflects the resources available to the researcher, the rationale for the study, and the research tradition within which the work is done.

IR research has traditionally been strong in terms of construct validity, but rather weak in terms of external validity. The advent of workplace IR surveys has introduced a stronger element of external validity into the field, albeit at the (for some unacceptable) expense of construct validity. A key problem for the field, however, lies in the area of internal validity, especially the ability of researchers to distinguish between cause and effect, for example, to determine whether the often-found positive association between HR practices and performance runs from the former to the latter, or vice versa.

Construct validity is particularly important for researchers in psychology, but less so for economists. It is more significant for policy-oriented than for theoretical researchers. Internal validity has been a particularly important concept for economists, and it is notable that much econometric research is concerned with ensuring that a statistical model has internal consistency. External validity is important for policy-based researchers, given that their work is intended to influence policies affecting general populations. By contrast, much theoretical research explicitly focuses on extreme or atypical cases to test whether theoretical ideas are widely applicable. If they apply in extreme cases, presumably they will also apply in cases which are less extreme.

Research methods: qualitative and/or quantitative

Most inductive research is qualitative and most deductive research is quantitative, but this isn't always the case. Sometimes quantitative researchers will analyze a set of available data with no hypotheses in mind, hoping that an interesting pattern will emerge – 'magic computer on the wall, what's the meaning of this all?' Only then is an attempt made to explain this pattern logically. Though sometimes sneeringly called the 'kitchen sink' approach, quantitative inductive research occasionally yields unexpected results, just as random testing of drugs sometimes provides unexpected cures. In contrast, qualitative methods may be employed in a deductive fashion when, having completed one case study, the researcher undertakes another with the intent of determining whether the same relationships hold in both cases. Often they do not, and this may lead the researcher to look for explanations of the difference. This is a common approach in comparative international studies.

Among the advantages of the quantitative approach is transparency: how the research is conducted is generally clear, others may replicate the study, and typically the data on which the conclusions are based are made publicly available. By contrast, the reported results of qualitative research may be affected by the researcher's biases and expectations. Surveys are less likely to be seen as biased. Another advantage of the quantitative approach is its ability to generalize. Conclusions based on qualitative research in a small number of situations may have limited external validity. While qualitative research may suggest hypotheses, quantitative research assists in determining how widely these hold and the general strength of the relationship.

Compared with the quantitative approach, qualitative research typically considers a broader range of variables and issues, many of which are difficult to quantify. This helps the researcher understand the dynamics of a relationship – how it actually operates (what some call 'getting into the little black box'). Although quantitative research may indicate that factors A and B are correlated, unless the data are longitudinal it may be hard to determine the direction of causation, thereby yielding low internal validity. Qualitative research can often tell us something about causation. Further, it typically yields a richer picture of actual behavior than quantitative research, and so may be more useful in policy making.

Disciplinary, theoretical, and national backgrounds

Industrial Relations, broadly defined, involves contributions from a variety of cognate disciplines and fields. Not only do researchers from different disciplinary backgrounds look at different questions, but they use different methods. Their methods influence the nature of their findings.

Methods change over time. The big change in IR in recent years has been the increasing use of quantitative methods. Psychologists were among the first to quantify, then economists, and, more recently, institutional IR researchers and labor historians. Early industrial sociologists specialized in ethnography and case studies; now they often use quantitative methods. Today, scholars in most areas studying employment engage in calculations.

Even within quantitative research there are differences among fields. Economists generally favor regressions, while psychologists are more likely to use techniques that identify patterns, such as factor analysis. Psychologists emphasize the need to validate proxy measures, that is, to ensure high construct validity; economists typically do not see this as a problem. Many younger IR scholars, who have been broadly trained in both economics and organizational behavior, feel comfortable with both econometric and psychometric techniques. Consequently, linear regression analysis, which was for a while the almost standard technique used in economic research, is being increasingly supplemented by factor, path, cluster, maximum likelihood, and meta-analysis.

There are national differences. American sociologists make greater use of quantitative techniques than do those elsewhere, while many continental European sociologists shun them altogether, arguing that these techniques merely deal with superficial aspects of underlying problems. Indeed, some IR researchers reject quantitative analysis as suggesting spurious and misleading exactitude. In other words, they argue that statistical relations lack external validity and do not accurately reflect the real world's complexity. A related approach argues that valid research should involve 'subjects' who participate in gathering and evaluating the data, such as in 'action research'.

This diversity complicates scholarly communication. The problem is no longer one of national languages, but of differences in frames of reference and theoretical paradigms. Though seemingly translated into English, much German sociology is virtually unintelligible to US readers, even to US sociologists. Furthermore, many of the technical terms that constitute the common discourse of postmodernists are meaningless to quantitative labor economists. Take for example Keenoy's (1999: 1) view of 'HRM as a Hologram' or his 'attempt to analyze the problem of HRM ... in terms of the intrinsic conceptual-theoretical, empirical, representative, and institutional ambiguities which characterize the discourse and practices of HRM [which, he argues] stem from the epistemological limitations of modernistic methodologies'. Few economists think in terms like this (and for some this language is almost undecipherable). The reverse is also true: most post-modernists are mathematically illiterate (and proud of it). Yet both deal with the world of work. They might learn from each other.

Values and personal interests

IR is a normative, value-oriented field. Many IR scholars identify with unions. Consequently, until recently, unions received more attention than management. By contrast, those who receive part of their income as management consultants are likely to deal with managerial problems and from a managerial perspective. And even those who try to be neutral are often charged with being pro-union (Brown, 1998).

One of the personal advantages of more traditional forms of face-to-face research, such as ethnography and interviewing, was that it provided the researcher with a sense of psychological involvement that may be largely lacking in the computerized study of data-sets. The passion and excitement that once characterized IR may be lost, and those who crave personal involvement or desire to change the world may pick other fields of study.

Journal preferences

In academia, it is increasingly the case, particularly for younger researchers, that they publish or perish. The preferences of journal editors carry great weight. Recent changes in British research funding arrangements, for instance, have increased the kudos for publishing in a small set of 'front-rank' journals. This editorial system generally encourages safe, narrow articles that can pass the scrutiny of often-hostile reviewers. Most journals today seem to prefer highly empirical studies, heavily buttressed with statistics, to think-pieces with unorthodox new ideas. Particularly in the US, few articles

without numerical data get published. Editors also want to publish 'new' research; mere replication of previous studies rarely gets into print. Consequently, favored articles are based on small 'advances' on previous studies which are heavily supported by statistics. The net effect is to discourage inductive research. On the other hand, in the US, the *Journal of Labor Research* and the *Labor Studies Journal* both publish significant numbers of qualitative articles, while the same is true of the *Industrial Relations Journal* in the UK and the *Journal of Industrial Relations* in Australia.

Technology

Computers have revolutionized the social sciences. They have made it possible to store and analyze large amounts of data cheaply, as long as these data can be reduced to symbolic (largely numerical) form. In recent years, there has been not only a phenomenal growth in the capacity of computer hardware, but also an increase in supporting software – particularly in statistical programs that allow a wider range of data to be analyzed. Calculations that previously might have taken hundreds of hours can now be done almost instantaneously. Given the availability of computers and the growing number of databases, quantitative research can be converted into article form without researchers ever leaving their offices. On the other hand, it discourages qualitative research, and it may lead to attempts to categorize squishy data into hard numbers, for example, by coding interviews into rigid categories. Despite its presumed objectivity, the coding process is very open to being influenced by research biases.

Availability of data

Data availability has a strong impact on the nature of IR research and on the methods used. National workplace surveys in Australia and the UK, as well as a series of somewhat similar but considerably less comprehensive US studies, have created a bonanza for scholars. These data have facilitated a growing interest in both workplace studies and the use of quantitative techniques which permit hypothesis testing. The ready availability of statistics showing votes in National Labor Relations Board (NLRB) elections contributed to a plethora of US research on voting behavior. Later, the decision to stop collecting data on all but large US strikes has inhibited studies of strike incidence. Similarly, the availability of surveys of the population generally (such as the Panel Study of Income Dynamics in the US and the Socio Economic Panel in Germany) has encouraged studies that can utilize these data and has discouraged other kinds of research. In other words, the availability of potential answers has encouraged questions.

A lamentable tendency among some researchers when good quantitative data are not available is to test a hypothesis by selecting the best alternative (technically 'proxy') around. Sometimes, this best alternative is bad, in other words, construct validity is low. This is like the drunk looking for lost keys under the street lamp because this is where the light is.

An unfortunate consequence of the greater availability of survey data (as well as of computers to analyze them) is that IR researchers are now less likely to go out into the field to talk to real workers and real managers. One danger, particularly for a problem-oriented field, is that important insights are lost and overly simplistic conclusions accepted. A second danger is that the IR literature will lose the colorful descriptions that were once common.

Level of analysis

Studies differ in the organizational levels they examine: the individual worker; the workplace; the enterprise, firm, industry, or country; or the entire world? Traditionally, the primary focus of IR has been on unions, management, and especially their collective bargaining relationships. A second stream of research dealt with the relationships between unions and companies, as aggregates, and the state.

The different disciplines related to IR focus on different levels: economics and psychology on individuals, sociology on groups and larger aggregations, and political science on countries. It should not be surprising, therefore, that the recent spurt in interest in comparative international relations has contributed to the fact that some of the most innovative IR work is being done by scholars who have backgrounds in political science (for example, Thelan, 2004).

Different techniques are more appropriate for research at each level. Further, different insights emerge depending on the level studied. Thus, if one is concerned with strikes at the individual level, one looks at phenomena such as workers' needs, attitudes, and frustrations. At the workplace level, the behavior of specific members of management, the social structure of the group, and perhaps the nature of technology may be most germane. To study these issues, ethnography may be appropriate. At the plant level, fine-grained ethnographic studies may be too difficult; hence, plant-level research may involve case studies. At higher levels, quantitative analyses of economic data (profits, changes in the cost of living, and the like) may be more relevant. And still other variables must be considered in comparing strike rates among countries, such as their histories, economies, and governmental institutions.

Interdisciplinary research

IR claims to be interdisciplinary. There are obvious advantages to utilizing several disciplines, in that each discipline can provide its own insights and so reduce the likelihood of narrow, single-dimensional perspectives on complex, multidimensional problems. Unfortunately, these advantages are rarely garnered in practice. Indeed, there are many examples of failure, despite highly laudable attempts to break down disciplinary barriers.

There are two main types of interdisciplinary research. The first involves a single researcher (or a research team from a common discipline) drawing on a variety of disciplines. The second involves several researchers, each from a different discipline. To date, neither type has been common in IR research, though this may be changing, especially as the training of IR students gets broader. Generally, the first type has been more fruitful. Researchers from different backgrounds may have trouble communicating, and could therefore produce what some have called 'the cross-sterilization of the social sciences'.

Among the few examples of research that extends beyond discipline-specific boundaries is Getman et al. (1976). In this study, two lawyers and a psychologist employed an attitude survey to test legal propositions regarding the impact of management behavior on workers' voting patterns. Similarly, some economists, such as Freeman and Medoff (1984) and Farber and Krueger (1993), have introduced attitudinal variables into their equations.

In some cases, IR scholars have borrowed from other fields. For example, the concept of 'union commitment', is derived from an analogous concept, 'organizational commitment', widely employed in organizational behavior (see, for example, Gordon et al., 1980). Somewhat similarly, Walton and McKersie (1965) drew on game theory and psychology, but applied its conceptual apparatus directly to collective bargaining. Kelly (1998) builds his analysis of union behavior partly on sociological theories of collective action. On the whole, however, IR researchers have been rather parochial. Some are uncomfortable with any conceptualization that treats IR as only one form of a broader socio-economic category. An example is the reluctance of researchers to follow up on Walton and McKersie's somewhat theoretical analysis of bargaining behavior, thus permitting the new academic field of negotiations and conflict resolution to develop with little IR participation (and few jobs for IR academicians). Similarly, IR has made little use so far of the highly relevant concepts of transaction cost economics or sociological theories of collective action.

A common problem is that researchers from different disciplines may deal with the same phenomena, but fail to communicate with each other because they use different languages and read different journals. Psychologists and economists, for example, study labor turnover, sometimes using equivalent data, yet they rarely cite each other. 'Organizational justice,' especially 'procedural justice,' is one of the most popular subjects in micro-organizational behavior (Greenberg, 1990). Much of the research in that field has involved IR issues, such as compensation, promotion, and discipline. Yet, despite its obvious relevance, little research in the procedural justice tradition has appeared in IR publications or has been cited by those who call their field IR.

One of the major factors inhibiting interdisciplinary research is that it takes research from the comfort of the shared assumptions and ways of seeing and doing that exists within disciplinary boundaries. In particular, the criteria used to judge a 'good' piece of research differ between disciplines, and few studies satisfy all of them. For example, Getman et al.'s highly policy-relevant study was criticized by economists on methodological grounds (Dickens, 1983), and by researchers outside of economics for lacking in realism (Siegel, 1998). Psychologists would no doubt regard the attitudinal variables in Freeman and Medoff's and Farber and Krueger's work as rather primitive.

The advent of workplace IR surveys was expected to encourage interdisciplinary analysis. Representative sample surveys, it was hoped, would interact complementarily with non-generalizable case studies. Yet the British experience is that little inter-disciplinarity has occurred. Much of the analysis of the early survey data has been conducted by economists using a narrow range of quantitative methods, and very little has been undertaken by IR specialists themselves (Millward, 1993). Indeed, some of the latter have been critical of survey data, arguing that it fails to capture the true complexity and dynamic character of British IR (McCarthy, 1994); in other words, that it lacks construct validity.

But there is some room for hope. There is, for example, a largely new approach to compensation and careers that links psychology, sociology, and economics, making use of such concepts as procedural justice; agency, tournament, expectancy, and equity theories; organizational ecology; and commitment. Few of the scholars contributing to this development identify their field as IR, however.

Multi-method research

A growing number of IR studies make use of more than one method. This has numerous advantages. First, through 'triangulation', it helps validate findings. If two methods lead to the same conclusion, the findings are more robust than if one method alone is used. If they disagree, more research may be necessary. The findings of the International Motor Vehicle Project were based largely on managers' responses to detailed questionnaires (McDuffie and Pil, 1995). But to ensure that the questions were understood and answered accurately, the researchers personally visited most of the plants around the world. Second, if several methods are employed, each may provide different nuances or insights. Consequently, the ultimate findings are richer. And if the results differ, totally new questions may be raised. Third, one method can be used to improve another. Focus groups, for example, can be used to help design survey questions. Case studies can help improve causal models used in quantitative studies. Experimental methods can be used to evaluate different econometric models.

Fourth, one method can lead to another when the techniques are used in sequence, one after another, rather than simultaneously. Thus, one study may be 'nested' within another. Case studies may be used at first to suggest relationships, and, afterward, surveys or other quantitative measures can be employed to determine the extent to which they can be 'generalized'. Alternatively, if a survey finds that X is correlated with Y, case studies can be used to get into 'the black box' and analyze the dynamics of this relationship. Case studies may be run on typical examples,

as revealed by surveys or on deviant ones (Lipset et al., 1956). Another approach is to administer surveys of workplace practices to key union and management leaders in a large sample of organizations and then survey the attitudes toward these policies of all the workers in a small sample of firms taken from the larger sample. In this way, the larger study can determine the extent of a practice, while the smaller ones look at its impacts.

Data sources

IR scholars gather their data from a variety of sources. Those who are interested in bargaining behavior may set up laboratory experiments or perhaps observe real union-management bargaining sessions (in the ethnographic tradition). Those whose research focuses on workers' attitudes favor attitude surveys. Institutional researchers examining union-management behavior traditionally engage in case studies (but more recently may also use workplace surveys). In doing research of this type, researchers typically gather their own data. Economists, by contrast, typically base their research on data collected by others, usually a government agency. However, a few economists have conducted carefully controlled field experiments designed to measure the impact of various forms of training and income supplements on the employment history of disadvantaged workers. And there is a growing field of experimental economics that utilizes laboratory experiments to study economic behavior, such as risk taking.

A hallmark of traditional IR research was that scholars tended to collect their own data. A major advantage of gathering one's own data is that the nature of the data collected and the data-collecting technique can be tailored to fit the questions being asked (in other words, there may be high construct and internal validity). On the other hand, it is generally cheaper to use data collected by others. Further, there is the advantage of transparency: if generally available data are used, other researchers can repeat and check on the original researcher's findings. Researchers who collect their own data may bias the questions they ask so as to get the answers they want. What ethnographers and case study collectors 'see' may be heavily influenced by their own expectations and values. This is a serious limitation.

SOME EVIDENCE OF CHANGE

Evidence as to how the nature of research is changing is provided by two studies, both of which looked at articles appearing in major academic IR journals. The first (Whitfield and Strauss, 2000) examined articles appearing at 15 year intervals (1952, 1967, 1982, and 1997) in two British journals, the *British Journal of Industrial Relations (BJIR)* and the *Industrial Relations Journal* (IRJ), two American ones, the *Industrial and Labor Relations Review* (ILRR) and *Industrial Relations* (IR) as well as one each from Canada, *Relations Industrielles* (RI) and Australia, the *Journal of Industrial Relations* (JIR). The second study, (Frege, 2005) looked at the same British and US journals, but instead of Canadian and Australian journals, to provide an illustration of continental European developments, it looked at *Industrielle Beziehungen* (IB). This study compared the entire set of articles appearing in the 1970s with those appearing in the 1990s. Both studies coded the articles under a number of headings, most of which are listed in the attached tables. Tables 9.1 and 9.2 are based on the Whitfield and Strauss paper (but only the four oldest of these journals (BJIR, ILRR, IR, and JIR). Table 9.3 is based on Frege's paper.

The findings of the two studies are broadly comparable. Some of the differences can be ascribed to differences in the years covered, though we suspect that important parts are due to differences in coding rules. Both studies found a marked trend away from inductive to deductive research, with the US journals moving further than those based in Australia, Britain, and Germany. Whitfield and Strauss found this trend to be somewhat stronger than did Frege; the proportion of articles published in the former's four longest running journals classified as deductive increased

from 17 per cent in 1967 to 57 per cent in 1997. According to both studies, articles which are purely descriptive or purely theoretical (without data) have become increasingly rare in Anglo–Saxon journals but, according to Frege, still common in IB.

Looking back to 1967, Whitfield and Strauss found a trend away from policy oriented research and toward discipline-building in both countries, the proportion of articles of the former type in the four main journals increasing from 34 per cent in 1967 to 65 per cent in 1997. Further, the proportion of papers using data which contained multivariate analysis grew quite rapidly so that, by 1997 they constituted the vast majority of papers published in US journals. Taking the four longest-running journals as a whole, the proportion of papers involving data that utilized multivariate analysis increased from 6 per cent to 47 per cent. This shift was more pronounced in the US-based journals, but less so in JIR.

The overall proportion of articles on what Whitfield and Strauss call 'union management relations' and Frege calls 'industrial relations topics' has remained roughly constant over the years. Whitfield and Strauss noted, however, a marked contrast between journals in this respect. ILRR witnessed a substantial decline in the proportion of articles on union-management relations from 58 per cent in 1967 to 20 per cent in 1997, whereas the other three journals all saw a corresponding increase. In short, IR resembled BJIR and JIR rather than ILRR in this area.

Frege classifies articles by 'analytic level', with one category being 'micro'. US journals had more micro articles during both of her chosen periods, and the proportion of these increased from the 1970s to the 1990s. Meanwhile, the proportion in Britain declined. The closest Whitfield and Strauss equivalent to Frege's 'micro' is 'individual/household'. The proportion of papers in this category has gone up in both countries; however, only in the ILRR did they constitute a majority of data-based articles.

Whitfield and Strauss discovered that only a small proportion (16 per cent) of studies used

Table 9.1 Nature of papers published in main IR journals

	1967					1982					1997				
	BJIR	ILRR	IR	JIR	Total	BJIR	ILRR	IR	JIR	Total	BJIR	ILRR	IR	JIR	Total
Articles coded	22	19	19	16	76	24	27	19	23	93	21	30	22	17	90
Basic approach															
Deductive	3 (14%)	4 (21%)	4 (21%)	2 (13%)	13 (17%)	8 (33%)	21 (78%)	16 (84%)	4 (17%)	41 (44.0%)	10 (48%)	26 (87%)	15 (68%)	0 (0%)	51 (57%)
Inductive	18 (82%)	14 (82%)	7 (37%)	10 (62%)	49 (65%)	13 (54%)	6 (22%)	2 (11%)	19 (83%)	50 (54%)	11 (52%)	4 (13%)	7 (32%)	17 (100%)	39 (43%)
Unclassified	1 (4%)	1 (5%)	8 (42%)	4 (25%)	14 (18%)	3 (13%)	0 (0%)	1 (5%)	0 (0%)	4 (4%)	0 (0%)	0 (0%)	0 (0%)	0 (0%)	0 (0%)
Primary Orientation															
Discipline orientation	10 (46%)	9 (47%)	5 (26%)	2 (13%)	26 (34%)	15 (63%)	18 (67%)	16 (84%)	9 (39%)	58 (62%)	9 (43%)	28 (93%)	17 (77%)	4 (23%)	58 (65%)
Policy orientation	11 (50%)	10 (53%)	6 (32%)	9 (56%)	36 (47%)	5 (21%)	7 (26%)	3 (16%)	13 (57%)	28 (30%)	9 (43%)	1 (3%)	4 (18%)	13 (77%)	27 (30%)
Unclassified	1 (44%)	0 (0%)	8 (42%)	5 (31%)	14 (18%)	4 (16%)	2 (7%)	0 (0%)	1 (4%)	7 (8%)	3 (14%)	1 (3%)	1 (5%)	0 (0%)	5 (5%)
Data															
Yes	12 (55%)	18 (95%)	11 (58%)	16 (100%)	57 (75%)	21 (87%)	27 (100%)	17 (90%)	21 (91%)	86 (92%)	20 (95%)	30 (100%)	20 (91%)	17 (100%)	87 (97%)
No	10 (45%)	1 (5%)	8 (42%)	0 (0%)	19 (25%)	3 (13%)	0 (0%)	2 (10%)	2 (9%)	7 (8%)	1 (5%)	0 (0%)	2 (9%)	0 (0%)	3 (3%)
Subject area															
Union-management relations	12 (55%)	11 (58%)	3 (16%)	6 (38%)	32 (42%)	15 (63%)	9 (33%)	7 (37%)	8 (35%)	39 (42%)	16 (76%)	6 (20%)	8 (36%)	11 (65%)	41 (46%)

Source: Whitfield and Strauss (2000).

Table 9.2 Type of data and methods of analysis used

	1967					1982					1997				
	BJIR	ILRR	IR	JIR	Total	BJIR	ILRR	IR	JIR	Total	BJIR	ILRR	IR	JIR	Total
Articles with data	12	18	11	16	57	21	27	17	21	86	20	30	20	17	87
Type of data															
Quantitative	6 (50%)	10 (56%)	8 (73%)	2 (13%)	26 (46%)	16 (76%)	23 (85%)	14 (82%)	12 (57%)	68 (79%)	13 (65%)	29(97%)	17 (57%)	3 (18%)	62 (71%)
Non-quantitative	6 (50%)	10 (56%)	8 (73%)	2 (13%)	26 (46%)	5 (24%)	4 (15%)	3 (18%)	9 (43%)	32 (37%)	7 (35%)	1 (3%)	3 (15%)	14 (82%)	38 (35%)
Multivariate analysis	0 (0%)	2 (11%)	1 (9%)	1 (6%)	4 (7%)	4 (19%)	20 (74%)	13 (76%)	4 (19%)	41 (48%)	6 (30%)	25(83%)	17 (85%)	2 (12%)	41 (47%)
Data collected by:															
Author	3 (25%)	3 (17%)	3 (27%)	11 (69%)	20 (35%)	10 (48%)	6 (22%)	7 (41%)	7 (33%)	41 (48%)	14 (70%)	6 (20%)	6 (30%)	7 (41%)	49 (56%)
Other	2 (17%)	8 (44%)	6 (55%)	5 (31%)	21 (37%)	7 (33%)	16 (59%)	10 (59%)	8 (38%)	38 (44%)	6 (30%)	24(80%)	15 (75%)	1 (6%)	39 (45%)
Case study	2 (17%)	4 (22%)	3 (27%)	5 (31%)	14 (25%)	7 (33%)	5 (19%)	4 (24%)	3 (14%)	24 (28%)	6 (30%)	1 (3%)	2 (10%)	6 (35%)	20 (23%)
Multi-method	0 (0%)	2 (11%)	3 (27%)	0 (0%)	5 (9%)	3 (14%)	2 (7%)	4 (24%)	4 (19%)	14 (16%)	5 (25%)	2 (7%)	4 (20%)	3 (18%)	18 (20%)

Source: Whitfield and Strauss (2000).

Table 9.3 Industrial Relations research methods

	1970					1990					
	BJIR	IRJ	ILRR	IR	Total	BJIR	IRJ	ILRR	IR	IB	Total
Broad research topics											
IR topics	42 (43%)	42 (62%)	57 (52%)	43 (36%)	184 (47%)	123 (63%)	143 (73%)	77 (32%)	71 (36%)	84 (92%)	498 (54%)
HR topics	27 (29%)	16 (24%)	19 (17%)	42 (36%)	104 (27%)	44 (23%)	36 (19%)	62 (26%)	54 (28%)	1 (1%)	197 (21%)
Labor market topics	25 (27%)	10 (15%)	33 (30%)	34 (29%)	102 (26%)	28 (14%)	16 (8%)	104 (43%)	70 (36%)	6 (6%)	224 (24%)
Total	94 (100%)	68 (100%)	109 (100%)	119 (100%)	390 (100%)	195 (100%)	195 (100%)	243 (100%)	195 (100%)	91 (100%)	919 (100%)
Nature of Article											
Empirical descriptive	20 (21%)	18 (26%)	20 (18%)	25 (21 %)	83 (21%)	56 (29%)	86 (44%)	10 (4%)	17 (9%)	12 (13%)	181 (20%)
Empirical inductive	30 (32%)	12 (17%)	33 (30%)	41 (35%)	116 (30%)	56 (29%)	37 (19%)	146 (60%)	94 (48%)	20 (22%)	353 (38%)
Empirical deductive	9 (9%)	11 (16%)	29 (27%)	15 (13%)	64 (16%)	38 (19%)	21 (11%)	71 (29%)	59 (30%)	5 (6%)	194 (21%)
Thinkpiece/essay	20 (21%)	19 (28%)	18 (17%)	25 (21%)	82 (21%)	40 (21%)	48 (25%)	12 (5%)	17 (9%)	39 (43%)	156 (17%)
Theory	15 (16%)	8 (12%)	9 (8%)	13 (11%)	45 (12%)	5 (3%)	3 (2%)	4 (2 %)	8 (4%)	15 (17%)	35 (4 %)
Total	94 (100%)	68 (100%)	119 (100%)	119 (100%)	390 (100%)	195 (100%)	195 (100%)	243 (100%)	195 (100%)	91 (100%)	919 (100%)
Methodology											
Qualitative	19 (32%)	20 (49%)	16 (20%)	19 (24%)	74 (28%)	58 (39%)	96 (67%)	11 (5%)	20 (12%)	24 (59%)	209 (28.6%)
Quantitative	40 (68%)	21 (51%)	66 (80%)	62 (76%)	189 (72%)	92 (61%)	48 (33%)	216 (95%)	150 (88%)	17 (41%)	523 (71.4%)
Total	59 (100%)	41 (100%)	82 (100%)	81 (100%)	263 (100%)	150 (100%)	144 (100%)	227 (100%)	170 (100%)	41 (100%)	732 (100%)
Dataset size											
Small	36 (61%)	36 (88%)	50 (61%)	49 (60%)	171 (65%)	89 (59%)	122 (85%)	51 (22%)	64 (38%)	30 (81%)	356 (49%)
Large	23 (39%)	5 (12%)	32 (39%)	32 (40%)	92 (35%)	61 (41%)	22 (15%)	176 (78%)	106 (62%)	7 (19%)	372 (51%)
Total	59 (100%)	41 (100%)	82 (100%)	81 (100%)	263 (100%)	150 (100%)	144 (100%)	227 (100%)	170 (100%)	37 (100%)	728 (100%)
Analytical level											
Macro	22 (37%)	9 (22%)	17 (21%)	18 (22%)	66 (25%)	27 (18%)	49 (34%)	20 (9%)	24 (14%)	6 (13%)	126 (17%)
Sector	11 (19%)	10 (24%)	21 (26%)	24 (30%)	66 (25%)	34 (23%)	31 (22%)	26 (11%)	30 (18%)	6 (13%)	127 (17%)
Firm	14 (24%)	16 (39%)	11 (13%)	17 (21%)	58 (22%)	73 (48 %)	51 (35%)	65 (29%)	60 (35%)	28 (62%)	277 (38%)
Micro	12 (20%)	6 (15%)	33 (40%)	22 (27%)	73 (28%)	16 (11%)	13 (9%)	116 (51%)	56 (33%)	5 (11%)	206 (28%)
Total	59 (100%)	41 (100%)	82 (100%)	81 (100%)	263 (100%)	150 (100%)	144 (100%)	227 (100%)	170 (100%)	45 (100%)	736 (100%)

Source: Frege (2005).

more than one method in 1997, and even fewer did in earlier years. They also found that, in 1997, data for the overwhelming majority of articles appearing in the two US journals was collected by 'others'. Outside the US, it was more typically collected by the authors themselves.

These two studies largely support our book's original observations. We see no reason to change them. Specifically, they indicate that our field is extremely hetero-geneous, which is possibly both its main strength and its main weakness. There are substantial cross-national differences in the way in which research is undertaken. The US has clearly seen the greatest move toward the more deductive, discipline-oriented approach, though ILRR seems to have reflected this more than IR. Of the non-US journals, both the Australian JIR and the German IB have remained more committed to publishing papers in the older Industrial Relations tradition than is the British BJIR.

Yet taking the field as a whole, there have been moves over time away from inductive, policy-oriented, macro-focused research and toward that which is deductive, discipline-oriented, and micro-focused in all countries studied. The use of multi-method approaches is still the exception rather than the rule, but does show signs of becoming more prominent. Secondary analysis of data-sets is becoming more common, reflecting the many changes in the nature of the subject and the broader environment.

There has therefore clearly been consider-able change in the nature of IR research in recent years, but whether this is a good or bad thing is debatable. Clearly, the field has adapted to the availability of powerful data-sets, and has made considerable use of the range of new analytical techniques that have emerged in the economic and social sciences. But, to some extent, this has been at the cost of losing its close connections both with the people and institutions studied and with the policy implications of the research findings. And there is a *prima facie* case that it has resulted in a failure to develop a broader, multi-method, approach to empirical research

that might have grown out of the field's more traditional approach (but which that approach did not itself encompass). Whatever the net effect of these changes, it is clear that IR scholars have still not settled on a way of undertaking research that is both distinctive and widely-accepted. The search for the Holy Grail goes on.

THE FUTURE

In 1998, we argued that the future advance-ment of IR as a field of study required that more attention should be paid to four main areas:

1) concepts;
2) scope;
3) title;
4) research design.

Conceptual developments

In our view, conceptual development in the IR area has stalled. If anything, scholars from other fields have increasingly studied topics which traditionally were considered to be in IR's balliwick, but now using these other fields' analytic tools. Further, as Jarley et al. (2001) document, a high percentage of the articles appearing in the main US IR journals are written by scholars whose identification is not with IR (at least they don't belong to the field's primary professional organization, then called the Industrial Relations Research Association). This causes the authors 'to question whether IR can sustain a unique scholarly community…[and whether] … IR journals will continue to provide a venue for sustaining a coherent, cumulative literature that will distinguish the field from other areas' (p. 343). But as Kaufman (2004) suggests, the IR field in the UK may be more cohesive than that in the US, and so less likely to change.

A key contribution to the discussion of conceptual tools is Paul Edwards' recent (2005) paper, which built on our original spec-ulations. The key theme of this paper is that one of IR's main strengths is its sensitivity to context. In short, this means that how Factor A influences Factor B depends on other Factors, C, D, and E (psychologists call them moderators). Greater context-sensitivity, Edwards argues, will facilitate further methodological progress, build stronger links with the other social sciences, and possibly result in greater policy relevance.

Context-specificity, however, comes at quite a cost. It inevitably fragments the subject-area. Studies undertaken in given settings help us to understand the complexity of relationships within that particular setting, but may provide few insights as to what is happening elsewhere. Often single-situation research is justified as contributing to the development of middle-range theory, but typically the theoretical contribution of such highly-focused studies is minimal. IR still lacks an overall theory. This may be strength, but on balance it may be even more a weakness. Consequently, IR people typically only have fragments of theory with which to work, and they lack the more all-embracing theoretical frameworks that those in related fields and disciplines have at their disposal.

Context-specificity also gives an air to the field that suggests that it is a second-order subject-area that uncovers uncomfortable facts that others explain and develop. For example, many of the key features of the so-called new institutional labor economics are based around stylized/simplified facts that have been developed from the work of IR researchers, such as those related to the internal labor market concept. While some IR scholars have attempted to develop alternative, more realistic, theoretical approaches around such context-specific research (most notably, for example, Michael Piore), these efforts have been overwhelmed by the work of those attempting to integrate their existing and less realistic theoretical frameworks with what is typically a narrow conception of the facts outlined by the context-focused researchers. The advent of Personnel Economics is a prime example of this in action (Lazear, 2000).

IR's scope

In 1998, we suggested that IR should return to its earlier emphasis on policy. To our mind, there has been little positive change in this respect, if anything the reverse. In terms of subject-matter, we have definitely seen a major expansion in the range of subjects examined in recent years, and IR research now covers far more than just union-management relations. However, much of this new research is done at arm's length from the concerns of key policy-makers. Indeed, the current political situation, at least in the US, makes it unlikely that academic policy recommendations would be reflected in practice. This reduces scholars' incentives to make them. In short, it would seem that IR research has broadened its scope, while not noticeably increasing its involvement with the real world that it seeks to understand.

The end of IR as a distinct field?

The trend toward abandoning the term 'Industrial Relations' has continued, especially in the US. Where it is not being displaced by *Human Resource Management*, it is being replaced by *Work Studies* or, more commonly, *Employment Relations*. Among the organizations changing their name are the former Industrial Relations Research Association in the US (now the Labor and Employment Relations Association) and the former British Workplace Industrial Relations Surveys (now Workplace Employment Relations Surveys). How long before the other leading institutions in the field follow suit? The new names imply that IR covers more than labor-relations. But does it all imply that IR is no longer a distinct field?

Research design

In 1998, we argued that IR should place greater emphasis on research design; for example, multi-method studies which permit triangulation should be encouraged. Some progress has definitely been made in this area. Younger scholars, in particular, are thinking more broadly about research design, and are crossing the qualitative/quantitative divide more often. This may reflect broader and more systematic research training, or merely a change in the background of those researching in the subject-area, away from those who enter from the practitioner domain. Purely descriptive work is being replaced by that which is avowedly analytical. In our view, this is the area in which greatest and positive change is occurring and which offers the most scope for the future advancement of a field that has made and continues to make major and distinctive contributions to our understanding of the world of work.

ACKNOWLEDGMENTS

The authors would like to thank all of the authors of *Researching the World of Work: Strategies and Methods in Studying Industrial Relations* (1998) for stimulating a lot of the ideas that have gone into this paper and Paul Blyton, Dan Cornfield, and Jack Fiorito for extremely perceptive comments on an earlier draft.

REFERENCES

Brown, William. (1998) 'Funders and Research: The Vulnerability of the Subject', in Keith Whitfield and George Strauss (eds) *Researching the World of Work: Strategies and Methods in Studying Industrial Relations.* Ithaca: ILR Press. pp. 267–86.

Cappelli, Peter. (1985) 'Theory Construction in IR and Some Implications for Research', *Industrial Relations,* 24 (1): 90–112.

Clawson, Dan. (2003) *The Next Union Upsurge: Labor and the New Social Movements.* Ithaca: ILR Press.

Commission on the Future of Worker-Management Relations. (1994). *Final Report.* US Department of Labor and US Department of Commerce.

Commons, John, R. (1909) 'American Shoemakers, 1648–1895', *Quarterly Journal of Economics,* 24 (November): 39–98.

Dickens, W.T (1983) 'The Effect of Company Campaigns on Certification Elections: Law and Reality Once Again'. *Industrial and Labor Relations Review,* 36 (4): 560–75.

Edwards, P. (2005) 'The Challenging but Promising Future of Industrial Relations: Developing Theory and Method in Context-Sensitive Research', *Industrial Relations Journal,* 36 (4): 264–82.

Farber, H. S. and Krueger, A. B. (1993) 'Union Membership in the United States: The Decline Continues', in Bruce Kaufman and Morris Kleiner, (eds) *Employee Representation: Alternatives and Future Directions.* Madison, WI: Industrial Relations Research Association.

Freeman, R.B and Medoff, J.L (1984) *What do unions do?* New York : Basic Books.

Frege, C. (2005) 'Varieties of Industrial Relations Research: Take-over, Convergence or Divergence?' *British Journal of Industrial Relations,* 43 (2): 179–207.

Getman, J.G., Goldberg, S.B., and Herman, J.B. (1976) *Union Representation Elections: Law and Reality.* New York: Russell Sage Foundation.

Gordon, M.E., Philpot, J.W., Burt, R.E., Thompson, C.A., and Spiller, W.E. (1980) 'Commitment to the Union – Development of a Measure and an Examination of its Correlates', *Journal of Applied Psychology,* 65: 479–99.

Greenberg, J. (1990) 'Organisational Justice: Yesterday, Today and Tomorrow', *Journal of Management,* 16 (2): 399–432.

Hancock, K.J. (1985) *Australian Industrial Relations Law and Systems: Report of the Committee of Review.* Canberra: AGPS.

Ichniowski, Casey, Levine, Davis, Olson, Craig, and Strauss, George (eds) (2000) *The American Workplace: Skills, Compensation, and Employee Involvement.* Cambridge: Cambridge University Press.

Jarley, Paul, Chandler, Timothy, and Faulk, Larry (2001) 'Maintaining a Scholarly Community: Casual Authorship and the State of IR Research', *Industrial Relations,* 40 (2): 338–43.

Kaufman, Bruce. (2004) *The Global Evolution of Industrial Relations.* Geneva: International Labor Office.

Keenoy, Tom (1999) 'HRM as Hologram: A Polemic', *Journal of Management Studies,* 36 (1): 1–23.

Kelly, J. (1998) *Rethinking Industrial Relations: Mobilization, Collectivism and Long Waves.* Routledge: London.

Lazear, E. P. (2000) 'The Future of Personnel Economics', *Economic Journal,* 110: 611–39.

Lipset, S.M., Trow, M.A., and Coleman, J.S. (1956) *Union democracy: the internal politics of the International Typographical Union.* New York: Free Press.

Marginson, P. (1998) 'The Survey Tradition in British Industrial Relations Research', *British Journal of Industrial Relations,* 36 (3): 361–88.

McCarthy, W. (1994) 'Of Hats and Cattle: or the Limits of Macro-survey Research in Industrial Relations', *Industrial Relations Journal*, 25(4): 315–22, December.

McDuffie, J. P. and Pill, F. (1995) *The international assembly plant study: update on round two findings.* Briefing paper, MIT International Motor Vehicle Program, Cambridge, MA.

Millis, Harry and Royal Montgomery. *The Economics of Labor.* Vol. 1. *Labor's Progress and Some Basic Labor Problems (*1938); Vol. II, *Labor's Risks and Social Insurance (1938);* Vol. III *Organized Labor* (1945). New York: McGraw-Hill.

Millward, N. (1993) 'Uses of the Workplace Industrial Relations Surveys by British Labor Economists'. *CEP Discussion Papers* 0145, Centre for Economic Performance, LSE.

Royal Commission on Trade Unions and Employers' Associations 1968). *Report* (London: HMSO).

Schwab, D. P. (2005) *Research Methods for Organizational Studies.* Mahwah, NJ: Lawrence Erlbaum.

Siegel, Jay. (1998) 'Industrial Relations Research and the American Policy-Making Process', In Keith Whitfield and George Strauss (eds) *Researching the World of Work: Strategies and Methods in Studying Industrial Relations.* Ithaca, NY: ILR Press.

Strauss, George and Peter Feuille (1978) 'Industrial Relations Research: A Critical Appraisal', *Industrial Relations*, 17 (3): 259–77.

Thelan, Kathleen. (2004) *How Institutions Evolve: The Political Economy of Skills in Germany, Great Britain, the United States and Japan.* Cambridge: Cambridge Universitry Press.

Voss, Kim and Sherman, Rachel. (2000) 'Breaking the Iron Law of Oligarchy: Union Revitalization in the American Labor Movement', *American Journal of Sociology*, 106 (2): 303–49.

Walton R. E. and McKersie R. B. (1965) *A Behavioral Theory of Labor Negotiation.* New York: McGraw-Hill.

Whitfield, K. and Strauss, G. (eds) (1998) *Researching the World of Work: Strategies and Methods in Studying Industrial Relations.* Ithaca, NY: ILR Press.

Whitfield, Keith and Strauss, George (2000) 'Methods Matter: Changes in Industrial Relations Research and their Implications', *British Journal of Industrial Relations*, 38 (1): 141–52.

PART TWO

The Actors in Industrial Relations

10

Trade Union Morphology

Jack Fiorito and Paul Jarley

Morphology (dfn): Any scientific study of form and structure. From *Webster's New World Dictionary, Second College Edition*, 1984.

morphology [mawr-fol-*uh*-jee] – *noun*; the study of the form or structure of anything [Origin: 1820–30; MORPHO- + -LOGY; first formed in G. Dictionary.com Unabridged (v 1.01) Based on the *Random House Unabridged Dictionary*, © Random House, Inc. 2006.

SCOPE

Union structure traditionally connotes external (or horizontal) and internal (or vertical) dimensions (Fiorito et al., 1991). External structure refers to the scope of membership, boundaries in terms of membership criteria and patterns distinguishing one union from another, etc. Internal structure refers to two sub-dimensions, governance (or representation) and administration. In addition to external and internal structure, this chapter considers the nature or 'soul' (Budd, 2004: 137–57) of union representation, encompassing the 'servicing model' vs. 'organizing model' debate, and in doing so, addresses

recent suggestions that unions may be conceptualized as networks that produce social capital.

We focus on national and local unions in English speaking Anglo-Saxon nations, particularly Britain and the US, with occasional references elsewhere. Unions are largely embedded within and shaped by national cultures, institutions, and legal systems (Ebbinghaus and Visser, 1999), such that attempts at broader comparisons tend to be limited to summary statistics, such as membership levels, that are most easily compared (for example, Visser, 1989, 2006). There are a few notable exceptions to this generalization, of course, studies that expressly address union structures across nations (for example, Visser and Waddington [1996] comparing Sweden, The Netherlands, and Britain). There are also collections of more in-depth analyses within specific nations, or that emphasize particular union effects across nations on such topics as productivity or employer innovation (for example, Addison and Schnabel, 2003). Other studies focus on federations of unions (for example, Ebbinghaus, 2003) or other structural units.

UNION GOALS AND STRATEGIC CHOICE

Structural functionalism suggests that any discussion of structure should start with function or purpose. Unions dedicated primarily to protecting and improving the well-being of their members or workers generally within an existing socio-economic order will likely choose different strategies and structures than those dedicated primarily to creating a new socio-economic order. The choice of who to serve (for example, members vs. workers generally) is also important. A union emphasizing its members' interests might have relatively less interest in works councils or protective legislation than one emphasizing broader interests. The choice of strategy itself may affect structure as well. For example, a strategy emphasizing collective bargaining might favor narrower craft unions while a strategy emphasizing political action or mutual aid might favor more general unions. This basic framework has been laid out previously (Fiorito et al., 1991).

Given that union strategy is addressed in another chapter, we only wish to point out that our discussion of morphology is embedded in a broader framework – it does not assume that a discussion of unions logically begins with structure.

As a further preliminary, we note that our emphasis on *choice* is deliberate. Others (for example, Strauss, 1993) challenge that emphasis, noting that union structures are in many instances most easily understood as historical accidents, highly idiosyncratic, affected by leader personalities and various other nearly random influences, or as *reactions* to environmental factors such as legislation affecting recognition, workforce feminization, and institutions such as mechanisms for union roles in providing government funded benefits (Ebbinghaus and Visser, 1999). All true! Strategic choices are not made in a vacuum or a laboratory free from 'contaminants.' Nonetheless choices are made and actions and consequences follow from those choices that differ from the actions and consequences of other choices. Although

noting various anomalies of union structure, Strauss concedes that 'it is the regularities that should prove of greatest interest' (1993: 2).

In this modest but important sense, choices matter. Ship captains and airline pilots have little control over currents, winds, and others' choices, yet their choices on courses, speed, and other variables are decisive, albeit not entirely deterministic. Union leaders and the members who ultimately choose and direct them may not enjoy the degree of control that ship captains and pilots do, but their choices are still decisive. Although the case of any given union at a particular moment may be best understood in terms of its idiosyncratic milieu, a more general understanding of union morphology requires appreciation for the role of choice.

EXTERNAL STRUCTURE

A primary distinction here is between craft vs. industrial unions, with craft unions emphasizing representation of particular skill groups regardless of product or service produced, and industrial unions emphasizing representation for workers producing a particular product or service without regard to worker skills. Other representation bases including enterprise, religion, ideology, geography, or ethnicity/tribe are important in some nations. Some of these bases have been or still are important in some nations or within some niches in advanced Anglo-Saxon nations at times (for example, Scottish teachers) and at different levels within labor movements (for example, the peak federation or local level). Further, there are occasional calls to reconsider establishing, or efforts to establish, unions on alternate bases (for example, Cobble (2001) on craft unions and other forms), recent efforts to unite US Wal-Mart workers (for example, Associated Press, 2005), community-based alliances or transformations for the British steel workers' union (now 'Community' but still mainly iron and steel workers (Trades Union Congress, 2005)); also see, for example, Jacoby and Verma (1992), ro 'company unions' in the US. The community-based union form may have particular appeal for industry-based unions in declining industries that traditionally dominated particular areas.

Historically, craft unions emerged by the early twentieth century as the dominant form in the nations of main interest, possibly due to an 'organic solidarity' arising from common training and skills and the ability of craft unions to wage successful strikes due to difficulty in replacing skilled workers. As industrialization proceeded, however, Taylorist and Fordist reorganizations of work in many industries undermined traditional craft distinctions, lending support to calls from Marxists and others for industry-based unions that were in socialist views better suited to a broader sense of class consciousness rather than craft consciousness (Strauss, 1993).

In the US, the craft vs. industrial debate exploded in the 1930s with pro-industrial unionism forces (what became the Congress of Industrial Organizations or CIO) seceding from the dominant labor federation, the American Federation of Labor (AFL), organizing millions of workers on an industrial basis and creating many well-known unions such as the United Auto Workers (UAW). At the same time, craft unions such as the International Brotherhood of Electrical Workers (IBEW) were in many instances compelled to accept a new reality and relax their opposition to industrial unionism in practice if not in principle. The AFL–CIO merger of 1955 reflected various influences but of greatest immediate significance was its meaning in terms of acceptance of industrial unionism. In fact, industrial unions and industrial unionism (even within some nominal craft unions) tended to dominate organized labor for much of the twentieth century.

The continued dominance of either form is in serious doubt. In theory, market forces in either product or labor markets remain a strong impetus for craft or industrial forms by influencing bargaining structures needed 'to take wages out of competition' (Commons, 1909), but the legal and perhaps sociological concept of 'community of interest' seems a less significant driver of union structure today than in past times. Many unions have clearly diversified their membership bases, often in response to employment declines within traditional jurisdictions (for example, autos and steel) coupled with opportunistic organizing or mergers (for example, Chaison, 2001). Although the assertion that many national unions today (in the US) are 'general' unions (Budd, 2005: 196) may be an overstatement, there is some merit in this as a description of tendencies. In Australia, the statutorily encouraged consolidation of unions via minimum size requirements for legal registration clearly pushed unions toward general forms.

Many of the more general unions have internalized formerly external structures, in effect preserving occupational or industrial identities within their union through divisions and similar sub-structures, making them a bit like mini-federations. In the past, unions have used similar internalization of external structure to address enterprise-specific issues (for example, GM and Ford 'departments' within the US' United Auto Workers). With bargaining increasingly decentralized from industry levels to enterprise levels (see Chapter 21), enterprise dimensions within union structures should grow in importance, and increasing roles for European works councils will likely add momentum to this trend.

Britain presents an interesting case in evolving union structures. Several national unions have made conscious efforts to 're-brand' themselves in response to membership composition changes and perceived opportunities for survival and growth. One of the first and better-known instances is Unison, the mainly public sector giant, but more recent examples include Community, Connect (mainly telecommunications), and Amicus (mainly manufacturing, printing, and finance). These are recently formed or re-branded unions that can still be linked in a 'union genealogy' sense to specific industries, occupations or firms, but their intent seems to be to evolve away from their roots. The GMB ('Britain's General Union') is also an interesting case in asserting that its three-initial 'name' doesn't stand for anything in particular in terms of craft or industry, although it once did (General, Municipal, and Boilermakers).

A further interesting British case for a slightly different reason is the construction union, UCATT. While its acronym is more traditional in not spelling anything that would be mistaken for a word, and reflecting words (for example, 'c' for construction) that reveal its base, it is notable as the modern descendant of various genuine *trade* unions in an industry (along with railroads) and nation famous for its narrow craft-based unions. In fact, some US writers still note that Britain's unique Industrial Relations (IR) characteristics include numerous narrow craft unions, but one could argue that British (or Australian) union consolidation toward general unions is considerably more advanced than that in the US.

Some American unions have taken smaller and sometimes faltering steps in this re-branding direction, notably in the cases of PACE and UNITE-HERE. In these cases, the letters used to form the new 'name' still link the union to its roots, but the union seems to have consciously chosen a name that can have more general appeal as an acronym. Some might argue that names are unimportant, but in these instances they seem to carry at least symbolic importance, reflecting trends toward union generality in external structure. PACE, however, was relatively short-lived as a national union, subsequently merging into the United Steel Workers of America. Thus the generality trend continued, but the re-branding trend was abandoned in this instance.

Intertwined with this trend toward general unionism is a distinct consolidation trend. In terms of membership, and more so in terms of organizing activity (Fiorito, 2003; Fiorito and Jarley, 2003), union membership is being concentrated in smaller numbers of national unions. (This despite the notable failure of the proposed merger between the UAW, IAM, and USWA that would have created a new 'superunion' roughly comparable to the German I.G. Metall.) The AFL-CIO had over 100 affiliates as recently as about 1980, but today claims about 60 affiliates (prior to the Change to Win Federation [CWF] secession). The recent creation through merger of

ver.di (United Services Union) in Germany illustrates that these trends extend beyond the focal nations (Keller, 2005; also see Streeck and Visser, 1997). In Britain, the number of 'major' national unions (say with 10, 000 or more members) is just over 30 (Trades Union Congress, 2006). Even within these respective numbers of unions, relatively small numbers account for a very substantial majority of union membership. These 'dominant players' have sometimes questioned whether 'one union, one vote'-type executive committee structures are appropriate, particularly in the US. To some extent the CWF secession reflected this tension (among other factors), with nearly all of the seceding unions coming from the ranks of the AFL-CIO's largest affiliates. The implications for worker choice of representative may be interesting. On one hand, consolidation suggests fewer choices and greater centralization of decision-making, but on the other, the CWF secession partly enabled by that consolidation may ultimately lead to more competition for membership and more responsive union leadership.

Is industrial unionism doomed? Around 1950, it appeared that industrial unionism had arrived to stay. Some may even have pointed to Marxian predictions of its inevitability and appropriateness. Now its future seems in doubt. The theoretical underpinnings in terms of market structure are still relevant (see Commons, 1909), but in many industries globalization has undermined the viability of *national* industrial unions. Cornfield (2006) recently argued that the CWF's formation represents resurgent 'universalistic' industrial unionism, but the CWF unions tend to represent workers in local and regional product and service markets and have generally not faced the full force of globalization. It is still conceivable that industrial unionism will resurge at a transnational level or through more closely co-ordinated national units (if that is truly different than transnational unionism). European economic integration and similar movements elsewhere will tend to push in that direction. The obvious anchor on these trends is limited 'like-consciousness' across national borders, limiting workers' sense of community of interest. This too may change as information technology and globalization become more pervasive (for example, as underscored by the ubiquitous Wal-Mart, McDonald's, and Starbucks). It may be apt to note that the Industrial Workers of the World have recently organized a few Starbucks shops in New York, although this may be of no real significance and merely an instance of 'boutique unionism' under a universalistic name (albeit a name with considerable historical significance in the US).

An interesting question is whether industrial unionism can resurge at a transnational level if its national counterparts evolve away from industrial forms. Some sort of 'matrix' structure that would allow functional linkages along industrial lines between sections of general unions would seem appropriate, perhaps something similar to the Building and Construction Trades Department within the AFL-CIO that links historically craft-based unions based on their common industrial interests. With international conglomerate giants, attention also is needed to linkages across industrial interests within firms. At least to some extent the International Confederation of Free Trade Unions' (ICFTU) 'Global Union Federations' (formerly 'Trade Secretariats') serve this role.

Amidst this discussion emphasizing industrial unionism and general unionism, it should be noted that 'craft' unionism (broadly defined to include occupation-based unions beyond traditional crafts) survives and thrives in certain quarters. Indeed, many of the public employee unions that have grown despite general union decline have a distinctly craft orientation (for example, nurses, teachers). Increasingly, craft-oriented unions are in fact professional worker unions. In part this reflects technological changes that have undermined some traditional crafts (for example, factory prefabrication of components formerly built on-site or technological advances such as paint spray-guns that have deskilled jobs in construction), while broader shifts in advanced industrial economies toward professional services have favored growth in professional worker ranks. In many cases

these professional unions are fairly small and sometimes uncomfortable about being labeled 'unions' (preferring terms such as 'professional association'). In contrast to the devastating impact of globalization on many industrial unions, however, these unions have generally benefited from restructuring of economies toward more professional work (Wilson, 2006).

Research in these areas is limited by ignorance regarding union membership composition. None of the focal nations can claim sufficient data to track changes in this over time. In the US case, the last time a government-sponsored survey solicited information on the industrial composition of membership was 1979 (US Bureau of Labor Statistics, 1980). Case studies both within nations (for example, Chaison, 2001; Keller, 2005) and across nations (for example, Chaison, 1996) have examined particular unions and small samples of cases that provide observable events through mergers. Frequently these studies suggest that while theory and norms emphasize synergies and resource rationales (for example, that larger unions can function more effectively and efficiently), opportunism and idiosyncrasies such as union internal politics and personalities play a large role. There have been very limited efforts to link external structure to outcomes, with limited success (for example, Fiorito et al., 1995; Heery et al., 2003b; Maranto and Fiorito, 1987).

INTERNAL STRUCTURE

As noted earlier, internal structure consists of two main dimensions, representation or governance (two sides of the same coin) and administration. The first focuses on the extent that union members control their union directly or through representative government, for instance, indirectly through their power to choose and change leaders. The second focuses on how efficient and effective the union is in achieving its goals.

The contours of representative and administrative structures may be the result of different contingencies (Jarley et al., 1997), but the everyday tension between these two features has long been noted (for example, Child et al., 1973) in expressions such as 'a union must at the same time be an army and a town meeting' (Muste, 1928). More recently, Heckscher (1988) alluded to unions as associations trying to act like organizations. At least in the focal nations, unions have a strong democratic tradition, often reinforced in statutes motivated by deviant cases or perceived abuses.

A long-standing union democracy debate revolves around the allegedly inherent tendency of organizations, including unions, toward oligarchy and conservatism, or Michels' 'Iron Law' (Voss and Sherman, 2000). Such tendencies have unquestionably been observed in some unions (for example, Moody, 1988). Their inevitability, however, has been repeatedly challenged by scholars studying union democracy and related matters. Notable recent contributions in this vein include works by Heery (2006), Kelly and Heery (1994), Knoke (1990), Moody (1988), and Voss and Sherman (2000).

Much of the literature presumes or concludes that union democratic traditions are frequently at odds with organizational effectiveness as suggested by the juxtaposition of oppositional concepts (for example, army vs. town meeting, organization vs. association, or bureaucracy vs. democracy). Alternatively, some argue that this tension may exist in the short term, but that long run suppression or neglect of democracy reduces member commitment and consequently the union's capacity for mobilization and effectiveness in the long term (Kochan, 1980). Also, some would argue that democracy is itself a union goal, and thus a union cannot be effective or efficient if it is not democratic as a matter of definition, aside from any adverse goal achievement effects from autocracy (Strauss, 1991). The other side of the argument stresses that even autocratic unions can have a democratizing influence at the workplace, and that members are far more concerned with that influence than participating in the democracy of their union (Bok and Dunlop, 1970).

A more extreme form of this debate contrasts spontaneous worker actions with organizationally sanctioned activity. Batstone (1988: 86) summarizes this debate within the context of British workplace reforms and shop steward roles in the 1970s:

> The bureaucratization thesis is part of a larger ethos of 'workerism' or 'rank-and-filism' which assumes that the spontaneous actions of workers are to be applauded while those of formal worker organizations are to be condemned; pre-reform shop stewards were an expression of spontaneity. Or, to put the matter another way, the thesis accepts that there exists a tension between the 'movement' and 'organization' features of trade unions and believes that the former is the more valid. While accepting the high premium (apparently) placed on democracy in this approach, I would wish to argue that the extent to which worker interests can be promoted without formal organization is limited and the extent to which stewards could ever be seen as simply part of the 'rank-and-file' is open to question.

As Batstone's comments suggest, there is a tendency in some quarters to see only the coercive, disempowering face of bureaucracy. This myopia neglects the enabling or empowering face (Adler and Borys, 1996).

Democracy or governance studies typically examine behavioral indicators such as member participation, election closeness, and leader turnover, attitudinal indicators such as members' perceived influence, and structural indicators from union constitutions including provisions on election and convention frequency, concentration of authority, potential power bases for leadership challenges, and member ability to recall incumbents (Strauss, 1991). No single indicator stands out. Rather, researchers seem to agree that there are many possible ways to measure democracy and none that is clearly superior despite some efforts to identify *the* key indicator (for example, Gamm, 1979). There has been some effort to move away from a simple democracy vs. autocracy perspective toward a broader focus on governance structures (Jarley et al., 2000). Consistent with the multiple indicators view but with a configurational emphasis, evidence suggests that certain combinations of structural variables recur such that one can identify distinctive union governance types, at least among US national unions (Jarley et al., 2000).

New issues continue to be added to the union democracy and governance mix. A growing issue is the role of 'identity groups' such as women, ethnic groups, gays and lesbians, and disabled workers. Nominally 'color-blind' (and similar) policies have often been judged insufficient to give effective voice to large segments of workers who have traditionally been minorities in many unions. Based on data from as recently as 2002, Heery called the absence of ethnic minorities in UK union officer ranks 'truly striking' (Heery, 2006: 464). 'Reserved seats' and similar devices have been offered as partial solutions, but there are differing views on the desirability and efficacy of these and alternatives (Colgan and Ledwith, 2003; also see Chapter 30).

Varied conceptions of democracy, its intertwining with centralization, and mixed results make it difficult to summarize findings on the long-standing debate on democracy and effectiveness. That said the evidence appears to favor those arguing for democracy as a prerequisite for effectiveness (for example, Charlwood, 2004; Fiorito et al., 1995; Maranto and Fiorito, 1987). It may be premature to summarize evidence on governance structure links to outcomes, but at least some of the findings suggest promise in this approach (see Jarley et al., 2000).

Studies focused on union effectiveness *per se* and those that examine unions as organizations tend to draw their inspiration from earlier work based in other organizational settings, notably businesses. Researchers have established that many bureaucracy concepts are somewhat transplantable. That is, one can speak of centralization of decisions, and a cluster of 'rationalization' measures (US sense; Barbash, 1969) or 'structuring of activities' (Warner, 1975) including specialization of functions, hierarchy of authority, formalization of procedures, and standardization of tasks within unions, or at least in larger unions including most nationals, in much the same way that these concepts

are used in other organizations. Warner (1975) noted this parallel for unions and other organizations, and further that several bureaucracy dimensions tended to correlate positively with each other and size in both settings but that centralization stood apart and decreased with size.

A notable qualifier arises for centralization, however, as centralization of decisions often means control by *elected* leaders relative to *non-elected* staff, and in this sense is confounded with democracy (Warner, 1975). In theory, a union could be highly centralized and highly democratic (in at least some regards), but in practice the two may be closely related and difficult to distinguish. A further complication arises because of the distinctions between staff, elected officials, and members within unions. In most organizations, virtually all members are employees. There is no staff vs. elected officer distinction, and 'members' (employees) do not have rights to elect organizational leaders. Although the staff vs. officer division in unions has some parallels in staff vs. line division within other organizations, the latter division does not entail such clear bureaucracy vs. democracy overtones unless one adopts the somewhat strained assumption that shareholders are analogous to union members and exercise their democratic control (at least in so far as a share is comparable to a citizen) via top line employees, for instance, top executives.

In sum, the parallels between unions and most other organizational forms exist at a fairly broad level. They begin to break down upon closer examination. While something may be learned by transplanting concepts and measures, there are clearly limitations. Some progress has been made in understanding union effectiveness and its antecedents, in some cases paralleling findings from other settings, but at the same time there have been notable discrepancies and poor performance for some measures (for example, Charlwood, 2004; Delaney et al., 1996; Fiorito et al., 1995; 2001; 2002; Heery et al., 2003b; Jarley et al., 1997). Failings may partly reflect such limitations, incomplete models (for example,

inadequate environmental influence conceptualizations or indicators), or both.

Qualifiers aside, it appears that the 'logic
of organizations' more generally applies
somewhat to unions. Decentralization and
innovation were linked with positive union
outcomes such as organizing or overall
effectiveness in various studies (for example,
Fiorito et al., 1995; 2002; Maranto and Fiorito,
1987) but results were sometimes mixed (for
example, Charlwood, 2004). Rationalization
was positively linked to innovation (Delaney
et al., 1996; Jarley et al., 2002; Fiorito
et al., 2000a), but its linkage to downstream
effectiveness outcomes has been more elusive
and perhaps even contrarian in some instances
(for example, Charlwood, 2004; Fiorito et al.,
1995; 2002). Some concepts closely linked
to rationalization have demonstrated expected
positive impacts on union outcomes such as
organizing (for example, Heery et al., 2003b;
Voss and Sherman, 2000). Clark and Gray
(2005) and Heery (2006) recently offered
some of the first published evidence regarding
longitudinal changes in administrative practices within unions, and suggests that unions
are improving their practices (rationalizing).
As yet little published work has linked
these changes to those in outcomes such as
organizing effectiveness (but see Fiorito et al.,
2007).

UNION CRISIS AND THE CONFUSED
SEARCH FOR UNION RENEWAL

Several studies of 'union renewal' and related
assessments or suggestions of new directions
for unions emerged in the late 1990s and
early 2000s with important implications for
union morphology research (for example,
Fairbrother, 2000; Heery, 2003; Heery et al.,
2003a; Kelly, 1998; Masters, 1997; Nissen,
2003a; Rose and Chaison, 2001; Turner et al.,
2001). Many of these reflected a sense of
crisis, a sense that unions are at a critical
juncture. It is a mildly interesting coincidence
that writers in both the UK (Fairbrother,
2000) and US (Masters, 1997) authored
books entitled 'Unions at the Crossroads.'

Unions themselves joined (often friendly and
constructively-minded) critical observers in
recognizing a crisis; of course, prescriptions
vary, but there are some common themes in
much of this work. Central among these is the
familiar debate on the 'organizing model' vs.
'servicing model' of unionism.

The organizing (mobilizing) model
and the servicing model

In caricatures, the traditional servicing model
union, the union type that came to dominate
unionism in the focal countries by the
latter half of the twentieth century, is a
vending machine, roadside auto service, or an
insurance policy. Members pay their dues in
exchange for union representation services,
for when they have a need, breakdown,
or claim, respectively. The servicing union
employs staff to provide these services more
effectively and efficiently, in theory, than
members can provide services to themselves.
Notice that in the servicing model, the focus
of union morphology research at least in terms
of internal structure, is on staff. Staff members
are employees of the union and in examining
how unions structured their activities it was
natural for union morphology research to
borrow heavily from the literature on businesses. Efforts to understand rationalization,
innovation, and even the conflict between
bureaucracy and democracy within unions
and their links to union effectiveness can all be
viewed as a product of the dominance of the
service model of unionism and recognition of
the key role of staff in carrying out the day-to-
day activities of servicing model unions. (See
Kelly and Heery's book *Working for the Union*
(1994) on union staff and officer roles.)

Citing the growing evidence of union
decline, concessionary bargaining, increasing
management ability to work the 'system' to
its advantage, and general union malaise,
organizing model proponents attacked the
servicing model as not merely broken, but
fundamentally flawed. In seminal pieces
outlining the debate, Banks and Metzgar (for
example, Metzgar, 1991) and Muehlenkamp
(1991) argued that unions need to return to

their self-help roots. Kelly's (1998) recent effort to advance mobilization theory and highlight the importance of workers' injustice perceptions in motivating collective action is in many ways another effort to underscore the importance of activating members in pursuit of union goals. The importance of member activism has long been recognized: 'The strength of a union depends, in part, upon its ability to *mobilize* its members not only in strikes, but also in policing the collective agreement, filing grievances, and serving in the capacity of union stewards or committee members' (Gallagher and Strauss, 1991: 139, emphasis added).

Union members generally cannot, or at least will not, pay a dues 'price' that provides the expected services adequately (see also Fiorito et al., 1993), perhaps due to reasons involving Wachter's (2003) assertion that (servicing model) union workplace governance is much more expensive than non-union human resource management governance (but see Turnbull, 2003: 513). What workers are often willing to do, however, and can do very efficiently in many instances, is supplement their dues payments with their own services that collectively can provide very substantial benefit to the individual member. For example, a group acting in concert may be able to achieve a grievance settlement much more quickly and on more satisfactory terms than can their contract's formal procedure. In some ways, the organizing model is a call to resume the 'fractional bargaining' (Kuhn, 1961) that institutionalized, mature IR sometimes likened to anarchy on the shop floor.

Just how often and to what extent members are willing to mobilize as activists is unclear, however. Insufficient activism has long been a concern: 'In early research, participation was found to be low, wherever it was studied' (Gallagher and Strauss, 1991:154). This presents a major challenge to, or question for, the organizing model. Data from the World Values Survey in the early 1980s showed that fewer than 10 per cent of union members were willing to volunteer for unpaid union work in the vast majority of advanced industrial nations, with fewer than 8 per cent in Canada and the UK and fewer than 5 per cent in Australia and the US (Kuruvilla and Fiorito, 1994: 550). Gallagher and Strauss (1991: 166) acknowledged limited evidence, but suggested that a potential consequence of steady union decline of recent decades is diminished activism, not simply in terms of a shrinking activist base, but because activism is motivated in part by perceived effectiveness or union instrumentality. Some recent studies present an admittedly haphazard sampling, but suggest still lower activist cadres, fewer than 2 per cent among US manual worker members in two large and diverse locals (Nissen, 1998: 136–138), and fewer than 3 per cent among UK union members in a back office check processing operation (Hartley, 1996: 339). Reviewing her activism findings, Hartley concluded that among her subjects, 'union membership is more like an insurance policy rather than membership of a social group' (1996: 340). Nissen observed that the activist numbers are 'way too small, even in the best cases' (1998: 149) and that '... locals are not getting even the mildly motivated members to volunteer. Instead, the volunteers are the most devoted members' (1998: 140). Both Hartley and Nissen stressed the importance of individuals' feelings of union commitment as the key influence on activism. To some degree such feelings are based on ideologies that are relatively immutable among adults. Kuruvilla and Fiorito (1994) also noted activism-enhancing roles for social referents (for example, co-workers) and job dissatisfaction, however, respectively underscoring the importance of: (1) one-on-one efforts and social networks (see below); and, (2) Kelly's (1998) stress on injustice perceptions as a cause of mobilization. Nissen also offered some hope for union influence in describing success from conscious efforts by unions to bolster activism, and in finding a key role for democracy and transparency within the union as key influences on commitment. Our focus on union morphology requires that we leave this interesting topic aside for now. Still, the potential importance of union structural considerations for individual union commitment and activism, and their importance in turn for the 'very fabric of unions' (Gordon et al., 1980: 480), or unionism's 'soul' (more on this later) are apparent.

More generally, the move from the servicing to the organizing model of unionism can be viewed as a form of decentralization and shift in responsibility away from paid staff and toward workplace rank-and-file activists. In a recent rephrasing, Banks and Metzgar, (2005: 27) argued: 'The focus needs to be on building rank and file committees for everything a union does.' From this very basic idea considerable confusion and controversy have followed both in understanding the basic logic and limits of this new (or should we say *old*?) approach to unions as well as in fashioning research to guide union policy makers interested in using organizational transformation as a primary vehicle for their union's renewal.

Understanding the organizing model of unionism requires new concepts and analytic tools. Very little research, especially quantitative research in English speaking countries, has focused on variations in union structure at the workplace level (but see Batstone, 1988, especially Chapter 3, for a thorough analysis of UK developments during the 1960s and 1970s). Yet, the servicing vs. organizing model distinction suggests very different contours and roles for union structures in the workplace. For one, the shift from a servicing to organizing model changes the role of stewards (for instance delegates) in the workplace. Their roles become less about bureaucratic grievance processing and more about education, relationship building, and mobilization. In essence stewards become internal organizers. More generally, the shift from the servicing to organizing model increases the need for co-ordination mechanisms to mobilize workers and as a result, we should observe more complex structures at the workplace in unions that have made the transformation. One might expect more stewards (or delegates), more frequent meetings among stewards in the workplace, and as Banks and Metzger's (2005) reference

suggests, a greater prevalence of rank-and-file or delegate committees in the workplace.

More fundamentally, the more complex union structures associated with the organizing model suggests a difference in the fabric of workplace interactions among union members and between union members and management on the shop floor. Here, union morphology research would benefit greatly from concepts and analytic tools developed in the burgeoning literature on social networks and social capital in the workplace. (See Putnam (2000) for more on social networks and an analysis that places US union decline in a broader context of social network decline.) Without getting into an extended discussion of social network terminology, whereas the servicing model suggests flat, sparse network structures composed of weak ties among members and between members and their union, the organizing model suggests dense networks of strong ties among members and between members and the union (Jarley, 2005).

Research on social networks and social capital suggests that dense interpersonal networks involving many frequently used ties generates the shared values, resilient trust and mutual understanding that make group cooperation and coordination possible (for a review see Adler and Kwon, 2002). Frequent interactions permit people to know and trust one another, share information and develop common goals, values, and points of view (Tsai and Ghoshal, 1998). Collective goal congruence reduces the possibility for opportunistic behavior (Ouchi, 1980) and increases the likelihood that people will share knowledge and resources (Tsai and Ghosal, 1998). Dense networks contain many redundant contacts who can observe each others' behavior, thereby lowering transaction costs by making it more difficult for people to engage in undetected social loafing (Lazega, 1999). Dense networks also facilitate the free circulation of resources throughout the system promoting the creation of resilient trust based on generalized reciprocity norms – the willingness to do something for someone today knowing that someone else will return the favor at a later date. Generalized reciprocity norms improve the durability of social capital, making it less vulnerable to erosion through exit of any single individual.

To put all of this in more familiar language to students of the labor movement, dense networks facilitate the formation of a sense of a community of interests (or class consciousness). More frequent interaction breeds solidarity and redundancy in network ties, and reduces free-riding. The result is that members are more willing to mobilize in support of one another because an injury to one is seen as an injury to all. Very preliminary work by Johnson and Jarley (2005) suggests that among a sample of young union members of the United Food and Commercial Workers, those members with denser workplace networks knew more about their union and developed greater trust and reciprocity norms toward it than workers with sparse workplace networks.

Jarley (2005) has gone so far as to argue that by themselves, the conflict escalation methods associated with the traditional organizing model are unlikely to sustain a dense network among union members in the workplace. He argues that unions should engage in a variety of social capital building activities that will maintain and enhance network density as well as solidarity between the union and its members in times of labor peace so that they can be more effectively tapped to mobilize workers in times of need. Jarley's discussion is highly speculative, but the key point is that an examination of union social structure in the workplace offers a promising new approach to union morphology research and union renewal. Peetz et al.'s (2002) examination of Australian workplace delegate activism also supports the importance of social network concepts within unions.

Different 'models' of unionism (be they service, organizing, value added or social capital) may be associated with different patterns of interaction among union members and between union members and their union (as well as management). We have stressed network density here, but other features of these networks may be important as well, for example, the degree of centrality of union representatives in the network. These different patterns are themselves important features of union structure and differences in them may very well be linked to differences in union member satisfaction, commitment, participation, and mobilization, the very outcomes often associated with union effectiveness and renewal.

Banks and Metzgar (2005) acknowledge, as many have suggested, that the contrast between servicing and organizing has been overplayed. Members value services, and unions often 'organize around services', that is by touting the service that union representation will provide when members have a need, breakdown, or claim, as well as representation's value on an ongoing non-crisis basis. Further, Banks and Metzgar were really speaking of organizing in the sense of *mobilization* rather than in the sense of recruiting new members or winning representation rights. These latter ends can of course be served through mobilization or activism, as can grievance settlements, bargaining gains, or legislative influence, and in that sense the phrase 'organizing for everything we do' (Butler, 1991) has clear meaning. From the standpoint of union morphology research, this recognition of the parallel importance for unions of servicing and mobilizing members makes it clear that a full understanding of union effectiveness requires an examination of staff, activist, and member structures in the workplace and beyond.

Much work needs to be done here, chief among it is assessing the degree to which unions have systematically adopted the key elements of the organizing model and how they have attempted to reconcile the need to mobilize members with the need to service them. We have several interesting case studies, but little systematic evidence (but see Heery et al., 2000a; 2000b). More fine-grained analysis is also needed to understand the relationship between various elements of national union bureaucracy (for example, professionalization, centralization, coordination, and communication), member networks in the workplace and activism. Carter (2000) noted the contradictions and consequent difficulty in a top-down approach to implementing the organizing model in Britain's MSF. Lévesque and Murray (2002) and Voss and Sherman (2000) offered some interesting insights in these regards as well. Exploring the relationship between workplace activism, innovation and democracy in unions is another important area for future work. All of this will require new data sets that allow us to match national union structures and practices with data from individual locals and workplaces, a daunting but necessary task.

Organizing-driven unions

To add confusion to the debate about the evolving nature of unionism, the emergence of the organizing model coincided with increased recognition of the need for recruiting and organizing non-union workers and the two have been understandably confounded. Note that Bronfenbrenner's work on rank-and-file-intensive organizing tactics (for example, 1997) appeared at this time. Given its emphasis on member activism to organize non-union workers (for example, one-on-one organizing; large rank-and-file organizing committees) it is understandable that organizing and the organizing model are often conflated despite the fact that Banks and Metzgar were focusing on mobilization rather than external organizing per se. There is also evidence that some unions consciously made the link by believing that the increases in member activism brought about by the organizing model would substitute for paid administrative staff in contract administration, freeing staff resources for greater external organizing (Fletcher and Hurd, 1998). (Information technology was also seen as offering significant potential to redirect resources toward organizing (Fiorito et al., 2000b.)

In Britain, the confusion may be multiplied by historically lower reliance on the servicing model, consistent with lower dues and staffing levels, and lower employer opposition, as compared to the US. The shop stewards' movement of the 1960s illustrates a stronger British tradition of self-help, 'an indigenous

union tradition of promoting active workplace trade unionism' (Heery, et al., 2003a: 81; also see Batstone, 1988 regarding government-backed efforts to 'domesticate' the shop stewards' movement). Thus the face validity of a call for greater mobilization and less reliance on staff servicing might have been less compelling than in the US. Coupled with severe membership declines (although less dramatic than in the US) and rising employer opposition (Gall, 2003), British unions and union scholars might more readily interpret calls for an 'organizing model' as calls for greater organizing commitment or for a specific set of organizing tactics relating to mobilization in varying degrees (see Heery et al., 2000a).

As Fletcher and Hurd (1998; 2001) noted, however, there is no inevitable link between activating workers in an organizing model sense and external organizing. Mobilized workers may, despite their activism, see little gain in spending their efforts and dues on organizing non-union workers. Fletcher and Hurd coined the term 'organizing-driven' unions to distinguish those unions that placed a high priority on organizing non-union workers from the organizing model and its emphasis on member mobilization; the term 'recruiting union' is used similarly in the UK. They argued that external organizing, rather than membership mobilization per se, is the more pressing matter for unions.

As with the organizing model, there is little systematic evidence on the extent to which unions have adopted an organizing-driven approach and what this means for union structure. With respect to external structure there is a temptation to equate an organizing-driven approach with the afore-mentioned trend toward general unionism and re-branding of the resulting unions with names that emphasize the collective nature of unions (for example, Unison, Connect, and even UNITE-HERE) without reference to industry or occupation. Although merger activity may play a larger role in union re-branding than adoption of an organizing-driven approach, the more generic names also suggest a broader sense of union jurisdiction and a more opportunistic approach to organizing. If such a broadening is associated with an organizing-driven approach, it brings with it obvious questions about the potential need to form divisional structures to accommodate a variety of potential sectional interests within the union based on industry, occupation, geography, or identity. Even the 'One Big Union-ism' philosophy of the Industrial Workers of the World was modified to incorporate industrial divisions as problems of neglecting these distinctive interests became apparent.

With respect to internal structure, the most visible innovations consistent with movement toward organizing-driven unions have been at the federation level with the creation of the Organizing Institute in the US (see Foerster, 2001), its counterpart Organising Academy in the UK, and Organizing Works in Australia. The development of these federation-level entities suggests a recognition among peak union leaders that many affiliates are unable to make the transition to organizing-driven unions on their own and need a new source of trained professional organizers who not only bring the newest organizing techniques to the national unions that employ them, but serve as agitators for change within their employing unions by pushing union staff and officers attuned to servicing members to adopt a more organizing-driven approach (Foerster, 2003). The reliance on paid professional organizers, many of whom are young college graduates or drawn from the ranks of political or community activists by the peak federation bodies that have trained them, has drawn criticism from some commentators who argue that organizing new members is best left to volunteer rank-and-file activists. Volunteer organizers, they argue, are likely to be more effective because they have more in common with the workers they are attempting to orga-nize. They may also be less susceptible to the burnout that often accompanies professional organizers because they remain attached to a local union where they have more manageable geographic jurisdiction that allows them to spend time with their families as well as the opportunity to rotate back onto the shop floor after each organizing campaign to

'recover' before receiving another assignment (Early, 1996; 1998). (One might speculate that increasing emphasis on specialist organizers is a manifestation of a broader specialization trend in union staff roles that extends to equality or diversity issues, among others. See Heery (2006)).

Foerster (2003) noted that backgrounds may be a source of tension between Orga-nizing Institute-type graduates and organizers who rise up through the ranks. There are other potential tension sources in terms of goal conflict, with functionally dedicated organizers' performance linked closely to membership and organizing gains rather than satisfying current members or being re-elected. That may be a necessary tension, as current members will always prevail in commanding leaders' attention (Strauss, 1993: 24). Similarly, Heery et al. (2003a: 82) allude to 'organizing initiatives being derailed through the demand for servicing of existing members'. There is another element of tension in terms of what has been called the 'high octane atmosphere' of an organizing campaign versus the routine of day-to-day union activism. Echoing Early's (1998) point on burnout but in a slightly different way, it is unlikely that a workgroup can sustain for long the sort of energy level that can accompany short-term campaigns.

In some ways the debate about the relative wisdom and efficacy of using professional (for instance, highly formally trained staff spe-cialist) organizers vs. volunteer (for instance, trained rank-and-file generalists) activists is a variant of the servicing vs. organizing debate recast around external organizing rather than servicing issues. It involves both debates about centralization (national vs. local control over the organizing function) and member vs. staff ownership of the day-to-day organizing function. There is some evidence to suggest that decentralization is associated with greater organizing success (Fiorito et al., 1995). From an internal structure standpoint, however, the debate about the proper approach to the organizing function might be as illusory a distinction as in the servicing context. A renewed emphasis on external organizing may lead to both an increase in the number of professional organizers (and rationalization of the organizing function; see Heery et al., 2000b; 2003a) as well as the development of an extensive network of local volunteer activists to support the organizing function. In short the task may require both greater professionalization (and rationalization) and more membership activation.

What seems clear is that any push to a more organizing-driven approach should result in an increase in the proportion of union resources, financial and human, devoted to organizing and a corresponding increase in organizing activity. At least in the US, despite considerable rhetoric advocating more resources for organizing there is as yet little evidence that these calls have been heeded in practice, at least in the aggregate (see Farber and Western, 2002), and even for many unions often cited as among those truly committed to organizing (Fiorito, 2003; Fiorito and Jarley, 2003). Masters (1997) pointed out that the financial commitment required may exceed realistic union capacity, and Rose and Chaison (2001) raised similar questions regarding both Canadian and US unions. In Britain, an apparent increase in organizing commitment may have waned as political exclusion eased with the return of a Labour Government (Heery et al., 2003a). If the resources have not been allocated and organizing activity has not increased, significant changes in internal union structure to support organizing are doubtful. More definite conclusions require better data.

Union 'soul' and union renewal: configurational approaches

The term 'union renewal' is sometimes attributed to Fairbrother (2000) in his call for revitalization and renewed rank-and-file activism among moribund UK public sector unions. Many of these unions could be said to have been put on their back foot and doubly damned in over a decade of Conservative government hostility to both unions and public sector workers. Although one could argue that organizing model concepts were at the

heart of Fairbrother's call for union renewal, the union renewal term has taken on broader and varied meanings, including not only activism or mobilization, but also organizing commitment and partnerships with employers among others (Heery, 2003).

In a sense, Heery (2003) encourages appreciation for the view that there are different problems and opportunities facing various unions. Bringing unions back to life in the sense of asserting renewed or greater influence on behalf of workers therefore involves various paths, what the business strategy and organizational theory literatures refer to as 'equafinality.' A relatively universal problem is activating members, but passive servicing model unionism is not the only problem and thus the organizing model does not constitute a sufficient solution (Fiorito, 2004, Fletcher and Hurd, 2001).

Budd (2004: 137–157) proffered the 'soul' terminology in suggesting that union strategy is a combination of union soul (servicing vs. organizing model orientation) and scope of representation (business unionism focused on the workplace vs. social unionism focused on broader social issues). We are hesitant to accept Budd's implicit definition of union strategy. First, another chapter will address union strategy in more depth. Second, a simple but useful distinction is that goals are about 'what' and strategy is about 'how.' The soul issue (organizing model versus servicing model) is fairly clearly about *how*, but the scope of representation issue (workplace versus broader) is arguably about *what*.

That said, Budd's juxtaposition of soul and scope does suggest some meaningful union types. Combining an organizing soul with a broad scope yields 'social movement unionism,' while an organizing soul with a narrow scope yields 'employee empowerment unionism.' A servicing soul combines with a broad scope to suggest European-style 'social partnerships,' while a narrow scope and servicing soul produce 'business unionism' (job control). Budd introduces additional factors to draw finer distinctions, for example, between efficiency-enhancing unionism (see Masters, 1997 on value-added unionism and

Fiorito et al., 1991 for related discussion), solidarity unionism, and other subtypes.

As in some other areas (for example, Jarley et al., 2000 on union governance), this approach emphasizes that configurations of multiple factors rather than the level of a particular factor may be critical. In effect this is a *configurational* rather than *contingency* approach. It has been popular in the business strategy literature for many years, and has a long tradition in industrial relations as well, arguably dating to Hoxie's (1917) time if not earlier. Configurational approaches are often useful pedagogical devices, but frequently disappoint as quantitative research tools. Here as in other applications the types may resonate with prior knowledge and provide a readily understandable way to view union differences, for instance, a way to approach union morphology. They may also serve prescriptive purposes, ideal types that highlight an underlying logic toward union renewal that should guide efforts to align strategy with external and internal structure and union practice. Yet, from a research perspective if the types truly add value, they must explain variance in some important outcome, above and beyond that explained by reference to the underlying dimensions that form the types. If not, a contingency approach is suggested even though the configurational approach may remain useful in some regards.

Nissen (2003b) recently illustrated the use of the configurational approach in assessing two contrasting future strategic directions for the US labor movement, value-added unionism (VAU) and social movement unionism (SMU). Here too, goals and strategy are entwined, with VAU corresponding closely to Budd's efficiency-enhancing type and SMU matching closely to Budd's like-named type. Nissen acknowledged that each type may fit a particular niche. For example, where unions are strongly rooted in companies, they may be able to leverage their strength into genuine partnerships where their contributions to firm performance are effectively traded for acceptance of unionism, much like some recognition deals in the UK based on 'the "business case" for unionism' (Gall and McKay, 1999: 610). VAU was portrayed as a logical successor to business unionism that has lost its ability to deliver the goods via more oppositional approaches in the face of increased management resistance. There is a strong 'top down' element to this approach, with relatively little need for mobilization and relatively much need for servicing by officers and staff. Nissen (2003b) asserted a much greater potential for SMU, with such unions forming the workplace-centered wing of broader social movements. But here too, he acknowledged limitations, seeing SMU as particularly suited to low wage workers, notably women and immigrant workers, where calls for social justice are most credibly linked to union efforts to improve their members' well-being.

This seems to leave much unclaimed 'turf,' unless we assume that globalization will inevitably greatly expand the ranks of low-wage workers (as often seems to be the case.) Some of Budd's other types may help to fill in some of that turf, but is the rest left to allegedly more efficient (Wachter, 2003) non-union human resource management, or worse, 'black holes' (Guest and Conway, 1999)? This conundrum of matching union types to workplace settings is one of the problems raised by approaches stressing union configurations. It is not insurmountable, but it does call into question, with previously noted concerns about the value added by types, the utility of a configurational approach relative to more general contingency approaches, or perhaps the need to consider both. We remain somewhat agnostic about configurational approaches from a quantitative research perspective, finding them useful in some regards but possibly too limiting.

CONCLUDING COMMENTS

With the crisis in union membership, consolidation and concentration of union membership in fewer and fewer unions, and the debate about the proper path to union renewal, understanding union morphology, especially the link between union structure, practices and effectiveness, is of paramount importance to both the study and practice of unionism. This chapter has argued that on balance the empirical evidence amassed to date suggests that structure matters. Some important findings relating to union renewal, on union outcomes such as organizing and effectiveness, appear fairly robust to setting, for instance, they emerge in broad cross-sections of unions. Notable in this vein are findings on decentralization and innovation (Fiorito et al., 1995; 2002; 2007) and to some extent on rationalization in terms of its effects on innovation, an intermediate outcome (Delaney et al., 1996; Fiorito et al., 2000). Other research corroborates some of these findings, at least in part (Charlwood, 2004; Fiorito 2004; Heery et al., 2003b; Voss and Sherman, 2000). Much of this was noted earlier in conjunction with our discussion on internal (or vertical) and external (or horizontal) structure, because the contingencies thus far examined have been internal or external structure measures or an outcome (for example, innovation) linked to structure measures.

Yet, the issue is far from settled. One persistent problem has involved a lack of systematic cross-sectional and time series data on union member characteristics, structures, and practices. This has left gaps in our knowledge and made it difficult to distinguish correlation from causality. Another, more subtle concern is that implicit in most of the quantitative research conducted to date has been adherence to a 'servicing model' of unionism. Recognizing the key role staff has played in carrying out the day-to-day activities of the union, union morphology research has borrowed heavily from the literature on businesses to construct measures of national union internal structures (for example, bureaucracy, centralization, and innovation) that are then linked to differences in national union outcomes. Yet, the recent decentralization of industrial relations in all English-speaking countries and the greater emphasis on member mobilization it has spawned suggests increased importance for formal and informal workplace structures.

Studying these phenomena requires new concepts and approaches and ultimately there is a need for a 'unified theory' that links structures and activities on the shop floor with national union morphology and union outcomes. Such a theory may or may not require a configurational, rather than contingency approach to unions. But at a minimum, the configurational approaches that are implicit in many prescriptive writings on the future of unions give us insights into the underlying logic of ideal union forms that highlight important linkages between union strategy, structure, and practice at multiple levels of the union movement.

Several of today's most pressing 'big questions' with respect to union morphology remain largely unanswered. For example, what workplace structures produce the greatest mobilization capacity? Have organizing model unions, those that have developed workplace mobilization structures and successfully activated members, fared better in organizing, bargaining, or politics than servicing model unions? What does it really mean to be an organizing-driven or recruiting union, and have those that have made this transition fared better than those that have not? The year 2005 witnessed a major fracturing of the US labor movement over this last issue (and others). It may be too soon to say whether the rebel unions of the Change to Win Federation are generating results such as organizing gains and increased influence for their members that will vindicate or legitimize their rebellion, or whether as the 'loyalists' argue, their secession has simply weakened the collective voice of labor. Of course, assessments will need to consider the environment and other organizational factors to provide persuasive evidence unless the simple (bivariate) evidence is overwhelming. As with union renewal itself, much work on union morphology remains to be done.

ACKNOWLEDGMENT

We thank Paul Blyton and Edmund Heery for helpful comments on an earlier draft.

REFERENCES

Addison, John T. and Schnabel, Claus, (eds) (2003). *International Handbook of Trade Unions.* Cheltenham, UK and Northampton, MA: Edward Elgar.

Adler, Paul S. and Bryan, Borys (1996) 'Two Types of Bureaucracy: Enabling and Coercive.' *Administrative Science Quarterly,* 41 (1): 61–90.

Adler, Paul S. and Kwon, Seok-Woo (2002) 'Social capital: Prospects for a new concept.' *Academy of Management Review,* 27 (1): 17–40.

Associated Press (2005) 'Alliance Aims to Organize Wal-Mart Workers.' On-line article at http://www.nytimes.com, August 23, 2005.

Banks, Andy, and Metzgar, Jack (2005) 'Response to 'Unions as Social Capital.' *Labor Studies Journal,* 29 (4): 27–35.

Barbash, Jack (1969) 'Rationalization in the American Union.' In Gerald G. Somers (ed.), *Essays in Industrial Relations Theory.* Ames, IA: Iowa State University Press. pp. 147–62.

Batstone, Eric (1988) *The Reform of Workplace Industrial Relations: Theory, Myth and Evidence.* Oxford, UK: Clarendon Press.

Bok, Derek and Dunlop, John T. (1970) *Labor and the American Community.* New York: Simon and Schuster.

Bronfenbrenner, Kate B. (1997) 'The Role of Union Strategies in NLRB Certification Elections.' *Industrial and Labor Relations Review,* 50 (2): 196–212.

Budd, John W. (2004) *Employment with a human face.* Ithaca, NY: Cornell University Press.

Budd, John W. (2005) *Labor Relations: Striking a Balance.* New York: McGraw-Hill Irwin.

Butler, Margaret (1991) 'Organizing for Everything We Do.' *Labor Research Review,* 17 (special issue on 'An Organizing Model of Unionism'): 7–17.

Carter, Bob (2000) 'Adoption of the Organising Model in British Trade Unions: Some Evidence from Manufacturing Science, and Finance (MSF).' *Work, Employment, and Society,* 14 (1): 117–36.

Chaison, Gary N. (1996) *Union Mergers in Hard Times.* Ithaca, NY: Cornell University Press.

Chaison, Gary N. (2001) 'Union Mergers and Union Revival.' In Lowell Turner, Harry C. Katz, and Richard W. Hurd (eds), *Rekindling the Movement.* Ithaca, NY: ILR Press. pp. 238–55.

Charlwood, Andy (2004) 'Influences on Trade Union Organizing Effectiveness in Britain.' *British Journal of Industrial Relations,* 42 (1): 69–93.

Child, John., Loveridge, Ray, and Warner, Malcolm (1973) 'Toward an Organizational Study of Trade Unions.' *Sociology* 7 (1): 71–91.

Clark, Paul F. and Gray, Lois S. (2005) 'Changing Administrative Practices in American Unions: A Research Note.' *Industrial Relations,* 44 (4): 654–58.

Cobble, Dorothy Sue (2001) 'Lost Ways of Unionism: Historical Perspectives on Reinventing the Labor Movement.' In Lowell Turner, Harry C. Katz, and Richard W. Hurd (eds), *Rekindling the Movement.* Ithaca, NY: ILR Press. pp. 82–96.

Colgan, Fiona and Ledwith, Sue (eds) (2003) *Gender, Diversity and Trade Unions: International Perspectives.* London: Routledge.

Commons, John R. (1909) 'American Shoemakers, 1648–1895: A Sketch of Industrial Evolution.' *American Economic Review,* 24 (1): 39–84.

Cornfield, Dan (2006) 'Immigration, Economic Restructuring, and Labor Ruptures: From the Amalgamated to Change to Win.' *Working USA,* 9 (2) (June): 215–223.

Delaney, John T., Jarley, Paul, and Fiorito, Jack. (1996) 'Planning for Change: Determinants of Innovation in US National Unions.' *Industrial and Labor Relations Review,* 49 (4) (July): 597–614.

Early, Steve (1996) 'New organizing should be membership-based.' *Labor Notes,* 205, April 12.

Early, Steve (1998) 'Membership-based organizing.' In G. Mantsios (ed.), *A New Labor Movement for the New Century.* New York: Monthly Review Press.

Ebbinghaus, Bernhard (2003) 'Ever Larger Unions: Restructuring and Its Impact on Union Confederations.' *Industrial Relations Journal,* 34 (5) (December): 446–60.

Ebbinghaus, Bernhard and Visser, Jelle (1999) 'When Institutions Matter: Union Growth and Decline in Western Europe, 1950–1995.' *European Sociological Review,* 15 (2) (June): 135–58.

Fairbrother, Peter (2000) *Unions at the Crossroads.* London: Mansell Publishing.

Farber, Henry S. and Western, Bruce. (2002) 'Ronald Reagan and the Politics of Declining Union Organization.' *British Journal of Industrial Relations,* 40 (3): 385–401.

Fiorito, Jack (2003) 'Union Organizing in the United States.' In Gregor Gall (ed.), *Union Organizing: Campaigning for Trade Union Recognition.* London: Routledge. pp. 191–210.

Fiorito, Jack (2004) 'Union Renewal and the Organizing Model in the United Kingdom.' *Labor Studies Journal,* 29 (2): 21–53.

Fiorito, Jack, Gramm, Cynthia L., and Hendricks, Wallace E. (1991) 'Union Structural Choices'. In George Strauss, Daniel G. Gallagher, and Jack Fiorito, (eds), *The State of the Unions.* Madison, WI: Industrial Relations Research Association. pp. 103–37.

Fiorito, Jack and Jarley, Paul (2003) 'Union Organizing Commitment: Rhetoric and Reality.' *Proceedings of the Fifty-fifth Annual Meeting of the Industrial Relations Research Association.* Champaign, IL: IRRA, pp. 283–93.

Fiorito, Jack, Jarley, Paul and Delaney, John T. (2000a) 'The Adoption of Information Technology by US National Unions.' *Relations Industrielles/Industrial Relations,* 55 (3): 451–76.

Fiorito, Jack, Jarley, Paul, and Delaney, John T. (2007) 'Change to Win: Can Structural Reform Revitalize the American Labor Movement?' *Advances in Industrial and Labor Relations,* 15: 359–91.

Fiorito, Jack, Jarley, Paul and Delaney, John T. (2002) 'Information Technology, Union Organizing, and Union Effectiveness.' *British Journal of Industrial Relations,* 40 (4): 627–58.

Fiorito, Jack, Jarley, Paul, and Delaney, John T. (1993) 'National Union Effectiveness.' *Research in the Sociology of Organizations,* 12: 111–37.

Fiorito, Jack, Jarley, Paul, and Delaney, John T. (1995) 'National Union Effectiveness in Organizing: Measures and Influences.' *Industrial and Labor Relations Review,* 48 (4): 613–35.

Fiorito, Jack, Jarley, Paul, and Delaney, John T. (2001) 'National Unions as Organizations.' In Gerald R. Ferris (ed.), *Research in Personnel and Human Resources Management,* 20: 231–68.

Fiorito, Jack, Jarley, Paul, Delaney, John T., and Kolodinsky, Bob (2000b) 'Unions and Information Technology: From Luddites to Cyberunions?' *Labor Studies Journal,* 24 (1): 3–34.

Fletcher, Bill, Jr. and Hurd, Richard W. (1998) 'Beyond the Organizing Model: The Transformation Process in Local Unions.' In Kate Bronfenbrenner, Sheldon Friedman, Richard W. Hurd, Rudy A. Oswald, and Ronald Seeber (eds) *Organizing to Win.* Ithaca, NY: ILR Press. pp 37–53.

Fletcher, Bill, Jr. and Hurd, Richard W. (2001) 'Overcoming Obstacles to Transformation: Challenges on the Way to a New Unionism.' In Lowell Turner, Harry C. Katz, and Richard W. Hurd (eds), *Rekindling the Movement.* Ithaca, NY: ILR Press. pp. 182–208.

Foerster, Amy (2001) 'Confronting the Dilemmas of Organizing: Obstacles and Innovations at the AFL-CIO Organizing Institute.' In Lowell Turner, Harry C. Katz, and Richard W. Hurd (eds) *Rekindling the Movement.* Ithaca, NY: ILR Press. pp. 155–81.

Foerster, Amy (2003) 'Labor's Youth Brigade: What Can the Organizing Institute and Its Graduates Tell Us About the Future of Organized Labor?' *Labor Studies Journal,* 28 (3): 1–31.

Gamm, Sarah (1979) 'The Election Base of National Union Executive Boards.' *Industrial and Labor Relations Review,* 32 (3): 295–311.

Gall, Gregor (2003) 'Employer Opposition to Union Recognition.' In Gregor Gall (ed.), *Union Organizing: Campaigning for Trade Union Recognition.* London: Routledge. pp. 79–96.

Gall, Gregor and McKay, Sonia (1999) 'Developments in Union Recognition and Derecognition in Britain, 1994-98.' *British Journal of Industrial Relations,* 37 (4): 601–4.

Gallagher, Daniel G. and Strauss, George (1991) 'Union Membership Attitudes and Participation.' In George Strauss, Daniel G. Gallagher, and Jack Fiorito, (eds) *The State of the Unions.* Madison, WI: Industrial Relations Research Association. pp. 139–74.

Gordon, Michael E., Philpot, John W., Burt, Robert E., Thompson, Cynthia A. and Spiller, William E. (1980) 'Commitment to the Union: Development of a Measure and an Examination of Its Correlates.' *Journal of Applied Psychology,* 65 (4): 479–99.

Guest, David, and Conway, Neil (1999) 'Peering into the Black Hole: The Downside of the New Employment Relations in the UK.' *British Journal of Industrial Relations,* 37 (3): 367–89.

Hartley, Jean (1996) 'The 'New' Service Sector: Employment Status, Ideology and Trade Union Participation in the UK.' In Patrick P. Pasture, Johan J Verbeckmoes, and Hans H. de Witte (eds), *The Lost Perspective? Trade Unions Between Ideology and Social Action in the New Europe.* Avebury Press: Aldershot, England and Brookfield, VT. pp. 326–352.

Heckscher, Charles C. (1988) *The New Unionism.* New York: Basic Books.

Heery, Edmund (2003) 'Evolution, Renewal, Agency: Developments in the Theory of Trade Unions.' In Peter Ackers and Adrian Wilkinson (eds), *Understanding Work and Employment.* Oxford: Oxford University Press. pp. 278–304.

Heery, Edmund (2006) 'Union Workers, Union Work: A Profile of Paid Union Officers in the United Kingdom.' *British Journal of Industrial Relations,* 44 (3): 445–71.

Heery, Edmund, Kelly, John and Waddington, Jeremy (2003a) 'Union Revitalization in Britain.' *European Journal of Industrial Relation,* 9 (1): 79–97.

Heery, Edmund, Simms, Melanie, Delbridge, Rick, Salmon, John and Simpson, Dave (2003b) 'Trade Union Recruitment Policy in Britain: Forms and Effects.' In Gregor Gall (ed.), *Union Organizing: Campaigning for Trade Union Recognition.* London: Routledge. pp. 56–78.

Heery, Edmund, Simms, Melanie, Delbridge, Rick, Salmon, John, and Simpson, Dave (2000a)

'Union Organizing in Britain: A Survey of Policy and Practice.' *International Journal of Human Resource Management,* 11 (5): 986–1007.

Heery, Edmund, Simms, Melanie, Simpson, Dave, Delbridge, Rick and Salmon, John (2000b) 'Organizing Unionism Comes to the UK.' *Employee Relations,* 22 (1): 38–57.

Hoxie, Robert F. (1917) *Trade Unionism in the United States.* New York: D. Appleton.

Jacoby, Sanford M., and Verma, Anil (1992) 'Enterprise Unions in the United States.' *Industrial Relations,* 31 (1): 137–58.

Jarley, Paul (2005) 'Unions as Social Capital: Renewal through a Return to the Logic of Mutual Aid?' *Labor Studies Journal,* 29 (4): 1–26.

Jarley, Paul, Fiorito, Jack and Delaney, John Thomas (1997) 'A Structural Contingency Approach to Bureaucracy and Democracy in US National Unions.' *Academy of Management Journal,* 40 (4): pp. 831–61.

Jarley, Paul, Fiorito, Jack and Delaney, John T. (2000) 'Union Governance: An Empirically-grounded Systems Approach.' *Journal of Labor Research,* 21 (2): 227–46.

Jarley, Paul, Harley, Bill and Hall, Richard (2002) 'Innovation in Australian Trade Unions.' *Industrial Relations,* 41 (2): 228–48.

Johnson, Nancy B. and Jarley, Paul (2005) 'Unions as Social Capital: The Impact of Trade Union Youth Programmes on Young Workers' Political and Community Engagement.' *Transfer,* 11 (4): 605–16.

Keller, Berndt (2005) 'Union Formation Through Merger: The Case of Ver.di in Germany.' *British Journal of Industrial Relations,* 43 (2): 209–32.

Kelly, John (1998) *Rethinking Industrial Relations: Mobilization, Collectivism, and Long Waves.* Routledge: London.

Kelly, John, and Heery, Edmund (1994) *Working for the Union: British Trade Union Officers.* Cambridge: University Press.

Knoke, David (1990) *Organizing for Collective Action.* New York: de Gruyter.

Kochan, Thomas A. (1980) *Collective Bargaining and Industrial Relations: From Theory to Policy to Practice.* Homewood, IL: Irwin.

Kuhn, James W. (1961) *Bargaining in Grievance Settlements: The Power of Industrial Work Groups.* New York: Columbia University Press.

Kuruvilla, Sarosh C. and Fiorito, Jack. (1994) 'Who Will Help? Willingness to Work for the Union.' *Relations Industrielles/Industrial Relations,* 49 (3): 548–75.

Lazega, E. 1999. 'Generalized Exchange and Economic Performance: Social Embeddedness of Labor Contracts in a Corporate Law Partnership.' In Roger Th.

A.J Leenders and Shaul M. Gabbay (eds) *Corporate Social Capital and Liability.* Norwell MA: Kluwer Academic Publishers.

Lévesque, Christian, and Murray, Gregor (2002) 'Local Versus Global: Activating Local Union Power in the Global Economy.' *Labor Studies Journal,* 27 (3): 39–65.

Maranto, Cheryl L. and Fiorito, Jack (1987) 'The Effect of Union Characteristics on NLRB Certification Election Outcomes.' *Industrial and Labor Relations Review,* 40 (2): 225–40.

Masters, Marick F. (1997) *Unions at the Crossroads.* Westport, CT: Quorum Books.

Metzgar, Jack (1991) 'Introduction' *Labor Research Review,* 17 (special issue on 'An Organizing Model of Unionism'): vi–viii.

Moody, Kim (1988) *An Injury to All: The Decline of American Unionism.* London and New York: Verso.

Muehlenkamp, Robert (1991) 'Organizing Never Stops.' *Labor Research Review,* 17 (special issue on 'An Organizing Model of Unionism'): 1–5.

Muste, A.J. (1928) 'Factional Fights in Trade Unions,' In J.B.S. Hardman (ed), *American Labor Dynamics.* New York: Harcourt and Brace. pp. 332–33.

Nissen, Bruce (2003a) 'Alternative Strategic Directions for the US Labor Movement: Recent Scholarship.' *Labor Studies Journal,* 28 (1): 133–55.

Nissen, Bruce (2003b) 'The Recent Past and Near Future of Private Sector Unionism in the US: An Appraisal.' *Journal of Labor Research,* 24 (2): 323–38.

Nissen, Bruce (1998) 'Utilizing the Membership to Organize the Unorganized.' In Kate Bronfenbrenner, Sheldon Friedman, Richard W. Hurd, Rudolph A. Oswald, and Ronald L. Seeber (eds), *Organizing to Win.* Ithaca, NY: Cornell University Press. pp. 135–49.

Ouchi, Walter, G. (1980) 'Markets, Bureaucracies, and Clans' *Administrative Science Quarterly,* 25 (1): 129–41.

Peetz, David, Webb, C. and Jones, M. (2002) 'Activism Amongst Workplace Union Delegates'. *International Journal of Employment Studies,* 10 (2), October 2002, 83–108.

Putnam, Robert D. (2000) *Bowling Alone: The Collapse and Revival of American Community.* New York: Simon and Shuster.

Rose, Joseph B., and Chaison, Gary N. (2001) 'Unionism in Canada and the United States in the 21st Century: Prospects for Revival.' *Relations Industrielles/Industrial Relations,* 56 (1): 34–65.

Strauss, George (1993) 'Issues in Union Structure.' In Samuel B. Bacharach, Ronald Seeber, and David Walsh (eds), *Research in the Sociology of Organizations,* 12: 1–49. Greenwich, CT: JAI Press.

Strauss, George (1991) 'Union Democracy.' In George Strauss, Daniel G. Gallagher and Jack Fiorito (eds), *The State of the Unions* Madison, WI: Industrial Relations Research Association. pp. 201–36.

Streeck, Wolfgang and Visser, Jelle (1997) 'The Rise of the Conglomerate Union.' *European Journal of Industrial Relations*, 3 (3): 305–332.

Tsai, W. and S. Ghoshal (1998) 'Social Capital and Value Creation: The Role of Intrafirm Networks.' *Academy of Management Journal*, 41 (4): 464–477.

Trades Union Congress (2005) 'Britain's Unions.' On-line directory at http://www.tuc.org.uk/tuc/unions_main.cfm#C

Trades Union Congress (2006) *TUC Directory 2006.* London: TUC.

Turnbull, Peter (2003) 'What Do Unions Do Now?' *Journal of Labor Research,* 24 (3): 491–527.

Turner, Lowell, Katz, Harry C. and Hurd, Richard W. (eds) (2001) *Rekindling the Movement: Labor's Quest for Relevance in the 21st Century.* Ithaca, NY: ILR Press.

US Bureau of Labor Statistics (1980) *Directory of US National Unions and Employee Associations, 1979.* Washington, DC: US Government Printing Office.

Visser, Jelle (1989) *European Trade Unions in Figures,* Deventer, The Netherlands: Kluwer.

Visser, Jelle (2006) 'Union Membership Statistics in 24 Countries.' *Monthly Labor Review,* 129 (1) (January): 38–49.

Visser, Jelle and Waddington, Jeremy (1996) 'Industrialization and Politics: A Century of Union Structural Development in Three European Countries.' *European Journal of Industrial Relations,* 2 (1): 21–53.

Voss, Kim and Sherman, Rachel (2000) 'Breaking the Iron Law of Oligarchy: Union Revitalization in the American Labor Movement.' *American Journal of Sociology,* 106 (2): 303–349.

Wachter, Michael L. (2003) 'Judging Unions' Future Using a Historical Perspective: The Public Policy Choice between Competition and Unionization.' *Journal of Labor Research,* 24 (2): 339–57.

Warner, Malcolm (1975) 'Unions as Complex Organizations.' *Relations Industrielles/Industrial Relations,* 30 (1): 43–59.

Wilson, Tom, TUC Director of Organisation and Services (2006). Interviews with first author, June and July.

11

Trade Union Strategy

Peter Boxall

INTRODUCTION

Over the last ten years, against a backdrop of a long period of union decline, discussion of union strategy has become increasingly common in the English-language industrial relations (IR) literature. The goal of this chapter is to offer a framework for conceptualizing and analyzing union strategy, situating it within its wider contexts. The chapter adopts a strategic choice perspective and uses the notion of 'organizational life cycles' to make sense of existing studies of union strategy. One of the advantages of the life cycle model is that it helps us to critically review the present arguments surrounding the strategic challenges that unions face in the Anglo-American world. Some degree of caution must be exercised, however, when borrowing concepts from management theory. There are important parallels with business firms, but trade unions as organizations also have distinctive features which need to be carefully incorporated into the analysis. We begin with a discussion of what we mean by 'strategy' in trade unions.

Strategic choice in trade unions

'Strategy can be viewed as the set of consistent behaviors by which the organization establishes for a time its place in its environment' (Mintzberg, 1978: 941).

When we say that trade unions have strategies, we are saying that they have 'characteristic ways' of interacting with their environments (Boxall and Purcell, 2003: 28). Strategy is the pattern of critical choices about ends and means that we see unfolding in an organization's behavior. As we observe trade unions over time, we can come to discern their typical intentions or goals and the resources they typically build or mobilize to try to reach these goals.

Two misconceptions about the notion of strategy must be dealt with straight away. First, as with business organizations, none of this implies that unions will use *formal* methods of strategic planning. Strategies exist irrespective of whether formal planning takes place (Mintzberg, 1978, 1990). Like other organizations, unions use a range of administrative structures and political processes to evolve strategy – standing committees, annual conferences, informal 'deals' among power-brokers, management directives, direct action by those in the front-line, and so on (Boxall and Haynes, 1997). Rituals of formal planning, where they exist, may be useful in helping to theorize strategic issues and develop creative recommendations for change. On the other hand, they might amount to little more than a 'talkfest' and make very little impact on a union's characteristic modes of behavior.

Second, nothing in the notion of strategy assumes that unions will be particularly effective in dealing with the strategic problems they face. Like other organizations, unions exhibit strengths and weaknesses in relation to their environment. In the worst case, the weaknesses of existing structures and processes expose unions to the risk that their strategies – their characteristic ways of behaving – will drift further and further away from the challenges actually presented by their environments: a syndrome known in the business management literature as 'strategic drift' (Johnson and Scholes, 2002: 76). In time, this will undermine, and may fatally compromise, a union's economic viability and its social legitimacy.

Meaningful discussion of strategy does, however, imply a 'strategic choice' perspective (Child, 1972, 1997). Both words are important: 'strategic' means that some actions are critical or consequential for the survival of organizations and, if they survive, their relative degree of performance (Boxall and Purcell, 2003: 30–2). The word 'choice' underlines the fact that deciding to do one thing usually implies deciding not to do another: strategies involve heading down one path, with all that this implies about opportunities for learning, both good and bad, while denying ourselves the option of heading down another.

The notion of 'choice' also reminds us that organizations are rarely totally 'determined' by their environments: there is always some element of discretion in the hands of leaders and other actors in the organization (Child, 1972, 1997). In this sense, it is fair to describe unions as 'strategic actors' (Boxall

and Haynes, 1997; Heery, 2005; Lange et al., 1982) but what varies is the *extent* of their strategic choice. In environments where workers readily act in collective ways and where employers can, and will, reach accommodations, unions enjoy an extensive realm of strategic choice (Boxall and Haynes, 1997). On the other hand, unions restricted to organizing workers in the secondary labor market among hostile employers face a much less favorable environment. They retain a degree of strategic choice but some aspirations, such as organizing low-skilled, vulnerable groups of workers on small sites, may simply be unattainable in the absence of explicit state support (Boxall and Haynes, 1997: 569–70).

Even though many, if not most, unions are currently facing difficult environments, it would be unhelpful to adopt a hyper-deterministic stance which casts them as a hopelessly reactive and powerless class of organizations. Ann C. Frost's (2001) work on the different responses of three union 'locals' to restructuring in the North American steel industry usefully illustrates this point. Faced with very similar and serious threats to the competitive viability of their plants (and thus to their memberships), union leaders adopted a much more engaging, multi-level interaction with management in two plants than in the third. In the former cases, union members were fully involved in developing proposals for change while, in the latter, the local union president centralized decision-making in the union. Because of the need to use the deep technical knowledge of workers to bring about productivity gains, it is not surprising that restructuring was much more successful in the cases where union members were deeply involved. In fact, in the case where only the union president engaged with management, restructuring proposals were unworkable: neither the branch president nor management had sufficient knowledge of what was workable. The point here is that *how* a union engages with its own members is one of the principal dimensions of strategic choice (Boxall and Haynes, 1997). In this respect, the union locals in Frost's (2001) study were not simply determined by their environment: even in such difficult circumstances, there were strategic options available to union leaders and the different strategic choices they took around activating and expressing membership participation led to markedly different outcomes.

The contexts of union strategy

Reviews of trade union structures and strategies regularly note that unions are located within a network of actors and the strategies they form are influenced by a range of critical factors expressed through the behavior of the actors in this network and through wider economic and socio-political influences (for example, Charlwood, 2004; Fiorito et al., 2001; Fiorito, 2004; Heery, 2005; Hyman, 1994; Masters and Atkin, 1999). Figure 11.1 depicts the way in which unions act as mediating organizations between employers and workers while being embedded in this wider context.[1] Most of their strategic behavior is oriented to organizing workers and negotiating with employers. In playing this mediating role in industries, occupations and workplaces, however, unions are engaged with wider economic and socio-political forces. They typically operate not only at the level of employer-employee interactions but 'at the level of the society' where they seek 'to defend workers both as workers and as citizens' (Levesque and Murray, 2002: 47). Powerful union movements play an important role in the political economy. Individual unions often affiliate with a national union federation which plays some role in evolving strategies designed to influence the national (and international) political economy, including the framework for regulating interest conflicts in the workplace. Links with political

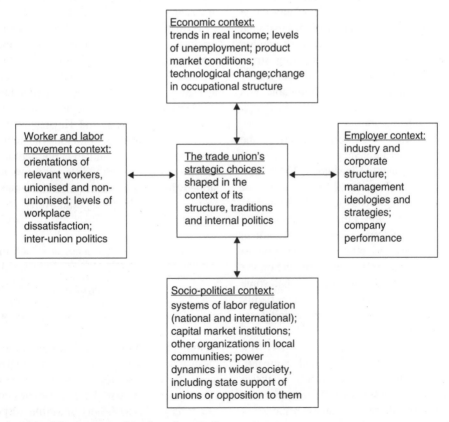

Figure 11.1   The context of trade union strategy

parties – and the various ways this influence can be exerted – are very important to many, if not most, trade unions (for example, James, 2004). On a more local basis, unions may also develop strategies to engage with community-based organizations (for example, in the pursuit of 'living wage' campaigns (for example, Nissen, 2000).

The box in Figure 11.1 symbolizing union strategic choices notes the way that these choices are inevitably shaped by the union's structure, its traditions (or 'culture') and its internal politics (for example, Fiorito et al., 2001; Heery, 2005; Hyman, 2001; Voss and Sherman, 2000). It is unhelpful to see a union's structure as something devolving straightforwardly from its strategy. This would be an overly simplistic reading of Alfred Chandler's (1962) famous dictum that 'structure follows strategy'. As Mintzberg's (for example, 1978) work argues, it is more helpful to understand strategy and structure as interactive: new strategies can give rise to new structures (as, for example, when a union decides to represent another occupational group and does so by merger with another union). On the other hand, existing structures tend to condition what is strategically possible, making some goals 'thinkable' and others virtually impossible. Thus, in 'large, merged "super unions"', existing structures and established roles seriously affect the possibilities for implementing certain kinds of espoused strategy (Charlwood, 2004: 383). For example, Carter's (2000) analysis of attempted strategic change in the Manufacturing, Science and Finance Union (UK) shows how regional officials and branch representatives are often in a position to resist the dictates of national officials on the grounds of strongly-held beliefs that some ideas will simply not work and certainly not without their willing cooperation (see, especially, pp. 128–9).

Saying that union strategy is influenced by a range of actors and contextual factors are not, however, saying very much. Analysis takes a step forward when studies or frameworks help us to identify patterns of strategic behavior as unions interact with these contextual factors.

In the US context, for example, 'business unionism' connotes a pattern in which unions came to focus on 'instrumental goals' at the workplace and had little truck with class politics or revolutionary ideals (Fiorito et al., 2001). Business unionism represented a pattern of union strategic choices that fitted the economic, ideological and political context of US industrial relations, particularly from the 1950s through to the late 1970s, but which many now argue has become part of an ill-fitting and failing pattern of behavior (see, for example, Voss and Sherman, 2000).

In parallel with the literature on 'varieties of capitalism' (Gospel and Pendleton, 2003; Hall and Soskice, 2001), which notes that the labor strategies of firms tend to be heavily shaped by the surrounding set of economic and political institutions, the literature on union strategies is now locating unions in a similar way (see this Handbook, Chapter 7). Unions develop 'histories of action' within 'particular national institutional environments' (Frege and Kelly, 2004: 38). In Hyman's (2001) terms, 'market-oriented' unionism, typical in the Anglo-American world, needs to be distinguished from 'class unionism', prevalent in Italy and Spain, and from the social dialogue model found in Germany. Union strategy in neo-liberal environments (Boxall and Haynes, 1997) – where unions must rely on industrial strategy unsupported by corporatism or political sponsorship – is significantly different from union strategy in societies where unions have social-partner status. As Heery and Adler (2004: 63–4) put it,

> where states accord the status of social partner to unions and allocate resources to support their functions there is less incentive to organize but where states pursue a policy of union exclusion the need to cultivate internal resources of power through organizing is correspondingly stronger.

Dominant institutional features in societies mean that unions tend to focus in different ways, creating significant variation in the extent to which workplace organizing is a key strategic thrust (Heery and Adler, 2004). Besides key differences around the integration

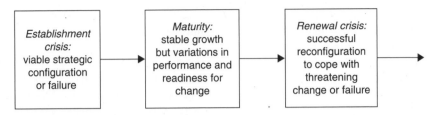

Figure 11.2   Phases of industry evolution
Source: Boxall and Purcell, 2003: 189.

of unions into the political economy, competition between union federations is a major difference across different national contexts, something which occurs in Italy and Spain but which has been relatively rare in the English-speaking world (Behrens, Hamann, and Hurd, 2004), at least until the recent split-up of the AFL-CIO in the United States (see this Handbook, Chapter 10).

This brief review of the wider context means that we must recognize significant diversity in union strategy across different societies. While influencing the direction of labor legislation and political settlements is important to all union movements, some are much more focused on strategies at national political levels than are others. As Turner (2004: 6–7) notes, there is currently an important distinction between 'labor movements that (are) focus(ing) revitalization efforts on *mobilization*, and those … focus(ing) on *institutional position* and/or reform' (emphasis in original). Preferences and the balance of energy can, of course, change over time within a single labor movement as one avenue becomes problematic or faces a crisis. Having said this, this chapter must make some strategic choices of its own. While recognizing the importance of both workplace and wider political strategies, and their interconnectedness, the chapter will direct its analysis to studies within the Anglo-American 'market-oriented' tradition of trade unionism.

Strategy and the life cycle of trade unions: organic and mature phases

Organizational ecology is a school within organizational studies which starts from the premise that organizations are typically located in industries and industries are subject to evolutionary forces (Carroll and Hannan, 1995).

Industries emerge at particular points in time and evolve through a 'life cycle': periods of establishment, maturity, and renewal/decline (as summarized in Figure 11.2). The organic or establishment phase involves high levels of start-ups with founding leaders of organizations experimenting with a range of business models (what set of product features or services to offer, which technologies to adopt, how to organize work and employment systems, how to fund the organization, how to gain official sanction, etc.). This process of experimentation and jostling for influence eventually leads to the creation of one or more 'dominant designs' for organizations in the industry (Boxall and Purcell, 2003; Suarez and Utterback, 1995). Dominant designs are *systems* of choices which are economically and socially sustainable. Individual organizations, while inevitably building their own idiosyncrasies, either mould their strategies around one of these dominant designs or fail. Organizations that successfully perceive and adopt a dominant design enjoy the growth opportunities, and room for elements of variation, that come with the mature phase. However, nothing lasts forever and the mature phase is eventually challenged by serious change (economic, technological, social or political) in the environment. At this point, dominant designs are either reformed in functional ways or organizations fail. As this suggests, strategic choices are typically laid down by founding leaders and solidify in periods of growth but then become subject to challenge by subsequent coalitions of actors when the dominant design is underperforming or shown to be failing.

Despite variations in rates of change, the three-phase model of industry evolution is well supported by research in industrial economics (Mueller, 1997). It provides a useful structure to analyze all sorts of organizations, including trade unions (Hannan, 1995; Kearney, 2003; Lester, 1958).

The organic phase

Unions began as 'social movement organizations' (Hannan, 1995: 121). The great surge of union formation in the US took place in the nineteenth century while the largest growth of membership took place in 'great spurts' at the end of the First World War, throughout the Great Depression of the 1930s, and during the Second World War (Hannan, 1995; Kaufman, 2004). Here, and elsewhere in the English-speaking world, trade unions sprang from serious interest conflicts between workers and employers: conflicts over safety, pay levels, employment security, working hours and the pace of work: over the whole relationship between what is given and what is asked for in the wage-work bargain.

At the outset, then, trade unionism was a grassroots-driven, collective worker response to objectively poor conditions. Its fundamental goal was to significantly improve the experience of work and the returns to labor and to ensure that organized labor could play an ongoing role in the regulation of working conditions. Union organizations were more 'militant and turbulent, with internal factionalism and vigorous external opposition' (Lester, 1958: 21). Membership participation was high. Working-class communities – in which people lived nearby and frequently traveled to and from work together – created dense networks of 'social capital' (Jarley, 2005). In the context of a surging social movement, we must understand trade union 'strategy' as something organic rather than manufactured: something driven by evident needs for change, heavy with crusading rhetoric and with notions of righting injustice.

The mature phase

Success in the organic phase meant that unions matured into organizations which could no longer rely on grassroots' spontaneity but required some kind of permanent structure of officials and management committees (for example, Hyman, 1989; Lester, 1958). The dominant design of unions became heavily laced with bureaucratic features. It is in the mature phase that we need to apply a more sophisticated understanding of unions as organizations if we are to interpret union strategy.

In organizational terms, maturity meant that unions came to exhibit a conflict between the 'administrative rationality' needed in an efficient bureaucracy and the 'representative rationality' of an organization of volunteers (Child et al., 1973: 77). The hiring of permanent administrators or paid officials inevitably created a tension between hierarchical control by the managerial elite and democratic decision-making by the members. It opened up the possibility for 'agency issues' (Fiorito et al., 2001: 242): for the goals of leaders to diverge from those of members (Lester, 1958: 56–8). While there are similar tensions in business organizations, the ambiguity around leadership in unions as *voluntary* organizations – the members pay to belong and are not employees of the union – is a distinctive characteristic.

The ways in which this tension is worked out vary across different unions and across the same union at different times (Boxall and Haynes, 1997). Some mature unions appear to behave as official-led organizations in which members consume a standard diet of services in exchange for their subscriptions: the 'servicing' model. Others seek to embrace the 'organizing' model or 'empower' the members.[2] Such a strategic choice appears as a decision taken by the managerial elite, much as might be expected in a corporation. However, it is entirely possible that the members themselves are seeking to shift the implicit model of union behavior, that *they* lead their officials into a more grassroots, shop floor–driven style of unionism. As Turnbull (1988: 113) puts it, 'trade union structure and behavior involves a *two-way* process of internal control' (emphasis in original). At various times, paid and/or lay officials may be pulling in one direction while strong groups of members pull in another, albeit within a context of long-term interdependence (Crouch, 1982: 187–9; Heery, 2005). In all mature unions, then, there is a 'politics of leadership' which requires sensitive analysis if strategic decision-making is to be understood (Boxall and Haynes, 1997: 571).

In terms of workplace strategies, mature unions can exhibit a range of styles. In Boxall and Haynes' (1997) typology, union strategy is understood as a conjunction of choices in relation to workers and employers. The worker face of union strategy is concerned with the extent to which the union *blends* servicing and organizing models. Boxall and Haynes (1997) argue that servicing and organizing are wrongly portrayed as dichotomous choices,[3] that all unions provide some services to members, which are particularly important when members seek protection against management actions directed at them as individuals (Masters and Atkin, 1999; Terry, 1994). Given this reality, the strategic question in terms of the worker dimension of union strategy is the extent to which unions build organizing capabilities which *complement* their servicing activities. The logical starting place is the creation of networks of activists, while another is associated with incorporating or fostering strong cells of workers. More powerful forms of organizing presuppose the presence of activists and/or cells but add the propensity to mobilize the total membership around key issues, generating episodes of mass organization or 'surges of participation' when important worker interests are threatened (Fosh, 1993: 580). To the extent that unions naturally encompass or complement their servicing roles with these more powerful forms of worker participation, they are a threat to employer control in the workplace.

Similarly, Boxall and Haynes (1997) argue that the employer face of union strategy does not rest on a simple dichotomy between adversarialism and cooperation but rests on blends of the two. Any form of sustainable engagement with an employer involves some level of co-operation and carries the risk of incorporation (see, for example, Craft, 1991; Hyman, 1989). Some unions go little further than they must to secure the best contract they can, assiduously avoiding identification with the sort of employer decisions that could subsequently prove unpopular with members. Other unions adopt an approach which involves classical bargaining while simultaneously exploring the possibilities of 'concertation' (Crouch, 1982: 109–17) or closer integration with the employer's business. One strategy involves union officials in a kind of 'attitudinal structuring' (Walton and McKersie, 1965: 184–280) where they offer their ideological support on the shop floor. Again, this can back-fire if officials misinterpret the mood of members on key issues. More robustly participative options involve the pursuit of joint working parties in which activists, rather than paid officials, are engaged (as, for example, in two of Frost's (2001) case studies). The most extensive option involves seeking to raise the level of participation to that of the firm's 'strategic activities' (Kochan et al., 1986: 15–8), such as business portfolio choices and plant location decisions, a strategy which carries heightened risks of incorporation (Terry, 1994).

Combining the employer and worker dimensions leads to four patterns of union strategic choice (see Figure 11.3) (Boxall and Haynes, 1997). 'Classic unionism', the style most associated with the historical rise of workforce struggle for improved conditions, depends on a conjunction of classical choices. On the worker side, classic unions are not simply organizations of consumers but pose a threat to employers through activism and mobilization. On the employer side, the approach is vigorously oppositional: the engagement does not extend beyond the explicit wage-work bargain, although an intensive amount of job regulation may occur. 'Paper-tiger unionism'

Classic unionism	Partnership unionism
Worker relations: servicing plus solid organizing	Worker relations: servicing plus solid organizing
Employer relations: robust adversarialism, no incorporation	Employer relations: credible adversarialism with extensive cooperative practices
Paper-tiger unionism	Consultancy unionism
Worker relations: servicing only	Worker relations: mostly servicing, limited organizing
Employer relations: formalistic adversarialism	Employer relations: routine adversarialism with some cooperative practices

Figure 11.3   Four patterns of trade union strategic choice in neo-liberal environments
Source: Boxall and Haynes, 1997: 576.

entails a stance of 'formalistic adversarialism' toward employers without building a base of worker activism. Without strong state support compelling employers to deal with them, paper tiger unions wither away. 'Consultancy unionism' is distinguished from 'paper tigerism' through an ability to carry out routine collective bargaining (at enterprise and/or establishment levels) and some basic attempts to stimulate organization, typically through a selective network of activists. This enables limited expressions of co-operation with employers. 'Partnership unionism' is a style now widely discussed in which unions seek a more constructive engagement in the strategic management of firms and industries. Boxall and Haynes (1997) contrast this from consultancy unionism, arguing that partnership unionism is best launched from a position of workplace strength in which the union presents both a threat and an opportunity to the employer's business. Management is far more inclined to respect partners with power (see also Belanger et al., 2002: 66–7).

While fieldwork shows that some unions fall into one of the main categories in Figure 11.3, other unions exhibit greater complexity resulting from amalgamations of diverse worker groups into 'general unions', or because of size and the resulting diversity of employers encountered, or because of significant ideological differences between officials and members (Boxall and Haynes, 1997). It is thus important to distinguish between specific unions and patterns of unionism. A large union may exhibit more than one pattern of unionism.

Large unions are, in certain ways, analogous to conglomerate firms (Willman, 2001): 'head office' officials preside over clusters or portfolios of bargaining units, in which the economics of organizing differ and across which variegation in strategy is inevitable. Willman (2001: 98) defines a 'viable bargaining unit … as one that is capable of sustaining collective bargaining with an employer without long-term support from elsewhere in the union'. His framework identifies four broad types of bargaining unit (Figure 11.4). In the most desirable condition (A), the employer is co-operative and members are active, reducing union costs per member and enabling other units to be subsidized. In condition B, members are willing to pay dues but not so willing to participate in union activities

Employer

Membership	Cooperative	Recalcitrant
	A	**C**
Active	Lay representation Facilities agreements Check-off Exporter of funds Politically powerful within union	Low facilities High official involvement High potential for conflict Importer of funds
	B	**D**
Passive	Full facilities Low lay representation High official involvement Exporter of funds	De-recognition potential Politically low profile Importer of funds

Figure 11.4　Willman's 'Union Portfolio'
Source: Willman, 2001: 103.

(perhaps because of time demands). Like A, however, this condition enables some cross-subsidization. The problematic categories are C and D: in the former, members are prepared to take action but conflict is costly because the employer is oppositional while, in the latter, the combination of a recalcitrant employer and a passive membership is likely to lead to de-recognition.

The implication of Willman's (2001: 114) framework is that it is important to analyze unions as 'portfolios of viable and inviable bargaining units'. This casts quite a different light on the dynamics of union growth and decline. It is possible for a union to grow in membership numbers but if this is heavily loaded toward risky bargaining units (types C and D); the union's financial viability is undermined. On the other hand, a union could experience membership decline but consolidate around a cluster of highly viable sites (types A and B) and, thus, become stronger. This perspective 'helps to explain the size distribution of unions in the UK, with the persistence of viable small unions during a long period of increasing union concentration' (Willman, 2001: 105). Larger scale is not always beneficial. We might also note that official-driven expansion strategies that involve acquiring and cross-subsidizing

inviable sites are not always popular with existing members.

The Boxall and Haynes (1997) framework indicates the way in which unions tend to adapt their workplace strategies to the context they face. As mentioned, paper-tiger unionism is a failing strategy outside a state-enforced system of union recognition and contract negotiation. Consultancy unionism poses little threat and thus depends on an employer seeing the efficiency and legitimacy value in negotiating a collective contract. Where not pressed by strong activism, the majority of employers now prefer a regime of individual contracts and direct forms of worker voice (Boxall and Purcell, 2003), albeit with strong elements of standardization which help to demonstrate equity of treatment. In Anglo-American societies, classic union-ism has become a common pattern in public sector services, such as public health and education. Health and education professionals have increasingly responded with force to a context in which rising community needs and new technologies have escalated work demands while governments have struggled to improve funding or have deliberately constrained it for broader reasons of economic or political management (Boxall and Haynes, 1997; Charlwood, 2004). Classic unionism is also common in those parts of the private sector where it first emerged but which now represent a much lower share of national employment: mining, large-scale manufacturing and the transport infrastructure. Workers in these sectors may be quiescent during periods of high unemployment but still generally show a capacity to mobilize when they consider important interests are threatened.

It goes without saying that unions cannot initiate the partnership pattern without a willing management. Management can be interested in situations where significant change is required to stay or become competitive (Boxall and Purcell, 2003), as shown in the British partnership arrangements studied by Haynes and Allen (2000) and Tailby and Winchester (2000). Firms with highly unionized workforces whose managers wish to restructure work to build 'high-performance work systems' have an obvious incentive to work co-operatively with their unions when union leaders and activists can help to legitimate and facilitate change. For their part, union leaders in these situations often have an incentive to do so because there are 'positive aspects of the new model, which workers themselves naturally espouse (expression of tacit skills, teamwork and reduced supervision)' (Belanger et al., 2002: 41). However, the tension for unions lies in the fact that the new work systems simultaneously involve a degree of challenge to worker interests: obviously to employment security and, some would argue, to employee stress levels through work intensification (see, for example, Godard, 2004; Ramsay et al., 2000). This latter point is currently a matter of some debate: other evidence on the impacts of new work systems finds that it is possible to create a pathway to higher performance which works through involvement without intensification (see, for example, Appelbaum et al., 2000; Mackie et al., 2001).

Where the degree of change needed is severe, however, management will typically pursue a blend of what Walton et al. (1994) call 'forcing' (imposed change) and 'fostering' (facilitated, cooperative changes in working styles). Increasingly, management

also wants to exercise what Walton et al. (1994) call 'escape': shifts of production sites to lower cost and less troublesome locations (nowadays, the seemingly ubiquitous 'outsourcing' and 'offshoring'). In these contextual conditions, partnership unionism is inherently fragile: 'even where management is ideologically supportive, unions cannot easily alter the wider politics of restructuring and rationalization in large organizations' (Boxall and Haynes, 1997: 587). A recent study of an aerospace firm in the UK by Danford et al. (2004) confirms this assessment: union-management partnerships are unlikely to survive in product market contexts characterized by intense margin competition where managers are unable to make any meaningful commitment to job security because of corporate requirements to secure cost reductions. In these situations, played out frequently in Anglo-American capital market regimes, management is instinctively resistant to growth in union power, an attitude which inevitably becomes apparent over time. It seems likely that only in rare situations will contemporary Anglo-American management be willing and able to sustain a joint philosophy respecting the union's institutional security *and* protecting existing union jobs. Lesser forms of partnership can, of course, be pursued where management does not directly undermine the union but declines to promise strong forms of job security and this may appeal to union leaders who feel they can sustain their internal legitimacy in these conditions.

Strategy and the life cycle of trade unions: the renewal crisis

This last comment brings us naturally to the current debate over union strategy. Unions in the Anglo-American world have moved past their prime into an era of crisis, characterized by serious decline in union density, loss of workplace relevance and political marginalization. There is an outpouring of writing on how unions might renew themselves, including important edited collections by Bronfrenbrenner et al. (1998), Fairbrother and

Yates (2003), Harcourt and Wood (2004), Healy et al. (2004), Milkman and Voss (2004), Verma and Kochan (2004), and Frege and Kelly (2004), among others. The 'dominant designs' of trade unions are currently the subject of extensive critique.

As we have just seen, one avenue for renewal lies through the pursuit of partnership unionism but union leaders adopting this strategy must make a very careful assessment of their context and the direction in which it is evolving. Helping management *renew companies* is not the same as *renewing trade unions*. For example, when labor-substituting technological changes become irreversible in an industry, as has been happening in Canadian metal-mining, unions might secure a high skill-high pay contract for the workforce remnant but cannot protect the 'vast majority' of their membership who are 'simply displaced' (Chaykowski, 2002: 600). In these conditions, 'reinventing' the union is a reality for only a small proportion of members. The logical strategy for the vast bulk of members is to 'milk till dry' the wages and benefits available under traditional contracts and the redundancy compensation offered to buy out their jobs as these contracts are restructured. What workers do after they are paid out – whether they retrain or whether they ever work again – is up to them.

Studies of union revitalization thus need to consider not only the employer face of strategy but *simultaneously* examine the impacts on workers. Since unions are voluntary organizations of workers, the question of the prospects for union renewal turns very critically on the analysis of worker needs and how these have evolved. One prominent line of analysis has been that associated with the renewal of unions as 'social movements' (for example, Johnston, 1994; Juravich and Hilgert, 1999; Nissen, 2003) or through rediscovery of the organizing model (for example, Bronfenbrenner and Juravich, 1998; Hurd, 1998). Social movement unionism has re-emerged in situations of low wages, poor conditions and social exclusion, where unions have 'constructed broader coalitions of workers and identity-based community groups' to

effect change (Belanger et al., 2002: 67). Where it has been successful, it has often entailed a blend of old and new tactics including

> focusing on issues such as dignity and fairness in addition to material concerns; using 'corporate campaigns', which involve interfering in the employer's relations with lenders, clients, shareholders, and subsidiaries; strategically targeting industries and workplaces to be organized; staging frequent direct actions; pressuring public officials to influence local employers; allying with community and religious groups; using the media to disseminate the union's message; and circumventing the NLRB election process to demand 'card-check recognition' (Voss and Sherman, 2000: 311–2).

Voss and Sherman's (2000: 309) study of a group of 14 Californian union locals identifies three important conditions for unions to break out of bureaucratic business unionism into a 'revitalized' mode: first, 'an internal political crisis that fosters the entry of new leadership'; second, these new leaders having 'activist experience in other social movements'; and, third, the new leaders having the political and resource backing of the national leadership in the relevant union. Such transitions are not victim-less because some 'resistant staff in some of the fully revitalized locals have been let go or encouraged to quit'[4] (Voss and Sherman, 2000: 324).

This study helps to make the point that we should avoid creating the picture that a simple return to organic unionism is generally occurring or is generally feasible. While organic unionism can, and does, re-emerge in some situations of objective exploitation, the challenge for unions is generally one of rebalancing the roles of officials, activists and members, finding new ways to integrate centralized decision-making and servicing with grassroots' democracy and involvement. Unless they willingly dissolve themselves into cells of workers, unions will remain bureaucracies in which the management of staff and their role-relations with members remain critical. Union renewal involves some kind of reform of union bureaucracy, not a repudiation of it. In this regard, the model emerging in the UK is more accurately called 'managed activism' in which 'management skills and processes are directed at promoting activism while activists themselves are encouraged to "manage" their own activity' (Heery et al., 2000: 1004). In the US, Lustig (2002: 8) has described the 'successor to services-unionism that provides for increased activism and recruitment but retains centralized control' as a 'mobilizing model', one which 'embraces grassroots activity but still directs it from above'. Nissen's (2000: 47) study of the living wage campaign in Miami, for example, underlines the importance of building a social movement *organization*, one in which a small staff of highly-skilled, paid organizers coordinates and maintains the agenda:

> ... the living wage issue is not really the product of a genuine, more spontaneous 'organic' social movement. Low wage workers play a very small role (or no role) in most living wage coalitions ... Building the coalition is a long, hard organizing process. Given that, there is seldom a substitute for competent, paid staff to organize the work and get 'grassroots leaders' involved.

There is growing recognition that current union renewal strategies might help to make unions more externally focused on recruitment and more internally concerned with membership involvement but will hardly usher in an era of mass worker mobilization (see, for example, Hurd, 2004). As Kaufman (2004: 52) points out, the 'growth prospect of unions is directly tied to the breadth and depth of labor problems affecting wage earners': absent such conditions, great spurts do not occur in union density (see also Charlwood, 2004). Similarly, de Turberville (2004: 785) comments that it is 'questionable whether, in periods of economic expansion, with increasing job opportunities, the organizing model could generate a sustainable membership and stewards system let alone a wider social movement'.

There are, as noted, significant pockets of worker discontent where a traditional union strategy is wanted and needed. This is demonstrated by studies of union representation gaps: around a third of US workers in non-unionized firms in the private sector have frustrated demand for unionism (Freeman and Rogers, 1999), a pattern mirrored elsewhere in the Anglo-American world (Boxall et al., 2007). The representation gap is highest among young workers, those on low incomes, and those whose workplaces have lots of labor problems.

If most of this frustrated demand could be effectively organized (and many workers who experience it are in small, hard-to-reach workplaces), union movements would be stronger and more politically powerful in all Anglo-American societies. However, they would still be irrelevant to most workers in the private sector who no longer identify with trade unionism. For example, studies of worker identities show how some workers are opposed to what they perceive as the leveling strategies of trade unions. Milton (2003: 41) explains how the North American high-tech workers he studied regard 'unions as anti-creative and opposed to the meritocracy system that anchors excellence in technology-based industries'. Strategies of organizing around discontent at a particular workplace are relevant to some worker groups but alienate others who want non-conflictual forms of voice (Freeman and Rogers, 1999) and 'express strong interest in having a job environment that supports continued learning and development' (Verma and Kochan, 2004: 7). For Verma and Kochan (2004: 14), the implication is that unions should 'adopt strategies and organizational structures that allow them to retain members as they move across jobs and through different stages of their life cycle'. Similarly, Bryson (2004: 22), in his analysis of the British Worker Representation and Participation Survey, argues that unions need to grow the 'aspirational agenda' while simultaneously having enough power to be credible on the adversarial agenda, when that is needed.

In sum, research on the prospects for union renewal increasingly cautions against any kind of 'one-size-fits-all' prescription for union revitalization and has moved on from simplistic appeals to the organizing model. Studies suggest that while unions still have a traditional or classical role to play where workers are exploited, are vulnerable to restructuring or are experiencing serious imbalance in the wage-work bargain, their chances of generating broader social appeal depend on whether they can find a non-traditional role that engages with the developmental aspirations that now characterize many workers (Rose, 2000). What is not clear is the basis on which workers who are pursuing self-development in and across workplaces might want support from trade unions, would be prepared to pay for it and would be prepared to participate in sustaining it. While unions need a 'proactive', 'autonomous' agenda (Levesque and Murray, 2002: 50), they need processes capable of keeping pace with the way worker interests, and attitudes to representation, have been evolving. If they cannot develop such processes, the 'dominant designs' of trade unions will continue to exhibit 'strategic drift'.

CONCLUSIONS

Unions are voluntary organizations mediating the different but overlapping interests of workers and employers and expressing a broader voice for workers in society. Their strategic choices, influenced by their own structures, traditions and internal politics, are shaped within the context of workplace interactions and within a much larger economic and socio-political context. In comparative terms, there are major differences between unions within labor movements which enjoy 'social partner' status and those that must survive with minimal state support. While recognizing these and other key variations, this chapter has focused on trade union strategy within the Anglo-American tradition of trade unionism and analyzed patterns of union strategy across establishment, maturity and renewal/decline phases of the organizational life cycle.

At the workplace level, union strategy can be understood as a conjunction of postures toward workers and employers. Servicing and organizing models are helpful for understanding the worker face of union strategy but do not constitute a simple dichotomy: the strategic question in terms of the worker dimension of union strategy is the extent to which unions build organizing capabilities which *complement* their servicing activities. Similarly, the employer face of union strategy does not rest on a simple dichotomy between adversarialism and cooperation but rests on blends of the two. A certain level of cooperation is necessary in any union bargaining engagement if a workable collective agreement is going to result. Union choices along worker and employer dimensions, evolved in particular contexts, create various patterns of unionism, each carrying different risks and advantages. It is important to distinguish unions from patterns of unionism and it helps to analyze union growth and decline not simply in terms of membership numbers. Trade unions are usefully analyzed as portfolios of viable and inviable bargaining units, particularly if we bring into such analysis the politics of portfolio decisions.

Understanding the particular tensions that unions face as mature bureaucracies is important to understanding their strategic behavior. Anglo-American unions have now moved from maturity into a renewal crisis brought about by a long period of decline. They are confronted with major evolution in employer strategies, elements of which appeal to workers while other parts pose threats. Questions of union revitalization turn not only on the employer face of strategy but also – and very critically – on the analysis of worker needs and how these are evolving. Research indicates that while some worker groups need and want traditional union representation, others have moved on to a more developmental orientation to work based on self-help and personal growth. Whether union movements can renew themselves through simultaneously responding to these two sets of needs is currently a very open question.

ACKNOWLEDGMENTS

I am very grateful to Jack Fiorito and Ed Heery for their comments on an earlier draft. The usual disclaimer applies.

NOTES

1 To save space, representative sources for each of these influences are not included in the chapter. Suffice to say, the factors identified are not controversial.

2 Hurd (1998) notes that the contrast between 'servicing' and 'organizing' models was first used in an AFL-CIO teleconference in 1988 and published in the resulting manual, 'Numbers That Count'.

3 A view very much reinforced by the respondents to Fiorito's (2004) survey of British trade union officials (see, especially, pp. 37–40).

4 One might note that vigilant unions grieve against such 'constructive dismissals' when companies instigate them.

REFERENCES

Appelbaum, E., Bailey, T., Berg, P. and Kalleberg, A. (2000) *Manufacturing Advantage: Why High-Performance Work Systems Pay Off*, Ithaca: ILR Press.

Behrens, M., Hamann, K. and Hurd, R. (2004) 'Conceptualizing labor union revitalization'. In Frege, C. and Kelly, J. (eds) *Varieties of Unionism: Strategies for Revitalization in a Globalizing Economy*, Oxford: Oxford University Press.

Belanger, J., Giles, A. and Murray, G. (2002) 'Towards a new production model: potentialities, tensions and contradictions'. In Murray, G., Belanger, J., Giles, A. and Lapointe, P. (eds) *Work and Employment Relations in the High-Performance Workplace*. London and New York: Continuum.

Boxall, P. and Haynes, P. (1997) 'Strategy and trade union effectiveness in a neo-liberal environment'. *British Journal of Industrial Relations*, 35 (4): 567–91.

Boxall, P. and Purcell, J. (2003) *Strategy and Human Resource Management*, Basingstoke and New York: Palgrave Macmillan.

Boxall, P., Haynes, P. and Freeman, R. (2007) 'Conclusions: what workers say in the Anglo-American world'. In Freeman, R., Boxall, P. and Haynes, P. (eds) *What Workers Say: Employee Voice in the Anglo-American Workplace*, Ithaca: Cornell University Press.

Bronfrenbrenner, K. and Juravich, T. (1998) 'It takes more than house calls: organizing to win with a comprehensive union-building strategy'. In Bronfrenbrenner, K., Oswald, R., Friedman, S., Seeber, R. and Hurd, R. (eds) *Organizing to Win: New Research on Union Strategies*, Ithaca: ILR Press.

Bronfrenbrenner, K., Oswald, R., Friedman, S., Seeber, R. and Hurd, R. (1998) (eds) *Organizing to Win: New Research on Union Strategies*, Ithaca: ILR Press.

Bryson, A. (2004) *A Perfect Union? What Workers Want From Unions*, London: TUC.

Carroll, G.R. and Hannan, M. T. (eds) (1995) *Organizations in Industry: Strategy, Structure and Selection*, New York & Oxford: Oxford University Press.

Carter, B. (2000) 'Adoption of the organizing model in British trade unions: some evidence from Manufacturing, Science and Finance (MSF)'. *Work, Employment and Society*, 14 (1): 117–36.

Charlwood, A. (2004) 'Annual review article 2003: the new generation of trade union leaders and prospects for union revitalization'. *British Journal of Industrial Relations*, 42 (2): 379–97.

Chaykowski, R. (2002) 'Reinventing production systems and industrial relations: technology-driven transformation in the Canadian metal-mining industry'. *Journal of Labor Research*, 23 (4): 591–613.

Chandler, A. (1962) *Strategy and Structure: Chapters in the History of Industrial Enterprise*, Cambridge, Mass.: MIT Press.

Child, J. (1972) 'Organizational structure, environment and performance: the role of strategic choice'. *Sociology*, 6 (3): 1–22.

Child, J. (1997) 'Strategic choice in the analysis of action, structure, organizations and environment: retrospect and prospect'. *Organization Studies*, 18 (1): 43–76.

Child, J., Loveridge, R. and Warner, M. (1973) 'Towards an organizational study of trade unions'. *Sociology*, 7 (1): 71–91.

Craft, J. (1991) 'Unions, bureaucracy, and change: old dogs learn new tricks very slowly'. *Journal of Labor Research*, 12 (4): 393–405.

Crouch, C. (1982) *Trade Unions: the Logic of Collective Action*, Glasgow: Fontana.

Danford, A., Richardson, M., Tailby, S. and Upchurch, M. (2004) 'Partnership, mutuality and the high-performance workplace: a case study of union strategy and worker experience in the aircraft industry'. In Healy, G., Heery, E., Taylor, P. and Brown, W. (eds) *The Future of Worker Representation*, Basingstoke: Palgrave Macmillan.

De Turberville, S. (2004) 'Does the "organizing model" represent a credible union renewal strategy?' *Work, Employment and Society*, 18 (4): 775–94.

Fairbrother, P. and Yates, C. (2003) *Trade Unions in Renewal: A Comparative Study*, London and New York: Routledge.

Fiorito, J. (2004) 'Union renewal and the organizing model in the United Kingdom'. *Labor Studies Journal*, 29 (2): 21–53.

Fiorito, J., Jarley, P. and Delaney, J. (2001) 'National unions as organizations'. *Research in Personnel and Human Resources Management*, 20: 231–68.

Fosh, P. (1993) 'Membership participation in workplace unionism: the possibility of union renewal'. *British Journal of Industrial Relations*, 31 (4): 577–92.

Freeman, R. B. and Rogers, J. (1999). *What Workers Want*, Ithaca: Cornell University Press.

Frege, C. and Kelly, J. (2004) 'Union strategies in comparative context'. In Frege, C. and Kelly, J. (eds) *Varieties of Unionism: Strategies for Revitalization in a Globalizing Economy*, Oxford: Oxford University Press.

Frege, C. and Kelly, J. (2004) (eds) *Varieties of Unionism: Strategies for Revitalization in a Globalizing Economy*, Oxford: Oxford University Press.

Frost, A. (2001) 'Reconceptualizing local union responses to workplace restructuring in North America'. *British Journal of Industrial Relations*, 39 (4): 539–64.

Godard, J. (2004) 'A critical assessment of the high-performance paradigm'. *British Journal of Industrial Relations*, 42 (2): 349–78.

Gospel, H. and Pendleton, A. (2003) 'Finance, corporate governance and the management of labor: a conceptual and comparative analysis'. *British Journal of Industrial Relations*, 42 (3): 557–82.

Hall, P. and Soskice, D. (2001) 'An introduction to varieties of capitalism'. In Hall, P. and Soskice, D. (eds) *Varieties of Capitalism: the Institutional Foundations of Comparative Advantage*, Oxford: Oxford University Press.

Hannan, M. (1995) 'Labor unions'. In Carroll, G. R. and Hannan, M. T. (eds) (1995) *Organizations in Industry: Strategy, Structure and Selection*, New York & Oxford: Oxford University Press.

Harcourt, M. and Wood, G. (eds) *Trade Unions and Democracy*, Manchester and New York: Manchester University Press.

Haynes, P. and Allen, M. (2000) 'Partnership as union strategy: a preliminary evaluation'. *Employee Relations*, 23 (2): 164–87.

Healy, G., Heery, E., Taylor, P. and Brown, W. (2004) (eds) *The Future of Worker Representation*, Basingstoke: Palgrave Macmillan.

Heery, E. (2005) 'Sources of change in trade unions'. *Work, Employment and Society*, 19 (1): 91–106.

Heery, E. and Adler, L. (2004) 'Organizing the unorganized'. In Frege, C. and Kelly, J. (eds) *Varieties of Unionism: Strategies for Revitalization in a Globalizing Economy*, Oxford: Oxford University Press.

Heery, E., Simms, M., Delbridge, R., Salmon, J. and Simpson, D. (2000) 'Union organizing in Britain: a survey of policy and practice'. *International Journal of Human Resource Management*, 11 (5): 986–1007.

Hurd, R. (1998) 'Contesting the dinosaur image: the labor movement's search for a future'. *Labor Studies Journal*, 22 (1): 5–30.

Hurd, R. (2004) 'The rise and fall of the organizing model in the US'. In Harcourt, M. and Wood, G. (eds) *Trade Unions and Democracy*, Manchester and New York: Manchester University Press.

Hyman, R. (1989) *The Political Economy of Industrial Relations*, Basingstoke: Macmillan.

Hyman, R. (1994) 'Changing trade union identities and strategies'. In Hyman, R. and Ferner, A. (eds) *New Frontiers in European Industrial Relations*, Oxford: Blackwell.

Hyman, R. (2001) *Understanding European Trade Unionism*, London: Sage.

James, P. (2004) 'Trade unions and political parties'. In Harcourt, M. and Wood, G. (eds) *Trade Unions and Democracy*, Manchester and New York: Manchester University Press.

Jarley, P. (2005) 'Unions as social capital: renewal through a return to the logic of mutual aid?' *Labor Studies Journal*, 29 (4): 1–26.

Johnson, G. and Scholes, K. (2002) *Exploring Corporate Strategy: Text and Cases*, Harlow: Pearson Education.

Johnston, P. (1994) *Success While Others Fail: Social Movement Unionism in the Public Workplace*, Cornell: ILR Press. Juravich, T. and Hilgert, J. (1999) 'UNITE's victory at Richmark: community-based union organizing in communities of color'. *Labor Studies Journal*, 24 (1): 27–41.

Juravich, T. and Hilgert, J. (1999) 'UNITE's victory at Richmark: community-based union organizing in communities of color'. *Labor Studies Journal*, 24 (1): 27–41.

Kaufman, B. (2004) 'Prospects for union growth in the United States in the early 21st Century'. In Verma, A. and Kochan, T. (eds) *Unions in the 21st Century*, New York: Palgrave Macmillan.

Kearney, R. (2003) 'Patterns of union decline and growth: an organizational ecology perspective'. *Journal of Labor Research*, 24 (4): 561–78.

Kochan, T.A., Katz, H.C. and McKersie, R.B. (1986) *The Transformation of American Industrial Relations*, New York: Basic Books.

Lange, P., Ross, G and Vannicelli, M. (1982) *Unions, Change and Crisis: French & Italian Union Strategy and the Political Economy 1945–1980*, London: Allen and Unwin.

Lester, R. (1958) *As Unions Mature: An Analysis of the Evolution of American Unionism*, Princeton: Princeton University Press.

Levesque, C. and Murray, G. (2002) 'Local versus global: activating local union power in the global economy'. *Labor Studies Journal*, 27 (3): 39–65.

Lustig, J. (2002) 'New leadership and its discontents'. *Social Policy*, 33 (1): 4–10.

Mackie, K.S., Holahan, C.K. and Gottlieb, N.H. (2001) 'Employee involvement management practices, work stress, and depression in employees of a human services residential care facility'. *Human Relations*, 54 (8): 1065–92.

Masters, M. and Atkin, R. (1999) Union strategies for revival: a conceptual framework and literature review. *Research in Personnel and Human Resources Management*, 17: 283–314.

Milkman, R. and Voss, K. (eds) (2004) *Rebuilding Labor: Organizing and Organizers in the New Union Movement*, Ithaca: Cornell University Press.

Milton, L. (2003) 'An identity perspective on the propensity of high-tech talent to unionize'. *Journal of Labor Research*, 24 (1): 31–53.

Mintzberg, H. (1978) 'Patterns in strategy formation'. *Management Science*, 24 (9): 934–48.

Mintzberg, H. (1990) 'The design school: reconsidering the basic premises of strategic management'. *Strategic Management Journal*, 11 (3): 171–95.

Mueller, D. (1997) 'First-mover advantages and path dependence'. *International Journal of Industrial Organization*, 15 (6): 827–50.

Nissen, B. (2000) 'Living wage campaigns from a 'social movement' perspective: the Miami case'. *Labor Studies Journal*, 25 (3): 29–50.

Nissen, B. (2003) 'Alternative strategic directions for the US labor movement: recent scholarship'. *Labor Studies Journal*, 28 (1): 133–55.

Ramsay, H., Scholarios, D. and Harley, B. (2000) 'Employees and high-performance work systems: testing inside the black box'. *British Journal of Industrial Relations*, 38 (4): 501–31.

Rose, M. (2000) 'Work attitudes in the expanding occupations'. In Purcell, K. (ed.) *Changing Boundaries in Employment*, Bristol: Bristol Academic Press.

Suarez, F. and Utterback, J. (1995) 'Dominant designs and the survival of firms'. *Strategic Management Journal*, 16 (6): 415–30.

Tailby, S. and Winchester, D. (2000) 'Management and trade unions: towards social partnership?' In S. Bach and K. Sisson (eds) *Personnel Management: A Comprehensive Guide to Theory and Practice*, Oxford: Blackwell.

Terry, M. (1994) 'Workplace unionism: redefining structures and objectives'. In Hyman, R. and Ferner, A. (eds), *New Frontiers in European Industrial Relations*, Oxford: Blackwell.

Turnbull, P. (1988) 'An economic theory of trade union behavior: a critique'. *British Journal of Industrial Relations*, 26 (1): 85–118.

Turner, L. (2004) 'Why revitalize? Labor's urgent mission in a contested global economy'. In Frege, C. and Kelly, J. (eds) *Varieties of Unionism: Strategies for Revitalization in a Globalizing Economy*, Oxford: Oxford University Press.

Verma, A. and Kochan, T. (2004) 'Unions in the 21st century: prospects for renewal'. In Verma, A. and Kochan, T. (2004) (eds) *Unions in the 21st Century*, New York: Palgrave Macmillan.

Verma, A. and Kochan, T. (2004) (eds) *Unions in the 21 st Century*, New York: Palgrave Macmillan.

Voss, K. and Sherman, R. (2000) 'Breaking the iron law of oligarchy: union revitalization in the American labor movement'. *American Journal of Sociology*, 106 (2): 303–49.

Walton, R. and McKersie, R. (1965) *A Behavioral Theory of Labor Negotiations*, New York: McGraw-Hill.

Walton, R., Cutcher-Gershenfeld, McKersie, R. (1994) *Strategic Negotiations: A Theory of Change in Labor-Management Relations*, Boston: Harvard Business School Press.

Willman, P. (2001) 'The viability of trade union organization: a bargaining unit analysis'. *British Journal of Industrial Relations*, 39 (1): 97–117.

12

Employer Organizations

Franz Traxler

As with any other kind of interest association, employer organizations are burdened with the problem of collective action (Olson, 1965). The primary goal of interest associations is to provide collective goods the benefits of which nobody interested in these goods can be excluded from. Hence, there is a strong incentive for rational, self-interested actors to take a free ride (not to contribute), with the consequence that associational action may be suboptimal in terms of effectiveness or may even fail. This line of reasoning presupposes that the members of the interest group share a basic interest in the common good, although they may vary in the degree of their interest. This assumption does not fully match the situation of employers, since their interest in associational action as such is dubious. This follows from the structural power asymmetry in the labor market (Offe, 1985). Their control over the means of production equips the employers with a much broader range of options for advancing their labor market interests compared to the options at the disposal of employees. This power asymmetry explains why employers and employees differ in their preference between individual and collective forms of industrial relations

(Traxler, 1995). Employers will generally prefer bilaterally individual exchange relations with labor, since they can deploy their strategic advantages in the labor market most effectively in these circumstances. In contrast to this, initiatives for collective exchange relations come from the employees, since it is only a collective approach which can enable them to improve their strategic capacities. The historical sequence of the formation of trade unions and employer organizations clearly reflects this configuration of power and interests. Unions were usually formed first. The employers responded by embarking on collective action only after the unions had proved their capacity to exert pressures upon them.[1]

However, even when unions have been formed, employers may refrain from collective action. If there is no notable union presence in their company, employers will see no need to set up or join an employer association. Generally, union density increases with firm size (Visser, 1991). As a result, smaller companies are not pressurized by union presence to join employer organizations. Large companies may also regard joining employers' organizations as pointless if they have sufficient resources to adopt a systematic strategy of union avoidance. Alternatively, they may recognize a union for single-employer bargaining instead of resorting to multi-employer bargaining which involves employer organizations. If employer organization membership is actually seen as a reasonable option, then the standard problem of free riding in collective action becomes relevant. There is good reason to believe that employers rationally follow their self-interest more consistently than any other interest group. This is because inter-firm competition continuously forces them to weigh the costs of their decisions against their benefits. Large companies, in particular, can rely on considerable in-house expertise, so as to be able to carefully examine the cost–benefit ratio of associational membership. The upshot of these considerations appears as a paradox. The special dilemma of employer organizations is that they have to organize the most powerful interest group in society. This power superiority diminishes the need of employers to rely on associational action. Multinational enterprises for example, have more resources than employer organizations and also surpass them in terms of their territorial scope of action. This means that employer organizations are condemned to cope with a double problem of collective action. On the one hand, the benefit of their activities is far more uncertain than in the case of other interest associations. On the other hand, their potential membership is more able to pursue its rational self-interest, such that there is a higher risk of free riding, as compared to most other interest groups. At worst, these problems may be so overwhelming that employer organizations fail to establish themselves as noticeable actors in industrial relations. Most importantly, this holds true for the US and Canada.[2] Likewise, the role of employer organizations as bargainers is negligible in the UK. In the transformed economies of Central and Eastern Europe, the newly formed associations usually lack a bargaining mandate, single-employer bargaining prevails and collective bargaining coverage is very low.[3]

In contrast to the US, the UK and Canada, employer confederations of these countries participate in national tripartite boards which deal also with labor market issues. However, their policy inputs are symbolic rather than providing governance because of the volatility of the party system and the absence of organized business in the collective bargaining process. More than any other labor relations arrangement, the existence and tasks of employer organizations are thus subject to a strategic choice, as made by their constituency.

Adopting a cross nationally comparative perspective, the structure of this chapter is as follows. It begins with an overview of the activities of employer organizations and then analyzes multi-employer bargaining as a key determinant of membership strength. The next section turns to the structures of employer organizations. The chapter concludes with the implications exogenous changes such as internationalization have for the future of employer organizations.

ACTIVITIES OF EMPLOYER ASSOCIATIONS

Interest representation

Businesses have interests not only in relation to labor but also vis-à-vis other businesses with which they have exchange relations: customers and the suppliers of power, raw materials, intermediate goods, finance and manifold services. Any of these interests may be taken up by associations which may advance them either directly vis-à-vis the market counterparts of their members or indirectly vis-à-vis the state. The state is an important target of interest politics, since any kind of markets are framed by state regulation, such that interest groups will seek to lobby for regulations of benefit to them. Hence, employer associations in the narrow sense relate only to a certain segment of business interests that originates in the labor market. However, this does not rule out the possibility that they also organize other interests which will be captured here as 'product market interests'. We thus differentiate between three basic types of business interest associations (Schmitter and Streeck, 1981): pure employer organizations process only labor market interests; 'mixed' associations combine the representation of labor and product market interests; and pure trade associations are specialized in product market interests. In the following, pure employer organizations and mixed associations are subsumed under the category of employer organization.

In the vast majority of countries pure employer associations co-exist with mixed associations. From a historical perspective, however, employer organizations usually emerged as pure associations for two main reasons. First, trade associations were set up earlier. Second, the logic of representing product market interests differs from that dealing with labor market interests. The labor market interests of business are far less divisive than its product market interests. The product market interests of a certain business group usually need to be advanced in relation to other business groups, whereas the counterpart in matters of labor market interests is labor. Therefore the conflicts of interest originating in product markets are endogenous to business as a class, while such conflicts ensuing from the labor market are exogenous to business. This results in distinct requirements for domain demarcation. When it comes to representing labor market interests, it is reasonable to establish rather encompassing associations, since controlling a broader labor market segment than one's counterpart means a strategic advantage. This contrasts with the strategic imperatives of representing product market interests which imply delimiting the membership domain so narrow that all kinds of product market interests conflicting with those of the association's constituency can be externalized. Comparative empirical studies show that pure trade associations significantly outnumber pure employer organizations and cover far narrower domains (Traxler, 1993). Regardless of these distinct logics of associational action, there has been a long-term trend toward merging the representation of labor

market interests and product market interests (Traxler et al., 2001; Traxler, 2004a). This trend gathered momentum during the 1980s, with mergers between lower-level (sectoral) associations and spilled over to the peak level afterwards. Peak organizations are understood as being not a subordinate member of another national employer organization. They were involved in mergers in the following countries: Norway (in 1989), Finland, Ireland (both in 1993), Sweden (in 2001) and Japan (in 2002) all saw amalgamations of their principal pure employer peak with trade peak associations. The Portuguese employer confederation, CIP, extended its activities from labor to product market interests during the 1980s. In 1992 the principal employer confederation of Denmark, DA, incorporated product market interests through the merger of its largest association for industry with its trade association counterpart. Likewise, the NZ Employers Federation (renamed Business New Zealand in 2001) has changed its profile from a pure to a mixed employer confederation as a result of mergers at lower levels and the enlargement of its confederal activities to product market interests. As a consequence of these developments at peak level, Germany and Switzerland remain the only countries in Table 12.1, where the principal employer peak organization is still a pure form.

The tendency to replace pure with mixed employer organizations can be traced to three main factors. First, labor relations have increasingly lost their status as a relatively isolated policy area. Growing interdependence of policy fields thus more and more cross-cuts the traditional boundaries of employer organizations and trade associations. Second, bargaining tasks have been curtailed due to bargaining decentralization. Hence, the shift of pure employer organizations to product market interests aims to reinforce their status as a voice of business. Third, mergers between employer organizations and trade associations are devised to economize on resources. This follows from intensified market competition which has induced the companies to curb costs. The driving force behind mergers has

Table 12.1 The largest employer peak organization: Basic data (1994–96)

Country	Name	Density*	Bargaining role**	Predominant level of collective bargaining	Extension practices***
A	WKÖ	100	3	MEB	2
AUS	CAI (1994–95), ACCI	75[c]	3	MEB	3
B	VBO/FEB	72	3	MEB	3
CDN	—	0	—	SEB	0
CH	ZSAO, SAV[a]	37	2	MEB	1
D	BDA	72[d]	1	MEB	1
DK	DA	39	3–2	MEB	0
E	CEOE	72	2	MEB	3
F	CNPF[b]	74	2	MEB	3
FIN	TT	44	3	MEB	3
I	C	39	2	MEB	0
IRL	IBEC	39	3	MEB	0
JP	Nikkeiren	40[g]	2	SEB	0
N	NHO	31	3	MEB	0
NL	VNO (1994), VNO-NCW	79	2	MEB	3
NZ	NZEF	90	0	SEB	0
P	CIP	34	2	MEB	3
PL	KPP	20–25[e]	0	SEB	0
S	SAF	55	1	MEB	0
SI	GZS	100	3	MEB	3
UK	CBI	54	0	SEB	0
USA	—	0	1	SEB	0

Notes:

* In terms of employees covered, period means or most recent data

** Recurrent involvement in wage bargaining: 0 = no substantial role; 1 = indirectly only, via member associations; 2 = co-ordination of member associations; 3 = direct involvement as a bargainer

*** Compulsory membership included; 0 = non-existing/irrelevant; 1 = limited; 2 = pervasive

MEB = multi-employer bargaining; SEB = single-employer bargaining

[a] ZSAO renamed in SAV in 1996, [b] CNPF renamed in MEDEF in 1998, [c] 1997, [d] West Germany, [e] 2002

For abbreviations, see Appendix.

Source: Traxler et al. (2001), Franz Traxler data set.

thus been the companies themselves, so as to overcome multiple membership and multiple payment of dues.

Employer organizations differ in their involvement in collective bargaining. Table 12.1 documents the role of the principal cross-sectoral national peak organizations in wage bargaining on a regular basis. Excluding the US and Canada from consideration, one finds that they are directly engaged in wage bargaining in approximately one third of the countries. In comparison to previous periods, the peaks negotiate collective agreements less frequently, since bargaining has become more decentralized since the late 1970s. In most countries, however, this process has assumed the form of 'organized decentralization' in the course of which the bargaining parties at higher levels set the framework for the negotiations at lower levels (Traxler et al., 2001). Hence, the tasks of the peaks have tended to shift from negotiation to cross-sectoral co-ordination of the bargaining activities of their member associations which then formally conclude the collective agreements. This pattern applies to the majority of the 20 peaks listed in Table 12.1. This contrasts with the situation in Germany and Sweden, where the peaks lack a direct role in wage bargaining and are only indirectly involved in the bargaining process via collective bargaining conducted by their member associations. It should be noted that the bargaining role of the peaks somewhat varies with issues and over time. In Sweden, for instance, the peak still negotiates with the union confederations over non-wage issues. The German BDA is autho-rized to co-ordinate its affiliates in matters of principle so as to prevent precedents to the disadvantage of the employers. In countries, such as Italy, Portugal and Spain, the employer confederations have occasionally negotiated central-level pacts on incomes policy. On a regular basis, however, the main responsibil-ities for bargaining remain with the sectoral associations in most of the 20 countries.

In all cases, representing the labor market interests of their members vis-à-vis the state forms an essential part of the activities of the peaks. In the UK and New Zealand their representational tasks have been limited to these activities, after single-employer bar-gaining supplanted multi-employer bargain-ing in the 1980s and early 1990s, respectively. The same profile characterizes the employer organizations in the USA and Canada, where neither cross-sectoral peaks exist nor multi-employer bargaining figures prominently. In the case of the US, for example the sectoral employer organizations are involved in lob-bying for labor law issues and sometimes deal with law suits. Cross-national comparison shows that the bargaining system significantly determines the extent to which the state incorporates the peaks into public policy-making (Traxler, 2004b). The scope of partic-ipation of the peaks in public policy diverges along the divide between co-ordinated and uncoordinated wage policies. In this respect co-ordinated bargaining is understood in the broad sense, insofar as cross-sectoral co-ordination may rely on peak-level bargain-ing, peak-level co-ordination or co-ordination by a lower-level pattern setter under the umbrella of the peak.

In countries with co-ordinated wage poli-cies, the peaks enjoy significantly more participation rights than their counterparts in countries where wage bargaining is uncoordinated. This is because attempts at cross-sectoral wage co-ordination matter in macro-economic terms and thus set a strong incentive for governments to seek the co-operation with the bargaining parties also in policy areas other than incomes policy. Conversely, such an incentive for governments is absent, if wage bargaining is so unco-ordinated, that none of the wage agreements has a noticeable impact on the economy. It is worth emphasizing that this correlation between co-ordination activities and associational participation in public policy holds regardless of how effective the co-ordination activities are. In the case of peak-level co-ordination, their effectiveness is uncertain because it is impossible for the peaks to make their affiliates comply by fiat.

In addition to the unions and the state as the classic interlocutors of employer organi-zations, their peaks have increasingly targeted the public by means of political lobbying, opinion formation and campaigning.[4] On the one hand, this reflects the above changes in tasks, namely the shift to mixed associations and the curtailed role in bargaining. On the other hand, this trend follows from the fact that organized business is the vanguard of what may broadly be captured as the neoliberal agenda: deregulation, privatization and welfare state retrenchment. Against this background, political campaigning becomes a key activity. It can serve as a means of downplaying the considerable conflicts of interests within more complex, mixed associ-ations; and it also aims to generate legitimacy needed for the far-reaching restructuring of society.

Service activities

Aside from interest representation, the range of activities performed by employer organi-zations also includes service activities. The difference between interest representation and services is that the former is a collective good, whereas the latter are private goods. Since private goods are excludable, they can be traded. Interest associations like employer organizations use private goods as selective incentives, for instance they trade their provision against membership, so as to overcome the problem of collective action. This implies that the members get the associational services free of charge or at relatively cheap rates. Moreover, associations may sell their services also to non-members on a commercial basis. The pattern most common to employer organizations is that they concentrate on providing non-payable services for members. One can, however, observe a growing tendency of commercialization (selling products and services on the market). New Zealand's employer organizations, for instance, have taken this route in response to the dismantling of multi-employer bargaining by the 1991 labor law reform (Carrol and Tremewan, 1993). In the Netherlands many employer organizations have set up special, commercial subunits to offer services to members and also non-members.

Services are generally seen as becoming more important as a way of attracting employers (Visser and Wilts, 2006). Services may include such activities as dissemination of information, advice on legal questions and management problems, consultancy, training and further training. What kind of services an association provides depends mainly on its representational profile. Hence, the services of pure employer organizations are geared to industrial relations, while they address also product market interests in the case of mixed associations. Services specific to employer organizations are assistance of members in matters of single-employer bargaining, representation of members in labor court proceedings and financial support in case of a labor conflict. These three services are borderline cases of the distinction between private goods and collective goods, as the members for which they are provided are the direct beneficiaries; at the same time, however, these services contribute to processing collective employer interests. In the case of mixed associations, advice and support regarding public programmes to aid business constitute a very important incentive for membership in the European countries, since organized business generally participates in their implementation there.

Although the relative importance devoted to representational activities and services varies with the associations, interest representation usually prevails in that most of their resources are allocated to this type of activity. In comparison to this, the priorities of the companies themselves vary more markedly, since the need for services clearly decreases as firm size increases. Associational services are of special importance to small companies due to their limited resources. Large companies can easily buy or make themselves all the services offered by associations, with the exception of the protection against strikes, as provided by a dispute fund run by employer organizations. This means that services work as a selective incentive for membership primarily in the case of the smaller companies. In addition to the existence of a dispute fund, it is the opportunity to participate in the association's decision-making process, which sets the strongest selective incentive for the large companies to associate. This is because they are more vulnerable to strike actions due to their higher levels of unionization; and they have more power to exert influence on their employer organization as a result of their superior resources.

MULTI-EMPLOYER BARGAINING AND MEMBERSHIP

As outlined above, there is hardly a reason for employers to associate, as long as unions do not enter the labor relations scene. Therefore the basic incentive to form employer association is unionization on the side of labor. Unionization, however, is not a sufficient precondition for gathering in employer organizations. Alternatively, employers may either try to do away with union presence in their company, if this presence is rather weak; or they may embark on single-employer bargaining, if unions are strong. As an implication, the appeal of employer organizations directly hinges on the power of multi-employer bargaining.[5] Power means two things. On the one hand, this refers to positive incentives, for instance special benefits multi-employer bargaining offers in comparison to single-employer bargaining. On the other hand, multi-employer bargaining may create negative incentives which more or less force the employers to join.

Positive membership incentives from multi-employer bargaining

In the literature one finds four main kinds of positive incentives (Clegg, 1976; Sisson, 1987; Traxler et al., 2001). First, multi-employer bargaining reduces transactions costs of the employment relationship. In this respect, the difference to single-employer bargaining is gradual, since any kind of collective agreement helps economize on transaction costs. However, this effect is larger in the case of multi-employer bargaining, as certain areas of employment regulation can be externalized to the signatory employer organization and its union counterpart. Second, multi-employer bargaining may perform a cartelizing function. Above all, this means taking wages out of inter-firm competition. This cartelizing effect becomes even more powerful if the standardization of wages helps employers reduce inter-firm competition in their product markets. Under these circumstances, the standard rate works as a means of passing wage increases on to consumers and forcing low-cost 'sweat shops' out of the market. Third, multi-employer bargaining may enable employers to neutralize the workplace from trade union activity. This is because multi-employer agreements are forced to set out provisions which are applicable to any company covered. As a consequence, these provisions are rather general in content and often set merely minimum standards, thus restricting management prerogatives less than single-employer settlements. Fourth, access to benefits in areas other than labor relations may be tied to membership in an employer organization. When employer organizations are mixed, businesses may join for the reason of product market interests, and may then become roped into the organizations' representational activities in labor relations. Conversely, business associations may engage in multi-employer bargaining even when this is not their primary concern. This is because the role of a bargainer is the key to participation in public policy, as noted above.[6]

Negative membership incentives from multi-employer bargaining

Negative incentives may be set either by the unions or the state. Unions can exert strong pressures on employers to accept multi-employer bargaining, if they pursue 'whipsawing' tactics aimed at confronting the employers individually. A related reason to associate is that employer organizations can work as 'strike insurance', in particular when they run a dispute fund. Membership in the employer organization thus diminishes the risk of becoming a target of strikes. If, nevertheless, a labor conflict occurs, the companies can rely on financial support from their employer organization. This protective function of multi-employer bargaining may be backed by statutory provisions, imposing a peace obligation on the parties to collective bargaining as long as their collective agreement is in force.

This brings us to the impact of state regulation on the strategic choice of employers. This choice is strongly conditioned by the way in which labor law regulates the legal effects of multi-employer agreements. In principle, a collective agreement applies only to those companies which are members of the signatory employer organization. Labor law, however, may provide for an extension scheme (Traxler, 1994). The first variant of such extension schemes makes a multi-employer agreement generally binding within the membership domain of the signatory employer organization, thus covering also companies not affiliated to the respective employer organization. A less widespread form of extension is devised to bind employers and employees in certain sectoral or geographical areas outside the domain of the multi-employer agreement, if these areas resemble those covered originally by the agreement, and if there are no parties conducting collective bargaining. The standard extension procedure is that the responsible authority declares a collective agreement as generally binding at the request of either or both of the bargaining parties.

Both extension mechanisms set a strong incentive for employers to associate provided there is a notable practice of application. As regards the first mechanism, employers have good reason to expect that a collective agreement will bind them even if they remain outside of the employer organization. Hence, it is rational especially for the larger companies to join in order to be entitled to participate in the bargaining process, the outcome of which may bind them in any case (Gladstone, 1984). The smaller companies (which have lesser capacities to influence the bargaining process) will become members of the employer organization, since they need its services for implementing the collective agreements. Likewise, the second extension mechanism fosters the formation of employer organizations, since employers will prefer regulating the employment relationship themselves over regulation by third parties.

In some countries (Belgium, France and the Netherlands) the unions and employer organizations use the extension mechanism as a vehicle for performing public functions (health and safety, vocational training, unemployment schemes) and raising financial resources. In this case the agreement imposes a levy on the employers which is designed to finance the public task as well as the signatory parties as such, since they keep a certain share for their own organization. Unaffiliated companies are also charged via the application of the extension provision (Traxler et al., 2001). This establishes a practice of compulsory dues payment which comes close to compulsory membership. In Austria and Slovenia, one finds formalized compulsory membership in employer organizations in that all firms belonging to the domain of the chambers of business are legally required to be their members. While chambers based on compulsory membership act as trade associations in many European countries, the situation of Austria and Slovenia is special, since their chambers of business perform the tasks of both a trade association and an employer organization.[7] In fact, they prevail over their voluntary counterparts and operate as the principal employer organizations. In addition, employer organizations and multi-employer bargaining enjoy special protection

in Austria, since labor law – with the exception of a few explicitly listed businesses – forbids single-employer bargaining and authorizes only associations (employer organizations and unions at multi-employer level) to conclude collective agreements. The case polar opposite to these manifold regulations conducive to employer organizations is represented by US and Canadian labor law. Its provisions rather discourage from entering multi-employer bargaining and, concomitantly, the formation of employer organizations, since they focus on the single employer when it comes to determining the scope of a bargaining unit and to certifying a union as the unit's bargaining agent for the employees. The US National Labor Relations Board (NLRB), for instance, defines a bargaining unit as a group of employees sharing a 'community of interest' that is usually seen as the result of performing similar types of work, and being employed by the same company.

The determinants of employer density

As these statutory provisions for bargaining and employer organizations markedly vary across countries, so does the relevance of the other incentives for multi-employer bargaining outlined above. In line with this, cross-national comparison shows a high degree of variation in employer density, measured as the ratio of the number of employees working in the member firms under the umbrella of the largest employer peak to the total number of employees of the firms covered by the peak's domain (Table 12.1).[8] This variation ranges from zero to 100 per cent. Employer density is zero in the case of the US and Canada, as there is no country-wide cross-sectoral employer peak. Austria's and Slovenia's peaks record 100 per cent, because of compulsory membership. Even though employer organizations remain invisible in two cases, density averaged over the 20 countries where membership is voluntary is rather high, with an unweighted mean of 48.4 per cent. Where does this high capacity to attract membership come from? As comparative quantitative analysis shows (Traxler et al., 2001; Traxler, 2004a), the incidence of extension practices most strongly affects employer density and even dominates the effect of the level of unionization. Accordingly, union density has a significant impact on employer density only when there is no practice of extending collective agreements. This is because the enactment as well as the application of extension provisions is fairly independent of union strength.

Extension practices are pervasive in countries with comparatively high union density (Belgium and Finland) and in countries with very low unionization (France and Spain). Aside from this, comparative analysis also suggests that the high employer density in terms of employees emanates from a generally stronger propensity of the large firms to associate, as compared to their smaller counterparts (Traxler, 1995). This implies that extension practices provide a weaker incentive for the small companies to join their employer organization. As comparative analysis shows (Traxler et al., 2007), labor regulation constitutes the divide between 'large' and 'small' companies by exempting what is legally defined as a small firm from the purview of certain employee rights. Furthermore, available data on unionization and collective bargaining coverage by firm size (Visser, 1991; Traxler, 1994) indicate that large and small companies differ far more in their associability, if extension practices are absent. While the large firms therefore represent the membership stronghold of the employer organizations in terms of firm size, manufacturing in particular the metalworking industry does so in sectoral respects (Traxler et al., 2007).

THE STRUCTURE OF EMPLOYER ORGANIZATIONS

Membership domains and hierarchical differentiation

The way in which employer organizations demarcate their potential membership lays the cornerstone of their structures, since this not only defines the businesses eligible for membership but also pre-determines the range of interests incorporated by the organizations. Branch or sectoral affiliation is most frequently used for demarcating the membership domain. Other relevant criteria are firm size, the production system and ownership/business orientation. In this respect, one finds associations specialized in organizing small and medium-sized firms; small-scale craft production; co-operatives and not-for-profit organizations. Public ownership of companies has widely lost its relevance for domain specification in Western Europe, in the wake of extensive privatization and deregulation.[9] If the public-sector employees have the right of collective bargaining, the state has formed separate employer organizations in countries like Sweden and Norway, whereas the authorities themselves negotiate in other cases. It should be noted that the employer groups complementary to these characteristics (large firms, privately-owned companies, profit-oriented businesses) rarely form special organizations. This is because they represent the mainstream of business interests that normally dominates the politics of employer organizations.[10]

In countries, where employer organizations have a notable role in industrial relations, a multiplicity of them exists. For instance, around 1000 employer organizations are under the umbrella of the German BDA. This is not outstanding, as the smaller countries of Western Europe appear to count no fewer organizations in relation to the size of their labor force, as available data suggest. According to the respective national statistical offices the Portuguese employer organizations totaled 436 in 1996, and there were around 100 employer organizations in Sweden in the early 2000s. This multiplicity of associations emanates from the specific power relationship between employer organizations and their member firms. Since the large companies tend to be more powerful than their associations, the latter are forced to suit their domains to the special interests of the former. This results in rather narrow demarcations. This tendency is especially pronounced in the case of mixed associations which have to accommodate to the high diversity of product market interests across the distinct business groups.

The large number of organizations goes hand in hand with an elaborate hierarchical differentiation that ranges from the primary associations (which organize the businesses themselves) up to the peaks. In some countries like Germany this complex pyramid of associations covers no less than four hierarchical levels. This pyramid is designed to unify powerful special interests in a step-wise process, so as to equip the employer organizations with strategic capacity when it comes to interacting with the state or the unions at higher levels of interest aggregation.

Table 12.2 lists all national employer peaks of the 22 countries in Table 12.1, as far as they exceed a certain threshold of cross-sectoral encompassment, covering at least two complete one-digit ISIC sectors. Recalling the distinct parameters of domain demarcation, as outlined above, one finds that the hierarchical structures are more able to unify the various sector and branch interests than the other categories of interest differentiations. There are only three countries, where the unification of employer interests along sectoral lines remains incomplete. In Australia, industry entertains a special organization, whereas the service sector does so in Norway and Portugal. Other characteristics of domain specialization more often feed through to distinctive peaks. In particular, separate organization applies to small and medium-sized firms and craft production. The fact that craft production correlates with small size indicates that the interest cleavages along firm size are most difficult to reconcile. Interests distinct from the predominant interests of the large companies, prompt their smaller counterparts to form separate associations.

Table 12.2   The system of employer organization (1991–98)*

Country	Total number	Number of peak organizations by main parameter of demarcation			
		General (business sector)	Firm size, production system	Ownership/business orientation	Sector
A	1	1	0	0	0
AUS	2–3	1	1	0	0–1
B	1	1	0	0	0
CDN	0	0	0	0	0
CH	2	1	1	0	0
D	1	1	0	0	0
DK	1	1	0	0	0
E	2	1	1	0	0
F	3	1	2	0	0
FIN	2	1	0	0	1
I	11–10	1	5	5–4	0
IRL	1	1	0	0	0
JP	1	1	0	0	0
N	2	1	0	0	1
NL	4–2	2–1	2–1	0	0
NZ	[1]	[1]	0	0	0
P	1–2–3	1	0–1	0	0–1
PL	[3]	[2]	[1]	0	0
S	3	1	0	2	0
SI	4	2	2	0	0
UK	[1]	[1]	0	0	0
USA	0	0	0	0	0

Note:
* National employer peak organizations covering at least two complete one-digit ISIC sectors. Peak organizations lacking a notable role in collective bargaining are put in parentheses.
Source: Traxler et al. (2001), Franz Traxler data set.

Most frequently, one general employer organization co-exists with one or more special peaks for small and medium-sized companies, crafts, etc. This pluralism is most accentuated in Italy. However, a large number of countries register only one single peak. It should be noted, however, that Table 12.2 somewhat downplays the degree of associational fragmentation, since it records only those peaks which play a notable role in bargaining matters either directly (through bargaining themselves or co-ordination activities) or indirectly via extensive involvement of their affiliates in bargaining).[11] In addition to the listed associations, further cross-sectoral national employer peaks exist in several countries (Austria, Ireland, Portugal, Denmark, Sweden and Finland) which confine their activities to lobbying the authorities (Traxler et al., 2007). In all cases but Austria, they are specialized in organizing crafts or small and medium-sized enterprises. In Ireland and Finland, their restriction to lobbying is not voluntary, as their efforts to join the tripartite peak-level negotiations taking place recurrently in these countries have been vetoed by the associations of business and labor which participate in this process. If more than one peak has a bargaining role, the general peak is always the principal actor. The role of the peaks in the bargaining process is relatively weak, as compared to their member associations. The peaks can build their co-ordination activities merely upon non-binding recommendations and their negotiations are overshadowed by the formal or informal power of their affiliates to either veto peak-level agreements or opt out. Analogous problems emerge when peaks are expected to formulate joint positions vis-à-vis the state. In this case they often limit themselves to taking up only those issues and interests which are not controversial among their members. Alternatively, their position may echo the interests of their largest affiliates. Sweden provides a striking example of the predominance of one single member over its peak. Despite resistance from other employer groups, the powerful association of the engineering industry, by threatening to secede otherwise, enforced the withdrawal of SAF from centralized bargaining as well as internal reforms that dismantled the bargaining capabilities of SAF (Swenson and Pontusson, 2000). Such predominance rests on marked asymmetry in resource distribution, as anecdotal evidence shows. An extreme case is Denmark where the largest affiliate, representing the industry, has accounted for around 50 per cent of the total wage sum covered by DA (Jørgensen and Traxler, 2007). In the early 2000s the staff of the Dutch VNO-NCW consisted of 160 employees (Kenis and Traxler, 2007), as compared to 225 employees of its most important affiliate, organizing the metal-working industry (Visser and Wilts, 2006).

The unit of membership and its legal effects

Finally, the structures of the employer associations are shaped by how their statutes define the unit of membership and its legal effects. As far as the primary associations are concerned, the standard definition of the membership unit is the company, as compared to the individual person as the owner of the respective business. At higher hierarchical levels, one can differentiate between associations which have solely lower-level associations as members and associations which organize associations as well as the companies themselves. This even includes the peak level, although direct firm membership is not standard at this level. Eight of the 20 principal confederations listed in Table 12.1 accept this kind of membership.[12] In all these cases direct firm membership is designed to attract very large firms. Obtaining the privileged status of a direct affiliate to the confederation, these firms play a key role in associational affairs and also significantly contribute to the confederation's budget (Traxler et al., 2007). The most important legal effect of membership relates to the bargaining role of the employer organizations. In this respect, the distinction is between conforming and non-conforming members. In contrast to non-conforming members, conforming members are regularly bound by the collective agreement concluded by their organization. In the vast majority of countries, membership always implies the conforming status. This may be traced to widespread extension practices in most countries where multi-employer bargaining prevails. Under these circumstances non-conforming membership does not make sense. This, however, does not necessarily rule out the possibility that either large member companies may be entitled to conclude their own collective agreements, as is the case of some Dutch companies (Kenis and Traxler, 2007), or the employer organization signs a single-employer agreement on behalf of one of its members, if wished by the respective member.[13] In comparison to this, non-conforming membership is formally established as a special type of membership, such that a company can choose to be either a conforming or a non-conforming member. This duality of membership status was important in some sectors in the UK, such as the chemical industry (Armstrong, 1984), as long as multi-employer bargaining was practiced. Since the mid-1990s, a growing number of primary employer associations in Germany have introduced the status of a non-conforming member in response to the decline in membership (Grote et al., 2007). As in the British case, non-conforming members have full access to the services provided by the associations. It is primarily the smaller companies which become a non-conforming member, while the larger companies still prefer conforming membership that includes protection against strikes. In Denmark a special kind of non-conforming membership has developed as the result of some mergers between trade associations and employer organizations, when the formerly independent associations continued to exist as distinctive subunits with separate membership under the new common umbrella. In this case, the companies which are solely members of the trade subunit are not bound by the collective agreements concluded by the association (Jørgensen and Traxler, 2007). This arrangement, however, differs from the British and German pattern in that any member of the employer subgroup of the mixed Danish

associations is covered by the collective agreements to which the association is a party. In Germany even pure employer organizations have adopted the principle of non-conforming membership, and have usually done so against the warnings by their sectoral umbrella associations. This includes the largest affiliate of BDA, Gesamtmetall, which in 2005 counted 2000 companies with 200,000 employees obtaining non-conforming membership under its umbrella, as compared to around 4,800 conforming members employing 1.9 million employees. The German development corroborates the limited control the higher-level associations have over their member associations. Likewise, the option of non-conforming membership underscores the weakness of employer organizations in governing their members, unless they are backed by such exogenous, legally-based mechanism as the extension provision.

CONCLUSIONS

If it is true that the *raison d'etre* of employer organizations is bargaining, then almost all of the incentives for employers to join them have markedly declined. Economic internationalization has eroded the cartelizing effect of multi-employer agreements. In Europe the extension of the statutory rights of the employee workplace representatives which started with national legislation in the 1970s and continued with the Directive on the European Works Councils in the 1990s has undermined the possibility of using multi-employer settlements as a means of excluding the union from workplace influence, since these representatives are formally or informally linked to the union organization (Traxler et al., 2001). As unionization has strongly dwindled in most countries since the late 1970s, so the risks of being targeted by whipsawing have declined. The pressures which the employers have put upon the unions and the employer associations to decentralize bargaining since the 1980s, so as to hand over bargaining tasks to the companies themselves, reflects this development. Furthermore, the structure of the economy has changed in a way detrimental to the recruitment capacities of employer organizations. Manufacturing as their traditional membership stronghold has been shrinking, as compared to the service sector. Likewise, the small companies which are harder to organize than larger units have expanded in terms of both their number and employment.

Since time series data on membership in employer associations are sparse, it is difficult to assess the scale of effects these adverse changes in exogenous conditions have had. Available comparative studies suggest that employer density (in terms of employees) has remained rather stable since the early 1980s (Traxler et al., 2001; Traxler, 2004a; Traxler, 2005).[14] As it seems, employer organizations have been able to accommodate to the new circumstances in most countries, by undergoing functional and structural adjustments. Functionally, there has been the gradual re-orientation from labor to product market interests. In cooperation with their union counterpart and backed by labor law, the employer organizations have usually managed to retain an organized approach to bargaining decentralization, which enables them to set a framework for bargaining within the companies by their higher-level agreements, and to retain a co-ordinating role in the overall bargaining process. Furthermore, they have commercialized their services in some cases. These functional adjustments fit well into the structural changes aimed mainly at economizing on resources. Aside from mergers (including those between associations of the same type) and commercialization of services, staff reductions have helped lower costs. In several countries, namely Austria, Denmark, Finland and Sweden, restructuring of this kind has resulted in substantial cuts in dues. The fact that these reforms were enforced by the member companies indicates that they resort to 'voice' rather than 'exit' when they feel uncomfortable with their association. This is because they have enough power to enforce real change, something which the individual employees cannot expect to bring about in relation to their union.

The problem with these reforms is that they threaten to replace old difficulties with new ones. The formation of mixed associations magnifies the centrifugal forces by incorporating divisive product market interests whose lines of conflict may spill over to the area of labor relations. Organized decentralization may turn into disorganization when reaching a scale that makes the parties to multi-employer bargaining lose their control over the process. Cuts in dues and the shift from free to payable services create new internal inequalities, since the members differ in their dues burden and their demand for services.[15] Commercialization is also conflict-provoking, since this means that the employer organizations compete with service companies which may form part of their own domain or the domain of their umbrella organization. Most of these conflicts crystallize in the divide between large and small companies. The latter are often the suppliers of the former in product markets, are generally less interested in organized decentralization, pay less dues, need more services and they may also produce some of those services (consultancy) the employer organizations are going on to sell.

Due to the tendency of these reforms to ever exacerbate internal cleavages, there is every reason to believe that employer organizations can continue to integrate their constituency primarily by means of state support. As noted above, statutory extension schemes are paramount. The rather high stability of employer organizations thus ensues from the fact that they can rely on pervasive extension practices in most countries (Table 12.1). Conversely, employer density strongly declined in each of the three countries where extension was rescinded. In Great Britain and New Zealand this happened in tandem with the collapse of multi-employer bargaining. Britain's lower-level employer associations lost around half of their density in terms of establishments over the 1980s (Millward et al., 1992). Density of the NZEF (in terms of employees) fell from 90 per cent to 67 per cent during the 1990s (Traxler, 2004a). In Germany the practice of extending multi-employer agreements has dwindled, in accordance with BDA efforts, since the early 1990s, while diversity in business interests has enormously grown as a result of unification. This has encouraged employers, especially those in East Germany, to escape from bargaining coverage by not joining or leaving their association. According to surveys by the Deutsche Institut für Wirtschaftsforschung density of firms in the East German manufacturing sector dropped from 36 per cent in 1993–4 to 10 per cent in 2005, and density in terms of employees did so from 74 per cent to 30 per cent over the same period. Lack of extension practices has not caused a decline of employer organization only in the case of the Scandinavian countries, where unionization levels are very high.

As noted above, employer associations are reactive undertakings insofar as they were set up in response to the rise of the union movement. Hence, the continued decline of the unions tends to qualify the interest of business in employer associations. This means that they have become increasingly reactive to the state, as their viability ever more depends on supportive national regulations.

LIST OF ABBREVIATIONS

Country Codes

A	Austria
AUS	Australia
B	Belgium
CDN	Canada
CH	Switzerland
D	Germany
DK	Denmark
E	Spain
FIN	Finland
F	France
I	Italy
IRL	Ireland
JP	Japan
NL	Netherlands
N	Norway
NZ	New Zealand
P	Portugal
PL	Poland
S	Sweden
SI	Slovenia
UK	United Kingdom
USA	United States of America

Associations and Parties

ACCI	Australian Chamber of Commerce and Industry
BDA	Bundesvereinigung der Deutschen Arbeitgeberverbände
C	Confindustria
CAI	Confederation of Australian Industry
CBI	Confederation of British Industry
CEOE	Confederación Española de Organizaciones Empresariales
CNPF	Conseil National du Patronat Français
DA	Dansk Arbejdsgiverforening
GZS	Gospodarska zbornica Slovenije
IBEC	Irish Business and Employers' Confederation
KPP	Konfederacja Pracodawcow Polskich
NHO	Næringslivets Hovedorganisasjon
Nikkeiren	Japan Federation of Employers' Associations
NZEF	New Zealand Employers' Federation
SAF	Svenska Arbetsgivareföreningen
SAV	Schweizerischer Arbeitgeberverband
TT	Teollisuus ja Työnantajat
VBO/FEB	Verband van Belgische Ondernemingen – Fédération des Entreprises Belgique
VNO	Verbond van Nederlandse Ondernemingen
VNO-NCW	Vereniging van Nederlandse Ondernemers – Nederlands Christelijke Werksgeversverbond

WKÖ   Wirtschaftskammer
           Österreich
ZSAO   Zentralverband
           Schweizerischer
           Arbeitgeber-
           Organisationen

NOTES

1 This sequence applies only to labor relations. The rise of trade associations designed to process business interests other than labor market interests (see below) preceded the unions.

2 In Canada multi-employer bargaining by employer associations generally prevails only in two provinces (Quebec and British Columbia) and a few sectors (trucking and construction) (Thompson and Taras, 2004).

3 It is only Slovenia and Slovakia which deviate from this pattern, with multi-employer agreements as the prevalent mode of bargaining (Marginson and Traxler, 2005).

4 For an instructive case study of Sweden, see Pestoff (1995).

5 When multi-employer bargaining attracts employers, their cooperation may be limited to joint negotiations instead of setting up a formal organization. This informality is rather unusual. In Hungary, however, this practice has spread among the larger companies (Marginson and Traxler, 2005).

6 For instance, in Spain only employer associations meeting the criterion of representativeness are vested with rights of consultation, in contrast to pure trade associations. The Portuguese employer organizations also enjoy legally-based preferential treatment.

7 In Slovenia voluntary associations may take over the bargaining tasks in the foreseeable future.

8 In principle, employer density can be measured in two ways, referring to either the firms themselves or the firms' employees. Measuring density of firms is difficult as we lack comparable statistics on the number of firms and their breakdown by the number of employees for many countries. Such statistics, however, are needed to disentangle employers from companies without employees. At any rate, density in terms of employees covered is the more appropriate indicator, when it comes to measuring associational power in the labor market. The figures presented in Table 12.1 are limited to density of a country's principal employer peak in terms of employees covered, because many narrower employer organizations usually exist outside the umbrella of the principal peak. It is hard to collect reliable data on the actual and/or potential membership of these narrower associations, because their domains rarely coincide with conventional statistical classifications of business activities.

9 In Italy, the employer organizations of the very large nationalised industry sector played a pioneering role in industrial relations, until they were dissolved as independent associations in the 1990s (Regalia and Regini, 1998).

10 A notable exception to this rule is the Business Council of Australia which was set up in 1983 by a group of larger employers because of their perception that CAI gave undue emphasis to their interests (Lansbury and Wailes, 2004). There are also special organizations for private companies in Eastern Europe against the background of a historically strong state-owned sector.

11 This does not hold true for the peaks in the UK, Poland and New Zealand. While put in parentheses for this reason, they are nevertheless listed, because they are the only cross-sectoral peaks of their countries.

12 KPP and the successor of Nikkeiren introduced direct firm membership in 2002.

13 For example, this is exceptional practice in Austria.

14 For instance, the expansion of the service sector does not negatively affect employer density, in stark contrast to union density.

15 Generally, the imperative to cut costs and dues restrains the possibility of the associations to substitute their declining role in bargaining for such services as the provision of specialist expertise, unless these services are made payable.

REFERENCES

Armstrong, E.G.A. (1984) 'Employers Associations in Great Britain', in J.P. Windmuller and A. Gladstone (eds), *Employers Associations and Industrial Relations*. Oxford: Clarendon Press.

Carrol, P. and Tremewan, P. (1993) 'Organizing Employers: The Effect of the Act on Employers and the Auckland Employer Association', in R. Harbridge (ed.), *Employment Contracts: New Zealand Experiences*. Wellington: Victory University Press.

Clegg, H. A. (1976) *Trade Unionism under Collective Bargaining*. Oxford: Blackwell.

Gladstone, A. (1984) 'Employers Associations in Comparative Perspective: Functions and Activities', in J. P. Windmuller and A. Gladstone (eds), *Employers Associations and Industrial Relations*. Oxford: Clarendon Press.

Grote, J., Lang, A. and Traxler, F. (2007) 'Germany', in F. Traxler and G. Huemer, (eds), *Handbook of Business Interest Associations, Firm Size and Governance: A Comparative Analytical Approach*. London and New York: Routledge.

Jørgensen, C. and Traxler, F. (2007) 'Denmark', in F. Traxler and G. Huemer, (eds), *Handbook of Business*

Interest Associations, Firm Size and Governance: A Comparative Analytical Approach. London and New York: Routledge.

Kenis, P. and Traxler, F. (2007) 'The Netherlands', in F. Traxler and G. Huemer, (eds), *Handbook of Business Interest Associations, Firm Size and Governance: A Comparative Analytical Approach.* London and New York: Routledge.

Lansbury, R.D. and Wailes, N. (2004) 'Employment Relations in Australia', in G.J., Bamber, R. D, Lansbury and N. Wailes, (eds) *International and Comparative Employment Relations.* London: Sage.

Marginson, P. and Traxler, F. (2005) 'After Enlargement: Preconditions and Prospects for Bargaining Coordination', *Transfer,* 3 (3): 423–38.

Millward, N., Stevens, M., Smart, D. and Hawes, W. R. (1992) *Workplace Industrial Relations in Transition.* Aldershot: Dartmouth.

Offe, C. (1985) *Disorganized Capitalism: Contemporary Transformations of Work and Politics.* Oxford: Polity.

Olson, M. (1965) *The Logic of Collective Action: Public Goods and the Theory of Groups.* Cambridge, London: Harvard University Press.

Pestoff, V. A. (1995) 'Towards a New Swedish Model of Collective Bargaining and Politics', in C. Crouch and F. Traxler (eds), *Organized Industrial Relations in Europe: What Future?* Aldershot: Avebury.

Regalia, I. and Regini, M. (1998) 'Italy: The Dual Character of Industrial Relations', in A. Ferner and R. Hyman (eds), *Changing Industrial Relations in Europe.* Oxford: Blackwell.

Schmitter, P.C. and Streeck, W. (1981) 'The Organization of Business Interests', Discussion Paper IIM/LPM 81–13. Berlin: Wissenschaftszentrum Berlin.

Sisson, K. (1987) *The Management of Collective Bargaining.* Oxford: Blackwell.

Swenson, P. and Pontusson, J. (2000) 'The Swedish Employer Offensive against Centralized Bargaining', in T. Iversen, J. Pontusson and D. Soskice (eds), *Unions, Employers and Central Banks.* Cambridge: Cambridge University Press.

Thompson, M. and Taras, D.G. (2004) 'Employment Relations in Canada', in G.J., Bamber, R. D, Lansbury and N. Wailes, (eds), *International and Comparative Employment Relations.* London: Sage.

Traxler, F. (1993) 'Business Associations and Labor Unions in Comparison: Theoretical Perspectives and Empirical Findings on Social Class, Collective Action and Associational Organizability', *British Journal of Sociology,* 44 (4): 673–91.

Traxler, F. (1994) 'Collective Bargaining: Levels and Coverage', in *OECD Employment Outlook.* Paris: OECD.

Traxler, F. (1995) 'Two Logics of Collective Action in Industrial Relations?', in C. Crouch and F. Traxler (eds), *Organized Industrial Relations in Europe: What Future?* Aldershot: Avebury.

Traxler, F. (2004a) 'Employer Associations, Institutions and Economic Change: A Crossnational Comparison', *Industrielle Beziehungen,* 11 (1–2): 42–60.

Traxler, F. (2004b) 'The Metamorphoses of Corporatism', *European Journal of Political Research,* 43 (4): 571–98.

Traxler F., Blaschke S. and Kittel B. (2001) *National Labor Relations in Internationalized Markets.* Oxford: Oxford University Press.

Traxler, F., Brandl, B. and Pernicka, S. (2007) 'Business Associability, Activities and Governance: Crossnational Findings', in F. Traxler, and G. Huemer, (eds), *Handbook of Business Associations, Firm Size and Governance: A Comparative Analytical Approach.* London and New York: Routledge.

Traxler, F. and Huemer, G. (eds) (2007) *The Handbook of Business Associations, Firm Size and Governance: A Comparative Analytical Approach.* London and New York: Routledge.

Visser, J. (1991) 'Trends in Trade Union Membership', in *OECD Employment Outlook 1991.* Paris: OECD.

Visser, J. and Wilts, A. (2006) 'Reaching Out and Fitting in: Dutch Business Associations at Home (and) in Europe', in W. Streeck, J. Grote, V. Schneider and J. Visser (eds), *Governing Interests: Business Associations Facing Internationalization.* London and New York: Routledge.

13

Management Strategy and Industrial Relations

Nicolas Bacon

INTRODUCTION

Since the 1980s managers rather than trade unions or the state have been responsible for the most important developments in industrial relations (IR). Industrial relations in many firms and countries have changed significantly as a result, as managers have become more reluctant to recognize, consult or negotiate with trade unions, and have made the contentious claim to be adopting a strategic approach to human resource management (HRM). Research on management strategy in industrial relations duly increased in order to track and understand the implications of these potentially important changes. Important questions included the extent to which managers were behaving strategically, the nature of the new strategies adopted and the reasons for changes in management approach? This chapter reviews the literature that emerged on management strategies within and beyond industrial relations to understand these critical issues. The insights generated from this research have gradually transformed the study of IR, according managers a central role and broadening the range of HRM practices now studied.

MANAGEMENT INDUSTRIAL RELATIONS STRATEGIES

The term 'strategy' is frequently used in an 'illusive and imprecise' manner when applied to IR (Hyman, 1987: 27). Lewin (1987: 8) similarly observed that IR researchers often fail to 'offer a consistent, clear or distinctive definition of strategy' and as a result 'strategy as applied to industrial relations is consistent with virtually any management action' (Lewin, 1987: 36). A careful definition is therefore required before we can begin to assess whether and when managers have a strategic approach toward industrial relations.

According to Thurley and Wood (1983: 198) 'Industrial relations strategies refer to long-term policies which are developed by the management of an organization in order to preserve or change the procedures, practices or results of industrial relations activities over time'.[1] Reflecting subsequent research conducted since the early 1980s, this chapter defines management industrial relations strategies as requiring formal plans that integrate employment practices; contain an underlying set of management values; involve significant managerial choice; integrate activities at different organizational levels; support the firm's operations; deliver effective outcomes and endure over the long-term. [2] As this exacting list of requirements implies, it is necessary to consider the separate elements of strategy in detail to illustrate why labor management strategies have proved so elusive.

First, it is reasonable to assume that industrial relations strategy requires a formal management plan. At the outset, it is important to note that many firms simply do not have a formal plan of any kind. The British Workplace Employment Relations Survey, for example, asks managers whether their workplace is 'covered by a formal strategic plan which sets out objectives and how they will be achieved', followed by show cards prompting them to indicate whether the plan includes any of seven issues (taking in three employment components) (Kersley et al., 2006: 62). In 2004, 30 per cent of British workplaces did not have a strategic plan and a further 10 per cent had a plan with no employment components (ibid.: 62).

In addition to a formal plan, industrial relations strategy also implies that employment practices are part of a consistent management approach. However, it is evident that managers rarely maintain consistent practices over time. At least in the short term, employment practices often seem *ad hoc* and opportunistic reactions to market changes (Sisson, 1994). For example, in the late 1980s managers introduced flexible staffing and changed the nature of contracts in response to labor market opportunities rather than developing far-sighted strategies or staffing plans (Hunter et al., 1993). Since the 1980s, firms often claim to have attached greater importance to labor management and to have adopted a strategic human resource management approach. This claim appears to lack real substance not least because new initiatives are frequently little more than opportunistic responses to economic and political liberalization (Legge, 1995; see also Purcell, 2001).

Emphasizing formal plans and consistent practices in labor management strategies also implies that managers should make long-term plans. Gospel (1992: 10–11 and 181) usefully distinguishes between intended and enacted strategies, rejecting the suggestion that most British employers had long-term and coherent strategies, but detecting a 'clear pattern of behavior over time'. As this implies, it may be difficult to assess whether managers have a long-term plan because management intentions may not be immediately obvious.

Further, not all observers agree that limited consistency between employment practices and a reliance on short-term adjustments indicate a lack of strategy. According to Edwards (1995: 14) 'strategy is not a neat package producing clear outcomes but necessarily contains several competing elements and has to be constantly reinterpreted as new results emerge and as the world changes'. Similarly, Streeck (1987: 285) argues that strategy does not imply a 'common and clear sighted vision', and matching IR to business needs requires experimentation. However, firms experimenting with apparently inconsistent practices, that reflect immediate circumstances, are involved in a process of searching for a strategy that they may or may not find, rather than necessarily engaging in strategy-formulation.

Strategy also appears to require an underlying set of management values guiding consistent choices over employment practices. Employment practices without these values in place are unlikely to result in consistent choices and a meaningful strategy. However, it is doubtful whether such underlying values exist and management values that support high commitment management practices may be especially rare. For example, Kochan and Dyer (1993) argue that managers did not make a strategic commitment to high commitment management practices in the late 1980s because they did not value investing in employees. In the second section of this chapter I will consider management style and values as potential explanations of differences in employment practices between firms and changes in approach over time.

Labor management strategies also require significant scope for management choice. The strategic choice theory of IR developed in the 1980s recognized managers as the critical actors initiating major workplace changes and exercising strategic choices in deciding on their approach (Kochan et al., 1986). In contrast to these claims however, many managers appear to lack the necessary freedom to make significant choices – in most circumstances employment practices are determined by markets that limit management options. The term 'strategy' has little substantive purchase if employment practices are severely restricted by labor and product markets. According to Thompson (2003) for example, shareholder pressure and global product markets increasingly restrict the options available to managers and prevent the provision of job security and high wages. This is an important point because managers themselves often claim they have little choice and competitive global markets force them to relocate overseas or reduce terms and conditions of employment (Lewin, 1987: 36; see also Brown, Chapter 6 in this volume). The degree of management choice is unfortunately difficult to establish not least because the choice of research method may influence the findings. Industrial or firm context often explain employment practices in surveys where it is possible to control these effects (Marginson, 1998). In contrast, case studies suitable for tracking decision-making often attribute too much choice and intention to managers rather than explaining employment practices by market pressures (Morris and Wood, 1991; Muller-Jentsch, 2004). The third section of the chapter looks at the extent to which managers deciding on employment practices have a degree of freedom to exercise strategic choice.

Labor strategies also require integration between management plans and activities at different organizational levels. Integration is often difficult to achieve because it involves managers from the corporate board down to the shop-floor, and it also involves a range of managerial functions from industrial relations to finance and operations managers (Hyman, 1987). Corporate structure and corporate strategies therefore affect integration between industrial relations strategies decided at different organizational levels. Section four considers the effects of corporate structure and corporate-level decisions on industrial relations as reasons why firms do not adopt a strategic approach to labor problems (Marginson et al., 1988; Purcell, 1993). The fifth section further considers the links between labor management and business strategy.

An alternative approach is to deduce a strategic approach *post hoc* if managers adopt best practices. Adopting high commitment management practices to take full advantage of employee effort and commitment (see the chapters by Delaney, Frost and Procter in this volume(Chapters 33, 22 and 8 respectively)) may require strategic action and a paradigm shift in managers' approach. Section six explores whether the adoption of high commitment management practices indicates a strategic approach to industrial relations. As we shall see, relatively few firms adopt these best practices.

The chapter will therefore discuss industrial relations strategies from these different standpoints – as reflecting an underlying management style, the exercise of managerial choice, shaped by corporate structure and strategy, linking employment practices to business strategy, and implementing high commitment management practices. Each research stream contributes important insights to understanding labor management strategy and, in addition to evaluating this work the chapter includes constructive ways forward to develop future research. The conclusion reflects on models and strategy types developed and tested in the research literature, the applicability of the strategy concept to the analysis of industrial relations and the degree to which strategies are empirically verifiable.

MANAGEMENT STYLE AND TYPOLOGIES

A common approach to understanding labor management strategy is to describe it as a broad management style. Management style is 'the existence of a distinctive set of guiding principles, written or otherwise, which set parameters to and signposts for management action in the way employees are treated and particular events handled' (Purcell, 1987: 79). A management style may guide industrial relations strategy, providing an 'underlying rationale' for discretionary managerial choices in employment policies (Purcell, 1987: 533; see also Kochan and Dyer, 1993: 573). Table 13.1 outlines alternative typologies of different management styles developed to help distinguish between industrial relations in different firms.

Fox (1966) who distinguished between unitary (anti-union) and pluralist (accepting unions) management frames of reference underlying general approaches to industrial relations (outlined in detail in Chapter 5 in this volume) made the first significant contribution. The assumption that firms adopt discrete bundles of employment practices, however, limited the usefulness of Fox's initial typologies (Edwards, 1995: 602). Clegg (1979: 163) identified three main problems with the simple unitarism-pluralism contrast: these frames of reference do not distinguish between firms with significant numbers of employees if most recognize trade unions;[3] neither type exists 'in pure form'; and on different issues managers shift between frames of reference. Fox (1974) also developed six typologies of labor management styles (traditional, classical conflict, continuous challenge, sophisticated modern, standard modern and sophisticated paternalism), subsequently refined and reclassified into five types of management style as listed in Table 3.1 (Purcell and Sisson, 1983). Typologies of labor management style are valuable for classifying a firm's general approach. The ensuing failure to find distinct approaches or styles in practice, however, suggested that rather than adopting strategic approaches to industrial relations, managers were mainly pragmatic and opportunistic (Deaton, 1985; Sisson and Sullivan, 1987: 429). After all, a consistent

Table 13.1   Management style industrial relations typologies

Authors	Areas covered	Key dimensions	Ideal Types
Fox (1966, 1974)	Trade unions and industrial relations	Unitarism (anti-union)/pluralism (accepts unions)	6 (traditional, classical conflict, continuous challenge, sophisticated modern, standard modern, sophisticated paternalism)
Purcell and Sisson (1983)	Trade unions and industrial relations	Unitarism/pluralism	5 (traditional, sophisticated paternalists, constitutionalists, consulters, standard modern)
Purcell (1987) Purcell and Ahlstrand (1994)	Industrial relations and human resource management	Individualism (labour control, paternalism or employee development)/collectivism (unitary, adversarial or cooperative relationship with employee representatives)	7 (traditional, paternalists, sophisticated human relations, bargained constitutional, sophisticated consultative, modern paternalist, co-option)
Storey and Bacon (1993)	Industrial relations (4 aspects), work organization (3 aspects) and human resource management (3 aspects)	Individualism/collectivism (defined differently according to each employment area)	8 according to the mixture across each employment area

management style is unlikely to exist if we cannot identify distinctive approaches. Recognition that management style is rather more fluid than initially suggested – changing in response to economic and political developments – subsequently led to further work on management style to produce alternative models.

It is helpful at this point to depart from a description of types in order to explain the early 1980s context, where UK and North American managers reassessed industrial relations strategies and in many cases withdrew support for trade unions and collective bargaining in response to product market competition. New management style models developed to describe changes in approaches and models expanded to account for greater interest in human resource management practices (Purcell and Ahlstrand, 1994). Influenced by non-union human relations firms, Japanese management practices and work redesign experiments in unionized firms, managers not only sought to delimit union influence but to engage individual employees in continuous performance improvements through a broader array of human resource management practices. Walton (1985) contrasted the 'control' approach of Taylorist job design with the 'commitment' approach to labor management in quality of work life and employee involvement experiments in the US during the 1970s. The labor process debate from the mid-1970s also studied management styles and strategies. In rejecting Braverman's (1974) argument that managers adopted a uniform Taylorist scientific management strategy, Friedman (1977) identified two broad labor management approaches – direct control (Taylorism) and encouraging responsible autonomy via employee involvement in the work process. Labor management style models gradually incorporated these insights from parallel fields.

Returning to a description of types of management style reflecting these changes, Purcell (1987) identified a more subtle range of management styles measured on the two dimensions of individualism and collectivism. Individualism was defined as the extent to which the firm invests in and develops employees (p. 536) usefully relabeled by others as 'investment orientation' (Marchington and Parker, 1990) and 'human resource management priority' (Guest, 2001). Whether managers recognize employee rights to have a say in decision-making was labeled collectivism (Purcell, 1987: 538) indicating 'management attitudes and behaviour toward trade unions in the workplace' (Marchington and Parker, 1990) and later 'industrial relations priority' (Guest, 2001). These two dimensions capture the varied ways in which firms combine approaches to industrial relations and human resource management as part of an overall management style. Storey and Bacon (1993) further classified management style as approaches emphasizing individualism or collectivism across three areas of industrial relations, work organization and human resources (see also Gospel, 1992). This framework covers a broad range of issues and captures multifaceted recipes of employment practices. However, including a complex range of employment practices produces many different combinations of practices that we cannot easily reduce to a small and parsimonious number of indicative management styles. As Table 13.1 indicates, over time the number of ideal types identified has steadily increased.

The enduring presence of simple typologies indicates management styles – unitarism and pluralism, direct control and relative autonomy, control and commitment, individualism and collectivism – remain useful reference points to describe different approaches to labor management. All such typologies inevitably simplify a complex reality: they collapse a range of approaches into a limited number of types; firms appear to use techniques associated with both typologies; and the typologies imply a coherent managerial attachment to one approach rather than a series of *ad hoc* practices. Nevertheless, the job of analysts is to simplify and this strand of theory is a commendable attempt to do this. Edwards (1995: 14) appropriately regards typologies 'as elements which can be combined in various ways', for example, with one employment practice developing control and reducing costs, and another maximizing commitment and potential (see Marchington and Harrison, 1991). Finding one practice used to exercise control and another to develop commitment clearly does not prevent classifying an overall management style (Edwards, 1995: 603).

Assessing practices across the three areas of industrial relations, work organization and human resource management practice is a useful way forward (Gospel, 1992; Storey and Bacon, 1993) because managers often seek to reduce costs in one area but invest in another. Broadly speaking, managers make basic industrial relations choices between unitarism restricting employee voice, or pluralism encouraging employee input into decision-making (often but not necessarily through trade unions). Work organization choices require the selection of practices to concentrate on mainly the direct control of employees conducting specified tasks or responsible autonomy encouraging a broader task contribution. The approach to human resources/personnel practices emphasizes either minimum cost or high investment (Table 13.2). This set of employment relations choices thus combines some of the parsimony of earlier models with the necessary breadth to capture some of the complexity of contemporary labor management. The intention is not to suggest labor management strategies must involve practices emphasizing only individualism or collectivism across each of the three policy areas, it allows for different recipes in reality.

The models discussed so far provide a framework to classify all firms. An alternative is to concentrate on a more sophisticated understanding of approaches in specific types of firms. Non-union firms and small and medium-sized enterprises are two areas where more work is still required. Management style models have already developed to some extent to allow for different approaches in non-union firms. Models have moved beyond Fox's (1974: 287) classic account that managers with a unitarist ideology enforce management prerogative by 'coercive power' and demand 'unquestioning obedience' from employees. Managerial attitudes toward trade unions are insufficient for studying non-union companies because strategies to remain non-union also involve different human resource management approaches from site to site (Roy, 1980). Purcell and Ahlstrand (1994) identified three non-union management styles or typologies on the basis of 'individualism' or use of human resource practices: 'sophisticated human relations' companies invest in employees; managers in the 'paternalist' firm care for employee welfare in return for loyalty; and in the 'traditional' approach managers minimize labor costs (see also Dundon and Rollinson, 2004). This clarifies human resource approaches in non-union firms but assumes a standard approach to the issue of employee representation. However, non-union employee representation takes a variety of forms (Gollan, 2006; Taras and Kaufman, 2006) and future work may usefully combine these forms with approaches to human resource management to develop typologies of non-union firms.

Management style in employment relations usually describes larger firms, but appears especially useful to categorize small and medium-sized firms (SMEs) and more work should be encouraged in this area. Labor management strategy is difficult to describe and classify in SMEs as few have formalized employment practices. In such firms, management style is a very useful

Table 13.2   Employment relations choices

		Management Approach	
		Individualism	Collectivism
Policy Areas	Industrial Relations	Unitarist	Pluralist
	Work Organization	Direct Control	Responsible Autonomy
	Human Resources/ Personnel	Minimum Cost	High Investment

concept because we can trace a direct link from management attitudes to management behaviors and employee experiences. It has therefore proved particularly insightful to identify such styles as 'fraternalism' in SMEs to manage highly skilled workers with significant levels of discretion and trust in the labor process. Among firms where we would expect to find fraternalism, Baron and Hannan (2002) found a wider range of labor management styles in small knowledge intensive firms and explained this by the entrepreneurs' organizational blueprints including 'the premises that guided their thinking about how to organize employment relations and manage personnel' (p. 10). Organizational blueprints are very similar to the concept of management style. In contrast, many SMEs adopt a 'sweating' strategy to manage unskilled employees (Goss, 1991). Rainnie (1989) argues that large dominant firms force many small supplier firms to adopt a 'sweating' strategy of authoritarian management, tight supervision and low wage levels. Management style in family-owned and run SMEs appears to be different again with 'negotiated paternalism' used and informal family loyalties generating a sense of mutual obligation (Ram and Holliday, 1993). Studies of SMEs are an important area for future research and returns attention to the importance of the enterprise founder's role in establishing labor management style (see Purcell and Sisson, 1983).

An alternative to developing increasingly sophisticated and differentiated types of management style is to use typologies as devices to identify the main trends and impose a framework on complex changes in management practices. For example, McKersie (1987) identified three main strategies adopted by US managers in the 1980s – the traditional or New Deal system of collective bargaining, the non-union system and transitional industrial relations (McKersie, 1987). In the UK, Guest (2001: 97) identified four broad patterns: traditional pluralism (similar to the New Deal system); individualism (non-union sophisticated HRM employers); partnership with unions; and the 'bleak house' or 'black

hole' (no unions and no sophisticated HRM practices). Cross-national studies of specific industries also generate management style typologies such as low wage, HRM, Japanese-orientated and joint-participatory approaches (Katz and Darbishire, 2000). This remains a useful and parsimonious way of imposing order on complex changes.

To develop the concept of management style, more work is required to establish the links between managerial values and specific employment practices. It would be helpful to develop reliable measurement instruments in order to do this. In one of the few attempts to do this so far, Osterman (1994: 179) assessed managerial values with a single survey question – 'In general, what is your establishment's philosophy about how appropriate it is to help increase the well-being of employees with respect to their personal or family situations'. He found managerial values measured in this way correlated with flexible work practices. The same variable relabeled 'humanistic values' was associated with more establishment-level training (Osterman, 1995). Other research provides less support for the management style concept. Godard (1997: 212) measured managerial ideology by three questions addressing 'values and beliefs about unions, employee involvement programs, and the participatory rights of workers in general'. Although managerial ideology thus measured correlated with employment practices, other context variables (for example, firm size, technology and market conditions) were more important. Reliable survey questions to capture a general labor management style connected to specific employment practices are yet to be developed.

An alternative approach worth developing in parallel in the future is to link managerial attitudes on individual issues to specific practices. The association between attitudes and practices is likely to be stronger if the attitude measured relates directly to specific employment practices.[4] For example, managers' attitudes toward work-life balance issues correlate with providing family-friendly practices (Kersley et al., 2006: 272; Woodland et al., 2003) and managers' attitudes toward unions are strongly related to workplace-level union density (Kersley et al., 2006: 114). Guest and Peccei (2001) reported a link between partnership principles and practices in UK companies with co-operative management-union relations, measuring 15 items on a five point scale of whether and how strongly the organization 'is believed to support or oppose each principle' (p. 218). Bacon and Blyton (2000) show that different management rationales correlate with quite different types of team working and that these types of teams produced contrasting outcomes for firms and employees.

One way forward may be to identify the required managerial attitudes and values for a range of different employment issues and then explore the relationship between these attitudes to build a more effective measure of management style. It is of course possible that management values on specific issues are unrelated and an underlying managerial ideology does not exist. If it does exist then developing tools to assess these values could have several important practical implications. For example, it may help firms select managers based on their orientation to labor management to support the effective implementation of practices. In addition, such tools could track the development of management values over time during a transition period when seeking to change employment practices.

Management style helps to conceptualize approaches to employment relations and highlights the importance of values and attitudes that explain managerial behavior as a sustained stream of relatively consistent decisions. The assumption that pressures from shareholders or from the firm's external environment do not easily deflect the underlying managerial philosophy will be questioned toward the end of the next section.

MANAGERIAL STRATEGIC CHOICE

Management values are also an important feature of the strategic choice theory of industrial relations. This theory marked a paradigm shift establishing managers, rather than unions, as the central industrial relations actor in the US (Strauss, 1984). Strategic choice theory makes several important assumptions. First, managers 'have discretion over their decisions; that is, where environmental constraints do not severely curtail the parties' choice of alternatives' (Kochan et al., 1984: 21). From the mid-1980s, the theory claims managers exercised an increasing degree of strategic choice in redesigning employment practices. As Kaufman (2003: 199) notes, in essence '"strategy" implies choice over alternative people management approaches', and strategic choice theory requires a (high) degree of managerial autonomy. Second, the theory assumes managers make important and significant decisions affecting the relationship between employers and employees, rather than routine decisions. Third, industrial relations decisions link across different levels from strategic business policy, to the collective bargaining and workplace levels of the firm. Section four will discuss the linking of industrial relations decisions across different organizational levels.

Managers have undoubtedly reshaped employment relations over the past 25 years but it is less clear that this is the result of greater strategic choice. Managers have limited latitude for strategic choice if economic conditions structurally determine many industrial relations decisions (Hyman, 1987). Lewin (1987: 8) for example argued that increased market competition in the 1980s reduced rather than increasing the scope for choice in labor management. Market competition may explain many developments including changes to working practices (Osterman, 1994, 2000), greater managerial control on the shop-floor (Edwards and Scullion, 1982) and wage restraint (Brown et al., 2003). Even arguments in much of the Total Quality Management/High Performance Work Practice literature that customers have become more demanding with the emergence of niche markets may offer managers little choice but to introduce flexible, high-quality work systems to meet changing customer requirements. Managerial choices may thus merely involve passive adaptation to short-term market pressures or long-term fundamental transitions in capitalism (Piore and Sabel, 1984; Thompson, 2003).

Although important, this argument has two problems. First, it leaves no room for managerial discretion in deciding between alternative employment practices to meet strategic aims. For example, should managers reduce labor costs by increasing work pace or reorganizing working methods? Second, it is not clear that market pressures have brought about an overall reduction in strategic labor management choice. The effects of market pressures on strategic choice are complex. Cost pressures do force managers to act to reduce labor costs although as stated such pressures do not direct managers in exactly *how* to act. At the same time cost pressures also increase management choice by reducing the abilities of employees to resist changes to working practices, protect jobs and negotiate pay increases (Osterman, 2000).

If we take into account factors other than the product market, it is even less clear that the degree of managerial strategic choice has declined. Labor market deregulation has offered managers greater labor flexibility including relocation, subcontracting, outsourcing and off-shoring work. We should not dismiss strategic choice simply because one factor may be forcing managers to make certain decisions. Rather than market liberalization restricting strategic options in labor management over the past 25 years, it has changed the nature of incentives surrounding different management choices. Many managers feel employment decisions have been liberated from trade union influence rather than more constrained by market pressures.

This leads on to a further criticism of strategic choice theory in industrial relations in that it provides only 'a framework that does not say what sorts of choice will be made' (Edwards, 1995: 599). As a result, Edwards (1995: 20) suggests that strategic choice theory is 'industrial relations with much of the politics removed' in that it does not stress the mainly negative implications for

workers of management choices made since the 1980s. The theory, for example, allows for a low cost or an investment approach to labor management and does not clarify the factors shaping various choices and identifying the most likely outcomes.

Hyman (1987: 30) reinserts the politics into strategic choice in offering an alternative Marxist explanation whereby strategic choice exists because the contradictions inherent in managing labor in capitalism make all employment practices 'different routes to partial failure'. Managers devise strategies and select appropriate courses of action, but the underlying requirement to both control employee behavior and develop their commitment creates a tension and class-based conflict that managers cannot resolve. Managers use diverse and varied practices for tactical reasons to manage this tension and bundles of employment practices as a result rarely conform to management style typologies (ibid.: 49). This is a useful insight but the term 'partial failure' is unhelpful. Acknowledging that managers are often unsuccessful at managing potential conflict and securing high levels of employee commitment does not necessarily imply managers always fail in this endeavor. It is important to identify the reasons why labor management choices are more or less successful. Both Hyman and Edwards tend to stress the unmanageability of capitalist firms when in many cases these firms seem to be very effective at surviving and generating streams of profit.

The emphasis on strategic choice did initially exaggerate the degree of managerial discretion to act without regard to structural constraints (Kochan and Dyer, 1993: 571). Intensified competition between firms due to globalization reduces the scope for managerial discretion in many respects given the imperative of reducing costs and increasing returns to shareholders. It is incorrect, however, to claim strategic choice is therefore necessarily reducing *per se* because globalization recreates new opportunities for strategic choices in other respects.

Strategic choice is a commendable attempt to simplify trends in labor management but it collapses a complex range of choices into two options: choice or determinism. Most authors conclude that strategies are a matter of contextualized choice, suggesting managers have 'considerable scope' (Sisson and Marginson, 2003: 182) or 'some degree' (Kessler and Purcell, 2003: 314) of choice. Should we therefore regard labor management as the result of constrained choices? Unfortunately, this does little to specify the precise degree of choice in different contexts.

CORPORATE STRATEGY AND STRUCTURE

As mentioned in the previous section, Kochan et al. (1984) argued that strategic choice in industrial relations requires managers to link decisions across different levels of the firm, from corporate to workplace levels. This requires the existence of industrial relations plans at both corporate and workplace levels for managers to link. Section one described the lack of a formal plan with employment components in many workplaces. Many firms also lack an overall industrial relations policy at corporate level. For example, Marginson et al. (1988) asked UK corporate personnel managers whether they had an overall human resource management policy. Although 80 per cent claimed they had an overall policy, few could describe it when asked, indicating such policies were informal aims rather than coherent plans. Even these descriptions of informal aims were not associated with the actual company practices used.

The failure to find corporate industrial relations policies suggests that industrial relations issues are unlikely to feature in many corporate strategies. Employment components or industrial relations strategies are indeed rarely principal ingredients of corporate strategy at boardroom level and are at best marginal rather than integral to corporate strategies (Purcell, 1983: 4). Labor management is therefore appropriately described as a 'third order' strategy involving decisions made after firms have developed and started to implement corporate and business

unit strategies (Purcell and Ahlstrand, 1994). This does not imply that corporate directors never consider labor management issues. The UK Company Level Industrial Relations Survey (Marginson et al., 1988) reported that company level directors often consider industrial relations issues in strategic decisions with employment implications. However, the personnel function is more likely to be involved at the implementation stage of key decisions rather than at the decision-making stage (Purcell, 1995: 77).

A number of factors increase the chance that managers consider employment issues in corporate strategy. Firms with a personnel director on the main board of directors are much more likely to consider labor management issues when deciding on business strategy. In addition, those firms are also more likely to have company-wide personnel policies and personnel policy committees (Sisson, 1995; 2001: 80). Workplace level findings are similar: workplaces in firms with a personnel director on the board are also more likely to include employment components in strategic workplace plans and involve managers responsible for employment relations matters in preparing these plans (Kersley et al., 2006: 62–64). However, at least in the UK, personnel functional representation has not increased at board level (Millward et al., 2000); there is no evidence that general workplace business strategies are currently more likely to include employment components than in the past; and the involvement of managers responsible for employment matters in preparing strategic plans has actually declined (Kersley et al., 2006: 67). The low status and marginal role of personnel managers clearly demonstrate that few firms adopt a strategic approach to labor management. As a result, corporate decisions restrict the range of strategic choices over employment practice available to managers.

Most research therefore points to severe restraints from 'beyond the workplace' imposed by corporate strategies and corporate structures on strategic industrial relations choices (Purcell, 1983). In addition, the growth of large diversified multi-divisional companies appears to deter managers from an investment or high road approach toward staff in a number of further ways. It decentralizes industrial relations strategies to business unit level (Purcell, 1989); industrial relations decisions are distant from corporate strategy-making (Purcell, 1995); and the financial control of business units in such companies appears to prevent long-term investments in high commitment management practices (Purcell, 1989).

Corporate and divisional managers frequently constrain and instruct workplace-level managers on a wide range of industrial relations decisions, restricting the autonomy of workplace industrial relations managers to make strategic decisions (Marginson et al., 1988; see also Kochan, 1980). Despite the formal decentralization of collective bargaining, few managers in workplaces belonging to large multi-establishment firms or in the public sector are able to make autonomous industrial relations decisions on such issues as union recognition and pay (Kirkpatrick and Hoque, 2005; Sisson, 2001). Corporate structure therefore continues to exert an important downward and restrictive influence on employment practices. Research highlights the importance of corporate trends toward diversification and divisionalization as especially pervasive pressures restricting the adoption of progressive employment practices (Sisson and Marginson, 2003). Briefly stated, it is less appropriate for diversified firms operating in a range of different product markets to make central employment relations decisions as the needs of different business units will most likely vary. Highly division-alised companies are also likely to exercise financial control from the center that restricts discretionary expenditure on employment matters at divisional level, notwithstanding the appearance of devolved decision-making.

It is clearly difficult for industrial relations managers to influence corporate decisions although recent corporate structure and ownership changes suggest possible ways in which corporate strategy and employment issues may be integrated. Management buy-outs, for example, have become an important mechanism to restructure organizations through a radical change in ownership. Buy-outs appear to reverse the process of corporate diversification and financial control that previously prevented investments in human resource management (Bacon et al., 2004; Bruining et al., 2005). Buy-out managers report an increase in high commitment management practices after buy-outs especially where existing managers and employees are involved in ownership, where buy-outs enter joint ventures, employment issues appear in strategic plans, and the buy-out prioritizes customer service. The extent to which buy-outs facilitate strategic labor management choices is still to be fully understood and requires further research.

As the structure of large diversified corporations makes strategic choices in industrial relations difficult, we might expect to find greater choice exercised in small and medium-sized enterprises (SMEs). Managers in SMEs certainly have strong views on employment issues, resist outside interference and advice, and few recognize trade unions. However, employment practices vary in a predictable manner within the SME sector suggesting that employment practices reflect the SME's context rather than managerial choice. Analysis of the 1998 British Workplace Employment Relations Survey, for example, reveals that SMEs adopt more sophisticated formal employment practices if they employ and need to retain highly skilled employees (Bacon and Hoque, 2005). The position of small firms in the supply chain also appears to explain labor management strategies. Rainnie (1989) argues that large customers tend to dominate small supplier firms, with 'dependent' SMEs forced to adopt authoritarian management, tight supervision and low wage levels. This implies that networks around small firms coerce managers to adopt specific practices and restrict strategic choices. However, small firms also proactively develop networks of contacts with other firms and business advisory organizations in order to learn how to develop more sophisticated employment practices (Bacon and Hoque, 2005; Erickson and Jacoby, 2003). The degree of strategic choice in labor management for SMEs appears to reflect whether they are proactive in developing networks to learn about employment practices, or whether larger dominant firms coerce them into certain activities. Research is still developing into the labor management implications of networks on SMEs.

Understanding the impact of corporate strategy and structure on the organization of management of industrial relations has explained the disconnection between corporate strategy and labor management. Recent work on buy-outs and SMEs is only starting to clarify the circumstances in which corporate strategy and labor management are connected.

BUSINESS STRATEGY AND LABOR MANAGEMENT

Rather than assuming corporate directors should take labor management strategy into account when designing broader corporate strategies, managers may of course be exercising limited choice but acting strategically if they develop employment practices that support business strategies that are already decided (Jackson et al., 1989; Guest, 1987; Miller, 1987; Purcell, 2001; Schuler and Jackson, 1987). Managers selecting appropriate employment practices to match business strategies may therefore be acting strategically (see Cappelli, 1999). For example, the following employment practices all appear appropriate: airlines providing innovative services pay higher wages (Johnson et al., 1989); workers in automobile assembly plants receiving less training in cost-driven mass production work systems (MacDuffie and Kochan, 1995); mini-mills producing differentiated steels investing in practices to develop employee commitment (Arthur, 1992); and hotels competing on service quality deploying high commitment employment practices (Hoque, 1999).

Matching employment practices to business strategy appears to imply at first glance limited scope for strategic labor management choices. It is, however, more difficult in practice to match specific employment practices to business strategies, not least because business strategies are only rarely straightforward or clear-cut (Legge, 1995; Whipp, 1992). Many firms seek to compete on several bases simultaneously pursuing more than one strategy at a time seeking, for example to improve quality and reduce costs (Wood, 1999: 374). In such cases, managers are likely to use a complex blend of some employment practices to reduce costs and others to increase employee commitment to producing quality products or services. This presents a series of difficult management choices.

HIGH COMMITMENT EMPLOYMENT PRACTICES

An alternative approach is to assume a strategic approach to labor management may exist if managers implement the best or most effective employment practices. Accumulated research from the mid-1990s shows a positive link between adopting a supporting bundle of high commitment management practices and firm performance (Wall and Wood, 2005). Chapters 33 (Delaney), 22 (Frost) and 8 (Procter) in this volume describe these practices and evaluate the evidence in detail. To the extent that the aim of management strategy is to maximize firm performance, and high commitment management practices maximize firm performance, then firms adopting these practices have effective labor management strategies.

Unfortunately, the limited adoption of high commitment management practices indicates an overall lack of labor management strategy according to the high commitment management paradigm. Between 1998 and 2004, for example, the number of UK workplaces reporting the bundle of high commitment management practices increased from only 13 to 16 per cent (Kersley et al., 2005: 40) and in the US only 10 per cent of workplaces reported three or more 'alternative work organization practices' (Gittleman et al., 1998). A similar picture emerges from single industry studies. Relatively few firms adopt the employment practices of their most successful competitors in the same industry. For example, Ichniowski and Shaw (1995) found only 11 per cent of steel processing lines had high commitment management practices and in MacDuffie's (1995) study of the auto industry only 25 per cent of workplaces reported the employment practices of the most productive sites. Most firms do not have a strategic approach to labor management if adopting high commitment management practices is a reasonable measure. If managers deploy opportunistic *ad hoc* collections of employment practices then it is ultimately more useful to analyze each practice individually rather than as part of a broader strategy.

CONCLUSION: THE STRATEGY CONCEPT AND IR ANALYSIS

This chapter has discussed several different ways of understanding labor management strategy. Labor strategies result from management choices with regard to some if not all of the following considerations: a strategic planning process; coherence; values; an assessment of the scope of choice; corporate structure and strategy; business strategy; and a practical assessment of employment practices that work. The applicability of the strategy concept to the analysis of industrial relations and the degree to which strategies are empirically verifiable depends on incrementally improving the conceptualization and measurement of labor management strategies with helpful suggestions provided in this chapter.

The most interesting work often emerges from exploring the connections between these issues. For example, managers may only adopt high commitment management practices if labor laws compel action and allow no strategic choice. Another example is the suggestion that high commitment management practices require business strategies emphasizing quality, management values that support investing in employees and gain-sharing, or an influential role for the HR function (Kochan and Dyer, 2001). Making

explicit links between the issues shaping management strategy are essential to generate more precise and interesting hypotheses and assess the likely direction of employment relations.

The increased study of management in industrial relations remains controversial for some researchers because it may make industrial relations research less scientific (Godard and Delaney, 2000; Sisson and Sullivan, 1987: 431). It may also result in work that is regarded as managerialist whereby 'labor management is made subservient to the needs of the firm' (Purcell, 1993: 523), incorporating the study of industrial relations into a management-driven agenda focused solely on firm productivity. This could occur because studying management may eclipse the traditional focus on trade unions, and displace labor movement values such as equality of treatment and wealth redistribution as legitimate aims of inquiry (Godard and Delaney, 2000).

Although it is always helpful to reflect on the values underpinning industrial relations research, Kochan (2000) is surely correct to argue that industrial relations researchers since the 1980s had little realistic choice other than to study management in greater detail in order to remain of practical relevance. To neglect the study of management in industrial relations over the past 20 years would have impoverished the subject because managers not trade unions were initiating major industrial relations changes (Kochan, 2000). Rather than diminishing the study of industrial relations, research on management has helped to ensure the continuing practical relevance of academic inquiry and enriched our understanding of the factors affecting employment (for example, see Gospel, 1992; and Sisson and Marginson, 2003). Furthermore, focusing on management should lead to increased rather than less criticism of managers. In many workplaces where managers deny trade unions influence, then it is managers who are solely responsible if labor problems such as low productivity persist. Labor problems are thus now clearly the result of mismanagement, requiring criticism of managers and consideration of ways to improve management practice including employment legislation.

Purcell's (1983: 6) argument that the inevitable broadening of the boundaries of industrial relations to encompass managers involved 'no more than a further twist to the multi-disciplinary nature of the subject' now predominates. Unless trade unions or governments start to initiate major changes in industrial relations, research studying the role of managers, developments in human resource management practices and the broader corporate context that shapes employment strategies, will continue to increase over the coming years.

NOTES

1 The detailed contents of industrial relations strategies, for example the decision whether to recognize unions, mechanisms for handling conflict and the level and scope of bargaining, will not be covered in detail here and are covered in other chapters in this book.

2 Other definitions stress that strategy also requires intention by decision-makers, proactive management, embedding in the firm's direction and history, espousal in plans and delivery in practice and variation in subject matter (see Marchington and Parker, 1990: 59).

3 Updating this point, the contrast is of limited help to classify firms in countries where a majority of firms do not recognize unions.

4 Dastmalchian in this volume makes a similar point that developing climate measures associated with specific practices is a useful way to increase the predictive capacity of industrial relations climate.

REFERENCES

Arthur, J.B. (1992) 'The link between business strategy and industrial relations systems in American steel minimills'. *Industrial and Labor Relations Review*, 45 (3): 488–506.

Bacon, N., and Blyton, P. (2000) 'High road and low road teamworking: Perceptions of management rationales and organizational and human resource outcomes'. *Human Relations*, 53 (11): 1425–58.

Bacon, N. and Hoque, K. (2005) 'HRM in the SME sector: valuable employees and coercive networks'. *International Journal of Human Resource Management*, 16 (11): 1976–99.

Bacon, N., Wright, M. and Demina, N. (2004) 'Management buyouts and human resource management'. *British Journal of Industrial Relations*, 42 (2): 325–47.

Baron, J.N., and Hannan, M.T. (2002) 'Organizational blueprints for success in high-tech start-ups: Lessons from the Stanford project on emerging companies'. *California Management Review*, 44 (3): 8–36.

Braverman, H. (1974). *Labor and Monopoly Capital*. New York: Monthly Review Press.

Brown, W., Marginson, P. and Walsh, J. (2003) 'The management of pay as the influence of collective bargaining diminishes'. In P. Edwards (ed.) *Industrial Relations: Theory and Practice*, Second Edition, Oxford: Blackwell. pp. 189–213.

Bruining, H., Boselie, P., Wright, M. and Bacon, N. (2005) 'HRM in Buyouts in the UK and the Netherlands'. *International Journal of Human Resource Management*, 16 (3): 345–65.

Cappelli, P. (ed) (1999) *Employment Practices and Business Strategy*. Oxford: Oxford University Press.

Clegg, H.A. (1979) *The Changing System of Industrial Relations in Great Britain*. Oxford: Basil Blackwell.

Deaton, D. (1985) 'Management style and large scale survey evidence'. *Industrial Relations Journal*, 16 (2): 67–71.

Drago, R. (1996) 'Workplace transformation and the disposable workplace: Employee involvement in Australia'. *Industrial Relations*, 35 (4): 526–43.

Dundon, T. and Rollinson, D. (2004) *Employment Relations in Non-Union Firms*. London: Routledge.

Edwards, P. (1995) 'Assessment: Markets and managerialism'. In P. Edwards (ed.) *Industrial Relations: Theory and Practice in Britain*. Oxford: Blackwell. pp. 599–613.

Edwards, P. and Scullion, H. (1982) *The Social Organization of Workplace Conflict*. Oxford, Basil Blackwell.

Erickson, C.L., and Jacoby, S.M. (2003) 'The effect of employer networks on workplace innovation and training'. *Industrial and Labor Relations Review*, 56 (2): 203–24.

Fox, A. (1966) *Industrial Sociology and Industrial Relations*. Research Paper 3, Royal Commission on Trade Unions and Employers' Associations. London: HMSO.

Fox, A. (1974) *Beyond Contract: Work, Power and Trust Relations*. London: Faber and Faber.

Friedman, A. (1977). *Industry and Labor*. London: Macmillan.

Gittleman, M., Horrigan, M. and Joyce, M. (1998) 'Flexible workplace practices: evidence from a nationally representative survey'. *Industrial and Labor Relations Review*, 52 (1): 99–115.

Godard, J. (1997) 'Whither strategic choice: Do managerial ideologies matter?' *Industrial Relations*, 36 (2): 206–29.

Godard, J. and Delaney, J.T. (2000) 'Reflections on the 'High Performance' paradigm's implications for industrial relations as a field'. *Industrial and Labor Relations Review*, 53 (3): 482–502.

Gollan, P.J. (2006) 'Editorial: consultation and non-union employee representation'. *Industrial Relations Journal*, 37 (5): 428–38.

Gospel, H. (1992) *Markets, Firms and the Management of Labor*. Cambridge: Cambridge University Press.

Goss, D. (1991). 'In search of small firm industrial relations'. In R. Burrows (ed.) *Deciphering the Enterprise Culture: Entrepreneurship, Petty Capitalism and the Restructuring of Britain*. London: Routledge. pp. 152–75.

Guest, D. (1987) 'Human resource management and industrial relations'. *Journal of Management Studies*, 24 (5): 503–21.

Guest, D. (2001) 'Industrial relations and human resource management'. In J. Storey (ed.) *Human Resource Management: A Critical Text*. London: Thomson Learning. pp. 96–113.

Guest, D.E. and Peccei, R. (2001) 'Partnership at work: Mutuality and the balance of advantage'. *British Journal of Industrial Relations*, 39 (2): 207–36.

Hoque, K. (1999) 'Human resource management and performance in the UK hotel industry'. *British Journal of Industrial Relations*, 37 (3): 419–43.

Hunter, L., McGregor, A., MacInnes, J. and Sproull, A. (1993) 'The "flexible firm": Strategy and segmentation'. *British Journal of Industrial Relations*, 31 (3): 383–407.

Hyman, R. (1987) 'Strategy of structure? Capital, labour and control'. *Work, Employment and Society*, 1 (1): 25–55.

Ichniowski, C. and Shaw, K. (1995) 'Old dogs and new tricks: Determinants of the adoption of productivity-enhancing work practices'. *Brookings Papers on Economic Activity, Special Issue Microeconomics*. pp. 1–65.

Jackson, S.E., Schuler, R.S. and Rivero, J.C. (1989) 'Organizational characteristics as predictors of personnel practices'. *Personnel Psychology*, 42 (4): 727–86.

Johnson, N.B., Sambharya, R.B. and P. Bobko (1989) 'Deregulation, business strategy, and wages in the airline industry'. *Industrial Relations*, 28 (3): 419–30.

Katz, H.C. and Darbishire, O. (2000) *Converging Divergences: Worldwide Changes in Employment Systems*. Ithaca, New York: Cornell University Press.

Kaufman, B.E. (2003) 'John, R. Commons and the Wisconsin school on industrial relations strategy and policy'. *Industrial & Labor Relations Review*, 57 (1): 3–30.

Kersley, B., Alpin, C., Forth, J., Bryson, A., Bewley, H., Dix, G. and Oxenbridge, S. (2005), *Inside the Workplace: First Findings from the 2004 Workplace Employment Relations Survey*, Department of Trade and Industry. London.

Kersley, B., Alpin, C., Forth, J., Bryson, A., Bewley, H., Dix, G. and Oxenbridge, S. (2006) *Inside the Workplace: Findings from the 2004 Workplace Employment Relations Survey*. London: Routledge.

Kessler, I. and Purcell, J. (2003) 'Individualism and collectivism in industrial relations'. In P. Edwards (ed.) *Industrial Relations*. Oxford: Blackwell. pp. 313–37.

Kirkpatrick, I. and Hoque, K. (2005) 'The decentralization of employment relations in the British public sector'. *Industrial Relations Journal*, 36 (2): 100–20.

Kochan, T.A. (1980) *Collective Bargaining and Industrial Relations*. Homewood, Illinois: Richard Irwin.

Kochan, T.A. (2000) 'On the paradigm guiding industrial relations theory and research: comment on John Godard and John, T. Delaney, "reflections on the 'high performance' paradigm's implications for industrial relations as a field"'. *Industrial and Labor Relations Review*, 53 (4): 704–11.

Kochan, T.A. and Dyer, L. (1993) 'Managing transformational change: the role of human resource professionals'. *International Journal of Human Resource Management*, 4 (3): 569–88.

Kochan, T. and Dyer, L. (2001) 'HRM: an American view'. In J. Storey (ed.) *Human Resource Management: A Critical Text*. London: Thomson Learning. pp. 272–87.

Kochan, T.A., McKersie, R.B. and Cappelli, P. (1984) 'Strategic choice and industrial relations theory'. *Industrial Relations*, 23 (1): 16–39.

Kochan, T.A., Katz, H.C. and McKersie, R.B. (1986) *The Transformation of American Industrial Relations*. New York: Basic Books.

Legge, K. (1995) 'HRM: Rhetoric, reality and hidden agendas'. In J. Storey (ed.) *Human Resource Management: A Critical Text*. London: Thomson Learning. pp. 33–59.

Lewin, D. (1987) 'Industrial relations as a strategic variable'. In M.M. Kleiner, R.N. Block, M. Roomkin and S.W. Salsburg (eds) *Human Resources and the Performance of the Firm*. Madison, WI: Industrial Relations Research Association. pp. 1–41.

MacDuffie, J.P. (1995) 'Human resource bundles and manufacturing performance: Organizational logic and flexible production systems in the world auto industry'. *Industrial and Labor Relations Review*, 48 (2): 197–221.

MacDuffie, J.P. and Kochan, T.A. (1995) 'Do U.S firms invest less in human resources? Training in the world auto industry'. *Industrial Relations*, 34 (2): 147–68.

Marchington, M. and Harrison, E. (1991) 'Customers, competitors and choice: employee relations in food retailing'. *Industrial Relations Journal*, 22 (4): 286–99.

Marchington, M. and Parker, P. (1990) *Changing Patterns of Employee Relations*. Hemel Hempstead: Harvester Wheatsheaf.

Marginson, P. (1998) 'The survey tradition in British industrial relations research: an assessment of the contribution of large-scale workplace and enterprise surveys'. *British Journal of Industrial Relations*, 36 (3): 361–88.

Marginson, P., Edwards, P., Martin, R., Purcell, J. and Sisson, K. (1988) *Beyond the Workplace*. Oxford: Basil Blackwell.

McKersie, R.B. (1987) 'The transformation of American industrial relations: The abridged story'. *Journal of Management Studies*, 24 (5): 433–40.

Miller, P. (1987) 'Strategic industrial relations and human resource management: distinction, definition and recognition'. *Journal of Management Studies*, 24 (4): 347–61.

Millward, N., Bryson, A. and Forth J. (2000) *All Change at Work?* London: Routledge.

Morris, T. and Wood, S. (1991) 'Testing the survey method: Continuity and change in British industrial relations'. *Work, Employment and Society*, 5 (2): 259–82.

Muller-Jentsch, W. (2004) 'Theoretical approaches to industrial relations'. In B.E. Kaufman (ed.) *Theoretical Perspectives on Work and the Employment Relationship*. Illinois: IRRA. pp. 1–40.

Osterman, P. (1994) 'How common is workplace transformation and who adopts it?' *Industrial and Labor Relations Review*, 47 (2): 173–88.

Osterman, P. (1995) 'Skill, training, and work organization in American establishments'. *Industrial Relations*, 34 (2): 125–46.

Osterman, P. (2000) 'Work reorganization in an era of restructuring: Trends in diffusion and effects on employee welfare'. *Industrial and Labor Relations Review*, 53 (2): 179–96.

Piore, M. and Sabel, C.J. (1984) *The Second Industrial Divide: Possibilities for Prosperity*. New York: Basic Books.

Purcell, J. (1983) 'The management of industrial relations in the modern corporation: Agenda for research'. *British Journal of Industrial Relations*, 21 (1): 1–16.

Purcell, J. (1987) 'Mapping management styles in employee relations'. *Journal of Management Studies*, 24 (5): 533–48.

Purcell, J. (1989) 'The impact of corporate strategy on human resource management'. In J. Storey (ed.) *New Perspectives on Human Resource Management*. London: Routledge. pp. 67–91.

Purcell, J. (1993) 'The challenge of human resource management for industrial relations research and practice'. *International Journal of Human Resource Management*, 4 (3): 511–27.

Purcell, J. (1995) 'Corporate strategy and its link with human resource management strategy'. In J. Storey (ed.) *Human Resource Management: A Critical Text*. London: Routledge. pp. 63–86.

Purcell, J. (2001) 'The meaning of strategy in human resource management'. In J. Storey (ed.) *Human Resource Management: A Critical Text*. London: Thomson Learning. pp. 59–77.

Purcell, J. and Sisson, K. (1983) 'Strategies and practice in the management of industrial relations'. In G. Bain (ed.) *Industrial Relations in Britain*. Oxford: Blackwell. pp. 95–120.

Purcell, J. and Ahlstrand, B. (1994) *Human Resource Management in the Multi-divisional Company*. Oxford: Oxford University Press.

Rainnie, A. (1989). *Industrial Relations in Small Firms*. London: Routledge.

Ram, M., and Holliday, R. (1993) 'Relative merits: family culture and kinship in small firms'. *Sociology*, 27 (4): 629–48.

Roy, D. (1980) 'Fear stuff, sweet stuff and evil stuff: Management's defences against unionization in the South'. In T. Nichols (ed.) *Capital and Labor: A Marxist Primer*. Glasgow: Fontana. pp. 395–415.

Schuler, R.S. and Jackson, S.E. (1987) 'Linking competitive strategies with human resource management practices'. *Academy of Management Executive*, 1 (3): 207–19.

Sisson, K. (1994) 'Personnel management: paradigms, practice and prospects'. In K. Sisson (ed.) *Personnel Management*. Oxford: Blackwell. pp. 3–50.

Sisson, K. (1995) 'Human resource management and the personnel function'. In J. Storey (ed.) *Human Resource Management: A Critical Text*. London: Routledge. pp. 87–109.

Sisson, K. (2001) 'Human resource management and the personnel function – a case of partial impact?'. In J. Storey (ed.) *Human Resource Management: A Critical Text*. London: Thomson Learning. pp. 78–95.

Sisson, K. and Marginson, P. (2003) 'Management: Systems, structures and strategy', in P. Edwards (ed.) *Industrial Relations*, Second Edition, Oxford: Blackwell. pp. 157–88.

Sisson, K. and Sullivan, T. (1987) 'Editorial: Management strategy and industrial relations'. *Journal of Management Studies*, 24 (5): 427–32.

Streeck, W. (1987) 'The uncertainties of management in the management of uncertainty: Employers, labor relations and industrial adjustment in the 1980s'. *Work, Employment and Society*, 1 (3): 281–308.

Storey, J. and Bacon, N. (1993) 'Individualism and collectivism: into the 1990s'. *International Journal of Human Resource Management*, 4 (3): 665–684.

Strauss, G. (1984) 'Industrial relations: Time of change'. *Industrial Relations*, 23 (1): 1–15.

Taras, D.G. and Kaufman, B.E. (2006) 'Non-union employee representation in North America: diversity, controversy and uncertain future'. *Industrial Relations Journal*, 37 (5): 513–42.

Thompson, P. (2003) 'Disconnected capitalism: Or why employers can't keep their side of the bargain'. *Work, Employment and Society*, 17 (2): 359–78.

Thurley, K. and Wood, S. (1983) *Industrial Relations and Management Strategy*. Cambridge: Cambridge University Press.

Wall, T. and Wood, S. (2005) 'The romance of human resource management and business performance, and the case for big science'. *Human Relations*, 58 (4): 429–62.

Walton, R. (1985) 'From control to commitment in the workplace'. *Harvard Business Review*, March–April: 77–84.

Whipp, R. (1992) 'Human resource management, competition and strategy: Some productive tensions'. In P. Blyton and P. Turnbull (eds) *Reassessing Human Resource Management*. London: Sage. pp. 33–55.

Wood, S. (1999) 'Human resource management and performance'. *International Journal of Management Reviews*, 1 (4): 367–413.

Woodland, S., Simmonds, N., Thornby, M., Fitzgerald, R. and McGee, A. (2003) *The Second Work-Life Balance Study: Results from the Employer Survey Main Report*. Employment Relations Research Series No. 22. DTI HMSO, London.

14

The State in Industrial Relations

Richard Hyman

In his pioneering attempt to develop a general theory of industrial relations (IR), Dunlop (1958) defined its essence in terms of three 'actors' (employers and managers, workers and their representatives and governmental agencies) and three 'contexts' (technology, market constraints and the distribution of power in society). One might assume from this that the role of government and the impact of politics (the dynamics of power) would have figured prominently in his analysis, and that of subsequent writers who embraced his systems model. However, this was not the case. In practice the main focus of Dunlop, and most subsequent writers in the English-speaking world, was on the rules negotiated between employers and unions. Dunlop placed key explanatory emphasis on the economic and (in particular) technological factors which influenced employment regulation: he devoted two central chapters of his book to a comparison of work rules in coal-mining and construction, arguing that cross-national similarities reflected common technical requirements. Politics, and government, were in effect treated as peripheral; collective bargaining

(mediating the uniform impact of technology) was central.

In part, this perspective reflected the specific realities of the North American institutional framework in the early postwar decades, together with an assumption that these would become the model elsewhere. The comparative study *Industrialism and Industrial Man* (Kerr et al., 1960), of which Dunlop was a co-author, established the dominant approach in Anglo-Saxon industrial relations analysis for much of the subsequent period. Diversity in national industrial relations systems was the product of the distinctive composition and priorities of the 'industrializing elites' who had driven the process of economic modernization; but common technologies and cross-national markets would create convergence toward a common model of regulation, which would match the contemporary Anglo-American pattern of 'pluralistic industrialism'. This was defined as a system in which employers and unions developed increasingly effective and non-conflictual bargaining relationships, making detailed state regulation unnecessary. Hence in this view, 'mature' industrial relations systems became detached from the political process. In Britain, similarly, Kahn-Freund argued that

> there exists something like an inverse correlation between the practical significance of legal sanctions and the degree to which industrial relations have reached a state of maturity. The legal aspect of those obligations on which labour-management relations rest is, from a practical point of view, least important where industrial relations are developed most satisfactorily (1954: 43–4).

This treatment long persisted in Anglo-American industrial relations writing: for example, in his influential textbook Kochan (1980: 1) defined industrial relations as 'an interdisciplinary field that encompasses the study of all aspects of people at work'; but his focus was almost exclusively on management-union relations, while the state was peripheral.

English-language writing in our subject has typically assumed, in effect, that 'politics' and 'industrial relations' are institutionally separate spheres (Giles, 1988). While the state may 'intervene' in employment relations, such intervention is (or should be) bounded and issue-specific. Similarly, the labor market and the welfare state are regarded as unrelated socio-economic subsystems: industrial relations scholars focus on the former, leaving the latter to social policy departments. This perspective contrasts markedly with the conceptions of employment regulation which prevail in many countries, and in literatures and languages other than English.

I will argue in this chapter that the notion of 'pluralistic' detachment between the state and industrial relations reflects a distinctive historical conjuncture in a limited number of countries; and that it stems from an empiricist tradition which reduces social relations to institutional interconnections. I also suggest that it is necessary to distinguish sharply between the concept of the state and the specific institutions of government; and that it is therefore misleading to speak in terms of 'state intervention', for the state is an integral element in any productive system and it is impossible to establish a clear separation between the 'economic' and the 'political'.

More specifically I insist, following Polanyi (1944) that markets including labor markets are politically constructed. My proposed analytical model points to a tension between three state functions relevant to industrial relations: accumulation, pacification and legitimation. This I explore by examining a variety of employment-relevant state functions in a wide range of national and historical contexts. I end by asking whether there can be a general theory of the role of the state in industrial relations.

WHAT IS THE STATE?

What do we mean when we speak of the state? It is essential to pose this question, even if it is impossible to give a definitive answer in the space available (indeed arguably, a definitive answer is in principle unattainable). As Held has argued (1983: 1), 'there is nothing more central to political and social theory than the nature of the state, and nothing more contested'. Part of the reason is that in English – unlike most continental European languages – to use the term 'state' implies a distinctive, 'theoretical' approach to the role of political institutions in socio-economic relations.

One common response is to reduce the concept to a set of empirical descriptors: the government, the parliament, the courts and so on. Some years ago the index of a well-known textbook on British industrial relations contained the entry: 'State, *see* government'. Yet if the term 'state' merely denotes a set of identifiable institutions, there is no obvious reason (except perhaps for brevity) to employ it at all. This is indeed the argument of Wilensky, who opens his impressive comparative study of 'rich democracies' with the statement (2002: xxv) that 'throughout I avoid vague discussion of "the state" or "society"; instead I examine the components of these grand abstractions ... The entire book is an attempt to specify the institutions – executive, legislative, judicial, military – that comprise the state ...'

Yet in any sphere of intellectual endeavor, abstraction serves a necessary purpose. Some abstractions (like capitalism, or indeed society, or an industrial relations system) may be 'grand'; others, like management, or productivity, or unemployment, may be more mundane and taken-for-granted. Even what we mean by an institution is complex and multi-faceted. Abstraction is the necessary link between simple description on the one hand and analysis and explanation on the other. When Hollingsworth and Boyer, for example, write (1997: 2) that 'markets and other coordinating mechanisms are shaped by and are shapers of social systems of production', they are employing three separate abstractions to assert the existence of a set of two-way causal interdependences. To move closer to our own theme, when Streeck refers (1997: 52) to 'state capacity' he is positing an *interrelationship* or *articulation* among institutions through which the whole may represent more than the sum of its parts.

Definitions of the state can embody many different emphases. For Weber, famously, it was 'that human community which successfully claims the monopoly of legitimate physical violence within a given territory'. As Skocpol has suggested (1979: 25), this conception underlies two more recent but opposing theoretical traditions, one highlighting legitimacy and consent, the other coercion and domination. Weber's reference to 'community' (*Gemeinschaft*) is also significant: the state comprises diffuse relationships which cannot be reduced to a set of formal institutions. As Jessop (1982: 221) insists, though from a very different theoretical background, 'state power is a complex social relation', subsequently adding (1990: 316) that 'the state does not exist as a fully constituted, organizationally pure, and operationally closed system but is an emergent, contradictory, hybrid and relatively open system'. Skocpol (1985: 28), though approaching from yet another perspective, writes that 'states may be viewed ... as configurations of organization and action that influence the meanings and methods of politics for all groups and classes in society'. For Mann (1986: 112), somewhat paradoxically, 'the state is merely and essentially an arena, a place, and yet this is the very source of its autonomy'. And Stråth (1996: 218) characterizes the state as 'a network structure with no permanent content. The state is constantly being recreated, in new forms, by the groups and structures active in society'.

Common to most approaches which transcend the institutional and descriptive is a rejection, as Crouch (1993: viii) puts it, of the 'view that sees a clear distinction between state and civil society'. Taken to the extreme, as for example in the writings of Poulantzas (1968), the state is so pervasive as to be omnipresent. Though his approach is very different, Mann (1986: 113) argues that there has been a transformation of state power from primarily 'despotic' to primarily 'infrastructural' forms, which he defines as 'the capacity of the state actually to penetrate civil society, and to implement logistically political decisions throughout the realm'. The corollary is that while governments may be regarded as 'actors' which 'intervene' in industrial relations, it is inappropriate to refer to the state in similar terms. Yet even if the state is not in any simple sense an 'actor', state power certainly shapes and conditions industrial relations. It does so, moreover, in ways which transcend the typical focus of academic industrial relations on the employment relationship narrowly defined: for crucially, the role of the state in creating (either actively, or by abstention) a regime of welfare provision, and a broader conception of citizenship, shapes in turn the basis on which workers enter the labor market.

STATE AND MARKET: THE FRAMEWORK FOR EMPLOYMENT REGULATION

Sidney and Beatrice Webb, the British pioneers of the study of industrial relations (though not of the term itself), wrote in the preface to their *History of Trade Unionism* (1894: vii–ix) that what they initially conceived as an investigation of economic issues turned out to encompass 'the political history of England'. More recent writers, as indicated above, have tended to reaffirm a division between politics and industrial relations: too great an overlap was evidence of 'immaturity'. More broadly, it has been normal to treat politics and economics as largely separate social worlds. Academic demarcations have run in parallel with ideological presuppositions. During the cold war, a close interconnection between state and economic life was seen as the hallmark of 'command economies', regarded as inefficient and definitely undesirable (Friedman, 1962; Hayek, 1960). Since the end of the Soviet empire, the 'Washington consensus' has insisted that those western (and even more so, Third World) governments which in the postwar decades had sought systematically to regulate the economy should abandon such attempts in order to 'free' the market. Such 'deregulation' should extend, in particular, to the labor market and the employment relationship.

Yet such arguments are misconceived: states and markets are not opposites but interdependent (Iversen, 2005). As Lindblom has insisted (1977: 8), 'in all political systems of the world, much of politics is economics, and most of economics is also politics'. Hence Crouch (1993: 299–300) contests the view that market processes are somehow 'natural', and that state involvement is an unnatural and problematic distortion of their functioning. 'To view the subject historically is to see it the other way round; states and organizations are enmeshed in the economy from the outset; it is how they were often driven out that needs explanation'. This was indeed the classic thesis of Polanyi (1944): the creation of 'free' markets in Britain in the early nineteenth century involved the massive deployment of state power to displace pre-existing economic relationships. 'Markets are themselves institutions', as Hall puts it (1986: 282–3) and hence 'ultimately artifacts of political action'.

This applies *a fortiori* to the arena of industrial relations. For Polanyi, labor was a 'fictitious commodity': since work was inseparable from the worker, it could never be bought and sold in the same way as say wool or potatoes. A labor market is

thus a distinctively artificial creation (and in some respects a contradictory idea), and its character reflects 'structures, conventions and practices' which vary with time and place (Peck, 1996: 266). State policy in turn does much to explain this variation: if 'the creation of the conditions under which labour power is sold has historically been one of the basic and unchanging functions of the capitalist state' (Coates, 2000: 225), *how* this function is performed is far from uniform or constant. Polanyi wrote of a 'double movement' in capitalist economies: the first involving the imposition of 'free' markets, the second (in the twentieth century) a countervailing process to impose some constraint on the disruptive social consequences of market liberalism. The creation of a regulatory web governing employment (whether through statute or collective agreement) – a process which Esping-Andersen (1990) terms 'decommodification' – can evidently be interpreted within this framework. And we can describe more recent trends as a *third* movement: the deliberate unraveling of this regulatory web – what Streeck (1987) has described as the re-imposition of 'contract' in place of 'status'. This process is commonly termed 'deregulation', but this is misleading: not only because markets are themselves regulatory institutions (Standing, 1997), but also because diverse experiences (Chile, Thatcher's Britain, much of Eastern Europe since the collapse of the Soviet empire and many countries of the Third World) suggest that, paradoxically, market intensification requires a strong state (Gamble, 1988) which suppresses resistance. This contrasts with the common assumption that market liberalization and political democracy go hand-in-hand.

Abstracting analytically from a diversity of national and historical experience, one may identify three broad and often contradictory (Offe, 1984) functions of state activity with a bearing on employment relations.

- Accumulation: encouraging economic performance, productivity and competitiveness. Obviously there are crucial debates whether this requires active state intervention and encouragement, or on the contrary the 'freeing' of markets. As suggested above, 'non-intervention' (or 'deregulation') must itself be viewed as a form of intervention (or regulation).

- Pacification: preserving the integrity of national territory, maintaining social order, defusing or suppressing conflict. Historically, in most countries, the boundaries between industrial conflict and social and political disorder have been uncertain, and in many countries this remains the case. Repression is a persistent feature of the evolution of industrial relations, though most academic literature is blind to this (Fusfeld, 1979; Kelly, 1998: 14, 56–7).
- Legitimation: maintaining popular consent by pursuing social equity (which typically requires 'market-correcting' interventions) and fostering citizenship and voice at work. Involving the 'social partners' in economic and social policy-making, as discussed below, may be a means of enhancing government legitimacy.

To speak of 'state functions' (a term also used by Mann, 1986), it should be emphasized, is not to imply that governments will necessarily pursue all three objectives consistently or will do so effectively. One reason is that there is almost inevitably a tension, or more strongly a contradiction, between these different policy goals, and this results in complex, and at times unstable, forms of interlinkage between government and industrial relations. For example, across Europe (and in many other parts of the world), the combination of an ageing population and a perceived need to curb public expenditure to sustain national competitiveness has resulted in efforts to cut back state pension systems; but such attempts risk provoking public disorder and undermining government legitimacy. And a second, interconnected reason is the role of political contingency. Governments – and indeed states – *do* deploy 'autonomous power'. Their policies are the outcomes of conflicts within and between political parties, and between ministers and state functionaries who may themselves be internally divided. For example, when the UK possessed a separate Ministry of Labour its officials were strongly committed to the maintenance of industrial peace through accommodation with the trade unions, whereas their counterparts in

the Treasury and the Department of Industry had no qualms at risking conflict in the interests of accumulation. A stark parallel can be seen in Germany under the Kohl government between 1982 and 1998, when the labor ministry was headed by a leader of the trade union wing within Kohl's own party, whereas the economics ministry was controlled by his business-oriented junior coalition partner. In both countries, the subsequent abolition of a separate employment ministry can be seen as a deliberate effort to reduce the influence of labor within the state machinery.

It is common to argue that the functionaries who occupy the state apparatus have their own distinctive interests and world-view, and often favor policies which enlarge their own influence and competence (Zeitlin, 1985: 26–7). As will be indicated below, historical experience in some countries certainly encourages such a thesis. Where does this leave the idea of a pluralist separation between politics and industrial relations? Miguélez and Prieto (1991: xvii) assert that an industrial relations system 'is a model based on the autonomy of the parties'. This is plausible, if we recognize that such autonomy is *relative*. If we assume two polar (and empirically scarcely conceivable) situations of absolute regulation of employment by market forces on the one hand, or by state prescription on the other, industrial relations as conventionally understood cannot exist. But because the 'autonomy of the parties' is always bounded, industrial relations involves an uneasy tension between state and market, voluntarism and prescription. Such a tension may even be regarded as a defining characteristic of industrial relations. One consequence is that the articulation between state and market varies across countries and may change over time.

CROSS-NATIONAL DIVERSITY

The literature on European industrial relations commonly proposes a triple classification of national systems according to the extent and character of state engagement with employers and (particularly) trade unions, and such analysis is applicable on a broader, global scale. Regini (1986: 61–2) distinguished between 'the concertation model', in which 'unions were closely involved in the formulation and implementation of economic policies' and regulation more generally was highly centralized; 'political isolation', where governments excluded labor from the policy process; and 'pluralistic fragmentation', where 'politics' and 'industrial relations' were institutionally demarcated and unions depended solely on their labor market power. Somewhat earlier, Hibbs (1978) had made a similar three-way distinction in classifying national patterns of industrial conflict according to whether governments tended to intervene to redistribute national income (in part through welfare provision) toward labor, or conversely reinforced the share of profits, or remained relatively aloof from distributional conflicts. More recently, Crouch (1993: 4) applied 'a threefold division between contestation, pluralism and corporatism'; while van Waarden (1995: 110–1) writes of 'three general kinds of state action, liberal pluralism: a passive state which upholds the principle of non-intervention, corporatism: active state interference, but usually in consultation with the social partners, [and] statism: active and direct state interference with terms of employment and working conditions'.

These different classifications overlap, but are far from identical. They differ, for example, in whether they focus on institutional interconnections and the policy process, or (as with Hibbs) on material outcomes; and whether the focus is on relations between the state and the labor movement (as with Regini and to a large extent Crouch), or more broadly (as with van Waarden) on the role of the 'social partners' in public policy. There are also differences in how far such classifications are taken as empirical descriptors or ideal types. For example, Regini cautioned against the mechanical application of his typology to specific national cases, and argued (1986: 62) that 'during the 1970s, the three models seemed even less applicable'. By contrast, Crouch suggests that his more recent classification 'emerged from the literature of the 1970s and 1980s'.

As seen above, Anglo-Saxon writing on industrial relations has traditionally taken 'pluralistic industrialism' as the norm. But pluralism was and is *not* typical; in most countries, political power is an overt feature of industrial relations though in ways which are contextually variable. 'In large parts of the world, the entire industrial relations system is dominated, directly or indirectly, by the government' (Sturmthal, 1973: 8).

First, there is continued national diversity of politico-economic regimes or 'varieties of capitalism' (Hall and Soskice, 2001), in which the state often performs important functions as economic actor and regulator or co-ordinator; and this diversity is often reflected in different forms of employment regulation. Hence convergence has not occurred (though note, as discussed below, that there are today frequent arguments that 'globalization' is a new, and more powerful driver of convergence).

Second, as a corollary, highly 'politicized' industrial relations systems which Anglo-Saxon writers have long considered an anachronism have tended to persist. This is the case in most of Africa, Asia, Latin America and even in many countries of Western Europe, for example France and Italy.

Third, new connections have arisen between industrial relations and political agendas even in countries where there was for a time considerable detachment. One argument would be that 'pluralist industrialism' was the outcome of a *temporary* and *contingent* interaction of social, political and economic forces. Typically this involved a 'post-war compromise' between unions and (nationally embedded) employers, which established a stable institutionalized relationship where mutual gains could be generated by rapid economic growth. Rising national income also funded expanding welfare states. In the very different economic conditions of the late twentieth and early twenty-first centuries, these compromises unraveled – or were sustained only by increasingly overt state action.

The next section discusses in more detail the ways in which the state can be seen as omnipresent in the dynamics of industrial relations. Thereafter I suggest a simple typology of three models of interconnection between states and industrial relations.

THE ROLE OF GOVERNMENT IN INDUSTRIAL RELATIONS: ARENAS OF REGULATION

The 'varieties of capitalism' literature which has become so influential in recent years (see Chapter 7 in this volume) insists that while all market economies may share certain core dynamics, their distinctive institutional configurations result in very different social and economic outcomes. Much of this literature assumes some form of functional interdependence between different elements of each nation's institutional architecture. For example, Dore (2000: 45–7) refers to 'institutional interlock' as typical of national economies and of the relationship between economy and broader society; Aoki (2001) writes of 'institutional complementarity'; Marsden (1999) argues that the institutions which constitute the 'employment system' within any country tend to 'cluster' over time, according to an underlying structural logic. As Hollingsworth and Boyer (1997: 2–3) put it, the industrial relations system and other institutional arrangements tend to be 'tightly coupled with each other' and thus 'coalesce into a complex social configuration'. The consequence, but also the reinforcing dynamic, is that 'firms will gravitate toward the mode of coordination for which there is institutional support' (Hall and Soskice, 2001: 9). While the last-cited authors find it useful to present a dichotomy between liberal and co-ordinated market economies (LMEs and CMEs), many other writers find this too broad-brush to make sense of the sheer diversity of institutional arrangements. And the state itself is central to any national institutional architecture: there are radical variations in the form, extent and depth of its role in industrial relations, both across countries and over time.

This section suggests (though such classifications are inevitably somewhat arbitrary) seven key respects in which the state shapes the national industrial relations regime:

- as an employer in its own right;
- through defining and delimiting the procedural status of the other 'actors' and prescribing the 'rules of the game';
- by legislating individual employment rights;
- by shaping the labor market through macroeconomic management;
- through 'supply-side' labor market policies which shape the capacities brought by employees;
- crucially, as a 'welfare state' limiting workers' dependence for survival on the employment relationship, and hence enhancing their bargaining power; and finally;
- as the matrix of ideas of citizenship which may (though not necessarily) shape the relationship between employers and employees.

All these arenas of state action operate to some degree in every country, but to very different degrees, and with stark contrasts in their relative importance. In consequence, there are multiple configurations in the role of government as an industrial relations actor (Amable, 2003).

The state as employer

All states are employers. Though the role of the state in LMEs is in theory more limited than in CMEs, and though in much of the world the last two decades have seen a process of privatization of public enterprises and contracting out of public services, almost universally the majority of those working in the military, law enforcement and public administration, and at least a substantial proportion in health, education and social services, are state employees (and those who are not are nevertheless typically subject to indirect state control of their employment conditions). This makes the state, broadly defined, the largest single employer in most countries. As a result, we may add, the simple notion of 'three actors' in industrial relations – workers, employers and government – is inadequate, since the state so to speak occupies two seats at the table.

As Chapter 16 in this volume indicates, state employment typically involves distinctive industrial relations regimes. In some respects, the rules are more restrictive than in the private sector. In very few countries are the armed forces allowed to unionize, and in many the exclusions are far wider. The right to collective bargaining may be constrained, either because some categories of public employee enjoy a distinctive status (such as the German *Beamte*), or because of the doctrine that this would infringe the sovereignty of the legislature in defining the terms of public employment. Often there are also prohibitions or tight limitations on strikes in 'essential services'. Conversely, however, there is widespread formal encouragement of collective representation for public employees. In Britain, this dates back to the Whitley Reports at the end of the 1914–18 war. In the US it stems from the Kennedy Executive Order 10988 of 1962, which authorized unionization and collective bargaining for federal employees, and was widely matched at state and local level. Partly because of the at least latent political leverage of public employees, in almost all countries their rate of unionization is today higher, and often far higher, than in the private sector. Job security in the public sector has often been high (which in many countries has made public employment a basis for political patronage). Secure employment has often been linked to ideologies of 'public service' and of the government as a 'good employer'. For these reasons, in many countries (though by no means all), public employment traditionally displayed peaceful industrial relations.

The dynamics of public-sector industrial relations are complex: does the state act as an imitator or innovator? In Britain, governments have tended to follow 'good practice' in the private sector (which in recent years has meant the importation of management styles and structures which critics consider inappropriate); in France and Italy, by contrast, the public sector has been the dynamo

of 'modern' employment relations. In most countries there were growing problems in public-sector industrial relations in the 1980s and 1990s. Growing budgetary deficits often led to efforts to cut public spending; in Europe, these pressures were reinforced by the constraints on public expenditure laid down by the EU in the 1991 Maastricht Treaty. In many countries, incomes policies were more rigorously enforced in the public than the private sector; the unequal impact led to feelings of inequity and a breakdown of the 'psychological contract' between the state and public employees. In addition, inter- and intra-union conflicts associated with public-sector collective bargaining became common. The growing weight of public sector unions within national confederations (notably in Sweden) shifted the balance of power, with challenges to established bargaining policy. In some countries (notably Italy) greater assertiveness by groups with key skills, who lost out from egalitarian wage policy, caused major tensions. Such factors have led in some countries to a rise in militancy, often at the same time as dispute numbers were falling sharply in the private sector.

Procedural regulation: defining the 'actors' and the 'rules of the game'

Even in 'voluntarist' systems (where the state supposedly 'abstains' from involvement in industrial relations) it has an unavoidable role in procedural regulation. This typically involves defining the status, rights and obligations of the 'actors', and prescribing and enforcing the 'rules of the game'. Such regulation can shape the major contours of the whole national system: for example, Howell (2005: 190) develops a powerful argument that at key moments of social and economic crisis, 'the British state ... played a central role in the construction, embedding and legitimization of new industrial relations institutions'.

One fundamental issue in any country is the legal status of collective agreements. Typically they are binding on the signatories and those they represent ('collective contracts') – though Britain is one of the most notable exceptions. Where this is the case (and in some countries where it is not) the law specifies who may negotiate such agreements, often linking this to the registration or certification of trade unions and employers' associations. Particularly in developing countries, such procedures can be used to privilege those organizations which the government favors politically. One fascinating European instance of selective certification is in France, where for historical reasons the law defines five trade union confederations as 'most representative', which gives them privileged access to peak-level dialogue, and to company-level recognition even where they have only one member. Much more generally, different approaches to the regulation of the 'actors' can encourage, or inhibit, collective organization in trade unions in particular, but also in employers' associations (Adams, 1993). Except for a brief period around WWII, US law and policy have offered little encouragement, in contrast to most of Western Europe. Shifts in policy from pro- to anti-collectivism can have dramatic effects, as in Britain under Thatcher and even more notably in New Zealand with the Employment Contracts Act 1991. Note that in most of Western Europe, even conservative parties (and governments) have tended to favor collective regulation of employment.

Another important issue is whether collective agreements apply only to firms (and indeed workers) who are members of the signatory organizations, or more generally. It is widely the case that employers are not permitted to discriminate between union members and non-members, and that the latter are therefore entitled to the terms and conditions contained in collective agreements. In the US, more broadly, the 'duty of fair representation' requires unions to represent the interests even of non-members where recognition exists. But what of firms which are not members of their appropriate employers' association and/or do not recognize trade unions? In countries like Britain or the US, multi-employer bargaining is a marginal phenomenon and the issue scarcely arises.

In many others, employers' associations have limited membership and non-members are not affected by their agreements. But elsewhere, notably in many Western European countries with strong traditions of 'employer solidarity', there exist 'extension mechanisms' (sometimes known as *erga omnes* rules) whereby multi-employer agreements apply, either automatically or in the case of explicit government determination to this effect, to non-member firms (Traxler and Behrens, 2002). Not surprisingly, such provisions can constitute quite an incentive to firms to join the relevant employers' association, so they can influence the outcome of agreements to which they will be subject.

In many countries, the state prescribes obligatory mechanisms (at least in firms over a certain size) for collective employee representation at company or workplace level, imposing an obligation on management to inform and consult the representatives over key business and personnel policies. In some cases, as in Germany, this gives the workforce a virtual veto over major decisions which threaten employment security.

A fourth, and very important, procedural role of the state is in handling (or avoiding) breakdowns in collective bargaining. Where there are disagreements over the interpretation of legally enforceable agreements ('disputes of right', in the American parlance), there typically exists dedicated machinery of adjudication such as labor courts. Most national systems also contain either voluntary or compulsory mechanisms of conciliation, mediation and arbitration applicable to 'disputes of interest' (where strikes and lock-outs are in principle permissible). There may also be powers enabling governments to delay, or even prohibit totally, stoppages in certain cases.

Substantive employment rights

How far are the terms of the contract of employment a private matter between employer and employee? The ideological debate noted in an earlier section can also be regarded as a conflict of organizing principles between LMEs and CMEs, reflected in the contrast between 'Anglo-Saxon' – or as Crouch (2005: 29–30) suggests is a preferable term, Anglophone – and (Western) continental European models of industrial relations (Hyman, 2004). In the former, the individual contract of employment is the primary point of reference; restrictions on the contractual liberty of employer and employee require special justification (or in extreme versions of liberal ideology, cannot be justified at all). In the latter, it is considered absurd to imagine that an individual employee can bargain on equal terms with an employer who may well be a giant corporation; the state therefore has the right and indeed duty to define standards which must be observed in all employment contracts, in order to prevent unequal bargaining power resulting in unreasonable conditions. (One interesting reflection of this clash of perspectives can be seen in the implementation of the EU Directive on working time. The UK was the only country to allow any individual employee to 'opt out' of the 48-hour limit on weekly working time. Elsewhere in Europe it was recognized that the idea of a 'voluntary' agreement to unlimited hours of work was fanciful.)

In practice, all states define some individual employment rights which limit the parameters of individual contracts, but there is great variation in the scope of such regulation and – an issue less commonly researched – the rigor of its enforcement. In most countries, employment law defines basic standards governing all contracts: minimum wages, maximum and 'abnormal' hours, annual leave; individual and collective dismissals; health and safety; equal opportunities; vocational and educational leave; parental leave. As indicated above, in LMEs the impact of such regulation tends to be relatively limited (though note that the US has some of the strongest legislation on equal employment opportunities in the world). Note also that there is considerable variation also within CMEs: whereas in some countries the law prescribes a wide range of contractual terms, in others most such issues are regulated by collective bargaining

(and the 'social partners' may strongly resist legislation).

As described above, there has been a recent trend in many countries toward what is misleadingly termed 'deregulation' but in fact entails a shift in regulatory mechanisms toward 'market forces' and the power asymmetries which these embody. 'Flexibility' has become the watchword (Ramaux, 2006), but there has been substantial variation in the fervor with which this has been pursued, the extent of the 'rigidities' addressed (in Europe, many changes have been limited to the liberalization of temporary contracts and of working time regimes), and in the extent to which governments have acted independently of the other industrial relations 'actors'. In some countries, indeed – as discussed below – modifications to existing legislative prescriptions have been negotiated with the 'social partners' and have been replaced, not by individualization but by collective bargaining.

Macroeconomic management: structuring the labor market

For much of the postwar period, at least in Western Europe, a widely accepted function of the state was in exercising macroeconomic management: in particular, using fiscal and monetary policy to raise aggregate demand in periods of recession and reduce it in periods of 'overheating'. This was consistent with the analysis of Keynes (1936), that the labor market was not a naturally self-equilibrating mechanism: in periods of demand deficiency, there would be high unemployment, and reducing wages (as orthodox economic theory recommended) would make matters worse. The resulting policy prescriptions were that governments should be prepared to run budget deficits when unemployment was high, and do the opposite when the economy was booming. This would be consistent with balanced budgets over the full economic cycle. Such macroeconomic management should be regarded as an 'industrial relations' issue, in that 'full' employment (on a strict definition, probably impossible to achieve) and economic growth affect the balance of power within the labor market, and also the margins for negotiation within 'free collective bargaining'. In addition, historical evidence shows that in most (though not all) countries, trade union membership tends to vary inversely with the level of unemployment.

Keynes wrote in an era of mass unemployment. In the postwar years when unemployment was lower and there was a scarcity of key skills, a dilemma emerged: economic expansion, generally seen as desirable in itself, created inflationary pressures which in turn threatened the stability of national currencies. In Britain, notoriously, this led to 'stop-go' economic policies: when inflation increased, governments applied restrictive measures which created a rise in unemployment and a brake on economic growth. An alternative which proved effective in some European countries with centralized bargaining regimes was the adoption of formalized incomes policies, whereby unions accepted the need for wage restraint in return for government commitment to maintain expansionary macroeconomic measures.

In this context it is important to note the role of central banks: in an increasing number of countries, independent of national governments but surely part of the state. These are rarely recognized by industrial relations analysts as relevant 'actors' but can exert a crucial role, as is increasingly argued (Iversen, 1999; Iversen et al., 2000). To take one notable instance, in Germany the *Bundesbank* has traditionally oriented its interest rate policies to the level of wage settlements; and unions have known that if they pursued, and won, over-ambitious increases they would be punished by restrictive policies which would result in unemployment. Since the introduction of the euro, many regard the European Central Bank as performing a similar role.

Since the 1970s, Keynesianism has been widely discredited as the basis for public policy, following the growing evidence that high inflation and economic stagnation ('stagflation') could coexist in a manner unpredicted by Keynes and his contemporaries – though there have been efforts to construct a 'neo-Keynesianism' which combines elements of Keynes' theories with those of classical economics which he attacked. Despite continued pressure by many national trade union movements for the continuation or revival of policies of demand management, government willingness to make full employment the primary target of macroeconomic policy has largely evaporated; the new orthodoxy involves a return to neoclassical assumptions that the labor market can and should regulate itself; or else, more pessimistically, that there is nothing that governments can do to shape the overall health of the labor market.

From demand to supply: the pursuit of 'employability'

Demand management may be a necessary but insufficient means to 'full' employment. Unless the supply and demand of different types of competence are in balance, there are likely to be shortages of certain types of labor (or in specific parts of a country) while unemployment remains relatively high among some occupational groups or regions. Typically, 'supply-side' intervention is seen as necessary to correct such imbalances.

Management of supply and demand can reasonably be seen as complementary. A good example in practice can be seen in Sweden. The social-democratic finance minister Wigforss introduced 'Keynesian' policies in the 1930s (some say he invented Keynesianism before Keynes), but these were subsequently supplemented by 'active labor market policy', targeted at the retraining and relocation of those who were unemployed, in addition to specific job creation schemes. Much more generally, vocational and educational training in many countries is provided on a free or subsidized basis by the state; alternatively or in addition, many governments provide incentives to employers to undertake in-house training. Such measures obviously enhance a country's skills base.

With the shift away from Keynesian policies, the principle of 'activation' has grown in importance, but typically as a substitute for demand management rather than a supplement. A clear example can be seen in the European Employment Strategy launched by the EU a decade ago, where 'employability' is a key policy theme. On the one hand this can be seen as an attempt to capitalize on the opportunities of a 'knowledge economy' by fostering the diffusion of new, up-market skills and qualifications. On the other, much of the focus is on providing basic literacy, numeracy and work discipline for those at risk of social exclusion. In this case, the notion of 'employability' can easily be seen as shifting responsibility for their situation to the unemployed themselves (Hyman, 2005).

Industrial relations and the welfare state

The 'decommodification' of labor which was mentioned earlier – the institutional protection of the labor force from total dependence for survival on the discretion of the employer – has two distinct dimensions. One is constituted by the complex of employment legislation, already discussed. Directly, laws which specify minimum wages or the length and organization of the working week and limit the circumstances in which a worker can be dismissed, if actually enforced, substantially limit the market dimension of the employment relationship. So, indirectly, do laws which give trade unions or works councils rights of joint regulation. The second dimension involves institutional support for workers who are sick or injured, unemployed, or past retirement age. Financial benefits in such circumstances, and services such as health care, again provide a buffer against the commodity status of labor. Those who are aged or incapacitated may be able to withdraw from the labor market without major loss of income; those who lose their job may not feel obliged to take the first available alternative, however unsuitable.

Some such protections may be derived from private insurance, or from collective agreements with employers, but universally they are provided to some degree by the state. The 'welfare state' should therefore be

considered an important part of industrial relations. By contrast (as indicated in the introduction), mirroring the predominant tendency in Anglo-Saxon industrial relations to see politics as a separate sphere, so the welfare regime is typically disregarded, its study left to specialists in social policy. This is in sharp contrast to most countries of continental Western Europe, where 'the equivalent term for "social policy" refers to both the welfare state and industrial relations' (Crouch, 1999: 437), and both are the responsibility of a single ministry and are studied by the same researchers. Here it is interesting to note the French term *rapport salarial*, the meaning of which cannot be captured by the banal English 'wage relationship': typically the concept encompasses skill formation, wage determination, collective bargaining, employment protection and labor market policies, and not least state welfare provision (Amable, 2003; Boyer, 1986).

The welfare regime takes very different forms in different countries, not only in terms of the balance between public and private provision (Arts and Gelissen, 2002; Esping-Andersen, 1990), but also in the nature and extent of integration between its governance and the industrial relations 'actors'. Outside Europe (and even in some European countries), state provision is often extremely limited. In Japan, major firms often provide extensive welfare benefits. The US is also notable for the existence of relatively generous provision by individual employers, often the outcome of collective bargaining (Jacoby, 1998); but such benefits, being company-based, have always been unevenly distributed, have recently been under widespread attack, and their coverage has declined in parallel with trade union membership. In much of the world, welfare depends on individual resources or (more commonly) on support from the extended family.

Any significant system of 'decommodification' strengthens the position of workers both individually and collectively, facilitating the emergence and stability of collectivized industrial relations (Korpi and

Esping-Andersen, 1984). For this very reason, in some countries early trade unions (particularly of skilled workers) provided their own 'friendly benefits' in order to shield members against the contingencies of their working lives. In general this function was displaced by the rise of the welfare state, but as part of this process the trade unions in some countries (sometimes together with employers) obtained a key role in the administration of public welfare (Ebbinghaus, 2002; Streeck and Hassel, 2003). Where this is the case, their institutional position in society is buttressed, and they may acquire a range of subsidies from the state which enable them to maintain their activities even in the absence of significant membership – as is most strikingly the case in France. In a small number of European countries, the historical decision to delegate to trade unions the running of publicly subsidized unemployment insurance funds (the so-called 'Ghent system') has a remarkably powerful effect in sustaining high union density (Western, 1998).

In many countries, in recent years established welfare systems have been under challenge, as a result of demographic changes, constrained public finances and an ideological shift toward liberalization and 'activation' (Esping-Andersen, 2002). Where welfare has been an accepted part of the industrial relations agenda, this has imposed serious challenges to the stability of the whole industrial relations system. The implications are considered in more detail below.

The construction of 'industrial citizenship'

The most fundamental influence of the state is in defining the status of labor in the polity, the economy and society as a whole. Crucially, is democracy a principle which applies only in a narrowly bounded political sphere, or is it of more general import? Over half a century ago, in his lectures on Citizenship and Social Class, Marshall (1950) explored the evolution of institutions linking rights, status and responsibilities in modern (and more specifically, British) society. He saw the key

achievement of the past two centuries as the rise, at national level, of universal citizenship. This process, he argued, occurred in three stages. The first, largely accomplished in the eighteenth and early nineteenth centuries, involved the institutionalization of the civil basis of citizenship: 'the rights necessary for individual freedom – liberty of the person, freedom of speech, thought and faith, the right to own property and to conclude valid contracts, and the right to justice'. The second, roughly 100 years later, saw the extension of political citizenship through electoral reform: 'the right to participate in the exercise of political power'. The third, a project of the twentieth century, was the creation of 'social citizenship': the right to at least minimum standards of 'economic welfare and security' and hence to enjoy 'the life of a civilized being' (1950: 10–11).

Though Marshall's central theme was the gradual 'civilization' of capitalism, he largely neglected the role of the citizen as worker. He noted that the success of trade unions in establishing their right to exist, to bargain, and if necessary to take industrial action, transformed the geography of social relations, creating 'a secondary system of industrial citizenship, parallel with and supplementary to the system of political citizenship' (1950: 42–4). This was, however, not for Marshall, a central component of the rise of 'social citizenship', which he identified rather with the rise of public education and the welfare state more generally; hence industrial relations does not figure prominently in his discussion. Yet does citizenship end at the workplace gates? Does the contract of employment give the employer an unbounded right to command, or does 'industrial citizenship' entail a right to employee voice, or, more grandly, 'industrial democracy'?

Here, the distinction between LMEs and CMEs can be mapped against the familiar contrast between shareholder and stakeholder capitalism (Albert, 1993; Dore, 2000; Hutton, 1996). In the former, company law requires managers to give (virtually) exclusive priority to the interests of shareholders; in the latter, management is required (or at least permitted) to consider the interests of other 'stakeholders', notably employees. Mandatory systems of employee voice express the same stakeholder conception: the 'social order' of the enterprise embodies the principle of employee as citizen (Kotthoff, 1994). To present the contrast starkly, in certain legal regimes the influence of labor through the industrial relations system is a conditionally tolerated anomaly, a qualification to the principle described in the US as 'employment at will'; whereas in others it is a natural expression of the status of the employee as a *member* of the employing organization. In codifying one or other of these conflicting understandings of the employment relationship, the state exerts its most profound and pervasive influence in industrial relations.

STATE, ECONOMY AND INDUSTRIAL RELATIONS: SOME STYLIZED MODELS

In the light of the preceding discussion, it is clear that there are almost infinitely possible permutations of the ways in which the state, directly and indirectly, shapes the industrial relations regime. In the earlier section on cross-national diversity I noted that it is common to seek to simplify complex reality by applying three-part classifications of such regimes. In this section I undertake a similar exercise, in this case suggesting a somewhat different three-part typology. It should be stressed that these are 'ideal types' rather than empirical descriptors; actually existing states involve some mix of the different elements.

The laissez-faire state: embedding market individualism

The notion of the laissez-faire state, as I use it here, overlaps closely with the concept of LME and partially with the 'English-speaking' world (only partially, because of the very different trajectories of Australia and New Zealand, which until recently have had much in common with aspects of the other two models I discuss).

Underlying this model is a 'civil law' tradition' which privileges individual contracts (van Waarden, 1995: 132), allied to a prevalent doctrine in the formative period of capitalist industrialization that the state should not 'interfere' in economic life. (*Laissez faire* means, literally, let people – and specifically, property-owners – do as they wish.) In fact the notion of state non-intervention is absurd. Every state defines what counts as property and what rights and responsibilities attach to it; establishes what may and may not be bought and sold; creates and underwrites the currency; and adjudicates complaints of breach of contract. In practice, laissez-faire means the creation of a distinct set of biases: bestowing specific privileges on capital (notably the invention of the principle of 'limited liability', freeing companies from the risks and responsibilities applying to ordinary citizens) and then permitting an imbalance of market power to operate with little or no hindrance: this might be described as 'non-intervention in favor of capital'.

This legal-ideological context has shaped employment regulation along the lines which Kahn-Freund (1954) termed 'collective laissez-faire'. When trade unionism and collective bargaining received (partial) protection from the common-law presumption of illegality,

> the easiest way to sanction the workers' right to collective action ... was to treat it as an extension of property rights and a corollary of the free market. The workers were entitled to sell their labor, or not to sell it, to the highest bidder as they wished. And if they were entitled to act in this manner as individuals, why not as a group, like other groups of property owners?' (Rimlinger, 1977: 224).

Such a foundation for industrial relations regulation is in practice 'internally contradictory' (Klare, 1981: 454). The model of the commercial contract implies that employment is a one-off transaction rather than a continuing relationship, implicitly underwriting managerial authority once a contract is reached (Collins, 1986). The circumstances under which employees can obtain the capacity to act collectively, and the boundaries of legitimate collective action, remain uncertain and thus open to determination by far from neutral courts. And 'collective laissez-faire' offers no protection to those outside the collective regulatory web. In reality, even in LMEs the property rights approach has been supplemented by other forms of procedural and substantive regulation, to an extent which makes the whole idea of 'non-intervention' fanciful (Howell, 2005). This approach also makes protections obtained by labor vulnerable to shifts in the economic balance of power, to judicial creativity or to relatively technical legislative changes: this is very apparent from experience in Britain, where in consequence, 'as the basis for a settlement between labour and capital, collective *laissez-faire* proved to be precarious' (Deakin and Wilkinson, 2004: 42).

Since administrative action by government can radically alter the effective rules of industrial relations (as, for example, through changes in the membership and operational procedures of the US National Labor Relations Board), unions may be able to defend a pre-existing industrial relations 'settlement' only through political mobilization. Here, though, an important obstacle is the phenomenon of 'state capture' – a concept developed with reference to post-communist Eastern Europe (Hellman et al., 2000) but particularly apposite in the case of the US, where only the ultra-rich can today expect to attain top political office, where successful electoral campaigns depend on massive corporate subsidies, and where trade unions' 'political action funds' are increasingly dwarfed by those of companies (Masters and Delaney, 2005), while the political agenda is shaped by media moguls with little affection for labor. 'State power in the United States is ... everywhere permeated by organized societal interests' (Skocpol, 1985: 12). To an important degree, a similar tendency can be seen in Britain. (When Marx and Engels wrote that 'the authority of the modern state is just a committee which administers the common affairs of the whole bourgeois class', perhaps they were showing some prescience!) The growing political power of employers virtually guarantees that in the contemporary laissez-faire state, the processes of industrial relations will be unfavorable to labor.

The social state: the decommodification of labor relations

The idea of a free market is an oxymoron, a fortiori in the case of the 'fictitious commodity' (Polanyi, 1944) of labor. The employment relationship is a social and political invention, and the rights and obligations of each party are necessarily defined by the state. As was seen in the previous section, the state has some role everywhere in the procedural and substantive regulation of the employment relationship, in structuring the labor market, in modifying the dependence of employees on the employer, and hence in negotiating the ambiguous interrelationship between the roles of citizen and of worker.

Nevertheless, it is in continental Western Europe that these functions are typically regarded as most developed. For this reason it is common to speak of a 'European social model'. This notion is misleading but contains an important element of truth. Western Europe comprises some 20 separate countries, 15 of which constituted the European Union (EU) before its 2004 enlargement, with distinctive national traditions and institutional arrangements. Nevertheless certain features are common to most of these. In important respects, it is accepted that 'labor is not a commodity'. Both socialist and catholic traditions, which inform the dominant political parties, reject the idea of work as primarily or exclusively a market transaction. Collective agreements have priority over individual employment contracts, while centralized bargaining and in some countries legal extension mechanisms result in high levels of coverage (even when union density is low). In most cases there is a standardized system of workplace representation at least partially independent of management (underwritten by law or peak-level agreement, or both). Most countries possess an extensive, publicly funded welfare system, and the 'social partners' often have a key role in its administration. One may add that government frequently rests on coalition politics, creating a bias toward compromise and an obstacle to radical institutional change.

Yet despite overarching commonalities, national distinctiveness – involving idiosyncratic 'state traditions' (Crouch, 1993) – results in an evident 'variable geometry' (Ebbinghaus, 1999). It is common to distinguish at least three groupings: the Nordic countries with an 'inclusive strategy of equality' (Palme, 2001) and particularly high levels of unionization; Mediterranean countries with detailed state regulation of substantive employment conditions but relatively undeveloped welfare systems; and a 'central' or 'Germanic' group with extensive but less egalitarian welfare systems and primarily procedural state regulation of industrial relations.

A central question for much of the recent literature is whether the 'European social model(s)' can survive the challenges of a more integrated global economy, or whether they will succumb to a kind of 'Gresham's law' (Crouch and Streeck, 1997) whereby 'bad' institutional arrangements drive out 'good'. Many argue that while EU policy is supposedly informed by the values of the social model, and is intended to consolidate it, in practice the liberal bias of economic integration embodies many of the priorities of LMEs (Chapon and Euzéby, 2002; Hodge and Howe, 1999; Hyman, 2001; Scharpf, 2002; Wickham, 2002). EU enlargement in 2004, encompassing countries from Central and Eastern Europe with inferior employment conditions and without the institutional foundations for wide-ranging collective regulation, is also seen as a threat of a downward spiral of 'deregulation' (Dauderstädt, 2003; Vaughan-Whitehead, 2003). Such concerns connect with the broader issue of the impact of 'globalization' and will be addressed in the last substantive section.

The developmental state: the ideal national capitalist?

Industrial relations systems, in the conventional sense of the term, evolved in parallel with industrial capitalism; in most nations of Western Europe and North America their contours were set in the early twentieth century or before, and consolidated half a century ago within the framework of 'postwar settlements' when the political and economic influence of labor movements was often at its peak. But in countries which developed 'modern' economic systems more recently, the evolution of industrial relations has followed different lines.

The notion of the 'developmental state', originally coined by Johnson (1982) with reference to Japan, has since been applied more generally to the 'newly industrializing' countries of East Asia and beyond (Haggard, 1986; Öniş, 1991; Weiss, 2004). The logic of the concept is that while state and economy are everywhere intertwined, 'late' industrialization within a world system already dominated by rich and hegemonic nations requires particularly overt and systematic state direction. The developmental state has typically involved an elite state bureaucracy with control over the financial system and a symbiotic relationship with private capital, able to give priority to the accumulation function and to determine the strategic priorities for growth. (One may note similarities with postwar industrial development in southern European countries.)

What are the implications for the evolution of industrial relations? While Kerr et al. (1960) placed considerable emphasis on the composition and ideology of national 'industrializing elites' in shaping the character of the labor force and the pattern of relationships with employers, analysis of the developmental state has tended to focus on political context and antecedents, and different modes of industrialization. In many post-colonial states, organized labor had played an important role in the struggle for independence and could not easily be excluded from influence in the polity and the workplace. In many dictatorships and other authoritarian regimes, labor exclusion could form an inherent part of the suppression of potential opposition. Another important political influence was the cold war: first in Japan, then in the later

East Asian industrializers, anti-communism helped legitimize an ethos of national unity and opposition to militant trade unionism, contributing strongly to what Öniş (1991: 124) terms the developmental state's 'key role in the promotion of cooperative labor-management relations'.

The literature on economic development makes a fundamental distinction between 'import substitution' and 'export-oriented' industrialization (ISI and EOI). Kuruvilla (1995) explores some of the industrial relations implications. In ISI, high tariff walls enabled the domestic production of basic industrial goods. Notably in Latin America, this enabled authoritarian regimes to develop domestic industry. In some cases (Argentina under Perón was the most obvious example), this was accompanied by a collaboration between the state and 'corporatist' trade unions (Cook, 1998). EOI occurred in part under external pressure for the reduction or removal of tariffs, and could occur in two phases. The first, price-competitive, involved exploiting the comparative advantage of a low-wage regime, the suppression of autonomous (or at least, militant) trade unionism, and in many cases the creation of 'export processing' or 'free enterprise zones' with even fewer worker protections than the rest of the economy. A second stage, visible in only a few (notably East Asian) countries involved value-added EOI. This strategy has offered scope for the company-level incorporation of labor, either through company unionism on the Japanese model (joint commitment to productivity) or (more likely) non-union HRM (Frenkel and Peetz, 1998).

A distinctive model of developmental state can be seen in China. While many, perhaps most newly industrializing countries have authoritarian regimes, China is exceptional in its disregard for the niceties of political democracy, and for the ruthlessness with which accumulation has been pursued (the concept of 'oriental despotism' which Marx used to characterize the 'Asiatic mode of production' is perhaps apposite). The rapid shift from a command to a market economy (though one with continuing state direction), ending the former security of employment (the 'iron rice bowl'), accentuated the disruptive force of economic transformation. China is also notable for the existence of a party-controlled 'transmission belt' trade union, of a kind previously common to the whole soviet bloc. A major uncertainty is whether this may evolve in the direction of greater independence, leading to the emergence of industrial relations at workplace level with affinities to experience elsewhere; for example, Howell (2006) suggests that moves toward more democratic electoral processes at grassroots level have resulted in an uneven process of invigoration of some local union branches.

If the developmental state has been a suitable framework for 'late development', what of the countries attempting to achieve '*late* late development'? In much of the 'Third World' (most notably Africa) there are problems of state-building, a weakness of civil society, extreme subjection to imperialist forms of external domination (today typically through the agency of multinational capital, though supported by the hegemonic nation-states), tensions between 'modern' and 'traditional' economic sectors. Is 'industrial relations' in any strong sense more than a marginal phenomenon?

In any event, the scope for the relative economic autarchy of the developmental state is today constrained by the liberalization of the world economic system. The 'Washington consensus', initially helping drive the shift from ISI to EOI strategies, has subsequently sought to eliminate the institutional arrangements which contributed to the success of EOI (Fernández Jilberto and Riethof, 2002). The structural adjustment program imposed by the World Bank have had disastrous effects in terms of worker insecurity and impoverishment. Such trends have however produced a reaction, notably in Latin America but also for example in Korea, with popular discontent provoking radical industrial and political protest. The implications for industrial relations are as yet unpredictable.

THE TRAJECTORIES OF 'MODERN CAPITALISM': THE RISE, DECLINE – AND REVIVAL? – OF 'CORPORATISM'

Writing 40 years ago, Shonfield sought to account for the superior economic performance of the 'modern capitalism' of many continental European countries compared to Britain or the USA. His explanation (1969: 66–7) centered on 'the vastly increased influence of the public authorities on the management of the economic system'. A combination of long-range planning and publicly funded national welfare meant that 'the violence of the market has been tamed'. He also commented on the, at first sight, surprising fact 'that full employment and the enhanced bargaining power of wage-earners have not resulted in the diversion of resources away from investment', and attributed this to 'the corporatist formula for managing the economy. The major interest groups are brought together and encouraged to conclude a series of bargains about their future behaviour' (1965: 5, 231).

The idea of corporatism became a popular theme of industrial relations analysis in the following decade. In many European countries, the 'post-war settlement' had resulted in a seeming contradiction (or as some writers have called it, a 'trilemma') between full employment, stable exchange rates and price stability. If full employment created the basis for strong trade unions, what was to prevent them using this strength to shift the distribution of income between labor and capital and also to press the government to increase the proportion of national income devoted to social welfare? If successful, such pressure could result in inflation and/or devaluation, and perhaps capital flight.

Yet as Shonfield intimated, this was not the universal experience. In particular, in the countries of Western Europe where unions were strongest there was commonly a trade-off in which they restrained their wage demands in return for government commitment to pursue an expansionary economic policy and to develop the welfare state. For Korpi and Shalev (1979), the organizational

strength of labor enabled unions to move from the (conflictual) defense of workers' interests in the industrial arena to the (non-conflictual) pursuit of their interests in the political arena. This could facilitate high investment, hence economic growth, hence subsequent increases in both wages and social expenditure: a virtuous circle. Such a trade-off was institutionalized immediately after the war in Austria and the Netherlands, but imitated elsewhere in the 1960s and 1970s. A corollary of such schemes was that unions and employers' associations achieved a privileged position in macro-policy formulation, which enhanced their own organizational status and in turn made it easier for them to enforce decisions on their constituents (particularly important where unions agreed to wage restraint). As Katzenstein (1985) noted, institutionalized solutions to the 'trilemma' were particularly necessary in the small, export-oriented states which comprised much of Western Europe – and also easier to achieve because of the density of networks between state functionaries and representatives of labor and capital (for the Swedish case see Svensson and Öberg, 2005).

Many academic analysts, following Shonfield, described such a relationship as 'corporatist'. This was slightly awkward, since the term was previously used as a label for Mussolini's fascist regime in Italy; and as described in the previous section, the concept was also associated with authoritarian regimes in Latin America. Hence some writers preferred the terms 'neo-corporatism' or 'concertation', others referred to 'political exchange' (Baglioni, 1987; Pizzorno, 1978; Regini, 1984). There were other problems with the theory of corporatism. For example, peak-level concertation on a rather similar agenda was consolidated in Sweden in the early 1950s and was widely seen as the basis for a long period of economic success; but the state was involved only in the background, since both unions and employers were anxious to preserve their own autonomous decision-making role. Or to take what was for several decades another success story, (West) Germany: here too the state was detached from the bargaining process (a detachment strongly valued as an expression of *Tarifautonomie* – roughly equivalent to 'free collective bargaining'); but in addition, the trade-off between wage moderation and economic growth was achieved not through central co-ordination but because the main trade unions were 'encompassing' (Olson, 1982) and could anticipate the macroeconomic consequences of their own bargaining activity. A further factor, as noted above, was that the *Bundesbank* pursued a rigorous anti-inflationary policy and unions were aware that high wage settlements would lead to deflationary monetary policy and unemployment. It could also be argued that 'corporatist' relationships between state and economic actors were not necessarily the outcome of trade union strength, and could arise without union involvement; for example, the postwar Japanese model was sometimes described as 'corporatism without labor', and the same might be said of 'developmental states' more generally.

By the 1980s, corporatist arrangements had come under increasing pressure and often unraveled. Corporatism had emerged as a mechanism for encouraging economic growth with positive-sum outcomes; now the economic situation was far less favorable, with inflation and unemployment both rising in many countries. In some countries, trade unions were weakened by recession and no longer needed to be 'bought off' by government; in others, their capacity to guarantee wage restraint had been undermined by rank-and-file revolts. In the main, corporatism – both as practice and as theory – fell out of fashion.

Yet in the 1990s, peak-level concertation again became widely practiced in Western Europe, though in a form very different from that of previous decades (Berger and Compston, 2002; Regini, 1997). The previous agreements had been reached, as has been seen, when unions appeared strong; in addition, employers were largely rooted in the national economy, and national governments had considerable autonomy in determining

fiscal and monetary policy. Now unions were far weaker, capital was more cosmopolitan and mobile, while financial liberalization constrained governments' economic policy discretion (formally so, within the eurozone) – issues which are considered further in the section which follows. The new 'pacts for employment and competitiveness' (PECs) have been primarily designed to reduce, or at least stabilize, unit labor costs and to reduce both corporate taxation and budget deficits (Fajertag and Pochet, 2000; Rhodes, 2001; Sisson et al., 1999). In the process, unions have been invited to maintain wage moderation but at the same time to accept cutbacks in the welfare state and often also some weakening of labor market regulation. The main rationale for such pacts has been that the outcome will be greater national economic competitiveness and more attraction to capital to invest in the country, thereby reducing unemployment. Governments, in many cases lacking the electoral base to push through unpopular policies unilaterally, have been keen to 'construct support coalitions' (Gourevitch, 1986: 239) as a means of blame avoidance.

In contrast to the positive-sum trade-offs of previous decades, if unions agree (and in some cases, notably in France and Germany, they have not) this has often been as a least-worst option and without specific compensation (except perhaps in bolstering their organizational status as 'social partners'). Hancké and Rhodes (2005) also suggest that while unions possessed significant bargaining power in the run-up to European monetary union, since they might have mobilized nationally against the project, once the new monetary regime was a reality the scope to affect government policy largely disappeared. However, national variations are important. In particular, unions in many countries have been able to ensure that 'deregulation' maintains a collective alternative to simple marketization. In Italy, for example, most relaxations of former statutory regulation has followed peak-level agreements between unions and employers, bolstering collective authority; in Belgium, 'derogation' from legislated rules is possible only by collective agreement; in the Netherlands, areas of public welfare have been delegated to sectoral collective bargaining (which, in contrast to the US model), ensures comprehensive coverage (Trampusch, 2006).

Some parallels can be seen in the countries of Central and Eastern Europe, in particular those which joined the EU in 2004. Here, even more starkly than in the west, there have been painful processes of restructuring in the transition to a market economy, in many countries involving the collapse of employment security and a lack of adequate welfare provision to cushion the blow. Transition has been widely associated with attempts to introduce tripartite concertation, with strong encouragement from the EU. However, trade unions in most cases are weak and divided, organization among employers is rudimentary, and governments often cling to the authoritarian reflexes of the old regime, and tripartism has generally achieved very limited success. Ost (2000) has referred to 'illusory corporatism', a hollow facade designed to sideline protest. Other assessments have however been somewhat less dismissive; for example, Avdagic (2005: 47) stresses nationally distinct paths: in Hungary, 'unstable bargaining with a rather low level of concessions for organized labor'; in Poland, 'labor cooptation with minimal concessions to the unions'; but in the Czech Republic, 'pragmatic institutionalized bargaining' of a kind familiar in the west.

'GLOBALIZATION' AND STATE CAPACITY

My discussion until now has assumed the (relative) autonomy of nation state. Is this reasonable in an era of 'globalization', seen by some as leading inevitably to 'the retreat of the state' (Strange, 1996)? I have reviewed elsewhere the debate on the eclipse of the nation state (Hyman, 1999, 2006), and this is a question which will be considered in greater detail in Chapter 34 of this volume. But it is necessary to address some of the issues here.

The 'strong globalization' argument can be simply summarized. Recent decades have seen, first, the liberalization of cross-national trade through the reduction or removal of tariff barriers; second, the cross-national integration of production within multinational companies (MNCs); third, the removal, sometimes forcible, of obstacles to cross-national investment and the more general liberalization of financial flows across borders, which in combination with advances in information technology and telecommunications render transactions in shares and currencies continuous and instantaneous. The corollary, it is often argued, is that individual companies are increasingly free – and given the pressures of competitiveness, are obliged – to escape the regulatory force of national industrial relations systems and establish employment regimes which suit their distinctive market strengths and weaknesses (Katz and Darbishire, 2000; Kochan et al., 1997). Concurrently, the increasingly autonomous dynamic of financial flows destabilizes material economies and allows capital-holders to 'punish' national regimes and governments the policies of which fail to match the criteria of rectitude embraced in financial markets. Taken together, the cross-national extension of production chains, product markets, corporate structures and financial flows makes national boundaries and the nation-state largely irrelevant. The only option for the latter is to accommodate to the new international regime: fostering competitiveness by pursuing labor market flexibility; reducing tax burdens by shifting from welfare to 'workfare' (Handler, 2004; Jessop, 1999) or 'competitive solidarity' (Streeck, 2001); stimulating, or at least permitting, increased income inequality (Iversen and Wren, 1998); and more generally reducing the role of the state from 'steering' the economy to the piecemeal correction of discrete 'market failures' (Majone, 1994).

The thesis of the irresistible imperatives of globalization is sometimes dismissed as little more than ideology (Hirst and Thompson, 1996). Other counter-arguments stress unevenness (Carter, 2005; Mann, 1997), contradiction and/or contingency, including political contingency (Hamann and Kelly, 2003; Kitschelt et al., 1999; Streeck, 1998). The corollary is that 'deregulation' is as much a matter of political choice as of economic necessity; even if 'competitiveness' is an increasingly coercive objective, how it can be achieved is far from self-evident. The 'social' or 'developmental' state may remain as successful as the 'laissez faire' alternative; if Gresham's law really applied, there would be no point in international treaties mandating liberalization.

The elusive nature of the challenge of 'globalization' helps explain the diversity of national responses, which contradict the thesis of universal 'Anglo-Saxonization' of industrial relations. For example, Kwon (2004: 92), while identifying some common themes in the reorganization of motor manufacturing in Germany and the US, found that the trends 'did not confirm the rejuvenation of market liberalism'; market relations remained socially structured in nationally distinctive ways. In respect of the reconfiguration of 'social models', Iversen and Pontusson (2000) argue that if continental European systems are converging, it is toward a 'Germanic' rather than an American model. Crouch (1995) has insisted that while the forms of decommodification may need to alter, it remains possible to preserve the principle: a thesis supported by Falkner and Tálos (1994) and Hemerijk and Schludi (2001). Along similar lines, Lane (1995: 195) points out that 'despite much deregulationist activity in labour and capital markets, re-regulation or alternative forms of state regulation have often occurred', adding that 'new modes of response remain strongly determined by pre-existing forms of state organization'. Much of the analysis of Germany and Japan in Streeck and Yamamura (2001) and Yamamura and Streeck (2003) develops an analogous interpretation. This is consistent with Jacoby's thesis (2004: 19) of 'weak-path-dependence', whereby countries 'adapt to common environmental changes in a similar way' but 'fashion those adaptations to preexisting institutions'. It seems plausible to conclude that no systematic elimination

of state capacity to shape industrial relations in nationally distinctive ways has occurred (Boyer, 1996; Boyer and Drache, 1996; Wade, 1996).

The very intensity of the 'globalization' debate suggests that what is occurring is multi-faceted and contradictory. Levy (2006) argues, indeed, that challenges to the traditional roles of the state offer new options for shaping the economy – and may indeed require them.

> Although economic, technological, social, and ideological changes may produce demands for reduced state intervention, such forces also create opportunities for new kinds of state intervention. There is a Janus-faced or dual-edged quality to these forces; they can push state intervention up as well as down. In other words, state activism can be renewed and replenished, rather than simply eroded.

Similarly, Weiss (1998: 5, 11) challenges the view that laissez faire is the only option: 'state capability has today become an important advantage in international competition .... The ability of nation-states to adapt to internationalization (so-called 'globalization') will continue to heighten rather than diminish national differences in state capacity, as well as the advantages of national economic coordination'.

A caveat is necessary however. First, some political choices may be virtually irreversible. Some domestic restructuring – 'freeing' the central bank from government control, large-scale privatization of public enterprise – can only be undone with immense difficulty if at all. Signing up to supranational treaties which prohibit controls over investment or require the marketization of public services irrevocably constrains the capacity for economic steering (unless, like the US, one is large and powerful enough to disregard such rules with impunity). As Ruggie (2003: 106, 116) puts it,

> the rights enjoyed by transnational corporations have increased manyfold over the past two decades, as a result of multilateral trade agreements, bilateral investment pacts and domestic liberalization ... Globalization was a one-way bet for the business community: governments were needed to create the space within which business could expand and integrate, but they were not otherwise welcome.

Second, the bias of global market forces and the sheer power of the new agglomerations of international capital entail some choices possible only through an uphill struggle, and almost certainly require the very strong counter-force of broad public and labor movement mobilization.

CONCLUSION

Can we have a general theory of the state in industrial relations? Probably not, if only, because there does not exist *a* general theory of the state or of industrial relations. The best we can expect to do is to provide accurate maps of diversity, seek explanations for recurrent patterns and present plausible accounts of causal dynamics.

Three broad points can, however, be asserted. First, in the words of Bordogna and Cella (1999: 28), 'all models of industrial relations, and not just the more "statist" ones, have been characterized throughout their history by complex and sometimes difficult relationships with the state'.

Second, modern states are all embedded, nationally and internationally, within the economic dynamics of capitalism (Jessop, 2002; Kelly, 1998). This does not mean that all governmental action is economically determined (not least because the electoral cycle is shorter than the business cycle), but the overarching influence of a capitalist logic cannot be ignored. 'Industrial battles are fought on the bourse floor as well as the foundry floor: industrial relations as an academic study is trivialized if such connections are not emphasized' (Guille, 1984: 492). This is even truer in an era when the bourse is global and electronic (though when foundries have almost disappeared, at least in the old industrial economies).

Third, universally there are continuing tensions which underlie the priorities of state action: there is always a trade-off between accumulation, pacification and legitimation (or to use a different vocabulary, efficiency, equity and stability) and never 'one best way'.

REFERENCES

Adams, R (1993) 'Regulating Unions and Collective Bargaining: A Global, Historical Analysis of Determinants and Consequences', *Comparative Labor Law Journal* 14 (3): 272–301.

Albert, M. (1993) *Capitalism against Capitalism*. London: Whurr.

Amable, B. (2003) *The Diversity of Modern Capitalism*. Oxford: OUP.

Aoki, M. (2001) *Information, Corporate Governance, and Institutional Diversity: Competitiveness in Japan, the USA, and the Transitional Economies*. Oxford: OUP.

Arts, W. and Gelissen, J. (2002) 'Three Worlds of Welfare Capitalism or More?', *Journal of European Social Policy* 12 (2): 137–158.

Avdagic, S. (2005) 'State-Labour Relations in East Central Europe', *Socio-Economic Review* 3 (1): 25–53.

Baglioni, G. (1987) 'Constants and Variants in Political Exchange', *Labour* 1 (3): 57–91.

Berger, S. and Compston, H. (eds) (2002) *Policy Concertation and Social Partnership in Europe*. New York: Berghahn.

Bordogna, L. and Cella, G.P. (1999) 'Admission, Exclusion, Correction: The Changing Role of the State in Industrial Relations', *Transfer* 5 (1–2): 14–33.

Boyer, R. (1986) *La théorie de la régulation: une analyse critique*. Paris: la Découverte.

Boyer, R. (1996) 'The Convergence Hypothesis Revisited: Globalization but Still the Century of Nations?', in S. Berger and R. Dore (eds), *National Diversity and Global Capitalism*, Ithaca: Cornell UP. pp. 29–59.

Boyer, R. and Drache, D. (1996) 'Introduction', in R. Boyer and D. Drache (eds), *States Against Markets: The Limits of Globalization*, London: Routledge. pp. 1–27.

Carter, B. (2005) 'The Restructuring of National States in the Global Economy' in P. Fairbrother and A. Rainnie (eds), *Globalization, State and Labour*, London: Routledge. pp. 136–150.

Chapon, S. and Euzéby, C. (2002) 'Towards a Convergence of European Social Models?', *International Social Security Review* 55 (2): 37–56.

Coates, D. (2000) *Models of Capitalism: Growth and Stagnation in the Modern Era*. Cambridge: Polity.

Collins, H. (1986) 'Market Power, Bureaucratic Power and the Contract of Employment', *Industrial Law Journal* 15 (1): 1–13.

Cook, M.L. (1998) 'Toward a Flexible Industrial Relations? Neo-Liberalism, Democracy and Labor

Reform in Latin America', *Industrial Relations* 37 (3): 311–36.

Crouch, C. (1993) *Industrial Relations and European State Traditions.* Oxford: Clarendon Press.

Crouch, C. (1995) 'Exit or Voice: Two Paradigms for European Industrial Relations after the Keynesian Welfare State', *European Journal of Industrial Relations* 1 (1): 63–81.

Crouch, C. (1999) 'Employment, Industrial Relations and Social Policy: New Life in an Old Connection', *Social Policy and Administration* 33 (4): 437–57.

Crouch, C. (2005) *Capitalist Diversity and Change: Recombinant Governance and Institutional Entrepreneurs.* Oxford: Oxford UP.

Crouch, C. and Streeck, W. (1997) 'Introduction: The Future of Capitalist Diversity', in C. Crouch and W. Streeck (eds), *The Political Economy of Modern Capitalism: Mapping Convergence and Diversity*, London: Sage. pp. 1–18.

Dauderstädt, M. (2003) 'EU Eastern Enlargement: Extension or End of the European Social Model?' in R. Hoffmann, O. Jacobi, B. Keller and M. Weiss (eds), *European Integration ans a Social Experiemnt in a Globalized World*, Düsseldorf: Hans-Böckler-Stiftung. pp. 69–95.

Deakin, S. and Wilkinson, F. (2004) 'The Evolution of Collective *Laissez-Faire*', *Historical Studies in Industrial Relations* 17: 1–43.

Dore, R. (2000) *Stock-Market Capitalism, Welfare Capitalism: Japan and Germany Versus the Anglo-Saxons.* Oxford: Oxford UP.

Dunlop, J.T (1958) *Industrial Relations Systems.* New York: Holt.

Ebbinghaus B. (1999) 'Does a European Social Model Exist and Can It Survive?' in G. Huemer, M. Mesch and F. Traxler (eds), *The Role of Employer Associations and Labour Unions in the EMU*, Aldershot: Ashgate. pp. 1–26.

Ebbinghaus B. (2002) *Varieties of Social Governance: Comparing the Social Partners' Involvement in Pension and Employment Policies.* Max-Planck-Institut Working Paper. http://www.mpi-fg-koeln.mpg.de/people/es/papers/Ebbinghaus_SocGov_2002.pdf

Esping-Andersen, G. (1990) *The Three Worlds of Welfare Capitalism.* Cambridge: Polity Press.

Esping-Andersen, G. (2002) *Why We Need a New Welfare State.* Oxford: Oxford UP.

Fajertag, G. and Pochet, P. (eds) (2000) *Social Pacts in Europe: New Dynamics.* Brussels: OSE/ETUI.

Falkner, G. and Tálos, E. (1994) 'The Role of the State within Social Policy', *West European Politics* 17 (3): 52–76.

Fernández Jilberto, A.E. and Riethof, M. (2002) 'Labour Relations in the Era of Globalization and Neo-liberal Reforms' in A.E. Fernández Jilberto and M. Riethof (eds), *Labour Relations in Development*, London: Routledge. pp. 1–25.

Frenkel, S. and Peetz, D. (1998) 'Globalization and Industrial Relations in East Asia', *Industrial Relations* 37 (3): 282–310.

Friedman, M. (1962) *Capitalism and Freedom.* Chicago: Chicago UP.

Fusfeld, D. (1979) *The Rise and Repression of Radical Labor, 1877–1918.* Chicago: Kerr.

Gamble, A. (1988) *The Free Economy and the Strong State.* Basingstoke: Macmillan.

Giles, A. (1988) 'Industrial Relations Theory, the State and Politics' in J. Barbash and K. Barbash (eds), *Theories and Concepts in Comparative Industrial Relations*, Columbia: University of South Carolina Press. pp. 123–53.

Gourevitch, P. (1986) *Politics in Hard Times.* Ithaca: Cornell UP.

Guille, H. (1984) 'Industrial Relations Theory: Painting By Numbers?', *Journal of Industrial Relations* 26 (4): 484–95.

Haggard, S. (1986) 'The Newly Industrializing Countries in the International System', *World Politics* 38 (2): 343–70.

Hall, P.A. (1986) *Governing the Economy.* Oxford: Oxford UP.

Hall, P. A. and Soskice, D. (eds) (2001) *Varieties of Capitalism: The Institutional Foundations of Comparative Advantage.* Oxford: Oxford UP.

Hamann, K. and Kelly, J. (2003) 'The Domestic Sources of Differences in Labour Market Policies', *British Journal of Industrial Relations* 41 (4): 639–63.

Hancké, R. and Rhodes, M. (2005) 'EMU and Labor Market Institutions in Europe', *Work and Occupations* 32 (2): 196–228.

Handler, J.F (2004) *Social Citizenship and Workfare in the United States and Western Europe: The Paradox of Inclusion.* Cambridge: Cambridge UP.

Hayek, F.A. (1960) *The Constitution of Liberty.* Chicago UP.

Held, D. (1983) 'Introduction: Central Perspectives on the Modern State' in D. Held (ed.), *States and Societies*, Oxford: Blackwell. pp. 1–55

Hellman, J. Jones, G., Kaufmann, D. and Schankerman, M. (2000) *Measuring Governance, Corruption, and State Capture: How Firms and Bureaucrats Shape the Business Environment in Transition Economies.* World Bank Policy Research Working Paper 2312, April.

Hemerijck, A. and Schludi, M. (2001) 'Welfare Adjustment in Europe: The Transformation of the European Social Model?', in L. Magnusson and J. Ottosson (eds), *Europe: One Labour Market?*, Brussels: PIE - Peter Lang. pp. 21–105.

Hibbs, D.A. (1978) 'On the Political Economy of Long-Run Trends in Strike Activity', *British Journal of Political Science* 8 (2): 153–75.

Hirst, P. and Thompson, G. (1996) *Globalization in Question: The International Economy and the Possibilities of Governance*. Cambridge: Polity.

Hodge, S. and Howe, J. (1999) 'Can the European Social Model Survive?', *European Urban and Regional Studies* 6 (2): 178–84.

Hollingsworth, J. R. and Boyer, R. (1997) 'Coordination of Economic Actors and Social Systems of Production', in J. R. Hollingsworth and R. Boyer (eds), *Contemporary Capitalism: The Embeddedness of Institutions*, Cambridge: Cambridge UP. pp. 1–47.

Howell, C. (2005) *Trade Unions and the State: The Construction of Industrial Relations Institutions in Britain, 1890–2000*. Princeton: Princeton UP.

Howell, J. (2006) *New Democratic Trends in China: Reforming the All-China Federation of Trade Unions*. IDS Working Paper 263. Brighton: IDS.

Hutton, W. (1996) *The State We're in: Why Britain Is in Crisis and How to Overcome It*. London: Vintage.

Hyman, R. (1999) 'National Industrial Relations Systems and Transnational Challenges', *European Journal of Industrial Relations* 5 (1): 89–110.

Hyman, R. (2001) 'The Europeanisation – or the Erosion – of Industrial Relations?', *Industrial Relations Journal* 32 (4): 280–94.

Hyman, R. (2004) 'Is Industrial Relations Theory Always Ethnocentric?' in B.E Kaufman (ed.), *Theoretical Perspectives on Work and the Employment Relationship*, Madison: IRRA. pp. 265–92.

Hyman, R. (2005) 'Trade Unions and the Politics of European Integration', *Economic and Industrial Democracy* 26 (1): 9–40.

Hyman, R. (2006) 'Structuring the Transnational Space: Can Europe Resist Multinational Capital?' in A. Ferner and J. Quintanilla, (eds), *Multinationals, Institutions and the Construction of Transnational Practices*, London: Palgrave Macmillan. pp. 239–54.

Iversen, T. (1999) *Contested Economic Institutions*. Cambridge: Cambridge UP.

Iversen, T. (2005) *Capitalism, Democracy and Welfare*. Cambridge: Cambridge UP.

Iversen, T., Pontusson, J. and Soskice, D. (eds) (2000) *Unions, Employers and Central Banks: Wage Bargaining and Macroeconomic Regimes in an Integrating Europe*. Cambridge: CUP.

Iversen, T. and Pontusson, J. (2000) 'Comparative Political Economy: A Northern European Perspective', in T. Iversen, J. Pontusson and D. Soskice (eds), *Unions, Employers, and Central Banks: Macroeconomic Coordination and Institutional Change in Social Market Economies*, Cambridge: Cambridge UP. pp. 1–37.

Iversen, T. and Wren, A. (1998) 'Equality, Employment and Budgetary Restraint: The Trilemma of the Service Economy', *World Politics*, 50 (4): 507–546.

Jacoby, S.M. (1998) *Modern Manors: Welfare Capitalism since the New Deal*. Princeton: Princeton UP.

Jacoby, S.M. (2004) *The Embedded Corporation: Corporate Governance and Employment Relations in Japan and the United States*. Princeton: Princeton UP.

Jessop, B. (1982) *The Capitalist State*. Oxford: Martin Robertson.

Jessop, B. (1990) *State Theory*. Cambridge: Polity.

Jessop, B. (1999) 'The Changing Governance of Welfare', *Social Policy and Administration* 33 (4): 348–59.

Jessop, B. (2002) *The Future of the Capitalist State*. Cambridge: Polity.

Johnson, C. (1982) *MITI and the Japanese Miracle: The Growth of Industry Policy 1925–1975*. Stanford: Stanford UP.

Kahn-Freund, O. (1954) 'Legal Framework' in A. Flanders and H.A. Clegg (eds), *The System of Industrial Relations in Great Britain*, Oxford: Blackwell. pp. 42–127.

Katz, H. and Darbishire, O. (2000) *Converging Divergences: Worldwide Changes in Employment Systems*. Ithaca: ILR Press.

Katzenstein, P.J. (1985) *Small States in World Markets*. Ithaca: Cornell UP.

Kelly, J. (1998) *Rethinking Industrial Relations: Mobilization, Collectivism and Long Waves*. London: Routledge.

Kerr, C., Dunlop, J.T., Harbison, F.H. and Myers, C. (1960) *Industrialism and Industrial Man*. Cambridge: Harvard UP.

Keynes, J.M. (1936) *The General Theory of Employment, Interest and Money*. London: Macmillan.

Kitschelt, H., Lange, P., Marks, G. and Stephens, J. D. (eds) (1999) *Continuity and Change in Contemporary Capitalism*. Cambridge: Cambridge University Press.

Klare, K. E. (1981) 'Labor Law as Ideology: Toward a New Historiography of Collective Bargaining Law', *Industrial Relations Law Journal* 4 (3): 450–82.

Kochan, T. (1980) *Collective Bargaining and Industrial Relations*. Homewood: Irwin-Dorsey.

Kochan, T. A., Lansbury, R. D. and MacDuffie, J. P. (eds) (1997) *After Lean Production: Evolving Employment Practices in the World Auto Industry*. Ithaca: Cornell UP.

Korpi, W. and Esping-Andersen, G. (1984) 'Social Policy as Class Politics in Post-War Capitalism' in J.H. Goldthorpe (ed.) *Order and Conflict in Contemporary Capitalism*, Oxford: Clarendon. pp. 179–208.

Korpi, W. and Shalev, M. (1979) 'Strikes, Industrial Relations, and Class Conflict in Industrial Societies', *British Journal of Sociology* 30 (2): 164–87.

Kotthoff, H. (1994), *Betriebsräte und Bürgerstatus: Wandel und Kontinuität betrieblicher Mitbestimmung*. Munich and Mering: Rainer Hampp.

Kuruvilla, S. (1995) 'Economic Development Strategies, Industrial Relations Policies and Workplace IR/HR Practices in Southeast Asia' in K. Wever and L. Turner (eds), *The Comparative Political Economy of Industrial Relations*, Madison: IRRA. pp. 115–50.

Kwon, H.-K. (2004) 'Markets, Institutions and Politics under Globalization', *Comparative Political Studies* 37 (1): 88–113.

Lane, C. (1995) *Industry and Society in Europe: Stability and Change in Britain, Germany and France*. Aldershot: Edward Elgar.

Levy, J.D. (2006) 'Introduction: The State also Rises' in J.D. Levy (ed.), *The State after Statism: New State Activities among the Affluent Democracies*. Cambridge: Harvard UP.

Lindblom, C.E. (1977) *Politics and Markets*. New York: Basic Books.

Majone, G. (1994) 'The Rise of the Regulatory State in Europe', *West European Politics* 17 (3): 77–101.

Mann, M. (1986) 'The Autonomous Power of the State' in J.A. Hall (ed.), *States in History*, Oxford: Blackwell. pp. 109–36.

Mann, M. (1997) 'Has Globalization Ended the Rise and Rise of the Nation-State?', *Review of International Political Economy* 4 (3): 472–96.

Marsden D. W. (1999), *A Theory of Employment Systems: Micro-foundations of Societal Diversity*. Oxford: Oxford UP.

Marshall, T. H. (1950) *Citizenship and Social Class*. Cambridge: Cambridge UP.

Masters, M.F. and Delaney, J.T. (2005) 'Organized Labor's Political Scorecard', *Journal of Labor Research* 26 (3): 365–92.

Miguélez, F. and Prieto, C. (eds), (1991) *Las relaciones laborales en España*, Madrid: Siglo XXI.

Offe, C. (1984) *Contradictions of the Welfare State*. London: Hutchinson.

Olson, M. (1982) *The Rise and Decline of Nations*. New Haven: Yale UP.

Öniş, Z. (1991) 'The Logic of the Developmental State', *Comparative Politics* 24 (1): 109–26.

Ost, D. (2000) 'Illusory Corporatism in Eastern Europe: Neoliberal Tripartism and. Postcommunist Class Identities', *Politics and Society* 28 (4): 503–30.

Palme, J. (2001) 'Will Social Europe Work?' in M. Kohli and M. Novak (eds), *Will Europe Work? Integration, Employment and the Social Order*, London: Routledge. pp. 35–51.

Peck, J. (1996) *Work-Place: The Social Regulation of Labor Markets*. New York: Guilford.

Pizzorno, A, (1978) 'Political Exchange and Collective Identity' in C. Crouch and A. Pizzorno (eds), *The Resurgence of Class Conflict in Western Europe Since 1968*. London: Macmillan.

Polanyi, K. (1944) *The Great Transformation: The Political and Economic Origins of our Times*. New York: Farrar and Rinehart.

Poulantzas, N. (1968) *Political Power and Social Classes*. London: NLB.

Ramaux, C. (2006) *Emploi, éloge de la stabilité: L'État social contre la flexicurité*. Paris: Mille et une nuits.

Regini, M. (1984) 'The Conditions for Political Exchange' in J.H. Goldthorpe (ed.), *Order and Conflict in Contemporary Capitalism*, Oxford: Clarendon. pp. 124–42.

Regini, M. (1986) 'Political Bargaining in Western Europe during the Economic Crisis of the 1980s' in O. Jacobi, B. Jessop, H. Kastendiek and M. Regini (eds), *Economic Crisis, Trade Unions and the State*, London: Croom Helm. pp. 61–76.

Regini, M. (1997) 'Still Engaging in Corporatism? Recent Italian Experience in Comparative Perspective', *European Journal of Industrial Relations* 3 (3): 259–78.

Rhodes, M. (2001) 'The Political Economy of Social Pacts: "Competitive Corporatism" and European Welfare Reform' in P. Pierson (ed.), *The New Politics of the Welfare State*, Oxford: OUP. pp. 165–94.

Rimlinger, G.V. (1977) 'Labor and the Government: A Comparative Historical Perspective', *Journal of Economic History* 37 (1): 210–25.

Ruggie, J.G. (1982) 'International Regimes, Transactions, and Change: Embedded Liberalism in the Postwar Economic Order', *International Organization* 36 (2): 379–415.

Ruggie, J. G. (2003) 'Taking Embedded Liberalism Global: The Corporate Connection', in D. Held and M. Koenig-Archibugi (eds), *Taming Globalization: Frontiers of Governance*. Cambridge: Polity. pp. 93–129.

Scharpf, F.W. (2002) 'The European Social Model: Coping with the Challenges of Diversity', *Journal of Common Market Studies* 40 (4): 645–70.

Shonfield, A. (1965) *Modern Capitalism: The Changing. Balance of Public and Private Power*. Oxford: OUP.

Sisson, K., Freyssinet, J., Krieger, H., O'Kelly, K., Schnabel, C. and Seifert, H. (1999) *Pacts for Employment and Competitiveness* http://www.eurofound.eu.int/publications/files/EF9960EN.pdf

Skocpol, T. (1979) *States and Social Revolutions*. Cambridge: Cambridge UP.

Skocpol, T. (1985) 'Bringing the State Back in: Current Research' in P.B. Evans, D. Rueschmeyer and T. Skocpol (eds) *Bringing the State Back in*, Cambridge: Cambridge UP. pp. 3–37.

Standing, G. (1997) 'Globalization, Labour Flexibility and Insecurity', *European Journal of Industrial Relations* 3 (1): 7–37.

Strange, S. (1996) *The Retreat of the State: The Diffusion of Power in the World Economy*. Cambridge: Cambridge UP.

Stråth, B. (1996) *The Organization of Labour Markets*. London: Routledge.

Streeck, W. (1987) 'The Uncertainties of Management in the Management of Uncertainty', *Work, Employment and Society* 1 (3): 281–308.

Streeck, W. (1997) 'German Capitalism: Does it Exist? Can it Survive?' in C. Crouch and W. Streeck (eds), *The Political Economy of Modern Capitalism: Mapping Convergence and Diversity*, London: Sage. pp. 33–54.

Streeck, W. (1998) 'Public Power Beyond the Nation-State', in R. Boyer and D. Drache (eds), *States Against Markets: The Limits of Globalization*, London: Routledge. pp. 299–315.

Streeck, W. (2001) 'International Competition, Supranational Integration, National Solidarity: The Emerging Constitution of "Social Europe"' in M. Kohli and M. Novak (eds), *Will Europe Work? Integration, Employment and the Social Order*, London: Routledge. pp. 21–34.

Streeck, W. and Hassel, A. (2003) 'Trade Unions as Political Actors' in J.T. Addison and C. Schnabel (eds), *International Handbook of Trade Unions*, Cheltenham: Edward Elgar. pp. 335–65.

Streeck, W. and Yamamura, K., (eds) (2001) *The Origins of Nonliberal Capitalism: Germany and Japan in Comparison*. Ithaca: Cornell UP.

Sturmthal, A. (1973) 'Industrial Relations Strategies' in A. Sturmthal and J. Scoville (eds), *The International Labor Movement in Transition*, Urbana: University of Illinois Press. pp. 1–33.

Svensson, T. and Öberg, P.O. (2005) 'Power and Trust: The Mechanisms of Cooperation' in P.O. Öberg and T. Svensson (eds), *Power and Institutions in Industrial Relation Regimes: Political Science Perspectives on the Transition of the Swedish Model*, Stockholm: Arbetslivsinstitutet. pp. 127–59.

Trampusch, C. (2006) 'Industrial Relations and Welfare States: The Different Dynamics of Retrenchment in the Netherlands and Germany', *Journal of European Social Policy* 16 (2): 121–33.

Traxler, F. and Behrens, M. (2002) Collective Bargaining Coverage and Extension Procedures, http://www.eiro.eurofound.eu.int/2002/12/study/tn0212102s.html

van Waarden, F. (1995) 'Government Intervention in Industrial Relations' in J. Van Ruysseveldt, R. Huiskamp and J. van Hoof (eds), *Comparative Industrial and Employment Relations*, London: Sage. pp. 109–33.

Wade, R. (1996) 'Globalization and Its Limits: Reports of the Death of the National Economy Are Greatly Exaggerated', in S. Berger and R. Dore (eds), *National Diversity and Global Capitalism*, Ithaca: Cornell UP. pp. 60–88.

Vaughan-Whitehead, D. (2003) *EU Enlargement Versus Social Europe?: The Uncertain Future of the European Social Model*. Cheltenham: Edward Elgar.

Webb, S. and Webb, B. (1894) *History of Trade Unionism*. London: Longmans.

Webb, S. and Webb, B. (1897) *Industrial Democracy*. London: Longmans.

Weiss, L. (1998) *The Myth of the Powerless State*. Ithaca: Cornell UP.

Western, B. (1998) *Between Class and Market: Postwar Unionization in the Capitalist Democracies*. Princeton: Princeton UP.

Wickham, J. (2002) *The End of the European Social Model: Before it Began?* Dublin: ICTU.

Wilensky, H.L. (2002) *Rich Democracies: Political Economy, Public Policy and Performance*. Berkeley: University of California Press.

Yamamura, K. and Streeck, W. (eds) (2003) *The End of Diversity? Prospects for German and Japanese Capitalism*. Ithaca: Cornell UP.

Zeitlin, J. (1985) 'Shop Floor Bargaining and the State: A Contradictory Relationship' in S. Tolliday and J. Zeitlin (eds) *Shop Floor Bargaining and the State*, Cambridge: CUP. p. 145.

15

The Legal Framework of Employment Relations

Simon Deakin and Wanjiru Njoya

INTRODUCTION

The field of labor law grew up alongside that of industrial relations and they have generally been closely aligned. Industrial or 'employment relations' research has had a major, perhaps even predominant influence, in shaping labor law scholarship. In the first half of the twentieth century, legal scholars and practicing lawyers in Europe and North America looked to industrial sociology to provide them with concepts and data which could be used to challenge the pre-existing legal order, which they saw as restrictive and outdated. This is the approach associated, most notably, with 'legal realism' in the US and the work of the 'social jurists' in Weimar Germany. Labor law continues to reflect these origins and, as a legal sub-discipline, is uniquely open to the influence of the social sciences. Today labor lawyers are taking on the task of engaging not just with the broad sociological tradition as it relates to employment relations, but with political science, gender theory, social psychology, and, above all, economics. Social

scientists are, in turn, devoting increased resources to exploring the impact of legal and related regulatory changes on the issues which concern them, which include organizational performance, labor market outcomes in terms of indicators such as unemployment, poverty and inequality, national economic competitiveness, and cross-national diversity.

To speak of alignment or engagement between labor law and the social sciences is not to assume that the process is without difficulties. In the immediate post-war years, 'industrial pluralism' provided a theoretical framework that united the various aspects of what became known in the Anglophone world as 'industrial relations'. Labor law was part of that field, its place acknowledged, for example, by Kahn-Freund's chapter in the first (1954) edition of *The System of Industrial Relations in Britain*, which was entitled 'Legal Framework'. This contained the influential observation that 'there is, perhaps, no major country in the world in which the law has played a less significant role in the shaping of [collective labor relations] than in Great Britain' (Kahn-Freund, 1954: 47).

Kahn-Freund's belief in the peripheral role of law was not, however, confined to his analysis of the British case; in his 1972 Hamlyn lectures, *Labour and the Law*, in the context of a broad comparative synthesis, he continued to insist that law was a 'secondary force in human affairs, and especially in labour relations' (Kahn-Freund, 1977: 2). This can be read, at one level, as a methodological point: a reminder that there are limits to how far the law can be used in an instrumental way to shape social and economic outcomes. But it was also, implicitly, a reaffirmation of a particular version of the pluralist position, namely the idea that industrial relations systems rested on an autonomous or 'extra-legal' arrangement of social forces. The law, and the state more generally, could support that arrangement of forces in various ways, as it did when it intervened to maintain or extend collective bargaining ('auxiliary' legislation), or to set wages and terms of employment in areas of the economy where collective agreements were weak or non-existent ('regulatory' legislation), but it could not fundamentally alter it.

That view, as we now know, did not long survive the ending of the policy consensus around support for collective bargaining which occurred in most systems, in varying forms, in the course of the 1980s and 1990s. Yet labor law has 'fragmented' as a field not simply because the state no longer supports collective bargaining as the principal or pre-ferred mechanism for regulating employment to the same degree that it did, but also because many additional interests to those of 'subordinated' or dependent labor are taken into account in the framing of labor legislation (Collins, 1997). The expansion of anti-discrimination legislation and the related orientation of labor law toward human rights discourses offer one illustration (Fredman, 1997); another is provided by attempts to use law as a mechanism for ensuring economic 'competitiveness' (Collins, 2001, 2002, 2003), raising employment levels (Ashiagbor, 2005) and bringing about a 'more flexible labor market' (Davies and Freedland, 2007). Labor law, understood as a set of

regulatory techniques, has to accommodate a greater range of objectives, at the same time that its use as an instrument of social and eco-nomic policy is contradicting the 'pluralist' methodological precepts around which many of those techniques were initially developed.

Under these circumstances it is no surprise that labor lawyers regularly talk about the 'crisis' of their discipline and seek to develop new conceptual frameworks for use in legal discourse. One option, increasingly gaining ground, is to widen the scope of the subject so that it in effect becomes 'the law of the labor market', encompassing the variety of mechanisms currently being used, in a legal context, to regulate labor supply and demand. At one level this involves greater attention being paid to the links between labor law and other fields of regulation such as social security law, company law, taxation and active labor market policy. More fundamentally, those who take this view argue that 'a broader focus on "labour market regulation" has a stronger chance of holding the subject together than the existing framework' (Mitchell and Arup, 2006: 16). This is not just about redrawing boundaries, but moving away from

> a traditional labor law subject [which] is still largely organized around *legal* categories (the contract of employment, the law pertaining to bargaining and conciliation and arbitration, the law on trade unions and industrial action, health and safety law and so on), and applies mainly to *legal* reasoning and to generally *legal* materials,

to one in which 'our inquiry will inevitably be directed to key issues in regulatory scholarship – the constitutive role of regu-lation, types of regulatory norms, regulatory techniques, regulatory institutions, and their effectiveness, responsiveness and coherence'. This necessitates a greater recognition of 'the importance of interdisciplinary studies in understanding the need for particular legal modifications in labor markets, and understanding the evolution of labor law' (Arup and Mitchell, 2006: 17–18).

In one sense this simply takes us back to the origins of labor law which was, after all, founded in a similar spirit of interdisciplinary openness (Finkin, 2006). However, opening up legal discourse and analysis to outside influence was only part of the process which took place in the first decades of the twentieth century; the refashioning of legal concepts in the light of what were then seen as new social policy goals was also important, and this, paradoxically perhaps, focused attention back on to those very doctrinal structures which formed the core of 'formalist' legal analysis.

Kahn-Freund famously enjoined labor lawyers to follow the example of Sinzheimer in going 'through' not 'round' the law, by which he meant that legal studies should not seek to abandon conceptual exposition as one of its core tasks (Kahn-Freund: 1981: 77). It is indeed difficult to see how labor law could survive as a discrete field if this were not one of its central objectives; and it is therefore appropriate that the conceptual reformulation of labor law's basic categories, including the employment contract or relationship, is currently the focus of a considerable body of work (Freedland, 2003; Collins et al., 2007). For sociologists, economists, and others who are concerned with the social operation or functioning of legal rules and institutions, the internal structure of labor law might seem to be less of a pressing issue. Yet, a unified approach to the subject would recognize that labor law is not simply a cipher for wider social or economic forces, but an autonomous institutional phenomenon, which influences the way in which policy is translated into formal legislation, and the way in which rules operate in practice. To that extent, many of the internal workings of the labor law system – not simply the institutional processes by which disputes are resolved, but the forms of legislation and the conceptual categories which are used by lawyers to frame their own discourse – are, in principle, of importance to social scientists seeking to understand the implications of legal regulation for their own areas of inquiry.

In the context of a collection of papers designed to provide an overview of research in the employment relations field, our aim, as labor lawyers, is to reassess the place of labor law in that wider area of study and to argue the case for labor law's importance

to social scientists. We will not attempt to review the vast empirical literature, mostly consisting of work by social scientists, which examines aspects of the operation of legal rules in practice. This is, indeed a huge field. The study of the way legal rules work in practice has a very long tradition in industrial relations scholarship, which, if we just consider the British context, can be traced right back to the pioneering work of the Webbs and their contemporaries on the poor law (Webb and Webb, 1910; 1927a; 1927b), factory legislation (Hutchins and Harrison, 1911), and the first minimum wage laws (Tawney, 1914; 1915). After a mid-century lull during the period of collective laissez-faire, increasing statutory intervention in the labor market in the 1970s led to seminal analyses of the operation of the *Industrial Relations Act* 1971 (Weekes et al., 1975) and the unfair dismissal legislation of the 1970s (Dickens et al., 1985), as well as a series of studies carried out under the auspices of the (then) Social Science Research Council's program on 'monitoring labour legislation' (see Hepple and Brown, 1981). In the course of the 1990s and 2000s this type of work, in many cases sponsored by the Department of Employment and the Department of Trade and Industry, became both more quantitative and more explicitly policy-orientated, and it is now normal practice for Parliamentary legislation to be accompanied by regulatory impact assessments of considerable detail and sophistication. A survey of empirical work concerning the operation of labor laws since 1997, carried out in 2005, provided an overview of the findings of a large number of academic papers on subjects ranging from working time regulation, the national minimum wage, trade union recognition, European works councils, non-standard work, and work-life balance legislation. But this study also found that 'there is a relatively limited amount of interdisciplinary/multi-disciplinary research bringing together academic lawyers and those trained in social science'. This was because, on the one hand, 'labor law research and writing has been constrained by traditional methods', while, on the other, industrial relations scholars 'still investigate labour markets and workplace relations focusing on areas where legal regulation is intended, or could be expected, to play a role (for example, employers' labour use strategies; worker representation) without actively exploring or commenting on this aspect' (Dickens and Hall, 2005: 32).

Against this background, our objective is to give an analytical account of the principal institutional features of labor law as a form of legal regulation, from an interdisciplinary perspective which takes into account both the internal workings of the labor law system and the social and economic context within which it has evolved. To that end we will seek to analyze, in the manner of an internal or 'immanent' critique (Supiot, 1994), the categories which are generally used within labor law discourse to describe the social and economic relations of employment; to account for their emergence and evolution in historical terms; to consider the origins of their diversity across different national systems; and to consider future prospects for convergence or divergence.

We begin by tracing the historical emergence of the contract of employment as the basic building block of labor law in different jurisdictions. We then look at current developments in relation to the individual employment relationship, before turning to a consideration of collective labor relations. This approach is justified by the continuing relevance of some of the core concepts, and by the need to consider just how far they are changing as a consequence of external pressures, and why. We conclude by offering some observations on the prospects for labor law in a period of organizational and institutional transition.

ORIGINS OF THE MODERN LABOR MARKET: THE EVOLUTION OF THE CONTRACT OF EMPLOYMENT

One way in which labor law maintains its boundaries with other subjects is captured by the proposition that labor law is principally concerned with relationships of so-called 'dependent' or 'subordinated' labor, that is, relations between *employers* and *employees*. The concept of 'subordination' is most explicit in civil law systems but is present in the common law too under different terminology (such as the 'control', 'integration', and 'economic reality' tests used to denote employee status). This concept defines the legitimate scope of managerial prerogative – the employer's right to give orders and to require loyalty of the employee – while also providing protection to employees against certain risks. These include physical risks (the domain of early factory legislation and now of occupational health and safety) and economic risks (such as interruptions to earnings and employment from sickness, unjust dismissal, termination on economic grounds, or old age). The genuinely *self-employed* are excluded from this type of regulation, on the grounds that they enjoy autonomy over the form and pace of work and over arrangements for their own economic security. In this way, labor law is closely aligned with social security law and tax law, which share with it many of the same risk-shifting functions.

The focus on the relationship of employment seems self-evident as the basis for labor law, but it is in fact both a controversial idea and an historically contingent concept. The twin ideas that work relations under capitalism are 'contractual', and that they can be captured using the term 'employment', are more recent than is often supposed. There is evidence that in the first phases of industrialization in Europe and America, labor was not uniformly or even generally 'free' and that contractual concepts played a limited role in defining the parties' mutual obligations. The employment model, as we have since come to know it, was initially confined to a small segment of the wage- or salary-dependent labor force. The manner of the emergence of the 'contract of employment' to occupy a central place in modern labor law systems is of interest from the point of view of the relationship between law and industrialization, and from the perspective of comparative legal development under capitalism.

The common law: Britain and America

The institutional roots of a market economy in Britain can be found in the later middle ages and in the early modern period; the stimulus provided to innovations in governance by such events as the Black Death (Palmer, 1993) and the dissolution of the monasteries (Woodward, 1980) have been extensively documented. England already had a mature *national* legal system at this stage, the significance of which for its economic development is only now beginning to be understood. However, wage labor in the modern sense of that term did not exist at this point. The terms used by the pivotal Statute of Artificers of 1562 and the poor law legislation of this period, including 'servant' and 'laborer', have to be treated with care; it would be a mistake to see them as simply the functional equivalents of the much later concept of the 'contract of employment' (Deakin and Wilkinson, 2005: Chapter 2).

The century after 1750 which is conventionally associated with the period of the 'industrial revolution' in Britain was, in addition to being a time of rapid technological and social change, also a period of legal innovation; hence Toynbee's suggestion, made in the 1860s, that the essence of the industrial revolution was not to be found in the adoption of steam power or the advent of factory labor, but in 'the substitution of competition for the medieval regulations which had previously controlled the production and distribution of wealth' (Toynbee, [1864] 1969: 92). Competition in the labor market was promoted through the repeal of the wage-fixing laws and apprenticeship regulations which had contained in the Statute of Artificers (in 1813 and 1814 respectively). It might be thought that this would have led to the contractualization of labor relations and hence to the recognition in the courts of the concept of the contract of employment as the paradigm legal form of the work relationship. However, this is not what happened. For some

occupational groups, a type of employment contract did indeed emerge, to which the courts attached status obligations in the form of implied contractual terms. The common law action for wages due as earned under the contract, and the action for damages for wrongful dismissal, can be identified in cases from the early decades of the nineteenth century (Freedland, 1976). However, these decisions were almost without exception based on the employment of managerial, clerical, or professional workers. Manual workers fell under the distinctive legal regime of the *Master and Servant* Acts, under which breach of the service contract was a criminal offence, for which thousands of workers were fined or imprisoned each year up to the 1870s (Deakin and Wilkinson, 2005: 61–74).

The master-servant model was not a hold-over from the corporative regime of the Statute of Artificers and old poor law. On the contrary, most of the disciplinary powers used by employers and courts were additions from the mid-eighteenth century and early nineteenth century, the result of parliamentary action to bolster the prerogatives of the new employer class. The nature of the paradigm legal form of the labor relationship under early industrial capitalism in England was statutory and hierarchical, rather than common law and contractual. The legal influence of the master-servant regime was just as far reaching as its considerable social and economic impact. The model of a command relation, with an open-ended duty of obedience imposed on the worker, and reserving far-reaching disciplinary powers to the employer, spilled over into the common law, so that long after the repeal of the last of the *Master and Servant* Acts in 1875, not just the terminology of master and servant but also many of the old assumptions of unmediated control were still being applied by the courts as they developed the common law of employment (Hay and Craven, 2004).

US employment law took a divergent path at this point, but one which also resulted in the emergence of a general model for the employment relationship based on contract. By the early twentieth century almost all states had adopted an 'employment at will' rule, under which the contract of employment could be terminated by either party on a moment's notice, without giving a reason. This conferred almost no job security upon the employee. Where the British and American systems diverged in the final decades of the nineteenth century was over the question of whether *all* employment relationships should be presumed to be at will unless the contrary were stated. The American courts, following *Payne* v. *Western & Atlantic Railroad*[1] and in particular *Martin* v. *New York Life Insurance Co.*[2] which concerned a middle-class employee, began to apply just such a general presumption. The extension of the at-will model was primarily a product of a constitutional debate over the legitimacy of social legislation. The question of the construction of the terms of employment contracts took on a general significance, far beyond the immediate question of rights under the wage-work bargain between employer and employee (Njoya, 2007). No such presumption developed in Britain, principally because there was no equivalent to the constitutional dimension to the issue which arose in the US.

In Britain, the advent of the welfare state and the extension of collective bargaining, neither of which was subject to constitutional constraints, saw employment law taking a different path (see Deakin and Wilkinson, 2005: 86–100). However, the persistence of the master-servant model, and the enduring influence of the principle of less eligibility in the long transition from the poor law to social security, which was completed only in the 1940s, delayed the advent of the modern 'contract of employment'; if that idea is identified, above all, with a classification of labor relations which incorporates the 'binary divide' between employees and the self-employed, we have to look to the middle of the twentieth century to find it in British labor law. The first statutes to adopt the binary divide in a clear form were concerned with income taxation and social insurance. The *National Insurance Act* 1946, which incorporated Beveridge's plan for social security, marked the turning point; its clear division between those

employed under a 'contract of service', a term which gradually became interchangeable with the term 'contract of employment', and those who were 'self-employed' or independent contractors, was then carried over into early employment protection statutes in the 1960s. The term 'contract of employment' is a recent innovation in British labor law, just as it is in civil law jurisdictions.

The civil law: French and German models

There is evidence from the civil law systems to support the suggestion that the modern contract of employment is an invention of the late nineteenth and early twentieth centuries, associated with the rise of the integrated enterprise and the beginnings of the welfare or social state. The emerging forms of wage labor were grafted on to the traditional Roman law concept of the *locatio conductio* in the post-revolutionary codes of the early 1800s. The adoption of contractual forms and language was more explicit than in the British case at this time. In adapting the model of the *locatio*, the drafters of the codes were grouping labor relationships with other types of contracts, the effect being to stress that, in common with them, they were based on exchange (Veneziani, 1986: 32). Labor, or in some versions labor power – as, for example, in the German term *Arbeitskraft* – thereby became a commodity which was linked to price (not necessarily the 'wage'), through the contract. The notion of the personal 'subordination' of the worker was absent from the formulae used by the codes (Simitis, 2000). The reality was rather different, since more or less all systems acknowledged the power of the employer to give orders, to issue rules which had binding force (in the form, for example, of the French *livret* or work book), and to retain the worker in employment, without a testimonial, until they considered the work to be complete. However, this body of legislation and practice was formally separated from the general private law of the codes, and administered by police authorities and specialized labor tribunals; as a result, it remained under-developed from a conceptual point of view.

The term contract of employment or, in France, *contrat de travail*, only entered general usage in the 1880s. The main impetus for its adoption was an argument by employers in larger enterprises that the general duty of obedience should be read into all industrial hirings. However, once the term became established, it was used in turn of the century legislation on industrial accidents (Veneziani, 1986: 64), and its adoption was promoted and systematized by commissions of jurists charged with developing a conceptual frame-work for collective bargaining and worker protection (ibid.: 68). At the core of the concept was a notion of 'subordination' in which the open-ended duty of obedience was traded off in return for the acceptance and absorption by the enterprise of a range of social risks (see Cottereau, 2000, 2002; Petit and Sauze, 2006). In Germany, a similar process of evolution can be traced, through which adaptations of the *locatio* model in the codes of the nineteenth century, culminating in the German Civil Code of 1896 (on which, see Sims, 2002), were in their turn modified to produce the modern employment relationship or *Arbeitsverhältnis* in the legislation of the Weimar period, with the advent of legal recognition for collective bargaining and social legislation.

Both France and Germany, then, experienced the late development of the contract of employment. What emerged, however, were forms which reflected the distinctive legal cultures of the two systems (Mückenberger and Supiot, 2000). In the French-origin systems, the power of the state to regulate conditions of work was instantiated within the legal system through the concept of *ordre public social*, that is, a set of minimum, binding conditions which applied as a matter of general law to the employment relationship. The implicit logic of this idea was that in recognizing the formal contractual equality of the parties to the employment relationship, the state also assumed, by way of symmetry, a responsibility for establishing a form of protection for the individual worker who was thereby placed in a position of 'juridical subordination'. In German-influenced systems, on the other hand, a 'communitarian' conception of the enterprise qualified the role of the individual contract. In contrast to the French approach, German law came to recognize the 'personal subordination' of the worker in the form of 'factual adhesion to the enterprise' (*Tatbestand*), a process which conferred 'a status equivalent to membership of a community' (Supiot, 1994: 18).

THE CONTRACT OF EMPLOYMENT TODAY: CONCEPTUAL EVOLUTION AND CHANGE

Although the emergence of a coherent model of the contract of employment was a considerable achievement, and a progressive one, for its time, its legacy has been problematic. We will consider two main challenges currently facing the law in its attempt to regulate individual aspects of the employment relationship. First, we look at why the heavy reliance on the notion of 'contract' poses difficulties in regulating the termination of employment. We note the special case of the employment relationship in the large, publicly held company. Second, we consider the question of balancing job security with flexibility, profitability, and competitiveness, a key issue in determining the scope of employment protection legislation. Economic dismissals remain largely unregulated by law in the UK, on the basis that such regulation would impose rigidity and exacerbate unemployment. We consider the social implications of this approach, contrasting it with some of the approaches in continental Europe and the US, and suggest that redefining the conceptual basis of the employment relationship may provide a means of ensuring a better balance between job security and economic flexibility.

Shifts in the contractual foundations of the employment relationship

One of the principal regulatory difficulties currently facing labor law is that of identifying the concepts best suited to defining and describing the employment relationship at a time when organizational form is in flux. As the organization and social context of work change, so does the nature of the employment relationship and the law constantly faces the challenge of adapting its own conceptual framework in response to these changes. As we have seen, the law generally conceives of the employment relationship as a *contract* between employer and employee. This is coupled with the notion of freedom of contract (based on the assumptions of perfect rationality, foresight, and information on the part of both employer and employee) as well as the assumption that both parties have equal bargaining power. These assumptions are particularly influential in the context of individual aspects of labor law – it is usually only in the context of collective action that these assumptions can be more directly addressed, and mitigated. In terms of the individual employment relationship one of the most pressing concerns is that of job security. In theory freedom of contract allows both parties to agree on terms that grant employment security to the worker, but in practice inequality of bargaining power and the prevalence of 'standard form' contracts mean that most workers are not in a position to enter into an independent negotiation of the terms and conditions of employment. Moreover, many atypical workers and semi-dependent workers are left outside the framework of the 'contract of employment' altogether. They do not fall within the strict legal definition of 'employee', and so are often not covered by employment protection laws.

As we have seen, the conceptual framework of labor law is shaped both by private law concepts, principally that of contract, and by social legislation. In relation to job security, the common law action for 'wrongful dismissal' is an action for breach of contract. 'Wrongful' in the common law refers simply to the failure to give reasonable notice of dismissal, and does not include any general notion of unfairness. The traditional rule in common law jurisdictions

was that the employer would be within its rights in terminating the contract for any reason or none at all, subject to giving the requisite notice or paying a monetary sum to the employee in lieu of notice. The only exception would be where the terms of the contract specify that there will be no dismissal except for just, or specified, causes.

Yet, the common law is not static. In the US, there have been recent suggestions that the common law might develop to allow breaches of contractual terms other than the notice term to give rise to a wrongful dismissal claim, overcoming or at least qualifying the concept of employment at will (Stone, 2007). In the UK, the implied term of 'mutual trust and confidence', under which the employer has an obligation to deal with the employee in good faith, has been seen as a potential way forward in developing norms preventing dismissal without just cause (Brodie, 1996). Similarly, in the US, most states have developed limited modifications or exceptions to the at-will rule on the basis of an implied covenant of good faith and fair dealing stone.

At the same time, there are limits to how far the common law can go. In English law, although the implied obligation to maintain mutual trust and confidence has had a considerable impact on the interpretation of the employer's duty in the course of a *continuing* employment relationship, so far this obligation has had little, if any, discernible effect on job security in terms of preventing dismissals. The main reason for this is that the scope of the implied term of mutual trust and confidence is limited, so that it applies during the continuing employment relationship but does not extend to the 'manner of dismissal'. The courts continue to draw a careful distinction between the action for damages for breach of the implied term of mutual trust and confidence as an ordinary action for breach of contract, on the one hand, and the action for wrongful dismissal on the other. Hence, as Freedland writes (2005: 361), 'the view that wrongful dismissal is wrongful, and remediable in damages, only because of its prematurity, its denial of a promised period of notice or fixed term of employment, has been and continues to be the dominant approach of English common law'.

Unfair dismissal legislation

The notion of 'unfairness' in dismissal had to be introduced by legislative intervention in virtually all systems; it was not a natural offshoot or development of private law norms or concepts. Unfair or unjust dismissal legislation originated in continental European systems in the inter-war period and in the decade immediately after 1945, and has since been adopted in some form by most systems with the exception of the US. ILO Convention No. 158 defines its core elements which include a requirement that the employer should normally have a valid reason for terminating the employee's employment. Only one US state (Montana) has enacted an unjust dismissal statute, even though a model code is available in the form of the *Model Employment Termination* Act (1991) which was drafted under the auspices of the National Conference of Commissioners for Uniform State Laws. However, at the federal level there is significant legislation in the area of human-rights dismissals; this includes federal statutes governing discrimination on the grounds of sex, race, age, and disability. The levels of compensation payable by employers to victims of discrimination often contain punitive elements, and far outstrip the sums which could be paid in most European jurisdictions.

In Britain, unfair dismissal legislation dates from 1971. Although this legislation was informed by the standards laid down by the ILO, it was also heavily influenced by a perceived need to streamline industrial relations procedures at plant level and to encourage employers to put in place disciplinary procedures for dealing with individual disputes, one effect of which would be to reduce unofficial strikes over dismissals. The subsequent evolution of unfair dismissal law was influenced by the growing debate over flexibility, although deregulatory legislation of the 1980s made only a marginal impact on the main body of unfair dismissal protection, which more or less remained intact. Over time, certain aspects of protection have been strengthened, in particular those relating to the category of inadmissible reasons or 'human rights' dismissals (Deakin and Morris, 2005: Chapter 5).

At the outset of the debate over labor flexibility in the early 1980s, most of the civil law systems began from a position of having strong dismissal laws, in contrast to those in the common law world which were less highly developed. As efforts to increase flexibility in the labor market intensified, the civil law systems have, in varying degrees, loosened controls over managerial decision-making, but have done so not through changes of a far-reaching nature to the core of dismissal law, but through limited exemptions in favor of 'atypical' forms of work. A number of legislative initiatives throughout the 1980s and 1990s sought to encourage the growth of part-time and fixed-term employment by exempting employers from dismissal protection in these cases and by subsidizing hirings under these contracts through other means such as the tax-benefit system. The balance of opinion is that these reforms may have had a positive but minor overall impact on employment levels (OECD, 2004); but they have also led to an increase in the numbers employed in flexible or 'atypical' forms of work, and hence to growing segmentation between a secure 'core' and a less secure 'periphery' of workers. In reaction to this negative development, several recent EU initiatives have sought to strengthen protection against inequality and structural discrimination at work. These include measures aimed at enhancing opportunities for temporary and part-time work at the same time as entrenching a principle of equality of treatment between these forms of work and full-time, long-term employment, and recognition at EU level of a wider principle of non-discrimination in employment.

Economic dismissals

The dismissal of workers for 'economic' reasons is one of the most controversial areas of legal intervention into the employment relationship. The justification for limiting the protective role of the law in this context is that when employing entities undergo organizational restructuring, the sustainability of the enterprise must take priority over job security. Thus the law generally respects the 'managerial prerogative' to dismiss workers as a cost-cutting measure. This approach is reflected across international law, European law, and UK law. For instance the ILO acknowledges that the 'operational require-ments of the undertaking' may justify termi-nation of employment (ILO Recommendation No 119 of 1963, Art 2(1) and Art 12). EU law, in the context of the Acquired Rights Directive, allows dismissal for 'economic, technical or organizational reasons' as a defense to an unfair dismissal claim. At common law, in the words of Lord Hoffmann, 'employment law requires a balancing of the interests of employers and employees, with proper regard not only to the individual dignity and worth of the employees but also to the general economic interest'.[3] Similarly, in the US economic dismissals are justifiable in the context of collective bargaining law on grounds of 'business necessity'.[4] The current law governing employment security therefore contains ample scope for flexibility, often to the detriment of job security.

It may be questioned why the law governing termination of the employment contract offers workers virtually no protection to the individual worker when the dismissal is for economic reasons. Economic dismissals during corporate restructuring geared toward boosting short-term share value arguably impose significant social costs on workers and their communities with knock-on effects for other industries and the economy as a whole. Concerns about job security in this context are heightened where there is no suggestion of 'fault' on the part of the workers – blame is laid instead on impersonal market forces, which may intensify the sense of social displacement felt by those affected particularly where the job cuts are not perceived to be inevitable. In response to these concerns, the suggestion that job security

should be enhanced is countered on the basis that job security for the employed would allow core workers to become entrenched in their positions, resulting in rigid labor markets in which certain marginalized groups, the peripheral and atypical workers referred to earlier, are perpetually unemployed. A related argument is that employment protection legislation may impede the creation of new jobs, as such legislation potentially 'increases the costs for the employer of adjusting their workforce and can create a barrier to hiring' (OECD, 2006: paragraph 3.3). These perspectives suggest that job security should therefore be understood as simply extending to the availability of jobs in the economy as a whole and especially widening access to employment opportunities, rather than being concerned with job protection for the employed in their specific or current positions. However, while the concerns about the entrenchment of secure core workers is legitimate, recent empirical studies published by the OECD 'generally have not found robust evidence for a significant direct effect of [employment protection legislation] on unemployment' (ibid.). The risks of adverse effects on opportunities for the unemployed appear to arise only when job protection is 'too strict', and not simply from the mere existence of job protection. The OECD therefore recommends that the implementation of such legislation should be 'quick, predictable and distort labor turnover as little as possible', and 'should be carefully coordinated with reforms to the unemployment benefits system … so as to reconcile so far as is possible labor market flexibility with security for workers' (ibid.).

The differences in levels of job protection in different jurisdictions partly reflect varia-tions in the overall economic, political, and institutional context of each country. This context has in turn given rise to different responses to the issue of how to regulate the employment relationship. Despite the fact that industrialization and the increasing sophistication of production methods have brought about a shift in the organization of work globally, labor relations and labor laws continue to diverge sharply in different jurisdictions and so far there is no reason to expect this trend to change. The UK and US have among the lowest levels of employment security legislation in the world (Botero et al., 2004). This is largely attributable to the continuing influence of private law concepts, in particular freedom of contract, as already noted. Conversely, in most EU member states employment protection has its origin in industrial traditions which, while they conceptualize employment as being founded upon a private law contract, *also* define it, as we have seen, as a special relationship regulated by principles of public law or mandatory public regulation (*ordre public social*), which grant workers a form of quasi-constitutional entitlement to remain in their jobs unless there is just cause for their dismissal. For instance in German law dismissal, even with notice, must be 'socially justified' otherwise it is 'illegal'; selection of employees for redundancy 'must take into account so called "social aspects" [so] that those who suffer the most from the effects of the dismissal should be the last ones to be dismissed … social justice for each individual case' (Weiss, 1998: 86–8, discussing the Act on Dismissal Protection of 1951 (s.1)).

Criticisms that the European approach to job security is too rigid have prompted reform proposals by the European Commission. Although the Commission still refers to 'full employment' as one of the goals of its employment agenda, this is now giving way to concepts such as adaptability, responsiveness, and employability. Flexibility on the workers' side is understood as the workers' capacity to anticipate change and move readily from one type of job to another. As European employment policy emphasizes the creation of 'more and better jobs' the focus is on ensuring that workers who lose their jobs will find alternative opportunities within a dynamic and vibrant economy.

Yet there are inherent difficulties in this focus on flexibility. For many highly skilled workers who have invested years of work in a particular firm or trade it may prove impossible to find an alternative of *comparable worth*, an effect often felt for the remainder of the worker's career. Where the worker is compelled to take the next best alternative, empirical studies demonstrate 'substantial and long-lasting effects of job loss on annual earnings and wages' over the long term, from which many workers never recover (Topel, 1990: 181). This has been defined as the real cost of job loss, that is, 'the difference between the utility value of being in the current job and that of the next best alternative' (Green and McIntosh, 1998: 365–6). The question then becomes whether the overall social cost of job loss is necessary in the interests of efficiency or overall wealth benefits to society. In situations where jobs are cut in order to boost short-term gains for the firm's shareholders it could be said that the corporation is 'effectively transferring to the public sector the costs of maintaining these displaced workers' (Singer, 1993: 496).

Alternatives to contract: the use of property-based concepts to enhance legal job security

Several commentators have noted that there are inherent difficulties in relying on the concept of 'contract' to define the employment relationship, and that there is a good case to be made for moving beyond contract. In the context of job security in the firm the concept of property may prove more helpful than that of contract, in the following way. Understood as an analogy rather than as a 'category' of property rights as such, the notion of property implies that the employee has a claim of 'ownership' in the form of an expectation of continued employment without fear of arbitrary dispossession (Meyers, 1964). Compensation for wrongful or unfair dismissal would be based not simply on the 'notice period' defined by the contract, but on the real value of the job lost. This approach is particularly helpful in understanding the employment relationship in the large firm. The dominant presumption is that the corporation is owned exclusively by its shareholders (who have rights of property in the firm) and that the workers' interests are fully defined by and limited to the terms of their employment contracts. However, a historical analysis of the employment relationship reveals that property rights have not traditionally been associated *exclusively* with the rights or status of the employer. Notions of respect for private property have long been invoked to support the rights of *employees* (Njoya, 2007).

Recognition of the value of firm-specific human capital has come to acquire important implications for law reform. The statement in the European Commission's *Employment in Europe* (2006, at 81 *et seq*), that 'workers feel better protected by a support system in case of unemployment than by employment protection legislation' presents only part of the picture. It remains the case that job security in the job actually held is paramount: 'a secure job is still an essential aspect, for most individuals, of their long-term economic security' (Deakin and Morris, 2005: 569). In drawing the boundaries of its regulatory scope the law already recognizes that not all dismissals which take place during corporate restructuring are justifiable, and that in certain situations employees may have property-like claims on the firm, for instance interests which go beyond the terms of their employment contracts. The best example of this in the UK is the *Transfer of Undertakings (Protection of Employment) Regulations* 2006, which recognize that workers have a claim to remain in their jobs with a particular firm when it is sold. Such a proprietary approach is more compatible with an understanding of employment security as much more than ensuring that workers are 'adaptable' and 'employable' in different jobs. It goes further by understanding employment security as 'a form of regulatory intervention designed to protect workers against arbitrary managerial decision-making', a protection which recognizes the valuable long-term relationships which arise between employees and the firms for which they work (Deakin and Morris, 2005: 388; Njoya, 2007).

COLLECTIVE LABOR RELATIONS: WORKER REPRESENTATION AND CORPORATE GOVERNANCE

Worker representation and the coverage of labor standards

Representation of workers through independent trade unions which negotiated pay and conditions of employment on their behalf with an employer or groups of employers became the predominant model around which the collective labor law of the twentieth century developed. It is reflected in the core principles of freedom of association of the ILO and in the practice of many systems. However, systems differ in the nature and extent of state encouragement for collective bargaining provided, the levels at which bargaining takes place, and the mechanisms for determining the representativeness of unions.

There is a case for seeing a division of systems along the lines suggested by the 'varieties of capitalism' approach (Hall and Soskice, 2001). In so-called 'liberal market' systems, the predominant form of employee representation is collective bargaining between employers and trade unions. From a legal perspective, collective bargaining operates in manner akin to setting up a contractual mechanism for negotiation. This can be done by the employer voluntarily recognizing a particular union or unions, or through various regulatory mechanisms which, as in the US since the 1930s, have required the employer to negotiate with a certified bargaining agent which can demonstrate that it has majority support in the relevant bargaining unit. On the face of it, the US system offers strong legal support for a union which can demonstrate in a workplace election that it has majority support in a bargaining unit. The union becomes the certified bargaining agent for that unit, and as a result has a statutory monopoly over bargaining for pay and conditions in respect of the employees in question. However, this arrangement, put in place by the federal *National Labor Relations* (or Wagner) Act of 1935 and subsequently amended by the

Taft-Hartley Act of 1947, is less favorable to unions than it might seem. Enforcing the employer's duty to bargain is often problematic, and employers are permitted to deploy a powerful array of weapons in frustrating unionization drives and in pressing for decertification. Attempts to reform the law so as to allow alternative forms of employee representation to emerge and to soften the rigidly adversarial quality of the certification process have failed. The deficiencies of the law are thought to be a contributing factor in the decline of union density in the US to its current level of only 7 per cent in the private-sector, compared with 36 per cent in the public sector where institutional support for collective bargaining is stronger (Kolins Givan, 2007).

In Britain, for most of the twentieth century, the 'recognition' of trade unions by employers – agreement to enter into collective bargaining over pay and conditions, among other things – was a matter of consent rather than of statutory imposition. The law imposed no duty to bargain and, conversely, played no role in certifying unions as bargaining agents, hence Kahn-Freund's insistence on seeing its role as 'marginal' in relation to autonomous sources of regulation. The law preserved a wide freedom to strike, and to lock-out, by granting unions and individuals immunities from liability in tort for organizing strike action. The absence of direct legal intervention was seen to be the system's principal strength. However, since the 1970s, the system of collective bargaining has undergone a process of decline, with falling coverage of collective agreements (down to below 40 per cent from over 80 per cent in 1979) and falling union density (now below 30 per cent from a peak of nearly 60 per cent in 1979). It is not entirely clear that the legal reforms of the 1980s, which cut back on the freedom to strike and encouraged decentralization of collective bargaining, were the critical factor in precipitating this decline, but there is some evidence that they were (Freeman and Pelletier, 1990). Since 2001 Britain also has had a system of compulsory recognition, based superficially on aspects of the US model, but with some

critical differences, in particular the greater role accorded to encouragement for voluntary agreements outside the framework of the legislation (Wood and Godard, 1999).

Whatever the degree of state compulsion used to bring about recognition or certification, there are strict limits to how far collective bargaining can go in relation to the core areas of managerial 'prerogative', so that it stops short of co-decision making or codetermination (for the US, see Weiler, 1990; for Britain, Wedderburn, 1986: Chapter 4). Outside those areas where employers concede collective bargaining or have it forced on them by public regulation, there is no legal obligation to deal with employee representatives. In their emphasis on collective bargaining as a form of regulated contractual co-ordination, these systems may continue to be characterized as *voluntarist*.

Voluntarism at the level of the enterprise tends to go hand in hand with a partial approach to regulation at market level. Thus although both Britain and the US have national minimum wage laws and some legislation governing basic terms and conditions such as working hours, the tendency has been for statutory regulation to impose only minimal constraints on the employment contract outside those sectors which are governed by collective bargaining. As collective bargaining has shrunk, since the 1950s in America and the late 1970s in Britain, so the uneven and *partial* character of labor market regulation has been accentuated within these systems (for the US, see Weiler, 1990; for the UK, see Deakin and Wilkinson, 1991).

'Co-ordinated market' systems, on the other hand, tend to combine an *integrative* approach to the role of employees in the enterprise with *universalism* in labor market regulation. 'Integration' implies the incorporation of employee voice directly into the decision-making structures of the firm. In many civil law systems, particularly those located in Western Europe, sectoral bargaining ensures that a basic floor is set to terms and conditions of employment, with legal support. In addition, legislation normally mandates some form of collective employee representation at plant or enterprise level.

The function of works councils (in Germany, in particular) is not (on the whole) to enter into collective bargaining, but rather to engage in the explicitly cooperative goal of 'codetermination' of the working process. This involves representing employee voice to the employer and monitoring the application of laws and agreements within the workplace, functions which are intended to complement collective bargaining operating at a multi-employer level. In Germany, collective bargaining between trade unions and associations of employers to set basic terms and conditions mostly takes place at industry or sector level; in that sense, codetermination within the enterprise is complementary to trade union autonomy both from management interests and from state interference at industry level. The effects of collective agreements can be extended to non-federated employers by statutory order. In France, where enterprise committees and other representative bodies operate at enterprise level in rather different fashion from the German works council (they have fewer legal powers and also have employer representation), we again find strong multi-employer bargaining at sectoral level. France also has a statutory minimum wage which is linked to wage (and not just price) increases and legislation on working time and other aspects of terms and conditions of employment which is enforced by a well-resourced labor inspectorate.

Information and consultation of employee representatives

A key element of the continental European model is the obligation of the employer to enter into processes of 'information and consultation' with the workforce representatives. This principle is incorporated in Article 27 of the European Charter of Fundamental Rights and has now been embodied in a series of European Union directives. This has the effect of institutionalizing a role for employee representation when decisions are taken which affect the form and operation of the enterprise, such as large-scale restructurings leading to dismissals and transfers of businesses between employers. Transnational enterprises are required to enter into regular consultation with employee representatives under the terms of the European Works Councils Directive of 1995, a model which was extended to other companies above a certain size threshold by the Information and Consultation of Employees Directive of 2002 (ICE). The ICE Directive has introduced significant changes to collective labor law in systems such as the UK and Ireland which had traditionally relied on a 'single channel' model of collective representation in which the sole mechanism for consulting workers was the recognized trade union. This left non-unionized workers unable for a while to benefit from rights of information and consultation granted by European law. Moreover, in the absence of any general framework for consultation, even those workers who were unionized would only have such rights in specific situations such as redundancies and transfers of undertakings. For these reasons, in so far as it goes against the pre-existing tradition of collective representation, the possible impact of the ICE Directive in Ireland and the UK is likely to prove more controversial and problematic than in other member states.

One of the difficulties in assessing the role of the ICE Directive within the legal framework of liberal market economies is that strong rights of employee consultation and representation in decision-making in the firm are perceived as incompatible with the notion that a company's directors are solely accountable to their shareholders, not the employees, for the decisions they make. Decision-making is an essential attribute of ownership and control. Within a legal tradition in which ownership and control are assumed to vest exclusively in shareholders (and in managers as the shareholders' agents), the general understanding has been that employee decision-making rights should not be prescribed by legislation. As we saw above, in view of the limits on how far collective bargaining can go in relation to the core areas of managerial prerogative the tradition in both the UK and the US has been to limit the scope of mandatory collective bargaining to wages, hours, and terms and conditions of work. In contrast, the emerging European framework of information and consultation extends to core managerial matters. For instance under Article 12 of the Works Councils Directive the matters over which workers have information and consultation rights include the firm's 'structure, economic and financial situation, the probable development of the business and of production and sales ... investments and substantial changes concerning organiza- tion ... [and] transfers of production, mergers, cut-backs or closures of undertakings, estab- lishments or important parts thereof'. Critics of this approach argue that while it is good managerial practice to consult employees and listen to their ideas and suggestions, any rights of information and consultation should be limited to an opportunity for employees to express their viewpoint (understood as rights of 'voice') but should not extend to a right to influence the final decision. As expressed by the US Supreme Court, in introducing a 'duty to bargain' with employee representatives under the NLRA 'Congress had no expectation that the elected union representative would become an equal partner in the running of the business enterprise in which the union's members are employed'; ultimately, 'management must be free from the constraints of the bargaining process to the extent essential for the running of a profitable business'.[5]

This perspective has nevertheless been challenged as overlooking the fact that in the modern knowledge and skills based economy employees who make valuable investments of firm-specific human capital are just as entitled to participate in decision-making as shareholders who invest finance capital (Njoya, 2007). If ownership of the firm is understood as a 'bundle of rights' which includes the right to participate in controlling the firm's operations and strategy, then such ownership may be understood as shared between employees and shareholders. This would imply that employee participation in decision-making goes beyond 'voice' rights, extending to a role in determining outcomes for instance by sitting on the firm's board of

directors. Employee membership of corporate boards is not mandated by European Union law, and is also the exception at national level; Germany is the most prominent system to make this a requirement. However, many systems have some combination of two- tier board structures and employee consul- tation requirements. Rights of information and consultation which fall short of board membership may still be understood within the framework of ownership rights, but only where they are coupled with sanctions which ensure that failure to observe these rights will invalidate the managers' unilateral decision. This is the case in some member states such as Germany and France, where a managerial decision arrived at without prior consultation with employee representatives is generally (subject to specified conditions) voidable or even void (Laulom, 2001). By contrast, in the UK the regulations implementing the ICE Directive impose a maximum financial penalty of £75,000 for non-compliance with the consultation requirement, payable not to the affected employees but to the Secretary of State. In the absence of any direct remedy available to workers for the firm's failure to consult them the regulations fall far short of conferring proprietary rights on employees.

The question may be posed whether participatory rights falling short of property or ownership rights are sufficient to protect employees' firm-specific human capital. One perspective is that 'voice' rights respect the dignity of workers by allowing their views to be heard, and if job security is understood simply as the need to respect the dignity and autonomy of workers while dismissing them (Collins, 1992) then the existing framework of information and consultation under the UK regulations would appear to meet this need. Another argument is that there is nothing to prevent employees bargaining for rights of ownership and control, so that there is no need for prescriptive legislation. This perspective accepts that employees make valuable investments in the firm but reasons that 'all are left to protect themselves through contract' (Easterbrook and Fischel, 1991: 38). In practice, however, such bargaining is inevitably incomplete (Kim, 1997; Stone, 2002).

This is not to suggest that the property-rights model is necessarily more effective at protecting human capital investments than a contractual model. There are potential governance costs associated with participatory decision-making. However, controls over restructuring which impede management and reduce financial returns also provide the basis for long-term co-operation between management and labor in systems reliant on investments in firm-specific human capital. In this context it is significant that in German debates about the benefits and costs of codetermination, there does not appear to be any conclusive view on whether the arms-length contractual model associated with the Anglo-American firm is superior in terms of efficiency: 'there have been no undisputed econometric studies on the (negative or positive) correlation between co-determination and company performance' (Baums, 2003: 185). Germany's 1998 Codetermination Commission considered that empirical evidence pointed to efficiency gains as well as costs (Addison et al., 2004: 394).

Corporate governance and its interface with labor law

A further aspect of the apparent divergence between 'liberal' and 'co-ordinated' market systems concerns the interaction of collective labor law with the predominant structures of corporate ownership and control ('corporate governance') in systems. In liberal market systems, dispersed ownership and market liquidity enable outside investors to diversify their holdings, thereby spreading the risk of being subject to managerial opportunism, while at the same time using the capital market to hold management to account, via the mechanism of the hostile takeover bid. In different systems, different institutions have evolved which facilitate these processes. In the US, a range of mechanisms, including shareholder litigation and an intensively regulatory regime of securities law, serves to protect minority shareholder interests (Coffee,

1999). In Britain and other common law countries such as Australia, the model of the takeover code, originating in the city of London, plays a key role, and shareholder litigation is rare. This reflects, to a large degree, the collective voice exercised by institutional investors in the British context, which is not matched to the same degree, historically, in the US (Black and Coffee, 1994; Armour and Skeel, 2007). Shareholder litigation and takeover codes therefore appear to be substitutes in providing a mechanism for protecting minority shareholders; the presence of one means that there is less need for the other.

By contrast, in the case of 'insider-orientated' or 'co-ordinated market' systems, the concentration of ownership allows for direct monitoring and observation of managerial performance, thereby overcoming some of the agency problems which are inherent in the separation of ownership and control in outsider-based régimes (although this need not imply the absence of laws protecting shareholder interests, which are often quite strong in civil law countries: see Siems, 2005). Concentration or 'blockholding' takes different forms, depending on context; in varying degrees, corporate cross-shareholdings, bank-led governance and the residue of family-based control and state control can be observed (see the contributions in Hopt et al., 1997). Again, specific legal institutions have developed to complement the presence of mechanisms of direct control (Rogers and Streeck, 1994). In German-influenced systems, there is a role for employee-nominated directors on a supervisory board as part of a two-tier board structure. Employee representation within company organs is by no means the general rule, however. In France, most companies have not taken up the option, provided in legislation, of having a dual board, and employee voice, while significant, mostly operates outside corporate structures (Goyer and Hancké, 2003). In Japan, a highly integrative approach to the participation of employees in the firm almost entirely takes the form of social norms rather than legal prescription (Learmount, 2002: Chapter 7).

In the context of co-ordinated market economies, this more direct form of employee involvement appears to be complementary to concentrated share ownership. Employee representatives may aid investors in the process of monitoring managers, and may also bring valuable information on organizational processes to bear on the decision-making process, notwithstanding possible costs arising from more extended or protracted decision-making processes (Pistor, 1999). Employee representation may also provide a more broadly-based mechanism for building trust between workers and investors and in particular for encouraging mutual investments in firm-specific assets (Rogers and Streeck, 1994). Either way, institutionalized employee involvement in the firm may be said to be complementary to blockholding as a particular form of corporate ownership and control.

There is evidence of enterprises and sectors which go against the trend in all varieties of system; British and American pharmaceutical firms behave very much along the lines predicted for stakeholder-orientated systems (Gospel and Pendleton, 2003), as do many utilities and service providers in regulated sectors (see Deakin et al., 2002). Conversely, some German and Japanese companies have begun to adopt shareholder value metrics and the business strategies associated with them (Lane, 2003; Learmount, 2002). Thus legal institutions do not rigidly dictate firm-level practices. However, the balance of evidence suggests that a good case can be made for the existence of complementarities across the linked domains of corporate governance and labor law, and for the continuing influence of these linkages at firm level. (Parkinson, 2003: 491).

In Germany and Japan, internal labor markets, constructed around implicit promises of job security and high levels of investment in firm-specific training, have remained in place during the 1990s and early 2000s, when they have become a rarity in the private sector in US and Britain. There is also evidence that Japanese and German companies have adjusted to the growing role of external investors and to increased capital market pressures in a way which has left intact (so far at least) the social compromises embodied in those systems (Jacoby, 2005; Höpner, 2005). Thus it is far from clear that a tendency to convergence of either form or function is being observed (Amable, 2003). Even during a period when national systems are increasingly exposed to the effects of transnational capital flows, regulatory competition and the growing acceptance, among policy makers and business elites of a 'shareholder value' norm (see Hansmann and Kraakman, 2001), governance mechanisms remain matched to local conditions and reflect particular trajectories of economic development.

CONCLUSIONS: THE PROSPECTS FOR LABOR LAW IN A TIME OF TRANSITION

In this chapter we have sought to explain some of the structures and concepts which distinguish labor law as an autonomous institutional phenomenon; autonomous, that is from the industrial relations system, and from labor market relations more broadly. The idea that labor law possesses this autonomy and so is not a mere appendage or expression of social and economic forces is one which labor law scholars increasingly look to in an attempt to give shape to their discipline (Rogowski and Wilthagen, 1994). This is not to argue that labor law can be studied in isolation from the social sciences. Rather, it represents a return to labor law's methodological roots, and to a tradition which sought co-existence between what we might now describe as an 'internal' (or juridical) perspective on the conceptual language of legal discourse and an 'external' (or social science) understanding of labor law as impacting on, and being impacted by, social and economic relations. The essence of this approach is that it is only by recognizing that positive legal analysis, on the one hand, and the sociological or economic analysis of law, on the other, are *distinct* techniques, that they can be effectively integrated in the study of labor law; one should not be dissolved into the other (Kahn-Freund, 1981: 97).

From this point of view, labor law can be identified with the emergence of conceptual forms for defining the employment relationship, the business enterprise and structures of worker representation. These forms were at one and the same time the product of certain prior legal categories (those of contract and property in private law, and the rationalization of governmental power in public law), and the result of the influence on the law of the social and economic changes which accompanied the rise of industrial societies. Divergence across labor law systems is in part the legacy of the common law/civil law divide, but it also reflects variations in the timing of industrialization, the forms of worker organization and the nature of industrial enterprise in different countries. Yet, there is also a high degree of functional continuity across labor law systems, not least in the common identification of 'subordinated labor' within an 'employment relationship' as the focal point of labor law regulation.

According to Sinzheimer (1922; cited in Kahn-Freund, 1981: 101), 'in times of sudden change, where the old disappears and the new craves recognition, a purely technical insight into the existing legal order is not sufficient'. At the start of the twenty-first century, labor law seems to be going through just such a period, when changes to organizational forms, coupled with the delocalization of production, are undermining familiar conceptual categories. It is not surprising therefore that some scholars identify at the core of labor law a 'failing paradigm' (Hyde, 2006: 45), which has to be corrected by a fundamental re-evaluation of core concepts. In this chapter we have provided concrete examples of the way in which these concepts have constrained the capacity of labor law to address contemporary problems, while also pointing out how even such foundational notions as those of contract and property are being adapted to new conditions. A methodology which seeks to understand how labor law's conceptual core came to be as it is, when allied to the techniques of the social sciences in explaining

the law's wider operation and impact, might help us in understanding its likely future development.

NOTES

1 81 Tenn. 507 (1884).
2 148 NY 117 (1895).
3 *Johnson v Unisys* [2003] 1 A.C. 518 at para. 37.
4 National Labor Relations Act, 29 U.S.C. 151–69.
5 Justice Blackmun in *First National Maintenance Corporation v NLRB* 452 U.S. 666, at 676 (1981).

REFERENCES

Addison, J., Bellmann, L., Schnabel, C. and Wagner, J. (2004) 'The reform of the German Works Constitution Act: a critical assessment', *Industrial Relations*, 43 (2): 392–420.

Amable, B. (2003) *The Diversity of Modern Capitalism.* Oxford: Oxford University Press.

Armour, J. and Skeel, D. (2007) 'Who writes the rules for hostile takeovers, and why? – the peculiar divergence of US and UK takeover regulation', *Georgetown Law Journal*, 95: forthcoming.

Ashiagbor, D. (2005) *The European Employment Strategy: Labour Market Regulation and New Governance.* Oxford: Oxford University Press.

Barmes, L., Collins, H. and Kilpatrick, C. (eds) (2007) 'Reconstructing Employment Contracts', special edition, *Industrial Law Journal*, 36: 1–140.

Baums, T. (2003) 'Company law reform in Germany', *Journal of Corporate Law Studies*, 3 (?): 181–9.

Black, B. and Coffee, J. (1994) 'Hail Britannia? Institutional investor behavior under limited regulation', *Michigan Law Review*, 92: 1997–2087.

Brodie, D. (1996) 'The heart of the matter: mutual trust and confidence', *Industrial Law Journal*, 25: 121–36.

Botero J., Djankov S., La Porta R., Lopez-de-Silanes F. and Shleifer A. (2004) 'The regulation of labor', *Quarterly Journal of Economics*, 119: 1340–82.

Coffee, J. (1999) 'The future as history: prospects for convergence in corporate governance and its implications', *Northwestern University Law Review*, 93 (?): 641–747.

Collins, H. (1997) 'The productive disintegration of labour law', *Industrial Law Journal*, 26: 295–309.

Collins, H. (2001) 'Regulating the employment relation for competitiveness', *Industrial Law Journal*, 30: 17–47.

Collins, H. (2002) 'Is there a third way in labour law?' in J. Conaghan, R.M. Fischl, and K. Klare (eds) *Labor Law in an Era of Globalisation: Transformative Practices and Possibilities*. Oxford: Oxford University Press. pp. 449–69.

Collins, H. (2003) *Employment Law*. Oxford: Oxford University Press.

Cottereau, A (2000) 'Industrial tribunals and the establishment of a kind of common law of labour in nineteenth century France', in W. Steinmetz (ed.) *Private Law and Social Inequality in the Industrial Age. Comparing Legal Cultures in Britain, France, Germany and the United States*. Oxford: Oxford University Press. pp. 203–26

Cottereau, A. (2002) 'Droit et bon droit. Un droit des ouvriers instauré, puis évincé par le droit du travail (France XIXe siècle)' *Annales HSS*, novembre-décembre no. 6: 1521–1557.

Davies, P. and Freedland, M. (2007) *Towards a Flexible Labour Market: Labour Legislation and Regulation since the 1990s*. Oxford: Oxford University Press.

Deakin, S., Hobbs, R., Konzelmann, S. and Wilkinson, F. (2002) 'Partnership, ownership and control: the impact of corporate governance on employment relations', *Employee Relations*, 24: 335–52.

Deakin, S. and Morris, G. (2005) *Labour Law* 3rd edn. Oxford: Hart Publishing.

Deakin, S. and Wilkinson, F. (1991) 'Labour law, social security and economic inequality', *Cambridge Journal of Economics*, 15: 125–48.

Deakin, S. and Wilkinson, F. (2005) *The Law of the Labour Market: Industrialization, Employment and Legal Evolution*. Oxford: Oxford University Press.

Dickens, L. and Hall, M. (2005) 'The impact of employment legislation: reviewing the research', in L. Dickens, M. Hall and S. Wood (eds), *Review of Research into the Impact of Employment Relations Legislation* Employment Relations Research Series No. 45 (London: DTI).

Dickens, L., Weekes, B., Jones, M., and Hart, M. (1985) *Dismissed: A Study of Unfair Dismissal and the Industrial Tribunal System*. Oxford: Blackwell.

Easterbrook, F. and Fischel, D. (1991) *The Economic Structure of Corporate Law*. Cambridge, MA: Harvard University Press.

European Commission (2006) *Employment in Europe* (Luxembourg: OOPEC).

Finkin, M. (2006) 'Comparative labour law', in M. Reimann and and R. Zimmermann (eds) *Comparative Law*. Frankfurt: Springer.

Fredman, S. (1997) *Women and the Law*. Oxford: Oxford University Press.

Freedland, M. (1976) *The Contract of Employment*. Oxford: Oxford University Press.

Freedland, M. (2003) *The Personal Employment Contract*. Oxford: Oxford University Press.

Freeman, R. and Pelletier, J. (1990) 'The impact of industrial relations legislation on British union density', *British Journal of Industrial Relations*, 28: 141–64.

Gospel, H. and Pendleton, A. (2003) 'Finance, corporate governance and the management of labour: a conceptual and comparative analysis', *British Journal of Industrial Relations*, 41: 557–82.

Goyer, M. and Hancké, B. (2003) 'Labour in French corporate governance: the missing link', in H. Gospel and A. Pendleton (eds) *Corporate Governance and Labour Management: An International Comparison*. Oxford: Oxford University Press.

Green, F. and McIntosh, S. (1998) 'Union power, cost of job loss and workers' effort' *Industrial and Labor Relations Review*, 51: 363–83.

Hansmann, H. and Kraakman, R. (2001) 'The end of history for corporate law', *Georgetown Law Journal*, 89: 439–68.

Hay, D. and Craven, P. (eds) (2004) *Masters, Servants and Magistrates in Britain and the Empire*. Chapel Hill, NC: University of North Carolina Press.

Hepple, B. and Brown, W. (1981) 'Tasks for labour law research', *Legal Studies*, 1: 56–67.

Höpner, M. (2005) 'What connects industrial relations and corporate governance? Explaining institutional complementarity', *Socio-Economic Review*, 3: 331–57.

Hopt, K. and Wymeersch, E. (eds) (1997) *Comparative Corporate Governance: Essays and Materials*. Berlin: Walter de Gruyter.

Hutchins, B. and Harrison, A. (1911) *A History of Factory Legislation* 2nd edn. London: P.S. King & Son.

Hyde, A. (2006) 'What is labor law?', in G. Davidov and B. Langille (eds) *Boundaries and Frontiers of Labour Law*. Oxford: Hart Publishing.

Jacoby, S. (1985) 'The duration of indefinite employment contracts in the United States and England: an historical analysis', *Comparative Labor Law*, 5: 85–128.

Jacoby, S. (2005) *The Embedded Corporation: Corporate Governance and Employment Relations in Japan and the United States*. Princeton: Princeton University Press.

Kahn-Freund, O. (1954) 'Legal framework', in A. Flanders and H. Clegg (eds) *The System of Industrial Relations in Britain*. Oxford: Blackwell.

Kahn-Freund, O. (1977) *Labour and the Law* 2nd edn. London: Stevens.

Kahn-Freund, O. (1981) 'Hugo Sinzheimer 1875–1945', in O. Kahn-Freund, *Labour Law and Politics in the*

Weimar Republic (eds R. Lewis and J. Clark). Oxford: Blackwell.

Kim, P. (1997) 'Bargaining with imperfect information: a study of worker perceptions of legal protection in an at-will world', *Cornell Law Review*, 83: 105–60.

Kolins Givan, R. (2007) 'Side by side we battle onward? Representing workers in contemporary America', *British Journal of Industrial Relations* 45: forthcoming.

Lane, C. (2003) *Changes in the corporate governance of German corporations: convergence on the Anglo-American model?* Centre for Business Research Working Paper No. 259, University of Cambridge.

Laulom, S. (2001) 'The European Court of Justice in the dialogue on transfers of undertakings: a fallible interlocutor?', in S. Sciarra (ed.) *Labour Law in the Courts: National Judges and the European Court of Justice*. Oxford: Hart Publishing.

Learmount, S. (2002) *Corporate Governance: What Can We Learn from Japan?* Oxford: Oxford University Press.

Mitchell, R. and Arup, C. (2006) 'Labour law and labour market regulation', in C. Arup, P. Gahan, J. Howe, R. Johnstone, R. Mitchell, and A. O'Donnell (eds) *Labor Law and Labor Market Regulation*. Sydney: Federation Press.

Mückenberger, U. and Supiot, A. (2000) 'Ordre public social et communauté. Deux cultures du droit du travail', in B. Zimmermann, C. Didry and P. Wagner (eds) *Le travail et la nation*. Paris: Éditions de la Maison des Sciences de l'Homme. pp. 81–105

Njoya, W. (2007) *Property in Work: The Employment Relationship in the Anglo-American Firm*. Aldershot: Ashgate.

OECD (2004) *Employment Outlook*. Paris: OECD.

OECD (2006) *Employment Outlook*. Paris: OECD.

Palmer, R. (1993) *English Law in the Age of the Black Death, 1348–1381: A Transformation of Governance and Law*. Chapel Hill, NC: University of North Carolina Press.

Parkinson, J. (2003) 'Models of the company and the employment relationship', *British Journal of Industrial Relations*, 41: 481–509.

Petit, H., and Sauze, D. (2006) 'Une lecture historique de la relation salariale comme structure de repartition des aléas. En partant du travail de Salais', in F. Eymard-Duvernay (ed.) *L'économie des conventions : méthodes et résultats. Tome II : Développements*. Paris: La Découverte. pp. 303–16.

Pistor, K. (1999) 'Codetermination in Germany: a socio-political model with governance externalities', in M. Blair and M. Roe (eds) *Employees and Corporate Governance*. Washington, DC: Brookings Institution.

Prothero, I. (1979) *Artisans and Politics in Early Nineteenth Century London: John Gast and His Times*. Folkestone: Dawson.

Rogers, J. and Streeck, W. (1994) 'Worker representation overseas: the works council story', in R. Freeman (ed.) *Working Under Different Rules*. Washington, DC: NBER.

Rogowski, R. and Wilthagen, T. (1994) *Reflexive Labour Law*. Deventer: Kluwer.

Siems, M. (2005) 'What does not work in securities law: a critique of La Porta *et al.*'s methodology' *International Company and Commercial Law Review*, 7: 300–5.

Simitis, S. (2000) 'The case of the employment relationship: elements of a comparison', in W. Steinmetz (ed.) *Private Law and Social Inequality in the Industrial Age. Comparing Legal Cultures in Britain, France, Germany and the United States*. Oxford: Oxford University Press. pp. 181–202.

Singer, J. (1993) 'Jobs and justice: rethinking the stakeholder debate', *University of Toronto Law Journal*, 43: 475–531.

Sims, V. (2002) *Good Faith in Contract Law: A Comparative Analysis of English and German Law*. PhD. Thesis, University of Cambridge, 2002.

Stone, K. (2002) 'Knowledge at work: disputes over the ownership of human capital in the changing workplace', *University of Connecticut Law Review*, 34: 721–764.

Stone, K. (2007) 'Revisiting the at-will employment doctrine: imposed terms, implied terms, and the normative world of the workplace', *Industrial Law Journal*, 36: 84–101.

Supiot, A. (1994) *Critique du droit du travail* (Paris: PUF).

Tawney, R.H. (1914) *The Establishment of Minimum Rates in the Chainmaking Industry under the Trade Boards Act of 1909*. London: Bell.

Tawney, R.H. (1915) *The Establishment of Minimum Rates in the Tailoring Industry under the Trade Boards Act of 1909*. London: Bell.

Tawney, R.H. (1967) *The Agrarian Problem in the Sixteenth Century*. L. Stone, New York: Harper & Row.

Topel, R. (1990) 'Specific capital and unemployment: measuring the costs and consequences of job loss', in A. Meltzer and C. Plosser (eds) *Studies in Labour Economics in Honor of Walter Oi*. Amsterdam: Elsevier.

Toynbee, A. (1969) *Lectures on the Industrial Revolution in England*, in T.S. Ashton. (ed.) Newton Abbott: A.M. Kelley.

Veneziani, B. (1986) 'The evolution of the contract of employment', in B. Hepple (ed.) *The Making of Labour Law in Europe*. London: Mansell.

Webb, S. and Webb, B. (1910) *English Poor Law Policy*. London: Longmans, Green & Co.

Webb, S. and Webb, B. (1927a) *English Poor Law History: Part I. The Old Poor Law*. London: Longmans, Green & Co.

Webb, S. and Webb, B. (1927b) *English Poor Law History Volume II: The Last Hundred Years*. London: Longmans, Green & Co.

Wedderburn, Lord (1986) *The Worker and the Law* 3rd edn. Harmondsworth: Penguin.

Weekes, B., Mellish, M., Dickens, L. and Lloyd, J. (1971) *Industrial Relations and the Limits of Law*. Oxford: Blackwell.

Weiler, P. (1990) *Governing the Workplace*. Cambridge, MA: Harvard University Press.

Weiss, M. (1988) 'Individual employment rights: focusing on job security in the Federal Republic of Germany', *Nebreska Law Review*, 67 (?): 82–100.

Wood, S. and Godard, J. (1999) 'The statutory union recognition procedure in the Employment Relations Bill: a comparative analysis', *British Journal of Industrial Relations*, 37: 203–45.

Woodward, D. (1980) 'The background to the Statute of Artificers: the genesis of labour policy, 1558-63' *Economic History Review (NS)*, 33: 32–44.

16

The State as Employer

Marick F. Masters, Ray Gibney,
Iryna Shevchuk, and Tom Zagenczyk

The state's role as employer depends on several aspects of governance, including questions regarding the functions of the state, the organizations through which the state operates, and the adopted management approach (Lane, 2000). The functions a state chooses to undertake affect the scope of its employment both directly and indirectly. Organizationally, states may opt to employ workers directly or contract services through private entities. Government decides how it will manage its workforce, selecting a model of staffing, compensation, and employee involvement that it wants to follow. The nature of any given state's role as employer reflects a confluence of economic, legal, political, and social factors. States may also use their role as employer to engineer important public-policy and societal goals. The role of the state thus manifests the realities of interacting forces and choices made in response to a changing environment.

The state as employer varies widely in function, organization, and management across countries (Bordogna, 2003). Diverging patterns of culture, history, and ideology contribute to the variation evident in policy and practice. Amid such diversity, however, emerge recognizable cross-national trends. The globalization of economic and political affairs creates common pressures to adjust the role of the state at both the macro and micro levels (Kettl, 2005). Events in one part of the world may rapidly influence considerations in distantly located areas as the communication of new ideas and practices is nearly instantaneous given today's technology. Formal structures of economic and political integration, such as the European Union, intensify existing tendencies for convergence. New models of public management emerge to challenge the traditional within a complex mosaic.

In this chapter, we address developments and practices relevant to the multifaceted role of the state as employer. We focus mainly on activities at the central level of government in countries associated with the Organization for Economic Cooperation and Development (OECD), highlighting those nations that have been at the cusp of change and influence on a cross-national scale.

We organize this paper into several sections. The first presents a conceptual framework to guide the analysis of trends and developments in the role of the state as employer on a cross-national basis. Section two examines trends in the role and size of the public sector, focusing on privatization and the scope of public employment. We examine key trends in human resource management (HRM) practices in section three. Section four addresses the public governance initiatives undertaken in the US as an illustration of recent public management trends. We focus not only on the reinvention initiative of the Clinton-Gore years (1993–2000) but also on President George W. Bush's Management Agenda and the major reforms of his administration. We conclude in section five with a brief overview of how well the new public management has performed at what needs to be addressed in the future.

AN INDUSTRIAL RELATIONS (IR) FRAMEWORK OF THE STATE AS EMPLOYER

We present an industrial relations (IR) systems framework to examine the role of the state as employer (see Figure 16.1). The framework focuses on three main elements, of which governance is at the center. Various environmental contexts influence decisions about

governance issues and affect the resources available to finance governmental operations, including personnel. Governance involves decisions about

1) functions and size of government and the allocation of responsibilities across different levels of the public sector;
2) how the state organizes its operations in terms of being a direct provider or contractor; and
3) the management policies and practices which it chooses to follow.

These decisions are highly interrelated, and the choices available are not necessarily mutually exclusive. The other aspect of this framework focuses on results, that is, the outputs and outcomes of what government does. Public financing links the environment to governance. Performance links governance to those it serves. In this framework, variation exists in the functions of government, how government should provide its operations, and the manner in which it should manage those who perform its work.

Environmental contexts

Several major environmental trends have impacted the role of the state as employer on a transnational basis: democratization and

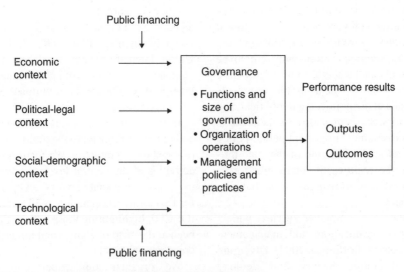

Figure 16.1   IR systems framework of the state as employer

privatization; economic globalization; and demography. First, the collapse of the Soviet Union and the concomitant end of the Cold War has unleashed the forces of democracy and free markets. Previously state-controlled societies have established democratic institutions and de-nationalized industries. The shift to market-based economies has meant the role of the state as owner and employer has shrank. In addition, the end of the Cold War has subdued international pressures to build up enormous national defenses with a supporting civilian sector, either publicly employed or contracted. At the same time, however, the international wave of terrorism has created a new set of defense burdens which have required a global response. In the US especially, the interrelated requirements of homeland and national security have changed how government proposes to operate large segments of its civilian federal workforce.

Second, economic globalization has required that nations become more competitive in order to sustain and promote prosperity. Globalization has encouraged states to reduce governmental barriers to competition. For example, the European Union has guidelines on acceptable levels of government deficits. Societies must examine how the state can facilitate markets rather than regulating them to conform to social-welfare, redistributionist models of governance.

Third, in many societies, the changing demographic composition of the population and workforce has stimulated rather than dampened demand for public services, with attendant employment implications. Across Europe, Japan, and in the US, for example, aging populations have resulted in growing health care needs, much of which have been traditionally met through public organizations. Similarly, retiree pensions and health care costs have grown and absorbed a growing share of overall public expenditures in many societies.

These environmental trends, with their competing implications, put many states in a difficult crosswind. On the one hand, they must respond to the requirements of intense global competition by relieving markets of the burdens of excessive taxation and regulation. On the other hand, political realities make it impossible for societies to abandon major segments of social-welfare support, particularly with aging populations. Increasingly, states must find ways to navigate these challenges. A wave of governmental reforms, accelerated globally by the instantaneous communication of new ideas, is a major result of the changing environment.

Governance

As mentioned, governance involves three basic sets of questions for societies and their policymakers in particular (see Table 16.1). The first concerns the function and size of the state. States decide which functions to perform, how extensively they want to undertake them, and the degree to which responsibility will be centralized or decentralized across various levels of government (for example, national or central; regional or state; local or municipal). The range and scope of functions a state chooses directly affects its size as employer, with obvious public-financing consequences.

We may distinguish between two basic types of governmental activities: inherently governmental, or public, and commercial. The former are those activities which provide genuine public goods and therefore cannot be expected to be sufficiently served by private markets. Common examples include national defense, police and fire, primary and secondary education and income maintenance. The second set includes activities that produce benefits more directly tied to the user, and they may thus also be met via the private sector. Airlines, railroads, energy, and telecommunications fall into this category. There are arguably many 'commercial' activities in which there is a public interest. In addition, there are many commercial activities (for instance health care, post-secondary education) which serve government. Thus, the line between inherently governmental and commercial is often unclear. The choices a state makes as to how much to cross the line – on one side or the other – reflects

Table 16.1 Dimensions of governance

Function, size, distribution	Organizational type	Management model
Inherently governmental and commercial	Publicly owned and provided	Bureaucratic civil service
Share of GDP and total employment	Contracted or outsourced	Collective bargaining
Central or federal distribution	Public-private hybrid	Business process or reinvention
		New public management

its prevailing political ideology and notions of efficiency.

A second aspect of governance concerns the form of organization adopted. The critical issue is whether the state intends to own and operate the means of production. Three conceptually distinguishable possibilities exist. First, government may choose to own the assets of production and directly employ those who provide the relevant good or service. This approach seems consistent with those inherently governmental functions. This is a core sphere of governmental operations in which workers and managers are employees of the state.

Second, government may choose to contract out or outsource the actual work of producing goods and delivering services while still maintaining ownership of the final product. Privately owned firms receive payment for fulfilling the government's requisition. They also employ those who do the work, though government may impose more labor-related regulations because the work is being paid for by taxpayers.

A third organization type is a hybrid public-private entity, of which there are several variants, some of which are similar to an outsourced function. One example is a jointly owned and operated enterprise in which profits are shared (Lane, 2000; Trebilock, 1995). Another is a franchise in which the work is contracted but paid for by users, not general revenues. The state may also choose to establish a government-owned corporation that runs on a for-profit basis and that is not part of the general budget.

In short, there are several different types of organizational structures that can be used

by government to perform its functions. The degree to which the state plays a role directly as employer varies, though it may influence employment practices through its regulatory powers where it is not the direct employer. Regardless, through governmental charter, employment, or subsidization, the state may exert a significant role on a nation's employment picture across these organization types.

Finally, in choosing a managerial model, the state makes additional choices since any model encompasses a set of policies and practices which give the model its conceptual distinction. We identify several models to capture the breadth of approaches a state may take:

- bureaucratic-civil service;
- collective-bargaining;
- business-process or reinvention; and
- the New Public Management (NPM) (see Godine, 1951; Kettl, 2005; Lane, 2000).

These approaches are not mutually exclusive. They differ, however, in focus and the extent to which they define the functions and size of government as employer.

The bureaucratic-civil service model relies on a permanent employment contract in which rewards are based largely on longevity; hiring is based on merit; and work duties are carefully defined within a hierarchical structure. Political entities establish budgets with funds earmarked for specific activities over which there is limited discretion. The collective-bargaining model involves labor unions in setting various terms and conditions of employment as opposed to a centralized civil service personnel agency issuing employment regulations. Unions may participate in compensation, work schedule, and job classification decisions. They may also enjoy, in some instances, access to dispute resolution procedures, or the right to strike, though the latter is much more restricted than in the private sector. By delegating collective-bargaining powers to unions and managers, the state arguably voids claims of exclusive sovereignty over such matters (for a discussion of sovereignty, see Godine, 1951; Rosenbloom, 1971).

The business-process, or reinvention, model focuses on applying modern personnel practices to maximize performance. These include employee involvement, incentive-based pay systems, job flexibility, and increased training and skill development. The objective is to make government more efficient and productive, with the focus being on *how* government works not *what* it does.

The NPM model takes reinvention a step further. It focuses not only on *how* but *what*. It questions the role of government, whether functions should be privatized or outsourced. It also introduces more flexibility into the work systems; incentives; short-term contracts; and performance management (at the individual and budgetary levels). In essence, NPM is more encompassing than the business-process, or reinvention, model.

The final dimension of the IR framework focuses on results (Figure 16.1), or the outputs and outcomes of governmental activities. Outputs are the immediate effects, such as patients served by a governmental hospital, the number of tax returns processed, etc. Outcomes concern the quality and cost effectiveness of governmental operations; whether government achieves the fundamental public-policy goals that were intended in an efficient manner.

The framework provides a basis for examining recent trends in governance. We begin with an examination of the role and size of the state.

TRENDS IN THE ROLE AND SIZE OF GOVERNMENT

Globalization, international competition, and advances in technology during the past 25 years have led to higher levels of downsizing, outsourcing, and restructuring in today's organizations (Csoka, 1995), resulting in changes in the relationship between employer and employee (Kissler, 1994). The state has not been immune to pressures faced by private-sector organizations. Since 1990, the state's role as an employer in OECD countries has changed in important ways, such as the size of government, which functions government performs, the number of individuals employed, and increased privatization and outsourcing of government services.

Trends in the size of government

One important trend that affects the role of the state as an employer is the size of the government, measured using the percentage of government expenditure relative to GDP (Gwartney et al., 1998; OECD, 2005b). Although the US economy performed well in the 1990s, the growth in GDP was less than half that achieved during the 1960s. Some argue that economic growth has been slower than possible because the size of government is growing at a rate that restricts economic performance (Gwartney et al., 1998). Gwartney et al. (1998) contend that the government should provide two main functions: (1) legal and physical infrastructure for the operation of a market economy, and (2) a limited set of goods. Economic growth will be adversely affected when governments provide services beyond these core functions because such involvement creates disincentives due to higher taxes. Freeman (2002), parenthetically, offers a different perspective, suggesting that institutional arrangements associated with labor protections may not hinder economic performance. He (2002:19) argues that 'once a country has a strong tradition of basic market freedoms ... it has considerable leeway in the precise way it structures institutions.' Moreover, markets can be more efficient in finding new ways to create value.

Despite these arguments, government size has grown consistently between 1960 and the present. In recent years (1995–2004), even though reducing the size of government has been identified as a priority and privatization and outsourcing have increased (OECD, 2005b), the size of government relative to GDP has grown in 17 of 30 OECD countries (see Table 16.2). For example, in the UK, government expenditures as a percentage of GDP grew from 19.6 per cent in 1995 to 21.1 per cent in 2001.

Government functions

Changes in size naturally affect the functions governments of OECD countries provide for their citizens. Across the OECD member countries, a core set of functions provided by government includes the provision of defense, education, health, police, and social services (OECD, 2002b). However, the provision of these core functions varies by the level of administration across countries, except for the provision of defense. As is evident in Table 16.3, national defense is provided by the central or federal administration in all reporting OECD member countries. The provision of other core functions, however, varies by country. For example, France has centralized the education process at the national level, while the administration of education is maintained at the municipal or local and 'state' levels, for instance California, in the US.

Public sector employment

The past 20 years have brought important changes to the employer-employee relationship for public sector employees (OECD, 2005b). Demands to reduce the size of government and increase efficiency and responsiveness have led to questions regarding the nature of employment in the public sector. First, due to privatization and outsourcing, many jobs that had traditionally

been held by public sector employees are now in the realm of the private sector. Second, reformers have attempted to make the employment relationship between public sector employees and their employers more like the relationship between private sector employees and their employers: long-term job security has been reconsidered, public sector jobs have become increasingly competitive, and site or individual wage bargaining has become increasingly prevalent relative to collective bargaining (OECD, 2005b).

During the 1990s, many governments attempted to reduce the size of government by reducing the number of public sector employees. In some cases, public sector employment has been reduced at the central or federal administrative levels. In Japan, Spain, and the US, however, public sector employment has been cut at local and regional levels (OECD, 2005b). Table 16.4 shows public employment for OECD countries for the years 1995 through 2003. The number of public sector employees has decreased in 8 of the 14 countries, while it has increased in 6 countries. However, when the percentage of public sector jobs is considered relative to total jobs (Table 16.4), public sector jobs comprise a smaller portion of total jobs in 9 of 14 countries. For example, in the UK overall employment increased from 5,368,000 in 1995 to 5,634,000 in 2003, but public sector employment as a percentage of total employment decreased from 21 per cent to 20 per cent over the same time span. Overall, these numbers indicate that the relative number of public sector jobs is decreasing. However, the results presented in Table 16.2 suggest the size of government, as a percentage of GDP expenditures, is growing in the majority of OECD countries. Thus, the size of government is growing with respect to government expenditures as a percentage of GDP, but is decreasing in terms of relative employment levels. At the same time, there is some evidence that governments experience difficulty in contracting out work when governmental agencies may bid for this work (Gansler and Lucyshyn, 2004).

Table 16.2 General government final consumption expenditure (percent of GDP)

	1995	1996	1997	1998	1999	2000	2001	2002	2003	2004
Australia	18.5	18.1	18.1	18.3	18.1	17.9	17.8	17.8	–	–
Austria	20.4	20.3	19.7	19.5	19.8	19.2	18.9	18.6	18.7	–
Belgium	21.4	21.7	21.2	21.1	21.2	21.2	21.7	22.3	22.8	–
Canada	21.5	20.7	19.7	19.8	19.2	18.6	19.0	19.2	–	–
Czech Republic	21.7	21.2	21.8	21.0	22.3	22.1	22.2	23.0	24.0	22.8
Denmark	25.8	25.9	25.5	26.0	25.8	25.3	25.9	26.3	26.5	–
Finland	22.8	23.2	22.3	21.6	21.6	20.6	21.0	21.7	22.1	–
France	23.9	24.2	24.2	23.4	23.3	23.2	23.2	23.9	24.3	–
Germany	19.8	19.9	19.5	19.2	19.1	19.0	19.0	19.2	19.3	–
Greece	15.3	14.5	15.1	15.3	15.4	15.7	15.3	15.7	15.5	–
Hungary	11.0	10.2	10.5	10.2	10.2	9.7	10.2	10.8	10.8	10.5
Iceland	22.3	22.2	22.0	22.5	23.4	23.9	23.8	25.5	26.4	–
Ireland	16.4	15.8	15.1	14.4	14.0	13.9	14.8	15.1	–	–
Italy	17.9	18.1	18.2	17.9	18.0	18.3	18.8	19.0	19.5	–
Japan	14.6	14.8	14.8	15.3	15.9	16.4	17.1	17.7	17.5	–
Korea	11.2	11.6	11.6	12.8	12.3	12.1	12.9	12.9	13.3	–
Luxembourg	18.4	18.9	17.9	16.8	16.8	15.7	17.0	17.8	18.6	–
Mexico	10.4	9.6	9.9	10.4	11.0	11.1	11.8	12.1	12.4	11.7
Netherlands	24.0	23.1	22.9	22.7	22.9	22.7	23.4	24.5	–	–
New Zealand	17.7	17.5	18.3	18.3	18.6	17.6	17.6	17.6	–	–
Norway	21.6	20.9	20.5	21.9	21.4	19.1	20.6	22.1	22.6	–
Poland	19.8	19.6	19.2	18.7	18.8	19.0	19.0	19.0	18.5	17.7
Portugal	18.6	18.9	19.0	18.9	19.7	20.5	20.8	21.1	–	–
Slovak Republic	21.2	23.0	22.0	22.4	20.7	20.7	21.0	20.9	20.8	20.3
Spain	18.1	17.9	17.5	17.5	17.4	17.6	17.5	17.8	17.9	–
Sweden	27.2	27.8	27.2	27.4	27.4	26.6	27.1	28.1	28.3	–
Switzerland	11.7	11.8	11.5	11.3	11.1	11.1	11.6	11.7	–	–
Turkey	10.8	11.6	12.3	12.7	15.2	14.1	14.2	14.0	13.6	13.1
UK	19.6	19.2	18.3	17.9	18.4	18.7	19.2	20.1	21.1	–
US	15.3	15.0	14.5	14.3	14.3	14.4	14.8	15.2	–	–

Source: World Bank national accounts data, and OECD National Accounts data files.

Table 16.3   Core government functions of selected OECD member countries

Sector	Central or federal administration	Regional administration	Local administration
Defense	France Finland Greece Hungary Italy Luxembourg Netherlands Spain US		
Education	France Hungary Italy Netherlands Luxembourg	Australia Germany Ireland Spain US	Finland Greece Hungary Mexico US
Health	France Hungary Spain US	Australia France Germany Ireland Japan Spain US	Finland Germany Greece Hungary Mexico US
Police	Finland Hungary Italy Luxembourg Netherlands Spain	Ireland Japan	France Greece
Social	Hungary Spain	Australia France Germany Ireland Japan US	Finland France Germany Greece US

Source: OECD (2002b).

Privatization

Privatization, the transfer of assets from the public to the private sector in terms of ownership, management, finance, or control, can occur in a number of ways, including

(1) the sale of assets from public to the private sector, the most common form of privatization;
(2) the state contracting out services that it had previously provided;
(3) internal market arrangements in which the purchase of services is separated from their provision;
(4) the assessment of user fees for state-provided services;
(5) private-public partnerships, in which the government finances, manages, and shares risk with the private sector on joint projects; and

(6) liberalization, or the removal of statutory provisions which keep private sector firms from entering public sector markets (Bach, 2000).

Trends including pressures for effective and efficient public services, technological change, and public finance problems led to an increase in the privatization of public services between 1995 and 2000 (see Table 16.5). During these years, approximately US$650 billion worth of state-owned enterprises were transferred to the private sector in OECD countries alone. Telecom companies were the largest source of privatization revenue during this time period, although manufacturing, banking, defense, energy, transportation, and public

Table 16.4 Public employment

Country	Public employment (thousands)									Public employment as a percentage of total employment								
	1995	1996	1997	1998	1999	2000	2001	2002	2003	1995	1996	1997	1998	1999	2000	2001	2002	2003
Australia	1545.9	1537.3	1457.8	1433.7	1427.5	1437.8	1427.5	1457.5	1468.6	19	19	17	17	17	16	16	16	16
Austria	545.9	526.6	525.1	525.4	519.1	518.3	503.4	490.1	484.2	22	21							
Canada	2957.8	2851.3	2789.4	2779	2769.9	2785.8	2813.5	2847	2912.9			20	20	19	19	19	19	19
Czech Republic			1170	1110.7	1065.7	1110.9	1083.6	1058.4				24	23	23	23	23	22	
Denmark		927.7	938.4	934.8	947.4	946	937.9	946.8	926.6		35	35	35	34	34	34	34	34
Finland	549.1	557.5	569	567.1	570.1	576.6	584.8	597.5	602.8	27	27	26	26	25	25	25	25	26
Germany	7116	6991	6846	6726	6631	6534	6259	6185	6079	19	19	18	18	17	17	16	16	16
Greece	825.4	842.6	841.4	845.5	849.6	841.7				22	22	22	21	22	21			
Hungary	820.4	1063	967.9	947.1	933.8	837.7	839.4	863	876	35	47	44	42	37	31	31	31	31
Italy	3670.2	3633.9	3584.5	3543.3	3531.5	3508.2				16	16	16	15	15	15			
Luxembourg			26.8	28	28.8	30.1												
Mexico	4595.2	4626.6				4812.7	4812.1	4796.2	4785.3	17	16				15	15	15	15
Netherlands	1471.4		1500			1583.9	1648.8	1662.9	1704.8	26		25			25	25	26	26
New Zealand	245.6	251.2	247.2	247.7	244	216.3	223.6	233.2	239.2	19	19	18	18	18	20	20	20	20
Norway	798.3	814.8	836.1	850.1	861.5	854.8	847.5	866.1	865.1	38	38	38	37	38	37	37	37	38
Poland	5623.1	5412.5	5072.8	4671.3	4338.8	4318.1	4027.7	3905.1	3780.2	37	35	32	29	28	28	27	30	30
Slovakia	879.1	818.6	747.8	707.3	676.4	657.1	631.3	591.3	552.6	44	40	37	35	34	33	31	29	27
Spain	2219.5	2319.7	2359.4	2322.4	2354.2	2437	2495.2	2566.2	2687.6	18	18	18	17	16	16	15	15	16
Sweden	1263.1	1257.1	1237.1	1230.6	1246.3	1208.9	1203.7	1214.6	1235.2	41	39	37	36	36	34	34	34	34
Turkey	2888	2979	2881	3046	3103	3109	3157	3225	3213	14	14	14	14	14	14	15	15	15
UK	5368	5269	5175	5163	5206	5288	5378	5484	5634	21	20	20	19	19	19	19	20	20
US	19432	19539	19664	19909	20307	20790	21118	21513	21583	17	16	16	16	16	16	16	17	17

Source: ILO/ LABORSTA.

Table 16.5 Country breakdown of amounts raised by privatization (Billions of $US)

	1990	1991	1992	1993	1994	1995	1996	1997	1998	1999	2000
Australia	19	1,042	1,893	2,057	2,055	8,089	9,052	16,815	7,146	15,220	6,273
Austria	32	48	49	142	700	1,035	1,302	2,438	2,537	70	2,086
Belgium	–	–	–	956	548	2,745	1,222	1,842	2,288	10	–
Canada	1,504	808	1,249	755	490	3,998	1,768	–	11	–	–
Czech Republic	–	59	877	837	1,065	976	902	395	437	737	520
Denmark	644	–	–	122	229	10	366	45	4,502	19	111
Finland	–	–	–	229	1,120	363	911	835	1,999	3,716	1,827
France	–	–	–	12,160	5,479	4,136	3,096	10,105	13,597	9,478	17,438
Germany	11	351	–	73	678	191	1,421	3,125	11,357	2,754	1,750
Greece	–	–	–	35	73	44	558	1,395	3,960	4,880	1,384
Hungary	102	385	705	1,308	955	2,645	849	647	197	88	66
Iceland	–	–	21	10	2	6	–	4	128	228	1
Ireland	–	515	70	274	–	157	293	0	0	4,846	1,458
Italy	–	–	759	3,039	9,077	10,131	11,230	23,945	15,138	25,594	9,729
Japan	–	–	–	–	13,875	–	2,039	–	6,641	15,115	–
Korea	–	–	–	1,451	3,782	643	3,091	645	201	2,153	18
Luxembourg	–	–	–	–	–	–	–	–	–	–	–
Mexico	3,124	10,747	6,864	2,531	766	170	73	2,670	988	279	406
Netherlands	716	179	–	780	3,766	3,993	1,239	842	335	1,481	310
New Zealand	3,895	17	967	630	29	264	1,839	–	441	1,331	–
Norway	73	–	–	–	118	521	660	35	–	454	1,039
Poland	23	171	373	433	725	1,101	1,442	2,043	2,079	3,422	6,262
Slovak Republic	–	–	–	63	415	1,004	486	11	–	–	1,313
Spain	172	–	830	3,222	1,458	2,941	2,680	2,532	11,618	1,128	1,079
Sweden	–	–	378	252	2,313	852	785	2,390	172	2,071	8,082
Switzerland	–	–	–	–	–	–	–	–	6,442	–	–
Turkey	486	244	423	566	412	572	292	466	1,020	38	2,712
UK	4,219	5,346	7,923	8,114	4,632	5,648	2,426	4,500	–	–	–
US	–	–	–	–	–	–	–	3,650	3,100	–	–
Grand Total	16,112	20,925	25,586	40,461	55,885	54,599	53,022	96,282	100,633	96,735	67,119

Source: ILO/ LABORSTA.

utilities sectors were also affected. European Union countries which sought to meet the conditions of the Maastricht Treaty, including Italy, Austria, France, Spain, Portugal, and the UK, were responsible for nearly 60 per cent of privatization revenues (OECD, 2001).

While privatization activity was high in the 1990s, it decreased considerably following the turn of the century. A number of factors were responsible for the slow down in privatization, including a downward slide in equity markets, poor economic performance, and the fact that OECD countries have sold off the majority of saleable assets (OECD, 2002c). In fact, in 2001, privatization revenues of OECD countries dwindled to only US$20 billion. The decline of privatization in the telecom sector in the 1990s was particularly important to the reduction of privatization revenues, as it was previously responsible for nearly one-third of all privatization revenues. For a breakdown of the privatization initiatives of selected countries, see Table 16.6.

Outsourcing or contracting government services

One of the key mechanisms through which the state is able to privatize its operations is through outsourcing, 'the process whereby governments contract with private sector providers for the provision of services to government ministries and agencies or directly to citizens on behalf of the government' (OECD, 2005b: 131). Outsourcing is utilized because introducing competition for the provision of services, in theory, increases efficiency, usually through

- cost reduction;
- access to expertise unavailable in-house;
- access to quantity and diversity of expertise over time; and
- replacement of poor-performing government operations (OECD, 2005b).

Outsourcing has increased in OECD countries in recent years. A 2005 OECD (OECD, 2005b) report observes that differences in utilization of outsourcing across countries results from differences in public sector labor markets. In particular, countries with less flexible public services, such as continental European countries, are less apt to use outsourcing as it is particularly expensive to downsize public servants. On the other hand, English-speaking and Nordic countries such as the UK, the US, Norway, and Sweden utilize outsourcing more extensively.

In addition to considering the extent to which different countries outsource, it is also important to examine what services or activities are outsourced. Generally, these activities/services can be classified into three groups:

(1) blue-collar support services, which include janitorial services, facilities and waste management, food service, and guard service provision;
(2) high-value services that are ancillary to an agency's core mission, such as information technology, human resources management, banking, and financial services; and
(3) activities viewed as inherently governmental, such as prisons, emergency rescue/fire services, food inspection, audit services, health, education, and welfare services (OECD, 2005b).

Table 16.6 Privatization initiatives in selected countries

Austria	Banking, oil and gas
Belgium	Banking, insurance
Canada	Transport and telecommunications
Denmark	Banking and transport
Finland	Power generation, telecommunications, air traffic
France	Banking
Germany	Automobiles, chemicals
Ireland	Telecommunications
Italy	Banking and insurance
Netherlands	Banking, chemicals, steel, public utilities
New Zealand	Privatization of may state enterprises
Portugal	Utilities and communications
Spain	Iron, steel, textiles, public utilities
Sweden	Some privatization of elderly care
UK	Telecommunications, gas, airways, water and sewage, rail, electricity, energy
US	Limited sales of state assets

Source: ILO (2001).

Overall, available evidence indicates that outsourcing is positively related to service quality and negatively related to costs (see OECD, 2005b for a review of studies conducted on outsourcing and outcomes).

Despite the fact that empirical evidence suggests that outsourcing is advantageous, obstacles often make it difficult to implement. Generally, these obstacles stem from public concerns regarding the private sector's participation in activities that have traditionally been provided by the government. In particular, when outsourcing threatens traditional governmental service provision, government employees, unions, and political allies may present resistance (OECD, 2005b). Accountability is also an issue that arises with respect to outsourcing, especially when a service is provided from a private sector source on behalf of the government directly to citizens (OECD, 2005b).

HRM TRENDS

With regard to common trends, OECD member countries are not significantly different with respect to the public sector. While each organization or state may address the situation differently based upon its culture (OECD, 2005a), common trends in human resource practices across institutions are evident in both the public and private sectors.

Labor relations and unions

Three broad categories of labor relations in OECD member countries are:

(1) the same employment laws cover public and private sector employees;
(2) civil servants covered under separate civil service employment laws; and
(3) some civil servants covered under separate laws and others covered under private sector employment laws (OECD Observer, 2004).

However, under all three conditions, labor unions exert a strong influence on civil servants' working conditions and pay levels, but have a limited role in employee performance, recruitment, and staffing levels (OECD Observer, 2004).

Union density is the percentage of unionized workers in the labor force and can be aggregated based upon different characteristics of the labor force. Union density is higher in the public sector than in the private sector throughout OECD member countries and public sector union density in most OECD countries has declined from 1980s levels (see Table 16.7). For example, in the US 36 per cent of public sector employees were unionized in 2004, but only 8 per cent of private sector employees were unionized. France's 10 per cent differential in public and private sector density was the smallest reported difference in 2003. However, between 1981 and 2003, public sector union density in France declined by nearly two-thirds. Austria, Canada, Norway, and Spain reported increases in public sector union density with Norway's 9 per cent gain being the largest. In comparison, Australia, Belgium, Germany, Italy, and the UK all reported decreases of 10 per cent or greater.

Performance management

Most OECD member countries have performance management systems in place (OECD, 2005a). Systems commonly include three elements: performance management objectives, performance appraisal methods, and pay-for-performance plans (OECD, 2004a). Countries vary on the degree of HR delegation and the strength of the link between an individual's performance appraisal and pay (OECD, 2004a). For example, New Zealand has a high degree of HR delegation and a strong link between pay and performance, whereas Japan does not.

There appear to be three objectives for these performance management systems:

- improving internal functioning and performance;
- improving mechanisms to distribute and clarify responsibilities and control; and
- reducing budgets (OECD, 1997).

Each member country's system emphasizes a specific objective. The different objectives require different techniques for

Table 16.7   Union density, private and public sector (percent of unionized workers)

Country	Year	Private	Public	Year	Private	Public
Australia	1982	39	73	2004	17	46
Austria	1980	49	68	1998	30	69
Belgium	1982	41	79	1991	45	67
Canada	1984	28	64	2004	18	72
France	1981	18	44	2003	5	15
Germany	1980	29	67	1997	22	56
Italy	1980	48	60	1997	36	43
Japan	1980	29	75	2003	18	58
Netherlands	1980	26	60	2001	22	39
Norway	1980	47	74	1998	43	83
Spain	1991	14	26	1997	15	32
Switzerland	1980	24	71	1987	22	71
United Kingdom	1980	45	69	2004	17	59
United States	1980	17	37	2004	8	36

Source: ILO, 2000; Visser, 2006.

managing performance, however, the required techniques are complementary and mutually reinforcing (OECD, 1997).

Most member countries are utilizing a form of management by objectives, wherein managers and employees agree upon performance evaluation criteria (OECD, 2005b). In addition, quantifiable numerical criteria are being employed less often. Job analyses are also broader in nature.

Recruitment and selection

As is noted in Table 16.8, HRM systems have unique implications for recruitment and selection policies (OECD, 2005a). A career-based system allows employees to enter public service only at the early stages of their careers, while position-based systems allow employees to enter public service at different points in time and make lateral transfers. For example, France most closely approximates a career-based system. The recruitment practices in France tend to utilize competitive examination and education to gain access to entry level positions with limited access to some middle level posts, and no outside access to more senior positions. In contrast, New Zealand's recruitment and selection process emphasizes competitive posting for positions utilizing professional experience, with both senior and middle level management positions being open to outside competition.

In addition, recruitment and selection policies are also influenced by the new focus on organizational and individual performance (OECD, 2005b). The new focus on individual performance has lessened the differences between private and public sector employment which has created increased competition for employees (OECD Observer, 2004).

OECD member countries generally utilize four different staffing approaches. The traditional public sector employment includes guaranteed lifelong employment protected by law (OECD, 2005b). However, in many countries, civil servant employment laws have been abolished and the same laws cover public and private sector employees. A second approach provides employment protection but employees remain in a certain position only as long as their performance is sufficient. A third approach utilizes short-term contracts with no guaranteed employment following the term of the contract. The final approach utilizes contract employees instead of internal employees. The loss of lifelong employment protection has reduced the attractiveness of public sector employment and made it more difficult to recruit qualified employees (OECD Observer, 2004).

Compensation

Staffing level reductions were undertaken to decrease the central or federal administrations

Table 16.8 Characteristics of career-based, department-based, and position-based civil systems

	Career-based public services	Department-based public services	Position-based public services
Tendencies of status	Covered by civil service employment laws.	Some covered by public employment laws and other covered by civil service employment laws.	Covered by public employment laws.
Trend toward term contracts within the civil service	No	No	Yes
Recruitment	Competitive examination. Mix of individual and pool recruitment early in career. Few lateral entries.	Mix of recruitment of pools and individuals depending on country, but early in career. Few lateral entries.	Recruitment of individuals. Very open systems to lateral entries.
Emphasis on entry training versus lifelong training	Emphasis on training at entry in the civil service.	Mix	Lifelong training
Existence of a senior civil service with differential management rules	Yes	No	Mix – yes and no.
Existence of central HRM body and line ministries autonomy vis-à-vis central HRM body	Limited or very limited autonomy vis-à-vis central HRM body.	Large autonomy or absence of central HRM body.	Large autonomy or absence of central HRM body.
Career development, promotion, incentives	Performance incentives/sanctions on promotion. Few pay based incentives.	Emphasis on promotion incentive/sanction. Some pay incentive.	Emphasis on pay and promotion as incentive/sanction.
Decentralization of pay	Centralization of pay systems. Little individualization.	Partial delegation of pay. Little individualization of pay.	Partial or extensive delegation of pay. Extensive individualization of pay.
Examples	France, Greece, Hungary, Ireland, Japan, Korea, Luxembourg, Spain.	Austria, Belgium, Germany, Italy, Mexico, Netherlands, Poland, Portugal.	Australia, New Zealand, Norway, UK, US.

Source: OECD.2005a; 2005b.

wage bill (OECD, 2005b). Overall, this appears to have been a successful strategy since the ratio of compensation costs to GDP of OECD member countries has decreased since 1990 (OECD, 2002a). Interestingly, public sector employment in most OECD countries (Table 16.4) and compensation levels have been decreasing (OECD, 2002a), but the overall size, expressed as the ratio of government expenditures to GDP, of government has been increasing (Table 16.2).

The major trend regarding compensation in the OECD member countries is the use of performance-related pay (PRP) (OECD, 1997; 2002a; 2004b). The main reasons for introducing PRP include:

- attracting and retaining talent;
- improving motivation;
- creating more visible accountability; and
- facilitating management change (OECD, 2004b).

Motivation for implementation of PRP plans varies by country, but is strongly linked to the degree of authority delegated to line managers to make personnel decisions (OECD, 2005a).

There is a general trend in most OECD countries to focus on individual performance and decentralize HRM decisions. The decentralization has been accomplished by (a) transferring responsibility for HR activity to line managers, (b) simplifying rules and procedures by developing the main policy in the central HRM office and leaving details to the line managers, or (c) developing more flexible policies. By focusing on individual performance and decentralized decision-making, line managers can more closely link employee's pay with their performance (OECD, 2005a). In contrast to position-based systems, career-based systems foster cohesiveness by utilizing rewards based on group performance (OECD, 2005a). The proportion of pay-for-performance relative to total compensation is, on average, less than 10 per cent for employees and 20 per cent for managers (OECD, 2005a), proportions that are rather small. Bonuses are being used to supplement or replace merit increments and are generally larger than merit increments.

NEW PARADIGMS OF PUBLIC GOVERNANCE

In *The Global Public Management Revolution*, Kettl (2005) argues that recent government change has been rapid and widespread. The global revolution in public management generally follows the 'reinvention' model adopted by the Clinton-Gore administration in the US and new public management model adopted in the mid-1980s in New Zealand. While Kettl (2005) argues that these are distinct, these models share commonalities.

Key points/trends related to NPM and reinvention

Important similarities exist between reinvention and NPM. Fundamentally, the purpose of reinvention and NPM is to apply proven business practices to maximize the performance of large, often inefficient governments. Reinvention relies on employee involvement, incentive-based pay systems, job flexibility, and increased training and skill development. These practices are intended to increase the efficiency and productivity of government. The objective is to make government more efficient and productive. However, reinvention centres on how the government operates, not on what it does.

This illustrates the key difference between reinvention and NPM. Unlike reinvention, NPM is concerned not only with how the government operates, but also on what it does. NPM questions the fundamental role that government plays in society, such as whether functions should be privatized or outsourced. NPM also provides greater flexibility in work systems than does reinvention; incentives; short-term contracts; and performance management (at the individual and budgetary levels). While reinvention and NPM utilize similar means, such as employee involvement, NPM is more encompassing than the reinvention model.

The US provides an interesting illustration of public management reform. It embraced reinvention under the Clinton-Gore administration, pushing toward a NPM conceptualization. However, the Bush II administration has reversed many of these initiatives. It has focused on managing for results, with HR reforms tied to improving performance and reducing costs.

The US: reinvention and beyond reinvention

In the US reinvention encapsulated a set of reforms in governance that gained considerable popularity across all levels of government, particularly the federal, in the 1990s. Osborne and Gaebler's (1992) *Reinventing government* focused on improving the management of government, or *the how* of government, rather than *the what* of government. In the US, reinvention became a program to save, not eviscerate, the public sector. Focusing on the application of business practices to governance, it gained ready acceptance by the Clinton-Gore administration immediately after assuming office in 1993. Clinton-Gore embraced reinvention as a means of simultaneously promoting popular reforms to make government more efficient and less costly while at the same time dampening political pressures to scale back the domestic programs that served the needy and subsidized improvements in the public infrastructure.

As originally conceived, reinvention focused on making government more business-like in its processes, infusing an entrepreneurial spirit into traditionally staid bureaucracies. Osborne and Gaebler's (1992) purpose was not to make government a for-profit business, but to make it more efficient and effective by using proven business methods. They defined their entrepreneurial model as one in which public sector institutions 'constantly use their resources in new ways to heighten both their efficiency and their effectiveness' (Osborne and Gaebler, 1992: xix). An entrepreneurial government followed 10 operating principles, including injecting competition into service delivery; transforming rule-driven into mission-driven organizations; focusing on results or outcomes, not inputs; meeting the needs of the customer not the bureaucracy; decentralizing power and authority; and making government market-oriented.

When President Clinton assumed office in 1993, he faced three then-chronic deficits: budget, performance, and public confidence (Kettl, 1994). To address these issues, he created the National Performance Review (NPR) 'to redesign, to reinvent, to reinvigorate the entire national government' (NPR, 1993:1). The 1993 *From Red Tape to Results: Creating a Government that Works Better and Costs Less* embraced the philosophy of reinvention with its entrepreneurial spirit. It distilled the core operating principles to four in number:

(1) cutting red tape;
(2) putting customers first;
(3) empowering employees to get results; and
(4) cutting back to basics: producing better government for less.

The Republican victory in the 1994 congressional elections produced heated debates over federal spending (Kettl, 1998; 2005) and broadened the initial focus of reinvention on how government works eventually to include what government should do. In reality, reinvention at the federal level concentrated on the 'costs less' rather than 'works better.' Downsizing the federal workforce became the principal way of cutting costs. During the Clinton White House years, federal civilian employment dropped by over 300,000 positions and to its lowest levels since John F. Kennedy was president.

In terms of the employment relationship, the most significant aspect of reinvention concerned promoting labor-management cooperation. The NPR (1993) reported that adversarial labor-management relations in the federal service had hindered performance and impeded positive change. To change this situation, NPR recommended establishing a governmental labor-management partnership policy, citing the success of such partnerships in transforming private sector organizations (NPR, 1993: 87). As per the NPR recommendation, President Clinton issued Executive Order 12871, on October 1, 1993, which mandated federal agency heads to create partnerships at appropriate organizational levels to 'involve employees and their union representatives as full partners with management representatives to identify problems and craft solutions to better serve the agency's customers and mission.' Partnerships proliferated throughout the federal service, where 60 per cent of the workforce is represented by unions (Masters, 2001). These partnerships helped improve the quality of labor-management relations. In selected cases, they also improved organizational performance (Masters, 2001; Masters et al., 2006; US Office of Personnel Management, 2000). Philosophically, EO 12871 represented the most significant shift in federal labor-management programs since President Kennedy granted federal employees the right to unionize and bargain collectively through his 1962 EO 10988.

Beyond reinvention: Bush's management agenda and homeland security

Shortly after President Bush took office in January 2001, he began dismantling the reinvention apparatus of the Clinton-Gore era. Among other things, he rescinded the labor-management partnership order. In August 2001, through his Office of Management and Budget (OMB), Bush unveiled his own Management Agenda. It promoted a citizen-centered, results-oriented, and market-based government. Its goals ranged from strategic human resource management to expanded electronic government (e-government). As mentioned, managerial flexibility received special attention as a means of facilitating intended reforms.

Competitive sourcing has emerged as central to President Bush's approach to management. It has widely encouraged that much of what government does is subject to competitive bidding. Competitive sources were intended to make government more market-based. OMB (2001:17) stated that 'By rarely subjecting commercial tasks performed by the government to competition, agencies have insulated themselves from the pressures that produce quality service at reasonable cost.' In July 2003, OMB (2003) identified 416,000 federal positions, or 26 per cent of the total civilian workforce, as available for competition.

For the most part, the President's Management Agenda was silent on the types of managerial reforms it sought with regard to employees. It advocated competitive sourcing as a means of reducing costs, including payroll. September 11, 2001, however, led to a dramatic emphasis on personnel reform in the civilian part of the federal service. In response to the terrorist attacks, President Bush recommended, after considerable Congressional prodding, creating a new Department of Homeland Security (DHS). In his recommendation, he originally proposed to exempt DHS employees from the law granting the right to bargain collectively (for instance, the Federal Service Labor-Management Relations Statute, FSLMRS, or Title VII of the 1978 Civil Service Reform Act). While Congress eventually put most DHS employees under Title VII when creating the DHS in 2002, it gave the Secretary of DHS wide authority to create a new, more flexible personnel system. The goal was to enable the agency to frame the managerial flexibility it needed to protect the homeland.

For similar reasons, Congress gave the Secretary of the Department of Defence (DoD) similar authority in 2003. By 2005, the DHS and DoD had issued regulations establishing new personnel systems. While the implementation of these regulations has been at least temporarily stalled by court injunctions, the proposals have far-reaching impacts. Both DHS and DoD recommended significant changes in job classification, compensation, performance management, and labor-management relations. They have proposed giving management more flexibility to classify workers into jobs; introducing pay-for-performance systems; and substantially shrinking the bargaining rights and powers of labor unions. These changes have led to considerable labor-management confrontation. Federal-employee unions have aggressively opposed the DHS and DoD reforms in both Congress and the courts.

A coalition of unions representing federal employees filed legal challenges to the Bush administration's proposed personnel reforms in DHS and DoD. In August 2005, a federal district judge issued a ruling that enjoined the plan to reform the collective bargaining system at DHS. A federal court of appeals upheld this ruling in 2006, and the DHS decided not to make a further appeal in September 2006. In February 2006, another federal district judge enjoined DoD by implementing the collective bargaining provisions of its proposed National Security Personnel System. This decision is on appeal. As another example of how things can change as a result of political and legal challenges, and newly installed 110th Congress, which is controlled by Democrats, is considering legislation to grant airport screeners the right to unionize, which the Transportation Security Administration has denied by an agency memorandum.

CONCLUSION

Globally sweeping economic, political, and technological changes have caused organizations of all kinds to change. Organizations that produce goods and provide services have had to become more efficient and effective, while still satisfying the customer. Public sector organizations in particular have had to transform, squeezed by growing political demands, on the one side, to shrink government and intensifying needs, on the other side, for efficient public services given demographic realities.

New models of public management and governance have emerged. Societies have had to rethink the role of government and the distribution of resources and functions between the private and public sectors. In addition, governments have had to revamp managerial and HR practices to respond to these demands.

The global wave of public sector changes cannot be gainsayed, though it may not have lived up to expectations. Privatization and outsourcing (contracting out or competitive sourcing, etc.) have swept across societies. Managerial flexibility, pay-for-performance, and more contingent workforces have become widely accepted. The line between government and industry has become increasingly blurred. More is expected of government, yet less will be given willingly for it to do the job. Government today suffers the consequences of its past failures. Further, it lacks the allure and financial reward of business. Nonetheless, governments perform *essential* functions, from national defense and education to public health. The battles against terrorism, including the omnipresent fear of biological or chemical warfare, and the thread of pandemic flu make the relevance of government inescapable, no matter how much we may worship the dogma of free markets.

This burst of public sector reform energy has produced results, albeit mixed. Focusing attention on better performance and greater results merits commendation. But there are drawbacks.

First, the public sector reforms almost invariably demand more from both managers and employees. The luxury of 'cushy' government jobs has gone by the wayside. Marsden (1999) reports that the pay-for-performance efforts in the UK have caused managers to experience greater and more intense work loads. Schouteten (2004) has found that a team-based approach among UK home care workers did not yield a relatively higher quality of work life, partly because of expansion in work load. There are obviously limits to how much more one can do no matter how 'incentivized.'

Second, privatization, outsourcing, devolution, pay-for-performance, downsizing, and contracted employment have no doubt undermined confidence in the legitimacy of public service among some in government as well as the wider society. Indeed, new public management, or its country-specific variants, has often represented a political response to avoid more draconian cutbacks in the public sector. To some, it may represent a stopgap measure at best. A political psychology of doubt may surround the public sector, with the doubt being the inherent capacity of government to perform effectively. Witness the widespread criticisms of how the US government, at all levels, responded to Hurricane Katrina in New Orleans especially. This sentiment could hamper government's ability to attract qualified employees, a dangerous proposition in societies where huge bubbles of retirement are on the horizon.

Third, the excitement with the NPM has appeared to vaporize. Such is the case with all 'experiments' in reform. Reality eventually sets in, as limitations become clear. The intrinsic complexities of existing working relationships are often underestimated (for example, Bach et al., 2004).

The difficulties inherent in governing become inescapable, not the least of which are the political pressures on public servants.

The conceptualization and implementation of public management reforms, no matter how antiseptically phrased are political judgments. Changes in the political winds shift emphasis in managerial reform. The transfer of power from Clinton-Gore to Bush-Cheney demonstrated this reality. Emphasis went from reinventing government to managerial flexibility, not mutually incompatible schemes but different ones. One encouraged employee involvement and labor-management cooperation while the other disbanded it with remarkable alacrity. One focused on shrinking the workforce while the other encouraged disembarking governmental functions of a commercial nature. In democratic societies, it is hard to plan for the future.

Last, challenges facing government in the future are no less foreboding than those of the past. They will demand more from those who serve, both in terms of capability and performance. The role of government will undergo continually redefinition. Should vouchers replace public schools or should education be outsourced (Cottrell, 2006; O'Reilly and Boorstin, 2002). Relatedly, the ability of government to fund new initiatives is often doubtful. Is there enough money for government to fund meaningful pay-for-performance systems? Or, more fundamentally, should monetary incentives replace 'public service' as a driver of performance.

We can only say a few things with absolute certainty. Governments across the globe will face serious challenges. How they perform will directly affect public confidence in public institutions. Failure to perform will demand new reforms and invite unrest. Before long, a new mantra of change will replace the NPM wave.

REFERENCES

Bach, Stephen, Kessler, Ian, and Heron, Paul (2004) 'Support Roles and Changing Boundaries in the Public Services: The Case of Teaching Assistants in British Primary School,' paper presented at the *22nd Annual Labour Process Conference, Amsterdam*, April 5–7.

Bach, Stephen (2000) *Decentralization and Privatization in Municipal Services: The Case of Health Services.* Sectoral Activities Programme Working Paper 164. Geneva: ILO.

Bordogna, Lorenzo (2003) 'The Reform of Public Sector Employment Relations in Industrialized Democracies,' in Jonathan Brock and David B. Lipsky, (eds), *Going Public: The Role of Labor-Management Relations in Delivering Quality Government Services.* Champaign, IL: IRRA: pp. 23–68.

Cotterell, Bill (2006) Legislature may regulate privatization. *Tallahassee Democrat.* March 27, 2006.

Csoka, Louis, S. (1995) 'A New Employer-Employee Contract?' *Employment Relations Today*, 22 (2): 21–31.

Dunleavy, Patrick, Margetts, Helen, Bastow, Simon, and Tinkler, Jane (2006) 'New Public Management Is Dead-Long Live Digital-Era Governance'. *Journal of Public Administration Research and Theory*, 16 (3): 467–94.

Freeman, Richard, B. (2002) *Institutional Differences and Economic Performance Among OECD Countries.* London: Centre for the Economics of Education, October.

Gansler, Jacque, S. and William Lucyshyn (2004) *Competitive Sourcing: What Happens to Federal Employees?* Washington, D.C.: IBM Center for the Business of Government, October.

Godine, Morton Robert (1951) *The Labor Problem in the Public Service.* Cambridge, MA: Harvard University Press.

Gwartney, James, Lawson, Robert, and Holcombe, Randall (1998) *The Size and Functions of Government and Economic Growth.* Joint Economic Committee Report, Congress of the United States, May 1998.

International Labour Organization (2001) *The Impact of Decentralization and Privatization on Municipal Services.* Geneva: ILO, October.

Kettl, Donald, F. (1994) *Reinventing Government* Washington, D.C.: Brookings Institution Press.

Kettl, Donald, F. (1998) *Reinventing Government: A Fifth-Year Report Card.* Washington, D.C.: Brookings Institution Press.

Kettl, Donald, F. (2005) The *Global Public Management Revolution*, 2nd edn. Washington, D.C.: Brookings Institution Press.

Kissler, G.D (1994) 'The New Employment Contract.' *Human Resource Management*, 33 (3): 335–52.

International Labour Office (2000) *Trends in unionization and collective bargaining.* Geneva: ILO.

Lane, Jan-Erik (2000) *New Public Management.* New York, NY: Routledge.

Marsden, David (1999) 'Managing Performance Now Developments: A Senior Organized by IPD's Public Sector Forum,' July 1st.

Masters, Marick, F. (2001) *A Final Report to the National Partnership on Evaluating Progress and Improvements in Agencies' Organizational Performance Resulting From Labor-Management Partnerships.*

Masters, Marick, Albright, Robert, and Eplion, David (2006) 'What do Partnerships Do? Evidence from the Federal Sector.' *Industrial & Labor Relations Review*, 59 (3): 367–85.

NPR (National Performance Review) (1993) *From Red Tape to Results: Creating a Government that Works Better and Costs Less.* Washington, D.C.: Government Printing Office.

OECD (1997) *In Search of Results: Performance Management Practices.* Paris: OECD Publications.

OECD (2001) 'Recent Privatisation Trends.' *Financial Market Trends*, 79 (June): 43–65.

OECD (2002a) *Assessing Performance-oriented HRM Activities in Selected OECD Countries.* Paris: OECD Publications.

OECD (2002b) *Highlights of Public Sector Pay and Employment Trends: 2002 Update.* Internet resource available at www.oecd.org/gov/hrm. Last verified September 2006.

OECD (2002c) Recent Privatization Trends in OECD Countries. *Financial Market Trends*, 82 (June): 43–58.

OECD (2004a) *The Learning Government: Introduction and Draft Results of the Survey of Knowledge Management Practices in Ministries/Departments/Agencies of Central Government.* Paris: OECD Publications.

OECD (2004b) *Performance-related Pay Policies for Government Employees: Main Trends in OECD Member Countries.* Paris: OECD Publications.

OECD (2005a) *Trends in Human Resources Management Policies in OECD Countries An Analysis of the Results of the OECD Survey on Strategic Human Resources Management.* Paris: OECD Publications.

OECD (2005b) 'Organising and Motivating Public Servants: Modernising Public Employment' in *Modernising Government: The Way Forward.* Paris: OECD Publications. pp. 157–84.

OECD Observer, July 2004. *Policy Brief Public Sector Modernisation: Modernising Public Employment.* Internet resource available at www.oecd.org/publication/Pol_brief. Last verified September 2006.

OMB (Office of Management and Budget) (2001) *The President's Management Agenda.* Washington, D.C.: Government Printing Office.

OMB (Office of Management and Budget) (2003) *Competitive Sourcing: Conducting Public-Private Competition in a Reasoned and Responsible Manner.* Washington, D.C.: Government Printing Office.

O'Reilly, Brian and Boorstin, Julia (2002) Why Edison doesn't work. *Fortune*, 146 (12): 148–54.

Osborne, David and Gaebler, Ted (1992) *Reinventing Government: How the Entrepreneurial Spirit is Transforming the Public Sector.* Reading, MA: Addison-Wesley.

Rosenbloom, David, H. (1971) *Federal Service and the Constitution.* Ithaca, NY: Cornell University Press.

Schouteten, Roel (2004) 'Does Group Work Improve the QWL in the Home Care Sector?' Paper presented to the 22nd *Annual Labour Process Conference*, Amsterdam, April 5–7.

Trebilock, Michael (1995) 'Can Government Be Reinvented?' in Jonathan Boston (ed.), *The State Under Contract.* Wellington, New Zealand: Bridget Williams Brooks Ltd. pp. 1–35.

US Office of Personnel Management (2000) *A White Paper: A Fresh Start for Federal Pay: The Case for Modernization.* Washington, D.C.: Government Printing Office.

Visser, Jelle (2006) Union membership statistics in 24 countries, *Monthly Labor Review*, January, 129 (1) 38–49.

17

International Actors and International Regulation

Rebecca Gumbrell-McCormick

INTRODUCTION

Industrial relations (IR), as a field of study, is oriented around the nation-state. When Dunlop (1958) proposed the concept of an industrial relations system, this was nationally bounded; though his aim was in part to compare and contrast different national systems, the idea of an international system was not addressed. Yet can we speak of an international industrial relations system? Writing of developments within the European Union (EU), Jensen et al. (1999) argue that we can identify supranational equivalents of Dunlop's three actors – representative organizations of workers and employers, and government agencies – and that their interactions are creating a supranational body of rules. Hence, they conclude, a European industrial relations system exists. The same might be said of the global level, as this chapter explains. But how far do the international 'actors' match our understanding of trade unions, employers' associations and governments at national level? And how far do the rules they create match the laws and collective agreements normally seen as typical of national employment regulation? My aim is to suggest answers to these questions.

When academic industrial relations became established in the mid-twentieth century, the main collective actors and the main arena of regulation were clearly nationally based. But this primacy of the national level has been challenged in recent years, both practically and analytically. The spread of multinational companies (MNCs), and other aspects of economic internationalization, are widely seen as weakening or undermining the capacity for regulation at a national level. While my intention is not to focus on the debates over the concept and extent of globalization (the theme of Chapter 6 in this volume), these processes have stimulated a growing interest in the possibility of international regulation of the employment relationship. But despite a growing body of international law and other forms of regulation, and an expanding academic literature documenting and interpreting the implications of supranational action, this remains relatively unfamiliar to most students of mainstream industrial relations.

For this reason, this chapter needs to present considerable empirical detail as well as to review existing theoretical debates. I shall begin by addressing some key conceptual and definitional issues, before outlining the background and structure of the international industrial relations system and the actors within it. I will then discuss some of the motives for organization and action at this level, exploring similarities and differences as against national industrial relations. Next I will address some of the main instruments of supranational regulation, again comparing and contrasting with their national analogues. My conclusion will be that it is indeed meaningful to speak of international industrial relations, but that it is a mistake to interpret it as a national system writ large.

DEFINITIONS, CONCEPTS AND ANALYSIS

Most literature on the international level of IR tends to apply concepts and theoretical approaches originally developed at national level. Before I consider how far this is appropriate, it is necessary to clarify what we *mean* by the international level in the context of industrial relations. This question has probably been more extensively addressed in the EU than the global context (Böröcz and Sarkar, 2005; Dølvik, 1997; Schmidt, 2002; Wallace, 2000).

There is a continuum in the division of powers between national and international levels. At one extreme is *supranational* authority, where higher-level institutions can impose rules on national actors, at the other is *internationalism*, where higher-level competence is conditional on consensus among the national actors. In between are *federal* structures, with a clear functional division between the autonomy retained at national level and that of supranational authorities, which may itself depend on a large majority of support from lower-level actors.

In IR, with very few exceptions: the *international* form of organization is the norm. Nation-states tend to delegate very few of their powers: much of the tension within the United Nations (UN) system, and more recently within the World Trade Organization (WTO), has to do with the extent of supranational authority. This is also the case for national unions taking part in trade union internationals: they agree to pay dues and accept the collective choice of leadership, although not always with good grace, but in practice have rarely agreed to delegate substantial powers of policy-making or negotiation. Employers' associations have been even more restrictive.

National and international: parallels and differences

As noted above, much analysis of the international level of industrial relations has proceeded by analogy with the national. This is misleading. The state has *citizens*; despite the occasional rhetoric of 'world citizenship', individuals do not possess an analogous set of rights and responsibilities *vis-à-vis* international institutions. Trade unions have *members*, who directly contribute to union funds and possess corresponding rights and obligations; international union organizations (leaving aside the special case of those unions which bridge the US-Canadian border) possess members only indirectly, through the affiliation of national bodies. The same is also true of most national confederations; but union internationals are one step further removed from individual members. This distance has been an important area of debate, with some arguing that this has allowed trade union internationals to misrepresent the concerns of individual members (Thompson and Larson, 1978). Likewise, international employers' associations often affiliate national organizations rather than individual companies.

A related issue is the *basis of legitimacy* and *nature of decision-making* at international level. I will cover the issue of governance within intergovernmental organizations below. Looking at the other actors, while there are few expectations for individual employers to operate democratically, their associations are expected to do so, much like international trade unions. But the distance from their base makes this difficult; moreover international bodies must deal not only with the core issues which affect members at national level, but also with world politics and political rivalries between nations. For employers' associations, this is not necessarily a problem; for trade unions it is, because the labor movement relies on its members and their capacity to act (Coates and Topham, 1980: Chapter 11; Hyman, 2005a). For unions, authority depends on democratic accountability to the members – their 'internal authority' (Martin, 1980); yet to be effective, unions must be regarded as representative by outside bodies, such as employers and governments. This external authority can be closely linked to internal authority: if members support the union, employers and governments will take it seriously. Yet some argue that if unions pay too much attention to the agenda set by external interlocutors, they may cease to represent their members' interests effectively and may thus lose internal authority – which in turn may erode their external representative capacity. This issue has been discussed by Dølvik (1997) as a tension between the 'logic of membership' and a 'logic of influence'.

The nature of international regulation

At international as at national level, the industrial relations actors operate within a *regulatory system* which constrains their actions. To some extent, the governmental actors overlap with the regulatory system itself – national governments, for example, are actors within intergovernmental institutions such as the International Labour Organization (ILO), and these intergovernmental bodies themselves formulate policies and programmes that in turn have an effect on the nature and scope of international regulation, but it is important to maintain a conceptual distinction between their role as actors and as components of the supranational system.

The international regulatory system is not identical to that at the national level: the type of structures and their internal decision-making processes, the time-scale of their development, the type of governance and the extent of their regulatory powers are very different, although questions of legitimacy and authority show many similarities. Since the Treaty of Westphalia in 1648, the sovereignty of nation-states has been a fundamental principle of international politics; in normal circumstances, the right of self-determination can only be voluntarily abrogated. In general, nations have been willing to assign only tightly bounded powers to intergovernmental institutions, imposing decision-making rules which restrict the chances that they will be bound by policies to which they object. Similar constitutional limitations apply in the case of international organizations of unions and employers. This principle of 'subsidiarity' is reinforced by the long time gap between the consolidation of nation-states and the creation and development of an international system (from approximately the mid-nineteenth to mid-twentieth centuries).

Governance and government

Even those international organizations with relatively strong sets of competence lack key defining characteristics of governments. National states, in Weber's definition (see Chapter 14), hold the monopoly of the legitimate use of violence within a given territory. International organizations lack this capacity (although the UN, in exceptional circumstances, may be empowered to intervene forcefully if one state threatens the security of another, or collapses into civil war). The international institutional order, as expressed in the title of the study by Rosenau and Czempiel (1992), is a matter of 'governance without government'; while Bulmer (1998: 366) has argued, in the context of the EU, that the latter 'does not resemble, or have, a government, so governance offers some descriptive purchase on the character of the polity'.

The elusive concept of *governance* – 'an archaic term become newly fashionable' (Leisink and Hyman, 2005: 277) – is also commonly used with reference to decision-making by companies – 'corporate governance' – and other bodies. Its practical meaning is often unclear, since the concept leaves open questions of power relations, means of enforcement and implementation. There is also a tension between the descriptive or analytical use of the term 'global governance', and the normative or programmatic usage which calls for a regulatory order to compensate for a presumed loss of national capacity (Dingwerth and Pattberg, 2006).

Precisely because international organizations rarely possess the ultimate sanction of force to implement their decisions, the distinction between government and governance links to that between 'hard' and 'soft' law (Abbott and Snidal, 2000). 'Soft' law indicates decisions which those to whom they are addressed are expected to observe but which cannot be juridically enforced; their efficacy depends on peer pressure and the possibility of less formalized means of retaliation, and on the extent to which the underlying norms of conduct are 'internalized' by decision-makers at national level (Koh, 1999). Much international regulation in the field of industrial relations is precisely of this nature. There is considerable disagreement as to whether non-binding norms can exert hard effects; those who assert the value of such approaches insist that 'soft' law may help 'frame' the political debate at national as well as international level, providing an important resource for those actors pressing for stronger national regulation (Zeitlin and Pochet, 2005).

THE INTERNATIONAL SYSTEM: THE MAJOR ACTORS AND INSTITUTIONS

This section gives a 'snapshot' of the international industrial relations system. I identify the key characteristics of the international level of industrial relations; its actors and the relations between them; its structure and its regulatory setting and its evolution over time. I focus on the three actors comprising Dunlop's model but also refer more briefly to a putative fourth actor, non-governmental organizations (NGOs) or

'civil society actors'. Of key significance are the institutions that have been established to regulate the international economy and polity. These include the ILO, the Bretton Woods institutions and the rest of the UN system, the Organization for Economic Cooperation and Development (OECD) and the WTO, which are both actors *and* major components of the regulatory framework or structure of the international system. I conclude this section by considering the regional dimension of international industrial relations, with particular attention to the EU.

States and intergovernmental organizations

There has been much recent debate on the supposedly declining powers of nation-states in the era of globalization (Berger, 2000; Strange, 1996; Weiss, 1998). My focus here, however, is not on the autonomy of states to regulate their own internal affairs, but rather on their role at the international level.

International organizations of states and governments were formed after the first and then after the second world wars. The oldest major organization still in existence is the ILO, founded in 1919 as part of the League of Nations and incorporated in the UN system in 1946 (Alcock, 1971; Hughes, 2005; ILO, 1931; Shotwell, 1934). Most international organizations discussed here are formally intergovernmental, that is, they represent the governments of national states directly, although the forms of representation and selection may vary. The ILO is distinctive, representing workers and employers as well as states in a tripartite system.

Intergovernmental organizations, while acting on behalf of nation-states, do not enjoy analogous powers or legitimacy. The UN system is recognized by and represents the largest number of nation-states on a permanent basis and is granted the legitimate right to use force under very limited conditions. No other intergovernmental body — at least at the world level – enjoys such powers, and nation-states are rarely willing in practice to grant the UN the freedom in theory to act in the way that is allowed in emergency situations. The UN system has been rife with inter-state and interregional rivalries and has been subject to the veto power of individual states, in particular the US.

The ILO has a direct influence on national industrial relations practices, but possesses fewer powers than the UN system as a whole. Much of the literature focuses on its effects rather than its structure, functions and gover-nance, with debate polarized between those who emphasize its positive achievements (Kyloh, 1998; Langille, 2005; Sengenberger, 2002) and those who stress its limitations (Elliott and Freeman, 2003; Standing, 2004). I explore the efficacy of the ILO regulatory instruments in a later section.

Many would argue that an even greater impact on industrial relations is exerted by the international financial institutions (IFIs) which define the rules of the global economic game. The Bretton Woods agreements of 1944 resulted in the creation of the International Monetary Fund (IMF) and what was to become the World Bank (WB). Their orig-inal mission, as integral parts of the new UN system, was the reduction of poverty and inequality between nations; but from the 1950s, financial support to developing countries was made conditional on 'structural adjustment programmes'. With the advance of the neo-liberal 'Washington consensus', these involved radical measures of privatization, reduction in public expenditure, removal of barriers to external trade and investment and flexible labor market policies. Such policies have been widely blamed for causing unem-ployment, insecurity, reduced living standards and increased poverty (Cammack, 2005; Chorev, 2005; Germain, 2002); critics have included the former WB chief economist, Joseph Stiglitz (2002). However both institu-tions, especially the WB, may now be moving towards closer co-ordination within the UN system (with the ILO) and the pursuit of their original goals (Panić, 2003; Toye, 2003).

The Bretton Woods conference also led to the General Agreement on Tariffs and Trade (GATT), which promoted trade liberalization and was transformed into the WTO in 1995. The latter is not part of the UN system but functions in some respects in parallel with the WB and IMF. With some 150 members, it has a cumbersome governance structure and positions are often polarized, as is evident from the deadlock in a number of recent attempts to achieve further trade liberalization. Also separate from the UN system is the OECD, the predecessor of which was established in 1948. Today it includes some 30 of the world's richest countries, and while it possesses fewer formal powers that the UN institutions, it is often seen as a vehicle of 'soft' law;[1] by its own description it 'produces internationally agreed instruments, decisions and recommendations to promote rules of the game in areas where multilat-eral agreement is necessary for individual countries to make progress in a globalized economy'. It is notable for possessing an element of tripartism in its governance, with Advisory Committees representing both employers and trade unions. The Trade Union Advisory Committee (TUAC) is independent of the ITUC but works closely with it.

The international economy is, inevitably, strongly influenced by the policies of its most powerful actors; and since the collapse of the Soviet empire, this has given the US a hegemonic role in the functioning of the IFIs, accelerating the liberalization of trade in both goods and services and of cross-national flows of finance and investment. In other words, those dynamics characterized as globalization, and their impact on employ-ment conditions at national level, are to an important extent the outcome of the policies of the IFIs and those nation-states which dominate their governance.

Employers' associations and multinational corporations

The International Organization of Employ-ers (IOE), formed in 1920 after the ILO was established (Rojot, 2006), represents employers' interests within the ILO and the UN system as a whole. It comprises national associations in some 140 countries and cooperates with a variety of regional employers' organizations, and also with the Business and Industry Advisory Committee to the OECD (BIAC). Another influential body is the International Chamber of Commerce (ICC), established in 1919. It is a strong advocate of neo-liberalism. While it lacks the legitimacy as a 'social partner' enjoyed by the IOE, it has nevertheless been allowed a significant role within the UN system (Kelly, 2005). Numerous organizations also represent employer interests in individual industries and sectors.

One reason for the low profile of international employers' organizations is that individual employers are important international actors in their own right, especially (but not exclusively) if they are large MNCs. They are often seen as acting with more power and autonomy at the international level than many national governments, and as exerting a significant influence on the actions of such governments. As an example, Balanyá et al. (2003: 3) report that over 200 corporations have European government affairs offices in Brussels, alongside some 500 corporate lobby groups. There is a much-quoted statistic that just over half of the 100 largest economic entities in the world are MNCs, not nation-states (Hertz, 2001). The growth in mergers and acquisitions (facilitated by the liberalization of takeover rules) has accelerated the trend.

MNCs are not 'embedded' in the norms and institutions of most of the countries in which they operate, they often ensure frequent mobility of key managers across countries to prevent them 'going native', and they have the capacity to pursue international strategies while most trade unions and other employee representative institutions are nationally bounded. Many writers see their dominance in the global economy, not only in manufacturing but increasingly in service industries, as undermining both the practical and theoretical coherence of national industrial relations systems (Katz and Darbishire, 2000). Leading international trade unionists – for example, Fimmen (1924)

and Levinson (1971, 1972) – have long regarded MNCs as a serious threat. For some contemporary writers, they impose irresistible downwards pressure on national employment regulation through their ability to shift production to low-cost and weakly regulated locations (Gray, 1998). Others argue that there is little evidence that MNCs give priority in their investment decisions to low labor costs: they want a productive and efficient labor force, and also need infrastructure, possibly access to local markets, as well as political stability and secure property rights – all of which are typically associated with countries with advanced labor standards. However, there is compelling evidence that MNCs shift labor-intensive, low valued-added activities to low-wage countries; and though there is little evidence that they frequently close down existing operations to move to low-wage locations (which in some fields of economic activity is difficult), they may well successfully threaten to do so in order to force workers and their unions to make concessions on pay and working practices.

Workers and trade unions

National unions are sometimes important actors at the international level, generally those based in the wealthiest countries or those with the highest union density, but it is dedicated international trade union bodies that carry out most union action and policy-making at the international level. These organizations can be classified by structure, geographical coverage and ideology. Structurally, we can distinguish between organizations based on industrial sectors and those based on national centers. The earliest trade union internationals, founded at the end of the nineteenth century, were industry-based, becoming known as International Trade Secretariats (ITSs), and recently renamed Global Union Federations (GUFs). The first cross-sectoral body was founded in 1901 and reconstituted as the International Federation of Trade Unions (IFTU) in 1913. There developed a division of labor, with the ITSs concentrating on practical organizing and solidarity work within their sectors, and the confederations of national centers addressing broader political issues (Reinalda, 1997; Van Goethem, 2000).

Geographically, we can distinguish between regional and global bodies. The first international organizations were almost exclusively European in coverage, and the weight of membership and financial resources has always ensured strong European influence in global unionism. After the Second World War, decolonization gave a spur to the creation of regional union organizations in the rest of the world. The split in international trade unionism in 1949 reinforced this trend as three confederations competed for membership across the globe. From the 1950s, the process of European integration led to the establishment of formal regional trade union structures in Europe.

Ideological divisions have received the most attention in studies of international trade unionism. The IFTU mainly encompassed unions with a social-democratic orientation, together with more 'business unionist' affiliates in Britain and the US. After 1920 it faced two smaller rivals, the mainly catholic International Federation of Christian Trade Unions (IFCTU) and the communist Red International of Labour Unions. A new global organization, the World Federation of Trade Unions (WFTU), was founded as a unitary confederation in 1945, but never included the Christian unions. In 1949, most non-communist affiliates broke away to form the International Confederation of Free Trade Unions (ICFTU). In 1968 the IFCTU 'deconfessionalized' and became the World Confederation of Labour (WCL) (Pasture, 1994). Meanwhile WFTU, consisting mainly of national centers from communist and/or developing countries, lost membership rapidly with the rise of 'Eurocommunism' followed by the fall of the Berlin Wall in 1989.

Ideological differences remain important despite the foundation at the end of 2006 of a new unitary organization, the International Trade Union Confederation (ITUC), bringing together the ICFTU and WCL along with a number of independent centers, some of which had formerly belonged to WFTU. It is worth noting that the split in WFTU in 1949 reflected *both* a political confrontation between communists and anti-communists, *and* a conflict over plans to subordinate the ITSs to the control of the Confederation (MacShane, 1992). Within the new ITUC, ideological frictions overlap with regionalism, most notably whether Latin American unions should enjoy regional autonomy (as in the WCL) or be part of a broader pan-American structure in which the US unions exert major influence (as in the ICFTU).

Non-governmental organizations

There is a growing literature on the role of 'civil society', 'social movements' or 'non-governmental organizations' (NGOs) as a fourth category of industrial relations actor (Heery and Frege, 2006; Chapter 19 in this book). Such bodies are particularly important at the international level of industrial relations, where arguably some NGOs have acquired a greater impact than trade unions or employers' organizations (Elliott and Freeman, 2003). We are concerned here with NGOs working in industrial relations areas, such as the relatively worker-oriented War on Want, Amnesty and Oxfam, faith-based charities and development bodies. Certain NGOs can be considered more employer-oriented, devoted to corporate social responsibility and related themes. Others, not specifically oriented to employment issues, also have an impact in this area, for example feminist or environmental NGOs (Cockburn, 1997; Waterman, 1998).

Much recent literature suggests that NGOs are able to campaign more forcefully and effectively than trade unions against the adverse impact of neo-liberal globalization on work and employment. It is widely argued that individuals are increasingly likely to define themselves in a number of ways – as consumers, citizens, women or members of other particular groups – rather than in terms of their role in the production process (Munck, 2002). Most of the older democracies have seen to a decline in membership and activism within trade unions and political parties, and an increased role of 'single-issue' or 'pressure' groups (Koenig-Archibugi, 2003). Many of these have a direct or indirect concern with industrial relations issues.

Waterman (1998) argues that trade union internationals have become 'institutionalized' and have been captured by the official institutions whose policies they seek to influence. Organizational demarcations and administrative procedures have to be transcended in order to create a 'new' labor internationalism within which social movements play an equal role. However, official union representatives typically respond that NGOs and social movements, whether operating nationally or internationally, are often small and unrepresentative, and lack the stability, accountability and transparency of trade unions or political parties. Yet many NGOs do possess clearer representative structures and greater accountability. A good example is Amnesty, which has played a significant role in highlighting abuses of human and social rights, both within nations and at the international level. It has often cooperated with UN bodies and with the ICFTU and other trade union bodies (Gumbrell-McCormick, 2000: 454–8). More generally, it is clear that 'social-movement'-oriented campaigns have been important in shifting the international trade union agenda towards more serious attention to issues such as gender equality, home-working and the 'informal sector' more generally. Significantly, the Self Employed Women's Association, an Indian organization with a bridging role as trade union and campaigning NGO, was given a platform slot at the ITUC founding congress.

Thus we can see a growing rapprochement between international trade unionism and international NGOs as actors in a 'global civil society' (Waterman and Timms, 2005). This can be seen, for example, in the experience of the annual World Social Forum, first convened, mainly by Third World NGOs, in Porto Alegre, Brazil in 2001 as a movement for 'globalization from below' (Sen et al., 2004). Initially the official trade union organizations largely held aloof, but have become increasingly active participants; the same is true of the European Social Forum, first held in Florence in 2002.

The regional dimension

Some critics of the globalization thesis insist that the most notable feature of international economic restructuring has been the intensification of trade relations and corporate activity within regional blocs. Few of these have an explicit industrial relations competence, though their role in trade liberalization has obvious industrial relations consequences. The North American Free Trade Area (NAFTA), as its name indicates, is essentially a free trade zone: its main function is to eliminate cross-national obstacles to trade and investment. It has a minimal 'social dimension' (the 'side agreements' on labor and environmental standards) and establishes no significant supranational institutions with the important exception of the dispute adjudication machinery. The Asia-Pacific Economic Cooperation (APEC), which groups 21 countries in or bordering on the Pacific, is a purely intergovernmental organization with no independent powers. Its membership partly overlaps with that of the Association of Southeast Asian Nations (ASEAN), comprising 10 South-East Asian countries, which is designed to encourage trade but also the coordination of social (including labor) policies. It has few effective supranational powers. There is also a variety of regional trading blocs in Latin America (Mercosur), Africa and the Middle East.

The one regional entity with a substantial industrial relations role is in Europe. The European Economic Community (EEC), created with six member states in 1957, has developed into the contemporary European Union (EU) with 27 members. From one perspective it constitutes a free trade area, underpinned by the principle of the free movement of goods and services, capital and labor. Yet unlike NAFTA it is more than a 'common market': it has an elaborate politico-institutional framework, even if it lacks many of the key attributes of national states, with governing powers divided between the Commission, appointed for a five-year term, and the Council, comprising ministers from each of the member states. There is a parliament, though with weaker powers than national legislatures, a supreme court (the European Court of Justice, ECJ) and a European Central Bank which largely controls monetary policy. Economic integration is accompanied by a 'social dimension', and the legal competence of the EU to regulate employment issues has increased considerably over time. This has had a notable impact on industrial relations in the UK, for example triggering legislation on such issues as equal opportunities, working time and information and consultation. I discuss EU employment regulation in more detail below.

Two employers' organizations have an important formal role in EU policy-making and legislation. UNICE (Union of Industrial and Employers' Confederations of Europe) was founded 1958; since renamed BusinessEurope, it comprises national business and employer confederations, and is as much (or more) concerned with issues of trade and business as with employment. It is resistant to social regulation, and its national affiliates are often reluctant to give it a mandate to negotiate. CEEP (*Centre européen des entreprises à participation publique*) covers public enterprises and has shown more support than UNICE for the 'social dimension' of European integration. There are also representative bodies for commercial undertakings and the small-firm sector.

On the trade union side there is just one major player, the ETUC (European Trade Union Confederation). Founded in 1973 by ICFTU affiliates, it soon admitted the main European members of the WCL, and subsequently all main (ex-)communist confederations were allowed in. It has a dual structure, including national confederations and European Industry Federations (EIFs); hence national trade unions have a dual channel of representation. It covers the large majority of unionized workers in EU countries, and in the 1990s it admitted members and associates from Eastern Europe. It is strongly in favor of enhanced social regulation at EU level; but arguably there is a lack of internal consensus on what, and how, to regulate. It is interesting to note that the ETUC superseded the former European structures of the ICFTU and hence escaped the authority of the global organization; it retains its autonomy despite the creation of the new ITUC.

The notion that trade unions and employers' organizations are 'social partners' is familiar in most European countries. This does not necessarily mean that unions and employers cooperate in a spirit of mutual friendship; rather, that the organizations of capital and labor are 'partners' of the state in formulating and administering social policy. This conception was reflected at EU level in the creation of what is now the European Economic and Social Committee (EESC), representing a wide variety of economic interest groups but with no real power and little influence.

The concept of 'social dialogue' was invented, and strongly promoted, by the Commission in the run-up to the Single Market of 1992 and Economic and Monetary Union which was launched by the 1991 Maastricht Treaty. The 'constitution' of the EU states that 'the Commission shall endeavour to develop the dialogue between management and labour at European level which could, if the two sides consider it desirable, lead to relations based on agreement'. Maastricht boosted the role of the social partners: as well as being guaranteed consultative input during the framing of Commission legislative proposals, they acquired a new right to opt to deal with an issue by means of European-level agreements. Some EU legislation has indeed been adopted through this route.

INTERNATIONAL ORGANIZATION: MOTIVES AND CONSTRAINTS

There is an influential argument in industrial relations (first expounded by Commons in 1909) that the expansion of product markets results in a parallel extension of employment regulation. Yet this never occurs automatically: the actors concerned must regard higher-level (in our case, international) regulation as in their mutual interest, or those who favor such an extension must have the power to impose their will. Hence it is necessary to examine the purpose or motivation for the actions of the key international actors. Much of the literature which addresses this question adopts a rational-choice approach, though this has serious limitations. We may also distinguish 'bottom-up' and 'top-down' perspectives. The former asks why national actors agree to transfer some of their sovereignty to supranational bodies; the latter, starting from the fact that such bodies *do* exist, explores how institutional self-interest can encourage those who manage these to expand their own authority and competence. This has been an important theme in the literature on EU governance. I should also note that much of the writing on the international level of industrial relations concentrates on trade unionism. The discussion below reflects this, but first I consider the other parties.

Governments may participate in intergovernmental bodies for negative and defensive or positive and constructive reasons (as will be seen, a similar distinction applies to the other actors). Many international agencies or treaties are designed to prevent the destructive consequences of the unregulated pursuit of national interests: from war to global warming to retaliatory tariff barriers. Others may be intended to facilitate commonly desired objectives which single states lack the capacity to achieve, or even to establish a 'new world order' – a goal proclaimed at the end of both world wars (and reiterated after the collapse of communism). The ILO, and the whole UN system, were explicitly assigned such idealistic aims.

One common view is that the bias of international economic regulation is negative (reducing or removing barriers to cross-national trade and financial movements) whereas the thrust of employment regulation is positive (enhancing the conditions of working life). Scharpf (1999) refers to a tension between these two aspects of European integration; in his view the negative dynamic of market liberalization has overridden the positive goal of upward harmonization of employment conditions. Many critics of globalization argue similarly: a neo-liberal project of eliminating inhibitions to international trade and investment is antagonistic to the creation of new international labor standards and indeed implies the weakening of those which currently exist at national level. A rather different distinction is proposed by Langille (2005), who contrasts a negative view of international labor standards as a defense against a 'race to the bottom' with a positive conception of high standards as economically productive. The conflict between these two perspectives is central to much academic, and public policy, debate.

Given the very limited academic attention to international employers' organizations (partly because of the limited transparency of their operations), it is impossible to analyze their motivations in detail. One should also note that many of these bodies are primarily representatives of companies' commercial interests with only a subsidiary concern for industrial relations issues. Often their function seems negative in the strong sense of resisting projects of transnational regulation, or at least those seen as threats to employers' interests. Yet we should note that those who represent employers at international level may be inspired by the more positive visions indicated above, and may also absorb the progressive culture of bodies such as the ILO. In addition, sectoral employers' organizations – in the maritime industry, for example – may be powerfully motivated by the need to establish rules of the game essential for international industries to thrive.

Trade unions are most likely to articulate positive, idealistic reasons for internationalism. Skeptics argue that more mundane interests have typically inhibited purely idealistic projects of international solidarity, and that the real foundations of international trade unionism are more pragmatic. What divides most analysts, however, is whether these interests are primarily economic or political.

The economic self-interest approach has taken many forms. Fimmen (1924), writing in an early era of 'globalization', believed that trade unions would organize internationally because the development of capitalism obliged them to do so. Logue (1980), in an essay highly influential among students of the international labor movement, saw trade unions as organizations representing the short-term economic interests of their members. More subtly, Ramsay and Haworth looked in detail at the changing patterns of ownership and control of individual companies and industrial sectors, exploring the varying interests of workers in different sectors at different times (Haworth and Ramsay, 1986, 1988; Ramsay, 1997, 1999). Anner et al. (2006) argue that contrasts in the form and extent of cross-national union solidarity in shipping, textiles and car manufacturing can be explained by differences in production organization and product and labor market competition. Yet this does not explain why workers such as typographers, who were scarcely exposed to international competition, were among the pioneers of international trade unionism (van der Linden, 2000: 526–7).

Political self-interest has been seen by many students of the labor movement as the primary motivation for international trade union action. Studies of the international labor movement in the post-war period have either concentrated on the motivations of labor leaders themselves, growing out of their ideological convictions or war-time experience (Carew, 1987; MacShane, 1992), or on the motivations of governments, in explaining their support to international trade union activities (Logue, 1980; Thompson and Larson, 1978). Most of the debate on this issue has been between those who see labor as an unwitting tool of the great powers and those who see it as a willing participant, even an initiator of the Cold War. Wedin's study of the ICFTU in the early 1960s stands out in its portrayal of the complex interdependence between political and trade union leaders and interests (Wedin, 1974). While the nature of this debate is ideological, empirical research, such as Carew's study of labor under the Marshall Plan (1987), has shown the subtle interpenetration of political and trade union elites in the post-war world, and the degree to which the values and

hence the perception of self-interest of leaders have been intermingled. Here we may note Hyman's argument (2005a) that political logic seems best to explain the development of international trade unionism at cross-sectoral level, while a more economic logic is reflected in the history of industrial organizations.

A third consideration is institutional self-interest, whereby trade unions (or their leaders) seek to defend their own interests as institutions. It is understandable that leaders of the international union organizations should seek to protect their own institutional self-interest, but why do national centers feel the need to defend them? The answer to this question is usually linked to the protection of political self-interest, by which small elites in control of national centers seek to maintain their control over the international sphere. We may also note Visser's discussion (1998) of 'push' and 'pull' factors in transnational union organization: national unions may be 'pushed' towards supranational activity by the factors mentioned previously, but they may also be 'pulled' by the opportunities and resources (material assistance or status and legitimacy) available though a role on the international stage. For example, it is widely remarked that the European Commission is anxious to cultivate interlocutors at EU level and thus provides significant resources to the ETUC (Gobin, 1997; Hyman, 2005b). More recently, it may be added, parallel assistance has been given to a range of European NGOs.

While economic, political and institutional self-interest all have some explanatory value in the study of the *purpose* of action and organization at the international level, all three confront the problem of how interests are to be identified, and hence run the risk of circularity (Devin, 1990: 72–3). Lorwin, who wrote one of the first studies of international trade unionism (1929), took a different approach by concentrating on the efforts of the international labor movement to regulate labor at the international level, through its role as a major component in an international industrial relations system. Reinalda (1997: 18–23) makes a similar point when he identifies participation in an international industrial relations system as a dimension beyond the simple accumulation of different individual and national interests.

The capacity to act and the means of action available to trade unions provide the most striking contrast between the national and international levels. Commonly it is assumed that a union exerts leverage through the threat to withdraw its members' labor; its goal is to reach a satisfactory deal for its members through collective bargaining. This model does not apply in many national situations; often, action such as lobbying of public opinion and government is more important. This observation applies *a fortiori* to action at the international level. While there have been a few cases of international strike action and, more rarely, of international collective bargaining, these are exceedingly rare and limited in scope (Etty and Tudyka, 1974; Northrup and Rowan, 1979). Even the possibilities that have been created for international collective bargaining at EU level have been limited (Dølvik, 1997; Martin and Ross, 1999; Visser, 1996). The GUFs have a stronger collective bargaining orientation, but despite their focus on industrial issues they also are obliged to act politically within a largely international and intergovernmental system.

Neither Fimmen nor Lorwin regarded international collective bargaining as imminent, but Levinson (1971, 1972), head of the chemical workers' ITS, made this the focus of his influential writings; and such authors as Northrup and Rowan evaluated international trade unionism negatively against this yardstick. However, even without collective bargaining there is considerable potential for international solidarity action, such as assistance in industrial disputes, and for greater coordination of action, for example of national collective bargaining demands. Lorwin (1929: 468) made an interesting comparison of these instruments of action, referring to early successes in preventing workers from one country being brought in as strike-breakers in a dispute in another country as the 'international equivalent of picketing'. Fimmen promoted the organization of international boycotts, but Lorwin and others have since pointed out limitations to this form of action. International strikes have been even rarer, a leading example being European-wide solidarity with striking workers at Ford in Belgium and the UK in the early 1970s (Piehl, 1974b) although the provision of assistance to workers on strike in other countries has been fairly widespread, alongside attempts to put pressure on the head offices of the companies involved. Regarding collective bargaining as a key function of international trade unionism demonstrates the danger of false analogies with national trade unionism.

The function and means of action of international organizations are closely related to their purpose. One of the main functions is to represent the interests of the national constituency at world level, to provide a *voice,* whether for workers or employers or citizens, within intergovernmental bodies, and to organize or coordinate any other actions that may be taken in pursuit of their interests (Devin, 1990). This latter point is rather different for trade unions and for employers' organizations. While employers often do act together, whether through trade or employers' associations or informal groupings, they have many means of action at their disposal within their own corporations and in political connections at the national or international level. Trade unions tend to have fewer opportunities.

Trade unions (like employers' organizations) face particular difficulties at the international level. At national level, capacity is ultimately determined by members' willingness to act, the internal cohesion of the organization and its responsiveness to members' concerns. This cannot apply in the same way to the international level, which is composed of organizations of organizations. While national action must depend ultimately on individual members, in practice for the international organization the main question is the willingness to act of the national affiliates, based on their view of the legitimacy and representativity of the international body and their estimate of the advisability of the action proposed. National rivalries proved a major obstacle to international action in the Cold War period, particularly for the trade unions, but also for employers and intergovernmental organizations (Etty, 1978a; Piehl, 1974a). Differences between national organizations in the industrialized and developing countries have also created many problems for internal cohesion (Haworth and Ramsay, 1988: 311–21; Olle and Schöller, 1987: 37–9). International organization is clearly necessary for representation within intergovernmental institutions, but only international workers' or employers' organizations that are seen as truly representative have the legitimacy required and the capacity to develop common strategies out of disparate interests.

Another key function for any international organization is information and representation to members or constituent groups. Again, the means available to employers and trade unions are very different, but the function itself is the same. As with the external function discussed above – voice and representation to outside bodies, this internal function – servicing and informing members – is particularly difficult at international level, because of the greater difficulties in communicating, achieving cohesion and representing a larger variety of interests when covering a greater area of the globe. Observers of the international labor movement claim that its capacity has expanded radically with the advent of modern communications technology (Lee, 1997); it has been used to great effect in the coordination of international disputes, such as those at the international mining concern Rio Tinto, but it is often used more effectively by small, single-issue NGOs than by large, heterogeneous international organizations. The open access and essentially non-governable nature of the internet creates new possibilities for international action, but challenges existing chains of communication and authority within international bodies.

The main factors in the effectiveness of the international labor movement were well summarized by Windmuller (1967): the importance of internal cohesion, on the basis of shared ideology and goals; recognition and legitimacy, from the movement itself

and from other actors in the international system; and access to appropriate instruments of action. These factors apply equally to employers' and some other types of international organizations.

INSTRUMENTS AND OUTCOMES

The major international actors form a network of relationships, norms, rules and regulations that provide the basis for the international industrial relations system. But as I have shown, the international actors are not endowed with the same powers or sense of legitimacy as national actors; international law is not enforceable in the same way as national law; and the main instruments of action are not always directly comparable. However, an international industrial relations system with at least some instruments of action and some rules does exist. Below, I consider three types of international regulation: international law, including conventions of the major intergovernmental institutions; voluntary forms of regulation, such as codes of conduct; and international framework agreements based on collective bargaining. Together these three mechanisms shape, or at least influence, the operations of the international economy in all areas related to industrial relations.

International law and international labor standards

Prior to the creation of the ILO in 1919, a small number of international legal instruments adopted by the major European nations regulated certain health and safety issues (Shotwell, 1934: 492–6). These set the precedent for international standards in industrial relations matters alongside those governing the actions of states in wartime and other international issues, and marked an important step in the development of the intergovernmental system as a whole. From the beginning, government ministers and other industrial relations actors were conscious of the difficulties of assuring the implementation of international law by nation states without infringing their sovereignty; for this reason, international law generally requires transposition into national law and enforcement by national governmental agencies. The nature, purpose and means of enforcement of international legal instruments have been much debated by legal and industrial relations scholars (Langille, 2005; Valticos, 1998; Wedderburn, 2002).

Not all international legal instruments need concern us here: some ILO conventions are purely technical in nature or narrow in scope, and many other international instruments have no direct link to industrial relations issues. The most important for this discussion are the group of conventions adopted by the ILO that have won international recognition as essential for the protection of the legal and social rights of workers and their representatives. These 'core' conventions were first identified at the World Social Summit in Copenhagen in 1995 and were formally adopted in the ILO's Declaration on Fundamental Principles and Rights at Work (1998).

These conventions are significant, not only because they have been recognized as 'core' by the ILO itself, but because of the legitimacy they have acquired within world public opinion. They form the basis of most of the voluntary codes of conduct adopted by individual companies or industries and are accepted by governments in north and south alike. Further, the implementation of these conventions is not considered to affect the comparative advantage of countries with low labour costs (Elliott and Freeman, 2003: 11–13; Sengenberger, 2002), as could other

---

Box 17.1 Core ILO Conventions

No Forced Labour (No. 29, 1930; No. 95, 1957)
Freedom of Association (No. 87, 1948)
Free Collective Bargaining (No. 98, 1949)
Equal Pay and Equal Treatment (No. 100, 1951; No. 111, 1958)
No Child Labour (No. 138, 1973; No. 182, 1999)

---

social regulations, for example concerning health and safety standards or a living wage.

Like all ILO conventions, these have the force of international law, and must be adopted through legislation by all member states that have ratified them; they are given added weight by the 1998 Declaration, which requires states to observe them irrespective of formal ratification. As with other ILO conventions, the means of ensuring implementation are limited, and rely mostly on the carrot of technical assistance and the stick of 'naming and shaming'. However, the ILO considers one core convention, that on Freedom of Association (no. 87), so important that it created a Committee on Freedom of Association in 1951 to monitor its implementation, whether or not member states had ratified it, on the basis of complaints raised by recognized representatives of workers or employers as well as by other states. Cases have been taken against governments in every region of the world and have often led to substantial improvements in such areas as union organizing rights (as with Japan in 1973: see Gumbrell-McCormick, 2000: 434). Other governments have been ostracized as a result of condemnation by the Committee, including that of Chile under Pinochet, sometimes contributing to change towards democracy.

Some other international legal instruments outside the ILO conventions are relevant to our purposes. The most influential are probably the guidelines on the conduct of MNCs included in the 1976 OECD Declaration on International Investment and Multinational Enterprises (Gumbrell-McCormick, 2000: 392–3; Murray, 2001). These guidelines, updated in 2000, allow OECD member states, recognized trade unions and employers' representatives to ask for 'clarification' of their implementation by individual MNCs. A number of high-profile cases were brought in the first years after their adoption, such as the successful complaint brought by the government of Belgium against the Badger company, a subsidiary of a US multinational (Blanpain, 1977). Here, too, the main form of implementation has been 'naming and shaming', and the guidelines have been hampered by applying to OECD member states only. The influence of TUAC has no doubt played a role in the successful use of these guidelines. The ITUC has also long pressed for a more general application of codes of conduct (Keohane and Ooms, 1975: 200).

The inclusion of 'social clauses' in international trade agreements is not strictly speaking a legal instrument, but is closely related in that such clauses require implementation by intergovernmental organizations such as the WTO, or through international or regional agreements, such as NAFTA or ASEAN. As with most international instruments, social clauses are based on ILO core conventions, but the mode of implementation and enforcement is different. The threat of exclusion from an international trade agreement is potentially more persuasive than any of the sanctions available to the ILO or OECD, but it is also more controversial and difficult to adopt. Originally an initiative by the International Metalworkers' Federation and the ICFTU during the negotiations for trade liberalization in 1973 (Gumbrell-McCormick, 2000: 508–11), the concept was soon taken up by leading NGOs, trade unions in many industrial countries and some social-democratic governments.

The 'social clause' was not welcomed, however, by most developing country governments or by unions in those countries. The main bone of contention has been the argument that the quest for international labor standards is 'protectionist' (Gumbrell-McCormick, 2004: 44–6; Tsogas, 2001). The ITUC, ILO and many academics have challenged this argument, and Elliott and Freeman (2003: 17–22, 80–3) have provided convincing evidence that protectionism has not been a motive for most actors, yet this contention has been a powerful obstacle to the adoption of social clauses. As a result, a shifting coalition of developing country governments and conservative western governments has always managed to block the inclusion of a social clause in GATT and subsequently in WTO agreements

(Tsogas, 2001). Some clauses have been inserted in regional agreements, such as those of NAFTA (Elliott and Freeman, 2003: 84–9; Stanford, 2003) and in EU external trade agreements.

As indicated earlier, the EU has a major role in adopting supranational labor standards. One of the key instruments is the directive, which as its name implies has stronger regulatory force than ILO conventions: directives are instructions to member states, which retain discretion in how they transpose them into national law. The EU explicitly lacks competence to adopt directives on general levels of pay or on trade union rights (though the ill-fated Constitutional Treaty did include references to both issues). Regulation on other employment issues (except those relating to health and safety) formerly required unanimous support in Council, but Treaty changes in the 1990s increasingly enabled legislation by qualified majority. Before then, most directives reflected a 'lowest common denominator' of existing law in continental Europe – though the UK, with its 'voluntarist' traditions, was more often obliged to make legislative changes. From the 1990s there have been more substantial developments in EU law, covering in particular equal employment opportunities (covering issues of gender, race, disability, age and sexual orientation); the treatment of 'non-standard' work situations; working time; and employee information and consultation. The latter has created a new industrial relations institution, the European Works Council, obligatory if employee representatives so demand in all larger European MNCs. There is by now a large literature on the impact of this legislation (Fitzgerald and Stirling, 2004). The obligation to introduce formal mechanisms of employee information and consultation at national level has also required a major change in UK legislation.

Many observers feel that the era of extensive EU employment regulation is now past. For a decade the Commission appears to have adopted a more neo-liberal, de-regulationist stance; while achieving even a qualified majority in the Council for new directives has become more problematic, particularly after the major enlargement of EU membership in 2004. The emphasis has shifted to the 'open method of coordination' (OMC) and other forms of soft law, exemplified by the European Employment Strategy which sets guidelines for member state policy but has no explicit binding effect.

Voluntary measures – codes of conduct

Recent years have seen a rapid growth of voluntary forms of regulation, usually by individual companies or groups within an industrial sector. There is now a substantial body of academic and practitioner literature on these measures, which include corporate codes of conduct, corporate social responsibility initiatives and other company-led schemes (Elliott and Freeman, 2003; Tsogas, 2001). This growth has accompanied the rise of neo-liberalism and the focus, by academics as well as employers and governments, on the agenda of 'deregulation' and increased autonomy of the firm. These voluntary codes are usually based on the ILO core conventions (although significantly less often on conventions 87 and 98). They are most common in high-profile industries, especially the garment, textile and food industries, where brand names play a large role in consumer choice.

Some academics and practitioners have stressed the self-interest of the firms involved, seeking to avoid mandatory regulation by international or national legal instruments and often responding to campaigns by trade unions and NGOs that threaten bad publicity for the brand (Elliott and Freeman, 2003; Justice, 2003). Others emphasize altruistic motives in the adoption of a CSR agenda, the leadership of committed individual entrepreneurs, or the firm's own benefits from higher labor standards (Jenkins, 2002; Murray, 2002). Examples can be found to suit both arguments, and indeed motives are often complex and interwoven, and enlightened self-interest often bridges the gap between altruism and selfishness. In any event, corporate social responsibility was an important element

in the 'Global Compact' proclaimed by UN secretary-general Kofi Annan in 1999 (Ruggie, 2003; Thérien and Pouliot, 2006), and has also been strongly supported by the EU (European Commission, 2001).[2]

The effectiveness of codes is another important area of debate. The wording is often vague and the content limited, excluding support for rights to union organization and collective bargaining. They are concentrated in consumer industries, while less high-profile industries are rarely covered. They are uncoordinated, leading to multiple codes in some industries and companies, each with its own detailed, sometimes conflicting, provisions. Monitoring is left to a number of agencies, mainly private accounting and auditing firms, and is therefore inconsistent and often weak, too closely linked to the employer's interest (Justice, 2002; for a detailed study of monitoring and application in Mexico and Guatemala see Rodríguez-Garavito, 2005.) One possible solution has been proposed by Kyloh (1998), that the ILO should become the monitoring body for the implementation of all international labor standards and codes. A centralized inspectorate would have the potential of improving the coordination and implementation of the current plethora of different codes, a problem for employers as well as workers, as Elliott and Freeman also point out (2003: 132–3). This would require a degree of cooperation between individual corporations, the ILO and the IFIs that does not yet exist (Verma, 2003; Vosko, 2002).

International framework agreements and international collective bargaining

International collective bargaining is the basis for the third form of international regulation we consider here. As noted above, this was strongly advocated in the 1970s by Levinson and other international trade union leaders. Many academic observers indeed insisted that international trade unionism would only be effective in so far as it was able to engage in international collective bargaining

(Ramsay, 1997, 1999). This was largely ineffectual: almost universally, MNCs refused to bargain cross-nationally on core issues such as rates of pay.

However, from the late 1980s a number of international 'framework' agreements have been concluded between the ICFTU and ITSs (or GUFs) and leading MNCs, mainly in the food, hotel, textile and other consumer industries. One of the first was with the French multinational BSN-Danone in 1988 (Justice, 2003: 97–8). Such framework agreements are usually based, like corporate codes, on the ILO core conventions. Unlike corporate codes, they do include references to conventions 87 and 98, on union representation and collective bargaining. They also tend to provide for independent monitoring, by NGOs or by the trade unions themselves. Framework agreements – which have been endorsed by the EU – are a potentially important form of regulation combining the best features of international labor standards and voluntary codes of conduct. There are still too few of them in operation to be able to judge their effectiveness, though numbers are increasing (Miller, 2004; Wills, 2002).

CONCLUSION AND FUTURE DIRECTIONS

I conclude with brief reflections on both the theory and the practice of international industrial relations, but first return to my opening point, that there is at least the beginning of an international industrial relations system, but it is a mistake to see it as a national system writ large.

The preceding pages have introduced the reader to international industrial relations actors – trade unions, NGOs, employers and their organizations. To be sure, these actors operate primarily at the national level, but they have by now built up a set of institutions at the international level that has remained intact throughout most of the past century. These actors, along with those at the national level, possess a limited common set of norms, on the basis of the ILO core conventions, and these appear to be shared by wide sectors of public opinion. Further, there are international institutions involved in regulating industrial relations matters: the ILO and the rest of the UN system, the WTO and OECD. These too have proved fairly stable over the past 50 years, and in the case of the ILO, nearly over a century. But these international institutions lack key characteristics of states – democratic accountability (if not legitimacy), the ability to monitor compliance and the power to impose sanctions on those who breach the requirements.

If an international industrial relations system simply means a larger version of national systems, we would have to conclude that it does not (yet) exist. But as I have argued, the two are not analogous. Trade unions at the international level may not carry out collective bargaining or strikes (although they sometimes do), but they pursue much the same ends through other means: international campaigns, coordination of national or sectoral demands, coordinated approaches to corporate head offices. International employers' associations are weak, but individual employers do operate on an international scale, with more flexibility, greater means and a higher degree of coordination than trade unions. The most problematic element here is the state: the ILO cannot simply send in international inspectors any more than the UN can send in peace-keeping forces, without the consent of member states. But, as Langille argues (2005, 20–2), international law does not have to be enforceable in the same way as national law – the implementation of ILO conventions, for example, depends on employers and states understanding that this is in their best interests. This is essentially the European approach of 'soft' law or OMC applied on a world scale.

Until recently at least, academic analysis of the field has been weakened by a triple set of demarcations. In terms of analytical approach, there have been valuable contributions by those working in the disciplines of international relations, constitutional and labor law, trade union history and labor economics; but their work has rarely interconnected to any substantial degree. The problem of separate worlds applies equally in terms of language: most academics writing in English are unfamiliar with the considerable literature written in other languages; in the reverse direction the problem is less serious but still exists. Ideologically, there has tended to be a polarization between 'optimists' and 'defeatists' regarding the possibilities of consensual regulation of the global economy and its employment outcomes. Hence the future of the theory of international industrial relations requires further development of cross-disciplinary research and analysis, greater familiarity with the linguistic variety of existing literatures and more sophisticated exploration of ways in which the governance of globalization, though difficult, may yet be possible.

In the world of practice, it is inevitable that regulation at international level remains highly contested. There is some basis for the criticism that the official trade union institutions have been too ready to pursue a 'composite resolution' approach (Hyman, 2005b) which locks them into the dominant logic of the IFIs and of neo-liberal governments. Conversely, anti-capitalist social movements have more frontally challenged the main drift of globalization but have offered few persuasive visions of how to shift the outcomes. There are however signs of a new accommodation, in which international trade unionism recognizes the need for a more combative stance, while many international NGOs prepare for the long march through the institutions. If such a synthesis evolves, perhaps a new world – or a new international industrial relations system – is possible?

NOTES

1 http://www.oecd.org/dataoecd/15/33/34011915.pdf

2 Promoting a European framework for corporate social responsibility http://ec.europa.eu/employment_social/soc-dial/csr/greenpaper_en.pdf

REFERENCES

Abbott, K.W. and Snidal, D. (2000) 'Hard and Soft Law in International Governance', *International Organization* 54 (3): 421–56.

Alcock, A. (1971) *History of the International Labour Organization*. London: Macmillan.

Anner, M., Greer, I., Hauptmeier, M., Lillie, N. and Winchester, N. (2006) 'The Industrial Determinants of Transnational Solidarity: Global Inter-Union Politics in Three Sectors', *European Journal of Industrial Relations* 12 (1): 7–27.

Balanyá, B., Doherty, A., Hoedeman, O., Ma'anit, A. and Wesselius, E. (2003) *Europe Inc.*, 2nd edn. London: Pluto Press.

Berger, S. (2000) 'Globalization and Politics', *Annual Review of Political Science* 3 (?): 43–62.

Blanpain, R. (1977) *The Badger Case and the OECD Guidelines for Multinational Enterprises*. Deventer: Kluwer.

Böröcz, J. and Sarkar, M. (2005) 'What is the EU?', *International Sociology* 20 (2): 153–73.

Bulmer, S.J. (1998) 'New Institutionalism and the Governance of the Single European Market', *Journal of European Public Policy* 5 (3): 365–86.

Cammack, P. (2005) 'The Governance of Global Capitalism: A New Materialist Perspective' in R Wilkinson, ed., *The Global Governance Reader*. London: Routledge. pp. 156–73.

Carew, A. (1987) *Labour under the Marshall Plan*. Manchester: Manchester UP.

Chorev, N. (2005) 'The Institutional Project of Neo-liberal Globalism: The Case of the WTO', *Theory and Society* 34 (3): 317–55.

Coates, K. and Topham, T. (1980) *Trade Unions in Britain*. Nottingham: Spokesman.

Cockburn, C. (1997) 'Gender in an International Space: Trade Union Women as European Social Actor', *Women's Studies International Forum* 20 (4): 459–70.

Commons, J.R. (1909) 'American Shoemakers, 1648–1895: A Sketch of Industrial Evolution', *Quarterly Journal of Economics* 24 (1): 39–84.

Devin, G. (1990) 'La Confédération Internationale Des Syndicats Libres: Exploration d'un Réseau' in G. Devin, *Syndicalisme: Dimensions Internationales*. La Garenne-Colombes: Editions Européennes ERASME. pp. 69–99.

Dingwerth, K. and Pattberg, P. (2006) 'Global Governance as a Perspective on World Politics', *Global Governance* 12 (2): 185–203.

Dølvik, J.E. (1997) *Redrawing Boundaries of Solidarity? ETUC, Social Dialogue and the Europeanisation of Trade Unions in the 1990s*. Oslo: Arena.

Dunlop, J.T (1958) *Industrial Relations Systems.* New York: Holt.

Elliott, K.A. and Freeman, R.B. (2003) *Can Labor Standards Improve under Globalization?* Washington: Institute for International Economics.

Etty, T. (1978a) 'Gewerkschaftliche Weltkonzernausschüsse: Ein Überblick', in W. Olle (ed.), *Einführung in die internationale Gewerkschaftspolitik*, 1, Berlin: Olle & Wolter, pp. 68–78.

Etty, T. and Tudyka, K. (1974) 'Wereldkoncernraden: Vakbonden en hun "kapitaalgerichte" Strategie Tegen Multinationale Ondernemingen', in T. Etty, K. Tudyka and P. Reckman (eds), 'Naar een Multinationale Vakbeweging', *Kosmodok* 7 (2): 3–39.

Fimmen, E. (1924) *Labour's Alternative: The United States of Europe or Europe Limited.* London: Labour Publishing Co.

Fitzgerald, G. and Stirling, J. (eds) (2004) *European Works Councils: Pessimism of the Intellect, Optimism of the Will.* London: Routledge.

Germain, R.D. (2002) 'Reforming the International Financial Architecture: The New Political Agenda' in R. Wilkinson and S. Hughes, eds, *Global Governance, Critical Perspectives.* London: Routledge. pp. 17–35.

Gobin, C. (1997) *L'europe Syndicale.* Brussels: Labor.

Gray, J. (1998) *False Dawn: The Delusions of Global Capitalism.* London: Granta.

Gumbrell-McCormick, R. (2000) 'Facing New Challenges: The International Confederation of Free Trade Unions (1972–1990s)' in A. Carew, M. Dreyfus, G. Van Goethem, R. Gumbrell-McCormick and M. van der Linden, (eds) *The International Confederation of Free Trade Unions.* Bern: Peter Lang.

Gumbrell-McCormick, R. (2004) 'The ICFTU and the World Economy: A Historical Perspective', in R. Munck, (ed.) *Labour and Globalisation*, Liverpool: Liverpool University Press. pp. 34–51.

Haworth, N. and Ramsay, H. (1986) 'Matching the Multinationals: Obstacles to International Trade Unionism', *International Journal of Sociology and Social Policy* 6 (2): 55–82.

Haworth, N. and Ramsay, H. (1988) 'Workers of the World United: International Capital and Some Dilemmas in Industrial Democracy', in R. Southall (ed), *Trade Unions and the New Industrialisation of the Third World.* London: Zed, pp. 308–21.

Heery, E. and Frege, C. (2006) 'New Actors in Industrial Relations', *British Journal of Industrial Relations* 44 (4): 601–04.

Hertz, N. (2001) *The Silent Takeover: Global Capitalism and the Death of Democracy.* London: Heinemann.

Hughes, S. (2005) 'The International Labour Organization', *New Political Economy* 10 (3): 413–25.

Hyman, R. (2005a) 'Shifting Dynamics in International Trade Unionism: Agitation, Organization, Diplomacy, Bureaucracy', *Labour History* 46 (2): 137–54.

Hyman, R. (2005b) 'Trade Unions and the Politics of European Integration', *Economic and Industrial Democracy* 26 (1): 9–40.

Ietto-Gillies, G. (2005) *Transnational Corporations and International Production.* Cheltenham: Edward Elgar.

ILO (1931) *Dix ans d'Organisation Internationale du Travail.* Geneva: ILO.

Jenkins, R. (2002) 'The Political Economy of Codes of Conduct' in R. Jenkins, R. Pearson and G. Seyfang, eds, *Corporate Responsibility and Labour Rights.* London: Earthscan. pp. 13–30.

Jensen, C.S., Madsen, J.S. and Due, J. (1999) 'Phases and Dynamics in the Development of EU Industrial Relations Regulation', *Industrial Relations Journal* 30 (2): 118–34.

Justice, D. (2003) 'The International Trade Union Movement and the New Codes of Conduct' in R. Jenkins, R. Pearson and G. Seyfang, (eds), *Corporate Responsibility and Labour Rights.* London: Earthscan. pp. 90–100.

Katz, H. and Darbishire, O. (2000) *Converging Divergences: Worldwide Changes in Employment Systems.* Ithaca: ILR Press.

Kelly, D. (2005) 'The International Chamber of Commerce', *New Political Economy* 10 (2): 259–71.

Keohane, R.O. and Ooms, Van D. (1975) 'The Multinational Firm and International Regulation', *International Organization* 29 (1): 169–209.

Koenig-Archibugi, M. (2003) 'Global Governance' in J. Michie, ed., *The Handbook of Globalisation.* Cheltenham: Edward Elgar. pp. 318–30.

Koh, H.H. (1999) 'How Is International Human Rights Law Enforced?', *Indiana Law Journal* 74 (?): 1397–17.

Kyloh, R. (1998) 'The Governance of Globalization: The ILO Contribution' in R. Kyloh, ed., *Mastering the Challenge of Globalization: Towards a Trade Union Agenda.* Geneva: ILO. pp. 1–35.

Langille, B. (2005) *What is International Labour Law For?* Geneva: IILS.

Lee, E. (1997) 'Globalization and Labor Standards: A Review of the Issues', *International Labour Review* 136 (2): 173–89.

Leisink, P. and Hyman, R. (2005) 'Introduction: The Dual Evolution of Europeanization and Varieties of Governance', *European Journal of Industrial Relations* 11 (3): 277–86.

Levinson, C. (1971) *Capitalism, Inflation and the Multinationals.* London: Allen & Unwin.

Levinson, C. (1972) *International Trade Unionism.* London: Allen & Unwin.

Logue, J. (1980) *Toward a Theory of Trade Union Internationalism*. Gothenburg: University of Gothenburg.

Lorwin, L. L. (1929) *Labour and Internationalism*. London: Allen & Unwin.

MacShane, D. (1992) *International Labour and the Origins of the Cold War*. Oxford: Clarendon.

Martin, A. and Ross, G. (1999) 'In the Line of Fire: The Europeanization of Labor Representation' in A. Martin and G. Ross et al., *The Brave New World of European Labor*. New York: Berghahn. pp. 312–67.

Martin, R. (1980) *TUC: Growth of a Pressure Group*. Oxford: Clarendon.

Miller, D. (2004) 'Negotiating International Framework Agreements in the Global Textile, Garment and Footwear Sector', *Global Social Policy* 4 (2): 215–39.

Munck, R. (2002) *Globalisation and Labour: The New 'Great Transformation'*. London: Zed.

Murray, J. (2001) 'A New Phase in the Regulation of Multinational Enterprises: The Role of the OECD', *Industrial Law Journal* 30 (3): 255–70.

Murray, J. (2002) 'Labour Rights/Corporate Responsibilities: The Role of ILO Labour Standards' in R. Jenkins, R. Pearson and G. Seyfang, (eds), *Corporate Responsibility and Labour Rights*. London: Earthscan. pp. 31–42.

Northrup, H. and Rowan, R. (1979) *Multinational Collective Bargaining Attempts: The Record, the Cases and the Prospects*. Philadelphia: Wharton School.

Olle, W. and Schöller, W. (1987) 'World Market Competition and Restrictions upon International Trade Union Policies', in R. Boyd, R. Cohen and P. Gutkind (eds), *International Labour and the Third World*, Aldershot: Avebury.

Panić, M. (2003) 'A New Bretton Woods?' in J. Michie, ed, *The Handbook of Globalisation*. Cheltenham: Edward Elgar. pp. 370–82.

Pasture, P. (1994) 'Christian Trade Unionism in Europe Since 1968'. Aldershot: Avebury.

Piehl, E. (1974a) 'Multinationale Konzerne und die Zersplitterung der internationalen Gewerkschaftsbewegung', *Argument-Sonderbände* AS2: 230–55.

Piehl, E. (1974b) 'Gewerkschaftliche Basismobilisierung kontra multinationale Kapitalstrategie: am Beispiel Ford', in O. Jacobi, W. Müller-Jentsch and E. Schmidt (eds), *Gewerkschaften und Klassenkampf: Kritisches Jahrbuch 1974*. Frankfurt: Fischer. pp. 235–48.

Ramsay, H. (1997) 'Solidarity at Last? International Trade Unionism Approaching the Millennium', *Economic and Industrial Democracy* 18 (4): 503–37.

Ramsay, H. (1999) 'In Search of International Union Theory' in J Waddington (ed.), *Globalization and Patterns of Labour Resistance*. London: Mansell.

Reinalda, B. (1997) 'The ITF in the Context of International Trade Unionism' in B. Reinalda (ed.), *The International Transportworkers' Federation 1914–1945: The Edo Fimmen Era*. Amsterdam: IISG.

Rodríguez-Garavito, C.A. (2005) 'Global Governance and Labor Rights: Codes of Conduct and Anti-Sweatshop Struggles in Global Apparel Factories in Mexico and Guatemala', *Politics and Society* 33 (2): 203–33.

Rojot, J. (2006) 'International Collective Bargaining' in M.J. Morley, P. Gunnigle and D.G. Collings, eds, *Global Industrial Relations*. London: Routledge. pp. 254–72.

Rosenau, J.N. and Czempiel, E.-O., (eds) 1992. *Governance without Government: Order and Change in World Politics*. Cambridge: Cambridge UP.

Ruggie. J.G. (2003) 'The United Nations and Globalization: Patterns and Limits of Institutional Adaptation', *Global Governance* 9 (3): 301–21.

Scharpf, F. (1999) *Governing in Europe: Effective and Democratic?* Oxford: Oxford University Press.

Schmidt, V.A. (2002) *The Futures of European Capitalism*. Oxford: OUP.

Sen, J., Anand, A., Escobar, A. and Waterman, P. (eds) (2004) *World Social Forum: Challenging Empires*. New Delhi: Viveka Foundation.

Sengenberger, W. (2002) *Globalization and Social Progress: The Role and Impact of International Labour Standards*. Bonn: Friedrich Ebert Stiftung. pp. 30–70.

Shotwell, J.T., ed. (1934) *The Origins of the International Labour Organization*. New York: Columbia UP.

Standing, G. (2004) 'Global Governance: The Democratic Mirage?', *Development and Change* 35 (5): 1065–72.

Stanford, J. (2003) 'The North American Free Trade Agreement: Context, Structure and Performance' in J. Michie, (ed.), *The Handbook of Globalisation*. Cheltenham: Edward Elgar. pp. 261–82.

Stiglitz, J. (2002) *Globalization and its Discontents*. London: Allen Lane.

Strange, S. (1996) *The Retreat of the State: The Diffusion of Power in the World Economy*. Cambridge: Cambridge UP.

Thérien, J.-P. and Pouliot, V. (2006) 'The Global Compact: Shifting the Politics of International Development?', *Global Governance* 12 (1): 55–75.

Thomson, D. and Larson, R. (1978) *Where Were You Brother?* London: War on Want.

Toye, J. (2003) 'The International Monetary Fund and the World Bank' in J. Michie, ed., *The Handbook of Globalisation*. Cheltenham: Edward Elgar. pp. 358–69.

Tsogas, G. (2001) *Labor Regulation in a Global Economy*. Armonk: M.E. Sharpe.

Valticos N (1998) 'International labour standards and human rights: approaching the year 2000' *International Labour Review*, 137 (2): 135–47.

van der Linden, M (2000) 'Conclusion: The Past and Future of International Trade Unionism' in A Carew, M Dreyfus, G Van Goethem, R Gumbrell-McCormick and M van der Linden, *The International Confederation of Free Trade Unions.* Bern: Peter Lang.

Van Goethem, G (2000) 'Conflicting Interests: The International Federation of Trade Unions (1919–1945)' in A Carew, M Dreyfus, G Van Goethem, R Gumbrell-McCormick and M van der Linden, *The International Confederation of Free Trade Unions.* Bern: Peter Lang.

Verma, A. (2003) 'Global Labor Standards: Can We Get from Here to There?', *International Journal of Comparative Labor Law and Industrial Relations* 19 (4): 515–34.

Visser, J. (1996) 'Internationalism in European Trade Unions' in Patrick Pasture, Johan Verberckmoes and Hans De Witte (eds), *The Lost Perspective? Vol 2.* Aldershot: Avebury. pp. 176–99.

Visser, J. (1998) 'Learning to Play: The Europeanisation of Trade Unions' in P. Pasture and J. Verberckmoes (eds), *Working-Class Internationalism and the Appeal of National Identity.* Oxford: Berg. pp. 231–56.

Vosko, L.F. (2002) '"Decent Work": The Shifting Role of the ILO and the Struggle for Global Social Justice', *Global Social Policy* 2 (1): 19–46.

Wallace, H. (2000) 'Europeanisation and Globalisation: Complementary or Contradictory Trends?', *New Political Economy* 5 (3): 369–82.

Waterman, P. (1998) *Globalization, Social Movements and the New Internationalisms.* London: Mansell.

Waterman, P. and Timms, J. (2005) 'Trade Union Internationalism and a Global Civil Society in the Making' in H. Anheier, M. Glasius and M. Kaldor, (eds), *Global Civil Society 2004/5.* London: Sage. pp. 175–202.

Wedderburn, K.W. (2002) 'Common Law, Labour Law, Global Law' in B. Hepple, ed., *Social and Labour Rights in a Global Context.* Cambridge: CUP. pp. 19–54.

Wedin, Å (1974) *International Trade Union Solidarity: ICFTU 1957-1965.* Stockholm: Prisma.

Weiss, L. (1998) *The Myth of the Powerless State.* Ithaca: Cornell UP.

Wills, J. (2002) 'Bargaining for the Space to Organise in the Global Economy: A Review of the Accor–IUF Trade Union Rights Agreement', *Review of International Political Economy* 9 (4): 675–700.

Windmuller, J P (1967) 'International Trade Union Organizations' in S Barkin (ed.), *International Labor.* New York: Harper & Row.

Zeitlin, J. and Pochet, P., eds (2005) *The Open Method of Co-ordination in Action: The European Employment and Social Inclusion Strategies* Brussels: P.I.E.-Peter Lang.

18

Works Councils

Jean Jenkins and Paul Blyton

INTRODUCTION

Works councils continue to attract considerable interest from industrial relations (IR) scholars. As the fortunes of other IR arrangements have faltered in many countries – notably the coverage of collective bargaining and levels of trade union membership – other forms of employee representation, such as works councils, have gained an added significance. Indeed, Frege (2002: 221) goes so far as to assert that works councils have come to be 'widely regarded as the most prominent, widespread and powerful form of industrial democracy in contemporary capitalist societies'. It is certainly the case that this prominence has been further advanced in Europe over the recent period by the promotion of works council structures by the European Union (EU) as the way to secure more extensive employee information and consultation, both within transnational corporations and in nationally-based organizations.

Works council arrangements of one form or another act as vehicles for employee workplace representation in many countries, particularly within Europe but also elsewhere, such as South Korea and (on a more

limited scale) South Africa (Kim and Kim, 2004; Rogers and Streeck, 1995; Wood and Mahabir, 2001). There has also been interest, though limited progress, in the potential for 'intermediate organizations' such as joint committees and works council arrangements as possible mechanisms for workforce representation and mutual gains in the US (see Freeman, 2005: 663). If every form of representation-based worker consultation is included, the list of countries operating such arrangements is a comparatively long one. However, as Marginson and Sisson (2006: 46) note in their discussion of European industrial relations, even within those European contexts where works councils operate at workplace level, the precise arrangements vary considerably from country to country, making direct comparisons hazardous. The most notable variations include whether the councils are trade union or employee based, whether they are underpinned by voluntary or statutory provision and what their different rights and responsibilities cover. For example, in Austria, Germany, Luxembourg and the Netherlands, legislation has led to works council systems that involve elections of representatives by all employees and also that the works councils form the main vehicle for local worker representation. Elsewhere, however, in countries such as Belgium, France, Portugal and Spain, works councils operate alongside union committees as parallel local-level representation systems (ibid). In the UK and Ireland, the general absence in the past of a statutory requirement for consulting employees is reflected in a lack of any uniform pattern of consultation, though consultative arrangements of one form or another are long established. For example in the UK, workplace consultation structures can be traced back almost a century, and in 2004 just over two-fifths (42 per cent) of all employees were located in a workplace with a workplace-level joint consultation committee (Kersley et al., 2005: 14). In addition, the UK has long standing, issue-specific consultation arrangements in the area of health and safety, as well as requirements on employers to consult over redundancy and transfer.

Of the different works council systems in operation, those operating in parts of Europe remain more highly developed than elsewhere. Of these, the most extensive rights to information, consultation and joint decision-making exist in Austria and Germany. Given the more detailed evaluative literature available on the latter, we will consider the German experience in more detail (for a discussion of the Austrian system, see Traxler, 1998). It is worth noting, however, that even by narrowing the focus to a single country (and one where the works council system has been strongly supported and shaped by legal regulation) the diversity in how works councils function in practice, and their varying impact on management activity, have frequently been acknowledged and hamper generalized conclusions (see for example, Haipeter and Lehndorff, 2005; Jirjahn and Smith, 2006: 650–2; and Kotthoff, 1994 cited in Frege, 2002). Such diversity is less surprising when one considers the very large number of works councils in operation in Germany – over 40,000 in the private sector alone in the 1990s, for example (Jacobi et al., 1998: 211). Nevertheless, a review of recent German evidence on the developing role and

outcomes of works councils will act as a useful starting point not only for considering future challenges to works council arrangements more generally, but also the prospects for higher level (transnational) works council systems that have been shaped, in part, by the German experience.

WORKS COUNCIL DEVELOPMENT IN GERMANY

Within Europe, the German system of industrial relations continues to represent a prime example of one where legal regulation underpins worker representation. Germany conforms to Hall and Soskice's classification of a co-ordinated market economy (2003: 241), where the 'insider' model of corporate governance prevails. Within such systems, far more scope exists for influence to be exerted by different stakeholder interests in the firm, including workers and their representatives, than prevails in less regulated, 'outsider' models of liberal market economies (such as the US and UK), where shareholder interests dominate. In Germany, the roots of worker representation in the workplace are long established. During and immediately after the First World War, official union structures were supplemented at the workplace by *Arbeiteratte* or unofficial workers' councils (Hyman, 2001: 24). To varying degrees, these councils challenged official trade union policies (in a similar way that early shop steward systems did in Britain) and were viewed as a source of disorder – even potential social revolution – both by employers and official trade unions (Clegg, 1976: 58–60; Hyman, 2001: 44). In different national contexts various 'solutions' to grass-roots worker militancy evolved, and in 1920s Germany this involved enacting laws which separated workers' representation at the workplace from the sectoral, regional or national collective bargaining system, and channeled local activities into formal works councils. After the Second World War the works councils, which had originally been a means of containing socialist revolutionary fervor, became a vehicle for safeguarding democracy and preventing a return of fascism. It was judged as important to have trade union involvement and worker participation enshrined in the constitution for the rebuilding of Germany, and indeed, Europe (Hyman, 2001: 116–7).

The system of dual channels of representation for workers became increasingly formalized: one channel by means of collective bargaining by trade unions, the other by consultation and co-determination via works councils. The Works Constitution Act (*Betriebverfassungsgesetz*, 1952, amended 1972/1988/2001) gave employees at establishments with more than five employees the right to a works council where three employees (or a union represented in the establishment) initiated an election (French, 2001: 560). Works council functions are legally distinct from areas of union activity and works council representatives are elected by all workers, not just union members. The same Act also provides for worker representation on the supervisory boards of companies. The activities of supervisory boards will not be considered in this chapter, however.

The upshot of the development of laws on employee representation is a highly juridified system of management-worker relations in Germany. As part of this, works councils have rights to information, consultation and co-determination over different areas of organizational activity. Crucially, in return, they are charged with supporting the employer in achieving the aims of the enterprise. In this way, distributive collective bargaining is left to trade unions while works council representatives are charged with representing workers' interests in a spirit of 'mutual trust' with employers. Works councils cannot lawfully lead or organize industrial action; peaceful negotiations only are permitted, with any disputes settled by labor courts or an arbitration committee.

The dual system has served Germany well. Despite tensions during different periods, and problems of achieving full coverage (see below), works councils and unions have generally maintained a symbiotic relationship.

Unions have typically provided works councillors with training and legal advice, while works councillors (who in most cases are themselves trade unionists) have contributed to union membership by recruiting on the unions' behalf (French, 2001: 562; Jacobi et al., 1998: 191–2). However, as we will discuss, the dual system has come under increasing pressure in more recent years as a result of growing international competition, as well as other factors (see Frege, 2002: 241; and Hassel, 1999).

Yet, despite the way in which the German works council system has been widely celebrated as a model to emulate, within Germany its coverage is far from comprehensive. Despite the mandatory nature of establishing a works council where a small number of employees initiate an election, in practice it is estimated that only between one-half and three-fifths of employees in eligible workplaces are covered by a work council (Addison et al., 2004b: 402; Frege, 2002: 234; Weiss, 2006). While works council presence is very high in larger establishments (councils are present in over 95 per cent of workplaces with more than 1,000 employees, for example) it is very much lower in small workplaces. Addison (2005: 428) notes that in firms with between five and twenty employees, less than one in ten has a works council. In many respects, this lack of coverage in small workplaces is not surprising. Not only is the threshold for eligibility set comparatively low (5 employees) but also the power of works councils, and specifically their statutory rights to information, become significantly stronger in establishments with over 21, and particularly over 100 employees. Likewise, resources to support the activities of the works council (for example, additional rights to time off for councillors) become operable in establishments with more than 200 employees (Addison et al., 2004b).

Probably of more concern for the future of the works council system in Germany, however, is not their low frequency in small firms, but the indications of declining coverage since the 1980s. Addison et al. (2004b) for example, to quote national statistics indicating that between the mid-1980s and mid-1990s the proportion of employees not enjoying works council coverage rose by more than a quarter. Haipeter and Lehndorff (2005: 141) note a similar decline occurring in even the well-organized engineering and metal-working sector: a fall in works council coverage from 77 to 63 per cent of employees between 1980 and 2000. The tendency toward smaller company sizes appears to be one factor accounting for this reduced works council presence (Keller, 2004: 226).

Works councils in Germany face challenges not only in maintaining and extending their coverage in medium and smaller enterprises, but also in retaining an influential presence within the organizations in which they are present. Both coverage and influence of works councils have also been relevant issues in former Eastern German enterprises following reunification. While Frege (1999) points to the success of the works council system in gaining widespread acceptance in the former Eastern regions, Gumbrell-McCormick and Hyman (2006), together with Frege herself and others, question the degree to which works councils have been able to develop their role and influence employers in a similar way to their counterparts in Western German. The particularly difficult economic conditions and high redundancy and unemployment rates that have faced many enterprises and communities in the former Eastern regions appear to have severely hampered the ability of many newly-constituted works councils to exert an independent influence within their workplaces. More generally in Germany, the growth of international competition and the influence of incoming foreign multinational companies, represent further challenges to the status and representation of worker interests in Germany, as they have proven to be elsewhere. These challenges manifest themselves in various ways. Royle (1998) for example, highlights the extent to which those multinational firms entering Germany that are averse to co-determination, have been able successfully to deploy avoidance strategies to minimize works council development (see also Ferner and Edwards, 1995).

A series of other developments acting to reduce collective organization and increase more individualized employment systems are also evident in Germany. One example of these is the increasingly widespread use of individual working time accounts where hours worked in excess of contractually-agreed hours are 'banked' and converted into time off at a later stage, rather than paid as overtime (Haipeter and Lehndorff, 2005; Croucher and Singe, 2004). These individual time accounts have acted not only to reduce overtime costs for employers, but at the same time have reduced works council rights to co-determination in respect of overtime (Haipeter and Lehndorff, 2005: 145) and generally undermined the collective organization of working time in those organizations using the time banking arrangements (see also Chapter 27 Working Hours and Work-Life Balance, in this volume). This is not to deny the possibility of works councils playing an active part in the regulation of time-banking arrangements, particularly on issues relating to the limits of employer or employee influence over the use of time credits (for examples in engineering, see Haipeter and Lehndorff, 2005; and financial services, see Croucher and Singe, 2004). However, it is also evident that in other situations, a less effective works council response to problems arising from time banking has diminished the role of the works council in certain sectors (Croucher and Singe, 2004) and occupational groups (Haipeter and Lehndorff, 2005).

Yet while some working time developments appear to be challenging the role of many works councils in Germany, other working time issues can be seen to have enhanced the role of works councils in the recent period. In part, these developments reflect a more general issue that pressures to decentralize industrial relations (pressures that are noted at several points throughout this volume) can work in favor of extant local IR institutions, such as works councils. In Germany, this is exemplified in the expanded role of works councils over certain aspects of working hours. Historically, works councils have played a role in the determination of actual working time patterns, including the shift arrangements, the scheduling of paid leave and the regulation of overtime (Addison et al., 2004c: 128). However, working time settlements in the 1990s – most notably the negotiation of a 35-hour week in the metal-working industry in former Western Germany – were accompanied by agreement that implementation of the shorter week would be subject to detailed local negotiations between management and works councils (Haipeter and Lehndorff, 2005). In subsequent local negotiations, management have sought increased working time flexibility as a means to offset the cut in hours. The metal-working settlement for example, provided scope not only for local agreement over the proportion of the workforce who could hold contracts exceeding 35 hours (up to a 40-hour limit) but also over the length of the averaging period (up to 6 months and in certain cases 1 year) within which the agreed 35-hours could be achieved.

The upshot of these developments has been that the decentralization of important aspects of working time negotiation has significantly enhanced the potential role of works councils in determining this aspect of work, buttressing the councils' role in a period when other temporal developments (such as individual time accounts) have the potential to erode collective relations between management and worker representatives. Further, the importance to employers of securing greater temporal flexibility has, in some cases at least, given works councils a wider ability to exercise influence in other areas of work organization and arrangement. The overall effect, according to Haipeter and Lehndorff, (2005: 141) has been that, 'Collective agreements on working time gradually gave the actors in the workplace increased scope for bargaining and thereby helped to make the firm or establishment an important locus within the German industrial relations system' (see also French, 2001: 563). The overall picture therefore is that while there have been some pressures to de-collectivize aspects of the employment relationship within many workplaces, other

moves to decentralize industrial relations activities in Germany have bolstered the role and scope of works councils.

In terms of any evaluation of the impact or outcomes of works councils in Germany, three problems are evident at the outset. First, as Frege (2002: 237) points out, a general methodological problem is the distribution of works council activity: almost all large workplaces have a works council, which therefore restricts comparisons of those with or without a works council mainly to medium and smaller establishments. Second, the outcomes that have been considered have tended to be primarily issues relating to firm performance – the effect of works council presence on productivity, wage levels, investment and so on. As Frege points out, however (ibid: 239) these outcomes fail to reflect the central reasons why works councils were introduced and supported by the state in Germany in the first place: to increase the level of employee participation and industrial democracy in the workplace. Yet, overall there has been little enquiry into the impact of works councils on the distribution of influence between management and workforce. The third problem, and related to the previous point, is that there has been an overall lack of study of how the presence of a works council affects individual worker perceptions of their working environment (though exceptions include Bartölke et al., 1982; and Wever, 1994).

In terms of the main focus of evaluation in recent years – the impact of works councils on firm performance – the findings offer a mixed picture, but overall suggest that the impact has been a fairly modest one. In a series of studies drawing on large-scale survey data, Addison and colleagues (Addison, 2005; Addison and Teixeira, 2006; Addison et al., 2004a, 2004b, 2004c, 2007) have found works council presence to be associated with, among other things: lower quit rates and dismissals, reduced employment growth, and a higher level of plant closures, but with no identifiable effect on investment patterns. In terms of the impact on productivity, Addison's analyses detect a small positive effect of works council presence on productivity (see also Hübler and Jirjahn, 2003). As Addison et al. (2004a) point out, however, different periods of investigation and different types of study have tended to produce different results regarding productivity and works councils. Given the nature of most of this enquiry, based on cross-sectional surveys – further investigation is needed to establish under what circumstances and in what ways works councils can impact on firm outcomes, either positively or negatively. Further, given the changing role of works councils (for example, in relation to working time issues; see above) there would be value in further study that focuses on the functioning of works councils in particular contexts – examining more extensively, for example the circumstances where works councils have successfully exerted influence over emerging agenda, and those where they have been less successful (Croucher and Singe, 2004).

In addition to the continuing significance of the works council system in Germany and several neighboring countries including Austria and the Netherlands, in latter years the German works council model has acted as 'the prototype of works councils in Europe' (Frege, 2002: 222) and a key vehicle for developing a European social model that acknowledges the need for independent worker representation (Hyman, 2001: 118–9; Gumbrell-McCormick and Hyman, 2006: 474) A brief overview of these Europe-wide developments will provide a broader platform for assessing some of the issues facing works councils in the coming period.

EUROPEAN WORKS COUNCILS

In Europe, attempts to introduce measures to support employee rights to information and consultation were first made in the early 1970s, though concerted employer opposition prevented significant progress (Burchill, 1997: 196). Hence, in the following two decades, whilst European regulations did place consultation requirements on companies contemplating redundancies and the transfer of undertakings, overall workers' representatives did not gain rights 'to alter substantially the position taken by managements' (Waddington, 2006: 682).

The European Works Council Directive in 1994 sought to increase the pressure on employers, and in particular transnational employers, to consult with employee representatives over a range of cross-national issues including restructuring and employment developments. The Directive requires that undertakings employing more than 1,000 people in member states, of which 150 must be employed in each of two member states, should establish a European-wide Works Council (EWC Directive, 1994, Article 2). Though information and consultation were at the heart of the Directive, the notion of exactly what the terms meant was left 'loosely defined' (Lorber, 2004: 191).

Assessments of the operation of EWCs broadly concur on several general features evident during the first decade of the Directive's existence. First, compliance with the national legislation passed to implement the Directive has been patchy. Overall, approximately one-third of companies covered by the Directive have established EWCs (Kerckhofs, 2002; Marginson et al., 2004). Compliance is higher among larger companies and in certain sectors such as financial services and hotels and catering (Addison and Belfield, 2002). Second, it is clear that EWCs vary considerably in how they operate in practice. Waddington (2006: 683), for example, refers to a continuum ranging from highly restricted consultation and information practices, to much more extensive involvement of worker representatives in company decision-making. Similarly, Marginson et al.'s (2004: 223) results underline the variation in activity across the cases they studied, as do Weiler (2004) and Voss (2006). Factors associated with different levels of information and consultation activity include the strength of employee-side organization; country-of-origin effects (particularly the influence of companies from countries with a tradition of worker involvement and cooperative industrial relations) and a company industrial relations effect (for example the positive effect of companies having a longer tradition of works councils and where the EWC is more integrated with extant IR structures) (Weiler, 2004: 96–97; see also Gilman and Marginson, 2002).

Third, notwithstanding the diversity of operation noted above, the vast majority of studies point to the very limited impact of EWCs on company decision-making. The patchiness of compliance (see above) is relevant here, but even where compliance has been secured, it is clear that this has frequently been at a minimal level. In her overview of more than forty case studies drawn from five countries for example, Weiler (2004) highlights widespread limitations reflected in, among other things, the (in)frequency of meetings, the inadequacy of much of the training provision for worker representatives and language barriers impeding communication, particularly outside the formal council meetings. More significant still, however, is the apparent widespread use of EWCs by management to inform worker representatives of decisions already taken, and to gain legitimacy for those decisions. Where consultation does take place, it is more likely to be over the processes of implementation of decisions rather than consulting over decisions yet to be made (Marginson et al., 2004; Waddington, 2006). As Weiler (2004: 81) concludes, 'All the case studies [that formed the basis for her report] reveal that the EWCs had little or no influence on general management practices and on transnational decisions'. A subsequent analysis of companies in new EU member states by Voss (2006) largely mirrors this finding of the overall paucity of the consultative process, and the quality and timing of information made available to employee representatives. Further, as Voss points out, in countries such as the Czech Republic, Hungary, Poland and Slovakia, this generally minimalist strategy toward information and consultation is given added significance by the scale of company relocation and restructuring occurring between older and newer EU members, and the resulting implications for

the workforces in different locations (Voss, 2006: 43).

The tendency for management to minimize the role of the EWC and consult after rather than before decisions are taken, underlines the widespread absence of a clear managerial commitment to effective consultation (a lack of commitment that also finds expression in the small number of managerial representatives that are present on many EWCs). As Weiler (2004) points out, however, this lack of commitment is not only identifiable within management. It is evident too that employee representatives frequently demonstrate a limited willingness to develop joint European positions on issues, with the prioritizing by representatives of their own locality tending to be more prominent than any development of a common sense of purpose (ibid: 62,97; for a notable exception, see Whittal, 2000).

Overall, the weakness of regulation governing the nature, scope and function of EWCs, coupled with the ambivalent view of the parties to the arrangements established, has resulted in EWCs generally operating in a way that varies considerably from the prototypical German works councils discussed earlier. Among other things, the restricted nature of much EWC activity highlights the difficulties that the EU faces in seeking to advance consultative employment mechanisms that apply across member states, whose national systems of provision for employee consultation vary considerably.

RECENT NATIONAL-LEVEL DEVELOPMENTS

To complement the EWC Directive's requirements in respect of transnational corporations, the possibility of an EU framework to support provisions for information and consultation within nationally-based undertakings, was first raised by the European Commission in 1995. After much negotiation and opposition on various grounds from several member states, the EU Information and Consultation Directive (ICD) was eventually adopted in 2002. The aim of this Directive is to require employers to: inform employees on the recent and probable development of the establishment's activities and economic situation; inform and consult with employees on the situation and probable development of employment in the establishment; and inform and consult with employees on decisions likely to lead to substantial changes in work organization or in contractual relations (from Article 4 of the Information and Consultation Directive).

The EC allowed member states discretion and flexibility in the introduction of the regulations in the interests of not challenging or supplanting existing mechanisms for consultation or bargaining (Hall, 2005: 107–8). The resulting variation, however, in how member states are able to implement the Directive, coupled with the lengthy period allowed for compliance (up to 2008 for smaller establishments; see Blyton and Turnbull, 2004: 266–7) makes any generalized analysis of the impact of the Directive to date difficult. The ICD's potential significance is greater in those countries such as the UK and Ireland, where statutory requirement for informing or consulting with employees was largely absent (other than over certain specific issues such as redundancy) (Dundon et al., 2006; Sisson, 2002). But, just as the assessments of the development of European Works Councils have generally pointed to only very restricted development of effective consultation, there is considerable potential for a similarly minimalist development of national works council systems under the ICD, particularly in those countries lacking any existing regulatory foundation for consultation. Indeed, in the UK, the initial signs are not particularly encouraging in terms of building a more comprehensive consultation architecture. The UK government has not provided a strong lead in the development of a consultation culture: not only did it support a diluted rather than a more extended version of the ICD, but has subsequently established considerable scope for employers to rely on forms of workforce consultation other than through

worker representatives (Hall, 2005, 2006; Truter, 2003).

This last point is an issue for commentators concerned about the independent representation of workers' interests in an era of relative union weakness. In this context, the question is whether works councils offer a new opportunity for a stronger labor voice to develop, or whether they provide employers with greater scope to marginalize and undermine unions and incorporate worker representatives. For Kelly (1996: 54–7) the dangers for labor (and a factor in the evident union ambivalence toward works councils in many contexts) lie in the ideological and power issues underpinning the operation of works councils, namely: their lack of independence in comparison with unionized representation; their relative unassertiveness; their foundation in employee obligations to engage with employers in a spirit of peace, trust and co-operation; and finally, their potential for encouraging employees to identify their interests 'ever more closely with employers' and to therefore be attractive to employers as a 'roadblock to union growth' (ibid: 57). There is also the associated issue, in the context of the decentralization of collective bargaining, for works councils to reinforce the tendency towards 'company egoism' (see French 2001: 563–4; Gumbrell-McCormick and Hyman, 2006: 478–9; see also, Heery, 2002: 22), and to undermine wider solidarity between workers by focusing on the interests of established 'core' employees at a particular workplace. While acknowledging such dangers, however, Hyman (1996: 80–2), argues that *assertive* works councils could still offer an effective channel for employee voice in the context of union weakness, and could be one aspect of a set of 'positive rights' for employee representation that might provide a 'springboard for unionization'. Hyman makes the point that where unions have little opportunity to make advances in securing full collective bargaining rights, an institutional framework for works council might facilitate power as well as voice and represent 'the least worst option for British unions' (ibid: 65). To a very large extent, no conclusion can yet be drawn on these matters, and the detail of the operation of works councils established under the terms of the ICD, will require ongoing evaluation.

Thus, it would seem that in those European countries where legislation over consultation requirements has in the past been weak, or absent altogether, the recent regulation deriving from the ICD represents the beginning of a journey of consultation, rather than its end. In countries like Germany, the works council system has been effective precisely because it is embedded in a broader statutory framework of participation and collective representation. Also important has been the willingness of many employers actively to engage in workplace-based participation; and that works councils have been given sufficient statutory rights to maintain an independence from management (Truter, 2003; Wever, 1995). Elsewhere, these conditions are met to a greater or lesser extent. In this regard, the UK is an extreme case for none of these conditions currently prevail in the UK, and the ICD does not in itself provide any of them. Whether or not the consultation arrangements that stem from the ICD will initiate a significant degree of change, either in the UK or more widely, remains to be seen.

CONCLUSION

Workplace committees, involving either elected or nominated worker representatives, are a widespread form of management-workforce interaction. In those countries that have witnessed a decline in collective bargaining coverage in the recent period, such committees could well become yet more evident, together with other, direct forms of employee involvement (Lansbury and Wailes, in this volume; Pyman et al., 2006; Taras and Kaufman, 2006). Many of these workplace committees carry the title of works councils, or a similar term such as company council. Yet, in many cases, they remain a far cry from those works council structures that exist in contexts where the presence and powers of works councils are regulated

by statute. In the German case (and other similar European cases) what this has meant is that whilst the industrial relations system has experienced similar pressures to those exhibited elsewhere – in particular, pressures to decentralize and de-collectivize different parts of the employment relationship – the works council system has been sufficiently robust largely to withstand those pressures. Indeed, in more organized works council contexts at least, the pressures to decentralize the determination of industrial relations issues has stimulated a new and broader role for works councils within the local IR structure. Given the statutory requirement to involve works councils in decision-making, many companies in Germany have shown a preference for channeling more industrial relations activity through the integrative bargaining system represented by the works councils, rather than via more centralized bargaining involving negotiations with trade unions.

Elsewhere, however, and particularly in those contexts such as Australia, the US and the UK, where adversarial relations have been more evident in past industrial relations, the likelihood of any thoroughgoing development of representative employee participation looks a distant prospect (notwithstanding that in the UK, for example, employers have a statutory duty to consult over specific issues such as large-scale redundancies). The ICD has been significant for the UK (and Ireland) in introducing a statutory platform for employees to insist on being informed and consulted by management over a much broader range of issues than currently prevails (Hall, 2005: 103). However, the comparatively restricted nature of the directive, and the scope it allows management to minimize the extent to which they are required to embrace a more consultative approach to decision-making, is likely to mean that its effects will remain modest. In practice, this limited impact is likely to be the case not only in countries where no previous legislation exists, but also in many cases where a more regulatory framework has been in place, for in the main in these latter countries this extant regulation is likely to be more comprehensive than that represented by the ICD. A similar picture also appears to be the case in relation to European Works Councils. As we have discussed, though companies vary considerably in the extent to which they actively utilize the EWC structure to inform and consult with worker representatives, in the main EWCs have not so far fundamentally altered the pattern of corporate decision-making, nor led to significant consultation with worker representatives before important decisions have been taken.

Overall, in the absence of a regulatory requirement to engage in consultative behavior, managers have tended to express their interest in only very limited participatory devices. Such an attitude towards limiting the sharing of influence over decisions has been evident for example in various studies of management attitudes (see for example, Freeman and Rogers, 1999; and Poole and Mansfield, 1992). In Europe, it remains to be seen whether there is the political will to increase the degree of industrial democracy in organizations through extending the powers initially set down in directives relating to transnational and national works councils. Given the prominence of the political rhetoric on the importance of management having the 'flexibility' to compete internationally, however, for the foreseeable future it may well be the case that we have already witnessed the high-water point of works council development in terms of the influence they are able to wield. If so, future developments are more likely to be based on the expansion of forms of works council in which there is more emphasis on discussing how best to implement decisions already taken, and less opportunity for challenging management action or for shaping decisions before they have been taken in another place.

ACKNOWLEDGMENTS

The authors would like to thank Nicolas Bacon and Ed Heery for their useful comments on an earlier version of this chapter.

REFERENCES

Addison, J.T. (2005) 'The determinants of firm performance: unions, works councils and employee involvement/high-performance work practices', Scottish Journal of Political Economy, 52 (3): 406–50.

Addison, J.T. and Belfield, C.R. (2002) 'What do we know about the new European Works Councils? Some preliminary evidence from Britain', Scottish Journal of Political Economy, 49 (4): 418–44.

Addison, J.T., and Teixeira, P. (2006) 'The effect of works councils on employment change', Industrial Relations, 45 (1): 1–25.

Addison, J.T., Schnabel, C. and Wagner, J. (2004a) 'The course of research into the economic consequences of German works councils', British Journal of Industrial Relations, 43 (2): 255–81.

Addison, J.T., Bellmann, L., Schnabel, C. and Wagner, J. (2004b) 'The reform of the German Works Constitution Act: a critical assessment', Industrial Relations, 43 (2): 392–420.

Addison, J.T., Bellmann, L. and Kolling, A. (2004c) 'Works councils and plant closings in Germany', British Journal of Industrial Relations, 42 (1): 125–48.

Addison, J.T., Schank, T., Schnabel, C. and Wagner, J. (2007) 'Do works councils inhibit investment?', Industrial and Labor Relations Review, 60 (2): 187–203.

Bartölke, K., Eschweiler, D., Flechsenberger, D. and Tannenbaum, A.S. (1982) 'Workers' participation and the distribution of control as perceived by members of ten German companies', Administrative Science Quarterly, 27 (3): 380–97.

Blyton, P. and Turnbull, P. (2004) The Dynamics of Employee Relations, Third Edition, Basingstoke: Palgrave Macmillan.

Burchill, F. (1997) Labour Relations, Basingstoke: Macmillan.

Clegg, H. (1976) Trade Unionism Under Collective Bargaining: A Theory Based on Comparisons of Six Countries, Oxford: Basil Blackwell.

Croucher, R. and Singe, I. (2004) 'Co-determination and working time accounts in the German finance industry', Industrial Relations Journal, 35 (2): 153–68.

Dundon, T., Curran, D., Ryan, P. and Maloney, M. (2006) 'Conceptualising the dynamics of employee information and consultation: evidence from the Republic of Ireland', Industrial Relations Journal, 37 (5): 492–512.

Ferner, A. and Edwards, P. (1995) 'Power and the diffusion of organizational change within multinationals', European Journal of Industrial Relations, 1 (2): 1–35.

Freeman R.B. (2005) *'What do unions do? – the 2004 M-Brane Stringtwister edition'*, *Journal of Labor Research*, 26 (4): 641–68.

Freeman, R.B. and Rogers, J. (1999) *What Workers Want*, Ithaca: Cornell University Press.

Frege, C.M. (1999) 'Transferring labor institutions to emerging economies: the case of East Germany', *Industrial Relations*, 38 (4): 459–81.

Frege, C. M. (2002) 'A critical assessment of the theoretical and empirical research on German works councils', *British Journal of Industrial Relations*, 40 (2): 221–48.

French, S. (2001) 'Works councils in unified Germany: still loyal to the trade unions?', *International Journal of Manpower*, 22 (6): 560–78.

Gilman, M. and Marginson, P. (2002) 'Negotiating European Works Councils: contours of constrained choice', *Industrial Relations Journal*, 33 (1): 36–51.

Gumbrell-McCormick, R. and Hyman, R. (2006) 'Embedded collectivism? workplace representation in France and Germany', *Industrial Relations Journal*, 37 (5): 473–91.

Haipeter, T. and Lehndorff, S. (2005) 'Decentrailsed bargaining of working time in the German automotive industry', *Industrial Relations Journal*, 36 (2): 140–56.

Hall, M. (2005) 'Assessing the Information and Consultation of Employee Regulations', *Industrial Law Journal*, 34 (2): 103–26.

Hall, M. (2006) 'A cool response to the ICE Regulations? Employer and trade union approaches to the new legal framework for information and consultation', *Industrial Relations Journal*, 37 (5): 456–72.

Hall, P. and Soskice, D. (2003) 'Varieties of capitalism and institutional change: a response to three critics', *Comparative European Politics*, XX (1): 241–50.

Hassel, A. (1999) 'The erosion of the German system of industrial relations', *British Journal of Industrial Relations*, 37 (3): 483–505.

Heery, E. (2002) 'Partnership versus organising: alternative futures for British trade unionism', *Industrial Relations Journal*, 33 (1): 20–35.

Hubler, O. and Jirjahn, U. (2003) 'Works councils and collective bargaining in Germany: the impact on productivity and wages', *Scottish Journal of Political Economy*, 50 (4): 471–91.

Hyman, R. (1996) 'Is there a case for statutory works councils in Britain', in McColgan, A. (ed.) *The Future of Labour Law*, London: Cassell, pp. 64–84.

Hyman, R. (2001) *Understanding European Trade Unionism – Between Market, Class and Society*, London: Sage.

Jacobi, O., Keller, B. and Muller-Jentsch, W. (1998) 'Germany: facing new challenges', in Ferner, A. and Hyman, R. (eds) *Changing Industrial Relations in Europe*, Oxford: Blackwell, pp. 190–238.

Jirjahn, U. and Smith, S.C. (2006) 'What factors lead management to support or oppose employee participation – with and without works councils? Hypotheses and evidence from Germany', *Industrial Relations*, 45 (4): 650–80.

Keller, B. (2004) 'Employment relations in Germany', in G.J. Bamber, R.D. Lansbury and N. Wailes (eds) *International and Comparative Employment Relations*, 4th edn, London: Sage, pp. 211–53.

Kelly, J. (1996) 'Works councils: union advance or marginalization?' in McColgan, A. (ed.) *The Future of Labour Law*, London: Cassell, pp. 46–63.

Kerckhofs, P. (2002) *European Works Councils – Facts and Figures*, Brussels: European Trade Union Institute.

Kersley, B., Alpin, C., Forth, J., Bryson, A., Bewley, H., Dix, G. and Oxenbridge, S. (2005) *Inside the Workplace: First Findings from the 2004 Employment Relations Survey*, London: DTI.

Kim, D-O. and Kim, H-K. (2004), 'A comparison of the effectiveness of unions and non-union works councils in Korea: can non-union employee representation substitute for trade unionism?', *International Journal of Human Resource Management*, 15 (6): 1069–93.

Kotthoff, H. (1994) *Betriebsratte und Burgerstatus: Wandel und Kontinuitat betrieblicher Co-determination*, Munich: Rainer Hampp Verlag.

Lorber, P. (2004) 'Reviewing the European Works Council Directive: European progress and United Kingdom perspective', *Industrial Law Journal* 30 (2): 191–9.

Marginson, P. and Sisson, K. (2006) *European Integration and Industrial Relations*, Basingstoke: Palgrave Macmillan.

Marginson, P., Hall, M., Hoffman, A. and Müller T. (2004) 'The impact of European Works Councils on management decision-making in UK and US-based multinationals: a case study comparison'. *British Journal of Industrial Relations*, 42 (2): 209–33.

Poole, M. and Mansfield, R. (1992) 'Managers' attitudes to human resource management: rhetoric and reality', in P. Blyton and P. Turnbull (eds) *Reassessing Human Resource Management*, London: Sage. pp. 200–14.

Pyman, A., Cooper, B., Teicher, J. and Holland, P. (2006) 'A comparison of the effectiveness of employee voice arrangements in Australia', *Industrial Relations Journal*, 37 (5): 543–59.

Rogers, J. and Streeck, W. (1995) 'The study of works councils: concepts and problems', in J. Rogers and W. Streeck (eds) *Works Councils*, Chicago: University of Chicago Press. pp. 3–26.

Royle, T. (1998) 'Avoidance strategies and the German system of co-determination', *The International Journal of Human Resource Management*, 9 (6): 1026–47.

Sisson, K. (2002) 'The Information and Consultation Directive: Unnecessary "Regulation" or an Opportunity to Promote 'Partnership'?', *Warwick Papers in Industrial Relations No. 67*, Industrial Relations Research Unit, Warwick University.

Taras, D.G. and Kaufman, B. (2006) 'Non-union employee representation in North America: diversity, controversy and uncertain future', *Industrial Relations Journal*, 37 (5): 513–42.

Traxler, F. (1998) 'Austria: still the country of corporatism', in Ferner, A. and Hyman, R. (eds) *Changing Industrial Relations in Europe*, Oxford: Blackwell, pp. 239–61.

Truter, G.M. (2003) *Implementing the Information and Consultation Directive in the UK: Lessons from Germany*, London: Institute for Employment Rights.

Voss, E. (2006) *The experience of European Works Councils in new EU Member States*, Dublin: European Foundation for the Improvement of Living and Working Conditions.

Waddington, J. (2006) 'The performance of European Works Councils in engineering: perspectives of the employee representatives', *Industrial Relations*, 45 (4): 681–708.

Weiler, A. (2004) *European Works Councils in Practice*, Dublin: European Foundation for the Improvement of Living and Working Conditions.

Weiss, M. (2006) 'The effectiveness of labour law: reflections based on the German experience', *Managerial Law*, 48 (3): 275–87.

Wever, K. S. (1994) 'Learning from works councils: five unspectacular cases from Germany', *Industrial Relations*, 33 (4): 467–81.

Wever, K.S. (1995) *Negotiating Competitiveness: Employment Relations and Organizational Innovation in Germany and the United States*, Boston, MA: Harvard Business School Press.

Whittal, M. (2000) 'The BMW European Works Council: a cause for European industrial relations optimism?', *European Journal of Industrial Relations*, 6 (1): 61–84.

Wood, G. and Mahabir, P. (2001) 'South Africa's workplace forum system: a stillborn experiment in the democratisation of work?', *Industrial Relations Journal*, 32 (3): 230–43.

19

The Evolution of Stakeholder Regimes: Beyond Neo-Corporatism

Charles Heckscher

A central phenomenon of industrial relations (IR) since the 1960s has been the pluralization of the field – in practice, if not in theory. Where the Dunlopian paradigm envisioned a tripartite model, with unions and government as the sole representatives of non-market values, recent decades have seen a rapid expansion of the cast. Many of the emergent actors are 'new movements', formed around social identities such as race, gender, disability, and other markers of status; though not centered on the workplace, these groups have had enormous impacts on employment through civil rights legislation and publicity campaigns. Others are more clearly 'labor' groups, such as immigrant worker centers that have emerged, largely independent of unions, to meet the needs of temporary laborers (Fine, 2006). As the power of NLRA-framed unionism has declined, these diverse and mostly fragmented actors have tried to fill in the growing gaps in the system of employment representation.

Research and theory have not yet caught up with this sea change. The arena of new associational actors has been very poorly mapped: there is as yet little agreement even on the major categories, and still less on the numbers of people involved or the importance of these groups (Carré and Joshi, 2000). Although it is clear that the tripartite 'neo-corporatist' model is now a poor description of reality, no replacement has emerged.

I will make the case that to understand the current scene we need to abstract from the system described by classic IR theory, building a new theory that treats that approach as just one way of organizing the demands of multiple stakeholders.

STAKEHOLDER REGIMES

At times transition theory should help us pull back from the familiar ways of framing events to construct new ones. The traditional frame now keeps us within a narrow space: it suggests that since unions and the welfare state are in decline they should be strengthened again – so that things in the future might look more like they did in the 1950s. Yet the tripartite neo-corporatist model is merely one historical way of solving a more permanent problem: how to give voice to conflicting interests and values in the economy (Schmitter, 1983; Williamson, 1985).

Neo-corporatism (as I will use the term) has been a successful *stakeholder regime* that balanced multiple positions.[1] It is characterized by organized relations among three principal actors: large corporations, a state supporting some form of social-welfare model, and unions oriented to collective bargaining. Other actors are represented only through one of these 'primary' institutions and had to accept the results of negotiations among them. In the era before the dominance of large corporations, there was a different stakeholder regime with different actors – principally craft unions and guilds-based structures rather than industrial unions.

The concept of 'stakeholders' is relatively undeveloped. Most treatments are still based on Freeman's (1984: 46) strikingly vague definition of a stakeholder as 'any group or individual who can affect, or is affected by, the achievement of a corporation's purpose'. Two central problems are generally blurred or left unresolved. First, how can one *identify* a stakeholder? It is not too hard to identify individuals, but groups with shared values are much harder to pin down. In practice they ebb and flow, forming and dissolving, splitting and merging, depending on the particular constellation of problems. Some are more self-aware than others, some are more visibly powerful than others; yet those are not sufficient criteria in themselves, since it is often those who are not highly self-aware or influential who have the strongest claims to justice. Freeman's definition does nothing to tackle this problem; indeed, it leaves us with essentially infinite numbers of stakeholders, with no way to sort out who should or should not be part of the process.

Second, what decision-making process should be used? The notion of majority vote is not useful for a stakeholder analysis: the players are not equal individuals, but groups of varying degrees of stability and size. In general a notion of negotiation seems more on the mark than voting, but that leaves a huge range of problems: how to manage the differences in power and identity among the players, how to manage multilateral negotiations, how to deal with impasses, and so on.

These problems are the focus of institutionalization of stakeholder systems. While it is possible to create stakeholder dialogs 'on the fly', with no prior agreement on the nature of the process, this is not a reliable way to assure that consensus is reached and people accept the legitimacy of the outcomes. In order to achieve these two purposes there needs to be an accepted way of dealing with the issues just raised, with the backing of relevant authorities including courts and government regulators.

A regime (again, in my usage) is a set of societal institutions that involves stakeholders in decision-making, leading to legitimate and enforceable outcomes.[2] The concept covers a wide range of institutional forms, including collective bargaining but also, for example, regulatory negotiation or certain regional development mechanisms. It is not even specific to a capitalist society: in principle any complex system with multiple overlapping groups must consider how to define and involve stakeholders. Indeed, from this perspective, capitalism is defined simply as a regime in which owners are a dominant stakeholder group with strongly institutionalized legal rights.

The stakeholder literature has so far largely ignored the analysis of institutionalized decision-making regimes. The term 'stakeholder' has been used to help managers and policy-makers think about particular conflicts, but it has rarely been extended to the consideration of how these relations can be formed into systems that are stable and reflective of the full range of societal concerns and values. The field of IR, meanwhile, has remained fixated on a particular regime dating from the interwar period, and has not adopted the larger frame offered by the stakeholder perspective.

My core argument is that we are currently experiencing a transition between stakeholder regimes in employment relations, from the neo-corporatist system which dominated the industrial era to an as-yet uninstitutionalized and unnamed system for the future. This argument involves first the description of the prior regime, which is now coming apart but whose outlines are relatively clear; from there, an abstraction of the general characteristics of stakeholder regimes; and on that basis, an attempt to model some core characteristics of a regime responsive to the current configuration of needs.

THE NEO-CORPORATIST STAKEHOLDER REGIME AND ITS DECLINE

We can learn a good deal about the current situation by looking at the construction of the prior regime. Neo-corporatism, treated as an ideal-type, is characterized by particular answers to the problems described above.

- There are three institutionalized actors: employers, labor unions, and government.
- Decision-making processes are a mixture of two basic kinds: periodic bilateral negotiation between employers and unions, and regulation by government.
- The process seeks a balance of values between economic productivity and values of concern to the other stakeholders. That is, economic value is one key concern, but not the only one which measures the success of the outcomes. Non-economic values are legitimate in the process.
- The collective bargaining piece of the regime deals with issues of workplace governance; it has generally been restricted to issues of wages and working conditions. The government regulation piece deals with the concerns of other stakeholders and is far more open, with few predefined limits on the issues.

This pattern describes the institutional relations throughout the OECD nations and, to my knowledge, in all industrialized countries. There are important varieties within this framework: negotiation processes may range in character from cooperative to highly conflictual, and government can base regulations on dialog or on bureaucratic expertise. But all industrial democracies, from Sweden to the US, share the essential characteristics just sketched.

Although today many think of the US as purely econometric or managerial rather than neo-corporatist, that view is something of a retroactive reading of history. During the 1950s and 1960s unions reached densities of over 35 per cent, which would be considered quite respectable today and certainly large enough to set the basic standards for the economy. Large employers almost never tried to push their ability to operate during strikes or fire people during organizing drives; they widely accepted that the compromise was working and did not seek to rock the boat. And, as Jacob Hacker has calculated, the amount spent on welfare in the US in the post-WWII period has been very similar to that of European nations like the Netherlands and Denmark; only the method of provision was different, with a higher proportion provided through union-management negotiations and a smaller proportion through direct state programs and regulations (Hacker, 2002).

What was most distinctive to the US was a relatively decentralized image of the good society: the labor federation had relatively little power over its members, and employers never formed the kind of strong associations that were found in Scandinavia and elsewhere. Sweden and Germany adopted a much more centralized version of the neo-corporatist compromise. In general these highly centralized institutionalizations strove for direct dialog and consensus and had relatively low rates of conflict. In the less centralized forms – France or Italy, for example – it was more difficult to maintain consensus, and agreements could more easily be destabilized by shifting power alignments; thus there was more of a tendency for periodic large-scale clashes to erupt. In the most decentralized systems, such as the US or UK, conflict was nearly continuous and generally much more local, though in these countries occasional large-scale clashes served to define the parameters within which everyone worked as well. It should be emphasized, however, that even in these least stabilized institutions, conflict became highly ritualized and manageable – moving from the fierce and unconstrained battles of the 1930s to the periodic games of threats, counter-threats, brinkmanship, and eventual agreement.

The neo-corporatist regime in all its variants met the needs of the major active stakeholders well enough to last for many years. In particular, the most organized and entitled stakeholder, corporate management, found that this system helped to guarantee the stability and quality of the workforce and increase the reliability of the hierarchy – partly by forcing managers to be consistent and fair in dealing with employees. Many studies have shown that under conditions of mass production and bureaucratic management, economic performance is improved by unionization (Freeman and Medoff 1984; Slichter and Livernash, 1960). Though managers, like all those with power, never like having their authority challenged, they could 'live with' neo-corporatist institutions under those conditions. Meanwhile, the most organized social force, that of workers in large industrial workplaces, got improved wages and working conditions; and the society at large got a broad increase in purchasing power that helped drive economic expansion and the growth of a strong middle class (or skilled working class) during the postwar period.

Such a win-win compromise is not eternal, however, any stakeholder regime is essentially a concrete balance of forces rather than a tightly integrated system based on shared values. When conditions shift sufficiently that one party or another thinks it can better achieve its own interests and values without these institutions, there are few communal or moral bonds keeping it from trying to get out of the deal. Both worker movements and managers have for the most part held to the neo-corporatist frame because they saw it as the best they could do in the

circumstances not because they have felt it to be fundamentally the best way to organize society.

The last few decades have seen such a shift in conditions. The economic scene has increasingly moved away from mass production as the central motor of value; 'commodity production' is viewed in many industries as unprofitable and something to be avoided. In its place has arisen a growing sector of the economy for which profit is driven primarily by innovation and responsiveness. In this sector the neo-corporatist compromise, with its emphasis on stability and contractual rules, is a poor fit – to the degree that managers have felt it was more in their interests to break with the deal than to go along with it. They have had a relatively easy time doing so in the US because the legal framework supporting neo-corporatism is comparatively weak; employers who resist unionization or fire organizers suffer few legal penalties, so that when the economic incentive is lost there is nothing left. In other countries where the legal and institutional props of neo-corporatism are stronger, employers have been slower to show open hostility to unions; but the pendulum is swinging in this direction in virtually all industrial nations.

A GENERAL MODEL OF CHANGE IN STAKEHOLDER REGIMES

There is in these events a suggestive pattern. In the nineteenth century economy many stakeholders made claims, such as anarchist and communal models, but one regime became dominant: that of regularized negotiations between craft unions and employers. In the first decades of the twentieth century this relatively stable relation was blown apart by a profound economic transformation that destroyed the old relationships and bases of power. This led to a transitional era of low regulation, in which economic values became dominant at the expense of other important social values; this imbalance led to growing inequality, a rise in corruption and public cynicism, and a loss of community.

Finally, out of the turmoil there emerged a new stakeholder pattern, with government playing a more active role as a regulator and the union presence shifting from the craft to the industrial form.

It seems plausible that there is a greater universality to this pattern which can be put in the form of general propositions.

- Stakeholder regimes stabilize social orders by balancing values of diverse stakeholders, ensuring relative predictability and social stability.
- Stakeholder regimes can be disrupted by major economic or social change.
- Such disruption leads to a destabilization of communal norms such as public service and equity, and to a decline in the regulatory institutions that implement them. The result is an unbalanced focus on economic values driven by corporate interests.
- These shifts produce social and economic instability and pathology as many stakeholders feel that their concerns are ignored.
- There follows an assertion of new stakeholder claims appropriate to the existing situation, and the establishment of a new regime to institutionalize those claims.

Stakeholder regimes stabilize (modern) social orders

Some theories of modern society see no need for stakeholders – particularly neoclassical economic theory and, in the political realm, varieties of utilitarianism. But it has been a steady and growing theme of social theory that such individualist views lack something essential: a moral force that is vital both for the stabilization of personal identity and for the maintenance of social trust and motivation. Emile Durkheim showed a century ago that social order requires a sense of shared community and solidarity, and that intermediate groups between the state and individual were needed to build and institutionalize these solidarities. Economists have been reluctant to accept the importance of collective behavior, but in the last decades work on imperfect information has increasingly drawn out the significance of organizations and group norms in shaping economic behavior (Olson, 1971; Philips, 1989; Solow, 1990).

If we accept that preferences and values are shaped by groups, then the nature of these groups must be analyzed as a vital element in explaining social dynamics. The concept of 'interest groups' has become increasingly accepted as essential to political analysis. The authors of the US Constitution feared that such 'factions' would lead to fragmentation of the body politic; and insofar as there is no regularized relation among such interests, they are right. Sometimes interest fragmentation has caused major social disruption. One such period, in the US, was the late 1920s and early 1930s, when competing worker groups began fighting with each other, as much as with management, making it impossible to reach any stable agreements. The National Labor Relations Act was largely intended to organize those interests into a stable regime that could resolve conflicts and create consensus.

In the current phase, moreover, the importance of group claims is greater than ever for both social stability and economic productivity.

In advanced capitalist societies, effective stakeholder regimes are increasingly necessary for economic and social stability

As capitalism has advanced, group memberships have become both more plural and complex. In agricultural and early modern societies people had a single hierarchically-nested set of affiliations, from family through village to tribe or nation. Capitalism differentiated occupation from family, so that wage-earners were faced with often-conflicting loyalties (Parsons, 1971). Thus the first major stakeholder claim was historically that of occupations, organized in unions and professional groups. During the nineteenth century, regulatory systems and negotiating frameworks were created to stabilize the relation of these groups to firms and the rest of society.

In the last few decades these claims on individual loyalty have become far more differentiated, with gender, race, sexual preference, political orientation, and other dimensions creating a web of identities that are not by any means stably ordered. This explosion of claims to identity and rights has disrupted the rather simple stakeholder framework of collective bargaining: the democratic process is increasingly shaped by the growing role of interest groups, identity groups, and deliberate associations. Thus the stabilization of the political sphere requires ways to build agreements among complex and often overlapping stakeholders.

Stakeholder regimes are necessary to economic performance

Stakeholder regimes are also essential from the narrower perspective of economic production. Economies are always highly interdependent on other social institutions: They require workers who will commit their labor and who have sufficient education to perform effectively; they require consumers who believe in the value of what is offered and trust the offering; they require a general trust in the soundness of the legal system and regulatory mechanisms; and so on. These conditions for economic success involve the realization of values that are not in themselves economic.

One theory is that businesses should themselves represent these outside values: the Japanese model was once touted as one in which businesses have a sense of social responsibility which tempers the economic view (Vogel, 1979). The Japanese experience since then is one of many, however, which shows that one organization cannot effectively represent multiple competing values without distortion and loss of credibility (Shikawa, 2002). The Wagner Act, and the neo-corporatist order in general, are based on the opposite approach: encouraging a system of stakeholder representation and regular forums for discussion and negotiation among them.

As markets mature the dependence of firms on social institutions grows – educational needs increase, webs of interdependence with outside suppliers and contractors become more elaborate; firms need to draw on knowledge developed in universities and other non-economic institutions; customers become more demanding and willing to exercise choice. As a result an increasing

range of stakeholders is able to do harm to companies – not just unions, but identity groups, issue groups, consumer groups, and others. Conversely, an increasing range of stakeholders (though not always the same ones) can help in the co-ordination of resources: for example, universities, standards groups, and so on.

As this range of stakeholders grows, the possibility of management internalizing them all grows even more remote. Thus the ability to work with stakeholder groups becomes more central to the economic success of firms and to the overall productivity of the economy (Ramirez and Wallin, 2000). A relatively organized method for negotiation and building agreement among the main claimants – that is to say, a stakeholder regime – is essential to the predictability and risk-assessment on which successful businesses depend.

Stakeholder regimes can be disrupted by economic or social change

Major changes in the structure of the economy can disrupt established networks of stakeholder relations. Indeed, *any* major shift in stakeholder power or interests can be disruptive to a regime; but in advanced capitalist systems the most solidly established stakeholder, backed by legal rights and strong institutions, is always corporate management. Thus no stakeholder regime can succeed without at least persuading this key stakeholder that it is worth participating; and when management needs shift fundamentally this equation is likely to be invalidated.

Management's core interests as a stakeholder can be captured largely by an analysis of strategic imperatives. Until a century ago most companies focused on local markets and needed to maintain strong communal relationships, which was favorable to a regime which involved local players and craft unions. But the strategic shift toward scale and scope in a mass-production economy in the early twentieth century meant that the established relations no longer met corporate needs.

There followed a decades-long process of undermining craft unions and government legitimacy. For a few decades in the US, especially in the 1920s, companies operated virtually without needing to pay attention to competing stakeholder claims.

Such a disruption leads to a destabilization of public norms and to a decline in the regulatory institutions that spring from them

As stakeholder institutions are weakened, values that go beyond the narrowly economic, such as public service and equity, lose power. What was visible in the 1920s, and again today, is a lessening of corporate contribution to public welfare and even of business acceptance of fundamental values like integrity and honesty. The pressure of competition, without the counterweight of pressure from stakeholders representing other values, begins to drive behavior in a one-sided direction.

These declines produce instability and social pathology

Pursuit of one-sided values leads to a general loss of trust and public spirit. Growing inequality – again a feature of both the 1920s and the present period (Plotnick et al., 1998) – is disruptive economically and socially. Corruption tends to increase, leading to a vicious circle of increasing withdrawal from the public sphere. The loss of confidence in the long-run stability of the system leads to increasing degrees of short-term speculative risk, producing market bubbles. In the 1920s and1930s phase this contributed to the economic destabilization leading to the Depression.

There follows an assertion of new stakeholder claims appropriate to the existing situation, and the establishment of a new regime to institutionalize those claims

This follows from the first argument: that effective stakeholder regimes are necessary to

both societal and business success. In freeing themselves from the constraints of existing stakeholder regimes, managers may feel liberated for a time; but they will soon find problems on two fronts: the erosion of trust and the quality of social relations on which businesses depend; and the rise of uncoordinated and unpredictable attacks and claims for which no agreed-on method of negotiation and agreement exist.

THE DYNAMICS OF THE CHANGE PROCESS

The development of new claims into a new regime is not a smooth and predictable process. At least three complicated dynamics have to be worked through. First, old stakeholders, those whose positions were institutionalized in the old regime, must change their status – possibly by disappearing entirely, but possibly by shifting strategies and the nature of their interaction with other players. Second, new stakeholders must develop to a point where they can be reliable representatives in an institutionalized regime. Finally, a set of rules and procedures for negotiation and agreement must be established and accepted by all the players.

There are significant obstacles to these changes. The old players are generally far more organized and stable than the new, and are also likely to be 'locked into place' in the system by a combination of norms, habits, and formal legal supports. There is likely to be especially a heavy resistance to change from the weaker stakeholders – those who are most heavily 'propped up' by societal institutions and who would be most likely to lose position. As a result, existing regimes are highly sticky and slow to change, and players may maintain substantial social influence even when their real support from members and other constituencies erodes. To take one example, there is a good deal of evidence that even in Scandinavia the foundations of industrial unions have greatly weakened – they are having trouble in recruiting younger workers and in penetrating growing economic sectors. Nevertheless, they are such powerful players in the political arena, have such a large pool of resources, and in many cases have such links to critical social welfare programs such as unemployment insurance, that the weakness at the base has not yet shown itself in normal societal negotiations (Boeri et al., 2001; Hyman, 2001).

On the other side, 'new' stakeholders must go through a difficult process of development. In their early phases stakeholder groups necessarily lack elaborated and accepted internal processes for decision-making; thus they typically have significant problems in maintaining internal discipline, developing coherent strategies, and following through on commitments. This makes it difficult for any group to establish enough credibility either to convince other stakeholders – especially management – that they are worth dealing with, or to gain enough political weight to win formal rights. The process of building stable organizations to represent unstable social identities and issues can be long and painful. In the case of the US labor movement in the 1920s, as craft unionism declined, many groups contended for the representation of worker interests; John L. Lewis' charisma and his solid, long-established base in the mining industry combined to give him a substantial advantage over the others and contributed to the eventual success of industrial unionism.

The development of new stakeholders has an external as well as an internal dimension (though they are closely linked): their maturation involves getting more engaged in reliable links to other players, and participation in forums for reaching agreement. The ability to modify positions to win allies, without creating internal fissures, is vital to long-term success.

Finally, the building of an accepted framework of procedures may be equally a matter of lengthy trial-and-error. There are two basic ways this can be done: either through negotiation among the powerful stakeholder groups, or through the imposition of a government-defined framework. Given the realities of a democratic political system, the first is likely to take the lead before being formalized by the second. Craft unionism developed with very little government intervention and was almost entirely a pragmatic series of agreements between particular unions and companies, evolving slowly into a regime of informal norms and 'ways of doing business'. Industrial unionism developed for decades through battles inside and outside the framework of organized labor, until the Wagner Act gave it a formal institutional status.

One key problem in institutionalization is to decide which groups will participate in stakeholder discussions. In a turbulent transitional period, where new groups are emerging and shifting all the time, there is no formula for doing this. A few companies have tried to reach out to stakeholders to establish some kind of consensus-building forum on key issues – examples include Shell's environmental forums and efforts at Texaco or Coca-Cola to bring together groups around race issues; but such initiatives have trouble in reaching binding agreements, because anyone can say they disagree with the results and go off and battle with them. The other approach would be for government (legislatively or judicially) to determine which groups have been 'standing'. This has the advantage of putting the enforcement powers of government behind some particular configuration, but it also risks leaving out important emergent players; if government steps in too soon it may find its rules miss the 'real' social forces and create more trouble than they resolve.

Stages of development of stakeholder regimes

The emergence of new stakeholder regimes can be formalized in a sequence of stages, observable in the history of the development of industrial unionism and in the development of various movements for civil rights and other issues in the last century.

- Stakeholders emerge to represent issues that are not adequately dealt with through existing decision-making processes. In this first phase the stakeholder groups are driven by very concrete grievances or goals, and they have little internal stability; they are typically organized by charismatic leaders, which is in effect a very simple form of organization – but also one that is very prone to factionalization and splits. In the absence of institutionalized dialog, violence is a frequent element. The black Civil Rights movement formed around powerful leaders like Martin Luther King, and has since fragmented; today even the most developed organizations, like Jesse Jackson's Rainbow/PUSH Coalition, are still person-dependent and fragile.

- As stakeholders begin to stabilize – if they in fact represent social values with lasting constituencies – they become somewhat more predictable. They must generally broaden their self-definition in order to integrate a reasonable range of views and limit secessions, and they must elaborate their internal processes to gain reliable support from their members. In the US, the women's movement, and more recently the environmental movement, have begun exploring this terrain, trying to frame their issues more inclusively and as contributing to the good of all.

- At this point a series of battles with existing status groups is likely to lead to some sort of concrete *modus vivendi*, in which the various players have gotten to know and understand each other well enough that they can anticipate each other's moves and know which is likely to succeed. This is an unstable situation, though, because in the absence of binding agreements all parties are still looking for new ways to get an edge.

- The next stage is the development of regular discussions seeking binding agreements. The potential for instability remains in that there is not yet a way of preventing other groups from making other claims. Today the closest to this may be in the environmental realm, where some groups engage in regular dialog with companies and regulators and have developed some consistent influence, but there are no regularized ways of making and enforcing agreements.

- A fourth stage, not always reached, involves engaging social groups and values beyond the immediate stakeholders. Usually this means a successful political campaign, gaining support from the government, as a representative of the society as a whole, in establishing a regime that establishes standing for particular players and enforces agreement between them.

THE CURRENT DISCONTINUITY

The challenge to the neo-corporatist stakeholder regime since at least the 1970s has been driven in part by the economic shift away from mass and toward knowledge production (Piore and Sabel, 1984; Best, 1990). Mass production has increasingly declined as a source of profit – a victim of something very much like Marx's 'tendency of the rate of profit to fall' – with the result that in almost every industry large companies have fled that sector, passing it off to smaller subcontractors in lower-wage areas. But (something Marx did not foresee) knowledge production has moved to fill the void: profit can still be drawn from novelty, customization, and the ability to address customers' particular and changing problems. This has led to the rise of 'solutions' strategies, which aim to combine services and products flexibly around customer needs, and which draw profits mainly from the knowledge that they provide in helping customers navigate an increasingly complex and fast-changing market-place (Foote et al., 2001). Thus IBM, for example, is drawing less of its profit from selling equipment, and more from selling integrated solutions that may include its own equipment and that of others along with consulting and maintenance.

Solutions strategies and focus on knowledge-value bring deep changes to the organization of production. Large-scale bureaucratic integration, which is particularly strong on stability and reliability, is less important than before; more important is flexibility, the capacity to combine resources in changing ways from many sources. Thence the explosion of innovation around teams, task forces, alliances, supplier networks, and supply chain management.

The neo-corporatist stakeholder regime is a casualty of these fundamental shifts. Both industrial unionism and government regulation are essentially ways of bringing values of fairness and honesty to a bureaucratic structure; they rely heavily on rules and tight definition of responsibility through position and office. Industrial unions focus on drawing sharp job boundaries and establishing formal equality between equivalent jobs; government, similarly, assumes individualized liability for responsible positions, and they also depend on stable industries and companies.

These forms of regulation are increasingly unworkable for many reasons. The high level of turbulence due to industrial change means that government rules and union contracts are often equally ineffectual as forms of control. Flexible team structures are less amenable to control through job definition. Complex alliances and networks continually challenge the boundaries of contractual agreements (Heckscher, 2001).

This turbulence has also thrown up a set of new players making value claims on corporations. These fall into two main categories: issue groups and identity groups. Issue groups are simple to understand: the most important currently are probably those focused on environmental and consumer safety. They increase gradually in significance with social interdependence and political maturity. Identity groups are somewhat more complicated. It is empirically clear that in the last 40 years their impact has grown exponentially. This is particularly visible in the US, where while legal protection for collective bargaining has steadily retreated, laws guaranteeing rights to identity groups have equally steadily advanced – starting with the Civil Rights laws of 1964, to the women's rights amendments, to the Americans With Disabilities Act of 1990. States have passed many further laws protecting sexual orientation, religious beliefs, and other identities, and courts have also extended such protections through judicial rulings. The assertion of rights by identity groups has by now become visible in most industrialized nations. It is less clear *why* this increase has been occurring, and how deep its roots run; there is some disagreement among sociologists about whether they represent fundamental shifts in the nature of social movements (Castells, 1997; Touraine, 1985; Zald, 1988).

In any case the neo-corporatist regime is being attacked from two different angles. First, corporate managers see less reason

than before to support it; second, many other groups are less willing to fall in behind the labor movement in pressing their demands, preferring instead to break free and seek their own sources of power.

None of the existing solutions built up during the industrial era works very well in managing this new set of problems. Whether it be the strong systems of codetermination in Scandinavia, the decentralized regimes of the US, the decentralized-conflictual system of France, the managerial form in Japan, or the powerful welfare-state institutions of northern Europe and New Zealand, *all* are suffering from the same essential problems: loss of support for unions among the young, failure to penetrate new and growing economic sectors, and a delegitimization of government's role as regulator. The erosion is most visible in systems like the US which have relatively weak governmental mechanisms stabilizing the industrial system, but the most careful studies of the European scene have concluded that the same essential forces are acting there as well and will lead to a continuing decline of neo-corporatist institutions (Boeri et al., 2001; Hyman, 2001.)

Most analysts – that is, those who accept the need for stakeholder involvement – are looking to other forms of neo-corporatism to solve their problems: America may envy the seeming strength of Scandinavia, the French admire the effectiveness of pragmatic American collective bargaining, and so on. But it follows from this analysis that no solution from the existing portfolio will work; we need to be looking at the conditions for creation of a new regime.

REQUIREMENTS FOR AN EMERGENT REGIME

What can we say about the emergent stakeholder regime – or, to put it in the terms of this discussion, about the form of industrial democracy appropriate to this socio-economic moment?

The critical structural element is that the emergent regime will almost certainly involve more players than the current one. The tripartite structure of the past has been increasingly seen as too limiting by many important social actors who have felt their needs were not being adequately represented. More importantly, many of these actors are not centrally identified with the workplace; their claims on corporations come not from the perspective of workplace dignity but from that of broader societal values and identities. Given this focus, it is fundamentally implausible that these groups would subordinate themselves to the labor movement, as they did in the heyday of industrial unionism, using unions as the primary vehicle for expressing their concerns. The values of unions and new social movement groups may overlap, and may certainly allow for alliances, but they cannot be reduced to a tripartite structure as in the past.

It also seems certain that the emergent regime will need to move away from models of formalized rule-making, including strong work rules and job protections, toward more continuous engagement and negotiation. The pace of technological and social change seems unlikely to slow for the foreseeable future: the effects of the microprocessor are just beginning to make their way into the economy; the biotechnology revolution coming right behind will be equally powerful; the huge leap in global interdependence will take many decades to sort out. Thus, as many have noted, it is increasingly hard for any company in any industry to give long-term assurances of stable jobs and careers. A central feature of the emergent regime must therefore be the ability to continually review and discuss new challenges.

There are, to be sure, major parts of the economy where all this change is less visible – where the traditional strategic dynamics of cost, scale, and scope are still dominant or even becoming more dominant. Retail sales, for example, have historically been structured by relatively small and local companies; but Wal-Mart has transformed this pattern and is shifting the retail sector to something much more like the industrial production model. Similarly, health care

is moving from the model of independent professional entrepreneurs toward a far more bureaucratized structure with a heavy focus on cost and scale. To the extent that these developments continue in these extremely important sectors, the essential structure of industrial unionism continues to be appropriate. But there is reason to doubt that these sectors will continue along the classic industrial line. More complex knowledge-based services such as health care are less amenable than manufacturing by a scale/mass production approach, because they cannot escape ongoing interaction with end consumers; thus there is already great resistance to organizing health-care delivery on the basis of detailed rules. Though the industrial logic does seem to fit better with low-knowledge services such as Wal-Mart or McDonald's, even in those cases there is some tendency to move toward models emphasizing customer responsiveness and innovation. To the degree that such solutions approaches develop, unions and government will face the same problems of regulation as in other knowledge sectors.

THE CURRENT IMPASSE

The stakeholders of the neo-corporatist regime have varying relations to the change process. Management is, of course, a driver of change because it stands to benefit most from it. Unions, however, have almost universally dug in their heels and proclaimed the need to go back to the familiar forms of regulation. They have remained (with few exceptions) fundamentally ambivalent and ineffective in dealing with the spread of team-based work organizations, which necessarily challenge contractual regulations. They have failed to appeal to the growing sector of part-time and contingent workers. They have not penetrated branches of the economy based on solutions production, such as information technology and the rapidly-growing field of biotechnology. They have been unable to build effective alliances with identity and issue movements whose center is outside the workplace and they have been largely unable to broaden their scope beyond the national borders that have supported them in the past (Boeri et al., 2001).

Government, as the other main player in the neo-corporatist framework, is in a more contradictory position. In almost every country of the industrialized world there have been moves to weaken government regulation. Yet the size of governments everywhere continues to grow with the increased complexity of economic and social activity. Government regulation is widely perceived as necessary but distasteful; there is a casting-about for new roles and ways of performing the necessary kinds of co-ordination.

Many new stakeholder groups have been emerging – or more exactly, groups making claims to stakeholder status – but very few of them have moved beyond the stage of factionalism, charismatic leadership, and narrowness of issues characteristic of immature organizations. Even the most respected issue and identity groups remain fragile and have only begun to play more regular roles in societal debates. Overall the constellation looks somewhat like the American labor movement of the 1920s, which was characterized by many scattered organizations with uncertain prospects and extremely different agendas, often very narrow and partisan.

Thus we have reached a point of seeming impasse: existing stakeholder processes are inadequate to build an agreement in the current situation, and there are as yet only scattered indicators of what new ones might look like; old institutions still fighting for position and new ones not yet strong enough to make their way into the game.

The lack of a legitimate stakeholder regime at the moment is apparent in the growth of relatively uncontrolled conflict – that is, conflict that does not move toward a widely acceptable balancing of values. In the US, this has largely taken the form of employee rights litigation. Though there is clearly a growing sense that rights of citizenship – equal treatment, free speech, and so on – should apply to the workplace, this has led not to a unified set of norms but to particular laws

aimed at particular groups, often state-by-state or jurisdiction-by-jurisdiction. Groups that have backed and sought to enforce the laws have been unstable and unreliable. Thus managers on the one hand can often 'get away' with things that much of the society would see as unfair, and on the other hand they may 'get hit with' lawsuits that seem irrational. This has been going on long enough now that it has reached the second stage of development described above: some rough rules are beginning to emerge, drawn on all sides from pragmatic assessment of experiences, but since they are implicit and unenforceable they are frequently violated.

Another major unregulated conflict, even earlier in development and less structured, is the growing resistance to globalization. Here the groups and coalitions are extremely fluid and organizationally immature, and their views vary widely. So far there are far fewer forums for discussion of these issues and attempts to reach agreement than there is in the employee-rights area. The combination of anger and lack of reliable expression has led at times to open violence, as in the Seattle anti-globalization demonstrations of 1999 (comparable, in fact, to the early days of the civil rights movements which constituted stage one of the employee-rights development). Even more recently, immigration and employment have become in many countries a third area of growing conflict and instability.

WAYS FORWARD

The way forward, in terms of the analytic scheme proposed here, involves three main components: changing 'old' stakeholders; developing 'new' stakeholders; and formulating processes for discussion and agreement.

Old stakeholders

The issues are different for the main stakeholders in the neo-corporatist regime. Corporate management has made considerable strides in defining new kinds of organization that can support a solutions strategy: the level of invention around temporary task forces and process management has been impressive. But they have not successfully connected this to policies that will maintain employee commitment and ensure efficient labor markets in the long run. As a result they are moving toward a highly dualistic career system where everyone is fighting over a few valued employees and leaving the rest to fend for themselves. This will certainly undermine the ability to develop knowledge competencies and flexible resource allocation over time (Heckscher, 2000). To the extent that management comes to recognize this long-term interest, it will be more willing to engage in stakeholder discussion processes, which will make the transition easier.

Industrial unions are still oriented to stabilizing large bureaucratic corporations through job security and clear protective rules. To the extent that they can broaden this view to encompass a view of career development and flexibility, they will find more overlap both with management and with many other identity groups and will be better able to engage in stakeholder dialogs. This is, however, an extremely difficult prescription, since the structure of these unions – as well as their histories and identities – are built very strongly around the preservation of jobs *in situ* (Heckscher, 1988: introduction; Heckscher et al., 2003, Chapter 11).

Government in the neo-corporatist era took primarily the roles of rule-maker and arbitrator, standing 'above the fray'. Recently there have been some experiments with the relatively new role of convener – that is, establishing fora and inviting parties to work out agreements among themselves. 'Reg-neg' (regulatory negotiation) efforts have attempted to revise the rule-making process to engage the parties themselves in discussion of the rules. The advantage of this approach, at least potentially, is that it helps to stabilize the process of reaching agreements without rigidifying it through elaborate rule-making and enforcement bureaucracies. To the extent that the convener role can be

further developed it will make it easier to involve a wide range of stakeholder groups in a more flexible ways around different types of issues.

New stakeholders

For new stakeholders the problem has two related components: internal organization development and external involvement in processes of coalition-building and negotiation. Internally such groups need especially to be able to mobilize volunteer effort, a subject that has generated considerable research recently. There is less analysis, to my knowledge, of the problems involved in moving from the charismatic-founder stage to the 'routinization of charisma', or of the difficulties involved in shifting from purist focus on member concerns to engagement and consensus-building with other stakeholder groups. Such literature as there is seems to be split between those criticizing associations for being too democratic and egalitarian for their own good (Merton, 1966) and those who criticize them for being too bureaucratic (Cnaan, 1991), and in general is characterized by a sense of their fragility (Flament, 1991; Gittell, 1980; Scully and Segal, 2002; Smith and Freedman, 1972).

Processes for discussion and decision-making

There has been substantial recent experimentation and innovation with multiparty consensus-building processes. Over the last decades it has progressed from simple consensus-building within small work teams to processes for large-scale community discussions involving at times thousands of people or many groups (Weisbord, 1987; Dannemiller Tyson Associates, 2000). These techniques have emerged in large part because of the social factors described above: increases in the complexity of social actors, in the need for co-ordinated social co-operation, and in the need for flexibility. Shell is, at least among large companies, the one that has done the most to apply them to stakeholder management in the sense described here; they have begun to host frequent 'stakeholder forums' with 50 or more organizations, including NGOs (non-governmental organizations) and governmental agencies, in various countries, to try to build agreement on a sustainable approach to energy policy and the environment (Lawrence, 2002).

These processes are not sufficient: they essentially help move only to stage 2 of the stakeholder development process sketched above. That is, they move *understanding* forward and thus help to reduce conflicts born out of miscommunication or lack of foresight. But they do not have the leverage to produce real modifications of values on the part of different stakeholders that could help bring them together in agreements. In terms of the two major issues raised at the beginning of this essay, they have no clearly accepted way of defining who should be in or out, and they have no way to reach decisions when consensus is impractical. Since they are relatively unstructured and non-binding, they cannot sustain the longer-running kinds of relationships needed to bring together parties who start far apart.

To move to the third stage of a stakeholder regime, one where negotiations can be structured to produce agreements, more progress must be made around defining mechanisms of accountability and enforcement. This is traditionally the realm of governance rather than process management. It is likely to involve government authority, though this is not essential: professional associations have had binding accountability mechanisms for centuries independent of government.

passing through a period of destabilization, we have an interest in asking how the evident conflicts arising from economic transformation can be institutionalized in a new regime of negotiation and consensus.

The analysis of stakeholder regimes opens a number of complex problems that have been only been touched on in interest-group theories of modern democracy. The rules governing systems of negotiation must define the actors, the issues, and the codes of discussion and decision; in practice these rules are not eternal but rather adapted to concrete sets of actors and issues.

The key problem for any new regime will be to encompass new actors that have developed in the last few decades. This creates serious organizational problems: it is harder to organize relations among many players than among the three of the neo-corporatist model. There has been a good deal of learning in recent years about the management of multiparty systems, but not yet enough to resolve the problem.

The most difficult obstacles, however, may be attitudinal. Leaders of the old order have a hard time accepting new actors as legitimate: unions in particular have a tendency to think that other 'progressive' groups should follow their lead, as they did through much of the last century. It is equally hard for new actors, for their part, to give up their initial purity of purpose and to accept compromise with others who have different priorities. These attitudes are a constant source of friction and conflict among groups that should be allies in building a new stakeholder order to balance the economic values of corporations.

CONCLUSION

For all the power of the ideology of free markets, industrial societies have always been characterized by conflict among groups with different values. When these conflicts are unregulated they destabilize both economies and societies; when institutionalized they can lead to pragmatic balances that for a time meet most stakeholder needs. Since we are clearly

NOTES

1 The concept of 'neo-corporatism' is sometimes used to refer to systems with high levels of co-operation and partnership. I am using it more broadly to refer to all tripartite systems characteristic of industrial capitalism, of which the 'partnership' type is one variant.

2 The concept of 'regime' has been used in various fields, most relevantly by Esping-Andersen (1990) and others in studies of welfare states. I am in a sense

adapting that usage to IR, though I intend it more as an expression of institutional theory à la Parsons (1971).

REFERENCES

American Society of Association Executives and Chamber of Commerce of the United States (1975) *Principles of Association Management.* Washington, DC: ASAE & CCUS.

Boeri, Tito, Brugiavini, Agar and Calmfors, Lars (eds) (2001). *The Role Of Unions In The Twenty-First Century.* Oxford: Oxford University Press.

Best, Michael H (1990). *The New Competition: Institutions of Industrial Restructuring.* Cambridge, MA: Harvard University Press.

Carré, Françoise and Joshi, Pamela (2000) 'Looking for leverage in a fluid world: innovative responses to temporary and contracted work'. in Carré, Françoise; Ferber, Marianne; Golden, Lonnie; and Herzenberg, Stephen A. (eds) *Nonstandard Work: The Nature and Challenge of Changing Employment Arrangements.* Industrial Relations Research Association: pp. 313–39.

Castells, Manuel (1997). *The Power of Identity.* Oxford: Blackwell.

Cnaan, Ram A. (1991) 'Neighborhood-representing organizations: how democratic are they? A review of the literature'. *Social Service Review,* 65: 614–34.

Cobble, Dorothy Sue (1991) *Dishing It Out: Waitresses and Their Unions in the Twentieth Century.* Urbana, Ill: University of Illinois Press.

Dannemiller Tyson Associates (2000) *Whole-Scale Change: Unleashing the Magic in Organizations.* Berrett Kohler.

Durkheim, Emile (1947/1893) *The Division of Labor in Society.* NY: The Free Press, 1947; orig 1893.

Ebbinghaus, B (1990) 'Does a European social model exist and can it survive?'. in Huemer, G. et al. (eds) *The Role of Employer Associations and Labour Unions in the EMU.* Aldershot: Ashgate. pp. 1–26.

Esping-Andersen, Gosta. (1990) *Three Worlds of Welfare Capitalism.* Princeton: Princeton University Press, 1990.

Fine, Janice (2006) *Worker Centers: Organizing Communities at the Edge of the Dream.* NY: Cornell University Press, forthcoming (January).

Flament, Catherine (1991) 'Associations-réseaux et réseaux d'associations: une approche formelle de l'organisation réticulée'. *Sociétés Contemporaines,* 5 (March): 67–74.

Foote, Nathaniel W., Galbraith, Jay, Hope, Quentin and Miller, Danny (2001) 'Making solutions the answer'. *The McKinsey Quarterly* 3: 85–93.

Freeman, R.E (1984) *Strategic Management: a stakeholder approach.* Mass: Pitman, 1984.

Freeman, Richard B. and Medoff, James L (1984) *What Do Unions Do?* NY: Basic Books.

Gittell, Marilyn (1980) *Limits to Citizen Participation: the decline of community organizations.* Beverly Hills: Sage.

Hacker, Jacob (2002) *The Divided Welfare State: The Battle over Public and Private Social Benefits in the United States.* Cambridge, UK: Cambridge University Press.

Heckscher, Charles (1988) *The New Unionism: Employee Involvement in the Changing Corporation.* Cornell University Press, 1995 (second edition).

Heckscher, Charles (2000) 'HR strategy and contingent work: dualism vs. true mobility'. in Carré, Françoise; Ferber, Marianne; Golden, Lonnie; and Herzenberg, Stephen A. (eds) *Nonstandard Work: the Nature and Challenge of Changing Employment Arrangements.* Industrial Relations Research Association: pp. 267–90.

Heckscher, Charles C (1995) *The New Unionism: Employee Involvement in the Changing Corporation.* Cornell University Press, 1995 (second edition).

Heckscher, Charles, Maccoby, Michael, Ramirez, Rafael and Tixier, Pierre-Eric (2003) *Agents of Change: Crossing the Post-Industrial Divide.* Oxford: Oxford University Press.

Hyman, Richard (2001) *Understanding European Trade Unionism: Between Market, Class, and Society.* London: Sage Publications.

Lawrence, Anne T. (2002) 'The Drivers of Stakeholder Engagement: Reflections on the Case of Royal Dutch/Shell'. *Journal of Corporate Citizenship,* 6 (Summer).

Left Business Observer (2000) 'Income and Poverty.' 93, February; available at http://www.leftbusinessobserver.com/Stats_incpov.html (viewed 5/10/06)

Merton, Robert K (1966) 'Dilemmas of democracy in the voluntary associations'. *American Journal of Nursing,* May: 1055–61.

Olson, Mancur (1971) *The Logic of Collective Action: Public Goods and the Theory of Groups.* Cambridge, MA: Harvard University Press.

Parsons, Talcott (1971) *The System of Modern Societies.* Englewood Cliffs, NJ: Prentice-Hall.

Philips, Louis (1989) *The Economics of Imperfect Information.* Cambridge, UK: Cambridge University Press.

Piore, Michael J. and Sabel, Charles F. (1984) *The Second Industrial Divide: Possibilities for Prosperity.* New York: Basic Books.

Plotnick, R. D., Smolensky, E., Evenhouse, E. and Reilly, S. (1998) 'Inequality and poverty in the United States: The twentieth-century record'. *Focus* 19 (3): 7–14.

Ramirez, Rafael and Wallin, Johan (2000) *Prime Movers: Define Your Business or Have Someone Define It against You.* Chichester: John Wiley & Sons.

Schmitter, Philippe C (1983) 'Democratic theory and neocorporatist practice'. *Social Research* 50 (4) (Winter): 885–928.

Scully, Moreen and Segal, Amy (2002) 'Passion with an Umbrella: grass roots activism in the workplace'. *Research in the Sociology of Organizations*, 19: 125–68.

Shikawa, Akihiro (2002) 'Modernization: Westernization vs. Nationalism – a Historical Overview of the Japanese Case'. *Development and Society* 31 (2) (December): 281–88.

Slichter, Sumner H., Healy, James J. and Livernash, E. Robert (1960) *The Impact of Collective Bargaining on Management.* Washington: Brookings Institution.

Smith, Constance and Freedman, Anne (1972) *Voluntary Associations: Perspectives on the Literature.* Cambridge, MA: Harvard University Press.

Smolensky, Eugene and Plotnick, Robert (1992) *Inequality and Poverty in the United States: 1900 to 1990.* University of California, Berkeley, Graduate School of Public Policy: Working Paper #193 (July 8).

Solow, Robert (1990) *The Labor Market as a Social Institution.* Cambridge, MA: Basil Blackwell.

Touraine, Alain (1985) 'An introduction to the study of social movements'. *Social Research* 52 (4) (Winter): 749–87.

Vogel, Ezra F. (1979) *Japan as Number One: Lessons for America.* Cambridge, MA: Harvard University Press, 1979.

Weber, Max (1968) *Economy and Society.* New York: Bedminster Press, 1968/1921. Translated and edited by Guenther Roth and Claus Wittich.

Weisbord, Marvin R. (1987) *Productive Workplaces: Organizing and Managing for Meaning, Dignity, and Community.* San Francisco: Jossey-Bass.

Williamson, Peter J (1985) *Varieties of Corporatism: a Conceptual Discussion.* Cambridge: Cambridge University Press.

Zald, Mayer N (1988) 'The trajectory of social movements in America'. *Research in Social Movements, Conflicts and Change* 10: 19–41.

Industrial Relations Processes

20

Union Formation

John Godard

Research into the formation of unions has been conducted primarily in liberal market economies (especially the US, but also Canada and the UK), where union representation is determined chiefly by the level of worker support. It has involved four relatively disparate bodies of literature, addressing:

1) individual level propensities to vote for a union;
2) the organizing process;
3) labour law; and
4) macro-level economic and political conditions.

This chapter addresses each of these in turn.[1] It then discusses their implications for understanding the formation of unions and suggests a future direction for work in this area.

WORKER VOTING PROPENSITIES AND THE PRECONDITIONS FOR UNION FORMATION

The stated propensity to vote for a union by no means determines how workers will actually vote. However, the available evidence does suggest that voting propensity at the early stages of an organizing drive accounts for half or more of the variation in actual voting behavior (Getman et al., 1976; Premack and Hunter, 1988; Montgomery, 1989; Davy and Shipper, 1993). Even outside of an organizing drive, voting propensity may be seen as indicative of untapped union growth potential and hence of latent unionism (Fiorito et al., 1995). Analysis of variation in voting propensity is thus potentially useful for understanding the main reasons workers support unions and identifying the conditions under which they are more likely to do so. Below, I review the research relevant to each of these questions in turn, distinguishing between 'internal' (for instance, attitudes, and beliefs) and 'external' (for instance, demographic, contextual, and social) determinants. Because the literature is vast, I focus on studies employing large, representative data sets and multivariate analysis, as identified in Table 20.1; where a study does not meet these criteria but is referred to, the sample and method are noted.[2]

The internal determinants of voting propensities

There have been a number of attempts to theorize voting propensities, drawing on frustration-aggression (Klandermans, 1986),

Table 20.1 Major studies and data sets employed in voting propensity analyses

US studies and data sets

Kochan, 1979; Fiorito, 1987; Evansohn, 1989; Fiorito & Greer 1986.	1977 Quality of Employment Survey (QES), national survey of 804 union and 711 non-union workers, by the University of Michigan Survey Research Centre.
Getman et al., 1976; Farber & Saks, 1980; Dickens, 1983; Davy & Shipper, 1993.	Getman, Goldberg, and Herman data set (GG&H), collected by the University of Illinois Survey Research Laboratory in 1973, from 1004 employees subject to 31 NLRB elections in 1972 and 1973; merged with NLRB election data.
Cornfield et al., 1998.	1991 General Social Survey (GSS), national survey of 910 non-union and 517 union employees, by the National Opinion Research Centre (University of Chicago).
Deshpande & Fiorito, 1989; Jarley & Fiorito, 1989; Fiorito et al., 1987; Schur & Kruse, 1992; Cornfield & Kim; 1994	Union Image Survey, national survey of 830 non-union and 622 union workers, conducted in 1984 by Louis Harris & Associates for the AFL-CIO.
Fiorito & Young, 1998; Fiorito & Greer, 1986*.	1991 General Social Survey /National Organizations Survey, matched data from national surveys of 484 employees and employers (non-union = 383), by the National Opinion Research Centre and the University of Illinois Survey Research Lab.
Freeman et al., 2000; Fiorito 2001.	Worker Participation and Representation Survey, national survey of 1,929 non-union and 479 union employees in private or non-profit organizations, conducted in 1994 by Princeton Survey Research for R. Freeman and J. Rogers.
Youngblood et al., 1984.	Consumer panel survey in two southeastern states, n=400 non-union workers.

UK studies and data sets

Wood & Machin, 2005; Belfield & Haywood, 2004.	1998 Work Employee Relations Survey, national matched surveys of 2,191 employers and 28,237 employees, conducted by Social and Community Planning Research.
Wood & Machin, 2005.	Work and Industrial Relations Survey, national surveys of 3,312, 3,209, and 3,023 employers conducted in 1980, 1984, and 1990 by Social and Community Planning Research (UK) for the UK government; predecessor to WERS 98.
Charlwood, 2002; 2003.	1998 British Social Attitudes Survey, national survey of 3,146 adults (755 were in non-union employment, 653 in union employment), by the National Centre for Social Research (UK).
Charlwood, 2003.	2001 British Workers Representation and Participation Survey, national survey of 693 non-union and 662 union workers, designed by the Centre for Economic Performance, London School of Economics, conducted by BMRB International.

Canadian studies and data sets

Gomez et al., 2001.	1996 Lipset-Meltz survey, national survey of 1,495 adults, by the Angus-Reid Group.

Source: *Studies identified more than once are those using more than one data set.

cognitive dissonance (Wheeler and McClendon, 1991: 60), rational choice (Farber and Saks, 1980), and interactionist (Montgomery, 1989) theory, and on various other social science frameworks (see Wheeler and McClendon, 1991). But although the specific terminology employed may have varied, most have generally focused on one or more of three conventional explanations (for example, Kochan, 1979; Klandermans, 1986; Wheeler and McClendon, 1991):

1) dissatisfaction with one's job or aspects thereof;
2) general beliefs about unions; and

3) perceived benefits relative to costs of union formation, or union 'instrumentalities'.

I begin by considering these explanations, and then turn to alternative possible explanations that have generally received less attention in the literature.

Conventional explanations

Of the three conventional explanations, dissatisfaction is hypothesized to matter only if individuals believe that a union can address the sources of their dissatisfaction. Thus, its effects are often viewed as conditional on instrumentalities (Wheeler and McClendon, 1991). In contrast, union beliefs have typically been viewed as operating independently, although one study (Youngblood et al., 1984; also see Summers et al., 1986) has postulated that negative beliefs can have a 'veto effect,' negating the effects of dissatisfaction and instrumentalities, while another (Park et al., 2006) has argued that general beliefs operate in part through their implications for instrumentalities. Finally, instrumentalities have been viewed as operating independently as well as in interaction with dissatisfaction and, possibly, general beliefs.

Almost all of the relevant research has been in the US. In general, it has found global measures of all three general explanations to be associated with both voting propensities and voting behavior (Barling et al., 1992: 54), with instrumentalities generally bearing a larger coefficient than general beliefs, and general beliefs a larger coefficient than dissatisfaction (for example, Kochan, 1979: 25; Fiorito, 1987; Deshpande and Fiorito, 1989; Youngblood et al., 1984: 583). These results may be seen as consistent with the US tradition of business unionism and the instrumental orientation associated with it.

When the measures are broken into sub-components, however, the results become murkier. Results reported by Kochan (1979: 29) and by Fiorito (1987), both using 1977 Quality of Employment Survey (QES) data, revealed dissatisfaction with each of a number of facets of the employment relation (for example, pay and benefits) to have coefficient sizes that were in combination similar to that of for instrumentality. Their results also suggested a similar combined effect size for two sub-dimensions of dissatisfaction (with 'bread and butter' issues and with the 'nature of work'). Finally, Fiorito (1987), again using QES data, reported coefficient sizes for two sub-dimensions of general beliefs ('political instrumentality' and 'negative image') that were in combination equivalent to those for instrumentality. Such comparisons should be treated with caution. But they suggest that instrumentality may not be more important than the other two

conventional explanations once the latter are broken into sub-dimensions.

The evidence is also unclear as to the relative importance of specific issues encompassed within the three conventional explanations. In their analyses of the 1977 QES, Kochan (1979: 26) found dissatisfaction with bread and butter issues to have a somewhat larger effect than dissatisfaction with the nature of work, while Fiorito (1987) found dissatisfaction with working conditions and wages and benefits to bear relatively strong associations, yet dissatisfaction with supervision, job challenge, role support, and promotion opportunities to bear statistically insignificant ones. Again, these findings may be seen as consistent with the US tradition of business unionism. However, using the 1984 Union Image Survey (UIS) data set, Deshpande and Fiorito (1989) reported 'intrinsic' (that is, job content) issues to have an effect similar to that for their 'extrinsic' counterparts. In addition, Jarley and Fiorito (1991) found the importance of job content issues to be greater in this data set than in the QES data set, collected seven years earlier. They argued that this could reflect an ongoing shift in what motivates workers to support unions.

There is some evidence of different associations outside of the US. In an analysis of UK data collected in 1998, Charlwood (2002) found dissatisfaction with pay to matter only for manual workers reporting their pay to be 'very low.' He found no associations for other categories. This may reflect the weak bargaining power of UK unions as of the late 1990s (for example, Brown et al., 2000). It may also reflect a different traditional role for UK unions, one that focuses more on fairness and support at work (see Waddington and Whitson, 1997). However, an analysis of survey data from workers in two Canadian cities (Krahn and Lowe, 1984) found general instrumentality perceptions to have stronger effects than 'big labor image,' suggesting little difference from the US despite Canada's stronger tradition of social unionism.

Attempts to find support for the hypothesized relationships between the three general explanations have met with mixed success. Both Charlwood (2002: 481; 2003: 61) and Youngblood et al. (1984: 585) found little evidence of such relationships. In a meta-analysis of data from previous studies, Premack and Hunter (1988) found that dissatisfaction may have an indirect effect, operating through instrumentalities. But they also found strong direct effects for dissatisfaction, and evidence as to an indirect effect was based on correlation analysis and hence did not establish causality. Park et al. (2006) found general beliefs to have a significant effect on instrumentalities (labeled 'specific beliefs'), with no converse relationship, and the total (direct and indirect) effect of the former to be three times that of the latter. But their sample was comprised of pharmacists in the US, and so these results may not generalize.

There has been little research into the extent to which appealing to various attitudes and beliefs is likely to enhance the likelihood of union success. For example, high levels of dissatisfaction may be positively associated with voting propensity, but may not be sufficiently widespread to really matter (see Kochan, 1979: 25), and may be difficult to influence without union organizers appearing to be 'trouble makers' and hence enhancing the fear of conflict (see below). Yet the opposite may be the case for instrumentalities and general beliefs, which lend themselves to more positive appeals. If so, targeting the latter, rather than attempting to foster dissatisfaction, may be more effective for improving the rate of union formation.

In addition, there does not appear to have been any research specifically distinguishing between dissatisfaction with the job or facets thereof and dissatisfaction with the employer.[3] One might expect the latter to matter more, because it involves attribution and hence a belief that something can be done through collective representation (Kelly, 1998).

An underlying problem with analyses of these three general explanations and components thereof is that they have tended to abstract the decision to unionize from the institutional environment within which it is made, including not just the structure of the employment relation at law, but also the broader system of laws and norms that frame this relationship. As suggested by Charlwood's analysis of UK workers, differences in these environments have possible implications for the ability to generalize research findings across nations. Failure to address these environments may also limit the extent to which research findings actually contribute to our understanding of why workers do or do not vote for a union within a particular nation and how this may be related to matters of institutional design. In this regard, much may ultimately depend on national differences in union identities and perceptions of 'what unions do.' However, this possibility has not been considered.

Alternative explanations

Although researchers have tended to focus on the three general explanations as identified above, a number of alternative possible explanations have been addressed. Many of these explanations may be captured in part by the three general explanations. But they tend to be more specific and more institutionally informed.

Distrust. In capitalist economies, the employment relation is one of subordination under conditions of interest conflict (Godard, 1998, 2004c). As such, one would expect distrust and insecurity as to the exercise of authority to form an important rationale for union formation, with the union largely selling itself as a source of 'conflict insurance' (van de Vall, 1970; Adams, 1974). But only one study (Zalesny, 1985) has addressed the role of trust, and it relied on a single item measure and was based on a survey of faculty in a single university. It found a statistically significant but weak association with propensity.

Desire for voice and representation. In view of the nature of the employment relation, the desire for collective representation and voice should also form a major explanation for voting propensities – especially in liberal market economies, where alternative forms of representation are weak or non-existent. In this regard, US evidence reveals a high level of demand for such representation (Freeman and Rogers, 1999). Yet, there would appear to have been no research explicitly addressing how or the extent to which this desire matters to union formation. At least two analyses, one using UK (Charlwood, 2003) and one using US data (Kochan, 1979), have found 'desire for influence' to bear positive associations with voting propensity. The former found this association to be substantially smaller than for either instrumentality or general beliefs, while the latter found it to be roughly half that for instrumentality but roughly equivalent to that of general beliefs. These measures might be seen as proxies for the desire for representation and voice, but the extent to which they capture desire for collective influence rather than simply individual, job level influence is not clear.[4]

Perceived injustice.

Fairness has long been identified as important in the IR literature, especially in the UK (for example, Hyman and Brough, 1975), where there has been a tradition of 'informality' in the employment relation. Conversely, injustice perceptions have been considered critical prerequisites to collective action in IR (Kelly, 1998). Again, this likely reflects the nature of the employment relation in liberal market economies. However, there has been little attempt to specifically explore the importance of injustice and fairness perceptions on the propensity to vote for a union.[5] One US study did include a measure of pay equity (Kochan, 1979) and another of discrimination (Deshpande and Fiorito, 1989). Neither was found to have an effect. But whether these adequately capture perceptions of injustice is unclear.

Fear of reprisal.

Employer reprisal, or fear thereof, has been identified as perhaps the major factor influencing the outcome of a union organizing drive. This is especially so in the US, where employers have traditionally been hostile towards union recognition and labor law protections are weak (see appendix).

However, both Deshpande and Fiorito (1989) and Fiorito (2001) found employee expectations of union suppression activities to bear a positive rather than negative association with voting propensity, possibly because pro-union workers have a more negative view of their employer to begin with (Fiorito and Bozeman, 1997). More direct evidence of the importance of fear of reprisal may, however, be contained in a 2004 poll of Canadian workers, even though Canadian labor law protections are generally stronger than in the US. It found voting propensity to increase from 33 to 43 per cent when non-union respondents were asked how they would vote if they could be assured there would be no reprisal from the employer (CLC, 2004). Research into the implications of employer anti-union tactics, addressed below, also suggests that fear of reprisal matters.

Fear of conflict.

Employees may also fear increased conflict once a union has been organized (Cohen and Hurd, 1998). Again, this may be especially important in North America, where adversarial relations are the norm (Adams, 1993) and employers have been known to play on this fear in order to discourage workers from voting for a union. In a study of 320 NCR customer engineers subject to a recent organizing attempt, Cohen and Hurd (1998) found fear of conflict to be the most frequently identified reason not to join any employee organization and argued, based on corresponding case analysis, that it was more important than fear of employer retaliation. But only one multivariate study has addressed fear of conflict (Farber and Saks, 1980: 364), finding concern over a possible deterioration in worker-supervisory relationships to increase the likelihood of a negative vote in union certification elections.

Work orientations.

Worker orientations and consciousness of conflicts underlying the employment relation may be central to their willingness to challenge employer authority, which may in turn be critical to the unionization decision. For example, where workers possess oppositional orientations, they should be more likely to view unions as means to resist managerial domination. However, there have been only two studies that include measures of work values and orientations, both Canadian. Gomez et al. (2002) found traditional union values (for example, regarding seniority) to be positively associated with voting propensity, while Barling et al. (1991) found both 'Marxist' work beliefs (for example, about exploitation) and 'humanist' work beliefs (for example, about whether work should be gratifying) to be positively associated with student voting propensities.

Political beliefs and affiliations. Political beliefs and affiliations should be useful *a priori* predictors of voting propensity, especially to the extent that they reflect a consciousness of broader class relationships embedded in the employment relation. This relationship should be strongest in nations where unions have had stronger political party affiliations than otherwise (for example, Canada vs. the US). Yet, although a number of studies have found a general association (Fiorito and Young, 1998; Fiorito, 2001; Charlwood, 2002; Gomez et al., 2002), the measures employed have varied, and most have been single item and typically *ad hoc*. Perhaps as a result, they have yielded only weak associations. There has also been no attempt to explore for cross-national differences.

Overall

Overall, the research reveals that, each of the three general explanations for union propensity is important, even if their relative importance and the associations between them are not clear. However, there has been little research into the importance of alternative and more specific possible explanations, many of which can be said to derive from the institutional design of the employment relation and which may therefore provide for a more institutionally informed and nuanced understanding of the determinants of union formation. In addition, little attention has been

paid to the importance of national institutional environments, even though these may shape what unions do and ultimately the internal determinants of voting propensity.

External determinants

External explanations of voting propensities can be grouped into six categories:

(1) employer practices;
(2) job characteristics;
(3) pay;
(4) working conditions;
(5) social influences; and
(6) individual and demographic characteristics.

All may be hypothesized to operate through one or more of the internal explanations identified above, although attempts to explore the extent to which this is the case have been limited.

Employer practices

Initial interest in employer practices addressed whether a 'union substitution' approach (Kochan, 1980), involving practices similar to those negotiated by unions, lowered support for unions. However, although one study (Evansohn, 1989) found some support for this thesis, another (Fiorito and Young, 1998) found measures of individual practices believed to be associated with a union substitution strategy (for example, grievance systems) to bear weak and often insignificant associations, and a composite index of five such practices to be statistically insignificant.

More recently, focus has been on practices associated with the so-called 'high performance paradigm,' including team work, problem solving groups, direct forms of communication, and supportive selection, training, and reward practices (Godard, 2004c). These can be hypothesized to reduce propensity not only through their implications for union substitution, but also through selection processes that are biased towards workers with anti-union orientations and through work designs and practices that enhance satisfaction and lower instrumentalities.

The US research generally supports this argument. Freeman et al. (2000) found that only a quarter of non-union workers with an employee involvement scheme would vote for a union, compared with four in ten for those without. Fiorito (2001) found a statistically significant but modest association between an index of 12 high performance HRM practices and union voting propensity. Cornfield et al. (1998) found performance based pay raises to be associated with a 22 per cent lower propensity to join a union. Kochan et al. (1986) found high performance practices to lower the likelihood of union formation in recently opened establishments, although Fiorito et al. (1987), using the same data set, found mixed effects. Finally Bronfenbrenner (1997) found that, where a participation program is in place, the estimated likelihood of union organizing success declined by 22 per cent.

Results have been more uneven outside of the US. Gomez et al. (2002) found high performance practices to bear a negative association with voting propensity in Canada, but only for youth. Belfield and Heywood (2004) found only one of eight practices (performance-related pay) to bear a consistent negative association with desire for a union in the UK. One (problem solving groups) actually bore a positive association. Using UK workplace level data, Wood and Machin (2005) found high performance practices to bear no association with the likelihood of union recognition, and some evidence of a complementarity between unions and HRM practices.

The research on employer practices has, however, been of uncertain overall quality (also see Godard, 2004c). In a number of cases (for example Bronfenbrenner, 1997; Cornfield et al., 1998; Freeman et al., 2000; Gomez et al., 2002), researchers have relied on a single binary measure of employer practices. Where multiple items have been employed, these items often do not include key work or HRM practices (for example, Fiorito, 2001; Fiorito and Young, 1998; Belfield and Heywood, 2004; Wood and Machin, 2005) or controls (Kochan et al., 1986), or they are imprecise (see Fiorito et al., 1987: 116). In addition,

the two relevant UK studies are based on data collected prior to the introduction of recognition laws in 1999.[6]

It is also possible, once again, that the effects of these practices depend on institutional environments. For example, employer resistance towards unions, although not unheard of, has traditionally been less intensive in the UK than in North America, and a number of factors have combined to encourage more collaborative relationships with employers (Oxenbridge et al., 2003; Oxenbridge and Brown, 2004, 2005; Godard, 2008). If so, we would expect high performance practices in the UK to be more amenable to union representation and hence characterized by lower employer resistance to unions. Yet this possibility has received little attention in the literature.

A 2003–2004 telephone survey of 750 Canadian and 450 English workers (Godard, 2006a) was designed to address these limitations. Analysis of the data from this survey found:

1) high levels both of high performance work practices and of high commitment HR practices (both multi-item indices) to be positively associated with the propensity to vote for a union in Canada, but to bear no significant associations in England;
2) an index of more traditional HR practices to bear a strong negative association with voting propensity in Canada yet no association in England;
3) high commitment HR practices and union representation to bear no significant association between in Canada but a positive association in England, and
4) contingent pay schemes to bear a strong negative association with voting propensity in Canada, but no association in England.

The different findings across the two samples were argued to reflect an adversarial institutional logic in Canada compared to a more collaborative logic in England, especially in so-called 'best practice' workplaces.

Job characteristics

Job characteristics have been closely identified with the high performance model (for example, Appelbaum et al., 2000). Although the causal direction of this linkage is unclear (Handel and Gittelman, 2004: 90–94), they are also viewed as of major importance in the literature on job attitudes, and hence can be expected to have implications for voting propensity. The research on internal determinants indirectly supports this expectation, finding dissatisfaction with job content and intrinsic instrumentality to both be associated with voting propensity, as reported earlier.

The implications of three characteristics have been addressed: autonomy, complexity, and influence. Three studies (Cornfield et al., 1998; Evansohn, 1989; (Lowe and Raskin, 2000) have found the first to bear negative associations with propensity, although another study (Fiorito and Young, 1998) found no association. Studies addressing the importance of the second have found no significant association (Youngblood et al., 1984; Lowe and Raskin, 2000). Finally, the third has been found to bear a negative association with voting propensity (Kochan, 1979; Charlwood, 2003) and with union support (Belfield and Heywood, 2004). It would thus appear that autonomy and influence matter, but that job complexity does not. This may be because autonomy and influence convey trust, which is reciprocated by the employee (Fox, 1974), yet complexity does not.

Pay

In view of the traditional economic role of unions, it is plausible to expect low pay to be positively associated with voting propensity. Yet only a few studies have directly addressed the importance of pay, in some cases finding no association (Haberfield, 1995; Youngblood et al., 1984) and in others finding a negative but typically weak one (for example, Premack and Hunter, 1988; Cornfield and Kim, 1994: 528). It may, however, be relative rather than absolute pay levels that matter (Premack and Hunter, 1988). Consistent with this argument, Farber and Saks (1980) found workers at the low end of the intra-firm wage distribution to be more likely to vote for a union.

Studies of certification elections have also addressed the implications of pay for union success, but with mixed results. Fiorito et al., (1987) found absolute pay levels to bear a positive association with win rates, and Bronfennbrenner (1997) found low pay to bear a positive association. But Cooke (1983) and Bronfenbrenner and Juravich (1998) found no association. It is possible that low wage employers have more to loose if a union is successful and hence engage in stronger resistance, offsetting any direct implications low wages have for voting propensity.

Working conditions

The only working condition to receive attention in the literature has been workplace hazards. Using the QES data set, Kochan (1979; also see Fiorito, 1987) reported perceived job hazards to bear a strong positive association with voting propensity, smaller in magnitude than for instrumentality, but larger than for general beliefs. Using data from the US Young Men's/Women's Longitudinal Surveys, Robinson (1988) found a significant positive association for young women, but not for young men. Much likely depends, however, on whether a union is perceived as able to address hazards, which again may depend on workplace characteristics and on institutional differences, especially the role health and safety laws allow for unions.

Social influences

At least two studies, one using US data (Deshpande and Fiorito, 1989: 893), and one using Canadian data (Gomez et al., 2002) have found support for a union to be associated with whether a member of the respondent's immediate family is already represented by one. Perceptions that family and friends support a union have also been found to be associated with respondent support, especially for young workers, presumably because they have yet to form strong views of their own (Gomez et al., 2002). Canadian research (Barling et al., 1991; Kelloway and Watts, 1994) has also found student perceptions of parental union attitudes to be associated with voting propensity, and these perceptions to in turn be strongly associated with actual parental attitudes and participation.

Co-worker support for a union may be particularly important (Brief and Rude, 1981) given that union organizing is more likely to be successful if workers develop solidarity and 'come together as a group' (Weikle et al., 1998). A number of US studies (Dickens, 1983; Davy and Shipper, 1993, Youngblood et al., 1984) have found support for this argument. One of these (Davy and Shipper, 1993) found perceived co-worker support to not only have strong direct and indirect associations, but also to substantially reduce the observed independent effects for job satisfaction. Another (Youngblood et al., 1984) found it to matter more than general beliefs. Yet another, of 125 university employees, (Montgomery, 1989) found both perceived co-worker and family normative pressures, in interaction with the subjective importance of these pressures, to be associated with the intention to vote for a union.

Absent from the research literature has been analysis of how information provided by managers, union organizers, or co-workers alters attitudes or beliefs as they pertain to the various internal determinants discussed earlier. In their classic work on social information processing, Salancik and Pfeffer (1977) show that job satisfaction is strongly influenced by social information. Consistent with this argument, Davy and Shipper (1993) found perceived peer support for a union to be indirectly as well as directly linked to propensity, through a negative association with satisfaction. It is likely that other determinants can be similarly influenced, with potentially important implications for understanding how various employer or union tactics may alter union organizing success. This may be especially the case for general beliefs and instrumentalities, which for non-union workers are less likely to be based on direct experience (Devinatz and Rich, 1996). In this regard, Lopez (2004: 285) concluded, based on ethnographic analysis, that the ability to debunk negative general beliefs about unions and what it is like to be a union member can be important to organizing success.

Individual and demographic characteristics

Individual and demographic characteristics may be viewed as potentially important 'markers' for locating pockets of latent unionism. However, research findings have been uneven.

Research conducted in the US generally suggests that public sector workers and past union members are more predisposed to vote for a union, that white collar workers are less predisposed, and that seniority, marital status, and rural background do not make much difference (Kochan, 1979; Farber and Saks, 1980; Fiorito and Greer, 1986; Youngblood et al., 1984; Deshpande and Fiorito, 1989; Cornfield et al., 1998). Although most studies control for age, only a few have found it to matter (Farber and Saks, 1980; Dickens, 1983; Fiorito, 2001), and the observed effects have been weak. The findings have also been generally weak for gender, although at least one study (Friedman et al., 2006) has found women to be more favorable to unions, and another (Bronfenbrenner and Hickey, 2004) has estimated union success rates in National Labor Relations Board (NLRB) elections to be 70 per cent higher in predominantly female workplaces.

Results for race have been ambiguous. Some studies have found non-whites to be substantially more prone to vote for a union (Kochan, 1979; Farber and Saks, 1980; Cornfield and Kim, 1994: 528; Cornfield et al., 1998; Fiorito, 2001; Friedman et al., 2006) and union success to be higher in predominantly non-white workplaces (Bronfenbrenner and Hickey, 2004), but others have found little or no association for either dependent variable (Deshpande and Fiorito, 1989, Youngblood et al., 1984; Dickens, 1983).

Region of residence has been found to matter in some US studies (Kochan, 1979; Cooke, 1983; and Deshpande and Fiorito, 1989) and in the UK (Charlwood, 2002: 483), yet other US studies have found that it does not (Farber and Saks, 1980; Heneman and Sandver, 1989; also see Cornfield et al., 1998).

The same is true of education, with some studies (Deshpande and Fiorito, 1989; Fiorito, 2001) having found a negative association, yet others (Kochan, 1979; Dickens, 1983; Cornfield et al., 1998) having found no association.

It is possible that more refined categorizations, based on multiple characteristics, are necessary. For example, Schur and Kruse (1992) found that white collar women are twice as likely to support a union as are both their male and their blue collar counterparts, but only in the private sector. Fiorito and Greer (1986) found race to bear weaker associations with voting propensity among females than among males.

There is also evidence that individual and demographic characteristics matter for the importance of various internal determinants. For example, Kochan (1979) found dissatisfaction to matter for manual workers only with respect to supervision, yet for white collar workers only with respect to 'bread and butter' and 'nature of work' issues. Fiorito (1987) found union political instrumentality to matter more for public sector workers than for private sector workers, and workplace instrumentality to matter only for private sector workers. Fiorito et al. (1996) found instrumentalities and satisfaction to matter more for private than public sector workers, and general beliefs to matter less. Gomez et al. (2002) found social influences (labeled as 'social capital') to matter more for workers between 16 and 25 years of age than for those between 25 and 65 years of age.

Attempts to explore for these differences often border on little more than fishing expeditions and hence may suffer from type II errors. Nonetheless, they do suggest a case for more complex analysis. From a practical standpoint, they also suggest that research may be of limited value to union organizing unless it is tailored to the specific group that a union is targeting.

More generally, measures of individual and demographic characteristics are typically included in regressions with measures of the various internal determinants addressed earlier. To the extent that they operate through these determinants, the result may be to understate their combined (for instance indirect as well as direct) effects and hence to undermine their value as markers for latent unionism. This is confirmed by Cornfield and Kim (1994), whose results reveal that coefficient sizes on most demographic variables decline by a half or more once attitudinal variables are controlled.[7] A further, related problem is that this research may only be picking up representation gaps arising from unmet demand for unions at the time of data collection (for example, among public sector and white collar workers in the 1970s). Yet these gaps may either close or shift over time, potentially rendering research findings obsolete.

Overall

It would appear that individuals who perceive influence and autonomy in their job are less likely to support a union, and that the same is the case for workers in private sector and white collar jobs – possibly because the latter are likely to score higher on the former. Family and co-worker influences also matter. Finally, so-called high performance practices appear to be (negatively) associated with support for unions, but possibly only in the UA.

Overall, however, research on the external determinants of voting propensities would appear to yield surprisingly slim pickings. This is especially true with regard to individual and demographic characteristics, which may have substantively important effects, yet the findings for which often vary across studies and may operate in interaction with other variables. It is also possible that some of these findings reflect representation gaps that existed at the time of the research but have since closed. But a similar assessment applies with regard to employer practices, where research to date has typically suffered from a number of limitations, including a failure to account for the role of institutional environments in shaping employer motives or employee responses where various practices have been implemented. Finally, although the literature establishes that social influences matter (as one would expect), it does not address how social informational influences can be used to alter voting propensities.

THE ORGANIZING PROCESS

Research into the implications of the organizing process for union success may be considered as follows: 1) the immediate organizing context, including union, organizer, and bargaining unit characteristics, 2) union strategies and tactics, and 3) employer strategies and tactics. Again, almost all of this research has been conducted in North America, especially the US.

The immediate organizing context

A number of factors may enhance union success during the actual organizing process, beginning with the characteristics of the union itself. Using data from 111 national unions, Fiorito et al. (1995) found that national union decentralization, use of innovative organizing tactics, and specialization in particular industries were associated with union NLRB win rates, but that democratic union structures were not. In a subsequent study of 74 national unions, Fiorito et al. (2002) also found that union leaders reporting their union to have a broad message, to place considerable emphasis on new organizing, and to make extensive use of information technology were also likely to perceive higher levels of organizing effectiveness. However, none of these variables was associated with NLRB win rates.

Devotion of resources to new organizing has also been argued to enhance organizing success (Voos, 1984). In support of this view, Dickens et al. (1987) found that unions with higher levels of organizing effort, which may be seen as a proxy for resources, obtain a higher percentage of favorable votes. However, Heneman and Sandver (1989) found no relationship between the dollars spent per election and certification success in NLRB elections as of the late 1970s.[8]

Organizer characteristics may also matter. Using data from a survey of organizers in 195 NLRB elections, Reed (1989) found significant associations for a variety of personality characteristics. He also found organizers to be more successful if they had experienced downward mobility, were moderately educated, were former rank-and-file union members, and spent a higher percentage of their work time organizing. Bronfenbrenner and her colleagues (see below) found no association between organizer 'representativeness' and union win rates in one of three studies (Bronfenbrenner, 1997), an estimated 20 per cent increase in another (Bronfenbrenner and Juravich, 1998), and an estimated 110 per cent increase in another (Bronfenbrenner and Hickey, 2004). However, the latter study used a combined measure of number of organizers and representativeness.

Finally, a number of studies have explored the implications of bargaining unit size for union organizing success. Although some have revealed a negative association (Farber, 2001; Thomason, 1994: 222; Gilson and Wagar, 1995: 78; Scott et al., 1996), others have suggested little effect (Lawler and West, 1985; Bronfenbrenner and Juravich, 1998; Bronfenbrenner and Hickey, 2004). Still others have found size to have a curvilinear effect, increasing the likelihood of union success up to a point (65 workers or less, depending on the study), beyond which its effects diminish or even become negative (Cooke, 1983; Dickens et al., 1987; Florkowski and Schuster, 1987; Thomason and Pozzebon, 1998: 761). This has been interpreted as showing that group dynamics increasingly play a role up to a certain point, reflecting greater group cohesiveness, beyond which they make little further difference and may be offset by increased diversity (Thomason and Pozzebon, 1998) and more sophisticated employer opposition (Cooke, 1983).

Union organizing activities

There has been widespread advocacy for a more activist, 'organizing' model, one that involves workers themselves more fully in the organizing campaign, creating a sense of collective identity and support (also see Boxall, this volume, and Fiorito and Jarley, this volume). This model is largely consistent with mobilization theory, especially as advanced by Kelly (1998). However, it may be inconsistent with worker identities and norms, especially in the US, where 'bread and butter' unionism has been most prevalent and potential members may prefer a servicing model (Hurd, 2004). Consistent with this possibility, Cohen and Hurd (1998), in a case study analysis of US professional workers, found that such tactics may alienate workers. Based on three cases, Heery et al. (2000) find that, in the UK, this model may enhance the likelihood of union success, but tends to be resource intensive and as such may not be viable. Hurd (2004) has made a similar argument for the US.

There is also emergent evidence that an important tactic may be to build support outside of the election unit, through coalitions with various community groups and various tactics to place public pressure on employers. The paradigm case for this strategy has been the Justice for Janitors campaign conducted in Los Angeles in the mid-1990s (Erickson et al., 2002; Waldinger et al., 1998). However, in this case, there was a history of bargaining in the industry, which may limit the ability to generalize. Moreover, Rudy (2004) found that, even within California, local political contexts and histories may make an important difference to the success of community campaigns.

In a study of 211 NLRB elections involving a large national union, Peterson et al. (1992) found 'working closely with community leaders' to be positively associated with union success. But it was not associated with the percentage voting in favor of the union. They also found isolating the employer and conducting boycotts, both of which can be said to entail community support, to be negatively rather than positively associated with the percentage voting for the union. This suggests that some community tactics may actually backfire. Reed (1989) also found that building coalitions increased the likelihood of success, but that the use of paid advertising decreased it, again suggesting a backfire effect.

The three studies by Bronfenbrenner and her colleagues referred to earlier represent the most comprehensive attempts to explore the effects of union tactics. In the initial study, Bronfenbrenner (1997) obtained data on union and employer tactics from lead organizers for 261 NLRB elections held in 1986–1987. Of ten union tactics, she found five to be significantly associated with the likelihood of union success, in combination roughly doubling this likelihood. In the second study, Bronfenbrenner and Juravich (1998) used data from 165 campaigns conducted in 1994. Six of ten tactics were associated with statistically significant increases in union win rates, again in combination roughly doubling the likelihood of union success, and an additive index combining the ten tactics yielded an estimated 9 per cent increase in union success rates for each additional practice adopted. In the third study, Bronfenbrenner and Hickey (2004) used data collected from lead organizers involved in each of 412 organizing attempts in 1998–1999. Three of ten tactics were significantly associated with organizing success, in combination almost quadrupling the likelihood of union success, and an additive index combining all ten tactics yielded an estimated increase of 34 per cent in the likelihood of union success for each additional tactic adopted.

In Canada, Martinello and Yates (2004) found that union campaign strategies that could be classified as 'the maximum' did not win significantly more votes than those that eluded classification, while those that focused on small group meetings, house calls, or simply communications with workers, did. Only a 'house call' strategy was significantly associated with success rate.

There may be important limitations to this research. For example, the items included in the Bronfenbrenner studies varied considerably by study, making comparisons difficult. Their estimated effects were also uneven, which may reflect co-linearity problems. So the main conclusion to be drawn is from the findings for the indices. As one would expect, they reveal that the resources and effort put into a campaign and the ability to mobilize volunteers yield a higher likelihood of union success. Yet the estimated effect size in the third study is so large as to strain credulity, and it is not clear why it is so much greater than for the second, the data for which were collected only four years earlier. This could be explained if these tactics are synergistic (Sherman and Voss, 2000: 312) and if union organizers had discovered this and so had begun to adopt higher numbers of tactics. The former possibility is consistent with the main conclusion drawn by Bronfenbrenner and Hickey (2004: 53), which is that their results show the need for a 'multifaceted, comprehensive' campaign. However, possible synergies are not explored in this research. The latter possibility also does not appear to bear support: Bronfenbrenner and Hickey (2004: 41) report that even unions with national reputations for effective organizing used more than five tactics in only a third or less of their campaigns as of 1998–1999.

More generally, the data used in union tactics research have been retrospective. It is possible that organizers (from whom the data are collected) rationalize unsuccessful drives by discounting the extent to which various tactics were effectively used, biasing estimates upward.

In addition, the number of tactics may be higher where the chances of success justify the required resource expenditure per worker (which may often be high: Voos, 1983, 1984; Farber and Western, 2001), and where there is sufficient internal and external support for them to be effective – something that may only be determined during the course of a campaign and may be shaped by employer tactics (see Cooke, 1983).[9] Indeed, the adoption of these tactics may reflect (as much as determine) a successful drive, with unions adopting these tactics only as the drive proceeds and only if a win appears within reach. If so, this could result in further upward biases (and may explain why unions typically adopt only a limited number of tactics). In this regard, Bronfenbrenner's first study included a measure of per cent signing union cards prior to application, which may be

considered a proxy for the initial likelihood of success. The remaining significant tactics accounted, in combination, for slightly more than a 50 per cent increase in the likelihood of success. This is substantially below that suggested by her second and third studies, which did not include card sign-ups.

A further possible problem with the union tactics research is that unions may adopt different sets of strategies depending on employer tactics and internal support levels. For example, boycotts and advertising may be employed as external tactics where employers have successfully used intimidation and internal support remains weak. This would explain why some studies have observed apparent backfire effects for these tactics.[10]

Finally, it is again not clear how well US research generalizes to other institutional environments. It may be that limited campaign periods in Canada (see appendix) render comprehensive, US style strategies superfluous. This would be consistent with the Martinello and Yates findings. The US research also may not generalize to the UK. Because employers have tended to be less hostile towards unions in the UK, US-style strategies may actually alienate both employers and workers, lowering union success. However, there has been no multivariate research on this topic in the UK.

Employer activities

Employer tactics have long been held to have major implications for union success. Yet, research results have been mixed. The first major (and still most comprehensive) study of this question, by Getman, et al. (1976), found such practices to have only small effects on both voting intentions and voting behavior. In a re-analysis of their data, Dickens (1983) found employer tactics – especially employer threats and actions against union supporters, certain communications, and captive audience speeches – to bear negative associations, in combination reducing the likelihood of union success by 17 per cent or more. Lawler and West (1985) found only 3 of 12 practices (small group meetings, use of surveys, employee list irregularities) to have statistically significant negative effects, in combination lowering the likelihood of union success by 24 per cent. They also found discrimination for union activities to be associated with an 11 per cent increase, suggesting backfire effects. Peterson et al. (1992) also found that, of 15 employer tactics, only two (spreading rumors about store/plant closing and distributing right to work literature) bore significant negative associations with win rates of a large national union, and that two (delaying an election and shifting work elsewhere) bore positive associations, again suggesting backfire effects. Reed (1989) also found that, of twelve tactics, none was statistically significant. But none of these studies adequately controlled for union tactics, which may co-vary with their employer counterparts, thus potentially yielding downward biases.

The three US studies conducted by Bronfenbrenner and her colleagues did include union tactics, potentially addressing this problem. The first (Bronfenbrenner, 1997) revealed a number of employer tactics – including wage or benefit increases, promises, anti-union letters, captive audience meetings, and letters to employees – to bear negative associations with union certification success, in combination yielding a 42 per cent decrease in the likelihood of success.[11] The second and third (Bronfenbrenner and Juravich, 1998; Bronfenbrenner and Hickey, 2004) relied only on additive indices, yielding estimates of, respectively, a 7 per cent and a 13 per cent decline in the likelihood of union success for each practice adopted. The third study contained substantially more items than the second (22 compared to 12), and as such the differences in these two results suggest a major difference in overall effect size, as was also the case for the union effects results. Again, however, it is unclear as to why. It is also unclear as to why both of these studies suggest much larger effects than did the first study.

In Canada, where restrictions on employers are stronger and the campaign period more limited, Thomason and Pozzebon (1998) reported an index of ten practices to decrease union success rates by an estimated 14 per cent

per practice (computed by this author). Bentham (2002) found two practices (limiting employee-union communication and managerial training) to lower the likelihood of union success, two other practices (tightened supervision and contesting the bargaining unit) to increase it, and seven other practices to not matter (she did not compute an index). Neither study controlled for union tactics, again potentially resulting in downward biases. However, Martinello and Yates (see earlier) did. Their results reveal a simple 'communication strategy' to be associated with a 26 per cent decline in union success rates (as computed by this author) and to be about as effective as a more comprehensive, 'do everything' strategy.

As for the union tactics results, the retrospective nature of these studies may give rise to recall bias, especially where the data are collected from union organizers (see Thomason and Pozzebon, 1998: 755).[12] A further possible problem, also similar to one for union tactics research, is that employers may be less likely to engage in anti-union tactics where support for a union is either low (because the tactics are not needed and could backfire) or high (because there is little point and it could cause unnecessary antagonism), or where the union effort is tepid, hence posing little threat (see Cooke, 1985: 434).[13, 14] Thus, there is a possible endogeneity problem. In exploring this question, Freeman and Kleiner (1990) found strong evidence that firms with workforces having the greatest innate probability to vote for a union (measured by card sign-ups and by an index summing answers to a series questions asked of organizers) devote fewer resources to opposing a union, and some evidence that those with the lowest innate probability also devote fewer resources. They also found the sign for unfair labor practices to switch from positive to negative when they used an instrumental variable. Although neither the initial nor the instrumental variable estimate was significant, this not only suggests possible specification bias in other studies, but also that backfire effects found in some studies reflect such biases (also see Cooke, 1985: 433). Apparent backfire effects may also, however, once again reflect a tendency for some employer tactics to be adopted primarily where a union victory is already more likely.

Finally, the research on employer tactics may also be sensitive to the institutional environment within which organizing occurs. This is illustrated by the differences between the US and the Canadian results, though it is likely even more important for the UK, where there has traditionally been a greater expectation that employers will respect the right of workers to join a union and hence 'play by the rules.' This may not only mean that employers are less likely to resort to anti-union tactics, but also that any backfire effect could be much stronger.

Overall

Research on the organizing process yields some information on the importance of contextual factors such as union characteristics, organizer characteristics, and unit size. But the research on both union and employer tactics would appear to suffer from potentially significant methodological and interpretive problems. These problems are probably not sufficient to reject the main findings of this research, which are that union and employer activities generally have the expected effects and that these effects may be stronger with regard to union activities. But they do mean that the estimated effect sizes, both for individual tactics and for additive indices, should be interpreted with caution.

LABOR LAW

Almost all of the research undertaken on the differences in labor law has been in the US and Canada. In both countries, labor law is based on the 'Wagner' model (see appendix) and premised on the assumption of employer hostility (and may, paradoxically, perpetuate this hostility: see Adams, 1993). In Canada, there are eleven separate private sector labor law jurisdictions, compared to one in the US. This limits what can be said about Canada in general. But, as outlined in the appendix, Canadian labor law regimes have remained relatively strong in comparison to their US counterpart, providing the primary explanation for why density decline has been moderate in Canada yet catastrophic in the US (see Godard, 2003: 462).

There have been a number of analyses illustrating the importance of US-Canadian differences.[15] Rose and Chaison (1996: 83; also see Riddell, 2001: 401) found that, from 1976 to 1985, unfair labor practice complaints against employers in Canada were one-fourth to one-tenth (depending on the jurisdiction) the US rate, even though they were easier to file and win in Canada (Bruce, 1993, 1994). Meltz and Verma (1996: 6) computed that, from 1980 to 1995, union success rates for certification applications were almost 50 per cent higher in Canada than the USA (69 vs. 48 per cent). Finally, available estimates reveal that a third or more of all first negotiations failed to reach an agreement in the USA in the 1980s and early 1990s (Commission on the Future of Worker Management Relations, 1994; Weiler, 1983, 1984; Cooke, 1985), compared to less than 10 per cent as of the mid-1990s in Canada (Bentham, 1999: Chapter 4, lviii), where there was provision for first contract arbitration.

Lipset and Meltz (1998) reported that almost 50 per cent more US than Canadian non-union workers (47 per cent vs. 33 per cent) would have voted for a union as of 1996, suggesting a much higher untapped demand for unionism in the US (see Godard, 2003: 479–82). Both Godard (2003) and Gomez et al. (2001), using their data but relying on different methods of calculation, computed that US union density would have been roughly equivalent to Canadian density if US workers faced the same conditions as in Canada. Although a variety of explanations other than labor law (for example, Canada's 'social unionism' and cultural differences) have been advanced for these differences, they are not well supported by the available evidence (see Godard, 2003).

One aspect of labor law believed to be especially important has been provision for card certification, under which a ballot can be avoided and hence the opportunity for employer interference minimized. In a study comparing Canadian jurisdictions with and without card certification, Johnson (2000, 2002, 2004) estimated that mandatory ballot laws reduce union success rates by from 6 to 9 percentage points. She also estimated that, as of 1998, this alone accounted for 17 to 26 per cent of the US-Canada density gap. Bentham (1999: Chapter 7) found the availability of card certification to lower the probability of illegal employer tactics by 10 per cent, and increase the probability of certification by 11 per cent. Slinn (2004) found a shift to mandatory ballots in Ontario in the mid-1990s to be associated with a 21.7 percentage point decline in the probability of union success, while Riddell (2004) found a similar shift in British Columbia to be associated with a 19 per cent decline. He also found management opposition to be twice as successful as under card certification. Only one study (Martinello and Meng, 1992) has not found an effect for card certification.[16]

A number of multivariate studies have also investigated the implications of the length of time from application to election. Those measuring delays in months (Cooke, 1983; Prosten,1978; Thomason, 1994) have found each month of delay to be associated with only small declines (of 2.5 per cent or less per month) in union success rates. Of those measuring delays in days, at least three studies (Hurd and McElwain, 1988; Cooke, 1985; Cooper, 1984) have not found a significant effect. However, other studies have. Florkowski and Schuster (1987) found a 26 per cent greater change of winning if the election is held within 12 days, but that delays much beyond this period made little difference. In the first of her three studies, Bronfenbrenner (1997) found each day of delay to be associated with a 0.1 per cent lower likelihood of union success. Riddell (2001: 407) found an approximately 1 per cent lower probability of success for every two days of delay in British Columbia (Canada), though only where unfair labor practice charges had been filed.

A problem may be that employers are more likely to challenge the bargaining unit and introduce delays when union support appears to be moderate or high. This could result in downward biases. These biases are less likely for Riddell's study, because it is difficult for employers to introduce such delays in Canada. Yet shorter time delays, coupled with stronger restrictions on employers, may also lessen the implications of delays in Canada, limiting the generalizability of his results to the US.

Finally, longitudinal analyses have found changes in labor law in general to be associated with union density. Freeman and Pelletier (1990) found legal changes to be a major determinant of UK density from 1945 to 1986. Martinello found changes in labor laws to be more important than changes in either government or the economy for explaining variation in union density over time in three Canadian provinces (Martinello, 1996). In a subsequent analysis, Martinello (2000) found changes in labor law and in political party to have had significant effects on both union organizing activity and success in Ontario.

One limitation to research into the effects of labor law has been a failure to establish just why labor law matters. The assumption is that employers can be expected to engage in intimidation if allowed involvement in the organizing process. Yet proponents of laws that allow involvement – especially mandatory ballot requirements – claim that this only allows for a more informed decision on the part of workers and a more democratic decision process (Yager et al., 1998). The failure to test this argument has meant something of a lacuna for debates over labor law reform.

With the exception of the Freeman and Pelletier study, it is also not clear that this research generalizes beyond the North American environment. In the UK, recognition laws have (since 1999) been designed to build on the tradition of lower employer opposition to unions and to avoid the adversarial climate found in North America (Wood and Godard, 1999). Partly as a result, these laws allow substantial opportunity for employer involvement (see appendix). Yet, as of 2003, anti-union tactics remained much less pervasive than in North America (Gall, 2003: 92), and 88 per cent of new recognitions were still voluntary (Gall, 2005: 2).

It is also not clear how much specific labor laws and changes therein can matter. For example, in Canadian jurisdictions with even the most favorable laws, union density levels remain below 40 per cent overall, and 30 per cent in the private sector. In the UK, density has stalled at around 30 per cent despite the introduction of recognition laws. Thus, there may be a ceiling on what labor laws can do. The broader problem may be with the institutional regimes in which these laws are embedded, especially the requirement of formal certification and the decentralization of bargaining, but also broader institutional environments and norms, especially as these influence employer orientations towards unions (Godard, 2004d).

Overall

Differences in labor law regimes would appear to provide a key explanation for US-Canada differences in employer behavior (for instance, unfair labor practices), union success rates, and ultimately union density. It would also appear that specific provisions, especially for card certification, make a major difference in union success rates. This research may therefore be seen to provide some evidence not only that labor law matters to the prospects for union formation, but also that employer activities matter. However, it may not generalize beyond the North American environment, where there is tradition of intensive employer resistance to union formation. It is also possible that the effects of specific components of labor law are less important than, or conditioned by, the broader institutional environment within which they operate.

MACRO ECONOMIC, POLITICAL, AND INSTITUTIONAL DETERMINANTS

Beginning with Commons (1918), there has been a long history of attempts to establish the macro determinants of union growth (for example, see Chaison and Rose, 1991; Kochan, 1980: 133–142; Schnabel, 2003). Primary concern has been with changes in membership levels and union density rather than with union formation. But the tendency has been to assume that the former portends the latter.[17]

A variety of models have been proposed, typically based on arguments consistent with the conventional internal determinants identified earlier (also see Stepina and Fiorito, 1986). For example, Ashenfelter and Pencavel (1969) argued that price inflation and employment growth increase the benefits from union formation (for instance, obtaining wage gains to catch up to inflation) while lowering the costs (for instance, tight labor markets mean lower employer retaliation), that a higher unemployment rate in a preceding recession means a higher stock of worker grievances, and that the percentage of Democrats in the US House of Representatives captures pro-union sentiments. Based on a time series analysis of US data from 1904 to 1960, they found support for all of their arguments. Although their model did not perform well for the post-WWII period in the US (Moore and Pearce, 1976), Sharpe (1971) found similar results for Australia, as did Swidinsky (1974) for Canada. In addition, Adams and Krislov (1974) successfully applied their model to analyze new union organizing in the USA from 1949–1970, although political climate (Democratic Party membership) was not significant in this analysis.

Using a somewhat different specification and a longer time period (1897 to 1970) than Ashenfelter and Pencavel, Bain and Elsheikh (1976) found increasing wages, low employment, and high inflation to be associated with union density growth in an analysis of four different countries (the US, the UK, Sweden, and Australia). Their specification represented an improvement for the post war period up to 1970 in the US, although it did not perform well for the US for the decade after 1970 (Fiorito, 1982), and political variables were not significant for Sweden or the UK. However, using a different definition of union density and UK data for 1896 to 1984, Carruth and Disney (1988) found the election of Conservative governments to be associated with an average density decline of 2.5 percentage points. Finally, Booth (1983) developed a substantially different specification for the UK, finding business cycle variables to successfully account for short-term but not long-term growth.[18]

An obvious limitation of much of this research has been that it relies on a limited number of variables to capture complex economic, social, and political developments. A great deal depends on the operationalization of relevant constructs, the isolation of relevant variables' effects, and the time period examined (see Stepina and Fiorito, 1986: 262). As such, it has been criticized as *ad hoc* and deterministic (see Moore and Pearce, 1976; also see Schnabel, 2003: 21–22; Riley, 1997: 267–269). Nonetheless, this research generally appears to confirm that low inflation, low wage growth rates, high unemployment, and conservative governments are inimical to union formation, especially in liberal market economies. In view of the problems inherent to this research, it is surprising that researchers have been able to demonstrate consistent effects at all, and the ability to do so may demonstrate that these variables play a greater role than the findings themselves reveal. A more important criticism is that this research tends to be successful for periods of 'normal' growth, but it does not do a very good job of accounting for periods of rapid union growth, which is when union revitalization tends to occur.

There have been a number of attempts to account for these periods. For example, both Dunlop (1948) and Bernstein (1954, 1961) argued that they tend to occur during wars and social unrest, although the former explained this with reference to economic conditions (for example, high labor demand) and the latter with reference to labor policy (for example, labor law). Price and Bain (1983) argued that such periods reflect paradigm shifts that allow for radical change in the institutional environment. Freeman (1998) argued that growth spurts occur once density reaches (in effect)

a tipping point, at which unions have the resources to organize more aggressively and employer opposition declines. Kelly (1998) argued that density should grow fastest during strike waves, followed by the beginning of major economic (for instance, Kondratieffian) upswings or downswings, because these are most conducive to perceptions of injustice and hence mobilization.

These explanations offer possible insights into the preconditions for labor movement revitalization. However, they have not been well supported empirically. For example, Freeman draws on data from specific unions to establish the conditions for growth, but his analysis is not well linked to his initial theory. Kelly's explanation is not well supported by the historical data, although he argues that it may bear stronger support in non-corporatist countries (1998: 94). Price and Bain do not provide a test of their argument, nor do Dunlop or Bernstein.

Finally, Western (1997) has argued that, although economic conditions matter, the extent to which this is so depends on institutional conditions. He finds general support for his model across 18 OECD countries (1997:120–21). But his model essentially distinguishes between economies where unions grow through formal certification processes (the primary concern of this chapter) and those where they are more institutionally embedded (for instance with centralized bargaining, Ghent systems, and strong political ties). As such it does not provide much insight into union formation in liberal market economies.

One largely overlooked possibility is that major ruptures or changes do not just alter the rate of union growth, they may also change the way in which economic and political variables influence worker attitudes and behavior. For example, Stepina and Fiorito (1986) found considerably different results prior to the Wagner/Depression era in the US than after it. A similar shift may have occurred in recent decades, particularly within liberal market economies. Workers in these economies are not well insulated from market forces and so may be more susceptible to neoliberal globalization ideologies, which attribute economic hardship and insecurity to immutable economic forces that are beyond the reach of employers in particular (also see Clawson and Clawson, 1999: 101). It may as a result be increasingly difficult to successfully mobilize workers against employers, thus weakening the effects of economic and political conditions that would otherwise be positive for union growth, while strengthening the effects of negative ones.[19]

Also important may be the failure of this research to adequately address differences in institutional environments and the norms that underpin them (even across liberal market economies: see Godard, 2004d), especially as they pertain to the orientations and identities of both employers and unions (Locke and Thelen, 1995) and hence to worker expectations of unions and employer responses to union organizing. These differences may as a result condition the extent to which and ways in which changes in economic and political conditions, including historical ruptures, matter.

Overall

The research suggests that, at least until recently, 'normal' variation in union growth (and hence formation) can be accounted for in part by economic and political variables. But accounting for growth spurts and longer term trends is more difficult. To fully account for variation in union formation, including the conditions under which it occurs and how it occurs, it may ultimately be necessary to adopt a broader perspective, one that addresses the importance of institutional environments, norms, and traditions in accounting for the behavior of the parties.

CONCLUSIONS: WHAT CAN BE SAID?

Each of the bodies of research reviewed in this chapter has much to offer if judged as a specific area of empirical inquiry addressing specific empirical questions. But as is the case for most such research, any conclusions from it should be drawn with considerable caution (Godard, 1994). A number of gaps also remain – particularly as they apply to our *understanding* of union formation.

Research into voting propensity has been extensive and establishes the importance of three general internal determinants (dissatisfaction, instrumentalities, and union image). However, the relative importance of each remains unclear and little attention has been paid to a number of alternative, typically more specific, determinants arising from the nature of the employment relation in liberal market economies. These include distrust, injustice perceptions, oppositional work orientations, and others. The research on external determinants reveals that employer practices can affect union formation, as may job characteristics, pay, working conditions, various social influences, and individual and demographic characteristics. But the results are often weak, inconsistent, or methodologically suspect, and how these factors operate through internal determinants has for the most part been unexplored.

Research into the organizing process and the role of labor law both tell a somewhat more coherent story. Union and employer tactics matter, especially in the USA, where there tend to be lengthy and often acrimonious union election campaigns. However, possible specification problems and inconsistent findings limit both what can be said about specific tactics and the confidence that can be placed in overall effect sizes. Labor law also clearly matters, at least in North America. But even with substantial reforms, union density is not likely to reach much beyond a third of the labor force in the absence a major regime change.

Finally, there is evidence that macro economic, political, and institutional conditions matter, even if precisely how they matter may depend on the model used. But the importance of globalization ideologies and of broader institutional environments that shape the role of, and level of acceptance for, labor unions have been largely unexplored. Moreover, this research still does not (and perhaps cannot) provide much insight into the preconditions for a resurgence in union fortunes, although attempts to explain periods of rapid growth offer some promise in this regard.

A problem with much of the literature has been the failure to account for the role of institutional environments. To be sure, all modern capitalist economies *are* capitalist economies. Yet there is reason to think that, in general, institutional environments and norms matter. This may be so even within liberal market economies, as differences in the experience with the UK recognition system and with its North American counterparts would seem to suggest. Yet institutional differences do not just explain employer behavior. They also explain differences in union identities (Locke and Thelen, 1995), in the functions unions serve (Hyman, 2001), and in the organizing problems unions face (Heery and Adler, 2004: 63–65). These differences may have important implications for the attitudes, beliefs, and expectations of workers towards unions, for the reasons they join them (for instance internal determinants), and for the role of various external determinants of union formation (for example employer practices). They are also likely to have important implications for the organizing process, including the extent to which each party adopts various tactics and the likely effects of these tactics. These implications are likely to be greatest across different 'varieties' of capitalism (Hall and Soskice, 2001), but they cannot be ignored when comparing individual countries within the same variety (for instance, liberal market economies).

For those concerned with the future of unions, the critical question may not even involve differences in union identities, functions, or organizing problems. Rather, it may involve the broader institutional environments and norms within which unions operate and the possibilities they do or do not offer for increased rates of union formation. It would seem, for example, that the US institutional environment and the norms that have historically underpinned it (for instance, economism, individualism, and 'free' markets) have given rise to severe biases against union formation (Godard 2006b). If so, all that researchers can hope to capture,

and all that activists can hope to influence, may be short term variation on a longer path trajectory that is alterable only at the margins. This may substantially limit the possibilities for labor union formation in that country (Godard, 2006b), even in comparison to other liberal market economies. Of course, this argument is oversimplified and may underestimate the importance of union agency (Sherman and Voss, 2000; Clawson and Clawson, 1999) and of historic 'junctures' (Krasner, 1988) during which this agency may be particularly important. The point, however, is that there is a need to move beyond the empiricist orientation of much of the existing research to address these sorts of issues and explanations.

In short, a more comprehensive understanding of union formation and the conditions that give rise to it will likely require a more explicitly institutional approach. This approach might begin with the recognition of the nature of the employment relation in capitalist economies and its implications for the rationale underlying union formation. But it would then address the implications of different institutional environments and the norms that underpin them, and take into account differences in the identities, types, and problems of unions and of other representative bodies, seeking to establish the extent to which these matter and how. Rather than generating lists of determinants, the task would be to develop an institutionally informed approach to understanding and researching the *essential* conditions for union formation, how and why these may vary both within and across nations, and, ultimately, how these may be influenced.

APPENDIX

US, Canadian, and UK labor law regimes compared

These regimes are all based on the majority principle and administered by a labor relations board or, in the case of the UK, the Central Arbitration Committee (CAC). However, the assumptions and philosophy underlying the Canadian and US regimes differ considerably from those underlying the UK regime, and the Canadian regime is considered to be much stronger than its US counterpart. Focus here is on private sector laws, which in the US in particular differ from those for public sector workers. For more in-depth comparisons, see Godard (2004b: 11–37), Wood and Godard (1999) and Bogg (2004).

Both the US and Canadian systems are predicated on the assumption that the recognition process will be adversarial and that employers may engage in considerable resistance both during and immediately after this process. However, in the US, there is substantial opportunity for an employer to do so. A ballot is required in all cases, and may not be held until after the appropriate election unit is determined and any appeal of this determination has been held. This can mean substantial delays, providing an employer with considerable opportunity to dissuade workers from joining a union. While they are prohibited from threatening, disciplining, or dismissing individual union supporters during this period, the remedies tend to be weak, largely involving either injunctive relief or make whole remedies. Employers can also legally hold captive audience meetings and may submit employees to one-on-one meetings with supervisors. They may also resort to anti-union propaganda, even where this propaganda is untrue, and union organizers have no legal access to employer premises in order to respond. In addition, it is legal to 'predict' to workers that a union will render the workplace economically unviable and hence will result in its closure. Should a union succeed in winning a certification election, it is possible to instigate a lengthy appeals process, and there is no requirement to bargain with the union until this process has been completed. Moreover, the requirement to bargain is weak and virtually unenforceable. Finally, in the event of a strike or lockout, the employer may hire permanent replacement workers, subject to no time restrictions.

In Canada there are eleven separate jurisdictions, and there has been some deterioration of the law, beginning in the late 1980s, but especially after 1995. However, in six jurisdictions, covering roughly 50 per cent of the labor force, there is provision for automatic card certification, without a ballot. Where a ballot is required, there is no requirement for a final decision on the bargaining unit prior to a ballot, and the ballot must normally be held within 5 to 10 days of a union's application, depending on the jurisdiction, thus minimizing delays. Unfair labor practices are also more stringent. Although captive audience meetings are legal, one-on-one meetings are not, and there are strong restrictions on employer speech. It is extremely difficult for an employer to appeal a ruling of the board to the courts, and employers can be ordered to begin bargaining before any such appeal is settled. If a first agreement is not reached within a reasonable period and bargaining appears to have broken down, the union may in most jurisdictions request first contract arbitration, thus ensuring a settlement is achieved. Finally, it is illegal in all jurisdictions to hire permanent striker replacements, and temporary replacements are either banned or restricted in three.

In the UK, the underlying assumption is that the recognition process should essentially involve a negotiation by the union and the employer, and that this negotiation should give rise to a voluntary agreement in which the employer recognizes the union and the parties agree on the appropriate unit and both the procedure for and scope of bargaining. To encourage this, the legislation requires the union to first approach the employer (as is, technically, also required in the US), and allows for up to 38 days before the CAC subsequently becomes involved. The CAC may either certify the union if a majority of eligible workers has signed a union card, or call a ballot. However, it must first attempt to broker voluntary agreement between the parties. In total, there can be up to 6 stages and 86 days or more before the CAC decides to grant recognition, and another 20 days if it determines that a ballot is called for. The CAC may also specify the bargaining unit and the scope of bargaining if the parties cannot agree on these. But the CAC can only require the parties to bargain over wages, hours, and holidays. There is no provision for first contract arbitration, but in the event of a strike or lockout, the employer must wait eight weeks before hiring permanent replacement workers. Employers are subject to unfair labor practices (ULPs) similar to those in the US and Canada, but these only apply once a ballot has been formally arranged. In addition, the employer may require captive audience meetings, but if it does it is also required to grant the union equal time, during working hours. Finally, the grounds for appealing a CAC decision are narrow, as in Canada.

NOTES

1 This chapter does not address the determinants of union membership in non-majority, open shop systems predominant within Europe. In these systems, collective bargaining coverage may be as much a determinant of membership as vice versa, and union formation per se is not closely linked to membership levels. For recent reviews of this literature, see Riley (1997) and Schnabel (2003).

2 See Fiorito and Greer (1982), Wheeler and McClendon (1991), and Barling et al. (1992) for earlier reviews. These reviews also cover studies with small samples and that use only bivariate analysis.

3 In their meta analysis, Premack and Hunter (1988) did find "satisfaction with administration" to have a larger effect size than "extrinsic satisfaction." But the item content of these two measures was not reported and so it is unclear what they actually measured.

4 Another analysis, of UK data collected between 1991 and 1993 (Waddington and Whitston, 1997), found that almost three quarters of new union members (n=10,823) reported "support if I have a problem at work" – which may be seen to entail voice and representation – to be a major reason for joining, identified twice as often as "improved pay and conditions." However, at the time of this survey union membership in the UK was more likely to entail individual support at work than coverage by a union agreement (and hence improved pay and conditions). Thus, these findings may not generalize.

5 Charlwood (2003) explored the linkage between perceived injustice and the likelihood of joining a union, but his injustices measure addressed political rather than employment specific beliefs. Farber and Saks (1980: 364) found perceptions that a union will improve fairness at work, which may be seen as

reflecting justice but also instrumentality perceptions, to be positively associated with voting behavior.

6 This may be especially problematic for the Belfield and Heywood (2004) study, whose dependent variable measured perceptions of who would best represent the respondent about getting pay increases, and so may have captured union instrumentalities more than voting propensity per se. Wood and Machin address union recognition, which should be less problematic, but at the time their data were collected roughly a third of all workplaces with recognition in the UK did not even have bargaining over pay (Brown et al., 2000).

7 Their results are also of interest because they suggest that pro-union sentiment is strongest among socially diverse, low socio-economic status workers. They argue that this reflects the tendency for unions to legitimize themselves by appealing to the identities of these workers.

8 Bronfenbrenner and Hickey (2004: 56) include a variable referred to as "adequate and appropriate staff and financial resources," but it does not appear to include any information on financial resources, and "appropriate staff" refers to representativeness, limiting its value for present purposes.

9 Brofenbrenner's (1997) discussion of her theoretical framework also suggests that union tactics are endogenous, yet this is not addressed in any of her analyses.

10 I thank Jack Fiorito for this insight.

11 The estimates for captive audience meetings and company letters items referred to the number of each, yet both had a large range (0–200 and 0–5). I therefore multiplied the coefficient by twice the sample mean for each (5.50 and 4.5, respectively) to compute the combined effect score.

12 This may explain why Bentham's findings, which would appear to be the only ones based on employer data, are much weaker than those of other studies, although her surveys were not sent out until three to six years after the organizing drives in her study occurred, affecting recall. It is also possible that employer respondents are hesitant to admit to some tactics and/or that their recall is affected by the election outcome in ways that differ from organizer recall biases.

13 Against this possibility, Dickens argues that the latter tend to be less visible to employers than vice versa and that employer anti-union campaigns pretty much follow preset formulae provided by consultants and lawyers, minimizing any endogeneity (1983: 563–4). But there is widespread variation in reported employer tactics.

14 As noted earlier, Bronfenbrenner's first study included a measure of initial card sign-ups and hence a partial proxy for support. She found weaker rather than stronger effects for employer practices than in her other two studies. Both Reed (1989) and Dickens (1983) also included card sign-ups and reported weak effects. None of these studies explored for possible

curvilinearity. Also as noted earlier, the latter two also did not control for union tactics.

15 Most of this evidence is from the mid-1990s or before. However, it may actually provide a better indication of the importance of law than if it was more recent, because it predates a substantial weakening of labour laws in the largest Canadian jurisdiction (Ontario) during the second half of the 1990s.

16 There is also descriptive data as to the importance of card certification. In the US, a Wall Street journal article reported that only 73 per cent of those signing a union card vote in favor of the union by the time a ballot is held (Wall Street Journal, 1991: A16). In Canada, Riddell (2001) observed that success rates were substantially higher (92 vs. 73 per cent) in the province of British Columbia when card certification was allowed than when it was not, while Godard (2000: 299) reported similar evidence for the provinces of Ontario (77 vs. 59 per cent) and Manitoba (75 vs. 64 per cent). These statistics apply to the public as well as the private sector, and so may understate the implications of card certification for the latter.

17 I do not consider the literature on how compositional shifts account for density changes, as this literature really tells us little about union formation – rather, it likely picks up the effects of variables associated with sectoral differences (e.g., white collar vs. blue collar), as reviewed throughout this chapter. The evidence also suggests that compositional shifts are of less importance than sometimes assumed, although much may depend on how encompassing the definition of compositional shift is (e.g., see Green, 1992). See Western (1997: 150–155) and Goldfield (1987) for the USA, Meltz and Verma (1996) for Canada, and Carruth and Disney (1988) for the UK. For Europe, see Calmfors et al (2001: 26).

18 I do not address business cycle research on single, open shop European countries due to its limited relevance to union formation and to space limitations.

19 Reinforcing this dampening may be the weakened economic and political power of unions, in part because changed worker ideologies have meant less willingness to strike or to back pro-labor public policies. As a result, unions appear no longer able to achieve substantial gains during an upturn, thus lessening their "demonstration" effects.

REFERENCES

Adams, Avril V. and Krislov, Joseph (1974) 'New Union Organizing: A Test of the Ashenfelter-Pencavel Model.' *Quarterly Journal of Economics* 88 (May): 304–11.

Adams, Roy (1974) 'Solidarity, Self-Interest and the Unionization Differential Between Europe and North America.' *Relations Industrielles* 29 (3): 497–512.

Adams, Roy (1993) 'The North American Model of Employee Representational Participation: "A Hollow Mockery".' *Comparative Labor Law Journal* 15 (4): 4–14.

Appelbaum, E., T. Bailey, P. Berg and A. Kalleberg (2000) *Manufacturing Advantage: Why High Performance Work Systems Pay Off.* Ithaca, NY: Cornell University Press.

Ashenfelter, Orley and John Pencavel (1969) 'American Trade Union Growth, 1900–1960.' *Quarterly Journal of Economics* 83 (3): 434–48.

Bain, George, and Elsheikh, Farouk (1976) *Union Growth and the Business Cycle.* Oxford: Basil Blackwell.

Bain, George, and Robert Price (1983) 'Union Growth: Dimensions, Determinants, and Density.' In George Bain (ed.) *Industrial Relations in Britain.* Oxford: Basil Blackwell. pp. 3–33.

Barling, Julian, Fullagar, Clive and Kelloway, Kevin E. (1992) *The Union and its Members: a Psychological Approach.* New York: Oxford University Press.

Barling, Julian, Kelloway, Kevin E. and Bremmerman, Eric (1991) 'Pre-employment Predictors of Union Attitudes' *Journal of Applied Psychology* 76 (5): 725–31.

Belfield, Clive R. and Heywood, John S. (2004) 'Do HRM Practices Influence the Desire for Unionization?' *Journal of Labor Research* 25 (2): 279–300.

Bentham, Karen (1999) *The Determinants and Impacts of Employer Resistance to Union Certification in Canada,* Ph.D. diss. University of Toronto.

Bentham, Karen (2002) 'Employer Resistance to Union Certification: A Study of Eight Canadian Jurisdictions.' *Relations Industrielles* 57 (1): 159–85.

Bernstein, Irving (1954) 'The Growth of American Unions.' *American Economic Review* 44 (June): 301–18.

Bernstein, Irving (1961) 'The Growth of American Unions.' *Labor History* 2 (Spring): 131–51.

Bogg, Allan (2004) 'The Employment Relations Act 2004: Another False Dawn for Collectivism?' *Industrial Law Journal* 34 (1): 72–82.

Booth, Alison (1983) 'A Reconsideration of Trade Union Growth in the United Kingdom.' *British Journal of Industrial Relations* 21 (3): 377–91.

Brief, A. P. and Rude, D.H. (1981) Voting in Union Certification Elections: A Conceptual Analysis. *Academy of Management Review.* 6 (2): 261–68.

Bronfenbrenner, Kate (1997) 'The Role of Union Strategies in NLRB Certification Elections.' *Industrial and Labor Relations Review,* 50 (2): 195–212.

Bronfenbrenner, Kate and Juravich, Tom (1998) 'It Takes More than House Calls: Organizing to Win with a Comprehensive Union-Building Strategy,' in Kate Bronfenbrenner et al. (eds) *Organizing to Win.* Ithaca: ILR Press.

Bronfenbrenner, Kate and Hickey, Robert (2004) 'Changing to Organize: A National Assessment of Union Strategies.' in Ruth Milkman and Kim Voss (eds), *Rebuilding Labor.* Ithaca: Cornell University. pp. 17–61.

Brown, William, Deakin, Simon, Nash, David and Oxenbridge, Sarah (2000) 'The Employment Contract: From Collective Procedures to Individual Rights.' *British Journal of Industrial Relations* 38 (4): 611–30.

Bruce, Peter (1993) 'State Strategies and the Processing of Unfair Labor Practice Cases in the U.S. and Canada.' In *The Challenge of Restructuring: North American Labor Movements Respond.* Edited by Jane Jenson and Rianne Mahon, Philadelphia: Temple University Press. pp. 180–204.

Bruce, Peter (1994) 'On the Status of Workers Rights to Organize in the United States and Canada.' In *Restoring the Promise of American Labor Law.* Edited by Kate Bronfenbrenner, Sheldon Friedman, Richard W. Hurd, Rudolph A. Oswald, and Ronald Seeber, Ithaca, NY: Cornell University Press. pp. 147–72.

Calmfors, Lars, Booth, Alison, Burda, Michael, Checchi, Daniele, Naylor, Robin and Visser, Jelle (2001) 'The Future of Collective Bargaining in Europe.' in Tito Boeri, Agar Brugiavini, and Lars Calmfors (eds) *The Role of Unions in the Twenty-First Century.* Oxford: Oxford University Press. pp. 1–156.

Carruth, Alan, and Disney, Richard (1988) 'Where Have Two Million Trade Union Members Gone?' *Economica* 55 (?): 1–19.

Chaison, Gary, and Rose, Joseph (1991) 'The Macrodeterminants of Union Growth and Decline.' in George Strauss, Dan Gallagher, and Jack Fiorito (eds) *The State of the Unions.* Madison: IRRA. pp. 3–45.

Charlwood, Andy (2002) 'Why Do Non-union Employees Want to Unionize?' *British Journal of Industrial Relations.* 40 (3): 463–92.

Charlwood, Andy (2003) 'Willingness to Unionize Amongst Non-union Workers.' in Howard Gospel and Stephen Wood, (eds) *Representing Workers.* London: Routledge. pp. 51–70.

CLC (Canadian Labor Congress) (2004) *Canadians Talk about Unions.* Ottawa: CLC.

Clawson, Dan and Clawson, Mary Ann (1999) 'What Has Happened to the US Labor Movement? Union Decline and Renewal.' *Annual Review of Sociology* 25: 95–119.

Cohen Larry, and Hurd, Richard W. (1998) 'Fear, Conflict, and Union Organizing.' in Kate Bronfenbrenner, Sheldon Friedman, Richard Hurd, Rudoph Oswald,

and Ronald Seeber (eds) *Organizing to Win.* Ithaca: ILR Press.

Commission on the Future of Worker Management Relations (1994) *Report and Recommendations.* Washington: US Dept. of Labor and Dept. of Commerce.

Commons, John R. (1918) *History of Industrial Relations in the United States,* vol. I New York: Macmillan.

Cooke, W (1983) 'Determinants of the outcome of union certification elections.' *Industrial and Labor Relations Review* 36 (3): 402–14.

Cooke, W (1985) 'The Rising Toll of Discrimination Against Union Activists.' *Industrial Relations* 24 (3): 421–42.

Cooper, Laura (1984) 'Authorization Cards and Union Representation Election Outcome.' *Northwestern University Law Review* 79 (1): 87–139.

Cornfield, Dan, McCammon, Holly, McDaniel, Darren and Eatman, Dean (1998) 'In the Community or in the Union? The Impact of Community Involvement on Non-union Worker Attitudes about Unionizing.' in K. Bronfenbrenner, S. Friedman, R. Hurd, R. Oswald, and R. Seeber (eds), *Organizing to Win: New Research on Union Strategies.* Ithaca, NY: ILR Press. pp. 102–19.

Cornfield, Dan, and Hyunhee, Kim (1994) 'Socioeconomic Status and Unionization Attitudes in the United States.' *Social Forces* 73 (2): 521–32.

Davy, Jeanette A. and Shipper, Frank (1993) 'Voter behavior in union certification elections: A longitudinal study.' *Academy of Management Journal* 36 (1): 187–201.

Deshpande, Satish and Fiorito, Jack (1989) 'Specific and General Beliefs in Union Voting Models.' *Academy of Management Review* 32 (4): 883–97.

Devinatz, Victor and Rich, Daniel (1996) 'Information, Disinformation, and Union Success in Certification and Decertification Elections.' *Journal of Labor Research* 17 (1): 199–210.

Dickens, W (1983) 'The Effect of Company Campaigns on Certification Elections: Law and Reality Once Again.' *Industrial and Labor Relations Review* 36 (4): 560–75.

Dickens, William, Wholey, Douglas and Robinson, James (1987) 'Correlates of Union Support in NLRB Elections.' *Industrial Relations* 26 (3): 240–52.

Dickens, Linda, Hall, Mark and Wood, Stephen (2005) *Review of research into the impact of employment relations legislation.* Employment Relations Research Series No. 45, Department of Trade and Industry, UK Government.

Dunlop, John T. (1948) 'The Development of Labor Organization: A Theoretical Framework.' In Richard A. Lester and Joseph Shister (eds), *Insight into Labor Issues.* New York: Macmillan. pp. 163–93.

Erikson, Chris, Fisk, Catherine, Milkman, Ruth, Mitchell, Daniel and Wong, Kent (2002) 'Justice for Janitors in Los Angeles: Lessons from Three Rounds of Negotiation.' *British Journal of Industrial Relations* 40 (3): 543–68.

Evansohn, John (1989) 'The Effects of Mechanisms of Managerial Control on Unionism.' *Industrial Relations* 28 (1): 91–103.

Farber, H. (2001) 'Union Success in Representation Elections: Why Does Size Matter?' *Industrial and Labor Relations Review* 54 (2): 329–48.

Farber, H. and Saks, D. (1980) 'Why Workers Want Unions: The Role of Relative Wages and Job Characteristics.' *Journal of Political Economy*, 88 (2)BE: 349–69.

Farber, Henry, and Western, Bruce (2001) 'Accounting for the Decline of Unions in the Private Sector, 1973–1998.' *Journal of Labor Research* 22 (3): 459–85.

Fiorito, Jack (1982) 'Models of Union Growth: a Test of the Bain-Elsheikh Model in the US.' *Industrial Relations* 21 (1): 123–27.

Fiorito, Jack (1987) 'Political Instrumentality Perceptions and Desires for Union Representation.' *Journal of Labor Research* 8 (3): 271–89.

Fiorito, J. (2001). 'Human Resource Management Practices and Worker Desire for Representation.' *Journal of Labor Research* 12 (2): 334–54.

Fiorito, J. and Dennis P. Bozeman (1997) 'Fear and Loathing (and Bribery) in the Workplace: Worker Perceptions of Employer Responses to Union Organizing,' *Journal of Individual Employment Rights* 5 (2): 137-52.

Fiorito, Jack, and Greer, Charles R. (1982) 'Determinants of US Unionism: Past and Future Research Needs.' *Industrial Relations* 21 (1): 1–32.

Fiorito, Jack, and Greer, Charles R. (1986) 'Gender Differences in Union Membership, Preferences and Beliefs.' *Journal of Labor Research* 7 (2): 145–64.

Fiorito, Jack, Jarley, Paul and Delaney, John (1995) 'National Union Effectiveness in Organizing.' *Industrial and Labor Relations Review* 48 (4): 613–25.

Fiorito, Jack, Jarley, Paul and Delaney, John (2002) 'Information Technology, Union Organizing, and Union Effectiveness.' *British Journal of Industrial Relations* 40 (4): 627–58.

Fiorito, J., Lowman, C. and Nelson, F. (1987). 'The Impact of Human Resource Policies on Union Organizing.' *Industrial Relations* 26 (2): 113–26.

Fiorito, Jack, Stepina, Lee and Bozeman, Dennis (1996) 'Explaining the Unionism Gap: Public-Private Sector Differences in Preferences for Unionism.' *Journal of Labor Research* 27 (3): 463–78.

Fiorito, J., and Young, A. (1998). 'Union Voting Intentions: HR Policies, Organizational Characteristics, and Attitudes.' In Kate Bronfrenbrenner, S. Friedman, Richard W. Hurd, Rudolph A. Oswald, and Ronald Seeber (eds), *Organizing to Win.* Ithaca: ILR Press.

Florkowski, Gary and Shuster, Michael (1987) 'Predicting the Decisions to Vote and Support Unions in Certification Elections: An Integrated Perspective.' *Journal of Labor Research* 8 (2): 191–207.

Fox, Alan (1974) *Beyond Contract: Work, Power, and Trust Relations.* London: Farber.

Freeman, Richard (1998) 'Spurts in Union Growth: Defining Moments and Social Processes.' in Michael D. Bordo, Claudia Goldin, and Eugene White (eds) *The Defining Moment: The Great Depression and the American Economy in the Twentieth Century.* Chicago: University of Chicago Press.

Freeman, R. and Kleiner, M. (1990) 'Employer Behavior in the Face of Union Organizing Drives.' *Industrial and Labor Relations Review* 43 (4): 351–65.

Freeman, R., Kleiner, M. and Ostroff, C. (2000) *The Anatomy of Employee Involvement and its Effects on Firms and Workers.* Working Paper 8050, National Bureau of Economic Research, Cambridge, Mass.

Freeman, Richard and Pelletier, Jeffrey (1990) 'The Impact of Industrial Relations Legislation on British Union Density.' *British Journal of Industrial Relations* 28 (2): 145–64.

Freeman, Richard and Rogers, Joel (1999) *What Do Workers Want?* Ithaca: ILR Press.

Friedman, Barry A., Abraham, Steven B. and Thomas, Randall K. (2006) 'Factors Related to Employees' Desire to Join a Union.' *Industrial Relations* 45 (1): 102–10.

Gall, Gregor (2003) 'Employer Opposition to Union Recognition.' In Gregor Gall (ed.) *Union Organizing: Campaigning for Trade Union Recognition.* London: Routledge.

Gall, Gregor (2005) *Trade Union Recognition in Britain: A Corner Being Turned?* paper presented at the 2005 annual meetings of the Labor and Employment Relations Association, Philadelphia, PA.

Getman, J., Goldberg, S. and Herman, J. (1976) *Union representation elections: Law and Reality.* New York: Russell Sage Foundation.

Gilson, Clive and Wagar, Terry (1995) 'The US/Canada Convergence Thesis: Contrary Evidence from Nova Scotia.' *Relations Industrielles* 50 (1): 66–85.

Godard, J. (1994) 'Beyond Empiricism: Towards a Reconstruction of IR Theory and Research.' In David Lewin and Donna Sockell (eds) *Advances in Industrial and Labor Relations.* (JAI Press) VI: 1–36.

Godard, J. (1998) 'An Organizational Theory of Variation in the Management of Labor.' In David Lewin and Bruce Kaufman (eds) *Advances in Industrial and Labor Relations.* (JAI Press) VIII: 25–66.

Godard, John (2000) *Industrial Relations, the Economy, and Society* (2nd. edn) Toronto: Captus Press.

Godard, J. (2003) 'Do Labor Laws Matter? The Density Decline and Convergence Thesis Revisited.' *Industrial Relations* 42 (3): 458–92.

Godard, J. (2004a). 'The U.S. and Canadian Labor Movements: Markets vs. States and Societies,' In *Trade Unions and the Crisis of Democracy: Strategies and Perspectives*. ed. Geoffrey Wood and Mark Harcourt, Manchester: Manchester University Press. pp. 159–90.

Godard, John (2004b). *Trade Union Recognition: Statutory Unfair Labor Practice Regimes in the USA and Canada.* Employment Relations Research Series No. 29, Department of Trade and Industry, UK Government.

Godard, John (2004c). 'A Critical Assessment of the High Performance Paradigm.' *British Journal of Industrial Relations* 42 (2): 349–78.

Godard, John (2004d) 'The New Institutionalism, Capitalist Diversity, and Industrial Relations.' In Bruce Kaufman (ed.), *Theoretical Perspectives on Work and the Employment Relationship.* Urbana-Champaign: IL: Industrial Relations Research Association. pp. 229–64.

Godard, John (2006a) 'Institutional Environments, Work and Human Resource Practices, and Unions: Canada vs. England,' unpublished manuscript, the University of Manitoba.

Godard, John (2006b) 'Institutional Norms, Mobilization Bias and the Decline of the US Labour Movement,' unpublished manuscript, the University of Manitoba.

Godard, John (2008). 'An Institutional Environments Approach to IR?' In *Industrial Relations as an Academic Enterprise: Roads to Revitalization*, ed. Charles Whalen, Northampton MA: Edward Elgar, forthcoming.

Goldfield, Michael (1987) *The Decline of Organized Labour in the United States.* Chicago: University of Chicago Press.

Gomez, Rafael, Gunderson, Morley and Meltz, Noah (2002) 'Comparing Youth and Adult Desire for Unionization in Canada.' *British Journal of Industrial Relations* 40 (3): 521–42.

Gomez, Raphael, Lipset, Seymour Martin and Meltz, Noah (2001) 'Frustrated Demand for Unionization: The Case of the United States and Canada Revisited.' In *Proceedings of the 53rd Annual Meeting, Champaign IL: Industrial Relations Research Association.* pp. 163–72.

Green, Francis (1992) 'Recent Trends in British Trade Union Density: How Much of a Compositional Effect?' *British Journal of Industrial Relations* 30 (3): 445–58.

Haberfield, Yitchak (1995) 'Why do Workers Join Unions? The Case of Israel.' *Industrial and Labor Relations Review* 48 (4): 656–70.

Hall, Peter and Soskice, David (2001) 'An Introduction to Varieties of Capitalism.' In Peter Hall and David Soskice, eds, *Varieties of Capitalism: The Institutional Foundations of Comparative Advantage.* Oxford: Oxford University Press, pp. 1–68.

Handel, Michael, and Gittleman, Maury (2004) 'Is there a Payoff to Innovative Work Practices?' *Industrial Relations* 43 (1): 67–97.

Heneman, Herbert and Sandver, Marcus (1989) 'Union Characteristics and Organizing Success.' *Journal of Labor Research* 10 (4): 377–89.

Heery, Ed and Adler, Lee (2004) 'Organizing the Unorganized.' in Carola Frege and John Kelly (eds) *Varieties of Unionism: Strategies for Union Revitalization in a Global Economy.* Oxford: Oxford University Press. pp. 45–70.

Heery, Edmund, Simms, Melanie, Simpson, Dave, Delbridge, Rick and Salmon, John (2000) 'Organizing Unionism Comes to the UK.' *Employee Relations* 22 (1): 38–60.

Hurd, Richard (2004) 'The Rise and Fall of the Organizing Model in the US.' In G. Wood and M. Harcourt (eds) *Trade Unions and the Crisis of Democracy: Strategies and Perspectives.* Manchester: Manchester University Press.

Hurd, Richard and McElwain, Adrienne (1988) 'Organizing Clerical Workers: Determinants of Success.' *Industrial and Labor Relations Review* 41 (2): 350–73.

Hyman, Richard (2001) *Understanding European Trade Unionism.* London: Sage.

Hyman, Richard and Brough, Ian (1975) *Social Values and Industrial Relations.* Oxford: Blackwell.

Jarley, Paul and Fiorito, Jack (1991) 'Unionism and Changing Employee Views Toward Work.' *Journal of Labor Research* 12 (3): 223–30.

Johnson, Susan (2000) *The Growth and Decline of Unions in Canada and the United States* Ph.D. Thesis, Department of Economics, McMaster University.

Johnson, Susan (2002) 'Card Check or Mandatory Representation Votes? How the Choice of Union Recognition Procedure Affects Union Certification Success.' *Economic Journal* 112 (April): 344–61.

Johnson, Susan (2004) 'The Impact of Mandatory Votes on the Canada-US Density Gap: A Note.' *Industrial Relations* 43 (2): 356–63.

Kelly, John (1998) *Rethinking Industrial Relations.* London: Routledge.

Kelloway, Kevin and Watts, Laura (1994) Preemployment Predictors of Union Attitudes: Replication and Extension.' *Journal of Applied Psychology* 79 (4): 631–34.

Klandermans, B. (1986) 'Perceived costs and benefits of participation in union action.' *Personnel Psychology* 39 (2): 379–97.

Kochan, T. (1979) 'How American workers view labor unions.' *Monthly Labor Review* 102 (4): 23–31.

Kochan, T. (1980) *Collective Bargaining and Industrial Relations.* Homewood, IL: Irwin.

Kochan, T., McKersie, R. and Chalykoff, J. (1986) 'The Effects of Corporate Strategy and Workplace Innovations on Union Representation.' *Industrial and Labor Relations Review* 39 (4): 487–501.

Krahn, Harvey and Lowe, Graham (1984) 'Public Attitudes Towards Unions: Some Canadian Evidence.' *Journal of Labor Research* 5 (2): 149–63.

Krasner, Stephen D. (1988) 'Sovereignty: An Institutional Perspective.' *Comparative Political Studies* 121 (1): 66–94.

Lawler, John and West, Robin (1985) 'Impact of Union Avoidance Strategy in Union Representation Elections.' *Industrial Relations* 24 (3): 406–20.

Lipset, Seymour Martin and Meltz, Noah (1998) 'Canadian and American Attitudes Toward Work and Institutions.' *Perspectives on Work* 1 (3): 14–19.

Locke, Richard and Thelen, Kathleen (1995) 'Apples and Oranges Revisited: Contextualized Comparisons and the Study of Comparative Labor Politics.' *Politics and Society* 23 (3): 337–67.

Lopez, Steven (2004) *Reorganizing the Rust Belt: the Inside Story of the American Labor Movement.* Berkley, CA: University of California Press.

Lowe, Graham and Raskin, Sandra (2000) 'Organizing the Next Generation: Influences on Young Worker Attitudes.' *British Journal of Industrial Relations* 38 (2): 203–22.

Maranto, Cheryl and Fiorito, Jack (1987) 'The Effect of Union Characteristics on the Outcome of NLRB Certification Elections.' *Industrial and Labor Relations Review* 40 (2): 225–40.

Martinello, Felice (1996) 'Correlates of Certification Application Success in British Columbia, Saskatchewan, and Manitoba.' *Relations Industrielles* 51 (3): 544–62.

Martinello, Felice (2000) 'Mr Harris, Mr Rae and Union Activity in Ontario.' *Canadian Public Policy* 26 (1): 17–33.

Martinello, Felice and Meng, Ronald (1992) 'Effects of Labor Legislation and Industry Characteristics on Union Coverage in Canada.' *Industrial and Labor Relations Review* 46 (1): 161–75.

Martinello, Felice and Yates, Charlotte (2004) 'Union and Employer Tactics in Ontario Organizing Campaigns.' In David Lewin and Bruce Kaufman (eds) *Advances in Industrial and Labor Relations* 13: 157–90.

Meltz, Noah and Verma, Anil (1996) 'Beyond Union Density: Union Organizing and Certification as Indicators of Union Strength in Canada and the United States.' Paper presented at the *33*rd *annual meeting of the Canadian Industrial Relations Association,* Brock University, St. Catherines, Ont., May 29–31.

Montgomery, B. Ruth (1989) 'The Influence of Attitudes and Normative Pressures on Voting Decisions in a Union Certification Election.' *Industrial and Labor Relations Review* 42 (2): 262–79.

Moore, William and Pearce, D.K. (1976) 'Union Growth - A Test of the Ashenfelter-Pencavel Model.' *Industrial Relations* 15 (2): 244–47.

Oxenbridge, Sarah and Brown, William (2004) 'Developing Partnership Relationships.' in Mark Stuart and Miguel Martinez Lucio (eds) *Partnership and Modernization in Employment Relations.* London: Routledge.

Oxenbridge, Sarah and Brown, William (2005) 'Achieving a New Equilibrium? The Stability of Cooperative Employer-Union Relationships.' *Industrial Relations Journal* 35 (5): 388–402.

Oxenbridge, Sarah, Brown, William, Deakin, Simon and Pratten, Cliff (2003) 'Initial Response to the Statutory Recognition Provisions of the Employment Relations Act 1999.' *British Journal of Industrial Relations* 41 (2): 315–34.

Park, Heejoon, McHugh, Patrick and Bodah, Matthew (2006) 'Revisiting General and Specific Beliefs: the Union Voting Intentions of Professionals.' *Industrial Relations* 45 (2): 270–89.

Peterson, Richard, Lee, Thomas and Finnegan, Barbara (1992) 'Strategies and Tactics in Union Organizing Campaigns.' *Industrial Relations* 31 (2): 370–82.

Premack. S. and Hunter, J (1988) 'Individual unionization decisions.' *Psychological Bulletin* 103 (2): 223–34.

Price, Robert and Bain, George (1983) 'Union Growth in Britain: Retrospect and Prospect.' *British Journal of Industrial Relations* 21 (1): 46–62.

Prosten, Richard (1978) 'The Longest Season: Union Organizing in the Last Decade.' *Proceedings of the Thirty-First Annual Meetings of the Industrial Relations Research Association (IRRA).* Madison: IRRA.

Reed, Thomas (1989) 'Do Union Organizers Matter? Individual Differences, Campaign Practices, and Representation Election Outcomes.' *Industrial and Labor Relations Review* 43 (1) (Oct.): 103–19.

Riddell, C. (2001) 'Union Suppression and Certification Success.' *Canadian Journal of Economics* 34 (2): 396–410.

Riddell, Chris (2004) 'Union Certification Success Under Voting Versus Card-Check Procedures: Evidence from British Columbia, 1978–1998.' *Industrial and Labor Relations Review* 57 (4): 493–517.

Riley, Nicola-Maria (1997) 'Determinants of Union Membership: A Review.' *Labor* 11 (2): 265–301.

Robinson, James (1988) 'Workplace Hazards and Workers' Desires for Union Representation.' *Journal of Labor Research* 9 (3): 237–49.

Rose, Joseph and Chaison, G. (1996) 'Linking Union Density and Union Effectiveness: The North American Experience.' *Industrial Relations* 35 (1): 78–105.

Rudy, Preston (2004) 'Justice for Janitors,' Not 'Compensation for Custodians': The Political Context and Organizing in San Jose and Sacramento' in Ruth Milkman and Kim Voss (eds), *Rebuilding Labor*. Ithaca: Cornell University. pp. 133–50.

Salancik, G. and Pfeffer, J. (1977) 'An Examination of Need-Satisfaction Models of Job Attitudes.' *Administrative Science Quarterly* 22 (3): 427–56.

Schnabel, Claus (2003) 'Determinants of Trade Union Membership.' in John T. Addison and Claus Schnabel (eds) *International Handbook of Trade Unions*. Cheltenham, UK: Edward Elgar.

Schur, Lisa, and Kruse, Doug (1992) 'Gender Differences in Attitudes Towards Unions.' *Industrial and Labor Relations Review* 46 (1): 89–103.

Scott, Clyde, Seers Anson and Culpepper, Robert (1996) 'Determinants of Union Election Outcomes in the Non-Hospital Health Care Industry.' *Journal of Labor Research* 17 (4): 701–15.

Sharpe, Ian G. (1971) 'The Growth of Australian Trade Unions: 1907–1969.' *Journal of Industrial Relations* 13 (June): 144–53.

Sherman, Rachel and Voss, Kim (2000) 'Breaking the Iron Law of Oligarchy: Union Revitalization in the American Labor Movement.' *American Journal of Sociology* 106 (2): 303–49.

Slinn, Sarah (2004) 'The Effects of Compulsory Certification Votes on Certification Applications in Ontario: An Empirical Analysis.' *Canadian Labor and Employment Law Journal* 11: 259–99.

Stepina, Lee P. and Fiorito, Jack (1986) 'Toward a Comprehensive Theory of Union Growth and Decline.' *Industrial Relations* 25 (3): 248–64.

Summers, Timothy P., Betton, John H. and Decotiis, Thomas A. (1986) 'Voting for and Against Unions: A Decision Model.' *Academy of Management Review* 11 (3): 643–55.

Swidinsky, R. (1974) 'Trade Union Growth in Canada: 1911-1970.' *Relations Industrielles* 29 (3): 435–49.

Thomason, Terry (1994) 'The Effect of Accelerated Certification Procedures on Union Organizing Campaigns.' *Industrial and Labor Relations Review* 47 (2): 207–26.

Thomason, Terry and Pozzebon, Sylvana (1998) 'Managerial Opposition to Union Certification in Quebec and Ontario.' *Relations Industrielles* 53 (4): 750–71.

Troy, Leo (2000) 'U.S. and Canadian Industrial Relations: Convergent or Divergent?' *Industrial Relations* 39 (4)(December): 695–713.

van de Vall, Mark (1970) *Labor Organizations*. Cambridge: the University Press.

Visser, Jelle (2002) 'Why Fewer Workers Join Unions in Europe: A Social Custom Explanation.' *British Journal of Industrial Relations* 40 (3): 403–30.

Voos, Paula (1983) 'Union Organizing: Costs and Benefits.' *Industrial and Labor Relations Review* 36: 576–91.

Voos, Paula (1984) 'Does it Pay to Organize? Estimating the Costs to Unions.' *Monthly Labor Review* 107 (June): 43–44.

Voss, Kim and Sherman, Rachel (2000) 'Breaking the Iron Law of Oligarchy: Union Revitalization in the American Labor Movement.' *American Journal of Sociology* 106 (2): 303–49.

Waddington, J. and Whitston, C. (1997) 'Why do People Join Unions in a Period of Membership Decline?' *British Journal of Industrial Relations* 35 (4): 515–46.

Waldinger, R., Erikson, C., Milkman, R., Mitchell, D., Valenzuela, A. and Zeitlin, M. (1998) 'Helots no More. A Case Study of the Justice for Janitors Campaign in Los Angeles.' In K. Bronfenbrenner, S. Friedman, R. Hurd, R. Oswald, and R. Seeber (eds), *Organizing to Win: New Research on Union Strategies*. Ithaca, NY: ILR Press. pp. 102–19.

Wall Street Journal, April 25, 1991, A16, cited in Sexton, Patricia, *The War on Labor and the Left*. Boulder: Westview Press.

Weikle, Roger, Wheeler, Hoyt and McClendon, John (1998) 'A Comparative Case Study of Union Organizing Success and Failure: Implications for a Practical Strategy.' In K. Bronfenbrenner, S. Friedman, R. Hurd, R. Oswald, and R. Seeber (eds), *Organizing to Win: New Research on Union Strategies*. Ithaca, NY: ILR Press.

Weiler, Paul (1984) 'Striking a New Balance: Freedom of Contract and the Prospects for Union Representation.' *Harvard Law Review* 98 (2): 351–420.

Weiler, Paul (1983) 'Promises to Keep: Securing Workers' Rights to Self-Organization Under the NLRA.' *Harvard Law Review* 96 (8): 1769–1827.

Western, Bruce (1997) *Between Class and Market: Postwar Unionization in the Capitalist Democracies*. Princeton: Princeton University Press.

Wheeler, Hoyt and McClendon, John (1991) 'The Individual Decision to Unionize.' In George Strauss, Dan Gallagher, and Jack Fiorito (eds) *The State of the Unions*. Madison: IRRA.

Wood, Stephen and Godard, John (1999) 'The Statutory Recognition Procedure in the Employee Relations Bill: A Comparative Perspective.' *British Journal of Industrial Relations* 37 (2): 203–45.

Wood, Stephen and Machin, Steve (2005) 'Human Resource Management as a Substitute for Trade Unions in British Workplaces.' *Industrial and Labor Relations Review* 58 (2): 201–19.

Yager, D.V., Bartl, T.J. and LoBue, J.J. (1998) *Employee Free Choice: It's Not in the Cards*. Washington, D.C.: Labor Policy Association.

Youngblood, S., DeNisi, A., Molleston, J. and Mobley, W. (1984) 'The impact of work environment, instrumentality beliefs, perceived labor union image, and subjective norms on union voting intentions.' *Academy of Management Journal* 27 (3): 576–90.

Zalesny, Mary D. (1985) 'Comparison of Economic and Non-economic Factors in Predicting Faculty Vote Preference in a Union Representation Election.' *Journal of Applied Psychology* 7(2): 243–56.

21

The Changing Structure of Collective Bargaining

Robert J. Flanagan

The relative bargaining power that labor and management bring to the table is influenced by both the structure of collective bargaining negotiations and specific bargaining tactics, as conditioned by the prevailing economic and political environment. This chapter focuses on the determinants and effects of collective bargaining structure, which varies enormously around the world. After defining collective bargaining structure, the chapter explains how structure influences relative bargaining power, discusses evidence on the impact of bargaining structure on microeconomic and macroeconomic outcomes, and interprets the evolution of bargaining structures over time. Of particular interest is whether increased economic integration is producing a convergence of bargaining structures around the world.

THE CONCEPT OF BARGAINING STRUCTURE

Bargaining structures originate in the informal work groups of union members defined by technology and the organization of production. The aspirations of these work groups define a union's objectives, but the groups themselves often lack the power to conduct effective bargaining. As a result, informal work groups generally combine to establish broader negotiating units and those are the chief concern of this chapter. Negotiating units typically conduct collective bargaining and are bound by the terms of the resulting agreement. In Canada and the US, where union membership is normally decided by union representation elections, casual observers sometimes confuse the election unit – the group of workers eligible to vote in union representation elections – with the negotiating unit. Election units also may include several informal work groups in plants or companies, but they are usually smaller than the negotiating unit when there are industry wide or multi-plant collective bargaining agreements. Once an agreement has been negotiated, contract extension procedures or emulation by other firms or industries may produce a unit of direct impact that exceeds the scope of the negotiating unit (Weber, 1967). Indeed, in most countries, the number of workers covered by a collective agreement exceeds the number of union members. The gap between coverage and union membership is particularly large in several continental European countries with contact extension laws or procedures (OECD, 2004). Concerns that the economic impact of collective bargaining might spread beyond the negotiating unit have also stimulated an active literature, reviewed later in the chapter, on the relationship between bargaining structure and macroeconomic performance.

Collective bargaining occurs in an impressive variety of negotiating units around the world, but three concepts summarize the distinctions in bargaining level that have proved most important for analyzing how bargaining structure may influence bargaining outcomes. In *decentralized* collective bargaining structures (most common in North America, Japan, Korea, New Zealand, and the UK), most negotiations occur between employer and employee representatives in a company or plant. *Intermediate* level collective bargaining between industry wide unions and employers' associations historically was the dominant bargaining arrangement in continental Europe. These negotiations established a floor under working conditions within an industry. *Centralized* collective bargaining, common at times in Scandinavian countries, involves negotiations between national labor and employer federations to establish nationwide working conditions. Much of this chapter concerns how these distinctions in the bargaining level influence the relative power that labor and management bring to the bargaining table.

Detecting the effective collective bargaining structure can be a subtle business, requiring careful distinctions between the form and substance of bargaining arrangements. In some countries, seemingly decentralized bargaining may be so highly coordinated that one or two key negotiations effectively determine the contract terms agreed to in other negotiations. Understanding bargaining structure therefore requires an assessment of the degree of bargaining coordination as

well as the bargaining level. There is a further complication: Seemingly centralized bargaining systems usually include significant elements of decentralized determination of working conditions. These points receive more attention later in the chapter.

Bargaining structure is sometimes confused with the much vaguer concept of corporatism. Corporatism, in its many definitions, pertains to institutional arrangements and negotiating processes that facilitate bargaining between labor, management, and the government over economic policies and pay settlements that may support them. Centralized bargaining levels are one component of corporatist institutional arrangements, which may account for the confusion of terms. But the concept of bargaining structure excludes the government and focuses on labor-management negotiations.

DETERMINANTS OF BARGAINING STRUCTURE

Viewing the institutional differences as 'historical accidents' begs the question of what determines bargaining structure. Why the ubiquitous institution of collective bargaining should acquire so many different forms merits more research attention than it has received. Most institutions have some rational basis at the time of their development, although they may become less suitable as economic and political conditions change over time. Institutions may reflect social preferences and underlying cultural norms, for example. In a rare effort to consider influences on bargaining arrangements, Teulings and Hartog (1998, Chapter 3) examined how indices of corporatism, the concept that includes but is broader than bargaining structure, varied with measures of national cultures developed by Hofstede (1980).[1] They find that corporatist arrangements, which include relatively centralized collective bargaining structures, appear more often in societies that place high value on equality and the quality of life. This link between cultural attributes and collective institutions is consistent with the positive correlation between more centralized bargaining systems and pay equality that will be discussed later in this chapter.

Economic and legal influences supplement cultural predispositions. The balance between domestic and international competition can be an important economic influence on a country's bargaining structure. When competition is mainly domestic, broader bargaining structures that take the wage out of competition offer advantages to both employers and unions, as discussed more fully in the next section. For many years following WWII, industry wide and centralized bargaining – the most common bargaining arrangements – coexisted with relatively high, albeit declining, barriers to international trade. Later sections of this chapter describe and interpret a considerable decentralization of collective bargaining that has occurred in many countries since 1980, however. The spread of international competition in product markets appears to be an important element in this development.

Two aspects of the legal environment of collective bargaining condition bargaining structure. Laws governing the determination of union membership and the conduct of collective bargaining provide one influence. Legal systems in which union membership is usually determined by union representation elections at the place of employment (as in the US and Canada) encourage comparatively decentralized bargaining, for the representation elections tend to be held at the company or plant level. More subtle, and ultimately more important, are laws or policies that protect or provide opportunities for union rents on an industry or national basis. Regulatory policies in which prices to consumers are marked up a certain amount over costs provide a common example. By establishing a pricing rule that permits all producers in an industry to pass through costs, such regulatory policies facilitate the formation and maintenance of industry bargaining units. Later in this chapter, we shall see how changes in both types of legislation contributed to the decentralization of collective bargaining structures in the late twentieth century.

BARGAINING STRUCTURE AND BARGAINING POWER

Bargaining power is the ability to strike or take a strike. Most unions wish to raise the real wage of their members without reducing membership employment; hence the attraction of bargaining structures that produce an inelastic demand for the services of union members. Attaining that goal amounts to developing bargaining arrangements that limit (1) the ability of producers to substitute other inputs for the services of union members and (2) the ability of consumers to purchase cheaper substitutes for the goods or services provided by union labor. For most employers, the short-run ability to take a strike varies inversely with the ability of customers to shift (perhaps permanently) to similar products or services produced by other companies. Looking to the long-run consequences of a collective bargaining agreement, the employer's willingness to take a strike will also depend on whether non-union competition (or unionized competition from abroad) is likely to enter the market and undercut the company's prices.

The earliest analytical contribution to the debate over the relationship between bargaining structure and power in labor negotiations isolated the key role of the elasticity of demand for the services of union members. The most powerful unions face inelastic labor demand curves and incur small employment losses from their negotiated wage increases. Drawing on Alfred Marshall's (1923: 518–38) famous conditions for inelastic labor demand,[2] Milton Friedman (1951) argued that only craft unions – unions that organized workers with a particular skill – could have significant bargaining power. Friedman noted that unions of craft workers gain power because (a) it is difficult to substitute for their services and (b) they constitute a small percent of total costs (so that their wage increases have little impact on prices and sales). In contrast, he argued that industrial unions of dominantly unskilled labor, such as those that emerged in the auto and steel industries in the US during the

Great Depression, could never have much impact because they lacked these advantages. Presumably, the same reasoning would apply to general unions.

Lloyd Ulman (1955) countered that the application of labor demand elasticities in fact led to rather different conclusions when the institutional features of some unionized labor markets were fully considered. Noting the rigid relative wage relationships between many craft unions in the construction and printing trades, Ulman noted that patterns of wage emulation among crafts meant that a seemingly small wage negotiation could ultimately have a large impact on labor costs as other craft unions subsequently insisted on similar wage increases. Moreover, the 'importance of being unimportant' (a small percent of total costs) only holds when consumers can shift purchases from products made by union labor more easily than producers can substitute for union labor in production.

Industrial unions may create less elastic demand for their members' services when they limit the scope for consumer substitution by organizing all producers in a particular industry. When all domestic producers of a product or service are subject to the same labor agreement, consumers effectively have no (domestic) place to go to escape price increases that may follow union wage negotiations. Bargaining structures that effectively reduce the elasticity of product demand also suit employers' interests; labor agreements negotiated in those structures are less likely to produce a loss of customers. Industrial unions may also limit the scope for producer substitution when they broaden bargaining structures to encompass producers of capital goods or other potential substitutes for union labor. In short, the choice of bargaining structure can have a large influence on the relative bargaining power of employers and unions.

Beyond the specifics of the debate about craft vs. industrial union power, the exchange between Friedman and Ulman elevated the elasticity of labor demand to a central role in future discussions of the consequences of alternative bargaining structures. The sensitivity of the employment of union members to changes in their compensation influenced future reasoning and research into the relative merits of plant, multiplant, company, and industry wage agreements. As a rough rule of thumb, the demand for union labor becomes less elastic as the level of bargaining increases. Without clarity about the specific product and labor markets in which negotiations occur, however, it is difficult to reach definitive conclusions about the effects of a particular bargaining structure on the relative power of labor and management. Moreover, the goals of the bargaining participants regarding the scope of the labor agreement and the importance of wage equality or other distributional objectives may influence bargaining structures.

Company bargaining illustrates many of these points. Bargaining with a particular employer (and at the individual plants of an employer) characterizes decentralized collective bargaining systems. The appeal of company bargaining will vary with the company's market environment. In competitive industries, companies are in a weak position during a strike. Product demand is highly elastic, since consumers can easily shift their purchases to other companies producing identical products or very close substitutes. The possibly permanent loss of business to other firms is less threatening to the union, because members who lose their jobs can find jobs at the firms that captured the company's business. Industry employment will change little. These aspects of company bargaining provide employers in competitive industries with strong incentives to strengthen their position by seeking multi-employer bargaining units. Historically, many multi-employer bargaining structures have emerged in competitive industries even in countries with comparatively decentralized bargaining structures.

Single employer bargaining units have been more common in oligopolistic product markets, which offer less scope for substitution by consumers. Employers nonetheless remain in a relatively uncomfortable economic position.

On the one hand, they do not want to risk a permanent loss of market share to rivals by taking a strike alone. On the other, an expensive contract that avoids a strike may expose them to the same risk. The incentives to develop multiemployer bargaining arrangements remain strong.

Countering these general economic forces is the fact that bargaining at the plant or company level permits negotiators to address a wide range of company- or plant-specific issues that would be ignored in more centralized bargaining. Many non-monetary aspects of work life that influence a company's productive efficiency and workers' job satisfaction are unique to specific workplaces. Issues surrounding the introduction of new technology, changes in the organization of work, the pace of production and job safety vary substantially across companies and plants, and centralized bargaining systems are poorly suited to address the variety of conflicts that emerge over these issues. While raising the time devoted to negotiations, company bargaining permits joint resolution of many issues that influence the long-run viability of a firm. Company- and plant-specific efficiency issues become more important as industries encounter greater product market competition, for they govern the wages that a viable company can pay. The demand for decentralized bargaining arrangements should increase with the necessity of plant level solutions to workplace problems.

Multi-employer bargaining holds appeal for both unions and employers. Including all employers in the same negotiating unit reduces the elasticity of demand for labor by effectively reducing the opportunity for consumers to shift to less costly producers in the event of wage and price increases. A given increase in compensation should produce smaller employment losses for union members in multi-employer negotiating units than company units. Moreover, '[T]o have a common front throughout an industry also accords with the unionist's desire for solidarity, and his sense that it is only fair to have one and the same rate for the job wherever it is done.' (Phelps Brown, 1962, p.170)

Historically, European employers generally supported multi-employer bargaining units, which effectively took the wage out of competition and guaranteed that key competitors would also be shut down in the event of a strike. While such formal multi-employer bargaining arrangements exist in some competitive unionized industries in North America, a variant known as 'pattern bargaining' dominated oligopolistic industries for many years. Under pattern bargaining, a union first negotiated with a target company and then negotiated substantially similar agreements with other companies in the industry. Multi-employer contracts are also less constraining than company contracts. Faced with member companies who vary in their efficiency and needs, multi-employer negotiations often produce contracts whose terms permit the least efficient firms to remain solvent. Comparatively efficient companies may earn higher profits or pay higher wages than the contract requires. For both sides, broad units offer economies of scale in negotiations.

Multi-employer bargaining effectively creates a bilateral monopoly in the relevant labor market. The outcome of such bargaining is theoretically indeterminate, resting on the relative bargaining skill of labor and management. Whether multi-employer bargaining associations use their market power to resist union bargaining demands or to accept them and pass the higher costs on to consumers is an empirical question. Several studies indicate that relative to single employer bargaining, wages tend to be higher under multi-employer bargaining in local product markets (Hendricks and Kahn, 1984; Hendricks, 1975).

Centralized bargaining occurs in a few countries between nationwide labor and employer federations. The nationwide scope of such negotiations has a number of immediate consequences. The elasticity of labor demand is even lower, since labor agreements in principle cover all domestic substitutes. Nationwide collective bargaining is particularly well suited for pursuing greater wage equality, and empirical analyses report a robust negative cross-country correlation between bargaining level and wage dispersion (OECD, 2004). Greater equality emerges from central negotiations that restrain the bargaining power of the most powerful unions (that typically represent high-wage workers), while providing extra wage payments to low-wage workers. Sweden's postwar 'solidaristic wage policy' provides a clear illustration of how centralized bargaining can increase wage equality, and the internal tensions such policies can create.

More broadly, centralized collective bargaining inevitably produces contracts that address fewer issues than decentralized collective bargaining. (See previous discussion of company bargaining.) Negotiations must focus on issues that are common to the workplaces covered by an agreement. If company bargaining can address a wide array of compensation, health and safety, and work rule issues that are unique to an organization, nationwide bargaining must limit itself to issues shared by most workplaces. This largely limits bargaining to changes in compensation and work hours. In short, centralized contracts cannot address workplace-specific issues that may be of great concern to workers. Effectively, centralized bargaining raises the demand for additional levels of bargaining, and officially or unofficially, multiple tiers of bargaining typically emerge in centralized bargaining systems. (Multiple bargaining levels also can emerge in industry bargaining. In Germany, works councils, which are legally mandated to limit their negotiations to issues not addressed in industry collective bargaining negotiations, provide an example.)

As a result, centralized labor agreements provide a less reliable evolution of earnings than labor agreements under decentralized bargaining. 'Wage drift,' the tendency for actual earnings to increase more rapidly than negotiated wage rates reflects a variety of forces. Companies are free to pay more than the negotiated increase and some do in order to improve their recruiting prospects. On the union side, the centrally negotiated wage increase is often implemented in lower levels of bargaining, and there is a certain, regular tendency for the decentralized implementation to exceed the centralized intention. Wage drift has two main consequences in centralized bargaining systems. First, it adds uncertainty to the evolution of earnings. Second, it tends to reverse the greater wage equality that these systems try to establish in formal centralized negotiations. Work groups whose bargaining power is effectively restrained in central negotiations try to reassert their power during the implementation process. The most convincing evidence indicates that this effort is only partially successful; wage drift unwinds some, but not all, of the greater pay equality established in central negotiations (Hibbs and Locking, 1996).

Finally, nationwide negotiations produce macroeconomic concerns that are discussed more fully in the following section. Such negotiations have the potential to produce inflation or (under fixed exchange rate systems) balance of payments disequilibria, unless they are conducted with attention to a country's macroeconomic scope for non-inflationary pay increases. Union and employer negotiators must either internalize the macroeconomic concerns in their negotiating processes and outcomes or risk government intervention to restrain the full utilization of the power implicit in centralized bargaining. Over the years, examples of both private restraint and government intervention to protect macroeconomic objectives can be found in nations practicing centralized bargaining.

To summarize, a country's bargaining structure reflects the outcome of several distinct forces. Because the level of bargaining influences the elasticity of demand for the services of union labor, bargaining structure is a prime determinant of power in collective bargaining. As such, bargaining structure is vulnerable to economic developments – notably changes in product market competition – that alter the power implied by a given level of bargaining. The economic environment also influences bargaining structure through its influence on the range of issues that collective bargaining must address. Centralized structures can only address a short list of issues common to all participating units. When non-monetary issues involving the organization or restructuring of work and production processes become paramount, decentralized bargaining becomes more important. These topics grow in importance with increased product market competition.

Second, legal influences on both the conduct of collective bargaining and its economic environment influence the level at which bargaining can be sustained. Finally, bargaining structure may reflect a society's cultural attributes and particularly its goals regarding equality. As a public good, greater equality must be delivered by broad bargaining structures or by government action.

MACROECONOMIC OUTCOMES AND BARGAINING STRUCTURE

Governments periodically express concern with the potential macroeconomic consequences of collective bargaining. In industrial countries, such concerns have sometimes produced public policy efforts to restrain the advance of negotiated wages through the implementation of various forms of incomes policy. Most reviews of such policies express doubts about their long-term effectiveness (Ulman and Flanagan, 1971; Flanagan et al., 1983). A notable feature of the incomes policy approach is that it takes collective bargaining institutions as given.

In contrast, a significant theoretical and empirical literature (reviewed in Calmfors, 1993; Flanagan, 1999, 2003 and Boeri et al., 2001) examines the links between macroeconomic outcomes and the details of national industrial relations systems. Prominent among these details are the level and degree of coordination of collective bargaining. Several important ideas inform this literature.

Bargaining structure influences incentives for union negotiators to internalize the external (third-party) effects of negotiated wage pressures. If wage increases negotiated by a union with a company result in an increase in the prices of the goods and services produced by that company, there will be little impact on the real wage gains of union members. The company's price increase has a small impact on the national price level, and union negotiators can safely ignore that effect. Nationwide collective bargaining negotiations produce a very different calculus. Compensation increases in excess of productivity growth will now produce increases in the overall price level that limit the real wage gains that workers obtain from negotiations. With union negotiators facing stronger incentives to limit wage pressure in nationwide negotiations, countries with centralized bargaining arguably should have less inflation. In fact, this 'internationalization' hypothesis predicts that inflation and some other measures of macroeconomic performance should improve with the level of bargaining.

Of course, one must also consider the relationship between bargaining structure and bargaining power discussed earlier in this chapter. With the incorporation of bargaining power considerations, an inverted U-shaped relationship between macroeconomic performance and bargaining structure emerges. That is, intermediate level (industry wide) bargaining provides the worst macroeconomic performance (Calmfors and Driffill, 1988). Other analysts have stressed the importance of bargaining coordination, however, noting that some seemingly decentralized bargaining systems, such as Japan's, actually have highly coordinated bargaining, because a few key settlements set the pattern for most negotiations.

These predictions emerge from analyses of completely unionized, closed economies in which employers maximize profits and unions are concerned with both the real wage levels and employment of their members. Shifting to open economies or economies with a significant non-union sector complicates the analyses and alters the predicted relationship between bargaining structure and macroeconomic outcomes. With significant imports or a large non-union sector, the relationship between bargaining structure and economic performance weakens and may disappear. Centralized negotiators now face weaker incentives to restrain wage demands because overall consumer price increases (which include the prices of imports and domestic goods and services produce by non-union labor) will be smaller than the price increases of products made with union labor. That is, the real wage of union workers will increase because overall prices increase less rapidly than wages.

Empirical analyses of these hypotheses must rely on a rather limited database consisting of industrialized countries during the last third of the twentieth century. Institutions change infrequently within countries, so most of the variation in bargaining arrangements comes from differences between 15–20 countries. The possibilities for sharp tests are thus limited, and empirical findings have proven to be rather fragile. It seems likely that further progress in delineating the relationship between bargaining arrangements and macroeconomic outcomes will rest on more careful consideration of how interactions between the level of bargaining and the economic and political environments of collective bargaining interact to influence bargaining power.

MEASUREMENT OF BARGAINING STRUCTURE

Most efforts to characterize country's bargaining structures empirically utilize the levels of bargaining distinctions described in the previous section. Two difficulties confront such efforts. Some bargaining systems that appear decentralized in form may be more centralized in substance if most settlements closely emulate the outcome of one or a few key negotiations. Japan provides a key example of such 'pattern following' or coordinated bargaining. Although the formal structure of bargaining includes thousands of company negotiating units, in practice a few key settlements define the outcome of the Shunto each spring. In an effort to address this issue, some descriptions of bargaining

structure include indicators of both the level of bargaining and the degree of bargaining coordination.

The earlier discussion of centralized collective bargaining structures indicated the second difficulty. Formally centralized bargaining systems usually have several levels of negotiations – sometimes over similar issues, sometimes over different issues. The same may be said of 'tripartite' negotiations, invariably centralized, in which the government enters discussions with labor and management in an effort to limit the maximum compensation increase that emerges from collective bargaining (Katz et al., 2004). Tripartite bargaining typically emerges to confront particular 'emergencies' such as preventing or limiting inflation or meeting the requirements for entry into the European Union.

One finds examples of a variety of bargaining structures among the OECD club of mainly industrialized countries during the last three decades of the twentieth century (Table 21.1). At one extreme is the predominantly company and plant level bargaining in North America, Japan, Korea, and (in later decades) New Zealand and the UK. At the other extreme, Finland, Norway, and (in earlier decades) Sweden have had predominantly centralized agreements. For much of the twentieth century, there was no tendency for these structures to converge to a single institutional form. Countries coexisted with a variety of bargaining structure. Much the same may be said about the degree of bargaining coordination (Table 21.2).

Table 21.1 also shows a tendency for this stability to give way in several countries beginning in the 1980s and carrying forward into the early years of the twenty-first century. Looking across columns, one sees clear evidence of decentralization over the thirty-year period. Denmark, Portugal, Spain, and Sweden began the period with centralized agreements but entered the twenty-first century with predominantly industry level bargaining. Other countries (Australia, New Zealand, and the UK) moved from a variety of intermediate level bargaining structures

Table 21.1 Bargaining structures in OECD countries, 1970–2000

	1970–1974	1975–1979	1980–1984	1985–1989	1990–1994	1995–2000
Australia	4	4	4	4	2	2
Austria	3	3	3	3	3	3
Belgium	4	3.5	3	3	3	3
Canada	1	1	1	1	1	1
Denmark	5	5	3	3	3	2
Finland	5	5	4	5	5	5
France	2	2	2	2	2	2
Germany	3	3	3	3	3	3
Ireland	4	4	1	2.5	4	4
Italy	2	2	3.5	2	2	2
Japan	1	1	1	1	1	1
Korea	1	1	1	1	1	1
Netherlands	3	3	3	3	3	3
New Zealand	3	3	3	3	1	1
Norway	4.5	4.5	3.5	4.5	4.5	4.5
Portugal	5	4	3	3	4	4
Spain	5	4	4	3.5	3	3
Sweden	5	5	4.5	3	3	3
Switzerland	3	3	3	3	2	2
UK	2	2	1	1	1	1
US	1	1	1	1	1	1

1 = Company and plant level bargaining predominant.
2 = Combination of industry and company/plant bargaining.
3 = Industry level bargaining predominant.
4 = Industry bargaining with recurrent central agreements.
5 = Central bargaining predominant.
Source: OECD 2004 p. 151.

Table 21.2 Bargaining coordination in OECD countries, 1970–2000

	1970–1974	1975–1979	1980–1984	1985–1989	1990–1994	1995–2000
Australia	4	4	4.5	4	2	2
Austria	5	5	4.5	4	4	4
Belgium	4	3.5	4	4	4	4.5
Canada	1	3	1	1	1	1
Denmark	5	5	3	4	3	4
Finland	5	5	4	5	5	5
France	2	2	2	2	2	2
Germany	4	4	4	4	4	4
Ireland	4	4	1	2.5	4	4
Italy	2	2	3.5	2	3	4
Japan	4	4	4	4	4	4
Korea	1	1	1	1	1	1
Netherlands	3	4	4.5	4	4	4
New Zealand	4	4	4	4	1	1
Norway	4.5	4.5	3.5	4.5	4.5	4.5
Portugal	5	4	3	3	4	4
Spain	5	4	4	3.5	3	3
Sweden	4	4	3.5	3	3	3
Switzerland	4	4	4	4	4	4
UK	3	1	1	1	1	1
US	1	1	1	1	1	1

1 = Company and plant level bargaining predominant.
2 = Combination of industry and company/plant bargaining.
3 = Industry level bargaining predominant.
4 = Industry bargaining with recurrent central agreements.
5 = Central bargaining predominant.
Source: OECD 2004 p. 151.

closer to company and plant bargaining. Even the apparent stability of official industry bargaining in some countries obscures decentralizing tendencies. Employer participation industry wide bargaining arrangements declined in Germany (Thelen, 1998), and company level bargaining expanded in Italy:

> There has been a more or less strong tendency towards decentralization of collective bargaining in almost all countries that still have a dominance of intersectoral or sectoral bargaining. In many countries, such as Austria, Denmark, Finland, Germany, Italy, the Netherlands, Norway or Sweden, the higher-level agreements have widened the scope for additional bargaining at company level and/or have introduced opening clauses that allow companies to diverge from certain collectively agreed standards. Following this process of organized or controlled decentralization, many countries have seen the emergence of rather differentiated and flexible multi-level bargaining systems (EIRO, 2005).

Also not reflected in the tables is the decentralization implied by the continuing decline in union density in most industrialized countries. For countries without contract extension procedures, this trend signals a further shift toward non-union pay determination of working conditions through the human resource management policies and practices of individual companies. Finally, no country's collective bargaining structure became more centralized during this period. What accounts for the growing decentralization of bargaining in the last third of the twentieth century? What are the likely consequences of this development?

THE DECENTRALIZATION OF COLLECTIVE BARGAINING STRUCTURES

Collective bargaining structures weaken as economic, political, and legal developments limit a union's span of control over the relevant product market. Thus far, the discussion of bargaining structure pertains to control of domestic product markets, and for the period from the onset of WWI to the immediate post-WWII period, this was the appropriate frame of reference. The interwar period saw a general retreat from international economic integration with increased levels of trade protection that insulated many domestic product markets from significant import competition. Postwar trade negotiations under the auspices of the General Agreement for Tariffs and Trade (GATT) and its successor, the World Trade Organization (WTO), produced a sequence of reductions in tariff and non-tariff barriers to international trade that increased the exposure of most product markets to foreign competition. This development was particularly strong in industrialized countries, where tariff rates were lowest and where there were no special provisions to facilitate the development of 'infant industries.' (At the same time, most industrial countries retained restrictions on permanent international migration that had arisen in the late nineteenth and early twentieth centuries.)

The industry wide bargaining structures that protected firms from domestic labor cost competition also left entire industries vulnerable to foreign competition. As foreign companies captured domestic market shares, many domestic companies now found the wage floors of industry bargaining a competitive hindrance and sought discounts from the industry wage or other company-specific solutions.

Changes in the regulation of labor relations and the economic regulation of some industries provided an additional force for decentralization in several countries (Katz, 1993). After almost a century of collective bargaining in an environment of compulsory arbitration awards, Australia (in workplace reform statutes in 1988, 1993, and 1996) and New Zealand (with the *1991 Employment Contracts Act*) fundamentally revised their labor laws in ways that encouraged more decentralized collective bargaining. In the US and some European countries, the deregulation of transportation, communications, and other industries with competitive market structures provided another force for decentralization. Deregulation reduced barriers to entry and removed common regulated prices that had facilitated industry wide and even national bargaining structures. Increased domestic competition challenged the maintenance of such high labor cost arrangements and led many employers to seek company level bargaining. Moreover, in some countries many new entrants were able to remain non-union.

Increased pay dispersion is the most visible consequence of the decentralization of collective bargaining. In fact, the decentralization of pay determination in the late twentieth century actually exceeded the decentralization of bargaining, given the decline in union representation that accompanied the decentralization of bargaining in many countries. The growth of the non-union sector effectively decentralizes pay determination decisions to the company level. Yet, not all aspects of decentralization produce greater pay dispersion. A diminishing difference between average union and non-union wages should counter some of the increased pay dispersion among individual workers. On balance, dispersion increases, however. Whether the increased pay dispersion associated with decentralized collective bargaining provides stronger incentives for skill acquisition and production efficiency remains an important unresolved research question. Other consequences of decentralized bargaining are less visible to the public. The earlier discussion noted the necessarily limited scope of centralized collective bargaining agreements. Increasing decentralization of collective bargaining permits consideration of many non-monetary issues that concern workers and employers but are not sufficiently general to be addressed in more central negotiations. Decentralization may produce labor agreements of greater scope.

THE FUTURE OF BARGAINING STRUCTURE

Looking forward, economic pressures for decentralized bargaining are likely to continue for the foreseeable future, albeit at an abated pace. International negotiations to reduce trade barriers continue but take

longer to produce fewer achievements than in earlier decades. Globalization's critics notwithstanding, a reversal of the post-WWII trend toward greater international economic integration seems unlikely. Much the same may be said of national efforts to deregulate some industries. The economic conditions that support relatively centralized bargaining arrangements are increasingly rare.

Future interactions between the legal environment and bargaining structure are less predictable. To some extent, legal rules follow economic necessity, a pattern that would predict more of the same. Even so, political changes raise the odds of at least partial reversals in the legal environment, as evidenced by changes in labor legislation in the UK in the late 1990s. What bargaining structure responses to the future economic and legal environment might be expected?

TRANSNATIONAL BARGAINING STRUCTURES

The apparent connection between increased international trade and decentralization of collective bargaining in industrialized countries seems puzzling in historical perspective. Faced with expanding product and labor markets and the rise of multi-plant firms within countries in the late nineteenth and early twentieth centuries, many local labor unions formed national organizations to coordinate and implement similar labor standards across the relevant market areas and all units of a company. Whether by the development of industry wide bargaining structures or the coordination of multiple local negotiations, the national unions sought to thwart the incentive for employers to whipsaw unions with high-wage contracts by threatening to move business to low-wage areas of the country.

In the face of expanding international product and labor markets, the development of transnational collective bargaining – the coordination of collective bargaining demands among workers in the same industry but in different countries – would continue and extend this historical defensive tactic. Many difficulties confront such an extension of traditional union tactics to international markets, however, and after some 40 years of experimentation, transnational bargaining structures have failed to produce the durable coordination of contract terms associated with national industry level bargaining.

Two considerations motivate labor unions to form transnational bargaining structures. In the short-run, unions that bargain with many multinational companies worry that the companies will shift production to plants in other countries. In principle, unions in any country may share the concern that multinationals are better able to take a strike by shifting their production beyond the jurisdiction of any particular national union. Unions in high-wage countries have the further long-run interest in preventing the permanent reallocation of jobs to countries with lower labor costs per unit of output.

In principle, transnational collective bargaining structures could reduce the elasticity of demand for the services of a multinational's workers in a country by limiting the scope for substitution of production to other countries. While a few instances of strikes to resist production shifting have been recorded, coordinating labor resistance across national boundaries encounters much more resistance than coordination within a country. National labor movements differ significantly in their objectives. The single-minded focus on economic objectives so common in North American unions seems almost unique in international perspective, for example. On other continents, competing labor movements have their roots in political or religious beliefs that broaden the scope of their activity and limit their inclination to support unions with different, more narrowly focused goals. There are definite limits to international solidarity.

Transnational co-operation to prevent job reallocation seems even less likely. A lack of opportunity for reciprocity presents one significant problem. Potential job losses flow in one direction – from high-wage to low-wage countries. Labor unions in the latter countries understand that transnational bargaining has the potential to protect jobs in rich countries at the expense of jobs in poor countries. Unions in the rich countries have little to offer in return. Even if unions moved beyond the lack of reciprocity, the choice of international contract standards remains more challenging than the task of choosing contract standards within a country. Wage differences around the world are huge in comparison to differentials within a country. Moreover, international wage differentials rest on equally large international productivity differentials. Productivity levels in poor countries do not match the pay standards of rich countries, so that any effort to establish the latter through transnational bargaining would reverse the flow of jobs and diminish employment opportunities in poor countries. Transnational bargaining structures offer the same risks to countries with a comparative advantage in low-wage labor as international labor standards, and unions in poor countries are understandably wary of such proposals.

Recognizing this stance, unions in some rich countries, notably the United States, have abandoned serious efforts to develop transnational collective bargaining structures and instead have either opposed free trade agreements or insisted on the inclusion of labor clauses committing the signatories to enforce and improve their national labor laws. A bargaining strategy for unions in high-wage countries would be to facilitate productivity improvements that (at least) offset their relative wage. The decentralization of many collective bargaining structures provides an improved setting for lowering unit labor costs through productivity deals rather than wage concessions.

CONCLUSIONS

This chapter has reviewed the determinants and impacts of collective bargaining structure and offered interpretations of the widespread, if not unanimous, decentralization of bargaining structures that occurred beginning in the 1980s. The focus has been on developments in the private sector of industrialized nations, a choice mainly dictated by available evidence. The growing literature on collective labor action in developing countries has not yet isolated the nature and role of bargaining structures, and the applicability of the analysis of the relationship between bargaining power and the level of negotiations discussed in this chapter to labor markets dominated by agriculture and informal sectors remains uncertain.

Two analytical themes pervade this chapter. Most importantly, distinguishing between the form and substance of collective bargaining structure remains crucial for understanding the outcomes of collective bargaining. Descriptions of average bargaining level rarely capture the bargaining reality in a country. The second key theme pertains to the variety of bargaining structures that have survived in the world. Until recently, the historical record has not indicated an international convergence of bargaining structures that might be expected if one institutional arrangement were unambiguously superior. This chapter has tried to indicate why no bargaining structure offers a free lunch for all issues. Each offers different strengths and weaknesses. To the extent that the decentralization that began in the late twentieth century signals a convergence, it will be because countries increasingly face a common set of problems in labor markets and seek the institutional arrangement that best addresses those problems.

NOTES

1 In Hofstede's parlance, 'masculine' societies emphasize achievement over the quality of life; societies with high 'power distance' tolerate significant inequality in society; 'individualistic' societies prefer individual over collective activity; and societies with high 'uncertainty avoidance' have a low tolerance for risk. Updated values of national cultural norms are available at: http://www.geert-hofstede.com/index.shtml

2 The labor demand elasticity, a measure of the responsiveness of the demand for union labor to a change in its wage, is the percent change in the employment of union members, divided by the percent change in the union wage. Given the tradeoff between the wage and employment levels described by labor demand curves, labor demand elasticities are typically negative. As later refined by John Hicks (1966:241–47), the demand for the services of any group of union workers is more inelastic when (1) it is easy to substitute other inputs, such as capital, for the union workers, (2) efforts to use substitutes for union labor do not provoke large increases in the price of the substitute inputs, (3) union labor is a small percent of total costs, and (4) the price elasticity of the product that labor produces is low (meaning that most consumers lack acceptable substitutes for the product or service produced by union labor). Where these conditions exist, union bargaining power is relatively high.

REFERENCES

Boeri, Tito, Brugiavini, Agar and Calmfors, Lars (eds) (2001) *The Role of Unions in the Twenty-First Century*. Oxford: Oxford University Press.

Calmfors, Lars and Driffill, John (1988) 'Bargaining structure, corporatism and macroeconomic performance', *Economic Policy*, 3: 13–61.

Calmfors, Lars (1993) 'Centralization of wage bargaining and macroeconomic performance: A survey', *OECD Economic Studies*, 21: 161–191.

EIRO (2005) 'Changes in national collective bargaining systems since 1990.' http://www.eiro.eurofound.ie/2005/03/study/tn0503102s.html (accessed July 25, 2005).

Flanagan, Robert J. (1999) 'Macroeconomic performance and collective bargaining', *Journal of Economic Literature*, 37 (3): 1150–75.

Flanagan, Robert J. (2003) 'Collective bargaining and macroeconomic performance', in J. T. Addison and C. Schnabel (eds) *International Handbook of Trade Unions*. Northampton, MA: Elgar. pp. 172–96.

Flanagan, Robert J., Soskice, David W. and Ulman, Lloyd (1983) *Unionism, Economic Stabilization and Incomes Policies: European Experience*. Washington: Brookings Institution.

Friedman, Milton (1951) 'Some comments on the economic significance of labor unions for economic policy', in David McCord Wright (ed) *The Impact of the Union*. New York: Harcourt Brace. pp. 204–35.

Hendricks, Wallace E. (1975) 'Labor market structure and union wage levels', *Economic Inquiry*, 13 (3): 401–16.

Hendricks, Wallace E. and Kahn, Lawrence M. (1984) 'The demand for labor market structure', *Journal of Labor Economics*, 2 (3): 412–38.

Hibbs, Douglas A. and Locking, Håkan (1996) 'Wage compression, wage drift and wage inflation in Sweden', *Journal of Labor Economics*, 3 (2): 109–41.

Hicks, John R. (1966) *The Theory of Wages*. 2nd edn New York: St. Martins Press.

Hofstede, Geert H. (1980) *Culture's Consequences: International Differences in Work-related Values*. Beverly Hills, CA: Sage Publications.

Katz, Harry C. (1993) 'The decentralization of collective bargaining: A literature review and comparative analysis', *Industrial and Labor Relations Review*, 47 (1): 3–22.

Katz, Harry C. , Lee, Wonduck and Lee, Joohee (eds) (2004) *The New Structure of Labor: Tripartism and Decentralization*. Ithaca: Cornell University Press.

Marshall, Alfred (1923) *Principles of Economics*. 8th edn. London: Macmillan.

OECD (2004) *Employment Outlook*. Paris: OECD.

Phelps Brown, E. H. (1962) *The Economics of Labor*. New Haven: Yale University Press.

Teulings, Coen and Hartog, Joop (1998) *Corporatism or Competition? An International Comparison of Labor Market Structures and Their Impact on Wage Formation*. Cambridge: Cambridge University Press.

Thelen, Kathleen (1998) 'Why German employers cannot bring themselves to abandon the German Model', in Torben Iversen, Jonas Pontusson, and David Soskice (eds) *Unions, Employers, and Central Banks: Wage Bargaining and Macroeconomic Policy in an Integrating Europe*. Ann Arbor: U. Michigan Press.

Ulman, Lloyd (1955) 'Marshall and Friedman on union strength', *Review of Economics and Statistics*, 37 (4): 384–401.

Ulman, Lloyd and Flanagan, Robert J. (1971) *Wage Restraint: A Study of Incomes Policies in Western Europe*. Berkeley: University of California Press.

Weber, Arnold R. (1967) 'Stability and change in the structure of collective bargaining', in Lloyd Ulman (ed) *Challenges to Collective Bargaining*. Englewood Cliffs, N.J.: Prentice-Hall. pp. 13–36.

22

The High Performance Work Systems Literature in Industrial Relations

Ann C. Frost

Over the last decade and a half, the high performance work system literature has become a major stream of interest in the field of industrial relations (IR). Whether the new system of work organization is called high involvement, transformed, mutual gains, or high commitment, this body of work has generated much attention – both by researchers engaged in studying high performance workplace practices and by the parties themselves in trying to understand how to implement the new forms of work organization that are seen to be the way out of their competitive difficulties. The attention devoted to high performance work practices has sparked a renaissance and brought vibrancy to the field of IR, a field whose traditional focus of attention – unions and collective bargaining – have seen a great diminution in both numbers and relevance over this same time period.

However, this stream of literature has not been without its controversy. The field

of high performance work systems research has engendered a number of fair critiques. Is it redirecting attention away from more important things to be studied in IR? Does this research come from a unitarist perspective and has it taken on a managerialist tone? Are the prescriptive findings of this research good for workers? For unions? Are the largely American-based findings generalizable to the rest of the world and to other industrial relations systems?

There is little argument that the high performance work systems literature has been well-developed and considerable learning about 'what works at work'[1] has emerged as a result. We know much about the conditions that enable high performance forms of work organization in many organizations. We also know something about the outcomes of such work organization choices and supporting human resource practices not only for firms, but also for workers and their unions.

What has become clear though more recently is that the scenario of 'mutual gains' (Kochan and Osterman, 1994) is not at all as widespread as much of the early work in this stream argued. The high performance work system paradigm is not always the light shining at the end of the tunnel to take the parties into workplace and competitive nirvana. A much more critical view of the high performance paradigm has emerged. In some cases, so-called high performance practices are in fact 'mean' or coercive in nature, used to retaylorize the workplace and exert increased control over workers and take power and control away from their unions. Over time, a more tempered view of the high performance workplace and high performance practices has emerged. We have become much more muted in our assessments of the good that such systems at work can deliver.

In this chapter, I review the high performance work systems literature, tracing in a largely chronological way, the emergence and development of this stream of work. In the chapter I also highlight the development of the critique of the mainstream of this literature and argue here that the critique has served to strengthen this literature rather than to have detracted from it. I conclude the chapter with an overall assessment of this stream of literature and its contribution to the larger field of IR research.

LITERATURE REVIEW PART I – THE GENESIS AND EARLY KEY PIECES

Two books published in the mid-1980s laid the foundation upon which the subsequent high performance work systems literature would be laid: Piore and Sabel's (1984) *The Second Industrial Divide* and Kochan et al.'s (1986) *The Transformation of American Industrial Relations*. Piore and Sabel (1984) argued that the dominance of mass production was being severely challenged by a series of changes in the macro political economy. In its place, a new form of organization they termed 'flexible specialization' would become dominant. Characterized by decentralized networks of small firms, flexibly deployable technology, and multi-skilled artisanal workers, flexible specialization would be able to produce small lots of high quality, niche goods as mass markets fragmented and economic conditions became more unstable. In particular, the use of labor appeared quite distinct in contrast to the traditional use of labor under mass production. Workers were highly skilled, often worked in autonomous teams, and engaged in decentralized decision making on the job.

Kochan et al., (1986) similarly documented changes taking place in American industry in the late 1970s and early 1980s. Not only did they witness the breakdown in American manufacturing hegemony, but they recorded the changes management was leading in adjusting its workforce and manufacturing practices to compete in the new environment. In part, what was new about what Kochan et al. observed was that workplace changes were now managerially driven, seeking to change the post war labor accord – in contrast to the findings of much of the industrial relations research in the 1950s and 1960s in which union demands drove changes in employment practices.

Kochan et al. documented some of the earliest attempts at simplifying union collective agreements, moving to team forms of work organization, tying pay to performance outcomes, and implementing cross training and job rotation at firms such as General Motors, Xerox, TRW, and Corning. The authors also highlighted the positive outcomes that accrued to the parties who were able to make the transition successfully.

Kochan and Osterman (1994) in *The Mutual Gains Enterprise* argued that the emerging high performance model should become the standard new paradigm along whose lines organizations ought to be designed and work ought to be organized. Kochan and Osterman (1994) argued that through this model all parties stood to gain – firms to prosper and workers to enjoy better, more satisfying and secure work. Unions, too, would enjoy higher levels of influence in the workplace and face a more secure future under this system. The mutual gains enterprise the authors described was 'win-win'.

From the understanding provided by Piore and Sabel (1984) about why things on the shop floor had to change, the evidence provided by Kochan et al. (1986) that such changes were happening in the US and arguments from Kochan and Osterman (1994) for the positive outcomes to accrue to the parties as a result, research began in earnest to learn more about the phenomenon. In particular, researchers were eager to move beyond single case studies, to compile more convincing statistical evidence that such changes in work organization and human resource practices could make such a difference to performance outcomes. For the most part, this early statistically oriented work was highly concentrated in heavy manufacturing: autos and steel primarily. In part this was driven by the fact that both industries found themselves in competitive crises during the 1980s and 1990s, putting great pressure on these industries to restructure and to reorganize. As well, both were highly unionized industries making these workplaces attractive to industrial relations researchers. Finally, and not inconsequentially, both industries had inputs and outcomes that were easily measured.

The work from MIT's International Motor Vehicle Program (IMVP) led to the publication of *The Machine that Changed the World* (Womack et al., 1990), the work in which the contours of lean production were described and the mechanisms by which they served to increase productivity and quality (and thereby overall competitiveness) in the automotive industry were laid out. MacDuffie and Krafcik (1992) began to spell out the human resource practices side of the equation by specifying how human resources had to be used in conjunction with technology to enable high performance manufacturing. MacDuffie (1995) developed the human resource side of the high performance manufacturing paradigm even further in his later work in the automotive industry. Using survey evidence drawn from 62 IMVP-affiliated assembly plants around the world,

MacDuffie (1995) argued that particular human resource practices in isolation did not lead to better performance. Rather, only by 'bundling' groups of mutually reinforcing and complementary practices together did manufacturers see the benefits to outcomes. The notion of 'bundling' becomes a mainstay of the high performance work systems literature.

Ichniowski et al.'s (1997)[2] evidence on productivity in steel finishing lines solidified the 'bundling' argument. Their work, using a sample of 36 homogeneous steel finishing lines, found that lines employing a bundle of innovative human resource practices (such as incentive pay, teams, broadly defined and flexible job assignments, high levels of training, and job security) had substantially higher levels of productivity than did lines employing more traditional practices (such as narrowly defined jobs, strict work rules, close supervision, and hourly pay) (Ichniowski et al., 1997).

Arthur (1992) found similar results in the mini-mill sector of the US steel industry. Arthur (1992) linked mini-mill strategy to human resource strategy and found that those mills which adopted a flexible manufacturing strategy combined with human resource practices that encouraged decentralized decision making by shopfloor workers, employee participation in problem solving initiatives, and that provided general training outperformed their more traditional Taylorist, mass production oriented counterparts.

Huselid (1995), with careful econometric analysis, provided compelling evidence from a sample of 1000 US firms that managing workers with high performance human resource practices including comprehensive recruitment and selection procedures, contingent compensation, and extensive employee involvement and training positively impacted firm performance as measured by corporate financial performance, employee turnover, and productivity. Moreover, the effect size he found was substantial: a one-standard deviation increase in his index of high performance HR practices was associated with US$27,044 more in sales/employee, US$18,641 more in market value/employee, and US$3,814 more in profit/employee. This survey-based research examined firms of all sizes in a wide range of industries, helping to broaden the high performance work system literature beyond autos and steel and manufacturing in general.

Huselid's (1995) work capped off much of the early anecdotal and case-based evidence that high performance models of work organization and supporting HR practices had a real and significant impact on firm performance. So, if these models were so clearly superior, how widespread was the adoption of these practices in the broader US economy? Osterman (1994) sought to answer this question, using data from 694 US manufacturing establishments he surveyed in 1992. Focusing on what he termed the 'core workforce' – employees doing the main work of producing the firm's good or service – Osterman (1994) examined the incidence of the adoption of teams, job rotation, quality circles, and total quality management as well as the human resource practices supporting these new work models.

Osterman (1994) found surprisingly widespread adoption of these practices at a superficial level – if a given practice was adopted by any core employees. Over half of the survey respondents reported the use of teams and roughly one third reported using Total Quality Management (TQM) techniques (Osterman, 1994). However, requiring at least half of all core workers to be engaged in the practice before it was counted dropped the adoption rate by 15 percentage points (Osterman, 1994). What is also notable from Osterman's work is that the practices were not being adopted in bundles. Rather, employers appeared to be adopting single practices. Only 16 per cent of establishments surveyed reported having one HR practice in each of the four major HR areas (flexible job design, contingent pay, training, and employment security) (Ichniowski et al., 1996).

Osterman repeated his survey in 1997 and found that the practices continued to diffuse over the five-year interval (Osterman, 2000). In 1992, 24.6 per cent of establishments had

two or more practices at the 50 per cent level of penetration. In 1997, the figure had increased to 38.3 per cent. In this paper Osterman also investigated whether or not high performance work practices were able to deliver 'mutual gains' to both labor and management. He found that establishments that had adopted high performance practices in 1992 had a higher probability of layoffs in subsequent years and experienced no gain in real wages over that period (Osterman, 2000). Thus, no real evidence emerged of mutual gains.

DEVELOPMENTS IN THE STREAM

Much of the early work in the high performance work systems literature focused on outcomes for employers in terms of improved productivity, quality, and lower costs. Eventually interest emerged as to what these new models of work organization looked like for workers, how unions effected their efficacy, and their generalizability outside of manufacturing.

The impact on workers

An early and comprehensive review of the high performance work systems and workplace transformation literature by Appelbaum and Batt (1994) argued that two distinct models of transformed workplaces were emerging in the US. One form, American Lean Production, focused on quality and customer service and the re-engineering of work processes to ensure deliverables. The other model was American Team Production, characterized by the use of self-directed work teams, total quality management techniques, pay for performance, and labor-management partnership (Appelbaum and Batt, 1994). Best practice cases of lean production tended to be found in non-union settings, while best practice cases of team production appeared in unionized workplaces.

Performance effects of the two systems appeared, from the empirical evidence, to be comparable. Outcomes for workers, however, appeared to be different. Work organized around team forms of work organization provides more opportunities for employees to exercise discretion on the job and involves all workers in such activities. In contrast, under the lean production model, only a select number of chosen workers left the production floor to participate in off-line problem solving. Often, conflict emerged between those who left and those who were left behind to 'do the work' (Appelbaum and Batt, 1994).

Appelbaum et al. (2000), in their study of new models of work organization in steel, apparel, and medical electronic and imaging instruments, investigated five outcomes of interest to workers: trust in their employer, the intrinsic reward afforded by their work, organizational commitment, job satisfaction, and work-related stress. In all three industries, the authors found generally that high performance models of work organization enhanced levels of worker trust of their employer, the intrinsic reward they received from their jobs, organizational commitment, job satisfaction, and lowered levels of work-related stress (Appelbaum et al., 2000). Using data from the same study, Bailey et al. (2001) found high performance work practices to be positively associated with higher worker wages in the steel and apparel industries. In medical electronics and imaging, the positive association disappeared when a control for education was added suggesting that there is a strong link between formal education and high performance work systems in that industry (Baily et al., 2001).

Batt (2004) found that workers organized into self-managed teams in a large unionized telecommunications company reported significantly higher levels of perceived discretion, employment security, and satisfaction on the job. In contrast, participation in off-line problem solving teams had no statistically significant effect on outcomes for workers in this study (Batt, 2004). Quit rates are another indicator of worker satisfaction on the job. Batt (2002) found quit rates were lower for call centre workers in workplaces that emphasized high skills, organized workers into teams, and enabled workers to participate in workplace-related decisions.

Hodson (1996) assessed new models of work organization in terms of their effect on worker dignity. Participative forms of work organization, such as those found under high performance work systems, found workers working harder, but provided with greater dignity on the job. Workers experienced greater pride and job satisfaction, things that were diminished under earlier forms of work organization that were monitored through direct supervision, or paced by assembly-line technology, or governed by bureaucratic forms of organization (Hodson, 1996). However, the earliest model of work organization, that of craft production, still provided the highest levels of dignity at work in Hodson's (1996) assessment.

Generally, the evidence on the impact of high performance work practices on workers appears fairly positive – as long as the worker retains his or her job. Black et al. (2004) found that the implementation of high performance workplace practices, in particular the use of teams, was associated with greater reductions in employment. In contrast, the implementation of job rotation practices were associated with lower employment reductions. Of course the job losses may have been even larger if work organization had not been transformed; the counterfactual is not known.

The effects of unions

What about the effects that unions have on the implementation of high performance work systems? Early research in this stream indicated that most innovations occurred in non-union settings (Kochan et al., 1986). Later work determined that, in fact, work innovations were taking place equally across both union and non-union sectors (Eaton and Voos, 1994).

Much of the initial literature was interested in whether unions could be considered a barrier to successful implementation or whether they were supportive and useful in creating sustainable workplace changes. On the one hand, some argued that only with the discipline forced upon management by a union would a firm be able to satisfactorily implement the changes in work organization and supporting human resource practices that a high performance work system demanded (Kochan et al., 1986; Eaton and Voos, 1994). Eaton and Voos (1994) pointed out that unions helped support new forms of work organization because they are able to protect workers from job loss due to any resulting productivity improvements or from management reprisal; unions are able to provide workers with voice so their concerns are also addressed in any workplace undertakings so that outcomes are likely to be better balanced; and unions are able to extend the reach of high performance work system to a strategic level enabling the union voice to be heard at levels well beyond the shop floor.

On the other hand, others argued that union resistance to the proposed changes of a high performance work system would render the process impracticable. Either through blocking the changes outright, or by ignoring the program and waiting for it to die due to lack of uptake, unions were viewed as antithetical to the successful implementation of a high performance work system. Others still have taken a more nuanced view arguing that it depended on the union and its relationship with management whether the presence of a union would facilitate or inhibit the adoption of a high performance work system (Eaton and Voos, 1989; Frost, 2000).

Eaton and Voos (1989) identified a number of union responses to the implementation of high performance work practices: block and destroy; let the program proceed but not be involved with it; protective involvement meaning that the union seeks to maintain existing collective bargaining institutions without having the new work system impinge upon this area of the labor-management relationship; and finally, use the joint work around the implementation of the new work system to advance the interests of workers and the union. Similarly, Frost (2001) moved beyond the militant/co-operative dichotomy in describing union positions *vis a vis* the move to a high performance work system to conceptualize and describe three distinct union responses: apathetic, reactive, and

proactive. Only in the latter case did mutually beneficial outcomes emerge for the parties.

The empirical evidence is somewhat mixed. Osterman (1997) found no association between the adoption of high performance work practices and the presence of unions. In contrast, work by Bacon and Blyton (2000) in the UK found that managers were less likely to introduce team forms of work organization where trade unions were present. And, in contrast to the 'mutual gains' perspective (Kochan and Osterman, 1994), Bacon and Blyton (2000) reported that more conflict with unions appeared in the unionized enterprises where team forms of work organization had been introduced.

McNabb and Whitfield (1997), using data from the 3rd Workplace Industrial Relations Survey and the Employer Manpower Skills Practices Survey in the UK, reported variation even among unionized facilities. They found that the presence of a closed shop hindered the adoption of flexible work practices, but the presence of a union that management recognized (but that did not have a closed shop) facilitated the introduction of high performance practices (McNabb and Whitfield, 1997). Moreover, Cooke (1994) found from a survey of 841 manufacturing firms in Michigan that the performance benefits of high performance work systems in unionized plants were higher than those found in non-union firms.

Generalizability to industries outside of manufacturing

A great deal of the initial work in the high performance work system literature was conducted in manufacturing – in auto, in steel, and in manufacturing generally. The contours of what comprised a high performance work system emerged largely from these initial empirical investigations. The components that eventually came to be agreed upon were some form of job expansion (enlargement, enrichment, and often job rotation), skill enhancement (multi-skilling and skill upgrading), worker participation in workplace decision-making, the use of self-organized teams, and off-line problem solving of production-related problems (Wells, 1998). The set of supporting human resource practices consisted of pay for performance, some form of employment security, rigorous selection criteria, improved communication between labor and management, and a means of consultation between labor and management over workplace issues.

A great deal of evidence was amassed describing systems such as the ideal type described above in a range of manufacturing settings. But what about beyond that? Were there forms of high performance work systems in services, or in low-skilled occupations, or in the public sector? If so, what did they look like?

Batt (1999) was an early investigator of the high performance model outside of manufacturing, investigating the model and its effects in telecommunications services. She investigated the effects of total quality management and team forms of work organization for sales and customer service agents and found that team forms of work organization improved both reported service quality as well as increased sales per employee. TQM, in contrast, had no effect on performance (Batt, 1999). Worker participation in off-line problem solving groups and self-directed work teams also lowered quit rates in her sample of call centre workers (Batt et al., 2002).

Hutchinson et al. (2000) studied the implementation of a high performance work system in a UK call centre. They, too, found that the implementation lowered quit rates and absenteeism, while producing higher quality customer service, greater customer retention, and lower costs. The high performance work system in this instance involved the move to 10–15 member teams, a new pay-for-performance system, more sophisticated recruiting and selection procedures, an increase in training expenditures, and worker involvement in quality improvements at the workplace.

Hunter and Lafkas (2003) studied work practices and their effects on wages and the use of technology in the US banking industry. The use of high performance models of work organization (specifically the use of off-line

problem solving groups) in conjunction with IT that supported sales efforts was associated with higher wage levels for customer service representatives in bank branches. In contrast, where IT was used to automate processes and there were no high involvement work practices, wages of customer service representatives were lower.

In all three examples cited above, the workers possessed fairly high levels of skill and in both the telecommunications examples, the workforces were unionized. In contrast, Berg and Frost (2005) look for the existence of a high performance model in low skill services by exploring changes in work organization made to the jobs of food service workers, housekeepers, and nursing assistants in US hospitals. These workers are at or near the bottom of the US wage distribution. Turnover rates for these workers approach 100 per cent in some hospitals. The work they do is perceived to be low skilled and they are deemed to be virtually disposable.

In the late 1990s, on the recommendation of consultants, several hospitals adopted a Patient Care Associate (PCA) form of work organization that combined the nursing assistant, food service, and housekeeping roles. These PCAs were multi-skilled, worked as part of the patient care team, were afforded small wage increases, and were asked to participate in unit meetings and problem solving teams in their work areas.

For the most part, these experiments were a failure. Patients did not like the multi-skilled nature of the job (the person cleaning the toilet was the same person delivering lunch); nurses had little time to appropriately supervise the cleaning aspect of the PCA role, and the PCAs themselves often did not have the requisite level of social skills to interact with the patients and rest of the nursing team in ways that added value. Moreover, workers in these broadened jobs reported more job-related stress and lower levels of job satisfaction – in contrast to much of the earlier high performance work system research in which workers reported better outcomes being associated with the enhanced jobs (c.f. Appelbaum et al., 2000).

Instead, the more successful model in this setting appeared to be much more traditional: narrowly defined functional jobs in which the incumbent was adequately trained, in which pay was provided at a living wage level, and in which workers were provided enough resources (supplies, help, and time) to complete their work competently (Berg and Frost, 2005).

Once outside of manufacturing, the high performance work systems literature becomes more mixed in its assessment of how 'good' high performance models of work organization are – both for firms and for workers. Although from much of the earliest manufacturing-based research, it appeared that the adoption of high performance models of work organization and the necessary supporting HR practices were a singularly good way for firms (and unions where present) to assure their success in the now more competitive landscape, once researchers looked beyond manufacturing, the vision became much less clear. Not only was it less clear what the high performance model looked like outside manufacturing, but it was also less clear that the model was indeed good for workers.

THE CRITIQUES EMERGE

Critiques of the high performance work systems literature first emerged from studies conducted in the automotive industry studying the implementation of the lean production system and charting workers' experiences under it. Research of this kind took place in both union and non-union settings. In union settings, much of the initial concern was in regard to the effects of the new work system on the union as an effective institution for representing workers' interests – both narrowly in the workplace and more broadly in society as a whole.

Early fears in the American labor movement saw many unions refusing to participate in the negotiation and implementation of the high performance workplace. There is a long history of distrust in the US, in particular, about such employee-focused activities as quality circles and self-managed teams being used by management as a union substitute and the means by which to develop a company union. Very often, the move to implement a high performance work system in a unionized environment was seen as the first step in eradicating the union. First, the union would be marginalized in the workplace as management dealt directly with workers, bypassing the union to negotiate new terms and conditions of employment. Second, workers would soon adopt the same inward focus on outcomes of primary concern to management such as profit and productivity. Thus, union solidarity across workplaces would be left in ruins as workers and workplaces would be pitted one against another in a race for the bottom. (Parker and Slaughter, 1988). Empirically, Pulignano (2002) drew on evidence from the British and Italian auto industries, to argue that new high performance forms of work organization and the accompanying management strategies to support them, led to the marginalization of the union and its influence in the workplace.

The high performance workplace was also implemented in a number of non-union settings – in particular in the automotive industry in the Japanese transplants. These studies highlighted the potential downsides to workers from the implementation of the system. Graham (1995) wrote of her experiences as a participant observer employed as an Associate at Subaru-Isuzu, a non-union Japanese transplant built in Lafayette, Indiana. While there she documented her experiences and those of her co-workers under lean production and Japanese management. In particular, she sought to address the debate concerning the nature of lean production. Was it, on the one hand, a factory utopia in which the Japanese model will create a harmonious system of collaboration between management and workers in which workers willingly expand their responsibilities and increase their work loads by rotating jobs and revealing their hidden knowledge about work processes; in exchange for their collaboration they get job security and more challenging work (Graham, 1995: 131). Or, on the other hand, as labor process theorists claimed, was it nothing more than an extension of Fordism (Dohse et al., 1985)?

Graham (1985) found that the Subaru-Isuzu experience was something else. It certainly was not a factory utopia. Graham (1985) documented numerous repetitive strain injuries, constant peer pressure to keep up and to continue to work injured, the insecurity maintained through the use of a significant number of temporary workers, and the bitter reality associated with input to workplace decisions and process improvements (it was non-existent).

At Subaru-Isuzu there was no union to represent workers or to bargain with management over the implementation of the system. Perhaps the negative aspects of lean production in that case could be attributed to Subaru-Isuzu's non-union status. Research examining lean production in a unionized setting could assess whether this was the case. Work by Rinehart et al. (1997) carefully documented the experiences of workers at CAMI, the Suzuki-GM joint venture located in Ingersoll, Ontario and organized by the Canadian Auto Workers union (CAW).

The research team conducted one-week visits to the plant every six months for nearly two years (early 1990 through late 1991). In addition, they conducted surveys of workers about their experiences at four specific points in time. They also observed work throughout the plant and interviewed managers, union leaders, team leaders, and skilled trades representatives. On the basis of their data, the research team concluded, as Graham (1995) had, that lean production was not a transcendence of Fordist mass production. Rather than a committed workforce and harmonious labor-management relations, the researchers found a low and declining level of worker commitment over the two-year time frame and mounting work irritations that culminated in a five-week strike in 1992 (Rinehart et al., 1997). The authors found no evidence that worker knowledge under lean production was any greater than under mass production, that there was

any reunification of mental and manual labor, or that multi-tasking required any more skill than did work in a traditional plant (most jobs still were quickly learned and remained mind-numbingly repetitive). Work in a lean production plant was arduous and intense given the lean staffing ratios and an insatiable demand for overtime.

Both Graham (1995) and the CAMI research team (Rinehart et al., 1997) noted the important role played by teams in a lean production plant. But, both noted that teams were not needed for technical reasons; their role lay in their social function. Barker (1999) described and documented this phenomenon in great detail. Barker (1999) studied the implementation of teams in a non-union manufacturing plant. His work described the increasingly coercive nature of peer monitoring and control exerted by team members on one another. Barker documented how workers in self-managed teams developed a set of normative, value-based rules that controlled members' behavior more closely and completely than did the former bureaucratic control system.

Concertive control did not free the workers from the iron cage of rational control. Instead, the concertive system, as it became manifest in this case, appeared to draw the iron cage tighter and to constrain the organization's members more powerfully. (Barker, 1993: 408).

Lean production is also seen as a means of work intensification. Fairris (2002) linked transformed workplaces to worsened levels of health and safety, increased labor effort, and greater worker stress. He argued that the productivity improvements attributed to many high performance work systems are in fact due to the worsened conditions to which workers find themselves exposed (Fairris, 2002). In other writing, Fairris and Tohyama (2002) argued that the lean production model in Japan is mediated by important institutional measures that are missing when the system is imported to North America. As a result, lean production becomes 'mean' in the North American context, improving productivity and quality only through increased worker stress, additional effort, and reduced health and safety.

Work intensification is also associated with high performance models of work organization outside North America. In the UK, Green (2004), using establishment level data, argued that technological and organizational changes have been important sources of work intensification in Britain in the 1990. Green (2004) cited the use of high performance models of work organization, in particular, as stimulating work intensification. Bryson et al. (2005) used British data describing work organization, trade union representation, and financial performance. The authors found that high performance models of work organization had a positive effect on labor productivity, but only in unionized work-places. In these workplaces, however, the gains appeared to come from accompanying concessionary bargaining, rather than any 'mutual gains'.

Danford et al. (2004) used case study evidence from the aerospace industry in the United Kingdom to argue that high performance models of work organization and labor-management partnership failed to increase worker empowerment and participation. Rather, they found evidence of weakening workplace democracy and a deteriorating quality of work life in this setting.

Other scholars critical of the high performance work system model and its efficacy have highlighted a number of reasons why it has failed to deliver its promised outcomes in many cases. Godard (2001) argued that it is not incomplete implementation or flawed implementation (by not having all the appropriate supporting HR practices in place) that causes the variable success rates noted for high performance models of work organization. Rather, he argued using data from 78 Canadian workplaces, that pre-existing HR conditions and workplace context variables are associated with success. Similarly, Vallas (2003) found that implementation is difficult because management is often not willing to provide the very flexibility being demanded of workers in contexts where

high performance work systems are being implemented.

Another branch of research in the high performance work systems stream has explored the robustness and longevity of these new forms of work organization and labor-management relations. The levels of trust and co-operation needed to sustain these programs are significant and make these programs extremely fragile to maintain. There is considerable evidence that even the most successful programs eventually fail.

Early work indicated that this was indeed the case. Lawler and Mohrman (1985) noted that an early workplace innovation, quality circles, almost always, after implementation and some early successes, eventually declined and disappeared. Preuss and Frost (2003) charted the rise and decline over almost two decades of labor-management cooperation and workplace restructuring in health care in Minneapolis/St. Paul. The authors noted the inability of cooperative structures to adapt to new issues and challenges over time and the eventuality of conflict overwhelming the cooperation needed to sustain the joint initiatives (Preuss and Frost, 2003). Even the highly touted model of co-management at Saturn, has shown cracks in its shiny exterior. In 1999, the original leadership of the local union (that had supported and implemented the partnership model) was voted out by a two-to-one margin and replaced by a more traditional group of union leaders seeking to provide union members with more conventional union protections around scheduling, workload, and guaranteed (rather than partially contingent) pay (Hopp, 2000).

Despite this evidence from unionized settings, Voos and Eaton (1994) argue that union supported programs may in fact be more durable as the union's presence ensures workers' as well as managements' interests are taken into account and that changes in work systems are made without detriment to workers. The prognosis for the longevity of high performance work organization models in non-union settings would appear even more dismal.

DISCUSSION AND CONCLUSION

In contrast to what some critics have claimed, that the focus on high performance work system models in the field of industrial relations has been misplaced (Godard and Delaney, 2000), I believe that the high performance literature has been a very valuable area of focus in the field. The work, by and large, has displayed a continued interest in employers, in workers, their unions (where they exist), and many authors have addressed issues of policy concern – either policy barriers or recommendations for policy changes that would facilitate the transition to a high performance workplace.

The past nearly two decades worth of work in the high performance work system stream of research has produced a wealth of knowledge for both industrial relations researchers and for practitioners. This has been, and continues to be, a rich stream. Substantively, we can conclude a number of things.

First, new ways of organizing work in many cases do have positive performance effects for companies and beneficial effects for workers. Team forms of work organization and the opportunity to participate in workplace decision making and problem solving provide several benefits. Giving those closest to the work and who understand it best the authority to decide how that work gets done and how work-related problems should be resolved makes logical sense. In addition, granting additional authority, discretion, and providing outlets for the use of creativity and problem solving skills on the job often increases the intrinsic reward associated with people's work. Often, too, the resulting broadened and upskilled jobs are better paid, contributing as well to increased levels of extrinsic rewards.

Second, successful transformation appears to result from aligning the organization's structure and supporting HR practices with the new model of work organization. Adopting bundles of appropriately supportive HR practices appears central to successful implementation and sustainability of high performance work practices. The HR practices that appear especially important include employment security, extensive investments in training, relatively high pay contingent on performance, sharing of financial and performance information, and selective recruitment and selection of personnel into the new work system (Pfeffer, 1998).

Third, we also now know that this model is not generalizable across all work settings. It seems especially suited to manufacturing and to skilled, relatively well-paid service occupations. However, in conditions where pay is low (and is constrained to be low) the high performance model appears to have little success. Turnover in these situations is generally high, making the established work groups that are needed for productive team behaviors and for off-line problem solving exchanges to take place, difficult to maintain. Neither are workers in these workplaces persuaded to provide high levels of commitment to the employer – not the levels of commitment certainly that engagement in problem solving and to getting the job done right the first time would require.

Finally, we also now know that certain institutional contexts are more favorable for the development and sustainability of such models of work organization. Japan is the origin of many of these practices and its institutional landscape – which includes lifetime employment, enterprise unions, and a long-term investment focus – appears ideal to support these high performance models. Appelbaum and Batt (1994) and Kochan and Osterman (1994) all argue that critical changes in the American policy landscape are necessary to support and diffuse the implementation of high performance models of work organization throughout the American economy. Kochan and Osterman (1994) focus their critique on current American labor law in which employee committees that discuss workplace-related policies and issues with the employer are deemed illegal – a contravention of section 8(a)2 of the *National Labor Relations Act*. Appelbaum and Batt (1994) point to the need for publicly delivered worker training, institutional forms for employee and union participation in firm and workplace decision making, a decrease in the primacy of shareholders compared to other firm stakeholders, the construction of interfirm collaboration and cooperation, and institutional mechanisms by which the low wage path can be ruled out.

Similarly, much of the literature critical of the high performance workplace stream has also added considerable value to and has strengthened the industrial relations literature as a whole. It has brought with it a reminder to not be solely focused only on performance outcomes of consequence to firms. Later research in the high performance work systems stream examined in detail what high performance models of work organization meant for workers and for unions. Researchers interested in these questions explored the benefits, the downsides, and the conditions under which each occurred for both workers and unions. The critical literature also brought with it a healthy dose of cynicism about the 'win-win' nature of high performance models of work organization. It became quite clear that all high performance models of work organization were not universally good for all participants. In many cases, the benefits to employers came at significant costs to the work force through increased workloads, additional work-related stress, and more insecure employment.

So where does this leave us? Has this stream of work run its course? Have we learned all that we can and now find ourselves at a point from which we must move on? The answer, I think, is 'Perhaps'. We do know a lot about high performance models of work organization and their effects on various stakeholders. However, there is still much about the world of work that we do not know. The high performance literature has in fact pushed researchers to look past the traditional strongholds of industrial relations research in automobiles, steel, and other heavily unionized manufacturing industries to study non-manufacturing work – in services and the public sector and increasingly in non-union settings as well. As a greater portion of the workforce finds itself employed in settings such as these, such research is of considerable value. Studies in call centres in health care, in education, and in new media and the arts are all growing and are emerging, I would argue, in response to the growing desire to know 'what works at work' in a broad range of workplaces. This work has grown directly out of the high performance work systems stream. Although the research questions are evolving and the settings are changing, we owe much to the legacy of this very vibrant and important stream of research in the field of industrial relations.

NOTES

1 'What Works at Work' is the title of the lead paper in a 1996 special issue of *Industrial Relations* devoted to high performance work systems research and an assessment of what had been learned from the stream to date.

2 Although this piece is cited here as 1997 (when it appears in AER), this same work is often cited with dates ranging from 1993 to 1995 as it passed through various stages as a working paper. Its being so often cited in these earlier forms speaks to the paper's inherent value being so quickly perceived by those working in the field at the time.

REFERENCES

Appelbaum, E. and R. Batt. (1994) *The New American Workplace*. Ithaca, NY: Cornell University Press.

Appelbaum, E., Bailey, T., Berg, P. and Kalleberg, A. (2000) *Manufacturing Advantage: Why High Performance Work Systems Pay Off*. Ithaca, NY: ILR Press.

Arthur, J. (1992) 'The link between business strategy and industrial relations systems in American steel mini-mills', *Industrial and Labor Relations Review*, 45 (3): 488–507.

Bacon, N. and Blyton, P. (2000) 'Industrial relations and the diffusion of teamworking: Survey evidence from the UK steel industry', *International Journal of Operations and Production Management*, 20 (8): 911–31.

Bailey, T., Berg, P. and Sandy, C. (2001) 'The effect of high performance work practices on employee earnings in the steel, apparel, and medical electronics and imaging industries', *Industrial and Labor Relations Review*, 54 (2): 525–43.

Barker, J. (1993) 'Tightening the iron cage: Concertive control in self-managing teams', *Administrative Science Quarterly*, 38 (3): 408–38.

Barker, J. (1999) *The Discipline of Teamwork: Participation and Concertive Control*. Thousand Oaks, CA: Sage Publications.

Batt, R. (1999) 'Work organization, technology, and performance in customer service and sales', *Industrial and Labor Relations Review*, 52 (4): 539–65.

Batt, R. (2002) 'Managing customer services: Human resource practices, quit rates, and sales growth', *Academy of Management Journal*, 45 (3): 587–98.

Batt, R. (2004) 'Who benefits from teams? Comparing workers, Supervisors, and managers', *Industrial Relations*, 43 (1): 183–212.

Batt, R., Colvin, A. and Keefe, J. (2002) 'Employee voice, human resource practices, and quit rates: Evidence from the telecommunications industry', *Industrial and Labor Relations Review*, 55 (4): 573–94.

Berg, P. and Frost, A. (2005) 'Dignity at work for low wage, low skill service workers', *Relations Industrielles*, 60 (4): 657–83.

Black, S., Lynch, L. and Krivelyova, A. (2004) 'How workers fare when employers innovate', *Industrial Relations*, 43 (1): 44–67.

Bryson, A., Forth, J. and Kirby, S. (2005) 'High involvement management practices, trade union representation and workplace performance in Britain', *Scottish Journal of Political Economy*, 52 (3): 451–91.

Cooke, W. (1994) 'Employee participation programs, group-based incentives, and company performance: A union-nonunion comparison', *Industrial and Labor Relations Review*, 47 (4): 594–610.

Danford, A., Richardson, M., Stewart, P., Tailby, S. and Upchurch, M. (2004) 'High performance work systems and workplace partnership: A case study of aerospace workers', *New Technology, Work, and Employment*, 19 (1): 14–29.

Dohse, K., Jurgens, U. and Malsch, T. (1985) 'From 'Fordism' to 'Toyotaism'? The social organization of the labor process in the Japanese automobile industry', *Politics and Society*, 14 (2): 115–46.

Eaton, A. and Voos, P. (1989) 'The ability of unions to adapt to innovative workplace arrangements', *The American Economic Review*, 79 (2): 172–77.

Eaton, A. and Voos, P. (1994) 'The survival of employee participation programs in unionized settings', *Industrial and Labor Relations Review*, 47 (3): 371–90.

Fairris, D. (2002) 'Are transformed workplaces more productively efficient?', *Journal of Economic Issues*, 36 (3): 659–71.

Fairris, S. and Tohyama, H. (2002) 'Productive efficiency and the lean production system in Japan and the United States', *Economic and Industrial Democracy*, 23 (4): 529–55.

Frost, A. (2000) 'Explaining variation in workplace restructuring: The role of local union capabilities', *Industrial and Labor Relations Review*, 53 (4): 559–79.

Frost, A. (2001) 'Reconceptualizing local union responses to workplace restructuring in North America', *British Journal of Industrial Relations*, 39 (4): 539–64.

Godard, J. (2001) 'Beyond the high-performance paradigm? An analysis of variation in Canadian managerial perceptions of reform programme effectiveness', *British Journal of Industrial Relations*, 39 (1): 25–52.

Godard, J. and Delaney, J. (2000) 'Reflections on the 'high performance' paradigm's implications for industrial relations as a field', *Industrial and Labor Relations Review*, 53 (3): 482–501.

Graham, L. (1995) *On the Line at Subaru-Isuzu: The Japanese Model and the American Worker*. Ithaca, NY: ILR Press.

Green, F. (2004) 'Why has work effort become more intense?', *Industrial Relations*, 43 (4): 709–42.

Hodson, R. (1996) 'Dignity in the workplace under participative management: Alienation and freedom revisited', *American Sociological Review*, 61 (5): 719–39.

Hopp, T. (2000) 'Saturn workers get standard GM-UAW contract', *Labor Notes* (online), Feb. http://www.labornotes.org/archives/2000/0200/0200.html#story (accessed August 2, 2006.)

Hunter, L. and Lafkas, J. (2003) 'Opening the box: Information technology, work practices, and wages', *Industrial and Labor Relations Review*, 56 (2): 224–43.

Huselid, M. (1995) 'The impact of human resource management practices on turnover, productivity, and corporate financial performance', *Academy of Management Journal*, 38 (3): 535–70.

Hutchinson, S., Purcell, J. and Kinnie, N. (2000) 'Evolving high commitment management and the experience of the RAC call centre', *Human Resource Management Journal*, 10 (1): 63–79.

Ichniowski, C., Kochan, T., Levine, D., Olson, C. and Strauss, G. (1996) 'What works at work: Overview and assessment', *Industrial Relations*, 35 (3): 299–334.

Ichniowski, C., Shaw, K. and Prennushi, G. (1997) 'The effects of human resource management practices on productivity: A study of steel finishing lines', *American Economic Review*, 87 (3): 291–313.

Kochan, T., Katz, H. and McKersie, R. (1986) *The Transformation of American Industrial Relations*. New York, NY: Basic Books.

Kochan, T. and Osterman, P. (1994) *The Mutual Gains Enterprise.* Boston, MA: Harvard Business School Press.

Lawler III, E. and Mohrman, S. (1985) 'Quality circles after the fad', *Harvard Business Review*, 63 (1): 65–71.

MacDuffie, J.P. (1995) 'Human resource bundles and manufacturing performance: Organizational logic and flexible production systems in the world auto industry', *Industrial and Labor Relations Review*, 48 (2): 197–221.

MacDuffie, J.P. and Krafcik, J. (1992) 'Interacting technology and human resources for high performance manufacturing: Evidence from the international auto industry', in T. Kochan and M. Useem (eds), *Transforming Organizations.* New York: Oxford University Press.

McNabb, R. and Whitfield, K. (1997) 'Unions, flexibility, team working, and financial performance', *Organization Studies*, 18 (5): 821–39.

Osterman, P. (1994) 'How common is workplace transformation and who adopts it?', *Industrial and Labor Relations Review*, 47 (2): 173–88.

Osterman, P. (2000) 'Work reorganization in an era of restructuring: Trends in diffusion and effects on employee welfare', *Industrial and Labor Relations Review*, 53 (2): 179–97.

Parker, M. and Slaughter, J. (1988) *Choosing Sides: Unions and the Team Concept.* Boston, MA: South End Press.

Pfeffer, J. (1998) *The Human Equation.* Boston, MA: Harvard Business School Press.

Piore, M. and Sabel, C. (1984) *The Second Industrial Divide: Possibilities for Prosperity.* New York, NY: Basic Books.

Preuss, G. and Frost, A. (2003) 'The rise and decline of labor-management cooperation: Lessons from health care in the Twin Cities', *California Management Review*, 45 (2): 85–106.

Pulignano, V. (2002) 'Restructuring of work and union representation: A developing framework for workplace industrial relations in Britain and Italy', *Capital and Class*, 76 (Spring): 29–66.

Rinehart, J., Huxley, C. and Robertson, D. (1997) *Just Another Car Factory? Lean Production and its Discontents.* Ithaca, NY: ILR Press.

Vallas, S. (2003) 'Why teamwork fails: Obstacles to workplace change in four manufacturing plants', *American Sociological Review*, 68 (2): 223–50.

Wells, D. (1998) 'Are strong unions compatible with the new model of human resource management?', *Relations Industrielles*, 48 (1): 56–85.

Womack, J., Jones, D. and Roos, D. (1990) *The Machine That Changed the World.* Cambridge, MA: MIT Press.

23

Employee Involvement and Direct Participation

Russell D. Lansbury and Nick Wailes

INTRODUCTION

Employee involvement and direct participation by workers in decisions which affect their working lives have long been a focus of industrial relations (IR) scholarship. In the late 1960s and early 1970s, direct participation was promoted by state agencies in many developed countries as a means to 'humanize' work and reduce industrial conflict (Ramsay, 1977). Since the early 1980s there has been growing attention focused on the economic benefits of direct participation and management has been at the forefront of introducing employee involvement schemes in a number of countries. During the 1980s, for example, there was considerable experimentation with Japanese- style joint consultation in a number of countries (see Bradley and Hill, 1983). During the 1990s arguments that suggested that employee involvement and direct participation were central to creating high performance work systems (HPWS) produced heightened management interest in various forms of employee involvement

(Huselid, 1995; Becker and Gerhart, 1996). As Gill and Krieger (1999: 572) put it this 'rediscovery' of the human factor in work organizations can be seen as a response to the increasing competitive pressures in international product markets. Management increasingly recognized the need to involve employees, to grant them greater work discretion and great commitment in order to render organizations more flexible and productive.

While these arguments suggested that a common pattern of involvement and participation would diffuse across countries, the findings of empirical research show continued and persistent national differences in both the form and incidence of participatory practices. Thus, for example, recent studies estimate that almost 25 per cent of US workers are involved in some form of employee stock ownership plan, whereas less than nine per cent of firms in Europe have employee share ownership schemes (Blasi et al., 2003b; Poutsma and Huijgen, 1999). Moreover, despite efforts by the European Union (EU) to encourage financial participation, there are considerable differences in the extent and nature of financial participation adopted in countries across Europe (see, for example, Poutsma and de Nijs, 2003). In Japan, employee share ownership plans (ESOPs) are widespread but differ in character from those in the US and profit-sharing programs are more common (Kato and Morishima, 2003). Similarly there are considerable national differences in patterns of direct participation. In reviewing the findings of the 1996 European Participation in Organizational Change (EPOC) survey, Gill and Krieger (1999: 577–579) noted that while the incidence of direct participation in Europe was high, with 82 per cent of respondents to the survey reporting that they practiced at least one form of direct participation, there were significant differences between countries in both the forms of direct participation adopted and the involvement of employee representatives in their introduction (see also, Poutsma and Huijgen, 1999). Research in the US suggests that while some of the participative practices associated with HPWS diffused widely during the 1990s, the number of US organizations that have adopted a coherent bundle of participatory HR practices remains relatively limited (Osterman, 2000; Godard, 2004).

This chapter examines the contribution of a varieties of capitalism (VoC) approach to explaining divergent national patterns of involvement and participation despite seemingly common international pressures. The VoC approach argues that the practices adopted by organizations are influenced by the national institutional matrix within which they operate (see Hall and Soskice, 2001 and Hamann and Kelly, this volume). One of the implications of this argument is that some forms of participation and involvement will be more widely adopted and sustainable in some countries and less prevalent, or more difficult to sustain, in other countries where the institutional context is less favorable. In particular, it can be argued that the institutional matrix associated with liberal market economies (LMEs) is consistent with extensive financial participation and limited direct participation, whereas forms of direct and indirect participation linked to production systems are likely to more sustainable in co-ordinated market economies (CMEs). The VoC approach may also help explain why there appears to be much greater levels of experimentation with different forms of involvement and participation in LMEs than in CMEs.

The chapter is structured as follows. The next section briefly examines some of the different forms of employee involvement and direct participation and reviews theoretical explanations of involvement and participation. The third section outlines the VoC approach and its implications for understanding differences in national patterns of participation. Section four provides a historical overview of involvement and participation practices in the US and Australia which are two examples of LMEs. Section five examines involvement and participation in CMEs, focusing on Germany and Japan. The final section returns to current debates about employee involvement and HPWS and argues that, when viewed from a VoC perspective, there are reasons to question the sustainability of the participatory practices associated with HPWS especially in LMEs.

DIRECT PARTICIPATION: FORMS AND THEORETICAL FRAMEWORKS

Direct forms of employee involvement and participation are extremely diverse. They include both formal and informal modes of involvement, such as employee profit-sharing schemes and engagement in semi-autonomous work groups within an enterprise. Direct forms of participation are distinguished from indirect (or representative) forms which include employees being elected to works councils and other formal bodies involved in governance at the workplace or enterprise level. While the terms participation and involvement are often used interchangeably in the literature (and in this chapter), as Wall and Lisherson argue (1977), the concept of participation implies that workers share a degree of influence and power over decisions not implied by the concept of involvement. While many of the management-initiated practices which are the focus of the current literature, like employee share ownership, are often described as forms of participation, they appear to lack the degree of power and influence-sharing that this label implies and many would more accurately be described as forms of employee involvement.

It is possible to delineate two broad sets of approaches to historical developments in both direct and indirect forms of participation. The first are sociological and include evolutionary, cyclical and complex multivariate approaches. The second set of explanations are economic in character. Economic arguments underpin much of the contemporary management interest in HPWS. Debates about participation and involvement often turn on two interrelated and recurring issues: first, whether different forms of participation (direct, indirect and financial) reinforce or are antithetical to one another and; second, the extent to which participation or involvement is 'real' or not, in the sense of giving workers control over important aspects of their working lives.

The evolutionary approach to participation is closely linked to the notion of 'industrial democracy' and sees workers' direct and financial participation as a consequence of the spread of the 'democratic current' from political to economic and industrial life (Dachler and Wilpert, 1978). This approach suggests that forces such as a growing role for the state and legislature in industrial relations, advances in technology, the rise of a managerial elite well versed in human resource techniques and the changing values and aspirations of a more educated workforce will contribute to growing levels of participation and democracy. However, as Pateman (1970) argued, much of this thinking has been utopian, with little account being taken of the diverse patterns of power relations that, in practice, constrain the advance of employee involvement. It is particularly difficult for the evolutionary approach to explain the contemporary pattern of significant increases in the amount and variety of management-initiated direct and financial participation taking place in concert with the declining strength of organized labor and state provision of labor market protection.

The cyclical approach, which developed as a critique of evolutionary accounts, represents a second major explanation of patterns of participation and involvement and is closely associated with the work of Harvie Ramsay (1977, 1982, 1983). Ramsay disputed the extent to which participation was genuine and argued that management's interest in different forms of direct and financial participation followed a cyclical pattern: managers introduced participation in periods when labor had the power to challenge managerial prerogative and withdrew their support when labor's power waned or economic pressures increased. While the cyclical thesis countered the naivety of evolutionary accounts, and drew attention to the importance of understanding the historical and social context within which participation takes place, as Harley et al. (2005: 5) have recently argued 'participative practices have evolved in ways that the cycles theory has been unable to predict'.

More recent sociological approaches to participation reflect a more complex multivariate approach which differs from the evolutionary and cyclical positions in that it is based on the isolation of factors that help to explain the rise of employee participation (see, for example, Poole, 1986, 1989; Poutsma et al., 2003; and Strauss, 1986, 1990, 1996). This approach is consistent with traditional industrial relations approaches and with historical interpretations where the analyst focuses on how things come together at particular moments in time. Strauss (1986, 1996), for example, advocates a focus on the particular historical circumstances that have led to variations in participatory forms and an appreciation of the need to incorporate contingency and a role for agency in explaining the nature of participation. The emphasis is, thus, on a broad set of variables (including the power of the actors), on diverse initiating agents (labor and the state, as well as management) and on institutional forces *in addition to* the environment-enterprise linkages of a contingencies approach (see, for example, Poole et al., 2001).

While these multivariate approaches have drawn attention to the broad range of factors which might influence national patterns of participation and involvement, in general they stop short of developing causal hypotheses of the relationships between variables. Without this theoretical development there is a danger that multivariate theories of participation and involvement will become little more than elaborate contingency frameworks and, as a consequence, will provide little insight into contemporary cross national patterns of participation and involvement.

VARIETIES OF CAPITALISM, PARTICIPATION AND INVOLVEMENT

As Harley et al. (2005: 14) note, while issues of agency and contingency are important in explaining patterns of participation, institutional context 'shapes and constrains local contingencies'. This section elaborates on potential causal relationships between institutional context and forms and patterns of participation and involvement using the varieties of capitalism (VoC) framework, which distinguishes national capitalisms on the basis of institutional arrangements. While it is possible to identify a number of theories of capitalist diversity (see Hamann and Kelly, this volume; Crouch, 2005; Godard, 2005), the focus in this chapter is largely on Hall and Soskice's (2001) VoC approach. This is because it is the best known and because it is firm-centric and therefore has the potential to explain the relationship between institutional context and management-initiated participation practices.

Hall and Sosckice (2001: 6–9) argue that firms are faced with a series of co-ordination problems, both internally and externally. They focus on five spheres of co-ordination that firms must address: industrial relations; vocational training and education; corporate governance; inter-firm relations and relations with their own employees. Rejecting the idea that there is one best way to organize capitalism, they argue that there are at least two possible solutions to these co-ordination problems: liberal market economies (LMEs), in which firms rely on markets and hierarchies to resolve co-ordination problems, and co-ordinated market economies (CMEs), in which firms are more likely to use non-market mechanisms to co-ordinate external and internal relationships.

Central to Hall and Soskice's argument, and of particular significance for understanding the implications of this framework for involvement and participation, is the concept of *institutional complementarities*. Hall and Soskice (2001: 18) argue that 'nations with a particular type of co-ordination in one sphere in the economy should tend to develop complementary practices in other spheres as well' (see also Amable, 2003: 54–66). As Gospel and Pendleton (2005) have recently demonstrated, there appear to be close relationships between forms of firm financing and labor management practices. This suggests that patterns of participation and involvement are likely to vary systematically across varieties of capitalism. In LMEs, where there is a heavy reliance on equity markets for firm finance and outsider forms of corporate governance, labor management practices and production systems tend to be market-based and short term in character. Forms of financial participation, which give workers market-based rewards but limit the long-term commitment of the firm to workers, appear to be more consistent with the institutional matrix of LMEs than other forms of participation and involvement, which are predicated on a longer term relationship between workers and the firm. In CMEs, which are characterized by patient capital, insider forms of corporate governance and production strategies based on exploiting firm-specific skills developed over long periods of time, forms of participation which build on long-term commitment and elicit worker contribution to decision making and work design are likely to be more common than those which reduce the relationship to short-run, market exchanges. Thus, if the VOC approach holds, we would expect more evidence of long-term direct participation by workers in decision making in CMEs than is the case for LMEs. To the extent that there is evidence of ongoing employee involvement in LMEs, we expect that it is likely to be concentrated on financial participation, which will be less prevalent in CMEs.

Nonetheless, the VoC approach also implies that there are likely to be higher levels of experimentation with different forms of involvement and participation, both direct and financial, in LMEs than in CMEs. It has been widely argued that in CMEs competitive advantages are likely to arise from the development of firm specific assets associated with the long-term commitment of capital and labor (see Aoki, 2000). The institutional matrix of CMEs produces conditions for diversified quality production systems where the main focus is on incremental improvements to existing products and technologies (Streeck, 1991). Lacking certainty in the long-term financial commitment of investors, and unwilling to provide employees with the commitment necessary to encourage investment in firm specific human capital, the competitiveness of firms in LMEs are less likely to be based on the development of firm specific assets and more likely to be derived from innovation and experimentation (Jurgens, 2003). While the main focus of the literature has been on innovation in products and technologies, this argument can also be extended to management practices, including those associated with involvement and participation. Thus, we expect that LMEs are more likely to be characterized by high levels of experimentation with, and abandonment of, different forms of employee involvement and participation than is the case in CMEs. Research on the adoption of Japanese-style involvement processes by US and UK companies during the 1980s appears to provide empirical support for this proposition. While US and UK managers eagerly adopted participation based on Japanese quality control systems during the 1980s, the results were disappointing and these schemes were rapidly abandoned (see Ackroyd et al., 1988). As Bradley and

Hill (1983: 308) put it, this, in part, reflected the fact that Japanese 'management culture and worker behaviour is based on a different set of rules and institutions'.

This section has argued that patterns of participation and involvement are likely to vary systematically across varieties of capitalism, reflecting the impact of institutional context on the contingencies faced by social actors. The next section tests this argument by providing brief historical overviews of patterns of participation and involvement in two LMEs (the US and Australia) and two CMEs (Japan and Germany).

PARTICIPATION AND INVOLVEMENT IN LIBERAL AND CO-ORDINATED MARKET ECONOMIES

United States

The concept of employee participation in management has been perceived quite differently in the US than in the other countries covered in this chapter. Derber (1980:171) provided one possible explanation when he argued that 'the predominant view [in the US] is that industrial democracy has been widely achieved through the system of collective bargaining. Only a small minority of labor activists call for new routes to industrial democracy [by other means]'. Yet, as collective bargaining coverage has declined in the US, in parallel with shrinking union membership, there has been considerable experimentation with various forms of employee participation of a more direct kind.

The terms high-involvement workplaces and high-performance workplaces have gained currency in the US as descriptions of 'new' and 'innovative' approaches to the organization of work in which there is greater flexibility, co-operation between workers and management and worker participation in the decisions and financial well-being of the firm (Appelbaum and Batt, 1994; Appelbaum et al., 2000; Pil and MacDuffie, 1996). Kochan and Osterman (1994) coined the phrase 'mutual-gains enterprise' to describe organizations that have taken a comprehensive and integrated approach to implementing participatory practices and other activities designed to satisfy the needs of workers and management. Yet, while many US businesses have adopted some forms of innovative work practices aimed at enhancing employee participation, only a small percentage has adopted a full and integrated set of workplace innovations. Some of the reasons advanced to explain this situation include the problems encountered when changing from traditional work systems, resistance from those with a vested interest in retaining the former systems, and lack of a supportive institutional and public-policy environment (Ichniowski et al., 1996: 325–29).

The second category of participative programs concerns job redesign activities that change the nature of work organization and enable workers or groups of workers to exercise greater discretion in the way they conduct their work activities. New United Motor Manufacturing Inc. (NUMMI) is a joint venture between General Motors and Toyota, located at a former GM plant in Fremont, California, that had experienced major problems with productivity, quality and industrial relations. A new work system was devised, in which the UAW participated, that involved new workers being hired to operate in teams, responsible for planning and conducting work as well as engaging in *kaizen* ('continuous improvement') activities. Team leaders were chosen on the basis of recommendations of a joint union-management committee (Kochan and Rubenstein, 2001). Although the work teams could balance work assignments and rotate tasks, the fundamental assembly-line technology of repeated short job cycles was maintained. This caused some observers to describe NUMMI as 'humanized Taylorism' (see Adler and Cole, 1993). Nevertheless, NUMMI was hailed as a more participative and effective work system than the traditional mass-production assembly line (see Adler et al., 1997).

A third area of direct employee participation is through ownership of the means of production, such as stock ownership. Support for employee stock ownership plans (ESOPs) grew in the 1980s, in part because some thought that giving employees stock in a company would increase their sense of ownership and hence their participation in performance improvements. An ESOP is a benefit plan through which employees receive company stock either in trade for various wage and benefit concessions or as an addition to existing compensation. ESOPs cover over 11 million employees. Studies of the impacts of ESOPs yield mixed results, but research to date has not determined whether ESOP firms become more prosperous as a result of employee ownership or whether prosperous firms are more likely to establish ESOPs (for a review of recent research on ESOPs in the US see Blasi et al., 2003a). The empirical evidence suggests, however, that ownership and other forms of direct participation together do more to raise productivity than ownership does by itself. Furthermore, stock ownership alone is unlikely to stimulate worker commitment. Tying ESOP tax subsidies to worker representation, however, could establish this critical link. Meaningful employee participation occurs when appropriate structures are in place to provide the vehicle for participation (Eaton, 1994). Unions tend to argue, however, that stock ownership gives workers the illusion of ownership without any real control and that it is chiefly a management technique to replace superannuation plans, to reduce union influence, or to cut wages. In practice, however, stock ownership has little impact on industrial relations at the corporate level, and it does not appear to make unionists any less loyal to their unions. It simply does not have a major impact on employee involvement or participation at the workplace level (Strauss, 1996:190).

Australia

The ascendance of a neo-liberal agenda occurred somewhat later in Australia than in many other Anglo-Saxon countries. The Australian Labour Party (ALP) held power at the national level from 1983 to 1996, aided by an Accord between the Australian Council of Trade Unions (ACTU) and the Labor government (Lansbury and Wailes, 2004). Although the Accord underwent a number of modifications during this period, it emphasized union involvement in macroeconomic and social policy decision making. To this end, the government established various tripartite committees and councils at national and industry levels.

The election of a conservative Liberal-National Coalition government in 1996 ushered in new industrial relations reforms that ostensibly sought to increase deregulation. The new coalition government moved further away from a collectivist approach to industrial relations (and industrial democracy) in which there had been a strong role for unions and tribunals. Its *Work Choices Act 2006* privileges individual non-union agreements ahead of collectively bargained agreements between employers and employees (see Ellem et al., 2005). The unionized workforce has declined from around 40 per cent in 1990 to less than 25 per cent in 2005.

Data from the second (and last) Australian Industrial Relations Survey (AWIRS95) provides the best available data on participation and involvement practice in Australian workplaces (see Morehead et al., 1997). AWIRS95 demonstrated that direct forms of employee participation in Australia tend to be oriented around an employee's tasks and are designed to improve the performance of individuals and groups within the workplace. The most common direct form was found to be team building, reported in 47 per cent of workplaces. Semi- or fully-autonomous work groups were seen in 43 per cent of workplaces, whereas total quality management (TQM) was reported in 37 per cent of workplaces. As with indirect forms of participation, large workplaces tended to have more direct participation than smaller ones.

According to AWIRS95, the majority of managers believed that direct forms of employee participation led to improvements in workplace performance, the introduction of change and improved product or service quality. Most delegates in unionized workplaces believed that such schemes gave employees increased say at the workplace level. Yet when managers were asked whether they had consulted staff about important changes that had affected their workplaces during the previous year, only 29 per cent responded positively, and only 18 per cent said that employees had a significant input into decisions. This would appear to indicate that while the degree of participation by employees has increased (both in indirect and direct forms), there continues to be important issues on which they are not consulted by management (Morehead et al., 1997: 244).

This finding is reinforced by Harley (1999) who argues that there is little evidence of employee empowerment in Australia. Using AWIRS 1995 data he shows that while many of the practices associated with 'employee empowerment' are present in a substantial minority of Australian workplaces, there is little evidence to suggest that these practices increased employee autonomy or reduced the significance of organizational hierarchy. In particular Harley (1999: 53) finds that 'employees who work in workplaces with any of the empowerment mechanisms in place do not report any differences in their level of autonomy from employees who work in workplaces without the mechanisms'. Rather he finds continued close associations between measures of hierarchy and reported levels of autonomy.

Financial participation through employee share ownership and profit-sharing schemes has not increased as significantly in Australia as it has in some other countries. In 1990, only 16 per cent of private-sector workplaces offered share ownership schemes to their employees. By 1995, this had increased to 22 per cent. The likelihood of having a share ownership scheme was greater in private-sector workplaces that were part of a larger organization compared with single-workplace organizations (29 and 3 per cent, respectively). Of the 16 per cent of private-sector workplaces with schemes, fewer than 10 percent of employees actually held shares. Indeed, only 28 per cent of workplaces with share schemes had more than half their employees as shareholders (Morehead et al., 1997: 222).

An inquiry into employee share ownership in Australia by the House of Representatives Standing Committee on Employment, Education and Workplace Relations (2000) reported that the concept had been less enthusiastically embraced than in the US or the UK. This was despite support from both major political parties and shared views by successive governments that employee share ownership had the potential to improve net contributions to national savings. An investigation into two major corporations with considerable experience with employee share ownership, Lend Lease and Woolworths, found that they had achieved only limited success in these two firms. Rysiok (2004) argued that there appeared to be little sense of 'ownership' or genuine employee involvement by employees who participated in the share ownership schemes in both organizations.

Germany

Any account of German industrial relations in the recent period must take into account the momentous industrial relations consequences of reunification. The outcome has been the transfer of West Germany's industrial relations system to East Germany (Frege, 1999). Germany is characterized by a 'dual system of interest representation' that comprises collective bargaining between unions and employers at the industry level and co-determination at the level of the enterprise. Yet the system is under strain, particularly since unification between West and East Germany, which involved significant economic burdens for the 'new' Germany, increasing levels of unemployment and a waning of union influence in both the political and economic spheres.

New forms of production and work organization in German industry have created a number of new challenges for unions and works councils. Since the late 1980s, large enterprises and conglomerates (particularly in

the automobile industry) have undergone extensive organizational restructuring involving both the centralization and decentralization of decision-making structures. Some strategic decisions, such as the location of production facilities, have been centralized, whereas decisions dealing with arrangements at particular plants have been decentralized. This latter development has opened up possibilities for more employees at lower levels in the hierarchy to be involved in decision-making processes. On the other hand, regional union representatives who previously had served as a counterbalance to management no longer have an effective means of influencing decisions that have been moved from middle management to headquarters management. New forms of rationalization by firms also have created problems for works councilors. Management has used group or team work, quality circles and the like to enable employees to influence and directly participate in decision making, effectively bypassing the works councilors (Roth, 1997: 118).

New systems of production also have had consequences for direct participation. According to Auer (1996), German managers took up 'lean production' with great enthusiasm following publication of *The Machine that Changed the World* (Womack et al., 1990), arguing that it was necessary to abandon work practices that were inflexible and to combat 'overmanning' in automobile plants. German trade unions and works councils have been placed in a dilemma by lean production. While they have welcomed the opportunity for more participative work organization – as espoused by some proponents of lean production – unions have opposed rationalization that has led to 'downsizing' of the workforce. While works councils are entitled, under the *Works Constitution Act*, to be consulted on the introduction of lean forms of production, many employers have sought to use the opportunity to involve employees directly rather than through representative bodies. In any case, works councils are not empowered to refuse changes in work organization. Roth (1997) argues that unions have embraced direct forms of participation that have emphasized 'self-organization by improving skills or professional competence'. The unions have urged employers to introduce 'group work' based on Swedish experiences with semi-autonomous groups rather than 'team work' based on the Japanese or American approaches.

Wever (1995) notes that by acknowledging the growing importance of direct forms of participation and seeking to accommodate rather than oppose this trend, IG Metall risks conflict with some of its members as well as works councils because it will 'place into question past conceptualizations of worker interest representation'. However, this may not necessarily mean a ceding of power by the union but rather a shift of roles. By adapting to direct participation, the unions and works councils may provide an alternative to unilateral approaches by management.

Japan

During the rise of the Japanese economy in the late 1970s and early 1980s, considerable attention was focused on Japanese management and employment relations systems. In particular, cooperative approaches to labor-management relations were ascribed to several practices, which included: life-time employment, seniority-based wage systems and various forms of employee participation in enterprise-based activities such as quality circles and consultative committees. Japan's system of enterprise-based unionism was also regarded as contributing significantly to low-levels of industrial disputation and strong collaboration between management and workers in order to achieve high levels of productivity (Kuwahara, 2004). Much of the literature on high performance work systems (HPWS), in Western literature, implicitly draws upon Japanese experience with total quality management (TQM) practices, team work, multi-skilling of workers and information-sharing by management with the workforce (Faris and Varma, 1998). Yet some of the key elements in the so-called 'Japanese model', such as life-time employment and seniority-based wages, only ever applied to around one-third of the labor force in larger organizations. Similarly, trade union density in Japan declined from 31 per cent in 1980 to 19.6 per cent in 2003 and unionization is generally confined to large-scale industrial employers. Furthermore, many of the innovative workplace practices, such as TQM and quality circles, were imported from the West in the 1950s and 60s when Japan was not regarded as a leading economic power. Yet the 'Japanese model' was widely cited at evidence of the contribution which employee participation and involvement makes to economic performance at the enterprise level. The Japanese experience also illustrates that the effectiveness of participative practice is embedded in the political economy of a nation and its enterprise cultures.

Participation by employees in small group activities, such as quality control circles (QCCs) or total quality control (TQC), have long been associated with the Japanese system of management and employment relations. More recently, however, attention has focused on the Japanese bonus payment system and profit-sharing plans as a means by which employees can financially participate in enterprises. In addition to their regular monthly pay, most Japanese workers receive two large seasonal payments worth about 2.8 months' salary a year, although this varies between industries. The practice originated from the Buddhist 'bon festival' in summer and the lunar New Year celebrations which required extra expenditure. The amount of these payments fluctuates according to the financial performance of each company as well as the individual employee's contribution to the success of the enterprise. However, the size of the bonus has generally declined with economic stagnation in Japan over the past decade. Various studies have indicated that there is a modest productivity gain from the bonus system (Jones and Kato, 1995) and that bonuses tend to increase employees' interest in the operation and performance of their firm (Freeman and Weitzman, 1987). Yet other studies have viewed the bonus as a mixture of a disguised form of regular pay, investment in firm-specific human capital and a means of compensating effort (Hart and Kawasaki, 1995).

Recent studies have indicated that, contrary to the assumption that profit-sharing is almost universal among Japanese firms, only about one in four traded firms has a profit-sharing plan (PSP) in place. A PSP defined as a bonus payment system with a formal contract stipulating the presence of a profit-sharing scheme (Kato and Morishima, 2003). PSPs appear to be most popular among smaller firms, without unions but with employee participation at the grassroots. Such participation, it is argued, tends to promote an employment relations approach and a corporate culture that is conducive to labor-management cooperation and strong company loyalty by workers (Kato and Morishima, 2002).

Substantial changes in Japanese corporate governance are currently in progress, partly in response to the prolonged economic recession, which may introduce similar shareholder-based corporate governance systems to those which operate in US and European companies. Revisions to company law in 2001 and 2002 introduced committee-based systems for nominating director candidates, an audit committee and a directors' remuneration committee which nominates officers responsible for particular aspects of the business. Large companies are gradually changing, as illustrated by Matsushita and Toyota both decided to introduce a modified version of the new model in 2003. This may ultimately mean that Japanese companies move away from the traditional 'Illyria' model, which maximized the dividend or net income per worker, to the Western-style model which seeks to maximize profits and in which greater weight is given to 'shareholder prerogatives' (Kuwahara, 2004). However, it is likely that many elements of Japanese employment relations will persist while gradually changing. These include characteristics which have promoted direct forms of participation and are historically embedded in Japanese enterprises, such as: relatively vague and wide job descriptions, flexibility of workforce allocation, lack of rigid work rules compared with those found in other similar economies, long-term merit ratings for managers and employees and widespread use of annual bonus payments. Informal systems of employee involvement and participation, in combination with increased flexibilities of the labor market, will facilitate reforms of Japan's economic structure.

CONCLUSIONS

Recent decades have witnessed renewed interest in direct participation and employee involvement and their contribution both to improved productivity and increased flexibility in increasingly competitive markets. Despite an increase in the number of management-initiated participation and involvement schemes in many countries, empirical evidence suggests that there continues to be considerable diversity in patterns of participation at the national level. The previous section provided some brief summaries of patterns of participation in four countries, two of which are LMEs and two are CMEs. As these summaries indicate, the relationship between varieties of capitalism and forms of participation is not a simple one. It is apparent that labor market institutions play an important role, as does historical experience. Indirect forms of participation also influence direct forms, as illustrated by the importance of long-established systems of works councils and co-determination in Germany in fostering certain types of direct participation. Similarly, the century-old tradition of compulsory arbitration in Australia affected the degree to which direct forms of participation were given an opportunity to flourish. These findings are consistent with the view, advanced by Gospel and Pendleton (2005: 9) amongst others, that the VoC approach is too formal and simplistic to capture all of the factors that produce differences between and change within national patterns of labor management.

Despite these limitations, the empirical evidence presented in this chapter is broadly consistent with the propositions drawn from the VoC framework outlined above and suggest that the national institutional matrix has a significant impact on the adoption and sustainability of different forms of employee involvement and participation. There are two implications that can be drawn from these findings. First, it suggests that the adoption of employee involvement practices associated with HPWS in LMEs may be limited. Thus, despite evidence that elements of the HPWS have been widely adopted across a number of US industries (Osterman, 2000) and some initial findings which report positive associations between the adoption of key aspects of the HPWS model and firm performance (see Huselid, 1994 and Becker and Gerhart, 1996), more recent studies question both the extent to which US firms have derived improved performance from these practices (see Combs et al., 2006) and the extent to which any performance gains are associated with empowerment as opposed to work intensification (see Cappelli and Neumark, 2001). This is consistent with research on HPWS in two other LMEs, the UK and Australia, and suggests that the extent to which HPWS enhance productivity is achieved by increasing pressure on workers rather than empowering them (on the UK see, for example, Bryson et al., 2005 and, on Australia, see Harley, 1999. For a review of this research see Godard, 2004). Given the institutional matrix within which firms operate in LMEs, where investors focus on short-term performance and managers are encouraged to experiment with different forms of work organization in pursuit of short-term competitive advantage, these results suggest that many of the direct participatory practices associated with HPWS not producing the empowerment which their advocates claim and may be difficult to sustain.

Second, our survey of the literature on employee involvement in the four countries studied has revealed that where the conjunction of historical and institutional factors are favorable, direct forms of participation are more likely to be sustainable. In the past, this has characterized the co-ordinated market economies of Germany and Japan more than the liberal market economies of

Australia and the US. However, if labor market institutions continue to be weakened in Germany and Japan, and corporate governance reforms mean that managers in these countries become more susceptible to short-term investor pressure, they are likely to become less distinguishable from the liberal market economies of the US and Australia. Hence, the sustainability of their participative practices in the workplace will be less certain in the future unless there is stronger institutional support for their continuation and further development.

REFERENCES

Ackroyd, S., Burrell, G., Hughes, M. and Whittaker, A. (1988) 'The Japanisation of British industry?', *Industrial Relations Journal*, 19 (1): 11–23.

Adler, P. and Cole, R. (1993) 'Designed for learning: A tale of two auto plants', *Sloan Management Review*, 34 (3): 85–94.

Adler, P., Kochan, T.A., MacDuffie, J.P., Pil, F.K. and Rubenstein, S. (1997) 'United States: Variations on a theme', in T.A. Kochan, R.D. Lansbury, and J.P. MacDuffie (eds) *After Lean Production: Evolving Employment Practices in the World Auto Industry.* Ithaca, NY: ILR Press. pp. 61–83.

Amable, B. (2003) *The Diversity of Modern Capitalism.* New York: Oxford University Press.

Aoki, M. (2000) *Information, Corporate Governance and Institutional Diversity: Compeitiveness in Japan, the USA and the Transitional Economies.* Oxford: Oxford University Press.

Appelbaum, E. and Batt, R. (1994) *The New American Workplace.* Ithaca, NY: ILR Press.

Appelbaum, E., Bailey, T., Berg, P. and Kalleberg, A. (2000) *Manufacturing advantage: Why High Performance Systems Pay Off.* Ithaca, NY: Cornell University Press.

Auer, P. (1996) 'Co-determination in Germany: Institutional stability in a changing environment', in E. Davis and R.D. Lansbury (eds)*Managing Together: Consultation and Participation in the Workplace.* Melbourne: Addison-Wesley Longman. pp. 160–72.

Becker, B. and Gerhart, B. (1996) 'The impact of human resource management on organizational performance: progress and prospects', *Academy of Management Journal*, 39 (4): 779–803.

Blasi, J., Kruse, D. and Berstein, A. (2003a) *In the Company of Owners.* New York: Basic Books.

Blasi, J., Kruse, D., Sesil, J. and Kroumova, M. (2003b) 'An assessment of employee ownership in the United States with implications for the EU', *International Journal of Human Resource Management*, 14 (6): 893–919.

Bradley, K. and Hill, S. (1983) '"After Japan": The quality circle transplant and productive efficiency', *British Journal of Industrial Relations*, 21 (3): 291–311.

Bryson, A., Forth, J. and Kirby, S. (2005) 'High involvement management practices, trade union representation and workplace performance in Britain', *Scottish Journal of Political Economy*, 52 (3): 451–91.

Cappelli, P. and Neurmark, D. (2001) 'Do "high-performance" work practices improve establishment-level outcomes?', *Industrial and Labor Relations Review*, 54 (4): 737–75.

Combs, J., Lui, Y., Hall, A. and Ketchen, D. (2006) 'How much do high performance work practices matter? A meta-analysis of their effects on organizational performance', *Personnel Psychology*, 59 (3): 501–28.

Crouch, C. (2005) 'Models of capitalism', *New Political Economy*, 10 (4): 439–56.

Dachler, P.H. and Wilpert, B. (1978) 'Conceptual dimensions and boundaries of participation in organizations: A critical evaluation', *Administrative Science Quarterly*, 23 (1): 1–39.

Derber, M. (1980) 'Collective bargaining: The American approach to industrial democracy', in R.D. Lansbury (ed.) *Democracy in the Workplace*. Melbourne: Longman Cheshire. pp. 171–82.

Eaton, A. (1994) 'The survival of employee participation programs in unionized settings', *Industrial and Labor Relations Review*, 47 (3): 371–89.

Ellem, B., Baird, M., Cooper, R. and Lansbury, R.D. (2005) 'Work choices: Myth making at work', *Journal of Australian Political Economy*, 56: 13–31.

Faris, G.F. and Varma, A. (1998) 'High performance work systems: What we know and what we need to know', *Human Resource Planning*, 21 (2): 50–55.

Freeman, R. and Weitzman, M. (1987) 'Bonuses and employment in Japan', *Journal of the Japanese and International Economies*, 1 (2): 168–94.

Frege, C.M. (1999) 'Transferring labor institutions to emerging economics: The case of East Germany', *Industrial Relations*, 38 (4): 459–81.

Gill, C. and Krieger, H. (1999) 'Direct and representative participation in Europe: Recent survey evidence', *International Journal of Human Resource Management*, 10 (4): 572–91.

Godard, J. (2004) 'A critical assessment of the high performance paradigm', *British Journal of Industrial Relations*, 42 (2): 349–78.

Godard, J. (2005) 'The new institutionalism, capitalist diversity and industrial relations', in B.E. Kaufman (ed.) *Theoretical Perspectives on Work and the Employment Relationship*. Champaign, IL: Industrial Relations Research Association.

Gospel, H. and Pendleton, A. (2005) 'Corporate governance and labour management: An international comparison' in Gospel, H. and Pendleton A. (eds) *Corporate governance and labour management: An international comparison.* Oxford: Oxford University Press. pp. 1–32.

Hall, P. and Soskice, D. (2001) 'An introduction to varieties of capitalism', in P. Hall and D. Soskice (eds) *Varieties of capitalism: The Institutional Foundations of Comparative Advantage.* New York: Oxford University Press. pp. 1–69.

Harley, B. (1999) 'The myth of empowerment: Work organization, hierarchy and autonomy in contemporary Australian workplaces', *Work, Employment and Society*, 13 (1): 41–66.

Harley, B. (2005) 'Hope or hype? High-performance work systems', in B. Harley, J. Hyman and P. Thompson (eds) *Participation and Democracy at Work: Essays in Honours of Harvie Ramsay.* London: Palgrave. pp. 20–37.

Harley, B., Hyman, J. and Thompson, P. (2005) 'The paradoxes of participation', in B. Harley, J. Hyman and P. Thompson (eds) *Participation and democracy at work: Essays in honours of Harvie Ramsay.* London: Palgrave. pp. 1–19.

Hart, R.A. and Kawasaki, S. (1995) 'The Japanese bonus system and human capital', *Journal of the Japanese and International Economies*, 9 (3): 225–44.

House of Representatives Standing Committee on Employment, Education and Workplace Relations (2000) *Shared endeavours: An inquiry into employee share ownership in Australia,* Canberra: Parliament of the Commonwealth of Australia.

Huselid, M. (1995) 'The impact of human resource management practices on turnover, productivity and corporate performance', *Academy of Management Journal*, 38 (3): 635–62.

Ichniowski, C., Kochan, T.A., Levine, D., Olson, C. and Strauss, G. (1996) 'What works at work: Overview and assessment', *Industrial Relations*, 35 (3): 299–333.

Jones, D. and Kato, T. (1995) 'The Productivity Effects of Employee Stock Ownership Plans and Bonuses: Evidence from Japanese Panel Data', *American Economic Review*, 85 (3): 391–414.

Jurgens, U. (2003) 'Transformation and interaction: Japanese, US and German production models in the 1990s', in W. Streeck and K. Yamamura (eds) *The end of diversity? Prospects for German and Japanese capitalism.* Ithaca: Cornell University Press, pp. 212–39.

Kato, T. and Morishima, M. (2002) 'The productivity effects of participatory employment practices: Evidence from new Japanese panel data', *Industrial Relations*, 41 (4): 487–520.

Kato, T. and Morishima, M. (2003) 'The nature, scope and effects of profit sharing in Japan: Evidence from new survey data', *International Journal of Human Resource Managements*, 14 (6): 942–55.

Kochan, T.A. and Osterman, P. (1994) *The Mutual Gains Enterprise*. Boston: Harvard Business School Press.

Kochan, T.A. and Rubenstien, P.R. (2001) *Learning from Saturn*. Ithaca, NY: Cornell University Press.

Kuwahara, Y. (2004) 'Employment relations in Japan', in G.J. Bamber, R.D. Lansbury and N. Wailes (eds) *International and Comparative Employment Relations*. London: Sage. pp. 277–305.

Lansbury, R.D. and Wailes, N. (2004) 'Employment relations in Australia', in G.J. Bamber, R.D. Lansbury and N. Wailes (eds) *International and Comparative Employment Relations*. London: Sage. pp. 119–45.

Morehead, A. Steel, M., Alexander, M., Stephen, K. and Duffin, L. (1997) *Change at Work: The 1994 Australian Workplace Industrial Relations Survey (AWIRS 95)*. Melbourne: Addison-Wesley Longman.

Osterman, P. (2000) 'Work reorganization in an era of restructuring: trends in diffusion and effects on employee welfare', *Industrial and Labor Relations Review*, 53 (2): 179–96.

Pateman, C. (1970) *Participation and Democratic Theory*. Cambridge, England: Cambridge University Press.

Pendleton, A. (1997) 'The evolution of industrial relations in UK nationalized industries', *British Journal of Industrial Relations*, 35 (2): 145–72.

Pil, F.K. and MacDuffie, J.P. (1996) 'The adoption of high involvement workplaces', *Industrial Relations*, 35 (3): 423–55.

Poole, M. (1986) *Towards a New Industrial Democracy: Workers' Participation in Industry*. London: Routledge.

Poole, M. (1989) *The Origins of Economic Democracy*. London: Routledge.

Poole, M., Lansbury, R.D. and Wailes, N. (2001) 'A comparative analysis of developments in industrial democracy', *Industrial Relations*, 40 (3): 490–525.

Poutsma, E. and de Nijs, W. (2003) 'Broad based employee financial participation in the European Union', *International Journal of Human Resource Management*, 14 (6): 863–92.

Poutsma, E. and Huijgen, F. (1999) 'European diversity in the use of participation schemes', *Economic and Industrial Democracy*, 20 (2): 197–223.

Poutsma, E., Hendrickx, J. and Huijgen, F. (2003) 'Employee participation in Europe: In search of the participative workplace', *Economic and Industrial Democracy*, 24 (1): 45–76.

Ramsay, H. (1977) 'Cycles of control: Worker participation in sociological and historical perspective', *Sociology*, 11 (3): 481–506.

Ramsay, H. (1982) Evolution or Cycle? In Colin Crouch (ed.) *First International Yearbook of Organisational Democracy*. London: Wiley.

Ramsay, H. (1983) An International Participation Cycle: Variations on a Recurring Theme. In Stuart Clegg, Paul Boreham and Geff Dow (eds) *The State, Class and the Recession*. Canberra: Croom Helm.

Roth, S. (1997) 'Germany: Labor's perspective on lean production', in T.A. Kochan, R.D. Lansbury and J.P. MacDuffie (eds) *After Lean Production: Evolving Employment Practices in the World Auto Industry*. Ithaca, NY: Cornell University Press. pp. 117–36.

Rysiok, E. (2004) 'Shared endeavours: A case study of employee share plans at Woolworths and Land Lease', *Unpublished Honours Thesis*. School of Business, University of Sydney.

Strauss, G. (1986) 'Workers participation in management in the United States', in E.M. Davis and R.D. Lansbury (eds) *Democracy and Control in the Workplace*. Sydney: Longman Cheshire. pp. 313–31.

Strauss, G. (1990) 'Participation and gain sharing systems: History and hope', in M. Roomkin (ed.) *Profit and Gain Sharing*. Metuchen, NJ: Rutgers University Press. pp. 1–45.

Strauss, G. (1996) 'Participation in the United States: Progress and barriers', in E. Davis and R.D. Lansbury (eds) *Managing together: Consultation and Participation in the Workplace*. Melbourne: Addison-Wesley Longman. pp. 173–92.

Strauss, G. (1998) 'Comparative international industrial relations', in K. Whitfield and G. Strauss (eds) *Researching the World of Work*. Ithaca, NY: ILR Press.

Streeck, W. (1991) 'On the institutional conditions for diversified quality production', in E. Matzner and W. Streeck (eds) *Beyond Keynesianism: The Socio-Economics of Production and Full Employment*, Brookfield: Elgar, pp. 21–61.

Wall, T. and Lischeron, J (1977) *Worker Participation: a Critique of the Literature and Some Fresh Evidence*. Maidenhead: McGraw Hill.

Wever, K. (1995) *Negotiating Competitiveness: Employment Relations and Organizational Innovation in Germany and the United States*. Boston: Harvard Business School Press.

Womack, J., Jones, D.T. and Roos, D. (1990) *The Machine that Changed the World*. New York: Rawson Associates.

24

Resolving Conflict

David Lewin

RESOLVING CONFLICT

Conflict and the potential for conflict exists in all human relationships, including the employment relationship. Historically and contemporaneously, various approaches to and methods for resolving employment relationship conflict have been developed. How effective are these approaches and methods in actually resolving employment relationship conflict? That is the focal question addressed in this chapter, which is organized as follows. Section 1 briefly identifies key sources of employment relationship conflict, section 2 discusses main approaches to resolving employment relationship conflict, section 3 analyzes leading theories of employment relationship conflict and conflict resolution, section 4 examines both older and newer forms of employment conflict resolution and evidence of their effectiveness, and section 5 considers future directions for employment conflict resolution research. In these respects, this chapter focuses largely on formal individual employee-employer workplace conflict resolution rather than on more collective forms of conflict resolution, such as strikes,[1] and draws on theoretical and empirical research from North America, Europe, and other world regions.

Sources of employment relationship conflict

For employment relationship conflict to exist, an employment relationship must exist. While this may appear self-evident, underdeveloped, developing, and even some portions of developed economies feature small owner-operated businesses without specialization of function – as examples, the nineteenth century shoemaker (memorialized by Commons, 1919), the twentieth century small farmer or family-owned retail store, and the twenty-first century two-partner start-up financial consulting business. As small businesses grow, they hire paid labor to perform certain tasks that owner-operators previously performed, thereby creating an employment relationship. As these businesses grow further, they develop more specialized functions, promote some employees to serve as supervisors and managers, and hire more paid labor to perform specialized tasks. In this developmental stage, a separation of ownership from (direct) management has occurred, and there emerge clearly identifiable 'management' and clearly identifiable 'employees'.

If and as these businesses grow still larger, they may seek additional financial capital through public ownership. Once this occurs, the separation of business ownership from control deepens and both managers *and* employees become the agents of their principals. It is well known, however, that agents may not primarily serve the interests of their principals; instead, they may primarily serve their own interests (Jensen and Meckling, 1976). From this perspective, managers have certain interests, employees have certain interests, and the two sets of interests may well differ considerably even if they overlap in some respects. Such differing interests are a fundamental source of employment relationship conflict – but hardly the only source.

Another source of employment relationship conflict is a twin source, namely, hierarchy and specialization. Hierarchy refers to a pyramidal form of organization featuring several distinct levels in which those who occupy the top levels – executives and managers – co-ordinate and control the work of those who occupy the middle and lower levels (Weber, 1947). Specialization refers to the design of work such that any individual job features a few narrow, well-specified tasks that an employee repeats on a continuous basis and in which that employee takes instruction from a supervisor or manager (Taylor, 1911). In this organizational format, those at the upper levels ostensibly do the thinking and those at the lower levels do the work.

There is little question that the combination of organizational hierarchy and work specialization enabled business enterprises worldwide, indeed, entire national economies, to grow and prosper, especially during the twentieth century. But these same organizational characteristics often generated fundamental employment relationship conflict. Over time, workers expressed their dissatisfaction with orders that they received from 'on high', and sometimes openly rebelled against such orders, including through restricting their output or working to rule or absenteeism

(Mathewson, 1931). Further, to counter the dictates and power of business owners and managers, some workers went so far as to organize into labor unions and to withhold their labor (even without unions). For much of the twentieth century, employment relationship conflict largely meant union-management conflict, or collective conflict, with strikes and the prevention of strikes occupying the bulk of popular attention and public policy debates, respectively (see Gall and Hebdon, this volume, Chapter 31).

During the last quarter of the twentieth century, however, the economic environment for employment relationship conflict changed dramatically. The two 'oil shocks' that occurred during the 1970s signaled the growing importance of a global rather than a strictly domestic economic perspective, with the result that businesses in many nations became increasingly focused on global customers and competitors. For their part, national governments undertook the de-regulation of such key industries as airlines, trucking, telecommunications and financial services. Major advances in information and computing technology also occurred, with the advent of personal computing during the 1980s and the commercialization of the internet during the 1990s and continuing into the twenty-first century constituting watershed developments. Most notable for employment relationship conflict, the practice of 'continuous employment with the company' came undone as employer after employer sought to reorganize, restructure, downsize, and 'rightsize'. In this new economic environment, continuous employment with periodic layoff and recall was swiftly supplanted by outsourcing, including to offshore locations; by part-time, temporary and short-term employment; and by market-driven employability (Bognanno et al., 2007; Osterman, 1988).

The triplet of global economic competition, de-regulation and technological change has therefore contributed mightily to the reduction of concentrated power among employer *and* employee organizations. Today, most industries are characterized by competition rather than by oligopoly or monopoly, and most employees provide their labor individually and are neither members of nor represented by labor unions. Indeed, union membership has been declining globally during the last quarter century or so, and it appears that many more employees are party to individual employment contracts than to collective bargaining contracts (Lewin, 1994). These developments do not, however, mean that employment relationship conflict has faded from the scene or somehow been resolved. Rather, the focus of both research and practice has shifted from collective union-management conflict to individual conflict in the employment relationship.

One manifestation of this shifting emphasis is the rather widespread adoption by non-union companies of grievance and grievance-like procedures for dealing with employment relationship conflict. Several recent studies suggest that a majority, perhaps a large majority, of non-union companies have adopted one or more of these procedures (Lewin, 2005; Colvin, 2004, 2003). Another manifestation of this shifting emphasis is the work of organizational behavior scholars, who typically study conflict at the individual and team levels of analysis and who have importantly differentiated relationship conflict from task conflict in organizations (Bendersky, 2003; Jehn, 1997). Still another manifestation of this shifting emphasis is the voluminous litigation over claims by current and former employees that their employers violated one or another provision of laws aimed at preventing discrimination in employment (Stone, 1999; Donohue and Siegelman, 1991). In sum, there is much scholarly evidence and much practical experience to suggest that conflict in the employment relationship remains ever present, even as its particular forms and manifestations have changed over time in response to exogenous as well as endogenous forces.

Approaches to resolving employment relationship conflict

Surely the best known approach to resolving employment relationship conflict is the formal grievance procedure contained in collective bargaining agreements. This procedure typically specifies several formal steps, the first of which calls for an employee grievance to be put in writing and the last of which calls for arbitration of the issue or issues specified in the written grievance. Such grievance arbitration can be distinguished from contract arbitration in which the third-party arbitrator sets the terms and conditions of a new collective bargaining agreement between the two direct parties, union and management, to that agreement.

The collectively bargained grievance procedure has long been commended as a peaceful mechanism for resolving employee-management disputes. In the absence of a grievance procedure, according to this reasoning, disputes over existing terms and conditions of employment might lead to strikes, work slowdowns, absenteeism, lock-outs, and other overt behaviors that obviously interrupt the production and delivery of goods and services. From this perspective, the grievance procedure adds value to unionized businesses by mitigating the potential costs of employee-management disputes (Jacoby, 1986). Indeed, the grievance procedure provisions of collective bargaining agreements are almost always accompanied by (and thus traded for) provisions that explicitly ban employee strikes and employer lockouts during the life of those agreements. In addition to this efficiency benefit, the grievance procedure provides equity to unionized employees by serving as an institutionalized mechanism for addressing and (perhaps) resolving the workplace concerns voiced by these employees. In other words, there are both efficiency and equity (or voice) arguments for grievance procedures in unionized settings.

In non-union settings, the rationale for grievance and grievance-like conflict resolution procedures is rather different from that in unionized settings. According to both survey and field research-based studies, executives and managers of non-union businesses primarily view the grievance procedure as a mechanism for identifying workplace and organizational issues and as an information system for diagnosing, addressing and resolving such issues (Colvin, 2004; Feuille and Delaney, 1992; Delaney et al., 1989). From this perspective, the decisions by non-union businesses to adopt a grievance (or grievance-like) procedure are strategic or proactive decisions, which may be contrasted with the decisions of unionized businesses to adopt grievance procedures only when 'forced' to do so through collective negotiations with union representatives, that is, reactive decisions. Moreover and not widely recognized, grievance procedures in non-union businesses have a broader scope of employee coverage than grievance procedures in unionized businesses. In the latter, only those employees who are represented by a union are eligible to use the grievance procedure. In the former, there is no collective bargaining agreement so that employee eligibility to use the grievance procedure is bounded only by the specifications of the particular procedure adopted by a non-union business. Most non-union businesses have been rather expansive in this regard, and an instructive example is provided by Federal Express, a prominent global overnight delivery company. This company's formal three-step Guaranteed Fair Treatment (GFT) procedure applies to all employees except those who occupy top management positions (Lewin, 1997).

Whether in unionized or non-union settings, the presence of a formal grievance procedure implies that employee grievances are put in writing and then progress through the various steps of the procedure to settlement. In fact, however, most employee grievances never see the light of day, at least in terms of being reduced to writing. Instead, most employee grievances are taken up and 'settled' during informal discussions with management, typically with the employee's immediate supervisor. In this regard, research on unionized grievance procedures estimates that for every one grievance that is actually reduced to writing and that enters the formal grievance system,

about 10 grievances are settled informally in employee-supervisor (or manager) discussions (Lewin and Peterson, 1988). In the same vein, research on non-union grievance procedures estimates that the ratio of informal to formal grievance settlement is approximately 12:1 (Lewin, 2004). On the basis of these estimates, the dynamics of employment conflict resolution in business enterprises may be analogized to the dynamics of employee performance evaluation. While such formal evaluations are typically conducted annually or in some cases, semi-annually, researchers and practitioners emphasize that informal performance evaluation is a more or less continuous process, especially when it comes to supervisors and managers providing performance evaluation feedback to employees (Antonioni, 1994). Similarly, and despite the presence of formal grievance and grievance-like systems in business enterprises, most employment conflict resolution in such enterprises occurs informally in a more or less continuous process of information exchange, feedback, and settlement.

In unionized enterprises, the grievance procedure has evolved over a long period to the point where it may be characterized as 'mature'. In this procedure, the employee represents him or herself only at the first stage of and does so by putting the grievance in writing. Thereafter, at subsequent steps, the employee is represented by a shop steward or grievance committee person or other union official or combinations thereof depending on how far the particular grievance proceeds through the grievance process. At each of these steps, moreover, the company is represented by successively higher levels of supervisory and management personnel or combinations thereof. If a unionized employee's grievance is not settled at the lower or intermediate steps of the procedure, the grievance is taken to and settled in arbitration, which as noted earlier is the final step in virtually all unionized grievance procedures. In this setting, the costs of grievance handling, processing and arbitration are shared equally by (that is, split between) the union and the company.

In non-union enterprises, by contrast, grievance procedures are more varied and may be characterized as being in a 'developmental' stage of evolution. There are typically fewer steps in non-union than in unionized grievance procedures, a non-union employee is considerably more likely than a unionized employee to represent him or herself beyond the first step of the grievance procedure, arbitration constitutes the final step in approximately 20 per cent of non-union grievance procedures compared to about 97 per cent of unionized grievance procedures, and the non-union company typically pays all the costs of arbitration compared to the aforementioned split cost in unionized companies. The variation in non-union grievance procedures encompasses both between-company and within-company variation. Regarding between-company variation, some non-union company grievance procedures culminate in arbitration, others culminate in peer review, and still others culminate in an executive level decision, including in some instances by the Chief Executive Officer (CEO). Further, some non-union grievance procedures specify that a grievant may be represented by a third party, such as an attorney or a co-worker, at certain steps of the procedure. Regarding within-company variation, some non-union companies have adopted one grievance procedure covering all employees, while other non-union companies have adopted multiple grievance procedures, each of which covers a particular employee group or groups. A prominent example of the latter is TRW, a diversified manufacturer of automotive parts, advanced electronic technology, and information services, which has a peer review type grievance procedure for non-union employees of one of the company's major business units, and a grievance procedure culminating in arbitration for non-union employees of another of the company's major business units (Colvin, 2004).

By definition, non-union employees do not have union officials to represent them in grievance processing, and might therefore be presumed to be significantly less likely than unionized employees to file grievances.

Research on grievance filing in both unionized and non-union settings partially supports this presumption. Specifically, the grievance filing rate among unionized employees is approximately 10 per cent, while the grievance filing rate among non-union employees is approximately five per cent (Lewin and Peterson, 1988; Lewin, 1997). But in light of the decline of unionism and grievance procedure coverage of unionized employees and the growth of and scope of employee coverage by grievance procedures in non-union enterprises, the vast bulk of grievances are now actually filed by non-union rather than by unionized employees. When it comes to the progression of grievance cases through and the settlement of grievances at various steps of grievance procedures, there are no significant differences between unionized and non-union employees. In particular, about 60 per cent of both unionized and non-union employee grievances are settled at the first step of the grievance procedure, about 25 per cent are settled at the second step, about 13 per cent at the third step, and about two per cent at the final step (Lewin and Peterson, 1999; Lewin, 1997).

On balance, the fact that most grievances filed by both unionized and non-union employees are settled at the early steps of the grievance procedure seems to accord closely with notions of industrial justice, specifically that grievances should be settled swiftly and as close as possible to their sources of origin. This conclusion, however, is based largely on extant research into what might best be termed micro-level employment conflict resolution – that is, employee-employer conflicts that are resolved internally. A rather different conclusion emerges regarding what might best be termed macro-level or external employment conflict resolution. In North American, European, and Asian nations, numerous laws regulate certain aspects of private sector employment and employment relationships, including hiring, compensation, promotion, termination, and the workplace environment. Chief among these laws are those that seek to prevent employment discrimination on the basis of race, color, national origin, religion, gender, age, and disability. If an employee believes that he or she has been subject to discrimination on one or more of these bases, the employee may file a lawsuit alleging and seeking redress of such discrimination. This litigation could conceivably be pursued all the way to a court verdict.

The likelihood of such an external adjudication process actually occurring is quite low, however, and is becoming even lower. In the US, for example, the Supreme Court recently ruled that the entire range of anti-discrimination in employment laws is subject to arbitration provisions contained in employment contracts between employers and employees. So strong is this deferral to arbitration doctrine that it seemingly requires the 'diversion of all employment litigation...into an employer-designed arbitration procedure from which there is no right of appeal or only very limited possibility of court review' (Colvin, 2003). Such internal arbitration is the leading example of what has come to be known as alternative dispute resolution (ADR) – meaning an alternative to external litigation (Lipsky et al., 2003). It is therefore not surprising that non-union employers have increasingly adopted arbitration type internal employment conflict resolution procedures. Analytically, these adoption decisions can be seen to be primarily reactive, that is, taken in response to litigation or litigation threats, rather than being primarily strategic or proactive in nature.

Another type of ADR that has grown in popularity, especially in the US, Canada, and Britain, is grievance mediation. Here, a third party assists the two direct parties to an employment relationship conflict by

1) communicating settlement proposals from one to the other direct party;
2) posing one or another settlement proposal to both parties; or
3) offering an opinion about how a particular grievance would be settled if it were to be arbitrated.

The key difference between grievance mediation and grievance arbitration is that the mediator has no power to make or enforce a grievance settlement, whereas the arbitrator has exactly such power. The leading US example of grievance mediation occurred during the 1980s in the highly unionized coal mining industry. This initiative was undertaken in the wake of numerous wildcat strikes and widespread employee dissatisfaction with the industry's long-standing grievance arbitration process. With the assistance of the US Department of Labor, unions and coal companies in certain coalfield areas agreed to an experiment in which selected third-step grievances would be informally discussed with a mediator during a mediation conference. If these grievances were not settled during the conference, the mediator would then issue an on-the-spot advisory opinion indicating how the grievances would likely be settled in arbitration. The main results of this experiment were that some 90 per cent of mediated grievances were settled without arbitration, the time to decision and cost of decision were significantly lower in mediated than in arbitrated settlements, and the parties' satisfaction with grievance mediation was significantly higher than their satisfaction with grievance arbitration (Feuille, 1999; Goldberg, 1982).

This particular coal mining experience spurred additional grievance mediation experiments and activities in the US private and public sectors. Prominent in this regard are the non-profit Mediation Research and Education Project (MREP) and the US Federal Mediation and Conciliation Service (FMCS), which provide direct grievance mediation services to labor and management as well as training to union and management officials in how to resolve employment relationship conflict without third party intervention – so-called 'preventive mediation' (Feuille, 1999). Though data on grievance mediation in non-union settings are sketchy, it appears that grievance mediation is becoming more common in ADR procedures involving non-union companies and employees (Lipsky et al., 2003). This said, the available data indicate that grievance mediation remains much less prominent that grievance arbitration as a mechanism for resolving employment relationship conflict in the US.

In Britain, employees who believe that they have been unfairly dismissed from their jobs may seek redress by filing written claims with the Central Office of Industrial Tribunals or one of its regional offices within three months of dismissal. Under the 1999 *Employment Relations Act*, such complainants must have been continuously employed for a minimum of one year in an occupation covered by the law, and must also not have reached normal retirement age. Once registered, such claims are forwarded to the Advisory, Conciliation and Arbitration Service (ACAS), which is statutorily obliged to pursue a conciliated settlement between the parties and only thereafter (if conciliation is rejected by one or another party or is unsuccessful) conduct a full arbitration hearing. The volume of unfair dismissal claims filed with British industrial tribunals rose almost three-fold during the 1990s to more than 80,000 annually, and is likely to rise even more markedly in light of recent legislative relaxation of the criteria for filing such claims. Recent evidence shows about 37 per cent of British unfair dismissal claims were settled through conciliation, that another 30 per cent were withdrawn by complainants, and that most of the remainder, roughly one-third, were settled following a full tribunal hearing – meaning, arbitration. Moreover, these settlements were reached rather quickly, especially by US standards, with 52 per cent of all British unfair dismissal cases dealt with within 12 weeks and 92 per cent dealt with within 26 weeks of their receipt by the tribunals (Knight and Latreille, 2001).

By and large, conciliation is a synonym for mediation, and therefore the British and US approaches to employment conflict resolution or, more narrowly, claims of unfair dismissal from work seem identical. In fact, however, the British invest public authorities with the responsibility for and power to settle unfair dismissal claims involving private parties – employers and (former) employees – whereas in the US most such settlements are reached by the parties themselves or by arbitrators hired by the parties jointly in the case of unionized employees and by the employer alone in the case of non-union employees. Despite its foray into grievance mediation, the US FMCS continues to devote most of its mediation – conciliation – efforts to attempting to resolve strikes and lockouts over new collective bargaining agreements, though it has no mandatory settlement power in this regard. Probably the closest US analogy to the British public tribunal approach to unfair workplace dismissal is the set of individual wrongful termination cases that have been heard and decided by certain courts. Such cases, however, pale in comparison to the much larger volume of cases that US courts have deferred to private arbitrators for decisions – cases that largely involve non-union employees.

Theories of employment relationship conflict and resolution

While some scholars have criticized grievance procedure research, *per se*, for being largely atheoretical (Bemmels and Foley, 1996), there are in fact numerous extant theories of employment relationship conflict (Lewin, 1999). Chief among these are systems theory, exit-voice-loyalty theory, organizational justice theory, compensating differentials theory, due process theory, organizational punishment-discipline theory, displacement theory, and strategic human resource theory.

Grievance procedure systems theory focuses on interrelationships among key antecedent, process and outcome variables. As its name implies, research framed by this theoretical modeling has found systematic relationships among characteristics of union and management organizations, scope of grievance issues and stage of grievance settlement, and union (and management) grievance win-loss rates (Lewin and Peterson, 1988). This framework and related empirical research also show that the parties involved in grievance activity learn from this experience in that they alter their subsequent behavior based on 'feedback' from prior grievance dynamics and settlement (Knight, 1986).

Further, grievance procedure systems theory has been used to frame and measure post-grievance settlement outcomes, as examples, employee job performance, internal mobility (for instance, promotion), work attendance, and turnover.

Exit-voice-loyalty theory (Hirschman, 1970) leads to the provocative hypotheses that employee voice will be negatively correlated with employee exit from (for instance, quitting) the organization and that employee loyalty will be positively correlated with voice – and thus also negatively correlated with exit. Inferentially, therefore, it is relatively more loyal employees who will file grievances and be more likely to remain employed. Considerable empirical research has been conducted using exit-voice-loyalty theory (Freeman and Medoff, 1984), the main findings from which show that employee loyalty is indeed negatively correlated with exit but also that employee loyalty is negatively correlated with both exit and voice (Boroff and Lewin, 1997; Lewin and Boroff, 1996). Hence, some scholars have concluded that relatively more loyal employees are prone to suffer in silence even when they have experienced unfair workplace treatment (Rusbelt, et al., 1988). Despite these rather contrary findings, the notion that employees seek to exercise voice only after their employment relationships have deteriorated may be the most enduring insight drawn from exit-voice-loyalty theory (an insight that will be taken up again in the next section).

Organizational justice theory, which was first used in studies of the criminal justice system, importantly distinguishes between procedural justice and distributive justice (Lind and Tyler, 1988). The former refers to the extent to which a decision making process is perceived as fair or just by those subject to the decision, whereas the latter refers to the extent to which a decision outcome is perceived as fair or just by those subject to the decision. In the employment relationship, organizational justice theory has been used to analyze a wide range of decisions involving, as examples, work assignment,

performance evaluation, pay and promotion. An important finding from these studies is that employee perception of the fairness or justness of a decision process has a significantly stronger effect than employee perception of the fairness or justness of a decision outcome on employee perception of the overall fairness or justice of organizational decisions (Sheppard et al., 1992). Stated succinctly, the decision process matters more than the decision outcome when it comes to perceptions of organizational justice. This conclusion applies to and can be drawn as well from grievance procedure research which finds that, in both unionized and non-union settings, employee perceived fairness of the grievance process is significantly negatively associated with employee intent to exit, and significantly positively associated with employee satisfaction with the grievance procedure – and with the employer (Boroff and Lewin, 1997; Lewin and Boroff, 1996).

Compensating differentials theory basically argues that employees compare the cost and effectiveness of filing grievances with the cost and effectiveness of alternative behaviors, notably quitting (Ichniowski and Lewin, 1987). Empirical tests of this rational, utility maximization-based theory have shown that employee grievance filing is significantly positively associated with wage premiums paid by current employers and with local labor market unemployment rates (Cappelli and Chauvin, 1991). These findings can be readily integrated with exit-voice-loyalty theory by interpreting them to mean that employees will be more likely to file grievances – exercise voice – when the cost of exit is relatively high, as signaled by lower-paying and/or meager alternative employment opportunities. Further, these findings are consistent with those derived from organizational justice theory-based and also expectancy theory-based grievance procedure research, which similarly concludes that employees compare the costs and benefits of grievance filing with other alternatives in deciding whether or not to file grievances (Klass, 1989).[2]

Industrial relations-due process theory basically models grievance activity as a component of the larger collective bargaining relationship between union and management. In particular, grievance activity has been found to increase significantly as the time to renegotiate a collective bargaining agreement draws nearer, and to decline significantly after a new agreement has been reached (Lewin and Peterson, 1988; Chamberlain and Kuhn, 1965; Kuhn, 1961). Further, some of these grievances may be non-meritorious in the sense that they are fundamentally intended to influence or alter the parties' relative bargaining power. From this perspective, grievance activity represents a form of fractional or continuous bargaining between the parties in which due process objectives that were only partially achieved in collective bargaining are pursued through grievance filing, processing, and settlement. A limitation of this theory is that it de-emphasizes the conflict that occurs in day-to-day employment relationships and that can be distinguished from the periodic conflict that attends the negotiation of a new collective bargaining agreement.

Organizational punishment-industrial discipline theory basically treats the grievance procedure as a rule enforcement mechanism, with a marked emphasis on sanctions for 'deviant' workplace and organizational behavior (Arvey and Jones, 1985). This theory appears equally applicable to unionized and non-union employment contexts, and more than most other employment relationship conflict theories calls attention to post-grievance settlement behavior and outcomes. For example, research by Lewin and Peterson (1988), Lewin (1987) and Olson-Buchanan (1996) finds that, following grievance settlement, grievance filers are more likely than non-filers to experience higher turnover rates and lower job performance ratings, promotion rates and work attendance rates. US, Canadian, British, and Italian studies find that employees reinstated to their jobs following or as an explicit condition of grievance settlement subsequently experience lower job satisfaction and higher turnover rates than non-grievance filers (Malinowski, 1981; Barnacle, 1991; Dickens et al., 1984; Rocella, 1989). Still other research shows

that warnings to and dismissals of certain employees signal to employees and managers more broadly the types of workplace behavior that are inconsistent with or opposed to prevailing organizational rules and norms (O'Reilly and Weitz, 1980).

Displacement theory proposes that the time devoted to grievance activity – grievance filing, processing, and settlement – basically supplants productive work time. This theory is empirically supported by studies showing that grievance activity is significantly negatively associated with manufacturing plant productivity and product quality, and significantly positively associated with labor costs (Ichniowski, 1992, 1986; Katz et al., 1983; Kleiner et al., 1995). It is further supported by research showing that labor-management cooperation initiatives are significantly negatively associated with grievance filing rates (Katz et al. , 1985). The main weakness of this theory, however, is that it inferentially postulates that the optimum level of grievance activity is zero (because all grievance activity represents lost work time). Stated differently, this theory gives scant attention to the potential lost work time and productivity that may emanate from 'felt' grievances that are never made manifest.

Strategic human resource theory can be distinguished from other employment relationship conflict theories by its strong emphasis on progressive or 'high employee involvement' practices. These practices typically include selective hiring, employment continuity, team-based work, variable pay, and information-sharing with employees, which are modeled as a set, bundle or package that perforce reduces employment relationship conflict (Pfeffer, 1998). The underlying reasoning in this regard is that the more employees are involved in decision-making and managing their own work – self-management – the lower the likelihood that employment relationship conflict will occur. Indeed, some versions of high involvement human resource management include a grievance procedure as part of the package (Huselid, 1995). Several studies have found that high involvement management practices are significantly positively related to employee productivity, negatively related to employee turnover, and positively related to organizational performance, specifically, market value, return on invested capital, product quality, and production line 'up time' (Huselid, 1995; MacDuffie, 1995; Ichniowski et al., 1997; Arthur, 1994; Mitchell et al., 1990).

Among all of these theories of employment relationship conflict, strategic human resource theory most clearly envisions and positions the grievance procedure as a reactive voice mechanism, both in unionized and non-union settings (Kaminski, 1999). By contrast, strategic human resource theory envisions and positions high involvement management as a positive voice mechanism in which conflict either does not occur or, more realistically, occurs but can be anticipated and dealt with 'proactively'. Such proactive treatment may be rendered through work-centered teams or joint labor-management committees or informal discussions between supervisors and employees or employee forums and on-line chat rooms or even through grievance mediation. From a temporal perspective, therefore, strategic human resource theory emphasizes early stage conflict manifestation and resolution, in contrast to most other theories of employment relationship conflict that emphasize employment relationship deterioration, displacement, discipline and a late stage, reactive search for organizational justice.

Employment conflict resolution effectiveness

While there are myriad ways of assessing the effectiveness of employment conflict resolution systems, methods, and practices, there is not a firm consensus among researchers or practitioners about what exactly constitutes such effectiveness. To bring coherence to this matter, employment conflict resolution effectiveness will be considered in terms of grievance (and grievance-like) procedure dynamics as well as individual and organizational outcomes.

Grievance procedure dynamics

Conceptually and empirically, the existence or availability of a grievance procedure can be distinguished from the use of the procedure. From the perspective of employment conflict resolution, especially in North America and Europe, researchers and practitioners largely agree that a grievance procedure that is available but not used is an ineffective procedure, likely indicating that conflict is being suppressed or that employees fear retaliation from using the grievance procedure.[3] Similarly, a grievance procedure that is overused, that is, flooded with grievances, is regarded as an ineffective procedure, likely signaling the absence of workplace supervision/ management or employee misunderstanding of the scope and purposes of the procedure.[4]

Empirical evidence indicates that grievance procedure usage rarely displays either of the aforementioned extremes. Rather, in the US, the overall average grievance filing rate – the number of grievances filed annually by 100 employees – is approximately 10 per cent in unionized settings and five per cent in non-union settings. In terms of industry variation, Lewin and Peterson (1999, 1988) found annual average grievance filing rates among unionized US employees ranging between 7.8 per cent in retail trade (that is, department stores) and 16.3 per cent in steel manufacturing. Among unionized Canadian employees, Bemmels (1994) found annual average grievance filing rates ranging between 0.6 per cent in education and 48.2 per cent in railway transportation. Further, Cappelli and Chauvin (1991) found that grievance filing rates among US unionized employees varied significantly by industry labor market conditions but not by industry technology.

While grievance filing among non-union employees occurs about half as often as among unionized employees, there is also considerable variation in non-union employee grievance filing rates. For example, in a US-based five company study, Lewin (1997) found non-union employee annual grievance filing rates ranging between 3.8 and 6.2 per cent, and in a more recent single-company study (Lewin, 2005) found that non-union employee annual grievance filing rates ranged between 4.6 and 8.2 per cent over a 50-year period. These findings indicate not only that non-union grievance procedures are actually used by employees (rather then simply being available), but also that the volume of grievance activity is considerably greater among non-union than among unionized US employees. This is because of the continuing decline of US union membership and collectively bargained grievance procedures on the one hand, and the continuing growth of management-determined grievance procedures among non-union companies on the other hand. Hence, if actual grievance procedure usage is taken as a measure of employment conflict resolution effectiveness, then recent experience with both unionized and non-union grievance procedures indicates that these procedures are at least moderately effective.

A particularly widely used measure of grievance procedure effectiveness is speed of settlement. A standard maxim in the area of employment relationship conflict is that such conflict should be settled as quickly and as close as possible to its source of origin. From this perspective, quicker lower-level grievance settlement is preferable to slower, higher-level grievance settlement – though clearly speed and level of grievance settlement are highly correlated. Studies of grievance settlement in both unionized and non-union settings find that the vast bulk of formal grievances are settled at the first two (typically, out of four) steps of the grievance procedure, with only about two to three per cent of grievances settled at the final step. Regarding speed of grievance settlement, Lewin and Peterson (1999) found an average of 52 days to grievance settlement in four large unionized companies during the 1990s, with the average days to settlement having declined by about 25 per cent from the 1980s. Similarly, among non-union companies with grievance procedures most grievances are settled about 45 days after their initial filing (Lewin, 2004). Grievance settlements are reached more quickly when grievances are

subject to expedited arbitration, defined as the skipping of certain intermediate grievance processing steps, or when subject to grievance mediation.

While swifter justice may be preferable to slower justice in grievance settlement, speed of grievance settlement, *per se*, is a quite limited measure of grievance procedure effectiveness. Several scholars (for example, Gordon and Bowlby, 1988) have shown that perceived fairness of grievance processing and grievance decisions are significantly more important than speed of settlement to grievants' overall assessment of the grievance procedure. Clark and Gallagher (1988) found the perceived effectiveness of the grievance procedure in terms of workplace equity, fairness of grievance processing, and extent to which the grievance procedure represents employee interests to be significantly positively associated with employee attitudes toward the grievance procedure, whereas speed of settlement was unrelated to such attitudes. Clark et al. (1990) and Bemmels (1995) found that union member attitudes toward and assessment of grievance procedure effectiveness are strongly influenced by their commitment to the union, commitment to the employer, and dual commitment, but not by speed of grievance settlement.

Grievance procedure dynamics conclude with grievance decisions therefore the grievance decision win-loss rate may be considered a measure of employment conflict resolution effectiveness – but largely a one-sided measure. A priori, employee perceptions (ratings) of grievance procedure effectiveness can be expected to be positively correlated with the percentage of grievances decided in favor of employees, and management perceptions of grievance procedure effectiveness can be expected to be positively correlated with the percentage of grievances decided in favor of management. Surprisingly, there is scant empirical evidence that bears upon these propositions. Instead, empirical work in this area finds that the employee grievance decision win rate rises with the level of grievance settlement. For example, in a study of five non-union companies, Lewin (1997, 1992) found that the employee grievance decision win rate rose from about 40 per cent at the lowest step to about 60 per cent at the highest step of the grievance procedure. Moreover, in a study of four unionized companies, Lewin and Peterson (1999) found that grievances over disciplinary actions were far more likely than grievances over all other issues to be taken to and decided at the highest step of the grievance procedure (that is, arbitration), thereby suggesting a more parsimonious, issue-based framing of grievance decision win-loss rates in the parties' assessments of grievance procedure effectiveness. Even this framing, however, does not address the matter of whether employment conflict resolution is more effective when there is a 50-50 overall grievance decision win-loss rate than when a more unbalanced grievance decision win-loss rate prevails.

Post-grievance settlement outcomes

A broadened perspective on employment conflict resolution effectiveness is offered by extant research on post-grievance settlement outcomes. Much of this work focuses on employee performance, internal mobility and retention following grievance settlement, on management reprisal against grievants, and on the reinstatement of dismissed employees. Consequently, this research shifts the focus of grievance procedure study and practice from grievance procedure dynamics to the consequences of grievance procedure involvement for employees and to the behavior of management following grievance settlement.

In a series of studies, Lewin and Peterson (1999, 1988) analyzed post-grievance settlement outcomes in four unionized organizations over two separate three-year periods. The quasi-experimental research design used in these studies permitted comparisons between samples of grievance filers and non-filers of employee job performance ratings, promotion rates and work attendance rates during pre-grievance, grievance filing and post-grievance settlement periods as well as comparisons of post-grievance settlement

turnover rates among these two employee groups. The researchers found no significant between-group differences on these measures during the pre-grievance and grievance filing periods, but found significant differences during the one-to three-year post-grievance settlement periods. Specifically, and compared with non-filers, grievance filers had significantly lower job performance ratings and promotion rates (though not work attendance rates), during the period following grievance settlement.[5] Further, post-grievance settlement employee voluntary turnover rates were significantly higher among grievants than among non-grievants. Identical analyses conducted among samples of supervisors of grievance filers and non-filers in the same unionized organizations yielded closely similar results. That is, whereas as the two groups of supervisors did not differ significantly with respect to job performance ratings, promotion rates and work attendance rates during the pre-grievance and grievance filing periods, supervisors of grievants had significantly lower job performance ratings and promotion rates (though, again, not work attendance rates) and significantly higher turnover rates than supervisors of non-grievants during the period following grievance settlement. In particular, supervisors of grievants had significantly higher involuntary turnover rates than supervisors of non-grievants, meaning that supervisors of grievants were significantly more likely than supervisors of non-grievants to be terminated from employment following grievance settlement.

This same research design was used by Lewin (2005, 1997, 1992, 1987) to study post-grievance settlement outcomes in non-union organizations. The grievance procedures in these organizations varied in several respects, especially the final settlement step. Nevertheless, the findings from this research are strikingly similar to the aforementioned findings regarding post-grievance settlement outcomes in unionized organizations. In particular, and once again using matched samples of grievance filers and non-filers in each organization, there were no significant differences between these two employee groups in job performance ratings, promotion rates and work attendance rates during the pre-grievance and grievance filing periods. During the (one to three year) post-grievance settlement period, however, grievance filers had significantly lower job performance ratings and promotion rates and significantly higher voluntary *and* involuntary turnover rates than non-filers. A very similar pattern of post-grievance settlement outcome differences prevailed as between supervisors of grievants and supervisors of non-grievants in these non-union organizations. The supervisors of grievants, who did not differ significantly from the supervisors of non-grievants on any of the outcome variables measured prior to and during grievance filing, had significantly lower job performance ratings and promotion rates and significantly higher voluntary *and* involuntary turnover rates during the post-grievance settlement period.

This body of research accords most closely with employment relationship conflict systems theory, exit-voice-loyalty theory, and organizational punishment-discipline theory. In particular, the research supports the notion of systematic relationships among grievance procedure antecedent, process and outcome variables, indicates that grievance procedure involvement contributes to additional deterioration of employment relationships, and strongly implies that participants in the grievance process are punished for their involvement in such activity. Baldly stated, management appears ultimately to exercise reprisal against employee-grievants and the supervisors of grievants. This conclusion is further supported by Klass and DeNisi's (1989) research, which found that employees who file grievances against their direct supervisors subsequently receive significantly lower job performance ratings than employees who file grievances over management policies. Still further evidence for the management reprisal explanation of post-grievance settlement outcomes is provided by Boroff and Lewin's (1997) study of a large unionized telecommunications company, which found that employee fear of reprisal for filing grievances was significantly inversely related

to the probability of an employee filing a grievance (including when employee loyalty to the employer was controlled), and from Lewin's (2005) study of a large non-union aerospace company that found a similarly significant inverse relationship.

There is, however, an alternative to the management reprisal explanation of grievance filing and post-grievance settlement outcomes, which may be termed 'revealed performance'. The argument underlying this explanation is that grievants and their supervisors are systematically poorer performers than non-grievants and their supervisors. For this argument to hold sway, and recalling that grievants and their supervisors do not differ significantly from non-grievants and their supervisors in terms of job performance ratings, promotion rates and work attendance rates prior to grievance settlement, the actual filing and processing of grievances must cause management to pay closer attention to the assessment of employee and supervisor job performance. If and as this occurs, management discovers ex-post that grievants and their supervisors are (systematically) poorer performers than non-grievants and their supervisors.

There is some theoretical and empirical support for this alternative explanation. For example, the shock theory of unionism posits that the unionization of a firm's employees spurs the management of that firm to improve organizational performance, and to do so in such ways or to such an extent that the value added from improved organizational performance at least offsets the costs (typically, pay and fringe benefit costs) of unionization (Rees, 1977). By analogous reasoning, the filing of grievances by employees shocks management into taking actions that improve organizational performance, but in this instance by paying closer attention to performance evaluation and by terminating employees and supervisors whose 'revealed performance' is low. Experimental support for this alternative explanation is provided by Olson-Buchanan (1997, 1996), whose laboratory studies found that grievants had significantly poorer job performance after grievance settlement than comparably matched non-grievants. On the basis of this finding, Olson-Buchanan (1996) concludes that because conflict between an employee and her supervisor serves to reduce the employee's job performance, there may be 'a real difference between grievance filers' and non-filers' [job performance] behavior' (p. 62).

The literature on reinstatement of dismissed employees can be interpreted to support either the management reprisal explanation or the revealed performance explanation of post-grievance settlement outcomes. Most such reinstatement occurs as a result of arbitration awards in grievance cases, so that considerably more is known about the reinstatement and post-reinstatement experience of unionized than non-union employees. While reinstatement of dismissed employees occurs in about half of sampled arbitration awards, the proportion of dismissed employees actually returning to work following reinstatement decisions ranges widely, from negligible in Britain (Knight and Latreille, 2001; Dickens et al., 1984) to an estimated 46 per cent in a Canadian study, (Malinowski, 1981) to an estimated 88 per cent in a US study (Barnacle, 1991).[6] Reinstated employees are often reluctant to return to work and often have relatively low job performance and relatively high turnover after they return to work (Bemmels and Foley, 1996). In these respects, studies by Rocella (1989) and Shantz and Rogow (1984) found post-reinstatement employee turnover rates of 28 per cent and 55 per cent, respectively, during the two-year period following reinstatement of dismissed employees to their jobs, and a study by Labig et al. (1985) found that post-reinstatement job performance was significantly positively associated with employees' prior (pre-dismissal) job performance.

On balance, the extant literature on employee reinstatement to work following grievance settlement, as with the literature on post-grievance settlement employee job performance, internal mobility, and turnover, can be interpreted to support a management reprisal story or a revealed performance story, or both. On its face, employee reinstatement seems especially consistent with organizational justice theory, but on deeper reflection is perhaps most consistent with exit-voice-loyalty and organizational punishment-discipline theories. This is because reinstated employees appear for the most part to experience additional deterioration of their employment relationships, and to be more likely than continuing employees to be disciplined by *and* voluntarily quit (exit) their employers. More broadly, this reasoning is consistent with evidence drawn from North America and to a lesser extent Europe, which shows that monetary settlements of individual employment relationship conflict are far more prevalent, and perhaps more effective, than reinstatement to work and the intended resumption of original employment relationships.

Grievance procedures and organizational performance

Beyond their effects on individual employees, supervisors, and managers, grievance procedures have certain consequences for organizational performance. In this regard, the aforementioned distinction between the availability and use of a grievance procedure (or equivalent employment conflict resolution mechanism) is especially relevant. Succinctly stated, and to preview the main conclusion of this section, the availability of a grievance or grievance-like procedure as part of a bundle of high involvement type human resource management practices has been shown to be positively associated with such organizational performance measures as market value, rate of return on invested capital, productivity, and product quality, whereas the actual use of a grievance or grievance-like procedure has been shown to be negatively associated with these and other measures of organizational performance.

To illustrate, Katz et al. (1983) found the grievance rate to be significantly positively associated with labor costs and significantly negatively associated with productivity and product quality in a sample of US automobile manufacturing plants. These researchers interpreted their findings to support the concept of a displacement effect, meaning that time devoted to grievance filing and settlement is time taken away from productive activity, thereby resulting in lower plant performance. In a related longitudinal study of automobile manufacturing, Northsworthy and Zabala (1985) found the grievance rate to be significantly negatively associated with total factor productivity and significantly positively related to unit production costs. In studies of paper manufacturing that controlled for the effects of other variables, Ichniowski (1992, 1986) found a significant negative relationship between the grievance rate and monthly production in nine unionized paper mills over a six-year period. Instructively, Katz, et al. (1985) found that a quality of working life improvement program significantly reduced the grievance rate and thus the displacement effect in automobile manufacturing, and Ichniowski (1992) found that a labor-management cooperation initiative significantly reduced the grievance rate and significantly improved the labor relations climate and plant performance in paper manufacturing. These findings are closely consistent with those of Belman (1992), who concluded that employment relationship conflict measured by the grievance rate has significant negative effects on manufacturing performance, and with a case study of New United Motor Manufacturing, Incorporated (NUMMI), conducted by Levine (1995), that attributed improved manufacturing performance to lower grievance rates. Taken as whole, this research provides strong evidence that grievance procedure usage/activity is significantly negatively associated with organizational performance.

Another substantial body of research, however, indicates that the availability of a grievance or grievance-like employment conflict resolution procedure is significantly positively associated with organizational performance. To illustrate, Mitchell et al. (1990) constructed an index of human resource management practices that included the presence of a formal grievance procedure, and then analyzed the relationship between this index and several measures of financial performance among 495 US-based businesses. These researchers found significant positive relationships between the index and return on assets, return on investment and revenue per employee in these businesses. In a related study, Huselid (1995) included the percentage of employees covered by a grievance procedure in an index of high-involvement human resource management practices, and found a significant positive relationship between this index and employee productivity, a significant negative relationship between this index and employee turnover, and a significant positive relationship between this index and company market value and return on capital investment. In a study of steel manufacturing, Ichniowski et al. (1997) included the presence of a formal grievance procedure in their index of an innovative bundle of human resource management practices, and found significant positive relationships between this index and plant up time, productivity, and product quality. Similar findings have been produced by Arthur (1994, 1992) and MacDuffie (1995) in their studies of steel and automobile manufacturing, respectively, all of which are empirically consistent with conceptual arguments advanced by Levine (1995) and Eaton and Voos (1994, 1992) for the positive effects of innovative human resource management practices, especially enhanced employee participation in decision making, on organizational performance.

From this research on the grievance procedure as a mechanism for employment conflict resolution, one conclusion appears dominant, namely, the presence or availability of a grievance procedure is positively associated with organizational performance, whereas actual use of a grievance procedure – grievance activity – is negatively associated with organizational performance.

Future directions: a research roadmap

A major limitation of employment conflict resolution research is that some, perhaps most, employment relationship conflict is not made manifest through the filing of formal written grievances. In both unionized and non-union organizations, it appears that only relatively small proportions of actual conflicts enter into and are settled through formal grievance and grievance like-systems. This, in turn, suggests that even the strongest findings from employment relationship conflict research are fundamentally limited by what may be termed the omitted or unobserved variables problem. If formal grievance filing and settlement indeed represent only the tip of the employment relationship conflict iceberg, then a major research challenge is to make greater use of observation, participant-observation and other primary research methods that potentially permit greater documentation and analysis of the informal settlement of employment relationship conflict.

Following strategic human resource theory, low grievance rates imply that employment relationship conflict is anticipated and proactively managed through the use of high involvement practices which, in turn, positively contribute to organizational performance (see Gollan et al., 2007). From other theoretical perspectives, however, including exit-voice-loyalty theory, due process theory, compensating differentials theory, and displacement theory, the costs of making employment relationship conflict explicit through grievance filing exceed the benefits to be obtained there from. Consequently, employees who experience employment relationship conflict (that is, deterioration) may 'resolve' such conflict by quitting and taking jobs elsewhere, if in fact they have alternative employment opportunities. This line of reasoning underscores another important limitation of extant employment relationship conflict research, which is to have largely ignored the labor market as a protector of employee rights. In this regard, employment-at-will, which is most often characterized as a strongly management-oriented doctrine, can potentially serve the interests of employees who experience deteriorated employment relationships.

For employees who have few or no alternative employment opportunities, and for relatively long service employees who are tied to their employers through deferred compensation, pension benefit accumulation and other 'handcuffs', quitting and seeking alternative employment as a solution to deteriorated employment relationships is a limited or non-existent option. While, conceptually, such employees can seek redress of employment-related grievances through formal grievance filing, organizational justice and organizational punishment-discipline theory and research imply that these employees will choose silence – suffering in silence, as some put it – as the dominant response to employment relationship conflict.[7] In this regard, a challenge to researchers is to document and assess the extent to which silence in the face of employment relationship conflict is, on the one hand, an effective coping mechanism, and, on the other hand, a costly suppression mechanism that generates unanticipated deviant behavior, including workplace and family violence.

The argument that grievance filing shocks management into paying closer attention to performance evaluation – an argument offered as an explanation of empirical findings regarding post-grievance settlement outcomes – raises an important research issue. This issue is the validity and reliability of the performance evaluation systems, methods and techniques used by business (and non-business) enterprises. It has long been known that traditional performance evaluation in which a superior (boss or manager) alone periodically evaluates his or her subordinates leads to upwardly skewed rather than normally distributed performance evaluation ratings (Lewin and Mitchell, 1995). Newer 360 degree type performance evaluation is often claimed to generate relatively more valid and reliable performance assessments, but if this is so and given the widespread use of 360 degree performance evaluation by business and non-business organizations alike, the shock explanation of grievance filing and post-grievance settlement outcomes appears doubtful, perhaps even wrongheaded. A 'test' of this shock explanation could therefore be conducted by using performance evaluation ratings to predict employee grievance filing, with the operating hypothesis being that performance evaluation ratings will be significantly negatively correlated with (subsequent) grievance filing. Such a test could be refined and potentially produce more robust findings if it incorporated data from traditional as well as 360 degree type performance evaluation methods. Empirical confirmation of the aforementioned hypothesis would serve as evidence for the shock explanation of grievance filing, whereas empirical refutation of the hypothesis would serve as evidence against the shock explanation.

While, for some, quitting deteriorated employment relationships is a viable solution to employment relationship conflict, and, for others, suffering in silence may be an effective mechanism for coping with employment relationship conflict, still another response to employment relationship conflict has been invoked by a growing segment of the work force, namely, litigation. In this instance, employees and former employees seek to redress one or another type of employment discrimination or wrongful termination by suing their employers or former employers, and do so by 'employing' an agent – a plaintiff's attorney – to represent them. In the US, where separate laws ostensibly protect the employment rights of racial and ethnic minorities, women, older workers, and the disabled, litigation to redress employment-related actions, issues and grievances has grown enormously in recent years. While, in theory, such litigation is aimed at restoring or correcting severely deteriorated employment relationships, including by reinstatement to work, in reality, which is to say practice, most such litigation concludes with monetary settlements without (or in place of) reinstatement. An important research issue in this regard is determining the extent to which external litigation has supplanted internal grievance filing and settlement as an institutional mechanism for resolving employment relationship conflict.[8] As with the labor market as a potential protector

of employee rights, most employment relationship conflict research has ignored the potential for litigation to serve as a protector of employee rights.

While employment relationship conflict research has shifted from being dominated by industrial relations scholars to human resource management scholars and, more recently, organizational behavior scholars, and while research on labor law has largely become supplanted by research on employment law, insufficient research attention has nevertheless been paid to the vastly expanded scope of contemporary employment relationship conflict (Lewin, 2001). Today, such conflict involves not only lower-level employees ('organizational participants'), but middle- and especially upper-level employees as well. Most employees at all levels of organizations do not belong to unions and are therefore not covered by collective bargaining contracts. Ironically, however, non-union grievance procedures typically cover a far broader range of employees, up to and often including mid-level managers, than are covered by collectively bargained grievance procedures. In the US, moreover, and perhaps elsewhere, a far larger proportion of the workforce is covered by individual employment contracts than by collective bargaining contracts. Such individual employment contracts often contain procedures for the internal resolution of employment-related conflict, but also provide the basis for external litigation to settle claims of contractual violations brought by employee or employer. Researchers should therefore raise their sights a bit to focus attention on the dynamics and outcomes of employment relationship conflict that occurs at intermediate and higher levels of organizations irrespective of whether or not a grievance procedure is the mechanism through which such conflict resolution is pursued. In this regard, studies using samples of executive and professional employment contracts would be especially helpful and potentially illuminating.

The argument that unionized and non-union grievance procedures alike are reactive, ex-post type conflict resolution mechanisms that ultimately exacerbate rather than mitigate deteriorated employment relationships, and the contrasting companion argument that high involvement management enables employment relationship conflict to be anticipated and therefore dealt with ex-ante in a relatively more proactive fashion, requires broader and deeper empirical investigation. In this regard, researchers should document the specific ways in which employment relationship conflict is anticipated and resolved under varying degrees of high involvement management, and should also do so in comparison with conflict anticipation and resolution under conditions of low involvement management.[9] It would also be helpful for the purpose of advancing research on employment relationship conflict to know more about perceptions of organizational justice as well as employment relationship deterioration among employees who work under conditions of high involvement management. Finally, the claim that the presence or availability of a grievance procedure is positively associated with organizational performance while the actual use of a grievance procedure is negatively associated with organizational performance is hardly a robust claim. Further inquiry into this intriguing yet sobering claim is sorely needed lest it be concluded that, when it comes to employment conflict resolution, the 'best' grievance procedure is one that is least used!

NOTES

1 For a systematic treatment of collective forms of conflict, including strikes, see Gall and Hebdon, this volume, Chapter 31.

2 Compensating differentials theory (of grievance activity) is referred to by some scholars as efficiency theory, for example, Bacharach and Bamberger (2004), who also conclude that the effects on grievance filing of such labor market variables as the wage premium are moderated by work context and labor power variables.

3 The distinction between availability and use of a conflict resolution mechanism has been most pointedly made in studies of public sector contract arbitration (Lewin et al. 1988, Chapter 5).

4 Massive grievance filing sometimes occurs as a tactic intended to influence the power relationships and hence the results of collective negotiations over new contracts between union and management.

In this limited circumstance, the union (employees) would likely regard the grievance procedure as highly effective, whereas management would likely regard the grievance procedure as highly ineffective.

5 Other studies, however, find significant effects of grievance activity on employee work attendance. For example, Klass et al. (1991) report a significant positive relationship during an eight-year period between grievance filing over management policies and employee absenteeism in a unionized public sector organization, but a significant negative relationship between grievance filing over disciplinary issues and employee absenteeism.

6 A provocative finding from British and North American studies is that in cases of alleged unfair dismissal from work, arbitrators, who are predominantly male, are significantly more likely to render favorable decisions for female than for male grievants. These same studies, however, find no significant differences between 'successful' female and male grievants in the financial compensation awarded to them by arbitrators (Knight and Latreille, 2001; Bemmels, 1990; Bemmels, 1988).

7 Some researchers refer to such silence as 'neglect'. See Rusbelt et al. 1988.

8 The notion that litigation may be supplanting internal grievance and grievance-like procedures for the resolution of employment relationship conflict runs counter to a dominant theme in the literature on ADR, which is that ADR is, by definition, an alternative to litigation!

9 For a definition of low involvement management and evidence of its relationship to business performance, see Lewin and Dotan, 2007

REFERENCES

Antonioni, D. (1994) 'The Effects of Feedback Accountability on Upward Appraisal Ratings,' *Personnel Psychology*, 47 (2): 349–55.

Arthur, J.B. (1994) 'Effects of Human Resource Systems on Manufacturing Performance,' *Academy of Management Journal*, 37 (3): 670–87.

Arthur, J.B. (1992) 'The Link Between Business Strategy and Industrial Relations Systems in American Steel Minimills,' *Industrial and Labor Relations Review*, 45 (2): 488–506.

Arvey, R.D. and Jones, A.P. (1985) 'The Uses of Discipline in Organizational Settings,' in Staw, B.M. and Cummings, L.L. (eds), *Research in Organizational Behavior*, 7: 367–408.

Bacharach, S. and Bamberger, P. (2004) 'The Power of Labor to Grieve: The Impact of the Workplace, Labor Market, and Power-Dependence on Employee Grievance Filing,' *Industrial and Labor Relations Review*, 57 (4): 518–39.

Barnacle, P. (1991) *Arbitration of Discharge Grievances in Ontario: Outcomes and Reinstatement Experiences.* Kingston, ON: Industrial Relations Center.

Belman, D. (1992) 'Unions, the Quality of Labor Relations, and Firm Performance,' in Mishel, L. and Voos, P.B. (eds), *Unions and Economic Competitiveness.* Armonk, NY: Sharpe. pp. 41–107.

Bemmels, B. (1995) 'Shop Stewards' Satisfaction With Grievance Procedures,' *Industrial Relations*, 34 (1): 578–92.

Bemmels, B. (1994) 'The Determinants of Grievance Initiation,' *Industrial and Labor Relations Review*, 47 (2): 285–301.

Bemmels, B. (1990) 'Gender Effects in Grievance Arbitration,' *Industrial Relations*, 29 (3): 313–25.

Bemmels, B. (1988) 'Gender Effects in Discharge Arbitration: Evidence from British Columbia,' *Academy of Management Journal*, 31 (3): 251–62.

Bemmels, B. and Foley, J.R. (1996) 'Grievance Procedure Research: A Review and Theoretical Recommendations,' *Journal of Management*, 22 (3): 359–84.

Bendersky. C. (2003) 'Organizational Dispute Resolution Systems: A Complementarities Model,' *Academy of Management Review*, 28 (4): 643–56.

Bendix, R. (1956) *Work and Authority in Industry.* New York: Wiley.

Bognanno, M.F., Budd, J.W. and Kleiner, M.M. (2007) 'Symposium Introduction: Governing the Global Workplace,' *Industrial Relations*, 46 (2): 215–21.

Boroff, K.E. and Lewin, D. (1997) 'Loyalty, Voice and Intent to Exit a Union Firm: A Conceptual and Empirical Analysis,' *Industrial and Labor Relations Review*, 51 (1): 50–63.

Cappelli, P. and Chauvin, K. (1991) 'A Test of an Efficiency Model of Grievance Activity,' *Industrial and Labor Relations Review*, 45 (1): 3–14.

Chamberlain, N.W. and Kuhn, J.W. (1965) *Collective Bargaining*, 2nd ed. New York: McGraw-Hill.

Clark, P.F. and Gallagher, D.G. (1988) 'Membership Perceptions of the Value and Effect of Grievance Procedures,' *Proceedings of the Fortieth Annual Meeting. Madison, WI: Industrial Relations Research Association*, pp. 406–15.

Clark, P.F., Gallagher, D.G. and Pavlak, T.J. (1990) 'Member Commitment in an American Union: The Role of the Grievance Procedure,' *Labor Studies Journal*, 21 (2): 147–57.

Commons, J.R. (1919) 'American Shoemakers: 1648–1895: A Sketch of Industrial Evaluation,' *Quarterly Journal of Economics*, 25, reprinted and revised in Commons, J.R., (ed.), *A Documentary History of American Industrial Society, Vol. 3.* New York: Russell and Russell. pp. 18–58.

Colvin, A.J.S. (2004) 'Adoption and Use of Dispute Resolution Procedures in the Non-union Workplace,' in Lewin, D. and Kaufman, B.E., (eds), *Advances in Industrial and Labor Relations*, 13: 71–97.

Colvin, A.J.S. (2003) 'Institutional Pressures, Human Resources Strategies, and the Rise of Nonunion Dispute Resolution Procedures,' *Industrial and Labor Relations Review*, 56 (3): 375–92.

Delaney, J.T., Lewin, D. and Ichniowski, C. (1989) *Human Resource Policies and Practices in American Firms.* Washington, D.C.: US Department of Labor, BLMR #137.

Dickens, L., Hart, M., Jones, M. and Weeks, B. (1984) 'The British Experience Under a Statute Prohibiting Unfair Dismissal,' *Industrial and Labor Relations Review*, 37 (4): 497–514.

Donohue, III, J.J. and Siegelman, P. (1991) 'The Changing Nature of Employment Discrimination Litigation,' *Stanford Law Review*, 43 (4): 983–1033.

Eaton, A.E. and Voos, P.B. (1994) 'Productivity-Enhancing Innovations in Work Organization, Compensation, and Employee Participation in the Union versus the Nonunion Sectors,' in Lewin, D. and Sockell, D., (eds), *Advances in Industrial and Labor Relations*, 6: 63–109.

Eaton, A.E. and Voos, P.B. (1992) 'Unions and Contemporary Innovations in Work Organization, Compensation, and Employee Participation,' in Mishel, L. and Voos, P.B., (eds), *Unions and Economic Competitiveness.* Armonk, NY: Myron E. Sharpe. pp. 173–215.

Feuille, P. (1999) 'Grievance Mediation,' in Eaton, A.E. and Keefe, J.H., (eds), *Employment Dispute Resolution and Worker Rights in the Changing Workplace.* Champaign, IL: Industrial Relations Research Association. pp. 187–217.

Feuille, P. and Delaney, J.T. (1992) 'The Individual Pursuit of Organizational Justice: Grievance Procedures in Nonunion Workplaces,' in Ferris, G.R. and Rowland, K.M., (eds), *Research in Personnel and Human Resource Management*, 10: 187–232.

Freeman, R.B. and Medoff, J.L. (1984) *What Do Unions Do?* New York: Basic Books.

Gollan, P.J.; Poutsma, E. and Veersma, U. (2007) 'Editors' Introduction: New Roads in Organizational Participation?,' *Industrial Relations*, 45 (4): 499–512.

Goldberg, S.B. (1982) 'The Mediation of Grievances under a Collective Contract: An Alternative to Arbitration,' *Northwestern University Law Review*, 77 (1): 270–315.

Gordon, M.E. and Bowlby, R.C. (1988) 'Propositions About Grievance Settlements: Finally, Consultation With Grievants,' *Personnel Psychology*, 41 (2): 107–23.

Hirschman, A.O. (1970) *Exit, Voice and Loyalty.* Cambridge, MA: Harvard University Press.

Huselid, M.A. (1995) 'The Impact of Human Resource Management Practices on Turnover, Productivity, and Corporate Financial Performance,' *Academy of Management Journal,* 38 (2): 635–72.

Ichniowski, C. (1992) 'Human Resource Practices and Productive Labor-Management Relations,' in Lewin, D., Mitchell, O.S. and Sherer, P.D., (eds), *Research Frontiers in Industrial Relations and Human Resources.* Madison, WI: Industrial Relations Research Association. pp. 239–71.

Ichniowski, C. (1986) 'The Effects of Grievance Activity on Productivity,' *Industrial and Labor Relations Review,* 40 (1): 75–89.

Ichniowski, C. and Lewin, D. (1987) 'Grievance Procedures and Firm Performance,' in Kleiner, M.M., Block, R.N., Roomkin, R. and Salsburg, S.W., (eds), *Human Resources and the Performance of the Firm,* Industrial Relations Research Association. Washington, D.C.: Bureau of National Affairs. pp. 159–93.

Ichniowski, C., Shaw, K. and Prennushi, G. (1997) 'The Effects of Human Resource Management Practices on Productivity: A Study of Steel Finishing Lines,' *American Economic Review,* 87 (3): 291–313.

Jacoby, S.M. (1986) 'Progressive Discipline in American Industry: Origins, Development, Consequences,' in Lipsky, D.B. and Lewin, D., (eds), *Advances in Industrial and Labor Relations,* 3: 216–60.

Jehn, K. (1997) 'A Qualitative Analysis of Conflict Types and Dimensions in Organizational Groups,' *Administrative Science Quarterly,* 42 (4): 530–57.

Jensen, M.C. and Meckling, W.H. (1976) 'Theory of the Firm: Managerial Behavior, Agency Costs, and Ownership Structure,' *Journal of Financial Economics,* 3 (2): 305–60.

Kaminski, M. (1999) 'New Forms of Work Organization and Their Impact on the Grievance Procedure,' in Eaton, A.E. and Keefe, J.H., (eds), *Employment Dispute Resolution and Worker Rights in the Changing Workplace.* Champaign, IL: Industrial Relations Research Association. pp. 219–46.

Katz, H.C., Kochan, T.A. and Gobeille, K.R. (1983) 'Industrial Relations Performance, Economic Performance, and QWL Programs: An Interplant Analysis,' *Industrial and Labor Relations Review,* 37 (2): 3–17.

Katz, H.C., Kochan, T.A. and Weber, M.R. (1985). 'Assessing the Effects of Industrial Relations and Quality of Work Life Efforts on Organizational Effectiveness,' *Academy of Management Journal,* 28 (2): 509–27.

Klaas, B. (1989) 'Determinants of Grievance Activity and the Grievance System's Impact On Employee Behavior: An Integrative Perspective,' *Academy of Management Review,* 14 (3): 445–58.

Klass, B. and DeNisi, A. (1989) 'Managerial Reactions to Employee Dissent: The Impact of Grievance Activity on Performance Ratings,' *Academy of Management Journal,* 32 (4): 705–18.

Klass, B., Heneman, H.G. and Olson, C. (1991) 'Effects of Grievance Activity on Absenteeism,' *Journal of Applied Psychology,* 76 (6): 818–24.

Kleiner, M.M., Nickelsburg, G. and Pilarski, A. (1995) 'Monitoring, Grievances and Plant Performance,' *Industrial Relations,* 34 (2): 169–89.

Knight, T.R. (1986) 'Feedback and Grievance Initiation,' *Industrial and Labor Relations Review,* 39 (4): 585–98.

Knight, K.G. and Latreille, P.L. (2001) 'Gender Effects in British Unfair Dismissal Tribunal Hearings,' *Industrial and Labor Relations Review,* 54 (4): 816–34.

Kuhn, J.W. (1961) *Bargaining in Grievance Settlement: The Power of Industrial Work Groups.* New York: Columbia University Press.

Labig, Jr., C.E., Helburn, I. and Rogers, R. (1985) 'Discipline History, Seniority, and Reason for Discharge as Predictors of Postreinstatement Job Performance,' *The Arbitration Journal,* 40 (1): 44–52.

Levine, D.I. (1995) *Reinventing the Workplace.* Washington, D.C.: Brookings.

Lewin, D. (2005) 'Unionism and Employment Conflict Resolution: Rethinking Collective Voice and its Consequences,' *Journal of Labor Research,* 26 (2): 209–39.

Lewin, D. (2004) 'Dispute Resolution in Non-union Organizations: Key Empirical Findings,' in S. Estreicher and D. Sherwyn, (eds), *Alternative Dispute Resolution in the Employment Arena.* New York: Kluwer. pp. 397–403.

Lewin, D. (2001) 'IR and HR Perspectives on Workplace Conflict: What Can Each Learn from the Other?,' *Human Resource Management Review,* 11 (Fall): 453–85.

Lewin, D. (1999) 'Theoretical and Empirical Research on the Grievance Procedure and Arbitration: A Critical Review,' in Eaton, A.E. and Keefe, J.H., (eds), *Employment Dispute Resolution and Worker Rights in the Changing Workplace.* Champaign, IL: Industrial Relations Research Association. pp. 137–86.

Lewin, D. (1997) 'Workplace Dispute Resolution,' in Lewin, D., Mitchell, D.J.B. and Zaidi, M.A., (eds), *The Human Resource Management Handbook, Part II.* Greenwich, CT: JAI Press. pp. 197–218.

Lewin, D. (1994) 'Explicit Individual Contracting in the Labor Market,' in Kerr. C. and Staudohar, P.D., (eds), *Labor Economics and Industrial Relations: Markets and Institutions.* Cambridge, MA: Harvard University Press. pp. 401–28.

Lewin, D. (1992) 'Grievance Procedures in Non-union Workplaces: An Empirical Analysis of Usage, Dynamics, and Outcomes,' *Chicago-Kent Law Review*, 66 (3): 823–44.

Lewin, D. (1987) 'Dispute Resolution in the Non-union Firm: A Theoretical and Empirical Analysis,' *Journal of Conflict Resolution*, 31 (3): 465–502.

Lewin, D. and Boroff, K.E. (1996) 'The Role of Loyalty in Exit and Voice: A Conceptual and Empirical Analysis,' in Lewin, D., Kaufman, B.E. and Sockell, D., (eds), *Advances in Industrial and Labor Relations*, 7: 69–96.

Lewin, D. and Dotan, H. (2007) 'The Dual Theory of HRM and Business Performance,' Working Paper, UCLA Anderson School of Management.

Lewin, D. and Mitchell, D.J.B. (1995) *Human Resource Management: An Economic Approach*, 2nd ed. Cincinnati, OH: South-Western.

Lewin, D. and Peterson, R.B. (1999) 'Behavioral Outcomes of Grievance Activity,' *Industrial Relations*, 38 (4): 554–76.

Lewin, D. and Peterson, R.B. (1988) *The Modern Grievance Procedure in the United States.* New York: Quorum.

Lewin, D., Feuille, P., Kochan, T.A. and Delaney, J.T. (1988) *Public Sector Labor Relations: Analysis and Readings.* Lexington, MA: Heath.

Lind, E.A. and Tyler, E.R. (1988) *The Social Psychology of Procedural Justice.* New York: Plenum.

Lipsky, D.B., Seeber, R.L. and Fincher, R.D. (2003) *Emerging Systems for Managing Workplace Conflict.* San Francisco, CA: Jossey-Bass.

MacDuffie, J.P. (1995) 'Human Resource Bundles and Manufacturing Performance: Organizational Logic and Flexible Production Systems in the World Auto Industry,' *Industrial and Labor Relations Review*, 48 (2): 197–221.

Malinowski, A.A. (1981) 'An Empirical Analysis of Discharge Cases and the Work History of Employees Reinstated by Labor Arbitration,' *Dispute Resolution*, 36 (1): 31–46.

Mathewson, S.B., (ed.), (1931) *Restriction of Output Among Unorganized Workers.* Carbondale, IL: Southern Illinois University Press, reprinted 1969.

Mitchell, D.J.B., Lewin, D. and Lawler, III, E.E. (1990) 'Alternative Pay Systems, Firm Performance, and Productivity,' in Blinder, A.S., (ed.), *Paying for Productivity: A Look at the Evidence.* Washington, D.C.: Brookings. pp. 15–89.

Norsworthy, J.R. and Zabala, C.A. (1985) 'Worker Attitudes, Worker Behavior, and Productivity in the US Automobile Industry, 1959–1976,' *Industrial and Labor Relations Review*, 38 (4): 544–57.

Olson-Buchanan, J. (1997) 'To Grieve or Not to Grieve: Factors Relating to Voicing Discontent in an Organizational Simulation,' *International Journal of Conflict Management*, 8 (2): 132–47.

Olson-Buchanan, J. (1996) 'Voicing Discontent: What Happens to the Grievance Filer After the Grievance?,' *Journal of Applied Psychology*, 81 (1): 52–63.

O'Reilly, C.A. and Weitz, B.A. (1980) 'Managing Marginal Employees: The Use of Warnings and Dismissals,' *Administrative Science Quarterly*, 25 (2): 467–84.

Osterman, P. (1988) *Employment Futures: Reorganization, Dislocation, and Public Policy.* New York: Oxford University Press.

Pfeffer, J. (1998) *The Human Equation: Building Profits by Putting People First.* Boston, MA: Harvard Business School Press.

Rees, A. (1977) *The Economics of Trade Unions*, 2nd ed. Chicago: University of Chicago Press.

Rocella, M. (1989) 'The Reinstatement of Dismissed Employees in Italy: An Empirical Analysis,' *Comparative Labor Law Journal*, 10 (2): 166–95.

Rusbelt, C.E., Farrell, D., Rogers, G. and Mainous, III, A.G. (1988) 'Impact of Variables on Exit, Voice, Loyalty and Neglect: An Integrative Model of Responses to Declining Job Satisfaction,' *Academy of Management Journal*, 31 (3): 599–627.

Shantz, E. and Rogow, R. (1984) 'Post-reinstatement Experience: A British Columbia Study,' Paper presented at the annual meeting of the Canadian Industrial Relations Association.

Sheppard, B.H., Lewicki, R.J. and Minton, J.W. (1992) *Organizational Justice.* New York: Lexington.

Stone, K.V.W. (1999) 'Employment Arbitration Under the Federal Arbitration Act, in Eaton, A.E. and Keefe, J.H., (eds), *Employment Dispute Resolution and Worker Rights in the Changing Workplace.* Champaign, IL: Industrial Relations Research Association. pp. 27–65.

Taylor, F.W. (1911) *The Principles of Scientific Management.* New York; Harper and Bros.

Weber, M. (1947) *The Theory of Social and Economic Organization.* Henderson, A. and Parsons, T., translators. New York: Free Press.

PART FOUR

Industrial Relations Outcomes

25

Contingent Work Arrangements

Daniel G. Gallagher

During the past few decades there has been a gradual international trend toward a fundamental restructuring of the employment contracts between organizations and workers. At the broadest level there has been the suggestion that the 'normal' or 'standard' work arrangements of most workers during the twentieth century has increasingly been replaced with 'alternative' or 'non-standard' work arrangements (Bergstrøm and Storrie, 2003; Gallie et al., 1998; Kalleberg et al., 2003; Quinlan and Bohle, 2004; Smith, 2001; Voudouris, 2004; Zeytinoğlu, 1999). One such growing form of non-standard employment, by contemporary standards, is the hiring of workers on 'contingent' or 'fixed-term contracts.'

The objective of this chapter is to provide a brief description, explanation, and evaluation of the growing worldwide presence of contingent employment contracts as part of the worker-organization relationship. As part of this objective, an initial effort will be made to define the meaning of contingent work and how such arrangements are distinct from other forms of non-standard or alternative employment arrangements. The chapter will then identify organization-, worker-, and public policy-based factors which, to varying degrees, have contributed to the growth (or resurgence) of fixed-term contracts. An overview will be provided to describe the scope and focus of research that has been conducted and published on the individual and organizational consequences associated with contingent work contracts, as well as the underlying theoretical perspectives which have driven such research. The chapter will conclude with observations concerning theoretical and methodological issues found within the literature on contingent work and specify issues which should be addressed in future research.

THE MEANING OF CONTINGENT WORK

The US Bureau of Labor Statistics uses the following definition to delineate contingent employment from other forms of alternative or non-standard employment. The bureau's definition characterizes contingent work as '…any job in which an individual does not have an explicit or implicit contract for long-term employment or one in which the minimum hours worked can vary in a nonsystematic manner' (Polivka and Nardone, 1989: p11). Gallagher (2002) mentions that some definition inaccuracy or variability may exist over the interpretation of the meaning of 'long-term employment.'

From both organizational and worker perspectives, the meaning of long-term has an indeterminate value. For such reasons, contingent work has more frequently been referenced in the context of the absence of an *ongoing* employment relationship rather than as *long term* (Hipple, 1998). Moreover, Polivka and Nardone's (1989) effort at defining contingent work realizes that contracts may be both emphatic (for example, 'explicit' verbal or written terms) or involve an element of individualized perception (for example, an 'implicit' understanding). The inclusion of these elements into contractual definitions suggests the possibility that equally situated workers could reach different understandings about the perceived permanency of their relationships with employer organizations (Gallagher, 2002). However, as reflected in much of the psychological contract research (Guest, 1998; Rousseau, 1995), how an individual perceives the arrangement or 'the deal' may be more important to understanding the attitude and behavior of a worker than the ability to precisely slot a worker into a well-defined employment category (McLean Parks et al., 1998).

Consideration of the extent to which 'minimum hours can vary in a non-systematic manner' is another important component of contingent work. For example, a worker could have an agreement with a local school district to work as a substitute or supply teacher and be called into work on an *ad hoc* or as-needed basis. There may be a long-standing or ongoing relationship between the substitute/supply teacher and the school, but there is no guarantee of work hours or a reasonably predictable schedule. In effect, the level and regularity of work is entirely dependent on the variable needs of the employer organization (Gallagher, 2002).

Accordingly, there are three broad groupings of work arrangements that fit the contingent work definition, including temporary-help staffing firm arrangements, direct-line temporaries, and independent contractors.

Temporary-help staffing firm arrangements

First, and perhaps one of the most visible contractual arrangements fitting the parameters of contingent work, is fixed-term employment established through the use of an intermediary organization such as a temporary-help service firm or temporary staffing agency (Adecco, Manpower, Olsten, Randstad, for example). Through the utilization of temporary-help staffing firms, an organization contracts labor either for a specified period of time or until a particular event or project is complete. Within these staffing arrangements, there is a contractually explicit understanding that workers will be dispatched to the client organizations for fixed durations. In many countries, there are statutory limitations placed on how long a particular worker may be continuously assigned to a user or client organization by a temporary firm. Furthermore, the contractual and compensation agreement that a worker has with a temporary-help staffing firm lasts for a fixed duration and depends on the availability of assignments for which the worker is qualified (Gallagher, 2002; Gallagher and Sverke, 2005). There are rare exceptions in some countries where temporary workers may hold an ongoing employee status with the staffing firm.

There are two trends within the temporary-help services industry that are important to note. First, although the percentage of workers actually hired through temporary-help firms is a small share of total employment in most economies, the temporary-help service industry and the employment of agency-based temps has been one of the fastest growing segments of the workforce in many countries over the past few decades (Delsen, 1999; Gallie et al., 1998; Kalleberg and Marsden, 2005). Second, the image of temporary workers as legions of unskilled day laborers, receptionists, and conference staff is no longer universally applicable. Often overlooked in the economic literature are the increasing number of staffing agencies that focus on the short-term placement of professional workers such as accountants, engineers, information technology experts, nurses, and other medical and scientific personnel (Carnoy et al., 1997).

Direct-hire temporaries

A second and expanding category of contingent workers is comprised of individuals who are employed through direct-hire or in-house temporary staffing arrangements with the immediate employer organization (Gallagher, 2002; Connelly and Gallagher, 2004b). Direct-hire arrangements are most often found in large organizations where irregular staffing requirements result in the frequent use of workers for short-term assignments. These temporary workers may be hired on a specified fixed-term basis or on a more *ad hoc* or casual basis. The organization chooses to hire temporary workers directly rather than exclusively using the services of a temporary-help service firm. In practice, many direct-hire temporary workers may have an implicit or explicit understanding of an ongoing relationship with the same employer (for example, future temporary assignments). However, direct-hire temporary employment assignments are characterized as 'contingent' because they meet the second defining characteristic of contingent work which states that '…the minimum hours worked can vary in a nonsystematic manner' (Polivka and Nardone, 1989: p 11). A further and often overlooked variation of direct-hire contingent contracts entails hiring-hall arrangements in unionized sectors of the construction and entertainment industries. Although the union may operate as an intermediary, the resulting employment relationship is directly between the employee and the employer.

A subcategory of direct-hire contingent workers includes individuals directly hired by an organization for seasonal contracts (for example, resorts, tourism, etc.) (Polivka and Nardone, 1989). Because the number of assigned or contracted weeks of employment suggests the absence of a long-term contractual arrangement, many types of seasonal work can be viewed as fitting the aforementioned definition of contingent work. However, in some industries, as McDonald and Makin (2000) point out, seasonal work may be viewed as an opportunity for future fixed-term contracts (next season) or as the port of entry for long-term employment. Most seasonal contracts are short-term in duration and thus within the realm of contingent work (Aronsson et al., 2002; Connelley and Gallagher, 2004b).

Independent contractors

The diversity of occupational types and arrangements which have been incorporated under the scope of contingent work includes organizational hiring of independent contractors. Within most countries, independent contractors or freelance workers are legally defined as self-employed persons who contract or sell their services to a client organization on a fixed-term or project basis. Most often, independent contractors are well educated and professionally trained with skills that are either in short supply or for which the organization has an immediate but not long-term need (Gallagher, 2002). Independent contractors generally set their own hours and decide how to complete a project. They are directly compensated on the basis of a negotiated or bid contract with a prospective client organization. The client organization often has very limited, if any, responsibility for non-direct compensation (for example, healthcare, insurance, superannuation, etc.), and the client organization is not responsible for employment-related taxes and levies. Such responsibilities rest with the independent contractor as a form of sole proprietorship.

In recent years, there has been increasing evidence of organizational downsizing, which has led to the termination of employees who are then rehired by their organizations as independent contractors. Similarly, other organizations are relying on the large and growing percentage of independent contractors who are trained in knowledge-based occupations and areas requiring substantial craft and technological skills (for example, information technology). These organizations have used the independent contracting arrangements as a means of extending their pool of technical knowledge without making an implicit or explicit guarantee of ongoing employment (Matusik and Hill, 1998).

As evidenced in a 1996 US Federal Tax Court ruling with the Microsoft Corporation, there is a concern that client organizations may overly structure or control the duties and responsibilities of independent contractors to the point that the contractors are more akin to employees than contingent workers (Fragoso and Kleiner, 2005; Kondrasuk et al., 2001). Under the US Tax Code, the Internal Revenue Service (IRS) has established detailed guidelines concerning the proper legal classification of independent contractors. The IRS guidelines are based on the common law principle of the worker's 'right to control' how, where, and when work is performed to some extent (Fragoso and Kleiner, 2005). If a client organization exercises an exorbitant amount of control over an individualized contractor's work, the individualized contractor's relationship with the client organization may exceed stipulations of an independent contractor arrangement to become a more traditional employer-employee relationship or direct-hire temporary arrangement. Both the IRS and international labor experts share the concern that independent contractors who are heavily reliant upon a single client organization as a source for contracting income may constitute a form of *dependent* rather than independent contracting. (Greene, 2000; International Labour Office, 2000; Marlin, 2000). For governmental purposes, single client dependency is likely to move an independent contractor to employee status with all organizational employment protections and taxation requirements associated with traditional employees. Within the context of a broader ethical principle, organizations that incorrectly classify employee workers under the category of independent contractor may be using the occupational classification as

a shield against the application of rights and benefits provided to non-contingent workers (Marlin, 2000).

STRUCTURAL DIFFERENCES IN CONTINGENT WORK ARRANGEMENTS

The utilization of a commonly accepted definition of contingent work can result in the identification of fundamentally different classifications or groupings of contingent work. The three primary groupings, temporary-help staffing firms, direct-hire temporaries, and independent contractors, fit under the realm of contingent work and can exist in most industrialized countries, although the relative proportions of the three groupings may differ among countries' employment profiles (Booth et al., 2002a; Brewster et al., 1997).

It is also important to note that each of the three groupings of contingent work represents varying degrees of departure from the structure of the prevailing twentieth century 'employer-employee' relationship. Furthermore, the structure of the work relationship across each of the groupings contributes to potential differences regarding the status and rights of individual contingent workers.

Looking across the groupings of contingent work, the notion of an identifiable employer-employee relationship is not always immediately apparent. For example, in the case of contingent or 'fixed-term' workers hired through the intermediary services of a temporary-help staffing firm, the question may arise as to which entity is the 'employer' organization. If an employer is characterized as the organization that does the hiring and provides the compensation, then it would appear that the temporary-help firm holds the employer status. Conversely, if an employer is defined in terms of the organization that sets the work and job responsibilities, then the temporary-help staffing firm's client organization may hold the status of employer. Under different legal regimes, it is possible to argue that the temporary-help staffing firm and the client organization share co-employer obligations pertaining to the employment of the temporary workers (Gonos, 1997). The hiring of contingent workers through the use of temporary-help staffing firms establishes a 'triangular' employment relationship consisting of three principle parties, including the worker, the temporary-help staffing firm, and the client organization. The first side of the triangle signifies that while a worker is employed, he or she usually holds a contractual relationship with the temporary-help firm rather than the client organization where the work is being performed. Meanwhile, the second side involves the contractual relationship that exists between the temporary-help staffing firm and the client. The third side of the triangle represents the day-to-day working relationship that exists between the temporary worker and the client organization to which they have been dispatched. In circumstances where the temporary-help staffing firm dispatches a large number of workers to a single client location, the temporary-help firm may actually take direct on-site responsibility for the day-to-day tasks performed by the temporary workers. Gallagher and McLean Parks (2001) note that a further level of *disidentification* with the employer-employee concept may exist for contingent workers associated with temporary-help staffing firms because of the mechanics of the industry. Temporary workers will not only rotate between client organizations, but they may also be associated with and dispatched by multiple temporary-help firms. As a result, the contingent workers hired through temporary-help staffing firms may have an unclear notion of who represents their employer and what has been issued as their job.

In contrast, the employment of contingent or fixed-term workers through direct-hire arrangements is similar in structure to the traditional employer-employee relationship. Despite the insecurity that is still associated with contingent worker status, direct-hire temporaries are, in most countries, included under the umbrella of statutory projections provided to other 'employees' of the organization. Differentials, including wage levels and scope of compensation and benefit coverage, are likely to occur between contingents and more traditional workers in the same organization.

There is also the question of the applicability of labor law practices to the employment of contingent workers directly hired through independent contractor arrangements. Independent contractors represent a particular challenge to the traditional employer-employee relationship because independent contractors are not employees but rather are 'self-employers.' In this context most, if not all independent contractors, fall outside the scope of statutory definitions of employer-employee relations. Ironically for independent contractors, the importance of the traditional employer-employee relationship may become prominent to them if and when independent contractors hire support staff workers, thereby becoming employers.

The 'self-employer' status of independent contractors and the triangular nature of temporary-firm contingent work arrangements raise questions relating to the applicability of contemporary Industrial Relations (IR) and behavioral theories of employment to the understanding of work-related attitudes and behaviors of independent contractors.

CONTINGENT Vs. STANDARD WORK ARRANGEMENTS

Making the claim that contingent work represents a variation or departure from the standard employment contract requires some clarification on the customary interpretation of standard work arrangements. As Kalleberg (2000) writes, the standard arrangement during most of the twentieth century stipulated that work was performed full-time, would continue indefinitely, and was performed at the employer's place of business under the employer's supervision. Using such criteria, it is clear that the forms of contingent employment fall outside the definition of standard employment. Furthermore, most forms of part-time employment are more characteristic of the image of 'normal' employment than contingent work.

However, there are other types of organizational staffing arrangements that fall outside the realms of contingent and standard work arrangements. In particular, employee leasing, outsourcing, and subcontracting are increasingly popular means for organizations to meet staffing needs while emphasizing their core functions. In the case of outsourcing or subcontracting, a client or customer organization achieves flexibility by contracting services or production to a third party organization (Greer et al., 1999; Lepak and Snell, 2002). The *employees* of the third-party organization (outsource firm or subcontractor) have a more traditional arrangement; they have a clear and identifiable employer and the expectation of an ongoing work relationship subject to satisfactory individual performance and organizational survival. Even in the case of more complicated employee leasing arrangements, there is often an intermediary or professional employee organization (PEO). The employment relationship is open to long-term employment with a single, identifiable employer, and transfer between clients still retains an ongoing contractual relationship between the leasing firm and the worker (Drucker, 2002). Similarly, increased organizational interest in focusing on core competencies has led many organizations to turn over non-core functions to subcontracting organizations (Hamel and Prahalad, 1994; Nesheim, 2003). Although subcontractors are providers of services for client organizations, they are themselves employer organizations, and in most cases they employ their own workers on more traditional and ongoing employer-employee based arrangements.

FORCES DRIVING THE GROWTH OF CONTINGENT WORK

There is considerable international literature exploring the growth of contingent work arrangements (Bergstrøm and Storrie, 2003; Brewster, et al., 1997; Kalleberg, et al., 2003; Quinlan and Bohle, 2004; Zeytinoğlu 1999). As well as some research which questions

the extent to which long-term employment is on the decline (Doogan, 2001). Efforts to explain this growth have looked at the relative importance of demand vs. supply-based factors. Demand-side explanations have emphasized the role of changing market forces. These forces influence the desire of organizations to increase their reliance on contingent workers. Using time-series data on US based establishments, Golden and Appelbaum (1992) found that the demand for temporary workers was closely associated with three major factors: cyclical fluctuations in output, increased foreign competition, and the magnitude of non-wage labor costs. These findings comply with prescriptive and case-based studies which indicate that employers turn to contingent work contracts as a means of increasing flexibility in not only the number but also the types of workers which are hired on an 'as needed' basis (Barley and Kundra, 2004; Cully et al., 1999; Geary, 1992; Kalleberg and Marsden, 2005; Klein and vanVuuren, 1999; Nollen and Axel, 1996; Reilly, 1998). Many organizations' strategies for restructuring include an increasingly larger share of variable cost workforces over fixed cost labor (Cappelli and Neumark, 2003). Evidence also suggests that the use of temporary workers, particularly those hired through temporary-help staffing firms, remain a major resource used by employers to replace workers on short-term absences (Galup et al., 1997; Houseman, 2001).

Moreover, the literature points to an increasing employer emphasis on contingent work for functional flexibility, which is associated with the desire of employers to achieve a balance between the changing skill needs of an organization and the skills possessed by an organization's workforce. In workplaces where technology is rapidly changing, locating a match between the work demands and the skills of the standard workforce may be increasingly difficult. For many organizations, turning to technologically savvy independent contractors may represent an efficient approach for gaining immediate access to necessary skills without adding to the organization's long-term labor costs (Nishikawa, 2000). Such a finding fits well with prior observations that there is a growing cadre of professional temporaries and independent contractors who are appealing to employers because they provide technical services to employers without organizations having to invest in human resource development. The use of independent contractors is also attractive to organizations as a means of gaining access to intellectual capital and first-hand knowledge of industry trends which may offer a competitive advantage to the employing organization (Matusik and Hill, 1998).

Studies have also enhanced the understanding of the growth of contingent work arrangements by seeking to identify firm characteristics and organizational practices which either contribute to or limit the use of contingent workers. Davis-Blake and Uzzi (1993) studied the relationship between firm-level characteristics and the use of temporary workers and independent contractors, finding that firm-specific training, government oversight, bureaucratic practices, establishment size, and ongoing requirements for high-level technical skills have negatively affected the demand for temporary workers. Meanwhile, their results indicate that bureaucratic structures, establishment size, and participation with multi-site organizations had a positive impact on the use of independent contractors. These findings help link organizational characteristics with the use of contingent workers theoretically and empirically. The findings also indicate that different forms of contingent work may have different organizational level determinants (Gallagher, 2002). Uzzi and Barsness (1998) performed a similar study on British establishments and found that the intensity of fixed-term contracts was positively related to organizational size. In terms of organizational control mechanisms, Uzzi and Barsness found that organizations capable of systematically measuring and monitoring performance were more inclined to employ temporary workers. They also observed that there was a higher use of fixed-term hires in organizations that

implemented major changes in job-related computer technology.

With regard to the relationship between unionization and firm use of contingent workers, the results are rather ambiguous. Davis-Blake and Uzzi (1993) reported a positive effect of unionization on the use of direct-hire temporaries in the US. Within a study of British organizations, Uzzi and Barsness (1998) found that the level of union-management conflict was positively related to the use of contingent workers. Abraham (1998) reported a positive effect of unionization on the use of contractors and a negative effect on the use of temporary help workers in the US. Meanwhile, many other studies reported no effect of unionization on flexible staffing in the US (Houseman, 2001; Kalleberg et al., 2003). In a study of the UK and Norway, Gooderham and Nordhaug (1997) determined that organizations that perceived unions as being powerful were less prone to implement strategies for staffing flexibility. More recent research by Olsen (2003) of Norwegian organizations concluded that unionization was negatively related to the use of temporary workers for longer term staffing and positively related to the use of temporaries to fill short-term vacancies.

Surveys of organizational managers and human resource professionals show that they tend to believe that contingent workers hired through temporary-help firms are sought primarily to fill short-term vacancies due to leave time or the need to adjust to seasonal or unexpected changes in staffing needs (Galup et al., 1997; McAllister, 1998; Nollen and Axel, 1996). Similarly, there is limited survey feedback that indicates that some organizations employ temporary workers as part of an elongated interview process for more permanent positions (Bernasek and Kinner, 1999; Hardy and Walker, 2003). Again, reflective of differences among the various types of contingent work arrangements, employer reliance on independent contractors tends to be tied with an expressed need to gain short-term access to skill sets which may not immediately be available within the organization or as means to quickly resolve an immediate crisis (Barley and Kunda, 2004; Reilly, 1998; Wheeler and Buckley, 2000).

There also exists some opinion that employer demand for contingent worker arrangements may, in part, be driven by governmental policy. In particular, among studies that address the growth and consequences of temporary employment in many European countries, incidental commentary has often been made that contingent work contracts have been used by employers as a means of circumventing governmental polices which restrict the ability of employers to lay off or discharge workers or impose a high economic cost associated with such actions (Alba-Ramirez, 1998; Segal and Sullivan, 1997). Along similar lines, Olsen (2003) has suggested that social rights, including extensive worker access to paid absences from work, are particularly generous in many Scandinavian countries, thus creating a short-term demand for labor necessary to staff the positions of absent workers. In contrast, there is research indicating that the role of government regulation may have a negligible systematic impact on the use of contingent and alternative work arrangements (Brewster et al., 1997). Such research generally implies that contingent and short-term employment are more sensitive to market forces than government regulation. Within the US, the paucity of government programs guaranteeing workers periods of paid leave, combined with the legal principle of 'employment at will' suggest limited employer interest in contingent work arrangements from a regulatory perspective. However, contrary to this expectation, contingent work is a thriving form of contractual arrangement in the US

Consideration of the supply-side of the equation is also necessary when discussing the growth of contingent work. In many respects, parallel to the growth of part-time work, some portion of the contingent work phenomenon has been spurred on by the number of people who are actively seeking work outside of the traditional single employer-employee relationship. As Daniel Pink (2001) points out in *Free Agent Nation*, for some workers, the selection of contingent or fixed-term work arrangements represents a deliberate career decision to adopt a more personally flexible work schedule, allowing for a better work-family balance. Furthermore, contingent work may be appealing to more *boundaryless* workers who are interested in avoiding the restraints of being employed by a single employer organization (Marler et al., 2002). However, it is important to realize that the voluntary supply-side choice to work through contingent contracts is more pronounced among more educated and skilled professionals and craft workers than among marginally skilled workers. For workers with skills in high market demand (for example, information technology, medical services, etc.), independent contracting often represents a financially more lucrative career path while also enhancing personal control over work schedules (Kunda et al., 2002). Conversely, among less skilled workers, contingent employment is viewed as the better strategy so that they may re-enter the workforce or attain work experience to barter for more permanent or traditional types of employment.

CONSEQUENCES OF CONTINGENT WORK

An effort to fully understand the individual and organizational consequences associated with the growth of contingent work arrangements is constrained because contingent work covers a range of contractual arrangements and encompasses an array of reasons for which individuals undertake such work. Furthermore, individual worker responses to contingent work arrangements are likely to be functions of organizational practices pertaining to the management of contingent workers. However, economic and behavioral research supports a number of broad observations which provide some useful insights into the world of contingent employment arrangements.

As Cohany (1998) explains, the most disadvantaged workers laboring under contingent employment contracts work through the services of temporary-help firms. The traditional vision of clerical and day-laborers performing work at low hourly rates at less than full-time hours is actually affirmed (Cohany). The lower end or 'dark side' of contingent work is also characterized by extremely limited access to employment benefits. Within the US, contingent workers employed through intermediary firms have very limited direct access to health insurance, and when such access is available, it is often at a prohibitive cost. Among direct-hire temporaries, access to employer-operated benefit plans also tends to be limited or offered on a costly pro-rata basis. As Cohany notes, when workers in less stable and lower skill contingent jobs have access to insurance coverage in the US, it is usually through family-based insurance. While a partial solution to insurance coverage for some low-wage contingent workers, the absence or associated costs of benefit coverage can be seen as a particular economic burden for single or self-supporting temporary workers.

Investing in personal human resource development represents another economic consequence for workers employed in contingent contracts. As a result, throughout the lower and higher echelons of the contingent workforce, responsibility for skill maintenance and development rests with the individual worker (Hanratty, 2000; Heckscher, 2000; Virtanen et al., 2003; Zeytinoğlu, 1999). When training is provided to these workers by employer organizations, the level tends to be significantly less than what is provided to more permanent employees (Booth et al., 2002b). The extent to which an individual worker may feel compelled to invest in his or her skill development may, in large part, be a function of his or her career objectives. In the situation where a worker undertakes contingent work as a short-term arrangement or as a means of gaining access to the internal labor market of the firm, self-investment may be limited to achieving a level of technical competence which makes

the worker a qualified candidate for more permanent employment. However, among many of the top-end forms of fixed-term employment, in particular for many independent contractors, the desire to remain self-employed and appeal to potential clients depends on the currency of their skills sets. Barley and Kunda (2004) explain that among highly-skilled independent contractors in the area of information technology, there is a continuous need for skill upgrading which is contingent on the personal time and financial resources of individual workers rather than the client organizations.

In addition to the economic consequences of contingent work, a considerable amount of research attention has been given to the psychological impact of contingent work contracts on worker well-being. At the level of workers employed through the services of temporary staffing firms, there exists considerable case-based and anecdotal evidence to suggest that contingent workers are frequently subject to adverse working conditions (Henson, 1996). Research by Rogers (2000) indicates that lower-skill temporary workers are often physically, and more often psychologically, distanced from the standard workforce in the organizations to which they have been assigned. Rogers adds that in addition to being assigned demeaning tasks with low motivating potential, these workers are most often excluded from organizationally-based social events. However, it is important to note that exclusionary treatment of contingent workers can also be evidenced in the more prestigious independent contracting arrangements. For example, Carnoy et al. (1997) found that among top-end independent contractors in information technology, it was not unusual for contractors to be denied access to organizational meetings or proprietary data, even when such information affected the performance of their jobs.

Over the past decade there has been a dramatic increase in the number of empirical research studies which have sought to examine the job-related attitudes and behaviors of contingent workers. Often the research designs have focused on comparative analysis of contingent workers versus workers on more standard employment contracts. The research has covered a scope of issues such as organizational commitment, job satisfaction, organizational citizenship behaviors, and well-being role conflict and ambiguity. For example, many studies found contingent workers to be as committed to their client organizations and work as more permanent counterparts in the same organization (De Witte and Näswall, 2003; Linden et al., 2003; Pearce, 1993; and Van Dyne and Ang, 1998).

Although research findings may be fragmented, and at times contradictory, two important and closely-related findings consistently surface. First, workers vary in their motivations for undertaking contingent or short-term work assignments. Research indicates that workers who undertake temporary assignments as a means of gaining access to more permanent or ongoing work in organizations are more likely to maintain positive work attitudes and, most importantly, express more positive and supportive work behaviors than temporary workers with limited interest in securing ongoing employment contracts. Second, there is support for the importance of volition in understanding the attitudes of contingent workers. Workers who voluntarily choose to work on fixed-term contract bases are significantly more positive in their job-related attitudes than those who work as contingents due to the absence of more standard employment opportunities (Di Natale, 2001; Ellingson et al., 1998; Krausz et al., 1995). Collectively, the motivation and volition arguments may seem contradictory, but a distillation of the literature suggests that motivation is closely related to reported worker behaviors, while volition is more broadly tied to overall work attitudes.

Although there is a tremendous amount of prescriptive literature pertaining to the benefits of fixed-term or contingent employment contracts, empirical research of the relationship between organization performance and reliance on contingent work arrangements is virtually absent from the assessment of benefits and limitations of contingent work arrangements (Nollen and Axel, 1996).

A THEORETICAL PERSPECTIVE

Behavioral research on contingent work has focused on the comparative attitudes and behaviors of contingent vs. standard workers, or variations in attitudes and behaviors among samples of contingent workers. However, most research on individual and organizational consequences of contingent work is based on well-established theories of organizational behavior. Almost two decades ago, Pfeffer and Baron (1988) raised the concern that organizational theory was primarily developed in a context when organizational models of bureaucratic control were prevalent and, as such, may not have been fully applicable to less structured organizations and workers outside of more traditional employment arrangements. Similarly, some researchers have commented that much of our academic knowledge, organizational strategies, and public employment policy are based on the assumption of a stable and ongoing employer-employee relationship (Brewster et al., 1997; Gallagher, 2002; Kochan et al., 1994). Implicit within the prevailing view of the employment relationship is the accepted assumption that employees hold varying levels of attachment to a single identifiable employer and that work roles, attitudes, and behaviors are nested within the organization, the department, and the work group. Based on Gallagher and McLean Parks (2001), many of these underlying assumptions, as well as the meaning of employer's role, can be more complex and ambiguous within the context of contingent contract relationships (especially workers dispatched through temporary-help staffing firms and independent contractors).

Similar to Pfeffer and Baron (1998), Beard and Edwards (1995) recognize the need to reconsider the framework accounting for conditions under which contingent workers view and react to their work status. Beard and Edwards point out five key areas in which the contingent work experience may differ from standard or core workers, including

1) job insecurity;
2) predictability concerning job performance and associated outcomes;
3) control over how and when the work is performed;
4) the nature of the psychological contract; and
5) the social comparison process with non-contingent workers.

Of Beard and Edwards' five, the first three, are limited because they are characteristics which are present in all employment relationships. For example, while traditional workers may not hold contingent or fixed-term contracts, they do hold perceptions of job insecurity. Some research suggests that in certain circumstances, core workers may feel more insecure about their employment status than contingent workers. Ironically, this may reflect that security is measured in terms of finding replacement work rather than simply losing current positions for many types of contingent workers. Hence, it may not so much be a function of insecurity but rather how different groups of workers define job security (DeWitte and Näswall, 2003; Mauno et al., 2005). Similarly, the dimensions of predictability and control can vary as much among contingent workers as there is variability between contingent and standard workers. This point is well demonstrated when low-skill workers who are dispatched through temporary-help firms are more often assigned to simple and well-structured job tasks while contingent workers employed as independent contractors usually exercise a great deal of control over when, where, and how they complete their work.

Beard and Edward (1995) also suggest that psychological contracts and social comparison processes may be useful constructs for improving the understanding of individual reactions to contingent work and associated consequences. Psychological contracts have been viewed as unwritten contracts which exist between a worker and his or her employer organization (Rousseau, 1995). Broadly defined, the psychological contract

represents the 'idiosyncratic set of reciprocal expectations held by employees' concerning their obligations (what they expect to do for the employer) and their entitlements (what they expect to receive in return) (McLean Parks et al., 1998: 698). Psychological contracts can exist with or without the presence of more formally written employment contracts. They specify how the worker defines the perceived deal with the employer and whether or not the worker feels that the deal has been honored or violated. According to Rousseau (1995), psychological contracts can be both transactional and relational. Transactional-based contingent contracts are characteristic of employment relationships where a worker has a basic understanding of his or her responsibilities and anticipates that if these expectations are met then the employer will reciprocate with the agreed upon rewards. In the context of contingent employment, such a transactional contract could exist among workers dispatched by temporary-help firms who anticipate delivering a fixed number of hours of work in exchange for an agreed upon compensation and the expectation of future assignments from the temporary firm (De Cuyper et al., 2005; Krausz et al., 1995; Marler et al., 2002; Smith, 2001). Guest and Conway (2003) point out that professional and knowledge workers on fixed-term contracts may report more positive evaluations of the state of their psychological contracts because the contracts tend to be more transactional due to the explicit and bounded nature of the tasks which they perform for client organizations.

In contrast, psychological contracts that are more relational indicate that workers believe that positive changes in their behavior (extra-role behaviors, co-worker support, organizational citizenship) should be reciprocated by positive employer responses. In many respects, relational contracts are less focused on the employment relationship, are more fluid in nature, and are based on expectations and rewards that gradually evolve between the worker and employer. With direct-hire temporary workers, it is conceivable that a worker may come to expect that his or her willingness to regularly accept assignments on short notice, work beyond scheduled hours, and perform at above-average levels should be reciprocated by an employer through not only expected compensation but also the eventual reassignment of the worker to a permanent position within the organization. McLean Parks et al. (1998) report on the dimensions on which psychological contracts may differ (for example, scope, stability, tangibility, duration, etc.) and suggest that a better understanding of 1) differences in behaviors between contingent and traditional workers, 2) different forms of contingent work, and 3) differences among workers performing similar types of contingent work can be achieved with a more thorough knowledge of the formal contractual terms of employment, as well as the psychological contract forged by individual contingent workers (De Cuyper et al., 2005; Guest, 2004). As also noted by Drucker and Stanworth (2004), among workers dispatched through staffing firms, the nature of the psychological contract is even more complex due to the presence of a three-way relationship.

The underlying notion of reciprocity, which is a foundation of psychological contracts, is the theoretical underpinning of social exchange theory (Blau, 1964). According to Connelly and Gallagher (2004a), social exchange theory has been one of the most applied theories used-to-date to understand the attitudes and behaviors of contingent workers. Although well developed in the context of traditional employment relationships, social exchange theory suggests that worker support to an organization is a function of the extent to which a worker feels that an organization is supportive. Based on the social exchange theory, contingent workers' responses to assignments and their willingness to undertake additional role responsibilities may be a function of how supportive they perceive the actions of their employing organizations to be (Ang and Slaughter, 2001; Liden et al., 2003).

According to Beard and Edwards (1995), 'social comparison theory' also has promise for better understanding contingent work arrangements. Social comparison theory is based on the principle that individuals evaluate their own situations by comparing themselves to others both within and outside of an organization (Kruglanski and Mayseless, 1990). Workers are more likely to hold more positive attitudes toward their jobs when they see themselves being treated similarly to other workers doing comparable work. Social comparison theory suggests that contingent workers who see themselves as being treated the same as core workers in employing organizations or better than contingent workers in other work settings are more likely to hold positive attitudes toward their assignments. In past research, social comparison theory was viewed as a framework for understanding the job-related attitudes of part-time workers in comparison to full-time workers (Barling and Gallagher, 1996). However, the extent to which contingent workers are able to make meaningful social comparisons may be limited by organizations' strategies to deliberately isolate contingent workers rather than integrate them with core employees (Lautsch, 2003).

Volition and motivation also contribute to the theoretical framework of contingent worker attitudes and behaviors. Research has consistently supported the finding that workers who are involuntarily working on contingent contracts are significantly more negative toward their work experiences (Connelly and Gallagher, 2004a; Ellingson, et al., 1998; Krausz et al., 2000). Such a finding supports the principle of status congruency, which suggests that workers who are employed in work arrangements that are inconsistent with their personal preferences (full-time vs. part-time; contingent vs. permanent) are more likely to hold negative views toward their employer organizations and work experiences. Therefore, contingent workers who seek contingent work contracts and find such contracts consistent with their personal or professional interests are more likely to hold positive attitudes and demonstrate positive behaviors in the workplace.

Although research on contingent work could be criticized for over-relying on existing behavioral theories that were developed in the context of standard employment arrangements, there is no evidence that these theoretical perspectives do not apply to contingent work arrangements. It appears more reasonable for researchers to question how existing theoretical frameworks can adequately fit the context of contingent work. Furthermore, Gallagher and McLean Parks (2001) state that one of the more crucial theoretical issues that needs to be addressed is the extent to which common constructs developed in the context of more traditional employer-employee relationships is relevant to contingent work. For example, contingent work assignments, which are established through temporary-help staffing firms, raise theoretical and practical questions about the meaning of a 'job' and perceived 'job satisfaction.' It is conceivable that some contingent workers who attain employment through temporary-staffing firm based may perceive their jobs as temporary worker while others may identify their jobs as tasks that they are currently performing for their client organizations. In the latter case, workers' attitudes toward their jobs may evidence dramatic differences as the temporary worker moves between client organizations. Similarly, the meaning of 'employer' and the commitment to an employer organization may be questionable in the context of contingent workers who are employed as independent contractors. These contractors may have different levels of commitment, or even different attitudes toward their employers, because, unlike other workers, independent contractors may hold simultaneous client relationships.

In sum, as noted by McLean Parks et al. (1998) the tasks at hand may not necessarily be to invent new theoretical frameworks of study for contingent work but rather to give careful attention to how the existing theoretical frameworks may, to varying degrees, be modified to adjust to the nuances of the various forms of contingent employment.

SOME ISSUES FOR FUTURE CONSIDERATION

Many of the topical issues which have been addressed in this chapter are in the early stages of development and will require additional academic attention and eventual public policy debate. However, as part of the conclusion to this chapter, an effort will be made to identify a short list of contemporary issues related to the growth of contingent work arrangements which are in need of further academic and practitioner attention.

Contingent work and high performance work systems

In recent years, a considerable amount of research and practitioner attention in literature and seminars has been directed to the organizational development of 'High Performance Work Systems' (HPWS). The advocacy of HPWS as an effective and established means of enhancing firm performance is well established by Pfeffer (1994) in *Competitive Advantage Through People*. In a more recent articulation of the underlying principles of HPWS and commitment-based models, Pfeffer and Veiga (1999) suggest that workers are more involved and committed when they have greater control and responsibility placed in their hands. One of the more interesting aspects of the work of Pfeffer (1994) and Pfeffer and Veiga (1999) is their identification of human resource management practices that are essential ingredients in the development of high performance work environments. Listed among these strategies is enhanced organizational performance through the more effective use of human resources including selective hiring, increased employment security, self-managed teams, higher compensation based on organizational performance, extensive training investments, reduction in status differences within the organization, and the sharing of information within the organization.

Using contingent workers as resources for facilitating organizational flexibility seems to contradict the advice found in the commitment-based and HPWS models of human resource management. Such a contradiction raises several questions. How can organizations rely on an increasing number of temporary workers and at the same time espouse a philosophy of employment security? To what extent are organizations likely to extend the principle of extensive training investment or information sharing to workers on temporary or fixed-term contracts? And are not contingent work contracts a form of intra-organizational status differentials? In effect, either contingent work is inconsistent with the principles of HPWS, or HPWS models are exclusive to an organization's core workforce. From a research and practical perspective, attention should be given to the long-term consideration of the extent to which marginalization practices and HPWS models can effectively co-exist.

Spillover or unexpected consequences

Much of the early literature on the growth of contingent work contracts, as well as literature on the use of alternative employment arrangements (leasing, subcontracting, etc.), offered the promise that the use of non-standard employment arrangements could also be viewed as a layer of protection from fluctuations in market demand for the organization's regular or standard workforce (Nollen and Axel, 1996). However, within empirical literature there are some suggestions that, contrary to intent, standard workers who are part of a core organization could view the organization's increased usage of contingent workers as a threat to both existing job responsibilities and their own employment security.

In particular, as Pearce (1993) and Ang and Slaughter (2001) note, the introduction of contingent workers, especially independent contractors, as staffing alternatives to hiring workers under more standard contracts often results in core employees taking on duties and responsibilities which organizations wish to omit from the job duties of peripheral workers on contingent contracts. In effect, the question arises as to whether or not organizational policies that restrict the scope of contingent worker access to information have the unforeseen effect of increasing the obligations of non-contingent workers and negatively impacting their attitudes toward the organization (Pearce, 1993).

Organizational migration toward increased use of contingent workers may also raise concern among standard workers regarding organizational intentions and the extent to which their own jobs are secure. Such a concern could be particularly salient in organizations where standard workers have been terminated and rehired as independent contractors (Ho, Ang, and Straub, 2003). Although such workers would certainly be placed into the status of objectively insecure employment (fixed-term), the question arises concerning the extent to which the use of contingent staffing arrangements ultimately impact the subjective feeling of job insecurity among standard workers (Davis-Blake et al., 2003). Perhaps what is needed is a greater understanding of the extent to which contingent employment strategies adopted by organizations have a 'spillover' effect on the attitudes and behaviors of the traditional workforce. Mauno et al. (2005) suggest that insecurity among workers on more allegedly permanent contract terms may have more negative effects on worker well-being than is the case for workers who hold objectively insecure jobs.

Contingent work and unionization

From both the workplace and broader public policy perspectives, issues can be raised concerning what, if any, relationship exists between labor unionism and the increased organizational utilization of contingent workers. There tends to be rather limited evidence as to whether or not increased organizational use of contingent workers is systematically related to the workplace presence of unions or if unionization is itself a spur to organizational reliance on contingent workers as a staffing strategy (Olsen, 2003). However, there is objective data to suggest that the rate of union representation among temporary workers (and part-time workers) is significantly lower than the rate of standard or core workers (Gallie et al., 1998; Riley, 1998; Sverke et al., 2004; Zeytinoğlu, 1999). As Cobble and Vosko (2000) observe, difficulty in organizing contingent workers may stem in part from their mobility or frequent transition from one employer to another or the movement from temporary worker status to standard or ongoing employee status. Unionization is further complicated because the distinction between employer and employee is less definitive (Cobble and Vosko, 2000). Such an observation appears to be particularly relevant to the large segment of contingent workers who are self-employed as independent contractors and by definition, under many national labor laws, may fall outside the scope of the right to union representation. Furthermore, there is no substantial evidence to support that contingent workers have a particular interest or propensity to embrace unionization as it is currently structured. In fact, among contingent workers in more professional jobs, the relationship with unionism has been rather bleak (Benner and Dean, 2000).

Building upon research by Hyman (1994) on the typologies of union strategic choices, Heery (2004) and Heery and Abbott (2000) suggest that unions may choose to take one of a variety of responses to the growing presence of 'insecure jobs' or contingent working arrangements. These strategies are diverse and include such options as exclusion where the union seeks to exclude contingent workers from employment in organizations where unions have representational rights. Such a strategy would not be unlike initial union opposition to the growth of part-time work in many industries. The exclusion strategy implies the presence of a fundamental union belief that contingent work represents a threat to traditional jobs. Alternatively, Heery and Abbot (2000) and Cobble (1994) explain that unions may recognize the representational needs of contingent workers but, as a reflection of the casual nature of many contingent jobs, may seek to provide assistance through a servicing model of representation which helps provide contingent workers with collective access to benefits, assistance, and professional resources which they need to maintain their careers. Heery et al. (2004) suggest that among freelance workers, unions can help maintain the human capital of members through systems of vocational education and training. However as Cobble (1994) notes, such forms of professional self-help in organizations that are most often organized on a collectivist principle, but outside the mainstream structure of unionism, have been a past method for the representation of non-standard workers.

Further extending the application of Hyman's typology of union strategies, Heery and Abbott (2000) write that unions may respond to the growth of insecure and contingent work by entering in partnerships with management to seek ways to make work less secure. On a broader basis, unions may also undertake the strategy of entering into a social dialogue or mobilization to respectively protect union jobs while simultaneously seeking to achieve greater protection for the security of contingent workers and further informing society at large about the potential negative consequences of insecure employment.

The study of contingent work can benefit from future research if it makes the effort to determine the types of strategies, if any, union movements are utilizing in response to the growth of contingent work arrangements on an international basis (Heery, 2004). Of particular interest would be the consideration of the degree to which union responses are a function of the structure of union representation at the national level and extent of growth of contingent work within various industries. Inherent within such an examination would be consideration of how international differences in basic labor legislation influence the potential impact of contingent work. It would also be especially useful to determine if union responses are different based on the form of contingent employment of concern. Most notably, the focus should be on how unions perceive differences in both threat and strategic responses with regard to the presence of direct-hire temporaries compared with displaced workers from temporary-help firms.

CONCLUSION

A fundamental objective of this chapter has been to provide a broad overview of the issues pertaining to the concept of contingent employment. Although contingent employment contracts have, for a variety of reasons, become an increasingly common aspect of the employment landscape, there exists a large number of definitional, legal, theoretical, and practical IR-based issues that are in need of more systematic research attention. It is hoped that this chapter has provided readers with not only commentary pertaining to past issues and research but also some seedlings for future research and subsequent policy debate on the merits and dangers of contingent employment as a means of achieving organizational flexibility and competitive advantage.

REFERENCES

Abraham, K. G. (1988) Flexible staffing arrangements and employers' short-term adjustment strategies. In R. A. Hart (ed.), *Employment, Unemployment, and Labour Utlization*. London: Hyman. pp. 288–311.

Alba-Ramirez, A. (1998) 'How temporary is temporary employment in Spain?' *Journal of Labor Research*, 19 (4): 675–710.

Ang, S. and Slaughter, S. A. (2001) 'Work outcomes and job design for contract versus permanent information systems professionals on software development teams'. *MIS Quarterly*, 25 (3): 321–50.

Aronsson, G., Gustafsson, K. and Dallner, M. (2002) 'Work environment and health in different types of temporary jobs'. *European Journal of Work and Organizational Psychology*, 11 (2): 151–75.

Barley, S. R. and Kunda, G. (2004) *Gurus, hired guns, and warm bodies: Itinerant experts in the knowledge economy*. Princeton, NJ: Princeton University Press.

Barling, J. and Gallagher, D. G. (1996) Part-time employment. In C.L. Cooper and I.T. Robertson (eds), *International Review of Industrial and Organizational Psychology*, 11: 243–277. John Wiley and Sons Ltd.

Beard, K. M., and Edwards, J. R. (1995) Employees at risk: Contingent work and the psychological experience of contingent workers. In C. L. Cooper and D. M. Rousseau (eds), *Trends in organizational behavior*, 2: 109–26. Chichester, UK: Wiley.

Benner, C. and Dean, A. (2000) Labor in the new economy: Lessons from labor organizing in Silicon Valley. In F. Carré, M. Ferber, L. Golden and S. Herzenberg (eds) *Nonstandard work: The nature and challenge of changing employment arrangements*. Champaign, IL: IRRA.

Bergstrøm, O. and Storrie, D. (2003) *Contingent employment in Europe and the United States*. Cheltenham, UK: Edward Elgar.

Bernasek, A. and Kinnear, D. (1999) 'Workers' willingness to accept contingent employment'. *Journal of Economic Issues*, 33 (2): 461–70.

Blau, P. (1964). *Exchange and power in social life*. New York: Wiley.

Booth, A. L. Dolado, J. J. and Frank, J. (2002a) 'Symposium on temporary work introduction'. *The Economic Journal*, 112 (2): F181–F188.

Booth, A. L., Francesconi, M. and Frank, J. (2002b) 'Temporary jobs: Stepping stones or dead ends?' *The Economic Journal*, 112 (2): F189–F213.

Brewster, C., Mayne, L. and Tregaskis, O. (1997) 'Flexible working in Europe: A review of the evidence'. *Management International Review*, 37 (1): 85–103.

Cappelli, P. and Neumark, D. (2003) 'External churning and internal flexibility: Evidence on the functional flexibility and core-periphery hypotheses'. *Industrial Relations*, 43 (1): 148–82.

Carnoy, M., Castells, M. and Benner, C. (1997) 'Labour markets and employment practices in the age of flexibility: A case of Silicon Valley'. *International Labour Review*, 136 (1): 27–48.

Cobble, D. S. (1994) Making postindustrial unionism possible. In S. Friedman et al. (eds) *Restoring the promise of American labor law*. Ithaca, NY: Cornell University Press.

Cobble, D. S. and Vosko, L. F. (2000) Historical perspectives on representing non-standard workers. In F. Carré, M. Ferber, L. Golden, and S. Herzenberg (eds) *Nonstandard work: The nature and challenge of changing employment arrangements*. Champaign, IL: IRRA. pp. 291–312.

Cohany, S. (1998) 'Workers in alternative employment arrangements: A second look'. *Monthly Labor Review*, 121 (?): 3–21.

Connelly, C. E. and Gallagher, D. G. (2004a) 'Emerging trends in contingent work research'. *Journal of Management*, 30 (6): 959–83.

Connelly, C. E. and Gallagher, D. G. (2004b) Managing contingent workers: Adapting to new realities, In R. Burke and C. Cooper (eds) *Leading in turbulent times.* Malden, MA: Blackwell.

Cully, M., Woodland, S., O'Reilly, A. and Dix, G. (1999) *Britain at work.* London: Routledge.

Davis-Blake, A., Broschak, J. P. and George, E. (2003) 'Happy together? How using nonstandard workers affects exit, voice, and loyalty among standard employees'. *Academy of Management Journal,* 46 (4): 475–85.

Davis-Blake, A. and Uzzi, B. (1993) 'Determinants of employment externalization: A study of temporary workers and independent contractors'. *Administrative Science Quarterly,* 38 (2): 195–223.

De Cuyper, N., Isaksson, K. and De Witte, H. (eds) (2005) *Employment contracts and well-being among European workers.* Aldershot, Ashgate.

Delsen, L. (1999) Changing work relationships in the European union. In I. Zeytinoğlu (ed.) *Changing work relationships in industrialized economies.* Amsterdam: John Benjamins. pp. 99–114.

DeWitte, H. and Näswall, K. (2003) '"Objective" vs "subjective" job insecurity: Consequences of temporary work for job satisfaction and organizational commitment in four European countries'. *Economic and Industrial Democracy,* 24 (2): 149–88.

DiNatale, M. (2001) 'Characteristics of and preference for alternative work arrangements, 1999'. *Monthly Labor Review,* 124 (3): 28–49.

Doogan, K. (2001) 'Insecurity and long-term employment'. *Work, Employment and Society,* 15 (3): 419–41.

Drucker, P. F. (2002) 'They're not employees, they're people'. *Harvard Business Review,* 80 (2) February: 70–77.

Druker, J. and Stanworth, C. (2004) 'Mutual expectation: A study of the three-way relationship between employment agencies, their client organizations and white-collar agency "temps"'. *Industrial Relations Journal,* 35 (1): 58–75.

Ellingson, J. E., Gruys, M. L. and Sackett, P. R. (1998) 'Factors related to the satisfaction and performance of temporary employees'. *Journal of Applied Psychology,* 83 (6): 913–21.

Fragoso, J. L. and Kleiner, B. H. (2005) 'How to distinguish between independent contractors and employees'. *Management Research News,* 28 (2/3): 136–49.

Gallagher, D. G. (2002) Contingent work contracts: Practice and theory. In C. Cooper and R. Burke (eds) *The new world of work: Challenges and opportunities.* Oxford: Blackwell Publishers. pp. 115–36.

Gallagher, D. G. and McLean Parks, J. (2001) 'I pledge thee my troth…contingently: Commitment and the contingent work relationship'. *Human Resource Management Review,* 11 (3): 181–208.

Gallagher, D. and Sverke, M. (2005) 'Contingent employment contract: Are existing employment theories still relevant?' *Economic and Industrial Democracy,* 26 (2): 181–203.

Gallie, D., White, M., Cheng, Y. and Tomlinson, M. (1998) *Restructuring the employment relationship.* Oxford: Oxford University Press.

Galup, S., Saunders, C., Nelson, R. E. and Cerveny, R. (1997) 'The use of temporary staff and managers in a local government environment'. *Communication Research,* 24 (6): 698–730.

Geary, J. F. (1992) 'Employment flexibility and human resource management: The case of three American electronics plants'. *Work, Employment and Society,* 6 (2): 251–70.

Golden, L. and Appelbaum, E. (1992) 'What was driving the 1982–1988 boom in temporary employment?' *American Journal of Economics and Sociology,* 51 (4): 473–93.

Gonos, G. (1997) 'The contest over 'employer' status in the postwar US: The case of temporary help-firms'. *Law and Society,* 31 (1): 81–110.

Gooderham, P. M. and Nordhaug, O. (1997) 'Flexibility in Norwegian and UK firms: Competitive pressures and institutional embeddedness'. *Employee Relations,* 19 (6): 568–80.

Goslinga, S. and Sverke, M. (2003) 'Atypical work and trade union membership'. *Economic and Industrial Democracy,* 24 (2): 290–312.

Greene, B. (2000) 'Independent contractors: An attractive option?' *New Zealand Journal of Industrial Relations,* 25 (2): 183–204.

Greer, C. R., Youngblood, S. A. and Gray, D. A. (1999) 'Human resource management outsourcing: The make or buy decision'. *Academy of Management Executive,* 13 (6): 85–96.

Guest, D. E. (1998) 'Is the psychological contract worth taking seriously?' *Journal of Organizational Behavior,* 19 (1): 649–64.

Guest, D. E. (2004) 'Flexible employment contracts, the psychological contract and employee outcomes: An analysis and review of the evidence'. *International Journal of Management Reviews,* 5/6 (1): 1–20.

Guest, D. E. and Conway, N. (2003) The psychological contract, health and well being. In M. J. Schabracq, J. A. M. Winnubst and C. L. Cooper (eds) *The handbook of work and health psychology.* Chichester: John Wiley and Sons, Ltd. pp. 143–58.

Hamel, G. and Prahalad, C. K. (1994) *Competing for the future.* Boston, MA: Harvard Business School Press.

Hanratty, T. (2000) 'The impact of numerical flexibility on training for quality in the Irish manufacturing sector'. *Journal of European Industrial Training*, 24 (9): 505–12.

Hardy, D. J. and Walker, R. J. (2003) 'Temporary but seeking permanence: A study of New Zealand temps'. *Leadership and Organization Development Journal*, 24 (3): 141–52.

Heckscher, C. (2000) HR strategy and nonstandard work: Dualism versus true mobility. In F. Carré, M. Ferber, L. Golden and S. Herzenberg (eds) *Nonstandard work: The nature and challenge of changing employment arrangements*. Champaign, IL: IRRA. pp. 267–90.

Heery, E. (2004) 'The trade union response to agency labour in Britain'. *Industrial Relations Journal*, 35 (5):434–50.

Heery, E. and Abbott, B. (2000) Trade unions and the insecure workforce. In E. Heery and J. Salmon (eds) *The insecure workforce*. London: Routledge. pp. 155–80.

Heery, E., Conley, H., Delbridge, R. and Stewart, P. (2004) Beyond the enterprise: Trade union representation of freelances in the UK. *Human Resource Management Journal*, 14 (2): 20–35.

Henson, K. D. (1996) *Just a temp*. Philadelphia: Temple University Press.

Hipple, S. (1998) 'Contingent work: Results from the second survey'. *Monthly Labor Review*, 121 (11) November: 22–34.

Ho, V. T., Ang, S. and Straub, D. (2003) 'When subordinates become IT contractors: Persistent managerial expectations in IT outsourcing'. *Information Systems Research*, 14 (1): 66–86.

Houseman, S. N. (2001) 'Why employers use flexible staffing arrangements: Evidence from an establishment survey'. *Industrial and Labor Relations Review*, 55 (1): 149–70.

Hyman, R. (1994) Changing trade union identities and strategies. In R Hyman, R. and A. Ferner (eds) *New frontiers in European industrial relations*. Oxford: Blackwell.

International Labour Office (2000) Meeting of experts on workers in situations needing protection. MEWNP/2000, Geneva: International Labour Office.

Kalleberg, A. L. (2000) 'Nonstandard employment relations: Part-time, temporary and contract work'. *Annual Review of Sociology*, 26 (1): 341–65.

Kalleberg, A. L. and Marsden, P. V. (2005) 'Externalizing organizational activities: Where and how US establishments use employment intermediaries'. *Socio-Economic Review*, 3 (3): 389–415.

Kalleberg, A. L., Reynolds, J. and Marsden, P. V. (2003) 'Externalizing employment: Flexible staffing arrangements in US organizations'. *Social Science Research*, 32 (4): 525–52.

Klein Hesselink, D. J. and van Vuuren, T. (1999) 'Job flexibility and job insecurity: The Dutch case'. *European Journal of Work and Organizational Psychology*, 8 (?): 273–93.

Kochan, T. A., Smith, M., Wells, J. C. and Rebitzer, J. B. (1994) 'Human resource strategies and contingent workers: The case of safety and health in the petrochemical industry'. *Human Resource Management*, 33 (1): 55–77.

Kondrasuk, J .N., Reed, L. J. and Jurinski, J. J. (2001) 'The dangers of misclassifying 'employees': Microsoft litigation emphasizes distinctions between employees and nontraditional workers'. *Employee Responsibilities and Rights Journal*, 13 (4): 165–73.

Krausz, M., Brandwein, T. and Fox, S. (1995) 'Work attitudes and emotional responses of permanent , voluntary, and involuntary temporary-help employees: An exploratory study'. *Applied Psychology: An International Review*, 44 (3): 217–32.

Krausz, M., Sagie, A. and Biderman, Y. (2000) 'Actual and preferred work schedules and scheduling control as determinants of job-related attitudes'. *Journal of Vocational Behavior*, 56 (1): 1–11.

Kruglanski, A. W. and Mayseless, O. (1990) 'Classic and current social comparison research: Expanding the perspective'. *Psychological Bulletin*, 108 (2): 195–208.

Kunda, G., Barley, S. R. and Evans, J. (2002) 'Why do contractors contract? The experience of highly skilled technical professionals in a contingent labor market'. *Industrial and Labor Relations Review*, 55 (2): 234–60.

Lautsch, B. A. (2002) 'Uncovering and explaining variance in the features and outcomes of contingent work'. *Industrial and Labor Relations Review*, 56 (1): 23–43.

Lautsch, B. A. (2003) 'The influence of regular work systems on compensation for contingent workers'. *Industrial Relations*, 42 (4): 565–88.

Lepak, D. P. and Snell, S. A. (2002) 'Examining the human resource architecture: The relationships among human capital, employment and human resource configurations'. *Journal of Management*, 28 (4): 517–43.

Liden, R. C., Wayne, S. J., Kraimer, M. L. and Sparrowe, R. T. (2003) 'The dual commitments of contingent workers: An examination of contingents' commitment to the agency and the organization'. *Journal of Organizational Behavior*, 24 (5): 609–25.

Marler, J. H., Barringer, M. W. and Milkovich, G. T. (2002) 'Boundaryless and traditional contingent employees: Worlds apart'. *Journal of Organizational Behavior*, 23 (4): 425–53.

Marlin, E. (2000) The perspectives for a new and comprehensive vision of the protection of workers. *Proceedings of the 12th World Congress of the International Industrial Relations Research Association Tokyo, Japan.* Champaign: IRRA. pp. 151–59.

Matusik, S. F. and Hill, C. W. L. (1998) 'The utilization of contingent work, knowledge creation, and competitive advantage'. *Academy of Management Review*, 23(4): 680–97.

Mauno, S., Kinnunen, U., Mäkikangas, A. and Nätti, J. (2005) 'Psychological consequences of fixed-term employment and perceived job insecurity among health care staff'. *European Journal of Work and Organizational Psychology*, 14 (3): 209–37.

McAllister, J. (1998) Sisyphus at work in the warehouse: Temporary employment in Greenville, South Carolina. In K. Barker and K. Christensen (eds) *Contingent work: American employment relations in transition.* Ithaca, NY: ILR Press.

McDonald, D. J. and Makin, P. J. (2000) 'The psychological contract, organizational commitment and job satisfaction of temporary staff'. *Leadership and Organizational Development Journal*, 21 (2): 84–91.

McLean Parks, J., Kidder, D. L. and Gallagher, D. G. (1998) 'Fitting square pegs into round holes: Mapping the domain of contingent work arrangements onto the psychological contract'. *Journal of Organizational Behavior*, 19 (S1): 697–730.

Nesheim, T. (2003) 'Using external work arrangements in core value-creation areas'. *European Management Journal*, 21 (4): 528–37.

Nishikawa, M. (2000) Diversification in the use of atypical workers in Japanese establishments. *Proceedings of the 12th World Congress of the International Industrial Relations Research Association. Tokyo: Japan.* Champaign: IRRA. pp. 160–68.

Nollen, S. D. and Axel, H. (1996) *Managing contingent workers: How to reap the benefits and reduce the risks.* New York: AMACOM.

Olsen, K. M. (2003) *Contingency reversed: The role of agency temporaries and contractors in client-organizations.* Presented at Academy of Management meeting in Seattle, WA.

Parker, S. K., Griffin, M. A., Sprigg, C. A. and Wall, T. D. (2002) 'Effect of temporary contracts on perceived work characteristics and job strain: A longitudinal study'. *Personnel Psychology*, 55 (3): 689–719.

Pearce, J. L. (1993) 'Toward an organizational behavior of contract laborers: Their psychological involvement and effects on employee coworkers'. *Academy of Management Journal*, 36 (5): 1082–96.

Pfeffer, J. (1994) *Competitive advantage through people: Unleashing the power of the workforce.* Boston: Harvard University Press.

Pfeffer, J. (1998) *The human equation: Building profits by putting people first.* Boston, MA: Harvard Business School Press.

Pfeffer, J. and Baron, N. (1988) Taking the work back out: Recent trends in the structures of employment. In B. M. Staw, and L. L. Cummings (eds) *Research in organizational behavior*, 10, 257–303.

Pfeffer, J. and Veiga, J. F. (1999) 'Putting people first for organizational success'. *The Academy of Management Executive*, 13 (2): 37–48.

Pink, D. H. (2001) *Free agent nation.* New York: Time Warner.

Polivka, A. E. and Nardone, T. (1989) 'The definition of contingent work'. *Monthly Labor Review*, 112 (12): 9–16.

Quinlan, M. and Bohle, P. (2004) Contingent work and occupational safety. In Barling, J. and Frone, M.R. (eds) *The psychology of workplace safety.* Washington: American Psychological Association. pp. 81–105.

Reilly, P.A. (1998) 'Balancing flexibility, meeting the interests of employer and employee'. *European Journal of Work and Organizational Psychology*, 7 (1): 7–22.

Rogers, J. K. (2000) *Temps: The many faces of the changing workplace.* Ithaca: Cornell University Press.

Rousseau, D. M. (1995) *Psychological contracts in organizations: Understanding written and unwritten agreements.* Thousand Oaks: Sage Publications.

Segal, L. M. and Sullivan, D. G. (1997) 'The growth of temporary services workers'. *Journal of Economic Perspectives*, 11 (2): 117–36.

Smith, V. (2001) *Crossing the great divide: Worker risk and opportunity in the new economy.* Ithaca: Cornell University Press.

Sverke, M., Hellgren, J., Näswall, K., Chirumbolo, A., De Witte, H. and Goslinga, S. (2004) *Job insecurity and union membership: European unions in the wake of flexible production.* Brussels: P.I.E. Peter Lang.

Uzzi, B. and Barsness, Z. I. (1998) 'Contingent employment in British establishments: Organizational determinants of the use of fixed-term hires and part-time workers'. *Social Forces*, 76 (3): 967–1007.

Van Dyne, L. and Ang, S. (1998) 'Organizational citizenship behavior of contingent workers in Singapore'. *Academy of Management Journal*, 41 (6): 692–703.

Virtanen, M., Kivimaki, M., Virtanen, P., Elovainio, M. and Vahtera, J. (2003) 'Disparity in occupational training and career planning between contingent and permanent employees'. *European Journal of Work and Organizational Psychology*, 12 (1): 19–36.

Voudouris, I. (2004) 'The use of flexible employment arrangement: Some evidence from Greek firms'. *International Journal of Human Resource Management*, 15 (1): 131–46.

Wheeler, A. R. and Buckley, M. R. (2000) 'Examining the motivation process of temporary employees'. *Journal of Managerial Psychology*, 16 (5): 339–54.

Zeytinoğlu, I. U. (1999) *Changing work relationships in industrialized economies*, (ed.) Amsterdam: John Benjamins Publishing.

26

The Theory and Practice of Pay Setting

Alex Bryson and John Forth[1]

INTRODUCTION

In modern economies employers purchase labor power from workers who, in general, obtain their income from the sale of their labor. For the employer, the wage is the price of labor: the cost of securing the worker's productive capacity. However, as management theorists (and efficiency wage theorists before them) tend to emphasize, pay can also be used to elicit greater worker effort. As Marx (1976) emphasized, employers generally purchase units of workers' time rather than discrete units of effort. Employers can create incentives for workers to work more intensively over a given period – what Marx termed the 'real subsumption of labour'– or to work more extensively, by increasing their working hours over a given day, or even over a career (through increased tenure). From the employee's perspective, pay is the reward for labor, that is, the actual effort of producing goods or services. The nature of the payment varies greatly across workers, and may include not only monetary

income paid as labor is supplied, but also deferred payments, such as pensions, together with non-monetary rewards such as health insurance, which employees often rate as more valuable than their monetary equivalents (Dale-Olsen, 2006).

Despite these complexities, this characterization nonetheless implies that 'pay' is the outcome of a relatively straightforward, private, economic transaction in which workers receive pay in return for effort. But this is not the case for three reasons. First, social norms govern what is considered to be the appropriate trade-off between effort and reward. There is, for instance, a strong tradition of what constitutes a 'fair day's work for a fair day's pay'. Moreover, governments may intervene when market-set wages do not meet the subsistence needs of workers, either requiring certain minimum pay levels or supplementing pay from public funds (for example, through tax credits).

A second reason is that employers are often judged by what they pay and employees by what they receive. Again, social norms play a role, since employers may gain plaudits for socially responsible behavior. But equally their stock price may respond positively to a lowering of labor costs. For employees, one's social status is often bound up with one's wage and even how it is paid (hourly, weekly or as an annual salary). It may bear directly upon well-being, not only in terms of what workers can wear and eat, but in terms of what they can borrow, and how they are perceived by colleagues, friends and relatives. Workers' well-being is highly correlated with perceptions of their pay relative to their peers (Brown et al., 2005).

Third, employers and employees sometimes involve others in wage setting. Employees may join together to bargain with an employer, typically through a trade union. Similarly, employers may act collectively if they wish to avoid outbidding one another for scarce labor, thus 'taking wages out of competition' by setting single rates in particular industries, localities or occupations.

This chapter focuses on pay variance across workers, employers and across time and illustrates how theories of pay determination can shed light on this variance. We discuss the limitations of the orthodox economic approach to pay-setting and emphasize the importance of labor market imperfections, the role of institutions and the uniqueness of the labor contract in determining wage outcomes. Two broad conclusions emerge: first that no single theory has an overriding claim to virtue; and, second, that in spite of the knowledge generated within the field of industrial relations (IR), as will become apparent, much remains to be understood.

The chapter begins by examining the degree of variance in pay levels.

PATTERNS OF PAY

Any cursory examination of earnings is likely to indicate some of the factors that play either a direct or indirect role in pay setting. Earnings statistics illustrate how wages vary by occupation or skill level; they point toward the role of collective bargaining in raising wages for unionized employees; and they reveal the earnings differentials that exist between men and women.

Table 26.1 presents summary statistics on gross hourly earnings in the UK.[2] The table shows a gender wage differential of around 20 per cent in favor of male employees, an advantage for full-time workers over part-time employees of around 30 per cent and extensive variation between employees with different academic achievements. There is also considerable wage variation within each of these groupings. The employee at the 90th percentile of the distribution typically has gross hourly earnings that are around twice those of the median worker and around four times those of the employee at the 10th percentile. This partly reflects variations in the way the employment relationship is formulated. Wages set in a purely competitive market would solely reflect a worker's productivity and would be independent of the firm. However, as discussed later, there are many reasons why workers' pay may vary across firms, such as the acquisition of firm-specific human capital, union bargaining or the desire of employers to pay above market wages to capture the rents that 'good' workers generate. Table 26.1 shows, for example, that employees whose pay is negotiated by trade unions have wages that are 10 per cent higher, on average, than non-unionized employees.

This raises the question of how much wage variance occurs within workplaces, and how much occurs across workplaces? The answer has important implications for labor mobility and productivity. If, for the sake of argument, all workers in a firm are paid the same wage, but all firms pay a different wage – that is, all variance is across workplaces – workers would have to move to obtain higher wages, and they may be particularly concerned about which firm they join when first entering the labor market. At the other extreme, say all firms are identical in the distribution of wages they pay their workers – that is, all variance is within firms – it would matter very little which firm the worker joins since the rewards for advancement will be equivalent. Our own analysis of linked employer-employee data for

Table 26.1   Gross hourly earnings in the UK, Autumn 2005

	Mean	Percentiles		Percentile ratios		
		10th	50th	90th	50:10	90:10
All employees	10.90	5.00	8.84	19.22	1.77	2.17
Gender:						
Men	12.21	5.40	10.32	21.92	1.91	2.12
Women	9.70	4.80	8.00	16.99	1.67	2.12
Hours worked per week:						
Full-time (30 or more)	11.75	5.54	10.00	20.51	1.81	2.05
Part-time (1-29)	8.21	4.33	6.42	14.73	1.48	2.29
Highest qualification:						
Degree or equivalent	16.16	7.00	14.58	27.03	2.08	1.85
Higher education	12.49	6.18	11.74	19.67	1.90	1.68
GCE A-level or equivalent	10.05	5.00	8.66	16.83	1.73	1.94
GCSE grades A-C or equivalent	8.67	4.69	7.56	14.16	1.61	1.87
Other qualifications	8.39	4.69	7.29	13.23	1.55	1.81
No qualifications	7.12	4.50	6.25	11.11	1.39	1.78
Unionization:						
Collective bargaining	11.72	5.78	10.35	19.22	1.79	1.86
No collective bargaining	10.65	4.80	8.21	19.24	1.71	2.34

Source: UK Labor Force Survey, Autumn 2005.

Britain shows that workplace characteristics can account for at least as much of the variation in hourly wages as differences in employees' educational achievements and work experience, indicating a major role for firm-specific factors.[3]

The figures in Table 26.1 take no account of non-pecuniary rewards, such as subsidized or free health care, or employers' pension contributions. These tend to increase the differential between higher- and lower-paid workers, widening the gap between men and women (Joshi and Paci, 1998; Anderson et al., 2001) and increasing the premium associated with collective bargaining (Forth and Millward, 2000; Budd, 2004). For employers, the picture is further complicated by the addition of indirect labor costs, such as social security contributions. These account for around 13 per cent of total hourly labor costs in the UK, compared with 25–30 per cent in the EU as a whole (Eurostat, 2001).

Returning to the pattern of direct earnings, there have been notable changes in wage dispersion over time. Inequality in gross earnings grew in Britain in the 1980s after a century of relative stability (Gregg and Machin, 1994). Klondylis and Wadsworth (2006) show that, during the 1980s, there was rising wage inequality between middle and top earners (the 90:50 percentile ratio), and between middle and low earners (the 50:10 percentile ratio). The trend was apparent for men and women. In the first half of the 1990s, the male wage distribution continued to widen, though more slowly, driven by increases among top earners. Women, on the other hand, experienced some wage compression. Under the recent Labour governments, male wages have compressed a little whereas, among women, there has been further compression at the top and some compression between middle and low earners.[4]

Attempts to explain variations in wages across workers and over time are only partially successful. Statistical analyses which account for differences in individual, job and employer characteristics can typically explain little more than 50 per cent of the cross-sectional variation in gross hourly earnings. This partly indicates the difficulties in devising adequate proxies for important factors such as employee productivity or bargaining power. But it also indicates the limitations of our ability to understand the complexity of pay setting. The rest of the chapter discusses what is generally known about this complexity.

NEO-CLASSICAL LABOR MARKET THEORY

A conventional starting point in economics is the neo-classical model of the labor market under which wages, like other prices, are determined by the forces of supply and demand. Faced with a supply of workers (each with their own preferences about how much labor they will supply at given wage levels), the employer decides how many and which types of workers to employ at wage levels at which it can trade profitably. The firm will hire increasing numbers of workers up to the point where their wage is equal to their marginal product. Workers, for their part, will offer themselves for employment until the next potential recruit considers the wage an insufficient inducement. Under perfect competition, and with freedom of entry and exit for firms and workers, these market forces produce a single wage at which supply and demand are in equilibrium. In this situation, employers and employees are 'price takers' without the power to set wages. A state of disequilibrium may arise from time-to-time, in which wages do not lie on the intersection of the supply and demand curves. But this is expected to be a short-run phenomenon whilst prices adjust to changes in levels of demand or supply.

The theory predicts higher wages for workers who generate more output given a fixed amount of capital. But it says little about what determines worker productivity, although there is a broad notion of 'skill' which implicitly equates with it in many instances. Adam Smith (1982) noted that output and wages were related not only to innate abilities but also to acquired skills, but human capital theory has more recently formalized the conception of education and training as investments which could generate returns, both to employers through increased output and to employees through higher wages (Becker, 1964).[5] Estimates of the wage returns to educational investments are widespread. Recent estimates for the UK indicate that possession of a degree raises wages by 26–29 per cent (McIntosh, 2006).

However, some argue that educational attainment acts primarily as a signal of unobserved ability, which is then rewarded appropriately in the labor market, rather than serving as a productivity-enhancing investment (Arrow, 1973; Spence, 1973).

Estimates of the wage returns to 'skills' are less common. Human capital theory distinguishes between generic skills, which can be applied in a wide range of jobs or industries, and firm-specific skills. Using a detailed questionnaire covering a wide range of generic skills, Green and Dickerson (2004) showed that computing skills and high-level communication skills attract higher wages, as do the ability to act without close supervision and the capacity to manage varied tasks. Others have identified returns to industry-specific skills, which become apparent when displaced workers take lower-paid jobs in other sectors (Neal, 1995).

If wages are related to skill, changes in the skill distribution within the economy should affect wage differentials. McIntosh finds no recent change in the return to academic qualifications, despite the expansion of higher education (ibid). But others point to a wider process whereby technological change has increased demand for skill and automated intermediate low-skilled jobs, resulting in congestion at the lower end of the labor market, which, in turn, pushes down wages in low-skilled jobs that cannot be automated. This is consistent with developments in the 1980s in the US (Autor et al., 2003). However, in the 1990s the US experienced growing demand for both high-skilled jobs and non-automated lower-skilled jobs (Autor et al., 2006) which, coupled with the passing of the 'glut' of displaced routine labor, resulted in wage increases at the bottom end of the labor market. The net effect is stabilization in the lower half of the pay distribution and continuing growth in pay disparities in the upper half of the distribution. Goos and Manning (2003) and Spitz (2005) also point to a 'polarization of work' over the last 25 years in the UK and West Germany respectively. Although this story seems plausible, one might wonder, since technological innovation is all-pervasive, why these forces have not produced increasing wage inequality in more countries.

CRITICISMS OF THE NEO-CLASSICAL APPROACH

Commentators have rejected the neo-classical model to different degrees. Almost all consider it an abstraction from reality, since few markets are perfectly competitive and firms and workers are rarely free to enter and leave markets without delay. Some see it as a simplification which nonetheless provides a good indication of general tendencies (Hicks, 1932: 5). Others are more categorical in rejecting it as a meaningful approximation of the wage-setting process which overplays the market's invisible hand (for example, Rubery, 1997; Manning, 2003).

Critics point to a range of empirical facts that appear to contradict the neo-classical depiction of the labor market. First, they point to long-term unemployment and wage rigidities as evidence that markets do not clear. So whilst real wages of the lowest decile fell between 1979 and 2000 in North America and Australia, this is virtually unheard of elsewhere (Glyn, 2001). The combination of low unemployment and low wage inflation in the US and UK in the late 1990s also cast doubt on the mechanics of the disequilibrium adjustment process, depicted by Phillips (1958). Furthermore, Blanchflower and Oswald (2003) have demonstrated that, contrary to theoretical expectations whereby higher wage levels are associated with greater unemployment (all other things being equal), it is common to observe the reverse. Dunlop (1988), for his part, asserts that unemployment has little if any role to play in influencing wage reduction, except in small establishments.

A second empirical challenge comes from studies indicating a range of indeterminacy in wage-setting (Lester, 1952). The theory suggests that a perfectly-competitive labor market will be characterized by a single wage for a particular type of labor. Instead, studies of similar occupations in specific localities suggest that there may be considerable variation between firms (for example, Dunlop, 1957; Mackay et al., 1971; Brown et al., 1980; Nolan and Brown, 1983; Gilman et al., 2002). Whilst the theory allows for some short-term variance, as employers and employees adjust to changes in the demand for labor, longer-term differences should be imperceptible (Hicks, 1932: 24–27). However, the evidence suggests that differences may be more pervasive and do not simply reflect returns to firm-specific skills. Rather, it is suggested that the reality of wage setting rejects the neo-classical model in favor of a more complex account in which employers and employees may both play an active part.

IMPERFECTLY COMPETITIVE MARKETS

Relaxing the assumption of perfect competition leads to different predictions of the outcomes of pay setting and some plausible explanations of wage variation. Imperfections in product and labor markets are both relevant; in either arena, some level of concentration or collaboration among either buyers or sellers can generate a degree of control over the price of labor which may enable wages to sustain departures from employees' marginal products.

Monopoly or oligopoly

If a firm is a monopolist or oligopolist in its product market, its control over product pricing enables it to generate 'excess' profits, which in turn provide the freedom to pay wages above the level that would maximize profits under perfect competition. The degree of concentration among producers tends to be capped by regulatory bodies, but the thresholds are set fairly high. In a wide range of industries in the UK, the top five businesses currently account for at least one-third of gross output and in some this proportion is above two-thirds (Mahajan, 2005), suggesting at least the potential for some control over prices.

Although such product market power means that the firm has less need to minimize labor costs, there is no guarantee that any share of the additional income will be passed on to employees. However, this does happen to some degree, with a number of empirical studies having demonstrated a positive association between wages and past profitability (for example, Blanchflower et al., 1996; Van Reenan, 1996; Hildreth and Oswald, 1997). There may be a number of alternative rationales for this behavior. The monopolist or oligopolist may pay higher wages of its own volition, perhaps to demonstrate fairness, reduce turnover or boost recruitment. Alternatively, it may be induced to do so by a trade union representing some or all of its employees.[6]

Evidence points to a sizeable union wage premium in many countries (Blanchflower and Bryson, 2003). Unions also raise non-pay fringe benefits (Forth and Millward, 2000) so that the full costs of unionization are higher than those associated with pay alone. The size of this premium is correlated with unions' ability to monopolize labor supply, often proxied in empirical investigations by the presence of a closed shop (Stewart, 1987), union density (for example, Hirsch and Schumacher, 2001) or collective bargaining coverage (Forth and Millward, 2002). Indeed, unions seem to procure no premium where they have no monopoly power (see, for example, Stewart, 1987).

Changes in unions' monopoly power may also bring about changes in the union wage premium. Stewart (1995) attributes part of the decline in the premium in Britain to the demise of the closed shop. However, despite declining union density in developed countries and the ability to out-source production to non-unionized labor in less developed countries, there is little empirical evidence to support a secular decline in the union wage premium in Britain and the US. Instead, there has been counter-cyclical movement in the premium arising from unions' ability to resist the downward wage flexibility experienced by non-union workers in recession (Blanchflower and Bryson, 2004). There is also no evidence that increased competition induced by higher import penetration has lowered union wage premia. In fact, quite the reverse: Bratsberg and Ragan (2002) and Blanchflower and Bryson (2004) show higher import penetration raises the premium, perhaps because organized workers can resist the downward wage pressure this induces in non-union firms, at least in the short-term.

Unions can exert power over wage-setting in perfectly competitive markets, but neo-classical theory would predict that these firms would have to raise product prices above market levels and would eventually go out of business. However, some firms have a greater 'ability to pay' above-market rates than others. Slichter (1950) illustrated the point by drawing attention to the positive rank correlation between industries with high profit-to-sales ratios and those with high unskilled earnings. There is conflicting evidence as to whether unions affect the longevity of firms (Bryson, 2004a) and no direct evidence that any negative effect is attributable to union-induced labor costs. However, unions are associated with lower employment growth (Bryson, 2004b).

Union involvement in wage setting can also be expected to affect wage inequality. A priori, the direction is ambiguous. Unions' pursuit of 'standard' rates for jobs promotes pay equalization, as does the threat of unionization which forces non-union employers to raise pay or benefits to keep unions out (Rosen, 1969). Nevertheless, unions bargain for higher rates for their members. Thus their impact on the wage distribution will depend, in large part, on how many and which workers they organize, and on any variation in the wage premium across workers. Freeman (1980) found that unions tended to reduce wage inequality among men because the effect of bargaining higher rates for members was smaller than the effect of standardizing pay within the union sector. This remained so for the last 30 years of the twentieth century in the US, Britain and Canada (Card et al., 2003). However, unions do not reduce wage inequality for women in these countries because unionized women are concentrated in the upper end of the wage distribution, the union wage premium tends to be larger for women than it is for men and, whereas the premium is higher for lesser-skilled than higher-skilled men, this is not the case for women.

There are also gender differences in the effect of unionization on trends in pay dispersion. Declining unionization among men explained a significant fraction of the growth in wage inequality in the US and UK whereas the decline in unionization was more modest for women and had little impact on female wage inequality (Card et al., 2003; Gosling and Lemieux, 2004). Of course, declining unionization is not a universal phenomenon: countries such as Belgium, Denmark, Finland, Ireland, Norway and Sweden have experienced increased union density in recent decades and declining pay dispersion.

MONOPSONY AND OLIGOPSONY

Whilst product or labor market monopolies are a common feature of the wage-setting literature, the role of monopsony or oligopsony – where significant power is held by the buyer rather than the seller – is less extensively discussed. Product market monopsony, in particular, is given little attention. The industrial relations literature offers examples of how dependence relationships between small firms and large retailers may affect work organization and the exercise of management authority (Moule, 1998), but there is little documented evidence of an impact on wages, despite the potential implications for suppliers' cost structures.

One would expect the effect of product market monopsony to be equivalent to that of labor market monopsony, where the dominance of a single firm or small group of firms may drive down wages within a locality. The commonly-cited examples are company towns. These are a distant memory to most, but labor market monopsony may explain the present-day reduction in earnings that can accompany the arrival of large retailers into local labor markets (as described by

Neumark et al., 2005). It may also be a feature of the labor markets for nurses (Sullivan, 1989) and university professors (Ransom, 1993). Each example serves to indicate that restricted mobility among employees can consolidate employers' power in the wage setting process. Employers may use this power to different degrees. The discriminating monopsonist may practice wage discrimination, paying each employee at their individual reservation wage, whilst the simple monopsonist will instead pay a uniform wage that is just sufficient to fill all vacant posts. The theory predicts that simple monopsony will result in levels of wages and employment that are both lower than in a competitive market (a further feature described in Neumark et al.'s retail study), so monopsony has implications beyond wages alone.

If monopsony power is depressing wages, one would expect any action which reduces the power of the employer to consequently raise wages. Illustrations in the US literature focus on the removal of the reserve clause in professional baseball, which tied players indefinitely to the team for which they first signed; the change led to a significant income transfer from owners to players in the form of higher wages (Kahn, 1993). An equivalent European example is the Bosman ruling which, since 1995, has allowed professional soccer players to negotiate their own deals with a new employer once the contract with their current club expires. In cases of simple monopsony, a restriction on employer power may also result in greater employment without lowering wages. Indeed, monopsonistic labor markets are said to explain why the introduction of regulations governing wage setting, such as the Equal Pay Act and the National Minimum Wage, in the UK, have not brought about wide-scale job losses (Manning, 2003).

THE UNIQUENESS OF THE LABOR CONTRACT

In the discussion thus far, the basic approach to wage determination has differed little from the approach that might be applied in commodity pricing. However, a richer understanding of wages relies on recognizing the uniqueness of the labor contract. The open-ended nature of the employment contract is a key feature, bringing uncertainty and potential controversy over the terms of the exchange. Wages can then feature among the devices that employers may use to raise effort levels. The personal aspect of the exchange also means that wages may be critically influenced by norms, social institutions and political processes. An appreciation of these factors – which is one feature that sets the discipline of industrial relations apart from some parts of mainstream economics – means giving lower priority to the process of market clearing, accepting that the formal economic analysis of supply and demand is too narrow and that the social aspect of wages must also be carefully considered (Brown and Nolan, 1988; Dunlop, 1988). This leads to an emphasis on the context in which wages are determined and skepticism regarding the degree of apparent rationality that might be accorded to wage outcomes. In the following sections, we review a number of approaches that view pay setting from this general perspective.

EFFICIENCY WAGES

Efficiency wage theory abandons the conception of the spot market with a single wage for a given type of labor, acknowledging that employers can choose different wage levels to elicit different levels of effort. It therefore provides one potential means of explaining variations in wages among like workers.

If wages fall short of what the worker considers a fair reference wage (for example, the rate set in other firms) the theory posits that a wage increase will raise workers' effort (Akerlof, 1982, 1984; Akerlof and Yellen, 1990). It might also allow a firm to recruit higher-quality workers (Weiss, 1980), reduce turnover (Salop, 1979) and improve employee morale, all of which can enhance productivity. But the wage must not be set too high since effort can only rise so far. Accordingly, a wage

exists – the efficiency wage – where the marginal cost of increasing the wage equals the marginal gain in productivity. The notable implication, from the perspective of this review, is that this wage is set independently of labor market conditions outside the firm: the principal determinant is the influence of wage changes on worker effort within the firm.

The incentive to pay above the competitive market rate will differ according to production technologies, which imply different gains from reduced turnover, higher-quality labor and so on. For instance, organizations reliant on extensive firm-specific training will benefit from pay policies that lower voluntary quits. Since production technologies differ across industries, some point to efficiency wages as a reason for inter-industry wage differentials (Krueger and Summers, 1988; Gibbons and Katz, 1992). Others argue that such wage differentials are largely due to unmeasured differences in worker quality (Murphy and Topel, 1990; Abowd et al., 1999). Nevertheless, Fehr et al.'s (1996) laboratory experiments identify a clear causal relationship between efficiency wages and effort.

Shapiro and Stiglitz's (1984) version of efficiency wage theory focuses on the use of high wages to reduce shirking among employees. As employment contracts are incomplete, employees have some discretion over their effort. Where effort monitoring is costly, firms may choose instead to pay higher wages, thus increasing the cost of job loss to the worker. Krueger (1991) suggests that pay is lower in franchised burger outlets than in company-owned outlets within the same firm because local franchise owners monitor their employees more easily, thus having less need to 'buy' worker co-operation. Freeman et al. (2006) have similarly shown that US workers are more likely to intervene when co-workers are shirking if they believe that pay is at or above the market level.

This leaves the question of whether marginal wage increases raise productivity sufficiently to pay for themselves. Levine (1992) and Wadhwani and Wall (1991) found that they did.[7] Levine also found lower productivity effects of high wages in the presence of unions, consistent with the proposition that unions push wages above the optimum efficiency level. Earlier evidence comes from Henry Ford who described the doubling of wages to five dollars a day as 'one of the finest cost-cutting moves we ever made' because it dramatically reduced turnover and absenteeism and raised labor discipline and output quality (Raff and Summers, 1987: s59). Nevertheless, some have questioned how much effort managers devote to devising incentive pay systems. Others have questioned the whole basis of efficiency wage theory, contending that there is no necessary relationship between pay and productivity (Brown and Nolan, 1988: 352). This latter position raises substantial questions over the continued efforts of employers to link the two.

LINKING PAY TO PERFORMANCE

Paying a higher time-based wage is only one way in which firms might tackle shirking when effort is difficult to monitor. An alternative is to offer a piece rate, which allows the worker to decide how much to work and thus how much to get paid.

For economists, this induces greater effort by equating the marginal value of an extra unit of output with the marginal cost of producing it (Weitzman and Kruse, 1990). Sociologists, on the other hand, tend to view piecework – and other forms of performance-based pay – as mechanisms for managerial control when management cannot provide adequate supervision (Gallie et al., 1998: Chapter 3). Either way, one might anticipate less need for monitoring under piecework since, as Marx remarked, the 'superintendence of labour becom[es] to a great extent superfluous' (Marx, 1976: 695).

The originators of the British Workplace Industrial Relations Surveys reported their findings on payments-by-results (PBR) under the heading 'Systems of payment and control' alongside methods for controlling time keeping and payments while sick (Daniel and Millward, 1983: 200). In the Donovan tradition, PBR was treated as part of the problem of shop floor bargaining and a cause of industrial unrest (Daniel and Millward, 1983: 292). As Blanchflower and Cubbin (1986: 26) note, PBR is often included in analyses of strike propensities since the need for regular adjustments to pay increases opportunities for disagreement.

Marx (1976: 698–9) reports Factory Inspectorate figures showing that, in the mid-1800s four-fifths of employees in British factories were paid by the piece. Marx notes that it is 'the form of wage most appropriate to the capitalist mode of production'. Today pure piece-rate pay is rare, confined to occupations where outputs can easily be observed, such as sales or fruit picking. Nevertheless, in Britain in 2004, one-third of workplaces used some form of individual payments-by-results, 16 per cent used subjective merit pay and one-quarter used group-based payments-by-results (Bryson and Freeman, 2006).

In the US shared forms of compensation (share ownership plans, stock options, profit and gainsharing) have been rising since the 1980s, a trend that has seemingly accompanied greater employee involvement in decision-making (Dube and Freeman, 2006). The trends are very different in Britain. Task discretion declined in the 1990s (Gallie et al., 2004) and, in any event, shared compensation schemes are not strongly associated with employee decision-making (Bryson and Freeman, 2006). Both profit-related pay and share-ownership schemes grew in the 1980s, with government tax incentives playing some part, but their incidence has remained fairly static since then (Bryson, 2006).

In theory, performance-based pay will generate inequalities in output and thus earnings where workers are heterogeneous in effort and ability, but this relies upon a direct link at individual level between output and earnings. This is not always present, as some forms of performance-related pay (particularly profit-sharing and share-ownership) measure output at group or even firm level. Belfield and Heywood (2001) and Bryson and Freeman (2006) find that individual performance-related pay increases wage dispersion at workplace level whereas profit-sharing and share-ownership do not.

In large firms employers may reward effort through promotion, rather than directly through performance pay. In these internal labor markets (Doeringer and Piore, 1971) pay varies little within grades but increases with job changes. Limited promotion slots motivate workers to supply effort by virtue of the wage increases they would earn if promoted, with the competition for promotions then resembling a form of tournament where 'winner takes all' (Lazear and Rosen, 1981). The advantage to an employer is that it is often easier to observe relative performance than absolute performance. Additionally, it may suit some companies to structure pay so that the winner makes very large sums, as a way of spurring on those lower in the hierarchy as well as the CEO. Tournament theory therefore provides one possible explanation for the high wages of CEOs and, more generally, wage inequality within firms. Tournaments might be viewed as one form of 'deferred compensation' whereby worker and firm commit to each other. Under schemes of deferred compensation, workers are paid below their marginal product when young and above it when older. This may be because firms want to limit costly labor turnover (Salop and Salop, 1976) or because distinguishing good from poor workers takes time. Lazear (1979) shows how the common upward-sloping age-earnings profile can discourage workers from shirking.

However, tournaments may inhibit worker collaboration. Freeman and Gelber's (2006) laboratory experiment shows that total tournament output depends on pay inequality according to an inverse-U shaped function. Thus inequality can be too high as well as too low for efficiency. One fruit farm registered a 50 per cent increase in worker productivity after moving away from relative incentives to piece rates, the apparent explanation being the shift away from a system in which workers' individual efforts could have negative effects on co-workers' earnings (Bandiera et al., 2005). One implication is, however, that where a system generates positive externalities – as in the case of group incentive schemes – this should generate still greater productivity. A further implication is that notions of fairness are clearly important in the labor market.

FAIRNESS, NORMS AND RECIPROCITY

In standard neo-classical economics actors are driven by self-interest and decisions are made to maximize financial gain. However, exchanges between people are often conducted according to shared social norms of fairness and reciprocity. These notions are formalized in equity theory where the 'target relationship' sought by individuals is equality between their own reward per unit of input and their cognition of others' rewards. Employee perceptions of what they contribute to the organization and what they get in return, and how this ratio compares to others inside and outside the organization, determines how fair they perceive their employment relationship to be (Adams, 1963). Others in the same work-group, workplace or firm are likely to be the most salient comparators (Brown et al., 1998), which may explain why employees' pay satisfaction is so strongly associated with their wage rank within the workplace (Brown et al., 2005). However, employees may also make comparisons with similar workers in the external labor market, as is common in union bargaining. And when the union is dominated by less skilled employees, as with general rather than craft unions, the pressure from the union is generally to favor the lower paid and to compress wage differentials among covered workers.

The 'inputs' to the equity calculation vary across occupations. In manual occupations it is common to prioritize physical effort, dexterity and skill in using tools and machines, whereas in non-manual occupations greater priority is accorded to literacy, communication, information processing, and responsibility and so on. There is a broad correspondence between the 'inputs' forming the foundation of social norms of equity and the 'investments' that increase human capital. The pay premium for supervisory and managerial jobs, compared with the workers they supervise, also rests upon a widely-held norm that responsibility for other peoples' work should be rewarded.

These concepts first came to the fore among economists with Akerlof's (1982) partial gift exchange model of the labor contract which argues that worker effort depends on work norms of a relevant reference group and that the firm can alter these norms and thus effort by paying workers a wages 'gift' in excess of the minimum required in return for greater effort. Akerlof and Yellen's (1990) 'fair wage-effort' hypothesis suggests that, if the actual wage is lower than the workers' notion of the fair wage, they will withdraw their effort in proportion. The fair wage thus plays a role in wage bargaining where entitlements are fashioned by reference points. More broadly, notions of fairness can underpin the role of custom and practice in wage determination (Brown and Nolan, 1988; Rubery, 1997) though, as Hicks (1932) points out, forces of supply and demand can occasion changes in customary structures.

Greenberg (1990) presents evidence in support of the fair wage-effort model, recording employee thefts from a company in response to proposed pay cuts. Where management explained the reasons for pay cuts and expressed remorse, subsequent employee thefts were significantly lower than the situation where management provided inadequate information and showed no remorse. Greenberg suggests that perceptions of inequity caused employees to take actions to restore equity. Often what matters are employee perceptions of distributive justice. Thus Cowherd and Levine (1992) link a negative association between customer perceptions of quality and pay differentials between hourly paid employees and top management to a diminution in citizenship-type behavior.

Laboratory experiments repeatedly show individuals and firms behaving in accordance with norms of fairness and reciprocity, leading to outcomes that would not otherwise be predicted by neo-classical theory. For instance, experiments support Solow's (1990) contention that wage rigidity may be partially due to conformity with social norms. Falk et al. (2006) show that the introduction of a minimum wage law changes perceptions of a fair wage, forcing firms to increase wages above the minimum wage and retain them even when the minimum wage is rescinded. This helps to explain why fast food restaurants in the US increased wages for workers by more than was necessary following increases in the minimum wage (Card and Krueger, 1995; Katz and Krueger, 1992) and why the opportunity to pay sub-minimum wages to youth workers has no discernible effect on teenage workers' wages (Katz and Krueger, 1992).

Wade et al. (2006) also show that norms of fairness are salient to top decision makers and that over or underpayment of the CEO cascades down to lower organizational levels, partly due to CEOs using their own power not only to increase their own salaries but also those of their subordinates. Further, CEOs serve as a key referent for employees in determining whether their own situation is 'fair'. They find that when lower-level managers are underpaid relative to the CEO (that is, underpaid more than the CEO or overpaid less), they are more likely to leave the organization.

This discussion of fairness has focused on the ways in which levels of pay are influenced by the earnings of co-workers in the firm or wider labor market. But pay may also be influenced by comparisons of working conditions.

COMPENSATING WAGE DIFFERENTIALS

The concept underlying 'compensating wage differentials' is the idea that wages are not simply the reward for effort or skill, but that the context in which that effort is delivered is important in determining the price of labor. Thus one should not necessarily expect wage equality between jobs of equal value, but rather equality in the overall 'job package', which includes not only money wages but also non-pecuniary benefits and the whole range of working conditions. The principle also departs from the traditional framework of supply and demand by according workers some preference over issues other than monetary rewards.

The theory is often expressed in terms of the wage compensation for dangerous work. Most workers can be expected to value both higher wages and greater levels of safety, but some are presumed willing to accept additional risk in exchange for a higher wage that is sufficient to maintain the same overall level of utility. Equally, a firm can choose to invest in procedures that offer workers greater safety, or obtain the same level of profitability by economizing on safety and distributing the savings to workers through higher wages. Yet the principle of compensating differentials can be extended beyond the issue of workplace risk. This was clearly acknowledged in the writings of Adam Smith (1982: 202):

> The wages of labour vary with the ease or hardship, the cleanliness or dirtiness, the honorableness or dishonorableness, of the employment.... A journeyman blacksmith, though an artificer, seldom earns so much in twelve hours, as a collier, who is only a labourer, does in eight. His work is not quite so dirty, is less dangerous, and is carried on in day-light, and above ground.

One might therefore expect higher wages to be explained, in some instances, by the presence of negative job attributes such as dirt and insecurity. Similarly, one might expect lower wages to be associated with positive job attributes such as hours, flexibility or meaningful work.

Empirical studies find evidence of wage premia that appear to compensate workers for unsociable hours (Lanfranchi et al., 2002; Kostiuk, 1990), greater levels of job stress (French and Dunlap, 1998) and job insecurity (Moretti, 2000). McNabb (1989) finds a wage premium for unfavorable working conditions among manual workers in Britain. But he accepts (pp. 328–30), as do others (for example, Purse, 2004; Gunderson and Hyatt, 2001), that reliable estimation is difficult

because workers are not randomly allocated across jobs of varying quality. One must therefore account for biases arising from worker selection into good or bad jobs when evaluating the compensating differentials hypothesis. Compensating differentials are underestimated where employees with high earnings potential are able to secure 'better' jobs (Viscusi, 1978). Alternatively, if workers may sort into jobs according to their productivity under particular conditions (Garen, 1988) – perhaps possessing experience or a 'cool head' which enables them to be productive when others may panic – then estimates may overstate the size of any compensating differential, which is instead a 'return for skill'. One implication is that someone in a non-risky job may not necessarily be able to attain the higher wage of someone in a risky job simply by choosing to accept a higher level of risk; equally, it does not necessarily follow that seemingly underpaid employees undertaking meaningful work in the voluntary sector could necessarily raise their earnings by moving to equivalent jobs in the business sector.

A further area of empirical investigation has been the extent to which lower wages accompany the provision of fringe benefits. Olson (2002) finds that married women in the United States accept a wage penalty of around 20 per cent in return for employer-provided health insurance. However, higher wages are more usually found in conjunction with favorable levels of non-wage benefits (for example, Dale-Olsen, 2006, for Norwegian workers). Similarly, various studies find that the degree of wage inequality between low and high-wage groups tends to increase when one considers the complete compensation package (Joshi and Paci, 1998; Pierce, 2001). The co-existence of high wages and good conditions might arise through trade unions' bargaining power (see Fairris, 1989) while the co-existence of low wages and poor conditions could indicate employers' monopsony power. However, a positive correlation between wages and working conditions might also imply some segmentation of the labor market.

requests to change from full-time to part-time working, or to work some form of flexible work hours. Despite the apparent weakness in the wording, however, early assessments of the provision show the large majority of such requests being accommodated by employers (Holt and Grainger, 2005). I return to this below in the discussion of work-life balance.

A third European example of statutory working time development is recent legislation in several Nordic countries to extend paternity leave and father's parental leave, to encourage greater sharing of childcare responsibilities. Parental leave legislation is long established in Nordic countries; Norway for example, has had parental leave since 1936 and paternity leave since 1977 (Hardy and Adnett, 2002: 166). In recent years, 'father's leave' provisions have been further extended, ranging from six weeks in Norway to three months in Iceland (Moss and O'Brien, 2006). Early evaluations in Norway found that when this leave was introduced on a transferable basis (that is, available to either parent) it was primarily utilized as additional maternity leave. To stimulate a more equitable sharing of early childrearing, this father's leave has subsequently been made non-transferable; this has resulted, in a very short time period, in high rates of take-up by fathers in Norway (Brandth and Kvande, 2003).

A final example of statutory developments in the working time field in Europe has been the introduction (by two laws and despite strong employer opposition) of a 35-hour working week in France in 2000. Introduced as part of the socialist government's measures to address persistent high levels of unemployment, this legislation has resulted in a significant reduction in actual working hours in France, though the net effect on job creation and job retention is much less clear (Durand and Martin, 2004; Fagnani and Letablier, 2004: 554). In addition, as I discuss below, these working time laws in France have acted as a major stimulus to local negotiations over working time by leaving much of the detail of the implementation of shorter weekly hours undetermined.

Yet, as well as highlighting these different initiatives that have extended statutory coverage of aspects of working time, it is also important to note the presence of other factors that act to limit the impact of different working time laws. These include the exempting of particular groups from different pieces of legislation (McCann, 2005: 25, 27) and also the degree to which statutory regulations are effectively enforced. A further factor that can mute the impact of any legislation is the length of the reference period over which work hours are calculated (statutory limits on weekly hours typically include an averaging period within which the limits must be achieved). These averaging or reference periods vary considerably; for example, they are typically thirteen weeks in the Netherlands, but up to one year in Japan and Spain (McCann, 2005: 7). Where reference periods extend as long as a year (and thus in effect become annual hours contracts), this provides considerable scope for employees to be working much longer than the weekly statutory limits on hours for a considerable period of time.

Union-management relations

As noted earlier, working time issues have been a common focus of union-management relations over a long period. This continues, despite the substantial changes in the scope and coverage of those relations in many countries over the past two decades. In the UK in 2004, for example, working hours remained the second most frequent topic (after pay) that managers negotiated with trade unions; holidays represented the third most frequent topic (Kersley et al., 2006: 194). In those UK workplaces where unions were recognized, just over half (53 per cent) normally negotiated over hours, and a similar proportion (52 per cent) over holidays. A further 20 per cent of workplaces with recognized unions normally consulted over hours (ibid). Similarly in Germany, as Haipeter and Lehndorff (2005: 141) comment, apart from wages, working time has traditionally been the most prominent area of industrial relations regulation. A partial exception to this pattern is the US where as Berg and colleagues comment, 'working time has not been a high bargaining priority' for the majority of unions in recent times (Berg et al., 2004: 341). Elsewhere, however, working time negotiations in different countries have involved not only weekly and annual hours, but also the length of working lifetimes, with the negotiation of early retirement provisions. As Ebbinghaus (2006) describes, in recent periods of restructuring and recession, both employers and trade unions have sought agreements on early retirement as a way of securing a more popular means of workforce reduction than by compulsory redundancies.

While working time remains a prominent topic in most countries where managers continue to negotiate and consult with trade unions, what *has* changed in the joint regulation of hours is the level at which this regulation normally occurs: in particular, there has been an evident decentralization and a growing degree of local agreement and regulation of working time. In the past, three things went together in the area of working time: a lower level of differentiation of working hours than currently exists; a primary emphasis on duration (weekly hours and length of paid holidays) as the key issue in working time and a trade union aim of securing both standardization in relation to any working time changes, and overtime payments for hours worked in excess of basic weekly hours. Each of these elements acted both to simplify the treatment of working time issues, and facilitate a more centralized handling of many working time issues by both parties, away from the particularities of the workplace. However, build into this picture not only a growing tendency for managers to utilize a wider range of working time patterns, but also a growing emphasis on issues other than simple duration, and the effect has been that the ability (and motivation) of the parties to handle working time issues at a more distant, centralized level, has become considerably restricted. What has resulted has been a growing tendency for a decentralized approach to the regulation of working time,

but also a working time agenda at the local level which has become more wide ranging than hitherto.

Examples of this growing decentralization are widespread. In several European countries for example, decentralization has accompanied national framework agreements on weekly hours. In France, the introduction of a statutory 35-hour week has been accompanied by a major growth in company and local collective bargaining to increase temporal flexibility. Alis (2003) for example, reports that between 1998 and 2002, over 128,000 collective agreements on working hours were signed in France. Under the working time laws, collective agreements became the only means of implementing the 35-hour week, other than by a simple reduction in hours. Most commonly, these local collective agreements have focused on increasing the flexibility of working time to offset the cost implications of the aggregate hours reduction. In the main, this flexibility has taken the form of annual hours agreements (around an annual level of 1600 hours) and amending work time structures to cover longer operating or trading hours (ibid).

Similarly in Germany, the staged introduction of a 35-hour working week in the metalworking industry by 1995 was accompanied by an agreement that the implementation of the reduction would be subject to local negotiations between management and works councils. Management increasingly sought to offset the cost of the hours reduction by increasing the degree of temporal flexibility. In the event, the main forms of flexibility agreed related to: the proportion of the workforce who could voluntarily opt to work longer than the 35-hour week (up to 18 per cent of the workforce); the length of averaging periods to achieve the 35-hour norm (typically up to six months, and in some cases one year or even longer) and the use of individual time accounts to enable extra hours worked to be 'banked' and converted to time off (rather than overtime payments) at a later stage (Haipeter and Lehndorff, 2005: 143, 145). As Haipeter and Lehndorff point out, in highly unionized sectors such as automobile manufacture, where works councils coverage is comprehensive and well organized, this growth in the local determination of actual working time patterns has resulted in a process of 'regulated flexibility' (ibid: 154). However, in other areas, where unionism is weaker and works councils less powerful – or not in existence at all, as is the case in many smaller establishments (see Addison et al., 2001) – the upshot of the decentralization has been a growth in managerial power over the determination of actual working time patterns.

In the UK, a substantial decentralization of working time determination has also occurred over the past two decades, involving in part a shift away from multi-employer agreements and toward organization-based arrangements (either at company or workplace level) (Arrowsmith and Sisson, 1999). As these authors point out, however, this has not been a universal trend; national frameworks have continued to exist in some sectors (such as health) whilst elsewhere (for example, engineering) such frameworks were dismantled in the late 1980s and 1990s. Further, even where such dismantling has taken place, Arrowsmith and Sisson found that a standard working time pattern often remained identifiable, or at least a significant clustering around a small number of patterns. What is also evident in their study, however, is the widespread nature of the changes occurring in working time arrangements, principally to enable employers to secure greater flexibility and reduce costs, through for example increased shift working and the expansion of part-time schedules (Arrowsmith and Sisson, 1999: 63).

Outside Europe, changes in the employment relations of working time are particularly evident in Australia. The increased importance of workplace agreements in Australia from the mid-1990s onwards and the weakening of former sector-wide bargaining, has been accompanied by a widening range of working time patterns, including both very short and very long shift patterns (Barrett et al., 2005; Loudoun and Harley, 2001). More generally, several commentators have highlighted the growth of long hours working in recent years in Australia, made easier

by the relatively weak statutory framework governing working time, and the reduced significance of industry-wide regulation of work hours (Barrett et al., 2005; Berg et al., 2004: 339–341; Lee, 2004: 41).

In general, more localized regulation of hours has been associated with the growth of working time trade-offs, or 'something for something' agreements: for example, a reduction in duration being conceded by management either in return for greater flexibility over the scheduling of those hours, or in exchange for a broader definition of 'standard' hours not attracting overtime premia. In this way the working time agenda has broadened, and become more closely related to the particular working time requirements of individual organizations.

Management and employees

Any discussion of the regulation of working time by statutory instruments and employment relations agreements runs the danger of exaggerating the influence of each (and both, in combination) compared to other influences shaping actual patterns of work time. Here we briefly examine not only the influence of management, but also – less common in employment relations' discussions – the influence of workers on their own work time patterns.

In terms of managerial influence, though evidence is somewhat patchy, it is nevertheless clear that in many situations and over many aspects, managers unilaterally regulate their employees' working time patterns. This influence manifests itself in a variety of ways, from the initial determination of work time arrangements associated with job vacancies (for example whether the job vacancy is advertised as full- or part-time), to the determination of work periods and shift systems, the demand for overtime working, the availability of flexible working hours and any restrictions on the periods when staff can take paid leave. Further, as well as any formal authority to determine work time patterns, it is clear that managers also exert considerable informal powers of regulation.

Different studies have shown, for example, the influence of immediate line managers on the working time culture within their area of responsibility: whether employees feel under pressure to work long hours or work without taking their rest breaks in full, or whether they feel they would receive support if they requested flexible working, for example (Batt and Valcour, 2003: 211; BRMB Social Research, 2004; Houston and Waumsley, 2003: 36; Thompson et al., 1999). Other studies have also shown that over and above any formal flexible work time arrangements in operation (such as a flexitime system) much *ad hoc* adjustment of actual work time patterns occurs as a result of informal requests by management, for example for workers to stay on at work to complete a particular task (Marsh, 1991).

In the UK, the evidence from the WERS 2004 investigation underlines the extent of managerial influence in the working time area. For while, as noted earlier, hours and holidays figure prominently as items for joint regulation in those workplaces with recognized trade unions, in practice not only are large numbers of workplaces devoid of a recognized union presence but as we also noted, even in establishments where unions are present, only in just over half of these do management negotiate over working hours. Indeed, in approaching one-in-five (18 per cent) of workplaces with union representatives, there was no union involvement at all in work hours issues, and in a further 10 per cent of such workplaces, union involvement was restricted to being informed by management of any changes (Kersley et al., 2006: 194). Overall, the WERS 2004 results show that in over seven out of ten workplaces in Britain (71 per cent) management did not engage with unions or other employee representatives on any issues relating to working hours (ibid). A similar picture is portrayed by Berg et al. in relation to the US, where a lack of union coverage, coupled with a tendency for unions to prioritize issues other than working time, has resulted in 'Control over working time rest[ing] largely with employers' (Berg et al., 2004: 341).

Yet, while these findings underline the extent of managerial influence over work time issues and the restricted influence of trade unions in this area, it is also important to recognize that employees themselves exercise a significant degree of influence and control over their working time. We have noted already in the discussion for example, how recent legislation has, in different countries, provided individual employees with a greater measure of influence – for instance to take leave at the birth of their children, or to seek changes in their work patterns. Further, arrangements such as flexitime and time-banking, act to extend individual control over the work period. In addition, however, there are a variety of ways in which employees can act to influence their work time patterns. Indeed, in the field of work sociology, there is a history of studies documenting the many and varied ways that workers regulate aspects of their working time. These include taking time off through voluntary absence, a work behavior that may be individual and unorganized or more collaborative and organized (Edwards and Scullion, 1982; Heyes, 1997). Also significant are the many ways of 'fiddling' time at work, ranging widely from arriving at work late, leaving early and covertly extending rest breaks, to sabotaging equipment in order to create pauses in the work process (Ditton, 1979; Noon and Blyton, 2007). In their turn, managers deploy a variety of means to control some of these employee behaviors, including direct surveillance, bell-to-bell working and the close monitoring of absence behavior, to attendance bonuses and other rewards for accurate time-keeping. Yet the picture remains one of a considerable ability on the part of many employees to modify the standard work time pattern to gain some control over their working period. What is more, a number of studies of employee attitudes highlight the contribution to overall job satisfaction of this access to some discretion or control over working time (see for example, Baltes et al., 1999; Berg 1999; Macan, 1994). Indeed, it is evident that for many workers, it is not the overall length of the working period that is felt most keenly, nor even the timing of that work, but the degree to which these constraints are open to some degree of worker influence and control.

To sum up this part of the discussion, it is evident that working time continues to be regulated in several ways: partly by statute, setting various maxima and minima relating to hours, holidays and rest periods; partly by employment relations, increasingly through local rather than national agreements; partly by management, both by formally establishing working time structures and by more informal ways that influence both the working time culture and the actual patterns of hours worked and partly by employees themselves, both overtly (for example, via the use of flexitime arrangements) and also by more covert means that act to modify the formal work time structure. The relative influence of each of these appears to have shifted significantly in the recent past: there has been a somewhat enhanced role for statutory regulation in many countries; a reduced (and certainly a decentralized) role for trade unions and joint regulation (reflecting in important part the widespread decline in influence of trade unions) and an increased role for management in environments less subject to trade union influence. Overall, as a result of a growing fragmentation of work time patterns and a decline in standardization, together with an increased emphasis on the arrangement and flexibility of work hours, management appear to have gained significantly greater control over the work time agenda, despite any extension in statutory provision. At the same time, workers themselves continue to exert an important influence on their own work time patterns, an influence that is constrained by managerial action, but far from eliminated.

WORK-LIFE BALANCE

In many recent discussions on working time, much has been made of the link between aspects of work time and the ability of individuals to achieve a successful reconciliation of work and non-work demands: a better 'work-life balance'. Though criticized for its confused terminology (work being a major part of life rather than something separate, as implied in the expression 'work-life') nevertheless 'work-life balance' has come to refer to individuals' 'ability to pursue successfully their work and non-work lives, without undue pressures from one undermining the satisfactory experience of the other' (Noon and Blyton, 2007: 356). The work-life balance debate represents, in many respects, a broadening of discussions in the 1980s and 1990s surrounding 'family friendly' work policies. The now widely-preferred expression of 'work-life balance' is a recognition that all those in paid work, not just those with family responsibilities, have an interest in reconciling competing work and non-work demands.

For the large majority of those in different studies reporting a work-life imbalance, the source of that imbalance is a negative spill-over from work to non-work life, rather than the reverse. However, even among the former, what in practice constitutes 'balance' will vary considerably from person to person, depending on a wide range of factors including individuals' economic and domestic circumstances, their age, the nature, demands and security of their job and the characteristics of their non-work life. Indeed for some, a key source of imbalance may lie in excessive work, while for others (those under- or unemployed) any imbalance is likely to be the result of too little paid work. However, it is the former aspect of the work-life balance issue that is most relevant to the present discussion: the 'time squeeze' that many experience between their work and non-work lives. This includes working parents with paid work and family responsibilities, and the working time demands of many jobs reducing the time available for life outside work.

The association between work time and life outside work has been a long running theme in workers' demands for better terms and conditions. Various early calls for an eight-hour working day, for example, adopted as their campaign slogan the nineteenth century maxim that advocated 'eight hours of work, eight hours of rest, eight hours of recreation'. However, in recent years several coinciding factors have brought the issue of work-life balance more to the fore both in public policy and popular debate. These factors include the substantial growth in rates of women's economic activity (in part reflecting public policies to stimulate higher levels of labor force participation); the resulting rise both in dual-earner households and in levels of employment of women with dependent children; elements of working time patterns, particularly the continuation (and in some countries the expansion) of long hours working and the changing experience of work, particularly the growing experience among many workers of increased work intensification (Green, 2004; Johansson, 2002).

Responses to concerns over work-life balance are identifiable at societal, community, organizational and individual levels, and range from statutory childcare and nursery provision to individual decisions to 'downshift' to a simpler lifestyle. Within work organizations, three types of response are most in evidence: policies that provide employees with leave for child-bearing and care; arrangements that provide more choice and flexibility over working time (how much, when and where work hours are fulfilled) and workplace provision to support parents, such as child-care facilities or subsidies (Glass and Estes, 1997). With only very limited provision of the third of these in most countries (in the UK in 2004 for example, only 3 per cent of workplaces provided a workplace nursery; see Kersley et al., 2006: 254–5), the two main forms of organizational response to work-life balance concerns are closely connected with aspects of working time. This is also reflected in Heery's (2006) study of different work-life issues pursued by trade unions: of the 20 work-life issues that union representatives in the study had negotiated over, three-quarters were work hours related (Heery, 2006: 51). Wood et al's analysis of family-friendly management practices in Britain indicates that it tends to be larger organizations, with personnel departments, an equal-opportunity approach and/or a high proportion of women in the workplace, that are more likely to have implemented flexibility and other time-related policies (Wood et al., 2003).

Several of the aspects of working time that are most relevant to work-life concerns have displayed significant change in recent years. We have noted a number of these already and include first, a widespread and continuing growth in part-time working, with many working couples choosing to balance life in and out of paid work by one member (mainly women) working part-time. Second, there are various indications that the provision of more flexible work schedules is increasing. In Britain for example, the number of workplaces operating flexitime arrangements grew significantly between 1998 and 2004 (Kersley et al., 2006: 252), though as Hyman and Summers (2004) note, the actual provision of flexible work schedules is often characterized by a lack of formalization. However, in recent years, this access to flexible hours has been bolstered by statutory rights to request flexible working by parents of young children (see above). Elsewhere too, flexitime has become extensive; indeed, in Germany over four out of five larger organizations (over 500 employees) have introduced flexible working time systems (Croucher and Singe, 2004: 153) and a growing number are experimenting with far-reaching flexitime systems in which employees decide their own work patterns (Trinczek, 2006).

A third example of work time developments relevant to work-life balance relates to the area of leave policies, particularly child-care leave (less so in relation to caring for adults). Following an extensive review of leave provisions in 22 countries, Moss and O'Brien (2006: 7) conclude that 'leave policy is receiving much attention at present with most countries reporting significant recent changes or future changes'. As noted earlier, Nordic countries have been particularly prominent in this development, substantially extending both maternity and particularly paternity leave provision in recent years.

A final example of a working time development with significant work-life implications is the spread of retirement practices which provide a greater flexibility than a fixed and final retirement date. As discussed above, early retirement provision became more prominent in the 1980s and 1990s as employers, trade unions and many older workers viewed a voluntary early exit as a more acceptable means of workforce reduction than compulsory redundancy. As Ebbinghaus (2006) points out, the growth of early retirement provision has since slowed as the cost of such schemes has become a more prominent issue. However, provisions for retiring before the age that state pensions become payable remains widespread, and represents for many an important source of choice over work-life balance decisions.

The work-life aspects of retirement could potentially be increased further by greater opportunities for older workers to make a more gradual transition from work to retirement. Yet, whilst various partial retirement initiatives have been attempted in several European countries (allowing employees to continue working a reduced workweek and have access to a partial pension), such schemes have to date been of limited success due primarily to the inadequacy of supporting funding arrangements, and restrictions imposed by different occupational pension rules (Delsen, 1996; Ebbinghaus, 2006). This may change in the future, however, at least in Europe. The spread of age discrimination legislation, together with the increased right among other groups to secure (or at least request) more flexible working, could improve the future access of older workers to modifying their work time patterns, thereby creating a more gradual transition between work and retirement.

Yet at the same time various other employer policies on working time, as well as other aspects of work experience, are likely to continue to clash with a work-life agenda. In part this represents a divergence over flexibility: employers' desire for the variable availability of labor potentially conflicts with employees seeking greater choice and discretion over their own working time in order to coordinate their paid work more

effectively with non-work demands. Further, moves to increase productivity through the implementation of 'high performance' practices could add further work pressures that spill over negatively into non-work life. This is one finding of the study by White et al. (2003) which found individuals reporting a negative effect on home life not only associated with the number of hours worked, but also related to the presence of various high performance practices including appraisal systems, group-working and performance related pay (see also Hochschild, 1997, and for a contrasting view see Berg et al., 2003).

Thus, while work-life balance concerns continue to be raised, and while certain steps are taken to alleviate certain work-life pressures – particularly in relation to time off to care for young children – at the same time other aspects of organizational life, such as increased work pressures and greater work intensification, represent potentially significant obstacles for more adequately reconciling the demands of work and non-work life for many workers.

CONCLUSION

The foregoing discussion has identified shifts both in the overall working time agenda and in the patterns of regulation of working time. Overall, the agenda has broadened considerably in the recent period, away from a primary focus on duration – though this remains critical in certain contexts – to encompass a wider range of issues relating to the scheduling of work time, the degree of temporal flexibility available to both employers and employees and the scope for individuals to adjust their work time arrangements to achieve a more satisfactory work-life balance.

These features of working time are likely to remain prominent on employer, trade union and employee agendas in coming years. Further, the contested nature of many aspects of working time – the competing demands by employers and employees for greater flexibility, for example, the conflicting interests over the definition of standard and non-standard work hours and the potentially conflicting interests over workers' retirement decisions – highlight the continuing relevance of joint regulation in this important area of employment conditions. Yet, without a significant revival of trade union coverage and influence, many employees will need to rely more than hitherto on the power deriving from their own labor market position and – for those whose position is less strong – on statutory provision to bolster their influence over working time, and secure work time arrangements that more satisfactorily reconcile the demands of work and non-work life.

NOTES

1 Basic working hours is the term frequently used to refer to the contractually-agreed work period; this is distinct from 'usual' working hours which includes periods of paid or unpaid overtime.

2 Within the EU, directives are binding agreements but require legislation in each member state to comply with the objectives of the directive; see Gennard and Judge, 2005.

REFERENCES

Adam, B. (1990) *Time and Social Theory*. Cambridge: Polity.

Addison, J.T., Schnabel, C. and Wagner, J. (2001) 'Works councils in Germany: their effects on establishment performance', *Oxford Economic Papers*, 53 (4): 659–94.

Adnett, N. and Hardy, S. (2000) 'Reviewing the working time directive: rationale, implementation and case law', *Industrial Relations Journal*, 32 (2): 114–25.

Alis, D. (2003) 'The 35-hour week in France: the French exception?', *Personnel Review*, 32 (4): 510–26.

Anxo, D., Fagan, C., McCann, D., Lee, S. and Messenger, J.C. (2004) 'Introduction: working time in industrialized countries', in J.C. Messenger (ed.) *Working Time and Workers' Preferences in Industrialized Countries: Finding the Balance*. London: Routledge. pp. 1–9.

Arrowsmith, J. (2002) 'The struggle over working time in nineteenth and twentieth-century Britain', *Historical Studies in Industrial Relations*, 13: 83–117.

Arrowsmith, J. and Sisson, K. (1999) 'Pay and working time: towards organization-based systems?', *British Journal of Industrial Relations*, 37 (1): 51–75.

Arrowsmith, J. and Sisson, K. (2000) 'Managing working time', in S. Bach and K. Sisson (eds) *Personnel Management*, 3rd edition. Oxford: Blackwell. pp. 287–313.

Baltes, B. B., Briggs, T. E., Huff, J. W., Wright, J. A. and Neuman, G. A. (1999) 'Flexible and compressed workweek schedules: a meta-analysis of their effects on work-related criteria', *Journal of Applied Psychology*, 84 (4): 496–513.

Barrett, S., Burgess, J. and Campbell, I. (2005) 'The Australian labour market in 2004', *Journal of Industrial Relations*, 47 (2): 133–50.

Batt, R. and Valcour, P.M. (2003) 'Human resources practices as predictors of work-family outcomes and employee turnover', *Industrial Relations*, 42 (2): 189–220.

Berg, P. (1999) 'The effects of high performance work practices on job satisfaction in the United States steel industry', *Relations Industrielles*, 54 (1): 111–35.

Berg, P., Appelbaum, E., Bailey, T. and Kalleberg, A.L. (2004) 'Contesting time: international comparisons of employee control of working time', *Industrial and Labor Relations Review*, 57 (3): 331–49.

Berg, P., Kalleberg, A.L. and Appelbaum, E. (2003) 'Balancing work and family: the role of high-commitment environments', *Industrial Relations*, 42 (2): 168–88.

Bienefeld, M.A. (1972) *Working Hours in British Industry: An Economic History*. London: Weidenfeld and Nicolson.

Bittman, M. and Rice, J. (2001) 'The spectre of overwork: an analysis of trends between 1974 and 1997 using Australian time use diaries', *Labour and Industry*, 12 (3): 5–26.

Blyton, P. (1985) *Changes in Working Time: An International Review*. London: Croom Helm.

Blyton, P. (1994) 'Working hours', in K. Sisson (ed.) *Personnel Management*, 2nd edition. Oxford: Blackwell. pp. 495–526.

Blyton, P. and Trinczek, R. (1995) 'Working time flexibility and annual hours', *European Industrial Relations Review*, No. 260, September: 13–4.

Bouffartigue, P. and Bouteiller, J. (2001) '"Our own worst enemy" – French management and the 35-hour week', *Transfer*, 1 (2): 211–26.

Brandth, B. and Kvande, E. (2003): *Fleksible Fedre*[Flexible Fathers]. Oslo: Universitetsforlaget.

BRMB Social Research (2004) *A survey of workers' experiences of the Working Time Regulations*, Employment Relations Research Series No. 31, London: Department of Trade and Industry.

Burgess, K. (1975) *The Origins of British Industrial Relations: The Nineteenth Century Experience.* London: Croom Helm.

Campbell, I. (2002) 'Extended working hours in Australia', *Labour and Industry*, 13 (1): 91–110.

Croucher, R. and Singe, I. (2004) 'Co-determination and working time accounts in the German finance industry', *Industrial Relations Journal*, 35 (2): 153–68.

Deery, S. J. and Mahony, A. (1994) 'Temporal flexibility: management strategies and employee preferences in the retail industry', *Journal of Industrial Relations*, 36 (3): 332–52.

Delsen, L. (1996) 'Gradual retirement: lessons from the Nordic countries and the Netherlands', *European Journal of Industrial Relations*, 2 (1): 55–67.

Ditton, J. (1979) 'Baking time', *Sociological Review*, 27 (1): 157–67.

Durand, M. and Martin, J. (2004) 'The 35-hour week: portrait of a French exception', *OECD Observer*, 244: 10–12.

Duxbury, L. and Higgins, C. (2006) 'Work-life balance in Canada: rhetoric versus reality', in P. Blyton, B. Blunsdon, K. Reed and A. Dastmalchian, (eds) *Work-Life Integration: International Perspectives on the Balancing of Multiple Roles.* Basingstoke: Palgrave Macmillan. pp. 82–112.

Ebbinghaus, B. (2006) *Reforming Early Retirement in Europe, Japan and the USA.* Oxford: Oxford University Press.

Edwards, P. K. and Scullion, H. (1982) *The Social Organisation of Industrial Conflict.* Oxford: Blackwell.

EIRO (European Industrial Relations Observatory on-line) (2005) 'Working time developments – 2004', http://www.eurofound.ie/2005/03.

Fagnani, J. and Letablier, M-T. (2004) 'Work and family life in balance: the impact of the 35-hour laws in France', *Work, Employment and Society*, 18 (3): 551–72.

Freyssinet, J. (1998) 'France: a recurrent aim, repeated near-failures and a new law', *Transfer*, 4/98: 641–56.

Gennard, J. and Judge, G. (2005) *Employee Relations*, 4th edition. London: Chartered Institute of Personnel and Development.

Glass, J.L. and Estes, S.B. (1997) 'The family responsive workplace', *Annual Review of Sociology*, 23: 289–313.

Green, F. (1997) 'Union recognition and paid holiday entitlement', *British Journal of Industrial Relations*, 35 (2): 243–55.

Green, F. (2004) 'Why has work effort become more intense?', *Industrial Relations*, 43 (4): 709–41.

Haipeter, T. and Lehndorff, S. (2005) 'Decentralized bargaining of working time in the German automobile industry', *Industrial Relations Journal*, 36 (2): 140–56.

Hardy, S. and Adnett, N. (2002) 'The Parental Leave Directive: towards a "family-friendly" Social Europe?', *European Journal of Industrial Relations*, 8 (2): 157–72.

Heery, E. (2006) 'Bargaining for balance: union policy on work-life issues in the United Kingdom', in P. Blyton, B. Blunsdon, K. Reed and A. Dastmalchian, (eds) *Work-Life Integration: International Perspectives on the Balancing of Multiple Roles.* Basingstoke: Palgrave Macmillan. pp. 42–62.

Hewitt, P. (1993) *About Time: The Revolution in Work and Family Life.* London: Rivers Oram.

Heyes, J. (1997) 'Annualized hours and the "knock": the organization of working time in a chemicals plant', *Work, Employment and Society*, 11 (1): 65–81.

Hill, R. (2000) 'New Labour Force Survey questions on working hours', *Labour Market Trends*, January: 39–47.

Hochschild, A.R. (1997) *The Time Bind: When Work Becomes Home and Home Becomes Work.* New York: Metropolitan Books.

Holt, H. and Grainger, H. (2005) *Results of the Second Flexible Working Employee Survey*, Employment Relations Research Series No. 39, London: Department of Trade and Industry.

Houston, D. and Waumsley, J.A. (2003) *Attitudes to flexible working and family life.* Bristol: Policy Press.

Hyman, J. and Summers, J. (2004) 'Lacking balance? Work-life employment practices in the modern economy', *Personnel Review*, 33 (4): 418–29.

ILO (International Labor Organization) (2004) *Yearbook of Annual Statistics*, Geneva: ILO.

IMF (International Metalworkers' Federation) (1997) *Metalworkers and Working Time in the World*, Geneva: International Metalworkers' Federation.

Iskra-Golec, I., Folkard, S., Marek, T. and Noworol, C. (1996) 'Health, well-being and burnout of ICU nurses on 12- and 8-h shifts', *Work and Stress*, 10 (3): 251–56.

Johansson, G. (2002) 'Work-life balance: the case of Sweden in the 1990s', *Social Science Information*, 41 (2): 303–17.

Kersley, B., Alpin, C., Forth, J., Bryson, A., Bewley, H., Dix, G. and Oxenbridge, S. (2006) *Inside the Workplace: Findings from the 2004 Employment Relations Survey.* London: Routledge.

Lee, S. (2004) 'Working-hour gaps: trends and issues', in J.C. Messenger (ed) *Working Time and Workers' Preferences in Industrialized Countries: Finding the Balance.* London: Routledge. pp. 29–59.

Loudoun, R. and Harley, B. (2001) 'Industrial relations decentralization and the growth of 12 hour shifts in Australia', *Journal of Industrial Relations,* 43 (4): 402–21.

Macan, T. H. (1994) 'Time management: test of a process model', *Journal of Applied Psychology,* 79 (3): 381–91.

Marsh, C. (1991) *Hours of Work of Women and Men in Britain.* London: HMSO.

McCann, D. (2005) *Working Time Laws: A Global Perspective.* Geneva: Internal Labor Organization.

Moss, P and O'Brien, M. (2006) *International Review of Leave Policies and Related Research 2006,* Employment Relations Research Series No. 57, London: Department of Trade and Industry.

Noon, M. and Blyton, P. (2007) *The Realities of Work,* 3rd edition. Basingstoke: Palgrave Macmillan.

OECD (Organisation for Economic Cooperation and Development) (2005) *Employment Outlook,* Paris: OECD.

OECD (Organisation for Economic Cooperation and Development) (2006) *Employment Outlook,* Paris: OECD.

Office for National Statistics (2006) *Social Trends 36: 2006 edition.* London: Office for National Statistics.

Owen, J.D. (1979) *Working Hours: An Economic Analysis.* Lexington, MA.: D.C. Heath.

Presser, H.B. and Gornick, J.C. (2005) 'The female share of weekend employment: a study of 16 countries', *Monthly Labor Review,* August: 41–53.

Roediger, D.R. and Foner, P.S. (1989) *Our Own Time: A History of American Labor and the Working Day.* London: Verso.

Schor, J.B. (1991) *The Overworked American: The Unexpected Decline of Leisure.* New York: Harper Books.

Sparks, K., Cooper, C., Fried, Y. and Shirom, A. (1997) 'The effects of hours on health: a meta-analytic review', *Journal of Occupational and Organizational Psychology,* 70 (4): 391–408.

Thompson, C.A., Beauvais, L.L. and Lyness, K.S. (1999) 'When work-family benefits are not enough: the influence of work-family culture on benefit utilization, organizational attachment and work-family conflict', *Journal of Vocational Behavior,* 54 (3): 392–415.

Trinczek, R. (2006) 'Work-life balance and flexible work hours – the German experience', in P. Blyton, B. Blunsdon, K. Reed and A. Dastmalchian, (eds) *Work-Life Integration: International Perspectives on the Balancing of Multiple Roles.* Basingstoke: Palgrave Macmillan. pp. 113–34.

White, M., Hill, S., McGovern, P., Mills, C. and Smeaton, D. (2003) '"High-performance" management practices, working hours and work-life balance', *British Journal of Industrial Relations,* 41 (2): 175–95.

Wood, S.J., de Menezes, L.M. and Lasaosa, A. (2003) 'Family-friendly management in Great Britain: testing various perspectives', *Industrial Relations,* 42 (2): 221–50.

28

Worker Well-Being

David Guest

In recent years, the outcomes of employment relations in advanced industrial societies have broadened, reflecting a number of cultural and economic changes as well as changes in the make-up of the workforce, changes in the kind of work that people do and changes in the nature of the employment relationship. One consequence of this broader focus has been an increasing interest in worker well-being and a number of allied concepts such as work-related stress, job satisfaction and even happiness. This broader focus does not imply that the importance of the traditional substantive outcomes of employment relations has diminished. But it does mean that in any comprehensive analysis of employment relations, these rather different outcomes merit specific attention. This chapter will therefore explore worker well-being and related issues in the context of employment relations. It starts by setting out some of the issues that have influenced the shift towards a concern for worker well-being as an outcome of employment relations. It briefly considers the implications of this shift in emphasis for traditional pluralist perspectives on employment relations. The concept of well-being is explored in some detail. There are then sections on job satisfaction, job insecurity, and workload and stress, which have been identified as key indicators of work-related well-being. Finally, there is a consideration of the aspects of employment relations and the employment relationship that appear to support worker well-being and some discussion of the implications for contemporary employment relations.

WHAT EXPLAINS THE GROWING INTEREST IN WORKER WELL-BEING IN EMPLOYMENT RELATIONS?

The focus on a wider range of workers' outcomes of employment relations is shaped by a number of changes in the contexts in which employment relations is played out.

The changing nature of the workforce

The workforce has changed in a number of important ways in recent decades in all advanced industrial societies. Firstly, it is better-educated. Secondly, it contains a large number of female workers. Thirdly, there is a wider age spread. Fourthly, in some countries and in some sectors in particular, there is a large ethnic mix. More generally, and despite some considerable inequalities, the workforce has become more affluent. The changing make-up of the workforce brings with it a change in priorities among the potential outcomes of employment relations. Indeed, it means we need to re-define 'the worker' in employment relations from a stereotype of a blue-collar, semi-skilled, male, full-time worker to a new stereotype of a public-sector, professional, female and possibly part-time worker. If we adjust our stereotype in this way, then it is easy to accept that the orientations and the priorities among work outcomes may also have shifted.

The changing nature of work

The changing make-up of the workforce is closely associated with the changing nature of work. Over many years, employment in manufacturing and the primary sector has been declining while work in the service sector has been rapidly expanding. This has been accompanied by a reduction in the physical demands of work; even the majority of jobs that remain in the manufacturing sector are likely to be less physically demanding than in the past. For those with an interest in health and safety at work, this has meant a change in focus from physical to mental health and well-being. By the year 2000, stress-related illnesses had become the second most common cause of absence from work in the UK (Jones et al., 2003). One of the areas of work that has seen the most rapid expansion, the helping professions such as teaching, nursing and social work, has attracted particular concern because of the risk of what has become known as burnout, manifested in emotional exhaustion and depersonalization (Schaufeli and Buunk, 2003) which can lead to long-term stress-related absence from work. Stress and mental health are core features of the contemporary concern for well-being at work.

The shift from collective to individual deals

The decline in collective arrangements in many countries, captured in the UK through the data provided in the Workplace Employment Relations Surveys (Cully et al., 1999; Kersley et al., 2006), has been widely noted. However this does not mean the end of employment relations. Allied to the growing concern for flexibility, deriving in part from the changing composition of the workforce, there has been a growth in individual 'deals'. This has been captured in the concept of the psychological contract. Rousseau (2005) has argued that there has been a shift from what she terms collective and positional deals to idiosyncratic or individual deals. Whereas collective deals were typically highly visible and often written, the idiosyncratic deals are likely to be more informal, implicit and based on a local arrangement between the worker and her boss. There may therefore be an understanding that someone can have an extended lunch break on two days of the week to check on an elderly relative but that this will be made up on other days with a shorter lunch break. Someone else will want to arrange to attend a college course and miss a day of work each week, but only in term-time. An analysis of the working hours arrangements in many supermarkets will reveal dozens of different deals that suit both the many part-time workers but also meet the needs of the store to ensure that that staff are present in appropriate numbers to match the varying levels of customer demand. This recognition of the need to make a range of individual deals, even if there is a collectively agreed framework, reflects the growing priority given to personal concerns and personal well-being.

Despite the apparent decline in collective arrangements, the growth in individual deals indicates that workers have not lost all their power. This is illustrated by recognition of the need to offer a degree of flexibility and consideration for workers' concerns as a basis for attracting and retaining the right quality of worker. The growth of knowledge workers and the related concept of the boundaryless career (Arthur and Rousseau, 1996) has resulted in debates about the 'war for talent'. Much of this reflects a tight labor market, or at least tight pockets in the labor market, and one outcome is the choice made by some knowledge workers to become either self-employed or to work on temporary contracts to maintain their independence and employability and, by extension, their well-being (Barley and Kunda, 2004; De Cuyper et al., 2005).

The shift from protection of workers to promotion of good work

The last decades of the twentieth century saw the promotion of a European social program to protect workers from the vagaries of the labor market and exploitation by employers. Indeed, despite the language of social partnership, it was recognized that employers could not be trusted to act responsibly and therefore that legislation was necessary. The result has been a series of steps to promote equal opportunities, to ensure communication and consultation, to limit working hours and to protect those on fixed term contracts.

More recently, the emphasis has begun to switch from protecting workers to promoting good work. The Lisbon meeting of the Council of Europe in 2000 set as one of its long-term aims the promotion of the quality of work. Echoing this, the OECD in 2003 called for 'more and better' jobs. These recent concerns for good work have strong echoes of the 'quality of working life' movement that flourished in the early 1970s. This was an evidence-based approach to the promotion of certain features of work. One illustration of this is the recent emphasis placed by the UK Health and Safety Executive on specific steps to improve well-being at work in an attempt to reduce the rapid growth in stress-related absence (HSE, 1999; 2003).

A wider societal concern for a healthy life-style

Outside the workplace, but serving also to create more employment in the service economy, and heavily promoted by some governments, there has been a considerable concern for a healthy life style. The concern for physical and mental well-being is promoted as an end in itself but also has implications for management and control of health costs. In so far as work is a central life interest, then workplaces are not immune from this trend. As a result, there has been much more concern for healthy eating at work, for bans on smoking in workplaces and for the provision of gyms and health checks. All these developments reflect recognition of the importance of promoting or being seen to promote worker well-being in the workplace.

WORKER OUTCOMES, WORKER WELL-BEING AND TRADITIONAL EMPLOYMENT RELATIONS

The focus on well-being has emerged in a context where the traditional pluralist industrial relations has arguably given ground in the face of the emphasis on human resource management and partnership and the greater management dominance of the employment relationship allied to the increase in the proportion of non-union workplaces. However the decline of a pluralist emphasis in industrial relations should not be taken to imply a unity of interest or shared priorities for the outcomes of contemporary employment relations. This can be captured in an analysis of what might constitute these outcomes from the perspective of employer and employee, illustrated in Table 28.1.

Contemporary human resource policy and practice is largely geared towards achieving the outcomes that reflect the employer's perspective. A key question is how far the pursuit of these employer outcomes is compatible with promotion of worker outcomes. This is an issue I return to below.

What this analysis implies is that we can conceive of a range of worker outcomes of the contemporary employment relationship. Firstly, there is what we can term the traditional issues associated with collective

Table 28.1   Perspectives on the outcomes of contemporary employment relations

Employer perspective	Employee perspective
Employee flexibility	Job security
Knowledge sharing/learning organization	Knowledge/skill protection
Low absence	Positive physical and mental health
Performance-related pay	Fair/equitable pay
Low conflict/strike-free	Fairness of treatment; trust
Achieve high performance targets	Reasonable autonomy and workload
Retaining valued employees	Employability/potential for mobility
Low accidents	Low stress/manageable pressures
Hours that meet work requirements	Hours that suit personal requirements
Organizational commitment	Work-life balance

arrangements that address the terms and conditions of employment. These include job security, knowledge/skill protection, fair treatment and reward and health and safety. These are a set of long-standing concerns that may have altered in character but which continue to be important. Secondly, there are issues that have recently gained more prominence and are more likely to be concerned with worker well-being. These include work-life balance, flexibility of working arrangements, and autonomy and stress in the workplace. In practice all these 'new' issues have always been addressed to some extent in some organizations. What *is* new is the changes in the wider context that have meant that these issues receive a higher priority.

Another implication of this change in emphasis is that employment relations become a more diffuse and complex activity. If there is a shift from the transparent, collective exchange covering substantive, concrete and relatively easily monitored issues to a series of more implicit, local, idiosyncratic deals over less tangible and less easily monitored issues, the control of employment relations slips away from the employment relations specialists. They can set the context and, to some extent the boundaries of the employment relationship. But in a world where work-life balance and local flexibility become important, much more emphasis is placed on the local manager to deal with these issues, often on a one-to-one basis. These idiosyncratic arrangements, particularly if agreed in a context of constant turbulence and change, run all sorts of risks unless a great deal

of attention is paid to fairness of treatment and maintenance of mutual trust. In short, there is more risk of violation of the psychological contract (Conway and Briner, 2005). There are also distinctive challenges at both the general establishment level and the more local boss-subordinate level in managing the employment relationship to ensure an acceptable level of both performance and well-being. With this in mind, I turn to a closer examination of the concept of well-being.

THE NATURE OF WORKER WELL-BEING

The term 'worker well-being' is widely and loosely used to describe a range of possible outcomes. Danna and Griffin (1999) in a review of the literature define well-being as 'comprising the various life/non-work satisfactions enjoyed by individuals, work-related satisfactions, and general health' (p. 358). Despite embracing health in the definition, they also distinguish it as 'a sub-component of well-being and comprises the combination of such mental/psychological indicators as affect, frustration and anxiety and such physical/physiological indicators as blood pressure, heart conditions and general physical health' (p. 358). There is a risk that these definitions can become circular since the World Health Organization defines health as 'a state of complete physical, mental and social well-being and not merely the absence of disease or infirmity' (World Health Organization, 1998, cited in Danna and Griffin, op cit). By implication, health and well-being overlap. However Danna and Griffin also cite the well-known study by Steffy and Jones (1988) which revealed only a low association between subjective measures of well-being and more objective indicators of health.

Possibly the most rigorous analysis of the concept of work-related well-being has been provided by Warr, in a series of publications (see, for example, Warr, 1987; 1990; 2002). Specifically, he has sought to operationalize and measure work-related well-being. He views well-being as essentially psychological rather than physical and therefore concerned more with feelings than with physical symptoms, although he recognizes that there may be some association between them. Warr acknowledges that the traditional way to measure psychological reactions to, or feelings about, work is through a measure of job satisfaction. He argues that well-being needs to go beyond job satisfaction by additionally taking into account the level of mental arousal. This then provides three dimensions; satisfaction – dissatisfaction, which he labels pleasure – displeasure; enthusiasm – depression and comfort – anxiety. Enthusiasm combines high satisfaction and high arousal and is likely to be associated with strong motivation and involvement. Depression combines dissatisfaction with low arousal and is likely to be associated with low effort and possibly boredom. Comfort combines satisfaction with low arousal while anxiety combines dissatisfaction with high arousal and may be linked to stress.

Warr notes that well-being may be general or context-specific and that there is the possibility of spill-over from one domain to another. Indeed, he cites the research by Judge and Watanabe (1993) suggesting that work-related well-being and well-being in life as a whole mutually influence each other but that life well-being has a slightly stronger influence on work-related well-being than vice-versa. Despite this, there is good evidence of some spillover from work-related well-being to life well-being (for example Roxburgh, 1996).

Danna and Griffin (1999) identify three main types of antecedent of work-related well-being. These are the work-setting, broadly defined, the potential stressors in the specific job a person does and individual personality characteristics. Employment relations can have an impact on the first two of these sets of factors. Personality is less clearly related and there is good evidence that a variable such as positive or negative affect – the tendency to see the glass as half full or half empty – can have an influence on satisfaction and other attitudes (Watson and Clark, 1984). Danna and Griffin also address the consequences of well-being, suggesting that the pursuit of well-being has implications for individuals, for organizations and for society. With respect to society, they cite the potential benefits to society of policies at work that address smoking, drug habits and obesity, all of which are increasingly included in workplace well-being programs.

Economists have begun to take considerable interest in well-being both in the context of work and more broadly in life as a whole (see, for example, Layard, 2005). In the context of work, the measure they have often used as an indicator of well-being is job satisfaction (Blanchflower and Oswald, 1999) while the broader societal indicator has been some measure of happiness or life satisfaction. The factor that has sparked this interest is the failure to find an association between increased affluence and increased satisfaction or happiness. In other words, a core element of classic economic theory does not appear to work. Economists have discovered what many organizational psychologists have argued for a number of decades, namely that money has only a very tenuous link to job satisfaction and happiness.

Researchers have been using a variety of measures to compare and to track well-being at the societal level for a number of years. A typical question would be 'Taking all things together, would you say you were very happy, fairly happy or not very happy?' Such questions have been asked regularly in the Eurobarometer surveys across the member countries of the European Union (EU).

There have also been major international surveys across considerably more countries (see, for example, Veenhoven, 1999). These studies broadly confirm that there is a difference in well-being and happiness between the poor and the affluent countries in the world. But once countries enter the affluent group, an increase in affluence ceases to have any impact on happiness. Within affluent countries such as the US and UK, the rich generally report higher levels of happiness than the poor; but as the country as a whole becomes more affluent, the gap between the rich and the poor largely remains. By implication, an important basis for happiness is social comparison, a point reported in many studies by social psychologists and highlighted in particular in the work of Marmot and his colleagues (Marmot, 2004). How large the gap remains in the happiness of the more and less well-off within an affluent country is a subject of debate. Veenhoven (2005) has produced longitudinal data to suggest that the size of the gap in happiness has been slowly declining in many countries.

If income levels do not easily explain happiness in advanced industrial countries, what does? Research in America (Helliwell, 2003), based on large-scale national surveys of life satisfaction, and cited by Layard (2005, p. 63), highlights five factors, in order of importance. These are:

- family relationships;
- financial situation;
- work;
- community and
- friends and health.

Personal freedom and personal values are also important. Surveys in Europe reveal broadly similar results (Di Tella et al., 2001). Researchers such as Veenhoven also place some emphasis on cultural values in explaining national differences in life satisfaction. For example, there are consistent differences between the happier north European countries and the less happy southern European countries around the Mediterranean. These findings place work and well-being at work in some context. Helliwell's (2003) analysis of international work values in over 40 countries identifies key factors likely to reduce happiness, although the survey is likely to be unable to capture more than a small number of these. The three work-related factors that are identified are being unemployed, a sense of job insecurity and the level of national unemployment. We must be cautious in accepting these factors, all related to unemployment, as necessarily comprehensive. However what they do indicate is that having work is important for general well-being, a point also strongly emphasized by Warr (1987).

With this in mind, we return to the more specific focus on well-being at work. Warr, (2002) identifies ten antecedents of work-related well-being. They include several features of job design and in addition he cites 'availability of money', 'physical security', 'environmental clarity', 'supportive supervision' and 'valued social position' (p. 6). As we have indicated, work-related well-being can cover a wide range of issues. To explore the topic in more depth, we will select three for particular attention. First, we will consider the nature and antecedents of job satisfaction, since this comes closest to the general measure of work-related well-being. Secondly, we will explore job insecurity since, as we have noted above, this appears to be a key element affecting wider well-being. Thirdly, we will explore the nature and antecedents of work-related stress since this has become a major source of absence and shows some relation to health which, as we have seen, is a core component of general well-being. In each case, we will explore the evidence, using comparative research where possible, and consider the role that employment relations, broadly defined, plays in shaping the level of job satisfaction, job insecurity and work-related stress.

JOB SATISFACTION AND THE ROLE OF EMPLOYMENT RELATIONS

Job satisfaction is typically defined as 'an emotional state resulting from one's appraisal of the job' (Arvey, 2004, p.200). It is recognized as having a number of facets which are often divided into intrinsic and extrinsic categories. The intrinsic elements are concerned with the content of the job while the extrinsic are concerned with the context including the social context, the working conditions and the rewards. There are many well-validated scales that measure these various facets and also single more global measures of job satisfaction based on either a single item or a small number of items asking about general job satisfaction. Reviews of the evidence (see, for example, Wanous et al., 1997) suggest that a global measure, and even a single item, serves almost as well as a more sophisticated and more lengthy scale. However Wanous et al. also conclude that where feasible, it is preferable to use a scale rather than a single item.

The theory of job satisfaction is potentially important in this context. There are four perspectives that are worth highlighting. Person-environment fit theory suggests that if you can find a job that matches what you want, then you will be satisfied. Need fulfillment theory suggests that if you have a job that fulfils a set of pre-determined needs or requirements, then you will be satisfied. Expectations theories suggest that if a job meets your expectations, then you will be satisfied. Finally, effort-reward models suggest that when your outputs or gains are greater than your inputs, then satisfaction will occur and the greater the advantage of outputs over inputs, the greater the satisfaction. Concepts such as expectations, inputs and outputs can be socially determined and are potentially dynamic. Therefore social comparisons need to be taken into account, resulting in a form of dynamic discrepancy model whereby the gap between what you have and what you expect to have is constantly changing, usually in the light of rising expectations. This can help to account for the failure to show an association between rising affluence and higher job satisfaction.

Job satisfaction is a component of life satisfaction. How important a component is likely to depend on individual orientations and priorities and in particular whether work is a central life interest. Since we know that there are variations in this, we are not able to state with any certainty how much influence it is likely to have and, as noted above, the influence process is likely to be two-way. Job satisfaction also has to take into account individual differences in personality. For this and other reasons, economists who have become interested in job satisfaction as one indicator of well-being argue that it is essential to focus as far as possible on longitudinal data sets that can monitor changes over time after allowing for these influences.

The focus of research on job satisfaction has been changing. In the past, much of the interest lay in the association between satisfaction and outcomes of interest to organizations. These included job performance, absence and labor turnover. There have been interesting debates about cause and effect, particularly in relation to the link between job satisfaction and performance at firm level. In one of the most convincing longitudinal studies, which has relevance to the current context, it was found that the evidence supported the view that performance shapes satisfaction at least as strongly as the alternative and more traditional assumption that satisfaction influences performance (Schneider et al., 2003). By implication, and leaving aside any role for employment relations, working in a high performance organization is an important source of satisfaction. The focus on well-being shifts the debate from a concern for job satisfaction as a means to an end to job satisfaction as an end in itself. This in turn leads to an interest in its antecedents.

A number of international studies provide comparative information on job satisfaction and on trends in job satisfaction. Within Europe, the Eurobarometer provides a regular source of information for EU countries. However, probably the largest international data set is the International Social Survey Programme (ISSP) which collects data from 21 countries and has been conducted approximately every five years since 1985. The content varies from survey to survey, but in both 1989 and 1997 there was a single seven-point question asking for overall job satisfaction. The 1997 survey provides information from over 15,000 workers across 21 countries. This material has been analyzed by Sousa-Poza and Sousa-Poza (2000). There are a number of key findings that they highlight. Firstly, in all countries, the great majority of workers report that with varying degrees of enthusiasm, they are satisfied with their jobs. Those reporting dissatisfaction range from 4 per cent in Switzerland to 16 per cent in Russia. Secondly, while the East European countries reported some of the lowest levels of job satisfaction, the link between national wealth and satisfaction was weak. Thus Denmark reported the highest level of satisfaction, the US ranked seventh, Great Britain ranked fifteenth and Japan ranked nineteenth. Thirdly, in making comparisons between 1989 and 1997, they report a clear decline in job satis-faction in West Germany and in Norway and a slight decline in the US, while only Holland shows a clear increase in job satisfaction over this period. In most other countries, there was little or no change. Finally, Sousa-Poza and Sousa-Poza explored the factors associated with job satisfaction which might help to explain some of the variations. They found that the largest proportion of the variation was explained by having an interesting job followed by good relations with management. These were followed by a high income and working independently. Fifth was having an exhausting job, which was particularly likely to reduce job satisfaction. Job security has a very modest positive association with job satisfaction. There were some interesting national variations. For example, in the US and Great Britain, a high income had no significant association with job satisfaction while in Russia it was as important as interesting work.

Some of the key trends in job satisfac-tion have been analyzed by Green (2006). He reports that according to the European Community Household Survey, no country reported higher satisfaction in the year 2000 than in the early 1990s. Looking at survey data from within certain countries rather than the comparative data, he notes that the

long-term American data shows a decline in job satisfaction from the mid-1970s to the early 1990s followed by a reversal in the trend in the decade up to 2002. In contrast, the UK data show a decline in job satisfaction throughout the 1990s. A similar pattern has been found in Germany. Most other European countries show a slight decline in job satisfaction during the 1990s but the results vary a little across the different surveys. Given the rise in affluence in most advanced industrial countries in the decades up to 2000, how are we to explain the apparent decline in job satisfaction?

Green (2006), in his excellent analysis of UK trends, concludes that half the decline in job satisfaction during the 1990s can be accounted for by the decline in task discretion, a further third is accounted for by increased intensification and associated effort and a small amount is accounted for by a decreased fit between job demands and skills. No other personal or structural variables had any impact including union membership, bar-gaining arrangements or size of establishment. On this basis, we cannot seek an explanation by associating the decline in job satisfaction with a decline in trade union influence in the workplace. Germany shares with Britain a decline in job satisfaction and Green has reported an attempt to determine whether the causes are the same (Green and Tsiksianis, 2005). In practice, the different data sets make any direct comparison impossible. The key results are that the British data confirm the role of reduced autonomy and increased effort while the German data do not provide any significant explanation. However this may be partly because the German longitudinal data do not include measures of discretion and effort.

The evidence reported by Green indicates no association between any standard employ-ment relations indicators and job satisfaction. A wider body of research has consistently failed to find any evidence of an association between a trade union presence and collective bargaining and job satisfaction. Some of this research goes further in suggesting that union membership is associated with greater job dissatisfaction. There is a logic to this if we assume that dissatisfied workers are more likely to look to union membership to provide them with a voice (Freeman and Medoff, 1984). However it would only apply in the short term, since unions should either address the source of dissatisfaction or, by implication, fail to provide an effective voice. Analysis of the 1998 Workplace Employee Relations Survey by Guest and Conway (2004a) and by Bryson et al. (2004) confirm that using conventional bivariate analysis and regressions with a range of controls, union members report higher dissatisfaction whether we consider job satisfaction as a whole or separate pay satisfaction from other factors. Bryson et al. also consider the possibility that unions provide a voice for dissatisfied workers by comparing union activists and non-active members and find no evidence of greater dissatisfaction among activists. By implication, dissatisfaction is not leading to voice or different degrees of union membership and involvement. Bryson et al. extend their analysis, using a series of highly complex statistics, to argue that the association between union membership and job dissatisfaction is not a causal link but, rather, that both are caused by some other unexplained variable. In other words, the factors that cause people to belong to trade unions also cause them to be more dissatisfied. Despite this, the negative association remains and there is no evidence that unions contribute to well-being, as defined by satisfaction.

Leaving aside the specific role of trade unions, another step in the analysis is to explore other aspects of employment relations that might be associated with worker satisfaction and well-being. One of the best sources for this in Great Britain is the Workplace Employee Relations Survey. The 1998 survey (Cully et al., 1999) collected information about employment relations practices from a management representative and collected information on employee attitudes from about 28,000 workers. This included data on job satisfaction. An analysis by Guest et al. (2000) found that the four items on job satisfaction and the three on commitment

to the organization were very highly inter-correlated and emerged from factor analysis as a single factor. They therefore combined them into a single measure. They then explored the presumed antecedents of this broad satisfaction measure in both the public and private sectors using the data collected from managers. Responses on the four job satisfaction items were broadly similar in the public and private sectors with the exception of the item on sense of achievement which was slightly higher in the public sector. However the antecedents in the two sectors are rather different. In the public sector, higher satisfaction/commitment was associated with an increase in employee involvement over the past three years but it was negatively associated with a more sophisticated HR strategy. In the private sector, it was positively associated with the presence of more HR practices, with a more sophisticated HR strategy, with a stronger consultative climate and with the greater influence of the consultative process over decisions. However in both the private and public sectors, job satisfaction was lower where trade union density was higher. To add a level of complexity, trade union density was positively associated with the presence of more HR practices in both the public and private sectors, independently of the size of establishment. What these findings indicate is that employee involvement, perhaps through consultation and not necessarily with trade union representatives, is associated with higher satisfaction.

Cully et al. (1999) undertook a some-what similar analysis but using only the responses of the non-managerial employees. These revealed that satisfaction was strongly associated with higher levels of discretion and autonomy at work and where managers are perceived to be good at involving employees, where they show an understanding of family responsibilities and where they treat workers fairly. This again reinforces the importance of job autonomy, an understanding and supportive management, opportunities for development and fair treatment. These all lie at the heart of what is often advocated as good contemporary employee relations and are supported by the wider and well-established literature on the antecedents of job satisfaction (Spector, 1997; Wright and Boswell, 2002).

In summary, job satisfaction is a core indicator of work-related well-being. Despite rising affluence, which has been one of the traditional goals of the trade union movement, job satisfaction has been static or even declining in recent years in many advanced industrial countries. One major reason for this appears to be that pay and extrinsic rewards are not closely associated with this core dimension of work-related well-being in advanced industrial societies. This assertion requires some qualification; high earners tend to be more satisfied than low earners. But as the earnings of both groups improve, neither becomes more satisfied. Instead, job satisfaction appears to be more closely associated with the job content and in particular the demands of the job, the scope to develop and use knowledge and skills and the degree of involvement and autonomy. There are doubts about whether these have been improving in recent years. There is no evidence that trade unions are associated with job satisfaction, perhaps as an inevitable consequence of their role in raising awareness of sources of dissatisfaction and in raising expectations. On the other hand, a work climate that encourages participation and involvement and a work setting where high commitment HR practices are applied is associated with higher job satisfaction. These findings are very much in line both with Warr's review of the antecedents of work-related well-being and with what is often advocated as best practice contemporary employment relations.

JOB INSECURITY

Helliwell's (2003) analysis of factors associated with lower happiness highlighted the importance of unemployment and the fear of job loss. In other words, job insecurity appears to be a key factor associated with well-being at work and more widely in life. Despite the emphasis placed by Helliwell on the level of national unemployment, most research on well-being focuses on subjective insecurity. Job insecurity can then be defined as 'the subjectively perceived likelihood of involuntary job loss' (Sverke et al., 2005). Standing (1999) has reminded us that there are a wide variety of sources of employment-related insecurity including income insecurity and working time insecurity. Job loss incorporates many of these other aspects of insecurity and its impact on well-being appears to be the result of a sense of helplessness and loss of control. It can also be exacerbated by uncertainty and there are a number of studies of what is often termed the 'survivor syndrome' that have shown that those who remain in an organization after redundancies can also report a loss of well-being. For this reason, De Witte (2005) argues that we need to consider both quantitative and qualitative job loss in any analysis of job insecurity. The topic has been widely studied and there have been a number of books bringing together much of the evidence (see Burchell et al., 2002; De Witte, 2005; Hartley et al., 1991; and Heery and Salmon, 2000).

The impact of job loss or the fear of job loss on various indicators of well-being is widely supported in the literature, as Sverke et al. (2002) confirm through a meta-analysis of existing research. Much of the research undertaken by Warr and his colleagues (Warr, 1987) confirms that the experience of unemployment is associated with significantly reduced well-being, measured on standard scales of mental health. There is also some indication that as uncertainty about possible job loss extends over time; well-being continues to decline (Van den Berg and Masi, 2005). This is confirmed by Roskies and Louis-Guerin (1990) who support a broader definition of insecurity and report that the long term prospect of job loss, demotion and poorer working conditions are all associated with reduced well-being.

Objective indicators of job insecurity such as the level of national unemployment or the proportion of workers on various types of temporary contract are relatively easy to produce on a comparative and longitudinal basis. Subjective indicators require comparative attitude survey data, and this is harder to come by. One source of evidence cited by Burchell (2002) is the 1996 European Survey of Working Conditions which asked people to respond yes or no to the statement 'You have a secure job'. Across the 15 members of the European Union, an average of 70 per cent said 'Yes'. This ranged from 85 per cent in Luxembourg, 83 per cent in Denmark and 73 per cent in the UK to 59 per cent in Germany, 61 per cent in France, 63 per cent in Portugal and, somewhat surprisingly, 64 per cent in Sweden. Green (2006) cites evidence from the International Social Survey Programme. In 1989 and 1997 it asked whether respondents agreed that their job was secure. Insecurity can be measured by the proportion who disagreed that their job was secure. In 1997 this ranged from 28 per cent in the UK to 12 per cent in Norway. Job insecurity had increased during the period between 1989 and 1997 in six of the eight countries covered, including the UK, the US, West Germany and The Netherlands. It had decreased in Israel and Norway. The comparative evidence from Green and the more recent UK evidence from skills surveys and elsewhere suggests that subjective perceptions of insecurity quite closely track the levels of unemployment in most countries. Given the strong evidence that insecurity is associated with a lower score on indices of job satisfaction, mental health and well-being, for those experiencing chronic job insecurity and uncertainty, this must be a matter of concern.

While there has been extensive research on redundancies and the role of trade unions in the redundancy process, there has been much less research linking unions and the wider issue of job insecurity. This point is noted by De Witte (2005) who observes that 'Since unions have a crucial position in defending the interests of workers, it is remarkable that so little research has been devoted to analyse whether unions can reduce job insecurity or mitigate its negative consequences for individuals (and organizations)'. (op cit p. 3). His edited book is devoted to an analysis of this issue. More broadly, Wickert (2002)

suggests that the concept of social support provides a useful analytic framework. There are then a series of questions about the type of support and the source of support. A number of studies of job insecurity also use Hirschman's (1970) exit, voice and loyalty model as a framework within which to explore these issues.

Research evidence from Finland (Natti et al., 2005) and The Netherlands (Steijn, 2005) confirms the importance of information and notes the increase in information-seeking that occurs as job insecurity and the possible threat of job loss increases. In the Dutch study, workers tended to turn to the union in particular for information and advice. A study by Isaksson et al. (2005) of downsizing in a large retail store, in which staff with different outcomes (stay, retire, leave and unemployed, leave and find another job) were compared. The results confirm that the social support and advice of the union was valued. However those who obtained employment were no more positive about the union role than those who remained unemployed; indeed satisfaction with the union among both groups was rather low. Although the union adopted a collaborative role in managing the process, it did not appear to have been thanked for this or to have enhanced the levels of commitment among its members as a result. A Swedish study of attitudes towards the union in the context of downsizing (Hellgren et al., 2005) found that almost irrespective of the union role, the experience was likely to damage attitudes towards the union as well as the organization among those who stay as well as among those who lose their jobs.

Evidence from another Dutch study (Goslinga, 2005) found that faced with job insecurity, workers preferred individual to collective help from the union. In other words they wanted advice and support that helped them to cope with and ameliorate or address their personal situation; but they accepted the circumstances and did not want to support collective action to change it. The implication of the analysis is that the first reaction of a trade union is to try to change the situation. In practice this may just prolong the uncertainty which constitutes one of the more negative aspects of job insecurity. However there is strong evidence that union involvement in the change process has positive consequences. Firstly, as the study by Hellgren et al. (2005) suggests, potentially negative attitudes towards the union were considerably ameliorated if there was scope for extensive employee involvement and participation in the process, so that workers felt they were kept fully informed about what was happening and why and were given a chance to express views and influence the process. In other words, voice has a positive impact on attitudes towards the union, even if it cannot prevent job loss. Secondly, the evidence from research on participation reported by Heller et al. (1998) confirms the positive impact of participation in the process. Thirdly, a detailed study by Parker et al. (1997) found that those who reported an opportunity for involvement and who felt well-informed reported higher levels of well-being following workforce reductions.

The body of evidence supports the case that participation and involvement in decisions affecting workforce reductions, as a specific and identifiable example of job insecurity, has a positive impact on the well-being of both those who leave the organization and those who stay. The research evidence quite consistently shows that although the process of participation may be collective, and the union needs to be heavily involved, what workers want is support at an individual level rather than any idea of collective action. This confirms the social support model. That support will be informational but it may also include more emotional support to help to cope with the experience. This extends to the survivors. There is also a suggestion that the wider societal context will be able to buffer the effects of potential job loss. Therefore these effects should be less in a country like Sweden with its strong social security system. A comparative study of Sweden and Canada (van den Berg and Masi, 2005) failed to support this. However what they did find was that a co-operative industrial relations climate, with a strong union involvement was

more likely, in Hirschman's (1970) terms, to lead to loyalty. Specifically, in a context where there was uncertainty and the strong possibility of job loss, union members tended to stay with the organization while non-union members chose exit. Although this study did not directly address well-being, it suggests that in the context of job insecurity, a cooperative climate may provide some benefits for workers, union and employer.

WORK-RELATED STRESS AND WELL-BEING

There is a longstanding tradition of union involvement in the promotion of health and safety at work in most countries. In the UK, the Health and Safety at Work Act, 1974, enshrined this in legislation and managers have been required to consult with trade union representatives, where they are present, about health and safety. Since an extension to the act in 1996, managers have been required also to consult with non-union representatives or directly with the workforce. The 1998 UK Workplace Employee Relations Survey (Cully et al., 1999) reported that only 2 per cent of managers admitted that they failed to consult or inform workers in any way about these issues. They were more likely to negotiate on health and safety with non-union representatives and more likely to do nothing by way of involving representatives where there was a union presence. The same survey revealed that 64 per cent of representatives had dealt with a health and safety issue in the past year, more than any other topic, but it was only listed as the third most important issue they dealt with after fairness of treatment of employees by management and aspects of employment security.

In the past, the main focus of attention in the arena of workplace health and safety was the prevention of accidents and illness in the context of difficult and often unsatisfactory physical working conditions. However the nature of work-related illness has changed along with the changing nature of work and in the past decade, stress-related illnesses have begun to dominate. These often 'invisible' illnesses present distinctive challenges for employment relations and indeed for researchers who have for many years studied the evidence for a link between stress, particularly work-related stress and illness (for a brief review, see Cooper et al., 2001).

The importance of the growing problem of work-related stress, and its link to well-being and absence, as well as the soaring health-care costs associated with stress-related problems, has resulted in work-related stress becoming a priority issue for the UK Health and Safety Executive which has produced a set of management standards in an effort to limit the scale of the problem (Cousins et al., 2004). These standards are evidence-based and have at their centre the demand – control model of stress developed by Karasek (Karasek, 1979; Karasek and Theorell, 1990). This proposes that stress is likely to be at its highest among those who face high demands over which they have little control.

Both work demands and control over work are traditional issues at the heart of employment relations. Work demands are closely allied to the concern about 'a fair day's work for a fair day's pay' that has formed the core of the traditional effort-reward bargain, while control is central to the traditions of craft and professional jobs. Green (2006) has brought these two issues together in his analysis of contemporary work, focusing on increases in effort and work intensification and reductions in autonomy at work. Intensification can be operationalized in two ways, namely though increases in working hours and through working harder during each hour at work.

The evidence on working hours does not at first sight support the case for intensification. Throughout the advanced industrial world, average working hours have been coming down. The figures cited by Green (op cit p. 46) show that comparing 1983 and 2004, hours have reduced everywhere. Korea, the highest with an annual average of 2390 hours in 2004 has nevertheless come down from 2734 in 1983. The other two countries with the longest hours, Greece and Australia, show reductions from 1990 to 1938 and 1853 to 1814 respectively. In this context, the working hours in the UK, down from 1713 to 1673 and the USA, down from 1819 to 1792, look relatively modest. However they are still some distance from West Germany on 1429 and Norway on 1337 average annual hours in 2004. We need to be cautious about these figures since they can hide considerable variations and leave open the possibility that a sizeable minority are still working extremely long hours. They can also be distorted by the proportion of part-time workers.

Shorter hours may be compensated by more intense working. The evidence amassed by Green is convincing in demonstrating that subjective reports of effort levels have increased over a number of years in the UK. The comparative EU data using standard questions about working at high speed and working to tight deadlines also show a rise between 1991 and 2000 across all countries. Interestingly, in a number of countries, including the UK, there is some indication that this increase has slowed or even reversed more recently, though it is too early to tell whether this is a temporary phenomenon or an indication of some sort of peak of input. In 2000, the countries reporting the highest levels of intensity of work were Sweden, Finland and the Netherlands while workers in Spain and Portugal reported the lowest. In the UK, despite a large jump between 1990 and 1996, by 2000 the levels of intensity of effort were close to the EU average and the UK ranked fifth equal with Austria (Green, op cit p. 60).

There is very limited evidence linking intensity of work to employment relations. Green reports that the UK 2001 Skills Survey found no link between work intensity and union representation. On the other hand, Green and McIntosh (2001) found that in the early 1990s work intensification was greatest in those EU countries which saw the greatest decline in union membership. In contrast Gallie (2005) reports that union membership was associated with higher reported levels of work pressure across a number of European countries and that the association had grown stronger between 1996 and 2001. The picture is therefore rather confused and any associations are open to a variety of interpretations (Gallie, 2005, p. 363).

The second dimension in the demand – control model concerns the level of discretion or control over work. Some of the most compelling work on the importance of control, allied to level in the organizational hierarchy, has been produced by Marmot (2004) and his colleagues in what are known as the Whitehall I and II studies. These are longitudinal studies of large samples of UK civil servants and they show a clear association between position in the organizational hierarchy and both objective and subjective indicators of level of control and, in turn, a link between these and all forms of illness as well as longevity. In other words, those employed in low status positions, with less control over their work, are more likely to be ill in both the short and the long term.

The civil service may be an extreme example of hierarchy and there has been some discussion – though rather less evidence – about reductions in hierarchy and increased autonomy at lower levels, allied to the importance of providing a flexible, customized service. However, as Green (2006) again illustrates, the European evidence, based on Europe-wide data from 1996 and 2000, shows that the level of discretion at work appears to be declining across Europe. Indeed, during this short period it declined in 11 of the 15 countries, with Portugal, Belgium and the UK leading the way. Only Germany, Austria, the Netherlands and Sweden bucked the trend. Green (2006, p. 103) also draws attention to a direct comparison of rather better quality data between Finland and the UK. It shows that over a number of years, discretion in the UK has consistently declined while in Finland it has consistently increased. The decline in discretion is therefore not an inevitable trend. In the UK, the decline was sharpest among professional workers. Although Marmot cites data from the US and Sweden that indicates that the interaction of job demand and control

affects health and well-being more generally, he found in the Whitehall studies that control mattered rather more than demand. This fits with the notion that people may work long and hard and not experience too much stress if they are in control and choose to work this way. The problem becomes greater when the demand lies outside their control.

Although it seems plausible that trade unions should help to limit the challenge to workers' discretion, the evidence that they have done so is hard to find. While they have traditionally been more likely to represent those lower grade workers who have less control, some of the more powerful contemporary unions, allied to crafts or professions have among their objectives the maintenance of professional control and autonomy and protection of status differentials. Unions outside Scandinavia have also tended to be suspicious of job redesign programs that could increase local control. One response of the unions is likely to be to ensure that if job demands increase, workloads remain reasonable and employees are trained to meet these demands. Despite union reservations, there is some evidence that increased control over the job through job redesign can reduce stress and illness at work. There is also evidence that worker participation can increase the sense of control at work (Cooper et al., 2001). The 1998 UK Workplace Employee Relations Survey (Cully et al., 1999) found an association between influence in the job and experience of participation in decision-making across all levels of worker.

The employment relations context can also be important in other ways. The Management Standards promulgated by the UK Health and Safety Executive emphasize a number of areas that require attention. In addition to demand and control, these include support, relationships at work, role clarity, change management and an organizational culture reflecting fairness and openness. The standard set for the first three, demands, control and support, have been set at 85 per cent. In other words, when staff are surveyed, at least 85 per cent should provide a positive response. This level was determined on the basis of a large-scale UK study of stress at work (Smith, 2001) which concluded that just over 20 per cent of the working population reported very or extremely high levels of stress at work. The aim was to get below this level.

A survey in 2004 of a random sample of 1000 UK workers explored both the level of these standards and some of the antecedents (Guest and Conway, 2004). Very similar to the larger sample of Smith, they found that 21 per cent reported that their job was very or extremely stressful. With respect to the management standards, they found that, taking the average response of two items covering each of the standards, 42 per cent were uncomfortable with the demands of their job and 34 per cent reported low levels of control. 26 per cent said they did not receive much support from their supervisor though only 11 per cent said they did not receive the help and support they needed from work colleagues. In other words, the results fall well short of the HSE standard of 85 per cent positive responses. Those scoring higher on the management standards and therefore reporting a higher quality of workplace also reported much lower levels of stress. The presence of a high quality workplace was, in turn, associated with more high commitment HRM practices in place and more flexible employment practices; but it was also less likely to be reported by union members. Those working longer hours reported a poorer quality of workplace and higher levels of stress.

In summary, stress at work and stress-related illnesses are manifestations of low levels of work-related well-being. They are provoked in particular by high demands, low discretion and low social support. There is little evidence that traditional employment relations has done much to address this aspect of worker well-being. For example, unions have become less effective than in the past in limiting workload or maintaining control. In the UK, the most powerful trade unions today are probably those in the public sector representing professional groups; yet it is among these workers that the loss of perceived discretion and control has recently been

greatest. Set against this, the 'new' industrial relations may be more effective in addressing some of these concerns. The study by Guest and Conway suggests that the presence of high commitment HRM is associated with a higher quality workplace, where there is less intensification, more discretion and less stress. There is also evidence from this and other research, that higher levels of workers' participation in decision-making can result in higher levels of perceived influence and control and consequently in lower levels of work-related stress.

DISCUSSION AND CONCLUSIONS: WORKER WELL-BEING IN THE CONTEXT OF THE 'OLD' AND 'NEW' EMPLOYMENT RELATIONS

This chapter has focused on workers as stakeholders in employment relations and on outcomes associated with workers' well-being. It has explained and charted the growing interest in work-related well-being and has explored the levels of well-being and some of the determinants of well-being by focusing on job satisfaction, job insecurity and work-related stress. Despite this growing interest, there is little evidence of improvements in well-being.

In an earlier section, the potentially competing goals of employers and workers under the 'new' employment relations were highlighted. This review has revealed areas of persisting conflict which can restrict improvements in workers' well-being. In particular, the search for efficiency through labor force reductions and the intensification of work alongside reductions in autonomy are associated with lower satisfaction and higher work-related stress.

Set against these areas of conflicting interests, there is evidence of greater alignment where high commitment human resource practices are in place. Patterson et al. (1997) showed an association between the greater use of these practices and employee satisfaction in UK manufacturing firms. Guest (2002) using large UK data sets reported an association between a range of specific practices, notably those allied to job design, involvement and work-life balance and both work and life satisfaction. Wright and Boswell (2002) and Wright et al. (2005) review literature showing a link between greater use of human resource practices and more positive attitudes among workers and between these practices and attitudes and outcomes such as lower absence and labor turnover. One of the few negative findings is reported by Ramsay et al. (2000), who find some indication that certain HR practices may be associated with higher stress. However Appelbaum et al. (2000) explicitly considered this in their study of US manufacturing workers and found no evidence to support it.

These results based on studies of human resource management highlight the potential for mutual gains. They are very much in line with the findings of Green and others who show the negative effects of reducing autonomy. Despite the potential for mutual gains, the evidence from the UK Workplace Employee Relations Survey and other sources (Cully et al., 1999) shows that relatively few organizations are seeking to implement these practices on a large scale; and Guest and Peccei (2001) find that even in contexts where there has been some move towards partnership working, the balance of advantage tends to lie very much with management. To date, therefore, there is little evidence that a mutual gains model is gaining ground as a basis for promoting workers' well-being.

In the past, trade unions have made a major contribution to the improvement of working conditions and to the health of workers. However, there is little direct evidence that the traditional institutions of industrial relations have made a marked contribution to contemporary workers' well-being, largely because very little research has explored this relationship. The absence of evidence is largely the result of research directly exploring this relationship. Furthermore the rather gloomy picture that emerges about unions and job satisfaction and commitment to the union in the context of labor force

reductions may hide the indirect but much more positive role played by the unions at a higher level in promoting well-being at work. For example, as social partners in Europe, they have promoted pan-European legislation to protect and advance aspects of well-being. Through processes of co-determination, consultation and communication, they can help to safeguard aspects of well-being. There is scope to go further in promoting the aim of 'more and better' jobs; but as Leonard (2005) observes, the processes of concerted action between the social partners at national level in the EU are currently in a state of considerable flux.

The studies cited in this chapter illustrate how the unions help to promote dialogue and involvement in workforce reductions; and the processes of information sharing and involvement helped to mitigate some of the negative effects. There is also some evidence that a union presence is associated with greater adoption of high involvement human resource practices which, in turn, have been associated with higher levels of well-being. We should therefore be careful not to under-estimate the influence of trade unions on workers' well-being.

In summary, processes of direct participation and involvement, a sense of personal control and autonomy, and clear supervisory and organizational support, reflected in the organizational climate, are all associated with higher job satisfaction, higher levels of job security and lower levels of stress. High commitment human resource management appears to support these practices, which appear to have a similar association with well-being in union and non-union settings. There is a risk that given a choice, most managers will prefer not to deal with trade unions and their representatives; and the drift away from union membership suggests that unions will face major challenges in gaining and retaining the commitment of the next generation of workers. Given the pressures outlined at the start of this chapter, contemporary employment relations is likely to be increasingly concerned with workers' well-being. The evidence presented here confirms that managers, faced with a wide range of competitive challenges, may be tempted to give a relatively low priority to workers' well-being unless it can be clearly demonstrated that it is in their best interest to promote it. This creates both an opportunity and a threat for trade unions; an opportunity if they can successfully promote well-being and at the same time demonstrate their value to employees; and a threat if they are unable to do so. Addressing worker well-being will be one of the challenges facing the social partners as they seek to meet the interests of both the organization and the workforce in the future.

REFERENCES

Appelbaum, E., Bailey, T., Berg, P. and Kalleberg, A. (2000) *Manufacturing advantage*. Ithaca, NY: Cornell University Press.

Arthur, M. and Rousseau, D. (eds) (1996) *The boundaryless career: a new employment principle for a new employment era*. Oxford: Oxford University Press.

Blanchflower, D. and Oswald, A. (1999) *Well-being, insecurity and the decline of American job satisfaction*. Mimeo. www.andrewoswald.com.

Bryson, A., Cappellari, L. and Lucifora, C. (2004) Does union membership really reduce job satisfaction? *British Journal of Industrial Relations*, 42: 439–59.

Burchell, B. (2002) The prevalence and redistribution of job insecurity and work intensification. In B. Burchell, D. Lapido, and F. Wilkinson (eds) *Job insecurity and work intensification*. London: Routledge. pp. 61–76.

Burchell, B., Lapido, D. and Wilkinson, F. (2002) *Job insecurity and work intensification*. London: Routledge.

Conway, N. and Briner, R. (2005) *Understanding psychological contracts at work*. Oxford: Oxford University Press.

Cooper, C., Dewe, P. and O'Driscoll, M. (2001) *Organizational stress*. Thousand Oaks, CA.: Sage.

Cousins, R., Mackay, C., Clarke, S., Kelly, C., Kelly, P. and McHaig, R. (2004) 'Management Standards' and work-related stress in the UK: Practical development. *Work and Stress*, 18: 113–36.

Cully, M., Woodland, S., O'Reilly, A. and Dix, G. (1999) *Britain at work*. Routledge: London.

Danna, K. and Griffin, R. (1999) Health and well-being in the workplace: a review and synthesis of the literature. *Journal of Management*, 25: 357–84.

De Cuyper, N., Isaksson, K. and De Witte, H. (eds) (2005) *Employment contracts and well-being among European workers*. Aldershot, Hants: Ashgate.

Di Tella, R., MacCullough, R. and Oswald, A. (2001) Preferences over inflation and unemployment: Evidence from surveys of happiness. *American Economic Review*, 91: 335–41.

De Witte, H. (ed.) (2005). *Job insecurity, union involvement and union activism*. Aldershot: Ashgate.

Freeman, R. and Medoff, J. (1984) *What do unions do?* New York: Basic Books.

Gallie, D. (2005) Work pressure in Europe 1996–2001: Trends and determinants. *British Journal of Industrial Relations*, 43: 351–75.

Goslinga, S. (2005) Job insecurity, union participation and the need for (new) union services. In H. De Witte (ed.) *Job insecurity, union involvement and union activism*. Aldershot: Ashgate. pp. 81–96.

Green, F. (2006) *Demanding work*. Princeton: Princeton University Press.

Green, F. and McIntosh, S. (2001) The intensification of work in Europe. *Labour Economics*, 8: 291–308.

Green, F. and Tsitsianis, N. (2005) An investigation of national trends in job satisfaction in Britain and Germany. *British Journal of Industrial Relations*, 43: 401–29.

Guest, D. (2002) Human resource management, corporate performance and employee well-being: Building the worker into HRM. *Journal of Industrial Relations*, 44: 335–58.

Guest, D. and Conway, N. (2004a) Exploring the paradox of unionised worker dissatisfaction. *Industrial Relations Journal*, 35: 102–21.

Guest, D. and Conway, (2004b) *Employee well-being and the psychological contract*. London: CIPD.

Guest, D., Michie, J., Sheehan, M. and Conway, N. (2000) *Employment relations, HRM and business performance*. London: CIPD.

Guest, D. and Peccei, R. (2001) Partnership at work: mutuality and the balance of advantage. *British Journal of Industrial Relations*, 39: 207–36.

Hartley, J., Jacobson, D., Klandermans, B. and Van Vuuren, T. (1991) *Job insecurity: coping with jobs at risk*. London: Sage.

Health and Safety Executive (1999) *Managing stress at work*. DDE 10. Sudbury: HSE Books.

Health and Safety Executive (HSE) (2003) *Real solutions, real people: a managers' guide to tackling work-related stress*. Sudbury: HSE Books.

Heery, E. and Salmon, J. (eds) (2000) *The insecure workforce*. London: Routledge.

Heller, F., Pusic, E., Strauss, G. and Wilpert B. (1998) *Organizational participation: myth and Reality.* Oxford: Oxford University Press.

Hellgren, J., Sverke, M., and Stjernstrom, C. (2005) The union side of downsizing: Investigating members' union attitudes. In H. De Witte (ed.) *Job insecurity, union involvement and union activism.* Aldershot: Ashgate. pp. 117–34.

Helliwell, J. (2003) How's life? Combining individual and national variables to explain subjective well-being. *Economic Modelling,* 20: 331–60.

Hirschman, A. (1970) *Exit, Voice and Loyalty.* Cambridge, MA: Harvard University Press.

Isaksson, K., Hellgren, J. and Pettersson, P. (2005) Union involvement during downsizing and its relation to attitudes and distress among workers. In H. De Witte (ed.) *Job insecurity, union involvement and union activism.* Aldershot: Ashgate. pp. 97–116.

Jones, J., Huxtable, C., Hodgson, J. and Price, M. (2003) *Self-reported work-related illness in 2001/02: Results from a household survey.* Sudbury: HSE Books.

Judge, T. and Watanabe, S. (1993) Another look at the job satisfaction – life satisfaction relationship. *Journal of Applied Psychology,* 78: 939–48.

Karasek, R. (1979) Job demands, job decision latitude, and mental strain: implications for job design. *Administrative Science Quarterly,* 24: 285–308.

Karasek, R. and Theorell, T. (1990) *Healthy work.* New York: Basic Books.

Kersley, B., Alpin, C., Forth, J., Bryson, A., Bewley, H., Dix, G. and Oxenbridge, S. (2006) *Inside the workplace: findings from the 2004 workplace employment relations survey.* London: Routledge.

Layard, R. (2005) *Happiness.* London: Penguin.

Leonard, E. (2005) Governance and concerted regulation of employment in Europe. *European Journal of Industrial Relations,* 11: 307–26.

Marmot, M. (2004) *The status syndrome.* New York: Times Books.

Natti, J., Happonen, M., Kinnunen, U. and Mauno, S. (2005) Job insecurity, temporary work and trade union membership in Finland 1977–2003. In H. De Witte (ed.) *Job insecurity, union involvement and union activism.* Aldershot: Ashgate. pp. 11–48.

Parker, S., Chmiel, N. and Wall, T. (1997) Work characteristics and employee well-being within a context of strategic downsizing. *Journal of Occupational Health Psychology,* 4: 289–303.

Patterson, M., West, M., Lawthom, R. and Nickell, S. (1997) *Impact of people management practices on business performance.* London: IPD.

Ramsay, H., Scholarios, D. and Harley, B. (2000) Employees and high performance work systems: testing inside the black box. *British Journal of Industrial Relations,* 38: 501–31.

Roskies, E. and Louis-Guerin, C. (1990) Job insecurity in managers: antecedents and consequences. *Journal of Organizational Behavior,* 11: 345–59.

Rousseau, D. (2005) *I-deals: idiosyncratic deals employees bargain for themselves.* M.E. Sharpe.

Roxburgh, S. (1996) Gender differences in work and well-being: effects of exposure and vulnerability. *Journal of Health and Social Behavior,* 37: 265–77.

Schaufeli, W. and Buunk, B. (2003) Burnout: an overview of 25 years of research and theorizing. In M. Schabracq, J. Winnubst and C. Cooper (eds). *The handbook of work and health psychology.* New York: Wiley.

Schneider, B., Hanges, P., Smith, B. and Salvaggio, A. (2003) Which comes first: employee attitudes or organizational financial and market performance? *Journal of Applied Psychology,* 88: 836–51.

Sousa-Poza, A. and Sousa-Poza, A. (2000) Well-being at work: a cross-national analysis of the levels and determinants of job satisfaction. *Journal of Socio-Economics,* 29: 517–38.

Smith, A. (2001). Perceptions of stress at work. *Human Resource Management Journal,* 11 (4): 74–86.

Spector, P. (1997) *Job satisfaction: application, assessment, causes, and consequences.* London: Sage.

Standing, G. (1999) *Global labour flexibility: seeking distributive justice.* London: Macmillan.

Steijn, B. (2005) The insecure middle class and unionisation: an empirical investigation of class, job insecurity and union membership. In H. De Witte (ed.) *Job insecurity, union involvement and union activism.* Aldershot: Ashgate. pp. 49–62.

Steffy, B. and Jones, J. (1988) Workplace stress and indicators of coronary heart-disease risk. *Academy of Management Journal,* 31: 686–98.

Sverke, M., Hellgren, J. and Naswall, K. (2005) We get by with a little help from our unions: psychological contract violations and downsizing. In H. De Witte (ed.) *Job insecurity, union involvement and union activism.* Aldershot: Ashgate. pp. 135–54.

Van den Berg, A. and Masi, A. (2005) Responses to downsizing under different adjustment regimes: a two-country comparison. In H. De Witte (ed.) *Job insecurity, union involvement and union activism.* Aldershot: Ashgate. pp. 155–86.

Veenhoven, R. (1999) Quality-of-life in individualistic society: a comparison of 43 nations in the early 1990s. *Social Indicators Research,* 48: 157–86.

Veenhoven, R. (2005) Return of inequality in modern society? Test by dispersion of life-satisfaction across time and nations. *Journal of Happiness Studies,* 6: 351–55.

Wanous, J., Reichers, A. and Hudy, M. (1997) Overall satisfaction: How good are single item measures? *Journal of Applied Psychology*, 82: 247–52.

Warr, P. (1987) *Work, unemployment and mental health*. Oxford: Oxford University Press.

Warr, P. (1990) The measurement of well-being and other aspects of mental health. *Journal of Occupational Psychology*, 63: 193–210.

Warr, P. (2002) The study of well-being, behaviour and attitudes. In P Warr, (ed.) *Psychology at work*. (5th ed). London: Penguin. pp. 1–25.

Watson, D. and Clark, L. (1984) Negative affectivity: The disposition to experience negative emotional affective states. *Psychological Bulletin*, 96: 465–98.

Wickert, I. (2002) Job insecurity and work intensification: the effects on health and well-being. In B. Burchell, D. Lapido and F. Wilkinson (eds) *Job insecurity and work intensification*. London: Routledge. pp. 92–111.

World Health Organization (1998). *Definition of health*. http://www.who.ch/aboutwho/definition.htm

Wright, P and Boswell, W. (2002) Desegregating HRM: a review and synthesis of micro and macro human resource research. *Journal of Management*, 28: 247–76.

Wright, P., Gardner, T., Moynihan, L. and Allen, M. (2005) The relationship between HR practices and firm performance: examining causal order. *Personnel Psychology*, 58: 409–47.

29

Industrial Relations Climate

Ali Dastmalchian

The term industrial relations climate is generally used to describe the nature and quality of relationships between labor and management in the organization (for example Katz et al., 1983). More precisely, industrial relations climate reflects the perceptions of organizational members about the norms, conduct, practice and atmosphere of union-management relations in the workplace (Blyton et al., 1987).

In the last two decades, in response to increased levels of competition in the economic environment, organizations have been forced to restructure their work arrangements and introduce changes in labor-management relations in an attempt to improve organizational performance. In this context, there has been a renewed interest among academics and practitioners in finding ways in which management and unions can develop more co-operative relationships in the hope of leading to more mutually beneficial industrial relations arrangements (for example Deery and Iverson, 2005; Wagar, 1997a). For this to happen, and for the workplace changes and innovations to succeed, there is a need for the creation of a more co-operative industrial relations climate in the workplace

(for example Katz et al., 1983; 1985). A co-operative industrial relations climate not only relates to improved organizational performance (Cooke, 1992), it also has been shown to be associated with higher organizational commitment and union loyalty (Angle and Perry, 1986; Deery et al., 1999). Therefore, the role of industrial relations climate as a key variable that has an influence on performance and successful change, has gained a renewed centrality and importance.

In addition, in introducing and implementing workplace changes there is a need to appreciate and overcome the enduring relationships, attitudes and behaviors that have developed over time in workplaces and organizations. Industrial relations climate can provide a window to understanding and appreciating this and explain why apparently similar workplace innovations may have different outcomes in varied contexts. The work by Ichniowski et al. (1996) reviewing barriers to the successful adoption of high performance work practices identified union-management relationships as one of the key barriers. To reinforce the significance of industrial relations climate, it is appropriate to consider the co-operative industrial relations climates in workplaces of countries such as Japan and Germany to explain the greater successful adoption of high performance work practices and higher levels of labor productivity.

The use of the concept of industrial relations climate in explaining the performance, outcomes and processes of industrial relations in organizations and workplaces is therefore essential. The literature in industrial relations (for example Blyton et al., 1987; Deery et al., 1999; Wagar, 1997a) as well as in the organizational studies and social psychology areas (for example Dastmalchian et al., 1989; Iverson and Maguire, 2000; Redman and Snape, 2004; Tetrick and Fried, 1993) demonstrates this point.

In this chapter, I will review the development of the concept of industrial relations (IR) climate by providing a brief overview of the development of the climate concept in the broader organizational literature. I will then review the development of measuring IR climate and assess the empirical evidence regarding its relationship with other pertinent industrial relations concepts and variables, and examine its possible role in the future development of the field of industrial relations.

THE CONCEPT OF CLIMATE IN ORGANIZATIONS

The concept of organizational climate has its origins in the Gestalt psychology approach of Kurt Lewin in that it represents a characteristic of an organization as a whole which is greater, or different, from the sum of the specifics of individual perceptions (Lewin et al., 1939).

It has been employed by researchers to better understand the ways in which organizational structures affect the pattern of behaviors within organizations, or perhaps more generally to understand the context of the organization and representing the norms, attitudes, feelings and behaviors prevalent at the workplace (Litwin and Stringer, 1968; Tagiuri and Litwin, 1968; Pugh and Payne, 1977; Schneider and Bartlett, 1968; 1970; Denison, 1996). For many of these writers,

the concept seems to reflect the combined perceptions of organizational members of descriptive attributes of their organization. Some have viewed the concept of climate as an intervening variable in that it is affected by a set of external and structural variables, and at the same time has an influence on outcomes, such as firm performance and employee-related performance and behavior (for example Dastmalchian, 1986; Payne, 1971; Payne and Mansfield, 1973; Payne and Pugh, 1976).

There are a number of key conceptual and methodological issues and debates that have emerged regarding the concept of organizational climate, some of which have been resolved and others that are still the subject of debate. Each one of these issues has implications for IR climate that I will try and highlight in this section and or later in this chapter. The following is an outline of these key issues.

Level of analysis

This refers to the inappropriateness of focusing on an individual level of analysis for an 'organizational' concept (Schneider et al., 2000). Many researchers have addressed the individual vs. aggregate conceptualizations by referring to the individual climate and 'psychological' climate as distinct from 'organizational' climate (see Hellriegel and Slocum, 1974). Even though this issue seems to have been resolved, more recent research appears to call for more clarification (for example Parker et al., 2003). Clearly, whether a workplace or an organization can have an IR climate, or whether the perception of such climates is the property of the individuals and should be understood and studied as such, are considerations that would affect the way in which the concept and its implications are studied.

Climate and job satisfaction

The issue is whether climate merely measures the older concept of job satisfaction. The issue also seems to have been adequately addressed by researchers. Guion (1973), as well as a number of other researchers (for example Roberts et al., 1978; Rousseau, 1985; Schneider and Snyder, 1975) have shown the distinction between the concepts of work atmosphere and job satisfaction. For IR climate the same is true and, as will be seen later, most of the frameworks consider general satisfaction as an outcome of a particular climate.

Aggregation issues

The question is the reliability of aggregating individual measures to an organizational variable. This issue lies at the heart of the methodological and conceptual debate on climate and its utility and future direction as a concept (for example also see Dastmalchian et al., 1991; Glick, 1985; James et al., 1978; James, 1982; James et al., 1984; James et al., 1988). Aggregate concepts have a degree of ambiguity associated with them as the act of aggregation will introduce confusion regarding individual vs. organizational ownership of the information (Roberts et al., 1978). But it is suggested here that such ambiguity is more methodological than conceptual and that pursuing the debate over whether climate is an individual or an organizational construct is unlikely to be productive (Denison, 1996; Glick, 1988). On the methodological front, it has been suggested that one way of addressing the issue is to focus on within-organization variance which will provide an index tied to the organization rather than the individual (Roberts, 1978). In other words, an acceptable measure of organizational climate is obtainable where there is a relatively high agreement between individual respondents (Angle and Perry, 1986; Lincoln and Zeitz, 1980; Ansari et al., 1982; Kozlowski and Holts, 1987).

The work of Payne (1990) and Patterson et al. (1996) have also introduced the idea of the appropriate constituency for aggregation. Should, for instance, IR climate be based on sub-unit, department, similar locations, membership of different groups or unions interacting with one another, or the whole workplace? This is an issue that can be fairly

critical when one tries to understand, measure and analyze IR climate within a workplace or an organization.

On the whole, it does appear that as far as the aggregation issue is addressed well by the work of Roberts et al. (1978) and the detailed analysis of the level issues by Jones and James (1979) addressed the issue well. The procedure offered by James et al. (1984) for indexing the reliability of aggregated data and the methodological procedure suggestions by Dansereau and Alutto (1990) seem to have brought the aggregation issue into the light for resolution for quantitative researchers.

Volatility of climate

Another issue regarding the concept of climate is its volatility. According to Dastmalchian et al. (1991) if climate is viewed as subject to a great deal of turbulence, then its characterization and its measurement as an enduring construct is problematic. It appears that most studies have viewed climate as sufficiently broad to have a degree of endurance over time. Perhaps the comparison between climate and weather in meteorology is appropriate, in that one could attribute a description to the climate of a region despite the fact that in certain months or days the weather patterns might fluctuate away from the climate descriptions. How should one study IR climate in light of this issue? Should longer term, and longitudinal, designs be an appropriate approach to a better understanding of IR climate? Again, later in this chapter I will look at cross-sectional vs. longitudinal evidence on IR climate.

Climate and culture

Since the early discussions on organizational climate in the 1950s there have been numerous debates and discussions and many review articles on the subject (for example Argyris, 1958; Eckvall, 1987; James and Jones, 1974; Joyce and Slocum, 1979; Payne and Pugh, 1976; Rousseau, 1988; Schneider and Reichers, 1983; Pettigrew, 1990). Ironically, as the literature tried to resolve many of the key issues, organizational culture as an alternative way to look at the gestalt of organizations appeared on the scene, and has dominated the debates in this area (Pettigrew, 1979 and Trice and Beyer, 1993). Many articles have been devoted to exploring culture and climate similarities and differences (for example Ashforth, 1985; Ashkanasy et al., 2000; Denison, 1996; Rousseau, 1988; Schneider, 1990; Reichers and Schneider, 1990). At some level the distinction is fairly clear: climate is about feelings, thoughts and behavior, it is temporal, subjective and is more likely to be subject to manipulation by organizational members with ability to do so; culture on the other hand is an evolved context (Denison, 1996), is based on shared beliefs and values, and is sufficiently embedded in the situation so that it may not be readily subject to manipulation. On the other hand, there are many similarities and inconsistencies in the treatment of the two concepts. Both are consensual in nature, in that they both seek to portray characteristics applicable across the organization, they are meant to be stable over time and they are both perceived by individuals. In addition, the quantitative (climate research) and qualitative (culture research) methods have become increasingly blurred in that several climate researchers have studied the evolution of social contexts from a social constructionist point of view (for example Ashforth, 1985; Poole, 1985; Poole and McPhee, 1983), and culture researchers have used quantitative, comparative, and Lewinian approaches thought to be associated more with climate research (Chatman, 1991; O'Rilley et al., 1991).

However, organizational culture does affect climate. Organizational climate can be changed only to the degree that the desired climate is congruent with the underlying culture. According to Schein (2000: xxix) 'One cannot create…. a climate of teamwork and cooperation if the underlying assumptions in the culture are individual and competitive, because those assumptions will have created a reward and control system that encourages individual competitiveness'. Given this, is it possible to create and sustain a co-operative

IR climate in a workplace when the underlying values of the actors are grounded in a history of confrontation, mistrust and the absence of respect for the other party's view point? As we will discuss later, this has significant implications for further research in terms of understanding IR culture in an organization, the role of leadership and a different perspective for unions and management.

A consensus seems to have emerged among many writers on climate and culture. The two are different, but they are and should be treated as closer to one another than we once thought (Payne, 2000, p.176). Denison (1996) similarly concludes that the two concepts and their research traditions 'should be viewed as differences in interpretation rather than differences in the phenomenon' (p. 645).

Climate and organizational models

There has been a lack of agreement on the status of climate in organizational models, or on how climate variables should be operationalized. Several authors have utilized climate as an intervening concept between organizational inputs and constraints on the one hand, and individual or group behavior on the other. That is, the impact of organizational and contextual factors such as structure and technology on the individual is mediated by the individual's perception of the situation (Rousseau, 1988). Such a position has been reinforced explicitly and implicitly by the work of many other researchers (for example Dastmalchian, 1986; Joyce and Slocum, 1979; Litwin and Stringer, 1968; Payne and Mansfield, 1973; Payne and Pugh, 1976; Mansfield and Payne, 1977). In reviewing the IR climate research in this chapter, we will see that the intervening nature of IR climate has been adopted by many researchers who have studied the concept directly. The key implication of this perspective is that in many ways it reinforces the impact of IR climate on successful IR arrangements in workplaces in that any new and negotiated programs and structures will be affected by the IR climate before they can be expected to lead to desired outcomes.

Climate and performance

The measurement-oriented climate literature has debated (and continues to debate) the relationships between climate and key organizational variables such as performance. Reviews by Payne and Pugh (1976), Hellriegel and Slocum (1974), Schneider (1975), Siehl and Martin (1990) and Campbell et al. (1970) did not find convincing support for associations between climate and organizational performance and effectiveness. The evidence in the IR climate literature largely supports this lack of relationship as well, as will be discussed later (Deery and Iverson, 2005; Wagar, 1997).

Issue specific climates

Most studies using this concept have used a generalized approach without relating the notion of climate to a particular set of organizational activities or issues. As Schneider and Reichers (1983) have pointed out 'to speak of organizational climate *per se* without attaching it to a referent is meaningless' (p. 21). They called for the inclusion of the idea of the concept of organizational climate that has a focus or target in that the researchers should be looking for climate for 'something'. This 'something' might involve issues such as a climate for safety (Zohar, 1980; 2000; Zohar and Luria, 2005), climate for sexual harassment (Fitzgerald et al., 1997), climate for justice (Liao and Rupp, 2005), climate for well-being (Burke et al., 1992), climate for service (Schneider, 1980; Schneider et al., 1998; Schneider and Bowen, 1995), a whistle blowing climate (Micelli and Near, 1985) or – as is the case of this chapter – IR climate (Dastmalchian et al., 1989; 1991). The principle is that organizational climate as a concept has many facets, and that researching it needs to focus on which of these facets is being studied. As in the case of personality and attitude literature, say Schneider et al. (2000), unless the predictor variable is conceptually and operationally linked to the criterion variable, the probability of a relationship between them is low. The same logic applies to climate. That is, unless the concept and measure of climate is based on 'something' of interest, the relationship between it and the other key organizational variables can be expected to be modest at best. Using this logic I now move more directly to the notion of industrial relations climate.

INDUSTRIAL RELATIONS CLIMATE

Nicholson (1979) was one of the first authors who identified the use of the concept of IR climate and pointed out the possibilities for an industrial relations climate concept that could provide both a theoretical bridge between the structural characteristics of organizations and outcomes such as conflict; and also act as a diagnostic concept in industrial relations, capable of recommending changes in the industrial relations system. In this study and in a small number of other studies in the 1970s and the 1980s the climate concept was used to underline the variety of attitudinal elements relevant to the study of IR climate, and relate climate to a number of individual and organizational outcomes (for instance Angle and Perry, 1986; Dastmalchian et al., 1982; Katz et al., 1983; Kelly and Nicholson, 1980; Nicholson, 1979; Warr et al., 1978).

Warr et al. (1978) conducted a broad study of employee relations in which they highlighted the importance of IR climate. One of the members of the research team, Nigel Nicholson, took the idea of IR climate a step further in a steel plant study in the UK (Nicholson, 1979). Using a case approach and collecting data from union and management representatives in the plant, Nicholson focused primarily on two dimensions of IR climate: the one relating to the flow of the problems at the workplace (issue-centered climate) and the other to shaping the quality of interpersonal dealings between union and management (people-centered climate) and the extent of satisfaction of the parties with each. In general, he found that in this particular plant, the overall climate was not dependent on the quality of interpersonal relations, and as a whole IR climate was more issue-centered than people-centered. He argued that

IR climate as a concept can be used to integrate organizational variables and IR outcomes including industrial conflict. He identified the potential for using issue-centered vs. people-centered IR climates as a means of diagnosing and addressing the quality and outcomes of industrial relations in the steel plant under study. He pointed out that for the predictive power of the notion of IR climate to be fully realized, research would have to consider at least three major problems and integrate them into the research design:

1) untapped organizational dimensions of IR climate at the workplace level;
2) external influences on IR climate and
3) the process of IR climate's formation, transmission and transformation (Nicholson, 1979, p. 25).

Kelly and Nicholson (1980) took this latter idea further and suggested the basis of a conceptual model to predict the incidence of strikes, with IR climate as an integral part of that model. Dastmalchian et al. (1982) also utilized Nicholson's idea of IR climate in a survey of manufacturing firms in Wales and found that IR climate was positively related to company effectiveness in terms of adaptability and readiness to change. These relationships were moderated by other factors such as scale of operation and the economic conditions of the firm.

These early studies took the first steps toward developing the concept of IR climate and its measurement. Even though other subsequent studies used this concept in different contexts, their measurements (reflecting the depth and complexity of the concept of IR climate) were often problematic. For example, Katz et al. (1983) studied the introduction of Quality of Work Life programs in 18 General Motors plants. They reported a positive relationship between IR climate (a 5-item measure reflecting union-management cooperation as perceived by less than half (N=65) of their total sample of 176 supervisors) and IR conflict, labor efficiency and product quality. However, in addition to a low response, the standard deviation of the measure as reported was very low (mean=2.9

out of 5, s.d.0.5) reflecting the possibility of managers and supervisors exaggerating the climate score.

In another study Angle and Perry (1986) examined dual union commitment and union-management relationships in 22 municipal bus companies in the US. They used 22 items, which were adapted from the Michigan Organizational Assessment Package (MOAP) (Institute of Social Research, 1975). They used a single aggregate dimension to operationalize IR climate without conceptually explaining this. They also did not provide evidence of the validity of the climate measure or specify the kinds of modifications they had made to MOAP (Dastmalchian et al., 1991: p.36).

In order for the concept of IR climate to be of more utility and a better foundation, there was a need to develop its concept more systematically. Dastmalchian et al. approached this in the 1980s and early 1990s by bridging the literatures from industrial relations and organization behavior/theory and establishing components of a model of IR climate in which not only the dimensions of IR climate were developed, but the model specified the factors affecting climate and the dimensions of IR systems and organization on which climate would impact.

DEVELOPING A MODEL OF IR CLIMATE: WORKPLACE INDUSTRIAL RELATIONS CLIMATE (WIRC)

The lack of IR theory and theory testing becomes evident when one considers the factors that influence IR processes and outcomes. Dunlop (1993) identifies the importance of such factors as technology, product and labor markets and financial and budgetary constraints, as well as power distribution in society. Even in this broad and relatively simple model, no serious attempts have been made to suggest the relative weight for different input or contextual variables. The work of Craig (1983) is another important example. The impressive list of input variables ranging from the legal system to the weather leaves us with the difficult task of adequately testing such a multi-variable and interactive model. Dastmalchian et al. (1991) and Blyton et al. (1987) have stressed the need to develop models that not only have useful and worthwhile taxonomies, but such models need to have the capacity to be operationalized. Since the primary purpose of their work was to improve understanding of how IR climate as a concept works in individual work organizations, it was necessary to create a more middle-range model, which could be treated rigorously in a sample of organizations (Blyton et al., 1987). This required a more organizational focus to the model which meant an expansion of the factors more relevant at the organizational level and not focusing on variables that were broader and more external and macro. The model developed by Dastmalchian et al. is shown in Figure 29.1.

DIMENSIONS OF IR CLIMATE

IR climate refers to the workplace norms and attitudes perceived by management and employees (and their representatives) about industrial relations and the nature of union-management relationships in the organization. Also, based on the work of Nicholson (1979) there is a clear expectation that the concept of IR climate and its measurement are not uni-dimensional. This belief in multi-dimensionality has its roots in the work of authors such as Fox (1974) who identified trust and distrust as containing important explanatory power in the analysis of IR and in the broader study of society. Other studies have also reinforced this notion that climate and attitude dimensions such as co-operation, hostility, aggression/resistance, apathy, support for trade unions, joint participation, goal identification, trust, fairness and power balance can all represent different facets of IR climate (Martin and Biassatti, 1979; Biassatti and Martin, 1979; Brett, 1980; Gandz and Whitehead, 1981; Dastmalchian et al., 1982; Osborne and Blyton, 1985).

Dastmalchian et al. (1986) conducted a pilot study involving a population of 258 IR/HRM managers, union officials and labor arbitrators. In a validation study involving two Canadian cases and a total of 728 respondents, Dastmalchian et al. (1989) refined the measures to 26 items and the five IR climate dimensions of: harmony, openness, hostility, apathy and promptness. Dastmalchian et al.

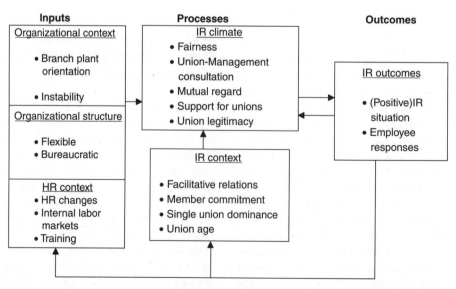

Figure 29.1   The industrial relations climate model and summary of relevant factors

(1989) also tested the appropriateness of the model as a whole using both quantitative and qualitative and case methods.

Based on the above, these authors embarked on a large-scale study of 51 organizations in Canada to test the model and finalize the IR climate measures (Dastmalchian et al., 1991). The organizations were from across the country belonging to both manufacturing and service sectors ranging in size from 19 to 7000 employees. The average firm was 63 years old. The data were collected by semi-structured interviews with various managers and union representatives, company records and questionnaires (for IR climate and other perceptual measures). The criteria used for questionnaire data collection was the distribution to a minimum of 10 per cent of the employees in each firm. Of the total 3000 questionnaires distributed, 1686 were received representing 35 organizations in the sample. After the analysis of validity and reliability of the scales and items, including interclass and agreement coefficient analyses, the final measure of IR climate consisted of 20-items measuring 5 dimensions of: fairness, union-management consultation, mutual regard, membership support for unions and union legitimacy. Appendix 29.1 shows the details and statistical properties of the final IR climate measure. Details of the 20 items and the final factor analysis results are shown in Appendix 29.2.

THE INPUT VARIABLES

Blyton et al. (1987) developed a comprehensive set of input variables that they argue had the most direct impact on the development of an IR climate. Based on the works of Dunlop (1993), Poole (1986) and others, they identified the broader environmental factors such as demographics, legal and social elements, in their earlier conceptualization. However in finalizing their model, they stayed closer to factors more immediately relevant at the organizational level. Many of these factors have been mentioned by a variety of other studies on IR climate. For example Deery et al. (1994) included external labor market and Wagar (1997) considered industry and product/service information in their studies, though not in a comprehensive fashion.

The first of the input variables was organizational context. This included organizational and workplace size (Payne and Mansfield, 1973), age (Ross and Hartman, 1960), ownership (Enderwick, 1985), technology (Eisele, 1974), environmental dependencies on owners, and labor markets (Dastmalchian, 1984; 1986), and the extent of turbulence and change, all of which have a potential impact on the IR climate. In the final stages of their study, Dastmalchian et al. (1991), drawing on factor analysis, used two dimensions to measure organizational context: (1) branch plant orientation where a higher score on this dimension represents the context of an organization which resembles a typical manufacturing or operating plant, with production technologies similar to that of an assembly line, relatively low skill requirement for labor (and thus likely to be less dependent on labor markets), owned by a larger group (and is a branch or a subsidiary of the large group), and relatively older as a unit. In contrast a lower score on this dimension represents a newer workplace with high interdependence among its various functions and units, less dependent on an owning group (not a branch or a subsidiary), and with higher skill requirements (and thus more dependent on labor markets); and (2) instability which refers to a context characterized by significant organizational change such as technological, ownership, products or market change. It was predicted that more branch plant orientation and instability would contribute to tension between union and management and thus adversely affect the IR climate dimensions of consultation, mutual regard and fairness.

The second group of organizational factors was organizational structure that has been shown in the literature to relate to organizational climate and industrial relations (Barbash, 1975; Brett, 1980; Brett and Goldberg, 1979; Payne and Pugh, 1976; Thompson, 1967). This group included the degree of centralization of decision making and formalization, which affect the nature of grievance handling, the resolution of labor disputes, attitudes toward unions and strikes. Research has shown that the more formalized and thus more bureaucratic the structure the less favorable the IR climate is likely to be. Ng and Dastmalchian (1989) have shown that centralization causing grievances to be settled at a higher level in organizations is associated with more delays and frustrations. Dastmalchian and Ng (1990) further showed that this relates to IR climates of less co-operation between union and management. One can make the argument that the existence of decentralization and participation would lead to a more co-operative IR climate, as Katz et al. (1983) have shown through their study of participation and quality of work life programs and their association with positive IR climates. Dastmalchian et al. (1991) used two dimensions to reflect aspects of organizational structure and design: (1) flexible design (referring to more participative, sharing and decentralized, as well as specialized, decision making); and (2) bureaucratic design (referring to a more formalized, centralized and complex, differentiated, organizational structure). It was predicted that more flexible organization structures would contribute to the development of more co-operative IR climates (consultation, fairness and mutual regard as well as union legitimacy and support).

The next category in the inputs for the model is human resource context. The composition of the labor force, existence of internal labor markets, provision of training and education and flexible HR practices are potentially influential on the formation of more positive IR climates (Dastmalchian and Blyton, 1992). Dastmalchian et al. (1991) finalized their measure of this category by focusing on: internal labor markets, training and HR changes.

Finally, the IR context is expected to exert a significant influence on IR climate. The extent and pattern of unionization (including the gender split, bargaining structure, history of recent settlements, union involvement, etc.) are expected to have a direct effect on the climate of union-management relationships. IR Climate also can be affected by the context and history of the interaction between management and unions (see Clegg, 1979; and Hyman, 1972 on the evidence on the impact of context on strike action). Dastmalchian et al. (1991) concentrated on a set of largely 'given' factors (for example bargaining structure) rather than the 'process' variable (for example process of dispute handling). Even though this latter group is not explicitly stated in the model, the authors have addressed the importance of process factors elsewhere (see Blyton, et al.,1987). The model used nine indicators to measure IR Context, and then clustered these into four factors:

1) Facilitative Relations (with higher score on this referring to a positive history, informal methods of grievance handling, higher rate of female membership and industry rather than local bargaining structures);
2) Membership commitment (attendance and commitment);
3) Single union dominance (high union density and a single or few union presence) and
4) Union age.

It was anticipated in this framework that more facilitative IR contexts would lead to the creation of more collaborative and harmonious IR climates. Single union dominance was expected to relate to more extreme situations (either very co-operative or conflictual). Membership commitment and union age were also expected to influence the formation of IR climates relating to more union support and union legitimacy.

IR outcomes

Following this proposed model, the question was how various IR climates impact upon the outcomes of industrial relations in the organization. The theoretical position was that the structure and context variables influence the IR climate, which in turn will impact on the outcomes of union-management relationships. That is, the relationships between structural and contextual variables and IR outcomes are mediated by the perception of the IR climate.

Viewing this in a broader context, one needs to consider the question of what constitutes the output of an IR system. Dunlop (1958: 1993) and his followers viewed the development of a web of rules (procedural and substantive) as outcomes of an IR system. Craig (1983, p.11) stated that rule making is the 'allocation of rewards to employees for their services and the determination of the conditions under which they work'. He then went on to suggest two types of outputs: one that related to the organization of work and trade unions, and a second type that focused more on wage-effort bargaining, rights and other worker-oriented bargaining. Craig (1983), however, did not recognize 'conflict' as an outcome of the IR system, which by implication emphasized the positive aspects of union-management and IR relationships. In their model, Dastmalchian et al. (1991) therefore incorporated two categories: consensual outcomes which refer to positive IR negotiations, effective grievance handling and agreements; and conflictual outcomes such as absence, turnover and strikes. The measures proposed in their model include both objective and subjective outcomes. These were: IR events, IR situation (management view), and success in negotiations, IR situation (union view), turnover, and absenteeism. These were then clustered into two factors: (1) IR situation (views of both sides about the positive outcomes, effective negotiation success and lack of major IR incidents); and (2) employee responses (turnover and absenteeism).

Testing the model: quantitative analysis

In testing their model, Dastmalchian et al. (1991) used quantitative and qualitative (longitudinal case analysis) approaches. The quantitative approach was concluded by a series of regression techniques (path analysis) examining the multi-variate associations among the key variables in the model (Dastmalchian et al., 1991: 112–14).

The results showed that the path model explained 65 per cent of the variation of the IR outcomes and between 36–38 per cent of the variation in IR climate. One important conclusion from this analysis was that the indirect paths of variables such as context (both IR and organizational) and organizational structure to outcomes are much stronger than their respective direct paths. That is, organizational context and structural variables impact more strongly on outcomes through their effects on perceived climate than by direct effects on those outcomes. Similarly, it can be argued that the context within which the interaction between the union and management takes place has its greatest influence on results through its potential impact on people's perceptions of the climate, rather than directly in the form of industrial actions, higher turnover and the like (pp.111 and 113). Appendix 29.3 shows the summary of the results by providing averages of the path coefficients across the path analyses provided by Dastmalchian et al. (1991: 112). The coefficients reported in Appendix 29.3 are path coefficients, and E refers to R^2 or the per cent of variance in dependent variables explained by each path.

Testing the model: case study analyses

Dastmalchian et al. (1991) also offer empirical evidence for their model in a more qualitative fashion by using six longitudinal case studies (over a period of 18 months – between 1987–1989) and three cross-sectional case studies. The purpose was to further validate their model and also to provide insights into the dynamics of IR climate, or what they referred to as Workplace Industrial Relations Climate (WIRC).

Longitudinal case study analysis
This was conducted in six Canadian organizations:

1) A sports and recreational facility employing professional people which reduced its size from 160 to 100 people;

2) A public library with high union density employing about 105 people in 1987 and experiencing a healthy growth of its unionized professional staff to a 160 strong staff by 1989;
3) and (4) Two breweries both branches of larger organizations employing some 121 and 153 people respectively which represented a 20–5 per cent decline for its heavily unionized employees compared to 1987;
5) An large agricultural co-operative business employing some 2600 people in 1987 growing to 2824 in 1989; and
6) A private graphic and printing firm which due to a merger went through downsizing and reduced its employees from 170 to 70 in 18 months.

Table 29.1 summarizes their findings. In four of the six cases, the findings of the quantitative analyses were confirmed. That is, the impact of change in inputs on IR outcomes can better be understood through their effects on IR climate perceptions than by examining their direct impacts on IR outcomes. In three of the cases (the sports and recreation facility – Western Recreation Facility, the City library and a brewery – Merton Brewery) a decline in flexibility of organizational design and decrease in participation, coupled with a reduction in extent of training, growth in size and increased dependency on the parent company, led to a deterioration of the IR climate (in terms of co-operation and trust) and resulted in a reduction in favorability of IR outcomes. In another brewery (Clark Brewery), an increase in structural flexibility and a greater emphasis on training had contributed to improvements in climate and outcomes. In the other two cases, the authors noted the complexity of the model and the possible interrelationships among the variables. For example, in the case of the printing company (Graphica), a merger with another firm in the same industry during the period under study resulted in a substantial change in the role of the main union and thus a decline in positive IR climate perceptions. But as the financial performance of the merged organization was strong and the merger had allowed access to different labor markets and the prosperity of the firm had improved, the decline in

climate was not associated with a decline on outcomes.

Therefore the case studies as well as the quantitative analysis provided by Dastmalchian et al. (1991) showed the value of the general model proposed in their work for understanding the determinants of workplace IR climate and its possible consequences at the level of the organization. The longitudinal case studies have also brought to bear the complexities of the relationships between various external and internal factors that could have a substantial impact on the process of climate formation and change. Overall, based on their work, IR climate does appear to provide a useful vehicle to better understand the factors involved in the processes of industrial relations and their outcomes. With the potential of a much wider range of influences than one can incorporate in any model or framework designed to understand attitudes and behaviors regarding firms' industrial relations, it is important to be able to utilize concepts such as climate both to evaluate the significance of individual input and to compare the industrial relations scene across diverse settings.

The utility of the concept of IR climate

Since the work by Dastmalchian, Blyton, Adamson and colleagues was published in the late 1980s and early 1990s, there have been a fairly large number of studies that have employed the concept and measures of IR climate to explore issues relating to industrial relations, dual commitment, high performance work practices, teamworking and a series of other changes and innovations in the workplace. An overview of the empirical and conceptual evidence shows that the concept of IR climate has been accepted as a legitimate variable that can gauge the context within which labor-management interactions take place.

Following on the suggestion made by Thornicroft (1993) that the quality of the labor-management relationship is a

Table 29.1 A Summary of the six longitudinal case studies

Cases	Change in key input variables	Change in workplace IR climate	Change in outcome variables
Western Recreational Association	• A sharp decline in structural flexibility • Declines in training and ILM (internal labour market)	Climate deteriorated (particularly union support and legitimacy)	An increase in conflictual outcomes.
City Library	• An increase in size • A decrease in structural flexibility • Moderate increase in ILM and technical training	Climate deteriorated (particularly fairness and mutual regard)	An increase in conflictual outcomes, and decrease in actors' ratings of IR situation.
Merton Brewery	• A substantial drop in structural flexibility • A reduction in size • An increase in technical training • Change in ownership structure (merger)	Climate deteriorated (consultation, mutual regard and union support)	A decrease in favorability of negotiation outcomes from union's view.
Clark Brewery	• An increase in structural flexibility and slight decrease in bureaucracy • An increase in HR related practices (training and ILM) • A decrease in branch plant orientation	Improvement in climate (fairness, consultation and mutual regard)	Overall decrease in conflictual outcomes.
Canadian Co-Operative Services	• An increase in structural bureaucracy • A decrease in HR practices (training)	Deterioration of climate (fairness, consultation and mutual regard)	A slight improvement in positive aspects of outcomes (reductions in absenteeism and turnover)
Graphica	• Ownership changes (merger) • Increases in structural bureaucracy and size • Reduction in emphasis on HR practices (ILM and training)	Deterioration of climate (fairness, consultation and union support)	Improvement in positive aspects of outcomes (turnover, grievances and absenteeism)

more important determinant of organizational performance than unionization, Wagar (1997a) addressed the question 'Is Labor-Management Climate Important?' He conducted an empirical study of organizations and unions in Canada, by collecting data from a national sample of unionized firms (N=367), a sample of unionized organizations from the province of Nova Scotia (N=392), and a sample of union officials in Nova Scotia (N=280). He analyzed the three data sets separately and concluded that labor-management climate is important. The dependent variable

was perceptions of performance, and the main independent variable was six IR climate items drawn from Dastmalchian et al. (1991). Other control variables in the study were: market demand, technology/automation, investment, unionization rate, workforce reduction, existence of team-based programs, incidence of strikes, union concessions and major change in company strategy, size and industry sector. The data from the two employer samples and one union sample showed clearly that more favorable union-management climates were associated with more favorable perceptions of organizational performance (with a stronger relationship reported in case of 'present' performance rather than performance 'change' over time). This is despite the fact that the union sample rated the climates less optimistically than the employers. The study also showed that achieving a positive labor-management climate is not easy and requires long-term commitment on both sides. In a related study, using the employer data from 752 Canadian organizations, Wagar (1997b) reinforced the finding from the study referred to above in that a more co-operative relationship between labor and management was associated with a number of positive organizational outcomes (for instance employees' willingness to support change and innovation, and lower levels of conflict, turnover and absenteeism).

In another, more recent, study of labor-management climate in Canadian health care, Wagar and Rondeau (2002) collected data from 260 union officials/representatives in the health care sector. The results, again using an IR climate measure drawn from Dastmalchian et al. (1991), showed that climate is an important variable affecting the satisfaction of the union members, or change in their level of satisfaction (climate was as important in this respect as the presence of joint labor-management committees). Climate on the other hand, was not seen to be as important a predictor of workplace performance as was the adoption of joint labor-management committees (workplace performance refers to service quality and client satisfaction). This latter finding is not surprising. In the language of the model presented by Dastmalchian et al. (1991), the presence of the joint committees is a feature of organizational structure which impacts on climate which in turn affects outcomes.

Other researchers have also incorporated IR climate as an integral concept in their research framework and measures. Deery et al. (1994) studied dual commitment among a sample of Australian white-collar unionists and found that IR climate, measured using the six items from Hammer et al.'s (1991) investigation (where climate was measured as a uni-dimensional construct), was related to company commitment but not to union commitment. The dual commitment issue has attracted the interest of many researchers and its association with IR climate has also been studied by other authors (for instance Angle and Perry, 1986; Barling et al., 1990; Gallagher and Clark, 1989). Based on the assumptions of role theory, it argues that in tense and hostile climates, undue pressure is placed upon employees to choose their allegiance, whereas in positive climates those perceived role conflicts exist less strongly (Angle and Perry, 1986). It has been suggested that the reason for divergent findings on the impact of climate on organizational and union outcomes is that the role that management and unions play in employees' views their attachment to the company or the union, or their instrumentality in employees achieving valued goals, is underestimated. Deery et al. (1999) emphasizing this point developed a framework of antecedents and consequences on IR climate that is based on this notion of management and union's instrumentality and relates climate to outcomes such as dual commitment and absenteeism. One difference between this and Dastmalchian et al.'s (1991) framework is that in Deery et al.'s (1999) case, the level of analysis is individual rather than organizational. Similar to the model presented earlier, their framework also has a number of variables as inputs (demographic variables of individuals; work setting variables such as routinization, autonomy, job security and satisfaction; and environmental variables such as job market and union instrumentality). These affect the IR climate, which in turn impacts upon organizational commitment, union loyalty and absenteeism.

Deery et al. (1999) collected data from a random sample of 525 blue-collar employees in a large American auto manufacturer firm in Australia. For IR climate, they used Dastmalchian et al.'s (1989) ten-item 'harmony' dimension. They found that the more employees reported their unions as instrumental in achieving their valued goals, the more favorable they perceived the IR climate and the more loyal to the union and committed to the organization they were. That is, they demonstrated a greater likelihood of having dual commitment. Higher union instrumentality, through its effects on climate, also had a positive impact on reducing absenteeism. In short, they found that unions that provided effective workplace representation could, through the creation of positive IR climates, facilitate positive organizational outcomes.

In a more recent study Deery and Iverson (2005) developed their earlier framework and in addition to union instrumentality, included variables reflecting the structure and context of both management and union activities that are specific to union-management dealings. These included: the perception of procedural justice, and management's willingness to share information and facilitate union business; and on the union side, their interest in integrative bargaining approaches and union responsiveness to members. Thus union, management and individual-related variables (belief in co-operation and in good relationships) as inputs will impact upon the perception of IR climate, which in turn influence dual commitment as well as three additional types of outcomes (productivity, quality of service and absenteeism). Deery and Iverson's causal model and the direction of relationships found are summarized in Figure 29.2.

Deery and Iverson (2005) conducted a further study of 305 branches of a unionized Australian-based multi-national bank using a longitudinal design with data collected over three time periods from unionized and non-unionized employees, plus additional data on performance measures from company records. They found that a co-operative labor relations climate was associated with higher levels of branch productivity and service quality. Also, more positive climate perceptions were related to higher commitment to the organization and more loyalty to the union.

Bacon and Blyton also included IR climate in their study of the UK steel industry (Bacon and Blyton, 2004; 2006; Bacon et al., 2005). They used a four-item scale from Dastmalchian et al.'s (1991) measure and utilized it to determine co-operative and conflictual IR climate. Their findings showed that IR climate collected by survey from the unionized employees had significant relationships to co-operative and conflict behaviors during negotiations by managers and unions. Positive IR climates were shown to be associated with collaborations between union and management when introducing changes in teamworking, shift and work patterns (Bacon et al., 2005). Bacon and Blyton (2006) also showed that whereas most literature tends to favor positive IR climates, in such climates workers may actually fare worse when organizational changes are introduced.

In addition to the above studies, the concept of IR climate has been used in understanding the dynamics of industrial relations in Asian counties. Wan et al. (1997) used the concept in a study of 73 manufacturing firms in Singapore and a more in-depth

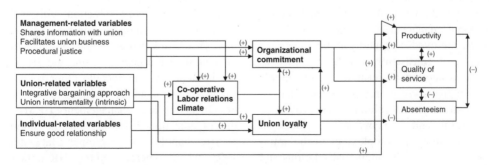

Figure 29.2 Simplified model of organizational performance
Source: Based on the findings of Deery and Iverson (2005), p. 603.

analysis of eight of the organizations in their sample. Their study revealed that positive industrial relations climates reflected the changes and improvement that had happened in Singapore's manufacturing sector. This had coincided with improved union membership and the perceived increase in the role and influence of unions in workplace industrial relations. They also found differences in the climate perceptions among union officials, management and employees and concluded that there is a need to strengthen the communication among the three parties. Wu and Lee (2001) examined the relationships between IR climate and participatory management approaches in Chinese-, Japanese-, and American-owned firms in Taiwan. Using data from 303 individual employees from 12 firms, they found that IR climate dimensions of harmony and openness had a significant relationship with the effective use of participatory management. Lee (2004) studied the association between dual commitment and IR climate by collecting data from 331 respondents in one automobile plant in Korea. Lee (2004) similar to Deery et al. (1994) he found that co-operative IR climate had a positive relationship with company commitment and a negative association with union commitment.

CONCLUSION

It does appear that over the past 25 years the concept of IR climate has made its way into the list of critical variables to be examined and paid close attention to in the field of industrial relations and human resource management. It has provided a much improved explanatory ability in various studies. It consistently has been shown to be associated with positive organizational and industrial relations outcomes. That is, the concept of IR climate has proved to be useful, and in many ways critical, in understanding the complexities of the atmosphere of workplace industrial relations and employee commitment to the organization and the union. At the same time, it is fair to

say that the field of industrial relations has not kept pace with those deeper conceptual and methodological issues surrounding the notion of IR climate that organizational studies have been grappling with. For example, none of the studies utilizing the concept has shown interest in looking more closely to examine the aggregation issues: how it should be aggregated to represent the IR climate at the plant level; what is the level of 'agreement' on climate; or which sub-groups should constitute the basis of aggregation – union types, departments, geographical regions and so on. The industrial relations field appears to have been less interested in these conceptual and methodological issues than in the utility of the notion of IR climate. However, one can argue that without due attention and care about such matters as level of 'agreement', and aggregation biases, what is being measured may not reflect what IR climate is intended to capture.

A related issue raised earlier in this chapter is the 'issue-specific' climate concept. It is clear from the evidence that an issue-specific concept of climate is more useful and can clarify the impact of climate on organizations, unions, management and employees. At a broader level, our focus on IR climate (rather than general organizational climate) has partly achieved this shift in attention. Looking ahead, there is a need to develop more specific IR climate constructs that deal with issues that are pertinent to the research questions. These include climates of safety (Zohar, 2000), harassment (Fitzgerald et al., 1997), grievances (Dastmalchian and Ng, 1990; Ng and Dastmalchian, 1989), absence (Iverson et al., 2003). Such a direction will likely result in studies and research frameworks that more clearly link the causes and consequences of a particular aspect of work and IR and the influence of the specific climate under study. Another example would be the climate of human resource management (HRM) in the organization. Building on the notion of HR 'bundles' (for example MacDuffie, 1995) where synergies among HR policies are the focus, the idea of HRM climate could provide insights into the role of climate in successful implementation of HR practices and bundles and be a fruitful research avenue to pursue for both unionized and non-unionized firms.

It clear from the review of the recent literature that IR climate has been used to better understand the dynamics of change in the workplace. IR climate has been an important variable included in a variety of different studies to explain either the impetus for change or the context within which change in organizational and employment practices has taken place (see for example, the work of Deery et al., 1999, and of Bacon and Blyton, 2006). In an attempt to better understand the dynamics of change and the outcome of interactions between unions and management and their changing relationships, IR climate has been shown to be a key factor to help understand the process and predict outcomes. The issue of climate vs. culture is an ongoing debate. In terms of the future direction of research, it is understood that the two concepts are connected, but differ in terms of what they represent – with culture signifying deeply rooted values, and climate referring to the atmosphere and the context of the relationships.

The early work by of Nicholson (1979) and the framework developed by Dastmalchian et al. (1989; 1991) have been shown to be useful and constructive concepts and measures in the development of the notion of IR climate. Many of the empirical studies conducted in the UK, Canada, Australia, the US and Asian countries (Singapore, Korea, China, Japan and Taiwan) have employed the concept, the measures and the suggested framework. The implication of the suggested framework by the above authors is far reaching. In order for new programs, new structures and new workplace arrangements to be successfully implemented, there needs to be an atmosphere, or an IR climate, created by the parties involved, their members and leaders. It is only then that innovative work practices will lead to the desired outcomes by both parties. This framework shows that the creation of new structures and new programs in isolation are unlikely to lead to the intended outcome unless the appropriate IR climate is created to facilitate their successful implementation. This has serious implications for the roles each party plays in the process of change. This also has direct implications for the leadership skills and perspectives of unions and management and their significance for any successful change and transformation – success as defined by all stakeholders. By accepting the concept of IR climate as a key factor in the study of industrial relations, we are also accepting the legitimacy and significance of behavioral and organizational concepts such as leadership, managing change and creativity, and the political model of organizations (Pfeffer, 1981) for industrial relations.

There is little doubt, based on research evidence, that co-operative IR climates contribute to firm performance (productivity levels, quality and service), higher levels of commitment to the organization and loyalty to unions (for example Deery and Iverson, 2005; Ichniowski et al., 1997; Katz et al.,1983; 1985; Wagar, 1997a; 1997b). The nature of the relationships and the resultant IR climate have been identified as significant facilitating factors for successful change and the adoption of innovative work practices (Ichniowski et al., 1996). This has important strategic implications for union and management IR strategies and for the future of IR climate research and its application. IR actors make choices about their approach and strategy. The discussion in this chapter shows that strategies based on creating IR climates rooted in trust, fairness and genuine desire to provide support and legitimacy for unions (and management) pay off and need to be an integral part of the process of IR development. Some recent evidence has suggested that perhaps co-operative IR climates may not always lead to better outcomes for the employees (Bacon and Blyton, 2006). Perhaps the underlying assumptions (for instance IR culture) on which the more temporal IR climate is based need also be changed and re-examined. This takes time and leadership on the part of both unions and management and a clear desire to recognize the importance of creating such enduring IR climates as a strategic direction for the future of industrial relations.

REFERENCES

Angle, H. and Perry, J. (1986) Dual commitment and labor management relationship climates, *Academy of Management Journal,* 29 (1): 31–50.

Ansari, M., Baumgartel, H. and Sullivan, G. (1982) The personal orientation – organizational climate fit and managerial success, *Human Relations,* 35: 1159–78.

Argyris, C. (1958) Some problems in conceptualizing organizational climate: a case study of a bank, *Administrative Science Quarterly,* 2 (4): 501–20.

Ashforth, B. (1985) Climate formation: issues and extensions. *Academy of Management Review,* 10 (4): 837–47.

Ashkanasy, N. M., Wilderom, C. P. M. and Peterson M.F. (eds), (2000) *Handbook of Organizational Culture and Climate.* London: Sage.

Bacon, N. and Blyton, P. (2004). Trade union responses to workplace restructuring: exploring union orientations and actions, *Human Relations,* 18 (4): 749–73.

Bacon, N. and Blyton, P. (2006) Union co-operation in a context of job insecurity: negotiated outcomes from teamworking, *British Journal of Industrial Relations,* 44 (2): 215–38.

Bacon, N., Blyton, P. and Dastmalchian, A. (2005) The significance of working time arrangements accompanying the introduction of teamworking: evidence from the employees, *British Journal of Industrial Relations,* 43 (4): 681–701.

Barbash, J. (1975) The unions as a bargaining organization: some implications to organizational behavior. *Proceedings of Industrial Relations Research Association.* Maddison Wis: IRRA Press.

Barling, J. Wade, B. and Fullager, C. (1990) *Journal of Occupational Psychology,* 63 (1): 49–61.

Biassatti, L. and Martin, J. (1979) A measure of the quality of union-management relationships. *Journal of Applied Psychology,* 64 (4): 387–90.

Blyton, P., Dastmalchian, A. and Adamson, R. (1987) Developing the concept of industrial relations climate, *Journal of Industrial Relations,* 29 (2): 207–16.

Brett, J. (1980) Behavioral research on unions and union management systems. In B. Staw and L. Cumming (eds), *Research in Organizational Behavior,* vol. 2. Greenwich, CT: JAI Press. pp. 177–213.

Brett, J. and Goldberg, S. (1979) Wildcat strikes in bituminous coal mining. *Industrial and Labor Relations Review,* 32: 465–83.

Burke, M., Borucki, C. and Hurley, A. (1992) 'Reconceptualizing psychological climate in a retail service environment: a multiple stakeholder perspective', *Journal of Applied Psychology,* 77 (5): 557–79.

Campbell, J., Dunnette, M., Lawler, E. and Weick, K. (1970) *Managerial Behavior, Performance, and Effectiveness.* New York, NY: McGraw-Hill.

Chatman, J. (1991) Matching people and organizations: selection and socialization in public accounting firms, *Administrative Science Quarterly,* 36 (3): 459–84.

Clegg, H. (1979) *The System of Industrial Relations in Great Britain.* Oxford, UK: Basil Blackwell.

Cooke, W.N. (1992). Product quality improvement through employee participation: the effect of unionization and joint union-management administration. *Industrial and Labor Relations Review,* 46 (1): 119–34.

Craig, A. (1983) *The System of Industrial Relations in Canada.* Scarborough, ON: Prentice-Hall.

Dansereau, F. and Alutto, J.A. (1990) Level of analysis issues in climate and culture research. In B. Schneider, (ed.) *Organizational climate and culture.* San Francisco: Jossey-Bass. pp.193–236.

Dastmalchian, A. (1984) Environmental dependencies and company structure in Britain, *Organization Studies,* 5 (3): 227–41.

Dastmalchian, A. (1986) Environmental characteristics and organizational climate: An exploratory study, *Journal of Management Studies,* 23 (6): 609–33.

Dastmalchian, A., Adamson, R. and Blyton, P. (1986) Developing a measure of industrial relations climate. *Relations Industrielles,* 41 (4): 851–59.

Dastmalchian, A. and Blyton, P. (1992) Organizational structure, human resource practices and industrial relations, *Personnel Review,* 21 (1): 58–67.

Dastmalchian, A., Blyton, P. and Abdollahian, R. (1982) Industrial relations climate and company effectiveness. *Personnel Review,* 11 (1): 35–9.

Dastmalchian, A., Blyton, R. and Adamson, R. (1989) Industrial relations climate: testing a construct. *Journal of Occupational Psychology,* 62: 21–32.

Dastmalchian, A., Blyton, P. and Adamson, R. (1991) *The Climate of Workplace Relations.* London, UK: Routledge.

Dastmalchian, A. and Ng, I. (1990) Examining the relationship between industrial relations climate and grievance outcomes, *Relations Industrielles,* 45 (2): 311–24.

Deery, S., Erwin, P. and Iverson, R. (1999) Industrial relations climate, attendance, behaviour and the role of trade unions, *British Journal of Industrial Relations,* 37 (4): 533–58.

Deery, S., Iverson, R. and Erwin, P. (1994) Predicting organizational and union commitment: The effect of industrial relations climate, *British Journal of Industrial Relations,* 32: 581–97.

Deery, S. and Iverson, R. (2005) Labor-management cooperation: antecedents and impact on organizational performance, *Industrial and Labor Relations Review,* 58 (4): 588–609.

Denison, D. (1996) What is the difference between organizational culture and organizational Climate? A native's point of view on a decade of paradigm wars? *Academy of Management Review,* 21 (3): 619–54.

Dunlop, J. (1958) *Industrial Relations System.* New York: Holt.

Dunlop, J. (1993) *Industrial Relations Systems: Revised Edition.* Boston, MA.: Harvard Business School Press.

Eckvall, G. (1987) The climate metaphor in organization theory. In B. Bass and P. Deneth (eds), *Advances in Organizational Psychology: An International Review.* Beverly Hills, CA: Sage. pp. 177–90.

Eisele, C.F. (1974). Organizational size, technology and frequency of strikes, *Industrial and Labor Relations Review,* 27 (4): 566–71.

Enderwick, P. (1985) Ownership nationality and industrial relations practices in British non-manufacturing industries, *Industrial Relations Journal,* 16 (2): 50–9.

Fitzgerald, L.F. , Drasgow, F., Hulin, C.L., Gelfand, M.J. and Magley, V.J. (1997) Antecedents and consequences of sexual harassment in organizations: a test of an integrated model, *Journal of Applied Psychology,* 82 (4): 578–89.

Fox, A. (1974) *Beyond Contract: Work, Power, and Trust Relations.* London, UK: Faber.

Gallagher, D. and Clark, P. (1989) Research on union commitment: Implications for labor, *Labor Studies Journal,* 14: 531–71.

Gandz, J. and Whitehead, J. (1981) The relationship between industrial relations climate and grievance initiation and resolution. *IRRA 34th Annual Proceedings,* Madison, Wis. pp. 320–28.

Glick, W. (1985) Conceptualizing and measuring organizational and psychological climate, *Academy of Management Review,* 10: 601–16.

Glick, W. (1988) Organizations are not central tendencies: shadowboxing in the dark, round 2, *Academy of Management Review,* 13 (1): 133–37.

Guion, R. (1973) A note on organizational climate, *Organizational Behavior and Human Performance,* 9 (1): 120–125.

Hammer, T., Currall, S. and Stern, R. (1991) Worker representation on boards of directors: a study of competing roles, *Industrial and Labor Relations Review,* 44 (4): 661–80.

Hellriegel, D. and Slocum, J. (1974) Organizational climate: measures, research and contingencies, *Academy of Management Journal,* 17 (2): 255–79.

Hyman, R. (1972) *Strikes.* London, UK: Fontana.

Ichniowski, C., Kochan, T., Levine, D., Olson, C. and Strauss, G. (1996) What works at work: overview and assessment, *Industrial Relations,* 35 (3): 299–333.

Ichniowski, C., Shaw, K. and Prennushi, G. (1997) The effects of human resource management practices on productivity: a study of steel finishing lines, *American Economic Review,* 87 (3): 291–313.

Institute of Social Research. (1975) *Michigan Organizational Assessment Package: Progress Report II.* Ann Arbor, MI: Survey Research Center, ISR.

Iverson, R., Buttigieg, D. and Maguire, C. (2003) Absence culture: the effects of union membership status and union-management climate, *Relations Industrielles,* 58 (3): 483–514.

Iverson, R. and Maguire, C. (2000) The relationship between job and life satisfaction: evidence from a remote mining community, *Human Relations,* 53 (6): 807–39.

James, L.A. (1982) Aggregation bias in estimates of perceptual agreement, *Journal of Applied Psychology,* 67 (2): 219–29.

James, L., Demaree, R. and Wolf, G. (1984) Estimating within-group interrater reliability with and without response bias, *Journal of Applied Psychology,* 69: 85–90.

James, L.R., Hater, J.J., Gent, M.J. and Bruni, J.R.(1978) Psychological climate: implications for cognitive social theory and interactional psychology, *Personnel Psychology,* 31 (6): 781–813.

James, L. and Jones, A. (1974) Organizational climate: a review of theory and research, *Psychological Bulletin,* 84 (12): 1096–112.

James, L., Joyce, W. and Slocum, J. (1988) Comment: organizations do not cognize, *Academy of Management Review,* 13 (1): 129–32.

Jones, A. and James, L. (1979) Psychological climate: dimensions and relationships of individual and aggregated work environment perceptions, *Organizational Behavior and Human Performance,* 23: 201–50.

Joyce, W. and Slocum, J. (1979) Climates in organizations. In S. Kerr (ed.), *Organizational Behavior,* Columbus, OH: Grid. pp. 317–33.

Katz, H.C., Kochan, T.A and Gobeille, K.R. (1983). Industrial relations performance, economic performance, and QWL programs: an interplay analysis, *Industrial and Labor Relations Review,* 37 (1): 3–17.

Katz, H.C., Kochan, T.A. and Weber, M.R. (1985). Assessing the effects of industrial relations systems and efforts to improve the quality of working life on organizational effectiveness, *Academy of Management Journal,* 28 (3): 509–26.

Kelly, J. and Nicholson, N. (1980) The causation of strikes: review of theoretical approaches and potential contribution of social psychology, *Human Relations,* 33 (12): 853–83.

Kozlowski, S. and Hults, B. (1987) An exploration of climates for technical updating and performance, *Personnel Psychology,* 40 (3): 539–67.

Lee, J. (2004) Company and union commitment: evidence from an adversarial industrial relations climate at a Korean auto plant, *Human Resource Management,* 15 (8): 1463–80.

Lewin, K., Lippitt, R. and White, R. (1939) Patterns of aggressive behavior in experimentally created social climates, *Journal of Social Psychology,* 10 (2): 271–99.

Liao, H. and Rupp, D.E (2005) The impact of justice climate and justice orientation on work outcomes: a cross-level multifoci framework, *Journal of Applied Psychology,* 90 (2): 242–56.

Lincoln, J. and Zeitz, G. (1980) Organizational properties from aggregate data: separating individual and structural effects, *American Sociological Review,* 45: 391–408.

Litwin, G. and Stringer, R. (1968) *Motivation and Organizational Climate.* Cambridge, MA: Harvard University Press.

MacDuffie, J.P. (1995) Human resource bundles and manufacturing performance: organizational logic and flexible production systems in the world auto industry, *Industrial and Labor Relations Review,* 48 (2): 197–221.

Mansfield, R. and Payne, R. (1977) Correlates of variance in perceptions of organizational climate. In D. Pugh and R. Payne (eds), *Organizational Behavior in its Context: The Aston Programme III.* Farnborough, Hants: Saxon House. pp. 149–59.

Martin, J. and Biassatti, L. (1979) A hierarchy of important elements in union-management relations, *Journal of Management,* 5 (2): 229–40.

McGregor, D. (1960) *The Human Side of Enterprise.* New York, NY: McGraw-Hill.

Micelli, M. and Near, J. (1985) Characteristics of organizational climate and perceived wrongdoing associated with whistleblowing, *Personnel Psychology,* 38 (3): 525–44.

Morse, N. and Reimer, E. (1956) The experimental change of a major organizational variable, *Journal of Abnormal and Social Psychology,* 52 (1): 120–29.

Ng, I. and Dastmalchian, A. (1989) Determinants of grievance outcomes: a case study. *Industrial and Labor Relations Review,* 42 (3): 393–403.

Nicholson, N. (1979) Industrial relations climate: a case study approach, *Personnel Review,* 8 (1): 20–5.

O'Rilley, C., Chatman, J. and Caldwell, D. (1991) People and organizational culture: a profile comparison approach to assessing person-environment fit, *Academy of Management Journal,* 34 (3): 487–516.

Osborne, D. and Blyton, P. (1985) Contrasting perspectives on productivity bargaining, *Journal of General Management,* 10 (3): 65–78.

Parker, C.P., Baltes, B.B., Young, S.A, Huff, R.W., Altman, H.A., LaCost, J. and Roberts, E. (2003) 'Relationships between psychological climate perceptions and work outcomes: a meta-analytic review', *Journal of Organizational Behavior,* 24 (4): 389–416.

Patterson, M., Payne, R. and West, M. (1996) Collective climates: a test of their socio-psychological significance, *Academy of Management Journal,* 39 (6): 1675–91.

Payne, R. (1971) Organizational climate: the concept and some research findings. *Prakseologia* 39/40, ROK. pp. 143–58.

Payne, R.L. (1990) 'Madness in our method: a comment of Jackofsky and Slocum's paper' A longitudinal study of climates, *Journal of Organizational Behavior,* 11 (1): 77–80.

Payne, R.L. (2000) 'Climate and culture: How close can they get?' In N.M., Ashkanasy, C.P.M. Wilderom, and M.F. Peterson (eds), *Handbook of Organizational Culture and Climate.* London: Sage. pp. 163–76.

Payne, R. and Mansfield, R. (1973) Relationships of perceptions of organizational climate to organizational structure, context and hierarchical position, *Administrative Science Quarterly,* 18 (4): 515–26.

Payne, R.L. and Pugh, D.S. (1976) 'Organizational structure and climate'. In M.D. Dunnette, (ed.), *Handbook of Industrial and Organizational Psychology.* Chicago: Rand-McNally. pp. 1125–73.

Pettigrew, A. (1979) On studying organizational cultures, *Administrative Science Quarterly,* 24 (4): 570–81.

Pettigrew, A. (1990) Organizational climate and culture: two constructs in search of a role. In B. Schneider (ed.), *Organizational Climate and Culture.* London: Sage. pp. 413–33.

Pfeffer, J. (1981) *Power in Organizations.* Marshfield, MA: Pitman Publishing.

Poole, M. (1985) Communication and organization climates. In R. McPhee and P. Thompkins (eds), *Organizational Communication: Traditional Themes and New Directions.* Beverly Hills, CA: Sage. pp. 79–108.

Poole, M. (1986) *Industrial Relations: Origins and Patterns of National Diversity.* London, UK: Routledge.

Poole, M.S. and McPhee, R.D. (1983) A structural analysis for organizational climates. In L. Putnam and M. Pacanowsky (eds), *Communication and Organizations: An Interpretive Approach.* Beverly Hills, CA: Sage. pp. 195–220.

Pugh, D. and Payne, R. (1977) *Organizational Behavior in its Context: The Aston Programme III.* Farnborough, UK: Saxon House.

Redman, T. and Snape, E. (2004) Kindling activism? Union commitment and participation in the UK fire service, *Human Relations,* 57 (7): 845–69.

Reichers, A. and Schneider, B. (1990) Climate and culture: an evolution of constructs. In B. Schneider (ed.), *Organizational Climate and Culture.* San Francisco, CA: Sage. pp. 5–39.

Roberts, K., Hulin, C. and Rousseau, D. (1978) *Developing an Interdisciplinary Science of Organizations.* San Francisco, CA: Jossey Bass.

Ross, A. and Hartman, P. (1960) *Changing Patterns of Industrial Conflict.* New York, NY: Wiley.

Rousseau, D.M. (1985) Issues of level in organizational research: multi-level and cross-level perspectives. In L.L. Cummings and B. M. Staw (eds), *Research in Organizational Behavior,* Vol. 7. Greenwich, CT: Jai. pp. 1–37.

Rousseau, D. (1988) The construction of climate in organizational research. In C. Cooper and I. Robertson (eds), *International Review of Industrial and Organizational Psychology.* Chichester, UK: Wiley. pp. 139–58.

Schein, E.H. (2000) Sense and nonsense about culture and climate. In N.M. Ashkanasy, C.P.M. Wilderom and M.F. Peterson, (eds), *Handbook of organizational culture and climate.* London: Sage. pp. xxiii–xxxiii.

Schneider, B. (1975) Organizational climate: individual preferences and organizational realities revisited, *Journal of Applied Psychology,* 60 (4): 459–65.

Schneider, B. (1980) The service organization: climate is crucial, *Organizational Dynamics,* 9 (2): 52–65.

Schneider, B. (1990) *Organizational Climate and Cultures.* San Francisco, CA: Jossey-Bass.

Schneider, B. and Bartlett, J. (1968) Individual differences and organizational climate I: the research plan and questionnaire development, *Personnel Psychology,* 21 (3): 323–33.

Schneider, B. and Bartlett, J. (1970) Individual differences and organizational climate II: measurement of organizational climate by the multitrait-multirater matrix, *Personnel Psychology,* 23 (4): 493–512.

Schneider, B. , and Bowen, D.E. (1995). *Winning the Service Game.* Boston, MA: Harvard Business press.

Schneider, B., Bowen, D.E., Ehrhart M.G. and Holcombe, K.M. (2000) 'The climate for service: evolution of a construct'. In N.M. Ashkanasy, C.P.M. Wilderom and M.F. Peterson (eds.), *Handbook of Organizational Culture and Climate.* London: Sage. pp. 21–36.

Schneider, B. and Reichers, A. (1983) On the etiology of climates, *Personnel Psychology,* 36 (1): 19–39.

Schneider, B. and Snyder, R. (1975) Some relationships between job satisfaction and organizational climate, *Journal of Applied Psychology,* 60 (3): 318–28.

Schneider, B., White, S.and Paul, M.C. (1998) Linking service climate and customer perceptions of service quality: test of a causal model, *Journal of Applied Psychology,* 83 (2): 150–63.

Schneider, B. (ed.) (1990) *Organizational Climate and Culture.* San Francisco, CA: Sage.

Siehl, C. and Martin, J. (1990) Organizational culture: a key to financial performance? In B. Schneider (ed.), *Organizational Climate and Culture.* San Francisco, CA: Jossey-Bass. pp. 241–81.

Tagiuri, R. and Litwin, G. (1968) *Organizational Climate: Exploration of a Concept.* Boston, MA: Harvard University Press.

Tetrick, L.E. and Fried, Y. (1993) Industrial relations: stress induction or stress reduction?, *Journal of Organizational Behavior,* 14 (5): 511–35.

Thompson, J. (1967) *Organizations in Action.* New York, NY: Wiley.

Thornicroft, K. W. (1993) Does labor climate matter? *1992 Canadian Industrial Relations Association Proceedings.* Fredericton, New Brunswick. pp. 69–81.

Trice, H. M. and Beyer, J.M.(1993) *The Cultures of Work Organizations.* Englewood Cliffs, NJ: Prentice Hall.

Trice, H. and Beyer, J. (1984) Studying organizational cultures through rites and ceremonials, *Academy of Management Review,* 9 (4): 653–69.

Wagar, T. (1997a) Is labor-management climate important? Some Canadian evidence, *Journal of Labor Research,* XVIII (1): 163–74.

Wagar, T. (1997b) The labor-management relationship and organization outcomes, *Relations Industrielles,* 52 (2): 430–46.

Wagar, T. and Rondeau, K. (2002) Labor-management forums and workplace performance. Evidence from union officials in health care organizations, *Journal of Management in Medicine,* 16 (6): 408–21.

Wan, D., Huat, O. and Yuee, L. (1997) Industrial relations climate in the manufacturing sector in Singapore, *Asia Pacific Journal of Management,* 14 (2): 123–41.

Warr, P., Fineman, S., Nicholson, N. and Payne, R. (1978) *Developing Employee Relations.* Farnborough, UK: Teakfield.

Wu, W. and Lee, Y. (2001) Participatory management and industrial relations climate: a study of Chinese, Japanese and US firms in Taiwan, *Human Resource Management,* 12 (5): 827–44.

Zohar, D. (1980) Safety climate in industrial organizations: theoretical and applied implications, *Journal of Applied psychology,* 65 (1): 96–102.

Zohar, D. (2000) A group-level model of safety climate: testing the effect of group climate on microaccidents in manufacturing jobs, *Journal of Applied Psychology,* 85 (4): 587–96.

Zohar, D. and Luria, G. (2005) A multilevel model of safety climate: cross-level relationships between organization and group-level climates, *Journal of Applied Psychology,* 90 (4): 616–28.

APPENDIX

Appendix 29.1 No. of items, reliability estimates, and within-organization agreement coefficients for Workplace Industrial Relations Climate Scales

Climate scales	Number of items	Cronbach's alpha	Within-organization agreement coefficient (ICC)
Fairness	6	0.926	0.904
Union-management consultation	6	0.931	0.875
Mutual regard	3	0.947	0.943
Membership support for unions	3	0.782	0.489
Union legitimacy	2	0.747	0.734
		Average	0.789

Source: Based on Dastmalchian et al. (1991), p.85.

Appendix 29.2 Factor analysis of the Workplace Industrial Relations Climate Items (with varimax rotation)

N = 1686	Climate items	Factor 1 (fairness)	Factor 2 (U/M consultation)	Factor 3 (mutual regard)	Factor 4 (member support)	Factor 5 (union legitimacy)
1	The collective agreement is regarded as fair by employees in this organization.	0.611				
2	A sense of fairness is associated with management dealings in this place.	0.592		0.452		
3	In this organization, negotiations take place in an atmosphere of good faith.	0.519				
4	The parties in the organization keep their word.	0.503		0.440		
5	Employees generally view the conditions of their employment here as fair.	0.496				
6	Grievances are normally settled promptly in this organization.	0.436				
7	Unions and management in this organization make sincere efforts to solve common problems.		0.551			

(Continued)

Appendix 29.2   Cont'd

N = 1686	Climate items	Factor 1 (fairness)	Factor 2 (U/M consultation)	Factor 3 (mutual regard)	Factor 4 (member support)	Factor 5 (union legitimacy)
8	Management often seeks input from unions before initiating changes.		0.532			
9	Management and unions cooperate to settle disputes in this organization.	0.474	0.496			
10	The parties exchange information freely in this organization.		0.453			
11	There is a great deal of concern for the other party's point of view in the union-management relationship.		0.429	0.403		
12	Joint union-management committees are a common means of implementing important changes in conditions.		0.421			
13	Unions and management work together to make this organization a better place to work.	0.404	0.601			
14	Unions and management have respect for each other's goals.		0.596			
15	In this organization, joint union-management committees achieve definite results.		0.439			
16	Generally, employees do not have much interest in the quality of the union-management relationship.				−0.529	
17	In this organization, unions have the strong support of their members.				0.495	

Appendix 29.2   Cont'd

N = 1686	Climate items	Factor 1 (fairness)	Factor 2 (U/M consultation)	Factor 3 (mutual regard)	Factor 4 (member support)	Factor 5 (union legitimacy)
18	Unions make a positive contribution to this organization.				0.408	0.401
19	Shop stewards in this organization generally play a helpful role.					0.490
20	People are encouraged to get involved in union activities here.					0.476
% Variance		37.6	44.6	49.1	53.5	57.3
Eigenvalue		9.030	1.665	1.077	1.029	0.939

Source: Dastmalchian et al. (1991), p.112.

Appendix 29.3   Tests of the overall model (path analysis)
Source: Dastmaclchian et al. (1991), p. 112.

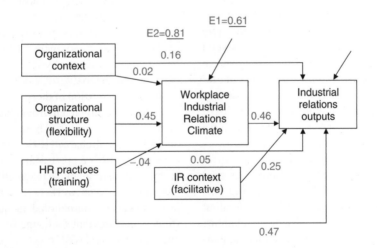

30

Equality at Work

Barbara Pocock

Equality – and its shadow, inequality – has long been a concern in the field of industrial relations (IR). Such inequality has many fault lines and some have received more attention than others. It is measured in several different ways, most commonly through wage outcomes, but also through differences in life-term earnings in retirement income, hours of work, the security of employment, employee voice at work, and access to promotion and a variety of other conditions and rights.

Inequality is at the heart of the employment relationship. Employers and employees generally exercise unequal power, and the outcomes of this inequality and its moderation are core concerns of employment relations, including regulation to mitigate this inequality, the collective organization of workers to 'rebalance' their power *vis a vis* their employers, and analysis of the perpetual contest between these two sides and its outcomes as reflected in the wage/effort bargain.

There are those who extract discussion of employer/employee inequality from their analysis (for example, the unitarist school and some proponents in human resources schools) but for the most part, the discipline

of industrial relations has been built around analysis of the practices and outcomes of a relationship between unequals.

The discipline has generally characterized the terms of the employment relationship, and its outcomes, as shaped by several factors: the personal characteristics of workers, the product or service location of those who buy labor, and the institutional environment in which their exchanges occur. These factors have distinct national characteristics and much of the study of IR – a great deal of it occurring at the national level – takes international inequality between workers as a naturalized fact. However, international inequality constitutes an important fault line of inequality, one that has received much less attention in the field than some other sources. Wide patterns of inequality exist at the international level between workers in different national systems of industrial relations, even where their effort, skill and contributions are broadly comparable. This inequality is expressed through wages most obviously, but is also reflected in rights at work, safety, employment security and other markers of work quality.

Workers in the footwear production zones of Asia are paid less than 5 per cent of the rates for US and Australian workers, while workers in large shoe production plants in China in February 2006 were paid US$ 0.40 per hour (National Labor Committee and China Labor Watch, February 2006). Given that the hours of these workers, their job security, voice at work and their occupational health and safety are also very inferior, this is inequality on an extraordinary scale, where equal pay for equal work has little real meaning. By any measure, such inequality in employment outcomes deserves close analysis. However, the national preoccupations of IR scholars (shaped by the national location of regulation and most data collection) mean that they receive all too little.

Further sources of work-based inequality lie between sub-groups of workers at national and regional levels, arising from their relative labor market power, including factors like skill, age, gender, 'race' and ethnicity. Some of these cross international bounds: in all countries, women are paid on average less than men, black workers less than white, and there are wide gaps in most countries between the top and the bottom of the labor market. These fault lines of inequality are not so under-attended by the discipline, and many have received a great deal of substantial and illuminating study, most significantly inequality structured around the personal characteristics of workers.

Despite this detailed study, legitimate critiques have been mounted of the field of industrial relations, about its blindness to the gendered character of the employment relationship and the embodied worker (Forrest, 1993; Pocock, 1997; Wajcman, 2000). Much remains to be done to deepen analysis in the field so that it accurately analyzes this aspect of employment and industrial life, as well as other sources of inequality like those arising from immigration, ethnicity, sexual orientation and age.

In this chapter, I canvass the current state of empirical evidence about some of the significant inequalities that are expressed around and through employment relationships, the ways in which national and international bodies have attempted to contain, moderate or redress

these, and some of the theoretical insights that have been generated along the way.

I focus on three aspects of inequality: inequality at the international level, between the top and bottom of the labor market, and gender inequality. These boundaries reflect my own research preoccupations rather than any defensible hierarchy of disadvantage. With growing international immigration, the question of the international movement of people, and the labor market fortunes of immigrants and workers of different ethnic and racial origins, are of growing importance in framing inequality. As the ILO notes 'the combined effect of global migration, the redefinition of national boundaries in some parts of the world, and growing economic problems and inequalities have exacerbated problems of xenophobia and racial and religious discrimination' (2003, p xi)

However, I put these complex questions – as well as other sources of labor market inequality such as sexual preference, age and perceived or actual HIV/AIDS status – to one side in the interests of giving some depth of discussion to other areas. It should be noted, however, that questions of multiple sources of inequality at work are of growing interest in many settings, encouraging research about intersecting inequalities as well as policy proposals like single equality statutes that address the 'mosaic' of inequality (Fitzpatrick, 2003).

INTERNATIONAL INEQUALITY

Wide employment-based inequalities remain at the international level. Growing global trade has been accompanied by widening inequality between countries over recent decades according to the United Nations (UN), as well as within many countries (United Nations, 2005). Work – or its absence – significantly shapes these inequalities with many citizens unable to find work, or enough of it, when they want it. Unemployment is high in many countries and as Kofi Annan puts it 'the best anti-poverty program is employment. And the best road to economic empowerment and social well-being lies in decent work' (Annan, 2004). Work can be a vehicle creating inequality whilst at the same time 'a privileged entry point from which to liberate society from discrimination' (ILO, 2003).

Around the world young people are especially affected by high levels of unemployment. Despite growing attention to the importance of transitional labor markets and the need to develop institutions which smooth transitions like that from education to work (Schmid, 1995), some transitions, especially for groups like youth, remain hazardous in many countries. In 2005 young people made up around 47 per cent of the 186 million unemployed people worldwide (United Nations, 2005). Unemployment is increasingly accompanied in many countries by growth in informal employment with very limited effective labor market regulation. Once again, young people are especially affected.

Debates about employment generation have fueled an ongoing debate between international agencies about the trade-offs between regulation of minimal labor standards on the one hand and employment and economic growth on the other. These debates have resonance in domestic politics and policy settings in many countries. The IMF has argued that regulation of employment relations through minimum wages, unemployment payments and employment security rights distort the market for labor and depress growth whilst increasing unemployment (IMF, 2003). On the other side of this international duel, the ILO has promoted core labor standards and regulation for 'decent work'.

This debate is sometimes cast as a contest between the regulation of work and its deregulation in favor of market forces. This is an inaccurate characterization in countries like Australia where current reforms are *re*-regulatory, designed to constrain and constrict past practices of collective bargaining and national and industry minima, and to make strikes, collective organization, rising minimum wages and protection against unfair dismissal more difficult. This is hardly 'deregulation' as thousands of pages of new industrial regulation make clear (Statement by a group of Australian Industrial Relations Academics, *Workchoices* Bill Submission, 2005).

The question of the true relationship between employment regulation (sometimes characterized as 'flexibility') and employment creation is critical in relation to inequality created through work. The nature of the trade-off remains controversial. Richard Freeman's recent analysis finds that 'the best summary of the data – what we really know – is that labor institutions reduce earnings inequality but that they have no clear relation to other aggregate outcomes, such as unemployment' (Freeman, 2005). Such institutions include, for example, minimum wage legislation or tribunals, active trade unions and industrial relations mediators or tribunals. The OECD have also recently agreed that 'a considerable number of studies' have found that evidence of an adverse impact of minimum wages on employment is 'modest or non-existent' and that there may be positive effects of minimum wages 'as one part of employment-centered social policy intended to mitigate poverty while fostering high employment rates' (OECD, 2006).

Scholars in employment studies have increasingly turned their attention to the issue of informal and precarious employment as it has grown apace, partly explaining the growth in the working poor and widening international inequality. Individual and household poverty – once certainly alleviated by entry to formal employment – is now growing in many locations around the world. A large majority of the working poor are in precarious or informal employment outside the agricultural sector, most of them in developing countries. According to UN estimates, in 2000 over 1,100 million people were living in absolute poverty on less than a dollar a day. While this is down from 1,237 million 10 years earlier, mostly through reductions in poverty in China and India, the numbers of very poor rose during the decade to 2000 in sub-Saharan Africa, Europe and Central Asia, and Latin America and the Caribbean (by 82, 14 and 8 million respectively (United Nations, 2005).

These changes, along with growth in the number of highly paid, help explain widening income inequalities in many countries. These have seen the ratio of the income of the richest 10 per cent of the world's population increase from 20 times that of the poorest 10 per cent in 1994, to 29 times in 2004 (United Nations, 2005). Even amongst the majority of higher income countries, gross earnings inequality widened in the decade to 2006 – and at a faster pace that the widening that occurred in the previous decade. Further, 'a persistent increase in the proportion of the working poor' is evident in OECD countries widened in the decade to 2006 (2006: 38–40).

International inequality is not, of course confined to incomes and wages, but also can be seen in the polarization around 'good' and 'bad' jobs and around levels of skills. Wage differentials in many countries have been widening between those with qualifications and those without (Ocampo, 2002; United Nations, 2005).

While the ILO holds as its founding principle the notion that labor is not a commodity and that the terms of its exchange should be regulated and moderated, growth in precarious employment and in forms of employment that are outside traditional employer/employee contracts has seen a recommodification of labor on terms that are regulated only lightly, if at all. The consequences for inequality are significant. For example, in Australia the proportion of workers employed as 'casuals' (that is, on an hourly hour contract with few formal rights and little job security at least in formal legal terms) has risen to over a quarter of the workforce at present (Campbell, 2000). This employment form allows employers to closely match their purchases of labor to production needs, but reduces those selling their labor to commodity status rather than assuring workers of a predictable, regular income or a 'living' wage. This has important implications for the dignity of labor and social reproduction (Pocock et al., 2004).

The traditional ILO approach of setting minimum standards through tripartite agreement, which countries then ratify, has been supplemented since 1998, with the adoption of four fundamental labor standards that ILO members are expected to support: freedom of association (including the right of workers to collectively organize and bargain), the abolition of forced labor, equality at work, and the elimination of child labor. The ILO system of exhortation and advocacy but weak 'name and shame' powers of enforcement has restricted the capacity of such international agencies to stem widening international employment-based inequalities. Increasing earnings at the top end of the labor market in many countries, and continuing inequalities in wage rates between countries, means that the international focus on minimal standards has had little effect on narrowing inequality either between nations or within them.

However, such attempts have at least given legitimacy to the notion that the employment relationship, in all its inequality, cannot be left to the market and that minimal rights should exist. That said, established employment standards in many countries are under powerful downward pressure and in some countries count for little – and not just in developing countries. The ILO's Committee on the Application of Standards is currently investigating Australia alongside Burma, Zimbabwe, Saudi Arabia, Nepal and Colombia for labor standard breaches. Indeed this committee has previously said that Australia's federal industrial law does not adequately protect from discrimination workers who choose to bargain collectively, a fundamental right according to the ILO. Further, more radical changes to Australian law in March 2006 create new grounds for investigation in relation to the minimal standards embodied in the ILO fundamental standards (Burrow, 2005).

Since 1999 employment analysts, including at the ILO, have turned their attention to the issue of 'decent work', widening policy goals from inequalities located around access to work to a broader discussion of the quality of work and the opportunities it creates. Questions of the security of work, and the conditions attached to it, are of critical importance to a full discussion of equality at work (Sennett, 1998; Standing, 2002). The ILO's decent work agenda has several strategic objectives: the provision for all of a productive job for fair pay; security and social protection; freedom of organization and voice and equal opportunities for women (ILO, 1999). The 'decent work' focus of the ILO responds to the outcomes of globalization and its effects on employment, social disruption and inequality (Ghai, 2002). It has profound implications for issues like working time and the larger work/effort bargain (Boulin et al., 2006; Messenger, 2004).

INEQUALITY BETWEEN THE TOP AND BOTTOM

Guy Standing has observed that the post-1945 era in many industrializing countries was an 'egalitarian age' when policy to narrow inequality through the regulation of employment as well as the provision of welfare support was seen as a valid goal (Standing, 1999). However, since the 1980s policy attention and discourse has moved away from direct discussion of inequality to analysis of 'exclusion', the basic premise being concern about those left behind or excluded, not the comparison between top and bottom. Analysts of the social effects of inequality however, argue that there are specific social consequences of widening inequality, much of it driven by changes at work, that are independent of growth in poverty alone (Wilkinson, 2005).

Interestingly, just as this focus on the excluded base strengthens, drawing attention away from analysis of the top and the bottom and the gap between them, these gaps are widening – in some cases on a breathtaking scale. This inequality is observable both between countries and within them. In the UK for example, inequality in the labor market has widened dramatically. In 1979 UK executives earned around ten times the pay of typical British workers but by 2002 executives of a FTSE company earned, on average, 54 times the pay of such workers, despite only very

modest increases in earnings and profit in many FTSE companies (Froud et al., 2006). The ratio is much wider in the US, with CEO pay in 2002, 281 times the rate of ordinary workers up from 50 times in 1980 (Elliott, 2006). In Australia, the average pay of chief executives in 2005 reached 63 times that of average workers compared to 18 times in 1989/90 (based on the earnings of Chief Executive who are members of the Business Council of Australia (Shields, 2005)).

This widening chasm between the top and bottom of pay scales occurs as greater dispersion in earnings generally characterizes pay outcomes in many locations in industrialized countries (OECD, 2006). Attention to inequality through employment in this environment has generally focused upon the minimum wage and containing poverty through small or larger movements in base rates. There is an accepted linkage between the characteristics of employment relations systems and their effects on wages and other industrial outcomes for workers in different countries as well as groups of workers such as women (Rodgers and Rubery, 2003). Richardson concludes in a recent survey that this relationship is now widely confirmed with 'clear evidence of the US, UK, Australia, New Zealand and several European countries that changes in the level of minimum wages are directly inversely correlated with the level of wage inequality' and 'where minimum wages fall, inequality increases and where it falls by a lot, inequality increases by a lot' (Richardson, 2005). She points to the growth in low paid jobs in most English-speaking member countries in recent years. The OECD suggests that rises have been especially sharp in the past decade in Germany (reaching 15.8 per cent in 2003/04), Hungary (24.4 per cent), the Netherlands (16.6 per cent), Poland (22.1 per cent) and the UK (23.4 per cent). Levels are also high in the US (23.3 per cent) (OECD, 2006 (see Statlink to Table 5.7)).

Awareness of the effects of different industrial systems and their implications for inequality is 'relatively rare' according to some (Almond and Rubery, 1998). This lack of awareness can result in important policy disconnects: for example, European Union (EU) activities to constrain minimum wages and contract the public sector to meet Maastricht convergence criteria in the 1990s ran counter to the EU policy goal of providing equal opportunities in all its activities (Almond and Rubery, 1998; Rubery, 2002). In contrast, the British move to create and lift the minimum wage was deliberately adopted as a means of increasing gender pay equity, and it did so with two-thirds of the beneficiaries of its 2004 increases being women (Low Pay Commission, 2005).

Employment and industrial relations analysis in general has established a connection between industrial systems and the equity of their outcomes. Systems providing relatively higher minimal wage protection, greater levels of centralism, collective instruments of pay setting and collective forms of worker representation, wider coverage of different types of employees and effective enforcement of standards and agreements, are generally associated with narrower dispersion of outcomes and a lower level of inequality. Such institutional arrangements and systems mediate the operation of raw power imbalances in the labor market that otherwise see poorer outcomes for weak or disadvantaged individuals or groups of workers.

Increasingly those who wish to understand employment-based inequalities must understand the intersections between pay rates and social security systems. Earned income tax credits (or their equivalent) mean that inequality analysis must now encompass both the work and social security spheres and cannot be understood only from an industrial relations or workplace perspective. Critics of wage supplements through the tax or welfare system make the point that such income supplements effectively subsidize low wage jobs and create positive incentives for their expansion and continuity, thus significantly shaping employment and industrial outcomes. Clearly the field of industrial relations has increasing incentive to understand the phenomena of labor market churning between low paid jobs and welfare systems, the

longitudinal dynamics of low pay, and the relationships between individual pay rates, taxes, benefits and household income (OECD, 2006).

Some international agencies would like to see policies to moderate inequality (where they see them as necessary at all) located outside national employment systems. However, employment primarily shapes social and economic standing for many citizens and is likely to do so for a long time. Having a job, a career and an identity through work are important signifiers of social status and citizenship, as well as sources of independence, dignity, pleasure and income. While this remains the case, employment remains a primary engine of inequality.

While international attention to narrowing inequality has waned in many countries, particular groups have been affected in consistent and negative ways by changes at work and I now turn to these. The effects of the engine of inequality are not randomly distributed.

LOW PAY AND INEQUALITY

The problem of low pay has been a central concern of employment analysis and inequality with general consensus that some form of regulation is necessary to ensure that the most disadvantaged citizens do not find themselves in employment relationships with unacceptable pay rates. While there are a variety of ways of defining low pay (see for example the discussion of Berstein and Hartmann (2000) in the US) the ILO conventionally define it as around 60 per cent of the median wage.

Four issues have recently received attention in relation to low pay: one is the perennial issue of the relationship between level of minimum wages and employment which I have referred to, second is the issue of labor market mobility and the opportunity for transitions out of low paid work, third is the issue of whether low pay afflicts individuals or households, and fourth is the need to take a broader look at the dimensions of 'bad' jobs beyond hourly pay, including especially the number of hours of employment, their security, work safety and the nature of working time.

For many workers, low hourly rates are compounded by limited labor mobility and a small number of paid working hours, as well as poor working-time predictability and job security. Defining low pay at the level of the household rather than the individual has important implications for individual autonomy. As Almond and Rubery have pointed out defining social justice at the level of the household rather than the individual 'undermines the case for equal pay and is indeed inimical to gender quality at a more general level ... and tantamount to putting employment rights at the level of the household rather than the individual' (1998: 676). As these writers observe such an approach is most common in countries where the remnants of the male-breadwinner wage model are strong, as in Australia. They are also resurgent at moments of political conservatism.

Low pay around the world affects particular groups of workers, with an over-representation of women, immigrant, low skilled, young and disabled workers amongst their number (Richardson, 2005). In industrialized nations, low pay especially affects workers in the service sectors most notably in the retail sector. For example, in the UK around three-quarters of the six million jobs that are low paid are in the retail and hospitality sectors (Low Pay Commission, 2005).

Low pay can be countered through strong collective bargaining or minimum wage arrangements that extend the results of collective bargains to categories of workers (Almond and Rubery, 1998). The gradual contraction of the reach of collective bargaining instruments to workers in growth sectors like the services sector has led some countries to adopt wage minima as a means of protecting the low paid.

Initiatives like the establishment of a national minimum wage in Britain in April 1999 provide interesting evidence in relation to the argument about the trade off between high minima and employment. While the initial UK minimum was set cautiously, its gradual improvement in recent years has been accompanied by strong growth in employment, including in sectors where the low paid are concentrated. Rates for the low paid have risen faster than average wages, but employment growth has continued to be robust and inflation low, allowing the Low Pay Commission to claim their interventions as a 'great success' (Low Pay Commission, 2005).

In other countries the effect of minimum wages remains rather more contentious. Low minima are, however, incontrovertibly linked to persistent employment-based inequality. For example, in the US, the federal minimum wage has remained at around US$ 5.15 per hour since 1997 (http://www.dol.gov/esa/minwage/america.htm), contributing to growth in the working poor and high levels of employment-based inequality in that country. Australia has traditionally had both relatively high minimum wage rates and until the late 1980s a relatively centralized system of industrial relations. As in Sweden, these arrangements have been associated with low dispersion in earnings and relatively more equal societies (including in relation to gender equity as I discuss below). Since the late 1980s, both Labor and conservative national Governments in Australia have facilitated a move away from centralized wage fixing towards enterprise-based bargaining, albeit in the presence of a national and regularly updated minimum wage. Widening dispersion in wage outcomes has been the result (Saunders, 2005). Since 1996, this de-centralization has been extended through a push towards individual bargaining in the presence of lowered general minimum standards. Very substantial legislative changes in March 2006 further restructure Australia's minimum wage system, encourage more individual contracts, lower minimum employment standards again, and focus a new 'Fair Pay Commission' upon the economic outcomes of minimum changes rather than fairness. The outcomes are likely to include widening wages dispersion.

GENDER INEQUALITY

Gender inequality is an international fact of employment life. Whilst its dimensions vary, women's disadvantage at work is profound around the world. Key outcomes that have been of interest to feminist analysis for decades include the questions of gender pay gaps, the gender segregation of the labor market, the sexual division of labor and the devaluation of women's work and skill (Bradley, 1998; Reskin and Padavic, 1994).

Existing data show that both gendered pay gaps and vertical and horizontal gender segregation remain entrenched with women confined to a relatively narrow range of occupations, industries and levels in many places. Unemployment rates are higher for women than men in many countries and women are disproportionately concentrated amongst the hidden unemployed (ILO, 2003). While the nature and trajectory of these indicators varies from country to country, the gender comparison remains consistently against women.

Pay inequality

Gender inequality is measured in persistent pay differentials, and scholars in the field of industrial relations have been particularly attentive to this issue (Wajcman, 2000). These gaps have narrowed in many countries but far from all, despite women's rapid increase in qualifications and experience. In countries like Britain, women at the top of the female employment hierarchy have increased the ratio of their earnings to average male incomes and this has resulted in greater gender pay equity overall, while at the same time widening inequality between women. This reflects the fact that in most countries women are concentrated in low status jobs that are poorly paid (Bruegel and Perrons, 1998).

The nature of industrial regulation is viewed as very important in explaining gender pay gaps. Where bargaining is centralized (either through legislated systems or patterns of collective bargaining), the gender pay gap is usually lower while it tends to be wider in decentralized systems where the market exercises greater effect (Gregory et al., 1989). Overall reductions in wages dispersion are generally associated with a lower gender pay gap (Blau and Kahn, 1996a). Higher levels of inequality are generally associated with the Anglo-Saxon 'firm-based voluntaristic systems' and the lowest with 'solidaristic bargaining' as in the Nordic countries (Almond and Rubery, 1998, p. 689). The kinds of decentralized fragmented systems of the US, Canada and the UK have traditionally been associated with relatively wide gender pay gaps. The weakening of Australia's centralized system of wage fixing has been associated with widening inequality in wages outcomes for workers, including in relation to gender (Heiler et al., 1999; Whitehouse, 2001). However, understanding gender pay gaps requires a more disaggregated analysis than broad averaged ratios allow, given that very different outcomes can be experienced by different groups of workers across the pay spectrum as several writers make clear (Bruegel and Perrons, 1998; Whitehouse, 2001).

Beyond the nature of pay fixing systems broadly, powerful cultures of direct and indirect discrimination, under-valuation of traditional feminized skills and cultures of traditional motherhood and femininity help explain wider gender pay gaps in places like Japan, though they are far from irrelevant in many other countries as well (Appelbaum, 2002; ILO, 2003).

Industrial systems – and wage bargaining in particular – are shaped by many factors and gender equality is not high on the list of framing ideas. However, these systems and their characteristics have important effects on gender outcomes. This has made the study of pay systems, the level at which bargaining occurs (individual, firm, industry), and the nature and pervasiveness of minimum standards of considerable interest to those trying to understand and remediate gender inequality.

Evidence suggests that the presence of properly enforced minimum wage systems have important effects on gender and broader inequality. For example, over the past 15 years economic restructuring in many Central and Eastern European countries has been associated with very significant falls in earnings for both women and men. In the case of the UK Low Pay Commission, as I have noted, most of those benefiting from sizeable increases in minimum wages are women workers (Low Pay Commission, 2005). In Australia, increases in minimum wages help explain the unchanging gender pay gap in the presence of more decentralized bargaining. Studies comparing the relative roles of anti-discrimination measures vs. centralized mechanisms suggest that anti-discrimination measures are relatively ineffective in narrowing the gender pay gap compared to the effects of more centralized systems (Kidd and Meng, 1997). This partly reflects the more generalized effects of system-wide measures like minimum wage increases compared to the weaker more partial ripples that might flow from individual, complaint-based, anti-discrimination cases.

THE CONTAGIOUS EFFECTS OF MINIMUM WAGE PROTECTION: GENDER, RACE AND ETHNICITY

Some US evidence suggests that the 'racial pay penalty' is higher for black men than black women (Bayard et al., 1999). Further that it is greater for men at the top of the employment hierarchy than towards the bottom, and increases with levels of education (ILO, 2003). However, evidence differs from country to country about the complex intersections of ethnicity, race and gender and the impact on employment outcomes (ILO, 2003).

Minimum wage protections have some important effects for groups beyond women. For example, in the UK low paid ethnic minorities have benefited from the minimum wage law, especially workers of Bangladeshi and Pakistani background, and these groups have suffered no obvious

negative employment effects (Low Pay Commission, 2005). Similarly, workers with work-limiting disabilities have been affected positively.

Participation rates and a supportive work/care regime

Participation rates of women have been increasing in most countries in the past three decades, with some exceptions; for example, in the transition economies of Europe and areas of sub-Saharan Africa (ILO, 2003).

However, participation rates vary widely from country to country reflecting in significant part the adequacy of support for workers who are also carers – most of whom are women. Jaumotte (2004) analyzes participation rates in 17 OECD countries over the period 1985–1999 controlling for education, proportion of married women, number of children and overall labor market conditions. She finds that the determinants of participation include the flexibility of working-time arrangements, the taxation of second earners, childcare subsidies, child benefits and paid parental leave. Employment-based supports like leave and employee say over working time arrangements help shape participation rates and affect under-employment and hidden unemployment. Their absence constructs gender inequality and closes down true choice for women around their labor market participation. They also have important policy significance. For example, Jaumotte calculates that providing a neutral tax environment for second earners, higher tax incentives to share paid work and an increase in public childcare spending to the highest level obtaining in the OECD would lift participation rates by an average of ten percentage points in OECD countries (2004: 12–15). This analysis is reinforced by recent analysis of work and family in a number of OECD countries (OECD, 2002, 2003, 2003, 2005). These studies show that high rates of female labor market participation and high fertility rates are possible in countries that implement effective care, leave and tax/benefit policies (OECD, 2006)

Rapid expansion in precarious forms of employment has occurred in many countries, simultaneous with women's rising participation (Fudge and Owens, 2006). In Australia and Spain – the extreme cases in the OECD – over a quarter of the workforce is now employed on casual or limited term contracts. Women (and youths) are disproportionately concentrated in these forms of employment. In Australia 42 per cent of all women work part-time (surpassed in the OECD only by the Netherlands with 61 per cent) (OECD, 2006), and these jobs are associated with high levels of insecurity with two-thirds of part-time jobs being casual (Pocock et al., 2004a). In addition, voluntary part-time employment has grown significantly and now affects many women (ILO, 2002).

In sum, over recent decades women across the world have joined men in paid work and found economic security through their employment, as well as enjoyment, social connection and a sense of contribution. However, on most measures they continue to be disadvantaged relative to men, not least in relation to their disproportionate share of unpaid work. Time use surveys in many countries record that women do twice as much domestic work as men on average, and their growing role at paid work has been met with little change on the domestic front (for Australian evidence, for example, see Baxter 2002 and for Swedish evidence see Lundberg 2002, SCB 1991, 2002). In Australia there are few signs that men are on average increasing their unpaid labor very significantly. The hours women spend on unpaid domestic work remain at around double those of men (33 hours on average a week compared to men's 17 in 1997 (ABS, 1999)). While men are spending a few minutes more a week on childcare, women are turning to the market to find relief from their overwork (buying in many services and prepared meals) or lowering their domestic standards. The decline of the breadwinner household in many countries where women's participation in paid work – as in many other countries – has increased rapidly in three decades has not been matched by the rise of a sensitive new age male partner, tea-towel in hand. This deeply inscribed sexual division of labor continues to shape women's place at work (Williams, 2000).

CONCEPTUALIZING GENDER INEQUALITY IN THE FIELD OF INDUSTRIAL RELATIONS

Not surprisingly gender inequality has been a concern of scholars in the field of industrial relations for some years. Wajcman (2000) argues that this concern and the sophistication of its analysis has been led by feminist scholars largely outside the discipline of industrial relations. However, the necessity to locate analysis of employment within the larger schema of households and social systems has now been more widely acknowledged (Hyman quoted in Hantrais and Ackers, 2005). The growing feminization of the workforce necessitates such a larger analysis, given the very different household locations of women over the life cycle and the depressing effect that having children creates upon women's earnings, especially in countries with conservative welfare states and strong traditions of maternal childcare and domesticity like Germany (see for example Lehndorff, 2006; Klammer, 2005). Women's growing presence at work disrupts the comfortable assumptions of male norms and advantage (Eveline, 1994) which lie at the centre of the workplace even if this has all too little disruptive effect upon the material effects of these norms.

At the same time, the significant contributions of women and men writing from within the discipline of industrial relations – criticizing its blind spots and 'bolt on' approach to gender analysis – have been increasing in number (Ackers, 2002; Cockburn, 1991; Dickens,1999; Forrest, 1993; Hantrais and Ackers, 2005; Pocock, 1997; Wajcman, 2000).

Several tensions are evident in research and policy around gender inequality at work: tension between legislation pursuing negative duties vs. legislation in favor of positive duties; tensions between focus on inequality vs. focus on diversity management and tension between specific direct action in response to inequality versus 'mainstreaming'. Each of these pairings is not necessarily mutually exclusive, and some like Dickens favor a multiple response including for example, state legislative action, union initiatives and voluntary employer action (Dickens, 1999). However, it is analytically helpful to consider these differences.

Negative duties versus positive action

Initially much concern around women's disadvantage was focused on discrimination against women (especially in relation to unequal pay and gender segregation by occupation). This resulted in early legal initiatives to create a 'negative duty' not to discriminate on the basis of sex. These important laws generally enable individual women to seek legal remedies to discrimination and harassment. Unfortunately these mechanisms are all too infrequently exercised by lower paid, lower status or non-unionized women.

Despite 30 years of anti-discrimination legislation in countries like the US, Australia, Britain and many others, gender inequality remains wide. Legal measures creating negative duties were always seen by many as inadequate to the systemic nature of discrimination, and so they have proved. 'An indispensable first step', as the ILO (2003) characterizes them, they have not shifted deep seated sources of inequality, and this can be said of such laws whether focused upon single grounds of discrimination as in the UK or various grounds as in Australia. Discrimination legislation has not had the effect of stamping out the raw expression of discrimination through behaviors like sexual harassment: in 1993, 54 per cent of British women reported experiencing sexual harassment at work but only 5 per cent had ever made a complaint (Institute of Employment Rights, 2003). The individual complaint-based legislative road to equality has proved slow and personally expensive for many complainants. It remains

a vital component of action but is far from an adequate basis for gender-based equality, creating strong arguments for more aggressive models of positive action.

As a result governments in several countries have taken further steps to establish 'positive duties' in relation to inequality, including regular audits of employment in larger companies (as in Australia). However, these positive duties have very variable traction in relation to systemic inequality, depending upon the nature and effect of penalties and enforcement, and upon the changing political environment. For example, Australia's experimentation with affirmative action – always confined to the public sector and larger companies – has been in hasty retreat in recent years (Summers, 2004) and was always weakly enforced through paltry penalties.

Alongside the positive actions of some governments, some unions have adopted more assertive positive measures in relation to women or other groups, including the organization of supported causes of particular groups, affirmative action positions, leadership quotas and so on, (Colgan and Ledwith, 2002). These have not been uncommon in the UK, Canada and Australia though they are less obvious in the US. Similarly, some employers have moved well ahead of their legislative obligations to create advanced paid leave, childcare, leadership development and other positive actions. They remain in the minority in most places, however, although many companies now have some kind of policy. Two-thirds of UK organizations had an equality or diversity policy targeting race and gender in 1998 (Cully et al., 1999). By the time of the 2004 Workplace Employment Relations Survey, 96 per cent of larger UK workplaces (with 100 employees or more) had an equal opportunity policy and most unionized and public sector workplaces had such policies (compared to 63 per cent of workplaces without recognized unions (Kersley et al., 2005)). Of course such policy is a long way from action (see for example Wajcman, 1998).

'Equal opportunities' policies essentially seek treatment of women on a par with men: that is, without discrimination. This analysis implicitly accepts male norms, which place women as 'disadvantaged'. Greater awareness and critique of 'male advantage' at work and the normalization of male advantage in practical terms in workplace and labor market cultures entered the literature in the 1990s, along with greater awareness about male resistance to female workers and their progress (Cockburn, 1991; Eveline, 1994). This line of analysis takes power differences, based significantly around gender, as core concerns that cannot be disrupted by individual women or by 'weak' equal opportunity measures, but require significant positive measures and the remaking of workplace norms to meet women's difference (Appelbaum, 2002). This 'sameness/difference' debate encourages a shift from discourses of 'equality with men', to new terms that recognize the different realities of women (Bacchi, 1990). This line of analysis insists that care work is work (a 'powerfully subversive' notion as Standing recognizes (2002: 268)), that understanding the sexual division of labor is vital to making sense of paid work, and that the terms of paid work need radical reform.

Enter diversity management

Conceptual differences have shaped policy proposals, ranging from the moderate anti-discrimination legislative reforms mentioned above through to recommendations for more general transformations of the terms of work, including the redistribution of unpaid labor. The more individualistic focus on discrimination was generally advanced by liberal claimants and included employers, government and some unions. Others who argued for greater systemic responses to deeply embedded gendered orders, recreated through both paid and unpaid work and industrial life, included feminists and activists within the labor movement who sought more collective responses to employment inequities rooted in class as well as gender.

More recently there have been further shifts in direction. One focus is towards analysis of equalities located around a broader range of characteristics including ethnicity, race and physical abilities – alongside gender – under the rubric of 'diversity'.

In policy terms, this line of analysis aligns itself with human resources policies and practices that recognize and celebrate diversity at work, and promulgate adaption to them as a source of profit and potential competitive advantage at the enterprise level, especially where the costs of recruitment and high labor turnover are high or labor shortages loom. Not surprisingly this individualistic approach to 'diversity' is especially promulgated by managers. Its origins lie mostly within the US (Green et al., 2005). Nonetheless the diversity literature and policy approach has grown in significance beyond the US to parts of Europe and Australia amongst other countries.

Green et al. define 'diversity' at three levels: as a mere descriptor of the workforce (diverse for example, in its gender, ethnicity, age and disability), as a particular management approach (which values a diverse workforce in order to make the best of it), and as a theoretical approach which moves away from traditional liberal or radical analysis of disadvantage defined around groups and finding equality between them, to a theoretical interest in the individual and multiple social identities (Green et al., 2005). They go on to point out that diversity policies can occur as individualizing responses, or deal with diversity at the group level within a more conventional equal opportunity approach oriented to address a broader set of social characteristics. They note that different social actors (unions, employers, government), employ discourses around diversity with more or less enthusiasm and at different levels of meaning in different countries. For example, UK unions remain skeptical about the individualized policies of managerially-led diversity initiatives that do not come to grips with deep structural inequalities around gender and class, while Danish unionists are much more comfortable with diversity management.

Essentially the diversity movement takes different forms in different hands. Union movements in many countries facing declining union density recognize that they must appeal to the diversity of the workforce, directly addressing the needs of women, immigrants, skilled and unskilled and ethnically diverse workers. Many recognize diversity as a meaningful descriptor and their policies also reflect this. At the same time in countries with declining birth rates and the prospect of labor market shortages, unionists readily mobilize notions of diversity and making the best of the workforce to secure traction for better workplace outcomes for their members, actual and potential. However, they do not support human resources policies that deliberately appeal to individual workers in order to draw them away from collective mobilization on the promise of an individual solution to discrimination or pay inequity or other sources of inequality.

The 'bottom line' arguments for diversity have developed some traction in some larger companies in particular. However, in many settings the connection between profits and fair practices is hard to measure within a time frame that has operational meaning. In some studies of motivations for good equal opportunity or 'diversity' practices, the commitment of a management 'champion' (who sees fair treatment and even positive action as simply the right thing to do) is much more significant to their adoption than any bottom line argument, and indeed in many locations managers do not make any real cost/benefit calculation about the merit of equal opportunity or diversity management before taking action (Charlesworth et al., 2005).

By contrast, another stream of gender analysis at work has focused on the embodied nature of gendered identities and the substantive and ethereal practices of 'doing gender' at work and at home, with the latter sphere significantly shaping the possibilities for both women and men in the former (Williams, 2000). This strain of analysis makes it increasingly evident that gendered realities at work cannot be understood – or changed – without careful attention to the embodied experience of the worker (increasingly selling her emotional labor and physicality – her thinness, her prettiness, her smilingness) and the conditioning possibilities of household life

along with the astonishing resilience of the gendered division of domestic labor (Bittman and Pixley, 1997). In policy terms this line of thinking continues the argument for structural and systemic responses to women's difference from men (rather than the need for mere equal treatment). It has led to a greater focus on work and family in industrial relations literature.

In many countries work and family issues draw into discussion some of the core ideas of employment relations, including the nature of working time and regulation, as well as the provision of rest and leave (OECD, 2006). New critical issues also emerge including the nature of care regimes provided by the state, employers, the family and the larger community. For example, the existence of quality, accessible, affordable childcare is a vital work support for many workers (OECD, 2005b).

Analysis of 'work and family' issues and the uneasy reconciliation of the two in many countries has spawned a significant strain of employment analysis (Harrington, 1999; Hochschild, 1997; Pocock, 2003; Williams, 2000). Some gender experts in the field of industrial relations regret the softening of a direct focus on women that this growth in work and family interest constitutes, with the category 'women' subsumed within the maternal identity. This focus is only likely to increase in strength, however, as policy regimes in industrialized countries, at least, come to grips with rising rates of female participation in paid work, a growing dependence upon the productive contribution of women and the prospect of an aging workforce and labor supply shortages (OECD, 2006). While trends like lower birth rates do not affect all countries evenly (the US being the outstanding case in the OECD area), these issues will remain significant policy concerns in many locations and are likely to continue as a significant strain of industrial research, if only because of their connection to core employment concerns like an adequate supply of suitably skilled workers. While the goal of gendered equality might remain a concern for feminist analysts in the field of industrial relations, adapting the terms of employment to better accommodate women workers and relieve their double day of paid and unpaid work, as well as the discrimination which holds them back occupationally or financially, is now more motivated by labor market factors than any devotion to alleviating gender inequality *per se*. This may not be all bad for the gender equality objective.

INEQUALITY AT WORK: WHAT HAVE WE LEARNED? WHAT MORE DO WE NEED TO KNOW?

Some important quandaries have arisen for scholars in the field. Looking ahead, inequality seems likely to remain a central fissure in the world of industrial relations, and scholars that ignore it handicap their analysis and its relevance. There are signs in some industrialized countries – at the policy level at least – that concern about unemployment and economic growth threaten to crowd out attention to policy and research about inequality, especially around gender, race and ethnicity. However, there are few signs that these categories of analysis do not, and will not, remain important lines of both empirical and theoretical significance. Indeed the feminization of paid work, and the growing and complex flows of labor across national borders, makes the pursuit of gender and ethnicity/'race' issues of growing importance in the field of industrial relations.

Inequality is also increasingly shaped by changes in employment that, for example, decollectivize employment relationships, create new large groups of informal and insecure workers, and foster increasingly porous boundaries around the wage/effort bargain and especially working time. In fact, analysis of each of these cannot proceed in a thorough way without attention to the ways in which they exacerbate and shape employment inequality and are gendered (Fagan et al., 2006).

Industrial relations began its scholarly life preoccupied with the formal regulation of work, conflict over its terms and the outcomes of that conflict – especially in relation to wages. It has traveled a great distance since. Understanding industrial life now demands a broad canvass that encompasses wages, working time, employment security, control over 'flexibility', paid and unpaid leave and the nature of the employment contract itself.

In understanding these questions, inequality remains of considerable theoretical and empirical importance, although the axes of analysis of inequality have multiplied, morphed and now often intersect in complex ways. Understanding inequality at work today demands analysis of both the top and bottom of the labor market, comparing the relative experiences of high and low paid workers and the factors that shape them – at both the national and international levels. This analysis must increasingly also embrace consideration of the embodied character of the worker including their gender, ethnicity/'race' and/or disability.

REFERENCES

ABS (1999) *How Australians Use Their Time. Cat No 4153.0.* Canberra, ABS.
Ackers, P. (2002) 'Reframing employment relations: The case for neo-pluralism.' *Industrial Relations Journal* 33 (1): 2–19.
Almond and Rubery (1998) 'The gender pay impact of recent European trends in wage determination.' *Work, Employment and Society* 12 (4): 675–93.
Annan, K. (2004) '*Secretary-General affirms commitment to achieving fair, inclusive globalization in remarks to headquarters event*,' Press Release, SG/SM/9487 , DEV/2487 New York, United Nations.
Appelbaum, E. (2002) 'Introductory Remarks: Shared work/valued care: New norms for organizing market work and unpaid care work. The Future of Work, Employment and Social Protection: The dynamics of change and the protection of workers.' P. Auer and P. Gazier. *Geneva, International Institute for Labour Studies. ILO.*
Bacchi, C. L. (1990) *Same difference: Feminism and sexual difference.* Sydney: Allen & Unwin.
Baxter, J. (2002) 'Patterns of Change and Stability in the Gender Division of Labour in Australia, 1986–1997.' *Journal of Sociology* 38 (4): 399–424.

Bayard, K., J. Hellerstein, et al. (1999) 'Why are racial and ethnic gaps larger for men than for women. Exploring the role of segregation using the new worker-establishment characteristics database.' Cambridge, MA.: National Bureau of Economic Research Working Paper No 6997.

Bernstein, J. and H. Hartmann. (2000) 'Defining and characterizing the low-wage labor market.' In K. Kaye and D. S. Nightingale (eds) *U.S. The Low-Wage Labor Market: Challenges and Opportunities for Economic Self-Sufficiency.* Department of Health and Human Services.

Bittman, M. and J. Pixley (1997) *The Double Life of the Family: Myth, Hope and Experience.* Sydney: Allen & Unwin.

Boulin, J.-Y., M. Lallement, et al. (2006) 'Decent working time in industrialized countries: issues, scopes and paradoxes. Decent working time.' In J.-Y. Boulin, M. Lallement, J. C. Messenger and F. Michon (eds) *New Trends, New Issues.* Geneva: ILO. pp. 13–40.

Bruegal, I. and D. Perrons (1998) 'Deregulation and womens' employment: The diverse experiences of women in Britain.' *Feminist Economics* 4 (1): 103–25.

Burrow, S. (2005) *'ILO decides to put Howard Government on trial over employee rights violations,'* Media Release, ACTU, 2 June 2005. Melbourne, ACTU.

Campbell, I. (2000) 'The spreading net: age and gender in the process of casualisation in Australia.' 45: 65–100.

Charlesworth, S., P. Hall, et al. (2005) *Drivers and Contexts of Equal Opportunity and Diversity Action in Australian Organizations.* Melbourne: RMIT Publishing.

Cockburn, C. (1991) *In the Way of Women. Men's Resistance to Sex Equality in Organizations.* London: Macmillan.

Colgan, F. and S. Ledwith (eds) (2002) *Gender, Diversity and Trade Unions: International Perspectives.* London: Routledge.

Cully, M., S. Woodland, et al. (1999) *Britain at Work: As Depicted by 1998 Workplace Employee Relations Survey.* London: Routledge.

Dickens, L. (1999) 'Beyond the business case: A three-pronged approach to equality action.' *Human Resource Management Journal* 9 (1): 9–19.

Elliott, L. (23 January 2003) *'Nice work if you can get it: cheif exectives quielty enrich themselves for mediocrity.'* The Guardian 23 January 2006 (www.guardian,co.uk/executives/story/0,,1692589,00. html accessed March 1 2006).

Eveline, J. (1994) 'The politics of male advantage.' *Australian Feminist Studies* 19 (Autumn): 129–54.

Fagan, C., A. Hegewisch, et al. (2006) *About Time: a new agenda for shaping working hours.* London: Trades Union Congress.

Fitzpatrick, B. (2003) *Foreword. Achieving equality at work.* In A. McColgan (ed.) *The Institute of Employment Rights.* London. pp. 1–2.

Forrest, A. (1993) *A view from outside the whale: the treatment of women and unions in industrial relations,* A. Forrest Women challenging unions: Feminism, democracy, and militancy Linda Briskin and P. McDermott. Toronto, University of Toronto Press

Freeman, R. (2005) *Labor market institutions without blinders: The debate over flexibility and labor market performance.* Working Paper 11286, NBER, April 2005.

Froud, J., S. Johal, et al. (2006) *Financialisation and strategy: Narrative and numbers.* London: Routledge.

Ghai, D. (2002) *Decent Work: Concepts, Models and Indicators.* Geneva: ILO.

Green, A.-M., G. Kirton, et al. (2005) 'Trade union perspectives on diversity management: A comparison of the UK and Denmark.' *European Journal of Industrial Relations* 11 (2): 179–86.

Hantrais, L. and P. Ackers (2005) 'Women's choices in Europe: striking the work-life balance.' *European Journal of Industrial Relations* 11 (2): 197–212.

Harrington, M. (1999) *Care and Equality. Inventing a New Family Politics.* New York: Alfred K. Knopf.

Heiler, K., B. Asovska, et al. (1999) 'Good and bad bargaining for women: Do unions make a difference?' *Labour & Industry* 10 (2): 101–28.

Hochschild, A. (1997) *The Time Bind. When Work Becomes Home and Home Becomes Wor.* New York: Metropolitan Books.

ILO (1999) *Report of the Director-General: Decent Work, 87th Session,* Geneva, June 1999. Geneva: ILO.

ILO (2002) *Key Indicators of the Labour Market 2001–2002.* Geneva: ILO.

ILO (2003) *Time for Equality at Work.* Geneva: ILO.

ILO (2004) *Fair Globalization: Creating Opportunities for All.* Geneva: ILO.

IMF (2003) *World Economic Outlook.* Washington, DC: IMF.

Institute of Employment Rights (2003) *Federation News.* London: Institute of Employment Rights.

Isaac, J. and R. D. Lansbury (eds) (2005)*Labour Market Deregulation. Rewriting the Rules.* Sydney: Federation Press.

Jaumotte, F. (2004) *Female Labour Force Participation: Past Trends and Main Determinants in OECD Countries.* Geneva: OECD Economics Department. p. 10.

Kersley, B., C. Alpin, et al. (2005) *Inside the Workplace: First Findings from the 2004 Workplace Employment Relations Survey (WERS 2004)*. London: Routledge.

Kidd, M. P. and Xin Meng (1997) 'Trends in the Australian gender wage differential over the 1980s: some evidence on the effectiveness of legislative reform.' *The Australian Economic Record* 30 (1): 31–44.

Low Pay Commission (2005) *National Minimum Wage, Low Pay Commission Report*. London: Low Pay Commission.

Lundberg, U. (2002) *Has the Total Workload of Swedish Men and Women Become More Equal during the Last Ten Years?* Stockholm: National Institute for Working Life.

Messenger, J. C. (ed.) (2004) *Working Time and Workers' Preferences in Industrialized Countries*. London: Routledge.

National Labor Committee and China Labor Watch (February 2006) *Workers in China: Facing an Olympian Struggle to Survive*. New York: China Labor Watch.

Ocampo, J. A. (2002) 'Rethinking the development agenda.' *Cambridge Journal of Economics*, 26 (3): 393–407.

OECD (2002) *Employment outlook*. Paris: OECD.

Pocock, B. (1997) 'Gender and Australian industrial relations theory and research practice', *Labour & Industry* 8 (1): 1–20.

Pocock, B. (2003) *The Work/Life Collison*. Sydney: Federation Press.

Pocock, B., J. Buchanan, et al. (2004a) *Securing Quality Employment: Policy Options for Casual and Part-time Workers in Australia*. Sydney: Chifley Foundation.

Pocock, B., R. Prosser, et al. (2004b) *Only A Casual... How Casual Work Affects Employees, Households and Communities in Australia*. Adelaide: Labour Studies, University of Adelaide.

Padavic, I. and Reskin, B. (2002) *Women and Men at Work*. Sage: London.

Richardson, S. (2005) *Are Low Wage Jobs for Life? Labour Market Deregulation. Rewriting the Rules*. Sydney: Federation Press. pp. 149–81.

Rodgers, J. and J. Rubery (2003) 'Perspectives: the minimum wage as a tool to combat discrimination and promote equality.' *International Labour Review* 142 (4): 543–59.

Rubery, J. (1998) *Part-time Work. A Threat to Labour Standards? Part-time Prospects*. J. O'Reilly and C. Fagan. London, Routledge: 137–55.

Rubery, J. (2002) 'Gender mainstreaming and gender equality in the EU: the impact of the EU employment strategy.' *Industrial Relations Journal* 33 (5): 500–22.

Rubery, J. (2004) '*The Dynamics of National Social Economic Models and the Lifecycle*.' Unpublished paper presented at 'Quality Part-time Work' Seminar, CASR, RMIT, Melbourne, June 2004.

Saunders, P. (2005) 'Reviewing recent trends in wage income inequality in Australia. Labour market deregulation. Rewriting the rules.' J. Isaac and R. D. Lansbury. *Sydney, Federation Press*: 68–89.

SCB (Statistics Sweden) (1991) *The Time Use Study*. Stockholm: Statistics Sweden.

SCB (Statistics Sweden) (2002) *The Time Use Study*. Stockholm: Statistics Sweden.

Schmid, G. (1995) 'A New Conribution to Labour Market Policy: A Contribution to the Current Debate on Efficient Employment Policies.' *Economic and Industrial Democracy* 16 (?): 429–56.

Sennett, R. (1998) *The Corrosion of Character. The Personal Consequences of Work in the New Capitalism*. New York: W.W. Norton and Company.

Shields, J. (2005) 'Setting the double standard: Chief executive pay the BCA way.' *Journal of Australian Political Economy* 56 (December): 299–324.

Standing, G. (1999) *Global Labour Flexibility: Seeking Distributive Justice*. London: MacMillan.

Standing, G. (2002) *Beyond Paternalism: Basic Security as Equality*. New York: Verso.

Statement by a Group of 151 Australian Industrial Relations, L. M. A. L. A. (2005) Research evidence about the effects of the 'Work Choices' Bill. A submission to the Inquiry into the Workplace Relations Amendment (Work Choices) Bill 2005, Unpublished.

Summers, A. (2004) *An End of Equality. Prospects for a Feminist Agenda?* Adelaide: University of Adelaide.

United Nations (2005) *Report on the World Social Situation 2005: the Inequality Predicament*. New York: United Nations.

Wajcman, J. (1998) *Managing like a man*. St. Leonards: Allen and Unwin.

Wajcman, J. (2000) 'Feminism facing industrial relations in Britain,' *British Journal of Industrial Relations* 38 (2): 183–204.

Whitehouse, G. (2001) 'Recent trends in pay equity: Beyond the aggregate statistics.' *Journal of Industrial Relations* 43 (1): 66–78.

Wilkinson, R. G. (2005) *The Impact of Inequality*. New York: New Press.

Williams, J. (2000) *Unbending gender. Why family and work conflict and what to do about it*. New York: OUP.

31

Conflict at Work

Gregor Gall and Robert Hebdon

INTRODUCTION

Just as 'industrial relations' is not the most appropriate term to encapsulate work relations in employment (Blyton and Turnbull, 1994), neither is 'industrial conflict' the most appropriate term to encapsulate both conflict at work and in employment.[1] Whilst 'industrial relations' has been superseded by the term 'employment relations', the term 'conflict at work' is superior to 'industrial conflict' because, *inter alia*, it would be wrong to imply conflict in employment is confined to industry, that is, workplaces of production and distribution. The term 'conflict at work' (Edwards, 1986) is thus able to generically encapsulate conflict both within employment and employment relations, and regardless of whether the conflict is to be found in agriculture, industry, manufacturing or the (public and private) service sectors and regardless whether it concerns managers, supervisors or blue-collar (manual), white-collar (non-manual), skilled, semi- or unskilled workers. Consequently, for industrialized or post-industrialized societies, the means of the provision of services and the exchange of goods and services are also encapsulated, along

with the traditionally understood means of production and distribution of goods, within the term 'conflict at work'. So the location of 'conflict at work' concerns where work is spatially performed, the social relations that surround work and those social relations that work gives rise to.

This more carefully framed definition would have been required even at the height of industrialization many decades ago because of the hitherto relative importance of agriculture and the private and state service sectors. Moreover, and following from this move away from the spatially-bounded implication of 'industrial conflict' to 'industry', another benefit of a temporal nature is evident, namely, that with the de-industrialization of western economies, the majority of employment in these economies is now service sector-based. However, several other benefits also accrue from deploying the term 'conflict at work' rather than 'industrial conflict'. Thus, it should not be assumed that conflict (at work) is necessarily predicated on collective conflict, primarily organized through trade unionism. Neither should it be assumed that societies which currently proclaim like China, or formerly proclaimed like the Soviet Union, to be socialist or communist – thus having theoretically abolished the historical antagonism between capital and labor – do not and did not, nonetheless, experience conflict at work. For some theorists, this confirmed the symmetry of capitalism with socialism or communism, while for other theorists, it confirmed that the 'actually existing socialism' was not socialist at all but a form of state capitalism.

The purpose of this chapter is to examine the definition, theory, basis, context, historical and contemporary trends and possible future direction of conflict at work. Thus, this chapter is concerned with not just strikes but the wider array of conflict at work as well as its scale, character and causation. Our underlying theoretical premise is that conflict, whatever its source, is a central, ever-present and ongoing dynamic of contemporary work and employment where conflict is both a 'means' and an 'end' in a cycle of perpetual motion. Thus, conflict at work should be viewed in a holistic, grounded manner, where a complex social relationship exists between latent and manifest conflict. A number of points, *inter alia*, flow from this.

One is that conflict at work is conventionally seen as an outcome of the interaction of two (or more) parties in the workplace. But it is not simply an outcome of employment or work relations. Conflict at work does not just have a 'process' by which the outcome is arrived at for conflict is also a process in itself reflecting subterranean dynamics. This situation is derived from the primary, underlying source of conflict, namely, differing or incompatible interests of different social groups, being a fundamental and quintessential component of work and employment relations. It is also because conflict, particularly of the more collective and conscious types, is an example of an act of agency whereby a particular actor does not just seek to indicate that there is conflict but in so doing change the balance of power between itself and the other party. So conflict is both reflective and creative, and of a systemic character.

A second point flows from the net effect of contemporary contextual changes.

The strengthening of management power, for example as a result of increasing capital mobility and union disorganization, has meant that management is able to bear down more on labor to extract more from it. In tandem, competitive globalization over the last few decades has increased tensions in the workplace and so the potential for conflict because workers are working harder for the same or less economic reward than before. A third is that the individualization of risk and workplace relations through the individualization of reward has led to a shift from more collective to more individualized conflict. A further point is that the relative, contemporary decline in strike activity is indicative of what we term 'method displacement', such that the inability to express grievances and discontent through strikes finds expression through other alternative or covert means. A final illustrative point here is that conflict at work is defined not just as open struggle or clashes between workers and employers but as also involving more hidden tensions and frictions, taking place between different and differing social groups. Thus, we pursue a radical, sociological line of enquiry in order to concentrate on issues of power resources, authority relations and interests of social groups.

DEFINING THE PARAMETERS OF CONFLICT AT WORK

Industrial relations scholars have agreed on the need for a wide definition of industrial conflict. When 'industrial conflict' was used as the common term some 20 or more years ago, the expressions of industrial conflict were taken to be 'as unlimited as the ingenuity of man' (Kerr, 1964), being a 'multifaceted phenomenon which was conceptually defined in broad terms to include such events as grievances, job actions, sabotage, and turnover' (Feuille and Wheeler, 1981: 290, see also Kornhauser, 1954). Fox (1966: 8) also adopted a broad definition that included individual expressions of conflict he labeled as 'unorganized conflict: ... labour turnover,

absenteeism, poor time-keeping and discipline, and negative attitudes'. Meanwhile,
Wheeler (1985: 4) offered three types of
collective expressions of industrial conflict
based on union organizing, striking and other
forms of industrial action.

In line with the direction of this thinking,
we suggest a holistic and comprehensive
definition of the parameters of conflict at work
in terms of 'conflict over what?', 'between
who?' and 'by what means?' The 'conflict
over what?' concerns differing (for example,
opposing, contradictory and incompatible)
interests over the material terms of the
wage-effort bargain (for instance, wages
and conditions of work and employment)
as well as clashes over values and ideologies, the exercise of managerial power
and the determination of organizational
goals. The 'conflict between who?' concerns different social groups within the
workforce, primarily arranged around the
subordinate-superordinate axis (for example,
worker/supervisor, worker/manager, supervi-
sor/manager). The 'conflict by what means?'
concerns any means chosen or used to
give expression to the conflict of interests.
Consequently, our boundary definition is
necessarily as wide as possible and includes
all forms of collective or organized conflict
and individual or unorganized actions.

Although conflict at work is commonly
perceived as conflict between workers and
employers or managers, there has been very
little focus on employer action being seen as a
form of conflict (for example, over industrial
accidents and injuries) or of employers
engaging pro-actively in conflict and taking
'industrial action'. This is derived from the
belief that the onus is on the wronged party
to take corrective action, otherwise there is no
evidence of conflict; that the power imbalance
at work means that it is only workers that
are compelled to take action; and that what
employers or managers do *vis-à-vis* coercion
and control of workers is legitimate and
part of a 'natural order'. If any or all of
these are stripped away, then there is ample
room to consider an array of managerial
actions as actions of conflict. These range

from threats and acts of dismissal, sacking,
victimization, suspension and lock-outs of
workers to closures, outsourcing, subcontracting as well as speed-ups, disciplinaries and
unsafe working conditions (see, for example,
Bronfenbrenner, 2000; Feuille and Wheeler,
1981; Hyman, 1980). What we are suggesting
here is two-fold: management actions in
employment relations should not just be seen
as the likely cause of conflict with workers
but these actions should be also seen as
expressions of management interests and thus
a fundamental, underlying conflict of interest
within the employment relationship between
management and workers. Thus, management
and management actions are also, in our
definitional terms, part and parcel of conflict
at work.

Moreover, conflict at work is normally
thought of as conflict between employers and
their agents (management or supervisors),
on the one hand, and employees or workers
and their agents (trade unions and other
representatives) on the other hand. And whilst
this is in the main correct, this should not
preclude recognition that conflict at work
can take place between different sections of
management and between different sections
of employees (Fox, 1971). Such conflict may
reflect occupational, job or status boundaries,
but even here management *per se* is still an
important actor because of the role it plays in
creating and influencing these boundaries as
well as mediating, resolving or subduing the
conflict. Conflict at work within or between
groups of workers or managers may not *prima
facie* seem to involve senior management.
However, senior management is implicitly
involved because either it has contributed to
the conflict by setting out the parameters in
which it exists or because it has the choice to
exercise the power of remedy.

Before moving on, it is important to
note that, despite general agreement on a
broader definition of conflict, research has
in practice focused on single expressions of
the variety of the means of conflict at any
one time (Feuille and Wheeler, 1981: 290;
Hyman, 1982). This narrowness of focus has
ignored the inter-linkages between different

forms of expressions and omitted to consider the impact of important processes, such as method displacement, thus causing errors of calculation of extant conflict in empirical work.

THE THEORIZING OF CONFLICT AT WORK

The setting out of the parameters or boundaries of conflict is essential to, but not synonymous with, defining conceptually the causation and dynamics of conflict at work. Thus, we briefly review the contending theoretical perspectives-but first we note that conflict at work can be conceived in a 'common sense', almost atheoretical, way. Here, the basis of conflict of interest thus concerns workers wanting to work less (intensively or extensively) for more pay and better terms of employment while employers want to pay less in remuneration for more intensive or extensive work. This is conventionally termed the 'wage-effort bargain'. Another type of 'common sense' explanation is that work requires social organization such as authority and discipline being established, whereby those who conceive of and direct are managers and those who execute are workers. This mere 'fact' and any accompanying social status and remuneration differentiation are believed to provide the basis for potential conflict along the manager–worker axis. However, no grander generalizations about wider social structuration are necessarily derived from these insights.

Extant conflict theories and theories of conflict at work may be distinguished along several dimensions. Two aspects of particular importance for this enquiry are the source and inevitability of conflict at work. The unitarist perspective explains conflict at work as derived from dysfunctionality, where order and harmony are the natural state of affairs. Conflict is deviancy and thus illegitimate and unproductive. Consequently, most conflict is derived from workers, in particular individual and pathological deviants and malcontents, be it over the nature of the subordinate–supervisor relationship, or material rewards and other conditions of employment. Where conflict is sometimes derived from management, it is the result of 'bad' or unenlightened management practices (Mayo, 1933; Taylor, 1911). This unitarist perspective denies the existence of an inherent conflict of interest between management and labor (see, for example, Godard, 1994). Thus, as long as sound management practices and policies are followed, conflict is neither necessary nor inevitable.

Although always a strain in management thought, the unitarist perspective has now come to dominate the managerialist paradigm over the last 20 years in the form of human resource management (HRM), albeit it has harder and softer versions where the softer version has pragmatic pluralist tinges. All other frames of references and perspectives such as pluralism, radicalism, materialism and Marxism recognize that conflict at work is a socialized process involving an array of social groups and their different and sometimes conflicting interests (see, for example, Jackson, 1991). However, thereafter this elementary degree of consensus ends.

A radical or materialist analysis focuses upon such conflict of interests but locates the dynamics of conflict in two specific arenas (Edwards, 1986). The first concerns a conflict over the distribution of an organization's resources between workers and employers or managers. The second concerns employers seeking to turn purchased labor time into (useful) labor power which requires managerial direction and control at the same time as providing for opportunities for insubordination and resistance. Meanwhile, a Marxist perspective would broadly concur with both the former but stress the collective nature of the workplace struggle between workers and employers with this merely being a microcosm of a wider, societal class struggle between the working class and the employing class (see, for example, Hyman, 1975). Therefore, for Marxists, the central dynamic revolves around the exploitation of workers or wage labor by the capitalist in the capitalist's search for generating surplus value (for instance, profit) in a competitive regime of accumulation. And here, the strike represents an important example of workers taking some control over their working lives, which may in turn build workers' own fighting capacity in terms of their class consciousness and mobilizing capability.

For a pluralist, albeit itself a broad school of thought, conflict at work can take place along a multiplicity of axes and between a multiplicity of groups, of which none are inherently more significant than others. Conflict at work, to a pluralist, is an indication of interchange, exchange and dialogue which can be healthy, functional and productive so long as it does not become endemic, widespread or embedded. Moreover, means of institutionalizing, and thus ameliorating, conflict into acceptable forms and levels are deemed a prerequisite for responsible management.

Whatever perspective is adopted in studying conflict at work (other than unitarism),[2] to one degree or another, all do not make the presence of overt, manifest symptoms of conflict at work synonymous with the existence of conflict at work *per se*. In other words, the articulation and expression of conflict at work is not the *sine qua non* for conflict itself because conflict of interest between groups can exist without manifest and deliberate attempts to pursue those interests. Of course, the point should not be pushed so far that the complete absence of expressed conflict would not then raise questions about the existence of conflict *per se*. However, the primary point here is that for manifest conflict, such as resistance to take place, requires the construction and mobilization of social agency, and attendant means and tools, for its expression. Thus, strikes, for example, are a symptom of conflict, not the cause of conflict.

This discussion has focused attention on power and authority relations (for a wider discussion, see Offe and Wiesenthal, 1985). For employers and management, these issues are less problematic in two senses. First, they have the means at their disposal to pursue their interests through owning and controlling the means of production, distribution and

exchange. Second, they normally have a legitimate right to do so as a result of the ideology of capitalism, the rights of private property and their experience and expertise. The latter are normally subsumed within the concept of the 'managerial prerogative'. However, for workers and employees not only must they construct a counter-authority and power resource which do not ordinarily exist, but they must do so in addition to their requirement to work. Therefore, it is misguided to interpret the absence of significant levels of strikes as evidence of the lack of conflict or evidence of harmony at work.

Depending on the opportunities for acting and the power resources available to each group, conflict of interests will be expressed in different ways and in different degrees at different points in time and space. Quite apart from stressing the contingent nature to their expression, this perspective suggests that conflict can be managed but not abolished within the existing social structuration of society and that management is not so omnipotent, omnicompetent, omniscient and omnipresent as to be able to abolish or prevent conflict. Thus, we contend that sophisticated HRM practices cannot end the conflict of interests at work, particularly of that between workers and managers, because of the maintenance of differing material interests. We also thus contend that 'method displacement' exists such that if workers are less able to strike, then there is likely to be, all other things being equal, a relative growth in the expression of grievance by other means. Consequently, later in this chapter we examine both semi-collective and individualized expressions of conflict.

THE CONTEXT OF CONFLICT

It is neither particularly contentious nor insightful to recognize that conflict is not the only feature of work and employment relations. A basic perspective would recognize that conflict has it anti-thesis, namely, co-operation. The foundation of co-operation is normally acknowledged to be common or compatible interests, particularly between employers and workers. The perceived need for both employers and workers to work together in pursuit of common or compatible goals is most readily observed in the belief that profitable operations are the best guarantor of security of employment. However, a fuller understanding of the context of conflict demands that we appreciate that co-operation is not the simple, zero sum anti-thesis of conflict. Both not only exist alongside each other in different measures and forms at any one point in time, but they also interact with each other to synthetically produce an array of outcomes (which Marxists, for example, conceptualize as a dialectical relationship between the two elements). One such outcome is termed 'accommodation', whereby neither party finds itself in agreement with the other's interests or goals but is compelled by the balance of power to accept, in part, the existence and pursuit of each others' interests. Conflict and co-operation are not just outcomes derived from the struggle by workers and employers to generate consent and commitment for their interests but they are also emblematic of attempts by management and workers to determine and resist each others' terms for wage-labor. Thus, workers with varying degrees of power may be subject to 'responsible autonomy' or 'direct control' (Friedman, 1977).

The ability to collectively mobilize to express conflict of interest requires a sequential process which involves the formation of interest definition, the construction of collective organization, analyzing the costs and benefits of the action and identifying the opportunity to act (Kelly, 1998). Paying attention to the latter components is particularly useful in recognizing that not all groups feel in a position to express their conflict of interest because of their 'poor' labor scarcity and 'poor' strategic work position. Indeed, difficulties in these areas may impede the formation of interest definition and construction of collective organization. Nonetheless, such a perspective is not entirely sufficient to explain the presence or absence of manifest expressions of conflict at work. Thus, the impact of the levels of workers' consciousness (sectional, class-for-itself) and ideologies (radical militancy, co-operative mutual-gains) held within labor movements must also be borne in mind (Gall, 1999b).

Conflict at work is more commonly concerned with the subordinate group negotiating the terms of its subordination with the superordinate group rather than seeking to end the subordination itself and the existence of the superordinate group (Edwards, 1986). This is because structures of power and ideology provide defenses for the *status quo*. Put another way, consent is bargained over and mixes with the use of commitment and coercion. Therefore, we can also say that order and control are also negotiated over. So, for example, unions seek to better the terms of exploitation or wage-labor rather than abolish the exploitation or wage-labor itself. For some Marxists, this indicates that trade unions are merely reformist organizations without the potential for revolutionary purposes.

TYPES AND FORMS OF CONFLICT AT WORK

Conventionally, conflict at work has been understood by way of a number of simple dichotomies: latent (hidden, covert)/manifest (open, overt), organized/unorganized and individualized/collectivized (Edwards, 1986; Hyman, 1977; Kornhauser, 1954). The latent/manifest dichotomy indicates that conflict is ever present in terms of interests and attitudes but is not always acted upon. When it becomes acted upon, through behavior, it becomes more visible. Here manifest instances of conflict at work are normative actions in the senses that the actions are reactions against the norms of employers and their managers and that the actions display the components of a different and contrasting set of norms. 'Unorganized' conflict has traditionally been used to denote individual means of withdrawing physically or mentally from the work situation while organized conflict has been used to denote collective conflict which seeks to change the existing situation without withdrawal. Another dichotomy is that the articulation of conflict inherently concerns *expressing* discontent or grievance. However, articulation may not necessarily also seek *resolution* of those causes. Nonetheless, both are deliberate, conscious human actions.

In addition to these elementary dichotomies, there are a number of other ways of classifying the different types of conflict at work. One is to group the types of conflict on a horizontal axis ranging from individual to semi-collective to collective conflict, where each of these clusters are viewed as poles of attraction for the purposes of locating cases of conflict. The function of this type of classification is to understand the underlying nature and character of the example of conflict without becoming fixated on the form of conflict. In other words, it is to try to comprehend elements of the social group dynamics involved, the means by which different actors pursue their interests as well as how one example relates to another. Under this classification, one could observe that what appears at first sight as an individual conflict between a worker and management may be symptomatic of a wider collective conflict between workers and management, because the individual is taking a *de jure* or *de facto* test case against management for other workers. This example could indicate a semi-collective or collective dimension. In other words, some actions have both individualized and collectivized components (see, for example, Dowding et al., 2000; Kelly, 1998; Morill et al., 2003). However, this type of simple continuum cannot shed much light on the nature and context of the actors' interests. For example, it is of little help in understanding why the conflict took a particular form, namely, individual, semi-collective or collective. Another way to view conflict at work is to regard all types of conflict as falling under two generic categories, namely, conflict over substantive and procedural outcomes. 'Substantive'

conflict concerns the outcomes of the way people are treated at work *vis-à-vis*, for example, pay rises while 'procedural' conflict concerns the way in which substantive outcomes are decided. An example would be the presence or absence of collective bargaining, as well as the nature of collective bargaining, over pay.

Collective expressions of conflict at work necessarily involve conscious and directed human action and interaction because the expressions of conflict are neither accidental nor inevitable. Two or more persons are required to act in concert for the action to become collective and this necessarily requires a degree of heightened cognitive awareness concerning identification of the grievance, recognition of a commonality of interests and attribution to another party. This then provides the basis for discussion, agreement and planning on the taking of an action. Consequently, one is able to understand why the majority of collective actions are organized by unionized workers or through trade unions, albeit the desire by workers to pursue their interests as workers may lead to unions being formed. Unions and their workplace organizations then represent a semi-permanent resource for workers who want, or may wish, to pursue their interests. The resource is not just a simple organizational one of connecting individual workers to each other for trade unionism also represents behavioral or attitudinal resources conducive to collectively prosecuting their interests inside the workplace. For this reason, the location of manifest collective conflict reflects the location of trade unionism, which is now increasingly a public sector phenomenon. However, trade unions are not the only organizations representing workers for non-governmental organizations like faith groups, secular community organizations and political parties can also assist workers in these regards. Nonetheless, it can be understood that the decline in unionization densities has significant implications for the ability of workers to express their discontent and grievances in a collective and purposeful manner.

'INDUSTRIAL' ACTION

Although the strike has traditionally constituted the dominant focus of industrial relations' study of conflict, the strike is far from the only means by which discontent can be collectively expressed. Traditionally, in Western societies, the term 'industrial action' has been used to describe conscious, proactive collective mobilizations of workers, primarily through unions, which involve not just strikes, but also 'industrial action short of a strike' comprising work-to-rules, go-slows and overtime bans. Work-to-rules, or the withdrawal of goodwill, involve only doing particular work or working in a certain way as laid down in a job specification, organizational rules or employment contract. Employing organizations commonly work more efficiently and effectively when workers do what is operationally required rather than what is laid down in their rules and regulations. This goodwill to do what is required is, thus, the 'oil' that lubricates the 'wheels'. Go-slows involve the restricting of the work rate from that which is commonly regarded by workers and management as a 'normal' (and higher) rate. Overtime bans involve the withdrawal of the willingness to work either compulsory or voluntary overtime and are predicated on the belief that working overtime is necessary to sustain the employing organization in meeting its goals and objectives. The former type of industrial action – work-to-rules, go-slows – concerns the intensity of work while the latter – overtime bans – concerns the extensity of work.

In addition to these well-known examples of industrial action, there are a host of lesser known forms ranging from sabotage, vandalism, fiddles, pilfering, output restriction, so-called 'restrictive practices', soldiering, absenteeism, turnover, grievance taking to individual and collective law suits and political (extra-workplace) actions (see, for example, Edwards and Scullion, 1982). These acts of resistance can be carried out by individuals and collectives and in individual, semi-collective and collective ways as laid out above. Moreover, these lesser known acts

and expressions of conflict vary according to their social visibility (for example, the degrees to which the acts are intended to be visible and the participant's identities known to authorities) and their outcome (for example, the potential for covert action to lead to wider, overt conflict) (Morill et al., 2003: 399).

Theft and sabotage are the most commonly studied forms of covert conflict which concern the 'subversion of organizational technologies and resources' (Morill et al., 2003: 394, see also Fortado, 2001; Robinson and Bennett, 1995). Studies have reported a wide array of means: mental health workers defacing and debilitating property in mental wards to 'protest' against managerial practices (Spector, 1975), construction workers breaking tools on construction sites to express their discontent with their working conditions (Tucker, 1993), and civil servants in public bureaucracies who subvert various policies (Brehm and Gates, 1997; Morill et al., 2003: 395). More recently, some of these types of more informal acts of 'deviancy' have been termed 'organizational misbehavior' (Ackroyd and Thompson, 1999; Thompson and Ackroyd, 1995).

However, it should not be assumed that all instances of resistance by workers are in direct and clear contradiction of management and employer's instructions or interests for in some instances, management and employers are complicit in these *prima facie* cases of conflict. This situation arises because it may be in the interests of management/employer to restrict output or work due to market or political conditions. More commonly, management and employers will tolerate expressions of worker conflict as a form of 'letting off steam' to prevent further or greater conflagration as well as to keep the wheels of 'industry' turning whereby clamping down on this right would, in fact, lead to conflagration. Furthermore, not all instances of absenteeism and turnover reflect conflict for some may be 'genuine', and absenteeism and turnover/quitting rates cannot be taken as straightforward measures because they are influenced by the opportunity to be absent and quit depending on organizational policy, labor market conditions and the social wage. But by the same token, it would be mistaken to conceptualize conflict as only existing where it finds some level of conscious expression by workers. Thus, for example, occupational ill-health and accidents at work of workers may indicate conflicting interests at work between workers and employers (Nichols, 1997).

DYNAMICS OF CONFLICT

The literature on the causes, frequency and dynamics of strikes on national, inter- and trans-national bases, let alone that on 'industrial' action and conflict, is sufficiently large and complex as to defy summary here. Suffice it to say, however, that considerable controversy has raged in this decades-old debate on this field of study, and this has often centered upon the consequences of the use of different levels or units of analysis as well as competing theories or hypotheses. For example, and particularly with regard to strikes, theoretical analysis has focused, *inter alia*, on the 'business cycle', the rise and fall of corporatism, institutionalization and paradigm shifts (for example, Fordism/post-Fordism, industrialism/post-industrialism) while determinant analysis has considered the influence of different economic conditions like unemployment or inflation, and workforce and economic sector compositions. A number of authors like Edwards and Hyman (1994), Hyman (1977), Jackson (1987, 1991) and Kelly (1998) have provided overviews of the salient debates.

Given that analysis of overt collective conflict, that is strikes, has tended to be the traditional focus of attention, it is also worth noting analysis of the dynamics of covert conflict has focused on the individual and organizational levels. With the former, the primary factors are perceived loss of control over the regulation of work and the wage-effort bargain (see Morill et al., 2003: 402), while for the latter attention has focused on 'substitution' and 'complementarity' hypotheses (Morill et al., 2003; Sapsford and Turnbull, 1994). The substitution hypothesis predicts

formal structures that facilitate 'voice' will reduce covert conflict and the complementarity hypothesis predicts that formally enabling voice is associated with 'corresponding increases in other forms of ... [submerged] conflict' (Sapsford and Turnbull, 1994: 250). Empirical research reveals support for the substitution hypothesis (Hebdon and Stern, 1998; Sapsford and Turnbull, 1994). And since much of the research that has analyzed more than one form of conflict at a time has either implicitly or explicitly employed the tradeoff or substitution hypothesis, it is worth recognizing that an apparent assumption is the notion that the total amount of conflict is fixed. But unless the amount of conflict is assumed to be constant, the tradeoff hypothesis cannot be rigorously tested. Hebdon (2005) has called this into serious question. For example, a decrease in strikes, that is associated with an increase in absenteeism, may be due to a change in total conflict that has unequal effects on strikes and absenteeism.

REGULATION OF CONFLICT

Conflict at work is regulated for a number of economic, political and social reasons and in a number of different ways (legal, voluntary, institutional, social, ideological). For example, collective expressions of conflict at work are commonly believed by mainstream commentators to be disruptive to economic efficiency and social cohesion at organizational and societal levels. If the disruption is viewed as unwarranted or disproportionate then state regulation is exercised. Thus, conflict at work can be 'political' even where there is not a party of organized labor. At the micro-level, such collective mobilizations are also regulated because of the challenges potentially posed to the managerial prerogative. That said, regimes of regulation are extremely varied. For example, arbitration is compulsory in some sectors like the US postal service while in Germany strikes are unlawful within the duration of a collective bargaining contract and works councils cannot call strikes.

Systems of macro-regulation (and attendant collective bargaining structures) are regarded as important determinants of the manner in which conflict at work is expressed in both intended and unintended ways. Thus, the institutionalization of conflict may channel it at certain times, but, as in contemporary Burma, China, Indonesia and South Korea, it may compel workers to step outside its confines by rioting where the strike option is curtailed.

STRIKES

The preoccupation of industrial relations scholars with strikes is well known (Feuille and Wheeler, 1981). This tendency to overly concentrate on the more visible expressions of conflict in both theory and empirical work is not limited to the field of industrial relations (see, for example, political science and social movement studies (Morill et al., 2003: 392)). The concentration on strikes as the 'premier' form of collective 'industrial action' arises for a number of reasons. Compared to the overtime ban or work-to-rule, strikes are regarded as being relatively more open, visible and important, in turn, making them more worthy of measurement and more measurable. The sense of importance is derived from the strike aiming to stop rather than just hinder work and from presenting a clear challenge to the managerial prerogative. So they are regarded as representing the starkest form of industrial conflict. Consequently, some like Olson (1988) attributed the narrow focus on strikes to the ease of obtaining data and the difficulty of researching other conflict expressions. However, it should be noted that the preoccupation of scholars with such a visible and measurable conflict expression results from the undeveloped state of conflict theory, particularly the lack of comprehensive frameworks of workplace conflict which take into account less visible expressions and their inter-relationships (Hebdon, 2005).

A strike is conventionally defined as a collective withdrawal of the willingness to work. Two basic types can be identified

in terms of who is the target of leverage. The first, the economic strike, is an attempt to exert leverage over an employer (or group of employers acting in concert through employers' federations) to better the terms and conditions of employment within the immediate workplace and as determined by the contract of employment. This type of strike is the most common in Anglo-Saxon countries. This does not mean that the economic strike does not and cannot have a political dimension. Every economic strike challenges, albeit it momentarily, the prevailing micro-political workplace order. By contrast, large or widespread economic strikes by many workers can present a political threat to employer control or government economic policy (particularly where the government is the *de facto* employer in the state or public sector).

The second, the political strike, is an attempt to exert leverage over an extra-workplace actor, like the government or a state regulatory body, and usually on an extra-workplace issue. In this attempt, the workers seek to change the course of behavior of the external actor which in due course is believed will either change, regulate or constrain the behavior of the employer over determining the terms and conditions of employment. For example, workers may strike to challenge a piece of employment law or change an element of the social wage. This type of strike is necessarily a multi-employer strike and mass strike. Such strikes, in the form of general strike, are relatively common in a number of southern European countries like Greece, Italy, Portugal and Spain. Here, there is some sense of an economic connection to the workplace and the workers seek to use the economic dislocation and disruption emanating from their strike as the means of political leverage. A more overtly political strike concerns those which attempt to influence the course of behavior of the external actor such a government on an issue without regard to trying to exert influence over employers. Examples concern attempts by pro-democracy movements to remove authoritarian governments or dictatorships as in Brazil (1987), Indonesia (1998), Poland (1980–2), South Africa (late 1980s), South Korea (1987, 1997) and the Ukraine (2004–5). As the former and latter lists of countries suggest, the political strike is not common in the Anglo-Saxon countries. However, this does not mean that the economic strike is not also common in non-Anglo-Saxon countries. The salient point here is that strikes can have different meanings and representations vis-à-vis demands, mobilization and targets depending on their spatial location. The same is true with regard to the temporal location of strikes. Suffice it so say that while strikes are an inter- and trans-national phenomenon, the specific context of the strike is important to understanding the character and nature of any particular strike.

Given this, it is worth briefly noting that for westernized economies, there has been a broad cross-national trend of decline in the extent and intensity of strike activity since the late 1970s. The major caveats are that the decline has taken place from different pre-existing levels for different countries and that there are some exceptions. This highlights that while cross-national trends can be discerned, these are subject to and expressed within differing national-based systems of industrial relations. However, the main conclusion drawn from the data is that whilst the late 1960s and early 1970s represented a period of rising strike activity, subsequently a period of quiescence (Shalev, 1992) has set in, leading some to speculate on the 'withering away' of the strike (again, see, Ross and Hartman, 1960).

DATA PROBLEMS

Throughout the world, in both developed and developing economies, statistical data for the annual frequency of different types of 'industrial action' are absent, incomplete and non-standardized. Annual statistics for one type, the strike, do exist in a more complete form but even here there are problems concerning the minimum threshold for inclusion (size, sector) and the obligation on parties concerned

(union, employer, state body) to register strike activity (see www.laborsta.ilo.org). Where statistical data do exist for instances of 'industrial action short of strike', this is derived from one-off, episodic surveys in a few particular countries making comparative work and generalization extremely difficult.

CONFLICT AT WORK: NORTH AMERICA AND EUROPE

We now turn to examine the decline in strikes in North America and Europe as well as consider evidence of other conflict expressions. Flowing from our conflict framework, we expect to see some evidence of increases in collective expressions other than strikes and in individual conflict forms. Given that we are considering conflict at work in these western economies, we are not in a position to offer any definite insights regarding the experience of conflict at work in Eastern Europe, South East Asia, India or China. Nonetheless, we would anticipate some broad similarities in terms of the underlying existence of conflict and the available menu of methods of expression but differences in the choice of which methods are utilized over time, reflecting national differences in systems and traditions of employment regulation.

North America

Much of the North American economic literature on strikes focuses on the incidence and duration of strikes in large bargaining units – in the US, usually units with 1,000 or more workers and in Canada, units with 500 or more, but sometimes upwards of 200. There is evidence, however, that these large unit samples are unrepresentative of all strikes (Harrison and Stewart, 1993; Skeels et al., 1988). Despite this data limitation, there is strong evidence of a long term decline in strikes in North America.

The Bureau of Labor Statistics (BLS) in the US only collect data on large strikes (involving n>1,000 workers), covering both public and private sectors. Despite the problem of the raising of the minimum threshold for inclusion in the BLS data, a long term decline in the US strike activity is evident, and is shown in Figure 31.1. Although subject to big swings, days not worked peaked in the immediate post-war period before peaking again in 1970 and experiencing a sharp and sustained decline thereafter. Without identifying the strict order of causation, there are two primary factors to explain the decline that stand out. The first is the well-documented decline in US union density from a peak of 32.5 per cent (1953) to just 12 per cent (2006) (BLS 2006b). The second is due to the more hostile context to

unions in terms of legal barriers and greater management power under globalization (see Piazza, 2005, and for Europe, Scheuer, 2006).

Over the same period, the long-term decline in strikes in Canada is similar to that seen in the US (Figure 31.2). As the Canadian data include work stoppages of bargaining units of all sizes, it is much more representative than the US data.[3] Union density is less of an explanatory factor here because Canada has not experienced the same decline (see Godard, 2003), remaining around 30 per cent for the last decade. After a decline from an annual average of 754 in the 1980s, to 394 in the 1990s, to 221 in 2003, work stoppages rose to

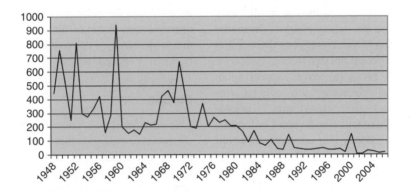

Figure 31.1   US – strike days per 1,000 workers, 1948–2006
Source: Computed from BLS (2006a).
Note: From 1984 onwards, the BLS data only measures strikes involving more than 1,000 workers. Previous to that it was 500 workers.

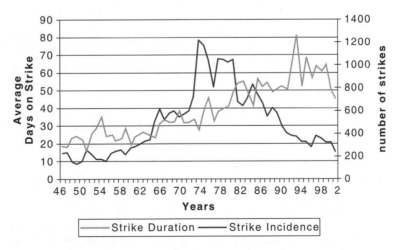

Figure 31.2   Canada – strike incidence and duration, 1946–2005

261 in 2004 and again in 2005. Alongside this, the duration of work stoppages have increased in Canada since the 1950s (Campoletti et al., 2005). Most work stoppages that commenced between 2003 and 2005 concerned wage and benefits. It is interesting that job security and subcontracting, issues that might be associated with the more manifest aspects of the recent business turn to globalization, represented only 9 per cent of all stoppages over this period (Statistics Canada, 2006).

The notion of method displacement suggests, *inter alia*, a trade-off between strikes and other forms of conflict (reviewed in Hebdon, 2005). When strikes are structurally blocked by laws or institutions, and capitalist globalization helps weaken organized labor, alternative expressions of conflict may increase. The prevailing wisdom from the covert conflict literature suggests that conflict may be redirected in two ways; collective actions will be more covert, appearing in the form of collective job actions (for example, sick-outs, slowdowns, work-to-rules), and there will also be more individual conflict expressions (for example turnover, absenteeism, grievances). These form two hypotheses, and while it is beyond this chapter's scope to rigorously test these, we can, however, highlight a body of work that is generally supportive of them.

The first is a study of unfair labor practices (ULPs) in the US from 1950–97 (McCammon, 2001). The creation of the offence of a ULP within the *National Labor Relations Act 1935* (commonly known as the 'Wagner Act' after it's creator, Senator Robert Wagner) was underpinned by an intention to channel conflict away from strikes and lockouts (see Hurd, 1976). ULPs are (overwhelmingly) union actions alleging employer violation of the National Labor Relations Act (bargaining in bad faith, management interference with a lawful union activity, etc.) (McCammon, 2001: 167). While initially ULPs concerned employers resisting a growing number of assertive organizing drives, under the decline in their strike capability, much weakened unions now file ULPs to pressurize employers to come to the table to discuss bargaining such that McCammon (2001: 145) argued ULPs now constitute 'a legalistic mode of struggle [which has] increasingly become labor's mainstay'. The second concerns absenteeism, and although it is difficult to isolate the conflict aspects, there is evidence from Canada that absenteeism rates have been rising and that increased on-the-job stress is a significant cause (Statistics Canada, 2005; Tomlinson, 2002). The third concerns quit rates. Statistics Canada (2007) found that 5.5 per cent of men and 7.0 per cent of women quit their jobs in 1984. By 2002, these were 7.7 per cent and 7.6 per cent, respectively. Whilst higher levels of unemployment impeded quitting in 1984, it is unlikely that the higher rates of quitting in 2002 can be fully explained by greater opportunities. Some of the increase is likely due to an increased demand to leave but more research is needed to settle this issue.

Europe

Like other Western economies, there has been a broad cross-national trend of decline in the extent and intensity of strike activity since the late 1970s in European economies, albeit subject to the caveats outlined above (see also Gall, 1999a). Given the number of economies within the European Union (EU) itself, the survey of strike activity here will merely focus on the four of the largest economies with the EU, namely, Britain, France, Germany and Italy between 1955 and 2005 using the relative measure of days not worked per 1,000 workers per annum (DNW/1,000W). Another reason for focusing on these four economies is that there is annual data for this entire half century unlike that for Greece or Spain. However, in both France and Germany, strike activity in public administration has been excluded for all or much of the period, this having an increased salience given the *de facto* shift in the location of most strike activity from the private to public sector in western economies.

At the low end is Germany, where from 1955 to the late 1980s, few years saw more than 150 DNW/1,000W, while subsequently it has been less than 15 per year. By contrast, in Britain, most years until the late 1980s experienced more than 250 DNW/1,000W, but since the early 1990s, the number has been considerably less than 100. Meanwhile, in France, most years until the late 1970s saw more than 250 DNW/1,000W whereupon almost all subsequent years experienced less than 100. From the mid-1960s, Italy experienced upwards of 1,000 DNW/1,000W until the early 1980s, and thereafter a fall to around 100 by 2005. (Although Italy has been by far the most strike prone of the four economies, relatively speaking, it has been put in the shade by Greece, which from the mid-1980s to mid-1990s experienced well in excess of 2,000 DNW/1,000W.) Nonetheless, what all four economies have in common is that their general patterns are punctuated by individual years of 'uncommonly' high strike activity. More generally, much strike activity has concerned resistance to government austerity measures, exclusions from the political process, retrenchment in public sector employment and pay rises.

When we turn to examine other instances of collective, non-strike 'industrial' action, available data is woefully incomplete and non-standardized. Nonetheless, focusing on Britain gives some indication of the processes at play. Milner (1993) and Gall (2006) found that 'industrial' action short of a strike and other means of collectively exerting influence (through balloting, collective conciliation) were prevalent and concluded that it was plausible that they have increased over the last 30 years. Several authors have noted the decline in the reach of trade unionism since the late 1970s and the likely attendant rise of individual workers' approaches to Citizens' Advice Bureaux – the state funded body for providing advice about legal and regulatory matters to private individuals – from below 0.2 million cases per annum then to more than 0.5 million cases in the last twenty years (Abbot, 2004: 245; Kelly, 1998: 45).

The main employers' federation, the Confederation of British Industry (CBI), has annually estimated, from an annual survey, the extent and cost of sickness/absence from the workplace since 1987. Annual estimates have remained broadly similar since 1989, being annually around 160–200 million days not worked, equating to between 6,000–9,000 days not worked per thousand workers and 'costing' £10–14 billion (www.cbi.org.uk). The CBI believes that between 10–20 per cent is not genuine sickness/absence, which does indicate conflict at work, and the degree of unauthorized absence is higher in unionized than non-unionized workplaces. Whatever the veracity of these figures, it is not possible to discern a trend in non-genuine sickness/absence given the absence of standardized data. Moreover, the CBI does not produce figures which show the extent of sickness/absence that is or may be attributable to mental stress, injury or accident at work or resulting from work, which would also indicate conflict at work. Nonetheless, given that employers believe much is not genuine sickness/absence, they are now dedicating more time and resources to trying to reduce it and to monitoring workers more stringently (Edwards and Whitston, 1989). Other than a few examples like British Airways in 1997, almost all these conflict-based sickness/absences have been conducted on an atomized, individual basis, even if the actions are commonly taken by many workers.

The union peak organization, the Trades Union Congress (TUC) has regularly published estimates of the amount of unpaid overtime that employers obtain from workers. These have averaged out in the last five years to constitute £23 billion per annum carried out by 5 million workers. And while not all unpaid overtime is forced overtime, for some workers may regard it as a career investment, and not all workers like professionals have set contractual hours, clearly employers are still extracting much coerced, unpaid work. Thereafter, there are scattered and isolated data on the extent of employer evasion of the statutory minimum wage and on the extent of theft and pilfering; for example, some 3 million workers were believed to be engaged in workplace theft in recent years in Britain (*Financial Times,* 7 March 2007).

Unfortunately, similar data, even of an incomplete, non-standardized type, on non-strike expressions of conflict is not readily available for the other three European economies through the European Industrial Relations Observatory or national-based studies. Although it is known that overtime bans and work-to-rules are sometimes used, the absence of inclusive survey data represents a major gap in our knowledge here. We also know that absenteeism, turnover and the like have a presence in these countries but again little is known of their specific extent and causation.

CONCLUSION

In discussing conflict at work, we concentrated on the workforce as workers or producers of goods and services rather than workers as citizens or consumers. This established an order and primacy of relationship even if the subsequent pursuit of the interests of workers may have involved workers as consumers (for example organizing a consumer boycott of their employer) or as citizens (for example using the services of a lawyer or citizens' advice bureau), and where either or both involve working in alliances with non-governmental actors such as pressure groups and political parties. In that sense, our use of the term 'conflict at work' was also preferable to the term 'conflict about work' for it focused attention on the workplace but, with our theoretical approach, without losing the sense of the totality. We also used the term 'employing organization' to denote our concern was with more than just companies and businesses or profit-seeking organizations. Thus, any organization which employs people as workers or managers was the subject of our analysis where our concern was conflict within an employing organization and not between employing organizations or the workforces thereof. That conflict is better conceived, at source, as being competition between different employing organizations over resources, market shares and profits. In a similar holistic vein, we used the term 'workers' rather than 'employees' as the act of work rather the contractual status

of employment creates the worker/employer divide. Thus, workers can perform paid work for an employing organization although they are not employed as such. We subsumed all these points within the framework of conflict of interests where conflict exists even if it is not consciously acted upon.

Given that overt and covert conflict at work is inherent and endemic in society, the salient substantive issues concern how it is expressed, at what volumes and what factors influence these. Indeed, the thrust of what we have argued is that it would be unwarranted to predict a genuine paradigm shift in the historically important method of expression through strikes. So rather than a secular trend – 'the withering way of the strike' – the notion of waves and cycles (for example, Kelly, 1998) stresses the contingent nature of their expression within a framework of conflict at work as an ever-present underlying dynamic. Here, the upswings and downswings in the bargaining power of labor, and organized labor in particular, are likely to be critical parts of an understanding and explanation, and these upswings and downswings also relate to the usage of political action and political parties by unions. And in historical terms, it is likely that the current period of 'labor quiescence' (Shalev, 1992) refers only to a single method of collective mobilization, namely, the strike, for the notion of method displacement has highlighted the prevalence of other semi-collective and individualized methods of conflict expression. Clearly, much more research is needed to put flesh on the bones of this hypothesis. Nonetheless, the reconfiguration of conflict at work continues to present unions and associated leftist political parties with a major conundrum given that they are both predicated, in different ways, on the collective association of workers. Finally, it is now becoming more apparent that where unions continue to exist, globalization has forced them to internationalize conflict. Although still in their early days, international union solidarity, coalition building with new social actors, global human rights campaigns and corporate campaigns are consequently on the rise around the world. So, to focus only on strikes as the primary form of the expression of conflict at work would be to ignore these important new directions in conflict.

More generally, and given that a major, explicit or implicit, cause of wider societal conflict under capitalism is the degree of income inequality and that the existence of wage labor has a role to play in explaining this inequality, political tensions and turmoil are likely in the future. Increasing trade through globalization, according to the theory of comparative advantage, ought to cause an increase in national incomes. But, without mediating institutions and policies to redistribute income, national income inequality will persist. Higher paid manufacturing jobs continue to be replaced by lower income service jobs. There is growing evidence that income inequality is, indeed, growing in North America and Britain (Bernstein and Gould, 2006; Hills and Stewart, 2005, Yalnizyan, 2007). Conflict about work and employment is, therefore, set to continue, even if it is not always or only based on conflict at work and in employment. Whether it is, in the traditional sense of manifest collective conflict, will be largely dependent upon the ability of workers to work in concert with each and mobilize through different forms of common organization.

NOTES

1 Although it should be noted that the term 'industrial' is synonymous with all non-agricultural workers in the eyes of many authorities.

2 The absence of manifest conflict is often mistakenly interpreted by those of a unitarist perspective as evidence of 'good management'.

3 The Canadian data also permit a close examination of strike duration. The duration variable shown in Figure 31.2 is simply the number of calendar days that the workers were on strike.

REFERENCES

Abbot, B. (2004) 'Worker representation through the Citizen's Advice Bureaux' in Healy, G., Heery, E., Taylor, P. and Brown, W. (eds) *The Future of Worker Representation.* Basingstoke: Palgrave. pp. 245–63.

Ackroyd, S. and Thompson, P. (1999) *Organizational Misbehavior.* London: Sage.

Bernstein, J. and Gould, E. (2006) *Working Families Fall Behind.* Washington, D.C.: Economic Policy Institute.

Blyton, P. and Turnbull, P. (1994) *The Dynamics of Employee Relations.* Basingstoke: Macmillan.

Brehm, J. and Gates, S. (1997) *Working, Shirking, and Sabotage: Bureaucratic Response to a Democratic Public.* Ann Arbor: University of Michigan Press.

Bronfenbrenner, K. (2000) 'Raw power: Plant-closing threats and the threat to union organizing' *Multinational Monitor,* 21 (12): 24–30.

Bureau of Labor Statistics (2006a) Press release. (<www.bls.gov/news.release/wkstp.nr0.htm>).

Bureau of Labor Statistics (2006b) Press release. (<www.bls.gov/news.release/union2.nr0.htm>).

Campoletti, M., Hebdon, R. and Hyatt, D. (2005) 'Strike incidence and strike duration: some new evidence from Ontario' *Industrial and Labor Relations Review,* 58 (4): 610–30.

Dowding, K., Peter, J., Mergoupis, T. and van Vugt, M. (2000) 'Exit, voice and loyalty: Analytic and empirical developments' *European Journal of Political Research* 37 (?): 469–95.

Edwards, P. (1986) *Conflict at Work: a Materialist Analysis of Workplace Relations.* Oxford: Basil Blackwell.

Edwards, P. and Hyman, R. (1994) 'Strikes and industrial conflict: peace in Europe?' in R. Hyman and P. Edwards (eds) *New Frontiers in European Industrial Relations.* Oxford: Blackwell, pp. 250–80.

Edwards, P. and Scullion, H. (1982) *The Social Organisation of Industrial Conflict.* Oxford: Blackwell.

Edwards, P. and Whitston, C. (1989) 'Industrial discipline, the control of attendance and the subordination of labour: towards an integrated analysis' *Work, Employment and Society,* 3 (1): 1–28.

Feuille, P. and Wheeler, H. (1981) 'Will the Real Industrial Conflict Please Stand Up?' in *US Industrial Relations 1950–1980: A Critical Assessment.* Madison, Wisconsin: IRRA. pp. 255–91.

Fortado, B. (2001) 'The Metamorphosis of Workplace Conflict' *Human Relations,* 54 (9): 1189–221.

Fox, A. (1966) *Industrial Sociology and Industrial Relations,* Research Paper No. 3, Royal Commission on Trade Unions and Employers' Associations. London: HMSO.

Fox, A. (1971) *A Sociology of Work in Industry.* London: Macmillan.

Friedman, A. (1977) *Industry and Labour: Class Struggle and Monopoly Capitalism.* London: Macmillan.

Gall, G. (1999a) 'A review of strike activity in Western Europe at the end of the second millennium' *Employee Relations,* 21 (4–5): 357–77.

Gall, G. (1999b) 'What is to be done with organized labour?' *Historical Materialism*, 5: 327–43.

Gall, G. (2006) 'Collective alternatives to striking' *Research Report No. 5.* Hatfield: Employment Research Service, Centre for Research in Employment Studies, University of Hertfordshire.

Godard, J. (1994) *Industrial Relations, the Economy, and Society.* Scarborough: McGraw-Hill Ryerson.

Godard, J. (2003) 'Do labor laws matter? The density decline and convergence thesis revisited', *Industrial Relations*, 42 (3): 458–92.

Harrison, A. and Stewart, M. (1993) 'Strike duration and strike size' *Canadian Journal of Economics*, 26 (4): 830–48.

Hebdon, R. (2005) 'Toward a theory of workplace conflict: The case of US municipal collective bargaining' *Advances in Industrial and Labor Relations*, 14: 35–67.

Hebdon, R. and Stern, R. (1998) 'Tradeoffs among expressions of industrial conflict: public sector strike bans and grievance arbitrations' *Industrial and Labor Relations Review*, 51 (2): 204–21.

Hills, J. and Stewart, K. (eds) (2005) *A More Equal Society? New Labour, Poverty, Inequality and Exclusion.* Bristol: Policy Press.

Hurd, R. (1976) 'New deal labor policy and the containment of radical union activity' *Review of Radical Political Economics*, 8 (1): 32–43.

Hyman, R. (1975) *Industrial Relations: a Marxist Introduction.* London: Macmillan.

Hyman, R. (1977) *Strikes.* second edition. Glasgow: Collins.

Hyman, R. (1980) 'Theory in industrial relations: towards a materialist analysis' in P. Boreham and G. Dow (eds) *Work and Inequality.* Melbourne: Macmillan. pp. 38–59.

Hyman, R. (1982) 'Pressure, protest, and struggle: some problems in the concept and theory of Industrial Conflict' in G. Bomers and R. Peterson (eds) *Conflict Management and Industrial Relations.* Boston: Kluwer. pp. 96–119.

Jackson, M. (1987) *Strikes: Industrial Conflict in Britain, USA and Australia.* Brighton: Wheatsheaf Books.

Jackson, M. (1991) *Introduction to Industrial Relations.* Routledge: London.

Kelly, J. (1998) *Rethinking Industrial Relations: Mobilization, Collectivism and Long Waves.* London: Routledge.

Kerr, C. (1964) *Labor and Management in Industrial Society.* New York: Doubleday.

Kornhauser, A. (1954) 'Human motivations underlying industrial conflict' in R. Dubin, A. Kornhauser and M. Ross (eds) *Industrial Conflict.* New York: McGraw-Hill. pp. 62–85.

Mayo, E. (1933) *The Human Problems of an Industrial Civilisation.* New York: Macmillan.

McCammon H. (2001) 'Labor's legal mobilization – Why and when do workers file unfair labor practices?' *Work and Occupations*, 28 (2): 143–75.

Milner, S. (1993) 'Overtime bans and strikes: Evidence on Relative Incidence' *Industrial Relations Journal*, 24 (3): 201–10.

Morrill C., Zald, M. and Rao, H. (2003) 'Covert political conflict in organizations: challenges from below' *Annual Review of Sociology*, 29: 391–415.

Nichols, T. (1997) *The Sociology of Industrial Injury.* London: Mansell.

Offe, C. and Wisenthal, H. (1985) 'Two logics of collective action' in C. Offe, (ed.) *Disorganised Capitalism: Contemporary Transformation of Work and Politics.* Cambridge: Polity Press. pp. 170–220.

Olson, C. (1988) 'Dispute resolution in the public sector' in *Public Sector Bargaining.* Madison, Wisconsin: Industrial Relations Research Association.

Piazza, J. (2005) 'Globalizing quiescence: globalization, union density and strikes in 15 industrialized countries' *Economic and Industrial Democracy*, 26 (2): 289–314.

Robinson, S. and Bennett, R. (1995) 'A typology of deviant workplace behaviors: A multi-dimensional scaling study' *Academy of Management Journal*, 38 (2): 555–73.

Ross, A. and Hartman, P. (1960) *Changing Patterns of Industrial Conflict.* New York: Wiley.

Sapsford, D. and Turnbull, P. (1994) 'Strikes and industrial conflict in Britain's docks: balloons or icebergs?' *Oxford Bulletin of Economics and Statistics*, 56 (3): 249–65.

Scheuer, S. (2006) 'A novel calculus? Institutional change, globalization and industrial conflict in Europe' *European Journal of Industrial Relations*, 12 (2): 143–64.

Shalev, M. (1992) 'The resurgence of labor quiescence' in M. Regini (ed.) *The Future of Labor Movements.* London: Sage. pp. 102–32.

Skeels, J., McGrath, P. and Arshanapalli, G. (1988) 'The importance of strike size in strike research' *Industrial and Labor Relations Review*, 41 (4): 582–91.

Spector, P. (1975) 'Relationships of organizational frustration with reported behavioral reactions of employees' *Journal of Applied Psychology*, 60 (5): 635–37.

Statistics Canada (2005) 'Fact Sheet on Work Absences', *Perspectives on Labor and Income*, April, 6/4.

Statistics Canada (2006) 'Increased Work Stoppages', *Perspectives on Labor and Income*, August, 7/8.

Statistics Canada (2007) 'Gender Differences in Quits and Absenteeism', *The Daily*, 23 February, p. 5.

Taylor, F. (1911) *The Principles of Scientific Management*. New York: Harper and Row.

Thompson, P. and Ackroyd, S. (1995) 'All quiet on the workplace front? A critique of recent trends in British industrial sociology' *Sociology*, 29 (4): 615–33.

Tomlinson, A. (2002) 'Healthy living a remedy for burgeoning employee absentee rates.' *Canadian HR Reporter*, 15/6, 25 March.

Tucker J. (1993) 'Everyday forms of employee resistance: How temporary workers handle conflict with their employers' *Sociological Forum*, 8 (1): 25–45.

Wheeler, H. (1985) *Industrial Conflict: An Integrative Theory*. Columbia, South Carolina: University of South Carolina Press.

Yalnizyan, A. (2007) *The Rich and the Rest of Us: the Changing Face of Canada's Growing Gap*. Ottawa: Canadian Centre for Policy Alternatives.

32

Skill Formation

Irena Grugulis

Skill has always been a central element of industrial relations (IR). In Britain many of the early trade unions and friendly societies formed around skilled trades, to negotiate pay levels, the differentials available for skill or experience and ensure the development of skills (see, for example Cockburn,1983; Penn, 1984; Thelen, 2004). Skill affects the way work is designed and organized and influences, or stems from, the levels of power, discretion and autonomy that workers have over work processes (Turner, 1962). It is also a key aspect in the way that firms, industrial sectors and nations compete. Indeed, high skills have the potential to both raise wages and improve firm and national competitiveness (Culpepper, 2001). Unsurprisingly then, what skills are formed, how they are developed and the way they are exercised in the workplace is a matter of key interest to all parties in the employment relationship.

It is also an area of enduring variation between nations with systems of skill formation and employment relations often differing dramatically from country to country (Crouch et al., 1999; Whitley, 1999). Nations vary greatly in the extent that they rely on the general education

system, provide specialist publicly-funded or subsidized vocational education and training (VET), or rely on individual firms to offer continuing development. Such differences seem to be stable; despite the rhetoric on globalization there seems to be little sign of convergence between states. Korea remains different to the US and France's system is not the same as that in Hungary. Nor do these differences in vocational training occur in isolation. Rather, each is embedded in systems of institutional structures and relationships, managerial strategies, market relations and national systems. Indeed, it is likely that these structures make the differences between the various systems of skill formation meaningful. After all, once a skill has been learned it must be put into practice in the workplace so the markets in which a firm competes, the way managerial authority is exercised and the discretion that is allowed to workers are all likely to be highly influential. According to Whitley (2003) there are five key elements in these differences (680):

- the extent and nature of the state's coordinating role in economic development;
- the organizational basis, and particularly the cohesion of business associations;

- the strength of the market for corporate control;
- the organization and effectiveness of the public training system;
- the extent and form of labour market regulation.

Ashton (2004) describes this far more concisely as the relationship between capital, labour and the state. Both of these authors are careful to emphasize that the skills that are developed and exercised depend on many more factors than the relative vocational education and training practices. Job design, employment security and inter-firm relations (among others) will influence and be influenced by the way firms compete, their ownership structures and the trust and authority that is delegated or withheld.

Accordingly, this chapter seeks to present various different skill formation systems in their national and institutional settings. It starts by describing practices in three very different systems: the US, Japan and Germany; noting particularly the nature and role of state involvement, the extent to which decisions are left to individual firms and the legacy of VET that exists; before exploring the reasons for the differences observed and considering the relative advantages and disadvantages of each system. It then focuses on the firms themselves and the choices they make (since firms within the same sector can and do make very different choices about the skills they require from, and are prepared to develop in, their workers). Finally it considers the impact that trade unions have on skill formation in both regulated economies (where unions are often pivotal and institutionalized elements of the system) and market ones (where individual firms choose whether or not to recognize a union presence).

THE US

In the US there is little state involvement in learning and the system of vocational education is market-led and decentralized (Rubery and Grimshaw, 2003). Almost all decisions on skills development are taken by individual firms or workers with little involvement from public institutions. Some states regulate particular industry sectors but this intervention is being abandoned rather than extended, as in the construction industry. Such a withdrawal of influence does little to encourage investment, indeed, training levels have slumped in the states which have deregulated, as has investment in physical capital and productivity (Bosch, 2003; Crouch et al., 1999). One brief attempt to devise national skill standards never got off the ground (Ashton, 2004). In the absence of nationally recognized qualifications most learning is by doing, quality is uneven and provision polarized. Workers who are not already qualified to degree level are unlikely to receive firm-sponsored training and, when they do, the opportunities they are presented with are often narrowly based, while firms complain that much of their training spend is remedial. Many organizations rely on outside training providers or immigration to supply them with skills (Rubery and Grimshaw, 2003). By contrast, employees who are already extremely highly educated may benefit from extensive (and expensive) provision (Crouch et al., 1999).

At firm level high turnover and low wages make investing in skills unattractive. The US is the only developed economy where wages have actually fallen over the last 20 years (Green, 2006). But as Crouch et al. (1999) point out, this seems to be a deliberate strategy rather than a pre-determined feature of the labor market. Organizations that seek to reduce turnover (by offering greater job security, linking pay to performance and involving employees in decision making) are generally successful. Yet these are, and remain, a minority. It seems that most US firms would rather treat labor as a variable cost, preserving numerical flexibility when demand slackens. Despite this, the US enjoys both high capital productivity and reasonably high labor productivity in most sectors and is particularly effective at producing highly skilled elites in financial services, aero engineering, entertainment, biotechnology and software. But the exceptional performance of those with most skills effectively conceals a far less impressive average performance and a wide distribution of skills, which is growing yet wider. More recently too, US job growth has been achieved by trading off skills against employment.

JAPAN

Japan, like the US, leaves VET decisions and activities to individual firms. State intervention took the form of encouraging large firms to develop, post war, then giving them free rein internally (Thelen, 2004). But while companies are free to decide their own strategies and set their own training standards both skill formation and employment practices are very different to those in the US. In Japan, large 'institutional companies' provide workers with employment security and put a great deal of effort into encouraging active social engagement and identity with the firm (Dore and Sako, 1989; Sako, 1999; Keizer, 2005). A high proportion of young people stay on in general education and this is then reinforced by a remarkable and extensive system of continuing education and development once in employment. Skill formation is broad and extends to the majority of the workforce (Cole, 1992). One study, cited in Crouch et al. (1999) calculated that the average Japanese firm provided newly recruited assembly workers with 310 hours of training, Japanese-owned subsidiaries in the US offer 280 hours while US plants provide only 48 hours.

This in-company training is key since some of the initial skills of Japanese workers compare poorly with those in Britain and Germany (particularly among engineering graduates). This formal learning is rarely accredited (since workers may expect to stay with one firm for most of their working lives) but is supplemented by extensive on-the-job training. Flexibility is ensured by moving workers between departments which has the added advantage of providing skills development beyond the traditional functional work areas so materially assisting workplace problem solving. Since pay and promotions are heavily based on seniority,

workers have further incentives to stay with the same employer and are not penalized for abandoning their specialism and learning new skills (Cole, 1992; McMillan, 1996).

GERMANY

The lynchpin of German VET is its rigorous system of three-year apprenticeships, which are long established in the old West Germany and were extended to the East after unification, a process which, as noted below, was not without problems. These are designed by consensus with input from employers' associations, trade unions and educationalists and costs are shared between all parties to the employment relationship (including the apprentices who accept a wage set at about a third of the adult wage for the duration of their studies, Crouch et al., 1999; Rubery and Grimshaw, 2003; Streeck et al., 1987). Time on the program is split between formal taught courses in colleges and on-the-job learning, generally structured around a series of problem solving activities that become progressively more challenging. Apprentices are taught by *Meister* (master craftspeople) who are both qualified experts in their occupation and still actively practicing so workplace innovations are incorporated into the program (Culpepper, 1999; Lane, 1987, 1989).

This intensive and highly regarded preparation for work is supported by several features: low turnover; employee involvement both directly in work design and process and indirectly through the trade unions and works councils; and comparative employment security once employees are in work. The state is involved in supporting apprenticeship but also, more directly, by regulating employment far more closely than do national governments in either the US or Japan. Because such regulation makes labor more expensive, it provides an incentive to employers to use it differently (Streeck, 1992). Lane's (1987) study of the banking and insurance industries shows how automation was used to eliminate almost all the low-skilled jobs. Other tasks were combined in a way that retained (and occasionally raised) skill levels, including a greater focus on customer service. In Britain, by contrast the introduction of technology in banks resulted in work being standardized with 91 per cent of clerks and 50 per cent of supervisors doing deskilled work (Crompton and Jones, 1984: 61).

These three national systems develop skills in very different ways, supporting dramatically different levels and distributions of skills in the economy. The US, as noted above, is highly successful at producing small numbers of expert elite workers, Reich's (1991) 'symbolic analysts' who compete against the best in the world, but in the process average and low-skilled workers are (often badly) neglected. In Japan, male workers in large firms receive continued and extensive skills development on- and off-the-job and the way those skills are learned ensures a competence that is very broadly based. While in Germany about two-thirds of the workforce are qualified to intermediate level in vocationally relevant skills (Bosch, 2003; Steedman, 2001). In the workplace these skills are harnessed to workplace innovations.

These variations stem from a range of different choices made by states, employers and occasionally trade unions on a range of factors including the form and nature of state intervention, the relations that exist between firms, the way those firms compete and the product markets in which they compete. These are worth exploring in more detail since they help to reveal both the depth of variation in the different systems and something about their relative prospects for the future.

ACCOUNTING FOR DIFFERENCES

Voluntarism and regulation

A key aspect in all skill formation systems is the role played by the state. This can be *voluntarist* (also known as liberal or market-based) or *regulated* (educational). The central assumption in a voluntarist system, as is broadly the case in the US and Britain, is that businesses operate most effectively when unfettered by regulation and that they are best placed to assess their own skill needs and react to changes as the market dictates. Competitive pressures will ensure businesses remain responsive and offer suitable training. The government's role is to minimize intervention and ensure that appropriate legal and other frameworks are in place to facilitate the free play of market forces.

Alternatively, in *regulated* systems, governments may take the view that skills development is a public good, that it is in everyone's interest to have a highly skilled population but that, left to themselves, individual businesses will be unable or unwilling to invest sufficiently in the long-term skills of their employees. Indeed, where a competitive market exists between firms, it may be rational for them to choose *not* to train since there is no obligation on their competitors to invest similar amounts of money and skilled workers may be poached by other firms. So activities that make sense at firm level may effectively sabotage the sector or the economy's chance of up-skilling. It then becomes the state's task to provide such skills or ensure that systems are in place which will guarantee that business provides them.

Regulation may take a variety of forms. The state can supply the necessary skills directly or put systems in place to ensure that businesses invest in development. Taiwan and Denmark provide interesting examples of both of these approaches. Both economies are dominated by small and medium sized enterprises (which are far less likely to train and develop workers than their larger competitors) and in both nations the state has intervened to ensure that VET takes place and that activities are of high quality but these interventions take very different forms. In Taiwan extensive technical and vocational skills were introduced into the education system. Despite the fact that most of the demand was for (high status) academic courses, and that these would have been cheaper to provide, the Taiwanese government invested extensively in the education of scientists and engineers. Access to academic courses was officially restricted, more than half of school-children were channeled into technical training and, at university level, more courses were made available for scientists and engineers and new Institutes of Technology launched. Student numbers, textbooks and curricula were state controlled and this meant that Taiwan succeeded in both increasing the numbers of low-cost industrial products for export and also managed the transition from this to higher value-added production across many if not all sectors without significant reported skills shortages (Green et al., 1999a). In Denmark, a long legacy of strong and collaborative trade unions meant that workplace learning programs could be set centrally (by both employers and unions) to ensure high standards and consistency, while state subsidy provided for a high uptake by firms and apprentices (Ashton, 2004). Elsewhere, state imposed levies and 'licenses to practice' for particular occupations help to ensure high skills and high competence. In France, employers are required to support training or pay a levy of 1.5 per cent of turnover plus an apprenticeship tax of 0.5 per cent of turnover to the state. While in Austria, Germany, Switzerland and the Netherlands there are systems of extensive and rigorous apprenticeships which attract high proportions of young people entering the labor market (Steedman, 2001).

Both voluntarist and regulated approaches can be successful. Regulation is particularly effective at ensuring that large sections of the working population acquire a broad range of vocationally relevant skills while Finegold's (1999) work in Silicon Valley demonstrates how this intensely competitive labor market can support a 'high skills ecosystem'. Silicon Valley is famously the site of a cluster of extremely high-tech computing firms. These are supported by the proximity of universities (University of California campuses in Berkeley, San Francisco, San Diego and Los Angeles and private institutions such as Stanford, USC and CalTech) that supply expert labor, share research and stimulate start-up companies. Stanford (whose graduates include

William Hewlett and David Packard) even set up the first university science park to provide fledgling firms with support services. The infrastructure is conducive to growth with good local transport, an international airport and a state-of-the-art telecommunications system while the availability of venture capital, low levels of regulation and limited penalties on bankruptcy encourage start-ups. These small and often highly focused firms prosper through inter-dependency forming partnerships with other organizations and participating in employer groups to pursue initiatives such as improving technical training in city colleges, that are to their mutual benefit. Individuals also collaborate through professional associations, continuing education courses and alumni associations. In firms there is little formal training but skills and expertise are developed through project work on cutting edge technical challenges. Even labor mobility, a point of concern elsewhere, assists knowledge diffusion and adds to personal and professional networks. However, these two ways of operating are successful at different activities and, with the very notable exception of Japan it is difficult to find an example of a market economy which provides high quality skills development for the majority of the workforce.

Such inactivity presents voluntarist economies with a dilemma. Most support high skills competition with other nations and believe this can best be achieved by market means, leaving firms unregulated so that the fittest survive to compete internationally. Yet in practice this lack of intervention may result in low-skills competition (Finegold and Soskice, 1988). Not only is such activity less desirable than knowledge-based, high skills competitiveness, since the margins earned are likely to be narrower; it may also, outside person-to-person services which are not readily sent off-shore, be a finite strategy for the developed world as India and China provide increasing access to cheap, highly skilled labor. When the hourly labor costs in inland China are 41 US cents an hour and those in Sri Lanka 40 US cents an hour (Freeman, 2005) it is difficult to imagine how the developed world can compete on labor cost alone. In Britain and Australia this dilemma has resulted in extensive official intervention to encourage and exhort employers to provide more skill development (Buchanan et al., 2004; Hampson, 2004; Keep and Mayhew, 1999; Keep and Stasz, 2004). However, these campaigns are often based on the assumption that the problem is one of information, that once firms know how positive VET can be and what programs are available they will invest in workforce skills. Yet, there is no evidence to suggest that non-training firms do not appreciate the potential advantages that training can confer (quite the contrary, as shown in Matlay, 1998). It may be, as noted above, that not training is a rational, economic decision. Moreover, interventions tend to be targeted only at the *supply* of skills, so this widespread activity does little to address the fact that firms may still compete on the basis of unskilled labor. More worryingly, by exempting employers from responsibility for VET, these interventions may mean that governments get stuck with both the role of skills provider and the need to subsidize the private sector, and all in the name of voluntarism (Felstead et al., 2002; Keep and Ashton, 2004).

Both voluntarism and regulation are simplifications. Few nations are prepared to completely abandon economic intervention and even regulated states will not legislate for every activity. The dominance of the market in the US does not preclude the extensive (if variable) mass education system (Whitley, 1999) and many of the most highly skilled are selected on the basis of their educational achievements or actively use their academic qualifications in the workplace (Estevez-Abe et al., 2001). While the British and Australian governments intervene extensively in attempts to improve the supply of skills (Keep and Ashton, 2004; Buchanan et al., 2004). German apprenticeships provide high quality and widely recognized qualifications for young people but, after that, much continuing development is as *ad hoc* and variable as in market economies (Culpepper, 1999).

Moreover, it is difficult to apply either label to Japan. Large firms are certainly given a great deal of freedom by the state to decide whether, when and what skills to invest in, but limited labor mobility ensures that their investments are far safer than those made by firms in other nations and it required extensive and active state regulations for earlier generations (including insisting on official approval for firms hiring experienced workers, approval which would only be granted with the consent of their previous employer) to limit this mobility (Thelen, 2004). This extensive employer-provided training is also limited to the large firms and (generally) the male employees. Kondo's (1990) account of the experiences of women and marginalized workers presents a very different picture of working life in Japan. Nonetheless, despite these reservations, it is still useful to know the extent to which states are market-led or regulated, particularly over issues of skill formation since it is here that many will intervene.

Competitive and co-operative relations

Another key area of difference is in the relations that exist between firms. In Japan there are strong collaborative inter-firm networks. Some of these are drawn together on a regional or craft basis but most are created and maintained by large corporations. Unlike large US firms, which may have thousands of suppliers, used for one-off contracts or switched when a price advantage is seen elsewhere, even the largest Japanese firms will have only a few hundred suppliers, but their (tiered) relations with these are generally close and stable. Members of networks provide high quality, just-in-time supply closely tailored to the needs of the central organization with products adapted to suit changes in demand where necessary. In return they receive security of contract and long-term partnership. Such close and sustained links mean that firms do not have to renegotiate contracts and prices every time an order is placed and processes, financial arrangements and management systems are often open to supply chain partners for collective discussion and improvement. Since the members of networks are also linked to one another they may combine to purchase expensive plant and equipment or help redistribute work when deadlines are tight while their central organizations are likely to invest in developing suppliers' skills or providing technology and expertise. Trust is strengthened and maintained by the fact that effort goes into keeping personal, as well as institutional, ties within the network with managers in the whole supplier community encouraged to socialize together and to develop and maintain friendships (Crouch et al., 1999; Dore and Sako, 1989; Nonaka and Takeuchi, 1995; Whitley, 1999).

In Germany links tend to be sectoral, rather than supply-chain based. Wage bargaining is still conducted sectorally with employer associations negotiating for all their members. Because of this, there is less incentive for newly qualified apprentices to gain a premium on their salary by moving employers (Rubery and Grimshaw, 2003). Such collective agreements also mean that firms do not compete by slashing wages and prices. Chambers of Commerce rigorously police apprenticeship programs to ensure that companies are not exploiting trainees or exempting themselves from the obligation to provide training, and that all provision is of high quality. This intervention is tolerated since the chambers are controlled by the employers themselves and they also provide a basis for sharing information on good practice; firms may come together to fund joint projects, invest in R&D or develop specific workplace innovations. Sanctions against firms that fail to train range from formally removing apprentice training powers or depriving them of access to technology transfer networks as well as (widely used) more informal deterrents (Culpepper, 1999).

In each of these networks the desire to be competitive drives firms to improve their products, enhance the performance of every member of their supply chain or invest in research and these positive reactions are fostered by the institutional structures, the expectation (and reality) of

long-term collaboration and close personal friendships between key workers. They are key elements in the success of VET provision and collaborative inter-firm developments. As Culpepper (2001) points out in his account of changes to youth training in France and the introduction of the apprenticeship system to East Germany after unification, many of the problems these interventions experienced could be directly attributable to weak employer associations. Such collaborations are not confined to nations that are 'institutionally dense' (Ashton, 2004). Networks do exist in Silicon Valley and the Los Angeles concentration of multi-media companies (Finegold, 1999); they may be created around Japanese transplants abroad (Brown, 2001a); supported by state and local authority initiatives (Edwards et al., 2002); or grow around strong employer associations (Grugulis et al., 2003). But they are far rarer in market-based economies where contracts respond largely to price. Indeed, in the US, legislation actively discourages collaborative inter-firm activities so shared interests generally result in mergers or competition (Whitley, 1999). In market systems, when small supplier firms adjust their processes to suit their larger customers there is no promise of contractual security (Blyton and Turnbull, 2004; Rainnie, 1988) and no expectation that developments will be mutual or gains shared. Some may be, albeit unequally but competition may also be zero sum with firms competing to drive others out of the market and small firms vulnerable to exploitation and insolvency.

These institutional links extend to the way firms are funded. Mutual shareholdings in Japan and long-term bank investment in Germany ensure that organizations are supported on a long-term basis (Rubery and Grimshaw, 2003). In the US and Britain, where many large firms are publicly quoted, shareholders are far more likely to demand short-term performance. To the extent that, as Cappelli (1995) notes, redundancy programs result in share price gains. Given the links noted elsewhere between job security and investment in skills it is easy to see why such regular rounds of 'de-knowledging the firm' have been criticized (Littler and Innes, 2003). As Lloyd (1999) demonstrates in her comparative study of the British and French aerospace industries, making skilled workers redundant during economic downturns (the option taken by the British firms) meant that they were far less well equipped to take on orders when conditions improved. More broadly, co-operative and collaborative relations between firms may encourage trust-based relations within them. Such collaboration may take very different forms. In Germany and Denmark for example it is common for employees to be involved in issues of job design and work process (Ashton, 2004), works councils and trade union representatives have a formal role in management and consultation has a statutory basis (French, 2001). In Japan, where work processes tend to be designed in detail, little worker input is expected but a great deal of effort is put into securing participation in detailed problem solving activities (Whitley, 1999). By contrast, in the market economies, even where formal consultation mechanisms exist there is far less evidence of constructive collaboration on workplace problems.

Products and product markets

The markets that firms choose to compete in are also significant since these have a key influence on the skills that are developed and the way they are used. Large numbers of standardized products mass produced require very different forms of labor to customized, small batch, high quality or innovative products. Thelen (2004) points out that since US companies have access to a large and reasonably homogeneous domestic market, many went into mass production early, deskilling workers and selling large numbers of standardized goods. In Germany, by contrast, an emphasis on quality, customized service and products in all areas of the economy creates a very different demand for and supply of goods. It also involves a very different way of organizing labor. Mason et al.'s (1996) detailed study of biscuit manufacturing shows how German firms concentrated on producing small batches of high quality foodstuffs with 90 per cent of the workforce skilled bakers and most concentrated in areas of production which would add value, such as decoration or adding fillings to the biscuits (as compared to British mass produced simple biscuits where most labor was unskilled). German workers were able to take on more tasks, with one worker often monitoring several production lines and accepting responsibility for quality (indeed, such a concern is an integral element of pride in the occupation or *Beruf*). Similarly, the German and Dutch construction sites studied by Clarke and Wall (2000) had higher numbers of skilled workers, fewer managers and far fewer faults reported than their British counterparts. Indeed repeated comparative studies of a range of different industries and services show that German firms employ more skilled workers and pay higher wages but that those workers are far more productive, take more individual responsibility for quality and work very differently to their counterparts elsewhere. Moreover, when work is reorganized or new technologies introduced the priority for automation is to eliminate low-skilled jobs and the remaining tasks are recombined in ways that often increase skills still further (Finegold et al., 2000; Jarvis et al., 2002; Lane, 1987).

Firm level choices

National systems of skill formation, employment and business are important. They provide the institutional and regulatory structures against which firms operate and they are, as noted above, comparatively stable. Yet the existence of these structures does not mean that choices at firm level are irrelevant nor that every organization is a mirror image of all its compatriots. The choices that firms make: to enter certain markets and withdraw from others; to compete on quality or compete on cost; to hire and fire workers as orders are lost and won or to multi-skill them so that they can contribute at all levels of the production process; are all important and all have implications for skill formation. The emphasis in all of these is on choice. As will be seen below, certain decisions make it more likely (or more rational) for organizations to invest in training but such choices are not pre-determined since employment practices do not arrive as pre-formed templates, to be 'read off' once decisions have been taken on products or strategies. Different firms can and do choose to enter the same market or adopt the same technology in very different ways (Ashton and Sung, 2006; Boxall and Purcell, 2003).

One choice that firms make is the market in which they compete and the products or services they compete on. Mason et al.'s (1996) study of biscuit manufacture, considered above, shows the links between such strategies and skills; high skill levels are generally associated with a high value added product strategy (Mason, 2004). Arthur's (1999) study of US steel mini-mills reinforces this. When production focused on small batches of different products workers' skills were an integral part of the process since the changeover between batches could be complicated. Firms engaged on large production runs, by contrast, required far less input and far fewer skills of their workers (who simply monitored the machinery). This intuitive link does not invariably hold true. High value added production can be undertaken by predominantly low-skilled employees and low cost production by highly skilled workers (Ashton and Sung, 2006). Aldi, the discount supermarket chain, employs comparatively few members of staff for the number of customers it serves but provides high levels of training and above average wages. By contrast Hannon (2005), in his study of the Irish dairy industry observes how some firms dramatically upgraded production but still kept tight control over work processes, ensuring that skill levels remained low.

Another much cited predictor of training levels is change at work and the introduction of new working practices since workers need to familiarize themselves with new procedures, technologies and ways of working (Ashton and Sung, 2006; Frazis et al., 2000; Leigh and Gifford, 1999; Lynch and Black,1998). With training particularly high

in organizations that introduced bundles of human resource practices such as 'lean production' or 'high performance work systems' (Whitfield, 2000). But again, while all these elements are positively linked with higher levels of training they are not deterministic. Firms can and do introduce new management practices without linking these to employee training.

It may be that these, and other, choices are inextricably intertwined with the way organizations choose to treat their employees, as dependable or disposable. Interchangeable unskilled laborers are likely to be engaged on very different types of work and have very different expectations of skill formation to trusted expert workers. As numerous studies note, higher levels of training are associated with higher than average salaries, generous fringe benefits, internal labor markets and promotions based on seniority (Fairris, 2004; Frazis et al., 2000; Arthur, 1999). These are generally explained by the fact that well-treated employees are more likely to stay with their employer, reducing the risk that training investments will be lost to rival firms. But, as Keep and Mayhew (1996) note, the causality is rather more complex than this as investments in skills and training may also justify others in sophisticated human resource practices, as workers contribute more to production and perks are devised to reward status.

Trade unions and skill formation within firms

There is also, particularly given this book's focus, another area over which firms make choices and which can significantly impact on skill formation and that is the role of trade unions. In Japan, Germany and Denmark unions' roles are institutionalized. Indeed, it is their co-operation which makes skill formation effective in each of these three nations. There is extensive consultation with establishment level unions in Japan and high levels of consensus and security in large firms; in Germany unions underpin sectoral bargaining, collaborate on the design and implementation of apprenticeships and contribute to workplace decision making through local representation and works councils; while in Denmark unions bring together workplace interests from numerous small and medium sized enterprises. Elsewhere, where unions are not automatically involved in the skill formation process, their role is more debatable.

In theory, unions can impact on skill formation and training in a number of ways. On the negative side they may reduce workplace flexibility, increase pay levels or distort the premia available for skills and so make it less viable, or less attractive, for employers to fund training. On the positive, they may increase workers' security, raising morale and commitment and so make training more attractive for employers (by reducing employee turnover and safeguarding investments in skill development), actively bargain with employers for skills, support skill formation practices such as apprenticeships and work with employers to justify higher wages via productivity improvements. According to Stevens (1996), higher wages may also bring advantages to firms because they stimulate productivity gains and productivity gains made through training (see, for example, Zwick, 2006) are likely to rise faster than wages.

So much then for the theory, what of the evidence? This is rather more mixed and there are distinct differences between the US and the British evidence. Several US studies have revealed positive links between trade unions and training. Parker's (1997) historical analysis of Milwaukee reveals how co-operation with trade unions made its successful adoption of the German apprenticeship possible between 1911 and 1933 (attempts to introduce apprenticeships into unorganized industries and areas met with repeated failure). More recently, Bilginsoy's (2003) research into apprenticeships in the construction industry shows dramatically higher success rates in schemes funded by both unions and employers than those run by employers alone (58 per cent as opposed to 30 per cent) and this despite the fact that the joint programs had significantly higher numbers of women and minority candidates who are less likely to complete their apprenticeships (see also Berik and Bilginsoy, 2000). Elsewhere however the evidence is less clear cut. Shibata (1999) contrasts the reluctance of unions in the US to let front-line workers acquire skills in basic maintenance (for fear that specialist maintenance workers would be laid off) with the attitude of Japanese unions (in matched plants), who had no such fears. Surveys have variously reported positive (Lynch, 1992), insignificant (Knoke and Kalleberg, 1994; Lynch and Black, 1998) and negative (Frazis et al., 2000) correlations between union presence and training levels.

In Britain the link between trade union recognition and training is both more consistent and more positive. Here, repeated studies reveal a strong, positive association with both the amount and the intensity of training (Boheim and Booth, 2004; Green et al., 1999b; Booth et al., 2003). Not only are workers in unionized workplaces more likely to receive training (and to receive more training) than their non-unionized peers, they are also more likely to be rewarded for this in the form of greater returns to training and higher wages (Booth et al., 2003). The reasons for this seem to be less that unions bargain over training or implement training schemes themselves (they do, but on a comparatively small scale) and more, as Green et al. (1999b) note, to do with the general environment for employee relations in these firms.

DISCUSSION AND CONCLUSIONS

These various and varying systems each boast very different advantages and disadvantages. The flexibility of the market allows firms to respond quickly to changing needs and may provide a stimulus for them to support the development of a 'skills elite' but it is also far more likely to be the reason for a problem in skill formation than the means of its solution. Organizations that compete against one another may save training costs by free-riding on the investments of their competitors and poaching skilled workers. But one of the consequences of this for the economy as a whole is that the workforce is likely to be under-trained since few employers will wish to risk their funds in developing skills (Bosch, 2004) and employers are likely to suffer from the problems of skills shortages and skills gaps (Hillage et al., 2002). This also creates problems for employees since poaching makes skill premia unpredictable so their investments of time or money may be at risk and, in the absence of training and development, unskilled work is rarely well paid, more likely to be casual or temporary and may not be linked to the sort of career ladders which could improve both work and life chances (Green, 2006).

By contrast, the consensus required for regulated systems makes institutions less responsive to the needs of individual employers (firms in Sweden complained repeatedly but without success, at the start of the 1990s that the vocational training system needed to be adapted to the shifts in technology and the market, Crouch, 2005). But they are far more successful in providing high-quality, vocationally-relevant skills for the majority of the working population. This allows firms to compete on the basis of quality goods, innovation or incremental customization; earning more in both domestic and international markets. Individual workers are more productive and are paid more, which improves their standard of living and has positive implications for society (Brown, 2001b; Lloyd and Payne, 2003, 2004).

It seems that, following Finegold and Soskice (1988), systems of skill formation may help to create 'path dependencies' which either enable nations to compete on the basis of skills and knowledge or restrict them to low-wage, low-skill markets. Small wonder then that the consensus among commentators was that some form of intervention was needed in national VET systems and that it was the role of the state to intervene through regulation, by supporting tertiary bodies of employer and employee associations, by developing and insisting on occupational qualifications or by supporting skills directly,

to ensure that workers acquired skills (Crouch et al., 1999). Yet recently this consensus has been challenged, not because of flaws in the various systems of skill formation but because increasingly integrated national economies may make individual divergence less viable and because the dramatic changes in technology and labor markets since the start of the 1990s may make formal systems of VET, which rely on stability and a consensus over which skills are needed and will be rewarded in the future, much less relevant.

Let us examine these two challenges. Surprisingly perhaps globalization seems to be the lesser one. Economies are connecting and international trade is growing (although this is not a new phenomenon) but different institutional frameworks mean that national economies develop very distinctive capabilities, competing in different sectors and with different technologies (Whitley, 2003). As Whitley (1999) notes, they are effectively competing by differentiating their goods, rather than by harmonizing practice against some universal template. Even multi-national companies, which might be expected to be the harbingers of shared practice generally remain rooted in their own national and cultural systems (Bradley et al., 2000), while employment practices are adapted to local circumstances (Edwards and Ferner, 2002; Ferner and Varul, 2000a, 2000b; Ramirez and Mabey, 2005). Markets are social as well as economic institutions and firms may shape the markets they are in as much as they respond to them (Djelic et al., 2005). As the descriptions of the various systems in this chapter have shown, differences are embedded in competition and are far more deeply rooted than simply divergent approaches to the same goal.

Set against this however, several of the regulated economies are struggling. The Japanese economy has been in a prolonged slump for more than a decade while Germany is beset by high levels of unemployment (Federal Statistical Office, 2005). Commentators vary in their reactions to this, and particularly in their predictions for the future health of the

German regulated system. None blame the country's ills on its skill formation practices but there are queries over whether, after the expenses and economic ills of unification, these are sustainable. According to Crouch (2005) 'many' employers are trying to free themselves from the costly VET system and French's (2000) study of IG Metall reveals how the firm's activities in old East German are effectively creating a dual market, undermining the whole system of collective bargaining. Yet elsewhere in East Germany, Culpepper (1999) notes how few firms are attempting to introduce low-wage or numerically flexible forms of labor (see also Bluhm, 2001). It may be that the service sector presents a greater danger here than unification. In the retail sector the old model of apprentice-trained assistants is being abandoned in favor of small numbers of key, functionally flexible 'anchor' workers who support larger numbers of lower paid, numerically flexible employees (Kirsch et al., 2000), while in hotels the highly skilled and multi-lingual qualified German employees are set against poorly paid East European domestics (Finegold et al., 2000).

Despite some claims (Sloane and Ertl, 2003) demand for apprenticeships by young people is still strong (and falls only slightly short of record-breaking levels) although the majority of East German trainees are on schemes subsidized by the state, which raises questions about employer commitment to co-funding (Culpepper, 1999). Encouragingly too the system for designing apprenticeships is becoming more adept at responding to change and technological innovation. In the past Germany certainly struggled to provide qualifications for developing industries such as ICT since the tri-partite arrangements for agreeing standards were so time consuming that qualifications in fast developing fields were out of date before they were launched. However, this development process has been considerably shortened and the dominance and longevity of systems like Microsoft mean that computing skills that do not date rapidly can be supported (Bosch, 2003). Four new technical apprenticeships were launched in 1997 and proved so popular that, even in work with no tradition of apprenticeships 60,000 young people were in training by the end of 2001, and this figure was in addition to the 10,000 apprentices enrolled on the 'old' ICT apprenticeship (Steedman et al., 2003:13).

By contrast, in the Anglo-American labor markets, where efforts have been put into reducing regulation and the focus is on numerically flexible workers (often employed on temporary or part-time contracts) job growth is healthy and unemployment low. It seems that skills-based competition no longer secures economic advantage.

Yet what such accounts neglect is the *quality* of the jobs that are available. Some years ago *The Economist*, a publication known for its support of deregulated labor (and other) markets greeted the news that 10,000 new jobs had been created in the US by publishing a joke that noted 'you need three of them to live'. As Green (2006) points out, in the US, alone among the developed world, real wages have declined over the last 20 years (elsewhere they have more than doubled). In Britain part-time work, undertaken predominantly by women working in the service sector, is significantly less well paid than its full time equivalent and part-time workers generally have little access to career ladders or job-related training. When an economy is dominated by such jobs it may be trapped in a 'low-skills equilibrium' where the existence of low-skilled, low-paid labor creates a demand for low priced products which themselves create a demand for low-skilled labor (Finegold and Soskice, 1988). Nor is there any evidence that future job generation will restrict the numbers of such undesirable jobs. As Brown (2001b) notes, sweatshops have been observed again in the US, and the existence of so many part-time workers provides a considerable economic advantage. Most of the new jobs being created are confined to front-line service work and characterized by low skill, low pay and low prospects (see, for example Nolan and Slater, 2003). Yet there is no requirement for these jobs to be poorly paid. In Sweden many person-to-person care services are undertaken by the public sector and workers enjoy reasonable earnings and good terms and conditions (Esping-Andersen, 1999). In opting for high numbers of badly paid jobs in the private sector employers and their governing states have noted the trade-off between skill and employment and embarked on the low road to prosperity (Crouch et al., 1999; Ebbinghaus and Kittel, 2005; Maurin and Postel-Vinay, 2005).

Any contrast between economies cannot be reduced to a simple headcount between the numbers employed or unemployed (although such headline figures are important). It is also significant that US firms pay low wages, provide few forms of social protection, invest little in skills and cope with high levels of employee turnover while their German counterparts treat workers very differently.

It may be more worrying to consider areas of job growth and skills change. As noted above, some of the most problematic developments for the German system can be observed in the service sector where long traditions of high skill, high quality and responsible autonomy are being abandoned in favor of low skill and direct control. This area has been the site of most dramatic job growth in recent years and in the US more people are now employed by McDonald's than US Steel (Macdonald and Sirianni, 1996). At the same time, manufacturing has been in decline, effectively, as Crouch (2005) observes, removing a major source of stable, middle skill occupations. Since many existing skill formation systems thrive on the stability of sectors, and many successful programes are located in manufacturing this may cause problems.

The model of skills development proposed by Crouch (2005) in response to this seems more of a problem than a solution. When no-one knows what skills are likely to be needed in the future because demand has become much more unpredictable, an absence of provision coupled with a tendency of governments to defer responsibility for skills acquisition to the young people entering the labor market (who need to be flexible and to 'learn to learn') means that many workers will be attempting to acquire skills and that some will succeed in acquiring the 'right' ones (whatever these turn out to be). He acknowledges that such a system is wasteful. While some workers will succeed in this blindfolded game of the survival of the fittest many will not and since those who fail to guess correctly may have education but few vocationally relevant skills he suggests that their alternative source of employment is the unskilled part of the service sector, work that is likely to prove alienating and unfulfilling.

Worryingly though it is these free-market approaches that seem to be being taken up by many rapidly developing economies. Russia's new market economy relies almost entirely on old Soviet-era skills or the vocational training carried out in what remains of the public sector. In the private sector poaching is the most widely used substitute for training, although some firms do hire highly educated graduates in the hope that they may be able to learn what is necessary on the job. On the rare occasions that training is provided it is seen as a privilege of rank, rather than an activity required to do work well, so those with high status in the firm may be sent on courses, regardless of whether they can benefit from them. One knitwear firm in Kemerovo got a new computerized knitting machine but sent the designer rather than the operator to be trained in how to use it, so were never able to deploy it to full capacity (Clarke and Metalina, 2000). Even in Hungary, which has attempted to support a gentle transition from a managed economy to capitalism, most up-grading of production and up-skilling of the workforce is observable in the foreign-owned firms. While Korea, although heavily influenced by the Japanese system in other ways, is heavily dependent on cheap, unskilled labor and firms provide little VET and very limited access to career ladders for these workers (Whitley, 1999). It seems unlikely that this is the result of free choice or due consideration over which skill formation system is most effective. Rather, the absence of strong intermediary bodies (including trade unions, professional bodies or employers' associations) and limited resources drive both firms and nations towards a *laissez faire* free market approach.

To some extent, this is simply a new gloss on an old problem. The dilemma of providing skills remains and, for the majority, it is likely that market systems will fail (there have always been a minority who have succeeded under these conditions). The rapid changes in technology, in skills required and the eternal impossibility of predicting the future may make the skills dilemma less easy to resolve than in times when policymakers and employers could assert with confidence what industry's requirements would be in 20 years time, but they do not change the fact that the skills available in the labor force are a major influence on the way companies use labor nor that markets can be and are constantly actively shaped. It may well be that in nations and sectors where young people are equipped with skills they will have to re-learn them or acquire new ones in the course of their careers but it is surely better to provide skills and decent jobs to go with these expectations of flexibility than to abandon the labor market entrants to their fate. As experience in Japan shows, skilled workers are not necessarily inflexible and gaining new skills may add to their abilities and capacity to problem solve. Whichever predictions on the future of the labor market prove correct it seems unlikely that skill formation systems will converge in the future.

REFERENCES

Arthur, J.B. (1999) 'Explaining variation in human resource practices in US steel mini-mills.' in P. Cappelli (ed.) *Employment Practices and Business Strategy.* Oxford and New York: Oxford University Press. pp. 11–42.

Ashton, D. (2004) 'The political economy of workplace learning.' in H. Rainbird, A. Fuller, and A. Munro (eds) *Workplace Learning in Context.* London and New York: Routledge. pp. 31–59.

Ashton, D. and Sung, J. (2006) 'How competitive strategy matters? Understanding the drivers of training, learning and performance at the firm level.' in *SKOPE Research Paper.* Warwick and Oxford: SKOPE, Universities of Warwick and Oxford.

Berik, G. and Bilginsoy, C. (2000) 'Do unions help or hinder women in training? Apprenticeship programs in the United States.' *Industrial Relations* 39 (4): 600–24.

Bilginsoy, C. (2003) 'The hazards of training: attrition and retention in construction industry apprenticeship programs.' *Industrial and Labor Relations Review* 57 (1): 54–67.

Bluhm, K. (2001) 'Exporting or abandoning the "German Model"? Labour policies of German manufacturing firms in Central Europe.' *European Journal of Industrial Relations* 7 (2): 153–73.

Blyton, P. and Turnbull, P. (2004) *The Dynamics of Employee Relations.* Basingstoke: Palgrave Macmillan.

Boheim, R. and Booth, A. (2004) 'Trade union presence and employer-provided training in Great Britain.' *Industrial Relations* 43 (3): 520–45.

Booth, A., Francesconi, M. and Zoega, G. (2003) 'Unions, work-related training, and wages: evidence for British men.' *Industrial and Labor Relations Review* 57 (1): 68–91.

Bosch, G. (2003) 'Skills and innovation – a German perspective.' Presented at The Future of Work/SKOPE/Centre for Organization and Innovation Conference on Skills, Innovation and Performance, 31 March–1 April, Cumberland Lodge, Windsor Great Park.

Bosch, G. (2004) 'Towards a new standard employment relationship in Western Europe.' *British Journal of Industrial Relations* 42 (4): 617–36.

Boxall, P. and Purcell, J. (2003) *Strategy and Human Resource Management.* London: Palgrave.

Bradley, H., Erickson, M., Stephenson, C. and Williams, S. (2000) *Myths at Work.* Cambridge: Polity Press.

Brown, A. (2001a) 'Supporting learning in advanced supply systems in automotive and aerospace industries.' Presented at Joint Network/SKOPE/TLPRP international workshop, 8–10 November, University College Northampton.

Brown, P. (2001b) 'Skill formation in the twenty-first century.' in P. Brown, A. Green, and H. Lauder (eds) *High Skills: Globalization, Competitiveness and Skill Formation.* Oxford: Oxford University Press. pp. 1–55.

Buchanan, J., Watson, I. and Briggs, C. (2004) 'Skill and the renewal of labour: the classical wage-earner model and left productivism in Australia.' in C. Warhurst, I. Grugulis, and E. Keep (eds) *The Skills that Matter.* Basingstoke: Palgrave Macmillan. pp. 186–206.

Cappelli, P. (1995) 'Rethinking employment.' *British Journal of Industrial Relations* 33 (4): 563–602.

Clarke, L. and Wall, C. (2000) 'Craft versus industry: the division of labour in European housing construction.' *Construction Management and Economics* 18: 689–98.

Clarke, S. and Metalina, T. (2000) 'Training in the new private sector in Russia.' *International Journal of Human Resource Management* 11 (1): 19–36.

Cockburn, C. (1983) *Brothers: Male Dominance and Technological Change.* London: Pluto Press.

Cole, R.E. (1992) 'Issues in skill formation in Japanese approaches to automation.' in P. Adler (ed.) *Technology and the Future of Work.* New York and Oxford: Oxford University Press. pp. 187–209.

Crompton, R. and Jones, G. (1984) *White Collar Proletariat: Deskilling and Gender in the Clerical Labour Process.* London: Macmillan.

Crouch, C. (2005) 'Skill formation systems.' in S. Ackroyd, R. Batt, P. Thompson, and P.S. Tolbert (eds) *The Oxford Handbook of Work and Organization.* Oxford and New York: Oxford University Press. pp. 95–115.

Crouch, C., Finegold, D. and Sako, M. (1999) *Are Skills the Answer? The Political Economy of Skill Creation in Advanced Industrialised Countries.* Oxford: Oxford University Press.

Culpepper, P.D. (1999) 'The future of the high-skill equilibrium in Germany.' *Oxford Review of Economic Policy* 15 (1): 43–59.

Culpepper, P.D. (2001) 'Employers, public policy and the politics of decentralized co-operation in Germany and France.' in P. Hall and D. Soskice (eds) *Varieties of Capitalism: The Institutional Foundations of Comparative Advantage.* Oxford and New York: Oxford University Press. pp. 275–306.

Djelic, M.-L., Nooteboom, B. and Whitley, R. (2005) 'Introduction: dynamics of interaction between institutions, markets and organizations.' *Organization Studies* 26 (12): 1733–1741.

Dore, R. and Sako, M. (1989) *How the Japanese Learn to Work*: Nissan Institute/Routledge. Japanese Studies Series. London: Routledge.

Ebbinghaus, B. and Kittel, B. (2005) 'European rigidity versus American flexibility? The institutional adaptability of collective bargaining.' *Work and Occupations* 32 (2): 163–95.

Edwards, P., Gilman, M. Ram, M. and Arrowsmith, J. (2002) 'Public policy, the performance of firms and the "missing middle": the case of the employment regulations and a role for local business networks.' *Policy Studies* 23 (1): 5–20.

Edwards, T. and Ferner, A. (2002) 'The renewed "American Challenge": a review of employment practices in US multinationals.' *Industrial Relations Journal* 33 (2): 94–111.

Esping-Andersen, G. (1999) *Social Foundations of Postindustrial Economies.* Oxford: Oxford University Press.

Estevez-Abe, M., Iversen, T. and Soskice, D. (2001) 'Social production and the formation of skills: a reinterpretation of the welfare state.' in P. Hall and D. Soskice (eds) *Varieties of Capitalism: The Institutional Foundations of Comparative Advantage.* Oxford and New York: Oxford University Press. pp. 145–83.

Fairris, D. (2004) 'Internal labor markets and worker quits.' *Industrial Relations* 43 (3): 573–94.

Federal Statistical Office, G. (2005) Press Release.

Felstead, A., Gaillie, G. and Green, F. (2002) *Work Skills in Britain 1986–2002.* Nottingham: DfES Publications.

Ferner, A. and Varul, M.Z. (2000a) 'Internationalisation of the personnel function in German multinationals.' *Human Resource Management Journal* 10 (3): 79–96.

Ferner, A. and Varul, M.Z. (2000b) ' "Vanguard" subsidiaries and the diffusion of new practices: a case study of German multinationals.' *British Journal of Industrial Relations* 38 (1): 115–40.

Finegold, D. (1999) 'Creating self-sustaining, high-skill ecosystems.' *Oxford Review of Economic Policy* 15 (1): 60–81.

Finegold, D. and Soskice, D. (1988) 'The failure of training in Britain: Analysis and prescription.' *Oxford Review of Economic Policy* 4 (3): 21–43.

Finegold, D., Wagner, K. and Mason, G. (2000) 'National skill-creation systems and career paths for service workers: hotels in the United States, Germany and the United Kingdom.' *International Journal of Human Resource Management* 11 (3): 497–516.

Frazis, H., Gittleman, M. and Joyce, M. (2000) 'Correlates of training: an analysis using both employer and employee characteristics'. *Industrial and Labor Relations Review* 53 (3): 443–62.

Freeman, R. (2005) 'What are the implications of globalization for worker well-being and trade unions?' Presented at British Universities Industrial Relations Association, 7–9 July, Northumbria University.

French, S. (2000) 'The impact of unification on German industrial relations.' *German Politics* 9 (2): 195–216.

French, S. (2001) 'Works councils in Germany. Still loyal to the trade unions?' *International Journal of Manpower* 22 (6): 560–78.

Green, F. (2006) *Demanding Work: The Paradox of Job Quality in the Affluent Economy.* Princeton and Oxford: Princeton University Press.

Green, F., Ashton, D., James, D. and Sung, J. (1999a) 'The role of the state in skill formation: evidence from the republic of Korea, Singapore and Taiwan.' *Oxford Review of Economic Policy* 15 (1): 82–96.

Green, F., Machin, S. and Wilkinson, D. (1999b) 'Trade unions and training practices in British workplaces.' *Industrial and Labor Relations Review* 52 (2): 179–95.

Grugulis, I., Vincent, S. and Hebson, G. (2003) 'The rise of the "network organization" and the decline of discretion.' *Human Resource Management Journal* 13 (2): 45–59.

Hampson, I. (2004) 'Training reform in a weakened state: Australia 1987–2000.' in C. Warhurst, I. Grugulis, and E. Keep (eds) *The Skills that Matter*. Basingstoke: Palgrave Macmillan. pp. 72–90.

Hannon, E. (2005) 'Prospects for the upskilling of general workers in liberal market economies.' Presented at British Universities Industrial Relations Association, 7–9 July, Northumbria University.

Hillage, J., Regan, J., Dickson, J. and McLoughlin, K. (2002) 'Employers Skill Survey 2002.' in *Research Report*. Nottingham: DfES.

Jarvis, V., O'Mahoney, M. and Wessels, H. (2002) 'Product quality, productivity and competitiveness: a study of the British and German ceramic and tableware industries.' in *Occasional Paper*. London: National Institute of Economic and Social Research.

Keep, E. and Ashton, D. (2004) 'The state.' Presented at SKOPE High Skills Vision Conference, 28–29 October, Lumley Castle.

Keep, E. and Mayhew, K. (1996) 'Evaluating the assumptions that underlie training policy.' in A. Booth and D.J. Snower (eds) *Acquiring Skills*. Cambridge: Cambridge University Press. pp. 305–34.

Keep, E. and Mayhew, K. (1999) 'The assessment: knowledge, skills and competitiveness.' *Oxford Review of Economic Policy* 15 (1):1–15.

Keep, E. and Stasz, C. (2004) 'The Employers.' Presented at SKOPE High Skills Vision Conference, 28–29 October, Lumley Castle.

Keizer, A.B. (2005) *The Changing Logic of Japanese Employment Practices: A Firm-Level Analysis of Four Industries*. Rotterdam: Erasmus Research Institute of Management.

Kirsch, J., Klein, M., Lehndorff, S. and Voss-Dahm, D. (2000) 'The organization of working time in large German food retail firms' in C. Baret, S. Lehndorff, and L. Sparks (eds) *Flexible Working in Food Retailing: A Comparison between France, Germany, the UK and Japan*. London and New York: Routledge. pp. 58–82.

Knoke, D. and Kalleberg, A.L. (1994) 'Job training in U.S. organizations.' *American Sociological Review* 59 (4): 537–46.

Kondo, D.K. (1990) *Crafting Selves: Power, Gender and Discourse of Identity in a Japanese Workplace*. Chicago: University of Chicago Press.

Lane, C. (1987) 'Capitalism or culture? A comparative analysis of the position in the labour process and labor market of lower white-collar workers in the financial services sector of Britain and the Federal Republic of Germany.' *Work, Employment and Society* 1 (1): 57–83.

Lane, C. (1989) *Management and Labour in Europe*. Aldershot: Edward Elgar.

Leigh, D. and Gifford, K.D. (1999) 'Workplace transformation and worker upskilling: the perspective of individual workers.' *Industrial Relations* 38 (2): 174–91.

Littler, C.R. and Innes, P. (2003) 'Downsizing and de-knowledging the firm.' *Work, Employment and Society* 17 (1): 73–100.

Lloyd, C. (1999) 'Regulating employment: implications for skill development in the Aerospace industry.' *European Journal of Industrial Relations* 5 (2): 163–85.

Lloyd, C. and Payne, J. (2003) 'What is the "high skills society"? Some reflections on current academic and policy debates in the UK.' *Policy Studies* 24 (2/3): 115–33.

Lloyd, C. and Payne, J. (2004) 'The political economy of skill.' in C. Warhurst, I. Grugulis, and E. Keep (eds) *The Skills that Matter*. Basingstoke: Palgrave Macmillan. pp. 207–24.

Lynch, L.M. (1992) 'Private sector training and the earnings of young workers.' *American Economic Review* 82 (1): 299–312.

Lynch, L.M. and Black, S.E. (1998) 'Beyond the incidence of employer-provided training.' *Industrial and Labor Relations Review* 52 (1): 64–81.

Macdonald, C.L. and Sirianni, C. (1996) 'The service society and the changing experience of work.' in C.L. Macdonald and C. Sirianni (eds) *Working in the Service Society*. Philadelphia: Temple University Press. pp. 1–26.

Mason, G. (2004) 'Enterprise product strategies and employer demand for skills in Britain: evidence from the employers skill surveys.' in *SKOPE Working Paper*. Warwick and Oxford: Universities of Warwick and Oxford.

Mason, G., Van Ark, B. and Wagner, K. (1996) 'Workforce skills, product quality and economic performance.' in A. Booth and D.J. Snower (eds) *Acquiring Skills*. Cambridge: Cambridge University Press. pp. 175–97.

Matlay, H. (1998) 'The paradox of training in the small business sector of the British economy.' *Journal of Vocational Education and Training* 49 (4): 573–89.

Maurin, E. and Postel-Vinay, F. (2005) 'The European job security gap.' *Work and Occupations* 32 (2): 229–52.

McMillan, C.J. (1996) *The Japanese Industrial System.* Berlin and New York: Walter de Gruyter.

Nolan, P. and Slater, G. (2003) 'The labour market: history, structure and prospects.' in P. Edwards (ed.) *Industrial Relations: Theory and Practice.* Oxford: Blackwell. pp. 58–80.

Nonaka, I. and Takeuchi, H. (1995) *The Knowledge Creating Company: How Japanese Companies Create the Dynamics of Innovation.* New York and Oxford: Oxford University Press.

Parker, E. (1997) 'Youth apprenticeship in a laboratory of democracy.' *Industrial Relations* 36 (3): 302–23.

Penn, R. (1984) *Skilled Workers in the Class Structure.* Cambridge: Cambridge University Press.

Rainnie, A. (1988) *Employment Relations in the Small Firm.* London: Routledge and Kegan Paul.

Ramirez, M. and Mabey, C. (2005) 'A labour market perspective on management training and development in Europe.' *International Journal of Human Resource Management* 16 (3): 291–310.

Reich, R. (1991) *The Work of Nations: Preparing ourselves for 21st century Capitalism.* New York: Vintage Books.

Rubery, J. and Grimshaw, D. (2003) *The Organization of Employment.* Basingstoke: Palgrave Macmillan.

Sako, M. (1999) 'From individual skills to organizational capability in Japan.' *Oxford Review of Economic Policy* 15 (1): 114–26.

Shibata, H. (1999) 'A comparison of American and Japanese work practices: skill formation, communications and conflict resolution.' *Industrial Relations* 38 (2): 192–214.

Sloane, P. and Ertl, H. (2003) 'Current challenges and reforms in German VET.' Presented at Vocational learning for the twenty-first century: international perspectives, 22–23 July, Oxford.

Steedman, H. (2001) *Benchmarking Apprenticeship: UK and Continental Europe Compared.* London: Centre for Economic Performance, LSE.

Steedman, H., Wagner, K. and Foreman, J. (2003) *The Impact on Firms of ICT Skill-Supply Strategies: an Anglo-German Comparison.* London: Centre for Economic Performance, LSE.

Stevens, M. (1996) 'Transferable training and poaching externalities.' in A. Booth and D.J. Snower (eds) *Acquiring Skills: Market Failures, Their Symptoms and Policy Responses.* Cambridge: Cambridge University Press. pp. 19–40.

Streeck, W. (1992) *Social Institutions and Economic Performance: Studies of Industrial Relations in Advanced Capitalist Economies.* London: Sage.

Streeck, W., Hilber, J. van Kevalaer, K. Maier, F. and Weber, H. (1987) 'The role of the social partners in vocational education and training in the FRG.' Berlin: CEDEFOP.

Thelen, K. (2004) *How Institutions Evolve: The Political Economy of Skills in Germany, Britain the United States and Japan.* Cambridge: Cambridge University Press.

Turner, H.A. (1962) *Trade Union Growth, Structure and Policy.* London: George Allen and Unwin Ltd.

Whitfield, K. (2000) 'High performance workplaces, training and the distribution of skills.' *Industrial Relations* 39 (1): 1–25.

Whitley, R. (1999) *Divergent Capitalisms: The Social Structuring and Change of Business Systems.* Oxford: Oxford University Press.

Whitley, R. (2003) 'The institutional structuring of organizational capabilities: the role of authority sharing and organizational careers.' *Organization Studies* 24 (5): 667–95.

Zwick, T. (2006) 'The impact of training intensity on establishment productivity.' *Industrial Relations* 45 (1): 26–46.

33

Industrial Relations and Business Performance

John T. Delaney

At the start of the twenty-first century, economic performance indicators seem to serve as society's ultimate scorecard. Much attention is paid to measures of the economy, wealth, and performance. Witness the prominence given to reports on the stock market in the media. Inevitably, it seems today that nations are judged by their economic output and firms by their revenues and profits. Only to a slightly lesser extent have people come to be evaluated in these ways. 'In a capitalist society,' as Alan Wolfe (1997: 566) has written, 'we value work to the degree that we establish a value for work.' That the value and cost to society of people (usually women) staying home to raise children is given less attention than the value of the minimum wage illustrates our desire to use metrics to summarize life. This makes it essential to examine links between industrial relations (IR) and business performance. After all, society will judge IR that way too. Such an analysis must begin, however, with a determination of the bounds of IR. Based on the bounds, it is possible to discuss

relevant research and report general IR effects on organizational performance. After the review, I consider whether studies of these IR-performance links can adequately capture the essence and nature of IR – for workers and society.

WHAT IS 'INDUSTRIAL RELATIONS?'

In this analysis, IR is viewed broadly as a field covering activities related to unions, collective bargaining, human resource (HR) policies, and workplace rules that have the potential to alter interactions between employers and employees. This approach reflects the origins of the field. As Kaufman (2004: 3) reported, 'the term industrial relations developed a broad, generic meaning connoting the tenor or state of relations between the different parties to the employment relationship.' Simultaneously, over time, the field also developed more specific meanings, such as 'the corporate employment department and personnel policies used to co-ordinate, control, and motivate labor,' and 'progressive labor policies' such as collective bargaining and employee voice (Kaufman, 2004: 3). Such an approach accepts the notion that the adoption of alternative work practices (AWPs), creation of works councils, or existence of systematic workplace discord may influence business performance. The approach also stipulates that IR is broader than the study of unions and collective bargaining.

Whereas this formulation claims that IR encompasses most aspects of work and employment, the measures of IR available for association with business performance are much more limited. For example, economists have long studied the relationship between unionization and firm performance. To get beyond theory, they examined measures of union representation (or coverage), union density, and collective bargaining coverage. The indicators have been aggregated and disaggregated, and cover one point in time or many years. Essentially, the approach treats unions as a 'black box' that influences employment and organizational outcomes. Conveniently, this allows the union effect to be summed up empirically in the parameter on the union measure in a regression equation. Unfortunately, in addition to failing to show how unions influence outcomes, studies like this often ignore other workplace factors that could be associated with performance. For example, the organizational rules adopted by employers influence the nature and effectiveness of workplace interactions. In recent years, this has been demonstrated most clearly by the attention devoted to examining AWPs. Research has used many names for AWPs, including innovative HR practices, high involvement management (HIM), high performance work practices (HPWPs), high performance work systems (HPWSs), sophisticated HRM, and so on. Regardless of the name used, researchers have spent much time trying to estimate the association of AWPs with firm performance (see Becker and Gerhart, 1996; Bryson et al., 2005; Combs et al., 2006; Delaney, 1996; Huselid, 1995).

Given the substantial decline in union density over the past 50 years, the association of AWPs and performance has become a more prominent indication of the effect of IR. For example, if used strategically by employers, such practices may shape and reflect the likelihood of unionization. AWPs may represent the firm's preferred work rules, in contrast to the terms of typical collective bargaining agreements, which reflect union and management preferences on many work rules. AWPs may also reflect workers' changing views and preferences regarding the organization of work and need for union representation.

Accordingly, the review presented below focuses on three streams of research. First, attention is devoted to studies of the relationship between indicators of unionization (including union and collective bargaining coverage) and measures of organizational performance ('Old IR'). This is the oldest and most traditional way to link IR and firm performance. Second, it is unsurprising that this research stream gave rise to examinations of the types of rules enacted in union and non-union workplaces. Accordingly, attention is given to the association of union status measures and the adoption of AWPs. This extension of 'Old IR' is important because it offers an opportunity to assess whether unions indirectly influence business outcomes through the creation of certain HR policies and work rules. Third, in an era of declining unionization, it is necessary to study the link between AWPs and firm performance. This 'New IR' view is premised on the notion that HR and organizational rules may be associated with performance. In particular, certain approaches, such as ones emphasizing teamwork and co-operation, may lead to stronger performance. And even if it is impossible to disentangle precisely the relationship among, unions, AWPs, and performance, it is critical to recognize that each component represents part of the effect of IR. Prior to beginning the research assessment, it is necessary to give attention to several methodological concerns and issues associated with studies of IR and business performance.

A NOTE ON METHODOLOGICAL ISSUES AND CONCERNS

One of the hallmarks of studies of IR and business performance is enduring criticism of research methods, designs, and results. Indeed, reviews of relevant literature, such as studies of unions and firm performance (see Hirsch, 2004) or AWPs and organizational outcomes (see Wright et al., 2005) pay significant attention to the methodological problems of covered studies. The criticisms are often so strong that it would seem necessary to discount results of much of the published research. Of course, in areas where theory is indeterminate – for example, economic theory suggests unions could raise or lower productivity – this provides little help. But the extent of the criticism needs to be kept in mind when assessing the research trends noted below. While specific problems will be mentioned, I spend little time reviewing methodological concerns. Instead, references are provided to reviews that closely examine these problems.

THE OLD IR AND BUSINESS PERFORMANCE

Although economists have discussed the effects of unions for many years (for a review, see Kaufman, 2004), studies linking unionization and organizational outcomes are a recent phenomenon. The new attention is due primarily to advances in computational power and the publication in 1984 of *What Do Unions Do?*, Richard Freeman and James Medoff's classic book on union effects. Freeman and Medoff's book provided empirical backing to their earlier assertion that unions have 'two faces' (Freeman and Medoff, 1979). The first face was a monopoly view that economists widely embraced. The other face was a collective voice view that, among other things, suggested unions helped organizations by improving circumstances for workers. Although based on Hirschman's (1971) book *Exit, Voice, and Loyalty*, this

view was new to IR. In general, Freeman and Medoff accepted that unions had monopolistic tendencies in some instances, but argued that the voice-enhancing aspects of unions outweighed the monopoly aspects. This view was contentious then and continues to be so now. Freeman and Medoff's new perspective inspired considerable research on the two faces of unionism. As much of the research sought to provide evidence of the effects of unions, it is relevant to an assessment of IR's effects on business performance. For the purpose of this review, research is divided into three streams covering union effects on productivity, financial performance, and other business outcomes, such as organizational stability and survival.

Unions and productivity

Union effects on productivity are controversial because economic theory does not provide clear guidance. Unions may lower productivity by raising wages and other costs, putting limits on work practices, promoting concerted activities (for example, slowdowns), reducing trust between managers and workers, and encouraging less investment in operations by the organization. At the same time, unions could increase productivity by encouraging better management practices (to overcome the potential negative effects), monitoring output quality, and enhancing employee morale. How these conflicting theoretical premises sort out is a matter for empirical analysis. Such analysis began in the late 1970s as data and technology combined to permit more careful studies than could be conducted in earlier years. Freeman and Medoff (1984) assessed available empirical studies on the association between unions and productivity and concluded that 'productivity is generally higher in unionized establishments than in otherwise comparable establishments that are non-union' (p. 180). Moreover, they asserted that the positive results were driven by good IR, for instance, the positive elements of voice promoted by unionism. Underlying Freeman and Medoff's conclusion, however, was the strong evidence marshaled in a single study (Brown and Medoff, 1978). That study suggested that unions were associated with greater total factor productivity of 10–25 per cent depending on capital usage assumptions. Other studies, such as Clark's (1980a, 1980b) examinations of the cement industry, suggested positive, albeit more modest, union productivity effects (about 6 per cent).

Freeman and Medoff's conclusion regarding productivity was assailed almost from the beginning. As Ashenfelter (1985: 247) cautioned in his generally positive review of Freeman and Medoff's book: 'Until better evidence is available, it may be more reasonable to conclude that unions have little or no effect on productivity.' To a large extent, Ashenfelter's admonition was prescient as the strong results presented by Freeman and Medoff have not been reproduced in subsequent work. Even Freeman (2005: 657) admitted that subsequent research reported union productivity effects much more modest in magnitude, though he felt the results were likely due to the nature of empirical production function methodologies and the reality that productivity effects are due to the 'interaction of unions and management, which can differ across industries, firms, and even establishments within a firm'.

In a 20 year assessment of Freeman and Medoff, Hirsch (2004) reviewed work on the relationship between unions and productivity. He concluded that 'the evidence produced since *What Do Unions Do?* suggests that the authors' characterization of union effects on productivity was overly optimistic' (p. 430). Although Hirsch suggested that Freeman and Medoff correctly identified several elements potentially related to unionization that affected productivity, he felt they were wrong in their assessment of union productivity effects. Based on his assessment of the literature, Hirsch (2004: 430) concluded that 'the average union effect [on productivity] is very close to zero, and as likely to be somewhat negative as somewhat positive.' In general, Hirsch's (2004) assessment is reflective of the general view taken by economists today.

This view was generally supported in a meta-analysis of 73 studies published between 1977 and 2002 (Doucouliagos and Laroche, 2003). The first panel of Table 33.1 presents general results from this meta-analysis. Although the general union productivity effect appeared to be close to zero, variation occurred across nations and industries. For example, small positive effects were evident in US studies. Larger effects were evident in US manufacturing studies. And negative effects were estimated using data from the UK and Japan.

Research on the association between unions and productivity *growth*, which is shown in the second panel of Table 33.1, suggests a negative relationship. These findings are drawn from another meta-analysis conducted by Doucouliagos and Laroche (2002). That assessment examined 26 empirical studies published between 1980 and 2000, including 20 from the US and others from the UK, Canada, Australia, and Austria. Doucouliagos and Laroche (2002: 15) concluded that 'taking all the studies together and for all time periods, the overall association between unions and productivity growth is negative.' The results were more negative in the US than in the other nations and more negative in studies relating changes in union density and changes in productivity growth. While Doucouliagos and Laroche stressed that the magnitude of the effect was small, and seemed to be less negative over time, their findings are consistent with the observed pattern in the US where large positive union productivity effects have declined over time. One explanation of the pattern may be the negative productivity *growth* results shown in the earlier Doucouliagos and Laroche (2002) meta-analysis. That meta-analysis also illustrates how the characteristics of individual studies – sample size, measurement of key variables, and comprehensiveness of control variables – can dramatically influence estimated results. Such variability has been cited by many researchers as influencing estimated union productivity effects.

For example, based on data generated in the US, Addison (2005: 416) concluded

Table 33.1   Summary of meta–analyses of union effects

	Number of studies	Total sample	Mean correlation[a]	Total union effect
1. Union effects on productivity				
All studies	73	58,403	.03	4%
US studies	55	47,549	.05	7%
US Mfg studies	10	5,004	.12	10%
UK studies	7	1,687	−.17	−11%
Japanese studies	5	4,045	−.01	−13%
2. Union effects on productivity growth				
All studies	26	25,965	−.19	
US studies	21	21,844	−.24	
Change in unionization	9	3,119	.02	
3. Union effects on profits				
All studies	37	29,771	−.12	
US studies	20	18,188	−.20	
Probit studies	20	12,122	−.08	
UK studies	14	9,313	−.06	
4. AWP effects on performance				
Overall SHRM	92	19,319	.15	
Individual practices	61	11,928	.11	
AWP systems	38	8,615	.21	
Mfg organizations	29	3,989	.24	
Service organizations	19	3,013	.13	

Notes: [a] Measure is the average correlation between union measures (for example, density) and the outcomes noted in panels 1–3 and the average correlation between AWPs and the performance measures noted in panel 4.
Sources: Panel 1) Doucouliagos and Laroche (2003); Panel 2) Doucouliagos and Laroche (2002); Panel 3) Doucouliagos and Laroche (2004–2005); Panel 4) Combs et al. (2006).

that: '*on average* union effects on productivity are small.' But, based on research using data from Germany, Addison simultaneously concluded that 'works councils and innovative practices may have favorable effects on productivity' (Addison, 2005: 446). Given such conclusions and the size of the estimates calculated in meta-analyses, discussions of union productivity effects will likely remain contentious.

Unions and profits

Whereas the literature on unions and productivity has been inconsistent (in results and interpretations), studies of the effects of unions on organizational profitability show remarkable agreement. Freeman and Medoff concluded that 'the evidence on profitability shows that, on average, unionism is harmful to the financial well-being of organized enterprises or sectors' (1984: 190). This conclusion has been generally accepted and confirmed in many studies. For example, Addison and Hirsch (1989: 160) concluded: 'the evidence points rather clearly to negative union effects on firm profitability, irrespective of the particular profit indicator used (rate of return on capital, Tobin's q, price-cost margin, etc.) and level of aggregation.'

The third panel of Table 33.1 reports data from a meta-analysis of studies of union effects on firm profits (Doucouliagos and Laroche, 2004–2005). In this meta-analysis of 57 studies of the union-profitability relationship in 9 countries, Doucouliagos and Laroche (2004–2005: 23) concluded that 'unions have a negative impact on financial performance and that this is strongest in US manufacturing.' Indeed, with one exception, no matter how the data in the Table are disaggregated, the association between unions and profits remains negative. The estimated association is positive and very small in France – one of the eight countries studied.

Although Metcalf (2003: 143) provided a similar assessment of the literature, he noted that some recent studies seemed to suggest a different picture. In particular, Batt and Welbourne's (2002) analysis of entrepreneurial firms (those going through an initial public offering) reported strong positive associations between unionization and measures of profitability. Metcalf's (2003: 145) surprise at this is suggested by his comment that 'the results are pretty remarkable.' In combination with some research conducted in Japan (Tachibanaki and Noda, 2000), which suggested positive profitability effects, Metcalf speculated that the union-profitability relationship might somehow be evolving. Perhaps because of the decline in union density, the increase in the use of innovative HR practices, and the reduction in labor-management conflict, unionization no longer reduces profits. At the same time, as Metcalf (2003: 145) opines, 'if unions really do boost profits, this begs the question of why firms are not asking to be unionized.'

Overall, evidence still points to a negative relationship between unionization and profitability. This is likely an indication that firms cannot completely recapture the increased labor costs that result from unionization among workers; in competitive markets, prices cannot be raised enough to offset cost increases, so shareholders receive lower profits in return. It is taken as a given in the literature that this lower profit stream fuels employer opposition to unionization (Kleiner, 2001).

Unions, employment, investment, and firm survival

If unions cause lower profits, managers might be less inclined to invest in unionized firms (or in unionized business lines within a firm). Two decades ago, Kochan et al. (1986) suggested that unionized firms dealt with such cost disadvantages by divesting and reducing their unionized operations while nourishing

and expanding their non-union ones. That approach is consistent with the steady erosion of union density in the US and also supports the notion that unionized firms could slowly go bankrupt as leaner non-union firms invade their territory. This idea has been studied by a variety of scholars.

Several US studies have indicated that unionized firms make smaller investments in capital (tangible and intangible) than similar non-union firms (Becker and Olson, 1992; Bronars and Deere, 1993; Bronars et al., 1994; Cavanaugh, 1998; Hirsch 1990, 1991, 1992). In addition, Fallick and Hassett (1999) suggested that union organizing victories led to substantial reductions in company investments in capital. Research conducted in Canada (Betts et al., 2001; Odgers and Betts, 1997) and Germany (Schedlitzki, 2002) suggested the same pattern of results, though evidence from the UK (Metcalf, 1993) and Japan (Benson, 1994) presents a mixed and more complex pattern. Studies examining R&D expenditures in union and non-union firms have also concluded that organized establishments invest less. Although these results are especially pronounced in the US, they appear to vary across nations (Blanchflower and Bryson, 2003; Menezes-Filho and Van Reenen, 2003; Menezes-Filho, et al., 1998). Evidence also suggests that unionized firms experience slower employment growth than non-union ones in Australia (Wooden and Hawke, 2000), the US (Leonard, 1992; Dunne and Macpherson, 1994), and the UK (Addison and Belfield, 2004).

Smaller capital and R&D investment does not translate into more bankruptcies among unionized firms than similar non-union ones, however, as research suggests that the union effect on organizational survival is negligible (DiNardo and Lee, 2002; Freeman and Kleiner, 1999; LaLonde et al., 1996). As Hirsch (2004: 437–38) noted, these results are potentially inconsistent. He interpreted them to indicate that unions act rationally in pushing firms towards the edge of bankruptcy but not into bankruptcy. Support for his view comes from evidence of concessions unions make when organizations experience significant economic problems. Certainly, developments in the US airline industry at the start of the twenty-first century have borne this out, as employees have made substantial concessions at United, Delta, and Northwest, among others.

THE NEW IR AND BUSINESS PERFORMANCE

Unions influence the rules used by organizations. The union effect occurs as a result of bargaining, as part of a union avoidance campaign, or as part of a concerted company effort to improve management effectiveness. As Kaufman (2004) carefully delineated, the personnel management (PM) wing of IR was established more than a century ago. Although PM researchers gradually shifted their allegiance from IR to HR, scholars provided substantial evidence showing that unions influenced organizational arrangements at work. Slichter et al.'s (1960) classic book served for many years as the benchmark assessment of unions and personnel management. During the 1980s and 1990s, however, researchers increasingly studied this area to estimate the relationship between organizational rules and firm performance. While early streams of this research treated union status measures as control variables in performance equations, subsequent studies examined the effects of unions on the adoption of AWPs and the effects of union status and AWP measures on performance outcomes.

Unions and the adoption of AWPs

Despite recognition that unions influence organizational structures and rules, few studies have examined the relationship holistically. In one of the earliest empirical studies, Jackson and her colleagues (1989) reported a mixed relationship. Unionization was positively associated with the existence of certain personnel policies and negatively associated with the existence of others. In addition, although unionized firms appeared to adopt personnel policies that were similar to those in non-union firms, innovative personnel policies seemed more likely in non-union firms. Subsequent research suggested a negative association between unions and AWPs (Delaney, 1991; Huselid and Rau, 1996; Ichniowski and Shaw, 1995; Osterman, 1994). Several explanations were given for the finding, including the inertial effects of existing HR systems in older union plants and the fact that many non-union plants with extensive AWPs were built on greenfield sites. And to the extent that AWPs were more likely to be adopted in new establishments, a negative association with unionization was unsurprising.

But some studies have suggested a more complex relationship. For example, recent work using British data indicated no relationship between unions and AWPs (Machin and Wood, 2005). Similarly, in an early evaluation of the literature on unions and HR policies, I concluded that union effects on many HR policies were inconsistent or inconclusive across studies (Delaney, 1991). In particular, there was no systematic evidence that unions resisted 'innovative HR practices' or that the non-union sector led the way in adopting AWPs. The latter point emerged clearly in an analysis of HR policies across business units of 'double-breasted' companies – firms that had unionized and non-union employees (Ichniowski et al., 1989).

To gain more insight into this inconsistent relationship, I calculated the association between unions and the introduction of AWPs, and then examined the effects of unions and AWPs on various performance measures (Delaney, 1996). The empirical results suggested that the extensiveness of AWPs was greater for non-union employees in non-union workplaces than for union or non-union employees in double-breasted workplaces. Neither industry nor company union density measures were significantly associated with the introduction of AWPs, but an inverse relation existed between a measure of 'opposition to unions' and AWPs (Delaney, 1996: 226). Additional analysis of double-breasted firms indicated that company union density was positively associated with the introduction of AWPs covering unionized workers and negatively associated with the introduction of AWPs covering non-union workers. Examinations of the relationship among unionization, AWPs, and performance produced mixed results. AWPs were negatively related to turnover and positively related to employees' support for change, ceteris paribus. But both turnover and support for change were higher among non-union employees in non-union firms than among union or non-union employees in double-breasted firms. The findings suggested that there is a systematic link among union status, AWPs, and performance outcomes, though the study could not disentangle completely the pattern of relationships. Overall, the nature of the relationship is still unclear, though it would appear to be necessary to include union status control measures in studies linking AWPs and organizational performance.

AWPs and firm performance

Over the past two decades, increasing attention has been paid to the existence and development of HR practices that promote superior organizational outcomes. As noted, the practices have been given many names, including several that presume a positive relationship with organizational outcomes (for example, high performance work practices). Some studies have identified the terminology issue as a serious problem (see Cappelli and Neumark, 2001; Wood, 1999). Nonetheless, despite the growing number of studies on this topic, consensus has not developed on what the construct should be called, how it should be measured or even what it means. Such conceptual problems are amplified by inconsistent results. For example, Wood's (1999) review of research on AWPs and performance reported diverse measures and mixed results. Still, the idea that AWPs might enhance performance has generated much credence. It has likely been propelled forward by estimation of favorable empirical results, narrow interpretation of results, and some wishful thinking. The research stream has to

some extent outrun its underlying theoretical basis.

AWPs reflect another way that IR influences business performance. While seldom acknowledged as IR, researchers have studied the practices and evaluated their association with various performance measures, including employee indicators (for example, turnover), establishment indicators (for example, productivity or profitability), and firm indicators (for example, stock price). To do so, research on this subject has adopted a variety of formulations. Initially, scholars examined the correlation between limited outcome measures and individual HR practices, such as training (Bartel, 1994), information sharing (Morishima, 1991), and grievance resolution systems (Ichniowski, 1986). Subsequently, studies examined HR practices more generally (for example, through an index, factor score, or some other combination) and estimated the association between HR and organizational outcome measures – stressing that the more extensive the practices, the stronger the performance effect (Delaney, 1996; Delaney and Huselid, 1996; Huselid, 1995; Ichniowski, et al., 1996). In this regard, AWP systems – combinations of practices that were in alignment – were seen as conceptually the most promising measures.

Simultaneously, another group of scholars followed a different conceptualization – focusing on 'bundles' of HR practices that complement each other – arguing that complementarities among the practices enhance performance and that non-complementary HR practices do not drive organizational results (MacDuffie, 1995; Pil and MacDuffie, 1996). As scholars examined the research approaches and offered constructive criticism of the underlying theory, samples, and methods, another group of researchers concluded that the role of HR practices is contingent and that innovative HR practices are more or less effective depending on the context into which they are introduced (Godard, 2001, 2004).

Other researchers suggested a more complex relationship in which the AWP-performance effect was moderated by an organization's business strategy (Huselid and Becker, 2000). From this view, optimal results occur when business strategy drives a set of HR practices that are internally consistent. Overall, regardless of the name given to these HR practices or the approach followed by researchers, the underlying notion is that certain HR practices or sets of practices affect performance outcomes. For example, organizations employ various types of teamwork and teams, engage in sophisticated recruitment and selection, share information, and provide communication and conflict management assistance. For various reasons, these approaches are believed to encourage good work habits, stimulate peer monitoring of work behavior, and promote peer pressure to avoid shirking. These factors represent the mechanisms through which the practices influence performance outcomes.

Studies of alternative work practices (AWP) and organizational outcomes suggest three general findings. First, there is tremendous variance in the approach used by researchers to operationalize AWPs. Not only are many different HR practice variables examined, but some practices are measured differently across studies. Cappelli and Neumark (2001: 743) cautioned that this contextualization across studies limits the validity and generalizability of the results. Second, many studies find significant positive relationships between AWP measures and organizational performance measures, though only one well-designed national study reported strong associations between AWP measures and firm financial performance (Huselid, 1995). While Cappelli and Neumark (2001) assert that the cost of enacting AWP measures may offset any value they produce, many studies of different indicators – with stronger and weaker study designs and empirical controls – report positive associations between AWP and performance indicators. It seems curious to dismiss the potential relationship, given the sheer number of studies reporting that AWPs enhance organizational performance.

Third, for reasons that are unclear, research on the link between AWPs and firm performance has generated an increasingly bitter debate about the true nature of AWP effects. The debate is framed around methodological and research design problems, though the critics seem to be more concerned with disparaging existing studies than producing better ones. This is apparent in the commentary and responses by Wright and his associates (Gerhart et al., 2000a, 2000b; Wright et al., 2001) on the work of Huselid and Becker (1996, 2000). Regardless of the merits of specific points raised in the debate, the nature of the arguments distracts from the purpose of the debate. For example, Wright and his associates (2005: 415) draw the following conclusion regarding the vast majority of research on the subject: 'it does make one wonder how such studies can legitimately suggest that HR practices "cause" performance.' Of course, few of the authors made any such suggestion and many made explicit efforts to address methodological issues, as well as simultaneity problems in the data. In general, the debate is reminiscent of the kinds of arguments made in response to Freeman and Medoff's (1984) suggestion of a positive relationship between unions and productivity. The hyper-negative commentary serves primarily to create competing camps, whose purpose in part seems to be to discredit each other rather than to identify the links and relationships among AWPs and performance.

A recent meta-analysis of research on the AWP-performance link by Combs and his colleagues (2006) reported strong positive effects in all instances. The fourth panel of Table 33.1 presents some of these findings. In addition to strong positive overall AWP-performance associations, findings suggest that AWP systems have significantly larger effects than individual HR policies and AWPs produce significantly greater benefits in manufacturing industries than in the service sector.

Even the critics of the AWP literature agree that research has reported consistent positive relationships between AWPs and performance measures (Wright et al., 2005: 416). Although the inclusion of longitudinal data has typically led to a reduction in reported AWP-performance effects (see Guest et al., 2003; Huselid and Becker, 1996; Ichniowski et al., 1997), such approaches have not caused the effects to disappear. This reinforces the need to understand more precisely any relationships among management, AWPs, and performance (Wright et al., 2005). In an increasingly competitive world, policies and processes that systematically enhance performance should be seriously considered.

A potential extension of research on AWPs and performance is the examination of how union status is related to AWPs and performance. As Addison (2005: 447) warned, because considerable research on the relationship between unions and performance outcomes suggests a small effect on average, it is important to 'look to factors such as innovative work practices in explaining the diversity in the effects of worker representation in different settings'. Based on an examination of US and German studies, Addison (2005: 447) concluded that 'combinations of innovative practices and worker representation can yield substantial productivity gains.'

Unions, AWPs, and performance

Research on the links among unions, AWPs, and performance has speculated that union effects operate through communication, cooperation, and monitoring (see Addison, 2005; Bryson et al., 2005; Kleiner, 2001; Metcalf, 2003). Partly because of this, some researchers have reported that certain AWPs work best in unionized workplaces (see Cooke, 1992; 1994). Similarly, other studies have suggested that co-operative relations between unions and employers could magnify the effects of AWPs. For example, Metcalf (2003) concluded that limited evidence from the US and UK was consistent with this argument. He cited a US study by Black and Lynch (2001) reporting that the best performance results occurred in establishments with AWPs *and* union representation. Based on an assessment of research in the UK,

Metcalf (2003: 158–159) reported a similar conclusion:

> A HRM [for instance, AWP] workplace with no union has a superior productivity and financial performance to a unionized workplace with no HRM. But when the workplace with union recognition also has the various HRM practices its performance is much enhanced, indeed in the case of labour productivity growth the best performing workplaces are those with both HRM and recognition.

Expanding on these notions, a recent review of research in the UK by Bryson and his colleagues (2005) suggested positive union productivity effects and negative performance effects in the 1990s (especially after the strength of the union was considered). The results suggested consistent cross-national patterns. In the UK, AWPs seemed to work better in union settings than non-union ones (Bryson et al., 2005: 483). Bryson and his colleagues interpreted this to be due to concession bargaining rather than some advantage accruing in the union sector. Given that studies of the US suggest a similar pattern but do not attribute it to concessions, further analysis of the associations among unions, AWPs, and performance outcomes is needed.

Interestingly, these findings are a natural extension of research reporting that union involvement in participation programs was positively associated with the longevity and success of such programs (see Eaton, 1990, 1994; Eaton and Nocerno, 2000). In many ways, the underlying driver of positive results in such studies is the 'voice' effect of unionism (Freeman and Medoff, 1984). Workers seem more inclined to co-operate when they feel a part of participative work arrangements. Although these conjectures suggest the need to examine the association between unionization and the enactment of AWPs and the effect of union representation and AWPs on organizational performance, studies have not consistently done so.

Research has, on an inconsistent basis, included various measures of union status in equations estimating the effect of AWPs on organizational performance (see for example, Huselid, 1995; Delaney and Huselid, 1996;

Addison and Belfield, 2001; Arthur, 1994; Huselid and Becker, 1996; Bae and Lawler, 2000; Guest et al., 2003). Coefficients on the union variables have been mixed, though the patterns generally conform to research on turnover and profitability (for instance, negative union effects). Results for AWP measures are also generally consistent across dependent variables when union status is included or excluded. For example, in an analysis of data from the UK, Guest and his associates (2003) reported strong positive associations between AWPs and productivity and performance outcomes and generally negative though rarely significant associations between different union measures (industry union density greater than 25 per cent and a single union deal at the workplace) and the same performance and productivity outcomes. Because Guest et al. (2003) did not examine the association between union measures and AWPs, however, their results don't address any potential indirect relationship among unions, AWPs, and organizational performance.

A SUMMARY OF IR EFFECTS ON BUSINESS PERFORMANCE

The research discussed above suggests several observations about the relationship between IR and the performance of business organizations. The observations must be considered in light of the caveats noted above, however, especially the methodological and estimation issues limiting research and the two ideological disputes roiling the field: between theorists and empiricists in economics and between advocates of competing methodologies in management and psychology.

First, studies examining the relationship between union measures (for example, union status, collective bargaining coverage, etc.) and business performance measures do not offer good news to supporters of unions. In particular, since the publication of Freeman and Medoff's (1984) classic book, research has consistently suggested that unions increase costs, have little effect on productivity, and lower profits. Unionization also appears to reduce employment and retard employment growth. The results are consistent with the reality that unions were not intended mainly to promote efficiency (Turnbull, 2003: 513). While evidence does not indicate that unions make enterprises insolvent, this combination of union effects offers a solid clue into the ardent employer opposition to unionization. That opposition has helped reduce union density in the US and other nations.

Second, while studies have suggested that unions foster a more formalized approach to HRM (see Ng and Maki, 1994; Slichter et al., 1960), some research on businesses in the US suggests a negative relationship between union status measures and AWPs. Various explanations for this pattern have been provided by researchers. Whether the result is due to inertia, as unionized workplaces seem to be older on average than non-union ones, or deliberate employer investment decisions, it is not good news for unions. Surveys have shown that workers prefer alternative workplace arrangements (see Freeman and Rogers, 1999), so negative union associations with AWPs may signal a disconnection between today's workers and traditional union approaches. Given that research suggests that non-union organizations are more likely to have AWPs than unionized ones, continued growth of the non-union sector seems likely.

Third, although substantial criticism has been voiced about the literature, evidence suggests positive relationships between AWP measures and firm performance. The association may be due to increased workplace co-operation or better communication or for some other reason, but it nonetheless suggests that organizational structures may affect outcomes. To the extent that union status is related to the adoption of AWPs and few studies have examined associations between union status and AWPs, indirect union effects may not be apparent in this research stream. The bulk of research on AWPs and performance fails to control for union effects on performance and very few studies have examined the link between unions and the adoption of AWPs.

At the same time, because union contracts are substantially affected by laws regulating the scope of mandatory bargaining, there has been little recent interest in examining links between unions and specific HR practice outcomes. In addition, in studies that have included measures of AWPs and unionization, little discussion is offered on the interaction among these measures and performance. More importantly, some of the most careful and comprehensive studies of AWPs and performance ignore union status and unionization altogether. In general, because non-union organizations are less likely than unionized ones to have AWPs, union performance effects may be even more disappointing than research shows.

Overall, on the dimensions noted, IR does not appear to enhance organizational performance. The effect does not appear to be large, but it is seemingly persistent. In addition, the effect seems consistent across nations (though it is most evident in the US). And whereas most research on the subject has been conducted using US data samples, the strongest data sets analyzed are government surveys conducted in Canada, the UK, and Australia. Based on this, it appears that IR detracts from or, at best, does not contribute to organizational performance. This finding explains the negative view of IR held by US managers and offers a rational explanation for explicit business opposition to unions and the tacit opposition to IR. Even within the scholarly community, IR has come to be viewed as more tangential and less important than other fields (see Kaufman, 2004).

SHOULD IR BE JUDGED BY BUSINESS PERFORMANCE ALONE?

The past three decades have not been kind to unions or IR. The union sector has declined nearly everywhere. The decline, in turn, raises questions about the future of unions and the field of IR. On the one hand, the decline may precipitate a Darwinian effect, causing a survival of the fittest. In such a case, weak unions will vanish and strong unions will survive. This may magnify the effects of unions, as the powerful are able to extract large concessions from employers (for example, US dock workers, New York City Transit Workers). At the same time, because the strong union cases are so unique, they may be the exception to the rule. After all, demand for unions has not grown when strong unions have achieved great bargaining results and in some instances, members of unions presumed to be strong (for example, US airline pilots) have been forced to make large concessions to keep their jobs. This may mean that union effects today are much more contingent than was the case in the past (Bryson, et al., 2005: 455). But it may also mean that unions and IR should *not* be judged by the metric of business performance. Other metrics may be more appropriate – ones that capture worker and societal interests. Societal wellbeing may be more dependent on employment, social justice, and equity than it is on organizational efficiency. In other words, IR's effect on business performance is just one indicator of its overall effect – just as a parent's earnings represent one possible indicator of his or her overall effectiveness in raising a child.

How should IR be measured?

Given what the data suggest about IR's effect on business performance, what should be concluded about the value of IR? On the basis of the data, IR seems to be more a cost than a benefit. Unions raise costs and there is no guarantee that the costs are offset by increased productivity, performance, or other outcomes. From the perspective of economic rationality, it seems that IR, at least as it is defined by unions, collective bargaining, and mediating institutions at work, does not help businesses maximize profits. In some but not all instances IR hinders business in the search for efficiency and performance. This is probably why so many economists see unions and bargaining as an impediment.

Underneath this, however, lies the question of whether business should be judged only by the concept of economic efficiency. While postulated as a rational, neutral approach, the framework of neoclassical economics contains its own biases. As Kaufman (2004) and Stiglitz (2002) have noted, the theory assumes away many of the aspects of work that really affect people. This leaves social scientists to ponder whether IR should be measured solely by metrics on which it can never prevail. If so, elimination of the institutions of IR will serve to make business more successful – at least in theory. Such elimination will also create real problems for millions of people who work for a living (see Godard and Delaney, 2000). If not, IR must be examined based on the extent to which it creates workplace justice – a concept that is loose and means different things to different people.

This creates another dilemma for the field. At a time when performance measurement is an accepted and expected way to assess institutions, IR is in a difficult position. On economic efficiency measures, it performs poorly. On workplace justice measures, it performs in an uncertain manner. Uncertainty occurs because there is no clear indicator of workplace justice. Is it necessary for a union or mediating institution to be present for workplace justice to occur? That is, can it ever occur in non-union firms? Because IR has focused so much on the role of unions, scholars have paid little attention to the possibility that justice can occur in other ways (at least other than laws). The field must identify performance measures that allow a systematic assessment of justice or democracy or sensibility at work.

Cross-national IR differences

Because of differences in labor legislation across nations, union engagement with management varies. For example, company unionism is illegal in the US, but permissible in many other nations. Where allowed, company unions have more latitude to bargain over any issue of concern to workers. This allows unions to be more responsive to changing conditions as the nature of bargaining can evolve more rapidly than is the case where the scope of bargaining is narrowly restricted.

The results presented in this study support the notion that some variation exists in union effects on business performance across nations. Because of methodological concerns and small differences in some instances, this pattern may be statistically significant but practically meaningless. Nonetheless, it demonstrates that IR may need to be judged differently in different nations. To do so, it is critical to examine data from many nations. Research shows that governments in other countries systematically collect much better data on unions and AWPs than occurs in the US

IR in a flat world

In his recent book, Thomas Friedman (2005) makes a compelling case that world-wide competition has escalated and will continue to grow. He also asserts that life in a 'flat world' can be better than life is today. But better is achieved only by the relentless press for innovations, improvements, and efficiencies. Friedman asserts that such a situation changes the competition that has characterized the last century from one of firms vs. firms to one of individuals vs. individuals. The reason for the change is that talent is not randomly distributed and that technologies increasingly allow organizations to seek out top talent wherever it is. The advantage currently enjoyed by people in the US or Western Europe evaporates in the flat world. Indeed, people who have long been held back by restrictive governments (for example, Russia, India, China) suddenly have opportunities that never before existed. As they choose those opportunities and compete in the global economy, they could swamp the westerners who take for granted a high standard of living. Put differently, in a flat world, people with talent who are hungry will outperform others. The talent advantage of the US has declined as its schools have performed at levels below many other nations, as the population has grown at slower rates, as the government has restricted immigration (for instance, to keep out future Bin Ladens, we've chosen to keep out future Einsteins and

Schwarzeneggers), and as the work ethic of Americans has dwindled. Regardless of what American politicians say, absent some change, our economic future is going to be more balkanized and societal inequality is going to grow.

Ironically, many of the problems shaping and reflecting a flat world are relevant to the subjects long studied by IR scholars. The field could be vibrant in a flat world, but it must change to be so. The change requires a new and clear thinking of the purpose of the field and its long accepted institutions. For example, in a flat world, mediating institutions may not offer security for workers. This is because competition is increasingly among individuals and therefore efforts to institute protections in companies, nations, and sectors are doomed to failure. Does this mean that unions are doomed? No. It does mean that organized labor may need to take a different path to aiding workers. For example, if collective bargaining is no longer successful, perhaps it should be de-emphasized. Instead, unions could focus on providing the highest level of skills to enrolled workers. A union movement that represents workers in the same way that professional athletes and entertainers are represented today is more likely to grow in a flat world than a movement that represents employees in the way that assembly line workers are represented. In the entertainment industry, unions seek to negotiate wage and benefit floors that can be exceeded by individuals with very high skills. Since the flat world will be ruled by skilled workers, it is possible that an entertainment industry model of unions would be accepted by workers.

This means that unions could be a strong force in a flat world. Strength will be derived from a new model that recognizes that skills are in demand and allows workers to receive different outcomes based on their skills. What I see instead, however, is an effort to promote barriers (for example, tariffs, immigration restrictions) that will ultimately fail. This is unfortunate as ample evidence of corporate scandals, unethical behavior throughout society (ranging from cheating in

school to crime), and dissatisfaction at work provide a huge opportunity for scholars and practitioners eager to shape a better world. That is after all what John R. Commons, Sidney and Beatrice Webb, and ironically, Karl Marx sought. Which of their visions will prevail? I don't know the answer. But I am sure that IR must move beyond a ritualistic acceptance of its traditional institutions and a narrow analysis of economic data if it is to make future contributions.

REFERENCES

Addison, John T. (2005) 'The determinants of firm performance: Unions, works councils, and employee involvement/high-performance work practices.' *Scottish Journal of Political Economy*, 52 (3): 406–50.

Addison, John T. and Hirsch, Barry T. (1989) 'Union effects on productivity, profits, and growth: Has the long run arrived?' *Journal of Labor Economics*, 7 (1): 72–105.

Addison, John T. and Belfield, Clive. (2004) 'Unions and employment growth: The one constant.' *Industrial Relations*, 43 (2): 305–23.

Arthur, Jeffrey B. (1994) 'Effects of human resource systems on manufacturing performance and turnover.' *Academy of Management Journal*, 37 (3): 670–87.

Ashenfelter, Orley. (1985) 'Comment on *What do Unions Do?*' *Industrial and Labor Relations Review*, 38 (2): 245–47.

Bae, Johngseok and Lawler, John J. (2000) 'Organizational and HRM strategies in Korea: Impact on firm performance in an emerging economy.' *Academy of Management Journal*, 43 (3): 502–17.

Bartel, Ann P. (1994) 'Productivity gains from the implementation of employee training programs.' *Industrial Relations*, 33 (4): 411–25.

Batt, Rose and Welbourne, Theresa. (2002) 'Performance growth in entrepreneurial firms: Revisiting the union–performance relationship.' In Jerome A. Katz and Theresa Welbourne (eds), *Research on Entrepreneurship*, Vol. 5. Greenwich, CT: JAI Press. pp. 1–29.

Becker, Brian and Gerhart, Barry. (1996) 'The impact of human resource management on organizational performance: Progress and prospects.' *Academy of Management Journal*, 39 (4): 779–801.

Becker, Brian E. and Olson, Craig A. (1992). 'Unionization and firm profits.' *Industrial Relations*, 31 (3): 395–415.

Betts, Julian R., Odgers, Cameron W. and Wilson, Michael K. (2001) 'The effects of unions on research and development: An empirical analysis using multi–year data.' *Canadian Journal of Economics*, 34 (3): 785–806.

Black, Sandra E. and Lynch, Lisa M. (2001) 'How to compete: The impact of workplace practices and information technology on productivity.' *Review of Economics and Statistics*, 83 (3): 434–45.

Blanchflower, David G. and Bryson, Alex. (2003) 'Changes over time in union relative wage effects in the UK and the US revisited.' In John T. Addison and Claus Schnabel (eds), *International Handbook of Trade Unions*. Northampton, MA: Edward Elgar. pp. 197–245.

Bronars, Stephen G. and Deere, Donald R. (1993) 'Unionization, incomplete contracting, and capital investment.' *Journal of Business*, 66 (1): 117–32.

Bronars, Stephen G., Deere, Donald R. and Tracy, Joseph S. (1994) 'The effects of unions on firm behavior: An empirical analysis using firm–level data.' *Industrial Relations*, 33 (4): 426–51.

Brown, Charles and Medoff, James. (1978) 'Trade unions in the production process.' *Journal of Political Economy*, 86 (3): 355–78.

Bryson, Alex, Forth, John and Kirby, Simon. (2005) 'High involvement management practices, trade union representation and workplace performance in Britain.' *Scottish Journal of Political Economy*, 52 (3): 451–91.

Cappelli, Peter and Neumark, David. (2001) 'Do 'high-performance' work practices improve establishment-level outcomes?' *Industrial and Labor Relations Review*, 54 (4): 737–75.

Cavanaugh, Joseph K. (1998) 'Asset specific investment and unionized labor.' *Industrial Relations*, 37 (1): 35–50.

Clark, Kim B. (1980a) 'The impact of unionization on productivity: A case study.' *Industrial and Labor Relations Review*, 33 (4): 451–69.

Clark, Kim B. (1980b) 'Unionization and productivity: Micro-econometric evidence.' *Quarterly Journal of Economics*, 95 (4): 613–39.

Combs, James G., Liu, Yongmei, Hall, Angela T. and Ketchen, David J., Jr. (2006) 'How much do high performance work practices matter? A meta–analysis of their effects on organizational performance.' *Personnel Psychology*, 59 (3): 501–28.

Cooke, William N. (1994) 'Employee Participation Programs, Group–Based Incentives, and Company Performance: A Union-Non-union Comparison.' *Industrial and Labor Relations Review*, 47 (4): 594–609.

Cooke, William N. (1992) 'Product quality improvement through employee participation: the effects of union-ization and joint union-management administration.' *Industrial and Labor Relations Review*, 46 (1): 119–34.

Delaney, John T. (1991) 'Unions and human resource policies.' In *Research in Personnel and Human Resource Management*, Vol. 9. Greenwich, CT: JAI Press. pp. 39–71.

Delaney, John T. (1996) 'Unions, human resource inno-vations, and organizational outcomes.' In *Advances in Industrial and Labor Relations*, Vol. 7. Greenwich, CT: JAI Press. pp. 207–45.

Delaney, John T. and Huselid, Mark A. (1996) 'The impact of human resource management practices on perceptions of organizational performance.' *Academy of Management Journal*, 39 (4): 949–69.

DiNardo, John and Lee, David S. (2002) 'The impact of unionization on establishment closure: A regression discontinuity analysis of representation elections.' National Bureau of Economic Research Working Paper 8993 (June).

Doucouliagos, Chris and Laroche, Patrice. (2004–2005) 'The Impact of Unions on Profits: A Meta-Analysis.' Université Nancy. Unpublished manuscript.

Doucouliagos, Chris and Laroche, Patrice (2003) 'What do unions do to productivity? A meta–analysis.' *Industrial Relations*, 42 (4): 650–91.

Doucouliagos, Chris and Laroche, Patrice (2002) 'Unions and Productivity Growth: A Meta–Analytic Review.' Deakin University. Unpublished manuscript.

Dunne, Timothy and Macpherson, David A. (1994) 'Unionism and gross employment flows.' *Southern Economic Journal*, 60 (3): 727–38.

Eaton, Adrienne E. (1990) 'The Extent and Determinants of Local Union Control of Participative Programs.' *Industrial and Labor Relations Review*, 43 (5): 604–20.

Eaton, Adrienne E. (1994) 'The Survival of Employee Par-ticipation Programs in Unionized Settings.' *Industrial and Labor Relations Review*, 47 (3): 371–89.

Eaton, Adrienne E. and Nocerno, Tom. (2000) 'The effectiveness of health and safety committees: Results of a survey of public sector workplaces.' *Industrial Relations*, 39 (2): 265–90.

Fallick, Bruce C. and Hassett, Kevin A. (1999) 'Investment and union certification.' *Journal of Labor Economics*, 17 (3): 570–82.

Freeman, Richard B. (2005) 'What do unions do? – The m-brane stringtwister edition.' *Journal of Labor Research*, 26 (4): 641–68.

Freeman, Richard B. and Rogers, Joel. (1999) *What Workers Want*. Ithaca, NY: Cornell University Press.

Freeman, Richard B. and Kleiner, Morris M. (1999) 'Do unions make enterprises insolvent?' *Industrial and Labor Relations Review*, 52 (4): 510–27.

Freeman, Richard B. and Medoff, James L. (1979) 'The two faces of unionism.' *The Public Interest*, 57: 69–93.

Freeman, Richard B. and Medoff, James L. (1984) *What Do Unions Do?* New York: Basic Books.

Friedman, Thomas L. (2005) *The World is Flat: A Brief History of the Twenty-First Century.* New York: Farrar, Straus, and Giroux.

Gerhart, Barry, Wright, Patrick M., McMahan, Gary C. and Snell, Scott A. (2000a) 'Measurement error in research on human resources and firm performance: How much error is there and how does it influence effect size estimates?' *Personnel Psychology*, 53 (4): 803–34.

Gerhart, Barry, Wright, Patrick M. and McMahan, Gary C. (2000b) 'Measurement error in research on the human resources and firm performance relationship: Further evidence and analysis.' *Personnel Psychology*, 53 (4): 855–72.

Godard, John. (2001) 'High performance *and* the transformation of work? The implications of alternative work practices for the experience and outcomes of work.' *Industrial and Labor Relations Review*, 54 (4): 776–805.

Godard, John. (2004) 'A critical assessment of the high performance paradigm.' *British Journal of Industrial Relations*, 42 (2): 349–78.

Godard, John and Delaney, John T. (2000) 'Reflections on the "high performance" paradigm's implications for industrial relations as a field.' *Industrial and Labor Relations Review*, 53 (3): 482–502.

Guest, David E., Michie, Jonathan, Conway, Neil and Sheehan, Maura (2003) 'Human resource management and corporate performance in the UK.' *British Journal of Industrial Relations*, 41 (2): 291–314.

Hirsch, Barry T. (2004) 'What do unions do for economic performance?' *Journal of Labor Research*, 25 (3): 415–55.

Hirsch, Barry T. (1990) 'Market structure, union rent seeking, and firm profitability.' *Economics Letters*, 32 (1): 75–79.

Hirsch, Barry T. (1991) *Labor Unions and the Economic Performance of US Firms.* Kalamazoo, MI: Upjohn Institute.

Hirsch, Barry T. (1992) 'Firm investment behavior and collective bargaining strategy.' In Mario F. Bognanno and Morris M. Kleiner (eds), *Labor Market Institutions and the Future Role of Unions.* Cambridge, MA: Blackwell. pp. 95–121.

Hirschman, Albert O. (1971) *Exit, Voice, and Loyalty.* Cambridge, MA: Harvard University Press.

Huselid, Mark A. (1995) 'The impact of human resource management practices on turnover, productivity, and corporate financial performance.' *Academy of Management Journal*, 38 (3): 635–72.

Huselid, Mark A. and Becker, Brian E. (2000) 'Comment on "Measurement error in research on human resources and firm performance: How much error is there and how does it influence effect size estimates?"' *Personnel Psychology*, 53 (4): 835–54.

Huselid, Mark A. and Becker, Brian E. (1996) 'Methodological issues in cross–sectional and panel estimates of the HR-firm performance link.' *Industrial Relations*, 35 (3): 400–22.

Huselid, Mark A. and Rau, Barbara L. (1996) 'The determinants of high performance work systems: Cross sectional and longitudinal analyses.' Unpublished paper, Rutgers University.

Ichniowski, Casey. (1986) 'The effects of grievance activity on productivity.' *Industrial and Labor Relations Review*, 40 (1): 75–89.

Ichniowski, Casey and Shaw, Kathryn. (1995) 'Old dogs and new tricks: Determinants of the adoption of productivity–enhancing work practices.' *Brookings Papers on Economic Activity*, 1–65.

Ichniowski, Casey, Shaw, Kathryn and Prennushi, Giovanna. (1997) 'The effects of human resources management practices on productivity: A study of steel finishing lines.' *American Economic Review*, 87 (3): 291–313.

Jackson, Susan E., Schuler, Randall S. and Rivero, J. Carlos (1989) 'Organizational characteristics as predictors of personnel practices.' *Personnel Psychology*, 42 (4): 727–86.

Kaufman, Bruce E. (2004) *The Global Evolution of Industrial Relations: Events, Ideas, and the IIRA.* Geneva: International Labour Office.

Kleiner, Morris M. (2001) 'Intensity of Management Resistance: Understanding the Decline of Unionization in the Private Sector.' *Journal of Labor Research*, 22 (3): 519–40.

Kochan, Thomas A., Katz, Harry C. and McKersie, Robert B. (1986) *The Transformation of American Industrial Relations.* New York: Basic Books.

LaLonde, Robert J., Marschke, Gérard and Troske, Kenneth (1996) 'Using longitudinal data on establishments to analyze the effects of union organizing campaigns in the United States.' *Annales d'Économie et de Statistique*, 41/42: 155–85.

Leonard, Jonathan S. (1992) 'Unions and employment growth.' *Industrial Relations*, 31 (1): 80–94.

MacDuffie, John Paul (1995) 'Human resource bundles and manufacturing performance: Organizational logic and flexible production systems in the world auto industry.' *Industrial and Labor Relations Review*, 48 (2): 197–221.

Machin, Stephen and Wood, Stephen (2005) 'Human resource management as a substitute for trade unions in British workplaces.' *Industrial and Labor Relations Review*, 58 (2): 201–18.

Menezes–Filho, Naercio and van Reenen, John (2003) 'Unions and innovation: A survey of the theory and empirical evidence.' Center for Economic Policy Research, Discussion Paper 3792 (January).

Menezes–Filho, Naercio, Ulph, David and van Reenen, John (1998) 'R&D and unionism: Comparative evidence from British companies and establishments.' *Industrial and Labor Relations Review*, 52 (1): 45–63.

Metcalf, David. (2003) 'Unions and productivity, financial performance, and investment: International · evidence.' In John T. Addison and Claus Schnabel (eds), *International Handbook of Trade Unions*. Northampton, MA: Edward Elgar. pp. 118–71.

Morishima, Motohiro (1991) 'Information sharing and firm performance in Japan.' *Industrial Relations*, 30 (1): 37–61.

Ng, Ignace and Maki, Dennis (1994) 'Trade union influence on human resource management practices.' *Industrial Relations*, 33 (1): 121–35.

Odgers, Cameron W. and Betts, Julian R. (1997) 'Do unions reduce investment? Evidence from Canada.' *Industrial and Labor Relations Review*, 51 (1): 18–36.

Osterman, Paul (1994) 'How common is workplace transformation and who adopts it?' *Industrial and Labor Relations Review*, 47 (2): 173–88.

Osterman, Paul (2000) 'Work Reorganization in an era of restructuring: Trends in diffusion and effects on employee welfare.' *Industrial and Labor Relations Review*, 53 (2): 179–96.

Pil, Fritz K. and MacDuffie, John Paul. (1996) 'The adoption of high involvement work practices.' *Industrial Relations*, 35 (3): 423–55.

Schedlitzki, Doris (2002) 'German works councils, employee involvement programmes and their impact on establishment profitability.' London School of Economics. CEP Working Paper No. 1191.

Slichter, Sumner H., Healy, James J. and Livernash, E. Robert (1960) *The Impact of Collective Bargaining on Management*. Washington, D.C.: Brookings Institution.

Stiglitz, Joseph E. (2002) 'Employment, social justice, and societal well–being.' *International Labour Review*, 141 (1–2): 9–29.

Tachibanaki, Toshiaki and Noda, Tomohiko. (2000) *The Economic Effects of Trade Unions in Japan*. Basingstoke: Macmillan Press.

Turnbull, Peter. (2003) 'What Do Unions Do Now?' *Journal of Labor Research*, 24 (3): 491–527.

Wolfe, Alan (1997) 'The moral meaning of work.' *Journal of Socio–Economics*, 26 (6): 559–70.

Wood, Stephen (1999) 'Human resource management and performance.' *International Journal of Management Reviews*, 1 (4): 367–413.

Wooden, Mark and Hawke, Anne (2000) 'Unions and employment growth: Panel data evidence.' *Industrial Relations*, 39 (1): 88–107.

Wright, Patrick M., Gardner, Timothy M., Moynihan, Lisa M., Park, Hyeon Jeong, Gerhart, Barry and Delery, John E. (2001) 'Measurement error in research on human resources and firm performance: Additional data and suggestions for future research.' *Personnel Psychology*, 54 (4): 875–902.

Wright, Patrick M., Gardner, Timothy M., Moynihan, Lisa M. and Allen, Matthew R. (2005) 'The relationship between HR practices and firm performance: Examining causal order.' *Personnel Psychology*, 58 (2): 409–46.

34

Labor Market Institutions Around the World

Richard B. Freeman

It was six men of Hindustan
To learning much inclined,
Who went to see the Elephant
(Though all of them were blind)
That each by observation
Might satisfy the mind. (Saxe)

At the turn of the twenty-first century, questions regarding labor market institutions replaced macro-economic policy at the center of much policy debate in advanced economies. By ascribing the high unemployment in European Union (EU) countries to labor institutions that reduced wage and employment flexibility, the OECD's 1994 Jobs Study (OECD, 1994a, 1994b) directed the attention of policy-makers and economists to institutions that mainstream economics had previously viewed as peripheral to aggregate economic performance. The Jobs Study recommended that countries deregulate labor markets to increase flexibility in working time; make wages and labor costs more responsive to market pressures; weaken employment security provisions and unemployment benefit systems; and introduce active labor market policies – training programs, job-finding assistance to workers, subsidies to employers to hire the long-term unemployed and special programs for youths leaving school.

This perspective marked a giant shift in the attitude of mainstream economics toward labor institutions. From the 1970s through to the mid-1980s or so, most economists favored macro-economic explanations and cures for economic problems (recall the battles between monetarist and Keynesian policies). They viewed labor institutions as peripheral to economic performance. In the 1990s, however, the higher employment rate and more rapid productivity growth of the US than of major European countries despite similar 'responsible' macro-economic policies directed attention to the possible role of labor market institutions in explaining differences in aggregate economic performance.

How much of the varying economic performance of capitalist economies can reasonably be attributed to labor institutions? Which outcomes do those institutions influence – the distribution of income, allocation of labor across sectors, productivity, inflation, economic growth? Through what channels do institutions affect outcomes?

This chapter reviews what economists know about these questions. Section I documents the large cross-country differences in labor institutions that make them a candidate explanatory factor for the divergent economic performance of countries. Section II examines the ways institutions can affect behavior and outcomes by altering incentives, enabling groups to engage in efficient bargaining per the Coase Theorem,[1] and by improving information, communication, and trust. Turning from what labor institutions *might* do to evidence on what they actually *do*, Section III shows that labor institutions reduce income inequality but has equivocal effects on other aggregate outcomes, such as employment and unemployment in the advanced countries on which most research has focused. Section IV considers three possible interpretations of the empirical findings and ways to improve our knowledge of how the institutional 'Elephant' affects economic performance.

VARIATION IN LABOR INSTITUTIONS AND ECONOMIC PERFORMANCE AMONG COUNTRIES

The starting fact for analyzing labor market institutions across countries is that countries evince widely varying institutional arrangements. The list at the outset of the paper can be easily extended: apprenticeship programs, occupational health and safety rules, defined benefit and defined contribution pension plans; mandated works councils; equal employment legislation; and so on. While economists do not have a single tight definition of an institution, per Justice Potter's famous statement about pornography, they know institutions when they see them, and they see them everywhere.[2]

Table 34.1 documents the variety of labor institutions among OECD countries and in the Asian 'Tiger' economies. It records quantitative rankings of country labor markets by their market vs. institutional orientation, measures

of specific institutional arrangements, and the share of social expenditures in GDP. Column 1 gives the ranking of countries by the market orientation of their labor market from the Fraser Institute's 'economic freedom' index. Since the 1980s the Institute has produced an index of economic freedom based on metrics for 'personal choice, voluntary exchange, freedom to compete, and protection of person and property' (Fraser Institute, 2003: 5). Beginning in 2001 the Institute included 6 indicators of labor institutions in its economic freedom index for 58 countries. The Fraser rankings give high rank (low numbers) to countries that rely more on markets, so that the rank1 implies that a country is the leading country in using market forces to set employment, wages, working conditions while a country with rank of, say 57, implies that that country relies greatly on institutions.

The conservative orientation of the Fraser Institute leads it to define economic freedom in a way that privileges the rights of capital compared to the rights of labor. The Institute regards protection of property as contributing to economic freedom but protection of labor as reducing that freedom (on the grounds that protective institutions limit the ability of businesses to make purely market-based decisions). As a result in 2003 countries with little or no labor protection, such as Uganda, the United Arab Emirates, Zambia, and Haiti, ranked at the top of its index of labor market freedom while countries with well-developed legal systems to protect workers, such as Germany and Sweden, ranked near the bottom.[3] But, nomenclature aside, the Institute's index measures the market vs. institutional orientation of economies in a way that fits with general observation for advanced countries, in that its index places the US higher in reliance on markets than European economies.

Column 2 gives the rankings of countries in the market orientation of their labor market from a very different survey – the Harvard Labor and Work Life Program's Global Labor Survey (GLS). This Internet-based survey asked union leaders, labor law professors, and other experts around the

Table 34.1 Measures of the variation of labor institutions across advanced countries

Country group	Fraser, 2003 labor index	GLS, 2005	Per cent union 2003	Per cent collective bargaining 2000	Employment protection legislation	Gov. social spending/ NNI, 2003
Anglo-American						
US	10	6	12	14	0.7	18.7
UK	19	13	29	30	1.1	23.3
NZ	38	16	22	25	1.3	22
Ireland	47	17	35	–	1.3	22.2
Australia	32	17	25	80	1.5	25.4
Canada	25	15	26	32	1.1	20.9
Other Advanced						
Switzerland	34	19	18	40	1.6	31.6
Netherlands	52	29	23	80	2.3	25.5
Finland	90	26	74	90	2.1	31.8
Denmark	71	26	70	90	1.8	34.3
Austria	83	25	35	95	2.2	32.3
Belgium	63	29	55	90	2.5	31.4
Germany	101	23	23	68	2.5	34.6
Portugal	77	–	24*	80	3.5	29
Sweden	96	29	78	90	2.6	36.3
Japan	28	17	20	15	1.8	22.9
Norway	89	27	53	70	2.6	31.3
Spain	54	–	16	80	3.1	24.3
Italy	95	24	34	80	2.4	30.8
France	58	26	6	90	2.9	33.7
Greece	94	–	27*	–	2.9	23.2
Four Asian Tigers						
Hong Kong	5	–				–
Singapore	42	9				–
Taiwan	61	7				–
Korea	81	10	11	11		9.2

Source: Column 1, Fraser Institute (2005) Economic Freedom of the World: 2005Annual Report. http://www.freetheworld. com/download.html; Column 2, Global Labor Survey (2005), Freeman and Chor (2005); Column 3 from Visser, J., "Union membership statistics in 24 countries", in *Monthly Labor Review*, Vol. 129, No. 1, January 2006, with * for 2000 from OECD 2004; Table 3.3; Column 4, OECD, 2004, Table 3.3 Column 5, OECD, 2004, Table 2. A2.4, version 2; Column 6, Society at a Glance: OECD Social Indicators 2006 Edition 2007 – Data GE1.2 Share of non-health and total social spending in national income, 2003. Note: the numbers in the ranking in columns 1 and 2 exceed the number of countries in the figure because the rankings include developing economies that I do not report in the table.

world to report on the *actual situation* of labor in their country. Because respondents were generally favorable to labor institutions (Chor and Freeman, 2005), it provides a useful counterpart to the Fraser index. The rankings in column 2 correspond closely to those in column 1, demonstrating that persons with differing ideological persuasions see the institution/market orientation of economies in analogous ways.

Columns 3 and 4 turn to measures of union density and collective bargaining coverage. Historically unions have been the major organization representing workers, and collective bargaining has been the main mechanism by which they raise wages. The density data show wide and increasing variation in the percentage of workers in unions among advanced countries. In 1980, the 5 countries with the highest union density averaged 67.8 per cent while the five countries with the lowest density averaged 18.9 per cent, for a ratio of 3.6 to 1.0. In 2000, the 5 most unionized countries had an average density of 66.2 per cent while the 5 least unionized countries had a density of 12.5 per cent, giving a ratio of 5.3 to 1.0 (data from Visser, 2006). The percentage of workers covered by collective bargaining in column 4 shows greater variation. In the US, UK, Canada, New Zealand, and Japan, the rate of collective bargaining coverage approximates the rate of unionization, so that declining union density produces commensurate declines in collective bargaining coverage. By contrast, many EU countries extend collective bargaining contracts to all workers and firms in a sector, so that the majority of workers are covered by collective bargaining regardless of union density. This pattern is most striking for France, whose collective bargaining coverage is among the highest in the world despite France having a rate of unionization below that in the US! In 1980, the 5 countries with the highest level of collective bargaining coverage had 2.8 times the coverage of the 5 countries with the lowest level of collective bargaining coverage. In 2000, the ratio of coverage in the five most highly covered countries to coverage in the five least covered countries had risen to 4.6.[4]

Column 5 records OECD measures of employment protection legislation (EPL) – legal rules protect workers against layoffs by requiring sizeable severance pay if the firm lays them off and in many cases require that the firm negotiate with a works council on a social plan for retraining. The Table shows that the US and the other Anglo-American countries (UK, Canada, Ireland, Australia, New Zealand) have weak employment protection legislation compared to other advanced economies. (Freeman et al., 2007). The Anglo-American economy with the strongest EPL regulations, Australia, had weaker regulations than the European countries with the weakest protection, Denmark, and Switzerland. The US, which operates in large part by employment-at-will has the lowest EPL score. In the US firms own jobs and can replace workers for any business or other (non-discriminatory) reason.

The last column of Table 34.1 gives the ratio of government social expenditures to net national income. High shares of national income going to social expenditures imply more extensive welfare states. The US and Japan have low ratios. The Anglo-American country with the highest social expenditure ratio is the UK, whose spending falls below all of the other countries save Japan and Spain. At the other end of the spectrum the Scandinavian countries have relatively high social expenditure shares of national income.

As a crude statistical test of the difference in labor institutions between the Anglo-American economies and other advanced economies, Freeman et al. (2007) calculated t-statistics of differences in the mean values of several measures of labor institutions between the Anglo-American and other advanced countries. Table 34.2 shows that most of the differences are large and statistically significant. Executives in the Anglo-American countries, for example, report greater control over wages, ability to link pay to productivity; and power over hiring and firing than do executives in the other advanced countries. Similarly, labor practitioners in the Anglo-American countries report a greater tilt toward business in labor market conditions and regulations, in government's attitude in labor disputes provision of employee benefits, and in forming unions than practitioners in the other advanced countries.

Classifying wage-setting institutions

From the 1970s through to the mid-1980s, analyses of labor institutions viewed the aggregate economic outcomes of countries with 'neo-corporatist' labor arrangements – centralized wage-setting between peak level national union organizations and employer associations – as superior to outcomes in countries where market forces or decentralized collective bargaining set wages and conditions of work. The studies explained the success of centralized bargaining in terms of the ability of national bargainers to adjust readily to aggregate economic shocks, notably the 1970s oil price increases. By contrast, from the late 1980s through to the mid-2000s, most studies focused on the superior employment and productivity growth of the US compared to the EU, with due allowance for high employment in Scandinavia.

Table 34.2   Mean values of ranks of Anglo-American and other advanced economies labor institutions (low value=market-oriented) and t-tests of their statistical significance

Panel A: Reports by executives on World Economic Forum 2003

Mean, t-test	Wage flexibility	Pay link to productivity	Hiring and firing	Delegation of authority	Co-operative labor-mgt relations
Mean, Anglo-American	26	11	27	11	25
Mean, Other Advanced	60	39	53	18	25
t-test	2.6	5.09	2.72	1.4	0.08
Implications	Anglo-American have more control over wages	Anglo-American firms link pay to productivity more than others	Anglo-American firms have greater power to hire and fire	Anglo-American delegate slightly more authority	No difference perceived in labor-mgt cooperation

Panel B: Reports by labor practitioners, Global Labor Survey 2004

Mean, t-test	Labor market conditions	Freedom of association/ collective bargaining	Labor disputes	Regulations and working conditions	Employee benefits
Mean, Anglo-American	16	15	12	13	13
Mean, Other	26	26	22	25	26
t-test	4.13	5.03	3.34	3.29	5.67
Implications	Labor market is more business-friendly in Anglo-American	Freedom of association and collective bargaining more difficult in Anglo-American	Anglo-American have more pro-business stance in disputes	Labor regulations are more pro-business in Anglo-American	Fewer benefits in Anglo-American

Source: Freeman, Boxall, Haynes, 2007, Chapter 1.

To measure country wage-setting institutions researchers developed indices of central-ization and/or co-ordination in wage setting. Although these indices relied on limited descriptive data on wage practices and varied among analysts, they gave a roughly similar picture of the role of institutions in wage set-ting (see *OECD Employment Outlook*, 1997, Table 3.4) – one that resembles the pattern in Table 34.1. All the indices rate the US as having one of the most decentralized systems of wage-setting and the Scandinavian coun-tries as among the most institution-driven. Analysts have, however, disagreed about the placement of some countries along the institutional/market scale (Kenworthy, 2001). For instance, some view Japan as 'corporatist'

on the basis of its Shunto offensive and strong business-government relations; while others view Japan as decentralized on the basis of its enterprise level unionism, bonus pay system, and lack of a centralized bargaining structure or strong government wage-setting regula-tions. Given Japan's success in overcoming wage and price inflation in the 1970s, whether analysts place Japan as corporatist or liberal colors how one assesses the relation between institutions and outcomes in that period.[5] Another country that has created problems is Switzerland, which has also had good aggregate economic performance.

In the ensuing years, the OECD has devel-oped new and improved measures of wage set-ting and other institutions in OECD countries over time. In 2004 it placed countries' wage setting into five categories reflecting the centralization of bargaining; and into five categories reflecting co-ordination of bargaining. Both categorizations resemble those in Table 34.1, albeit with changes over time. Looking at the Anglo-American economies, the OECD places the US, UK, Canada, and New Zealand in the most market determined wage group; Australia in the second most market determined group; and puts Ireland, which sets pay through a national wage pact, into the second most centralized wage-setting group (OECD, 2004, Table 3.5).[6] Still, there are problems with some classifications. The OECD categorized Italy in the 1980s as have company-based wage setting although during that period Italy set wages through the centralized *Scala Mobile*, which reduced dispersion of pay to Scandinavian levels (Erickson and Ichino, 1995). Taking a different approach, Botero, et al. (2004) coded laws regulating employment contracts, industrial relations, and the social security regulations of 85 countries to form indices of *de jure* regulation of labor procedures. This analysis extends the measures of institutions to many developing countries and links the institutions to the legal traditions of the country. But because countries differ in the way they implement legal statutes, the indices provide only a crude measure of the *de facto* institutions that can affect economic outcomes. Indices based on legal regulations are particularly suspect for developing countries, many of whom do not have strong rules of law. Consistent with this, the legal indices are more weakly correlated with other measures of the institutional orientation of countries than are the measures of actual practices correlated among themselves (Chor and Freeman, 2005). The legal indices show that the advanced Anglo-American countries rely less on labor regulation and have weaker protections for workers than other (non-Asian Tiger) advanced countries in industrial relations and employment laws but their measures of social security regulations miss the huge difference in social spending shown in Table 34.1.

Outside the advanced OECD countries, quantitative information on *de facto* differences in labor market practices is sparse. The *Global Competitiveness Report*, the *Global Labor Survey*, and the Fraser Institute include developing countries in their data sets. The ILO measured unionization and collective bargaining coverage for some developing countries in its World Labour Report 1997–1998, (ILO, 1997) and records the ILO conventions that countries have signed (http://www.ilo.org/ilolex/english/convdisp1.htm). But counts of union membership or coverage and conventions signed have different meanings in different countries. In 2007 the national union federation with the largest reported membership in the world is the All Chinese Federation of Trade Unions, which is a branch of the government/party rather than an independent union organization, though it may be moving more toward protecting workers in China's new labor market. Neither the ILO, World Bank, nor other organization concerned with economic development has studied labor institutions in developing countries with the depth that the OECD has done for advanced countries.[7] The biggest lacuna is in data for workers in the informal sector, where most developing country employees work, and where the government regulations and traditional unions that underlie most taxonomies are largely irrelevant.

Variation in economic performance among countries

The dependent variables in cross-country analyses of labor market institutions are measures of aggregate economic performance, such as rates of growth of GDP per capita, income inequality, employment and unemployment, productivity growth, inflation, and growth of real earnings. These outcomes have varied greatly among advanced and developing countries over time. Among advanced countries, much attention has been on employment differences between the US and Western Europe and on productivity growth differences between the US and Japan.

But, the US aside, there is wide variation in outcomes among other OECD countries. For instance, Ireland more than doubled its GDP per capita from 1979 to 2005 while France increased its GDP per capita more slowly. Spain had 20 plus per cent unemployment for two decades while unemployment was low in Japan. In the 1990s through to the mid-2000s small European Union countries had lower unemployment rates than Germany, France, and Italy, while in the 1990s through the mid-2000s Australia had lower unemployment and more rapid economic growth than New Zealand.

Economic performance has varied even more widely among developing countries (Easterly et al., 1993). In the 1960s and 1970s Africa had better growth experience than much of Asia, and higher GDP per capita than India or China. In the 1980s through to the mid-2000s, China and then India had rapid growth, albeit with different labor institutions and economic and political structures. In the Maoist era, China had essentially no labor market (Walder, 1986). Labor bureaus assigned jobs to workers in state-owned enterprises. Managers of firms had little right to hire and fire or determine pay. A national grid determined wages. Mobility of labor was restricted to local areas as the need to have *hukou* residence permits kept potential migrants from moving to the large cities. This situation changed when China began its market reforms so that by the early 2000s, the labor market determined wages and employment. Over the same period, many Latin American economies stagnated, and the share of the work force in informal sector employment grew. Within Latin America, however, some countries did well and others poorly. In Africa, many economies stagnated or deteriorated, though again with considerable cross-country variation.

Research on labor institutions in developing economies has largely focused on the danger that institutional interventions distort market outcomes and reduce growth. The Harris-Todaro model of unemployment and migration attributed high unemployment in African cities to high urban wages resulting from government policies and trade unions (http://en.wikipedia.org/wiki/Harris-Todaro_Model). In this analysis, institutions created excessively high wages in urban areas; which in turn drew rural migrants to cities where they would wait unemployed for jobs. In 1990, the World Bank warned countries that institutions designed to improve worker well-being in fact harmed those workers:

> Labor market policies – minimum wages, job security regulations, and social security – are usually intended to raise welfare or reduce exploitation. But they actually work to raise the cost of labor in the formal sector and reduce labor demand ... increase the supply of labor to the rural and urban informal sectors, and thus depress labor incomes where most of the poor are found (World Bank, 1990: 63).

In the ensuing years, the accumulation of evidence on these policies led the World Bank to modify its views (World Bank, 1995) but its 1990 statement still represents a widely held perspective.

SHOULD LABOR INSTITUTIONS MATTER?

The hypothesis that labor institutions are a prime determinant of aggregate economic outcomes is a flattering one to specialists in comparative labor analysis. But, flattery aside, is it reasonable to expect labor practices to have large effects on aggregate economies? There is an alternative perspective that institutions are largely veneer in a world dominated by fundamental economic forces. When I was in graduate school, John Dunlop – an institutionalist par excellence – used the fable of Cantillon's cock (which I believe he learned from John Hicks) to express this view. Every morning the cock awakens moments before sunrise and does what nature has programmed it to do: let out a mighty 'cock-a-doodle-do'. Observing the time sequence of cause and effect, the cock concludes that crowing induces the sun to rise. So too, warned Dunlop, might union leaders, business, and government officials believe that what they say or do, the way institutions operate, determines economic success. When you hear a union leader attribute trend growth of real wages to unionism, a politician credit prosperity to their stewardship, or a business leader attribute lucrative stock options in a rising share market to their productivity, you know there is truth to the fable.

Economic theory does not provide clear guidance to the effect of labor institutions on economic performance. Comparative static analyses based on optimizing behavior in competitive markets predict that institutions affect outcomes, usually in ways that reduce economic efficiency compared to what a perfect market would do. But analyses that posit efficient bargaining among economic decision-makers predict that institutions may affect distribution but not efficiency. When competition gives firms little discretion to set prices or quantities, institutions have little scope to affect allocation or distribution. By contrast, analyses that stress the role of information, communication, and trust in economic behavior, and that regard resolving prisoner's dilemma problems as critical in economic success, suggest that institutions can improve efficiency. I consider each of these perspectives in turn.

Institutions affect outcomes

Standard models in which decision-makers respond to price/wage incentives in market settings show that responses to institutionally determined incentives can substantially impact distribution and efficiency. Consider the traditional analysis of union wage effects. The union bargains for wages above the market level, but does not bargain over employment. Faced with higher costs of labor, firms in unionized sectors reduce employment, which reallocates labor to lower paid less productive activities in the non-union sector. The result is lower economic efficiency and higher inequality since otherwise similar workers now receive different pay depending on union status. Or consider labor supply analyses of unemployment insurance (UI) which predict that job losers raise their

reservation wages and reduce job search, increasing unemployment. The extent to which collective bargaining and UI 'distort' outcomes from what would exist in an ideal competitive market rests on the degree of responsiveness of decision-makers to the institutionally determined incentives. If firms have high elasticity of demand for labor, the change in the allocation of labor can be considerable. If the unemployed have a high elasticity of response to unemployment benefits, they may remain jobless for long periods, which will depreciate their skills and reduce supply-side pressures on wages to clear the labor market.

Institutions also affect market outcomes by changing the maximand of decision-makers. Since optimizing conditions equate marginal benefits from an action to the marginal costs of the action, an institution that changes the marginal benefit function will alter outcomes just as does an institution that changes the marginal costs. Institutions that alter marginal benefits can affect behavior in subtle ways. Compare for instance the predicted effects of employee ownership on labor demand relative to the predicted effects of profit sharing on demand behavior. Since both of these institutions are designed to increase the rewards to workers from capitalism, one might expect that they have similar effects on labor demand and employment, but analysis shows the opposite. In a price theoretic model of employee ownership, where the employee owned firm seeks to maximize net revenues per worker, comparative statics predicts that the firm will admit fewer members to the enterprise than a competitive firm would hire. Even more striking, the employee-owned firm will reduce employment when the price of output rises. This is because lower employment raises net revenues per worker when prices rise. But this is not the end of the story. The employee-owned firm can make more for its members by hiring additional workers without giving them ownership in the firm. By doing this, the employee owned firm will employ the same number of workers and respond similarly to prices as a competitive firm while creating a dual class of workers, employee-owners and standard wage-employees.

By contrast, consider labor demand by a profit-maximizing firm that shares profits with workers by paying them a fixed proportion of profits rather than fixed wages. Weitzman (1984) has shown that when a firm pays workers a fixed share of profits per worker, the firm seeks to hire more workers than would a competitive firm. In fact, the firm always tries to hire more workers, giving it an infinite demand for labor. Each additional worker adds to sales and profits, just as an additional commissioned salesperson adds to the profits of a marketing firm even if it cannibalizes some sales from existing salespersons. The firm's employment is limited by workers' alternative opportunities rather than by the cost of labor to the firm. As a result profit sharing can maintain full employment in the face of adverse economic shocks. To the extent that Japan's bonus compensation system – which pays of 4–6 months of earnings via winter and summer bonuses – operates as profit-sharing (Freeman and Weitzman, 1987), this can help explain Japan's more rapid recovery from economic shocks than countries that pay fixed wages.

Employee ownership and profit sharing also affect supply behavior. Most proponents of these institutions favor them because they give greater incentives to workers to work hard than do fixed wages. But to succeed, these modes of compensation must overcome the 'free rider' problem – the incentive that each worker has to shirk and live off the effort of other employees when all workers share the fruits of any individual's extra effort. In an N employee workplace this is often called the 1/N problem since the worker gets only 1/Nth of the reward for their effort. Overcoming the free rider problem may require institutions – work groups of different types, weekly team meetings and discussion of work problems – and a 'participative' corporate culture that complements the incentive system.

The bottom line is that by influencing both demand and supply, institutions have the potential for impacting the aggregate economy.

Institutions do not matter

Models of efficient bargaining predict that when firms/workers engage in bargaining, they 'leave no money on the table' and thus make the same decisions as a profit-maximizing firm. This is the Coase Theorem at work in the world of labor institutions (Freeman, 1993b). As long as transactions costs are negligible and someone has clear property rights to decisions, the bargaining parties produce efficiently and agree over some division of the rewards from their joint effort. The analysis suggests that institutionally determined rules, such as employment protection legislation, which some blame for European high unemployment by making firms leery of hiring workers they cannot readily lay off in the future in fact have no effect on employment. In the efficient bargaining model, the firm makes the efficient layoff regardless of whether the worker or the firm 'owns' the job. What EPL does is alter the division of the profits from the efficient choice. With EPL the firm pays some of the profit from a layoff to the worker to induce the worker to leave. Absent EPL the firm gets all of the profit from the decision. In this model, institutions alter the distribution of income but not the efficiency of production.

When market forces are so constraining that firms must choose profit-maximizing outcomes or go out of business, institutional arrangements affect neither distribution nor efficiency. If a firm has a U-shaped average cost curve and operates in a competitive market with free entry and exit, it either produces at the bottom of the U-shaped curve or loses money and goes out of business. The need to make non-zero or positive profits dictates decisions. Models of 'zero intelligent agents'(Gode and Sunder, 1993) – computer code that randomly selects the amount produced or price charged subject to the profits constraint – show the power of the profits constraint to produce competitive equilibrium rapidly absent any optimizing behavior. This argument has been applied to the adverse impact of employee ownership on employment. If an employee-owned firm makes large profits and limit entry, the workers whom the firm does not admit have an incentive to form a new firm and enter the market. As a result a market with worker-owned firms ends up in the same long run equilibrium as a market with profit-seeking firms. The logic also dictates that union wage effects do not persist over time, since the firm that pays a higher wage cannot survive competition from lower cost competitors. When firms do not have 'rents' to share with workers, institutions cannot affect distribution.

Situations when institutions improve outcomes

Institutions can increase information and communication flows inside firms, which can in turn improve decisions by management and labor (Freeman and Lazear, 1995). Unions or works councils, for instance, can facilitate the flow of information from workers to management because they give workers some control over how the firm uses the information that workers provide. These institutions can also increase the flow of information from management to workers by bargaining for open books, which raises the likelihood that workers will give wage concessions when the firm is truly in crisis and avoid being fooled into doing so when the firm cries 'wolf' while continuing to earn profits. In addition, workers with grievances will use firm-level institutions of voice to resolve problems rather than quit their employer, which should reduce turnover costs and lead to greater investments in firm-specific skills. In the Freeman-Lazear model, increasing the power of works councils raises output up to a point, after which increasing output falls. The reason is that in this analysis worker groups and management maximize their own income rather than their joint output, so that the worker-dominated firm would shortchange capital, just as the management-dominated firm would shortchange labor.

Institutions can also improve market outcomes if they enable real markets to come closer to the competitive ideal than those markets otherwise would have done. The belief that labor markets fall short of the competitive ideal is associated with evidence that the wages of workers in the same local labor market and occupation vary widely rather than cluster tightly around a single market wage. This result, found in diverse US data sets over the years greatly impressed US institutional economists (Slichter, 1950; Dunlop, 1956). To the extent that the large dispersion in pay reflects a failure of the competitive labor market to establish a single price of labor, institutionally determined reductions in dispersion could bring the market closer to the competitive ideal. Institutions can also make the dynamics of wage-setting closer to the competitive model. Looking at changes over time in pay across industries, analysts have noted that changes in countries with centralized bargaining more closely resemble the predictions of the competitive model than changes in the market-driven US. The competitive model predicts that exogenous changes in industrial productivity change the price of output but do not affect wages in an industry; while exogenous changes in output prices raise output and employment but also do not affect wages (Council of Economic Advisors, 1962; Salter, 1960). These predictions hold in the Nordic countries where centralized or co-ordinated bargaining link wages to national economic conditions rather than to sectoral conditions but do not hold in the US, where changes in wages depend substantively on changes in sectoral prices and productivity (Holmlund and Zetterberg, 1991; Teulings and Hartog, 1998).

At the macro-level, the case for institutions is that they deal better with macro-economic problems, such as inflation and balance of payments difficulties, than decentralized labor markets. The Nordic Model of the open macro-economy posits that peak level unions and employers' associations negotiate changes in wages equal to productivity growth in traded sectors and changes in world prices for those goods, which maintains fixed exchange rates (Aukrust, 1977; Milner and Wadensjö, 2001). By contrast, wage-setting in local labor markets risks inflationary spirals, with wage increases in non-traded sectors inducing wage increases in the traded goods sector that exceed productivity growth and increases in global prices for the traded goods. Mancur Olson (1990) argued that centralized collective bargaining in small open economies works because all-encompassing union organizations internalize the negative externalities from wage bargaining at the firm or industry level. The International Labor Organization goes further to claim that economic systems based on labor-management dialog improves aggregate efficiency: 'Successful social dialogue structures and processes have the potential to resolve important economic and social issues, encourage good governance, advance social and industrial peace and stability and boost economic progress'. (ILO, *Social Dialogue, 2007*) Finally, even if institutions reduce efficiency, they can still improve societal well-being if they redistribute income in ways consistent with the country's social welfare function.

In sum, there are arguments that institutions raise efficiency, reduce efficiency, and have no effect on outcomes beyond distribution. To determine which arguments are valid for which institutions under which economic conditions requires evidence on the actual link between institutions and outcomes, to which I turn next.

INSTITUTIONS AND OUTCOMES IN PRACTICE

'Give your evidence,' said the King; 'and don't be nervous, or I'll have you executed on the spot'. (*Alice's Adventures in Wonderland*, Chapter 11, 'Who Stole the Tarts?')

Since cross-country differences in performance motivate many studies of labor institutions, it is natural that the first wave of empirical analysis examined the cross-section relation between institutional arrangements and economic outcomes. These studies reported that countries with neo-corporatist arrangements did better in adjusting to the economic problems of the 1980s than countries with more market-oriented labor markets (Bruno and Sachs, 1985; Crouch, 1985; Tarantelli, 1986). But it is difficult to make strong statements about the effects of wage-setting institutions from cross-country data. Countries differ in many other dimensions and policies. Maybe income tax policy, or employment protection legislation, or product market regulations, or unemployment benefits rather than wage-setting mechanisms underlie differences in aggregate outcomes. Since the number of advanced countries is small relative to the number of institutions or policies, it is hard to estimate effects for particular institutions. This is one reason why many analyses link the *configurations* of institutions/policies captured in the taxonomies of the institutional/market orientation of countries to outcomes. But this still leaves open the possibility that an omitted cross-country factor outside the labor market underlies the pattern.

The second type of study looks at changes in institutions. A generic model would be:

(1) $Y_{ct} = a + b\, X_{ct} + T + I + u_{ct}$, where c refers to country and t refers to time; Y is the outcome variable of interest (or a vector of such variables); X are measures of institutions, T is a vector of year dummies; and I is a vector of country dummies.

By holding fixed country and year, this analysis infers the effects of policy by comparing the change in outcomes in the country that changed policy (the treatment) with the change in outcomes in countries that maintained policies (the controls). But developments in other countries are not necessarily a good measure of what might have happened for the country that changed policies. Abadie et al. (2007) have developed a more sophisticated counterfactual in which the analyst uses a composite of countries that give the best predictor of outcomes for the country prior to its change in policy. Evidence that the proposed counterfactual predicts what might have happened in the country before it changed policy increases the likelihood that the counterfactual is valid. Even if a given institutional change produced a particular outcome in one country, moreover, it is uncertain that it will produce the same outcome elsewhere. Institutions that work one way in one country may work differently in another country where it interacts with other institutions. Enact a law on temporary contracts in Spain and new entrants are hired under those contracts. Enact a similar law in Germany, and firms continue to hire apprentices for permanent jobs. To the extent that labor institutions form a unified consistent system, one cannot simply extrapolate the effects of changing a single institution in one labor system to another.

A third type of study compares outcomes between workers covered by different labor institutions within countries in which such intra-country differences exist. The virtue of this approach is that it holds fixed the factors that affect an economy in its entirety. Making within-country comparisons of union and non-union workers is how economists study the effects of unions in countries where union and non-union arrangements coexist – such as in the Anglo-American countries (Freeman and Medoff, 1984; Lewis, 1963). Such comparisons measure differences between institutionally determined and market determined outcomes but do not necessarily identify the structural impact of the institutions. They miss the potential spillover of institutionally determined outcomes on other workers, who can be helped or harmed depending on the nature of the interaction between the sectors.

In sum, determining how institutions affect outcomes across countries is difficult. Findings must be put through several sieves – cross-section analysis, before/after analyses, within-country analyses, and over different time periods – before one can hazard a generalization.

One strong finding and some problematic results

For all of the difficulties in pinning down the impact of institutions on aggregate economic performance across countries, analyses have found that institutions have a major impact on one important outcome: the distribution of income. As Table 34.3 shows, countries

Table 34.3   90/10 Wage differentials and Gini coefficients for advanced countries, circa 2000

	Dispersion	Gini
US	4.59	40.8
UK	3.45	36.0
NZ	3.28	36.2
Ireland	3.97	35.9
Australia	2.94	35.2
Canada	3.65	33.1
Switzerland	2.69	33.1
Netherlands	2.85	30.9
Finland	2.36	26.9
Denmark	2.16	24.7
Austria	3.56	30.0
Belgium	2.28	25.0
Germany	2.87	28.3
Portugal	3.76	38.5
Sweden	2.23	25.0
Japan	2.99	24.9
Norway	1.96	25.8
Spain	3.94*	32.5
Italy	2.40	36.0
France	3.07	32.7
Greece	3.62*	35.4

Source: Ratio of Wages, from OECD, 2004, Table 3.2, where the data are from 1995–99 with figures from Austria, Belgium, Denmark, Portugal are for 1990–94; Data for Spain and Greece from Pereira and Martins (2004), Table 1. Gini coefficients from United Nations 2005, Table 15.

that rely on institutions to set wages and working conditions have lower rates of inequality or dispersion of earnings – here measured by the ratio of the pay of persons in the 90th percentile of wages and salaries relative to the pay of persons in the 10th percentile – and lower levels of overall income inequality – here measured by the Gini coefficient for total income. The US, which ranks as the most market-driven labor market, has the highest dispersion of wages and the highest Gini. Other economies with relatively market-driven labor markets also have high levels of inequality. By contrast, Norway, where institutions set wages, has the lowest dispersion.

Studies that look at dispersion of pay when institutions change, ranging from declines in collective bargaining coverage as in the US or UK to the breakdown of centralized negotiations between the major union federation and major employer association in Sweden or the end of the Scala Mobile mode of centralized wage setting in Italy (Manacorda, 2004), show a comparable pattern. Movement toward market-determined pay widens earnings distributions. Movement toward more institutional wage determination narrows earnings inequality. Within-country data on the level of dispersion in union and non-union workplaces, also shows that inequalities are smaller in union settings and decline among workers who shift from non-union jobs to union jobs; and increase among workers who move in the other direction (Card et al., 2004; Freeman, 1984). What is true of collective bargaining also holds for government-mandated wage payments and taxation. Minimum-wage laws raise pay at the bottom of the distribution and are generally associated with lower dispersion of earnings.

By contrast, despite considerable effort, researchers have not pinned down the effects, if any, of institutions on other aggregate economic outcomes, such as unemployment and employment. This statement may seem surprising in light of the numerous policy pronouncements in the 1990s and 2000s that particular market-oriented changes would raise employment. The OECD Jobs Study was accompanied by two volumes of supporting research and followed by studies and reviews of studies, many given in the OECD's annual *Employment Outlook* (Layard et al., 1994). Nickell (1997) with various co-authors and diverse other economists estimated the effect of institutions on outcomes and asserted that they had nailed it down: In the January 2005 *Economic Journal* Nickell et al. (2005) summarized this work with the claim that 'the broad movements in unemployment in the OECD can be explained by shifts in labor market institutions' (p. 1).

But as economists have examined the evidence more critically, they have rejected these strong claims in favor of a more cautious stance about what the evidence shows about the impact of institutions on aggregate economic outcomes. Baker et al. (2005) documented that the time series models on which the OECD and independent researchers have relied to support their diagnosis that institutions adversely affect aggregate outcomes are not robust. The estimated coefficients on labor institutions become statistically insignificant with modest changes in the measures of institutions, countries covered, and time period. Models that cover more years, countries, and measures than the early studies did 'provide little support for those who advocate comprehensive deregulation of OECD labor markets' (p. 106). Baker et al. conclude that there is a 'yawning gap between the confidence with which the case for labor market deregulation has been asserted and the evidence that the regulating institutions are the culprits' (p. 198). Earlier Blanchflower (2001) told a similar story, noting 'only a weak positive relation in the OECD between unemployment and benefits (p. 390) and '*no* support (from a 1999 OECD report) ... for the belief that unions, benefits, the tax wedge, ALMP (Active labor market programs) spending or earnings dispersion influence unemployment ... contrary to the claims made in Layard et al. (1994), which appear to be based on mis-specified cross-country unemployment regressions (p. 392)'. Assessing results in the mid 2000s, Howell et al. (2006) and Baccaro and Rei (2005) come to a similar conclusion.

Given these studies and its own work, the OECD has backed away from the strong claims of the early 1990s. The 2004 *OECD Employment Outlook* argued for 'the *plausibility* (my italics) of the Jobs Strategy diagnosis that excessively high aggregate wages and/or wage compression have been impediments' to jobs, while admitting that 'this evidence is somewhat fragile', and that the effect of collective bargaining 'appears to be contingent upon other institutional and policy factors that need to be clarified to provide robust policy advice' (p. 165). The 2006 *Outlook* stressed that the institutions of low unemployment European countries differ greatly from those in the US and UK (Table 6.3). This implies that there is no single way to attain full employment and thus no single 'peak' form of capitalism to which each country should strive (Freeman, 2000). But the debate continues. In a study that takes account of many of the criticisms of earlier cross-country time series data, Bassanini and Duval (2006) estimated that changes in tax and labor policies explain about half of 1982–2003 changes in unemployment among countries, with tax policies playing a particularly important role.

The potential effect of employment protection legislation on employment and unemployment has attracted particular attention. Countries pass these laws to reduce layoffs and raise job security for existing workers. But by making layoffs more expensive to the firm, the laws also makes it more expensive to hire workers since the firm must factor in the greater expense of layoffs if it has to reduce output. The net effect of employment protection laws on aggregate employment thus depends on the degree to which they reduce layoffs compared to the degree to which they reduce hires. After over two decades of analysis, the consensus from studies of aggregate country data is that the regulations have little effect on the overall rate of unemployment. Rather, EPL shifts unemployment from older workers to younger jobseekers (*OECD Employment Outlook*, 2004). Micro-economic studies of the effect of EPL for Chile show little evidence of a negative impact on labor demand but find that EPL increases the within-firm gap between the marginal revenue product of labor and the wage, which it should since it creates a wedge between marginal product and the wage cost of employment (Petrin et al., 2006).

The disappearing inverse U

In the 1980s the pattern of unemployment among OECD countries changed. Whereas in the 1960s and 1970s, unemployment was lower in countries with highly centralized bargaining systems than in countries with decentralized wage-setting systems, in the 1980s unemployment was lower in both of those groups than in countries with collective bargaining institutions between the extremes, at least according to some measures of wage-setting institutions (Calmfors and Driffill, 1988). There is, moreover, logic to this pattern. Market wage setting presumably attains low unemployment through competitive pressures on firms and workers while centralized wage setting attains low unemployment by forcing bargainers to consider the impacts of wages on national unemployment, among other aggregate outcomes. The 'villain' in the story is industry or other intermediate level collective bargaining, which allow unions and firms to ignore the effects of their decisions on the aggregate economy (someone else pays the bulk of the unemployment compensation for workers whose jobs are lost due to high wages) and thus can produce high wages and unemployment.

But in ensuing years the inverse U relation disappeared. In the early 1990s Sweden's economic crisis reduced employment considerably. Two market-oriented economies, Canada and New Zealand, also experienced high unemployment. By contrast, the Netherlands, the archetype of a country with intermediate institutions, had modest wage settlements and altered some of its benefits to increase employment (Teulings and Hartog, 1998). Some other European countries, including those with industry bargaining, improved their economic performance. In its 2004 review, the OECD reported no indication of an inverse U in cross-country comparisons of wage institutions and unemployment in the 1990s. Rather, the data showed wide variation in aggregate outcomes among countries classified as highly centralized, decentralized, and intermediate that belies any simple generalization even in the earlier periods (OECD, 2004, Table 3.6). Soskice (1990) pointed out that analyses that adjust measures of wage setting for coordination of bargaining in countries with industry-wide bargaining produced no inverse U even in the 1980s. The inverse U appears to be more of a historical description of patterns at one period of time, rather than any general rule about the link between institutions and outcomes.

In short, the evidence is that institutions reduce inequality but have uncertain or time varying impacts on other aggregate outcomes, including those likely to be affected by wages.

INTERPRETATION

There are three possible interpretations of this evidence. First, it could be that labor institutions impact other outcomes substantially which extant measures of institutions and aggregate cross-section time series data are too weak to identify. From this perspective, the OECD's continual improvement of measures of institutions and the passage of time will eventually pin down the true relations. Doing more of the same with better and longer time series will surely add to our knowledge, but I am dubious that it will definitively uncover institutional effects beyond those on the dispersion of pay. Analyses of micro-data sets that focus on measuring labor practices – such as the UK's Workplace Employment Relations Survey (WERS) – offer a better chance for illuminating how institutions operate on the ground and their impact on outcomes. Adding measures of labor policies and practices to matched employee-employer panel data sets would create even greater potential for increasing knowledge. It would allow researchers to compare the behavior of the same worker under different practices, the effect of practices on selectivity of workers, and the effects of practices on productivity. Studies of firms that change labor practices (ideally under experimental conditions) or operate differently across countries due to country-specific rules and norms could also illuminate how institutions or policies work at workplaces.

The second possible interpretation of empirical results is that the effects of institutions on outcomes change over time due to changes in the economic environment or to changes in institutional responses to particular economic stimuli. The rough stability between US and advanced European institutions from the 1950s through the early 2000s when unemployment rose in the EU relative to the US rules out any simple causal link between institutions and outcomes. If essentially unchanged institutions caused this change in unemployment and other outcomes, the impact of institutions *must* have changed over time (Blanchard and Wolfers, 2000;

Lungquist and Sargent, 1998, 2004; OECD, 2006). In the case of unemployment, perhaps EU institutions were well suited to produce low unemployment in the 1960s–1980s while US institutions were better suited for low unemployment for the globalized digital economy of the 1990s and 2000s. Alternatively, perhaps the behavior of institutions changed over time as decision-makers learnt from experience what does or does not work. This would produce different responses to the same circumstances over time, shades of the Lucas critique of macro-economic models. While appealing, the 'changing economy/behavior interpretation' of the link between institutions and outcomes is difficult to test. It makes great demands on data and risks creating the social science equivalent of epicycles to account for observed patterns. A model that says EU style institutions helped attain full employment in the 1960s–1980s and reduced employment in the 1990s–2000s, or that posits that institutional decision-makers behaved differently in the latter period than in the former because they learned from their mistakes, can fit the observed experiences, but leaves little data to test the proposed explanations.[8] With enough interactions, one can readily over-fit any model.

A third reading of the evidence is that in fact labor institutions have a well-defined impact on income distribution but only modest effects on other outcomes. One reason their effects may be modest is that the political economy of institutional interventions rules out collective bargaining settlements and regulations that are truly expensive to an economy. No country would impose a minimum wage that disemployed a large fraction of the work force; and no union or employer would sign a collective bargaining agreement that forced the firm to close. If countries adopt only interventions with the most favorable benefit-cost ratios, one would observe reductions in dispersion only if they raise efficiency or produce minimal losses. In the same vein, it is possible that institutions have both the negative and positive effects hypothesized earlier, but that the two factors balance out, producing inconclusive results beyond those on distribution, again for political economy reasons via some form of bargaining among parties. Taking this line of thinking to its logical conclusion the economies that rely on institutions may have reduced the transactions costs of bargaining and developed long run relations among parties such that they produce efficient outcomes per the Coase Theorem more often than not.

To help assess these interpretations and increase our knowledge of institutions requires inputs from areas of research that have played little role in the debate over the link between labor institutions on aggregate outcomes. One such area is experimental economics. Evidence from laboratory experiments that people care about fair processes and outcomes and cooperate more than rational optimizing models of human behavior opens the door for studies of the conditions when institutions can improve market outcomes. Experiments that reflected real world institutions, such as group decisions, would at the minimum provide researchers with realistic priors about what to expect from those institutions outside the laboratory. Another area is game theory and the related field of implementation theory (Jackson, 2001). Theories of behavior under different bargaining rules could help illuminate the conditions under which European social dialogue institution can yield efficient bargains and direct attention at institutional reforms that would increase the potential for Coase-theorem bargains (Freeman, 2007). Finally, because labor institutions interact in ways that go beyond theory and experiments, artificial agent simulations could illuminate hypothesized interactions among institutions and between institutions and economic shocks and behavior, building on matching models of firms and workers (Pingle and Tesfatsion, 2003; Neugart, 2004). Roth and co-workers (1999, 2002) have shown the value of combining such modeling in analyzing the market for medical residents, which seemingly works better through a centralized allocative matching algorithm than through standard competitive behavior. In the spirit

of artificial agent modeling, analysts would ideally 'grow' artificial economies with specified institutional arrangements (Epstein, 2005) and then simulate the effects of institutional changes on economic outcomes.

In short, because the problem of determining whether labor institutions do more than reduce income inequality; and if so, whether they improve or worsen economic outcomes is such a hard one – on par with the six blind men trying to understand the elephant – we need all of the tools at our disposal. It is only by combining insights and observations from different perspectives that we will be able to capture the institutional reality and not:

> Rail on in utter ignorance
> Of what each other mean,
> And prate about an Elephant
> Not one of them has seen!
> (Saxe)

NOTES

1 The Coase Theorem holds that absent transaction costs, decision-makers will bargain to efficient outcomes regardless of the initial distribution of property rights. See http://en.wikipedia.org/wiki/Coase_Theorem

2 The Justice wrote, 'I shall not today attempt further to define the kinds of material I understand to be embraced within that shorthand description; and perhaps I could never succeed in intelligibly doing so. But I know it when I see it'. http://caselaw.lp.findlaw.com/scripts/getcase.pl?court=US&vol=378&invol=184

3 This scoring creates a negative relation between 'economic freedom' in the labor market and GDP per capita for all countries, while the overall freedom index is positively correlated with GDP per capita (Freeman, 2002).

4 The coverage for the top five was 87 per cent in 1980 and 91 per cent in 2000. The coverage for the bottom five was 31 per cent in 1980 and 20 per cent in 2000. *OECD Employment Outlook 2004*, Table 3.3. I have excluded the transition economy new entrants to the OECD from this analysis.

5 The range for Japan is from the 3rd or 4th most centralized or coordinated to among the most highly decentralized. Soskice 1990 finds that the categorization of countries changes some generalizations.

6 The six Anglo-American economies averaged 1.8 on the wage-setting centralization scale while the other advanced OECD countries averaged 2.8, where the scaling places lower value on more market-reliant systems.

7 Rama and Artetcona (2002) developed a World Bank labor database for all countries by gathering labor indicators from various sources into a single place, but the Bank did not pursue an on-going effort to improve the measures.

8 To illustrate, consider a model in which economies determine wages by collective bargaining or market forces and experience a price shock or competition from low wage countries or both. An experimental design to assess the link between shocks and institutions would require 16 (= 2^3) treatments If institutions reacted depending on which shock they faced first, the number of treatments would increase.

REFERENCES

Abadie, Alberto, Diamond, Alexis, and Hainmueller, Jens (2007) 'Synthetic control methods for comparative case studies: Estimating the effect of California's Tobacco Control Program', January. http://www.people.fas.harvard.edu/~jhainm/Paper/ADH2007.pdf

Aukrust, Odd (1977) 'Inflation in the open economy: A Norwegian model', in L.B. Krause and W.S. Salant (eds), *Worldwide Inflation; Theory and Recent Experience*. Washington, DC: Brookings Institution.

Baccaro, Lucio and Diego, Rei (2005) 'Institutional determinants of unemployment in OECD countries: a time series cross-section analysis (1960–98)', International Institute for Labour Studies Discussion Paper DP/160/2005, International Institute for Labour Studies, Geneva

Baker, D., Glyn, A., Howell, D., and Schmitt, J. (2005) 'Labour market institutions and unemployment: A critical assessment of the cross-country evidence', in David R. Howell (ed.), *Fighting Unemployment: The Limits of Free Market Orthodoxy*. Oxford: Oxford University Press.

Bassanini, Andrea and Duval, Romain (2006) 'Employment patterns in OECD countries: Reassessing the role of policies and institutions', OECD Economic Department Working Paper 486, June.

Blanchard, Olivier and Wolfers, Justin (2000) 'Shocks and institutions and the rise of European unemployment: The Aggregate Evidence', *Economic Journal*, 110 (1): 1–33.

Blanchflower, David G. (2001) 'Unemployment, well-being, and wage curves in Eastern and Central Europe', *Journal of the Japanese and International Economies*, 15: 364–402.

Botero, Juan, Djankov, Simeon, La Porta, Rafael, López de Silanes, Florencio, and Shleifer, Andrei (2004) 'The Regulation of Labor', *Quarterly Journal of Economics*, 119: 1339–82.

Bruno, Michael and Sachs, Jeffrey (1985) *Economics of Worldwide Stagflation*. Cambridge, MA: Harvard University Press.

Calmfors, Lars and Driffill, John (1988) 'Bargaining structure, corporatism, and. macroeconomic performance', *Economic Policy*, 6 (April): 14–61.

Card, David, Lemieux, Thomas, and Riddell, W. Craig (2004) 'Unions and wage inequality', *Journal of Labor Research*, 25 (4): 519–62.

Carroll, Lewis (2006) *Alice's Adventures in Wonderland*. Harold Bloom (ed.) NY: Chelsea House Publishers.

Chor, Davin and Freeman, Richard (2005) 'The 2004 global labor survey: Workplace institutions and practices around the world', NBER Working Paper 11598.

Council of Economic Advisors (1962) *Economic Report of the President*. Washington, DC: Government Printing Office.

Crouch, Colin (1985) 'Conditions for trade union wage restraint', in Leon N. Lindberg and Charles S. Maier (eds) *The Politics of Inflation and Economic Stagflation*. Washington, DC: Brookings Institution.

Easterly, William, Kremer, Michael, Pritchett, Lant, and Summers, Lawrence H. (1993) 'Good policy or good luck? Country growth performance and temporary shocks', *Journal of Monetary Economics*, 32 (3): 459–83.

Epstein, Joshua M. (2005) 'Remarks on the foundations of agent-based generative social science', Brookings, CSED, Working Paper 41 (July).

Erickson, Christopher L. and Ichino, Andrea (1995) 'Wage differentials in Italy: Market Forces, Institutions and Inflation', in Richard B. Freeman and Lawrence F. Katz (eds), *Differences and Changes in Wage Structures*. Chicago: University of Chicago Press for NBER.

Fraser Institute (2001) *Economic Freedom of the World: 2001 Annual Report*. Vancouver, BC: The Fraser Institute.

Fraser Institute (2003) *Economic Freedom of the World: 2003 Annual Report*. Vancouver, BC: The Fraser Institute.

Freeman, Richard B. (1984) 'Longitudinal analyses of the effects of trade unions', *Journal of Labor Economics*, 2 (1): 1–26.

Freeman, Richard B. (1993a) 'Labor market institutions and policies: Help or hindrance to economic development?' *Proceedings of the World Bank Annual Conference on Development Economics 1992*. Washington, DC: The World Bank.

Freeman, Richard B. (1993b) 'Labor markets and institutions in economic development', *American Economic Review*, 83 (2) (May): 403–8.

Freeman, Richard B. (2000) 'Single peaked vs. diversified capitalism: The relation between economic institutions and outcomes', in Richard B. Freeman (ed.), *Inequality around the World*. London, UK: Palgrave.

Freeman, Richard B. (2002) 'Varieties of labor market institutions and economic performance', presented at the *IRRA Session on Labor Market Institutions and Economic Outcomes*, January 4.

Freeman, Richard B. (2005) 'Labour market institutions without blinders: The debate over flexibility and labour market performance', *International Economic Journal RIEJ*, 19 (2): 129–45.

Freeman, Richard B. (2007) 'Searching for the EU social dialogue model', in Nicola Acocella and Riccardo Leoni (eds), *Social Pacts, Employment and Growth: A Reappraisal of Ezio Tarantelli's Thought*. Heidelberg: Physica-Verlag.

Freeman, Richard B., Boxall, Peter and Haynes, Peter (eds) (forthcoming, 2007) *What Workers Say: Employee Voice in the Anglo-American Workplace*. Ithaca, NY: Cornell University Press.

Freeman, Richard B. and Lazear, Edward P. (1995) 'An economic analysis of works councils', in Joel Rogers and Wolfgang Streeck (eds), *Works Councils: Consultation, Representation, Cooperation*. Chicago, IL: University of Chicago Press for NBER. pp. 27–50.

Freeman, Richard B. and Medoff, James (1984) *What do Unions Do?* New York: Basic Books.

Freeman, Richard B. and Weitzman, Martin L. (1987) 'Bonuses and employment in Japan', *Journal of the Japanese and International Economies*, 1: 168–94.

Gode, Dhananjay K. and Sunder, Shyam (1993) 'Allocative efficiency of markets with zero-intelligence traders: Market as a partial substitute for individual rationality', *Journal of Political Economy*, 101 (1): 119–37.

Holmlund, Bertil and Zetterberg, Johnny (1991) 'Insider effects in wage determination: Evidence from five countries', *European Economic Review*, July.

Howell, David, Baker, Dean, Glyn, Andrew, and Schmitt, John (2006) 'Are protective labour market institutions really at the root of unemployment? A critical perspective on the statistical evidence', July 14. http://www.cepr.net/documents/2006_07_unemployment_institutions.pdf

International Labour Office (1997) *World Labour Report 1997–98. Industrial Relations, Democracy and Social Stability*. Geneva: ILO.

International Labour Office (2007) *Social Dialogue*. http://www.ilo.org/public/english/dialogue/themes/sd.htm

Jackson, Matthew O. (2001) 'A crash course in implementation theory', *Social Choice and Welfare*, 18 (4): 655–708.

Kagel, John H. and Roth, Alvin E. (eds) (1995) *The Handbook of Experimental Economics*. Princeton, NJ: Princeton University Press.

Kenworthy, Lane (2001) 'Wage-setting measures, a survey and assessment', *World Politics* 55 (October): 57–98.

Layard, Richard, Nickell, Stephen, and Jackman, Richard (1994) *The Unemployment Crisis*. Oxford, UK: Oxford University Press.

Lewis, H. Gregg (1963) *Unionism and Relative Wages in the United States*. Chicago, IL: University of Chicago.

Ljungqvist, Lars and Sargent, Thomas J. (1998) 'The European unemployment dilemma', *Journal of Political Economy*, 106 (3): 514–50.

Ljungqvist, Lars and Sargent, Thomas J. (2004) 'European unemployment and turbulence revisited in a matching model', *Journal of the European Economic Association*, 2(2–3)(April/May): 456–68.

Manacorda, Marco (2004) 'Can the Scala Mobile explain the fall and rise of earnings inequality in Italy? A semiparametric analysis, 1977–1993', *Journal of Labor Economics*, 22 (3): 585–613.

Manning, Alan (2005) *Monopsony in Motion: Imperfect Competition in Labor Markets*. Princeton, NJ: Princeton University Press.

Martin, John Paul (1998) 'What works among active labour market policies: Evidence from OECD Countries' Experiences'. Available at: www.rba.gov.au/PublicationsAndResearch/Conferences/1998/Martin.pdf

Milner, Henry and Wadensjö, Eskil (eds) (2001) *Gösta Rehn, the Swedish Model and Labour Market Policies: International and National Perspectives*. Aldershot: Ashgate.

Neugart, Michael (2004) 'Endogenous matching functions: an agent-based computational approach', *Advances in Complex Systems*, 7 (2): 187–202.

Nickell, Stephen J. and Brian Bell (1996) 'Changes in the distribution of wages and unemployment in the OECD countries',*American Economic Review*, Papers and Proceedings, 86 (5): 302–08.

Nickell, Stephen, Nunziata, Luca, and Ochel, Wolfgang (2005) 'Unemployment in the OECD since the 1960s: What do we know?', *The Economic Journal*, 115 (January): 1–27, Royal Economic Society.

Nickell, Stephen (1997) 'Unemployment and labor market rigidities: Europe versus North America', *Journal of Economic Perspectives*, 11 (3) (Summer): 55–74.

Olson, Mancur (1990) *How Bright Are the Northern Lights?: Some questions about Sweden*

(Crafoord lectures). Lund, Sweden: Institute of Economic Research, Lund University.

Organisation for Economic Cooperation and Development (OECD) (1994a) *OECD Jobs Study, Evidence and Explanations, Part I: Labor Market Trends and Underlying Forces of Change.* Paris: OECD.

OECD (1994b) *OECD Jobs Study, Evidence and Explanations, Part II: The Adjustment Potential of the Labor Market.* Paris: OECD.

OECD (1995) *OECD Jobs Study, Taxation, Employment, and Unemployment.* Paris: OECD.

OECD (1996) *OECD Employment Outlook.* Paris: OECD.

OECD (1997) 'Economic performance and the structure of collective bargaining', *OECD Employment* Outlook (July). Paris: OECD.

OECD (1997) *Implementing the Jobs Study.* Paris: OECD.

OECD (2002) *OECD Employment Outlook.* Paris: OECD.

OECD (2004) *OECD Employment Outlook.* Paris: OECD.

OECD (2006) *OECD Employment Outlook.* Paris: OECD.

Pereira, Pedro Telhado and Martins, Pedro Silva (2004) 'Returns to education and wage equations', *Applied Economics*, 36 (6) (April): 525–31.

Petrin, Amil and Sivadasan, Jagadeesh (2006) 'Job security does affect economic efficiency: Theory, a new statistic, and evidence', NBER Working Paper 12757 (December).

Pingle, Mark and Tesfatsion, Leigh (2003) 'Evolution of worker-employer networks and behaviors under alternative non-employment benefits: An agent-based computational study', *Computing in Economics and Finance*, 7, Society for Computational Economics.

Rama, Martin and Artecona, Raquel (2002) 'A database of labor market indicators across countries', Washington, DC: World Bank, Development Research Group.

Roth, Alvin E. and Peranson, Elliott (1999) 'The redesign of the matching market for American physicians: Some engineering aspects of economic design', *American Economic Review*, 89 (4) (September): 748–80.

Roth, Alvin E. (2002) 'The economist as engineer: Game theory, experimentation, and computation as tools for design economics', Fisher-Schultz Lecture, *Econometrica*, 70 (4) (July): 1341–78.

Salter, Wilfred E.G (1960) *Productivity and Technical Change.* Cambridge, UK: Cambridge University Press.

Saxe, John Godfrey, 'Blind men and an Elephant', http://en.wikisource.org/wiki/The_Blindmen_and_the_Elephant

Slichter, Sumner H. (1950 'Notes on the structure of wages', *The Review of Economics and Statistics*, 32 (1) (February): 80–91.

Soskice, David (1990) 'Wage determination: The changing role of institutions in advanced industrialized countries', *Oxford Review of Economic Policy*, 6 (4): 36–61.

Tarentelli, Ezio (1986) 'The Regulation of Inflation and Unemployment', *Industrial Relations*, 25 (1): 1–15.

Teulings, Coen and Hartog, Joop (1998) *Corporatism or Competition? Labour Contracts, Institutions and Wage Structures in International Competition.* Cambridge, UK: Cambridge University Press.

Traxler, Franz (2002) 'Bargaining (de)centralization, macro-economic performance and control over the employment relationship', *British Journal of Industrial Relations*, 1(March): 1–27.

Traxler, Franz and Kittel , Bernhard (2000) 'The bargaining system and performance: A comparison of 18 OECD countries', *Comparative Political Studies*, 33 (?): 1154–90.

United Nations (2005) *United Nations Human Development Report 2005.* New York: UNDP.

Visser, Jelle (2006) 'Union membership statistics in 24 countries', *Monthly Labor Review*, 129(1)(January). Available at: http://www.bls.gov/opub/mlr/2006/01/art3abs.htm

Walder, Andrew (1986) *Communist Neotraditionalism: Work and Authority in Chinese Industry.* Berkeley, CA: University of California Press.

Weitzman, Martin L. (1984) *The Share Economy: Conquering Stagflation.* Cambridge, MA: Harvard University Press.

World Bank (1990) *World Development Report 1990.* New York: Oxford University Press.

World Bank (1995) *World Development Report.* Washington, DC: The World Bank.

World Economic Forum (2003) *Global Competitiveness Report.* Geneva, Switzerland: World Economic Forum.

Index